Lecture Notes in Computer Science 13432

More information about this series at https://link.springer.com/bookseries/558

Linwei Wang · Qi Dou · P. Thomas Fletcher ·
Stefanie Speidel · Shuo Li (Eds.)

Medical Image Computing and Computer Assisted Intervention – MICCAI 2022

25th International Conference
Singapore, September 18–22, 2022
Proceedings, Part II

 Springer

Editors
Linwei Wang
Rochester Institute of Technology
Rochester, NY, USA

Qi Dou (iD)
Chinese University of Hong Kong
Hong Kong, Hong Kong

P. Thomas Fletcher (iD)
University of Virginia
Charlottesville, VA, USA

Stefanie Speidel (iD)
National Center for Tumor Diseases
(NCT/UCC)
Dresden, Germany

Shuo Li (iD)
Case Western Reserve University
Cleveland, OH, USA

ISSN 0302-9743 ISSN 1611-3349 (electronic)
Lecture Notes in Computer Science
ISBN 978-3-031-16433-0 ISBN 978-3-031-16434-7 (eBook)
https://doi.org/10.1007/978-3-031-16434-7

This Springer imprint is published by the registered company Springer Nature Switzerland AG
The registered company address is: Gewerbestrasse 11, 6330 Cham, Switzerland

Preface

We are pleased to present the proceedings of the 25th International Conference on Medical Image Computing and Computer-Assisted Intervention (MICCAI) which – after two difficult years of virtual conferences – was held in a hybrid fashion at the Resort World Convention Centre in Singapore, September 18–22, 2022. The conference also featured 36 workshops, 11 tutorials, and 38 challenges held on September 18 and September 22. The conference was also co-located with the 2nd Conference on Clinical Translation on Medical Image Computing and Computer-Assisted Intervention (CLINICCAI) on September 20.

MICCAI 2022 had an approximately 14% increase in submissions and accepted papers compared with MICCAI 2021. These papers, which comprise eight volumes of Lecture Notes in Computer Science (LNCS) proceedings, were selected after a thorough double-blind peer-review process. Following the example set by the previous program chairs of past MICCAI conferences, we employed Microsoft's Conference Managing Toolkit (CMT) for paper submissions and double-blind peer-reviews, and the Toronto Paper Matching System (TPMS) to assist with automatic paper assignment to area chairs and reviewers.

From 2811 original intentions to submit, 1865 full submissions were received and 1831 submissions reviewed. Of these, 67% were considered as pure Medical Image Computing (MIC), 7% as pure Computer-Assisted Interventions (CAI), and 26% as both MIC and CAI. The MICCAI 2022 Program Committee (PC) comprised 107 area chairs, with 52 from the Americas, 33 from Europe, and 22 from the Asia-Pacific or Middle East regions. We maintained gender balance with 37% women scientists on the PC.

Each area chair was assigned 16–18 manuscripts, for each of which they were asked to suggest up to 15 suggested potential reviewers. Subsequently, over 1320 invited reviewers were asked to bid for the papers for which they had been suggested. Final reviewer allocations via CMT took account of PC suggestions, reviewer bidding, and TPMS scores, finally allocating 4–6 papers per reviewer. Based on the double-blinded reviews, area chairs' recommendations, and program chairs' global adjustments, 249 papers (14%) were provisionally accepted, 901 papers (49%) were provisionally rejected, and 675 papers (37%) proceeded into the rebuttal stage.

During the rebuttal phase, two additional area chairs were assigned to each rebuttal paper using CMT and TPMS scores. After the authors' rebuttals were submitted, all reviewers of the rebuttal papers were invited to assess the rebuttal, participate in a double-blinded discussion with fellow reviewers and area chairs, and finalize their rating (with the opportunity to revise their rating as appropriate). The three area chairs then independently provided their recommendations to accept or reject the paper, considering the manuscript, the reviews, and the rebuttal. The final decision of acceptance was based on majority voting of the area chair recommendations. The program chairs reviewed all decisions and provided their inputs in extreme cases where a large divergence existed between the area chairs and reviewers in their recommendations. This process resulted in the acceptance of a total of 574 papers, reaching an overall acceptance rate of 31% for MICCAI 2022.

In our additional effort to ensure review quality, two Reviewer Tutorials and two Area Chair Orientations were held in early March, virtually in different time zones, to introduce the reviewers and area chairs to the MICCAI 2022 review process and the best practice for high-quality reviews. Two additional Area Chair meetings were held virtually in July to inform the area chairs of the outcome of the review process and to collect feedback for future conferences.

For the MICCAI 2022 proceedings, 574 accepted papers were organized in eight volumes as follows:

- Part I, LNCS Volume 13431: Brain Development and Atlases, DWI and Tractography, Functional Brain Networks, Neuroimaging, Heart and Lung Imaging, and Dermatology
- Part II, LNCS Volume 13432: Computational (Integrative) Pathology, Computational Anatomy and Physiology, Ophthalmology, and Fetal Imaging
- Part III, LNCS Volume 13433: Breast Imaging, Colonoscopy, and Computer Aided Diagnosis
- Part IV, LNCS Volume 13434: Microscopic Image Analysis, Positron Emission Tomography, Ultrasound Imaging, Video Data Analysis, and Image Segmentation I
- Part V, LNCS Volume 13435: Image Segmentation II and Integration of Imaging with Non-imaging Biomarkers
- Part VI, LNCS Volume 13436: Image Registration and Image Reconstruction
- Part VII, LNCS Volume 13437: Image-Guided Interventions and Surgery, Outcome and Disease Prediction, Surgical Data Science, Surgical Planning and Simulation, and Machine Learning – Domain Adaptation and Generalization
- Part VIII, LNCS Volume 13438: Machine Learning – Weakly-supervised Learning, Machine Learning – Model Interpretation, Machine Learning – Uncertainty, and Machine Learning Theory and Methodologies

We would like to thank everyone who contributed to the success of MICCAI 2022 and the quality of its proceedings. These include the MICCAI Society for support and feedback, and our sponsors for their financial support and presence onsite. We especially express our gratitude to the MICCAI Submission System Manager Kitty Wong for her thorough support throughout the paper submission, review, program planning, and proceeding preparation process – the Program Committee simply would not have be able to function without her. We are also grateful for the dedication and support of all of the organizers of the workshops, tutorials, and challenges, Jianming Liang, Wufeng Xue, Jun Cheng, Qian Tao, Xi Chen, Islem Rekik, Sophia Bano, Andrea Lara, Yunliang Cai, Pingkun Yan, Pallavi Tiwari, Ingerid Reinertsen, Gongning Luo, without whom the exciting peripheral events would have not been feasible. Behind the scenes, the MICCAI secretariat personnel, Janette Wallace and Johanne Langford, kept a close eye on logistics and budgets, while Mehmet Eldegez and his team from Dekon Congress & Tourism, MICCAI 2022's Professional Conference Organization, managed the website and local organization. We are especially grateful to all members of the Program Committee for their diligent work in the reviewer assignments and final paper selection, as well as the reviewers for their support during the entire process. Finally, and most importantly, we thank all authors, co-authors, students/postdocs, and supervisors, for submitting and presenting their high-quality work which made MICCAI 2022 a successful event.

We look forward to seeing you in Vancouver, Canada at MICCAI 2023!

September 2022

Linwei Wang
Qi Dou
P. Thomas Fletcher
Stefanie Speidel
Shuo Li

Organization

General Chair

Shuo Li   Case Western Reserve University, USA

Program Committee Chairs

Linwei Wang   Rochester Institute of Technology, USA
Qi Dou   The Chinese University of Hong Kong, China
P. Thomas Fletcher   University of Virginia, USA
Stefanie Speidel   National Center for Tumor Diseases Dresden,
                                Germany

Workshop Team

Wufeng Xue   Shenzhen University, China
Jun Cheng   Agency for Science, Technology and Research,
                                Singapore
Qian Tao   Delft University of Technology, the Netherlands
Xi Chen   Stern School of Business, NYU, USA

Challenges Team

Pingkun Yan   Rensselaer Polytechnic Institute, USA
Pallavi Tiwari   Case Western Reserve University, USA
Ingerid Reinertsen   SINTEF Digital and NTNU, Trondheim, Norway
Gongning Luo   Harbin Institute of Technology, China

Tutorial Team

Islem Rekik   Istanbul Technical University, Turkey
Sophia Bano   University College London, UK
Andrea Lara   Universidad Industrial de Santander, Colombia
Yunliang Cai   Humana, USA

Clinical Day Chairs

Jason Chan   The Chinese University of Hong Kong, China
Heike I. Grabsch   University of Leeds, UK and Maastricht
                               University, the Netherlands
Nicolas Padoy   University of Strasbourg & Institute of
                               Image-Guided Surgery, IHU Strasbourg,
                               France

Young Investigators and Early Career Development Program Chairs

Marius Linguraru   Children's National Institute, USA
Antonio Porras   University of Colorado Anschutz Medical
                               Campus, USA
Nicole Rieke   NVIDIA, Deutschland
Daniel Racoceanu   Sorbonne University, France

Social Media Chairs

Chenchu Xu   Anhui University, China
Dong Zhang   University of British Columbia, Canada

Student Board Liaison

Camila Bustillo   Technische Universität Darmstadt, Germany
Vanessa Gonzalez Duque   Ecole centrale de Nantes, France

Submission Platform Manager

Kitty Wong   The MICCAI Society, Canada

Virtual Platform Manager

John Baxter   INSERM, Université de Rennes 1, France

Program Committee

Ehsan Adeli   Stanford University, USA
Pablo Arbelaez   Universidad de los Andes, Colombia
John Ashburner   University College London, UK
Ulas Bagci   Northwestern University, USA
Sophia Bano   University College London, UK
Adrien Bartoli   Université Clermont Auvergne, France
Kayhan Batmanghelich   University of Pittsburgh, USA

Hrvoje Bogunovic	Medical University of Vienna, Austria
Ester Bonmati	University College London, UK
Esther Bron	Erasmus MC, the Netherlands
Gustavo Carneiro	University of Adelaide, Australia
Hao Chen	Hong Kong University of Science and Technology, China
Jun Cheng	Agency for Science, Technology and Research, Singapore
Li Cheng	University of Alberta, Canada
Adrian Dalca	Massachusetts Institute of Technology, USA
Jose Dolz	ETS Montreal, Canada
Shireen Elhabian	University of Utah, USA
Sandy Engelhardt	University Hospital Heidelberg, Germany
Ruogu Fang	University of Florida, USA
Aasa Feragen	Technical University of Denmark, Denmark
Moti Freiman	Technion - Israel Institute of Technology, Israel
Huazhu Fu	Agency for Science, Technology and Research, Singapore
Mingchen Gao	University at Buffalo, SUNY, USA
Zhifan Gao	Sun Yat-sen University, China
Stamatia Giannarou	Imperial College London, UK
Alberto Gomez	King's College London, UK
Ilker Hacihaliloglu	University of British Columbia, Canada
Adam Harrison	PAII Inc., USA
Mattias Heinrich	University of Lübeck, Germany
Yipeng Hu	University College London, UK
Junzhou Huang	University of Texas at Arlington, USA
Sharon Xiaolei Huang	Pennsylvania State University, USA
Yuankai Huo	Vanderbilt University, USA
Jayender Jagadeesan	Brigham and Women's Hospital, USA
Won-Ki Jeong	Korea University, Korea
Xi Jiang	University of Electronic Science and Technology of China, China
Anand Joshi	University of Southern California, USA
Shantanu Joshi	University of California, Los Angeles, USA
Bernhard Kainz	Imperial College London, UK
Marta Kersten-Oertel	Concordia University, Canada
Fahmi Khalifa	Mansoura University, Egypt
Seong Tae Kim	Kyung Hee University, Korea
Minjeong Kim	University of North Carolina at Greensboro, USA
Baiying Lei	Shenzhen University, China
Gang Li	University of North Carolina at Chapel Hill, USA

Fuyong Xing	University of Colorado Denver, USA
Ziyue Xu	NVIDIA, USA
Yanwu Xu	Baidu Inc., China
Pingkun Yan	Rensselaer Polytechnic Institute, USA
Guang Yang	Imperial College London, UK
Jianhua Yao	Tencent, China
Zhaozheng Yin	Stony Brook University, USA
Lequan Yu	University of Hong Kong, China
Yixuan Yuan	City University of Hong Kong, China
Ling Zhang	Alibaba Group, USA
Miaomiao Zhang	University of Virginia, USA
Ya Zhang	Shanghai Jiao Tong University, China
Rongchang Zhao	Central South University, China
Yitian Zhao	Chinese Academy of Sciences, China
Yefeng Zheng	Tencent Jarvis Lab, China
Guoyan Zheng	Shanghai Jiao Tong University, China
Luping Zhou	University of Sydney, Australia
Yuyin Zhou	Stanford University, USA
Dajiang Zhu	University of Texas at Arlington, USA
Lilla Zöllei	Massachusetts General Hospital, USA
Maria A. Zuluaga	EURECOM, France

Reviewers

Alireza Akhondi-asl
Fernando Arambula
Nicolas Boutry
Qilei Chen
Zhihao Chen
Javid Dadashkarimi
Marleen De Bruijne
Mohammad Eslami
Sayan Ghosal
Estibaliz Gómez-de-Mariscal
Charles Hatt
Yongxiang Huang
Samra Irshad
Anithapriya Krishnan
Rodney LaLonde
Jie Liu
Jinyang Liu
Qing Lyu
Hassan Mohy-ud-Din

Manas Nag
Tianye Niu
Seokhwan Oh
Theodoros Pissas
Harish RaviPrakash
Maria Sainz de Cea
Hai Su
Wenjun Tan
Fatmatulzehra Uslu
Fons van der Sommen
Gijs van Tulder
Dong Wei
Pengcheng Xi
Chen Yang
Kun Yuan
Hang Zhang
Wei Zhang
Yuyao Zhang
Tengda Zhao

Yingying Zhu
Yuemin Zhu
Alaa Eldin Abdelaal
Amir Abdi
Mazdak Abulnaga
Burak Acar
Iman Aganj
Priya Aggarwal
Ola Ahmad
Seyed-Ahmad Ahmadi
Euijoon Ahn
Faranak Akbarifar
Cem Akbaş
Saad Ullah Akram
Tajwar Aleef
Daniel Alexander
Hazrat Ali
Sharib Ali
Max Allan
Pablo Alvarez
Vincent Andrearczyk
Elsa Angelini
Sameer Antani
Michela Antonelli
Ignacio Arganda-Carreras
Mohammad Ali Armin
Josep Arnal
Md Ashikuzzaman
Mehdi Astaraki
Marc Aubreville
Chloé Audigier
Angelica Aviles-Rivero
Ruqayya Awan
Suyash Awate
Qinle Ba
Morteza Babaie
Meritxell Bach Cuadra
Hyeon-Min Bae
Junjie Bai
Wenjia Bai
Ujjwal Baid
Pradeep Bajracharya
Yaël Balbastre
Abhirup Banerjee
Sreya Banerjee

Shunxing Bao
Adrian Barbu
Sumana Basu
Deepti Bathula
Christian Baumgartner
John Baxter
Sharareh Bayat
Bahareh Behboodi
Hamid Behnam
Sutanu Bera
Christos Bergeles
Jose Bernal
Gabriel Bernardino
Alaa Bessadok
Riddhish Bhalodia
Indrani Bhattacharya
Chitresh Bhushan
Lei Bi
Qi Bi
Gui-Bin Bian
Alexander Bigalke
Ricardo Bigolin Lanfredi
Benjamin Billot
Ryoma Bise
Sangeeta Biswas
Stefano B. Blumberg
Sebastian Bodenstedt
Bhushan Borotikar
Ilaria Boscolo Galazzo
Behzad Bozorgtabar
Nadia Brancati
Katharina Breininger
Rupert Brooks
Tom Brosch
Mikael Brudfors
Qirong Bu
Ninon Burgos
Nikolay Burlutskiy
Michał Byra
Ryan Cabeen
Mariano Cabezas
Hongmin Cai
Jinzheng Cai
Weidong Cai
Sema Candemir

Qing Cao
Weiguo Cao
Yankun Cao
Aaron Carass
Ruben Cardenes
M. Jorge Cardoso
Owen Carmichael
Alessandro Casella
Matthieu Chabanas
Ahmad Chaddad
Jayasree Chakraborty
Sylvie Chambon
Yi Hao Chan
Ming-Ching Chang
Peng Chang
Violeta Chang
Sudhanya Chatterjee
Christos Chatzichristos
Antong Chen
Chao Chen
Chen Chen
Cheng Chen
Dongdong Chen
Fang Chen
Geng Chen
Hanbo Chen
Jianan Chen
Jianxu Chen
Jie Chen
Junxiang Chen
Junying Chen
Junyu Chen
Lei Chen
Li Chen
Liangjun Chen
Liyun Chen
Min Chen
Pingjun Chen
Qiang Chen
Runnan Chen
Shuai Chen
Xi Chen
Xiaoran Chen
Xin Chen
Xinjian Chen

Xuejin Chen
Yuanyuan Chen
Zhaolin Chen
Zhen Chen
Zhineng Chen
Zhixiang Chen
Erkang Cheng
Jianhong Cheng
Jun Cheng
Philip Chikontwe
Min-Kook Choi
Gary Christensen
Argyrios Christodoulidis
Stergios Christodoulidis
Albert Chung
Özgün Çiçek
Matthew Clarkson
Dana Cobzas
Jaume Coll-Font
Toby Collins
Olivier Commowick
Runmin Cong
Yulai Cong
Pierre-Henri Conze
Timothy Cootes
Teresa Correia
Pierrick Coupé
Hadrien Courtecuisse
Jeffrey Craley
Alessandro Crimi
Can Cui
Hejie Cui
Hui Cui
Zhiming Cui
Kathleen Curran
Claire Cury
Tobias Czempiel
Vedrana Dahl
Tareen Dawood
Laura Daza
Charles Delahunt
Herve Delingette
Ugur Demir
Liang-Jian Deng
Ruining Deng

Yang Deng
Cem Deniz
Felix Denzinger
Adrien Depeursinge
Hrishikesh Deshpande
Christian Desrosiers
Neel Dey
Anuja Dharmaratne
Li Ding
Xinghao Ding
Zhipeng Ding
Ines Domingues
Juan Pedro Dominguez-Morales
Mengjin Dong
Nanqing Dong
Sven Dorkenwald
Haoran Dou
Simon Drouin
Karen Drukker
Niharika D'Souza
Guodong Du
Lei Du
Dingna Duan
Hongyi Duanmu
Nicolas Duchateau
James Duncan
Nicha Dvornek
Dmitry V. Dylov
Oleh Dzyubachyk
Jan Egger
Alma Eguizabal
Gudmundur Einarsson
Ahmet Ekin
Ahmed Elazab
Ahmed Elnakib
Amr Elsawy
Mohamed Elsharkawy
Ertunc Erdil
Marius Erdt
Floris Ernst
Boris Escalante-Ramírez
Hooman Esfandiari
Nazila Esmaeili
Marco Esposito
Théo Estienne

Christian Ewert
Deng-Ping Fan
Xin Fan
Yonghui Fan
Yubo Fan
Chaowei Fang
Huihui Fang
Xi Fang
Yingying Fang
Zhenghan Fang
Mohsen Farzi
Hamid Fehri
Lina Felsner
Jianjiang Feng
Jun Feng
Ruibin Feng
Yuan Feng
Zishun Feng
Aaron Fenster
Henrique Fernandes
Ricardo Ferrari
Lukas Fischer
Antonio Foncubierta-Rodríguez
Nils Daniel Forkert
Wolfgang Freysinger
Bianca Freytag
Xueyang Fu
Yunguan Fu
Gareth Funka-Lea
Pedro Furtado
Ryo Furukawa
Laurent Gajny
Francesca Galassi
Adrian Galdran
Jiangzhang Gan
Yu Gan
Melanie Ganz
Dongxu Gao
Linlin Gao
Riqiang Gao
Siyuan Gao
Yunhe Gao
Zeyu Gao
Gautam Gare
Bao Ge

Rongjun Ge
Sairam Geethanath
Shiv Gehlot
Yasmeen George
Nils Gessert
Olivier Gevaert
Ramtin Gharleghi
Sandesh Ghimire
Andrea Giovannini
Gabriel Girard
Rémi Giraud
Ben Glocker
Ehsan Golkar
Arnold Gomez
Ricardo Gonzales
Camila Gonzalez
Cristina González
German Gonzalez
Sharath Gopal
Karthik Gopinath
Pietro Gori
Michael Götz
Shuiping Gou
Maged Goubran
Sobhan Goudarzi
Alejandro Granados
Mara Graziani
Yun Gu
Zaiwang Gu
Hao Guan
Dazhou Guo
Hengtao Guo
Jixiang Guo
Jun Guo
Pengfei Guo
Xiaoqing Guo
Yi Guo
Yuyu Guo
Vikash Gupta
Prashnna Gyawali
Stathis Hadjidemetriou
Fatemeh Haghighi
Justin Haldar
Mohammad Hamghalam
Kamal Hammouda

Bing Han
Liang Han
Seungjae Han
Xiaoguang Han
Zhongyi Han
Jonny Hancox
Lasse Hansen
Huaying Hao
Jinkui Hao
Xiaoke Hao
Mohammad Minhazul Haq
Nandinee Haq
Rabia Haq
Michael Hardisty
Nobuhiko Hata
Ali Hatamizadeh
Andreas Hauptmann
Huiguang He
Nanjun He
Shenghua He
Yuting He
Tobias Heimann
Stefan Heldmann
Sobhan Hemati
Alessa Hering
Monica Hernandez
Estefania Hernandez-Martin
Carlos Hernandez-Matas
Javier Herrera-Vega
Kilian Hett
David Ho
Yi Hong
Yoonmi Hong
Mohammad Reza Hosseinzadeh Taher
Benjamin Hou
Wentai Hou
William Hsu
Dan Hu
Rongyao Hu
Xiaoling Hu
Xintao Hu
Yan Hu
Ling Huang
Sharon Xiaolei Huang
Xiaoyang Huang

Yangsibo Huang
Yi-Jie Huang
Yijin Huang
Yixing Huang
Yue Huang
Zhi Huang
Ziyi Huang
Arnaud Huaulmé
Jiayu Huo
Raabid Hussain
Sarfaraz Hussein
Khoi Huynh
Seong Jae Hwang
Ilknur Icke
Kay Igwe
Abdullah Al Zubaer Imran
Ismail Irmakci
Benjamin Irving
Mohammad Shafkat Islam
Koichi Ito
Hayato Itoh
Yuji Iwahori
Mohammad Jafari
Andras Jakab
Amir Jamaludin
Mirek Janatka
Vincent Jaouen
Uditha Jarayathne
Ronnachai Jaroensri
Golara Javadi
Rohit Jena
Rachid Jennane
Todd Jensen
Debesh Jha
Ge-Peng Ji
Yuanfeng Ji
Zhanghexuan Ji
Haozhe Jia
Meirui Jiang
Tingting Jiang
Xiajun Jiang
Xiang Jiang
Zekun Jiang
Jianbo Jiao
Jieqing Jiao

Zhicheng Jiao
Chen Jin
Dakai Jin
Qiangguo Jin
Taisong Jin
Yueming Jin
Baoyu Jing
Bin Jing
Yaqub Jonmohamadi
Lie Ju
Yohan Jun
Alain Jungo
Manjunath K N
Abdolrahim Kadkhodamohammadi
Ali Kafaei Zad Tehrani
Dagmar Kainmueller
Siva Teja Kakileti
John Kalafut
Konstantinos Kamnitsas
Michael C. Kampffmeyer
Qingbo Kang
Neerav Karani
Turkay Kart
Satyananda Kashyap
Alexander Katzmann
Anees Kazi
Hengjin Ke
Hamza Kebiri
Erwan Kerrien
Hoel Kervadec
Farzad Khalvati
Bishesh Khanal
Pulkit Khandelwal
Maksim Kholiavchenko
Ron Kikinis
Daeseung Kim
Jae-Hun Kim
Jaeil Kim
Jinman Kim
Won Hwa Kim
Andrew King
Atilla Kiraly
Yoshiro Kitamura
Stefan Klein
Tobias Klinder

Lisa Koch
Satoshi Kondo
Bin Kong
Fanwei Kong
Ender Konukoglu
Aishik Konwer
Bongjin Koo
Ivica Kopriva
Kivanc Kose
Anna Kreshuk
Frithjof Kruggel
Thomas Kuestner
David Kügler
Hugo Kuijf
Arjan Kuijper
Kuldeep Kumar
Manuela Kunz
Holger Kunze
Tahsin Kurc
Anvar Kurmukov
Yoshihiro Kuroda
Jin Tae Kwak
Francesco La Rosa
Aymen Laadhari
Dmitrii Lachinov
Alain Lalande
Bennett Landman
Axel Largent
Carole Lartizien
Max-Heinrich Laves
Ho Hin Lee
Hyekyoung Lee
Jong Taek Lee
Jong-Hwan Lee
Soochahn Lee
Wen Hui Lei
Yiming Lei
Rogers Jeffrey Leo John
Juan Leon
Bo Li
Bowen Li
Chen Li
Hongming Li
Hongwei Li
Jian Li

Jianning Li
Jiayun Li
Jieyu Li
Junhua Li
Kang Li
Lei Li
Mengzhang Li
Qing Li
Quanzheng Li
Shaohua Li
Shulong Li
Weijian Li
Weikai Li
Wenyuan Li
Xiang Li
Xingyu Li
Xiu Li
Yang Li
Yuexiang Li
Yunxiang Li
Zeju Li
Zhang Li
Zhiyuan Li
Zhjin Li
Zi Li
Chunfeng Lian
Sheng Lian
Libin Liang
Peixian Liang
Yuan Liang
Haofu Liao
Hongen Liao
Ruizhi Liao
Wei Liao
Xiangyun Liao
Gilbert Lim
Hongxiang Lin
Jianyu Lin
Li Lin
Tiancheng Lin
Yiqun Lin
Zudi Lin
Claudia Lindner
Bin Liu
Bo Liu

Chuanbin Liu
Daochang Liu
Dong Liu
Dongnan Liu
Fenglin Liu
Han Liu
Hao Liu
Haozhe Liu
Hong Liu
Huafeng Liu
Huiye Liu
Jianfei Liu
Jiang Liu
Jingya Liu
Kefei Liu
Lihao Liu
Mengting Liu
Peirong Liu
Peng Liu
Qin Liu
Qun Liu
Shenghua Liu
Shuangjun Liu
Sidong Liu
Tianrui Liu
Xiao Liu
Xingtong Liu
Xinwen Liu
Xinyang Liu
Xinyu Liu
Yan Liu
Yanbei Liu
Yi Liu
Yikang Liu
Yong Liu
Yue Liu
Yuhang Liu
Zewen Liu
Zhe Liu
Andrea Loddo
Nicolas Loménie
Yonghao Long
Zhongjie Long
Daniel Lopes
Bin Lou

Nicolas Loy Rodas
Charles Lu
Huanxiang Lu
Xing Lu
Yao Lu
Yuhang Lu
Gongning Luo
Jie Luo
Jiebo Luo
Luyang Luo
Ma Luo
Xiangde Luo
Cuong Ly
Ilwoo Lyu
Yanjun Lyu
Yuanyuan Lyu
Sharath M S
Chunwei Ma
Hehuan Ma
Junbo Ma
Wenao Ma
Yuhui Ma
Anderson Maciel
S. Sara Mahdavi
Mohammed Mahmoud
Andreas Maier
Michail Mamalakis
Ilja Manakov
Brett Marinelli
Yassine Marrakchi
Fabio Martinez
Martin Maška
Tejas Sudharshan Mathai
Dimitrios Mavroeidis
Pau Medrano-Gracia
Raghav Mehta
Felix Meissen
Qingjie Meng
Yanda Meng
Martin Menten
Alexandre Merasli
Stijn Michielse
Leo Milecki
Fausto Milletari
Zhe Min

Jorg Peters
Terry Peters
Eike Petersen
Jens Petersen
Micha Pfeiffer
Dzung Pham
Hieu Pham
Ashish Phophalia
Tomasz Pieciak
Antonio Pinheiro
Kilian Pohl
Sebastian Pölsterl
Iulia A. Popescu
Alison Pouch
Prateek Prasanna
Raphael Prevost
Juan Prieto
Federica Proietto Salanitri
Sergi Pujades
Kumaradevan Punithakumar
Haikun Qi
Huan Qi
Buyue Qian
Yan Qiang
Yuchuan Qiao
Zhi Qiao
Fangbo Qin
Wenjian Qin
Yanguo Qin
Yulei Qin
Hui Qu
Kha Gia Quach
Tran Minh Quan
Sandro Queirós
Prashanth R.
Mehdi Rahim
Jagath Rajapakse
Kashif Rajpoot
Dhanesh Ramachandram
Xuming Ran
Hatem Rashwan
Daniele Ravì
Keerthi Sravan Ravi
Surreerat Reaungamornrat
Samuel Remedios

Yudan Ren
Mauricio Reyes
Constantino Reyes-Aldasoro
Hadrien Reynaud
David Richmond
Anne-Marie Rickmann
Laurent Risser
Leticia Rittner
Dominik Rivoir
Emma Robinson
Jessica Rodgers
Rafael Rodrigues
Robert Rohling
Lukasz Roszkowiak
Holger Roth
Karsten Roth
José Rouco
Daniel Rueckert
Danny Ruijters
Mirabela Rusu
Ario Sadafi
Shaheer Ullah Saeed
Monjoy Saha
Pranjal Sahu
Olivier Salvado
Ricardo Sanchez-Matilla
Robin Sandkuehler
Gianmarco Santini
Anil Kumar Sao
Duygu Sarikaya
Olivier Saut
Fabio Scarpa
Nico Scherf
Markus Schirmer
Alexander Schlaefer
Jerome Schmid
Julia Schnabel
Andreas Schuh
Christina Schwarz-Gsaxner
Martin Schweiger
Michaël Sdika
Suman Sedai
Matthias Seibold
Raghavendra Selvan
Sourya Sengupta

Carmen Serrano
Ahmed Shaffie
Keyur Shah
Rutwik Shah
Ahmed Shahin
Mohammad Abuzar Shaikh
S. Shailja
Shayan Shams
Hongming Shan
Xinxin Shan
Mostafa Sharifzadeh
Anuja Sharma
Harshita Sharma
Gregory Sharp
Li Shen
Liyue Shen
Mali Shen
Mingren Shen
Yiqing Shen
Ziyi Shen
Luyao Shi
Xiaoshuang Shi
Yiyu Shi
Hoo-Chang Shin
Boris Shirokikh
Suprosanna Shit
Suzanne Shontz
Yucheng Shu
Alberto Signoroni
Carlos Silva
Wilson Silva
Margarida Silveira
Vivek Singh
Sumedha Singla
Ayushi Sinha
Elena Sizikova
Rajath Soans
Hessam Sokooti
Hong Song
Weinan Song
Youyi Song
Aristeidis Sotiras
Bella Specktor
William Speier
Ziga Spiclin

Jon Sporring
Anuroop Sriram
Vinkle Srivastav
Lawrence Staib
Johannes Stegmaier
Joshua Stough
Danail Stoyanov
Justin Strait
Iain Styles
Ruisheng Su
Vaishnavi Subramanian
Gérard Subsol
Yao Sui
Heung-Il Suk
Shipra Suman
Jian Sun
Li Sun
Liyan Sun
Wenqing Sun
Yue Sun
Vaanathi Sundaresan
Kyung Sung
Yannick Suter
Raphael Sznitman
Eleonora Tagliabue
Roger Tam
Chaowei Tan
Hao Tang
Sheng Tang
Thomas Tang
Youbao Tang
Yucheng Tang
Zihao Tang
Rong Tao
Elias Tappeiner
Mickael Tardy
Giacomo Tarroni
Paul Thienphrapa
Stephen Thompson
Yu Tian
Aleksei Tiulpin
Tal Tlusty
Maryam Toloubidokhti
Jocelyne Troccaz
Roger Trullo

Chialing Tsai
Sudhakar Tummala
Régis Vaillant
Jeya Maria Jose Valanarasu
Juan Miguel Valverde
Thomas Varsavsky
Francisco Vasconcelos
Serge Vasylechko
S. Swaroop Vedula
Roberto Vega
Gonzalo Vegas Sanchez-Ferrero
Gopalkrishna Veni
Archana Venkataraman
Athanasios Vlontzos
Ingmar Voigt
Eugene Vorontsov
Xiaohua Wan
Bo Wang
Changmiao Wang
Chunliang Wang
Clinton Wang
Dadong Wang
Fan Wang
Guotai Wang
Haifeng Wang
Hong Wang
Hongkai Wang
Hongyu Wang
Hu Wang
Juan Wang
Junyan Wang
Ke Wang
Li Wang
Liansheng Wang
Manning Wang
Nizhuan Wang
Qiuli Wang
Renzhen Wang
Rongguang Wang
Ruixuan Wang
Runze Wang
Shujun Wang
Shuo Wang
Shuqiang Wang
Tianchen Wang

Tongxin Wang
Wenzhe Wang
Xi Wang
Xiangdong Wang
Xiaosong Wang
Yalin Wang
Yan Wang
Yi Wang
Yixin Wang
Zeyi Wang
Zuhui Wang
Jonathan Weber
Donglai Wei
Dongming Wei
Lifang Wei
Wolfgang Wein
Michael Wels
Cédric Wemmert
Matthias Wilms
Adam Wittek
Marek Wodzinski
Julia Wolleb
Jonghye Woo
Chongruo Wu
Chunpeng Wu
Ji Wu
Jianfeng Wu
Jie Ying Wu
Jiong Wu
Junde Wu
Pengxiang Wu
Xia Wu
Xiyin Wu
Yawen Wu
Ye Wu
Yicheng Wu
Zhengwang Wu
Tobias Wuerfl
James Xia
Siyu Xia
Yingda Xia
Lei Xiang
Tiange Xiang
Deqiang Xiao
Yiming Xiao

Hongtao Xie
Jianyang Xie
Lingxi Xie
Long Xie
Weidi Xie
Yiting Xie
Yutong Xie
Fangxu Xing
Jiarui Xing
Xiaohan Xing
Chenchu Xu
Hai Xu
Hongming Xu
Jiaqi Xu
Junshen Xu
Kele Xu
Min Xu
Minfeng Xu
Moucheng Xu
Qinwei Xu
Rui Xu
Xiaowei Xu
Xinxing Xu
Xuanang Xu
Yanwu Xu
Yanyu Xu
Yongchao Xu
Zhe Xu
Zhenghua Xu
Zhoubing Xu
Kai Xuan
Cheng Xue
Jie Xue
Wufeng Xue
Yuan Xue
Faridah Yahya
Chaochao Yan
Jiangpeng Yan
Ke Yan
Ming Yan
Qingsen Yan
Yuguang Yan
Zengqiang Yan
Baoyao Yang
Changchun Yang

Chao-Han Huck Yang
Dong Yang
Fan Yang
Feng Yang
Fengting Yang
Ge Yang
Guanyu Yang
Hao-Hsiang Yang
Heran Yang
Hongxu Yang
Huijuan Yang
Jiawei Yang
Jinyu Yang
Lin Yang
Peng Yang
Pengshuai Yang
Xiaohui Yang
Xin Yang
Yan Yang
Yifan Yang
Yujiu Yang
Zhicheng Yang
Jiangchao Yao
Jiawen Yao
Li Yao
Linlin Yao
Qingsong Yao
Chuyang Ye
Dong Hye Ye
Huihui Ye
Menglong Ye
Youngjin Yoo
Chenyu You
Haichao Yu
Hanchao Yu
Jinhua Yu
Ke Yu
Qi Yu
Renping Yu
Thomas Yu
Xiaowei Yu
Zhen Yu
Pengyu Yuan
Paul Yushkevich
Ghada Zamzmi

Ramy Zeineldin
Dong Zeng
Rui Zeng
Zhiwei Zhai
Kun Zhan
Bokai Zhang
Chaoyi Zhang
Daoqiang Zhang
Fa Zhang
Fan Zhang
Hao Zhang
Jianpeng Zhang
Jiawei Zhang
Jingqing Zhang
Jingyang Zhang
Jiong Zhang
Jun Zhang
Ke Zhang
Lefei Zhang
Lei Zhang
Lichi Zhang
Lu Zhang
Ning Zhang
Pengfei Zhang
Qiang Zhang
Rongzhao Zhang
Ruipeng Zhang
Ruisi Zhang
Shengping Zhang
Shihao Zhang
Tianyang Zhang
Tong Zhang
Tuo Zhang
Wen Zhang
Xiaoran Zhang
Xin Zhang
Yanfu Zhang
Yao Zhang
Yi Zhang
Yongqin Zhang
You Zhang
Youshan Zhang
Yu Zhang
Yubo Zhang
Yue Zhang

Yulun Zhang
Yundong Zhang
Yunyan Zhang
Yuxin Zhang
Zheng Zhang
Zhicheng Zhang
Can Zhao
Changchen Zhao
Fenqiang Zhao
He Zhao
Jianfeng Zhao
Jun Zhao
Li Zhao
Liang Zhao
Lin Zhao
Qingyu Zhao
Shen Zhao
Shijie Zhao
Tianyi Zhao
Wei Zhao
Xiaole Zhao
Xuandong Zhao
Yang Zhao
Yue Zhao
Zixu Zhao
Ziyuan Zhao
Xingjian Zhen
Haiyong Zheng
Hao Zheng
Kang Zheng
Qinghe Zheng
Shenhai Zheng
Yalin Zheng
Yinqiang Zheng
Yushan Zheng
Tao Zhong
Zichun Zhong
Bo Zhou
Haoyin Zhou
Hong-Yu Zhou
Huiyu Zhou
Kang Zhou
Qin Zhou
S. Kevin Zhou
Sihang Zhou

Tao Zhou
Tianfei Zhou
Wei Zhou
Xiao-Hu Zhou
Xiao-Yun Zhou
Yanning Zhou
Yaxuan Zhou
Youjia Zhou
Yukun Zhou
Zhiguo Zhou
Zongwei Zhou
Dongxiao Zhu
Haidong Zhu
Hancan Zhu

Lei Zhu
Qikui Zhu
Xiaofeng Zhu
Xinliang Zhu
Zhonghang Zhu
Zhuotun Zhu
Veronika Zimmer
David Zimmerer
Weiwei Zong
Yukai Zou
Lianrui Zuo
Gerald Zwettler
Reyer Zwiggelaar

Outstanding Area Chairs

Ester Bonmati   University College London, UK
Tolga Tasdizen   University of Utah, USA
Yanwu Xu   Baidu Inc., China

Outstanding Reviewers

Seyed-Ahmad Ahmadi   NVIDIA, Germany
Katharina Breininger   Friedrich-Alexander-Universität
                       Erlangen-Nürnberg, Germany
Mariano Cabezas   University of Sydney, Australia
Nicha Dvornek   Yale University, USA
Adrian Galdran   Universitat Pompeu Fabra, Spain
Alexander Katzmann   Siemens Healthineers, Germany
Tony C. W. Mok   Hong Kong University of Science and
                       Technology, China
Sérgio Pereira   Lunit Inc., Korea
David Richmond   Genentech, USA
Dominik Rivoir   National Center for Tumor Diseases (NCT)
                       Dresden, Germany
Fons van der Sommen   Eindhoven University of Technology,
                       the Netherlands
Yushan Zheng   Beihang University, China

Honorable Mentions (Reviewers)

Chloé Audigier   Siemens Healthineers, Switzerland
Qinle Ba   Roche, USA

Pulkit Khandelwal	University of Pennsylvania, USA
Andrew King	King's College London, UK
Stefan Klein	Erasmus MC, the Netherlands
Ender Konukoglu	ETH Zurich, Switzerland
Ivica Kopriva	Rudjer Boskovich Institute, Croatia
David Kügler	German Center for Neurodegenerative Diseases, Germany
Manuela Kunz	National Research Council Canada, Canada
Gilbert Lim	National University of Singapore, Singapore
Tiancheng Lin	Shanghai Jiao Tong University, China
Bin Lou	Siemens Healthineers, USA
Hehuan Ma	University of Texas at Arlington, USA
Ilja Manakov	ImFusion, Germany
Felix Meissen	Technische Universität München, Germany
Martin Menten	Imperial College London, UK
Leo Milecki	CentraleSupelec, France
Lia Morra	Politecnico di Torino, Italy
Dominik Neumann	Siemens Healthineers, Germany
Chinedu Nwoye	University of Strasbourg, France
Masahiro Oda	Nagoya University, Japan
Sebastian Otálora	Bern University Hospital, Switzerland
Michal Ozery-Flato	IBM Research, Israel
Egor Panfilov	University of Oulu, Finland
Bartlomiej Papiez	University of Oxford, UK
Nripesh Parajuli	Caption Health, USA
Sanghyun Park	DGIST, Korea
Terry Peters	Robarts Research Institute, Canada
Theodoros Pissas	University College London, UK
Raphael Prevost	ImFusion, Germany
Yulei Qin	Tencent, China
Emma Robinson	King's College London, UK
Robert Rohling	University of British Columbia, Canada
José Rouco	University of A Coruña, Spain
Jerome Schmid	HES-SO University of Applied Sciences and Arts Western Switzerland, Switzerland
Christina Schwarz-Gsaxner	Graz University of Technology, Austria
Liyue Shen	Stanford University, USA
Luyao Shi	IBM Research, USA
Vivek Singh	Siemens Healthineers, USA
Weinan Song	UCLA, USA
Aristeidis Sotiras	Washington University in St. Louis, USA
Danail Stoyanov	University College London, UK

Ruisheng Su	Erasmus MC, the Netherlands
Liyan Sun	Xiamen University, China
Raphael Sznitman	University of Bern, Switzerland
Elias Tappeiner	UMIT - Private University for Health Sciences, Medical Informatics and Technology, Austria
Mickael Tardy	Hera-MI, France
Juan Miguel Valverde	University of Eastern Finland, Finland
Eugene Vorontsov	Polytechnique Montreal, Canada
Bo Wang	CtrsVision, USA
Tongxin Wang	Meta Platforms, Inc., USA
Yan Wang	Sichuan University, China
Yixin Wang	University of Chinese Academy of Sciences, China
Jie Ying Wu	Johns Hopkins University, USA
Lei Xiang	Subtle Medical Inc, USA
Jiaqi Xu	The Chinese University of Hong Kong, China
Zhoubing Xu	Siemens Healthineers, USA
Ke Yan	Alibaba DAMO Academy, China
Baoyao Yang	School of Computers, Guangdong University of Technology, China
Changchun Yang	Delft University of Technology, the Netherlands
Yujiu Yang	Tsinghua University, China
Youngjin Yoo	Siemens Healthineers, USA
Ning Zhang	Bloomberg, USA
Jianfeng Zhao	Western University, Canada
Tao Zhou	Nanjing University of Science and Technology, China
Veronika Zimmer	Technical University Munich, Germany

Mentorship Program (Mentors)

Ulas Bagci	Northwestern University, USA
Kayhan Batmanghelich	University of Pittsburgh, USA
Hrvoje Bogunovic	Medical University of Vienna, Austria
Ninon Burgos	CNRS - Paris Brain Institute, France
Hao Chen	Hong Kong University of Science and Technology, China
Jun Cheng	Institute for Infocomm Research, Singapore
Li Cheng	University of Alberta, Canada
Aasa Feragen	Technical University of Denmark, Denmark
Zhifan Gao	Sun Yat-sen University, China
Stamatia Giannarou	Imperial College London, UK
Sharon Huang	Pennsylvania State University, USA

Anand Joshi	University of Southern California, USA
Bernhard Kainz	Friedrich-Alexander-Universität Erlangen-Nürnberg, Germany and Imperial College London, UK
Baiying Lei	Shenzhen University, China
Karim Lekadir	Universitat de Barcelona, Spain
Xiaoxiao Li	University of British Columbia, Canada
Jianming Liang	Arizona State University, USA
Marius George Linguraru	Children's National Hospital, George Washington University, USA
Anne Martel	University of Toronto, Canada
Antonio Porras	University of Colorado Anschutz Medical Campus, USA
Chen Qin	University of Edinburgh, UK
Julia Schnabel	Helmholtz Munich, TU Munich, Germany and King's College London, UK
Yang Song	University of New South Wales, Australia
Tanveer Syeda-Mahmood	IBM Research - Almaden Labs, USA
Pallavi Tiwari	University of Wisconsin Madison, USA
Mathias Unberath	Johns Hopkins University, USA
Maria Vakalopoulou	CentraleSupelec, France
Harini Veeraraghavan	Memorial Sloan Kettering Cancer Center, USA
Satish Viswanath	Case Western Reserve University, USA
Guang Yang	Imperial College London, UK
Lequan Yu	University of Hong Kong, China
Miaomiao Zhang	University of Virginia, USA
Rongchang Zhao	Central South University, China
Luping Zhou	University of Sydney, Australia
Lilla Zollei	Massachusetts General Hospital, Harvard Medical School, USA
Maria A. Zuluaga	EURECOM, France

Contents – Part II

Computational (Integrative) Pathology

Semi-supervised Histological Image Segmentation via Hierarchical
Consistency Enforcement 3
  Qiangguo Jin, Hui Cui, Changming Sun, Jiangbin Zheng, Leyi Wei,
  Zhenyu Fang, Zhaopeng Meng, and Ran Su

Federated Stain Normalization for Computational Pathology 14
  Nicolas Wagner, Moritz Fuchs, Yuri Tolkach, and Anirban Mukhopadhyay

DGMIL: Distribution Guided Multiple Instance Learning for Whole Slide
Image Classification 24
  Linhao Qu, Xiaoyuan Luo, Shaolei Liu, Manning Wang, and Zhijian Song

ReMix: A General and Efficient Framework for Multiple Instance
Learning Based Whole Slide Image Classification 35
  Jiawei Yang, Hanbo Chen, Yu Zhao, Fan Yang, Yao Zhang, Lei He,
  and Jianhua Yao

S^3R: Self-supervised Spectral Regression for Hyperspectral
Histopathology Image Classification 46
  Xingran Xie, Yan Wang, and Qingli Li

Distilling Knowledge from Topological Representations for Pathological
Complete Response Prediction 56
  Shiyi Du, Qicheng Lao, Qingbo Kang, Yiyue Li, Zekun Jiang,
  Yanfeng Zhao, and Kang Li

SETMIL: Spatial Encoding Transformer-Based Multiple Instance
Learning for Pathological Image Analysis 66
  Yu Zhao, Zhenyu Lin, Kai Sun, Yidan Zhang, Junzhou Huang,
  Liansheng Wang, and Jianhua Yao

Clinical-Realistic Annotation for Histopathology Images with Probabilistic
Semi-supervision: A Worst-Case Study 77
  Ziyue Xu, Andriy Myronenko, Dong Yang, Holger R. Roth, Can Zhao,
  Xiaosong Wang, and Daguang Xu

End-to-End Learning for Image-Based Detection of Molecular Alterations
in Digital Pathology 88
    *Marvin Teichmann, Andre Aichert, Hanibal Bohnenberger,
    Philipp Ströbel, and Tobias Heimann*

S5CL: Unifying Fully-Supervised, Self-supervised, and Semi-supervised
Learning Through Hierarchical Contrastive Learning 99
    Manuel Tran, Sophia J. Wagner, Melanie Boxberg, and Tingying Peng

Sample Hardness Based Gradient Loss for Long-Tailed Cervical Cell
Detection 109
    *Minmin Liu, Xuechen Li, Xiangbo Gao, Junliang Chen, Linlin Shen,
    and Huisi Wu*

Test-Time Image-to-Image Translation Ensembling Improves
Out-of-Distribution Generalization in Histopathology 120
    Marin Scalbert, Maria Vakalopoulou, and Florent Couzinié-Devy

Predicting Molecular Traits from Tissue Morphology Through
Self-interactive Multi-instance Learning 130
    *Yang Hu, Korsuk Sirinukunwattana, Kezia Gaitskell, Ruby Wood,
    Clare Verrill, and Jens Rittscher*

InsMix: Towards Realistic Generative Data Augmentation for Nuclei
Instance Segmentation 140
    Yi Lin, Zeyu Wang, Kwang-Ting Cheng, and Hao Chen

Improved Domain Generalization for Cell Detection in Histopathology
Images via Test-Time Stain Augmentation 150
    Chundan Xu, Ziqi Wen, Zhiwen Liu, and Chuyang Ye

Transformer Based Multiple Instance Learning for Weakly Supervised
Histopathology Image Segmentation 160
    *Ziniu Qian, Kailu Li, Maode Lai, Eric I-Chao Chang, Bingzheng Wei,
    Yubo Fan, and Yan Xu*

GradMix for Nuclei Segmentation and Classification in Imbalanced
Pathology Image Datasets 171
    Tan Nhu Nhat Doan, Kyungeun Kim, Boram Song, and Jin Tae Kwak

Spatial-Hierarchical Graph Neural Network with Dynamic Structure
Learning for Histological Image Classification 181
    *Wentai Hou, Helong Huang, Qiong Peng, Rongshan Yu, Lequan Yu,
    and Liansheng Wang*

Gigapixel Whole-Slide Images Classification Using Locally Supervised
Learning 192
  Jingwei Zhang, Xin Zhang, Ke Ma, Rajarsi Gupta, Joel Saltz,
  Maria Vakalopoulou, and Dimitris Samaras

Whole Slide Cervical Cancer Screening Using Graph Attention Network
and Supervised Contrastive Learning 202
  Xin Zhang, Maosong Cao, Sheng Wang, Jiayin Sun, Xiangshan Fan,
  Qian Wang, and Lichi Zhang

RandStainNA: Learning Stain-Agnostic Features from Histology Slides
by Bridging Stain Augmentation and Normalization 212
  Yiqing Shen, Yulin Luo, Dinggang Shen, and Jing Ke

Identify Consistent Imaging Genomic Biomarkers for Characterizing
the Survival-Associated Interactions Between Tumor-Infiltrating
Lymphocytes and Tumors 222
  Yingli Zuo, Yawen Wu, Zixiao Lu, Qi Zhu, Kun Huang, Daoqiang Zhang,
  and Wei Shao

Semi-supervised PR Virtual Staining for Breast Histopathological Images 232
  Bowei Zeng, Yiyang Lin, Yifeng Wang, Yang Chen, Jiuyang Dong, Xi Li,
  and Yongbing Zhang

Benchmarking the Robustness of Deep Neural Networks to Common
Corruptions in Digital Pathology 242
  Yunlong Zhang, Yuxuan Sun, Honglin Li, Sunyi Zheng, Chenglu Zhu,
  and Lin Yang

Weakly Supervised Segmentation by Tensor Graph Learning for Whole
Slide Images 253
  Qinghua Zhang and Zhao Chen

Test Time Transform Prediction for Open Set Histopathological Image
Recognition 263
  Adrian Galdran, Katherine J. Hewitt, Narmin Ghaffari Laleh,
  Jakob N. Kather, Gustavo Carneiro, and Miguel A. González Ballester

Lesion-Aware Contrastive Representation Learning for Histopathology
Whole Slide Images Analysis 273
  Jun Li, Yushan Zheng, Kun Wu, Jun Shi, Fengying Xie, and Zhiguo Jiang

Kernel Attention Transformer (KAT) for Histopathology Whole Slide
Image Classification 283
  Yushan Zheng, Jun Li, Jun Shi, Fengying Xie, and Zhiguo Jiang

Joint Region-Attention and Multi-scale Transformer for Microsatellite
Instability Detection from Whole Slide Images in Gastrointestinal Cancer 293
    Zhilong Lv, Rui Yan, Yuexiao Lin, Ying Wang, and Fa Zhang

Self-supervised Pre-training for Nuclei Segmentation 303
    Mohammad Minhazul Haq and Junzhou Huang

LifeLonger: A Benchmark for Continual Disease Classification 314
    Mohammad Mahdi Derakhshani, Ivona Najdenkoska,
    Tom van Sonsbeek, Xiantong Zhen, Dwarikanath Mahapatra,
    Marcel Worring, and Cees G. M. Snoek

Unsupervised Nuclei Segmentation Using Spatial Organization Priors 325
    Loïc Le Bescond, Marvin Lerousseau, Ingrid Garberis, Fabrice André,
    Stergios Christodoulidis, Maria Vakalopoulou, and Hugues Talbot

Visual Deep Learning-Based Explanation for Neuritic Plaques
Segmentation in Alzheimer's Disease Using Weakly Annotated Whole
Slide Histopathological Images 336
    Gabriel Jimenez, Anuradha Kar, Mehdi Ounissi, Léa Ingrassia,
    Susana Boluda, Benoît Delatour, Lev Stimmer, and Daniel Racoceanu

MaNi: Maximizing Mutual Information for Nuclei Cross-Domain
Unsupervised Segmentation 345
    Yash Sharma, Sana Syed, and Donald E. Brown

Region-Guided CycleGANs for Stain Transfer in Whole Slide Images 356
    Joseph Boyd, Irène Villa, Marie-Christine Mathieu, Eric Deutsch,
    Nikos Paragios, Maria Vakalopoulou, and Stergios Christodoulidis

Uncertainty Aware Sampling Framework of Weak-Label Learning
for Histology Image Classification 366
    Asmaa Aljuhani, Ishya Casukhela, Jany Chan, David Liebner,
    and Raghu Machiraju

Local Attention Graph-Based Transformer for Multi-target Genetic
Alteration Prediction 377
    Daniel Reisenbüchler, Sophia J. Wagner, Melanie Boxberg,
    and Tingying Peng

Incorporating Intratumoral Heterogeneity into Weakly-Supervised Deep
Learning Models via Variance Pooling 387
    Iain Carmichael, Andrew H. Song, Richard J. Chen,
    Drew F. K. Williamson, Tiffany Y. Chen, and Faisal Mahmood

Prostate Cancer Histology Synthesis Using StyleGAN Latent Space
Annotation 398
Gagandeep B. Daroach, Savannah R. Duenweg, Michael Brehler,
Allison K. Lowman, Kenneth A. Iczkowski, Kenneth M. Jacobsohn,
Josiah A. Yoder, and Peter S. LaViolette

Fast FF-to-FFPE Whole Slide Image Translation via Laplacian Pyramid
and Contrastive Learning 409
Lei Fan, Arcot Sowmya, Erik Meijering, and Yang Song

Feature Re-calibration Based Multiple Instance Learning for Whole Slide
Image Classification 420
Philip Chikontwe, Soo Jeong Nam, Heounjeong Go, Meejeong Kim,
Hyun Jung Sung, and Sang Hyun Park

Computational Anatomy and Physiology

Physiological Model Based Deep Learning Framework for Cardiac TMP
Recovery 433
Xufeng Huang, Chengjin Yu, and Huafeng Liu

DentalPointNet: Landmark Localization on High-Resolution 3D Digital
Dental Models 444
Yankun Lang, Xiaoyang Chen, Hannah H. Deng, Tianshu Kuang,
Joshua C. Barber, Jaime Gateno, Pew-Thian Yap, and James J. Xia

Landmark-Free Statistical Shape Modeling Via Neural Flow Deformations 453
David Lüdke, Tamaz Amiranashvili, Felix Ambellan, Ivan Ezhov,
Bjoern H. Menze, and Stefan Zachow

Learning Shape Distributions from Large Databases of Healthy Organs:
Applications to Zero-Shot and Few-Shot Abnormal Pancreas Detection 464
Rebeca Vétil, Clément Abi-Nader, Alexandre Bône,
Marie-Pierre Vullierme, Marc-Michel Rohé, Pietro Gori,
and Isabelle Bloch

From Images to Probabilistic Anatomical Shapes: A Deep Variational
Bottleneck Approach 474
Jadie Adams and Shireen Elhabian

Opthalmology

Structure-Consistent Restoration Network for Cataract Fundus Image
Enhancement 487
*Heng Li, Haofeng Liu, Huazhu Fu, Hai Shu, Yitian Zhao, Xiaoling Luo,
Yan Hu, and Jiang Liu*

Unsupervised Domain Adaptive Fundus Image Segmentation
with Category-Level Regularization 497
*Wei Feng, Lin Wang, Lie Ju, Xin Zhao, Xin Wang, Xiaoyu Shi,
and Zongyuan Ge*

Degradation-Invariant Enhancement of Fundus Images via Pyramid
Constraint Network 507
*Haofeng Liu, Heng Li, Huazhu Fu, Ruoxiu Xiao, Yunshu Gao, Yan Hu,
and Jiang Liu*

A Spatiotemporal Model for Precise and Efficient Fully-Automatic 3D
Motion Correction in OCT 517
*Stefan Ploner, Siyu Chen, Jungeun Won, Lennart Husvogt,
Katharina Breininger, Julia Schottenhamml, James Fujimoto,
and Andreas Maier*

DA-Net: Dual Branch Transformer and Adaptive Strip Upsampling
for Retinal Vessels Segmentation 528
*Changwei Wang, Rongtao Xu, Shibiao Xu, Weiliang Meng,
and Xiaopeng Zhang*

Visual Explanations for the Detection of Diabetic Retinopathy from Retinal
Fundus Images 539
*Valentyn Boreiko, Indu Ilanchezian, Murat Seçkin Ayhan, Sarah Müller,
Lisa M. Koch, Hanna Faber, Philipp Berens, and Matthias Hein*

Multidimensional Hypergraph on Delineated Retinal Features
for Pathological Myopia Task 550
*Bilha Githinji, Lei Shao, Lin An, Hao Zhang, Fang Li, Li Dong,
Lan Ma, Yuhan Dong, Yongbing Zhang, Wen B. Wei, and Peiwu Qin*

Unsupervised Lesion-Aware Transfer Learning for Diabetic Retinopathy
Grading in Ultra-Wide-Field Fundus Photography 560
*Yanmiao Bai, Jinkui Hao, Huazhu Fu, Yan Hu, Xinting Ge, Jiang Liu,
Yitian Zhao, and Jiong Zhang*

Local-Region and Cross-Dataset Contrastive Learning for Retinal Vessel
Segmentation 571
    Rui Xu, Jiaxin Zhao, Xinchen Ye, Pengcheng Wu, Zhihui Wang,
    Haojie Li, and Yen-Wei Chen

Y-Net: A Spatiospectral Dual-Encoder Network for Medical Image
Segmentation 582
    Azade Farshad, Yousef Yeganeh, Peter Gehlbach, and Nassir Navab

Camera Adaptation for Fundus-Image-Based CVD Risk Estimation 593
    Zhihong Lin, Danli Shi, Donghao Zhang, Xianwen Shang,
    Mingguang He, and Zongyuan Ge

Opinions Vary? Diagnosis First! 604
    Junde Wu, Huihui Fang, Dalu Yang, Zhaowei Wang, Wenshuo Zhou,
    Fangxin Shang, Yehui Yang, and Yanwu Xu

Learning Self-calibrated Optic Disc and Cup Segmentation
from Multi-rater Annotations 614
    Junde Wu, Huihui Fang, Zhaowei Wang, Dalu Yang, Yehui Yang,
    Fangxin Shang, Wenshuo Zhou, and Yanwu Xu

TINC: Temporally Informed Non-contrastive Learning for Disease
Progression Modeling in Retinal OCT Volumes 625
    Taha Emre, Arunava Chakravarty, Antoine Rivail, Sophie Riedl,
    Ursula Schmidt-Erfurth, and Hrvoje Bogunović

DRGen: Domain Generalization in Diabetic Retinopathy Classification 635
    Mohammad Atwany and Mohammad Yaqub

Frequency-Aware Inverse-Consistent Deep Learning for OCT-Angiogram
Super-Resolution 645
    Weiwen Zhang, Dawei Yang, Carol Y. Cheung, and Hao Chen

A Multi-task Network with Weight Decay Skip Connection Training
for Anomaly Detection in Retinal Fundus Images 656
    Wentian Zhang, Xu Sun, Yuexiang Li, Haozhe Liu, Nanjun He, Feng Liu,
    and Yefeng Zheng

Multiscale Unsupervised Retinal Edema Area Segmentation in OCT Images ... 667
    Wenguang Yuan, Donghuan Lu, Dong Wei, Munan Ning, and Yefeng Zheng

SeATrans: Learning Segmentation-Assisted Diagnosis Model
via Transformer 677
    Junde Wu, Huihui Fang, Fangxin Shang, Dalu Yang, Zhaowei Wang,
    Jing Gao, Yehui Yang, and Yanwu Xu

Screening of Dementia on OCTA Images via Multi-projection Consistency
and Complementarity 688
    Xingyue Wang, Heng Li, Zunjie Xiao, Huazhu Fu, Yitian Zhao,
    Richu Jin, Shuting Zhang, William Robert Kwapong, Ziyi Zhang,
    Hanpei Miao, and Jiang Liu

Noise Transfer for Unsupervised Domain Adaptation of Retinal OCT
Images 699
    Valentin Koch, Olle Holmberg, Hannah Spitzer, Johannes Schiefelbein,
    Ben Asani, Michael Hafner, and Fabian J. Theis

Long-Tailed Multi-label Retinal Diseases Recognition via Relational
Learning and Knowledge Distillation 709
    Qian Zhou, Hua Zou, and Zhongyuan Wang

Fetal Imaging

Weakly Supervised Online Action Detection for Infant General Movements 721
    Tongyi Luo, Jia Xiao, Chuncao Zhang, Siheng Chen, Yuan Tian,
    Guangjun Yu, Kang Dang, and Xiaowei Ding

Super-Focus: Domain Adaptation for Embryo Imaging via Self-supervised
Focal Plane Regression 732
    Chloe He, Céline Jacques, Jérôme Chambost, Jonas Malmsten,
    Koen Wouters, Thomas Fréour, Nikica Zaninovic, Cristina Hickman,
    and Francisco Vasconcelos

SUPER-IVIM-DC: Intra-voxel Incoherent Motion Based Fetal Lung
Maturity Assessment from Limited DWI Data Using Supervised Learning
Coupled with Data-Consistency 743
    Noam Korngut, Elad Rotman, Onur Afacan, Sila Kurugol,
    Yael Zaffrani-Reznikov, Shira Nemirovsky-Rotman, Simon Warfield,
    and Moti Freiman

Automated Classification of General Movements in Infants Using
Two-Stream Spatiotemporal Fusion Network 753
    Yuki Hashimoto, Akira Furui, Koji Shimatani, Maura Casadio,
    Paolo Moretti, Pietro Morasso, and Toshio Tsuji

Author Index 763

Computational (Integrative) Pathology

Semi-supervised Histological Image Segmentation via Hierarchical Consistency Enforcement

Qiangguo Jin[1], Hui Cui[2], Changming Sun[3], Jiangbin Zheng[1], Leyi Wei[6], Zhenyu Fang[1], Zhaopeng Meng[4,5], and Ran Su[4(✉)]

[1] School of Software, Northwestern Polytechnical University, Xi'an, Shaanxi, China
[2] Department of Computer Science and Information Technology, La Trobe University, Melbourne, Australia
[3] CSIRO Data61, Sydney, Australia
[4] School of Computer Software, College of Intelligence and Computing, Tianjin University, Tianjin, China
ran.su@tju.edu.cn
[5] Tianjin University of Traditional Chinese Medicine, Tianjin, China
[6] School of Software, Shandong University, Shandong, China

Abstract. Acquiring pixel-level annotations for histological image segmentation is time- and labor- consuming. Semi-supervised learning enables learning from the unlabeled and limited amount of labeled data. A challenging issue is the inconsistent and uncertain predictions on unlabeled data. To enforce invariant predictions over the perturbations applied to the hidden feature space, we propose a Mean-Teacher based hierarchical consistency enforcement (HCE) framework and a novel hierarchical consistency loss (HC-loss) with learnable and self-guided mechanisms. Specifically, the HCE takes the perturbed versions of the hierarchical features from the encoder as input to the auxiliary decoders, and encourages the predictions of the auxiliary decoders and the main decoder to be consistent. The HC-loss facilitates the teacher model to generate reliable guidance and enhances the consistency among all the decoders of the student model. The proposed method is simple, yet effective, which can easily be extended to other frameworks. The quantitative and qualitative experimental results indicate the effectiveness of the hierarchical consistency enforcement on the MoNuSeg and CRAG datasets.

Keywords: Hierarchical consistency enforcement · Semi-supervised learning · Histological image segmentation

1 Introduction

Accurate segmentation of cells and glands from histological images is an essential yet challenging task in computer-aided diagnosis [3,9,17,18,21]. With a large amount of labeled data, deep learning has achieved state-of-the-art (SOTA) performance on histological image segmentation tasks [11]. A challenging issue in histological image analysis is that the data-hungry deep learning model requires high-quality and large amounts

© The Author(s), under exclusive license to Springer Nature Switzerland AG 2022
L. Wang et al. (Eds.): MICCAI 2022, LNCS 13432, pp. 3–13, 2022.
https://doi.org/10.1007/978-3-031-16434-7_1

of well-annotated data. Acquiring well-annotated data, however, is a time-consuming and labor-intensive task for specialists with domain knowledge. To tackle this issue, semi-supervised learning (SSL) is proposed to learn from a limited amount of labeled data and unlabeled data at the same time.

A challenging issue in SSL is to improve the consistency between labeled and unlabeled data. In recent medical image analysis, considerable effort has been devoted to this issue [6,19,20]. For instance, Yu et al. [20] utilized unlabeled data by restricting the consistent prediction of a Mean-Teacher [12] architecture under different perturbations. Furthermore, a transformation-consistent strategy to enhance the regularization in a self-ensembling model is introduced by Li et al. [6], where the perturbations in the input and output spaces were constrained. Xie et al. [19] proposed a segmentation network (S-Net) and a pairwise relation network (PR-Net) for gland segmentation. Xia et al. [16] jointed SSL and unsupervised domain adaptation (DA) in a unified network named uncertainty-aware multi-view co-training (UMCT) for 3D pancreas and multi-organ segmentation.

The consistency training approaches mentioned above showed promising performance in various medical image analysis tasks for leveraging unlabeled data under perturbations. However, existing consistency training approaches mainly focus on formulating perturbations applied to the input space and high-level feature space [6,15], which neglect perturbations in the hidden feature space of the hierarchical deep network architecture [8]. Besides, in the Mean-Teacher architecture, the teacher model is usually used for generating targets for the student. It is, however, difficult to determine whether the teacher model provides more accurate results than the student model or not [15].

To address these issues, we propose a Mean-Teacher based hierarchical consistency enforcement (HCE) framework (as shown in Fig. 1) for histological image segmentation. The HCE architecture consists of three major components: (1) a basic teacher-student model for semi-supervised segmentation, (2) an HCE module to enforce hierarchical consistency during training, and (3) a hierarchical consistency loss (HC-loss) function. The HCE module is designed to boost the learning ability of the student model via modeling the perturbations over the hierarchical hidden feature space in the encoder. The novel HC-loss, which consists of a learnable hierarchical consistency loss and a self-guided hierarchical consistency loss function, is proposed for two purposes. Firstly, the learnable hierarchical consistency loss encourages the teacher model to provide more accurate guidance for the student model. Secondly, the self-guided hierarchical consistency loss penalizes inconsistent predictions between the main decoder and the auxiliary decoders in the student model.

The contributions are three-fold: (1) we propose a hierarchical consistency enforcement architecture for semi-supervised segmentation, where the invariance of the predictions is enforced over perturbations from the hierarchical encoder; (2) we introduce a novel HC-loss with learnable and self-guided mechanisms for the HCE framework; and (3) experimental results show that the proposed HCE achieves competitive histological image segmentation performances on two benchmarks when compared to the supervised and semi-supervised methods.

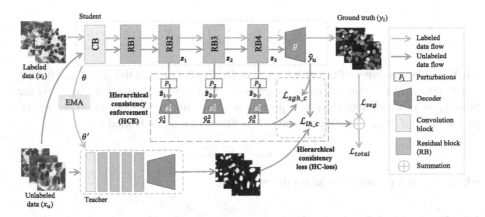

Fig. 1. Illustration of the proposed HCE framework. The HCE consists of a basic teacher-student model for semi-supervised segmentation and two innovations including a hierarchical consistency enforcement (HCE) module and a hierarchical consistency loss (HC-loss) function. HCE enforces hierarchical consistency during training. HC-loss consists of a learnable hierarchical consistency loss ($\mathcal{L}_{lh\_c}$) to provide more accurate guidance for the student model, and a self-guided hierarchical consistency loss ($\mathcal{L}_{sgh\_c}$) to penalize inconsistent predictions between the main decoder and the auxiliary decoders. EMA denotes exponential moving average. RB3 and RB4 are dilated residual blocks with dilation rates of 2 and 4 respectively.

2   Methodology

The proposed Mean-Teacher based HCE framework is given in Fig. 1. Our framework consists of a teacher-student framework, an HCE module, and an HC-loss. In the teacher-student framework, the teacher model guides the student model and evaluates predictions under perturbations for better performance. The weights θ'_t of the teacher model at training step t are updated as $\theta'_t = \alpha\theta'_{t-1} + (1 - \alpha)\theta_t$ by the exponential moving average (EMA) weights θ_t of the student model, where α is the EMA decay rate to update θ_t with gradient descent in a total of T training steps. The student model learns from the labeled data by explicitly penalizing the supervised loss. Apart from the limited supervision, the student model is regularized by a hierarchical consistency to exploit the unlabeled data. For the ease of description of our method, we firstly define the basic mathematical terms. Let $(\mathcal{X}_l, \mathcal{Y}_l) = \left\{(x_l^i, y_l^i)\right\}_{i=1}^M$ and $\mathcal{X}_u = \left\{(x_u^i)\right\}_{i=1}^N$ be the labeled dataset and the unlabeled dataset respectively, where M is the number of images with known segmentation results, each image x_l^i has a corresponding segmented mask y_l^i, N denotes the number of unlabeled images, and $\mathcal{X}_u$ represents images without labeled masks. Normally, M is assumed to be far less than N.

2.1   Basic Student Model for Supervised Learning

For the labeled dataset, we follow the previous work in [9] and optimize the dilated DeepLabV3+ [2] by the standard cross-entropy loss $\mathcal{L}_{ce}$ and the variance constrained cross loss $\mathcal{L}_{var}$. Formally, given a minibatch $B_l \subseteq \mathcal{X}_l$, the $\mathcal{L}_{var}$ is defined as [9]:

$$\mathcal{L}_{var} = \frac{1}{D} \sum_{d=1}^{D} \frac{1}{|B_d|} \sum_{i=1}^{|B_d|} (\mu_d - p^i)^2 \tag{1}$$

where D is the number of object instances in B_l, B_d denotes all the pixels that belong to instance d in the minibatch, $|B_d|$ represents the number of pixels in B_d, p^i is the probability of the correct class for a pixel i, and μ_d is the mean value of all the pixels' probabilities p^i in B_d. The segmentation loss function $\mathcal{L}_{seg}$ is defined as:

$$\mathcal{L}_{seg} = \mathcal{L}_{ce} + \lambda_{var}\mathcal{L}_{var}, \tag{2}$$

where λ_{var} is a parameter to adjust the weighting.

2.2 Hierarchical Consistency Enforcement (HCE) Module

For the unlabeled dataset, we design an HCE module to constrain the consistency over the hierarchical hidden representations from the encoder. Specifically, the hierarchical representation $(\mathbf{z}_h)$ is computed by the encoder at h-th block (as shown in Fig. 1). We hypothesize that the hierarchical consistency can provide stronger enforcement, thereby boost the generalization of the student network. Besides, the student network could be more generalized when we constrain the consistency over the variant representation $(\hat{\mathbf{z}}_h)$ instead of directly using the original representation $(\mathbf{z}_h)$.

Specifically, we introduce R stochastic perturbation functions, denoted by P_r with $r \in [1, R]$. With various perturbation settings, we generate perturbed variant $\hat{\mathbf{z}}_h$ (i.e., $\hat{\mathbf{z}}_h = P_r(\mathbf{z}_h)$) of its original representation $\mathbf{z}_h$ before feeding to the h-th auxiliary decoder g_a^h. By doing such, we enforce the output of the auxiliary decoders and main decoder in the student model to be consistent with the guidance generated by the teacher model. In our network, we randomly introduce the dropout and feature-level noise layers [8] as our perturbation functions before the auxiliary decoders. This consistency enforcement procedure can be formulated as follows:

$$\mathcal{L}_c = \frac{1}{|B_u|} \frac{1}{H} \sum_{i=1}^{|B_u|} \sum_{h=1}^{H} \mathrm{d}\left(\hat{y}_u^{i\prime}, g_a^h\left(\hat{\mathbf{z}}_h^i\right)\right) + \mathrm{d}\left(\hat{y}_u^{i\prime}, \hat{y}_u^i\right), \tag{3}$$

where B_u denotes the unlabeled minibatch with $B_u \subseteq \mathcal{X}_u$, $\mathrm{d}(,)$ is the distance measure between two output probabilities of the correct class, H represents the number of hierarchical blocks used in dilated DeepLabV3+. The probability target of i-th image generated by the teacher model is denoted as $\hat{y}_u^{i\prime}$. $\hat{y}_u^i$ is the probability prediction from the main decoder of the student model. $g_a^h\left(\hat{\mathbf{z}}_h^i\right)$ denotes the probability prediction of perturbed variant representation from the h-th auxiliary decoder. In this work, we set H to be 3 and use mean squared error (MSE) for distance measurement.

2.3 Hierarchical Consistency Loss (HC-Loss)

Learnable Hierarchical Consistency Loss. To prevent the teacher model from obtaining high uncertainty estimation and enforce the hierarchical consistency, we propose a learnable hierarchical consistency loss ($\mathcal{L}_{lh\_c}$). We modify the loss function $\mathcal{L}_c$ in Eq. (3) as:

$$\mathcal{L}_{lh\_c} = \frac{1}{|B_u|} \frac{1}{H} \sum_{i=1}^{|B_u|} \sum_{h=1}^{H} \mathcal{L}_{mse} \left(\hat{y}_{u\_t}^{i\prime}, g_a^h \left(\hat{\mathbf{z}}_h^i \right) \right) + \mathcal{L}_{mse} \left(\hat{y}_{u\_t}^{i\prime}, \hat{y}_u^i \right), \qquad (4)$$

where $\mathcal{L}_{mse}$ denotes the mean square error loss function, $\hat{y}_{u\_t}^{i\prime}$ represents the learnable prediction probabilities of the teacher model. $\hat{y}_{u\_t}^{i\prime}$ is capable of providing a more reliable prediction as guidance for the student model.

The learnable prediction probabilities $\hat{y}_{u\_t}^{i\prime}$ of the teacher model is inspired by [15], and is calculated as:

$$u_i' = -\hat{y}_u^{i\prime} \log \hat{y}_u^{i\prime}, \qquad \hat{y}_{u\_t}^{i\prime} = (1 - u_i') \hat{y}_u^{i\prime} + u_i' \hat{y}_u^i. \qquad (5)$$

When the teacher model generates unreliable results (high uncertainty), $\hat{y}_{u\_t}^{i\prime}$ is approximating to $\hat{y}_u^i$. On the contrary, when the teacher model is confident (low uncertainty), $\hat{y}_{u\_t}^{i\prime}$ remains the same as $\hat{y}_u^{i\prime}$ and provides certain prediction as targets for the student model to learn from.

Self-guided Hierarchical Consistency Loss. In HCE, we encourage the predictions of the student model to be consistent with the teacher model by $\mathcal{L}_{lh\_c}$. However, the consistency between the auxiliary decoders and the main decoder in the student model is neglected. Thus, we penalize the auxiliary predictive variance by a self-guided hierarchical consistency loss ($\mathcal{L}_{sgh\_c}$) to alleviate such inconsistency as:

$$\mathcal{L}_{sgh\_c} = \frac{1}{|B_u|} \sum_{i=1}^{|B_u|} \frac{1}{H} \sum_{h=1}^{H} \mathcal{L}_{mse} \left(g_a^h \left(\hat{\mathbf{z}}_h^i \right) - \hat{y}_u^i \right). \qquad (6)$$

By doing such, the student model takes its prediction of the main decoder as guidance, minimizes the inconsistency among all the decoders, thereby enforces a better feature representation ability.

In summary, the proposed HCE framework learns from both labeled data and unlabeled data by minimizing the following combined objective function:

$$\mathcal{L}_{total} = \mathcal{L}_{seg} + \lambda_{h\_c}(\mathcal{L}_{lh\_c} + \lambda_{sgh\_c}\mathcal{L}_{sgh\_c}), \qquad (7)$$

where λ_{h_c} and λ_{sgh_c} are weight factors to adjust the balance during training.

2.4 Dataset and Evaluation Metrics

Dataset and Preprocessing. Multi-organ nuclei segmentation dataset [5] (MoNuSeg) and colorectal adenocarcinoma gland [1] dataset (CRAG) are used to evaluate our HCE. The MoNuSeg dataset consists of 44 H&E stained histopathology images with 1000 × 1000 pixel resolution. The training set contains 30 histopathological images while the test set consists of 14 images. We use the randomly sampled 27 images as training data, and the remaining 3 images are used as validation data. The CRAG dataset is split into 173 training images, where 153 images are used for training and 20 images are used for validation, and 40 test images with different cancer grades. Most of the images are of 1512×1516 pixel resolution with instance-level ground truth.

We crop patches from each training image with a sliding window. For MoNuSeg, the patch size is 128×128, resulting in 1,728 patches. For CRAG, we extract 5,508 patches with 480×480 resolution from 153 images. We further perform online data augmentations including random scaling, flipping, rotation, and affine operations.

Evaluation Metrics. For MoNuSeg, we use F1-score (F1), average Dice coefficient (Dice), and aggregated Jaccard index (AJI) as introduced in [5,17] for evaluation. For CRAG, F1-score (F1), object-level Dice coefficient ($Dice_{obj}$), and object-level Hausdorff ($Haus_{obj}$) distance are used for detailed evaluation as described in [3,18].

2.5   Implementation Details

We implement HCE in PyTorch using a Tesla P100 graphics card. The batch size is set as 16 for MoNuSeg and 8 for CRAG. The Adam optimizer is used with a polynomial learning rate policy, where the initial learning rate 2.5×10^{-4} is multiplied by $\left(1 - \frac{iter}{total\_iter}\right)^{power}$ with $power$ at 0.9. The total number of training epoch is set to 500 for MoNuSeg and 300 for CRAG. We set the weight factor λ_{sgh_c} and λ_{var} as 0.1 and 1. Weight factor λ_{h_c} in Eq. (7) is calculated by the Gaussian ramp-up function $\lambda_{h\_c} = k * e^{\left(-5(1-t/T)^2\right)}$, as introduced in [6]. T is set to be equivalent to the total training epoch, and k is 0.1. The EMA decay rate α is set as 0.99 empirically. We use the ImageNet-pretrained ResNet34 [4] as our encoder. All the structures of the auxiliary decoders are identical, which include an Atrous Spatial Pyramid Pooling (ASPP) layer with sampling rates as $\{6,12,18,24\}$ [2] and an upsampling layer. The dilation rates of the last two residual blocks (as shown in Fig. 1) are 2 and 4.

3   Experiments and Results

3.1   Quantitative and Qualitative Comparison

Quantitative Comparison with Semi-supervised Methods. To demonstrate the effectiveness of our HCE, we implement several SOTA SSL methods for comparison, which include entropy minimization (Entropy) [14], Mean-Teacher (MT) [12], uncertainty aware Mean-Teacher (UA-MT) [20], interpolation consistency training (ICT) [13], and transformation-consistent self-ensembling model (TCSM) [6]. For a fair comparison, we used the same pretrained student network as shown in Fig. 1. The performances of all the methods are shown in Table 1.

For MoNuSeg, it shows that our model achieves the highest Dice and AJI over all the SSL methods. Comparing to the TCSM model on 5% labeled data that performs the second best, our model improves the Dice by 0.6% and the AJI by 2%. For CRAG, Table 1 shows that HCE significantly outperforms all the SOTA SSL methods by all the metrics.

Table 1. Performance comparison of the proposed HCE and SOTA SSL methods on the MoNuSeg and CRAG datasets. Note that 5%/10%/20% data consists of 1/3/5 and 8/15/31 labeled images on the MoNuSeg and CRAG datasets.

Labeled (%)	Method	MoNuSeg			CRAG		
		F1 (%)	Dice (%)	AJI (%)	F1 (%)	$Dice_{obj}$ (%)	$Haus_{obj}$
5%	SL	74.8	77.6	46.3	65.7	76.0	266.5
	Entropy [14]	74.3	78.1	47.3	63.8	71.7	342.0
	MT [12]	69.4	77.0	42.3	66.9	82.4	175.1
	UA-MT [20]	73.9	76.1	44.7	62.2	75.6	239.0
	ICT [13]	79.8	78.4	49.1	69.7	82.5	177.2
	TCSM [6]	**79.9**	79.1	50.3	67.1	79.9	200.4
	HCE	79.2	**79.7**	**52.3**	**74.4**	**84.4**	**152.7**
10%	SL	87.0	81.1	58.9	73.9	82.0	195.6
	Entropy [14]	86.2	82.4	60.0	76.1	84.1	180.3
	MT [12]	84.4	82.2	58.3	74.5	86.7	145.4
	UA-MT [20]	86.1	82.3	59.7	71.9	81.6	189.3
	ICT [13]	87.7	81.1	59.1	74.9	85.9	152.1
	TCSM [6]	87.9	81.0	59.0	75.0	85.3	152.1
	HCE	**88.0**	**82.6**	**61.9**	**78.8**	**87.4**	**130.2**
20%	SL	88.4	81.7	60.8	78.3	84.7	176.4
	Entropy [14]	87.6	82.6	60.9	81.0	85.9	169.7
	MT [12]	86.6	82.4	59.9	81.3	88.3	127.8
	UA-MT [20]	87.0	82.5	60.3	77.7	84.9	168.7
	ICT [13]	88.7	81.9	60.9	78.5	86.6	145.9
	TCSM [6]	71.0	81.8	60.4	80.6	87.7	140.4
	HCE	**89.7**	**82.8**	**63.2**	**82.4**	**88.5**	**122.9**

Our primary finding is that compared with the supervised dilated DeepLabV3+ (SL), most of the SSL methods improve the segmentation performance, as they can also learn from the unannotated data. Several SSL methods perform worse than the baseline model in some cases. A possible reason is that those methods are sensitive to the proportion of labeled samples. By encouraging consistency with our HCE, the segmentation performance and robustness are improved consistently. Secondly, with a smaller proportion of labeled data, the SSL methods could improve the performance by a large margin, which shows the power of learning from unlabeled data.

Quantitative Comparison with Fully-Supervised Methods. We evaluate the performance of HCE and recent fully-supervised methods. For MoNuSeg, three approaches are compared, including Micro-Net [10], Self-loop [7], and BiO-Net [17]. For CRAG, we compare HCE with MILD-Net [3], DSE [18], and PRS^2 [19]. As shown in Table 2, HCE consistently achieves the best performance in terms of all the metrics with only

50% labeled data on MoNuSeg. Although HCE achieves the second best on CRAG, the PRS^2 using 100% labeled data is much more complex and hard to train than our HCE.

Table 2. Performance comparison of the proposed HCE and fully-supervised methods on the MoNuSeg and CRAG datasets. Note that fully-supervised methods use 100% labeled data for training and HCE uses 50% labeled data.

Method	MoNuSeg		Method	CRAG		
	F1 (%)	Dice (%)		F1 (%)	Dice$_{obj}$ (%)	Haus$_{obj}$
Micro-Net [10]	–	81.9	MILD-Net [3]	82.5	87.5	160.1
Self-loop [7]	79.3	–	DSE [18]	83.5	88.9	120.1
BiO-Net [17]	–	82.5	PRS^2 [19]	**84.3**	**89.2**	**113.1**
HCE (50%)	**90.4**	**83.2**	HCE (50%)	84.1	88.9	118.7

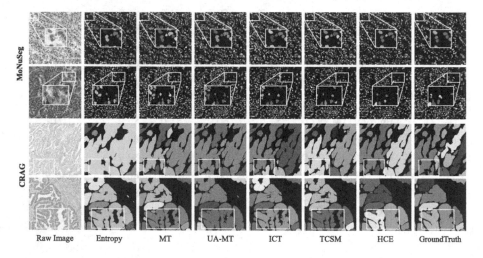

Fig. 2. Segmentation results on MoNuSeg/CRAG dataset using HCE and other SSL methods with 5%/10% labeled data. The first/second row of each dataset consists of 5%/10% labeled samples.

Qualitative Comparison with Semi-supervised Methods. As shown in Fig. 2, we provide the qualitative results of the segmentation on 5% and 10% labeled data of the two benchmarks. Comparing to the SOTA SSL models, HCE significantly improves the performance. Besides, we observe that the proposed HCE has better scalability to objects in different shapes, such as small cells and large glands. We speculate that it is because the hierarchical structures in the encoder may introduce uncertainties in predictions. With the hierarchical consistency enforcement, the proposed HCE rectifies the learning from such ambiguous predictions, yielding a more reasonable prediction.

3.2   Ablation Study of the Proposed Method

We perform ablation studies by gradually adding each component to the MT [12] framework to evaluate their effectiveness. As shown in Table 3, alleviating uncertainties obtained from the teacher network and enforcing a learnable consistency improve 2.6%/1.3%/0.1% AJI score with 5%/10%/20% labeled data. It is noted that without g_a^H, $\mathcal{L}_{lh\_c}$ is only applied to the prediction of the main decoder from the student model, which proves the effectiveness of $\hat{y}_{u\_t}^{i'}$ in Eq. (4). Then, we introduce HCE without perturbations in the encoder of the student model, which brings 0.2%/0.5%/1.7% improvements. After applying the perturbations, the performance consistently increases by 0.4%/0.1%/1.3% for AJI. Lastly, combining all the components in our framework achieves significant performance by 52.3%/61.9%63.2% for AJI.

Table 3. Ablation study on HCE using 5%/10%/20% labeled data on MoNuSeg. Imp denotes the improved AJI compared with the previous setting.

$\mathcal{L}_{lh\_c}$	g_a^H	P_R	$\mathcal{L}_{sgh\_c}$	5%	Imp (%)	10%	Imp (%)	20%	Imp (%)
				42.3	–	58.3	–	59.9	–
√				44.9	2.6	59.6	1.3	60.0	0.1
√	√			45.1	0.2	60.1	0.5	61.7	**1.7**
√	√	√		45.5	0.4	60.2	0.1	63.0	1.3
√	√	√	√	**52.3**	**6.8**	**61.9**	**1.7**	**63.2**	0.2

4   Conclusions

In this paper, we propose an HCE framework for semi-supervised learning. Our framework enforces the predictions to be consistent over the perturbations in the hierarchical encoder. Besides, we propose a novel HC-loss, which is composed of a learnable hierarchical consistency loss, and a self-guided hierarchical consistency loss. Comprehensive experimental results show that HCE achieves competitive performances using limited labeled data when compared with semi-supervised and supervised learning methods.

Acknowledgments. This work was supported by the Fundamental Research Funds for the Central Universities, the National Natural Science Foundation of China [Grant No. 62072329], and the National Key Technology R&D Program of China [Grant No. 2018YFB1701700].

References

1. Awan, R., et al.: Glandular morphometrics for objective grading of colorectal adenocarcinoma histology images. Sci. Rep. **7**(1), 1–12 (2017)
2. Chen, L.C., Papandreou, G., Kokkinos, I., Murphy, K., Yuille, A.L.: DeepLab: semantic image segmentation with deep convolutional nets, atrous convolution, and fully connected CRFs. IEEE Trans. Pattern Anal. Mach. Intell. **40**(4), 834–848 (2017)

3. Graham, S., et al.: MILD-Net: minimal information loss dilated network for gland instance segmentation in colon histology images. Med. Image Anal. **52**, 199–211 (2019)
4. He, K., Zhang, X., Ren, S., Sun, J.: Deep residual learning for image recognition. In: Proceedings of the IEEE Conference on Computer Vision and Pattern Recognition, pp. 770–778 (2016)
5. Kumar, N., et al.: A multi-organ nucleus segmentation challenge. IEEE Trans. Med. Imaging **39**(5), 1380–1391 (2019)
6. Li, X., Yu, L., Chen, H., Fu, C.W., Xing, L., Heng, P.A.: Transformation-consistent self-ensembling model for semisupervised medical image segmentation. IEEE Trans. Neural Netw. Learn. Syst. **32**(2), 523–534 (2020). https://doi.org/10.1109/TNNLS.2020.2995319
7. Li, Y., Chen, J., Xie, X., Ma, K., Zheng, Y.: Self-loop uncertainty: a novel pseudo-label for semi-supervised medical image segmentation. In: Martel, A.L., et al. (eds.) MICCAI 2020. LNCS, vol. 12261, pp. 614–623. Springer, Cham (2020). https://doi.org/10.1007/978-3-030-59710-8_60
8. Ouali, Y., Hudelot, C., Tami, M.: Semi-supervised semantic segmentation with cross-consistency training. In: Proceedings of the IEEE/CVF Conference on Computer Vision and Pattern Recognition, pp. 12674–12684 (2020)
9. Qu, H., Yan, Z., Riedlinger, G.M., De, S., Metaxas, D.N.: Improving Nuclei/Gland instance segmentation in histopathology images by full resolution neural network and spatial constrained loss. In: Shen, D., et al. (eds.) MICCAI 2019. LNCS, vol. 11764, pp. 378–386. Springer, Cham (2019). https://doi.org/10.1007/978-3-030-32239-7_42
10. Raza, S.E.A., et al.: Micro-Net: a unified model for segmentation of various objects in microscopy images. Med. Image Anal. **52**, 160–173 (2019)
11. Sahasrabudhe, M., et al.: Self-supervised nuclei segmentation in histopathological images using attention. In: Martel, A.L., et al. (eds.) MICCAI 2020. LNCS, vol. 12265, pp. 393–402. Springer, Cham (2020). https://doi.org/10.1007/978-3-030-59722-1_38
12. Tarvainen, A., Valpola, H.: Mean teachers are better role models: weight-averaged consistency targets improve semi-supervised deep learning results. In: Advances in Neural Information Processing Systems, pp. 1195–1204 (2017)
13. Verma, V., Lamb, A., Kannala, J., Bengio, Y., Lopez-Paz, D.: Interpolation consistency training for semi-supervised learning. In: Proceedings of the 28th International Joint Conference on Artificial Intelligence, IJCAI 2019, pp. 3635–3641. AAAI Press (2019)
14. Vu, T.H., Jain, H., Bucher, M., Cord, M., Pérez, P.: ADVENT: adversarial entropy minimization for domain adaptation in semantic segmentation. In: Proceedings of the IEEE/CVF Conference on Computer Vision and Pattern Recognition, pp. 2517–2526 (2019)
15. Wang, Y., et al.: Double-uncertainty weighted method for semi-supervised learning. In: Martel, A.L., et al. (eds.) MICCAI 2020. LNCS, vol. 12261, pp. 542–551. Springer, Cham (2020). https://doi.org/10.1007/978-3-030-59710-8_53
16. Xia, Y., et al.: Uncertainty-aware multi-view co-training for semi-supervised medical image segmentation and domain adaptation. Med. Image Anal. **65**, 101766 (2020)
17. Xiang, T., Zhang, C., Liu, D., Song, Y., Huang, H., Cai, W.: BiO-Net: learning recurrent bi-directional connections for encoder-decoder architecture. In: Martel, A.L., et al. (eds.) MICCAI 2020. LNCS, vol. 12261, pp. 74–84. Springer, Cham (2020). https://doi.org/10.1007/978-3-030-59710-8_8
18. Xie, Y., Lu, H., Zhang, J., Shen, C., Xia, Y.: Deep segmentation-emendation model for gland instance segmentation. In: Shen, D., et al. (eds.) MICCAI 2019. LNCS, vol. 11764, pp. 469–477. Springer, Cham (2019). https://doi.org/10.1007/978-3-030-32239-7_52
19. Xie, Y., Zhang, J., Liao, Z., Verjans, J., Shen, C., Xia, Y.: Pairwise relation learning for semi-supervised gland segmentation. In: Martel, A.L., et al. (eds.) MICCAI 2020. LNCS, vol. 12265, pp. 417–427. Springer, Cham (2020). https://doi.org/10.1007/978-3-030-59722-1_40

20. Yu, L., Wang, S., Li, X., Fu, C.-W., Heng, P.-A.: Uncertainty-aware self-ensembling model for semi-supervised 3D left atrium segmentation. In: Shen, D., et al. (eds.) MICCAI 2019. LNCS, vol. 11765, pp. 605–613. Springer, Cham (2019). https://doi.org/10.1007/978-3-030-32245-8_67

21. Zhou, Y., Onder, O.F., Dou, Q., Tsougenis, E., Chen, H., Heng, P.-A.: CIA-Net: robust nuclei instance segmentation with contour-aware information aggregation. In: Chung, A.C.S., Gee, J.C., Yushkevich, P.A., Bao, S. (eds.) IPMI 2019. LNCS, vol. 11492, pp. 682–693. Springer, Cham (2019). https://doi.org/10.1007/978-3-030-20351-1_53

Federated Stain Normalization
for Computational Pathology

Nicolas Wagner[1] , Moritz Fuchs[1(✉)] , Yuri Tolkach[2],
and Anirban Mukhopadhyay[1]

[1] Department of Computer Science, TU Darmstadt, Darmstadt, Germany
moritz.fuchs@gris.informatik.tu-darmstadt.de
[2] Institute of Pathology, University Hospital Cologne, Cologne, Germany

Abstract. Although deep federated learning has received much attention in recent years, progress has been made mainly in the context of natural images and barely for computational pathology. However, deep federated learning is an opportunity to create datasets that reflect the data diversity of many laboratories. Further, the effort of dataset construction can be divided among many. Unfortunately, existing algorithms cannot be easily applied to computational pathology since previous work presupposes that data distributions of laboratories must be similar. This is an unlikely assumption, mainly since different laboratories have different staining styles. As a solution, we propose BottleGAN, a generative model that can computationally align the staining styles of many laboratories and can be trained in a privacy-preserving manner to foster federated learning in computational pathology. We construct a heterogenic multi-institutional dataset based on the PESO segmentation dataset and improve the IOU by 42% compared to existing federated learning algorithms. An implementation of BottleGAN is available at https://github.com/MECLabTUDA/BottleGAN.

Keywords: Federated learning · Computational pathology · Deep learning

1 Introduction

Automatic processing of histological images has the potential to become an essential prerequisite for computer-assisted diagnosis, prognostication, and assessments in computational pathology (CP). If neural networks are to be used for this purpose, the standard deep learning methods need to be trained on a vast amount of labeled data. In reality, such data is hardly available in the public

---

N. Wagner and M. Fuchs—Equal contribution.

Supplementary Information The online version contains supplementary material available at https://doi.org/10.1007/978-3-031-16434-7_2.

domain. For instance, filtered by segmentation and histology, grand-challenge.org solely offers 15 datasets. Many of these are only of limited use. Considering the number of different dyes used in histopathology and different anatomies as well as tissue structures that are examined, many more labeled datasets are necessary. This problem is exacerbated because the style of staining can differ significantly between laboratories but also within a laboratory for a variety of reasons [26]. For instance, protocols, storage conditions, or reagents may vary. A neural network, however, should be reliable regardless of the staining style. To this end, a solution is to collect representative training data from many laboratories [3]. Unfortunately, creating large-scale datasets is only possible with an enormous effort, both in time and money.

The concept of federated learning (FL) appears to be a solution to this as it allows distributing the dataset creation work among many and captures the data diversity of multiple laboratories. Unfortunately, existing FL algorithms either expect a publicly available representative unlabeled dataset [4,19,25] or only work if participating clients are closely aligned in their data distribution [11]. It is fair to assume that neither requirement is fulfilled for computational pathology. Further, previous work does not integrate unlabeled clients out of the box [11,22], leading to high participation barriers.

In this study, we propose BottleGAN, a novel generative adversarial network architecture that makes FL applicable to CP by aligning the local data distributions of laboratories through stain normalization. We pair BottleGAN with an unsupervised federated learning procedure that makes no further demands on participating clients apart from minimal hardware requirements. We demonstrate how BottleGAN can seamlessly be integrated into federated learning algorithms based on weight aggregation (WA) [11,18,22] for solving downstream tasks. WA algorithms train a local neural network model per client and simply average the local model weights at a server to form a global model. After WA with BottleGAN, trained models are valid for the staining styles of all laboratories that participated in the unsupervised training of BottleGAN but did not necessarily contribute annotations to WA. We demonstrate on a heterogenic multi-institutional version of the PESO [2] dataset significant improvement through BottleGAN compared to existing work on federated learning.

2 Related Work

2.1 Weight Aggregation

Most WA algorithms are derived from the underlying idea of FEDAVG [22]. FEDAVG assumes that each client dataset is sampled i.i.d from a common data distribution. Many improvements have been developed to handle situations in which this assumption is not entirely fulfilled (i.e. client drift) [5,11,12,15,23]. The literature on federated learning in CP is very limited. Although evaluated on WSIs, Andreux et al. [1] use a more general adaptation of federated learning in that they learn different normalization statistics per client. Changing normalization layers has also been studied by others [8]. Lu et al. [20] are mainly concerned about the size of WSIs and use a pretrained model for embedding WSI patches. However, neither approach addresses the heterogeneity of participants in federated learning and goes significantly beyond standard weight aggregation algorithms. Recently, [21] have shown in a minimal setting with only three clients that FL can create robustness of deep learning in CP to multi-institutional heterogeneity.

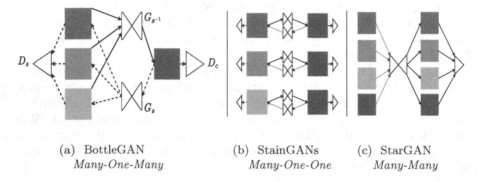

(a) BottleGAN
Many-One-Many

(b) StainGANs
Many-One-One

(c) StarGAN
Many-Many

Fig. 1. The BottleGAN architecture trains only two generators (cones) and two discriminators (triangles) for mapping between many staining styles (squares). For many StainGANs (b), the number of neural networks is linearly dependent on the number of staining styles. The number of mappings one StarGAN (c) must represent grows quadratic with the number of staining styles whereas BottleGAN achieves linear growth.

2.2   Stain Normalization

Lately, various versions of StainGAN [27] have become the dominant idea for stain normalization. StainGAN is an adaption of CycleGAN [29] and is able to learn the stain normalization task from small exemplary WSI crops while incorporating spatial variations. Unfortunately, CycleGANs, and hence StainGANs, are only able to handle one-to-one style mappings. In the FL setting under consideration in this work, the staining styles of all clients must be aligned. We are not aware of any work that is particularly intended to normalize various staining styles with only one or two neural networks. The most notable works for such many-to-many style transfers in the natural image domain, StarGAN [6] and StarGANv2 [7], use a framework akin to CycleGANs but deploys a single conditional generator for all transferred styles. BottleGAN can be used as an orthogonal mechanism to improve existing WA-based FL algorithms with federated stain normalization.

3   Method

In the following, we first give a problem statement of FL in CP and derive the necessity of BottleGAN. Afterward, we show how BottleGAN is constructed and how it can be trained with FL.

3.1   Problem Statement

In a standard deep learning setting for CP we have access to a dataset $D = \{(x_i, y_i)\}_{i=1}^N$ of N WSI-Label pairs. In the FL setting, however, we assume that there are clients K each owning a portion $D^k = \{(x_i^k, y_i^k)\}_{i=1}^{N^k}$ of $D = \bigsqcup_{k=1}^K D^k$ that can not be shared with others. For a simplified notation, we omit unlabeled clients which trivially can be integrated in the following derivations. As mentioned in the introduction, the success of WA-based FL is commonly dependent on the local distributions, from which the client datasets D^k were drawn, not diverging too much [11]. For CP, we can further decompose a WSI x into a destained content image c and staining style function s such that $s(c) = x$.[1] Given the staining style functions $S = \bigcup_{k=1}^K \{s_i^k\}_{i=1}^{N^k}$ of all clients, we define the decomposed dataset of a client as

$$\mathcal{D}^k = \bigcup_{s \in S} \{(s(c_i^k), y_i^k)\}_{i=1}^{N^k}. \tag{1}$$

In words, $\mathcal{D}^k$ contains the content images of a client in the staining styles of all clients. If we can create the decomposed set for each client in a privacy-preserving manner, we can also align the client data distributions much more closely.

3.2   Network Architecture

For creating the decomposed datasets, we introduce BottleGAN, a neural network architecture that is able to map between the staining styles of all clients. The BottleGAN architecture follows a *Many-One-Many* paradigm that differs conceptually from previous work as depicted in Fig. 1. BottleGAN consists of two generators that perform staining style transfers and two discriminators needed for training purposes. Generator G_s is responsible for approximating all staining style functions $s \in S$ whereas $G_{s^{-1}}$ is trained to approximate all inverse staining style functions s^{-1}. Hence, in contrast to a naive implementation of a *Many One-One* paradigm (Fig. 1 (b)), i.e. one StainGAN [27] per staining style transfer, we are significantly more computationally efficient as the number of neural networks to train remains constant. Additionally, compared to a StarGAN-based [6,7] *Many-Many* approach (Fig. 1 (c)), we avoid that the number of staining style transfers one network has to learn grows quadratic with the number of staining styles. Our architecture results in linear growth and, thereby, simplifies the training task considerably.

Generators. Both generators follow the same three major design choices that are novel in contrast to previous deep stain normalization networks [27]. First, we only use convolutions of size 1×1, no downsampling or upsampling techniques, and no skip connections that are usually used in common neural style transfer

---

[1] Without loss of generality we can assume that the content image is stained in a reference staining scheme rather than destained.

architectures like U-Net [24] or SB-Generators [16]. Contrary to changing the style of a pixel in a natural image, changing the staining style of a pixel in a WSI should only depend on the pixel's content and the globally prevalent staining style. Obviously, image capturing noise and other influences weaken this assumption. Nonetheless, in the federated setting, it is desirable to keep the communication and training costs of neural networks as small as possible for clients. For CP, both can be improved if parameter-efficient networks are used that avoid modeling long-distance correlations between pixels. Another advantage is that our architecture is entirely independent of the size of the input image. Phrased differently, as most WSIs can not be processed at once by neural networks due to their size, the standard solution is moving the networks across a WSI and processing one crop after the other. In this case, architectures like U-Net probably process a pixel differently depending on its position within a crop.

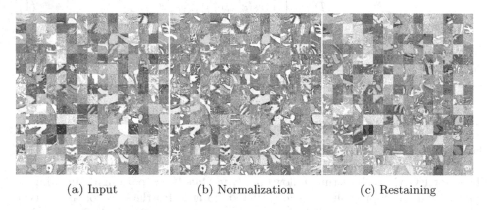

(a) Input   (b) Normalization   (c) Restaining

Fig. 2. A visual demonstration of BottleGAN capabilities. (a) shows 240 artificial stainings targets, (b) demonstrates the normalization of (a) by BottleGAN, and (c) displays the restaining from (b) to (a) by BottleGAN.

Second, we follow the current success of adaptive instance normalization (AdaIN) [7,13,16] to condition the BottleGAN generators on a particular staining style function. Although we implement all staining style functions with one BottleGAN and all inverse functions with another, we only use one trainable style code per staining style. Gaussian noise is added to style codes to represent ambiguities in staining style functions and make BottleGAN more robust.

Finally, both generators work directly in the optical density (OD) space, which is the negated logarithm of the image intensities. This is plausible since the staining matrix, which can describe all linear effects of staining, also acts in the OD space.

Discriminators. Looking at the discriminators now, both differ in their structure. The discriminator D_c decides whether an image is destained (or reference

stained). Hence, we can make use of a standard PatchGAN [17] discriminator
for this binary decision. The discriminator D_s, however, is ought to decide for
all staining styles if an image is stained in a particular style or not. For this, we
condition a PatchGAN discriminator by concatenating the respective style code
to the output of the last downsampling convolutional layer.

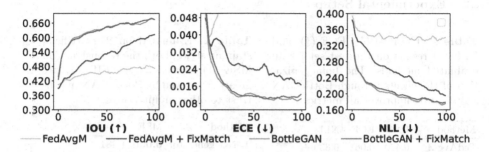

Fig. 3. Results on the test set of FEDAVGM and the variants with FIXMATCH as well as
BottleGAN over 100 communication rounds. FIXMATCH can seemingly improve client
homogeneity but by far not to the extent of BottleGAN.

3.3 Federated Learning

We train BottleGAN with FL based on knowledge distillation [10]. Given a
dataset $X = \bigsqcup_{k=1}^{K} X^k$ of WSIs as the union of non-shareable local datasets
X^k of clients K and a shareable dataset C of destained or reference stained
WSIs owned by a server. We start by asking all clients to train their own local
BottleGAN solely between their staining style and the reference staining style
defined by C. This requires a non-federated training similar to CycleGAN [29].
Afterward, the clients send their local models to the server. The server, in turn,
applies the collected client generators to its own dataset C to create a novel
dataset $\hat{X}$ that contains C in the staining styles of all clients. The server then
proceeds by training a global BottleGAN on $\hat{X}$ and C as a distillation of all
local BottleGANs. Finally, each client receives the global BottleGAN and is able
to create the decomposed dataset. The only assumption we make is that the
reference dataset C is public, and this assumption seems to be mostly fulfilled
based on public teaching examples alone.

An algorithmic description of the federated and the non-federated learning
of BottleGAN is given in the supplementary material. Due to the enormous size
of WSIs, an offline construction of the decomposed datasets might not be handy.
Therefore, we state an online integration of BottleGAN into WA-based FL in
the supplementary material, too.

4   Evaluation

4.1   Dataset

Most available CP segmentation datasets are either too small or lack a sufficient labeling quality for the evaluation of FL algorithms. Additionally, the

computational costs of simulating FL systems are massive. Hence, we limit ourselves to the PESO [2] dataset of prostate specimens. PESO comprises 102 hematoxylin and eosin stained whole slide images (WSI) and corresponding segmentation masks.

4.2 Experimental Setup

Table 1. The IOU (↑), ECE (↓), and NLL (↓) results on the test set for all evaluated methods. The homogenization of the clients through BottleGAN significantly improves all metrics.

Method	IOU	ECE	NLL
FedAvgM	0.470	0.061	0.339
+ FixMatch	0.613	0.016	0.193
BottleGAN	**0.671**	**0.011**	**0.177**
+ FixMatch	0.671	0.013	0.180

Table 2. Evaluated on 240 artificial staining styles, both the reconstruction MSE (↓) as well as the FID (↓) are greatly improved by BottleGAN in contrast to other architectures.

Method	MSE	FID
U-Net generator	**0.030**	1.281
Many-Many	0.034	1.385
Many-One	0.035	1.397
BottleGAN	**0.030**	**1.235**

Our experiments simulate a FL setup with 20 clients for 100 training rounds. Each client owns a training and a testing WSI, respectively. Both WSIs follow the same staining style, which we establish with the Macenko algorithm. The staining styles are unique per client and are random linear combinations of the styles defined in Schömig-Markiefka et al. [26]. To increase realism, we assume that not every client offers labels at all, and if they do, then the number of labels varies. For this purpose, we allow 60 labeled 300 × 300 px patches at a 10× magnification among the clients, whereby half of the clients can have between 1 and 11 patches. The other half does not have ground truth annotations at all and only contributes its staining styles. We always process random image crops of size 224 × 224 px.

Since BottleGAN can be paired with any WA-based FL algorithm, and in line with other recent work [5,14,19], we choose FEDAVGM [11] as a baseline comparison. Further, as BottleGAN should be considered a federated semi-supervised learning (FSSL) algorithm due to its capability to include unlabeled clients, we also compare against the naive combination of FedAvgM and the state-of-the-art semi-supervised learning algorithm FixMatch [28]. At this, we follow the implementation of Jeong et al. [14] but stick to the naive combination as other mechanisms are orthogonal to BottleGAN. The performance of all algorithms is compared with the help of the intersection over union (IOU), the expected calibration error (ECE), and the negative-log likelihood (NLL). Results are an average over two seeds and three folds. For each fold, the labeled patches are distributed differently among the clients. We will make the implementation publicly available.

4.3   Results

The test results after 100 simulated communication rounds of FEDAVGM can be read in Table 1. Further, we plot the development throughout training in Fig. 3. The findings are unambiguous. The worst result is achieved in all metrics when only FEDAVGM is applied, whereas the homogenization of client staining styles through BottleGAN seems to be a way to success for FL in CP. The addition of BottleGAN leads to significant improvements in all evaluated metrics. The IOU is increased by 0.21, the ECE is lowered by 0.50, and the NLL is reduced by 0.16. The addition of FixMatch can only improve plain FEDAVGM without BottleGAN and even leads to slightly worse performance in terms of NLL and ECE if combined with BottleGAN. Presumably, the consistency learning of Fix-Match also results in some sort of client homogenization but not to the extent BottleGAN can achieve.

4.4   BottleGAN Architecture

We validate major design choices of BottleGAN by training it in a non-federated setting to capture staining style transfer between 240 artificial staining styles. The staining styles are created as random linear combinations of the styles defined in Schömig-Markiefka et al. [26]. Additionally, the entries of the corresponding stain matrices and the pixelwise optical densities are augmented with independent Gaussian noise. Exemplary artificial staining styles are displayed in Fig. 2 (a), the normalization of BottleGAN in Fig. 2 (b), and the restaining in Fig. 2 (c). Even for so many challenging style transfers, both the normalization and the restaining visually appear to be successfully achieved. Further experiments are evaluated by the mean squared reconstruction error (MSE), and the Fréchet inception distance (FID) [9]. The results can be found in Table 2. First, we validate the novel generator design. BottleGAN achieves a MSE on par with the usually used U-Net [24,27] generator and even improves the FID while being translation invariant, using only half of the parameters, and avoiding upsampling artifacts. We also compare the novel *Many-One-Many* paradigm implemented by BottleGAN to the *Many-Many* paradigm of StarGAN [6] and a *Many-One* paradigm that implements BottleGAN with only one generator for both normalization and restaining. Considering the same training budget, BottleGAN greatly outperforms all other paradigms. Please note that we did not compare against the *Many-One-One* paradigm, which would train many StainGANs (see Fig. 1 (b)) due to the intractable computational costs.

5   Conclusion

In this work, we introduced BottleGAN, a novel generative model to unify heterogeneous histological slides from different pathology labs in their staining style. BottleGAN is built of a new architecture tailored explicitly to staining style transfer and paired with an unsupervised FL algorithm. Further, we integrated

BottleGAN into WA-based FL and demonstrated the superiority of our app-roach in contrast to existing FL algorithms developed for natural images. As BottleGAN allows for incorporating clients with unlabeled datasets, it becomes easier for laboratories to enter federated learning and share knowledge. In future work, we aim to incorporate uncertainty estimation into BottleGAN for building a bridge between FL and continual learning.

References

1. Andreux, M., du Terrail, J.O., Beguier, C., Tramel, E.W.: Siloed federated learn-ing for multi-centric histopathology datasets. In: Albarqouni, S., et al. (eds.) DART/DCL -2020. LNCS, vol. 12444, pp. 129–139. Springer, Cham (2020). https://doi.org/10.1007/978-3-030-60548-3_13
2. Bulten, W., et al.: Epithelium segmentation using deep learning in H&E-stained prostate specimens with immunohistochemistry as reference standard. Sci. Rep. **9**(1), 1–10 (2019)
3. Campanella, G., et al.: Clinical-grade computational pathology using weakly super-vised deep learning on whole slide images. Nat. Med. **25**(8), 1301–1309 (2019)
4. Chang, H., Shejwalkar, V., Shokri, R., Houmansadr, A.: Cronus: robust and hetero-geneous collaborative learning with black-box knowledge transfer. arXiv preprint arXiv:1912.11279 (2019)
5. Chen, H.Y., Chao, W.L.: Fedbe: making Bayesian model ensemble applicable to federated learning. arXiv preprint arXiv:2009.01974 (2020)
6. Choi, Y., Choi, M., Kim, M., Ha, J.W., Kim, S., Choo, J.: StarGAN: unified generative adversarial networks for multi-domain image-to-image translation. In: CVPR, pp. 8789–8797 (2018)
7. Choi, Y., Uh, Y., Yoo, J., Ha, J.W.: StarGAN V2: diverse image synthesis for multiple domains. In: CVPR, pp. 8188–8197 (2020)
8. Diao, E., Ding, J., Tarokh, V.: HeteroFL: computation and communication effi-cient federated learning for heterogeneous clients. arXiv preprint arXiv:2010.01264 (2020)
9. Heusel, M., Ramsauer, H., Unterthiner, T., Nessler, B., Hochreiter, S.: GANs trained by a two time-scale update rule converge to a local Nash equilibrium. In: Advances in Neural Information Processing Systems, vol. 30 (2017)
10. Hinton, G., Vinyals, O., Dean, J.: Distilling the knowledge in a neural network. arXiv preprint arXiv:1503.02531 (2015)
11. Hsu, T.M.H., Qi, H., Brown, M.: Measuring the effects of non-identical data distri-bution for federated visual classification. arXiv preprint arXiv:1909.06335 (2019)
12. Hsu, T.-M.H., Qi, H., Brown, M.: Federated visual classification with real-world data distribution. In: Vedaldi, A., Bischof, H., Brox, T., Frahm, J.-M. (eds.) ECCV 2020. LNCS, vol. 12355, pp. 76–92. Springer, Cham (2020). https://doi.org/10.1007/978-3-030-58607-2_5
13. Huang, X., Belongie, S.: Arbitrary style transfer in real-time with adaptive instance normalization. In: ICCV, pp. 1501–1510 (2017)
14. Jeong, W., Yoon, J., Yang, E., Hwang, S.J.: Federated semi-supervised learning with inter-client consistency & disjoint learning. arXiv preprint arXiv:2006.12097 (2020)
15. Karimireddy, S.P., Kale, S., Mohri, M., Reddi, S., Stich, S., Suresh, A.T.: Scaffold: stochastic controlled averaging for federated learning. In: International Conference on Machine Learning, pp. 5132–5143. PMLR (2020)

16. Karras, T., Laine, S., Aila, T.: A style-based generator architecture for generative adversarial networks. In: CVPR, pp. 4401–4410 (2019)
17. Li, C., Wand, M.: Precomputed real-time texture synthesis with Markovian generative adversarial networks. In: Leibe, B., Matas, J., Sebe, N., Welling, M. (eds.) ECCV 2016. LNCS, vol. 9907, pp. 702–716. Springer, Cham (2016). https://doi.org/10.1007/978-3-319-46487-9_43
18. Li, T., Sahu, A.K., Zaheer, M., Sanjabi, M., Talwalkar, A., Smith, V.: Federated optimization in heterogeneous networks. arXiv preprint arXiv:1812.06127 (2018)
19. Lin, T., Kong, L., Stich, S.U., Jaggi, M.: Ensemble distillation for robust model fusion in federated learning. arXiv preprint arXiv:2006.07242 (2020)
20. Lu, M.Y., et al.: Federated learning for computational pathology on gigapixel whole slide images. arXiv preprint arXiv:2009.10190 (2020)
21. Lutnick, B.R., et al.: A tool for federated training of segmentation models on whole slide images. BioRxiv (2021)
22. McMahan, B., Moore, E., Ramage, D., Hampson, S., Arcas, B.A.: Communication-efficient learning of deep networks from decentralized data. In: Artificial Intelligence and Statistics, pp. 1273–1282. PMLR (2017)
23. Reddi, S., et al.: Adaptive federated optimization. arXiv preprint arXiv:2003.00295 (2020)
24. Ronneberger, O., Fischer, P., Brox, T.: U-Net: convolutional networks for biomedical image segmentation. In: Navab, N., Hornegger, J., Wells, W.M., Frangi, A.F. (eds.) MICCAI 2015. LNCS, vol. 9351, pp. 234–241. Springer, Cham (2015). https://doi.org/10.1007/978-3-319-24574-4_28
25. Sattler, F., Korjakow, T., Rischke, R., Samek, W.: FedAUX: leveraging unlabeled auxiliary data in federated learning. arXiv preprint arXiv:2102.02514 (2021)
26. Schömig-Markiefka, B., et al.: Quality control stress test for deep learning-based diagnostic model in digital pathology. Mod. Pathol. **34**, 2098–2108 (2021)
27. Shaban, M.T., Baur, C., Navab, N., Albarqouni, S.: StainGAN: stain style transfer for digital histological images. In: 2019 IEEE 16th International Symposium on Biomedical Imaging (ISBI 2019), pp. 953–956. IEEE (2019)
28. Sohn, K., et al.: FixMatch: simplifying semi-supervised learning with consistency and confidence. arXiv preprint arXiv:2001.07685 (2020)
29. Zhu, J.Y., Park, T., Isola, P., Efros, A.A.: Unpaired image-to-image translation using cycle-consistent adversarial networks. In: ICCV, pp. 2223–2232 (2017)

DGMIL: Distribution Guided Multiple Instance Learning for Whole Slide Image Classification

Linhao Qu, Xiaoyuan Luo, Shaolei Liu, Manning Wang$^{(\boxtimes)}$, and Zhijian Song$^{(\boxtimes)}$

Digital Medical Research Center, School of Basic Medical Science, Shanghai Key Lab of Medical Image Computing and Computer Assisted Intervention, Fudan University, Shanghai 200032, China
{lhqu20,xyluo19,slliu,mnwang,zjsong}@fudan.edu.cn

Abstract. Multiple Instance Learning (MIL) is widely used in analyzing histopathological Whole Slide Images (WSIs). However, existing MIL methods do not explicitly model the data distribution, and instead they only learn a bag-level or instance-level decision boundary discriminatively by training a classifier. In this paper, we propose DGMIL: a feature distribution guided deep MIL framework for WSI classification and positive patch localization. Instead of designing complex discriminative network architectures, we reveal that the inherent feature distribution of histopathological image data can serve as a very effective guide for instance classification. We propose a cluster-conditioned feature distribution modeling method and a pseudo label-based iterative feature space refinement strategy so that in the final feature space the positive and negative instances can be easily separated. Experiments on the CAMELYON16 dataset and the TCGA Lung Cancer dataset show that our method achieves new SOTA for both global classification and positive patch localization tasks.

Keywords: Histopathological images · Multiple Instance Learning

1 Introduction

Histopathological image analysis is important for clinical cancer diagnosis, prognostic analysis and treatment response prediction [16]. In recent years, the emergence of digital Whole Slide Images (WSIs) facilitates the application of deep learning techniques in automated histopathological image analysis [4,8,11,18]. Two main challenges exist in deep learning-based WSI analysis. First, WSIs have extremely high resolutions (typically reaching $50{,}000 \times 50{,}000$ pixels) and thus are unable to be directly fed into deep learning models. Therefore, WSIs are commonly divided into small patches for processing. Secondly, fine grained manual annotations are very expensive and time consuming because of its big size, so

---

L. Qu and X. Luo—Contributed equally to this work.
Code is available at https://github.com/miccaiif/DGMIL.

© The Author(s), under exclusive license to Springer Nature Switzerland AG 2022
L. Wang et al. (Eds.): MICCAI 2022, LNCS 13432, pp. 24–34, 2022.
https://doi.org/10.1007/978-3-031-16434-7_3

patch-wise labels are usually not available, and only the labels of each WSI are known, leading to the inaccessibility of traditional supervised learning methods [17,19]. For these reasons, Multiple Instance Learning (MIL), an effective weakly supervised paradigm has become mainstream technique for deep learning-based WSI analysis, where each WSI is considered as a bag containing many patches (also called instances) [2,3,6,9,15,17,23,24]. If a WSI (bag) is labeled positive, then at least one patch (instance) in it is positive. On the contrary, if a WSI is negative, all patches in it are negative. Typically, WSI image analysis has two main objectives: global classification and positive patch localization. The first objective is to accurately classify each WSI into positive or negative and the second objective is to accurately classify each patch in a positive slide into positive or negative. In line with many recent studies [4,7,12,13,22], our approach is dedicated to accomplish both tasks.

Existing MIL methods for WSI analysis can be broadly classified into embedding-based methods [12,13,21,22,25] and key-instance-based [4,7] methods. In embedding-based methods, patches in a WSI are first mapped to fixed-length feature embeddings, which are aggregated to obtain the bag-level feature embedding. Then, a bag-level classifier is trained in a supervised way for slide-level classification. Aggregation parameters, such as attention coefficients are used to measure the contribution of different patches to the bag classification and thus to accomplish the patch-level classification task. The embedding-based methods focus on extracting and aggregating features of each instance. The approaches for feature aggregation in existing studies include attention mechanism [12,22], graph convolution network [25], masked non-Local operation [13] and Transformer [14,17,20]. Among them, most methods train a feature extractor and the feature aggregator end-to-end, while pretrained models are utilized for feature extraction in [13] and [25]. In the key-instance-based methods [4,7], some key patches are first selected and assigned pseudo-labels to train a patch-level classifier in a supervised manner, and both the key-patches with their pseudo-labels and the classifier are updated iteratively. During inference, the trained patch-level classifier can be directly used for patch-level classification and the classification results of all patches in a slide can be aggregated to perform slide-level classification.

We observed that existing methods do not explicitly model the data distribution, and instead they only learn a bag-level or instance-level decision boundary discriminatively by training a classifier. However, since the weak slide-level labels can only provide limited supervisory information, their performance is still limited. For example, in embedding-based methods, the model is mainly trained discriminatively by the bag-level loss so the model is not motivated to make accurate predictions for all instances after identifying some significant instances to accomplish bag classification. In key-instance-based methods, the positive pseudo labels may be wrong or the selected instances may be insufficient, both of which will result in an inferior classifier.

On the basis of the above observation, we propose DGMIL: a feature distribution guided deep MIL framework for WSI classification and positive patch localization. Instead of designing complex discriminative networks, we reveal that the inherent feature distribution of histopathological image data can serve as a very effective guide for classification. Therefore, different from existing MIL methods, we do not concentrate on designing sophisticated classifiers or aggregation methods, but focus on modeling and refining the feature space so that the positive and negative instances can be easily separated. To this end, we propose a cluster-conditioned feature distribution modeling method and a pseudo label-based iterative feature space refinement strategy. Specifically, we use the self-supervised masked autoencoders (MAE) [10] to map all instances into an initial feature space and iteratively refine it for better data distribution. In each iteration, we first cluster all the instances from negative slides in the training set and calculate positive scores for all instances from both negative and positive slides in the training set according to their Mahalanobis distance to each cluster. Then, the instances with the lowest and the highest positive scores are assigned negative and positive pseudo-labels, respectively, and are used to train a simple linear projection head for dynamic refinement of the feature space. This process iterates until convergence. For testing, we map all test instances to the final refined feature space and calculate the positive scores of each instance for the patch-level classification task. For bag-level classification, we only use the simple mean-pooling approach to aggregate the positive scores of all instances in a bag.

The main contributions of this paper are as follows:

- We propose DGMIL: a feature distribution guided deep MIL framework for WSI classification and positive patch localization. Instead of designing complex discriminative network architectures, we reveal that the inherent feature distribution of histopathological image data can serve as a very effective guide for instance classification. To the best of our knowledge, this is the first work that explicitly solves a deep MIL problem from a distribution modeling perspective.
- We propose a cluster-conditioned feature distribution modeling method and a pseudo label-based iterative feature space refinement strategy so that in the final feature space the positive and negative instances can be easily separated.
- Experiments on the CAMELYON16 dataset and the TCGA Lung Cancer show that our method achieves new SOTA for both global classification and positive patch localization tasks. Codes will be publicly available.

2   Method

2.1   Problem Formulation

Given a dataset consisting of N WSIs $W = \{W_1, W_2, \ldots, W_N\}$, and each slide W_i has the corresponding label $Y_i \in \{0, 1\}$, $i = \{1, 2, \ldots N\}$. Each slide W_i is divided into small patches $\{p_{i,j}, j = 1, 2, \ldots n_i\}$ without overlapping, and n_i is the number of patches in the ith slide. In the MIL formulation, all patches $\{p_{i,j}, j = 1, 2, \ldots n_i\}$ from a slide W_i constitute a bag, and the bag-level label is the label Y_i of W_i. Each patch is called an instance, and the instance label $y_{i,j}$ has the following relationship with its corresponding bag label Y_i:

$$Y_i = \begin{cases} 0, & \text{if } \sum_j y_{i,j} = 0 \\ 1, & \text{else} \end{cases} \tag{1}$$

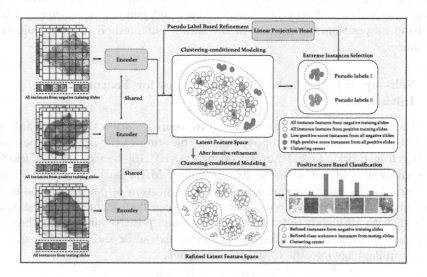

Fig. 1. The overall framework of DGMIL. (Best view in color.) (Color figure online)

That is, the labels of all instances in a negative bag are negative, while there is at least one positive instance in a positive bag but which ones are negative is unknown. We define a feature extractor $f : p_{i,j} \rightarrow z_{i,j}$, where $z_{i,j} \in R^d$, which maps the instances $p_{i,j}$ to a d-dimensional latent feature vector $z_{i,j}$. This feature extractor is typically parameterized by a deep neural network. There are significant differences in cell morphology between tumor and normal tissues, and therefore their distribution in the feature space should also be significantly different if a proper latent space can be found. We assume that the feature vectors of all negative instances and all positive instances are derived from the distribution $P_{z_{i,j}}^{neg}$ and $P_{z_{i,j}}^{pos}$, respectively, and the two distributions are significantly different from each other. On this basis, our goal is to model the feature space properly to make the negative and positive instances easily separable in the feature space. Since our methods are based on the features of instances, the instances we mention later in this paper all refer to their feature vectors.

2.2 Framework Overview

Figure 1 illustrates the overall framework of our proposed DGMIL. Specifically, we use masked autoencoders to perform self-supervised learning to train the Encoder to map all instances to an initial latent feature space, which will be iteratively refined. The iterative feature space refinement process is described in detail in Sect. 2.5, and the final refined latent feature space is used for instance classification. During inference, we map a test instance from a test slide to the refined latent feature space and calculate its positive score for instance-level classification. For bag-level classification, we only use the simple mean-pooling approach to aggregate the positive scores of all instances in a bag. Since both the training and the inference are based on each independent instance (i.e. without using its position information in the slide), our method is of permutation invariance.

2.3   Self-supervised Masked Autoencoders for Feature Space Initialization

It is crucial to learn an instance-level feature representation that is suitable for distribution modeling. We propose to use the state-of-the-art self-supervised learning framework masked autoencoders (MAE) [10] to extract the feature representations and initialize the feature space. MAE learns a robust feature representation by randomly masking a high proportion of patches of the input image and reconstructing the missing pixels using Transformer. We first train the MAE with all instances from the negative and positive slides, and then use the trained encoder as an instance-level feature extractor and map all instances in the training bags into the initial feature space.

2.4   Cluster-Conditioned Feature Distribution Modeling

We propose a feature distribution modeling method based on K-means clustering and Mahalanobis distance. Specifically, we first use the K-means algorithm to cluster all instances from negative slides in the training set into M clusters, where each cluster is denoted as C_m. Next, we compute the positive scores $s_{i,j}$ using the Mahalanobis distance for all instances from both negative slides and positive slides in the training set,

$$s_{i,j} = \min_m D\left(z_{i,j}, C_m\right) = \min_m \left(z_{i,j} - \mu_m\right)^T \sum_m^{-1} \left(z_{i,j} - \mu_m\right) \tag{2}$$

where $D(\cdot)$ denotes the Mahalanobis distance, and μ_m and Σ_m are the mean and covariance of all instances in the cluster. It can be seen that the positive score of an instance is actually the minimum of the distances from the instance to each cluster. A higher positive score indicates a higher probability that the instance is positive, and vice versa.

2.5   Pseudo Label-Based Feature Space Refinement

The direct use of the initial feature space based on MAE does not model the distribution of positive instances and negative instances well because the training of MAE is completely self-supervised and the bag-level supervision is not utilized. Therefore, we further propose a pseudo label-based feature space refinement strategy to refine it.

This feature space refine strategy is an iterative process. In each iteration, we first cluster all the instances from the negative slides in the training set using the K-means algorithm and calculate the positive scores of all instances from both positive and negative slides. A proportion of the instances with the highest positive scores from the positive slides and a proportion of instances with the lowest positive scores from the negative slides are called extreme instances, and they are assigned pseudo labels 1 and 0, respectively. With these extreme instances and their pseudo labels, we train a simple binary classifier consisting of a one-FC-layer Linear Projection Head and a one-FC-layer Classification Head in a supervised manner. Finally, we utilize the Linear Projection Head to remap the current instance feature into a new feature space to achieve the feature space refinement. The above process of feature space refinement iterates until convergence.

3   Experimental Results

3.1   Datasets

CAMELYON16 Dataset. CAMELYON16 dataset [1] is a widely used publicly available dataset for metastasis detection in breast cancer, including 270 training WSIs and 130 test WSIs. The WSIs that contained metastasis were labeled positive, and the WSIs that did not contain metastasis were labeled negative. The dataset provides not only the labels of whether a WSI is positive but also pixel-level labels of the metastasis areas. Following the MIL paradigm, we used only slide-level labels in the training process and evaluated the performance of our method in both the slide-level classification task and the patch-level classification task. We divided each WSI into 512×512 patches without overlapping under $5\times$ magnification. Patches with an entropy less than 5 are discarded as background. A patch is labeled as positive only if it contains 25% or more cancer areas; otherwise, it is labeled as negative. Eventually, a total of 186,604 patches were obtained, of which there were only 8117 positive patches (4.3%).

TCGA Lung Cancer Dataset. The TCGA Lung Cancer dataset includes a total of 1054 WSIs from The Cancer Genome Atlas (TCGA) Data Portal, which includes two sub-types of lung cancer, namely Lung Adenocarcinoma and Lung Squamous Cell Carcinoma. Only slide-level labels are available for this dataset, and patch-level labels are unknown. Following DSMIL [13], this dataset contains about 5.2 million patches at $20\times$ magnification, with an average of about 5,000 patches per bag.

3.2   Implementation Details

For the MAE, we only modified its input size of the ViT model in its encoder and decoder (from 224 to 512), and other model details are the same as those in [10]. For training the MAE, we set the mask ratio to 75%, use the Adam optimizer with a learning rate of 1.5e−4, a weight decay of 0.05, a batch size of 128, and train 500 epochs using 4 Nvidia 3090 GPUs. The number of clusters in Sect. 2.4 is set to 10 classes, and the proportion of extreme instances selected for refinement in Sect. 2.5 are set to 10%. For feature refinement, we use Adam optimizer with an initial learning rate of 0.01 and cosine descent by epoch. Both the Linear Projector Head and Classification Head are composed of one fully connected layer. Refinement convergence means that the decrease of the cross-entropy loss is below a small threshold in 10 consecutive epochs.

3.3   Evaluation Metrics and Comparison Methods

We report the AUC and FROC metrics for patch-level localization task and the AUC and Accuracy metrics for slide-level classification task. We compared our method with the latest methods in the field of MIL-based histopathological image analysis [4,7,12,13,22]. Among them, Ab-MIL [12], Loss-based-MIL [22] and DSMIL [13] are embedding-based methods and RNN-MIL [4] and Chikontwe-MIL [7] are key-instance-based methods.

Table 1. Results of patch-level and slide-level metrics on CAMELYON16 dataset and TCGA Lung Cancer dataset.

(a) Metrics on CAMELYON16 dataset.

Method	Patch AUC	Patch FROC	Slide AUC	Slide Accuracy
Ab-MIL (ICML'18)	0.4739	0.1202	0.6612	0.6746
RNN-MIL (Nat. Med.'19)	0.6055	0.3011	0.6913	0.6845
Loss-based-MIL (AAAI'20)	0.6173	0.3012	0.7024	0.7011
Chikontwe-MIL (MICCAI'20)	0.7880	0.3717	0.7024	0.7123
DSMIL (CVPR'21)	0.8873	0.4560	0.7544	0.7359
DGMIL (Ours)	0.9045	0.4887	0.8368	0.8018
Fully-supervised	0.9644	0.5663	0.8621	0.8828

(b)Metrics on TCGA Lung Cancer dataset.

Method	Slide AUC	Slide Accuracy
Mean-pooling	0.9369	0.8857
Max-pooling	0.9014	0.8088
Ab-MIL (ICML'18)	0.9488	0.9000
RNN-MIL (Nat. Med.'19)	0.9107	0.8619
DSMIL (CVPR'21)	0.9633	0.9190
DGMIL (Ours)	0.9702	0.9200

3.4   Results

Table 1 (a) shows the performance of our method and the competitors for both slide-level and patch-level classification tasks on CAMELYON16 dataset, and our method achieves the best performance on both tasks. Ab-MIL [12] used bag-level loss and used attention mechanism for patch classification, which can hardly classify the patches. Loss-based-MIL [22] utilized both a slide-level loss and a patch-level loss, and it achieved higher performances than Ab-MIL on both tasks. Both RNN-MIL [4] and Chikontwe-MIL [7] used the output probability of the instance classifier in the current iteration to select the key instances. However, the pseudo labels for some selected key instances may be wrong, and the true positive instances may not be fully selected, which lead to their limited performance. DSMIL [13] uses the contrastive self-supervised framework Simclr [5] for instance-level feature extraction and uses Masked Non-Local Operation-based dual-stream aggregator for both instance-level and bag-level classification, and it achieved the current SOTA performance on both tasks. However, its loss function is also defined at the bag-level and without extra guidance of data distribution, and the model is not motivated to make accurate predictions of all instances. In comparison, our proposed method DGMIL models the data distribution properly through iterative refinement of the feature space and achieve the highest performance on both tasks. Especially, the slide-level AUC of DGMIL is significant higher than that of DSMIL.

Table 1 (b) shows the performance of our method and the competitors for the slide-level classification task on TCGA Lung Cancer dataset, and our method also achieves the best performance.

Table 2. Results of ablation tests on CAMELYON16 dataset.

(a) Ablation tests of main strategies.

Method	Distribution Modeling	One-shot Refinement	Iterative Refinement	Patch AUC	Slide AUC
Baseline1				0.7672	0.7637
Baseline2	✓			0.8371	0.7355
One-shot DGMIL	✓	✓		0.8899	0.8267
DGMIL	✓		✓	0.9045	0.8368

(b) Further tests on feature space refinement.

Ratio	Patch AUC	Slide AUC
1%	0.8443	0.7649
5%	0.8903	0.8293
10%	0.9045	0.8368
20%	0.8911	0.8196
30%	0.8897	0.8280
Existing SOTA	0.8873	0.7544

4 Ablation Study

Table 2 (a) shows the results of our ablation tests on the CAMELYON16 dataset. **Baseline1** denotes that instead of using Cluster-conditioned Feature Distribution Modeling, an instance-level classifier is directly trained to predict all instances using a key-instance-based training approach similar to [4,22], where the key instances are selected according to the top 10% instances with the largest output probability and the top 10% instances with the smallest output probability. **Baseline2** denotes that only the initial feature space obtained by MAE is used to model feature distribution and calculate positive scores without feature space refinement. **One-shot DGMIL** indicates that the feature space refinement is done only once.

It can be seen that **Baseline1** does not achieve good performance because the key instances selected by the network are likely to be inaccurate. In addition, the direct use of the initial feature space based on MAE does not model the distribution of positive instances and negative instances very well, because the training of MAE is completely self-supervised and lacks the guidance of bag-level supervision information. Therefore, the initial feature space is not fully suitable for distribution modeling and the performance of **Baseline2** is not very high. On the other hand, one-shot refinement of the feature space (**one-shot DGMIL**) can improve the performance and multiple iterative refinement help DGMIL achieve the best performance.

Table 2 (b) shows the effect of the proportion of selected extreme instances on the final results during iterative feature space refinement. When too few extreme instances are selected, the feature space cannot be adjusted adequately. On the contrary, when too many extreme instances are selected, due to the low proportion of positive patches in the dataset itself, the number of false pseudo labels increases, resulting in distortion of the feature space. It can be seen that 10% is the optimal choice. At the same time, these results indicate that the proposed method is robust to the choice of the proportion of extreme instances. Using any proportion from 1% to 30%, the slide-level AUCs all exceed the current SOTA, and using any proportion from 5% to 30%, the patch-level AUCs all exceed the current SOTA.

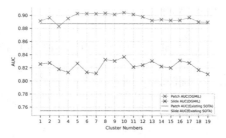

Fig. 2. Results of ablation tests on the number of clusters in Feature Distribution Modeling.

Figure 2 shows the effect of the number of clusters on the performance when performing feature distribution modeling, where a cluster number of one indicates that no clustering is performed. As can be seen, our method is not sensitive to the number of clusters, but performing clustering does work better than not performing clustering. The reason is that many different phenotypes exist in negative instances, such as normal cells, blood vessels, fat, and others in normal tissues, so the distribution of negative instances is fairly sparse. Clustering can divide different phenotypes into different clusters and help make the instance-to-cluster distance better reflect whether an instance is negative or not. It can be seen that clustering into 10 classes is the most effective choice.

5   Conclusions

In this paper, we propose DGMIL: a feature distribution guided deep MIL framework for WSI classification and positive patch localization. We propose a cluster-conditioned feature distribution modeling method and a pseudo label-based iterative feature space refinement strategy. Instead of designing complex discriminative classifiers, we construct a proper feature space in which the positive and negative instances can be easily separated. New SOTA performance is achieved on the CAMELYON16 public breast cancer metastasis detection dataset and the TCGA Lung Cancer dataset.

Acknowledgments. This work was supported by National Natural Science Foundation of China under Grant 82072021. The TCGA Lung Cancer dataset is from the TCGA Research Network: https://www.cancer.gov/tcga.

References

1. Bejnordi, B.E., et al.: Diagnostic assessment of deep learning algorithms for detection of lymph node metastases in women with breast cancer. JAMA **318**(22), 2199–2210 (2017)
2. Bi, Q., Qin, K., Li, Z., Zhang, H., Xu, K., Xia, G.S.: A multiple-instance densely-connected convnet for aerial scene classification. IEEE Trans. Image Process. **29**, 4911–4926 (2020)
3. Bi, Q., et al.: Local-global dual perception based deep multiple instance learning for retinal disease classification. In: de Bruijne, M., et al. (eds.) MICCAI 2021. LNCS, vol. 12908, pp. 55–64. Springer, Cham (2021). https://doi.org/10.1007/978-3-030-87237-3_6
4. Campanella, G., et al.: Clinical-grade computational pathology using weakly supervised deep learning on whole slide images. Nat. Med. **25**(8), 1301–1309 (2019)
5. Chen, T., Kornblith, S., Norouzi, M., Hinton, G.: A simple framework for contrastive learning of visual representations. In: International Conference on Machine Learning (ICML), pp. 1597–1607. PMLR (2020)
6. Cheplygina, V., de Bruijne, M., Pluim, J.P.: Not-so-supervised: a survey of semi-supervised, multi-instance, and transfer learning in medical image analysis. Med. Image Anal. **54**, 280–296 (2019)
7. Chikontwe, P., Kim, M., Nam, S.J., Go, H., Park, S.H.: Multiple instance learning with center embeddings for histopathology classification. In: Martel, A.L., et al. (eds.) MICCAI 2020. LNCS, vol. 12265, pp. 519–528. Springer, Cham (2020). https://doi.org/10.1007/978-3-030-59722-1_50
8. Cornish, T.C., Swapp, R.E., Kaplan, K.J.: Whole-slide imaging: routine pathologic diagnosis. Adv. Anat. Pathol. **19**(3), 152–159 (2012)
9. Couture, H.D., Marron, J.S., Perou, C.M., Troester, M.A., Niethammer, M.: Multiple instance learning for heterogeneous images: training a CNN for histopathology. In: Frangi, A.F., Schnabel, J.A., Davatzikos, C., Alberola-López, C., Fichtinger, G. (eds.) MICCAI 2018. LNCS, vol. 11071, pp. 254–262. Springer, Cham (2018). https://doi.org/10.1007/978-3-030-00934-2_29
10. He, K., Chen, X., Xie, S., Li, Y., Dollár, P., Girshick, R.: Masked autoencoders are scalable vision learners. arXiv preprint arXiv:2111.06377 (2021)
11. He, L., Long, L.R., Antani, S., Thoma, G.R.: Histology image analysis for carcinoma detection and grading. Comput. Methods Programs Biomed. **107**(3), 538–556 (2012)
12. Ilse, M., Tomczak, J., Welling, M.: Attention-based deep multiple instance learning. In: International Conference on Machine Learning (ICML), pp. 2127–2136. PMLR (2018)
13. Li, B., Li, Y., Eliceiri, K.W.: Dual-stream multiple instance learning network for whole slide image classification with self-supervised contrastive learning. In: Proceedings of the IEEE/CVF Conference on Computer Vision and Pattern Recognition (CVPR), pp. 14318–14328 (2021)
14. Li, H., Yang, F., Zhao, Yu., Xing, X., Zhang, J., Gao, M., Huang, J., Wang, L., Yao, J.: DT-MIL: Deformable Transformer for Multi-instance Learning on Histopathological Image. In: de Bruijne, M., Cattin, P.C., Cotin, S., Padoy, N., Speidel, S., Zheng, Y., Essert, C. (eds.) MICCAI 2021. LNCS, vol. 12908, pp. 206–216. Springer, Cham (2021). https://doi.org/10.1007/978-3-030-87237-3_20
15. Li, S., et al.: Multi-instance multi-scale CNN for medical image classification. In: Shen, D., et al. (eds.) MICCAI 2019. LNCS, vol. 11767, pp. 531–539. Springer, Cham (2019). https://doi.org/10.1007/978-3-030-32251-9_58

16. Lu, M.Y., Williamson, D.F., Chen, T.Y., Chen, R.J., Barbieri, M., Mahmood, F.: Data-efficient and weakly supervised computational pathology on whole-slide images. Nat. Biomed. Eng. **5**(6), 555–570 (2021)
17. Myronenko, A., Xu, Z., Yang, D., Roth, H.R., Xu, D.: Accounting for dependencies in deep learning based multiple instance learning for whole slide imaging. In: de Bruijne, M., et al. (eds.) MICCAI 2021. LNCS, vol. 12908, pp. 329–338. Springer, Cham (2021). https://doi.org/10.1007/978-3-030-87237-3_32
18. Pantanowitz, L., et al.: Review of the current state of whole slide imaging in pathology. J. Pathol. Inform. **2**, 2–36 (2011)
19. Rony, J., Belharbi, S., Dolz, J., Ayed, I.B., McCaffrey, L., Granger, E.: Deep weakly-supervised learning methods for classification and localization in histology images: a survey. arXiv preprint arXiv:1909.03354 (2019)
20. Shao, Z., Bian, H., Chen, Y., Wang, Y., Zhang, J., Ji, X., et al.: TransMIL: transformer based correlated multiple instance learning for whole slide image classification. In: Advances in Neural Information Processing Systems (NIPS), vol. 34 (2021)
21. Sharma, Y., Shrivastava, A., Ehsan, L., Moskaluk, C.A., Syed, S., Brown, D.: Cluster-to-Conquer: a framework for end-to-end multi-instance learning for whole slide image classification. In: Medical Imaging with Deep Learning (MIDL), pp. 682–698. PMLR (2021)
22. Shi, X., Xing, F., Xie, Y., Zhang, Z., Cui, L., Yang, L.: Loss-based attention for deep multiple instance learning. In: Proceedings of the AAAI Conference on Artificial Intelligence (AAAI), vol. 34, pp. 5742–5749 (2020)
23. Srinidhi, C.L., Ciga, O., Martel, A.L.: Deep neural network models for computational histopathology: a survey. Med. Image Anal. **67**, 101813 (2021)
24. Xu, Y., Zhu, J.Y., Chang, E., Tu, Z.: Multiple clustered instance learning for histopathology cancer image classification, segmentation and clustering. In: 2012 IEEE Conference on Computer Vision and Pattern Recognition (CVPR), pp. 964–971. IEEE (2012)
25. Zhao, Y., et al.: Predicting lymph node metastasis using histopathological images based on multiple instance learning with deep graph convolution. In: Proceedings of the IEEE/CVF Conference on Computer Vision and Pattern Recognition (CVPR), pp. 4837–4846 (2020)

ReMix: A General and Efficient Framework for Multiple Instance Learning Based Whole Slide Image Classification

Jiawei Yang[1,2], Hanbo Chen[1], Yu Zhao[1], Fan Yang[1], Yao Zhang[3,4], Lei He[2], and Jianhua Yao[1(✉)]

[1] Tencent AI Lab, Bellevue, USA
jianhuayao@tencent.com
[2] University of California, Los Angeles, USA
jiawei118@ucla.edu
[3] Institute of Computing Technology, Chinese Academy of Sciences, Beijing, China
[4] University of Chinese Academy of Sciences, Beijing, China

Abstract. Whole slide image (WSI) classification often relies on deep weakly supervised multiple instance learning (MIL) methods to handle gigapixel resolution images and slide-level labels. Yet the decent performance of deep learning comes from harnessing massive datasets and diverse samples, urging the need for efficient training pipelines for scaling to large datasets and data augmentation techniques for diversifying samples. However, current MIL-based WSI classification pipelines are memory-expensive and computation-inefficient since they usually assemble tens of thousands of patches as bags for computation. On the other hand, despite their popularity in other tasks, data augmentations are unexplored for WSI MIL frameworks. To address them, we propose ReMix, a general and efficient framework for MIL based WSI classification. It comprises two steps: reduce and mix. First, it reduces the number of instances in WSI bags by substituting instances with instance prototypes, *i.e.*, patch cluster centroids. Then, we propose a "Mix-the-bag" augmentation that contains four online, stochastic and flexible latent space augmentations. It brings diverse and reliable class-identity-preserving semantic changes in the latent space while enforcing semantic-perturbation invariance. We evaluate ReMix on two public datasets with two state-of-the-art MIL methods. In our experiments, consistent improvements in precision, accuracy, and recall have been achieved but with orders of magnitude reduced training time and memory consumption, demonstrating ReMix's effectiveness and efficiency. Code is available at https://github.com/TencentAILabHealthcare/ReMix.

J. Yang and H. Chen—Equally contribution.
J. Yang—Work done during an intern at Tencent AI Lab.

Supplementary Information The online version contains supplementary material available at https://doi.org/10.1007/978-3-031-16434-7_4.

L. Wang et al. (Eds.): MICCAI 2022, LNCS 13432, pp. 35–45, 2022.
https://doi.org/10.1007/978-3-031-16434-7_4

Keywords: Multiple instance learning · Whole slide image · Data augmentation · Deep learning

1 Introduction

Whole slide images (WSIs) are digital scans of pathology tissue slides that provide critical information for disease diagnosis [26]. Recently, many computer-aided WSI diagnostic systems have been developed upon deep learning (DL) methods [13,16,24]. However, some challenges in WSI classification still exist.

First of all, WSIs are huge and challenging to be processed at once by DL models. Given micron-size pixels and centimeter-sized slides, a WSI is usually of gigapixel size. Thus, it needs to be divided into thousands or tens of thousands of small "patches" for computational analysis. Current successful paradigms formulate WSI classification as a weakly supervised multiple instance learning (MIL) problem [13,16,17]. Under this setting, each WSI is regarded as a *bag* that contains many *instances* of patches. In practice, each bag is loaded into memory and fed into deep MIL models separately due to poor parallelization and large size. However, the number of instances in each bag can vary strikingly, leading to unstable input/output (I/O) stream. Besides, the different numbers of instances also make parallelizing MIL models hard as they cannot be directly composed into a batch. One naive solution is to select small random subsets of patches from each WSI [22]. Alternatively, Yao *et al.* [30] propose to cluster over the extracted features based on an ImageNet-pre-trained encoder to define phenotype groups and sample patches from those groups each time.

Second, DL models are usually data-hungry—they tend to perform better with diversified labeled data, which are expensive to collect. Data augmentation is a simple yet effective approach to improving data diversity [23]. Over the years, many augmentation methods have been proposed for different tasks. However, MIL problems' augmentations are unexplored, especially for WSI classification. Using image processing functions such as cropping, flipping, or color shifting for all instances is extremely inefficient. Therefore, developing efficient and effective augmentation methods for WSI classification is of significant interest.

To address the issues mentioned above, we propose `ReMix`, a general and efficient framework for MIL-based WSI classification. It consists of two steps: (1) Reduce and (2) Mix. Given the nature of WSIs that many tissues and contexts are similar, repetitive, and sometimes redundant, we hypothesize that using the clustered instance prototypes, instead of all available patches, to represent a WSI can still yield comparably well or even better performance. By doing so, `ReMix` *reduces* the number of instances inside a bag by orders of magnitude (*e.g.*, from 10^4 to $10^0 \sim 10^1$). After that, we propose a novel augmentation method called "Mix-the-bag." It contains several online, stochastic and flexible latent space augmentations that are directly applied on bags as well as on instance prototypes. It *mixes* different bags by appending, replacing, interpolating instance prototypes, or transferring semantic variations between different bags. This process is applied in the latent space via numerical addition, which is highly efficient. Our key contributions are:

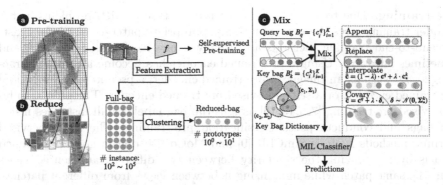

Fig. 1. ReMix's overview. (a) Patch encoder pre-training. (b) Reduce the number of instances by substituting them with prototypes (right); several patches can abstract a large-size whole slide image (left). (c) Mix the bags by appending, replacing, interpolating prototypes, or transferring intra-cluster covariance from other WSIs.

- Propose a general, simple yet effective method to improve the training efficiency of the MIL framework for WSI classification.
- Propose a novel and efficient latent augmentation method for MIL-based WSI classification, which is much underexplored in existing works.
- Improve previous state-of-the-art MIL methods on two public datasets by considerable margins but with orders of magnitude reduced budgets.

2 Method

2.1 Preliminary: MIL Formulation

In MIL, a dataset that has N bags is typically formulated as $\mathcal{D} = \{(B_i, y_i)\}_{i=1}^{N}$, where $B_i = \{x_k\}_{k=1}^{N_i}$ denotes the i-th bag that has N_i instances and y_i is the bag label. For binary classification, a bag is defined as positive if it contains at least one positive instance and negative otherwise. A general *spatial-agnostic* MIL classification process that does not rely on the spatial relationship between instances to make decisions can be expressed as $\hat{y}_i = g(f(x_1), ..., f(x_{N_i}))$, where $f(\cdot)$ is a patch instance encoder, and $g(\cdot)$ is an instances aggregator that aggregates information and makes final predictions.

2.2 ReMix

Overview. Instead of improving the performance of a specific dataset or model, our ReMix is a general framework that can accommodate most spatial-agnostic MIL methods. Figure 1 shows its overview. It consists of two efficient and effective steps, *i.e.*, reduce and mix, which we elaborate on below.

Pre-training. Due to the weakly supervision nature of MIL problems, patch encoder training faces the issue of lacking appropriate patch-level labels. Existing end-to-end training methods are usually expensive [7,20], inefficient, and sometimes infeasible. Using a pre-trained encoder has become a common practice [20,30], such as an ImageNet pre-trained encoder, a pseudo fully-supervised pre-trained encoder, or a self-supervised pre-trained encoder. The pseudo fully-supervised pre-training [7,8,13,16] assigns the bag labels to all instances inside the bags and conducts patch classification pre-training. The self-supervised learning methods such as SimCLR [9] and MoCo [14] obtain good pre-trained models by maximizing the similarity between two different augmented views from the same patch while minimizing it between views from different patches. Recent studies have witnessed the superiority of self-supervised pre-training on large-scale and imbalanced WSI patches over others [11,20,29]. We follow [20] to adopt a state-of-the-art self-supervised learning method—SimCLR [9] for patch encoder pre-training. Note that the choice of patch-encoder is orthogonal to the ReMix framework and downstream MIL models' training. We here briefly discuss available pre-training methods only for completeness. Thus their training budgets are not considered in this work.

Reduce. ReMix reduces the number of instances in each bag via clustering. Conventionally, all patches extracted from a WSI are assembled as a bag for downstream MIL classification [16,20]. However, the number of instances inside a bag can be huge (e.g., $N_i = 50{,}000$), leading to heavy I/O cost and high memory consumption during training. Given the nature of histological scans in mind that a large portion of tissues is usually similar, repetitive and, sometimes redundant, we propose to substitute instances with instance prototypes. Specifically, for each bag, we perform K-Means on the patches' representations to obtain K clusters and use their prototypes (centroids) to represent the bag, i.e., $B_i' = \{\mathbf{c}_k\}_{k=1}^{K}$, where $\mathbf{c}_k$ corresponds to the k-th prototype. Below, we denote the reduced-bags as B' and the full-bags as B. The WSI thumbnails in Fig. 1-(b) illustrate how several patches (reduced-bag) can provide sufficient information of the entire WSI (full-bag) for certain downstream tasks, e.g., whole-slide classification. The reduced-bag can be seen as a denoised abstraction of full-bag.

To fully exploit WSI information, inspired by [29], we construct a *bag dictionary* as $\Phi_i = \{(\mathbf{c}_k, \mathbf{\Sigma}_k)\}_{k=1}^{K}$ for each bag, where $\mathbf{\Sigma}_k$ corresponds to the intra-cluster covariance matrix of the k-th cluster. A bag dictionary captures how its instances distribute at a high level by modeling a multivariate Gaussian distribution $\mathcal{N}(\mathbf{c}_k, \mathbf{\Sigma}_k)$. Besides, the covariance can reflect the semantic directions inherent in each cluster, e.g., how features vary in that cluster.

Mix. ReMix applies latent space augmentation by mixing the bags to increase data diversity. DL models are prone to overfit with limited labeled training samples. Data augmentation can provide additional artificial data [10,12,23,25]. However, using image processing functions for bags can be extremely inefficient. Here we propose "mix-the-bag" augmentation that is illustrated in Fig. 1-(c).

At a high level, when a bag is fed into a MIL classifier, we randomly sample another bag of the same class and "mix" them. Without loss of generality, we define the former bag as a query bag $B'_q = \{\mathbf{c}^q_i\}^K_{i=1}$ and the latter bag as a key bag $B'_k = \{\mathbf{c}^k_i\}^K_{i=1}$. Their instances $\mathbf{c}^q$ and $\mathbf{c}^k$ are called query prototypes and key prototypes subsequently. For each query prototype $\mathbf{c}^q_i$, we find its closest key prototype $\mathbf{c}^k_{i*}$ and then augment the query bag with an applying probability of p by one of the following four augmentations:

- **Append:** append the closest key prototype $\mathbf{c}^k_{i*}$ to query bag B_q.
- **Replace:** replace the query prototype $\mathbf{c}^q_i$ with its closest key prototype $\mathbf{c}^k_{i*}$.
- **Interpolate:** append an interpolated representation

$$\hat{\mathbf{c}}_i = (1 - \lambda) \cdot \mathbf{c}^q_i + \lambda \cdot \mathbf{c}^k_{i*} \tag{1}$$

to the query bag B_q, where λ is a strength hyper-parameter.
- **Covary:** generate a new representation from the key covariance matrix by

$$\hat{\mathbf{c}}_i = \mathbf{c}^q_i + \lambda \cdot \boldsymbol{\delta}, \quad \boldsymbol{\delta} \sim \mathcal{N}(\mathbf{0}, \boldsymbol{\Sigma}^k_{i*}) \tag{2}$$

and append it to the bag B_q, where λ is a strength hyper-parameter and $\boldsymbol{\Sigma}^k_{i*}$ is the covariance matrix corresponding to the closest key prototype $\mathbf{c}^k_{i*}$.

It is vital to sample another bag from the *same class* and mix the query prototype with the *most similar* key prototype. It helps preserve critical class-related information and reduces the risk of losing original class identity. In addition to four individual augmentations, we propose to combine them sequentially as a "joint" augmentation.

2.3   Intuitions on ReMix's Effectiveness

Implicit Data Re-balance Behavior. Tissue imbalance is a common problem with WSIs. The majority of similar patches almost convey the same information about the WSI but could dominate in numbers over other distinct minority patches. Using the representative prototypes to assemble WSI bags can be seen as an implicit data re-balance mechanism that bridges the gap between the numbers of the majority and the minority. It alleviates the tissue imbalance problem to some extent. Besides, using the mean embedding of a group of similar patches could obtain a more accurate and less noisy tissue representation.

Efficient Semantic Consistency Regularization. Consistency regularization underlies many successful works, such as semi-supervised learning [5,6,25]. Usually, consistency regularization enforces models' predictions to be invariant under different data augmentations [25]. Instead of augmenting instances using image processing functions in the input RGB space, ReMix augments the bags by bringing diverse semantic changes in the latent space. Guided by bag labels and prototypes similarity, such changes are class-identity-preserving. The bag instance combination is no longer static and unaltered but diverse and dynamic, *i.e.*, different new bags can be fed into the MIL classifier every time. Our augmentations can be seen as efficient semantic consistency regularization methods.

Why Clustering and Additive Latent Augmentation Works. When learned properly, the deep representation space is shown to be highly linearized [3,27]. Consequently, the distance metrics could demonstrate the similarity between patches, making clustering meaningful. Moreover, in such a space, linear transformation, *e.g.*, interpolating features or adding semantic translation vector δ, is likely to provide plausible representations [10]. The mixed bag representations can serve as hard examples that help models generalize better [19,28,31].

3   Experiments

3.1   Datasets and Metrics

UniToPatho. UniToPatho [4] is a public dataset comprising 9536 hematoxylin and eosin (H&E) stained patches extracted from 292 WSIs. The slides are scanned at 20× magnification (0.4415 μm/px). There are six classes in this dataset. We use the official split of 204/88 slides for training/testing, respectively. For patch processing, we crop the provided images into 224 × 224 sized patches without overlapping. Under this setting, the average number of instances per bag is about 1.6k, with the largest bag having more than 20k instances.

Camelyon16. Camelyon16 [2] is a publicly available dataset consisting of 400 H&E stained slides from breast cancer screening. It contains two classes, *i.e.*, normal and tumor. We directly use the pre-computed features provided by DSMIL [20] without further processing. There are 271/129 slides in the training/testing set. The average number of instances per bag is around 8k, with the largest bag having more than 50k instances.

Metrics. We report class-wise averaged precision, recall, and accuracy. To avoid randomness, we run all experiments ten times and report the averaged metrics.

3.2   Implementation Details

Patch Encoder. For the Camelyon16 dataset [2], we use the pre-computed features provided by [20]. They pre-train a SimCLR patch encoder directly on the Camelyon16 dataset and use it for Camelyon16 patch encoding. To align with that setting, we also pre-train a ResNet-18 encoder [15] with SimCLR [9] on UniToPatho [4] dataset. More pre-training details are in Supplementary.

MIL Models. To demonstrate that ReMix can be MIL model-agnostic, we use two previous state-of-the-art deep MIL models, namely ABMIL [17] and DSMIL [20], for our experiments. ABMIL and DSMIL are both attention-based MIL methods that compute the attention-weighted sum of instances features as the bag representation. They differ in the way of attention computing. ABMIL [17] predicts the attention scores of each patch using a multi-layer perceptron (MLP) without explicit patch relation modeling. DSMIL [20] is a dual-stream method that comprises an instance branch and a bag branch. The instance branch identifies the highest scored instance. In addition, the bag branch measures the similarity between other patches and the highest scored instance and thereafter utilizes the similarity scores to compute attention.

We use DSMIL's codebase for implementation and training. Unless other specified, all MIL models are optimized for 50 epochs by Adam optimizer [18] with an initial learning rate of 2e−4 and a cosine annealing learning rate schedule [21]. The mini-batch size is 1 (bag) for a fair comparison, despite that ReMix can easily scale it up since the reduced bags have the same number of instances and thus can be composed into a batch for parallel computing.

ReMix Hyper-parameters. There are three hyper-parameters in ReMix, $i.e.$, number of prototypes K, augmentation probability p, and strength λ. To study the effects of different hyper-parameters, we first sweep K in $\{1, 2, 4, 8, 16, 32\}$ to find the optimal K for each method and dataset. For simplicity and bag diversity, we set $p = 0.5$ and uniformly sample λ from $(0, 1)$ in all individual augmentations. For "joint" augmentation, we set $p = 0.1$ since it comprises four augmentations and too strong augmentation is known to be harmful. Both MIL methods share the optimal K values: $K = 1$ for the UniToPatho dataset and $K = 8$ for the Camelyon16 dataset. Due to limited space, we postpone the empirical studies for each hyper-parameter to Supplementary, $e.g.$, studying the robustness to the choice of augmentation probability p and the choice of the number of prototypes K.

3.3 Comparisons

Main Results. Table 1 shows the main results. Even without "mix-the-bag" augmentations (no aug.), ReMix can improve previous state-of-the-arts by only the "reduce" step in both datasets, $e.g.$, +13.75% and +3.22% precision for ABMIL and DSMIL respectively in UniToPatho and +1.50%, +1.31% precision for them in Camelyon16. Overall, ABMIL benefits more from ReMix than DSMIL. DSMIL computes $self$-$attention$ that explicitly considers the similarity between different instances inside a bag, while ABMIL directly predicts attention scores using an MLP for all instances without such explicit inter-instance relation computing. For this reason, we conjure that ABMIL's attentions are more likely to overfit on redundant instances than DSMIL's, and thus it benefits more from the denoised reduced-bags. Using the representative prototypes can ease the recognition process and alleviate the overfitting problem. These results suggest that ReMix can reduce data noise in the bag representations to some extent and improve performance.

Applying "mix-the-bag" augmentations can further improve the performance of reduced-bags (no aug.) by a considerable margin, $e.g.$, +2.27% and +3.07% accuracy for ReMix-ABMIL and ReMix-DSMIL respectively, in UniToPatho. In general, append-augmentation fits more to DSMIL, while ABMIL favors covary-augmentation. Especially, covary-augmentation achieves the top-2 performance

Table 1. Main results. The "Average" columns report the mean of precision, recall and accuracy. Bold, underlined and italicized numbers are the first, second and third best entries. All results are averaged over 10 independent runs. Numbers are shown in percentage (%). "no aug." means no augmentation.

Methods\Metrics	UniToPatho Dataset [4]				Camelyon16 Dataset [2]			
	Precision	Recall	Accuracy	Average	Precision	Recall	Accuracy	Average
ABMIL [17] (baseline)	56.18	58.50	60.11	58.26	92.47	92.79	93.02	92.76
ReMix-ABMIL (no aug.)	69.93	72.85	68.75	70.51	93.97	93.15	93.95	93.69
ReMix-ABMIL (append)	71.81	74.54	69.09	71.81	94.59	93.38	94.34	94.10
ReMix-ABMIL (replace)	70.16	74.34	68.75	71.08	94.60	93.52	94.42	94.18
ReMix-ABMIL (interpolate)	71.55	75.54	70.23	72.44	94.65	93.49	94.42	94.19
ReMix-ABMIL (covary)	**72.32**	**76.71**	**71.02**	**73.35**	**94.75**	**93.55**	**94.49**	**94.26**
ReMix-ABMIL (joint)	72.13	76.00	70.91	73.01	94.69	93.45	94.42	94.18
Best Improvement Δ	+16.14	+18.21	+10.91	+15.09	+2.28	+0.76	+1.47	+1.50
DSMIL [20] (baseline)	72.92	79.41	76.36	76.23	94.37	93.39	94.11[†]	93.96
ReMix-DSMIL (no aug.)	76.14	79.26	77.95	77.78	95.68	93.44	94.80	94.64
ReMix-DSMIL (append)	77.91	80.56	**81.02**	79.83	96.39	**94.10**	**95.43**	**95.31**
ReMix-DSMIL (replace)	76.60	79.30	78.64	78.18	95.33	93.44	94.65	94.47
ReMix-DSMIL (interpolate)	76.99	80.26	80.00	79.08	96.39	93.96	95.35	95.23
ReMix-DSMIL (covary)	77.72	80.52	80.46	79.57	**96.51**	93.88	95.35	95.25
ReMix-DSMIL (joint)	**78.20**	**80.94**	80.68	**79.94**	96.18	93.97	95.27	95.14
Best Improvement Δ	+5.28	+1.53	+4.66	+3.71	+2.14	+0.71	+1.32	+1.35

† The reported accuracy for Camelyon16 in DSMIL [20] is 89.92%. We reproduce a better baseline.

across datasets, confirming our motivation that transferring others' covariance in the latent space could provide reliable and diversified variations for semantic augmentation. Using full-bags (baseline) can be seen as a special case of augmenting the prototypes with their own covariances. However, such bags are static and unaltered as discussed in Sect. 2.3. In contrast, with ReMix, the reduced and augmented bags can be more diverse and dynamic. Such augmentations are important for low-data applications, e.g., WSI classification. Using "joint" augmentation can further improve some of the results but not all. It is anticipated and in line with experience from other tasks and fields that too strong augmentation is not beneficial for training (e.g., Table 2 from [1]).

Overall, solid gains observed in Table 1 have confirmed the effectiveness of the proposed ReMix framework. We next demonstrate its efficiency.

Training Budgets. We compare the training budgets, i.e., average training time per epoch and the peak memory consumed during training, in Table 2. Although all models are trained with a batch size of 1 for a fair comparison, the ReMix framework significantly outperforms other entries in all training budgets. It costs nearly 20× less training time but obtains better results for both MIL methods in UniToPatho (e.g., +10.91% accuracy). Moreover, it takes about at least 200× shorter training time to achieve better results than the original ones in the Camelyon16 dataset, whose average bag size is about 5× as big as UniToPatho's. It can be expected that the training efficiency gains owned by ReMix would enlarge as the bag size increases. With more data collected in the real world, we argue that the training efficiency should be as important as the classification performance when scaling up to large datasets. Therefore, we emphasize the superiority of `ReMix` in being an extremely efficient framework.

More Studies. We provide more empirical studies, *i.e.*, the effect of the number of prototypes K, the effect of augmentation probability p, and the effect of training MIL classifier longer, in Supplementary to better understand `ReMix`.

Table 2. Comparison of training budgets. Numbers are estimated from 50-epoch training on the same machine with an 8 GB Tesla T4-8C virtual GPU. "Original/ReMix" rows show the multiplier between the original's and ReMix improved budgets.

	Average seconds/Epoch		Memory peak	
Methods\Datasets	UniToPatho	Camelyon16	UniToPatho	Camelyon16
ABMIL[†] (full-bag)	18.41″	235.72″	55.63 MB	332.12 MB
ReMix-ABMIL (no aug.)	0.84″	1.10″	6.45 MB	8.76 MB
Original/ReMix	21.93×	214.29×	8.61×	37.91 ×
DSMIL[†] (full-bag)	19.20″	255.14″	66.58 MB	364.72 MB
ReMix-DSMIL (no aug.)	0.85″	1.12″	6.46 MB	8.76 MB
Original/ReMix	22.57×	227.80×	10.31×	41.63×

[†] We have already improved the original DSMIL/ABMIL training by at least 2× faster speed and 2.4× less memory consumption. Note that, we use a distributed cluster storage platform (Ceph), so the data loading time might be longer than that in local disks.

4 Conclusion

This work presents `ReMix`, a general and efficient framework for MIL-based WSI classification. `ReMix` reduces the number of instances in WSI bags by substituting instances with instance prototypes, and mixes the bags via latent space augmentation methods to improve data diversity. Our `ReMix` can considerably improve previous state-of-the-art MIL classification methods, yet with faster training speed and less memory consumption, showing its effectiveness and efficiency.

References

1. Appalaraju, S., Zhu, Y., Xie, Y., Fehérvári, I.: Towards good practices in self-supervised representation learning. arXiv preprint arXiv:2012.00868 (2020)
2. Bejnordi, B.E., et al.: Diagnostic assessment of deep learning algorithms for detection of lymph node metastases in women with breast cancer. JAMA **318**(22), 2199–2210 (2017)
3. Bengio, Y., Mesnil, G., Dauphin, Y., Rifai, S.: Better mixing via deep representations. In: International Conference on Machine Learning, pp. 552–560. PMLR (2013)

4. Bertero, L., et al.: UniToPatho (2021). https://doi.org/10.21227/9fsv-tm25
5. Berthelot, D., et al.: ReMixMatch: semi-supervised learning with distribution alignment and augmentation anchoring. arXiv preprint arXiv:1911.09785 (2019)
6. Berthelot, D., Carlini, N., Goodfellow, I., Papernot, N., Oliver, A., Raffel, C.: MixMatch: a holistic approach to semi-supervised learning. arXiv preprint arXiv:1905.02249 (2019)
7. Campanella, G., et al.: Clinical-grade computational pathology using weakly supervised deep learning on whole slide images. Nat. Med. **25**(8), 1301–1309 (2019)
8. Chen, H., et al.: Rectified cross-entropy and upper transition loss for weakly supervised whole slide image classifier. In: Shen, D., et al. (eds.) MICCAI 2019. LNCS, vol. 11764, pp. 351–359. Springer, Cham (2019). https://doi.org/10.1007/978-3-030-32239-7_39
9. Chen, T., Kornblith, S., Norouzi, M., Hinton, G.: A simple framework for contrastive learning of visual representations. In: International Conference on Machine Learning, pp. 1597–1607. PMLR (2020)
10. Cheung, T.H., Yeung, D.Y.: Modals: modality-agnostic automated data augmentation in the latent space. In: International Conference on Learning Representations (2020)
11. Ciga, O., Xu, T., Martel, A.L.: Self supervised contrastive learning for digital histopathology. Mach. Learn. Appl. **7**, 100198 (2022)
12. Ghiasi, G., et al.: Simple copy-paste is a strong data augmentation method for instance segmentation. arXiv preprint arXiv:2012.07177 (2020)
13. Hashimoto, N., et al.: Multi-scale domain-adversarial multiple-instance CNN for cancer subtype classification with unannotated histopathological images. In: Proceedings of the IEEE/CVF Conference on Computer Vision and Pattern Recognition, pp. 3852–3861 (2020)
14. He, K., Fan, H., Wu, Y., Xie, S., Girshick, R.: Momentum contrast for unsupervised visual representation learning. In: Proceedings of the IEEE/CVF Conference on Computer Vision and Pattern Recognition, pp. 9729–9738 (2020)
15. He, K., Zhang, X., Ren, S., Sun, J.: Deep residual learning for image recognition. In: Proceedings of the IEEE Conference on Computer Vision and Pattern Recognition, pp. 770–778 (2016)
16. Hou, L., Samaras, D., Kurc, T.M., Gao, Y., Davis, J.E., Saltz, J.H.: Patch-based convolutional neural network for whole slide tissue image classification. In: Proceedings of the IEEE Conference on Computer Vision and Pattern Recognition, pp. 2424–2433 (2016)
17. Ilse, M., Tomczak, J., Welling, M.: Attention-based deep multiple instance learning. In: International Conference on Machine Learning, pp. 2127–2136. PMLR (2018)
18. Kingma, D.P., Ba, J.: Adam: a method for stochastic optimization. arXiv preprint arXiv:1412.6980 (2014)
19. Kuchnik, M., Smith, V.: Efficient augmentation via data subsampling. arXiv preprint arXiv:1810.05222 (2018)
20. Li, B., Li, Y., Eliceiri, K.W.: Dual-stream multiple instance learning network for whole slide image classification with self-supervised contrastive learning. In: Proceedings of the IEEE/CVF Conference on Computer Vision and Pattern Recognition, pp. 14318–14328 (2021)
21. Loshchilov, I., Hutter, F.: SGDR: stochastic gradient descent with warm restarts. arXiv preprint arXiv:1608.03983 (2016)
22. Naik, N., et al.: Deep learning-enabled breast cancer hormonal receptor status determination from base-level H&E stains. Nat. Commun. **11**(1), 1–8 (2020)

23. Shorten, C., Khoshgoftaar, T.M.: A survey on image data augmentation for deep learning. J. Big Data **6**(1), 1–48 (2019)
24. Sirinukunwattana, K., et al.: Gland segmentation in colon histology images: the GlaS challenge contest. Med. Image Anal. **35**, 489–502 (2017)
25. Sohn, K., et al.: FixMatch: simplifying semi-supervised learning with consistency and confidence. arXiv preprint arXiv:2001.07685 (2020)
26. Srinidhi, C.L., Ciga, O., Martel, A.L.: Deep neural network models for computational histopathology: a survey. Med. Image Anal. **67**, 101813 (2020)
27. Upchurch, P., et al.: Deep feature interpolation for image content changes. In: Proceedings of the IEEE Conference on Computer Vision and Pattern Recognition, pp. 7064–7073 (2017)
28. Wu, S., Zhang, H., Valiant, G., Ré, C.: On the generalization effects of linear transformations in data augmentation. In: International Conference on Machine Learning, pp. 10410–10420. PMLR (2020)
29. Yang, J., Chen, H., Yan, J., Chen, X., Yao, J.: Towards better understanding and better generalization of low-shot classification in histology images with contrastive learning. In: International Conference on Learning Representations (2022)
30. Yao, J., Zhu, X., Jonnagaddala, J., Hawkins, N., Huang, J.: Whole slide images based cancer survival prediction using attention guided deep multiple instance learning networks. Med. Image Anal. **65**, 101789 (2020)
31. Zhang, X., Wang, Q., Zhang, J., Zhong, Z.: Adversarial AutoAugment. arXiv preprint arXiv:1912.11188 (2019)

S³R: Self-supervised Spectral Regression for Hyperspectral Histopathology Image Classification

Xingran Xie, Yan Wang(✉), and Qingli Li

Shanghai Key Laboratory of Multidimensional Information Processing,
East China Normal University, Shanghai 200241, China
51215904112@stu.ecnu.edu.cn, ywang@cee.ecnu.edu.cn, qlli@cs.ecnu.edu.cn

Abstract. Benefited from the rich and detailed spectral information in hyperspectral images (HSI), HSI offers great potential for a wide variety of medical applications such as computational pathology. But, the lack of adequate annotated data and the high spatiospectral dimensions of HSIs usually make classification networks prone to overfit. Thus, learning a general representation which can be transferred to the downstream tasks is imperative. To our knowledge, no appropriate self-supervised pre-training method has been designed for histopathology HSIs. In this paper, we introduce an efficient and effective Self-supervised Spectral Regression (S³R) method, which exploits the low rank characteristic in the spectral domain of HSI. More concretely, we propose to learn a set of linear coefficients that can be used to represent one band by the remaining bands via masking out these bands. Then, the band is restored by using the learned coefficients to reweight the remaining bands. Two pretext tasks are designed: (1) S³R-CR, which regresses the linear coefficients, so that the pre-trained model understands the inherent structures of HSIs and the pathological characteristics of different morphologies; (2) S³R-BR, which regresses the missing band, making the model to learn the holistic semantics of HSIs. Compared to prior arts *i.e.*, contrastive learning methods, which focuses on natural images, S³R converges at least 3 times faster, and achieves significant improvements up to 14% in accuracy when transferring to HSI classification tasks.

Keywords: Self-supervised learning · Hyperspectral histopathology image classification · Low-rank

1 Introduction

Histopathology plays an important role in the diagnostic and therapeutic aspects of modern medicine [15,21]. As artificial intelligence is evolving rapidly, deep learning based image processing techniques have been extensively reported for histopathological diagnosis [15]. Nowadays, the microscopy hyperspectral imaging system has become an emerging research hotspot in the field of medical

L. Wang et al. (Eds.): MICCAI 2022, LNCS 13432, pp. 46–55, 2022.
https://doi.org/10.1007/978-3-031-16434-7_5

image analysis [17], benefited from the rich spatiospectral information provided by hyperspectral images (HSI). Thus, it provides a new perspective for computational pathology and precision medicine.

Supervised learning for histopathology image analysis requires a large amount of annotations [16]. Since both expertise and time are needed, the labeled data with high quality annotations are usually expensive to acquire. This situation is more conspicuous for annotating HSIs [22], whose appearances are different compared with RGB images, so pathologists may take longer time in recognizing cancer tissues on HSIs. Typically, an HSI is presented as a hypercube, such high spatiospectral dimensions make it difficult to perform accurate HSI classification, especially when the annotated data is limited, which may lead to overfitting problems. Thus, an appropriate HSI pre-training method is imperative.

In recent years, self-supervised pre-training has been successful in both natural language processing [6] and computer vision. Previous research of self-supervised learning mainly focuses on contrastive learning, e.g., MOCO [12], SimCLR [3], BYOL [9] and SimSiam [4], training encoders to compare positive and negative sample pairs. Among these methods, BYOL [9] and SimSiam [4] achieve higher performance than previous contrastive methods without using negative sample pairs. But, the training setup e.g., batch size in original papers is not always affordable for research institutions. More recently, masked image modeling (MIM) methods represented by MAE [11] have been proved to learn rich visual representations and significantly improve the performance on downstream tasks [18]. After randomly adding masks to input images, a pixel-level regression target is set as a pretext task. Almost all the MIM methods are designed based on transformers which receive and process tokenized inputs.

Different from natural images, HSIs analyze how light transmittance varies on different forms of tissues or cells, which infect the brightness of various regions [8]. This generates dozens even hundreds of narrow and contiguous spectral bands in the spectral dimension. Understanding the inherent spectral structure in self-supervised pre-training is non-trivial for the networks to conduct downstream tasks. To the best of our knowledge, there is not any self-supervised method designing the architecture tailored for microscopy HSI classification yet. In this work, we present **S**elf-**S**upervised **S**pectral **R**egression (S³R), an efficient and effective pre-training objective that takes advantage of low rankness in the spectral domain. More specifically, we assume that one band can be represented as a linear combination of the remaining bands, and propose to learn the linear coefficients by a Convolutional Neural Network (CNN) based backbone via masking out the remaining bands. We propose two alternative pretext tasks, which have different focuses. (1) **C**oefficients **R**egression (S³R-CR), which makes the network to directly regress the "groundtruth" linear coefficients learned beforehand. In this way, the pre-trained model acquires an adequate understanding of complex spectral structures and pathological characteristics of different morphologies. (2) **B**and **R**egression (S³R-BR), regressing the pixel intensity of the selected band by re-weighting the remaining bands. Since detailed information (edges, textures, etc.) is already stored in different bands of the HSI, our spectral

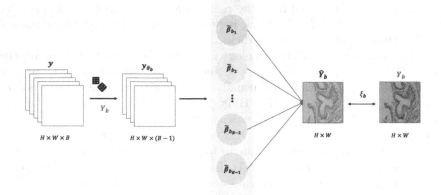

Fig. 1. Illustration of spectral regression in HSI. The whole process to estimate the coefficient $\tilde{\beta}_b$ can be optimized by back-propagation. $\hat{\mathbf{Y}}_b$ denotes the regression result. The dice icon refers to randomly sampling a band $\mathbf{Y}_b$ as the regression target.

regression approach will allow the model to focus more on the intrinsic association between spectral bands and the overall semantics of the masked image. Experiments show that our S^3R-CR and S^3R-BR perform better than contrastive learning and masked image modeling methods, and significantly reduces the cost of self-supervised task due to the faster convergence.

2   Method

2.1   Spectral Regression Based on Low-Rank Prior

Since the spectral correlation in HSIs is extremely high, HSIs can be well represented in a low-dimensional subspace [23]. Let $\mathcal{Y} \in \mathbb{R}^{H \times W \times B}$ denote an HSI presented in 3D tensor with $H \times W$ pixels and B spectral bands. We assume that $\mathbf{Y}_b \in \mathbb{R}^{H \times W}$, denoting the b-th spectral band in $\mathcal{Y}$, can be represented by a linear combination of the remaining $B - 1$ bands with a set of coefficients. This can be formulated as:

$$\mathbf{Y}_b = \boldsymbol{\xi}_b + \sum_{i=1}^{B} \mathbf{1}[i \neq b] \cdot \mathbf{Y}_i \cdot \beta_{b_i}, \tag{1}$$

where β_{b_i} denotes the linear coefficient corresponding to the ith band, and $\mathbf{1}[\cdot]$ is the indicator function. Let $\boldsymbol{\beta}_b = (\beta_{b_1}, \ldots, \beta_{b_{b-1}}, \beta_{b_{b+1}}, \ldots, \beta_{b_B})^{\mathsf{T}} \in \mathbb{R}^{(B-1) \times 1}$. Due to the existence of noise from hyperspectral imaging system, the linear regression process will generate a small error, $\boldsymbol{\xi}_b \in \mathbb{R}^{H \times W}$, which could not be eliminated completely. Equation 1 provides a linear regression model, which regresses a spectral band by the remaining bands.

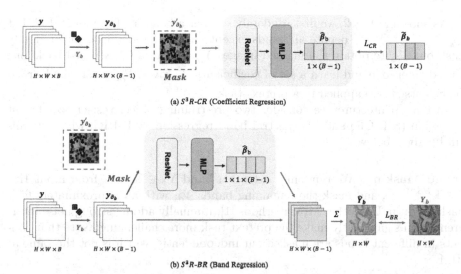

(a) S^3R-CR (Coefficient Regression)

(b) S^3R-BR (Band Regression)

Fig. 2. Our S³R architecture. During pre-training, we randomly select the bth band $\mathbf{Y}_b$ from the input HSI $\mathcal{Y}$. Then the remaining bands $\mathcal{Y}_{\partial_b}$ are masked out by random patches. The encoder is applied to learn a set of coefficients $\hat{\beta}_{b_i}$ from masked bands $\mathcal{Y}'_{\partial_b}$. The learned coefficients are then directly fit $\tilde{\beta}_b$ (a) or reweight $\mathcal{Y}_{\partial_b}$ to regress the initially selected band $\mathbf{Y}_b$ (b).

To find β_{b_i}, Eq. 1 can be estimated by minimizing the following loss function:

$$\mathcal{L} = \left\| \mathbf{Y}_b - \sum_{i=1}^{B} \mathbf{1}[i \neq b] \cdot \mathbf{Y}_i \cdot \beta_{b_i} \right\|_F^2. \tag{2}$$

One can simply obtain an estimation of the coefficient $\tilde{\beta}_{b_i}$ through back-propagation by deriving the partial derivatives of β_{b_i}:

$$\tilde{\beta}_{b_i} = \beta_{b_i} - \alpha \frac{\partial \mathcal{L}}{\partial \beta_{b_i}}, \tag{3}$$

or applying a closed-form solution. Let $\tilde{\beta}_b = (\tilde{\beta}_{b_1}, \ldots, \tilde{\beta}_{b_{b-1}}, \tilde{\beta}_{b_{b+1}}, \ldots, \tilde{\beta}_{b_B})^\mathsf{T} \in \mathbb{R}^{(B-1)\times 1}$. The overall process is shown in Fig. 1.

2.2 Model Based Spectral Regression

Previous section indicates that tensor low-rank prior is an inherent property of HSI which does not rely on any supervisory information. Inspired by the low-rank prior, we propose a Self-supervised Spectral Regression (S³R) architecture for hyperspectral histopathology image classification.

As shown in Fig. 2, we first randomly extract a band $\mathbf{Y}_b$ from an HSI $\mathcal{Y}$. Let $\mathcal{Y}_{\partial_b} \in \mathbb{R}^{H \times W \times (B-1)}$ denote all bands except the bth band. Next, we randomly mask out $\mathcal{Y}_{\partial_b}$ to obtain the masked images $\mathcal{Y}'_{\partial_b}$. Then, a CNN based backbone is used to encode and learn a set of coefficients $\hat{\beta}_{b_i}$ given $\mathcal{Y}'_{\partial_b}$. Last, the learned coefficients $\hat{\beta}_b$ are applied to a pretext task.

In our architecture, we consider two pre-training objectives: (1) coefficient regression (S^{3}R-CR) and (2) spectral band regression (S^{3}R-BR), whose details will be given below.

Image Masking. We randomly extract a band $\mathbf{Y}_b \in \mathbb{R}^{H \times W}$ from input HSI $\mathcal{Y} \in \mathbb{R}^{H \times W \times B}$, and mask the remaining bands $\mathcal{Y}_{\partial_b}$ with an approximately 65% masking ratio. Like other MIM methods [1], manually adding strong noise interference can significantly make the pretext task more challenging. Note that contents in different bands are masked out independently, which is not the same as MIM.

Coefficients Regression. The obtained $\tilde{\beta}_b$ from Eq. 3 can be treated as the groundtruth of the coefficients. Forcing the network to learn the coefficients via randomly masking out a portion of $\mathcal{Y}_{\partial_b}$ will make the network to understand the inherent structure of HSI. Residual architecture is proven to work well for HSI classification [14]. Thus, a vanilla ResNet is adopted to encode the masked tensor $\mathcal{Y}'_{\partial_b} \in \mathbb{R}^{H \times W \times (B-1)}$, followed by an MLP head which maps features to the predicted coefficient $\hat{\beta}_b$, where $\hat{\beta}_b = (\hat{\beta}_{b_1}, \ldots, \hat{\beta}_{b_{b-1}}, \hat{\beta}_{b_{b+1}}, \ldots, \hat{\beta}_{b_B})^\mathsf{T} \in \mathbb{R}^{(B-1) \times 1}$. Noted that the MLP head will not be involved in the downstream task. The loss function for optimizing coefficient regression is computed by:

$$\mathcal{L}_{CR} = \sum_{i=1}^{B-1} \left\| \hat{\beta}_{b_i} - \tilde{\beta}_{b_i} \right\|_1 . \tag{4}$$

Spectral Band Regression. As mentioned in Sect. 2.1, we assume that one band can be represented as a linear combination of the remaining bands. The selected band $\mathbf{Y}_b$ can be represented by the generated linear coefficients $\hat{\beta}_b$ and $\mathcal{Y}_{\partial_b}$. Then, we aim to minimize the following loss function:

$$\mathcal{L}_{BR} = \left\| \mathbf{Y}_b - \sum_{i=1}^{B} \mathbf{1}[i \neq b] \cdot \mathbf{Y}_i \cdot \hat{\beta}_{b_i} \right\|_1 , \tag{5}$$

where $\hat{\beta}_b$ does not require the supervision of $\tilde{\beta}_b$ learned from Eq. 3.

The two proposed pretext tasks are based on learning the inherent spectral structure, but they have different focuses. S^{3}R-CR tries to figure out the similarity between $\mathcal{Y}_{\partial_b}$ and $\mathbf{Y}_b$, i.e., $\hat{\beta}_b$, and focuses more on the pathological characteristics of different morphologies. S^{3}R-BR could be regarded as a novel MIM method, which focuses more on the holistic semantics of HSIs to recover $\mathbf{Y}_b$ and $\hat{\beta}_b$ is only regarded as a latent variable.

3   Experiments

3.1   Experimental Setup

Datasets. We verify the effectiveness of the proposed S³R on two hyperspectral histopathology image datasets, in which all histopathology samples are collected from the gastroenterology department of a hospital. During the process of capturing HSI, the light transmitted from the tissue slice was collected by the microscope with the objective lens of 20×. More details are as follows:

PDAC Dataset: It consists of 523 HSI scenes from 36 patients, which are split into 331 for training, 101 for validation, and 91 for testing. Noted that there is no overlap of patients between different splits. Among all the scenes, 255 of them belong to pancreatic ductal adenocarcinoma (PDAC), and the rest ones are normal. The wavelength is from 450 nm to 750 nm, which ends up with 40 spectral bands for each scene. The image size per band is 512 × 612.

PLGC Dataset: Clinically, intestinal metaplasia (IM) and dysplasia (DYS) are considered as precancerous lesions of gastric cancer (PLGC) [10] and there are 1105 HSI scenes (414 IM, 362 DYS and 329 normal cases) in the dataset. All samples are randomly split into 661 for training, 221 for validation, and 223 for testing. The wavelength is from 470 nm to 670 nm, which ends up with 32 spectral bands for each scene. The image size per band is 512 × 512.

Implementation Details

Pre-training: The pre-training process of all self-supervised algorithms is conducted on the training set, without any data augmentation. We adopt the ImageNet pre-trained model for all experiments unless otherwise specified. We set the initial learning rate to be 10^{-4}. The maximum training epoch for all the models are 200, and early stop strategy is adopted when training loss no longer drops. We use exponential learning rate decay with $\gamma = 0.99$. The learning rate, maximum training epochs, and learning rate decay for training are the same for other competing methods.

Downstream Task: All pre-trained models can be applied in downstream tasks directly after adjusting the first convolutional layer. During fine tuning, appropriate data augmentation (*e.g.*, scale rotation or gaussian noise) is added to training set. We evaluate the model on validation set after every epoch, and save the parameters when it performs best in current stage. At last, we measure the performance on the test set. Training configurations are consistent throughout the fine-tuning process to ensure fair comparisons. We use AdamW [13] as our optimizer and the learning rate is 10^{-4} with linear decline strategy. The maximum number of fine-tune epoch is 70. All experiments are implemented using Pytorch and conducted on a single NVIDIA GeForce RTX 3090.

Table 1. Ablation study on PLGC dataset.

Image masking	S^3-BR	S^3-CR	Backbone	Acc.
×	×	×	ResNet18	94.17
✓	×	×	ResNet18	93.72
✓	✓	×	ResNet18	94.62
✓	×	✓	ResNet18	**95.07**
×	×	×	ResNet50	95.07
✓	×	×	ResNet50	94.17
✓	✓	×	ResNet50	95.52
✓	×	✓	ResNet50	**96.41**

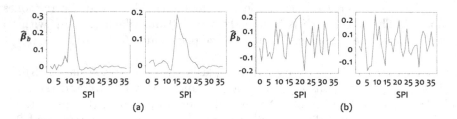

Fig. 3. Visualizations of $\hat{\beta}_b$. The images in figure (a) come from S^3R-CR, and the ones in figure (b) are from S^3R-BR. SPI indicates spectral band index. The regression targets from left to right are 10th and 15th band in both figures.

3.2   Ablation Study

The ablations are conducted on PLGC dataset with ResNet and the same pre-trained setup mentioned in Sect. 3.1. As shown in Table 1, we first evaluate a straightforward regression method. $\mathcal{Y}_{\partial_b}$ is first fed into a vanilla ResNet backbone. Next, a decoder consisting of five transposed convolutional layers is implemented to regress the target band $\mathbf{Y}_b$. This strategy only obtains 94.17% and 95.07% accuracy with two backbones. While masking the input HSI, the performance gets worse. This may due to the reason that directly regressing the missing band by feeding the remaining bands to a network does not use the inherent structure of HSIs. Thus, it leads to worse performance.

3.3   Comparison Between S^3R and Other Methods

In this section, we conduct comparisons between S^3R and three competitors: 1) contrastive learning (BYOL and SimSiam), 2) self-supervised models designed for remote sensing HSIs (Conv-Deconv [14]) and SSAD [20]), and 3) an MIM-like method [19], termed as Masked HyperSpectral Image Modeling (MHSIM). Vanilla siamese structure based on contrastive learning (*e.g.*, BYOL and Sim-Siam) is designed for natural images. Thus, we use two strategies to handle the input: randomly selecting 3 bands from HSIs or using all bands. For the MIM-like

Table 2. Performance comparison in Classification Accuracy (%) and Standard Deviation on our two datasets. Scratch means training-from-scratch and IN1K denotes ImageNet-1K. MHSIM is an MIM-like method mentioned in Sect. 3.3.

Method	Dataset	ResNet18	ResNet50
Scratch	PDAC	78.02 (2.28)	80.22 (1.10)
IN1K pre-trained	PDAC	83.52 (1.68)	85.71 (1.68)
BYOL [9] (3 bands)	PDAC	82.42 (1.68)	86.81 (2.28)
BYOL [9] (40 bands)	PDAC	83.52 (1.68)	85.71 (1.68)
SimSiam [4] (3 bands)	PDAC	86.81 (1.10)	86.81 (1.68)
SimSiam [4] (40 bands)	PDAC	85.71 (1.67)	87.91 (1.27)
SSAD [20]	PDAC	80.22 (2.29)	80.22 (2.20)
Conv-Deconv [14]	PDAC	79.12 (1.68)	80.22 (1.68)
MHSIM	PDAC	81.32 (1.10)	83.52 (0.64)
S³R-CR	PDAC	91.21 (2.23)	**91.21(1.68)**
S³R-BR	PDAC	**92.31(1.10)**	90.11 (1.27)
Scratch	PLGC	85.20 (1.58)	84.34 (2.87)
IN1K pre-trained	PLGC	93.27 (0.51)	94.62 (1.70)
BYOL [9] (3 bands)	PLGC	94.62 (0.90)	95.07 (0.69)
BYOL [9] (32 bands)	PLGC	94.62 (0.26)	94.17 (0.52)
SimSiam [4] (3 bands)	PLGC	94.62 (0.63)	95.07 (0.90)
SimSiam [4] (32 bands)	PLGC	93.72 (0.69)	92.38 (0.51)
SSAD [20]	PLGC	92.38 (2.99)	91.03 (0.68)
Conv-Deconv [14]	PLGC	90.13 (0.93)	90.13 (0.45)
MHSIM	PLGC	93.27 (1.44)	94.17 (0.52)
S³R-CR	PLGC	**95.07(0.21)**	**96.41(0.51)**
S³R-BR	PLGC	94.62 (0.42)	95.52 (0.26)

method, we first randomly mask out a portion of the input, and then reconstruct the missing pixels. Noted that DINO [2] and other transformer-based methods [5] need to be trained on large scale datasets, such as ImageNet. Our dataset contains only hundreds of HSIs. Moreover, due to the lack of computing resources, the batch size for training DINO is 25, which is far from enough. Thus, it is not suitable to compare with transformer-based self-supervised learning methods.

As shown in Table 2, our S³R performs significantly better than MHSIM and other contrastive learning based methods. In particular, on PDAC dataset, S³R-BR outperforms BYOL and SimSiam by 8.79% and 5.5% in classification accuracy with the ResNet18 backbone. On PLGC dataset, S³R-CR with ResNet50 backbone achieves best results. We can observe that, the performance of MHSIM is close to ImageNet pre-training, which is much lower than ours. This may caused by information leakage from CNN architecture in MIM method [7]. Restricted by computing resources, contrastive learning based methods require far more pre-training time (more than 8 minutes per epoch on PLGC) than S^{3}R (about 2 minutes per epoch on PLGC), even with 3-band image as input. Thus, our proposed method can effectively help improve the performance in HSI classification task with lower cost.

We also visualize $\hat{\beta}_b$ in Fig. 3 to further explore our method. We can see that, in Fig. 3 (a), with the coefficient regression, $\hat{\beta}_b$ exhibits a Gaussian-like distribution, which means restoring bth band (peak area in the figure) will be more dependent on its nearby bands. This may force the model to focus more on the inherent structures of HSIs. As shown in Fig. 3 (b), $\hat{\beta}_b$ learned as latent variable does not present a similar distribution, which illustrates that using pixel-level band regression as the target makes the encoder to extract features by the holistic semantics rather than detailed morphologies.

4 Conclusion

We first attempt to address the problem of self-supervised pre-training for hyperspectral histopathology image classification. We present self-supervised spectral regression (S^{3}R), by exploring the low rankness in the spectral domain of an HSI. We assume one spectral band can be approximately represented by the linear combination of the remaining bands. Our S^{3}R forces the network to understand the inherent structures of HSIs. Intensive experiments are conducted on two hyperspectral histopathology image datasets. Experimental results show that the superiority of the proposed S^{3}R lies in both performance and training efficiency, compared with state-of-the-art self-supervised methods in computer vision.

Acknowledgements. This work was supported in part by the National Natural Science Foundation of China under Grant 62101191, and in part by Shanghai Natural Science Foundation under Grant 21ZR1420800.

References

1. Bao, H., Dong, L., Wei, F.: BEiT: BERT pre-training of image transformers. In: ICLR (2022)
2. Caron, M., et al.: Emerging properties in self-supervised vision transformers. In: ICCV (2021)
3. Chen, T., Kornblith, S., Norouzi, M., Hinton, G.E.: A simple framework for contrastive learning of visual representations. In: ICML (2020)
4. Chen, X., He, K.: Exploring simple Siamese representation learning. In: CVPR (2021)
5. Chen, X., Xie, S., He, K.: An empirical study of training self-supervised vision transformers. In: ICCV (2021)
6. Devlin, J., Chang, M., Lee, K., Toutanova, K.: BERT: pre-training of deep bidirectional transformers for language understanding. In: Burstein, J., Doran, C., Solorio, T. (eds.) NAACL-HLT (2019)
7. Fang, Y., Dong, L., Bao, H., Wang, X., Wei, F.: Corrupted image modeling for self-supervised visual pre-training. CoRR arXiv:2202.03382 (2022)

8. Fu, Y., Zheng, Y., Zhang, L., Huang, H.: Spectral reflectance recovery from a single RGB image. IEEE Trans. Comput. Imaging **4**(3), 382–394 (2018)
9. Grill, J., et al.: Bootstrap your own latent - a new approach to self-supervised learning. In: NeurIPS (2020)
10. Gullo, I., Grillo, F., Mastracci, L., Vanoli, A., Fassan, M.: Precancerous lesions of the stomach, gastric cancer and hereditary gastric cancer syndromes. Pathologica **112**(3), 166–185 (2020)
11. He, K., Chen, X., Xie, S., Li, Y., Dollár, P., Girshick, R.B.: Masked autoencoders are scalable vision learners. In: CVPR (2022)
12. He, K., Fan, H., Wu, Y., Xie, S., Girshick, R.B.: Momentum contrast for unsupervised visual representation learning. In: CVPR (2020)
13. Loshchilov, I., Hutter, F.: Fixing weight decay regularization in Adam. CoRR arXiv:1711.05101 (2017)
14. Mou, L., Ghamisi, P., Zhu, X.X.: Unsupervised spectral-spatial feature learning via deep residual Conv-Deconv network for hyperspectral image classification. IEEE Trans. Geosci. Remote. Sens. **56**(1), 391–406 (2018)
15. Salvi, M., Acharya, U.R., Molinari, F., Meiburger, K.M.: The impact of pre- and post-image processing techniques on deep learning frameworks: a comprehensive review for digital pathology image analysis. Comput. Biol. Med. **128**, 104129 (2021)
16. Srinidhi, C.L., Kim, S.W., Chen, F., Martel, A.L.: Self-supervised driven consistency training for annotation efficient histopathology image analysis. Med. Image Anal. **75**, 102256 (2022)
17. Wang, J., Li, Q.: Quantitative analysis of liver tumors at different stages using microscopic hyperspectral imaging technology. J. Biomed. Opt. **23**(10), 1 (2018)
18. Wei, C., Fan, H., Xie, S., Wu, C., Yuille, A.L., Feichtenhofer, C.: Masked feature prediction for self-supervised visual pre-training. CoRR arXiv:2112.09133 (2021)
19. Xie, Z., et al.: SimMIM: a simple framework for masked image modeling. In: CVPR (2022)
20. Yue, J., Fang, L., Rahmani, H., Ghamisi, P.: Self-supervised learning with adaptive distillation for hyperspectral image classification. IEEE Trans. Geosci. Remote. Sens. **60**, 1–13 (2022)
21. Zhang, Q., Li, Q., Yu, G., Sun, L., Zhou, M., Chu, J.: A multidimensional choledoch database and benchmarks for cholangiocarcinoma diagnosis. IEEE Access **7**, 149414–149421 (2019)
22. Zhao, Z., Wang, H., Yu, X.: Spectral-spatial graph attention network for semisupervised hyperspectral image classification. IEEE Geosci. Remote. Sens. Lett. **19**, 1–5 (2022)
23. Zhuang, L., Ng, M.K.: FastHyMix: fast and parameter-free hyperspectral image mixed noise removal. IEEE Trans. Neural Netw. Learn. Syst. (2021). https://doi.org/10.1109/TNNLS.2021.3112577

Distilling Knowledge from Topological Representations for Pathological Complete Response Prediction

Shiyi Du[1], Qicheng Lao[2,3(✉)], Qingbo Kang[1], Yiyue Li[1], Zekun Jiang[1], Yanfeng Zhao[1], and Kang Li[1,3(✉)]

[1] West China Biomedical Big Data Center, Sichuan University West China Hospital, Chengdu, China
likang@wchscu.cn
[2] School of Artificial Intelligence, Beijing University of Posts and Telecommunications, Beijing, China
qicheng.lao@gmail.com
[3] Shanghai Artificial Intelligence Laboratory, Shanghai, China

Abstract. In breast radiology, pathological Complete Response (pCR) predicts the treatment response after neoadjuvant chemotherapy, and therefore is a vital indicator for both personalized treatment and prognosis. Current prevailing approaches for pCR prediction either require complex feature engineering or employ sophisticated topological computation, which are not efficient while yielding limited performance boosts. In this paper, we present a simple yet effective technique implementing persistent homology to extract multi-dimensional topological representations from 3D data, making the computation much faster. To incorporate the extracted topological information, we then propose a novel approach to distill the extracted topological knowledge into deep neural networks with response-based knowledge distillation. Our experimental results quantitatively show that the proposed approach achieves superior performance by increasing the accuracy from previously 85.1% to 90.5% in the pCR prediction and reducing the topological computation time by about 66% on a public dataset for breast DCE-MRI images.

Keywords: Knowledge distillation · Topological information · Persistent homology · Pathological complete response · Breast radiology

1 Introduction

Neoadjuvant chemotherapy (NAC) is routinely utilized as an early treatment for locally advanced breast tumors or breast cancers with certain molecular histotypes [5]. In breast radiology, the pathological Complete Response (pCR) indicates that there is no residual infiltrative disease or metastatic lymph nodes at the completion of the NAC duration, and the attainment of pCR can be perceived as an independent predictive factor for superior disease-free survival.

L. Wang et al. (Eds.): MICCAI 2022, LNCS 13432, pp. 56–65, 2022.
https://doi.org/10.1007/978-3-031-16434-7_6

Thus, it can be assumed that patients who achieve pCR after NAC will not require surgery in the future [23]. Therefore, early identification of patients who respond to NAC can facilitate personalized treatment planning, thus sparing patients from potentially invalid and/or poisonous treatment.

Recently, the predictive capabilities of deep learning in breast radiology continue to develop, raising the possibility of these methods being used for predicting tumor responses to therapy [7,17,20]. For example, Liu et al. [17] designed a convolution neural network (CNN) for pCR prediction of breast MRI images, and Comes et al. [7] proposed a transfer learning based method where a pre-trained CNN is utilized to extract low-level features. Although some of these approaches have achieved satisfactory performance, they are limited to complex pipeline of feature engineering, and (or) without direct spatial morphology (i.e., topological) guidance which has shown high correlation with pCR [15,25].

The remarkable success of persistent homology (PH)—an approach for determining topological features of a space at various spatial resolutions—in medical imaging [22,24–26] suggests that, specially-designed PH models can preserve important biological information with proper topological simplicity by extracting complex and subtle parenchymal structures in various diseases, which radiomics and deep learning models fail to capture explicitly. At the same time, significant improvements have been achieved after integrating topological information into the baselines in some of the deep learning based approaches. For example, Wang et al. [25] proposed to direct the neural network's attention to biologically relevant tissue structures by extracting multi-dimensional topological structures, successfully capturing complex and subtle parenchymal structures. However, there are still two main limitations in these approaches. Firstly, the topological representations that have been chosen in some of these approaches are too complex for practical applications, where the computational complexity and the time cost of topological representation extraction are relatively high, which is difficult to migrate to large-scale use cases. In addition, the performance improvement in previous studies is limited due to the adoption of shallow networks, restricting the powerful potential of deep neural networks.

To solve the above problems, in this paper, we propose a response-based knowledge distillation approach to distill computationally simple (less time-consuming) but effective topological representation (i.e., Betti curves) into the deep neural networks (e.g., DenseNet) for better pCR prediction performance. The topological knowledge distillation enables the large capacity deep network with better constraints in the solution space by using the topological information that is highly correlated with the disease. We evaluate our proposed approach on a public breast DCE-MRI dataset I-SPY-1 [14], and experimental results demonstrate that the proposed approach not only yields improved performance on the pCR prediction, but also has advantages on the convergence speed. Our main contributions are as follows:

1. We propose to use a simplified yet effective method to extract multi-dimensional topological representations from breast DCE-MRI images, making previously time-consuming topological representation extraction much quicker and more adaptable to large-scale use cases.

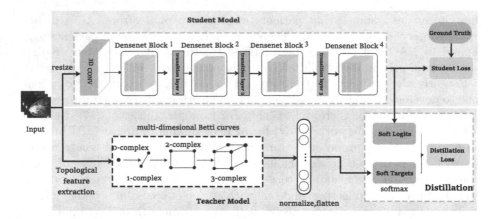

Fig. 1. Overview of the proposed model: a student model with a DenseNet backbone, and a teacher model consisting of soft targets from Betti curves. The multi-dimensional Betti curves are extracted from breast DCE-MRI scans.

2. We present a novel view of incorporating topological knowledge into deep neural networks by using response-based knowledge distillation, where the topological information can be better exploited.
3. We provide empirical evidence of the efficacy of the presented method on a public dataset by instantiating our proposed approach with DenseNet using Betti curves, where it achieves state-of-the-art performance in breast treatment response prediction after NAC with topology. A PyTorch implementation of our method can be found at our GitHub repository: DK_Topology_PCR.

2   Methods

The overall flow of our method is illustrated in Fig. 1. We first choose the middle half slices of the given 3D scans and extract their topological representations (i.e., Betti curves) of dimensions 0, 1 and 2 based on the theory of persistent homology [9]. Here, Betti curves record statistics of multi-dimensional topological structures during a filtration process which we will explain later in detail. Then, we distill the topological priors into a deep neural network for which we adopt the widely used DenseNet [13] via response-based knowledge distillation [11]. The main branch (i.e., the student model) learns from ground truth labels while the auxiliary branch (i.e., the teacher model) provides dark knowledge represented in Betti curves. After normalizing and flattening, the Betti curve representations are considered as soft targets, constraining the whole model through soft cross entropy with the soft logits from the student model.

In the following, we first introduce the theory of persistent homology in Subsect. 2.1. Then, we explain the computation of topological representations in Subsect. 2.2. Finally, we describe how we distill topological information into deep neural networks in Subsect. 2.3.

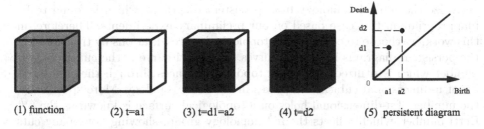

(1) function   (2) t=a1   (3) t=d1=a2   (4) t=d2   (5) persistent diagram

Fig. 2. Sublevel sets in filtration and its corresponding persistent diagram. (1) intensity function of a 3-dimensional image. (2)–(4) sublevel sets at time a1 < a2 = d1 < d2. (5) the persistent diagram of a 2D structure born at $a1$ and destroyed at $d1$ and a 3D structure born at $a2$ and destroyed at $d2$.

2.1 Persistent Homology

In this section, we introduce the basics of persistent homology in algebraic topology and for in-depth studies on this topic, we refer the readers to [9]. In computer vision, discretization of a volume is usually achieved by a cubic inlay where the use of cubical homology (a form of persistent homology) deals with the cubical structure directly unlike simplicial homology. Suppose the volume domain $\Omega \in R^3$ is discretized into a cubical complex K_Ω, which represents a set of composed vertices, edges, squares, and cubes. Given the volume, we can construct a sublevel set whose intensity value is no greater than the given threshold, $f_t = \{x \in \Omega | f(x) <= t\}$, where t is a threshold and $f : \Omega \to R$ is a real-valued function. A filtration is defined by a series of sublevel sets $S = \{S_t\}_{t \in R}$. Usually, we use two kinds of filtration, intensity filtration and density filtration. The intensity filtration is performed via voxel intensity values, while the density filtration softens the image by allocating the number of non-zero neighbors to each voxel within several voxel radius. The birth time of a structure is the threshold denoted by b where the structure appears in the filtration, while the death time of a structure is the threshold denoted by d where the structure disappears. Persistent homology tracks varying sublevel sets during the filtration process, and transforms the changes into a persistent diagram, i.e., a set of points, where each point (a, d) indicates a structure appears at a and disappears at d. Here the persistence of a topological structure can be represented by $(d - a)$. Meanwhile, the greater the persistence is, the more salient the topological structure appears.

For example, in Fig. 2, a cube with 12 edges totally black, 6 surfaces with lower intensity than edges and its inside space totally white is represented by a function f. The sublevel sets at different thresholds of f are shown in Fig. 2.

2.2 Topological Feature Representation and Its Computation

Here, we introduce the chosen topological representation computed by cubical homology. In recent years, various approaches have been proposed to transform the topological information into quantitative representations that can be integrated within deep learning frameworks [1–4,10,16,22]. One simple variant is to vectorize the cubical homology from persistent diagrams, which is found to be inappropriate in this case based on our preliminary experiments. Therefore, in this work, we choose to compute the topological representations by transforming the persistent diagrams into Betti curves. The Betti curve is the curve of Betti number which is utilized to identify topological spaces through the connectivity of n-dimensional cubical complexes in algebraic topology. More specifically, the number of n-dimensional holes on a topological surface is known as the nth Betti number, which reflects the nth homology group, showing how many cuts may be done before separating a surface into two sections or 0-cycles, 1-cycles, and so on. For 0-dimensional, 1-dimensional, and 2-dimensional cubical complexes, the Betti numbers have the following definitions: $B0$ is the number of connected components (i.e., 0-cycle); $B1$ is the number of one-dimensional holes (i.e., 1-cycle); and $B2$ is the number of two-dimensional voids (i.e., 2-cycle).

2.3   Distilling Betti Curves into DenseNet

In this section, we present our proposed approach to distill the topological priors (i.e., Betti curve) into the DenseNet via response-based knowledge distillation [11,12]. Response-based knowledge usually represents the neural response of the last output layer of the teacher model, which has been widely employed in a range of tasks and applications due to its simplicity and efficacy [6,19,27]. For the response-based knowledge distillation, there are several ways to incorporate topological information as a prior. The simplest one is to directly concatenate the Betti curves with the response from the DenseNet to conduct the prediction task, which we name as DenseNet-CONCATE. Another way is to utilize two separated branches, in which the DenseNet branch is mainly supervised by the task labels while being regularized by an auxiliary branch for the Betti curves. For the latter, we further introduce here various auxiliary branches we design. In the first model DenseNet-MSE, we transform the response logits from DenseNet to the same size as the flattened Betti curves, and apply the mean square error (MSE) loss between them. In the last model DenseNet-KD, we distill the topological priors (i.e., Betti curves) into the DenseNet through soft label regularization which will be detailed in the following. We will show later in our experiments that DenseNet-KD is preferable in terms of the final performance.

In our proposed model (i.e., DenseNet-KD), after extracting, normalizing, and flattening the topological features, we incorporate them into a linear layer to reduce their dimension to match that of the DenseNet logits. The output are then considered as the soft targets which are probabilities concerning which class the input belongs to, and they can be specified using a softmax function as:

$$prob(a_i, T) = \frac{exp(a_i/T)}{\sum_j exp(a_j/T)}, \tag{1}$$

where a_i is the logit of the i-th class, and the temperature factor T is introduced to control the importance of each soft target. Thus, the entire model loss can be defined as:

$$L_{total} = \alpha L_{RKD}(prob(a_t, T), prob(a_s, T)) + L_{CE}(y, prob(a_s, T = 1)). \tag{2}$$

where $prob(a_t, T)$ and $prob(a_s, T)$ indicates the softmax function of the teacher and student model logits under the temperature factor T, respectively, and L_{RKD} employs soft cross entropy loss. The student loss is specified as the cross-entropy loss between ground truth labels y and the softmax of student logits. α is the weight of distillation loss.

3 Experiments

3.1 Dataset and Experimental Setup

In this work, we evaluate the performance of our proposed approach on the I-SPY 1/ACRIN 6657 DCE-MRI dataset [14]. ACRIN 6657 is a prospective trial that aims to validate MRI imaging for the ability to predict response to treatment and recurrence in patients with stage 2 or 3 breast cancer who are undergoing neoadjuvant chemotherapy. A total of 162 women are considered in the dataset, with 42 achieving pCR (mean age = 48.8 years), 116 non-pCR (mean age = 48.5 years) and 4 missing. We use the contrast-enhanced MRI series in our experiments [14].

For image pre-processing, we resize the images from the original size of $256 \times 256 \times 60$ voxels into $96 \times 96 \times 60$ voxels for faster training. To keep a balance between the computation speed and adequacy of retained information, we use the middle half slices for the computation of Betti curves among the total 60 slices of each DCE-MRI scan. We randomly split the data into a training and a test set, and report the 10-fold cross-validation results. We adopt four commonly used evaluation metrics including accuracy, area under curve (AUC), specificity and sensitivity. All the models are trained for 100 epochs using the Adam optimizer with a batch size of 16 and a learning rate of 0.0005. Random rotations are utilized for data augmentation. The experiments are conducted on Nvidia Tesla V100 GPUs and implemented on PyTorch [21] and MONAI [8].

3.2 Visualization of Betti Curves of Breast MRI Scan

The Betti curve extraction are conducted using the GUDHI package [18]. We first produce bitmap, and then compute the cubical complex of the slices, from which the persistent diagrams are generated and transformed into Betti curves. We use intensity filtration to attain the final Betti curves with 254 filtration values. At the same time, we set the min persistence parameter to 10 (i.e., the minimum persistence of topological structures that is counted) to compute salient topological features. Figure 3 shows an example of the curves representing the Betti numbers of 0-cycle (b), 1-cycle (c) and 2-cycle (d), i.e., multi-dimensional topological structures, respectively from both pCR and non-pCR. It is obvious in the three diagrams that the peak value of the non-pCR scan usually arrives earlier than that of the pCR scan, which reveals topological differences between the two scans. In practice, it takes about a minute and a half for computing the Betti curves of a standard input scan of $256 \times 256 \times 60$, faster than the computation of

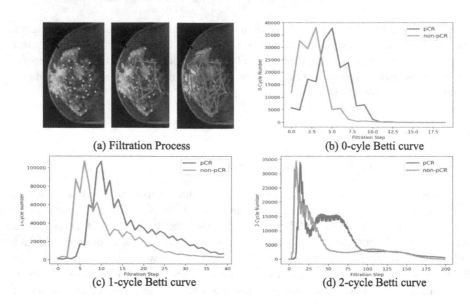

(a) Filtration Process

(b) 0-cyle Betti curve

(c) 1-cycle Betti curve

(d) 2-cycle Betti curve

Fig. 3. (*a*) visualizes the intensity filtration process of a DCE-MRI scan. The blue points have intensity values greater than those of the orange points. (*b*), (*c*), (*d*) are multi-dimensional Betti curves of both pCR and non-pCR scans. The blue curve is from pCR scan and the orange curve is from non-pCR scan. (Color figure online)

Table 1. Experimental results of pCR prediction on the I-SPY-1 dataset, including comparisons with the baselines*, TopoTxR [25], and our proposed method.

Method	Accuracy	AUC	Specificity	Sensitivity
Radiomics	0.563 ± 0.085	0.593 ± 0.098	0.552 ± 0.180	0.575 ± 0.081
PD	0.549 ± 0.081	0.567 ± 0.097	0.551 ± 0.167	0.547 ± 0.071
Radiomics+PD	0.563 ± 0.093	0.587 ± 0.099	0.592 ± 0.178	0.534 ± 0.087
Shallow Networks	0.633 ± 0.200	0.621 ± 0.102	0.570 ± 0.322	0.673 ± 0.354
DenseNet [13]	0.814 ± 0.057	0.821 ± 0.031	0.827 ± 0.023	0.816 ± 0.079
TopoTxR [25]	0.851 ± 0.045	0.820 ± 0.035	0.736 ± 0.086	0.904 ± 0.068
DenseNet-KD (ours)	**0.905 ± 0.021**	**0.874 ± 0.016**	**0.825 ± 0.043**	**0.923 ± 0.030**

*The baseline results are cited from [25].

topological cycles of a scan in [25] which needs about 5 min. Differences between the Betti curves of the two classes reveal topological disparity between them, indicating unique information that implies the pathological prediction can be hard to recognize even for experienced radiologists.

3.3 Results of Breast Cancer Treatment Response Prediction

In this paper, we compare our proposed method with previous state-of-the-art method TopoTxr [25], as well as methods based on radiomics features, persistent

Table 2. Performance comparisons of various strategies for knowledge distillation.

Method	Accuracy	AUC	Specificity	Sensitivity
DenseNet [13]	0.814 ± 0.057	0.821 ± 0.031	**0.827 ± 0.023**	0.816 ± 0.079
DenseNet-CONCATE	0.869 ± 0.041	0.838 ± 0.038	0.759 ± 0.052	0.916 ± 0.030
DenseNet-MSE	0.857 ± 0.036	0.794 ± 0.020	0.675 ± 0.109	0.913 ± 0.069
DenseNet-KD	**0.905 ± 0.021**	**0.874 ± 0.016**	0.825 ± 0.043	**0.923 ± 0.030**

Table 3. Epoch of convergence of the baseline model and its variants with topological priors (within 100 epochs).

Run	Method			
	DenseNet	DenseNet-CONCATE	DenseNet-MSE	DenseNet-KD
Average	>100	44.0 ± 4.3	55.0 ± 3.2	**43.3 ± 2.0**

diagram, and their combination. As shown in Table 1, our proposed DenseNet-KD achieves the best performance for pCR prediction on all evaluation metrics. As an ablation, DenseNet-KD also outperforms the backbone model DenseNet by a big margin, demonstrating the effectiveness of distilling topological prior knowledge into a deep network. It is also noted that compared to the shallow networks, deep networks alone can tremendously improve the performance.

Next, as explained in Subsect. 2.3, we explore a variety of strategies to guide the attention of the DenseNet backbone through topological priors. Table 2 presents the comparison results of the aforementioned strategies we design. From the results, it can be seen that it is most efficient to incorporate topological features into the model by knowledge distillation through soft labels from the teacher model. We speculate the undesirable performance of DenseNet-MSE is due to the strong constraint of the MSE regularization which expects the logits coming out of the student model to closely approximate the Betti curve values after flattening, thus impairing the optimization for the pCR prediction. The proposed DenseNet-KD, however, by using the branch containing topological priors as the teacher and the DenseNet branch as the student, makes it possible that the student branch learns the rich dark knowledge related to topology through soft cross entropy loss. At the same time, the soft cross entropy loss does not require the auxiliary branch to fit the Betti curves as perfectly as the DenseNet-MSE, but to impart the rich dark knowledge in the topological information to the main branch with relatively weaker constraint, so as to achieve the effect of better utilization of topological information.

Finally, we compare the convergence speed between the proposed method DenseNet-KD and its baseline DenseNet, and the variants including DenseNet-CONCATE and DenseNet-MSE. Based on the results shown in Table 3, the Betti curves can effectively promote the model converge speed, suggesting the proposed method can be more adaptive to large-scale dataset training.

4 Conclusion

In this paper, we extract topological representations of breast DCE-MRI scans in a simpler yet effective manner, which contributes to previous time-costing topological representation extraction in breast radiology with a much faster technique and more adaptive to large-scale dataset training. In addition, we incorporate topological information into a deep neural network using response-based knowledge distillation, which leverages morphological features from the topological dark knowledge in breast DCE-MRI scans, avoiding massive pre-trained models. To our best knowledge, we are the first to distill Betti curves of breast DCE-MRI into a deep neural network, reaching superior performance on the prediction of pathological complete response. Future work will be devoted to adapting the method to analysis of medical images with other diseases.

References

1. Adams, H., et al.: Persistence images: a stable vector representation of persistent homology. J. Mach. Learn. Res. **18**, 1–35 (2017)
2. Ahmed, M., Fasy, B.T., Wenk, C.: Local persistent homology based distance between maps. In: Proceedings of the 22nd ACM SIGSPATIAL International Conference on Advances in Geographic Information Systems, pp. 43–52 (2014)
3. Bendich, P., Cohen-Steiner, D., Edelsbrunner, H., Harer, J., Morozov, D.: Inferring local homology from sampled stratified spaces. In: FOCS, pp. 536–546. Citeseer (2007)
4. Bubenik, P., et al.: Statistical topological data analysis using persistence landscapes. J. Mach. Learn. Res. **16**(1), 77–102 (2015)
5. Cain, H., Macpherson, I., Beresford, M., Pinder, S., Pong, J., Dixon, J.: Neoadjuvant therapy in early breast cancer: treatment considerations and common debates in practice. Clin. Oncol. **29**(10), 642–652 (2017)
6. Chen, G., Choi, W., Yu, X., Han, T., Chandraker, M.: Learning efficient object detection models with knowledge distillation. In: Advances in Neural Information Processing Systems, vol. 30 (2017)
7. Comes, M.C., et al.: Early prediction of neoadjuvant chemotherapy response by exploiting a transfer learning approach on breast DCE-MRIs. Sci. Rep. **11**(1), 1–12 (2021)
8. Consortium, M.: MONAI: medical open network for AI. Zenodo, June 2022. https://doi.org/10.5281/zenodo.6639453
9. Edelsbrunner, H., Harer, J.: Computational Topology: An Introduction. American Mathematical Society (2010)
10. Frosini, P., Landi, C.: Persistent Betti numbers for a noise tolerant shape-based approach to image retrieval. Pattern Recogn. Lett. **34**(8), 863–872 (2013)
11. Gou, J., Yu, B., Maybank, S.J., Tao, D.: Knowledge distillation: a survey. Int. J. Comput. Vis. **129**(6), 1789–1819 (2021)
12. Hinton, G., Vinyals, O., Dean, J., et al.: Distilling the knowledge in a neural network, vol. 2, no. 7. arXiv preprint arXiv:1503.02531 (2015)
13. Huang, G., Liu, Z., Van Der Maaten, L., Weinberger, K.Q.: Densely connected convolutional networks. In: Proceedings of the IEEE Conference on Computer Vision and Pattern Recognition, pp. 4700–4708 (2017)

14. Hylton, N.M., et al.: Neoadjuvant chemotherapy for breast cancer: functional tumor volume by MR imaging predicts recurrence-free survival-results from the ACRIN 6657/CALGB 150007 I-SPY 1 TRIAL. Radiology **279**(1), 44–55 (2016)

15. King, V., Brooks, J.D., Bernstein, J.L., Reiner, A.S., Pike, M.C., Morris, E.A.: Background parenchymal enhancement at breast MR imaging and breast cancer risk. Radiology **260**(1), 50–60 (2011)

16. Kusano, G., Hiraoka, Y., Fukumizu, K.: Persistence weighted Gaussian kernel for topological data analysis. In: International Conference on Machine Learning, pp. 2004–2013. PMLR (2016)

17. Liu, M.Z., Mutasa, S., Chang, P., Siddique, M., Jambawalikar, S., Ha, R.: A novel CNN algorithm for pathological complete response prediction using an I-SPY TRIAL breast MRI database. Magn. Reson. Imaging **73**, 148–151 (2020)

18. Maria, C., Boissonnat, J.-D., Glisse, M., Yvinec, M.: The Gudhi library: simplicial complexes and persistent homology. In: Hong, H., Yap, C. (eds.) ICMS 2014. LNCS, vol. 8592, pp. 167–174. Springer, Heidelberg (2014). https://doi.org/10.1007/978-3-662-44199-2_28

19. Meng, Z., Li, J., Zhao, Y., Gong, Y.: Conditional teacher-student learning. In: ICASSP 2019–2019 IEEE International Conference on Acoustics, Speech and Signal Processing (ICASSP), pp. 6445–6449. IEEE (2019)

20. Ou, W.C., Polat, D., Dogan, B.E.: Deep learning in breast radiology: current progress and future directions. Eur. Radiol. **31**(7), 4872–4885 (2021). https://doi.org/10.1007/s00330-020-07640-9

21. Paszke, A., et al.: PyTorch: an imperative style, high-performance deep learning library. In: Advances in Neural Information Processing Systems, vol. 32 (2019)

22. Pun, C.S., Xia, K., Lee, S.X.: Persistent-homology-based machine learning and its applications-a survey. arXiv preprint arXiv:1811.00252 (2018)

23. Rustin, G.J., et al.: Re: new guidelines to evaluate the response to treatment in solid tumors (ovarian cancer). J. Natl. Cancer Inst. **96**(6), 487–488 (2004)

24. Saadat-Yazdi, A., Andreeva, R., Sarkar, R.: Topological detection of Alzheimer's disease using Betti curves. In: Reyes, M., et al. (eds.) IMIMIC/TDA4MedicalData -2021. LNCS, vol. 12929, pp. 119–128. Springer, Cham (2021). https://doi.org/10.1007/978-3-030-87444-5_12

25. Wang, F., Kapse, S., Liu, S., Prasanna, P., Chen, C.: TopoTxR: a topological biomarker for predicting treatment response in breast cancer. In: Feragen, A., Sommer, S., Schnabel, J., Nielsen, M. (eds.) IPMI 2021. LNCS, vol. 12729, pp. 386–397. Springer, Cham (2021). https://doi.org/10.1007/978-3-030-78191-0_30

26. Wu, P., et al.: Optimal topological cycles and their application in cardiac trabeculae restoration. In: Niethammer, M., et al. (eds.) IPMI 2017. LNCS, vol. 10265, pp. 80–92. Springer, Cham (2017). https://doi.org/10.1007/978-3-319-59050-9_7

27. Zhang, F., Zhu, X., Ye, M.: Fast human pose estimation. In: Proceedings of the IEEE/CVF Conference on Computer Vision and Pattern Recognition, pp. 3517–3526 (2019)

SETMIL: Spatial Encoding Transformer-Based Multiple Instance Learning for Pathological Image Analysis

Yu Zhao[2], Zhenyu Lin[1,2], Kai Sun[2,3], Yidan Zhang[4], Junzhou Huang[1,2,3,4], Liansheng Wang[1(✉)], and Jianhua Yao[2(✉)]

[1] Department of Computer Science at School of Informatics, Xiamen University, Xiamen 361005, China
lswang@xmu.edu.cn
[2] AI Lab, Tencent, Shenzhen 518000, China
jianhuayao@tencent.com
[3] School of Basic Medical Science, Central South University, Changsha 410013, China
[4] School of Computer Science, Sichuan University, Chengdu 610065, China

Abstract. Considering the huge size of the gigapixel whole slide image (WSI), multiple instance learning (MIL) is normally employed to address pathological image analysis tasks, where learning an informative and effective representation of each WSI plays a central role but remains challenging due to the weakly supervised nature of MIL. To this end, we present a novel Spatial Encoding Transformer-based MIL method, SETMIL, which has the following advantages. (1) It is a typical embedded-space MIL method and therefore has the advantage of generating the bag embedding by comprehensively encoding all instances with a fully trainable transformer-based aggregating module. (2) SETMIL leverages spatial-encoding-transformer layers to update the representation of an instance by aggregating both neighbouring instances and globally-correlated instances simultaneously. (3) The joint absolute-relative position encoding design in the aggregating module further improves the context-information-encoding ability of SETMIL. (4) SETMIL designs a transformer-based pyramid multi-scale fusion module to comprehensively encode the information with different granularity using multi-scale receptive fields and make the obtained representation enriched with multi-scale context information. Extensive experiments demonstrated the superior performance of SETMIL in challenging pathological image analysis tasks such as gene mutation and lymph node metastasis prediction.

Keywords: Multiple instance learning · Pathological image analysis · Transformer · Position encoding

Y. Zhao, Z. Lin, and K. Sun—Equally-contributed authors.

L. Wang et al. (Eds.): MICCAI 2022, LNCS 13432, pp. 66–76, 2022.
https://doi.org/10.1007/978-3-031-16434-7_7

1   Introduction

In modern healthcare, pathological image analysis plays a crucial role in the process of disease detection, interpretation, and is regarded as the gold standard for the diagnosis of almost all types of cancer [11,15,16,20,26,29]. The huge size of the WSIs draws a challenge for deep learning-based methods to comprehensively encode information of the entire WSI with conventional architecture. To tackle this issue, multiple instance learning (MIL) is usually leveraged to formulate pathological image analysis tasks into weakly supervised learning problems [1]. Generally, there exist two main categories of MIL methods in pathological image analysis, i.e., instance-space MIL and embedded-space MIL [1,23]. Instance-space MIL methods usually focus their learning process on the instance level and often achieve inferior performance compared to other MIL methods [1,8,9]. By contrast, embedded-space MIL methods attempt to extract information globally at the bag level, which can comprehensively exploit the entire WSI in pathological image analysis.

In embedded-space MIL methods, instances are firstly embedded into low-dimensional representations and then integrated to format a bag-level representation by an aggregating module, therefore transforming the multiple instance learning problem into a standard supervised learning problem [3,13,18,19]. Thus, developing an effective aggregating module to generate bag-level representation is a key step in embedded-space MIL methods, which remains a challenging problem for the following reasons. First of all, conventional fixed or parameterized pooling-based bag-embedding methods [23,25,30] are either fixed or partially trainable and therefore has limited ability to represent the bag information. Second, state-of-the-art attention-based MIL methods [6,7,13] represent the bag as a weighted sum of instance features, which is just a linear combination rather than a high-level feature embedding. Besides, these attention-based MIL methods lack sufficient consideration of position and context information of tiled patches (instances) in the WSI (bag). Third, recurrent neural network (RNN)-based MIL [2] or pioneering work employing transformer in image analysis [4] has considered position and context information. However, how to effectively and efficiently encode 2D positions of patches inside a WSI in the one-dimensional-sequence architecture is still an open question.

In this work, we aim at developing a MIL method to solve challenging pathological image analysis tasks, especially those needing comprehensive consideration of the tumour micro-environment on the entire WSI, such as metastasis and gene mutation prediction [5]. Taking into account that pathologists usually make diagnoses by leveraging both the context information locally around a single area and the correlation information globally between different areas, the developed MIL model should try to mimic this clinical practice. Therefore, we propose to update the representation of an instance by aggregating representations of both neighbouring instances (local information, a sub-region of WSI should have similar semantic information) and globally corrected instances simultaneously (similar sub-regions have similar semantic information). To summarize, we present a novel Spatial Encoding Transformer-based Multiple Instance Learning

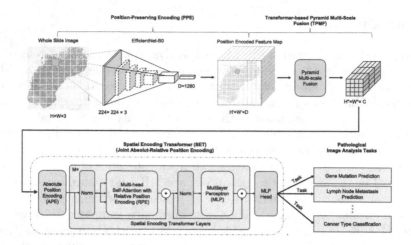

Fig. 1. The overall framework of the proposed spatial encoding transformer-based MIL (SETMIL).

method (SETMIL), which has a spatial encoding transformer-based bag embedding module, joint absolute-relative position encoding mechanism utilizing both absolute position encoding and relative position encoding, and a transformer-based pyramid multi-scale fusion module to comprehensively embed multi-scale information[1] The contributions of this paper include:

1) We present a novel embedded-space MIL method based on the transformer, which has a fully trainable transformer-based bag embedding module to aggregate the bag representation by comprehensively considering all instances.
2) We leverage the spatial encoding transformer to build a MIL method with the advantage of updating the representation of an instance by aggregating representations of both neighbouring instances and globally correlated instances simultaneously, which mimics the clinical practice.
3) We develop a transformer-based pyramid multi-scale fusion module to embed multi-scale information synchronously using multi-scale receptive fields and make the obtained representation enriched with multi-scale context information.
4) We demonstrate that joint absolute-relative position encoding outperforms either of them if utilized independently in transformer-based MIL.

2   Methods

2.1   Overview of the Proposed Method

As illustrated in Fig. 1, the proposed SETMIL consists of three main stages, i.e., position-preserving encoding (PPE), transformer-based pyramid multi-scale

---

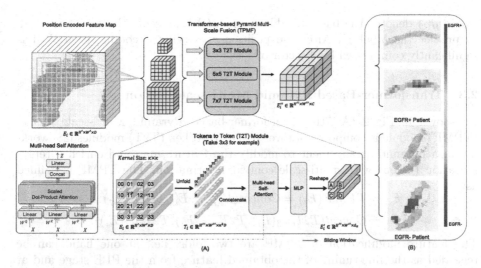

Fig. 2. Sub-figure (A) illustrates the transformer-based pyramid multi-scale fusion module. Sub-figure (B) shows a example heatmap for model interpretability. Colors reflect the prediction contribution of each local patch.

fusion (TPMF), and spatial encoding transformer (SET)-based bag embedding. First of all, in the PPE stage, SETMIL transforms input huge-size WSI to a small-size position-encoded feature map to simplify the following learning task. Second, the TPMF stage aims at modifying the feature map first and then enables each obtained representation enriched with multi-scale context information. Finally, the SET-based bag embedding module works for generating a high-level bag representation comprehensively considering all instance representations in a fully trainable way and leverages a joint absolute-relative position encoding mechanism to encode the position and context information. The details of these stages are introduced in Sects. 2.2, 2.3, and 2.4 respectively.

2.2 Position-Preserving Encoding

In pathological image analysis, assuming $B_i \in \mathbb{R}^{W \times H \times 3}$ is a WSI, tiled patches from B_i are instances denoted as: $B_i = \{p_i^{0,0}, p_i^{r,c}, \cdots, p_i^{H',W'}\}$, where $p_i^{r,c} \in \mathbb{R}^{\tau_h \times \tau_w \times 3}$, τ_h and τ_w represent the patch size, $H' = H/\tau_h$ and $W' = W/\tau_w$ are the raw and column number of obtained patches. To reduce the scale and facilitate the following learning task, we use a pre-trained EfficientNet-B0 [21] (trained on ImageNet) in the PPE module as the position-preserving encoder $f_E(\cdot)$ to embed each tiled path $p_i^{r,c} \in B_i$ into low-dimensional representations $e_i^{r,c} = f_E(p_i^{r,c}) \in \mathbb{R}^D$. Therefore, the MIL problem can be denoted as:

$$\hat{Y}_i = \phi(g(E_i)) = \phi(g(e_i^{0,0}, e_i^{r,c}, \cdots, e_i^{H',W'})), \tag{1}$$

where $g(\cdot)$ denotes the bag embedding and $\phi(\cdot)$ represents the transformation to predict the label Y_i. After the position-preserving encoding, each WSI is significantly compressed by a factor of $\frac{T_h \times T_w \times 3}{D}$.

2.3 Transformer-Based Pyramid Multi-scale Fusion

As shown in Fig. 2 (A), the Transformer-based Pyramid Multi-scale Fusion (TPMF) module is composed of three tokens-to-token (T2T) modules [28] working in a pyramid arrangement to modify the feature map and enrich a representation (token) with multi-scale context information. The TPMF is defined as:

$$E_i'' = TPMF(E_i) = Concat(E_{i,\kappa=3}', E_{i,\kappa=5}', E_{i,\kappa=7}')$$
$$= Concat(T2T_{\kappa=3}(E_i), T2T_{\kappa=5}(E_i), T2T_{\kappa=7}(E_i)). \tag{2}$$

The feature modification of TPMF are two-folds, i.e., at one hand can be regarded as the fine-tuning of the obtained feature from the PPE stage and at another hand to reduce the token length as instance-level feature selection. Each T2T module has a softsplit and a reshape process together with a transformer layer [22].

2.4 Spatial Encoding Transformer

The design of SETMIL's spatial encoding transformer (SET) component follows the following principles: (1) generating a high-level bag embedding comprehensively considering the information of all instances in a fully trainable way, (2) updating the representation of an instance by aggregating representations of both neighbour instances and globally correlated instances simultaneously mimicking the clinical practice, and (3) jointly leveraging absolute and relative position encoding to strengthen the context information encoding ability of SETMIL. As shown in Fig. 1, the SET has an absolute position encoding process at the beginning, M stacked spatial-encoding transformer layers (SETLs, $M = 6$) that jointly consider global correlation and local context information similarity to generate the bag embedding (as $g(\cdot)$) using relative spatial encoding, and a MLP to map the bag-embedding into the prediction (as $\phi(\cdot)$). We utilize the sinusoid procedure in standard transformer [22] as the absolute position encoding method. Besides, similar to [24,27], we apply the layer normalization (LN) before instead of after multi-head self-attention (MSA) operation and a multilayer perceptron (MLP) in each spatial encoding transformer layer. The prediction of SETMIL can be denoted as:

$$\hat{Y}_i = \phi(g(E_i'')) = \phi(SETL(\underset{M=6}{\cdots}, SETL(E_i''))), \tag{3}$$

where $SETL(\cdot)$ is defined as:

$$SETL(E_i'') = MLP(MSA^{SET}(LN(E_i''))). \tag{4}$$

The MSA^{SET} represents the multi-head self-attention in SETL, which is similar as MSA in [22] but with relative position encoding (Sect. 2.4) to embed the position and context information of each WSI. The self-attention mechanism in MSA is typical key-value attention. Assuming there is an input sequence $X = (x_1, x_2, \cdots, x_N)$, the output sequence of the self attention $Z = (z_1, z_2, \cdots, z_N)$ can be calculated as:

$$z_i = \mathcal{A}(X, W^Q, W^K, W^V) = \sum_{j=1}^{N} \frac{exp(\eta_{ij})}{\sum_{k=1}^{N} exp(\eta_{ik})} (x_j W^V), \tag{5}$$

where $x_i \in \mathbb{R}^{d_x}$, $z_i \in \mathbb{R}^{d_z}$, $W^Q, W^K, W^V \in \mathbb{R}^{d_x \times d_z}$ are the parameter projection matrices, η_{ij} is computed by a scaled dot-product attention:

$$\eta_{ij} = \frac{(x_i W^Q)(x_j W^K)^T}{\sqrt{d_z}}. \tag{6}$$

Relative Position Encoding. The mechanism of the $MSA^{SET}(\cdot)$ is demonstrated in Fig. 3. For two instance representations e_i'' and e_j'' in feature map $E'' = (e_1'', e_2'', \cdots, e_{H''W''}'')$ with 2D coordinate of $\rho_i = (r_i'', c_i'')$. The Euclidean distance μ between two instances can be calculated as:

$$\mu(\rho_i, \rho_j) = \sqrt{(r_i'' - r_j'')^2 + (c_i'' - c_j'')^2}. \tag{7}$$

To encode the position information, we refer the relative position encoding idea and assign a learnable scalar serving as a bias term in the self-attention module in formula (6). Therefor we have:

$$\eta_{i,j}'' = \frac{(e_i'' W^Q)(e_j'' W^K)^T}{\sqrt{d_z''}} + \lambda_{\mu(\rho_i, \rho_j)}, \tag{8}$$

where d_z'' is the dimension of SETL's output z_i'' and $\sqrt{d_z''}$ is used for appropriate normalization. $\lambda_{\mu(\rho_i, \rho_j)}$ is the learnable scalar indexed by $\mu(\rho_i, \rho_j)$, which is defined as: $\lambda_{\mu(\rho_i, \rho_j)} = \theta(\mu(\rho_i, \rho_j))$, where $\theta(\cdot)$ is learnable to adaptively assign weights for different spatial distances. As shown in Fig. 3, the first item in formula (8) is the same as a conventional transformer, which represents updating the representation of an instance referring to correlations between current instance and other instances globally. While, on the other hand, the second item assigns the same weight for instances with the same spatial distance to the current instance. This spatial-distance aware encoding strategy is similar to CNN but its kernel size is adaptively adjusted by $\theta(\cdot)$ and therefore has to potential to update the representation of an instance by aggregating neighbouring instances.

3   Experiments

Dataset: (1) Gene Mutation Prediction: The first task to evaluate the performance of SETMIL is gene mutation (GM) prediction. A total of 723 WSI slides

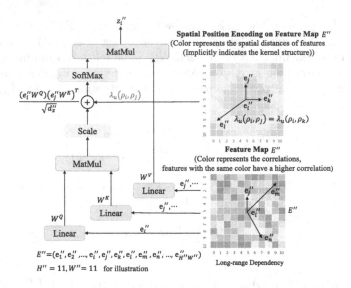

Fig. 3. Illustration of the spatial encoding transformer layer.

from patients diagnosed with LUAD were collected, where 47% cases included are with the epidermal growth factor receptor (EGFR) gene mutation. In this task, we use SETMIL to predict whether a patient is with EGFR gene mutation. (2) Lymph Node Metastasis Diagnosis: Another challenging task we would like to solve with SETMIL is the prediction of lymph node metastasis (LNM) status. 1274 WSI slides from patients with endometrial cancer (EC) were collected, among which 44% cases are diagnosed with lymph node metastasis. We apply this dataset to assess the potential of SETMIL in the prediction of LNM status.

Implementation Details: The samples in every dataset are randomly divided into the training, validation and test set with the percentages of $60\%, 20\%, 20\%$. We tile the WSI into patches using a 1120×1120 pixels sliding window without overlap. The proposed model is implemented in Pytorch and trained on one 32 GB TESLA V100 GPU. We utilize the Cross-Entropy Loss and the AdamW optimizer [12] with a learning rate of $2e^{-4}$ and a weight decay of $1e^{-4}$. The batch size is set to 4.

4   Results and Discussion

Comparison with State-of-the-Art Methods: The performance of SETMIL and other state-of-the-art (SOTA) methods including ABMIL [7,13], DSMIL [10], CLAM [14], RNN-MIL [2], ViT-MIL [4], TransMIL [17] and CNN-MIL are compared in Table 1. All methods are evaluated in two tasks, i.e., GM prediction (with/without EGFR) and LNM prediction (with/without LNM). Generally, the SETMIL achieves 83.84% AUC in the GM prediction task and 96.34% AUC in the LNM prediction task. From Table 1, we can also find that SETMIL outperforms other SOTA methods in the two tasks with over 1.51% and 5.19% performance enhancement (AUC), respectively. Figure 2 (B) shows a sample heatmap of the SETMIL reflecting the prediction contribution of each local patch. The top contributed patches for the prediction of EGFR mutation positive (EGFR+) and EGFR mutation negative (EGFR-) are indicated with red and blue colours, respectively.

Table 1. The performance of SETMIL compared with other state-of-the-art methods.

Models	LUAD-GM					EC-LNM				
	AUC (%)	Accuracy	Precision	Recall	F1-score	AUC (%)	Accuracy	Precision	Recall	F1-score
ABMIL [7,13]	52.44	54.55	47.83	13.10	20.56	64.30	53.33	53.33	**99.99**	69.57
RNN-MIL [2]	50.31	56.68	53.49	27.38	36.22	86.89	81.18	74.18	99.26	84.91
CNN-MIL	45.28	44.92	44.92	**99.99**	61.99	88.06	81.96	75.57	97.79	85.26
DSMIL [10]	78.53	71.53	**89.19**	47.14	61.68	88.51	85.10	79.88	96.32	87.33
CLAM-SB [14]	78.49	70.14	70.15	67.14	68.91	86.96	78.93	82.49	78.49	80.44
CLAM-MB [14]	82.33	75.70	73.97	77.14	75.52	87.62	81.31	83.24	82.80	83.02
ViT-MIL [4]	76.39	70.14	81.40	50.00	61.95	91.15	86.27	80.24	98.53	88.45
TransMIL [17]	77.29	74.45	68.74	69.02	68.87	82.76	74.78	74.58	73.98	74.16
SETMIL(Ours)	**83.84**	**76.38**	71.14	86.08	**78.24**	**96.34**	**92.94**	**92.75**	94.12	**93.43**

Ablation Studies: (1) Effects of Proposed Components: To evaluate the effectiveness of each proposed component in the SETMIL, we conducted experiments on the following configurations: (A) SETMIL (our proposed method): PPE + TPMF (T2T module & Pyramid Multi-scale Fusion (PMF) idea) + SET; (B) "w/o TPMF&SET": SETMIL without using both the TPMF and SET module, which is the same as the ViT-MIL [4]; (C) "w/o PMF&SET" SETMIL without using both the pyramid multi-scale fusion (PMF) idea and SET module but having a single 5 × 5 T2T module for feature modification and dimension reduction; (D) "w/o SET": SETMIL without using SET; (E) "w/o PMF": SETMIL without using PMF but having a single 5 × 5 T2T module for feature modification and dimension reduction; The ablation study results are illustrated in Table 2, where we can conclude that the SETMIL benefits from each proposed components. (2) Assessment of Different Position Encoding Strategies: To assess the performance of SETMIL by using different position encoding strategies, we also conducted experiments on the following two configurations: (A) "w/o Absolute": SETMIL without using absolute position encoding and (B) "w/o Relative": SETMIL without using relative position encoding (same as "w/o SET"). The experiment results are shown in Table 2, indicating that using both absolute position encoding and relative position encoding mechanisms jointly improves the performance compared to using either one of them.

Table 2. Ablation studies: effects of proposed components.

Methods	LUAD-GM					EC-LNM				
	AUC (%)	Accuracy	Precision	Recall	F1-score	AUC (%)	Accuracy	Precision	Recall	F1-score
w/o TPMF&SET	76.39 (-7.45)	70.14	81.40	50.00	61.95	91.15 (-5.19)	86.27	80.24	**98.53**	88.45
w/o PMF&SET	79.40 (-4.44)	70.83	65.56	84.29	**73.75**	92.84 (-3.50)	87.06	85.03	91.91	88.34
w/o SET	81.27 (-2.57)	72.92	78.18	61.43	68.80	95.42 (-0.92)	91.76	89.66	95.59	92.53
w/o PMF	80.41 (-3.43)	61.11	56.36	**88.57**	68.89	95.85 (-0.49)	89.41	87.59	93.38	90.39
w/o Absolute	75.56 (-8.28)	72.22	70.27	**74.29**	72.22	89.32 (-7.02)	80.39	85.25	76.47	80.62
w/o Relative	81.27 (-2.57)	72.92	78.18	61.43	68.80	95.42 (-0.92)	91.76	89.66	**95.59**	92.53
SETMIL(Ours)	**83.84**	**76.38**	71.14	86.08	**78.24**	**96.34**	**92.94**	**92.75**	94.12	**93.43**

5   Conclusion

In this paper, we comprehensively considered the characteristics of pathological image analysis and presented a novel spatial encoding transformer-based MIL method, which has the potential to be a backbone for solving challenging pathological image analysis tasks. Experimental results demonstrated the superior performance of the proposed SETMIL compared to other state-of-the-art methods. Ablation studies also demonstrated the contribution of each proposed component of SETMIL.

References

1. Amores, J.: Multiple instance classification: review, taxonomy and comparative study. Artif. Intell. **201**, 81–105 (2013)
2. Campanella, G., et al.: Clinical-grade computational pathology using weakly supervised deep learning on whole slide images. Nat. Med. **25**(8), 1301–1309 (2019)
3. Diao, J.A., et al.: Human-interpretable image features derived from densely mapped cancer pathology slides predict diverse molecular phenotypes. Nat. Commun. **12**(1), 1–15 (2021)
4. Dosovitskiy, A., et al.: An image is worth 16x16 words: transformers for image recognition at scale. In: International Conference on Learning Representations (2020)
5. Garrett, W.S.: Cancer and the microbiota. Science **348**(6230), 80–86 (2015)
6. Hashimoto, N., et al.: Multi-scale domain-adversarial multiple-instance CNN for cancer subtype classification with unannotated histopathological images. In: Proceedings of the IEEE/CVF Conference on Computer Vision and Pattern Recognition, pp. 3852–3861 (2020)
7. Ilse, M., Tomczak, J., Welling, M.: Attention-based deep multiple instance learning. In: International Conference on Machine Learning, pp. 2127–2136. PMLR (2018)
8. Kandemir, M., Hamprecht, F.A.: Computer-aided diagnosis from weak supervision: a benchmarking study. Computeriz. Med. Imaging Graph. **42**, 44–50 (2015)
9. Kather, J.N., et al.: Deep learning can predict microsatellite instability directly from histology in gastrointestinal cancer. Nat. Med. **25**(7), 1054–1056 (2019)

10. Li, B., Li, Y., Eliceiri, K.W.: Dual-stream multiple instance learning network for whole slide image classification with self-supervised contrastive learning. In: Proceedings of the IEEE/CVF Conference on Computer Vision and Pattern Recognition, pp. 14318–14328 (2021)
11. Li, R., Yao, J., Zhu, X., Li, Y., Huang, J.: Graph CNN for survival analysis on whole slide pathological images. In: Frangi, A.F., Schnabel, J.A., Davatzikos, C., Alberola-López, C., Fichtinger, G. (eds.) MICCAI 2018. LNCS, vol. 11071, pp. 174–182. Springer, Cham (2018). https://doi.org/10.1007/978-3-030-00934-2_20
12. Loshchilov, I., Hutter, F.: Decoupled weight decay regularization. In: International Conference on Learning Representations (2018)
13. Lu, M.Y., et al.: Ai-based pathology predicts origins for cancers of unknown primary. Nature **594**(7861), 106–110 (2021)
14. Lu, M.Y., Williamson, D.F., Chen, T.Y., Chen, R.J., Barbieri, M., Mahmood, F.: Data-efficient and weakly supervised computational pathology on whole-slide images. Nat. Biomed. Eng. **5**(6), 555–570 (2021)
15. Mehta, S., Mercan, E., Bartlett, J., Weaver, D., Elmore, J.G., Shapiro, L.: Y-net: joint segmentation and classification for diagnosis of breast biopsy images. In: Frangi, A.F., Schnabel, J.A., Davatzikos, C., Alberola-López, C., Fichtinger, G. (eds.) MICCAI 2018. LNCS, vol. 11071, pp. 893–901. Springer, Cham (2018). https://doi.org/10.1007/978-3-030-00934-2_99
16. Rubin, R., et al.: Rubin's Pathology: Clinicopathologic Foundations of Medicine. Lippincott Williams & Wilkins (2008)
17. Shao, Z., et al.: Transmil: transformer based correlated multiple instance learning for whole slide image classication. arXiv preprint arXiv:2106.00908 (2021)
18. Skrede, O.J., et al.: Deep learning for prediction of colorectal cancer outcome: a discovery and validation study. The Lancet **395**(10221), 350–360 (2020)
19. Song, Z., et al.: Clinically applicable histopathological diagnosis system for gastric cancer detection using deep learning. Nat. Commun. **11**(1), 1–9 (2020)
20. Srinidhi, C.L., Ciga, O., Martel, A.L.: Deep neural network models for computational histopathology: a survey. Med. Image Anal. 101813 (2020)
21. Tan, M., Le, Q.: Efficientnet: rethinking model scaling for convolutional neural networks. In: International Conference on Machine Learning, pp. 6105–6114. PMLR (2019)
22. Vaswani, A., et al.: Attention is all you need. In: Advances in Neural Information Processing Systems, pp. 5998–6008 (2017)
23. Wang, X., Yan, Y., Tang, P., Bai, X., Liu, W.: Revisiting multiple instance neural networks. Pattern Recogn. **74**, 15–24 (2018)
24. Xiong, R., et al.: On layer normalization in the transformer architecture. In: International Conference on Machine Learning, pp. 10524–10533. PMLR (2020)
25. Yan, Y., Wang, X., Guo, X., Fang, J., Liu, W., Huang, J.: Deep multi-instance learning with dynamic pooling. In: Asian Conference on Machine Learning, pp. 662–677. PMLR (2018)
26. Yao, J., Zhu, X., Huang, J.: Deep multi-instance learning for survival prediction from whole slide images. In: Shen, D., et al. (eds.) MICCAI 2019. LNCS, vol. 11764, pp. 496–504. Springer, Cham (2019). https://doi.org/10.1007/978-3-030-32239-7_55
27. Ying, C., et al.: Do transformers really perform bad for graph representation? arXiv preprint arXiv:2106.05234 (2021)
28. Yuan, L., et al.: Tokens-to-token vit: training vision transformers from scratch on imagenet. arXiv preprint arXiv:2101.11986 (2021)

29. Zhou, Y., Onder, O.F., Dou, Q., Tsougenis, E., Chen, H., Heng, P.-A.: CIA-Net: robust nuclei instance segmentation with contour-aware information aggregation. In: Chung, A.C.S., Gee, J.C., Yushkevich, P.A., Bao, S. (eds.) IPMI 2019. LNCS, vol. 11492, pp. 682–693. Springer, Cham (2019). https://doi.org/10.1007/978-3-030-20351-1_53
30. Zhou, Y., Sun, X., Liu, D., Zha, Z., Zeng, W.: Adaptive pooling in multi-instance learning for web video annotation. In: Proceedings of the IEEE International Conference on Computer Vision Workshops, pp. 318–327 (2017)

Clinical-Realistic Annotation for Histopathology Images with Probabilistic Semi-supervision: A Worst-Case Study

Ziyue Xu[1]([✉]), Andriy Myronenko[1], Dong Yang[1], Holger R. Roth[1], Can Zhao[1], Xiaosong Wang[2], and Daguang Xu[1]

[1] Nvidia Corp, Santa Clara, USA
ziyuex@nvidia.com
[2] Alibaba Group, Hangzhou, China

Abstract. Acquiring pixel-level annotation has been a major challenge for machine learning methods in medical image analysis. Such difficulty mainly comes from two sources: localization requiring high expertise, and delineation requiring tedious and time-consuming work. Existing methods of easing the annotation effort mostly focus on the latter one, the extreme of which is replacing the delineation with a single label for all cases. We postulate that under a clinical-realistic setting, such methods alone may not always be effective in reducing the annotation requirements from conventional classification/detection algorithms, because the major difficulty can come from localization, which is often neglected but can be critical in medical domain, especially for histopathology images. In this work, we performed a worst-case scenario study to identify the information loss from missing detection. To tackle the challenge, we 1) proposed a different annotation strategy to image data with different levels of disease severity, 2) combined semi- and self-supervised representation learning with probabilistic weakly supervision to make use of the proposed annotations, and 3) illustrated its effectiveness in recovering useful information under the worst-case scenario. As a shift from previous convention, it can potentially save significant time for experts' annotation for AI model development.

Keywords: Clinical-realistic annotation · Histopathology · Probabilistic semi-supervision · Worst-case study

1 Introduction

Supervised deep learning methods have shown state-of-the-art performances in many applications from natural images to the medical domain [9,14,17]. One of

Supplementary Information The online version contains supplementary material available at https://doi.org/10.1007/978-3-031-16434-7_8.

the major challenges of supervised methods is their reliance on the quantity and quality of the data and annotations. Using fully delineated segmentation masks for training has long been the common practice. Annotators need to first localize the object of interest from the image, then delineate its boundary. Thus the "annotation difficulty" can come from two sources: localization, and performing a specific type of annotation on the localized region.

For natural image tasks, localization is often less of a concern since our brains are trained to recognize objects from a natural scene. Therefore, the challenge comes mostly from the process of delineating the complex shapes from the background. To reduce the burden of manual boundary drawing, several "weak" annotation techniques have been proposed, mainly to replace the "strong" full-boundary delineation with easier alternatives, including points [1], bounding boxes [5,10,16], and scribbles [12].

In medical domain, there are similar attempts following this strategy [2,13, 18] to address the issue of tedious boundary delineation. However, performing accurate boundary delineation may not always be the most critical issue. Instead, the localization can pose a bigger challenge for annotators. This is because localization demands much higher expertise comparing to segmentation. In this work, we postulate that "weak" label alone may not be sufficient to make the annotation "easy" since the major difficulty can come from localization. Therefore, to accommodate for clinical-realistic annotation time, we would like to raise this issue to the attention of our society, and propose a shift from convention.

The major contributions of this work are: 1) We provide detailed analysis of the challenges, and simulated a "worst-case" scenario under clinical-realistic time constraint. 2) We proposed a more balanced annotation strategy to tackle the challenges from such time/resource limit, and to better model the difficulties in medical image annotation for AI model development. 3) To utilize the proposed annotations, we designed a semi-supervised learning strategy by using the probabilistic distribution information. With the candidate tasks of tumor detection from histopathology images, we illustrated the potential of the proposed strategies that may significantly ease the annotation burden. The implementation will be released under Project MONAI.

2   Method

In this work, we target at the task of lesion detection from histopathology images. In clinical routine, digital scanners capture the entire sample slide as whole slide image (WSI). Pathologists examine the WSIs carefully under different resolutions, searching for the patterns of cell appearance change indicating diseases. Each individual WSI can have a dimension of 100k × 100k pixels. At this scale, it can be very difficult for both disease region localization and delineation: small lesions can occupy less than 0.1% of the whole image, which is highly possible to be missed; while large lesions can occupy more than 50% of the slide, requiring tens of thousands of clicks if performing full boundary annotation. Hence, the annotation for AI model development often require much more time than what is acceptable in clinical routine [6].

To ease the difficulty of annotation for AI model development so that it can be achieved under a clinical-realistic setting, existing works proposed to use sparse point annotation [8], or diagnosis path [23] to replace full segmentation annotation. As the extreme of "weak" annotation category, a relatively common practice in histopathology domain is to learn from a single label for the entire WSI indicating the clinical findings. Most of time such problem is solved using multi-instance learning [22]. However, although a single label is the most simple from annotation input perspective, we argue that it does not directly relate to how "easy" the annotation is, and hence may not be sufficiently helpful to ease the annotation burden.

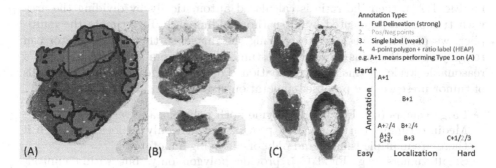

Fig. 1. Different difficulty levels in localization and performing 4 types of annotation: (A-C) give example of three common cases of tumor detection in histopathology: (A) distributed large tumor; (B) focal and medium-size tumor; (C) focal and small tumor. Different annotations illustrated in (A): single 4-point polygon (red), 10-point (5 positive yellow + 5 negative green), and full delineation (blue). (Color figure online)

Annotation Strategy. Figure 1 depicts a qualitative view of how "hard" and "easy" the tasks of detection and annotation can be for tumor regions of different sizes. As shown, the tumor region occupies 51%, 3%, and 0.01% of the foreground tissue for Case A, B, and C. Annotation difficulty can be derived directly from how many vertices are required by a particular scheme, from 0/few clicks to thousands of clicks (delineation for large tumors). And the localization difficulty comes from how "visually distinctive" the tumor region appears from normal tissue. By consulting pathologists, we believe it is generally true that smaller tumors are easier to miss (thus more difficult to locate). For Case A, the annotation challenge mainly comes from delineation. It is easy to capture the tumor site, but takes tedious work to segment it. For Case B, both localization and segmentation are moderately easy. In contrast, for Case C, the challenge mainly comes from localization: it takes pathologist significant effort to very carefully go over the WSI to identify the tiny region that has tumor, but once it is located, it is very easy to do the delineation. Therefore in clinical practice, "weak" label does not necessarily mean less effort. According to clinical studies, diagnosis can have 3.4% false negative, and 5.5% false positive [15]. With second opinion [21], 6.6% can have a change of diagnosis. Hence, "weak" label can be both "hard" and unreliable for cases like C. One aim of this work is to find such an annotation strategy that for different cases, the efforts are always **close to origin** in the 2D coordinate system shown at the right side of Fig. 1, while in the meantime provide as much information as possible for the AI algorithm training.

To tackle the above challenges, we propose a new annotation strategy to account for the difficulty arising from both localization and delineation. Annotators are expected to do two types of annotations: 1) a **single k-point polygon** on the **major** tumor site (if there are multiple tumors) as illustrated by the red polygon in Fig. 1(A), we set $k = 4$ in this study; 2) a rough (stride of 5%) estimation of the **tumor/tissue area ratio**. For large tumors, annotators will provide an estimated multiplier for the polygon area v.s. the whole tumor area(e.g. ×4 for Fig. 1(A)), then the ratio is calculated automatically by dividing the area with tissue area segmented by Otsu thresholding [11]. To estimate the multiplier, we provide a mesh grid overlaying the image, so that the annotator can roughly count the grids to make the estimation. With our experiments, 5% is a reasonable stride for this rough estimation. Then for images with different levels of tumor presence, the proposed annotation strategy is:

- Large tumors (e.g. Fig. 1(A)), provide both polygons and ratio
- Medium tumors (e.g. Fig. 1(B)), provide polygon only (if focal), or both if there are multiple tumors and only one is being annotated
- Small tumors (e.g. Fig. 1(C)), provide polygon only, but within clinical-realistic time limit. Note that in the worst-case scenario, most cases in this category will be considered "missed by annotators".

In this way, we provide decent polygon annotations for tumors of all sizes, and with area estimation for further probability modeling on large tumor regions.

Worst-Case Scenario. As compared with conventional annotation strategy where annotators need to take a lot of time and effort to either delineating the complex boundaries, or identifying the tiny region to provide/reject a positive label, in this work, we set the environment to be clinical realistic in that 1) large tumors are sparsely annotated, and 2) small tumors are located only if identified within time limit. Under this setting, we would like to design a training algorithm by considering both the available information from the above annotation strategy, and the potential uncertainty introduced by the missing tumor regions. To fully test the capability of the proposed method, we did our study under a worst-case scenario. In our experiment dataset of Camelyon 16 [6], out of 111 training cases, 55 are less than 1%, only 25 have tumor region greater than 10%. Given the statistics from [6], under "routine diagnostic setting", pathologists' sensitivity range from 58.9% to 71.9% with mean 62.8%. Hence, it is reasonable to simulate the worst-case scenario by considering all lesions under 1% as missing in annotation.

Semi-supervised Learning with Probabilistic Ratio Supervision. We design a semi-supervised method based on the proposed polygon and ratio annotations. We leverage semi- and self-supervised learning techniques to train a base model that can have high false positive rate, then make use of weak supervision from tumor proportional ratio under a probabilistic setting to refine the model.

Figure 2 illustrated the pipeline of the system. For Stage 1, we follow Mix-Match method similar to the one proposed in [8], but with the proposed polygon annotation. We split our dataset into the three categories following the strategy proposed above: WSIs with no annotated tumors, WSIs with both polygon and ratio annotations, and WSIs with polygon annotations only. For Stage 1, we generate positive samples by random sampling from the polygon regions, and negative samples by random sampling from WSIs with no annotations. Although it is possible to get positive patches from the latter, the possibility is low and can be regarded as noise during training.

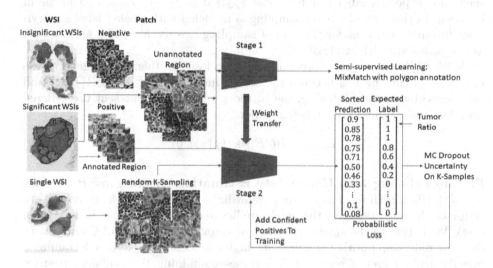

Fig. 2. Proposed semi-supervised pipeline with probabilistic ratio supervision.

With trained network from Stage 1, the learnt representation is transferred to Stage 2 and refined by probabilistic ratio supervision. Similar information has been recorded for diagnostic purposes in some clinical protocols. And existing work proposed to utilize such information [19] for subclass identification, where it is modeled as a pseudo label generation process in a deterministic way: the patches are pre-selected and fixed across the entire training process, only the pseudo labels will change according to the correct ratio. Hence, it needs a relatively good sampling strategy to begin with, and every step it need to perform inference over the entire dataset. Unfortunately for Camelyon dataset, 55/111 cases have tumor region less than 1%. It is thus neither realistic to correctly sample the potential tumor site, nor to do inference on all locations every step.

Due to this unique class imbalance issue, we propose to model the ratio information in a probabilistic manner. As shown in Fig. 2, at Stage 2, a batch x consists of a fixed number of K patches are randomly sampled from tissue region of a single WSI with rough ratio estimation $r\%$. From a probability perspective, it is expected that there will be around $K \times r\%$ cases of positive finding. Since r is a "rough" estimation, we model the uncertainty with a linear transition label. Specifically, we define a "fuzzy" range r_f around r, indicating that the positive ratio would be at least $r_{\min} = \max(0, r - r_f)$, and at most $r_{\max} = \min(r + r_f, 100)$. To reflect this fuzzy range, we generated a target prediction vector y with length K as:

$$y_i = 1 - \max(\min(i, r_{\max}) - r_{\min}, 0)/(r_{\max} - r_{\min}) \tag{1}$$

such that expected label is 1 for $i <= r_{\min}$, 0 for $i >= r_{\max}$, and linear in between. In this way, the fuzzy sampling is modeled with weaker label supervision. In our experiment for the ease of sampling, we set $K = 100$, and $r_f = 2$, as the ratios are with stride of 5%.

With CNN model f, the probabilistic ratio loss can then be designed as the binary cross entropy loss between the sorted model output $o = \text{sort}(f(x))$ and this "expected target vector" y, the sorted probabilities represent the ordered confidence of a random patch being tumor.

$$\mathcal{L}_{ratio} = BCE(\text{sort}(f(x)), y) \tag{2}$$

Pseudo Labeling with Uncertainty Estimation. In order to further make use of the data with ratio annotation, we utilized the Monte Carlo dropout [7] to estimate the uncertainty of the patch predictions from the K patch samples of every WSI. Due to the significant positive/negative imbalance of Camelyon 16 data, we only keep positive samples with high confidence for "feedback training". Specifically, we keep a queue of N samples containing the confident positive patches with their corresponding uncertainty U_N. At every step, out of the sorted predictions $\text{sort}(f(x))$, we select the first $K \times r\%$, which are expected to be positive. And according to the estimated uncertainty U_R, we replace k samples from N with the ones from R whose uncertainty is higher $U_R(i) < U_N(j)$, i.e. replacing the more uncertain ones with more confident ones. The loss of these N samples will be

$$\mathcal{L}_{feedback} = BCE(f(x_N), Y_+) \tag{3}$$

where Y_+ is the vector corresponding to positive. The total loss is

$$\mathcal{L} = \mathcal{L}_{ratio} + \lambda \mathcal{L}_{feedback} \tag{4}$$

As $r >= 10$ cases already have polygon annotations being used in Stage 1, we select only $r < 10$ cases in this feedback training. Also in this study, we use $N = 100$, and $\lambda = 1$.

3 Experiments and Results

We test our method using the publicly available Camelyon 16 dataset [6]. The length of the WSIs range from 50k to 200k pixels with two types of microns/pixel: 0.226×0.226 and 0.243×0.243. The training set consists of 111 tumor (with ground truth segmentations) and 159 normal WSIs. Testing set has 129 cases, and organizer provided the ground truth for 48 of them. All results below are tested on these 48 cases as the ground truth for other cases are unavailable. (Note that this can cause some discrepancies from the metric number reported in literature. For example, we used the code and model provided by [11], and on these 48 cases, the FROC score is 0.70, while in the paper [11], the reported FROC is 0.79. Also, the cases without ground truth can not be considered normal, because the result does not match.)

In this study, we compare the proposed annotation and learning strategy to several state-of-the-art alternatives, including fully-supervised, semi-supervised, and weakly-supervised methods with different levels of annotation. The methods include: 1) fully-supervised [11] with ground truth segmentation annotations. This is the expected "upper bound" for the experiments. For this baseline, we experimented with both customized (provided by [11]) and random sampling strategy in patch selection. Also, under our "worst-case" setting where the 55 cases with small tumors are all missed by annotators, we did an experiment with the training data selected from the other 56/111 cases with the customized sampling strategy. 2) SimCLR model [3] trained on both Camelyon and Patch Camelyon dataset in a self-supervised manner, and then fine-tuned using either 56 cases with polygon annotation, or 50% of the patch dataset [20]. 3) Mix-Match trained on 10-point or polygon annotations following [8]. 4) Weakly supervised model [4] using 0/1 label only, which is specifically designed and tuned on histopathology and Camelyon 16 data. All algorithms trained on Camelyon 16 data used 224×224 patches at level 0 ($40\times$), while Patch Camelyon network used 96×96 patch at level 2 ($10\times$). Note that these methods are one-stage, i.e. some of them are used as the base model for our Stage 2 finetuning.

We tried our best to reproduce the results by using the original code and model directly if they are available. For 1), we ran inference with the model provided with the customized sampling experiment. Further, we extracted all possible training samples with ground truth annotations at a stride of 128, and trained the model with the training code provided by the authors. For 2), we trained our model following [3], and perform inference under both common settings as other method, and the patch size and level as Patch Camelyon dataset [20]. For 3), we manually generated point annotations, unlabeled and extension sample sets, following the guidelines from [8] and train a model with the code provided by authors. For 4), we directly cite the metric number from the original paper (Table 1).

Table 1. Quantitative FROC evaluation of different methods in a one-stage manner.

Method	Training data	Annotation	Amount	Sampling	FROC
Fully-supervised [11]	Camelyon 16	Mask	Full	Customized	0.70
Fully-supervised [11]	Camelyon 16	Mask	Full	Random	0.51
Fully-supervised [11]	Camelyon 16	Mask	56/111	Customized	0.36
SimCLR [3]	Camelyon 16	Polygon	56/111	Random	0.38
SimCLR [3]	Patch Camelyon	0/1 patch	50%	Random	0.39
MixMatch [8]	Camelyon 16	10-point	56/111	Random	0.08
MixMatch [8]	Camelyon 16	Polygon	56/111	Random	0.10
Weakly-supervised [4]	Camelyon 16	0/1 WSI	Full	Random	0.31
Proposed	Camelyon 16	Polygon+ratio	56/111	Random	0.49

For ablation studies, we replaced the two components in the proposed pipeline with other alternatives. In this work, Stage 1 aims to learn a relatively good representation for histopathology images. Therefore, either self-supervised methods, e.g. SimCLR [3] with or without labeled fine-tuning, or semi-supervised method with limited annotation e.g. MixMatch [8], can be applied. We also did an experiment without Stage 1, start Stage 2 training with random initialization. For Stage 2, we choose to disable the uncertainty estimation and feedback strategy, using only the probabilistic ratio supervision. Also, we further relax the stride of ratio estimation from 5% to 10%, which allows for more estimation uncertainty (Table 2).

Table 2. Quantitative FROC evaluation of ablation configurations.

Stage 1	Annotation 1	Stage 2	Annotation 2	FROC
Skip	N/A	Probabilistic	Ratio at 5%	0.02
SimCLR [3]	N/A	Probabilistic	Ratio at 5%	0.34
SimCLR [3]	Polygon	Probabilistic	Ratio at 5%	0.44
MixMatch [8]	10-point	Probabilistic	Ratio at 5%	0.40
MixMatch [8]	Polygon	Probabilistic	Ratio at 5%	0.47
MixMatch [8]	Polygon	Probabilistic	Ratio at 10%	0.37
Proposed	Polygon	Probabilistic + feedback	Ratio at 5%	0.49

As shown in the two tables, the proposed probabilistic ratio supervision significantly promote the performance from Stage 1, (0.38 to 0.44 for SimCLR with labeled finetuning, and 0.08/0.10 to 0.40/0.47 for MixMatch). It is also better than other alternative semi- and weakly-supervised methods (0.31). Comparing the supervised method with full segmentation, it performs better than using the 25 annotated cases (0.36), and similar to using random sampling strategy on all annotations (0.51). We noticed that the performance of MixMatch with point annotations [8] seems to work a lot worse than what is presented in the original paper on different dataset. It could be due to that the original paper used customized data, which according to figures, seems to be much more balanced on the tumor/tissue ratio. This class imbalance issue is also raised in the weakly supervised paper [4].

For actual annotation time, the time of polygon + ratio is less than/ comparable to the time cost of the 10-point annotations [8] at around 1 minute per case: as shown in Fig. 1(A), the 10-points are preferred to cover all tumor sites (5 points), as well as normal regions (the other 5 points); while the polygon is 4 points, but preferred to cover a large portion of the major tumor. Thus their annotation complexity is comparable. As comparison according to [6], it takes 30 h to review the 129 testing cases for determining the presence of tumor, with an AUC 0.966. Regarding boundary delineation, although the precise time is not mentioned, there are on average 8800 vertices per WSI, indicating huge annotation effort. We performed an annotation experiment on the case shown in Fig. 1 (A), and it took us 5 h to finish a decent job.

4   Conclusion and Discussion

In order to reduce the annotation burden for medical AI model development, in this work, we proposed a shift from conventional annotate strategies where the localization cost is neglected, but can be highly difficult for medical applications. The proposed strategy take both localization and delineation into consideration. With the information annotated, we designed a semi-supervised learning method with probabilistic weak supervision and uncertainty-based feedback. Our results on Camelyon 16 dataset under worst-case clinical realistic setting showed that the proposed annotation and learning strategy achieved better performance than its semi-supervised counterparts, and is comparable to fully supervised method with random sampling strategy.

The major uncertainty of the proposed annotation strategy comes from the estimation of the "multiplier": we ask annotators to draw a polygon as big as possible, while fully contained inside the major tumor site. Under this request, for small/medium tumors, the polygon will not have significant variations because of limited size and shape irregularity. For large, irregular tumors, the polygon can have inter-observer variability issue. To cover such potential error, based on the observation from our repeated estimations, we chose a ratio with a stride of 5%. Fortunately, for this category of large tumors, the large polygon can already cover a significant area. Therefore, the contribution from the probability part is not as significant as the smaller ones. Adaptive stride beyond the fixed 5% will be a future direction.

References

1. Bearman, A., Russakovsky, O., Ferrari, V., Fei-Fei, L.: What's the point: semantic segmentation with point supervision. In: Leibe, B., Matas, J., Sebe, N., Welling, M. (eds.) ECCV 2016. LNCS, vol. 9911, pp. 549–565. Springer, Cham (2016). https://doi.org/10.1007/978-3-319-46478-7_34

2. Cai, J., et al.: Accurate weakly-supervised deep lesion segmentation using large-scale clinical annotations: slice-propagated 3D mask generation from 2D RECIST. In: Frangi, A.F., Schnabel, J.A., Davatzikos, C., Alberola-López, C., Fichtinger, G. (eds.) MICCAI 2018. LNCS, vol. 11073, pp. 396–404. Springer, Cham (2018). https://doi.org/10.1007/978-3-030-00937-3_46

3. Ciga, O., Xu, T., Martel, A.L.: Self supervised contrastive learning for digital histopathology. arXiv preprint arXiv:2011.13971 (2020)

4. Courtiol, P., Tramel, E.W., Sanselme, M., Wainrib, G.: Classification and disease localization in histopathology using only global labels: a weakly-supervised approach. CoRR arXiv:1802.02212 (2018)

5. Dai, J., He, K., Sun, J.: BoxSup: exploiting bounding boxes to supervise convolutional networks for semantic segmentation. In: Proceedings of the 2015 IEEE International Conference on Computer Vision (ICCV), ICCV 2015, USA, pp. 1635–1643 (2015)

6. Ehteshami Bejnordi, B., et al.: Diagnostic assessment of deep learning algorithms for detection of lymph node metastases in women with breast cancer. JAMA 318(22), 2199–2210 (2017)

7. Gal, Y., Ghahramani, Z.: Dropout as a Bayesian approximation: representing model uncertainty in deep learning. In: Proceedings of the 33rd International Conference on Machine Learning. Proceedings of Machine Learning Research, 20–22 June 2016, vol. 48, pp. 1050–1059 (2016)

8. Gao, Z., Puttapirat, P., Shi, J., Li, C.: Renal cell carcinoma detection and subtyping with minimal point-based annotation in whole-slide images. In: Martel, A.L., et al. (eds.) MICCAI 2020. LNCS, vol. 12265, pp. 439–448. Springer, Cham (2020). https://doi.org/10.1007/978-3-030-59722-1_42

9. He, K., Zhang, X., Ren, S., Sun, J.: Deep residual learning for image recognition. arXiv preprint arXiv:1512.03385 (2015)

10. Khoreva, A., Benenson, R., Hosang, J., Hein, M., Schiele, B.: Simple does it: weakly supervised instance and semantic segmentation. In: 2017 IEEE Conference on Computer Vision and Pattern Recognition (CVPR), pp. 1665–1674, July 2017

11. Li, Y., Ping, W.: Cancer metastasis detection with neural conditional random field. In: Medical Imaging with Deep Learning (2018)

12. Lin, D., Dai, J., Jia, J., He, K., Sun, J.: ScribbleSup: scribble-supervised convolutional networks for semantic segmentation. In: 2016 IEEE Conference on Computer Vision and Pattern Recognition (CVPR), pp. 3159–3167, June 2016

13. Maninis, K., Caelles, S., Pont-Tuset, J., Van Gool, L.: Deep extreme cut: from extreme points to object segmentation. In: 2018 IEEE/CVF Conference on Computer Vision and Pattern Recognition, pp. 616–625, June 2018

14. Milletari, F., Navab, N., Ahmadi, S.A.: V-Net: fully convolutional neural networks for volumetric medical image segmentation. In: 2016 Fourth International Conference on 3D Vision (3DV), pp. 565–571. IEEE (2016)

15. Ng, J.C., Swain, S., Dowling, J.P., Wolfe, R., Simpson, P., Kelly, J.W.: The impact of partial biopsy on histopathologic diagnosis of cutaneous melanoma: experience of an Australian tertiary referral service. Arch. Dermatol. 146(3), 234–239 (2010)

16. Papandreou, G., Chen, L.C., Murphy, K.P., Yuille, A.L.: Weakly-and semi-supervised learning of a deep convolutional network for semantic image segmentation. In: Proceedings of the 2015 IEEE International Conference on Computer Vision (ICCV), pp. 1742–1750 (2015)

17. Ronneberger, O., Fischer, P., Brox, T.: U-Net: convolutional networks for biomedical image segmentation. In: Navab, N., Hornegger, J., Wells, W.M., Frangi, A.F. (eds.) MICCAI 2015. LNCS, vol. 9351, pp. 234–241. Springer, Cham (2015). https://doi.org/10.1007/978-3-319-24574-4_28

18. Roth, H.R., Yang, D., Xu, Z., Wang, X., Xu, D.: Going to extremes: weakly supervised medical image segmentation (2020)

19. Tokunaga, H., Iwana, B.K., Teramoto, Y., Yoshizawa, A., Bise, R.: Negative pseudo labeling using class proportion for semantic segmentation in pathology. In: Vedaldi, A., Bischof, H., Brox, T., Frahm, J.-M. (eds.) ECCV 2020. LNCS, vol. 12360, pp. 430–446. Springer, Cham (2020). https://doi.org/10.1007/978-3-030-58555-6_26

20. Veeling, B.S., Linmans, J., Winkens, J., Cohen, T., Welling, M.: Rotation equivariant CNNs for digital pathology. In: Frangi, A.F., Schnabel, J.A., Davatzikos, C., Alberola-López, C., Fichtinger, G. (eds.) MICCAI 2018. LNCS, vol. 11071, pp. 210–218. Springer, Cham (2018). https://doi.org/10.1007/978-3-030-00934-2_24

21. Westra, W.H., Kronz, J.D., Eisele, D.W.: The impact of second opinion surgical pathology on the practice of head and neck surgery: a decade experience at a large referral hospital. Head Neck **24**(7), 684–693 (2002)

22. Xu, Y., Zhu, J.Y., Chang, E.I.C., Lai, M., Tu, Z.: Weakly supervised histopathology cancer image segmentation and classification. Med. Image Anal. **18**(3), 591–604 (2014)

23. Zheng, Y., Jiang, Z., Zhang, H., Xie, F., Shi, J.: Tracing diagnosis paths on histopathology WSIs for diagnostically relevant case recommendation. In: Martel, A.L., et al. (eds.) MICCAI 2020. LNCS, vol. 12265, pp. 459–469. Springer, Cham (2020). https://doi.org/10.1007/978-3-030-59722-1_44

End-to-End Learning for Image-Based Detection of Molecular Alterations in Digital Pathology

Marvin Teichmann[1]([✉]), Andre Aichert[1], Hanibal Bohnenberger[2], Philipp Ströbel[2], and Tobias Heimann[1]

[1] Digital Technology and Innovation, Siemens Healthineers, Erlangen, Germany
marvin.teichmann@siemens-healthineers.com
[2] Institute of Pathology, University Medical Center Goettingen, Goettingen, Germany

Abstract. Current approaches for classification of whole slide images (WSI) in digital pathology predominantly utilize a two-stage learning pipeline. The first stage identifies areas of interest (e.g. tumor tissue), while the second stage processes cropped tiles from these areas in a supervised fashion. During inference, a large number of tiles are combined into a unified prediction for the entire slide. A major drawback of such approaches is the requirement for task-specific auxiliary labels which are not acquired in clinical routine.

We propose a novel learning pipeline for WSI classification that is trainable end-to-end and does not require any auxiliary annotations. We apply our approach to predict molecular alterations for a number of different use-cases, including detection of microsatellite instability in colorectal tumors and prediction of specific mutations for colon, lung, and breast cancer cases from The Cancer Genome Atlas. Results reach AUC scores of up to 94% and are shown to be competitive with state of the art two-stage pipelines. We believe our approach can facilitate future research in digital pathology and contribute to solve a large range of problems around the prediction of cancer phenotypes, hopefully enabling personalized therapies for more patients in future.

Keywords: Digital pathology · Whole slide image (wsi) classification · Pan-cancer genetic alterations · Histopathology · End-to-end learning

As Whole Slide Imaging (WSI) is becoming a common modality in digital pathology, large numbers of highly-resolved microscopic images are readily available for analysis. Meanwhile, precision medicine allows for a targeted therapy of more and more cancer types, making the detection of actionable genetic alterations increasingly valuable for treatment planning and prognosis. Over the last few years, several studies have focused on the prediction of specific mutations, molecular subgroups or patient outcome from microscopy data of tumor tissue [3,5,11]. The large size of WSI images and the localized nature of information have led to the development of specific processing pipelines for this application.

L. Wang et al. (Eds.): MICCAI 2022, LNCS 13432, pp. 88–98, 2022.
https://doi.org/10.1007/978-3-031-16434-7_9

In a comprehensive review, Echele et al. [5] observe that the majority of work on WSI classification comprises two stages. Depending on the task at hand, the first stage selects a region of interest (ROI) of a certain type of tissue or high tumor content [4,11,14], while some tasks [21,30] and methods [7,22] require even more detailed localized annotation. This stage typically involves a separately trained segmentation model. In the second stage, tessellation of the ROI creates a set of smaller tiles (e.g. 224×244 pixels) that are well suited for processing with convolution neural networks (CNNs). For training, each tile is assigned the same target label corresponding to the whole slide. During inference, a subset or all of the tiles from a ROI are classified by the CNN. In order to obtain a slide-level prediction, all tile-level predictions are combined, e.g. by averaging the confidences [11], class voting [3] or by a second-level classifier [21]. We visualize a typical two-stage pipeline in Fig. 1. Some studies [5,13] omit the segmentation step and randomly choose tiles across the entire slide. This adds label noise to the classification step, since some areas (e.g. healthy tissue) do not contain any relevant information for the classification task at hand, which decreases the prediction performance.

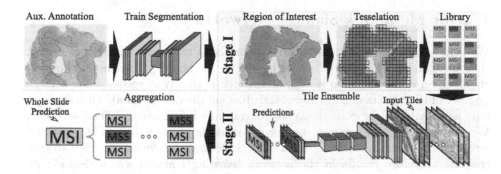

Fig. 1. Visualization of a typical two stage pipeline.

Recently, a few works which avoid auxiliary annotations have been presented. Weakly supervised methods aim to implicitly identify tiles with high information value without manual annotation [1,9,20]. In another line of work, clustering-based methods have been proposed for end-to-end WSI classification [17,26,27]. A recent benchmark [13] compares a number of state-of-the-art weakly supervised and end-to-end training methods for WSI classification. Their results indicate that the known weakly supervised and end-to-end methods are unable to outperform the widely used two-stage prediction pipeline. The existing methods therefore effectively trade annotation effort for prediction performance.

In this paper, we introduce a k-Siamese CNN architecture for WSI classification which is trainable end-to-end, does not require any auxiliary annotations, and is straight-forward to implement. We show that our method outperforms a reference two-stage approach in the clinically relevant task of microsatellite instability (MSI) classification in WSI of formalin-fixed paraffin-embedded (FFPE)

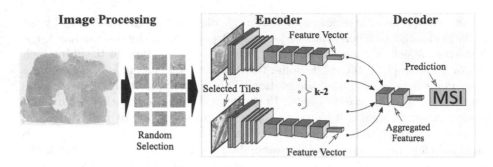

Fig. 2. An overview over our end-to-end learning pipeline.

slides with haematoxylin and eosin (H&E) stained tissue samples of colorectal cancer. In addition, we present competitive results on multiple tasks derived from a range of molecular alterations for breast, colon and lung cancer on the public Cancer Genome Atlas database (TCGA).

1   Our Method: k-Siamese Networks

We believe that the main reason for the success of two-stage approaches is that they mitigate the label noise issue inherent to tile based processing. Training a classifier on every tile from a WSI separately is disadvantageous since a large number of tiles do not contain any visual clues on the task at hand. Tiles showing only healthy tissue for example do not contain any information about the tumor. We know that CNNs are able to overfit most datasets, if this is the optimal strategy to minimize training error [32]. Utilizing uninformative tiles during training therefore results in the network learning features which degrade its generalization ability. We believe that this is the main reason that led to two-stage approaches becoming so popular for WSI analysis. However, for some tasks only a subset of the tumor area might contain the relevant information, for other tasks it might be required to combine visual information from multiple tiles before taking a decision. Both scenarios are not handled well by current two-stage pipelines.

We propose a novel encoder-decoder based pipeline to address these issues. Our encoder produces a latent representation for k randomly selected tiles from the input WSI. These tiles are processed simultaneously while sharing their weights. The resulting set of feature vectors is than aggregated by the decoder to output a single joined prediction. We call our approach k-Siamese networks, since it follows the idea of Siamese networks, but with k instead of just two encoders. We illustrate our approach in Fig. 2.

The feature vectors produced by the encoder are learned implicitly and can store any kind of information, including that the tile is not meaningful for the task at hand. The decoder can learn to interpret those feature vectors and combine the information found in multiple tiles. If k is chosen large enough, a sufficient number of the selected tiles contain task-relevant information, which eliminates the need for any auxiliary annotations.

Design Choices. Our encoder is based on Efficientnet-B0 [31], which offers high predictive capability with a relatively small computational and memory footprint. Our decoder performs average pooling over the feature vectors from all k patches, followed by a 1×1 convolution and a softmax layer. We have evaluated more complex designs however, we did not observe any significant performance boost. Utilizing adaptive average pooling for the feature vector aggregation step has the additional benefit that the model can be used with a variable number of encoders. This allows us to perform memory efficient training with as few as 24 tiles, while using more tiles for better prediction performance during inference.

Training and Inference. Our model is trained with stochastic gradient-descent using the Adam heuristic [12]. For training the encoder, we use a fine-tuning approach and start with the official EfficientNet weights, provided Tan et al. [31]. Unless otherwise specified, we use the following training parameters for all our experiments: base learning-rate (blr) of 2×10^{-5} and batch-size (bs) of 6.

Following the discussions in [8], we normalize our learning-rate (nlr) by multiplying the base-learning rate (blr) with our batch-size (bs): $nlr = bs \times blr$. We train the model for 72 epochs and report the scores evaluated on the final epoch. We use 12 warm-up epochs, during which the learning rate (lr) is linearly increased from 0 to nlr [8]. For the remaining 60 epochs, we use polynomial learning rate decay [2,16]. We use automatic mixed precision (amp) [19] training to reduce the memory and computational footprint. To improve generalization, we use the following regularization methods: We apply quadratic weight decay with a factor of 5×10^{-4} to all our weights. We use dropout [29] for the decoder and stochastic depth [10] for the encoder. We apply data-augmentation to each tile independently. We use the following common data-augmentation methods: (random) brightness, contrast, saturation, hue and rotation. In addition, tiles are not taken from a fixed grid, but their location is chosen randomly but non-overlapping. We exclude tiles which only contain background, which is estimated by using a threshold on the colour values.

During training, we use 24 tiles per slide, each with a spatial resolution of 256×256 pixel. We perform inference on 96 tiles. All tiles have an isometric resolution of 0.25 microns/pixel, which corresponds to a $10 \times$ optical magnification.

2 Data

2.1 The CancerScout Colon Data

For this study, we use 2085 diagnostic slides from 840 colon cancer patients. We have estimated the MSI status of all patients using clinic immunohistochemistry (IHC) based test. A total of 144 (17%) patients in the cohort are MSI positive. In addition, we have annotated tumor regions in 299 slides from 279 patients, with

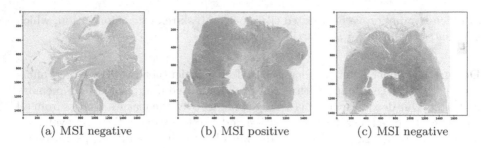

(a) MSI negative   (b) MSI positive   (c) MSI negative

Fig. 3. Three examples of diagnostic slides from the CancerScout Colon dataset. Slides are plotted with an optical magnification of 2.5.

the open-source annotation tool EXACT [18]. We use these annotations to train a segmentation model for our reference two-stage approach. Ethics approval has been granted by University Medical Center Goettingen (UMG).

Patient Cohort. The patient cohort was defined by pathologist from the UMG and consist of 840 colorectal cancer (CRC) patients. Patients were selected from those treated between 2000 and 2020 at UMG and who gave consent to be included in medical studies. Only patients with resected and histologically confirmed adenocarcinoma of the colon or rectum were included in this dataset. Among those, the pathologists manually selected samples for which enough formalin-fixed and paraffin embedded tumor tissue for morphological, immunohistochemical and genetic analysis was available. Patients of age 18 or younger and patients with neoadjuvant treatment were excluded from this study.

Image Data. The images are magnified H&E stained histological images of formalin-fixed paraffin-embedded (FFPE) diagnostic slides. Images are scanned with an isometric resolution of 0.25 microns/pixel, which corresponds to a microscopic magnification of $40 \times$. For all patients, a new slide was freshly cut, stained, and digitalized for this study. Figure 3 shows examples of those slides, we call them *cnew* slides. For 725 patients we have digitalized *cold* slides. These are archived slides which were cut and stained when the patient was initially treated. Each of the slides is from the same FFPE block as the corresponding *cnew*, located in very close proximity (about $2\,\mu m$). Those slides are used to augment training but not for evaluation. For 274 patients we have collected *hnew* slides. These are slides which only contain healthy tissue taken from the resection margins of the FFPE block. For 246 patients we have collected *hold* slides. These are slides which were cut and stained when the patient was initially treated, located in close proximity (about $2\,\mu m$) to the corresponding *hnew* slide We use those slides to increase the training data for our segmentation model.

2.2 TCGA Data

For additional experiments, we use three datasets based on The Cancer Genome Atlas (TCGA) data. The datasets are designed to perform mutation detection

Table 1. Results on the MSI prediction task (n = 672).

Method	AP	ROC AUC
Seg-Siam	0.83	0.94
k-Siam	0.83	0.94
Two Stage	0.77	0.91
CLAM [17]	0.73	0.90
ViT [13]	0.77	0.89
MIL [20]	0.69	0.88
EfficientNet	0.69	0.87

Table 2. Our default as well as the optimal hyper-parameters estimated for our models.

	Base learning rate (blr)	Batch size (bs)	Num epochs	Warm up epochs
Range	$[3 \times 10^{-6}, 10^{-4}]$	[4, 24]	[32, 96]	[0, 18]
Default	2×10^{-5}	6	72	12
Seg-Siam	7.5×10^{-5}	19	38	5
k-Siam	5.5×10^{-5}	21	81	16
Two Stage	8.8×10^{-5}	12	35	10
EfficientNet	9.3×10^{-5}	21	58	4

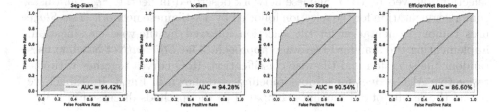

Fig. 4. RoC curves of the four models on the MSI prediction task (n = 672).

for breast invasive carcinoma, colon adenocarcinoma and lung adenocarcinoma patients and are based on the projects TCGA BRCA [24], TCGA COAD [23] and TCGA LUAD [25] respectively. We include all patients of the corresponding projects where the diagnostic slide images were publicly available in January 2022. TCGA diagnostic slides are WSIs from H&E-stained FFPE tissue of the primary tumor. The image data can be downloaded through the Genomic Data Commons Portal (https://portal.gdc.cancer.gov/).

We combine the slide images with somatic mutation data which serve as targets. For this, we utilize the omics data computed by the ensemble pipeline proposed in [6]. This data can be downloaded using the xenabrowser (https://xenabrowser.net/datapages/). We only include genes which are considered *Tier 1* cancer drivers according to the Cosmos Cancer Gene Census [28]. Of those, we consider the top 8 most prevalently mutated genes from each cohort for this study. We consider a gene mutated if it has a non-silent somatic mutation (SNP or INDEL). We exclude all patients from cohorts for which no somatic mutation data are provided. The individual genes, their respective mutation prevalence and the size of each cohort is given in Table 3.

3 Experiments and Results

3.1 MSI Prediction

We performed an ablation study on the CancerScout colon data to evaluate the quality and features of our model. In total, we compare the performance of

Table 3. RoC AUC scores for genetic mutation prediction on TCGA Data.

Gene	Prevalence	Ours [AUC]	Ref.[11] [AUC]	Gene	Prevalence	Ours [AUC]	Ref.[11] [AUC]	Gene	Prevalence	Ours [AUC]	Ref.[11] [AUC]
PIK3CA	35 %	**0.64**	0.63	APC	74 %	**0.66**	0.65	TP53	50 %	0.71	**0.72**
TP53	33 %	**0.80**	0.78	TP53	60 %	**0.74**	0.68	KRAS	29 %	**0.62**	<0.6
CDH1	13 %	**0.82**	—	KRAS	42 %	0.63	<0.65	FAT4	15 %	0.67	—
GATA3	12 %	**0.64**	<0.62	PIK3CA	32 %	0.54	<0.65	STK11	14 %	**0.65**	0.6
KMT2C	10 %	0.53	<0.62	FAT4	27 %	0.68	—	EGFR	13 %	**0.70**	<0.6
MAP3K1	8 %	0.47	0.62	KMT2D	17 %	0.74	**0.76**	KMT2C	13 %	0.49	<0.6
PTEN	6 %	**0.75**	<0.62	BRAF	17 %	**0.75**	0.67	NF1	12 %	0.57	<0.6
NCOR1	5 %	0.51	—	FBXW7	16 %	0.63	<0.65	SETBP1	10 %	0.59	<0.6

(a) Breast (n = 761)	(b) Colon (n = 268)	(c) Lung (n = 461)

four pipelines in the MSI prediction task. The first, *k-Siam*, uses random tile selection followed by the k-Siamese network described in Sect. 1. *Seg-Siam* uses tumor segmentation for tile selection followed by a k-Siamese network. *Two Stage* uses tumor segmentation for tile selection followed by tile-wise classification, implementing the standard two-stage approach. The *EfficientNet* baseline uses random tile selection and tile-wise classification. RoC curves together with the respective AUC values for all four pipelines are shown in Fig. 4. In Table 1 we report the results of our pipelines compared to the methods discussed in [13].

Experimental Setup. For the tumor segmentation, we use a PAN [15] based model with Efficientnet [31] backbone. This approach yields a validation Intersection over Union (IoU) performance of 98%. We use Efficientnet-B0 as base-classifier for all our experiments. Prediction aggregation is performed by averaging the confidences of all processed tiles. We use the same training and data-augmentation pipeline for all four models. For a fair comparison, we perform a random hyperparameter search with a total of 96 runs per model over the most influential training parameters. The parameters considered, their range and optimal values are given in Table 2.

We evaluate the performance of our models using a 5 fold patient-level cross-validation. We use fold 0 for the hyperparameter search and folds 1 to 4 as test-set for evaluation. No parameter-tuning, threshold selection or training decisions are done using those test folds. In particular, we did not do any early stopping based on the evaluation score, but rather train the model to the end and evaluate model performance after the final epoch.

3.2 Detecting Molecular Alterations

To gain further insights into the performance of our approach, we address the task of detecting molecular alterations from image features using the datasets discussed in Sect. 2.2 and compare our results to the study by Kather et al. [11]. For our study, we consider the top 8 most prevalently mutated genes in each cohort and report the AUC scores in Table 3. Note that this differs from the approach used in [11], who evaluate the prediction performance on a total of 95 known cancer driving genes and report the top 8 highest scoring results.

Experimental Setup. We employ a patient-level 5-fold cross-validation and use all folds as test-set. No parameter-tuning, thresholds or training decisions are done using those folds. We use the default parameters of our model discussed in Sect. 1 and train the model with these parameters only once on each of the 5 folds. In addition, we do not apply any early stopping based on test scores, but train the model for 72 epochs and evaluate the scores after the final epoch. We use a multi-label classification approach for this experiment. We train one network per dataset, each with 8 binary classification outputs. We apply a softmax-crossentropy loss on each of them and average them (without weights) for training. Note that this approach is different from [11] who train a separate network for each gene.

The datasets contain multiple slides for some patients. For training, we choose one slide during each epoch for each patient at random. For inference, we average the confidences over all slides per patient. We perform a patient-level split, i.e. all slides of a patient are part of the same fold.

We compare our results to Kather et al. [11], since the study also performs patient-level cross-validation on their entire cohort. We note, that our cohort is slightly different from the cohort used in the reference study [11] for a number of reasons. Note that Kather et al. manually inspect all slides in the cohort and remove slides of subpar quality. In addition, a number of diagnostic slides have been removed from the TCGA dataset in 2021, due to PII leaking in the images. Lastly, [11] uses a custom bioinformatics pipeline to compute the mutation information from the raw NGS data which yields target data for more patients. In summary, the reference study [11] uses a larger, higher quality dataset.

4 Discussion and Conclusion

This paper presents a novel k-Siamese convolutional neural network architecture for the classification of whole slide images in digital pathology. The method is trained end-to-end and does not require auxiliary annotations, which are tedious, time-consuming, and expensive to generate.

In our ablation study, we show that our method is able to clearly outperform commonly used two-stage approaches. We observe that adding a segmentation step to our model only leads to very minor improvement in the AUC score, which proofs that the k-Siamese model provides an efficient way of dealing with the label noise issue inherent to tile based processing. In addition, our experiments confirm the results shown in [13] that many recently proposed end-to-end methods are unable to outperform the widely used two-stage prediction pipeline. Those methods effectively trade annotation effort for prediction performance. In contrast, our approach is able to deliver state-of-the-art performance without requiring auxiliary annotations.

Further experiments on TCGA data reveal that our approach is also highly competitive with the published results by Kather et al. [11]: for most genes, our method is able to produce a higher response, painting a clearer picture which mutations have an impact on the morphology of the tumor. In contrast to [11], we are able to produce these results based exclusively on publicly available data, without the need for additional histological annotations. This makes it much easier to reproduce our results, but also allows to explore many more questions and tasks with minimal efforts.

We hope that the straight-forward implementation of our method, combined with its ability to outperform state-of-the-art approaches, will support further research on the identification of cancer phenotypes by digital pathology and ultimately enable personalized therapies for more patients in future.

Acknowledgements. The research presented in this work was funded by the German Federal Ministry of Education and Research (BMBF) as part of the CancerScout project (13GW0451). We thank all members of the CancerScout Consortium for their contributions, in particular Rico Brendtke and Tessa Rosenthal for organizational and administrative support as well as Sven Winkelmann and Monica Toma for performing various tasks in relation to data privacy, storage and transfer. In addition, we like to thank Christian Marzahl for his support during the installation and adaptation of the EXACT label server. Last but not least, we like to thank Matthias Siebert and Tobias Heckel for insightful discussions about the TCGA Dataset and the associated Omics data.

References

1. Chen, H., et al.: Rectified cross-entropy and upper transition loss for weakly supervised whole slide image classifier. In: Shen, D., et al. (eds.) MICCAI 2019. LNCS, vol. 11764, pp. 351–359. Springer, Cham (2019). https://doi.org/10.1007/978-3-030-32239-7_39
2. Chen, L.C., Papandreou, G., Kokkinos, I., Murphy, K., Yuille, A.: Deeplab: semantic image segmentation with deep convolutional nets, atrous convolution, and fully connected crfs. IEEE Trans. Pattern Anal. Mach. Intell. **40**(4), 834–848 (2018)
3. Coudray, N., et al.: Classification and mutation prediction from non-small cell lung cancer histopathology images using deep learning. Nat. Med. **24**(10), 1559–1567 (2018)
4. Echle, A., et al.: Clinical-grade detection of microsatellite instability in colorectal tumors by deep learning. Gastroenterology **159**(4), 1406–1416 (2020)
5. Echle, A., Rindtorff, N.T., Brinker, T.J., Luedde, T., Pearson, A.T., Kather, J.N.: Deep learning in cancer pathology: a new generation of clinical biomarkers. Br. J. Cancer **124**(4), 686–696 (2021)
6. Ellrott, K., et al.: Scalable open science approach for mutation calling of tumor exomes using multiple genomic pipelines. Cell Syst. **6**(3), 271–281 (2018)
7. Fu, Y., et al.: Pan-cancer computational histopathology reveals mutations, tumor composition and prognosis. Nat. Cancer **1**(8), 800–810 (2020)
8. Goyal, P., et al.: Accurate, large minibatch sgd: Training imagenet in 1 hour. arXiv preprint arXiv:1706.02677 (2017)
9. Hou, L., Samaras, D., Kurc, T.M., Gao, Y., Davis, J.E., Saltz, J.H.: Patch-based convolutional neural network for whole slide tissue image classification. In: Proceedings of the IEEE Conference on Computer Vision and Pattern Recognition, pp. 2424–2433 (2016)

10. Huang, G., Sun, Yu., Liu, Z., Sedra, D., Weinberger, K.Q.: Deep networks with stochastic depth. In: Leibe, B., Matas, J., Sebe, N., Welling, M. (eds.) ECCV 2016. LNCS, vol. 9908, pp. 646–661. Springer, Cham (2016). https://doi.org/10.1007/978-3-319-46493-0_39
11. Kather, J.N., et al.: Pan-cancer image-based detection of clinically actionable genetic alterations. Nat. Cancer **1**(8), 789–799 (2020)
12. Kingma, D.P., Ba, J.: Adam: a method for stochastic optimization. arXiv preprint arXiv:1412.6980 (2014)
13. Laleh, N.G., et al.: Benchmarking artificial intelligence methods for end-to-end computational pathology. bioRxiv (2021)
14. Lee, H., Seo, J., Lee, G., Park, J., Yeo, D., Hong, A.: Two-stage classification method for msi status prediction based on deep learning approach. Appl. Sci. **11**(1), 254 (2021)
15. Li, H., Xiong, P., An, J., Wang, L.: Pyramid attention network for semantic segmentation
16. Liu, W., Rabinovich, A., Berg, A.C.: Parsenet: Looking wider to see better. arXiv preprint arXiv:1506.04579 (2015)
17. Lu, M.Y., Williamson, D.F., Chen, T.Y., Chen, R.J., Barbieri, M., Mahmood, F.: Data-efficient and weakly supervised computational pathology on whole-slide images. Nat. Biomed. Eng. **5**(6), 555–570 (2021)
18. Marzahl, C., et al.: EXACT: a collaboration toolset for algorithm-aided annotation of images with annotation version control. Sci. Rep. **11**(1), 1–11 (2021)
19. Micikevicius, P., et al.: Mixed precision training. arXiv preprint arXiv:1710.03740 (2017)
20. Campanella, G., et al.: Clinical-grade computational pathology using weakly supervised deep learning on whole slide images. Nat. Med. **25**(8), 1301–1309 (2019)
21. Nagpal, K., et al.: Development and validation of a deep learning algorithm for improving gleason scoring of prostate cancer. NPJ Digital Med. **2**(1), 1–10 (2019)
22. Nazeri, K., Aminpour, A., Ebrahimi, M.: Two-stage convolutional neural network for breast cancer histology image classification. In: Campilho, A., Karray, F., ter Haar Romeny, B. (eds.) ICIAR 2018. LNCS, vol. 10882, pp. 717–726. Springer, Cham (2018). https://doi.org/10.1007/978-3-319-93000-8_81
23. Network, C.G.A., et al.: Comprehensive molecular characterization of human colon and rectal cancer. Nature **487**(7407), 330 (2012)
24. Network, T.C.G.A., et al.: Comprehensive molecular portraits of human breast tumours. Nature **490**(7418), 61–70 (2012)
25. Network, T.C.G.A., et al.: Comprehensive molecular profiling of lung adenocarcinoma: The cancer genome atlas research network. Nature **511**(7511), 543–550 (2014)
26. Shao, Z., et al.: Transmil: Transformer based correlated multiple instance learning for whole slide image classification. In: Advances in Neural Information Processing Systems, vol. 34 (2021)
27. Sharma, Y., Shrivastava, A., Ehsan, L., Moskaluk, C.A., Syed, S., Brown, D.: Cluster-to-conquer: a framework for end-to-end multi-instance learning for whole slide image classification. In: Medical Imaging with Deep Learning, pp. 682–698. PMLR (2021)
28. Sondka, Z., Bamford, S., Cole, C.G., Ward, S.A., Dunham, I., Forbes, S.A.: The cosmic cancer gene census: describing genetic dysfunction across all human cancers. Nat. Rev. Cancer **18**(11), 696–705 (2018)

29. Srivastava, N., Hinton, G., Krizhevsky, A., Sutskever, I., Salakhutdinov, R.: Dropout: a simple way to prevent neural networks from overfitting. J. Mach. Learn. Res. **15**(1), 1929–1958 (2014)
30. Ström, P., et al.: Pathologist-level grading of prostate biopsies with artificial intelligence. corr (2019) (1907)
31. Tan, M., Le, Q.: Efficientnet: rethinking model scaling for convolutional neural networks. In: International Conference on Machine Learning, pp. 6105–6114. PMLR (2019)
32. Zhang, C., Bengio, S., Hardt, M., Recht, B., Vinyals, O.: Understanding deep learning requires rethinking generalization (2016). arXiv preprint:1611.03530 (2017)

S5CL: Unifying Fully-Supervised, Self-supervised, and Semi-supervised Learning Through Hierarchical Contrastive Learning

Manuel Tran[1,3]($\boxtimes$), Sophia J. Wagner[1,3], Melanie Boxberg[1,2], and Tingying Peng[3]

[1] Technical University of Munich, Munich, Germany
`manuel.tran@helmholtz-muenchen.de`
[2] Pathology Munich-North, Munich, Germany
[3] Helmholtz AI, Helmholtz Munich – German Research Center for Environmental Health, Neuherberg, Germany

Abstract. In computational pathology, we often face a scarcity of annotations and a large amount of unlabeled data. One method for dealing with this is semi-supervised learning which is commonly split into a self-supervised pretext task and a subsequent model fine-tuning. Here, we compress this two-stage training into one by introducing S5CL, a unified framework for fully-supervised, self-supervised, and semi-supervised learning. With three contrastive losses defined for labeled, unlabeled, and pseudo-labeled images, S5CL can learn feature representations that reflect the hierarchy of distance relationships: similar images and augmentations are embedded the closest, followed by different looking images of the same class, while images from separate classes have the largest distance. Moreover, S5CL allows us to flexibly combine these losses to adapt to different scenarios. Evaluations of our framework on two public histopathological datasets show strong improvements in the case of sparse labels: for a H&E-stained colorectal cancer dataset, the accuracy increases by up to 9% compared to supervised cross-entropy loss; for a highly imbalanced dataset of single white blood cells from leukemia patient blood smears, the F1-score increases by up to 6% (Code: https://github.com/manuel-tran/s5cl).

Keywords: Contrastive learning · Self-supervision · Semi-supervision

1 Introduction

Pixel-wise annotation of histopathological data is highly time-consuming due to the large scale of whole-slide images (WSIs). Therefore, sparse annotations are commonly used [2], but this results in small amounts of labeled data and an abundance of unlabeled data – an ideal use case for semi-supervised learning.

Current semi-supervised methods often depend on self-supervised pre-training which applies domain-specific pretext tasks or contrastive learning techniques to extract useful features from the input data without relying on label

© The Author(s), under exclusive license to Springer Nature Switzerland AG 2022
L. Wang et al. (Eds.): MICCAI 2022, LNCS 13432, pp. 99–108, 2022.
https://doi.org/10.1007/978-3-031-16434-7_10

information [12,18]. Examples of methods that use domain-specific pretext tasks are COCO [23] and PC-CHiP [5] which utilize cross-stain prediction and tissue prediction on histopathological datasets, respectively. The quality of the learned representations, however, highly depends on the designed pretext task [11]. Sim-CLR [3], BYOL [7], and Barlow Twins [24], on the other hand, use contrastive techniques to learn feature representations that are invariant to various distortions of the input sample. These methods usually define positive pairs (two differently augmented versions of the same image) and negative pairs (two different images). A contrastive loss then pushes the representations of positive pairs toward each other while pushing the representations of negative pairs away. A common problem with this approach is that the extracted features can differ significantly from the ones learned through full-supervision [17]. Therefore, recent approaches in semi-supervised learning propose to train with both labeled and unlabeled images at the same time. S4L-Exemplar [25], for instance, combines a supervised cross-entropy loss on labeled images and a self-supervised triplet loss on the whole dataset. MOAM [25] and FixMatch [19] extend this approach by further applying pseudo-labels on unlabeled images. To overcome a confirmation bias toward large classes [1], Noisy Student [22] and Meta Pseudo Labels [16]

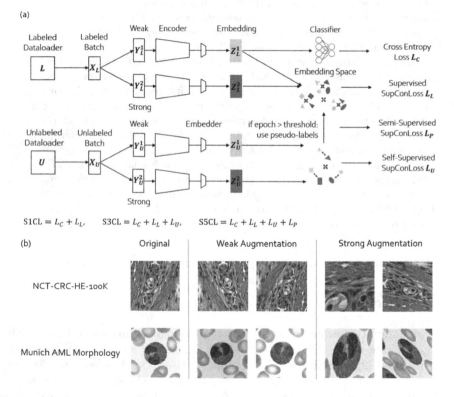

Fig. 1. (a) Overview of S5CL: Colors represent classes; shapes represent instances. Different shades or stretches indicate strongly and weakly augmented data points. (b) Examples of weak and strong augmentations on the two datasets we use.

use a teacher-student framework and additionally apply noise or a feedback system, respectively. Yet, these models still have difficulties with highly imbalanced datasets as they are usually biased toward the majority classes [15].

Contributions. To solve these issues, we propose a novel framework, called S5CL, that unifies fully-supervised, self-supervised, and semi-supervised learning through hierarchical contrastive learning. We train our models with three contrastive losses simultaneously to construct an embedding space that takes into account the hierarchy of distance relationships between images with respect to their class labels and consistency with different degrees of augmentations. The resulting framework is easy to use and highly flexible: We can omit unlabeled images and train fully-supervised; we can also set the weights of the supervised and semi-supervised loss to zero and train self-supervised; or we train with both labeled and unlabeled images in a semi-supervised way.

Unlike CoCo or PC-CHiP, S5CL does not require an artificially created pretext task. And different from SimCLR or BYOL, S5CL does not require, large batch sizes, long training times, and high-capacity networks [4]. Further, our approach does not need to be fine-tuned on labeled data in a second step like all self-supervised methods. In fact, as mentioned above, self-supervised training is even a special case of our framework. Similar to semi-supervised techniques like S4L or FixMatch, S5CL also learns from labeled and unlabeled images simultaneously, but neither applies a contrastive loss on labeled images directly: S4L treats labeled images as unlabeled instances in their triplet loss and FixMatch applies a consistency loss. It can be seen in Sect. 3 that a qualitative embedding space does indeed correspond with better classification performance.

We validate our method on two public datasets: a colorectal cancer dataset with H&E-stained image patches (NCT-CRC-HE-100K) [9] and a highly imbalanced dataset of single white blood cells from leukemia patients (Munich AML Morphology) [13].

2 Method

S5CL combines three contrastive losses as visualized in Fig. 1a. First, a supervised contrastive loss embeds images with the same class label into the same cluster and pushes images from other classes away. We improve this by adding weakly and strongly augmented images (see Fig. 1b for some examples) to the loss function (S1CL). Now, weak augmentations and similar images are embedded the closest, followed by different-looking images of the same class or strongly augmented views. Images from different classes are the furthest away. Next, a self-supervised contrastive loss additionally pulls the feature representation of unlabeled images and their augmentations toward each other (S3CL). Since both losses act on the same embedding space, the unlabeled image is also forced to have a representation close to its actual but not available class cluster. We further improve the performance by adding pseudo-labels. Instead of applying them to the supervised branch of our method, we add a semi-supervised contrastive loss to circumvent the confirmation bias mentioned above (S5CL). As contrastive loss, we choose the state-of-the-art SupConLoss [10]. It outperforms other losses like SimCLR [3], only has one hyperparameter, the temperature, and does not require hard negative mining like the triplet loss. However, our framework is more general and also works with other contrastive losses.

2.1 Description of S5CL

Given a labeled dataset L, we sample a batch X_L of labeled images. From X_L two batches of distorted images Y_L^1 and Y_L^2 are created via data augmentation. Y_L^1 is weakly augmented with simple color and geometric transformations. It is used for the supervised contrastive loss and the cross-entropy loss. The second batch Y_L^2, on the contrary, is strongly augmented and used for supervised contrastive learning only. Both batches are passed on to the encoder network. The last layer of the encoder is followed by a bottleneck layer called the embedder, producing embeddings Z_L^1 and Z_L^2. The labeled embeddings are then assessed by the supervised SupConLoss L_L [10]:

$$L_L(\tau) = \sum_{i \in I} \frac{-1}{|P(i)|} \sum_{p \in P(i)} \log \frac{\exp(\mathbf{z}_i \cdot \mathbf{z}_p / \tau)}{\sum_{a \in A(i)} \exp(\mathbf{z}_i \cdot \mathbf{z}_a / \tau)}. \tag{1}$$

Here, the anchor $\mathbf{z}_i \in Z_L^j$ is an embedding vector with class label y_i. As a measure of similarity, SupConLoss calculates the inner product of the anchor with all positive samples in the batch I that belong to the same class, $P(i) = \{p \in A(i) : y_i = y_p\}$. It then applies an exponential function that amplifies large values. The outputs are summed up and normalized over all samples $A = I \setminus \{i\}$. An important hyperparameter is the supervised temperature $\tau = T_L$ that helps distinguishing positive and negative samples. T_L controls the cluster density since intuitively, after training, we have $\mathbf{z}_i \cdot \mathbf{z}_p > T_L > \mathbf{z}_i \cdot \mathbf{z}_n$ with $n \in P(i)^C$.

Similar to the labeled dataset, given an unlabeled dataset U, a batch X_U of unlabeled images is sampled and two distorted views Y_U^1 and Y_U^2 of weakly and strongly augmented images are created. The unlabeled embeddings Z_U^1 and Z_U^2 are then processed by the self-supervised SupConLoss L_U. It has the same form as Eq. 1 but with a different temperature T_U. In L_U, the positive samples $\mathbf{z}_i'$ are the different augmented versions of the same image while the negative samples are different images. This could give rise to two contradicting loss objectives: two different samples from the same class are pulled together in the supervised loss L_L (as they belong to the same class) but get pushed away in the self-supervised loss L_U (as they are different samples). In S5CL, we solve this by choosing $T_U > T_L$ and achieve a hierarchy of distance relationships:

$$\mathbf{z}_i \cdot \mathbf{z}_i' > T_U > \mathbf{z}_i \cdot \mathbf{z}_p > T_L > \mathbf{z}_i \cdot \mathbf{z}_n. \tag{2}$$

After a fixed number t of epochs e, the classifier can be applied to Z_U^1, yielding pseudo-labels. This is passed on to L_U. The loss is now semi-supervised and called L_P with temperature T_P. The total loss function is thus

$$L_T = \mathbb{1}_{e<t} \cdot w_U L_U + \mathbb{1}_{e>t} \cdot w_P L_P + w_L L_L + w_C L_C, \tag{3}$$

where $\mathbb{1}_{e<t}$ and $\mathbb{1}_{e>t}$ are indicator functions. The positive parameters w_U, w_P, w_L, and w_C are the weights of each loss which are always one in our case.

2.2 Augmentations

Each input image is augmented weakly and strongly. Weak augmentations consist of rotations by $0°, 90°, 180°$, and $270°$; vertical and horizontal flipping; as well as color jitter (with brightness, contrast, saturation, and hue values all set to 0.1). We always apply rotations and color jitter while flipping is performed with a probability of 0.5.

Strong augmentations include all augmentations above except that color jitter is replaced by light HED jitter. Additionally, we apply Inception-crop for tissue images [20]. For single-cell images, we crop between 50% and 100% of the image around the center and re-scale the image to its original size. We lastly employ random affine linear transformations with interpolation (see Fig. 1b).

2.3 Competitive Methods and Implementation Details

We compare S5CL to the following baseline models: (i) a fully-supervised model that is trained with a cross-entropy loss only (CrossEntropy); (ii) another fully-supervised model that is trained with both a supervised contrastive loss and a cross-entropy loss (SupConLoss); (iii) a state-of-the-art semi-supervised learning method based on a teacher-student network, Meta Pseudo Labels (MPL) [16], which outperforms other frameworks such as BYOL [7] or Noisy Student [22].

All models use the same encoder – a ResNet18 [8] pre-trained on ImageNet without the final classification layer. The output of dimension 512 is fed into the embedder which consists of a linear layer without activation and batch normalization layer. The embedder is followed by a linear classifier. MPL uses the same architecture for both student and teacher networks. We employ the following training script for both S5CL and MPL: For each unlabeled batch sampled from the unlabeled dataloader, a labeled batch is sampled from the labeled dataloader.

We tune the hyperparameters, including all temperatures and batch sizes, for each model separately using an internal validation set that differs from the test set. Afterward, we fix the parameters and report the mean ± std over 5 runs. In particular, for MPL training, we use Adam with a learning rate of $1e{-}5$ for the student and a learning rate of $3e{-}5$ for the teacher. The weight decay is always $1e{-}4$. On NCT-CRC-HE-100K, the remaining models work well with Adamax while Adam is better on Munich AML Morphology. The learning rate and weight decay are set to $1e{-}4$.

3 Results and Discussions

3.1 Evaluation on the Colon Cancer Histology Dataset

The NCT-CRC-HE-100K dataset[1] contains 100,000 non-overlapping image patches from H&E-stained WSIs of colorectal cancer and normal tissue. The

---

[1] https://zenodo.org/record/1214456#.YhZI1ZYo-Uk.

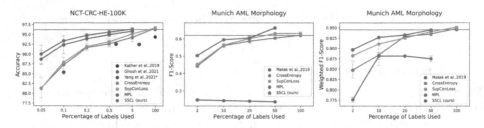

Fig. 2. Results for (a) NCT-CRC-HE-100K and (b, c) Munich AML Morphology. Percentages refer to the full dataset for NCT-CRC-HE-100K and to the majority classes in the case of Munich AML Morphology. Models depicted with a gray line are SOTA supervised models in the literature (Ghosh et al. [6] and Matek et al. [13]). *Yang et al. [23] is a SOTA semi-supervised baseline on the colon cancer dataset. They train with 8 labels without the background, here we assume 100% accuracy on that class.

images are 224×224 pixels large at 0.5 mpp and are color-normalized using Macenko's method. They are annotated into nine well-balanced classes.

We split the 100,000 images into a training set of 91,000 images and a validation set of 9,000 images (1,000 per class). Next, the original dataset is split into a labeled set containing 5, 10, 20, 50, and 500 images per class which are approximately 0.05%, 0.1%, 0.2%, 0.5%, and 5% of all labeled images. The remaining images are assigned to the unlabeled set. For the test set, we use CRC-VAL-HE-7K, an independent dataset with 7,180 patches from an external cohort [9].

The CrossEntropy and SupConLoss models are trained for 130, 30, and 5 epochs on the sets with 0.05%–0.2%, 0.05%–5%, and 100% labeled images. Both S5CL and MPL are trained for five epochs. The unlabeled set has a batch size of 128 while the labeled batch size is 32 (for 100% labeled images, the batch size is also 128). All the embedding spaces have a dimension of 64. The supervised temperature is set to 0.2, and both the self-supervised as well as the semi-supervised temperature are set to 0.7 (see Ablations 3.3 for details).

As shown in Fig. 2, on all reduced labeled sets, S5CL achieves higher accuracy than the three competitive models including MPL. With only 50 labeled images per class (0.5%), S5CL has an accuracy of 95%, which is already comparable to the two reference models in the literature [9] and [6] that are trained with the full dataset. With 500 labeled images per class (5%), S5CL almost reaches the accuracy of the full SupConLoss model with 96.6% accuracy.

In addition to improving the classification accuracy on small labeled datasets, S5CL also makes the feature embedding space more compact and explicable. To see this, we plot the feature representations as a UMAP in Fig. 3 and measure the embedding quality with the MAP@R score [14], where 100% implies perfect clustering and separation. S5CL achieves a MAP@R of 74% whereas CrossEntropy has a score of 67%. In Fig. 3, we can see that CrossEntropy, might split the representation of the same class (e.g. DEB = debris) into two different clusters – unlike S5CL. Within a cluster, S5CL also achieves more robust embeddings, i.e., images are ordered hierarchically: weakly augmented images and similar images

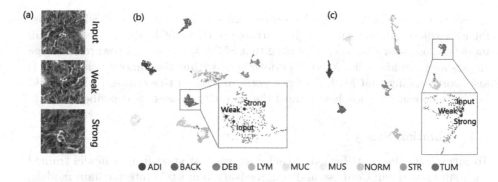

Fig. 3. UMAP of feature embeddings for the test set with 300 sampled images per class including weak and strong augmentations using (b) CrossEntropy and (c) S5CL.

are embedded the closest to their origins, then come strong augmentations as well as different looking images from the same class.

3.2 Evaluation on the Leukemia Single-Cell Dataset

The Munich AML Morphology dataset[2] contains 18,365 labeled single-cell images taken from peripheral blood smears of 100 patients diagnosed with acute myeloid leukemia (AML). All smears are scanned at 100× magnification with oil immersion at a resolution of 14.14 mpp and have a patch size of 400 × 400 pixels. The dataset's classes are heavily imbalanced, ranging from 8,484 images in the largest class to 11 images in the smallest class. In addition, some of the 15 cell types are morphologically similar as they are biologically related.

The dataset is split into a training set of size 11,025; a validation set of size 3,666; and a test set of size 3,674. The training set is further split into a labeled and unlabeled set. To preserve the class distribution, we sample 2%, 10%, 20%, 50%, and 100% images from the large classes for the labeled set and keep all labeled images from small classes that have less than 100 instances per class.

We train the CrossEntropy and SupConLoss models with a labeled batch size of 128; S5CL in addition has an unlabeled batch size of 64. Early stopping is used to avoid overfitting as in [13]. The number of epochs is thus 40, 25, 20, 15, and 15, respectively for each data subset. MPL models use smaller labeled and unlabeled batches of size 32 since training is very memory intensive. However, the batch size does not have a large effect on the results. Due to overfitting, we train the models for two epochs. In addition, we have to include the validation set into the training set, as otherwise, the student model would never see images from the minority class [16]. But we note the class proportions are still the same. For all models, the embedding dimension is 256. The supervised temperature is always set to 0.1 and the self-supervised, as well as the semi-supervised one, are both set to 0.6.

---

[2] https://wiki.cancerimagingarchive.net/pages/viewpage.action?pageId=61080958.

As shown in Fig. 2, S5CL also outperforms CrossEntropy and SupConLoss for all reduced labeled datasets. Remarkable is that S5CL also exceeds the full models in terms of F1-score, indicating that S5CL is less biased toward the large classes and can also achieve good performance within the minority classes. It is also worth noting that MPL does not perform well on this dataset, which could be due to a confirmation bias toward the majority classes, as described in [21].

3.3   Ablation Study

To investigate the contribution of each loss, we first start from a model trained with supervised SupConLoss and progressively build two intermediate models, S1CL and S3CL, to arrive at S5CL (please refer to Fig. 1a). We can see that as the model complexity grows, so does the test accuracy (Fig. 4a). Next, we analyze the effect of different augmentation techniques. We start with no augmentations, add weak augmentations and then vary different types of strong augmentations. Our results suggest that both weak and strong augmentations are important and different types of strong augmentations can change the accuracy by ~3% (Fig. 4b). We also investigate the choice of the self-supervised temperature T_U with respect to the supervised temperature T_L. We set $T_L = 0.2$ and vary the temperature T_U. As expected, a higher distance to T_L resolves the problem of conflicting loss objectives (Fig. 4c). The last ablation analyzes the effect of pseudo-labels. If no pseudo-labels are used after the first epoch, the accuracy drops (Fig. 4d). Also, if we use pseudo-labels for the classification loss, the accuracy decreases, possibly due to flawed pseudo-labels.

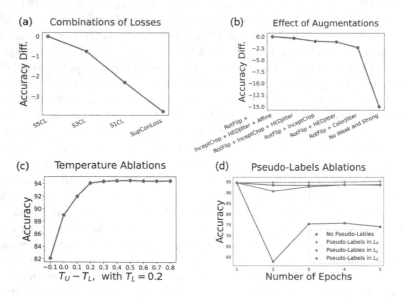

Fig. 4. Ablation study for different choices of hyperparameters and architectures.

4 Conclusion

We propose S5CL as a unified framework for supervised, self-supervised, and semi-supervised contrastive learning. It combines the cross-entropy loss with three contrastive losses for labeled, unlabeled and pseudo-labeled data. In particular, by altering the temperature of the SupConLoss, S5CL can simultaneously train supervised and self-supervised on both labeled and unlabeled data. We evaluate S5CL on two public datasets where it outperforms several baseline methods including Meta Pseudo Labels, a SOTA semi-supervised method. Due to its easy implementation and flexibility, we believe that S5CL can be employed in many problems in computational pathology with sparsely labeled datasets.

Acknowledgements. S.J.W. is supported by the Helmholtz Association under the joint research school "Munich School for Data Science - MUDS".

References

1. Arazo, E., Ortego, D., Albert, P., O'Connor, N.E., McGuiness, K.: Pseudo-labeling and confirmation bias in deep semi-supervised learning. Eprint arXiv:1908.02983 (2020)
2. Bokhorst, J.M., Pinckaers, H., van Zwam, P., Nagtegaal, I., van der Laak, J., Ciompi, F.: Learning from sparsely annotated data for semantic segmentation in histopathology images. In: Cardoso, M.J., et al. (eds.) Proceedings of the 2nd International Conference on Medical Imaging with Deep Learning, pp. 84–91. Proceedings of Machine Learning Research (2019)
3. Chen, T., Kornblith, S., Norouzi, M., Hinton, G.: A simple framework for contrastive learning of visual representations. Eprint arXiv:2002.05709 (2020)
4. Chen, T., Kornblith, S., Swersky, K., Norouzi, M., Hinton, G.: Big self-supervised models are strong semi-supervised learners. Eprint arXiv:2006.10029 (2020)
5. Fu, Y., et al.: Pan-cancer computational histopathology reveals mutations, tumor composition and prognosis. Nat. Cancer **1**(8) (2020). https://www.nature.com/articles/s43018-020-0085-8
6. Ghosh, S., Bandyopadhyay, A., Sahay, S., Gosh, R., Kundu, I., Santosh, K.: Colorectal histology tumor detection using ensemble deep neural network. Eng. Appl. Artif. Intell. **100**, 104202 (2021). https://www.sciencedirect.com/science/article/abs/pii/S095219762100049X?dgcid=rss_sd_all
7. Grill, J.B., et al.: Bootstrap your own latent: a new approach to self-supervised learning. Eprint arXiv:2006.07733 (2020)
8. He, K., Zhang, X., Ren, S., Sun, J.: Deep residual learning for image recognition. In: 2016 IEEE Conference on Computer Vision and Pattern Recognition (CVPR), pp. 770–778 (2016). https://doi.org/10.1109/CVPR.2016.90
9. Kather, J.N., et al.: Predicting survival from colorectal cancer histology slides using deep learning: a retrospective multicenter study. PLoS Med. **16**(1), 1–22 (2019). https://doi.org/10.1371/journal.pmed.1002730
10. Khosla, P., et al.: Supervised contrastive learning. In: Larochelle, H., Ranzato, M., Hadsell, R., Balcan, M.F., Lin, H. (eds.) Advances in Neural Information Processing Systems, vol. 33, pp. 18661–18673. Curran Associates, Inc. (2020). https://proceedings.neurips.cc/paper/2020/file/d89a66c7c80a29b1bdbab0f2a1a94af8-Paper.pdf

11. Koohbanani, N.A., Unnikrishnan, B., Khurram, S.A., Krishnaswamy, P., Rajpoot, N.: Self-path: self-supervision for classification of pathology images with limited annotations. IEEE Trans. Med. Imaging **40**(10), 2845–2856 (2021). https://doi.org/10.1109/TMI.2021.3056023
12. Le-Khac, P.H., Healy, G., Smeaton, A.F.: Contrastive representation learning: a framework and review. Eprint arXiv:2010.05113 (2020)
13. Matek, C., Schwarz, S., Spiekermann, K., Marr, C.: Human-level recognition of blast cells in acute myeloid leukemia with convolutional neural networks. Nat. Mach. Intell. **1**, 538–544 (2019). https://doi.org/10.1038/s42256-019-0101-9
14. Musgrave, K., Belongie, S.J., Lim, S.: A metric learning reality check. Eprint arXiv:2003.08505 (2020)
15. Oh, Y., Kim, D., Kweon, I.S.: Distribution-aware semantics-oriented pseudo-label for imbalanced semi-supervised learning. Eprint arXiv:2106.05682 (2020)
16. Pham, H., Dai, Z., Xie, Q., Le, Q.V.: Meta pseudo labels. In: 2021 IEEE/CVF Conference on Computer Vision and Pattern Recognition (CVPR), pp. 11552–11563 (2021). https://doi.org/10.1109/CVPR46437.2021.01139
17. Purushwalkam, S., Gupta, A.: Demystifying contrastive self-supervised learning: invariances, augmentations and dataset biases. In: Larochelle, H., Ranzato, M., Hadsell, R., Balcan, M.F., Lin, H. (eds.) Advances in Neural Information Processing Systems, vol. 33, pp. 3407–3418. Curran Associates, Inc. (2020). https://proceedings.neurips.cc/paper/2020/file/22f791da07b0d8a2504c2537c560001c-Paper.pdf
18. Sahito, A., Frank, E., Pfahringer, B.: Semi-supervised learning using Siamese networks. In: Liu, J., Bailey, J. (eds.) AI 2019. LNCS (LNAI), vol. 11919, pp. 586–597. Springer, Cham (2019). https://doi.org/10.1007/978-3-030-35288-2_47
19. Sohn, K., et al.: FixMatch: simplifying semi-supervised learning with consistency and confidence. In: Larochelle, H., Ranzato, M., Hadsell, R., Balcan, M.F., Lin, H. (eds.) Advances in Neural Information Processing Systems, vol. 33, pp. 596–608. Curran Associates, Inc. (2020). https://proceedings.neurips.cc/paper/2020/file/06964dce9addb1c5cb5d6e3d9838f733-Paper.pdf
20. Szegedy, C., et al.: Going deeper with convolutions. In: 2015 IEEE Conference on Computer Vision and Pattern Recognition (CVPR), pp. 1–9 (2015). https://doi.org/10.1109/CVPR.2015.7298594
21. Wei, C., Sohn, K., Mellina, C., Yuille, A., Yang, F.: CReST: a class-rebalancing self-training framework for imbalanced semi-supervised learning. In: 2021 IEEE/CVF Conference on Computer Vision and Pattern Recognition (CVPR), pp. 10852–10861 (2021). https://doi.org/10.1109/CVPR46437.2021.01071
22. Xie, Q., Luong, M.T., Hovy, E., Le, Q.V.: Self-training with noisy student improves ImageNet classification. In: 2020 IEEE/CVF Conference on Computer Vision and Pattern Recognition (CVPR), pp. 10684–10695 (2020). https://doi.org/10.1109/CVPR42600.2020.01070
23. Yang, P., Hong, Z., Yin, X., Zhu, C., Jiang, R.: Self-supervised visual representation learning for histopathological images. In: de Bruijne, M., et al. (eds.) MICCAI 2021. LNCS, vol. 12902, pp. 47–57. Springer, Cham (2021). https://doi.org/10.1007/978-3-030-87196-3_5
24. Zbontar, J., Jing, L., Misra, I., LeCun, Y., Deny, S.: Barlow twins: self-supervised learning via redundancy reduction. Eprint arXiv:2103.03230 (2020)
25. Zhai, X., Oliver, A., Kolesnikov, A., Beyer, L.: S4L: self-supervised semi-supervised learning. In: 2019 IEEE/CVF International Conference on Computer Vision (ICCV), pp. 1476–1485 (2019). https://doi.org/10.1109/ICCV.2019.00156

Sample Hardness Based Gradient Loss for Long-Tailed Cervical Cell Detection

Minmin Liu[1,2,3], Xuechen Li[1,2,3,4], Xiangbo Gao[5], Junliang Chen[1,2,3], Linlin Shen[1,2,3(✉)], and Huisi Wu[1,2,3]

[1] Computer Vision Institute, School of Computer Science and Software Engineering, Shenzhen University, Shenzhen, China
[2] AI Research Center for Medical Image Analysis and Diagnosis, Shenzhen University, Shenzhen, China
[3] Guangdong Key Laboratory of Intelligent Information Processing, Shenzhen University, Shenzhen 518060, China
llshen@szu.edu.cn
[4] National Engineering Laboratory for Big Data System Computing Technology, Shenzhen University, Shenzhen 518060, PR, China
[5] University of California, Irvine, USA

Abstract. Due to the difficulty of cancer samples collection and annotation, cervical cancer datasets usually exhibit a long-tailed data distribution. When training a detector to detect the cancer cells in a WSI (Whole Slice Image) image captured from the TCT (Thinprep Cytology Test) specimen, head categories (e.g. normal cells and inflammatory cells) typically have a much larger number of samples than tail categories (e.g. cancer cells). Most existing state-of-the-art long-tailed learning methods in object detection focus on category distribution statistics to solve the problem in the long-tailed scenario, without considering the "hardness" of each sample. To address this problem, in this work we propose a Grad-Libra Loss that leverages the gradients to dynamically calibrate the degree of hardness of each sample for different categories, and rebalance the gradients of positive and negative samples. Our loss can thus help the detector to put more emphasis on those hard samples in both head and tail categories. Extensive experiments on a long-tailed TCT WSI image dataset show that the mainstream detectors, e.g. RepPoints, FCOS, ATSS, YOLOF, etc. trained using our proposed Gradient-Libra Loss, achieved much higher (7.8%) mAP than that trained using cross-entropy classification loss.

Keywords: Long-tailed learning · Object detection · Cervical cancer

1 Introduction

Cervical cancer is the fourth most frequently diagnosed cancer and the fourth leading cause of cancer death in women [17]. Early diagnosis and screening of cer-

Supplementary Information The online version contains supplementary material available at https://doi.org/10.1007/978-3-031-16434-7_11.

vical cancer can effectively help its treatment. To solve the error-prone, tedious, and time-consuming problems of manual analysis of cervical smears, deep learning based CAD (Computer-Aided Diagnosis) has been introduced to cervical cancer screening. However, due to the difficulty of cancer samples collection and the cost of annotation, the number of cancer samples is far less than that of normal samples, which shows a typical long-tailed distribution and leads to a long-tailed class imbalance problem.

In this paper, we are mainly using object detectors to detect cancer cells in a WSI (Whole Slide Image) image captured from a TCT (Thinprep Cytology Test) specimen. The problem of training cell detectors on a long-tailed dataset mainly comes from two aspects. First, the categories are extremely imbalanced, which will cause the loss contributions of the tail classes to be easily overwhelmed by the head classes. Second, for the object detection framework, the background forms a large number of easy negative samples, which will also overwhelm the training process and degrade the training performance. Note that for a particular category, the samples belonging to the category are positive samples, while the samples of all the other categories and the background are negative samples. Most of the existing methods addressing long-tailed problem require additional statistics support [3,6–9,12] (e.g. data distribution statistics), or tedious operations [11,12,21] (e.g. fine-tuning and handcrafted head-tail class division). Data re-sampling methods [6–8] require the acquisition of pre-computed data distribution statistics, which may have the risks of over-fitting for tail classes and under-fitting for head classes. Loss re-weighting methods [3,9] also require data distribution statistics for up-weighting the tail classes and down-weighting the head classes at class level. Decoupled training schema [11,21] decouples representation and classifier learning but requires an extra fine-tuning stage. BAGS [12] divided all categories into several groups according to data distribution statistics during the training stage but the handcrafted division may block the sharing of information between the head and tail classes. In general, most existing methods focus on data distribution statistics to solve the class imbalance problem in the long-tailed scenario at class level, without taking into account the "**hardness**" of each sample at sample level. In fact, we cannot ignore the diversity of samples. A sample has different hardness (easy or hard) for the classification of different categories. It can be a hard positive sample of its category and a hard negative sample of other categories at the same time. Thus, there might be easy samples belonged to the tail classes get incorrectly up-weighted, or the opposite. To address this problem, we propose a Grad-Libra Loss that leverages the gradients to dynamically calibrate the degree of hardness of each sample for different categories, and re-balance the gradients of positive and negative samples.

To sum up, our contributions are as follows: (1) We propose a new perspective to describe the long-tailed samples, which defines the concept of sample hardness and calibrates the degree of hardness by gradients. (2) We provides a unified framework to take the hardness into account for both head and tail classes and present a novel Gradient Libra Loss that employs the gradients to adaptively re-weight samples of different hardness. (3) We conduct comprehensive experiments

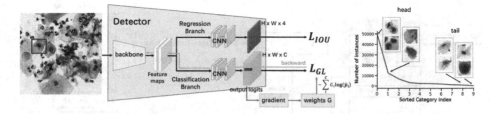

Fig. 1. The framework of the cell detector. We propose a novel Grad-Libra Loss for the classification branch. In the right part, we visualize the data distribution of the long-tailed dataset along with example instances.

using a long-tailed cervical cell image dataset. Our method consistently surpasses most existing methods and obtains a 7.8% mAP gain over the baseline model, increasing the AP of frequent, common, and rare categories by 7.3%, 5.6%, and 8.4%, respectively.

2 System Framework

Figure 1 shows the framework of our cell detector, which is based on mainstream object detectors like RepPoints, FCOS, ATSS, YOLOF, etc. During training, a batch of TCT WSI image patches is sampled from a dataset with the long-tailed distribution of cell categories and fed to the detector for loss calculation and gradient backpropagation. While Smooth L1 Loss [2,19,22,24] is usually used to train the regression of the bounding box, the cross-entropy loss is the main choice for the training of the classification branch. For the classification branch, we employ multiple binary classifiers for multi-class classification and design a novel Gradient Libra Loss. It employs the gradient to calibrate the degree of hardness of each sample at sample level and takes hardness as the weight term of the original cross-entropy loss function.

3 Gradient Libra Loss

To better explain our loss, we firstly analyze the connection between the gradients and positive-negative imbalance. Suppose we have a batch of samples $\mathcal{I}$ and their features for the classification branch, and their output logits are used to represent the attributes (e.g. easy or hard) of the samples. As shown in Fig. 2, for a sample $\mathbf{x}$ of class k, $\mathbf{z} = [z_1, z_2, ..., z_C]^T$ and $\mathbf{p} = [p_1, p_2, ..., p_C]^T$ are the output logits and probabilities for each class, respectively. The ground-truth label $\mathbf{y}$ of the sample is an one-hot vector, in which $y_i \in \{0, 1\}, 1 \leq i \leq C$ and $y_k = 1$ and $y_i = 0$ $(i \neq k)$. Its gradient with regard to the output logits $\mathbf{z}$ in the original cross-entropy L_{CE} is as follows:

$$\frac{\partial L_{CE}}{\partial z_i} = \begin{cases} p_i - 1, & if \ i = k \\ p_i, & if \ i \neq k \end{cases} \tag{1}$$

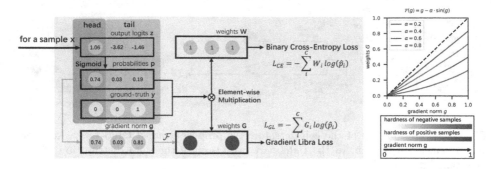

Fig. 2. Visualization of the detailed procedure of the classification loss function-Gradient Libra Loss, which takes hardness as the weight term of the original cross-entropy loss function. Note that the darker the color in the gradient bar, the stronger the hardness.

Equation 1 means that for the sample $\mathbf{x}$ of class k, it obtains the encouraging gradient $p_i - 1$ as positive sample but gets the penalty gradient p_i as negative sample for other class $i(i \neq k)$. As presented in [18], we choose the ratio r of cumulative gradients between positive and negative samples as an indicator to measure whether each category classifier is in a positive-negative balanced training state. For iteration $t+1$, the ratio r is defined as $r = \sum_{t^*=0}^{t} |\nabla_{z_i}^{+}(L)| \backslash \sum_{t^*=0}^{t} |\nabla_{z_i}^{-}(L)|$. The gradients of positive samples $\nabla_{z_i}^{+}(L)$ and gradients of negative samples $\nabla_{z_i}^{-}(L)$ of output logit z_i are formulated as: $\nabla_{z_i}^{+}(L) = \frac{1}{|\mathcal{I}|} \sum_{n \in \mathcal{I}} y_i^n (p_i^n - 1)$, $\nabla_{z_i}^{-}(L) = \frac{1}{|\mathcal{I}|} \sum_{n \in \mathcal{I}} (1 - y_i^n) p_i^n$. In general, for the head classes, the gradients of positive and negative samples have similar magnitudes, and the ratio r is close to or greater than 1. For the tail classes, the gradients of positive samples are often overwhelmed by the gradients of negative samples, resulting in the ratio r close to 0.

Our intention is to adopt the gradients to calibrate the hardness of the samples and re-weight the loss function. We define $\mathbf{g} = [g_1, g_2, ..., g_C]^T$, where $g_i = |\frac{\partial L_{CE}}{\partial z_i}|$. $\mathbf{g}$ is equal to the norm of gradient w.r.t output logits $\mathbf{z}$. $\mathbf{g}$ passes through a monotonically increasing function $\mathcal{F} : \mathbf{g} \rightarrow \mathbf{G}$, and $\mathcal{F}$ is defined as:

$$\mathcal{F}(\mathbf{g}) = \mathbf{g} - \alpha \cdot \sin(\mathbf{g}) \qquad (2)$$

$\mathbf{G}$ acts as the weight term of L_{CE}. $\alpha \in (0, 1]$ is a modulating factor to control the importance of samples. The integrated Grad-Libra Loss is expressed as follows:

$$L_{GL} = -\sum_{i}^{C} \mathbf{G}_i \log(\hat{p}_i), \; \hat{p}_i = \begin{cases} p_i, & if \; i = k \\ 1 - p_i, & if \; i \neq k \end{cases} \qquad (3)$$

Decouple the L_{CE} according to the positive and negative level: $L_{CE}^{+} = -y_i \log(p_i)$ and $L_{CE}^{-} = -(1 - y_i) \log(1 - p_i)$. L_{CE}^{+} and L_{CE}^{-} represent the positive and negative loss term in class i (omit the class index i for brevity), respectively. We set different modulating factors for positive samples and negative samples, i.e., α^+ and α^-. Grad-Libra Loss in class i is decoupled as follows:

$$\begin{cases} L_{GL}^+ = G^+ \cdot L_{CE}^+ \\ L_{GL}^- = G^- \cdot L_{CE}^- \end{cases}, \quad \begin{cases} G^+ = (1 - p_i) - \alpha^+ sin(1 - p_i) \\ G^- = p_i - \alpha^- sin(p_i) \end{cases} \qquad (4)$$

The unified framework of Grad-Libra Loss is written as:

$$L_{GL} = -\sum_{i}^{C} L_{GL}^+ + L_{GL}^- = -\sum_{i}^{C} \mathcal{F}(\mathbf{g}; \alpha^+) \cdot L_{CE}^+ + \mathcal{F}(\mathbf{g}; \alpha^-) \cdot L_{CE}^- \qquad (5)$$

The gradient norm $\mathbf{g}$ is nonlinearly transformed by the function $\mathcal{F}$ and then used as the weight of the loss function. In our unified framework, an appropriate function $\mathcal{F}$ can achieve excellent performance.

Implication 1 (Positive-Negative Balance). As shown in Eq. 4, α adjusts the weights of positive and negative samples. The overall weight $\mathbf{G}$ will increase according to the decrease of the α, as shown in the top right of Fig. 2. The overall importance of G^+ and G^- can be balanced by α^+ and α^-. Proper adjustment of α^+ and α^- can promote positive-negative balanced training. Notably, different detectors have different degrees of positive-negative imbalance. In order to achieve a more satisfactory effect, it is necessary to re-adjust α^+ and α^- when using different detectors.

Implication 2 (Hardness). $\mathbf{G}$ focuses on the hardness (easy or hard) of samples. G^+ and G^- adjust the weights of easy-hard positive and negative samples. When a sample's probability p_i for a category is closer to the ground-truth, it is more likely to be an easy sample of that category. The gradient norm g_i becomes smaller, and leads to a smaller weight G_i. Therefore, we use $\mathbf{G}$ to represent the hardness of the samples. As shown in Fig. 2, we visualize an example of loss computing for a tail sample and employ different colors to indicate the hardness. For a sample $\mathbf{x}$ belonging to a certain tail class i, its output logits $\mathbf{z}$ is transformed by the sigmoid function into estimated probabilities $\mathbf{p}$. The original cross-entropy loss does not consider the hardness of samples for different categories (the weight vector is set to 1), which seriously reduces the discrimination ability to of easy or hard samples. For the proposed Gradient Libra Loss, it calculates the gradient norm of the sample, obtains the degree of hardness through the function of $\mathcal{F}$, and uses it as $\mathbf{G}$ to weight the original cross-entropy loss. Through the weight $\mathbf{G}$ we can estimate the hardness of the samples for different classes. For example, as the positive sample (ground-truth is 1) of a certain tail class i, its probability of 0.19 is very small, so it tends to be a hard-positive sample of its own category (the weight G_i is marked by dark purple). As the negative sample (ground-truth is 0) of other categories, it has different probabilities and therefore different degrees of hardness (darker color represents higher hardness).

Table 1. The performance of Grad-Libra Loss compared with other methods. G means number of groups. * means adding the effect of α-balanced factor.

Method	Frequent	Common		Rare							mAP
	Inflammation	Normal	HSIL	Atrophy	bare_nucleus	SCC	Trichomonad	LSIL	ASC_US	ASC_H	
CBL [3]	20.2	65.0	24.7	30.1	26.7	0.0	26.9	27.2	17.2	0.0	23.8
Seesaw [20]	71.3	75.4	55.9	87.2	58.7	2.1	9.1	**61.3**	26.4	2.3	45.0
CE	72.8	76.3	57.2	88.0	56.0	6.6	16.0	59.8	18.9	1.9	45.3
EQLv2 [18]	74.7	77.1	54.7	87.1	62.6	4.4	19.7	56.7	23.2	0.7	46.1
BAGS (G3) [12]	80.3	77.1	61.2	87.2	69.7	0.9	22.4	55.9	21.9	0.9	47.8
BAGS (G2) [12]	**80.4**	77.5	54.8	87.4	70.1	3.0	29.4	59.1	27.1	0.9	49.0
Focal [14]	**80.4**	80.8	56.2	85.0	66.8	5.6	31.6	53.9	24.0	6.0	49.0
Focal* [14]	79.6	81.7	60.9	87.3	**72.7**	3.5	31.2	61.1	24.5	3.4	50.6
Grad-Libra (ours)	80.1	**83.2**	**61.6**	**88.3**	69.7	**10.3**	**40.6**	60.2	**27.3**	**9.6**	**53.1**

4 Experiments

4.1 Dataset and Evaluation Metrics

Public cervical cancer datasets [10,16] are small in scale, balanced in categories, which cannot represent the real distribution in clinical practice. Thus, we establish the CCA-LT dataset[1] that is closer to the actual long-tailed data distribution. We visualize the data distribution of the CCA-LT dataset along with example instances in Fig. 1. The CCA-LT dataset was captured by a whole-slide scanning machine. The specimens are prepared by Thinprep Cytology Test method with H&E staining [23] to give the image resolution of about 80000×60000 pixels. The dataset is divided into training-validation set and test set (7:3). The training-validation set is overlap-cropped for data augmentation, while the test set is not. Then we crop each whole slide digital image into patches of 512×512 pixels for training. To evaluate detection performance, we follow the PASCAL VOC evaluation criteria [4], i.e., mean average precision (mAP). We also report AP for each category, which is calculated with IoU threshold of 0.5. The AP and mean recall for rare, common, and frequent categories are denoted as AP_r, AP_c, AP_f, mR_r, mR_c, and mR_f, respectively.

4.2 Implementation Details

For a fair comparison, all experiments are performed on MMDetecion [1] platform in PyTorch [15] framework. We use 4 V100 GPUs for training. We choose the anchor-free detector RepPoints [22] with FPN structure [13] as the baseline model. The optimizer is stochastic gradient descent (SGD) with momentum 0.9 and weight decay 0.0001. The initial learning rate is set as 0.002, which is divided by 10 after 8 and 11 epochs. We employ the linear warming up policy [5] to start the training and the warm-up ratio is set as 0.001. The model is trained with batch size of 32 for 12 epochs.

---

[1] https://github.com/M-LLiu/Grad-Libra.

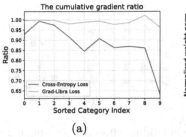
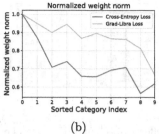

(a)   (b)

Fig. 3. The comparison of gradient balance between Grad-Libra and Cross-Entropy Loss. (a): The cumulative gradient ratio in the entire training process for each category. (b): The normalized L2 weight norm in the last classifier layer for each category.

4.3   Benchmark Results

We compare the performance of Grad-Libra Loss with other state-of-the-art methods and report the results in Table 1. Without any bells and whistles, Grad-Libra Loss achieves better results than all other losses and exceeds the CE baseline **7.8%** mAP. Without sacrificing the accuracy of the head classes, Grad-Libra Loss brings significant performance gains to the tail classes, e.g. increasing AP_f by 7.3%, AP_c by 5.6%, and AP_r by 8.4%, respectively. We further compare Grad-Libra Loss with recent designs, i.e., Class-balanced Loss (CBL) [3], Balanced Group Softmax (BAGS) [12], Equalization Loss v2 (EQLv2) [18], and Seesaw Loss (Seesaw) [20] in Table 1. Notably, CBL and Seesaw achieve 21.2% and 0.3% lower mAP than the CE baseline, respectively. CBL and Seesaw, which require data distribution information at class level or the number of samples in sample level, have poor robustness and drop sharply in performance. We follow BAGS and split the classes into 2 groups (0, 10000), (10000, +∞) and 3 groups (0, 5000), (5000, 10000), (10000, +∞) for group softmax computation, respectively. The division of 2 groups is better, which illustrates the necessity of sharing the head knowledge to reduce confusion between head and tail classes and enhances tail discrimination. Designed to address the extreme easy-hard imbalance problem, Focal Loss [14] can not effectively alleviate the tail classes problem. By employing the α-balanced factor in regulating the positive-negative imbalance, Focal* achieves 1.6% higher mAP, which confirms the importance of focusing on the positive-negative imbalance. In contrast, Grad-Libra Loss employs gradient information to re-balance positive-negative samples of different hardness and achieves the best 53.1% mAP performance. Grad-Libra Loss exceeds the second-best loss Focal* by 0.5% AP_f, 1.1% AP_c, and 3.2% AP_r in frequent, common, and rare categories, respectively.

4.4   Performance Analysis

Does our method balance gradients well? As shown in Fig. 3(a), for Cross-Entropy Loss, the tail classes obtain the gradient imbalance of positive and

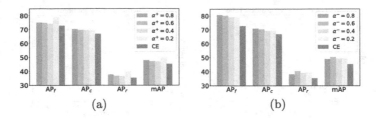

(a)   (b)

Fig. 4. The effects of α^+ and α^-. (a): The individual effects of α^+ from 0.2 to 0.8. (b): The individual effects of α^- from 0.2 to 0.8. CE means the original cross-entorpy loss.

Table 2. Effect of combining α^+ and α^- on head and tail classes.

α^+	α^-	mR_f	AP_f	mR_c	AP_c	mR_r	AP_r	mAP
-	-	83.8	72.8	80.6	66.8	54.3	35.3	45.3
0.2	0.6	96.3	80.3	94.6	71.9	81.1	42.3	52.0
0.6	0.6	96.9	80.7	97.2	72.5	83.2	44.2	52.5
0.8	0.8	96.8	80.1	98.0	72.4	89.9	43.7	**53.1**

negative samples, which means that the gradients of positive samples are overwhelmed by the gradients of negative samples. In contrast, our method rebalances the gradients of positive and negative samples in appropriate parameters. **Does our method balance classifiers well?** Decoupled training methods [11,25] demonstrate that if models are trained with long-tailed datasets, the head classes tend to learn a classifier with larger magnitudes and yields a wider classification boundary in feature space but it hurt data-scarce classes. As shown in Fig. 3(b), the normalized weight norm of the baseline model decreases sharply in tail classes. In contrast, our method provides more balanced classifier weight magnitudes, expands the classification boundary of the tail classes in feature space, and enhances the feature expression of the tail classes.

4.5   Ablation Study

Individual Parameter Contribution. We study the impact of the individual hyper-parameter in Fig. 4. Both α^+ and α^- can improve the performance of rare, common, and frequent categories. The effect of α^+ surpasses the baseline by 1.7 to 4.4 mAP. Up-weighting the hard positive samples makes the network focus on the tail classes. The effect of α^- exceeds the baseline by 3.7 to 5.2 mAP. α^- prevents vast easy negative samples from producing overwhelming loss and dominating the gradients. Notably, the effect of α^- is better than α^+. **Grad-Libra Loss.** By combining both α^+ and α^-, the classification performance is further improved, see Table 2. The performances on rare categories are significantly improved. $\alpha^+ = 0.8$ and $\alpha^- = 0.8$ work best overall, achieving a 53.1% mAP, increasing AP_f by 7.3%, AP_c by 5.6% and AP_r by 8.4% respectively. Our method also significantly increases the recall rate, increasing mR_f by 13%,

Table 3. Performance comparison when Grad-Libra Loss is applied to other detectors.

Detector	Grad-Libra	mR_f	AP_f	mR_c	AP_c	mR_r	AP_r	mAP
FCOS [19]		83.1	70.8	81.6	66.2	55.3	38.0	45.9
	✓	92.9	78.7	97.2	72.7	86.3	42.2	51.9
ATSS [24]		79.3	63.5	73.7	60.9	43.8	33.5	42.0
	✓	96.1	79.1	96.1	70.3	80.4	41.1	50.8
YOLOF [2]		84.9	64.9	82.6	66.1	42.7	38.3	46.5
	✓	88.4	68.5	97.3	67.8	85.5	41.0	49.1

mR_c by 17.4%, and mR_r by 35.6%, respectively. **Applied to other detectors.** To demonstrate the generalization ability of Grad-Libra across different detectors, it is applied to FCOS [19], ATSS [24], and YOLOF [2], separately. As presented in Table 3, Grad-Libra also performs well on all those detectors. The overall improvements for FCOS, ATSS, and YOLOF are 6%, 8.8%, and 3.5%, respectively. For rare categories, the mean recall of FCOS, ATSS, and YOLOF increases by 31%, 36.6%, and 42.8%, respectively.

5 Conclusion

In this work, we focus on the long-tailed class imbalance problem in cervical cancer detection scenario. We propose a Grad-Libra Loss that leverages the gradients to dynamically calibrate the degree of hardness of each sample for different categories and re-balance the gradients of positive and negative samples. Extensive experiments show that our method obtains better performance compared with other state-of-the-art methods.

Acknowledgments. This work was supported in part by the National Natural Science Foundation of China (Grant No. 91959108) and National Natural Science Foundation of China (No. 61973221).

References

1. Chen, K., et al.: MMDetection: open MMLab detection toolbox and benchmark. arXiv preprint arXiv:1906.07155 (2019)
2. Chen, Q., Wang, Y., Yang, T., Zhang, X., Cheng, J., Sun, J.: You only look one-level feature. In: Proceedings of the IEEE Conference on Computer Vision and Pattern Recognition (CVPR), pp. 13039–13048 (2021)
3. Cui, Y., Jia, M., Lin, T.Y., Song, Y., Belongie, S.: Class-balanced loss based on effective number of samples. In: Proceedings of the IEEE Conference on Computer Vision and Pattern Recognition (CVPR), pp. 9268–9277 (2019)
4. Everingham, M., Van Gool, L., Williams, C.K., Winn, J., Zisserman, A.: The pascal visual object classes (VOC) challenge. Int. J. Comput. Vision **88**(2), 303–338 (2010)

5. Goyal, P., et al.: Accurate, large minibatch SGD: Training imageNet in 1 hour. arXiv preprint arXiv:1706.02677 (2017)
6. Gupta, A., Dollar, P., Girshick, R.: LVIS: a dataset for large vocabulary instance segmentation. In: Proceedings of the IEEE Conference on Computer Vision and Pattern Recognition (CVPR), pp. 5356–5364 (2019)
7. Han, H., Wang, W.Y., Mao, B.H.: Borderline-smote: a new over-sampling method in imbalanced data sets learning. In: International Conference on Intelligent Computing (ICIC), pp. 878–887 (2005)
8. He, H., Garcia, E.A.: Learning from imbalanced data. IEEE Trans. Knowl. Data Eng. (TKDE) **21**(9), 1263–1284 (2009)
9. Huang, C., Li, Y., Loy, C.C., Tang, X.: Learning deep representation for imbalanced classification. In: Proceedings of the IEEE Conference on Computer Vision and Pattern Recognition (CVPR), pp. 5375–5384 (2016)
10. Jantzen, J., Norup, J., Dounias, G., Bjerregaard, B.: Pap-smear benchmark data for pattern classification. Nat. Insp. Smart Inf. Syst. 1–9 (2005)
11. Kang, B., et al.: Decoupling representation and classifier for long-tailed recognition. In: International Conference on Learning Representations (ICLR) (2019)
12. Li, Y., et al.: Overcoming classifier imbalance for long-tail object detection with balanced group SoftMax. In: Proceedings of the IEEE Conference on Computer Vision and Pattern Recognition (CVPR), pp. 10991–11000 (2020)
13. Lin, T.Y., Dollár, P., Girshick, R., He, K., Hariharan, B., Belongie, S.: Feature pyramid networks for object detection. In: Proceedings of the IEEE Conference on Computer Vision and Pattern Recognition (CVPR), pp. 2117–2125 (2017)
14. Lin, T.Y., Goyal, P., Girshick, R., He, K., Dollár, P.: Focal loss for dense object detection. In: Proceedings of the IEEE International Conference on Computer Vision (ICCV), pp. 2980–2988 (2017)
15. Paszke, A., et al.: Pytorch: an imperative style, high-performance deep learning library. Adv. Neural Inf. Process. Syst. **32**, 8026–8037 (2019)
16. Plissiti, M.E., Dimitrakopoulos, P., Sfikas, G., Nikou, C., Krikoni, O., Charchanti, A.: Sipakmed: a new dataset for feature and image based classification of normal and pathological cervical cells in pap smear images. In: IEEE International Conference on Image Processing (ICIP), pp. 3144–3148 (2018)
17. Sung, H., et al.: Global cancer statistics 2020: GLOBOCAN estimates of incidence and mortality worldwide for 36 cancers in 185 countries. CA: Cancer J. Clin. **71**(3), 209–249 (2021)
18. Tan, J., Lu, X., Zhang, G., Yin, C., Li, Q.: Equalization loss v2: A new gradient balance approach for long-tailed object detection. In: Proceedings of the IEEE Conference on Computer Vision and Pattern Recognition (CVPR), pp. 1685–1694 (2021)
19. Tian, Z., Shen, C., Chen, H., He, T.: FCOS: fully convolutional one-stage object detection. In: Proceedings of the IEEE Conference on Computer Vision and Pattern Recognition (CVPR), pp. 9627–9636 (2019)
20. Wang, J., et al.: Seesaw loss for long-tailed instance segmentation. In: Proceedings of the IEEE Conference on Computer Vision and Pattern Recognition (CVPR), pp. 9695–9704 (2021)
21. Wang, T., et al.: The devil is in classification: a simple framework for long-tail instance segmentation. In: Proceedings of the European Conference on Computer Vision (ECCV), pp. 728–744 (2020)
22. Yang, Z., Liu, S., Hu, H., Wang, L., Lin, S.: RepPoints: point set representation for object detection. In: Proceedings of the IEEE Conference on Computer Vision and Pattern Recognition (CVPR), pp. 9657–9666 (2019)

23. Zhang, L., et al.: Automation-assisted cervical cancer screening in manual liquid-based cytology with hematoxylin and eosin staining. Cytom. Part A **85**(3), 214–230 (2014)
24. Zhang, S., Chi, C., Yao, Y., Lei, Z., Li, S.Z.: Bridging the gap between anchor-based and anchor-free detection via adaptive training sample selection. In: Proceedings of the IEEE Conference on Computer Vision and Pattern Recognition (CVPR), pp. 9759–9768 (2020)
25. Zhou, B., Cui, Q., Wei, X.S., Chen, Z.M.: BBN: bilateral-branch network with cumulative learning for long-tailed visual recognition. In: Proceedings of the IEEE Conference on Computer Vision and Pattern Recognition (CVPR), pp. 9719–9728 (2020)

Test-Time Image-to-Image Translation Ensembling Improves Out-of-Distribution Generalization in Histopathology

Marin Scalbert[1,2(✉)], Maria Vakalopoulou[1], and Florent Couzinié-Devy[2]

[1] MICS, CentraleSupélec - Université Paris-Saclay, Gif-sur-Yvette, France
{marin.scalbert,maria.vakalopoulou}@centralesupelec.fr
[2] VitaDX International, Paris, France
f.couzinie-devy@vitadx.com

Abstract. Histopathology whole slide images (WSIs) can reveal significant inter-hospital variability such as illumination, color or optical artifacts. These variations, caused by the use of different protocols across medical centers (staining, scanner), can strongly harm algorithms generalization on unseen protocols. This motivates the development of new methods to limit such loss of generalization. In this paper, to enhance robustness on unseen target protocols, we propose a new test-time data augmentation based on multi domain image-to-image translation. It allows to project images from unseen protocol into each source domain before classifying them and ensembling the predictions. This test-time augmentation method results in a significant boost of performances for domain generalization. To demonstrate its effectiveness, our method has been evaluated on two different histopathology tasks where it outperforms conventional domain generalization, standard/H&E specific color augmentation/normalization and standard test-time augmentation techniques. Our code is publicly available at https://gitlab.com/vitadx/ articles/test-time-i2i-translation-ensembling.

Keywords: Test-time data augmentation · Image-to-image translation · Domain generalization · Generative adversarial networks

1 Introduction

Histopathology is the gold standard to diagnose most types of cancer. Sampled tissues are processed following specific protocols (fixation, staining, scanning) to obtain whole slide images (WSIs). It enables tissue types/cells structures differentiation and highlights abnormalities or cancer indicators. However, these protocols substantially vary across different medical institutions resulting in significant inter-hospital variability at the WSIs level. Such variability originating

Supplementary Information The online version contains supplementary material available at https://doi.org/10.1007/978-3-031-16434-7_12.

L. Wang et al. (Eds.): MICCAI 2022, LNCS 13432, pp. 120–129, 2022.
https://doi.org/10.1007/978-3-031-16434-7_12

from illumination and/or color variations or optical artifacts can even occur within the same hospital [11] as well as over time [18].

Intra and inter-hospital variability prevent models from generalizing well on unseen hospitals [21]. This makes domain generalization one of the primordial and studied task of computational pathology. To circumvent the drop of generalization performances in histopathology applications, recent methods have relied on standard color augmentations [21], H&E specific data augmentations [5,20,23], stain normalization [13,14,16,21] or domain generalization (DG) techniques [2,15,17,19]. In histopathology, data augmentation has proven to be one of the most efficient and simple technique to close the gap due to domain shift [21]. Some data augmentation/unsupervised domain adaptation (UDA) methods are even exploiting image-to-image translation methods to learn stain-invariant models [22,23]. However, UDA methods need access to unlabeled data from the target domain which is not the case in the DG setting and must be trained every time we want to predict on a new target domain. Currently, data augmentation methods only exploit image-to-image translation models at training which as shown by our study is not optimal.

In this paper, we propose for the first time, the use of image-to-image translation for test-time augmentation (TTA) designing a tailored ensemble strategy. In particular, the method is based upon the multi-domain image-to-image translation model StarGanV2 [3]. At test-time, it projects images from unseen domains to the source domains, classify the projected images and ensemble their predictions. Additionally, several ensembling strategies have been explored. The proposed TTA does not rely on any prior on the domain shifts, learning them directly from the training data. Our method, operating at test-time, can be easily combined with other DG and/or data augmentation techniques. To demonstrate its effectiveness, it has been evaluated on two different histopathology tasks and has shown better generalization over previous conventional DG, color augmentation/normalization, and standard TTA techniques [2,4,15,17,19,20].

2   Method

In the problem of multi-source DG, we are given S source domains $\{\mathcal{D}_1, \ldots, \mathcal{D}_S\}$. Each source domain $\mathcal{D}_i$ with domain label d_i contains $n_{\mathcal{D}_i}$ labeled examples $\{(x_j, y_j) \mid 1 \leq j \leq n_{\mathcal{D}_i}\}$. The goal is to learn a robust model from the S labeled source domains so that it generalizes well on an unseen target domain $\mathcal{D}_T$. In the following sections the different components of our method are detailed.

2.1   StarGanV2 Architecture

StarGanV2 is a multi-domain image-to-image translation model capable of translating an input image x into any source domain without requiring the input image domain label: this is what allows us to use it on unseen target domain. It is considered as a style based image-to-image translation model meaning that the generator takes as inputs the image that needs to be translated but also a domain-dependant style vector helping the generator to translate the input image into the corresponding domain. Style vectors can be extracted from a reference style image or from a random latent code (Fig. 1).

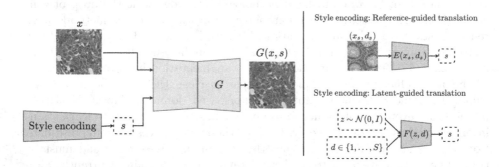

Fig. 1. The two different style encodings: on right top the reference-guided and right bottom the latent-guided image-to-image translation are presented.

More specifically, given an image x and a style vector s from a source domain d, the generator G translates the image x into an image $G(x, s)$ reflecting visual attributes of the domains d. s can be computed either from a style encoder E given a reference style image with its domain (x_s, d_s) (i.e. $s = E(x_s, d_s)$) or from a mapping network F given a random latent code z along with a domain label d (i.e. $s = F(z, d)$). Our proposed TTA method relies on latent-guided image-to-image translation due to the lighter size and lower computational overhead of F compared to E. Additionally, some of the explored ensembling strategies exploit the different domain discriminators used during the StarGanV2 training. To better preserve the structure of the input image in the translated images, the perceptual domain invariant loss [6] is added to the overall loss of StarGanV2. Examples of translated images are provided in Fig. 1 of supplementary material.

2.2   Test-Time Image-to-Image Translation Ensembling

Once a StarGanV2 and a classifier C have been trained separately on the source data, our TTA can be used at inference. An overview of our TTA method is presented in Fig. 2. Given a test image x, we sample S random latent code vectors $\{z_1, \ldots, z_S\} \sim \mathcal{N}(0, I)$ with respective domain label $\{d_1, \ldots, d_S\}$. Each latent code vector along with its domain label are fed to the mapping network F to produce the different style vectors $\{s_1, \ldots, s_S\} = \{F(z_1, d_1), \ldots, F(z_S, d_S)\}$. Then, the image x, along with each of the style vectors $\{s_1, \ldots, s_S\}$, are fed to the StarGanV2 generator G translating x into the images $\{x_1, \ldots, x_S\} = \{G(x, s_1), \ldots, G(x, s_S)\}$. From each x_i that should have now similar characteristics as real images from domain d_i, we compute the predictions of the classifier $\hat{y}_i = C(x_i)$ and the different StarGanV2 domain discriminators score $\hat{d}_i = D_i(x_i)$ reflecting how well the image x has been projected into domain d_i. Finally, from the classifier predictions $\{\hat{y}_1, \ldots, \hat{y}_S\}$ and the domain discriminators score $\{\hat{d}_1, \ldots, \hat{d}_S\}$, we propose three different strategies to ensemble the predictions into a final prediction $\hat{y}$.

Naive Ensembling. In this method, domain discriminators scores $\{\hat{d}_1, \ldots, \hat{d}_S\}$ are discarded and the predictions $\{\hat{y}_1, \ldots, \hat{y}_S\}$ are simply averaged.

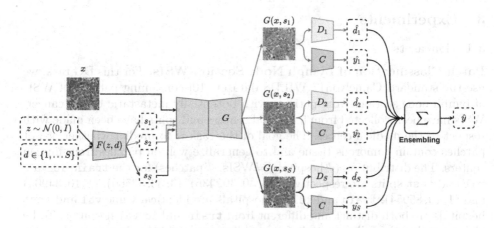

Fig. 2. Test-time data augmentation with latent-guided StarGanV2 image-to-image translation

Discriminator Based Top-k Ensembling. A domain discriminator score should reflect how well a test image has been projected into the corresponding source domain. Following this intuition, we propose to ensemble only k predictions associated to the images with the top-k domain discriminators scores:

$$\hat{y} = \frac{1}{S'} \sum_{s=1}^{S'} \hat{y}_s \quad ; \quad S' = \underset{\substack{I \subseteq \{1, \ldots, S\} \\ |I| = k}}{\arg\max} \sum_{i \in I} \hat{d}_i \tag{1}$$

Discriminator based weighted ensembling. In the discriminator based top-k ensembling, although the predictions associated to the lowest domain discriminator scores have been discarded from the ensembling, the k kept predictions contribute evenly even if there might be significant score disparities. Preferably, we would like to consider all the predictions to unlock the full power of ensembling while reducing the importance of predictions associated to badly projected images. That is why, we propose here to ensemble all the predictions $\{\hat{y}_1, \ldots, \hat{y}_S\}$ with respective weights $\{\alpha_1, \ldots, \alpha_S\}$ based on domain discriminators scores $\{\hat{d}_1, \ldots, \hat{d}_S\}$:

$$\hat{y} = \sum_{s=1}^{S} \alpha_s \hat{y}_s \quad ; \quad \alpha_s = \frac{e^{\frac{\hat{d}_s}{T}}}{\sum_{j=1}^{S} e^{\frac{\hat{d}_j}{T}}} \quad \forall s \in \{1, \ldots, S\} \tag{2}$$

The temperature T in Eq. 2 is a hyperparameter controlling how peaky the predictions weights distribution should be. When $T \to \infty$, predictions weights tend to be uniform ($\alpha_s = \frac{1}{S}$) which is equivalent to the naive ensembling. While, when $T \to 0$, predictions weights tend to be a one-hot encoded vector which is equivalent to the discriminator based top-k ensembling with $k = 1$.

3   Experiments

3.1   Datasets

Patch Classification of Lymph Node Section WSIs. For this DG task, we use the standard Camelyon17 WILDS dataset [10] containing patches of WSIs of lymph node sections from patients with potentially metastatic breast cancer. WSIs have been collected from 5 medical centers and splits have been made with respect to the medical center. The goal of the task is to predict whether or not patches contain tumorous tissue and to generalize well on patches from unseen centers. The distribution (#hospitals, #WSIs, #patches) for the train, id_val, val and test splits are respectively $(3, 30, 302436)$, $(3, 30, 33560)$, $(1, 10, 34904)$ and $(1, 10, 85054)$. train and id_val hospitals are identical while val and test hospitals are both distinct and different from train and id_val hospitals. To be able to exploit the full potential of ensembling, we decide to choose the different WSIs as the different source domains ($S = 30$) rather than the number of distinct hospitals. Moreover, considering WSIs as domain can be convenient when you have no more information than the WSI itself.

Tissue Type Classification in Colorectal Histological Images. For this DG task, we use 3 different datasets of colorectal cancer histological images namely: Kather16 [9], Kather19 [8] and CRC-TP [7]. Kather16 contains 5000 patches from 10 H&E WSIs spread into 8 classes. Kather19 includes 100000 patches from several H&E WSIs spread into 9 classes. CRC-TP comprises a total of 196000 patches extracted from 20 H&E WSIs and spread over 7 classes. Given that the hospital or slide information are not provided for Kather19 and CRC-TP, we only use Kather16 as the train set and Kather19 with CRC-TP as test sets. Because class definitions can vary from one dataset to another, we follow the class grouping suggested by [1]. Additionally, we remove the class *complex stroma* from Kather16 and CRC-TP which do not share the same definition. Finally, our problem consists in classifying patches from colorectal cancer histological images into 7 classes (*tumor, normal, stroma, lymphocytes, debris, adipose* and *background*) and to generalize well on unseen domains (Kather19, CRC-TP). Since our training set (Kather16) does not provide hospital information for each patch, we considered WSIs as source domains ($S = 10$).

3.2   Method Evaluation

In this section, the proposed TTA with the different ensembling methods are evaluated on the two different tasks. We report a baseline (base) corresponding to

Table 1. Accuracy on Camelyon17 WILDS, weighted F1-score on Kather19 and CRC-TP. *Naive ens*, *disc top-k ens* and *disc weighted ens* referred respectively to naive ensembling, discriminator based top-k ensembling and discriminator based weighted ensembling. Best performances are highlighted in **bold** and standard deviations are specified in parenthesis.

	Lymph node patch classification			Colorectal tissue type classification	
	id_val	val	test	Kather19	CRC-TP
Base	**98.5(0.1)**	80.3(4.4)	62.7(7.4)	70.8(1.8)	43.6(3.7)
SOTA domain generalization methods					
CORAL [19]		86.2(1.4)	59.5(7.7)		
IRM [2]		86.2(1.4)	64.2(8.1)		
Group DRO [15]		85.5(2.2)	68.4(7.3)		
FISH [17]		83.9(1.2)	74.7(7.1)		
Color normalization					
Macenko [13]		81.6(1.2)	92.5(1.8)	64.9(3.3)	51.6(1.2)
Train-time data augmentation					
Base + RandAugment [4]		90.6(1.2)	82.0(7.4)	72.6(3.2)	51.0(5.1)
Base + H&E staining color jitter [20]		88.0(4.2)	91.6(1.9)	72.4(3.3)	47.6(4.8)
Base + StarGanV2 data aug	**98.4(0.0)**	89.6(0.7)	76.4(4.5)	66.3(3.3)	37.7(6.1)
Test-time data augmentation					
Base + StarGanV2 data aug + geometric TTA	**98.5(0.1)**	90.0(0.6)	76.5(4.2)	66.2(3.5)	37.6(5.9)
Base + color jittering + color jittering TTA	97.4(0.1)	91.2(0.4)	77.2(1.2)	**74.5(2.5)**	**51.7(6.1)**
Our method					
Base + StarGanV2 data aug + naive ens	96.9(0.3)	**92.8(0.2)**	**94.0(1.2)**	**72.9(2.0)**	54.4(3.2)
Base + StarGanV2 data aug + disc top-k ens	97.3(0.2)	92.1(0.2)	**94.0(1.2)**	**72.9(2.0)**	54.4(3.2)
Base + StarGanV2 data aug + disc weighted ens	97.4(0.2)	**92.7(0.2)**	**94.0(1.2)**	**72.9(2.0)**	51.6(3.3)

cross-entropy minimization on the source domains. Additionally, we also evaluate a method named StarGanV2 data aug where StarGanV2 is used only for train-time data augmentation. The performances on Camelyon17, Kather19, CRC-TP are respectively averaged over 10, 5 and 5 independent runs and reported on Table 1. Implementation details about the StarGanV2 and classifier are provided in Table 1 of supplementary material.

State-of-the-Art Results on Camelyon17 WILDS. Our method obtains state-of-the-art results on Camelyon17 WILDS. Results of competing methods are reported in the "SOTA domain generalization methods", "Color normalization" and the two first lines of the "Train-time data augmentation" row. On the val and test splits, our TTA method with naive ensembling outperforms the previous best method by +2.2% and +1.5% respectively. It is worth mentioning that our method learns the domains variations from the data while the two previous best methods on test use expert priors (H&E staining color jittering and Macenko color normalization). Therefore, in theory, our method could generalize on other medical imaging modalities. Compared to the best DG method FISH, that do not use any priors on the domain change, our method leads to much better generalization with +8.9% and +19.3% accuracy improvements.

The TTA method performs also well on source domain data (id_val split) even if performances are slightly worse than the baseline.

Better Robustness on Kather19 and CRC-TP. The second task is more challenging as only 4400 images are available in Kather16 to train the StarGanV2 and the classifier. The experiments on these datasets have two objectives: show that our method generalizes on another problem/dataset and that it can work even with relatively small size datasets. Previous works usually use Kather16 for evaluation making performances comparisons impossible. However, the results on Kather19 and CRC-TP shows that our method increases the baseline results significantly: +2.1% and +11.8% respectively. These improvements are not as large as in Camelyon17 which is probably due to a less robust StarGanV2 model. This hypothesis is reinforced by the bad performances of train-time data augmentation using the StarGanV2.

3.3 Ablation Studies

Analyzing Data Augmentation Effects. We have studied independently the effects of the train-time and test-time data augmentations based on the same StarGanV2. The train-time data augmentation with StarGanV2 alone helps to make the model more robust on Camelyon17 (+9.3% and +13.7% for val and test splits). However, on Kather16, where the dataset is small, it leads to loss of performances (−4.5% and −5.9%). On both tasks, when train-time data augmentation based on StarGanV2 is combined with our TTA method, generalization performances improve considerably.

To evaluate the impact of our TTA, geometric TTA and color jittering TTA have been evaluated. Both perform quite well: in particular, the color jittering prior seems to be correct for 3 out of the 4 target datasets making it as good as our method on the colorectal datasets and nearly as good on the Camelyon17 val split. However, color jittering TTA fails on the Camelyon17 test split (−16.8% compared to our TTA method). This suggests that the augmented target domain distribution is not overlapping enough the source domains distributions and that projecting images onto source domains is a better approach to achieve generalization. A t-SNE [12] plot provided in Fig. 2 of supplementary material confirms that projecting target examples onto the different source domains is one of the key to achieve better generalization.

Comparison of the Ensembling Strategies. The naive ensembling has slightly better results than the two other proposed ensembling strategies. This seems counter-intuitive but two reasons might explain this result. Firstly, domain discriminators learned during the StarGanV2 training may not be adapted for the classification tasks. Secondly, the small number of WSIs in each training dataset (10 and 30) might be problematic: selecting a subset of projected images predictions when their number is already small, even if images are not well projected, might remove some of the advantages of standard ensembling. To explore this question, performances of discriminator based top-k ensembling and weighted ensembling with respect to their hyperparameters k and T are reported on Fig. 3. A small temperature T corresponds to top-1 ensembling while a large T is equivalent to naive ensembling or top-k with the biggest possible k.

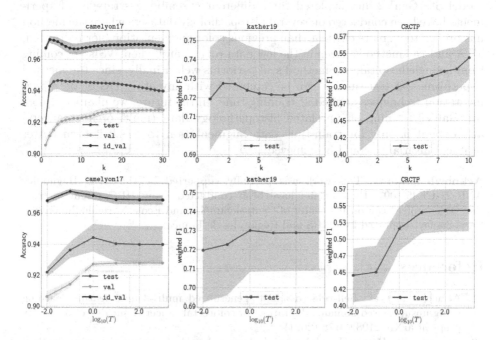

Fig. 3. Performances of *discriminator based top-k ensembling* with respect to k (1st row) and *discriminator based weighted ensembling* with respect to T (2nd row) for Camelyon17 WILDS, Kather19 and CRC-TP datasets.

On the four target datasets (`val`, `test` splits of Camelyon17, Kather19 and CRC-TP), the general trend is that the more predictions we consider in the top-k ensembling or the higher the temperature T for the weighted ensembling the better the performances are. Increasing k or T in the first steps enables significant gains while for higher values the performances continue to improve or decrease only slightly. It should be noted that the decrease in performances occurs on the Camelyon17 `test` split where the number of domains is the largest in our experiments (30). In this case, the naive ensembling does not lead to the best performance and it seems that predictions of badly projected images decrease the performance of the ensembling method. This observation suggests that when a bigger number of available domains (WSIs) is available, the top-k and weighted ensembling methods might generalize better.

Currently, when dealing with many domains our TTA can face a computational overhead. In Table 2 of supplementary material, time complexity, scalability of the approach are investigated and suggestions are proposed to limit such overhead.

4 Conclusion

To tackle problems of domain generalization in histopathology, we have proposed a new TTA technique based on the multi-domain image-to-image translation model StarGanV2 and explored three different ensembling strategies. Experiments have been conducted on several histopathology datasets where the method has proven to be more efficient than previous color augmentation/normalization, TTA and DG methods. Even in the low data regime and when WSIs are coming from a single hospital, our method still performs well. Finally, since the method is performed at test-time, it can be combined with any other DG or data augmentation techniques applied at training-time. In the future, we plan to explore StarGanV2 training on unrelated histopathology data (multi organs/cancers) and exploit it only for train-time data augmentation to check if even better protocol invariance could be achieved.

Acknowledgments. This work was partially supported by the ANR Hagnodice ANR-21-CE45-0007. Experiments have been conducted using HPC resources from the "Mésocentre" computing center of CentraleSupélec and École Normale Supérieure Paris-Saclay supported by CNRS and Région Île-de-France.

References

1. Abbet, C., et al.: Self-rule to adapt: generalized multi-source feature learning using unsupervised domain adaptation for colorectal cancer tissue detection. arXiv preprint arXiv:2108.09178 (2021)
2. Arjovsky, M., Bottou, L., Gulrajani, I., Lopez-Paz, D.: Invariant risk minimization. arXiv preprint arXiv:1907.02893 (2019)
3. Choi, Y., Uh, Y., Yoo, J., Ha, J.W.: Stargan v2: diverse image synthesis for multiple domains. In: Proceedings of the IEEE/CVF Conference on Computer Vision and Pattern Recognition, pp. 8188–8197 (2020)
4. Cubuk, E.D., Zoph, B., Shlens, J., Le, Q.V.: Randaugment: practical automated data augmentation with a reduced search space. In: Proceedings of the IEEE/CVF Conference on Computer Vision and Pattern Recognition Workshops, pp. 702–703 (2020)
5. Faryna, K., van der Laak, J., Litjens, G.: Tailoring automated data augmentation to h&e-stained histopathology. In: Medical Imaging with Deep Learning. PMLR (2021)
6. Huang, X., Liu, M.Y., Belongie, S., Kautz, J.: Multimodal unsupervised image-to-image translation. In: Proceedings of the European Conference on Computer Vision (ECCV), pp. 172–189 (2018)
7. Javed, S., et al.: Cellular community detection for tissue phenotyping in colorectal cancer histology images. Med. Image Anal. **63**, 101696 (2020)
8. Kather, J.N., et al.: Predicting survival from colorectal cancer histology slides using deep learning: a retrospective multicenter study. PLoS Med. **16**(1), e1002730 (2019)
9. Kather, J.N., et al.: Multi-class texture analysis in colorectal cancer histology. Sci. Rep. **6**(1), 1–11 (2016)

10. Koh, P.W., et al.: Wilds: A benchmark of in-the-wild distribution shifts. In: International Conference on Machine Learning, pp. 5637–5664. PMLR (2021)
11. Lafarge, M.W., Pluim, J.P.W., Eppenhof, K.A.J., Moeskops, P., Veta, M.: Domain-adversarial neural networks to address the appearance variability of histopathology images. In: Cardoso, M.J., et al. (eds.) DLMIA/ML-CDS -2017. LNCS, vol. 10553, pp. 83–91. Springer, Cham (2017). https://doi.org/10.1007/978-3-319-67558-9_10
12. Van der Maaten, L., Hinton, G.: Visualizing data using t-sne. J. Mach. Learn. Res. **9**(11) (2008)
13. Macenko, M., et al.: A method for normalizing histology slides for quantitative analysis. In: 2009 IEEE International Symposium on Biomedical Imaging: From Nano to Macro, pp. 1107–1110. IEEE (2009)
14. Reinhard, E., Adhikhmin, M., Gooch, B., Shirley, P.: Color transfer between images. IEEE Comput. Graph. Appl. **21**(5), 34–41 (2001)
15. Sagawa, S., Koh, P.W., Hashimoto, T.B., Liang, P.: Distributionally robust neural networks for group shifts: on the importance of regularization for worst-case generalization. arXiv preprint arXiv:1911.08731 (2019)
16. Shaban, M.T., Baur, C., Navab, N., Albarqouni, S.: Staingan: stain style transfer for digital histological images. In: 2019 IEEE 16th International Symposium on Biomedical Imaging (ISBI 2019). pp. 953–956. IEEE (2019)
17. Shi, Y., et al.: Gradient matching for domain generalization. arXiv preprint arXiv:2104.09937 (2021)
18. Stacke, K., Eilertsen, G., Unger, J., Lundström, C.: Measuring domain shift for deep learning in histopathology. IEEE J. Biomed. Health Inf. **25**(2), 325–336 (2020)
19. Sun, B., Saenko, K.: Deep CORAL: correlation alignment for deep domain adaptation. In: Hua, G., Jégou, H. (eds.) ECCV 2016. LNCS, vol. 9915, pp. 443–450. Springer, Cham (2016). https://doi.org/10.1007/978-3-319-49409-8_35
20. Tellez, D., et al.: Whole-slide mitosis detection in h&e breast histology using phh3 as a reference to train distilled stain-invariant convolutional networks. IEEE Trans. Med. Imaging **37**(9), 2126–2136 (2018)
21. Tellez, D., et al.: Quantifying the effects of data augmentation and stain color normalization in convolutional neural networks for computational pathology. Med. Image Anal. **58**, 101544 (2019)
22. Vasiljević, J., Feuerhake, F., Wemmert, C., Lampert, T.: Towards histopathological stain invariance by unsupervised domain augmentation using generative adversarial networks. Neurocomputing **460**, 277–291 (2021)
23. Wagner, S.J., et al.: Structure-preserving multi-domain stain color augmentation using style-transfer with disentangled representations. In: de Bruijne, M., et al. (eds.) MICCAI 2021. LNCS, vol. 12908, pp. 257–266. Springer, Cham (2021). https://doi.org/10.1007/978-3-030-87237-3_25

Predicting Molecular Traits from Tissue Morphology Through Self-interactive Multi-instance Learning

Yang Hu[2,3], Korsuk Sirinukunwattana[1,3], Kezia Gaitskell[4,6], Ruby Wood[1,3], Clare Verrill[5,6], and Jens Rittscher[1,2,3(✉)]

[1] Department of Engineering Science, University of Oxford, Oxford, UK
jens.rittscher@eng.ox.ac.uk
[2] Nuffield Department of Medicine, University of Oxford, Oxford, UK
yang.hu@ndm.ox.ac.uk
[3] Big Data Institute, University of Oxford, Li Ka Shing Centre for Health Information and Discovery, Oxford, UK
[4] Nuffield Division of Clinical Laboratory Sciences, Radcliffe Department of Medicine, University of Oxford, Oxford, UK
[5] Nuffield Department of Surgical Sciences, University of Oxford, Oxford, UK
[6] Department of Cellular Pathology, Oxford University Hospitals NHS Foundation Trust, Oxford, UK

Abstract. Previous efforts to learn histology features that correlate with specific genetic/molecular traits resort to tile-level multi-instance learning (MIL) which relies on a fixed pretrained model for feature extraction and an instance-bag classifier. We argue that such a two-step approach is not optimal at capturing both fine-grained features at tile level and global features at slide level optimal to the task. We propose a self-interactive MIL that iteratively feedbacks training information between the fine-grained and global context features. We validate the proposed approach on 4 subtyping tasks: EMT status (ovarian), KRAS mutation (colon and lung), EGFR mutation (colon), and HER2 status (breast). Our approach yields an average improvement of $7.05\% - 8.34\%$ (in terms of AUC) over the baseline.

Keywords: Histopathological subtyping · Genetic mutation detection · Limited data · Self-interactive learning · Fine-grained features

1 Introduction

The ability to predict specific molecular traits or biologically relevant subtypes of disease [19] from tissue morphology opens up new opportunities for computational pathology. The automated analysis of routinely acquired hematoxylin and eosin (H&E) images can so be used to generate more precise and informative diagnosis. Furthermore, such an analysis helps to identify cases which should be prioritised for detailed molecular testing, and hence holds the promise to link traditional histopathology with molecular medicine.

L. Wang et al. (Eds.): MICCAI 2022, LNCS 13432, pp. 130–139, 2022.
https://doi.org/10.1007/978-3-031-16434-7_13

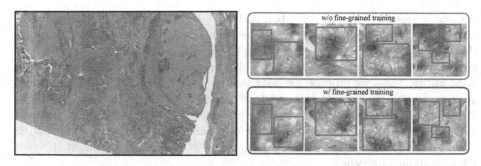

Fig. 1. Some examples of CNN attention regions comparing between the methods with/without fine-grained training. Left: green boxes are sample tiles from tumour regions. Top right: Grad-CAM [17]heatmaps of CNN without fine-grained training on the 4 sampled tiles. Bottom right: Grad-CAM heatmaps of CNN on the same sampled tiles, after fine-grained training by Inter-MIL. The green boxes locate tumour cells marked by our pathologist. (Color figure online)

Learning directly from entire whole slide images (WSIs) is challenging. Standard GPU memory limits the amount of data that can be processed by any deep learning models in a single run. Hence, WSIs are commonly split into numerous small tiles [1,6,10–13,15,18]. More importantly, disease-relevant features are often rare and subtle. In the absence of pixel-level annotations, weakly-supervised multi-instance learning where a WSI represents a bag consisting of multiple tile instances is a widely used learning paradigm.

Existing MIL methods in computational pathology generally separate the learning into two steps: 1) tile embedding and 2) integration of the feature embeddings for prediction. Tile embedding is based on pretraining a backbone network. The pretraining tasks can be ImageNet classification [3], self-supervised [2], or a related but easier task [10]. For feature aggregation, pooling is a preferred method. Ilse *et al.* [9] propose attention pooling (AttPool). Li *et al.* [13] integrate the encoding tiles from multiple resolutions in AttPool. Alternatively, it is possible to assign dynamic weights for features at different resolutions by using ensemble or dual-stream methods [6,11]. Clustering-constrained-attention MIL (CLAM) [15] uses clustering loss to reduce distance between tiles within clusters of similar features. Focal attention (FocAtt) [10] considers the prior context of the entire tissue when assigning attention to individual tiles. Transformers [4] which capture long-distance association between tiles have also been used to replace AttPool [12,18]. However, we hypothesise that all of these methods struggle to learn subtle rare features, which are optimal for morpho-molecular subtyping tasks. Furthermore, dividing the learning tasks into separate steps makes it extremely challenging to learn features that can simultaneously capture global and fine-grained tissue representations.

To address this problem, we present a novel MIL approach for morpho-molecular subtyping. Core to our approach is to learn fine-grained and task specific features iteratively. Let E denote tile-level embeddings, f_{cls} a joint pooling and a classifier, Y a target label, and $\mathcal{L}(Y, f_{cls}(E))$ a loss function between target Y and the prediction $f_{cls}(E)$. We wish to optimise for E and f_{cls} such that $E^*, f_{cls}^* = \arg\min_{(E, f_{cls})} \mathcal{L}(Y, f_{cls}(E))$. Simultaneous joint optimisation for both E and f_{cls} is not straightforward due to the hardware limitation as outlined above. Thus, we propose a self-interactive MIL (Inter-MIL) that iteratively optimises one variable at a time while keeping the other fixed, thereby searching for both optimal fine-grained tile-level features E^* and global-level features f_{cls}^*. Figure 1 compares examples of tile-level saliency heatmaps. In contrast to a model with no tile-level optimisation, Inter-MIL correctly highlight disease-relevant malignant cells.

Furthermore, we devise Inter-MIL as a means to tackle weakly-supervised learning in limited training data and/or severe class-imbalance settings. Inter-MIL constructs a representative tile-level feature pool to avoid tile encoder being swamped by more abundant features during training. This encourages learning of subtle rare features and, as a by-product, mitigates class-imbalance issue. Optimal tissue representations allow Inter-MIL to be more data efficient.

The main contribuitions of this paper are: (1) A novel self-interactive MIL framework capable of predicting molecular traits by combining a global context of WSIs with a tile-level optimisation. (2) A tile-level feature pool for fine-tuning the CNN encoder that contains several designated subsets of tiles. This feature pool is dynamically updated, making the CNN encoder learn some novel features from high-attention tiles while suppressing noise from low-attention tiles. (3) Validation of the proposed methodology on 4 subtyping tasks based on genetic and molecular analyses. Furthermore, the qualitative visualisation shows that Inter-MIL provides more discriminating feature representations.

2   Methodology

We describe the methodology in three parts. Firstly, we introduce the overall architecture of the Inter-MIL. Secondly, we explain the construction of the tile-level feature pool. Lastly, we describe adversarial training method to improve the learning of discriminate features.

Overall Framework. Inter-MIL consists of two learning modules: Module-1, attention pooling (AttPool) network and Module-2, trainable tile-level feature encoder. We optimise these modules alternately until the convergence conditions are met, as illustrated by Fig. 2.

Given a WSI with L tiles $\{x_i\}_{i=1}^L$ and the CNN encoder $f_{res}(\cdot)$, let $E = \{E_i\}_{i=1}^L$ be the set of tile embeddings such that $E_i = f_{res}(x_i)$. AttPool [9] receives tile embeddings E and outputs a classification result y:

$$y = \mathrm{softmax}\left(f_{mlp}\left(\sum_{i=1}^L att(E_i) \cdot E_i \right) \right), \tag{1}$$

where $f_{mlp}(\cdot)$ is the output layer for classification, the attention score $att(E_i) \in [0, 1]$ reflects the contribution of the ith tile to the classification, and $\sum_i^L att(E_i) = 1$. We train AttPool by optimising the slide-level prediction.

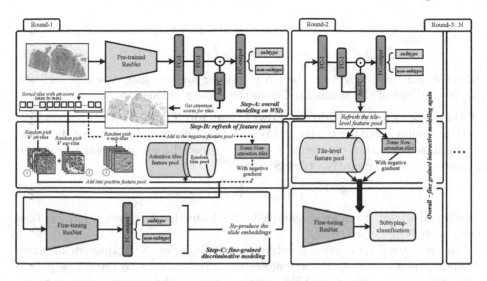

Fig. 2. Inter-MIL framework. Three steps in each round of interactive training: A. Train AttPool network with pre-calculated tile embeddings, and obtain the attention value for each tile; B. Construct tile-level feature pool with ① high-attention tiles and ② supplementary tiles as defined in (3), optionally introduce ③ non-attention tiles as defined in (5); C. Perform fine-grained training on CNN encoder (using ResNet) with tile-level feature pool, and re-produce the tile embeddings for training AttPool in the next round.

To model the fine-grained features and refresh tile embeddings E^{t-1} to E^t, where t is the training loop index, in Module-2, we use k representative tiles $\{x_i\}_{i=1}^k$ with high attention scores to fine tune $f_{res}^{t-1}(\cdot)$ to $f_{res}^t(\cdot)$. The training of $f_{res}^t(\cdot)$ optimises prediction loss at the tile level. Once completed, we regenerate the tile embeddings E^t using the fine-tuned CNN encoder $f_{res}^t(\cdot)$ and continue with the next training round for AttPool:

$$E^t = \left\{ E_i^t = f_{res}^t(x_i) \right\}_{i=1}^L.$$
(2)

Tile-Level Feature Encoder. We now elaborate on the details of the tile-level feature optimisation. Given a WSI, we rank tiles based on their attention scores in a monotonically decreasing order, i.e. $\{x_{d_1}, ..., x_{d_L} | att(x_{d_1}) \geq att(x_{d_2}) \geq ... \geq att(x_{d_L})\}$. We define a set of **attention tiles** S^{top} as a set of randomly sampled k^1 tiles out of the top K highest attention tiles, i.e. $S^{top} = \{x_i\}_{i=1}^{k^1} \subseteq \{x_{d_i}\}_{i=1}^K$. Similarly, we defined a set of **supplementary tiles** S^{sup} as a set of randomly sampled k^2 tiles out of the remaining $L - K$ tiles, i.e. $S^{sup} = \{x_i\}_{i=1}^{k^2} \subseteq \{x_{d_i}\}_{j=K+1}^L$. K is determined by the total number of tiles L separately for each WSI. S^{sup} increases the diversity of tile features that may not be captured by S^{top}. We construct the set S of tile-level feature pool as follows:

$$S = S^{top} \cup S^{sup}.$$
(3)

Thus, we optimise the CNN encoder $f_{res}(\cdot)$ using:

$$\theta_{f_{res}^t} = \theta_{f_{res}^{t-1}} + \gamma \cdot \nabla \mathcal{L}_{x_i \in S}\left(y_{x_i}, f_{res}^{t-1}(x_i)\right), \tag{4}$$

where θ and γ are weights of the CNN encoder and learning rate, respectively. y_{x_i} is the label of tile x_i inherited from the slide it belongs to.

Adversarial Optimisation for Low-Attention Tiles. We describe an alternative tile-level training strategy in this section. Without intervention in training, non-relevant tiles could end up being allocated high attention scores. We construct a set of **negative tiles** S^{neg} as

$$S^{neg} = \{x_i\}_{i=1}^n \subseteq \{x_{d_i}\}_{i=(L-N)+1}^L, \tag{5}$$

which consists of n randomly sampled tiles from the N lowest attention tiles from each WSI.

Inspired by [5], we leverage adversarial training on S^{neg} through negative gradient update. Essentially, we enforce the CNN encoder to predict as poorly as possible on samples from S^{neg}, which results in the low attention scores of these tiles. We extend the optimisation of the encoder $f_{res}(\cdot)$ in (4) to incorporate S^{neg} as follows:

$$\begin{aligned}
\theta_{f_{res}^t} = &\, \theta_{f_{res}^{t-1}} + \gamma \cdot \nabla \mathcal{L}_{x_i \in S}\left(y_{x_i}, f_{res}^{t-1}(x_i)\right) \\
&- \gamma^{neg} \cdot \nabla \mathcal{L}_{x_j \in S^{neg}}\left(y_{x_j}, f_{res}^{t-1}(x_j)\right),
\end{aligned} \tag{6}$$

where γ^{neg} denotes a negative learning rate.

3   Experiments and Results

Datasets. We evaluate the proposed framework on 4 subtyping tasks: 1) *OV-EMT*, 70 WSIs from TCGA-OV dataset with a binary epithelial-mesenchymal transition status (38 EMT-high vs 32 EMT-low); *COLU-KRAS*, a combined 112 WSIs with KRAS mutation status (44 mutated vs 68 wild-type) from TCGA-COAD and TCGA-LUAD datasets; *LU-EGFR*, 261 WSIs from TCGA-LUAD dataset for subtyping EGFR mutation status (75 mutated vs 186 wild-type); *BR-HER2*, 415 WSIs from TCGA-BRCA datasets with HER2 FISH expression (77 positive vs 338 negative). EMT status used in *OV-EMT* is available in [7,8] while the subtype labels for the rest of the tasks are available in the TCGA data repository [20]. For each WSI, we extract 256×256 tiles at $40\times$ magnification (0.25μ per pixel) from tissue regions. These morphomolecular subtyping tasks are challenging not only because of the nature of the problem but also the small sample size, combination of different tissue types (*COLU-KRAS*), and severe class imbalance (*LU-EGFR* and *BR-HER2*). To ensure enough training samples, we split the data into training/test sets with the following ratio: 0.7/0.3 for *OV-EMT* and *COLU-KRAS*, and 0.5/0.5 for *LU-EGFR* and *BR-HER2*.

Implementation. The following settings are used in all tasks unless specified otherwise. We use Gated-AttPool [14] as a pooling operator and ResNet-18 pretrained on ImageNet [3] as the CNN encoder. Weighted cross-entropy loss is

Table 1. Results on subtyping tasks with AUC $\pm$ variance (%). The best and the $2nd$ best results are marked in **bold** and **blue**, with ($\uparrow$ lift from baseline).

Methods	OV-EMT	COLU-KRAS	LU-EGFR	BR-HER2
CNN-MIL [1]	59.86 $\pm$ 1.11	50.56 $\pm$ 0.15	–	–
AttPool [9]	61.38 $\pm$ 1.35	61.41 $\pm$ 0.78	–	–
Gated-AttPool [9,14]	62.46 $\pm$ 1.13	59.94 $\pm$ 0.06	64.15 $\pm$ 0.39	54.84 $\pm$ 0.14
CLAM [15]	62.62 $\pm$ 1.10	62.18 $\pm$ 0.80	65.17 $\pm$ 0.25	54.17 $\pm$ 0.11
FocAtt-MIL [10]	56.89 $\pm$ 1.86	63.76 $\pm$ 1.05	64.19 $\pm$ 0.12	53.53 $\pm$ 0.15
Inter-MIL (ours)	**71.91 $\pm$ 0.50** ($\uparrow$ 9.45)	**64.78 $\pm$ 0.18** ($\uparrow$ 4.84)	**69.81 $\pm$ 0.12** ($\uparrow$ 5.66)	**63.08 $\pm$ 0.04** ($\uparrow$ 8.24)
– without S^{sup}	68.53 $\pm$ 0.21 ($\uparrow$ 6.07)	64.01 $\pm$ 0.3 ($\uparrow$ 4.07)	67.99 $\pm$ 0.02 ($\uparrow$ 3.84)	62.00 $\pm$ 0.07 ($\uparrow$ 7.16)
adInter-MIL (ours)	**74.55 $\pm$ 0.43** ($\uparrow$ 12.09)	**66.34 $\pm$ 0.31** ($\uparrow$ 6.41)	**70.65 $\pm$ 0.08** ($\uparrow$ 6.50)	**63.21 $\pm$ 0.03** ($\uparrow$ 8.37)

Table 2. Results on subtyping tasks with BACC $\pm$ variance (%). The best results are marked in **bold**, with ($\uparrow$ lift from baseline).

Methods	OV-EMT	COLU-KRAS	LU-EGFR	BR-HER2
Gated-AttPool [9,14]	70.45 $\pm$ 1.87	59.41 $\pm$ 0.08	60.34 $\pm$ 0.20	53.29 $\pm$ 0.02
CLAM [15]	69.00 $\pm$ 1.08	62.97 $\pm$ 0.27	61.11 $\pm$ 0.20	55.63 $\pm$ 0.11
FocAtt-MIL [10]	61.71 $\pm$ 0.72	61.74 $\pm$ 0.10	57.32 $\pm$ 0.02	53.56 $\pm$ 0.02
Inter-MIL (ours)	84.86 $\pm$ 0.45 ($\uparrow$ 14.41)	64.50 $\pm$ 0.45 ($\uparrow$ 5.09)	66.04 $\pm$ 0.33 ($\uparrow$ 5.70)	56.69 $\pm$ 0.07 ($\uparrow$ 3.40)
adInter-MIL (ours)	**85.45 $\pm$ 0.48** ($\uparrow$ 15.00)	**65.85 $\pm$ 0.24** ($\uparrow$ 6.44)	**69.56 $\pm$ 0.03** ($\uparrow$ 9.22)	**63.21 $\pm$ 0.03** ($\uparrow$ 9.92)

chosen to tackle the class imbalance. The Adam optimisation with the learning rate 0.0001 is used. We chose a batch size of 4 WSIs for training Gated-AttPool and 128 tiles for the CNN encoder. In addition, we set the following hyper-parameters. Each round consists of 5 epochs for AttPool and 2 epochs of ResNet training. The first round of AttPool training terminates when the loss reaches a threshold $\mathcal{L}_{init}$. We terminate the entire training when the loss converges to a threshold $\mathcal{L}_{final}$. The parameter K in (3) is set to 0.05L and N in (5) is set to 0.2L. The parameters k^1, k^2 and n in (3, 5) are set to 50, 20 and 10, respectively. We select the values of k^2 and n to maintain a reasonable amount of randomness and adversarial training examples. $\gamma^{neg} = 10^{-4} \cdot \gamma$. All experiments are conducted with PyTorch 1.6 on NVIDIA RTX 2080Ti GPUs. More details are available in the source code[1].

Evaluation. The following methods are used for comparison: CNN-MIL [1], AttPool [9], Gated-AttPool [9,14], CLAM [15], and FocAtt-MIL [10]. Gated-AttPool with fixed pretrained CNN encoder is selected as a baseline to provide a direct comparison with our trainable CNN encoder in Module-1. The training sets are selected randomly with no replacement for 10 folds in *OV-EMT* and 5 folds for the other tasks. For each evaluation fold, except for training set samples, the remaining samples are used as the test set. Due to limited amount of training data in *OV-EMT* and *COLU-KRAS*, we do not split the data further as a validation set. In all experiments, we use the last stage of the model for testing. We use the output of Module-1 as the final prediction of the Inter-MIL. The value of $\mathcal{L}_{final}$ is empirically determined based on the performance of the

---

[1] https://github.com/superhy/LCSB-MIL.

baseline model. $\mathcal{L}_{init}$ is set as $\mathcal{L}_{final}+0.15$. The performance is recorded in terms of the average and variance of the area under the receiver operating characteristic curve (AUC) and balanced accuracy (BACC) across multiple test folds.

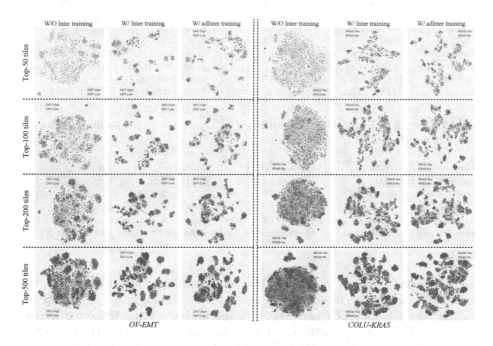

Fig. 3. The t-SNE [16] distribution maps of ResNet embeddings. The embeddings are generated from Top-k ($k = 50, 100, 200, 500$) tiles of all test WSIs in *OV-EMT* and *COLU-KRAS* tasks respectively. For each task, left: without Inter-MIL fine-tuning, mid: with basic Inter-MIL fine-tuning, right: with adversarial Inter-MIL fine-tuning.

Subtyping Performance. The results in Table 1 show that Inter-MIL consistently yields a better performance than comparison approaches across the tasks. The Inter-MIL with adversarial training using negative tiles (adInter-MIL) consistently performs better than Inter-MIL. We hypothesise that the use of negative tiles encourages the model to recognise examples negatively associated with the class, thus increasing the discriminative power of the model. Marked improvement of 12.09% in *OV-EMT* suggests the advantage of adInter-MIL over Inter-MIL in case of limited amount of training data. Interestingly, Inter-MIL shows an average of 5.63% improvement over the baseline when identifying KRAS mutation in both colon and lung tissues. This suggests that Inter-MIL is able to identify morphological signature associated with KRAS mutation agnostic to the tissue types. In addition, Inter-MIL shows to be resilient to the class imbalance issue in both *LU-EGFR* and *BR-HER2* tasks.

We also test the performance when removing the supplementary tiles from tile-level feature optimisation (without S^{sup}). Although AUCs decrease more or less on all 4 tasks, they are still higher than other comparison methods.

Table 2 lists the results of the main participating comparison methods on the BACC metric. Inter-MIL and adIner-MIL also achieve the best performance.

Visualisation. We give insightful interpretation to the proposed method with visualisation. Figure 3 shows the ResNet feature distribution for the k tiles with the highest attention values. In contrast to the mixed distribution generated by the fixed pretrained ResNet backbone, Inter-MIL generates tile features that are well separated between positive and negative classes. Moreover, such a separation is generalised to a higher number of tiles despite the fact that we only used 70 tiles per WSI in fine-tuning the backbone.

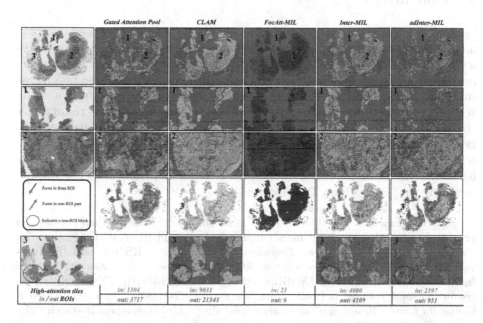

Fig. 4. Visualisation of attention on an example WSI from TCGA-OV dataset. The pathologist annotates the ROIs of the tumour with a red contour. ╱ and ╱ indicate magnified areas on 2 ROIs and a region of spurious attention assignments, respectively. **Columns left to right:** originals, Gated-AttPool, CLAM, FocAtt-MIL, Inter-MIL and adInter-MIL heatmaps. **Rows top to bottom:** entire WSI with blue-green-yellow-red colour map (low to high attention); Magnified areas 1 and 2; entire WSI with blue-white-red colour map (low to high attention); Magnified area 3. **Bottom:** the number of high-attention tiles falling inside/outside the ROIs. (Color figure online)

Figure 4 presents a comparison of attention heatmaps on an example WSI. Red contours demarcate tumour regions annotated by an expert pathologist. FocAtt generates a very sparse focal attention that consists of only a few tiles with high attention scores. The heatmap generated by Gated-AttPool does not fully match the pathologist's opinion. For instance, the region of high attention in the Magnified area 1 is consistent with the pathologist's annotation while it focuses on the exact opposite in Magnified area 2. CLAM attends to most areas covering spurious artefacts. The Magnified area 3 shows an example of a region corresponding to a staining artefact assigned by CLAM with high attention. On the opposite, Inter-MIL and adInter-MIL produce attention maps that are concordant with pathologist's annotation. Moreover, adInter-MIL's attention is less accentuated in some regions annotated by the pathologist, and it simultaneously reduces the attention on the regions outside the pathologist's Regions of Interest (ROIs).

4   Conclusion

We propose a self-interactive MIL framework, a weakly-supervised morpho-molecular subtyping approach that simultaneously optimises fine-grained tile-level features and slide-level global features. In the case of severely limited training data, the tile-level features that are optimal for specific subtyping task allows Inter-MIL to be more data efficient. Improved performance on 4 subtyping tasks suggests the effectiveness of the proposed method. The visualisation results show the high concordance between the model's attention and pathologist's annotation. Visualisation of the tile-level feature distribution also shows better discriminative representations. The feature aggregation tool in Module-1 and the backbone encoder in Module-2 can be flexibly replaced by any model of interest, including the latest Vision Transformer [4].

Acknowledgements. We thank Stefano Malacrino and Nasullah Khalid Alham for providing technical support. Financial support: YU, CV and JR - National Institute for Health Research (NIHR) Oxford Biomedical Research Centre; KS, CV, and JR - Innovate UK funded PathLAKE consortium; KG - Clinical Lectureship from the National Institute for Health Research (NIHR, grant no. CL-2017-13-001); RW - EPSRC Centre for Doctoral Training in Health Data Science (EP/S02428X/1) and Oxford CRUK Centre for Cancer Research. Computation used the Oxford Biomedical Research Computing (BMRC) facility.

References

1. Campanella, G., et al.: Clinical-grade computational pathology using weakly supervised deep learning on whole slide images. Nat. Med. **25**(8), 1301–1309 (2019)
2. Ciga, O., Xu, T., Martel, A.L.: Self supervised contrastive learning for digital histopathology. Mach. Learn. Appl. **7**, 100198 (2022)
3. Deng, J., Dong, W., Socher, R., Li, L.J., Li, K., Fei-Fei, L.: Imagenet: a large-scale hierarchical image database. In: 2009 IEEE Conference on Computer Vision and Pattern Recognition, pp. 248–255 (2009)
4. Dosovitskiy, A., et al.: An image is worth 16x16 words: transformers for image recognition at scale. In: International Conference on Learning Representations (2020)
5. Ganin, Y., et al.: Domain-adversarial training of neural networks. J. Mach. Learn. Res. **17**(1), 2096–2300 (2016)

6. Hashimoto, N., et al.: Multi-scale domain-adversarial multiple-instance CNN for cancer subtype classification with unannotated histopathological images. In: Proceedings of the IEEE/CVF Conference on Computer Vision and Pattern Recognition, pp. 3852–3861 (2020)
7. Hu, Z., et al.: The repertoire of serous ovarian cancer non-genetic heterogeneity revealed by single-cell sequencing of normal fallopian tube epithelial cells. Cancer Cell **37**(2), 226–242 (2020)
8. Hu, Z., et al.: The oxford classic links epithelial-to-mesenchymal transition to immunosuppression in poor prognosis ovarian cancers. Clin. Cancer Res. **27**(5), 1570–1579 (2021)
9. Ilse, M., Tomczak, J., Welling, M.: Attention-based deep multiple instance learning. In: International Conference on Machine Learning, pp. 2127–2136. PMLR (2018)
10. Kalra, S., et al.: Pay attention with focus: a novel learning scheme for classification of whole slide images. In: de Bruijne, M., et al. (eds.) MICCAI 2021. LNCS, vol. 12908, pp. 350–359. Springer, Cham (2021). https://doi.org/10.1007/978-3-030-87237-3_34
11. Li, B., Li, Y., Eliceiri, K.W.: Dual-stream multiple instance learning network for whole slide image classification with self-supervised contrastive learning. In: Proceedings of the IEEE/CVF Conference on Computer Vision and Pattern Recognition, pp. 14318–14328 (2021)
12. Li, H., et al.: DT-MIL: deformable transformer for multi-instance learning on histopathological image. In: de Bruijne, M., et al. (eds.) MICCAI 2021. LNCS, vol. 12908, pp. 206–216. Springer, Cham (2021). https://doi.org/10.1007/978-3-030-87237-3_20
13. Li, J., et al.: A multi-resolution model for histopathology image classification and localization with multiple instance learning. Comput. Biol. Med. **131**, 104253 (2021)
14. Lu, M.Y., et al.: Ai-based pathology predicts origins for cancers of unknown primary. Nature **594**(7861), 106–110 (2021)
15. Lu, M.Y., Williamson, D.F., Chen, T.Y., Chen, R.J., Barbieri, M., Mahmood, F.: Data-efficient and weakly supervised computational pathology on whole-slide images. Nat. Biomed. Eng. **5**(6), 555–570 (2021)
16. Van der Maaten, L., Hinton, G.: Visualizing data using t-sne. J. Mach. Learn. Res. **9**(11) (2008)
17. Selvaraju, R.R., Cogswell, M., Das, A., Vedantam, R., Parikh, D., Batra, D.: Grad-cam: visual explanations from deep networks via gradient-based localization. In: Proceedings of the IEEE International Conference on Computer Vision, pp. 618–626 (2017)
18. Shao, Z., et al.: Transmil: transformer based correlated multiple instance learning for whole slide image classification. Adv. Neural Inf. Process. Syst. **34** (2021)
19. Sirinukunwattana, K., et al.: Image-based consensus molecular subtype (imCMS) classification of colorectal cancer using deep learning. Gut **70**(3), 544–554 (2021)
20. Tomczak, K., Czerwińska, P., Wiznerowicz, M.: The cancer genome atlas (TCGA): an immeasurable source of knowledge. Contemp. Oncol. **19**(1A), A68 (2015)

InsMix: Towards Realistic Generative Data Augmentation for Nuclei Instance Segmentation

Yi Lin$^{(\boxtimes)}$, Zeyu Wang, Kwang-Ting Cheng, and Hao Chen

Department of Computer Science and Engineering,
The Hong Kong University of Science and Technology, Kowloon, Hong Kong
linyi.pk@gmail.com

Abstract. Nuclei Segmentation from histology images is a fundamental task in digital pathology analysis. However, deep-learning-based nuclei segmentation methods often suffer from limited annotations. This paper proposes a realistic data augmentation method for nuclei segmentation, named InsMix, that follows a Copy-Paste-Smooth principle and performs morphology-constrained generative instance augmentation. Specifically, we propose morphology constraints that enable the augmented images to acquire luxuriant information about nuclei while maintaining their morphology characteristics (e.g., geometry and location). To fully exploit the pixel redundancy of the background and improve the model's robustness, we further propose a background perturbation method, which randomly shuffles the background patches without disordering the original nuclei distribution. To achieve contextual consistency between original and template instances, a smooth-GAN is designed with a foreground similarity encoder (FSE) and a triplet loss. We validated the proposed method on two datasets, i.e., Kumar and CPS datasets. Experimental results demonstrate the effectiveness of each component and the superior performance achieved by our method to the state-of-the-art methods. The source code is available at https://github.com/hust-linyi/insmix.

Keywords: Data augmentation · Morphology constraints · Generative

1 Introduction

Nuclei segmentation is a crucial step for the analysis of computational pathology images. Cancer diagnosis and treatment are directly influenced by the distribution and morphology (e.g., size, shape, and location) of the nuclei [7]. Recent advances in deep learning [19,20,27] have led to remarkable success in nuclei instance segmentation tasks. For example, Micro-Net [17] utilized multi-resolutions and a weighted loss function to achieve robustness against the large inter-/intra-variability of the nuclei size. To separate the touching/overlapping nuclei, some

Supplementary Information The online version contains supplementary material available at https://doi.org/10.1007/978-3-031-16434-7_14.

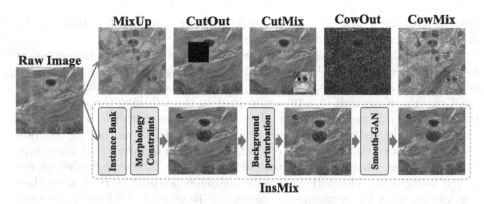

Fig. 1. Illustration of Mix-based data augmentation methods, and our InsMix method.

studies [1–3, 22, 29] incorporate the boundary information of the nuclei into the segmentation task. For example, TAFE [2] aggregated multi-scale information into two separate branches; one for the nuclei boundary and the other for the nuclei content. Some studies [11, 21] proposed to regress the distance map of nuclei to avoid predicting areas with indistinguishable boundaries. Some other methods tried to integrate nuclei detection and segmentation into one single network [28] where the segmentation results are used to refine the nuclei detection.

In spite of these advances in nuclei instance segmentation, one fundamental challenge of the current deep-learning-based methods is a lack of sufficient amount of annotated data for training. Accurate pixel-wise annotation of the nuclei, which requires clinical expertise, is a labor-intensive and time-consuming procedure. Data augmentation is the most straightforward way to overcome this limitation. In addition to the conventional data augmentation methods (e.g., flipping and rotation), several Mix-based methods have been proposed. For instance, as shown in Fig. 1, the MixUp method [26] is a data augmentation method that combines random samples of the input images. CutOut [4] augments an image by randomly masking a rectangular region to zero. CutMix [24] incorporates MixUp and CutOut that randomly crops a patch from one image and places it onto another one. CowOut and CowMix were proposed by French et al. [9] that extends CutOut and CutMix by introducing a random cropping mask.

Copy-Paste [5,6] is another way to combine multiple images' information, which can be viewed as a form of object-level CutMix, where foreground pixels from one image are copied and pasted onto another. The effectiveness of this type of method for the instance segmentation task has been successfully validated. In particular, Ghiasi et al. [10] performed a systematic study of the Copy-Paste method, and achieved state-of-the-art results on COCO instance segmentation [18] and LVIS benchmarks [12]. Nevertheless, there are still some limitations of this method, especially its application to nuclei instance segmentation. First, the Copy-Paste method simply copies instances from one image to another, which may result in some loss of clinical prior information, such as nuclei distribution and location. Second, the Copy-Paste method could result in obvious irregular appearance, due to the significant color variation between the original and template instances caused by staining.

To address these challenges, this paper proposes a novel data augmentation method, named InsMix, which performs Copy-Paste-Smooth, achieving more realistic data augmentation. The main differences of InsMix from the previous Copy-Paste methods [6,8,10] are at least in the following three aspects: 1) Instead of directly performing Copy-Paste, we propose morphology constraints (SSD, i.e., scale, shape, and distance) to maintain nuclei's morphology characteristics (i.e., location, clustering, etc.); 2) In addition to foreground augmentation, we propose a background perturbation method to fully exploit effective use of the background information for data augmentation and in turn strengthen the robustness of the segmentation model; 3) To generate realistic augmented images, we introduce smooth-GAN based on a triplet loss, where we design a foreground similarity encoder (FSE) to encode the original nuclei contextual information into the template nuclear instances. Extensive experiments on Kumar [16] and CPS [28] datasets show the proposed data augmentation methods substantially improve the nuclei instance segmentation performance compared with state-of-the-art techniques.

2   Method

As shown in Fig. 2, our InsMix aims at realistic instance augmentation in a Copy-Paste-Smooth manner. Specifically, the foreground instances are augmented under the morphology constraints, named SSD constraints. Then a background perturbation method is proposed to fully exploit the background information. Last, a smooth-GAN is proposed to eliminate the artifacts of template instances. In the following, we elaborate on each component in detail.

2.1   Foreground Augmentation with Morphology Constraints

As mentioned above, the Copy-Paste [6] method may lack the rationality of the pasted instances [8] by randomly copying the foreground from one image to another. To this end, we propose SSD constraints considering the morphology characteristics of the original instances, as shown in Fig. 2(a). Specifically, for more feasible augmentation, we first construct an instance bank by collecting all the instances from the training set as the templates. In this way, we can flexibly control the number of pasted instances, regarding the number of original instances. Then, for each instance I_o of the original image $\mathcal{I}_O$, and each template instance $I_t \in \mathcal{I}_T$, we apply the SSD constraints $f_{\text{SSD}}(I_o, I_t)$ as follows:

$$f_{\text{SSD}}(I_o, I_t): \ f_{scale}(I_o, I_t) \le \epsilon; \ f_{shape}(I_o, I_t) \le \rho; \ \delta \le f_{dis}(I_o, I_t) \le \gamma, \quad (1)$$

where f_{scale}, f_{shape}, and f_{dis} represent the functions for evaluating the scale difference, shape consistency, and centroid distance, respectively. The parameters ϵ, ρ, δ and γ are determined by cross-validation. Given the binary mask M_o and M_t of I_o and I_t, the function f_{scale} and f_{shape} can be formulated as:

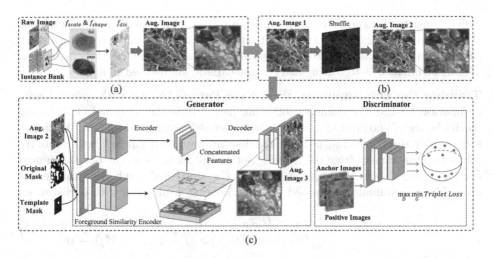

Fig. 2. Illustration of (a) morphology constraints (b) background perturbation, and (c) smooth-GAN.

$$f_{scale}(I_o, I_t) = \frac{\max(|M_o|, |M_t|)}{\min(|M_o|, |M_t|)}, f_{shape}(I_o, I_t) = \frac{|M_o - M_t|}{\max(|M_o|, |M_t|)}, \quad (2)$$

larger f_{scale} and f_{shape} indicate greater scale and larger shape inconsistency, respectively. To ensure that the position of template nuclei follows the original instance distribution, we further restrict the centroid distances of the two masks by δ and γ. By changing δ, we can easily obtain touching/overlapping nuclei instances; and by changing γ, the template instances can locate into the surrounding region of the target instance, avoiding clinically meaningless results.

2.2 Background Perturbation for Robustness Improvement

In practice, a common preprocessing step in nuclei segmentation is to split large pathology image into smaller patches. This may cause ambiguity regarding the sharp edges of the patches. Based on this observation, we introduce the background perturbation method to randomly shuffle the background patches. Specifically, as shown in Fig. 2(b) we first split the background region into 20×20 patches, and then randomly shuffle the patches with the ratio of α (which is empirically set to 0.2). In this way, the nuclei distribution would not be disordered, and the segmentation model would be robust to the distraction of the sharp edges, such as the irregular shape and incomplete texture of nuclei.

2.3 Smooth-GAN for Realistic Instance Augmentation

Due to the various stainings in the training set, there exists an obvious color shift between the template and original instances (as shown in Fig. 1). Thus, we introduce smooth-GAN to generate realistic and smoothed results. As shown in Fig. 2(c), our smooth-GAN adopts the image-to-image translation method [14], which consists of a generator and a discriminator. The generator is to translate the augmented images with a smoother appearance and boundary by borrowing the contextual information from the original instances to the template instances. The discriminator is to distinguish the unrealistic augmented images.

Training the Discriminator. We use the PatchGAN [14] with spectral normalization for the discriminator following [25]. Unlike conventional GAN-based methods, there's no ground-truth for the smoothed augmented images. We therefore employ the triplet loss to train the discriminator. Specifically, we randomly select two raw images from the training set as the anchor and the positive image (i.e., x_a and x_p), and the negative image is the smoothed result from the generator. The discriminator is trained by the following triplet loss with l_1 distance:

$$\mathcal{L}_D = \mathbb{E}_{x \sim P_{\text{ori}}, u \sim P_{\text{aug}}} (0, |D(x_a) - D(x_p)| \\ - |D(x_a) - D(G(u) \circ M + u \circ (1 - M))| + m), \quad (3)$$

where $D(\cdot)$ and $G(\cdot)$ denote the discriminator and generator, respectively. M denotes the binary mask corresponding to the template instance's region where $M_{xy} = 1$ indicates that pixel at $[x, y]$ belongs to the template instance. $\circ$ represents element-wise multiplication. The smoothed result $S(u) = G(u) \circ M + u \circ (1 - M)$ is composed by putting the generated template instance $G(u)$ in the original image while keeping the other region of u. The discriminator is trained to narrow down the perceptional distance between the anchor and positive samples and enlarge the distance between the anchor and negative samples with the margin m (which is empirically set to 1.0 in our experiments).

Training the Generator. The generative network adopts a typical autoencoder network [14]. We employ gated convolution [25] and dilated convolution in the network for a large receptive field [23]. The adversarial loss is defined as:

$$\mathcal{L}_{adv} = \mathbb{E}_{x \sim P_{\text{ori}}, u \sim P_{\text{aug}}}[|D(x_a) - D(S(u))| - |D(x_a) - D(x_p)|], \quad (4)$$

In addition, for maintaining the original image's information, we add the reconstruction loss (i.e., l_1 loss) to the adversarial loss as the final generative loss:

$$\mathcal{L}_G = \mathcal{L}_{adv} + \lambda|u - G(u)|, \quad (5)$$

where λ is the weight parameter, which is empirically set to 10 in our experiment.

Foreground Similarity Encoder (FSE). The generator, however, would collapse that it simply learns to apply background redundancy appearance to template instances' regions. To overcome this problem, we introduce an auxiliary encoder, named foreground similarity encoder (FSE), which borrows the appearance information (e.g., staining) from the original instances to the template instances. We first calculate the feature similarity between the original and template instances, and then integrate the original instance feature into the template feature space. As shown in Fig. 2(b), we first extract the 3×3 patches in the original instances' region. Then for each patch in the template instances' region, we calculate the cosine similarity for the original instance patches in a convolutional way as:

$$S_{i,j} = \frac{f(p_i)^\mathsf{T} s(p_j)}{|f(p_i)| \cdot |f(p_j)|}, i \in I_t, j \in I_o, \tag{6}$$

where $f(p_i)$ and $f(p_j)$ is the feature of the patches in the template and original instance's region, respectively. Then, we replace the template instance feature with the original instance feature, weighted by the normalized similarity as follows:

$$\bar{f}(p_i) = \sum_{j \in \mathcal{I}_A} \mathrm{softmax}(\mathcal{S}_{i,j}) \cdot f(p_j). \tag{7}$$

The obtained similarity encoding $\bar{f}(u)$ is then concatenated with the raw encoder feature as input for the decoder to generate the final augmented image. In this way, the augmented images would achieve global appearance consistency.

3 Experiments

Datasets and Implementation Details. The Kumar dataset [16] contains 30 H&E stained pathology images with a resolution of 1000×1000 pixels. We follow the same dataset splitting criterion as [2] that 16 images for training and 14 images for testing. In the test set, 8 images are from the same organs as the training set (denoted as seen organ), and 6 images are from 3 organs that are not in the training set (unseen organ).

For quantitative evaluation, we use Dice coefficient (Dice) and aggregated Jaccard index (AJI) as the evaluation metrics, which are the most commonly used evaluation metrics in nuclei instance segmentation at the pixel and object level, respectively. Note that this work focus on instance-level data augmentation, thus AJI would be more suitable for this work. During training, we crop 256×256 patches from the raw images. For a fair comparison, instead of the proposed InsMix augmentation, we also apply traditional data augmentation methods for all the compared methods, e.g., randomly scale, shift, rotation, flip, color jittering,

Table 1. Comparison with the state-of-the-art methods on Kumar.

Methods	Dice (%)			AJI (%)		
	Seen	Unseen	All	Seen	Unseen	All
CNN3 [15]	82.26	83.22	82.67	51.54	49.89	50.83
DIST [21]	–	–	–	55.91	56.01	55.95
NB-Net [3]	79.88	80.24	80.03	59.25	53.68	56.86
Mask R-CNN [13]	81.07	82.91	81.86	59.78	55.31	57.86
HoVer-Net [11] (*Res50)	80.60	80.41	80.52	59.35	56.27	58.03
TAFE [2] (*Dense121)	80.81	83.72	82.06	61.51	61.54	61.52
HoVer-Net + InsMix	80.33	81.93	81.02	59.40	57.67	58.66
TAFE + InsMix	**81.18**	**84.40**	**82.56**	**61.98**	**65.07**	**63.31**

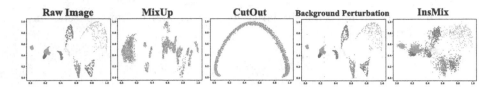

Fig. 3. T-SNE embedding of image patches with different data augmentations. Different colors indicate cropped patches from different images.

Table 2. Comparison with other Mix-based methods on Kumar.

	MixUp [26]	CutOut [4]	CutMix [24]	CowOut [9]	CowMix [9]	InsMix
Dice (%)	81.21	82.01	82.33	82.27	81.80	**82.56**
AJI (%)	61.68	62.29	61.61	62.87	61.19	**63.31**

Table 3. Ablation study on the Kumar dataset, where SSD, s-GAN, BgP denote SSD constraints, smooth-GAN, and background perturbation, respectively.

	Baseline	+ SSD	+BgP	+ SSD + s-GAN	+ SSD+BgP + s-GAN
AJI (%)	61.52	62.08	62.24	62.37	**63.31**

and blurring. We train the model in a total of 300 epochs, using the Adam optimizer with weight decay 10^{-4}. The initial learning rate is set to 10^{-3} with the cosine annealing schedule, resetting in every 50 epochs.

Comparison with SOTA. We compare the proposed method with the state-of-the-art methods [2,11,15,21,29] on the Kumar datasets. For the methods without public codes, we report the results from the original publications for a fair comparison. As depicted in Table 1, promising results in nuclei instance segmentation results are observed using the proposed data augmentation methods. Our InsMix significantly boosts the AJI by 2.23% and 0.63%, compared with TAFE [2] and HoVer-Net [11], respectively. And Our InsMix sightly improves the Dice score by 0.5%. We argue that our InsMix exploits the nuclei knowledge at the instance level, which hence improves the AJI by a large margin.

For comprehensive evaluation, we further compared our InsMix methods with other Mix-based data augmentation methods, including MixUp [26], CutOut [4], CutMix [24], CowOut [9], and CowMix [9]. The results are shown in Table 2. It can be seen that our InsMix outperforms other methods by 0.44%–2.12% in AJI. We believe that the improvement comes from the full exploration of both foreground and background information, without introducing distraction of the data distribution. A more intuitionistic explanation can be found in Fig. 3, where we conduct t-SNE for the augmented images. It can be seen that our InsMix could fill up the low density in data distribution, without introducing undesirable bias (e.g., CutOut) or distractions (e.g., MixUp).

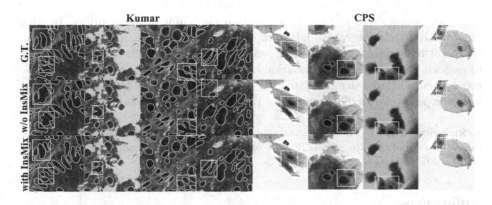

Fig. 4. Instance segmentation results on Kumar and CPS. Rectangles highlight differences among different methods.

Table 4. Comparison with other Mix-based methods on CPS. A 5-fold cross-validation is conducted.

	Baseline	MixUp [26]	CutOut [4]	CutMix [24]	CowOut [9]	CowMix [9]	InsMix
Dice (%)	69.29 ± 4.41	69.83 ± 3.87	69.79 ± 4.16	68.81 ± 3.03	61.91 ± 10.46	69.40 ± 4.30	**70.96** ± 4.59
AJI (%)	49.45 ± 4.44	49.833.82	50.23 ± 4.00	48.48 ± 2.43	39.77 ± 9.98	48.06 ± 4.79	**51.54** ± 3.93

Ablation Study. To validate each component in the InsMix method, we perform an ablation study on Kumar, taking TAFE [2] as the baseline. The results are presented in Table 3. The baseline method achieves an AJI of 61.52%, and the SSD constraints boost the AJI to 62.08%. We believe this is because the SSD constraints could take clinical prior into account to generate more meaningful results regarding the scale, shape, and distribution of the nuclei, which is different from the simple Copy-Paste method. Smooth-GAN could further improve the AJI to 62.37%. The visualization results of the smooth-GAN are shown in Fig. 1. Lastly, with background perturbation, the AJI increases to 63.31%.

Validation on Other Dataset. To evaluate the generality of the proposed method, we experiment on the cervical Pas smear (CPS) image dataset [28]. The dataset contains 82 Pap smear images with the size of 1000×1000 pixels. We adopt NB-Net [3] with ResUNet-34 as the baseline. We perform 5-fold cross-validation to evaluate the effectiveness of the proposed method, compared with baseline and other Mix-based methods. In Table 4, on average 5 folds, the InsMix improves the performance of the baseline method by 1.67% in Dice and 2.09% in AJI, respectively. Our InsMix also outperforms other Mix-based methods.

4   Conclusion

In this paper, we propose a novel data augmentation method, named InsMix, for nuclei instance segmentation. Our InsMix applies morphology constraints (SSD, i.e., scale, shape, and distance) to maintain the clinical nuclei priors. Besides foreground augmentation, we also propose background perturbation to exploit the pixel redundancy of the background. Further, a smooth-GAN is proposed to uniform the contextual information between the original and template nuclei. Experimental results demonstrated the effectiveness of each component and the superior performance of our model to the state-of-the-art methods.

Acknowledgments. This work was supported by Beijing Institute of Collaborative Innovation Funding (No. BICI22EG01) and HKSAR RGC General Research Fund (GRF) #16203319.

References

1. Chen, H., Qi, X., Yu, L., Dou, Q., Qin, J., Heng, P.A.: DCAN: deep contour-aware networks for object instance segmentation from histology images. Med. Image Anal. **36**, 135–146 (2017)
2. Chen, S., Ding, C., Tao, D.: Boundary-assisted region proposal networks for nucleus segmentation. In: Martel, A.L., et al. (eds.) MICCAI 2020. LNCS, vol. 12265, pp. 279–288. Springer, Cham (2020). https://doi.org/10.1007/978-3-030-59722-1_27
3. Cui, Y., Zhang, G., Liu, Z., Xiong, Z., Hu, J.: A deep learning algorithm for one-step contour aware nuclei segmentation of histopathology images. Med. Biol. Eng. Comput. **57**(9), 2027–2043 (2019). https://doi.org/10.1007/s11517-019-02008-8
4. DeVries, T., Taylor, G.W.: Improved regularization of convolutional neural networks with cutout. arXiv preprint arXiv:1708.04552 (2017)
5. Dvornik, N., Mairal, J., Schmid, C.: Modeling visual context is key to augmenting object detection datasets. In: Proceedings of the European Conference on Computer Vision, pp. 364–380 (2018)
6. Dwibedi, D., Misra, I., Hebert, M.: Cut, paste and learn: surprisingly easy synthesis for instance detection. In: Proceedings of the IEEE/CVF International Conference on Computer Vision, pp. 1301–1310 (2017)
7. Elmore, J.G., et al.: Diagnostic concordance among pathologists interpreting breast biopsy specimens. JAMA **313**(11), 1122–1132 (2015)
8. Fang, H.S., Sun, J., Wang, R., Gou, M., Li, Y.L., Lu, C.: InstaBoost: Boosting instance segmentation via probability map guided copy-pasting. In: Proceedings of the IEEE/CVF International Conference on Computer Vision, pp. 682–691 (2019)
9. French, G., Laine, S., Aila, T., Mackiewicz, M.: Semi-supervised semantic segmentation needs strong, varied perturbations. In: British Machine Vision Conference (2019)
10. Ghiasi, G., et al.: Simple copy-paste is a strong data augmentation method for instance segmentation. In: Proceedings of the IEEE/CVF Conference on Computer Vision and Pattern Recognition, pp. 2918–2928 (2021)
11. Graham, S., et al.: HoVer-Net: Simultaneous segmentation and classification of nuclei in multi-tissue histology images. Med. Image Anal. **58**, 101563 (2019)
12. Gupta, A., Dollar, P., Girshick, R.: LVIS: A dataset for large vocabulary instance segmentation. In: Proceedings of the IEEE/CVF Conference on Computer Vision and Pattern Recognition, pp. 5356–5364 (2019)
13. He, K., Gkioxari, G., Dollár, P., Girshick, R.: Mask r-cnn. In: Proceedings of the IEEE/CVF International Conference on Computer Vision, pp. 2961–2969 (2017)

14. Isola, P., Zhu, J.Y., Zhou, T., Efros, A.A.: Image-to-image translation with conditional adversarial networks. Proceedings of the IEEE/CVF Conference on Computer Vision and Pattern Recognition (2017)
15. Kumar, N., et al.: A multi-organ nucleus segmentation challenge. IEEE Trans. Med. Imaging **39**(5), 1380–1391 (2019)
16. Kumar, N., Verma, R., Sharma, S., Bhargava, S., Vahadane, A., Sethi, A.: A dataset and a technique for generalized nuclear segmentation for computational pathology. IEEE Trans. Med. Imaging **36**(7), 1550–1560 (2017)
17. Liao, M., et al.: Automatic segmentation for cell images based on bottleneck detection and ellipse fitting. Neurocomputing **173**, 615–622 (2016)
18. Lin, T.-Y.: Microsoft COCO: common objects in context. In: Fleet, D., Pajdla, T., Schiele, B., Tuytelaars, T. (eds.) ECCV 2014. LNCS, vol. 8693, pp. 740–755. Springer, Cham (2014). https://doi.org/10.1007/978-3-319-10602-1_48
19. Lin, Y., et al.: Label propagation for annotation-efficient nuclei segmentation from pathology images. arXiv preprint arXiv:2202.08195 (2022)
20. Litjens, G., et al.: A survey on deep learning in medical image analysis. Med. Image Anal. **42**, 60–88 (2017)
21. Naylor, P., Laé, M., Reyal, F., Walter, T.: Segmentation of nuclei in histopathology images by deep regression of the distance map. IEEE Trans. Med. Imaging **38**(2), 448–459 (2018)
22. Xie, X., Chen, J., Li, Y., Shen, L., Ma, K., Zheng, Y.: Instance-aware self-supervised learning for nuclei segmentation. In: Martel, A.L., et al. (eds.) MICCAI 2020. LNCS, vol. 12265, pp. 341–350. Springer, Cham (2020). https://doi.org/10.1007/978-3-030-59722-1_33
23. Yu, J., Lin, Z., Yang, J., Shen, X., Lu, X., Huang, T.S.: Generative image inpainting with contextual attention. In: Proceedings of the IEEE/CVF Conference on Computer Vision and Pattern Recognition, pp. 5505–5514 (2018)
24. Yun, S., Han, D., Oh, S.J., Chun, S., Choe, J., Yoo, Y.: Cutmix: regularization strategy to train strong classifiers with localizable features. In: Proceedings of the IEEE/CVF International Conference on Computer Vision, pp. 6023–6032 (2019)
25. Zeng, Y., Lin, Z., Lu, H., Patel, V.M.: CR-Fill: Generative image inpainting with auxiliary contextual reconstruction. In: Proceedings of the IEEE/CVF International Conference on Computer Vision, pp. 14164–14173 (2021)
26. Zhang, H., Cisse, M., Dauphin, Y.N., Lopez-Paz, D.: Mixup: Beyond empirical risk minimization. In: International Conference on Learning Representations (2018)
27. Zhou, Y., Chen, H., Lin, H., Heng, P.-A.: Deep semi-supervised knowledge distillation for overlapping cervical cell instance segmentation. In: Martel, A.L., et al. (eds.) MICCAI 2020. LNCS, vol. 12261, pp. 521–531. Springer, Cham (2020). https://doi.org/10.1007/978-3-030-59710-8_51
28. Zhou, Y., Chen, H., Xu, J., Dou, Q., Heng, P.-A.: IRNet: Instance relation network for overlapping cervical cell segmentation. In: MICCAI 2019. LNCS, vol. 11764, pp. 640–648. Springer, Cham (2019). https://doi.org/10.1007/978-3-030-32239-7_71
29. Zhou, Y., Onder, O.F., Dou, Q., Tsougenis, E., Chen, H., Heng, P.-A.: CIA-Net: Robust nuclei instance segmentation with contour-aware information aggregation. In: Chung, A.C.S., Gee, J.C., Yushkevich, P.A., Bao, S. (eds.) IPMI 2019. LNCS, vol. 11492, pp. 682–693. Springer, Cham (2019). https://doi.org/10.1007/978-3-030-20351-1_53

Improved Domain Generalization for Cell Detection in Histopathology Images via Test-Time Stain Augmentation

Chundan Xu, Ziqi Wen, Zhiwen Liu[✉], and Chuyang Ye[✉]

School of Integrated Circuits and Electronics, Beijing Institute of Technology,
Beijing, China
{zwliu,chuyang.ye}@bit.edu.cn

Abstract. Automated cell detection in histopathology images can provide a valuable tool for cancer diagnosis and prognosis, and cell detectors based on deep learning have achieved promising detection performance. However, the stain color variation of histopathology images acquired at different sites can deteriorate the performance of cell detection, where a cell detector trained on a source dataset may not perform well on a different target dataset. Existing methods that address this domain generalization problem perform stain normalization or augmentation during network training. However, such stain transformation performed during network training may still not be optimally representative of the test images from the target domain. Therefore, in this work, given a cell detector that may be trained with or without consideration of domain generalization, we seek to improve domain generalization for cell detection in histopathology images via test-time stain augmentation. Specifically, a histopathology image can be decomposed into the stain color matrix and stain density map, and we transform the test images by mixing their stain color with that of the source domain, so that the mixed images may better resemble the source images or their stain-transformed versions used for training. Since it is difficult to determine the optimal amount of the mixing, we choose to generate a number of transformed test images where the stain color mixing varies. The generated images are fed into the given detector, and the outputs are fused with a robust strategy that suppresses improper stain color mixing. The proposed method was validated on a publicly available dataset that comprises histopathology images acquired at different sites, and the results show that our method can effectively improve the generalization of cell detectors to new domains.

Keywords: Cell detection · Domain generalization · Test-time stain augmentation

1 Introduction

Automated cell detection in histopathology images can support pathologists in disease diagnosis, grading, and quantification, and methods based on deep

C. Xu and Z. Wen—Equal contribution.

© The Author(s), under exclusive license to Springer Nature Switzerland AG 2022
L. Wang et al. (Eds.): MICCAI 2022, LNCS 13432, pp. 150–159, 2022.
https://doi.org/10.1007/978-3-031-16434-7_15

learning have achieved promising cell detection performance [16]. However, histopathology images acquired at different sites may have different appearances due to stain color variation, and the detection model trained on a source dataset may not generalize well to a different target dataset [19]. It is necessary that this domain generalization problem is properly addressed so that cell detectors based on deep learning can be applied in real-world applications.

Previous work has addressed the domain generalization problem for histopathology image analysis by transforming the stain of the training images in the source domain during network training, so that the transformed training images are more representative of the test images in the target domain in terms of the stain color [4]. The stain transformation can be performed with stain normalization, where the stain of the source images is matched to the target domain. For example, the mean and standard deviation in the color space can be used for the normalization [12]. In [10] stain vectors are estimated and color deconvolution is performed to normalize the stain. In [20] histopathology images are decomposed into the stain color matrix and stain density map. Then, stain color variation is reduced by matching the stain color matrix of the source domain to the target domain with structure-preserving color normalization, and this method has achieved excellent stain normalization performance [14]. The stain transformation can also be achieved via stain augmentation, where a wide range of stain is generated for the training images and thus the stain of the target domain can be better represented by the training data. The augmentation can be performed by adjusting image brightness, hue, contrast, and saturation [9] or by perturbing the color channels and image pixels [2,18]. More recently, a more advanced approach stain mix-up is developed, where the stain color matrix of the source images is randomly mixed with that of the target images for stain augmentation [4].

Although the stain transformation applied to source images during network training can improve the generalization of the trained cell detector to a different domain, the transformed source images may still not be optimally representative of the target images, and we hypothesize that stain transformation for target images at test time may bring further benefits. Therefore, in this work, given a cell detector trained with or without consideration of domain generalization, we explore the use of test-time stain augmentation for the domain generalization problem. Since a histopathology image can be decomposed into the stain color matrix and stain density map, we choose to perform test-time stain augmentation by mixing the stain color of the target images with that of the source domain [4]. As it is difficult to determine the optimal amount of the contribution of each domain in the mixing, we propose to generate a number of different images with different mixing amounts. These augmented images are all fed into the given detection model, and their predictions are fused to obtain the final detection result with a robust averaging method that is less likely to be affected by improperly augmented stains. Since our method performs stain augmentation only at test time, it does not require retraining of the detection model. To validate the proposed method, experiments were performed on a publicly available dataset [21] for mitosis detection, which comprises histopathology images acquired at different centers. The results show that our method improves domain generalization for cell detection in histopathology images.

2   Method

2.1   Problem Formulation

Suppose we are given a set $\mathcal{I}^{\mathrm{s}} = \{I_i^{\mathrm{s}}\}_{i=1}^{N_{\mathrm{s}}}$ of histopathology images that are annotated with the cells of interest from a source dataset, where I_i^{s} is the i-th annotated image in the source dataset and N_{s} is the total number of these images. A cell detection model $\mathcal{M}$ based on deep learning can be trained with $\mathcal{I}^{\mathrm{s}}$ and applied to other test histopathology images without annotations for automated cell detection. However, in practice we may be interested in performing cell detection on a set $\mathcal{I}^{\mathrm{t}} = \{I_j^{\mathrm{t}}\}_{j=1}^{N_{\mathrm{t}}}$ of histopathology images from a different target dataset acquired at a different site, where I_j^{t} represents the j-th target image and N_{t} is the total number of target images. Due to the stain color variation at different sites, the appearance of the images in the target dataset can be different from that of the source images. In this scenario, the domain shift between the source and target datasets can degrade the cell detection performance, and the generalization of the cell detector to the target domain should be improved.

To address this problem, existing methods propose to apply stain transformation to the source training images [4]. For example, stain normalization [20] can be applied to $\mathcal{I}^{\mathrm{s}}$ during network training, so that the normalized images are more similar to $\mathcal{I}^{\mathrm{t}}$ in terms of the stain color. Stain augmentation [4] can also be applied to $\mathcal{I}^{\mathrm{s}}$, so that the augmented images with different stain colors are used for training, and it is likely that the stain of $\mathcal{I}^{\mathrm{t}}$ is better represented in network training.

2.2   Test-Time Stain Augmentation for Improved Domain Generalization

Although the stain transformation for source images applied during network training can reduce the domain shift between the training and test images, it may still not be optimal for the images in the target domain, because their stain may not be perfectly represented by the transformed source images. Therefore, we further explore the domain generalization problem and propose to transform the target images at test time, so that the transformed target images are better represented by the source images or their transformed versions used for training. In other words, given the detection model $\mathcal{M}$ trained with $\mathcal{I}^{\mathrm{s}}$ or its transformed versions, we only transform $\mathcal{I}^{\mathrm{t}}$ and feed the transformed images to $\mathcal{M}$ to obtain the detection results without retraining the detection model.

When $\mathcal{M}$ is trained with the original source images, its optimal domain—the domain on which $\mathcal{M}$ works best—is the source domain itself; if $\mathcal{M}$ is trained with transformed source images to improve the generalization to the target domain, then we assume that its optimal domain is between the source and target domains because of imperfect stain transformation during network training. In either case, $\mathcal{I}^t$ should be transformed towards the source domain.

Motivated by [20] and [4], we transform the target images based on their stain color matrices, which can be computed as follows. According to [1], a histopathology image—which is an RGB image and usually stained with hematoxylin and eosin—can be expressed as

$$I = I_0 \exp(-WH), \tag{1}$$

where $I \in \mathbb{R}^{3 \times n}$ represents the histopathology image with three color channels and n pixels, I_0 is the illuminating light intensity on the sample that is equal to 255 for 8-bit images, $W \in \mathbb{R}^{3 \times r}$ is the stain color matrix that determines the color appearance of the image with r representing the number of stains, and $H \in \mathbb{R}^{r \times n}$ is the stain density map. Equivalently, we have

$$V = \log \frac{I_0}{I} = WH, \tag{2}$$

where V is the relative optical density. Thus, given a histopathology image I, we can first obtain the relative optical density V and then separate its stain color matrix W and stain density map H. In this work, the separation is performed with sparse non-negative matrix factorization as in [20].

For a target image I_j^t that can be decomposed into the stain color matrix W_j^t and stain density map H_j^t, its transformation towards the source domain is achieved by mixing W_j^t with the stain color information from the source domain:

$$\tilde{W}_j^t = (1 - \alpha)W^s + \alpha W_j^t \quad \text{and} \quad \tilde{I}_j^t = I_0 \exp(-\tilde{W}_j^t H_j^t), \tag{3}$$

where $\tilde{W}_j^t$ and $\tilde{I}_j^t$ are the mixed stain color matrix and the transformed target image, respectively, W^s is a stain color matrix that is representative of the source domain, and $\alpha \in [0,1]$ determines the amount of the stain color information of I_j^t that is preserved in the transformed image. A smaller or greater α leads to a transformed image that is closer to the source or target domain, respectively. The designs of W^s and α are introduced below.

To determine W^s, we first compute the stain color matrix W_i^s of each source image I_i^s and obtain the mean color matrix W_{mean}^s as

$$W_{\text{mean}}^s = \frac{1}{N_s} \sum_{i=1}^{N_s} W_i^s. \tag{4}$$

Then, W^s is selected as the stain color matrix of the source image that is closest to W_{mean}^s in terms of the Mahalanobis distance $M(\cdot, \cdot)$:

$$W^s = \underset{W_i^s}{\arg\min}\, M(W_{\text{mean}}^s, W_i^s). \tag{5}$$

Since it is difficult to determine the value of α that corresponds to the optimal domain of $\mathcal{M}$, for each I_j^t various values of α ranging from zero to one are used to generate a set of transformed images, the domains of which are between (and include) the source and target domains, and it is likely that one or some transformed images are close to the optimal domain of $\mathcal{M}$. The transformation of the target images achieved with multiple values of α can be interpreted as test-time stain augmentation, and all the augmented images are fed into $\mathcal{M}$ to produce multiple predictions. Then, these predictions are fused to obtain the final detection result, where we emphasize the predictions associated with the augmented images that are possibly close to the optimal domain of $\mathcal{M}$ and suppress the other predictions. The fusion strategy is described next in Sect. 2.3.

Note that the computation of $\tilde{W}_j^t$ in Eq. (3) appears similar to the stain mixing in [4], but they are different in the following aspects. First, our framework applies stain transformation to the target images at test time, whereas in [4] the mixing is performed for the source images during network training. This also suggests that the proposed method can be integrated with [4], further matching test images to the optimal domain of the trained detector at test time. Second, the mixing in [4] involves all source images, whereas our method only selects the most representative source image in the transformation. The selection of the single source image can alleviate the problem of privacy concerns, where only a small part of the information in the source dataset needs to be accessed directly.

Also, the motivation of our method is different from existing *test-time augmentation* (TTA) methods. We generate multiple samples with different stain augmentation because the optimal stain transformation is unknown, and we need to identify the transformation that is potentially useful. Existing TTA methods are not suitable for our task because their operations are still in the native color domain.

2.3   Fusion of Augmented Detection Results

For each I_j^t, we use N different values of α to produce N augmented images. Thus, there are N detection results given by $\mathcal{M}$ that need to be fused. In this work, we consider modern object detectors, e.g., Faster R-CNN [13], where the detection results are represented by bounding boxes and the confidence of the boxes belonging to each category. We first group the detected cells in the N augmented images that represent the same cell with the grouping method in [3], where cells with high *Intersection over Union* (IoU) with each other are grouped. This grouping establishes the correspondence between the detected cells in the N augmented images, and the detected cells in the same group can be fused.

Since a wide range of α is used in the stain augmentation, there can be augmented images for which the detection model $\mathcal{M}$ performs poorly. Therefore, instead of directly fusing all cells (N at most) in each group, we propose a more robust fusion strategy by selecting a subset of the detected cells. Based on the assumption that the detection model tends to give higher confidence for images that better match its optimal domain, for each group the detected cells with the K ($K < N$) highest confidence scores are preserved. We denote the predicted location of the k-th preserved detected cell in each group by v_k, and its confidence vector is denoted by c_k. Then, the K preserved detected cells in the same group are fused as

$$v = \frac{1}{K} \sum_{k=1}^{K} v_k \quad \text{and} \quad c = \frac{1}{K} \sum_{k=1}^{K} c_k, \tag{6}$$

where v represents the location of the fused cell and c is the confidence vector indicating its class. Note that for different regions in the same image, the optimal stain transformation could be different. Thus, the detected cells preserved in different groups are not necessarily all associated with the same values of α.

2.4 Implementation Details

The proposed method is agnostic to the detection model, which can be trained with or without consideration of domain generalization, as long as the detection model produces bounding boxes and confidence like modern object detectors [13]. In this work, the set of the values of α is $\{0, 0.2, 0.4, 0.6, 0.8, 1\}$, leading to $N = 6$. Note that when $\alpha = 1$, no information in the source domain is used, and the transformed target image is simply the image reconstructed with the stain color and stain density of the original target image. Thus, in this case we use the original target image for detection instead of actually performing the reconstruction with $\alpha = 1$. We set $K = N/2$ to keep half of the predictions in the fusion.

The detection result on each augmented test image is processed with *non-maximum suppression* (NMS) [11] to remove duplicate detected cells before fusion. In the fused detection result, we keep the detected cells with a confidence score greater than 0.5 and apply NMS again to avoid duplicate detected cells.

3 Results

3.1 Data Description and Experimental Settings

We used the first auxiliary dataset provided by the TUPAC16 challenge [21] for evaluation. The dataset is publicly available[1] and aims to detect mitosis in breast cancer cells. The histopathology images in the dataset were collected from 73 cases at three centers, and mitosis annotations are provided for these cases.

The first 23 cases are from one center [23], and there are 606 images associated with them. The image size is 2000×2000. For convenience, we refer to these images as domain A, and they were used as the source dataset to train the cell detector. The remaining 50 cases are from two different centers [22], where 25 cases (cases 24–48) were collected at one center and the other 25 cases (cases 49–73) were collected at another center. Each of these 50 cases is associated with an image, the size of which is 5657×5657. We refer to the images associated with cases 24–48 and 49–73 as domain B and domain C, respectively, and they were used as two separate test sets (target domains) to evaluate the performance

---

[1] https://tupac.grand-challenge.org/.

of domain generalization. Since the original image size is large, we cropped all the images from the three centers into 500×500 patches.

Because in practice the cell detection model at hand may be trained on the source domain either with or without the consideration of domain generalization, we considered several possibilities for the integration of the proposed method with a trained cell detector. First, the detection model was trained without considering domain generalization, where the original images of domain A were used for network training. For convenience, this model is referred to as the baseline model. Second, the detection model was trained with stain normalization, where for demonstration the Vahadane normalization [20], which is one of the state-of-the-art stain normalization methods, was used. Third, the detection model was trained with stain augmentation, where the recently developed stain mix-up approach [4] was used.

For all cell detection models considered in the experiments, the Faster R-CNN [13] with FPN [7] and ResNet50 [6] implemented in MMDetection[2] was used as the backbone detection network, which is a popular choice for cell detection [17,24]. The weights of the Faster R-CNN had been pretrained on COCO [8] for a better initialization. To ensure training convergence, for each cell detection model 24 epochs were used for training. The other training configurations are set according to the default configurations of MMDetection.

3.2   Evaluation of Cell Detection Results

For convenience, the proposed test-time stain augmentation method is referred to as TTSA. Examples of detection results on test images are shown in Fig. 1, together with the annotation for reference. Here, we show the results of the three models described in Sect. 3.1 achieved with or without TTSA, and the results are shown for both domain B and domain C. In the given examples, when TTSA is applied, the mitosis is better detected or the false positive is reduced.

Next, we quantitatively compared the detection performance achieved with and without TTSA. We computed two typical evaluation metrics on the test images for each target domain. They are the AP_{50} (average precision computed for recall values over 0 to 1 at an IoU threshold of 50%) and the F1-score. Both metrics are commonly used for evaluating the performance of object detection [4, 5,15]. The results for each detection model and each target domain, as well as the average results of the two target domains, are shown in Table 1. In all cases, the use of TTSA improves AP_{50}; the use of TTSA improves F1-score in most cases, except for stain mix-up where the F1-score achieved with or without TTSA is comparable. The results of AP_{50} and F1-score together indicate that TTSA is beneficial to domain generalization for cell detection in histopathology images.

Finally, we investigated the necessity of using multiple values of α in TTSA, as well as the benefit of the proposed fusion strategy. To this end, we summarized the AP_{50} achieved with each individual α in TTSA for each target domain and each detection model, and the results are shown in Table 2. It can be seen that for

---

[2] https://github.com/open-mmlab/mmdetection.

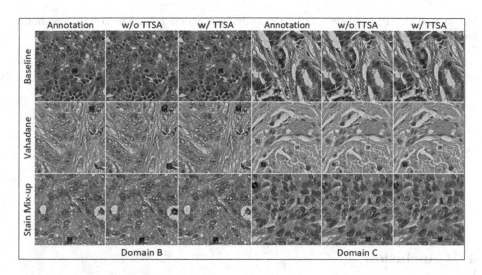

Fig. 1. Examples of detection results achieved with or without the proposed TTSA method on test images of domain B and domain C. The annotation is also shown for reference.

Table 1. The AP_{50} and F1-score achieved with or without the proposed TTSA. The results are shown for domain B and domain C with different detection models. The means of the results of the two domains are also listed. The results that are improved with TTSA are highlighted in bold.

Model	TTSA	Domain B		Domain C		Mean	
		AP_{50}	F1-score	AP_{50}	F1-score	AP_{50}	F1-score
Baseline	w/o	0.655	0.635	0.692	0.690	0.673	0.663
	w/	**0.745**	**0.718**	**0.716**	**0.692**	**0.730**	**0.705**
Vahadane	w/o	0.723	0.672	0.717	0.630	0.720	0.651
	w/	**0.759**	**0.723**	**0.739**	**0.663**	**0.749**	**0.693**
Stain Mix-up	w/o	0.704	0.717	0.733	0.682	0.718	0.700
	w/	**0.766**	0.710	**0.754**	**0.690**	**0.760**	0.700

images acquired at different sites and for different detection models, the optimal α can be different. Thus, it is difficult to predetermine a single best value of α. After we fuse the detection results achieved with individual values of α, the detection performance is better than the individual performance (with only one exception), which demonstrates the benefit of the fusion.

Table 2. The AP_{50} achieved with each individual α in TTSA. The results are shown for each target domain and each detection model. The results achieved with TTSA are listed again for comparison and highlighted in bold.

Domain	Model	α						TTSA
		0	0.2	0.4	0.6	0.8	1	
B	Baseline	0.742	0.714	0.688	0.667	0.640	0.655	**0.745**
	Vahadane	0.767	0.754	0.746	0.734	0.722	0.723	**0.759**
	Stain Mix-up	0.760	0.748	0.753	0.734	0.731	0.704	**0.766**
C	Baseline	0.700	0.684	0.666	0.653	0.628	0.692	**0.716**
	Vahadane	0.734	0.736	0.733	0.730	0.728	0.717	**0.739**
	Stain Mix-up	0.743	0.746	0.749	0.750	0.747	0.733	**0.754**

4   Conclusion

We have proposed a test-time stain augmentation method that improves domain generalization for cell detection in histopathology images. Multiple stain augmentations are performed for the images in the target domain at test time via stain color mixing with the source domain, and the predictions are fused with a robust averaging strategy. The experimental results on a public dataset show that our method improves the generalization of cell detectors to new domains.

References

1. Beer, A., Beer, P.: Determination of the absorption of red light in colored liquids. Annalen der Physik und Chemie **86**(5), 78–88 (1852)
2. Bug, D.: Context-based normalization of histological stains using deep convolutional features. In: Cardoso, M.J., et al. (eds.) DLMIA/ML-CDS -2017. LNCS, vol. 10553, pp. 135–142. Springer, Cham (2017). https://doi.org/10.1007/978-3-319-67558-9_16
3. Casado-García, Á., Heras, J.: Ensemble methods for object detection. In: European Conference on Artificial Intelligence, pp. 2688–2695 (2020)
4. Chang, J.-R., et al.: Stain mix-up: Unsupervised domain generalization for histopathology images. In: de Bruijne, M., et al. (eds.) MICCAI 2021. LNCS, vol. 12903, pp. 117–126. Springer, Cham (2021). https://doi.org/10.1007/978-3-030-87199-4_11
5. Chen, L., Strauch, M., Merhof, D.: Instance segmentation of biomedical images with an object-aware embedding learned with local constraints. In: Shen, D., et al. (eds.) MICCAI 2019. LNCS, vol. 11764, pp. 451–459. Springer, Cham (2019). https://doi.org/10.1007/978-3-030-32239-7_50
6. He, K., Zhang, X., Ren, S., Sun, J.: Deep residual learning for image recognition. In: IEEE Conference on Computer Vision and Pattern Recognition, pp. 770–778 (2016)
7. Lin, T.Y., Dollár, P., Girshick, R., He, K., Hariharan, B., Belongie, S.: Adaptive feature pyramid networks for object detection. In: IEEE Conference on Computer Vision and Pattern Recognition, pp. 2117–2125 (2017)

8. Lin, T.-Y.: Microsoft COCO: common objects in context. In: Fleet, D., Pajdla, T., Schiele, B., Tuytelaars, T. (eds.) ECCV 2014. LNCS, vol. 8693, pp. 740–755. Springer, Cham (2014). https://doi.org/10.1007/978-3-319-10602-1_48
9. Liu, Y., et al.: Detecting cancer metastases on gigapixel pathology images. arXiv preprint arXiv:1703.02442 (2017)
10. Macenko, M., et al.: A method for normalizing histology slides for quantitative analysis. In: International Symposium on Biomedical Imaging, pp. 1107–1110 (2009)
11. Neubeck, A., Van Gool, L.J.: Efficient non-maximum suppression. In: International Conference on Pattern Recognition, pp. 850–855 (2006)
12. Reinhard, E., Adhikhmin, M., Gooch, B., Shirley, P.: Color transfer between images. IEEE Comput. Graphics Appl. 21(5), 34–41 (2001)
13. Ren, S., He, K., Girshick, R., Sun, J.: Faster R-CNN: towards real-time object detection with region proposal networks. In: Advances in Neural Information Processing Systems, vol. 28 (2015)
14. Roy, S., Kumar Jain, A., Lal, S., Kini, J.: A study about color normalization methods for histopathology images. Micron 114, 42–61 (2018)
15. Schmidt, U., Weigert, M., Broaddus, C., Myers, G.: Cell detection with star-convex polygons. In: Frangi, A.F., Schnabel, J.A., Davatzikos, C., Alberola-López, C., Fichtinger, G. (eds.) MICCAI 2018. LNCS, vol. 11071, pp. 265–273. Springer, Cham (2018). https://doi.org/10.1007/978-3-030-00934-2_30
16. Song, T.H., Sanchez, V., Daly, H.E., Rajpoot, N.M.: Simultaneous cell detection and classification in bone marrow histology images. IEEE J. Biomed. Health Inform. 23(4), 1469–1476 (2018)
17. Sun, Y., Huang, X., Molina, E.G.L., Dong, L., Zhang, Q.: Signet ring cells detection in histology images with similarity learning. In: International Symposium on Biomedical Imaging, pp. 37–48 (2020)
18. Tellez, T., et al.: Whole-slide mitosis detection in H&E breast histology using PHH3 as a reference to train distilled stain-invariant convolutional networks. IEEE Trans. Med. Imaging 37(9), 2126–2136 (2018)
19. Torralba, A., Efros, A.A.: Unbiased look at dataset bias. In: IEEE Conference on Computer Vision and Pattern Recognition, pp. 1521–1528 (2011)
20. Vahadane, A., et al.: Structure-preserving color normalization and sparse stain separation for histological images. IEEE Trans. Med. Imaging 35(8), 1962–1971 (2016)
21. Veta, M., et al.: Predicting breast tumor proliferation from whole-slide images: the TUPAC16 challenge. Med. Image Anal. 54, 111–121 (2019)
22. Veta, M., Van Diest, P.J., Jiwa, M., Al-Janabi, S., Pluim, J.P.: Mitosis counting in breast cancer: object-level interobserver agreement and comparison to an automatic method. PLoS ONE 11(8), e0161286 (2016)
23. Veta, M.: Assessment of algorithms for mitosis detection in breast cancer histopathology images. Med. Image Anal. 20(1), 237–248 (2015)
24. Zhang, J., Hu, H., Chen, S.: Cancer cells detection in phasecontrast microscopy images based on Faster R-CNN. In: International Symposium on Computational Intelligence and Design, pp. 363–367 (2016)

Transformer Based Multiple Instance Learning for Weakly Supervised Histopathology Image Segmentation

Ziniu Qian[1], Kailu Li[1], Maode Lai[2,3], Eric I-Chao Chang[4], Bingzheng Wei[5], Yubo Fan[1], and Yan Xu[1(✉)]

[1] State Key Laboratory of Software Development Environment,
Key Laboratory of Biomechanics, Mechanobiology of Ministry of Education
and Beijing Advanced Innovation Centre for Biomedical Engineering, School of
Biological Science and Medical Engineering,
Beihang University,
Beijing 100191, China
xuyan04@gmail.com
[2] China Pharmaceutical University, Nanjing 210009, China
[3] Zhejiang University, Hangzhou 310058, China
[4] Microsoft Research, Beijing 100080, China
[5] Xiaomi Corporation, Beijing 100085, China

Abstract. Hispathological image segmentation algorithms play a critical role in computer aided diagnosis technology. The development of weakly supervised segmentation algorithm alleviates the problem of medical image annotation that it is time-consuming and labor-intensive. As a subset of weakly supervised learning, Multiple Instance Learning (MIL) has been proven to be effective in segmentation. However, there is a lack of related information between instances in MIL, which limits the further improvement of segmentation performance. In this paper, we propose a novel weakly supervised method for pixel-level segmentation in histopathology images, which introduces Transformer into the MIL framework to capture global or long-range dependencies. The multi-head self-attention in the Transformer establishes the relationship between instances, which solves the shortcoming that instances are independent of each other in MIL. In addition, deep supervision is introduced to overcome the limitation of annotations in weakly supervised methods and make the better utilization of hierarchical information. The state-of-the-art results on the colon cancer dataset demonstrate the superiority of the proposed method compared with other weakly supervised methods. It is worth believing that there is a potential of our approach for various applications in medical images.

Keywords: Weakly supervised learning · Transformer · Multiple Instance Learning · Segmentation

---

Z. Qian and K. Li—Contributed equally to this work.

L. Wang et al. (Eds.): MICCAI 2022, LNCS 13432, pp. 160–170, 2022.
https://doi.org/10.1007/978-3-031-16434-7_16

1   Introduction

Histopathology image segmentation is of great significance in computer-assisted diagnostics (CAD), which assists doctors quickly trace abnormal tissue areas. Recently, effective supervised methods always rely on a large amount of high-quality annotations [1–3]. However, it is time-consuming and labor-intensive for doctors to manually label regions of interest (ROIs) in histopathology images [4]. Therefore, there is a strong requirement of automated methods to segment and trace ROIs in histopathology images with weakly supervised methods. In this paper, we consider the design of weakly supervised segmentation methods with image-level annotations for their low cost and wide applicability [5].

Multiple instance learning (MIL) [6] is a subset of weakly supervised methods, which has demonstrated its effectiveness on segmentation tasks in previous studies [7–9]. Training datasets of MIL are set as several bags that contain multiple instances. The available labels are only assigned at the bag-level. MIL is able to predict instance-level labels except performing bag-level classification. In this work, cancerous images or not are regarded as bags, while pixels in images are regarded as instances. Labels of pixels can be predicted by MIL with the annotations of images so that semantic segmentation can be performed. However, MIL methods are all limited by the fact that the instances within the bags are independent of each other. The fact leads to a lack of relationships between instances with similar contextual information.

Transformer [10] has demonstrated its excellent performance both on Natural Language Process (NLP) and Computer Vision (CV). Different from convolutional neural networks (CNNs) that focus on the local receptive field at each convolution layer, Transformer can capture global or long-range dependencies with a self-attention mechanism [11]. Self-attention mechanism computes the response at a position in a sequence by attending to all positions and taking their weighted average in an embedding space. That is, self-attention mechanism aggregates contextual information from other instances in a bag in MIL. By weighting value with attention matrix, self-attention mechanism increases the difference between classes, which is the distance between foreground and background in semantic segmentation. Therefore, the feature maps from Transformer implicitly include relationships between instances in MIL. In previous studies, several researchers have proposed MIL methods integrated with Transformer that achieve superior performance over CNNs models [12–14]. However, existing studies in this field mostly focus on image classification, rarely addressing the challenge of segmentation. To the best of our knowledge, we are the first to attack semantic segmentation on histopathology images using Transformer combined with MIL.

Among the developed Transformer methods, Swin Transformer [15] constructs multi-scale feature maps and achieves state-of-the-art performance on several vision tasks. It is obvious that algorithms utilizing hierarchical information from multi-scale feature maps show better performance [16]. On the other hand, Swin Transformer provides higher resolution feature maps than other Transformer methods, which is benefit to facilitate prediction maps for lower upsampling ratio. Therefore, we explore adapting Swin Transformer in the MIL framework. In addition, it is difficult to constrain the learning process in the MIL method due to a lack of supervision. On the other hand, Transformer relies more on large datasets than CNNs methods, which are difficult to obtain in medical image analysis. To address these problems, we introduce deep supervision [9,17] to make better use of image-level annotations and strengthen constraints.

In this work, we introduce the Transformer into the MIL framework to perform histopathology image segmentation for the first time. We propose a novel MIL method leveraging Swin Transformer encoder, decoder and deep supervision to build a trainable bag embedding module for generating prediction masks. Swin Transformer encoder learns deep feature representations, where attention weights are assigned to features. To extend constraints, we introduce deep supervision by producing multi-scale side-outputs from the encoder which can be leveraged adequately by a fusion layer. Our code will be released on https://github. com/Nexuslkl/Swin_MIL. The contributions can be summarized as follows:

- We propose a novel Transformer based method for weakly supervised semantic segmentation. Deep supervision is leveraged in the framework to utilize multi-scale features and provide more supervised information.
- We explore the combination of Transformer and MIL for weakly supervised segmentation on histopathology images, which, to our best knowledge, is the first attempt at this task.
- Multi-head self-attention of Transformer builds long-range dependencies to solve the problem that instances in MIL are independent of each other.

2   Method

In this paper, the motivation is to introduce Transformer to solve the shortcoming of independent instances in MIL for histopathology image segmentation. The proposed Swin-MIL consists of Swin Transformer encoder, decoder and deep supervision. Swin Transformer encoder plays a role in assigning attention weights to features. By capturing global information, the self-attention module effectively highlights features that have better interpretability at each stage. Decoder of each stage generates pixel-level predictions as side-outputs, where the final segmentation maps are fused with side-outputs across all stages. Deep supervision is to constrain the training process with only image-level annotations. An overall framework of the proposed Swin-MIL is illustrated in Fig. 1.

Definition: Let $S = \{(X_n, Y_n), n = 1, 2, 3, ..., m\}$ donates our training set, where $X_n \in R^{H \times W}$ denotes the nth input image and $Y_n \in \{0, 1\}$ refers to the image-level label assigned to the nth input image. Here $Y_n = 1$ refers to a positive image and $Y_n = 0$ refers to a negative image.

Swin Transformer Encoder: MIL does not perform as well as fully supervised semantic segmentation methods. There is a problem that instances in the standard MIL maintain their independencies, which is in conflict with a characteristic named category consistency in semantic segmentation tasks. It means that pixels in the same class should have similar features, while those in a separate class should have dissimilar features [18]. To address the shortcoming of MIL, Swin Transformer encoder is introduced that incorporates the self-attention mechanism into the MIL setting. By introducing a shifted window partitioning approach which alternates between two partitioning configurations in consecutive Swin Transformer blocks, Swin Transformer encoder builds relationships between long-range tokens with an efficient computation. Therefore, similar features get high attention weights while dissimilar ones get low attention weights, which leads to an improvement in distinguishing foreground and background.

The image X_n is cropped into non-overlapping patches with patch size of 4×4 firstly. Each patch is treated as a "Token" and fed into several Swin Transformer blocks, which enhance the significant regions in feature maps and inhibit the influence of irrelevant regions through multi-head self-attention. The Swin Transformer blocks refer to as "Stage 1" together with a linear embedding layer, which projects the raw-valued feature to an arbitrary dimension. To produce a multi-scale feature representation, patch merging layers are introduced to reduce the number of tokens as the network gets deeper. The patch merging layers and several Swin Transformer blocks are denoted as "Stage 2" and "Stage 3", which output feature maps with resolution of $\frac{H}{8} \times \frac{W}{8}$ and $\frac{H}{16} \times \frac{W}{16}$, respectively. It is evident in our experiments that the backbone with three stages is sufficiently powerful to extract features. Then the output feature maps are fed into decoder.

Decoder: The channel size of the output feature map is squeezed to 1 by a 1×1 convolutional layer. After a bilinear upsampling operation, it is restored to the original size $(H \times W)$ and finally activated by the sigmoid to generate a predicted probabilistic map as side-outputs. A fusion layer is proposed to adequately leverage the multi-scale side-outputs across all stages to predict final segmentation maps. We can predict the classification of the image by each instance in the bag. $\hat{Y}_n(i, j)$ is denoted as the probability of the pixel p_{ij} in the nth image, where (i, j) denotes the position of the pixel p_{ij} in X_n. Therefore, a softmax function is often used to replace the hard maximum approach. Generalized Mean (GM) [19] is utilized as our softmax function, which is defined as:

$$\hat{Y}_n = \left(\frac{1}{|X_n|} \sum_{i,j} \left[\hat{Y}_n(i,j) \right]^r \right)^{\frac{1}{r}}, \tag{1}$$

where the parameter r controls the sharpness and proximity to the hard function: $\hat{Y}_n \rightarrow \max_{i,j} \hat{Y}_n(i,j)$ as $r \rightarrow \infty$.

Deep Supervision: To address the lack of supervision information in MIL and utilize hierarchical information effectively, we introduce deep supervision.

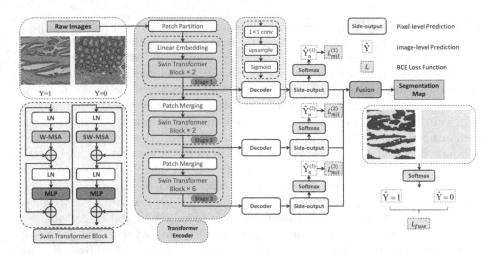

Fig. 1. An overview of our method. Under the MIL setting, we adopt the first three stages of the Swin Transformer encoder. At each stage, the deep supervision layer produces side-outputs which can be seen as predictions. In addition, a fusion layer is proposed to adequately leverage the multi-scale predictions across all side-outputs.

Our goal is to train the model by minimizing the loss between output predictions and ground truths, which is designed in the form of the cross-entropy loss function as follows:

$$L_{mil}^{(t)} = -\sum_{n} \left(\mathbf{I}\left(Y_n = 1\right) log\hat{Y}_n^{(t)} + \mathbf{I}\left(Y_n = 0\right) log(1 - \hat{Y}_n^{(t)}) \right), \tag{2}$$

$$L_{fuse} = -\sum_{n} (\mathbf{I}\left(Y_n = 1\right) log\hat{Y}_{n,fuse} + \mathbf{I}\left(Y_n = 0\right) log(1 - \hat{Y}_{n,fuse})), \tag{3}$$

where t is denoted to the number of stage, $\hat{Y}_n^{(t)}$ and $\hat{Y}_{n,fuse}$ are calculate by Eq. 1, and $\mathbf{I}(\cdot)$ is an indicator function.

Loss Function: The final objective loss function is defined as below:

$$L = \sum_{t=1}^{3} L_{mil}^{(t)} + L_{fuse}. \tag{4}$$

In each side-output and fusion layer, the loss function is computed in the form of deep supervision without any additional pixel-level label supervision. After that, the parameters are learned by minimizing the objective function via backpropagation using the stochastic gradient descent algorithm.

3   Experiment

3.1   Dataset

A hispathological tissue dataset was selected to evaluate the effectiveness of our approach. The dataset is a Haematoxylin and Eosin (H&E) stained histopathology image dataset of colon cancer reported by Jia et al. [9], which consists of 330 cancer (positive) and 580 non-cancer (negative) images. In this dataset, 250 positive and 500 negative images were used for training; 80 cancer and 80 non-cancer images were used for testing. These images were obtained from the NanoZoomer 2.0HT digital slide scanner produced by Hamamatsu Photonics with a magnification factor of 40, i.e. 226 nm/pixel. Each image has a resolution of 3,000 × 3,000. Due to memory limits, the original 3,000 × 3,000 pixels can not be loaded directly. Thus, in all experiments, images were resized to 256 × 256 pixels. For simplicity, we used Pos to refer to cancer images and Neg to refer to non-cancer images. The ground truths are pixel-level annotations which were provided by two pathologists. (1) If the overlap between the two cancerous regions labeled by the two pathologists is larger than 80%, we use the intersection of the two regions as the ground truth; (2) if the overlap is less than 80%, or if a cancerous region is annotated by one pathologist but ignored by another, a third senior pathologist will step in to help determine whether the region is cancerous or not.

3.2   Implementation

All experiments were implemented on the PyTorch framework and conducted on NVIDIA GeForce RTX 3090 GPUs with 24G memory. For training, the Adam optimizer is employed to train the model with a weight decay of 5e−4 and a fixed learning rate of 1e−6. The batch size is set to 4 per GPU, with an epoch of 60. The parameter r of the generalized mean function is set to 4. Learnable weights will cause over-segmentation problems and degrade performance. With the limited supervision of image-level annotation, MIL methods with learnable weights has a tendency to perform better classification but not segmentation. Thus, we adopt a strategy, using fixed weights, to preserve multi-scale information. The fixed weight values we set are optimal settings determined by experiments. Weights of 0.3, 0.4, 0.3 are selected for the three side-output layers. The learning rates of the side-output layers are set to 1/100 of the global learning rate. We used the pretrained model of Swin-T from ImageNet on our backbone and Xavier initialization [20] to initialize the side-output layers.

F1-score (F1) and Hausdorff Distance (HD) are employed to evaluate the quality of semantic segmentation and the boundary of prediction mask, respectively. Here, the F1-score in positive images is equivalent to the dice coefficient.

3.3   Comparisons

Attention mechanism is the core of Transformer to capture global or long-range dependencies. Hence, some attention-based MIL methods [21–23] which can

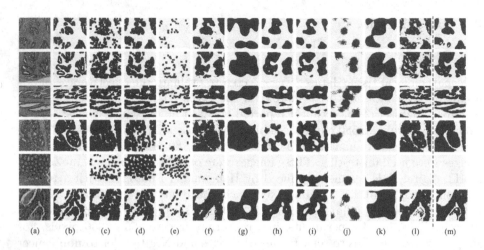

Fig. 2. Visualization results of all methods. (a) Raw Image. (b) Ground Truth. (c) DA-MIL. (d) DeepAttnMISL. (e) GA-MIL. (f) DWS-MIL. (g) OAA. (h) MDC-UNet. (i) MDC-CAM. (j) PRM. (k) VGG-CAM. (l) Ours. (m) U-Net. The rows 1–4 are the results on positive images. The row 5 are the results on negative images. The row 6 are the failure cases.

Table 1. Comparisons with weakly supervised methods and fully supervised methods. Pos and Neg means the results are conducted on positive images and negative images, respectively. WSL and FSL are denoted to weakly supervised learning and fully supervised learning, respectively.

Type	Method	$F1^{Pos}$	HD^{Pos}	$F1^{Neg}$	Running time(s)
MIL based WSL	**Swin-MIL (Ours)**	**0.850**	**10.463**	**0.999**	0.0226
	DA-MIL (2020) [21]	0.791	12.962	0.755	0.1635
	DeepAttnMISL (2020) [22]	0.772	11.111	0.634	0.1389
	GA-MIL (2018) [23]	0.355	16.289	0.939	0.1695
	DWS-MIL (2017) [9]	0.833	15.179	0.986	**0.0142**
CAM based WSL	OAA (2021) [24]	0.744	28.972	**0.999**	0.0190
	MDC-UNet (2018) [25]	0.744	17.071	0.998	0.0157
	MDC-CAM (2018) [25]	0.726	13.754	0.760	0.0167
	PRM (2018) [26]	0.561	24.468	0.995	0.9277
	VGG-CAM (2016) [27]	0.675	23.665	0.645	0.0160
FSL	U-Net (2015) [1]	0.885	7.428	0.997	0.0153

achieve patch-level segmentation by visualizing the attention map with image-level annotations, were conducted for comparison. Weakly supervised segmentation methods for natural images are also reimplemented on our dataset. Besides, we reimplemented DWS-MIL [9] framework using PyTorch instead of Caffe toolbox and introduced a batch normalization layer between convolutional layer and RELU for fair comparison. As shown in Table 1 and Fig. 2, compared with recent methods [22, 24] relied on image-level annotations, our method significantly outperforms those methods (state-of-the-art) and is close to the fully-supervised U-Net [1]. Attention-based MIL methods mainly focus on classification tasks, where the limitation of patch-level segmentation leads to a low-quality boundary. Accurate class activation maps (CAMs) are generated CAM-based weakly supervised methods [24–27], which are sensitive to the location of cancerous regions while ineffective in accurately segmentation. The MDC methods use dilated convolutional layers to obtain larger receptive fields, which achieve better performance than VGG-CAM. PRM and OAA can perform weakly supervised segmentation based on class activation maps to generate a complete mask prediction. However, it is obvious that these methods do not perform well in histopathology images. Because the natural image instance segmentation objects (people, vehicles, and animals) often have regular shapes and characteristics, the object regions are relatively complete. Nevertheless, the objects in the histopathology images are often of irregular shapes. It is difficult to generate accurate predictions by expanding which is sensitive to boundaries. Besides, we show the failure case in the row 6 of Fig. 1. Given the complexity and the diversity of the tissue appearance, our method misses the accurate segmentation boundary under the limited supervision with image-level annotation.

3.4   Ablation Study

Effect of Different Backbone: Table 2 shows the comparison results adopting CNN model (VGG-16 [28] & ResNet18 [29]) as the backbone. The VGG backbone can generate segmentation maps with higher boundary quality, while the ResNet backbone is able to extract more semantic information. However, because of the locality of convolution operations, the CNN backbones are unable to extract global or long-range dependencies, which can not solve the lack of relations between instances in MIL. By comparison, the Transformer backbone can learn global or long-range dependencies through multi-head self-attention, which leads to good performance both on F1-score and Hausdorff Distance.

Table 2. Effect of different backbone in MIL framework

Backbone	F1^{Pos}	HD^{Pos}	F1^{Neg}
Swin-T	**0.850**	**10.463**	**0.999**
VGG-16	0.833	15.179	0.986
ResNet-18	0.838	17.852	0.948

Table 3. Effect of the number of stages in backbone

Methods	F1^{Pos}	HD^{Pos}	F1^{Neg}
2 stages	0.814	12.980	0.998
3 stages	**0.850**	**10.463**	0.999
4 stages	0.759	37.738	**1.000**

Effect of the Number of Stages in Backbone: Table 3 summarizes the performances of the different number of stages in the Transformer backbone. It can be observed that the first two stages of Transformer backbone are unable to extract enough semantic information to perform segmentation accurately. On

Table 4. Effect of side-outputs and fusion

Methods	$F1^{Pos}$	HD^{Pos}	$F1^{Neg}$
Side-1	0.605	**10.383**	0.964
Side-2	0.810	10.413	0.995
Side-3	0.743	100.965	**1.000**
Fusion	**0.850**	10.463	0.999

the other hand, the fourth stage incorporates semantic information more than necessary, which affects the performance of the boundary accuracy and fails to achieve effective improvements. Thus, taking the first three stages as our backbone is the optimal option.

Effect of Side-Outputs and Fusion: To illustrate the effectiveness of deep supervision, Table 4 summarizes the performance of the different side-outputs. Due to the insufficient ability of feature extraction, the side-output of Stage 1 is limited in F1-score but gets the best boundary accuracy. The side-output of Stage 2 has the highest performance on F1-score and good boundary accuracy close to Stage 1. The side-output of Stage 3 contains most semantic information but lacks almost all boundary features. The fusion of three side-output feature maps can achieve optimal performance.

4   Conclusion

In this work, we propose a novel weakly supervised method for histopathology image segmentation, which combines Transformer with MIL to capture global or long-range dependencies. Multi-head self-attention in Transformer solves the independent instances of MIL by learning relations between instances, which significantly facilitates segmentation maps and makes the weakly supervised method more interpretable. It effectively utilizes hierarchical information from multi-scale feature maps through the introduction of deep supervision. The experiments demonstrate that our method achieves state-of-the-art performance on the colon cancer dataset. With a broad scope, the proposed method has the potential to be applied to a wide range of medical images in the future.

Acknowledgement. This work was supported by the National Natural Science Foundation in China under Grant 62022010, 81771910, the Fundamental Research Funds for the Central Universities of China from the State Key Laboratory of Software Development Environment in Beihang University in China, the 111 Project in China under Grant B13003, the high performancecomputing (HPC) resources at Beihang University.

References

1. Ronneberger, O., Fischer, P., Brox, T.: U-Net: convolutional networks for biomedical image segmentation. In: Navab, N., Hornegger, J., Wells, W.M., Frangi, A.F. (eds.) MICCAI 2015. LNCS, vol. 9351, pp. 234–241. Springer, Cham (2015). https://doi.org/10.1007/978-3-319-24574-4_28
2. Chen, H., Qi, X., Yu, L., Heng, P.A.: DCAN: deep contour-aware networks for accurate gland segmentation. In: Proceedings of the IEEE Conference on Computer Vision and Pattern Recognition, pp. 2487–2496 (2016)
3. Xing, F., Shi, X., Zhang, Z., Cai, J.Z., Xie, Y., Yang, L.: Transfer shape modeling towards high-throughput microscopy image segmentation. In: Ourselin, S., Joskowicz, L., Sabuncu, M.R., Unal, G., Wells, W. (eds.) MICCAI 2016. LNCS, vol. 9902, pp. 183–190. Springer, Cham (2016). https://doi.org/10.1007/978-3-319-46726-9_22
4. Yu, G., et al.: Weakly supervised minirhizotron image segmentation with MIL-CAM. In: Bartoli, A., Fusiello, A. (eds.) ECCV 2020. LNCS, vol. 12540, pp. 433–449. Springer, Cham (2020). https://doi.org/10.1007/978-3-030-65414-6_30
5. Zhou, Z.H.: A brief introduction to weakly supervised learning. Natl. Sci. Rev. 5(1), 44–53 (2018)
6. Dietterich, T.G., Lathrop, R.H., Lozano-Pérez, T.: Solving the multiple instance problem with axis-parallel rectangles. Artif. Intell. 89(1–2), 31–71 (1997)
7. Xu, Y., Zhu, J.Y., Chang, E., Tu, Z.: Multiple clustered instance learning for histopathology cancer image classification, segmentation and clustering. In: 2012 IEEE Conference on Computer Vision and Pattern Recognition, pp. 964–971. IEEE (2012)
8. Xu, Y., Zhu, J.Y., Eric, I., Chang, C., Lai, M., Tu, Z.: Weakly supervised histopathology cancer image segmentation and classification. Med. Image Anal. 18(3), 591–604 (2014)
9. Jia, Z., Huang, X., Eric, I., Chang, C., Xu, Y.: Constrained deep weak supervision for histopathology image segmentation. IEEE Trans. Med. Imaging 36(11), 2376–2388 (2017)
10. Vaswani, A., et al.: Attention is all you need. In: Advances in Neural Information Processing Systems, vol. 30 (2017)
11. Chen, J., et al.: TransUNet: transformers make strong encoders for medical image segmentation. arXiv preprint arXiv:2102.04306 (2021)
12. Li, H., et al.: DT-MIL: deformable transformer for multi-instance learning on histopathological image. In: de Bruijne, M., et al. (eds.) MICCAI 2021. LNCS, vol. 12908, pp. 206–216. Springer, Cham (2021). https://doi.org/10.1007/978-3-030-87237-3_20
13. Yu, S., et al.: MIL-VT: multiple instance learning enhanced vision transformer for fundus image classification. In: de Bruijne, M., et al. (eds.) MICCAI 2021. LNCS, vol. 12908, pp. 45–54. Springer, Cham (2021). https://doi.org/10.1007/978-3-030-87237-3_5
14. Shao, Z., et al.: TransMIL: transformer based correlated multiple instance learning for whole slide image classification. In: Advances in Neural Information Processing Systems, vol. 34 (2021)
15. Liu, Z., et al.: Swin Transformer: hierarchical vision transformer using shifted windows. In: Proceedings of the IEEE/CVF International Conference on Computer Vision, pp. 10012–10022 (2021)

16. Yi, J., et al.: Multi-scale cell instance segmentation with keypoint graph based bounding boxes. In: Shen, D., et al. (eds.) MICCAI 2019. LNCS, vol. 11764, pp. 369–377. Springer, Cham (2019). https://doi.org/10.1007/978-3-030-32239-7_41

17. Lee, C.Y., Xie, S., Gallagher, P., Zhang, Z., Tu, Z.: Deeply-supervised nets. In: Artificial Intelligence and Statistics, pp. 562–570. PMLR (2015)

18. Huang, Z., Wang, X., Huang, L., Huang, C., Wei, Y., Liu, W.: CCNet: Criss-Cross attention for semantic segmentation. In: Proceedings of the IEEE/CVF International Conference on Computer Vision, pp. 603–612 (2019)

19. Zhang, C., Platt, J., Viola, P.: Multiple instance boosting for object detection. In: Advances in Neural Information Processing Systems, vol. 18, pp. 1417–1424 (2005)

20. Glorot, X., Bengio, Y.: Understanding the difficulty of training deep feedforward neural networks. In: Proceedings of the Thirteenth International Conference on Artificial Intelligence and Statistics, pp. 249–256. JMLR Workshop and Conference Proceedings (2010)

21. Hashimoto, N., et al.: Multi-scale domain-adversarial multiple-instance CNN for cancer subtype classification with unannotated histopathological images. In: Proceedings of the IEEE/CVF Conference on Computer Vision and Pattern Recognition, pp. 3852–3861 (2020)

22. Yao, J., Zhu, X., Jonnagaddala, J., Hawkins, N., Huang, J.: Whole slide images based cancer survival prediction using attention guided deep multiple instance learning networks. Med. Image Anal. **65**, 101789 (2020)

23. Ilse, M., Tomczak, J., Welling, M.: Attention-based deep multiple instance learning. In: International Conference on Machine Learning, pp. 2127–2136. PMLR (2018)

24. Jiang, P.T., Han, L.H., Hou, Q., Cheng, M.M., Wei, Y.: Online attention accumulation for weakly supervised semantic segmentation. IEEE Trans. Pattern Anal. Mach. Intell. (2021)

25. Wei, Y., Xiao, H., Shi, H., Jie, Z., Feng, J., Huang, T.S.: Revisiting dilated convolution: a simple approach for weakly-and semi-supervised semantic segmentation. In: Proceedings of the IEEE Conference on Computer Vision and Pattern Recognition, pp. 7268–7277 (2018)

26. Zhou, Y., Zhu, Y., Ye, Q., Qiu, Q., Jiao, J.: Weakly supervised instance segmentation using class peak response. In: Proceedings of the IEEE Conference on Computer Vision and Pattern Recognition, pp. 3791–3800 (2018)

27. Zhou, B., Khosla, A., Lapedriza, A., Oliva, A., Torralba, A.: Learning deep features for discriminative localization. In: Proceedings of the IEEE Conference on Computer Vision and Pattern Recognition, pp. 2921–2929 (2016)

28. Simonyan, K., Zisserman, A.: Very deep convolutional networks for large-scale image recognition. arXiv preprint arXiv:1409.1556 (2014)

29. Targ, S., Almeida, D., Lyman, K.: Resnet in Resnet: generalizing residual architectures. arXiv preprint arXiv:1603.08029 (2016)

GradMix for Nuclei Segmentation and Classification in Imbalanced Pathology Image Datasets

Tan Nhu Nhat Doan[1], Kyungeun Kim[2], Boram Song[2], and Jin Tae Kwak[3]([✉])

[1] Department of Computer Science and Engineering, Sejong University, Seoul 05006, Korea
[2] Department of Pathology, Kangbuk Samsung Hospital, Sungkyunkwan University School of Medicine, Seoul 05505, Korea
[3] School of Electrical Engineering, Korea University, Seoul 02841, Korea
jkwak@korea.ac.kr

Abstract. An automated segmentation and classification of nuclei is an essential task in digital pathology. The current deep learning-based approaches require a vast amount of annotated datasets by pathologists. However, the existing datasets are imbalanced among different types of nuclei in general, leading to a substantial performance degradation. In this paper, we propose a simple but effective data augmentation technique, termed GradMix, that is specifically designed for nuclei segmentation and classification. GradMix takes a pair of a major-class nucleus and a rare-class nucleus, creates a customized mixing mask, and combines them using the mask to generate a new rare-class nucleus. As it combines two nuclei, GradMix considers both nuclei and the neighboring environment by using the customized mixing mask. This allows us to generate realistic rare-class nuclei with varying environments. We employed two datasets to evaluate the effectiveness of GradMix. The experimental results suggest that GradMix is able to improve the performance of nuclei segmentation and classification in imbalanced pathology image datasets.

Keywords: Nuclei segmentation and classification · Data augmentation · Data imbalance

1 Introduction

The assessment of nuclei is one of the primary tasks in digital pathology since nuclear features, including shape, size, and density, have known to be related to disease diagnosis and prognosis [1]. In order to analyze nuclear features in pathology images, an accurate and reliable segmentation and classification of nuclei is a pre-requisite. However, nuclei segmentation and classification remain a challenging task since there exists an enormous number of nuclei in a relatively small pathology image and there is a substantial intra- and inter-variability in the morphology, texture, and intensity among nuclei of differing cell types as well as within the same cell type. Hence, a robust nuclei segmentation and classification method is needed to expedite digital pathology analysis and to improve diagnostic decisions on pathology images.

© The Author(s), under exclusive license to Springer Nature Switzerland AG 2022
L. Wang et al. (Eds.): MICCAI 2022, LNCS 13432, pp. 171–180, 2022.
https://doi.org/10.1007/978-3-031-16434-7_17

Recently, several research efforts have made to develop deep learning-based nuclei segmentation and classification methods. Most of them focused on nuclei segmentation where one of the most challenging tasks is to separate touching or overlapping nuclei [2]. Some designed multi-resolution convolutional neural networks (CNNs) to preserve contextual information at multiple resolutions [3, 4]. Some others proposed to exploit morphology of nuclei. For example, [4, 5] utilized nuclear boundaries in identifying individual nuclei. [6] formulated nuclei segmentation as a regression of the distance map of nuclei. [7] exploited both the nuclear distance map and nuclear boundary for nuclei segmentation. Moreover, [8] utilized dense steerable filters to achieve rotation-symmetry within the network. Nuclei classification has been mainly studied as a downstream analysis of nuclei segmentation. For instance, [9] detected nuclear centroids and classified nuclei using CNN. [10] proposed RCCNet that classifies nuclei image patches into pertinent classes. [2] developed HoVer-Net that simultaneously performs nuclei segmentation and classification by utilizing horizontal and vertical distance maps of nuclei. Despite such recent advances, nuclei segmentation and classification still need to be improved. There exists a high variability in both segmentation and classification performance among different types of nuclei [2, 11]. This may be ascribable to imbalance in the datasets among different nuclei types. The lesser the annotated nuclei are available, the poorer the performance is in general. For nuclei segmentation, [12, 13] proposed to use a generative adversarial network (GAN) to synthesize pathology images with known nuclei annotations; however, GAN is not only computationally expensive but also requires a sufficient number of supervised datasets. Mixup [14], Cutout[15], and CutMix [16] are regularization techniques to generate new images from the existing images. These are computationally efficient and have been successfully applied to image classification and object detection. But, no prior work exists for image segmentation in digital pathology.

Herein, we propose a gradation mixup (GradMix) data augmentation technique for an improved nuclei segmentation and classification in imbalanced pathology image datasets. In the imbalanced datasets, there exist one or more major-classes of nuclei that are prevalent in the datasets and one or more rare-classes of nuclei that are underrepresented in the datasets. GradMix is a data augmentation technique that is tailored to nuclei segmentation and classification tasks. The technique aims at increasing the number of rare-class nuclei by generating realistic nuclei under various environments. GradMix generates a new rare-class nucleus by combining a major-class nucleus with a rare-class nucleus via a customized mixing mask $\mathcal{M}$. The rare-class nucleus is utilized as it is and placed at the center of the major-class nucleus. Then, the neighboring pixels of the rare-class nucleus and the corresponding pixels that are either major-class nucleus or its neighbors are combined with the corresponding weights in $\mathcal{M}$. The weights for the neighboring pixels of the rare-class nucleus are inversely related to the distance to the boundary of the rare-class nucleus. In this manner, we are able to generate a set of new, realistic rare-class nuclei with varying environments. This, in turn, aids in improving the performance of nuclei segmentation and classification.

2   Methodology

The overview of the proposed GradMix is illustrated in Fig. 1. Algorithm 1 provides the detailed algorithm for GradMix.

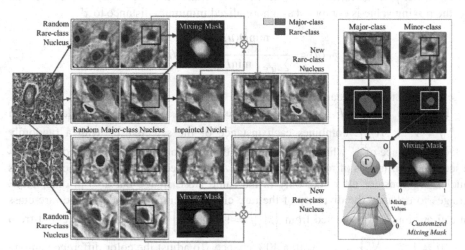

Fig. 1. Overview of GradMix. Major-class and rare-class nuclei are randomly selected and mixed to generate new rare-class nuclei.

2.1   GradMix

Let $I = \{(I_i, G_i)|i = 1, \ldots, N\}$ be a set of a H&E image and ground truth map where I_i is the ith H&E image, G_i is the ith ground truth map, and N is the number of image-ground truth map pairs. In an image I_i, there exist a number of major-class nuclei $\left\{x_{i,j}^m | j = 1, \ldots, N_i^m\right\}$ and a number of rare-class nuclei $\left\{x_{i,j}^r | j = 1, \ldots, N_i^r\right\}$ where $x_{i,j}^m \in \{1, \ldots, C^m\}$ and $x_{i,j}^r \in \{1, \ldots, C^r\}$ are the jth instances of major-class and rare-class nuclei, C^m and C^r are the cardinality of the major-class and rare-class nuclear types, and N^m and N^r are the number of major-class and rare-class nuclei, respectively. The objective of GradMix is to generate a new instance of rare-class nuclei $\hat{x}^r$ by combining one instance of major-class nuclei x^m and one instance of rare-class nuclei x^r. To combine the two instances, we define a mixing function as follows:

$$\hat{x}^r = \mathcal{M} \odot \rho(x^r) + (1 - \mathcal{M}) \odot x^m \tag{1}$$

where $\mathcal{M} \in [0, 1]$ is a customized mixing mask, $\odot$ is element-wise multiplication, and ρ is an image inpainting function [17]. The image inpainting function $\rho(x)$ replaces the intensity of the pixels inside x with the intensity that is similar to the neighboring pixels via interpolation, removing the color and texture of x.

To create the customized mixing mask $\mathcal{M}$ for the pair (x^r, x^m), we first conduct morphological dilatation for x^m with a 3×3 square kernel so as to include the neighboring pixels of x^m. The dilated instance is designated as $\tilde{x}^m$. x^r is translated to match the centroid of x^r to the centroid of x^m, forming $\tilde{x}^r$. Then, we define three mutually exclusive sets of pixels as $O = \{u | u \notin \tilde{x}^m\}$, $\Gamma = \{u | u \in \tilde{x}^r\}$, and $\Lambda = \{u | u \in \tilde{x}^m$ and $u \notin \tilde{x}^r\}$ where O, Γ, and Λ denote the sets of pixels that are corresponding to the outside of $\tilde{x}^m$, inside of $\tilde{x}^r$, and inside of $\tilde{x}^m$ excluding $\tilde{x}^r$, respectively. For the sets O and Γ, a mixing value is assigned per pixel as follows: $\forall u \in O$, $\mathcal{M}(u) = 1$ and $\forall u \in \Gamma$, $\mathcal{M}(u) = 0$. For the set Λ, the mixing value is computed as a normalized minimum distance to $\tilde{x}^r$:

$$\mathcal{M}(u) = \frac{\min_{v \in \tilde{x}^r} D(u, v)}{\sum_{u' \in \Lambda} \min_{v \in \tilde{x}^r} D(u', v)}, \forall u \in \Lambda \qquad (2)$$

where D denotes Euclidean distance.

For each image I_i, we randomly select 80% of the major-class nuclei $\{x_{i,j}^m | j = 1, \ldots, N_i^m\}$, combines each instance of the selected x^m with a randomly selected instance of x^r whose size is smaller than half of the size of x^m, and generates a set of new instances of rare-class nuclei $\tilde{x}^r$. As we select an instance of the rare-class nuclei, we consider all x^r not only in the same H&E image but also in other H&E images to enhance the diversity of the rare-class nuclei. Specifically, those rare-class nuclei are randomly selected from $\{x_{i,j}^r | j = 1, \ldots, N_i^r\}$ with a 60% chance and from $\{x_{k,j}^r | j = 1, \ldots, N_k^r\}_{k=1, k \neq i}^N$ with a 40% chance. To adjust the color difference among differing images, we compute the difference in the average color intensities of all the nuclei in I_i and the selected x^r. Then, the intensity difference is added to all the pixels in x^r.

2.2 Network Architecture and Optimization

Following [18], we build CNN for simultaneous nuclei segmentation and classification. The network contains one encoder and three decoders. The encoder has 2 convolution (Conv) blocks and 6 mobile inverted bottleneck convolution (MBConv) blocks with squeeze-and-excitation [19]. The three decoders, nuclear foreground (NF), nuclear ordinal regression (NO), and nuclear type (NT) decoders, share the identical structure that has three repetitions of an up-sampling block, a dilated convolution block with a factor of 1 and 2, and a 3×3 Conv block, followed by a series of a 5×5 Conv block, an up-sampling block, a 5×5 Conv block, and a 1×1 Conv block. NF and NT predict a nuclear foreground map and nuclear type map, respectively. NO predicts a nuclear ordinal regression map where each nucleus is subdivided into K layers with distinct ordinal labels. The ordinal labels are determined by the decreasing distance from the boundary to the centroid of the nucleus.

During training, the output of NO is utilized to obtain the two outermost layers (near boundary) that are corresponding to the most challenging regions since they determine the exact shape of nuclei. The two outermost layers are used to assign weights for NF and NT (2 for the outermost layer and 1 for the second outermost layer) so as to give more attention to the challenging regions at each iteration.

To optimize the network, we adopt cross-entropy loss for NO, cross-entropy loss and DICE loss for NF, and focal loss for NT. For NO, cross-entropy loss is computed for each ordinal layer. The weights of the two outermost layers are utilized for the computation of cross-entropy loss and focal loss for NF and NT, respectively.

Algorithm 1 GradMix

Inputs: A set of images $\{I_i | i = 1, ..., N\}$ with a set of major-class nuclei $\{x_{i,j}^m | j = 1, ..., N_i^m\}$, a set of rare-class nuclei $\{x_{i,j}^r | j = 1, ..., N_i^r\}$, ρ: an inpainting function

Outputs: A set of new instances of rare-class nuclei $\{x_{i,j}^r | j = 1, ..., N_i^{|\Phi|}\}$

1: **for** each image I_i **do**

2:     Select 80% of $\{x_{i,j}^m | j = 1, ..., N_i^m\}$ at random, forming Φ

3:     Compute $\mu_i \leftarrow Average(I_i(\Phi))$

4:     **for** each instance $x^m \in \Phi$ **do**

5:         Initialize $\mathcal{M} \leftarrow 0$

6:         Randomly select an instance x^r, subject to $size(x^r) < size(x^m)/2$, from $\{x_{i,j}^r | j = 1, ..., N_i^r\}$ and $\{x_{k,j}^r | j = 1, ..., N_k^r\}_{k=1, k\neq i}^{N}$ with 60% and 40% chances, respectively

7:         Compute $\mu^m \leftarrow Average(I_i(x^r))$

8:         Adjust color intensity: $x^r \leftarrow x^r + \mu^m - \mu_i$

9:         $\tilde{x}^m \leftarrow MorphologicalDilation(x^m)$ with a 3x3 square kernel

10:        $\tilde{x}^r \leftarrow Translation(x^r, x^m)$: Match the centroid of x^r to that of x^m

11:        Generate O, Γ, and Λ: O $\leftarrow \{u | u \notin \tilde{x}^m\}$, $\Gamma \leftarrow \{u | u \in \tilde{x}^r\}$, $\Lambda \leftarrow \{u | u \in \tilde{x}^m$ and $u \notin \tilde{x}^r\}$

12:        Assign mixing values: $\forall u \in O, \mathcal{M}(u) \leftarrow 1, \forall u \in \Gamma, \mathcal{M}(u) \leftarrow 0,$
$$\forall u \in \Lambda, \mathcal{M}(u) \leftarrow \frac{\min\limits_{v \in \tilde{x}^r} D(u,v)}{\sum_{u' \in \Lambda} \min\limits_{v \in \tilde{x}^r} D(u',v)}$$

13:        Synthesize a new mixed rare-class nucleus: $\tilde{x}^r \leftarrow \mathcal{M} \odot \rho(x^r) + (1 - \mathcal{M}) \odot x^m$

---

3 Experiments and Results

Table 1. Details of datasets.

Dataset		Lymphocytes/Inflammatory	Epithelial	Miscellaneous	Spindle	Total
GLySAC	Train	7409	7154	3386	–	17949
	Train+GradMix	9674	9383	16841	–	35898
	Test	4672	5133	3121	–	12926
CoNSeP	Train	3941	5537	371	5700	15549
	Train+GradMix	6911	8218	7234	8741	31098
	Test	1638	3214	561	3357	8770

3.1 Datasets

Two nuclei segmentation and classification datasets are employed in this study (Table 1). The GLySAC dataset [18] is composed of 59 H&E images of size 1000×1000 pixels that were obtained at 40x magnification from gastric adenocarcinoma WSIs (Aperio digital scanner). The dataset has 30875 nuclei that are grouped into three categories, including 12081 lymphocytes, 12287 epithelial nuclei, and 6507 miscellaneous. The miscellaneous category denotes any nuclei that do not belong to lymphocytes and epithelial nuclei categories such as stromal nuclei, endothelial nuclei, and etc. The 59 images are split into a training set (34 images) and a test set (25 images). The CoNSeP dataset [2] contains 24319 annotated nuclei from 41 H&E images of size 1000×1000 pixels. The nuclei are grouped into four types, including 5537 epithelial nuclei, 3941 inflammatory, 5700 spindle-shaped nuclei, and 371 miscellaneous. The 41 images are divided into a training stet of 27 images and a test set of 14 images.

3.2 Implementation Details

All the networks are implemented with the open-source software library Tensorflow version 1.12 on a workstation with two NVIDIA GeForce 2080 Ti GPUs. We train the networks for 50 epochs. During training, Adam optimizer is used with an initial learning rate of $1e^{-4}$, which is subsequently reduced to $1e^{-5}$ after 25 epochs. Several online data augmentation techniques are applied, including a random flip and rotation, a Gaussian blur, a Median blur, a Gaussian noise, and a random color change.

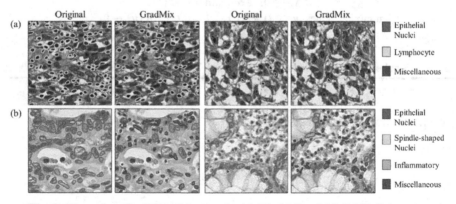

Fig. 2. Exemplary GradMix-ed images for (a) GLySAC and (b) CoNSeP datasets.

3.3 Results and Discussions

The simultaneous nuclei segmentation and classification network was separately evaluated on the two datasets (GLySAC and CoNSeP). To assess the effectiveness of GradMix, the network was trained on the combination of the original training set and GradMix-ed training set, and then tested on the test set of the two datasets. Figure 2 shows the exemplary input images and GradMix-ed images. Most of the major-class nuclei were replaced by the rare-class nuclei that were randomly chosen from the same and different images. The new mixed rare-class nuclei preserve the original texture and morphometry but possess a different neighboring environment. To quantitatively evaluate nuclei segmentation, dice coefficient (DICE), aggregated Jaccard Index (AJI), and panoptic quality (PQ) are utilized. PQ is composed of detection quality (DQ) and segmentation quality (SQ). As for nuclei classification, we quantified detection quality (F_d) and F1-score for each type of nuclei as described in [2]. In comparison to GradMix, we adopted CutMix [16] and repeated the same experiments by replacing the GradMix-ed images with the CutMix-ed images. Similar to GradMix, CutMix mixes two images to generate a new image. But, CutMix randomly samples a rectangular region in one image and replaces it by the corresponding region in the other image. To use CutMix, we randomly select x^r and x^m as described in Algorithm 1 and replace x^m by the rectangular region encompassing x^r.

Table 2. Results of nuclei segmentation.

	DICE	AJI	DQ	SQ	PQ
GLySAC	0.838	0.672	0.811	0.796	0.648
+CutMix	0.833	0.660	0.803	0.791	0.637
+GradMix (proposed)	**0.849**	**0.680**	**0.814**	**0.802**	**0.655**
CoNSeP	0.844	0.586	**0.698**	0.772	0.540
+CutMix	0.842	0.586	0.693	0.772	0.537
+GradMix (proposed)	**0.846**	**0.589**	**0.698**	**0.778**	**0.545**

Table 3. Results of nuclei classification.

	F_d	F^E	F^L	F^M	F^I	F^S
GLySAC	0.864	**0.557**	0.535	0.360	–	–
+CutMix	0.855	0.565	0.522	0.315	–	–
+GradMix (proposed)	**0.872**	0.556	**0.543**	**0.395**	–	–
CoNSeP	0.778	0.662	–	0.465	**0.659**	0.597
+CutMix	0.765	0.655	–	0.400	0.641	0.582
+GradMix (proposed)	**0.780**	**0.678**	–	**0.476**	0.651	**0.598**

F^E, F^L, F^I, F^S, and F^M denote F1-score for epithelial nuclei, lymphocytes, inflammatory nuclei, spindle-shaped nuclei, and miscellaneous nuclei, respectively.

Table 2 demonstrates the results of nuclei segmentation. For both GLySAC and CoNSeP datasets, the network equipped with GradMix was able to achieve the best segmentation performance, outperforming the ones using the original dataset only and the dataset with CutMix. The results of nuclei classification are available in Table 3. Similar to nuclei segmentation, we obtained the best classification performance by utilizing GradMix in general. The performance gain in nuclei classification is, in fact, (relatively) higher than that in nuclei segmentation. It is remarkable that we acquired a larger performance gain for rare-class nuclei, which are miscellaneous nuclei (F^M) for both datasets. With the help of GradMix, the F1-score for F^M increased by 0.035 and 0.011 for GLySAC and CoNSeP datasets, respectively. These results on the two datasets suggest that the proposed GradMix could aid in improving both nuclei segmentation and classification performance, in particular for rare-class nuclei. Moreover, the performance gain in nuclei classification will benefit the downstream analysis of differing cell/nuclei types in pathology images, leading to an improved decision making on them.

The network with CutMix was unable to improve neither nuclei segmentation nor nuclei classification, even inferior to the one with the original dataset only. Since CutMix simply replaces one nucleus by the other using a rectangular window, there is a substantial discontinuity around the boundary of a new nucleus. In particular, for overlapping nuclei, it cuts out parts of neighboring nuclei. Such discontinuity and artifacts obviously have an adverse effect on nuclei segmentation and classification. The results with CutMix also indicate that the performance gain by GradMix was not solely due to the increased number of the major- or rare-class nuclei.

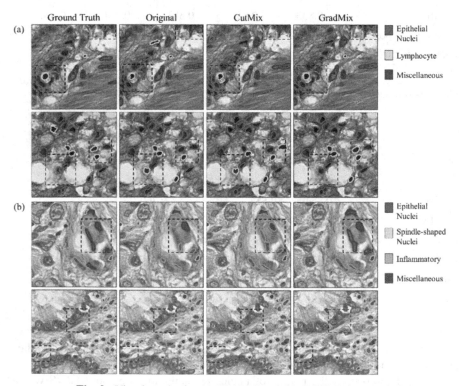

Fig. 3. Visual results for (a) GLySAC and (b) CoNSeP datasets.

Figure 3 demonstrates the visual results of nuclei segmentation and classification for the two datasets. Regardless of the datasets, the predictions by the network with GradMix was superior to others in handling overlapping nuclei as well as identifying the pertinent type of each instance of nuclei.

This study has several limitations. The experiments include a single model and two datasets. GradMix is only compared to CutMix. We will conduct an extended study to further validate GradMix by including more nuclei segmentation and classification models, external datasets, and data augmentation/generation techniques.

4 Conclusions

We present GradMix for an improved nuclei segmentation and classification in imbalanced pathology image datasets. GradMix is designed to mix the existing major-class nuclei and rare-class nuclei to generate new, mixed rare-class nuclei so as to increase the number of rare-class nuclei with varying conditions in an efficient and effective manner. The experimental results suggest that GradMix holds potential for resolving data imbalance issues in pathology image analysis.

Acknowledgements. This work was supported by the National Research Foundation of Korea (NRF) grant funded by the Korea government (MSIT) (No. NRF-2021R1A2C2014557 and No. NRF-2021R1A4A1031864).

References

1. Li, X., et al.: A comprehensive review of computer-aided whole-slide image analysis: from datasets to feature extraction, segmentation, classification and detection approaches. Artif. Intell. Rev. **55**, 4809–4878 (2021). https://doi.org/10.1007/s10462-021-10121-0
2. Graham, S., et al.: HoVer-Net: simultaneous segmentation and classification of nuclei in multi-tissue histology images. Med. Image Anal. **58**, 101563 (2019)
3. Raza, S.E.A., et al.: Micro-Net: a unified model for segmentation of various objects in microscopy images. Med. Image Anal. **52**, 160–173 (2019)
4. Vu, Q.D., et al.: Methods for segmentation and classification of digital microscopy tissue images. Front. Bioeng. Biotechnol. **7**, 53 (2019)
5. Zhou, Y., Onder, O.F., Dou, Q., Tsougenis, E., Chen, H., Heng, P.-A.: CIA-Net: robust nuclei instance segmentation with contour-aware information aggregation. In: Chung, A.C.S., Gee, J.C., Yushkevich, P.A., Bao, S. (eds.) IPMI 2019. LNCS, vol. 11492, pp. 682–693. Springer, Cham (2019). https://doi.org/10.1007/978-3-030-20351-1_53
6. Naylor, P., Laé, M., Reyal, F., Walter, T.: Segmentation of nuclei in histopathology images by deep regression of the distance map. IEEE Trans. Med. Imaging **38**, 448–459 (2018)
7. Liu, X., Guo, Z., Cao, J., Tang, J.: MDC-net: a new convolutional neural network for nucleus segmentation in histopathology images with distance maps and contour information. Comput. Biol. Med. **135**, 104543 (2021)
8. Graham, S., Epstein, D., Rajpoot, N.: Dense steerable filter cnns for exploiting rotational symmetry in histology images. IEEE Trans. Med. Imaging **39**, 4124–4136 (2020)
9. Sirinukunwattana, K., Raza, S.E.A., Tsang, Y.-W., Snead, D.R., Cree, I.A., Rajpoot, N.M.: Locality sensitive deep learning for detection and classification of nuclei in routine colon cancer histology images. IEEE Trans. Med. Imaging **35**, 1196–1206 (2016)

10. Basha, S.S., Ghosh, S., Babu, K.K., Dubey, S.R., Pulabaigari, V., Mukherjee, S.: RCCNet: an efficient convolutional neural network for histological routine colon cancer nuclei classification. In: 2018 15th International Conference on Control, Automation, Robotics and Vision (ICARCV), pp. 1222–1227. IEEE (2018)
11. Gamper, J., Alemi Koohbanani, N., Benet, K., Khuram, A., Rajpoot, N.: PanNuke: an open pan-cancer histology dataset for nuclei instance segmentation and classification. In: Reyes-Aldasoro, C., Janowczyk, A., Veta, M., Bankhead, P., Sirinukunwattana, K. (eds.) ECDP 2019. LNCS, vol. 11435, pp. 11–19. Springer, Cham (2019). https://doi.org/10.1007/978-3-030-23937-4_2
12. Hou, L., Agarwal, A., Samaras, D., Kurc, T.M., Gupta, R.R., Saltz, J.H.: Robust histopathology image analysis: to label or to synthesize? In: Proceedings of the IEEE/CVF Conference on Computer Vision and Pattern Recognition, pp. 8533–8542 (2019)
13. Gong, X., Chen, S., Zhang, B., Doermann, D.: Style consistent image generation for nuclei instance segmentation. In: Proceedings of the IEEE/CVF Winter Conference on Applications of Computer Vision, pp. 3994–4003 (2021)
14. Zhang, H., Cisse, M., Dauphin, Y.N., Lopez-Paz, D.: mixup: beyond empirical risk minimization. arXiv preprint arXiv:1710.09412 (2017)
15. DeVries, T., Taylor, G.W.: Improved regularization of convolutional neural networks with cutout. arXiv preprint arXiv:1708.04552 (2017)
16. Yun, S., Han, D., Oh, S.J., Chun, S., Choe, J., Yoo, Y.: CutMix: Regularization strategy to train strong classifiers with localizable features. In: Proceedings of the IEEE/CVF international conference on computer vision, pp. 6023–6032 (2019)
17. Telea, A.: An image inpainting technique based on the fast marching method. J. Graph. Tools 9, 23–34 (2004)
18. Doan, T.N.N., Song, B., Le Vuong, T.T., Kim, K., Kwak, J.T.: SONNET: a self-guided ordinal regression neural network for segmentation and classification of nuclei in large-scale multi-tissue histology images. IEEE J. Biomed. Health Inform. 26, 3218–3228 (2022)
19. Tan, M., Le, Q.: EfficientNet: rethinking model scaling for convolutional neural networks. In: International Conference on Machine Learning, pp. 6105–6114. PMLR (2019)

Spatial-Hierarchical Graph Neural Network with Dynamic Structure Learning for Histological Image Classification

Wentai Hou[1], Helong Huang[2], Qiong Peng[2], Rongshan Yu[2], Lequan Yu[3], and Liansheng Wang[2(✉)]

[1] Information and Communication Engineering Department at School of Informatics, Xiamen University, Xiamen, China
`houwt@stu.xmu.edu.cn`
[2] Department of Computer Science at School of Informatics, Xiamen University, Xiamen, China
`{hlhuang,qpeng}@stu.xmu.edu.cn`, `{rsyu,lswang}@xmu.edu.cn`
[3] Department of Statistics and Actuarial Science, The University of Hong Kong, Pok Fu Lam, Hong Kong SAR, China
`lqyu@hku.hk`

Abstract. Graph neural network (GNN) has achieved tremendous success in histological image classification, as it can explicitly model the notion and interaction of different biological entities (*e.g.*, cell, tissue and *etc.*). However, the potential of GNN has not been fully unleashed for histological image analysis due to (1) the fixed design mode of graph structure and (2) the insufficient interactions between multi-level entities. In this paper, we proposed a novel spatial-hierarchical GNN framework (SHGNN) equipped with a dynamic structure learning (DSL) module for effective histological image classification. Compared with traditional GNNs, the proposed framework has two compelling characteristics. First, the DSL module integrates the positional attribute and semantic representation of entities to learn the adjacency relationship of them during the training process. Second, the proposed SHGNN can extract rich and discriminative features by mining the spatial features of different entities via graph convolutions and aggregating the semantic of multi-level entities via a vision transformer (ViT) based interaction mechanism. We evaluate the proposed framework on our collected colorectal cancer staging (CRCS) dataset and the public breast carcinoma subtyping (BRACS) dataset. Experimental results demonstrate that our proposed method yield superior classification results compared to state-of-the-arts.

Keywords: Histological image classification · Graph neural network · Dynamic structure · Hierarchical representation · Vision transformer

---

W. Hou and H. Huang—Contributed equally to this work.

L. Wang et al. (Eds.): MICCAI 2022, LNCS 13432, pp. 181–191, 2022.
https://doi.org/10.1007/978-3-031-16434-7_18

1   Introduction

Histopathological examination is considered as the "golden standard" for diagnosis and treatment planning of many diseases [1,2]. For example, in clinical practice, gastroenterologists need to manually assess the histological images obtained by whole-slide scanning systems [3,4]. However, due to the complex morphology and structure of human tissues and the continuum of histologic features phenotyped across the diagnostic spectrum, it is a tedious and time-consuming task to manually classify the histological images [5,6]. Therefore, automatic histological image classification is highly demanded in clinical practice.

Over the years, convolutional neural networks (CNNs) [7,8] have greatly promoted the development of computational pathology. For example, Bai *et al.* [9] employed a pretrained google inception net (GoogLeNet) for learning high-level representations and further constructed a softmax classifier for patch-level classification of NHL histological images. Li *et al.* [10] proposed an atrous DenseNet (ADN) to integrate atrous convolutions with the dense block to extract multiscale features for histological image classification. However, one of the main shortcomings of CNN-based approaches is that convolution kernels only deal with regular pixel-wise regions and thereby ignore the notion of biological entities (*e.g.*, cell, tissue and *etc.*), which are essential for the histological image classification task and interpretability analysis [11].

Recently, graph neural networks (GNNs) [12–14] has shown great potential in modeling the notion and interaction of biological entities [11,15–19] for histological image classification. For example, Zhou *et al.* [19] first extracted the nuclei in histological images and constructed a cell-level graph according to the spatial relationship, and then designed an GNN to process the cell-level graph and performed image classification. In addition to cell-level graph, Pati *et al.* [11] proposed a HACT for pathological image analysis, where they introduced the tissue-level graph by the superpixel technique. Although the above GNN-based methods are able to improve the performance of histological image analysis, they still have two shortcomings that prevent them from achieving more satisfactory results. On the one hand, existing methods [11,19] connect the entities to generate a static graph representation according to the prior hypothesis, which lacks sufficient medical explanation and thus may degrade the representation capability of the graph. On the other hand, HACT [11] aligns multi-level entities and aggregates them by the add operation, resulting in the information loss and the insufficient interaction.

In this paper, we propose a novel spatial-hierarchical GNN framework (called SHGNN) equipped with dynamic structure learning (DSL) to explore the spatial topology and hierarchical dependency of the multi-level biological entities for improving histological image classification. We first design a DSL module to integrate the positional attribute and semantic feature representation of entities to automatically learn the adjacency relationship among different entities during the training process. By using such a dynamic learning scheme, the proposed framework is capable of capturing the task-related information for dynamic graph structure building, leading to more reliable message passing. More importantly,

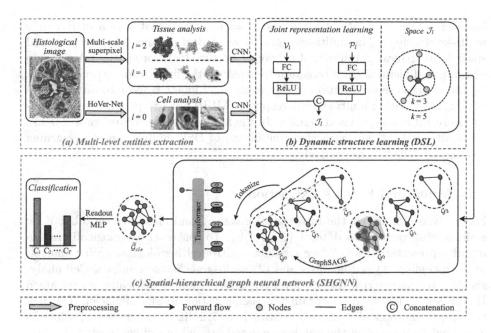

Fig. 1. Overview of the proposed framework. An analytical scheme with $L = 3$ levels is used for illustration. Multi-level biological entities are extracted and processed by our proposed SHGNN with DSL, to construct task-related graph structure and excavate spatial-hierarchical features for classification. Note that not all nodes and hierarchical relations are shown for visual clarity.

we adopt graph convolutional operations to mine the spatial features of different nodes (entities) and further design a novel vision transformer (ViT) paradigm to attentively aggregate the semantic of multi-level entities, obtaining more rich and discriminative features for high accurate classification. We conduct extensive experiments on our collected colorectal cancer staging (CRCS) dataset and the public breast carcinoma subtyping (BRACS) dataset to evaluate our proposed framework. The experimental results demonstrate that our method consistently outperforms state-of-the-art approaches on both datasets. Our code is made available at https://github.com/HeLongHuang/SHGNN.

2   Methodology

Figure 1 illustrates the pipeline of the proposed approach. We first extract the multi-level entities from the histological images, including the nuclei and the tissues with different scales (see Fig. 1(a)). Each entity is regarded as a node of the graph, for which the representation is extracted by the ImageNet [20] pretrained CNN encoder. For the DSL module (see Fig. 1(b)), we construct independent learning branches on the position attribute and feature representation of entities, and further combine their embedded representation as the judgment basis of adjacency relationship, so as to achieve the construction of dynamic multi-level graphs. The multi-level graphs are fed in parallel into the proposed spatial-hierarchical graph neural network (see Fig. 1(c)) for spatial relationship learning and hierarchical interaction to generate the final graph representation. The final graph representation of the histological image is fed into an attention pooling layer with a multi-layer perceptron (MLP) head to produce the classification result in a supervised manner. In the following subsections, we will detail the multi-level entities extraction, the design of DSL module, and the learning strategy of SHGNN, respectively.

2.1   Multi-level Entities Extraction

For a given sample, let the histological image X and classification label Y be a single observation in a dataset $\{X_i, Y_i\}_{i=1}^N$. To construct a biologically meaningful representation for X, we conduct multi-level histological entity analysis in X, including (1) *cell analysis* and (2) *multi-scale tissue analysis*. Cell analysis aims to characterize the low-level cell information. Specifically, a pretrained HoVer-Net [21] is used to obtain the segmentation masks of nuclei. The feature representation of each cell entities is a 512-dimensional vector, which is extracted by processing the patches centered around nuclei centroids via a pretrained ResNet34 encoder [7]. We denote the feature set of cell-level entities as $\mathcal{V}_0 \in \mathbb{R}^{|\mathcal{V}_0| \times 512}$, where $|\mathcal{V}_0|$ denote the number of cell-level entities. Multi-scale tissue analysis aims to effectively depict the high-level tissue microenvironments with different scales of shape (*e.g.*, stroma, vessel and *etc.*). Specifically, the SLIC superpixel [22] algorithms with different scales (the number of superpixels per image) are employed to obtain the segmentation masks of multi-scale tissues. The feature representation of each tissue is figured out by averaging the 512-dimensional deep features [7] of the patches cropped from the tissue. We denote the feature set of tissue-level entities at scale $s \in S$ as $\mathcal{V}_s \in \mathbb{R}^{|\mathcal{V}_s| \times 512}$, where $|\mathcal{V}_s|$ denote the number of tissue-level entities at scale s. After cell analysis and multi-scale tissue analysis, $L = S + 1$ levels of entities are extracted. According to the image size and hardware conditions, L can be appropriately increased to achieve more fine-grained hierarchical entity analysis.

2.2   Dynamic Structure Learning

Previous methods [11,19] often link the entities to generate a static graph representation based on the prior hypothesis, such as spatial distance adjacent matrix and k-nearest neighbor adjacent matrix. However, these methods lack medical explanation, which may degrade the representation capability of the graph. As shown in Fig. 1, we propose a DSL module to dynamically learn the adjacent relations between entities. Specifically, we comprehensively consider the feature representation $\mathcal{V}_l$ and position attribute $\mathcal{P}_l$ of l_{th} level entities as the judgment basis, where the position attribute $\mathcal{P}_l \in \mathbb{R}^{|\mathcal{V}_l| \times 2}$ is the 2D-spatial coordination of the centroid of the entity. We first align $\mathcal{V}_l$ and $\mathcal{P}_l$ to the embedding space by two projection layers and concatenate them to obtain the joint representation $\mathcal{J}_l$. This process can be written as:

$$\mathcal{J}_l = Concat[\sigma(\mathcal{P}_l^\top \mathbf{W}_1), \sigma(\mathcal{V}_l^\top \mathbf{W}_2)], \tag{1}$$

where $\mathbf{W}_1$ and $\mathbf{W}_2$ are learnable weight matrices of fully-connected (FC) layer. $Concat[\cdot]$ denotes the concatenation operation and σ denotes the activation function, such as LeakyReLU. Next, in the space $\mathcal{J}_l$, we use an online k-Nearest Neighborhood (k-NN) criteria to build the topology for each entity. Specifically, within a threshold distance d_{min}, an edge $e_{uv} \in \mathcal{E}_l$ is built for each entity $v \in \mathcal{V}_l$ if:

$$u \in \{w \mid ||v, w||_2 \le \min(d_k, d_{min}), \forall v, w \in \mathcal{V}_l\}, \tag{2}$$

where $||v, w||_2$ is the L2 distance of v and w in the space $\mathcal{J}_l$. $\min(\cdot)$ is the minimum operation. d_k is the k_{th} smallest distance in $||v, w||_2$.

The entities of each level are fed into the DSL module respectively to generate the adjacent matrix. Formally, the graph representation of multi-level entities can be represented as $\mathcal{G}_l = \{\mathcal{V}_l, \mathcal{E}_l\}$, $l \in \{0, 1, ..., L-1\}$. Specially, $\mathcal{G}_0$ denotes the cell graph while the others denote the tissue graphs. It is worth noting that the proposed DSL module is embedded into our model end-to-end, so that the multi-level graph structure can dynamically change and is able to autonomously capture task-related information for more reliable message passing.

2.3   Spatial-Hierarchical Graph Neural Network

Spatial Graph Convolution. As shown in Fig. 1, we adopt a graph convolution to extract the spatial features in the spatial dimension of multi-level graphs. Formally, the forward propagation rule of multi-level graphs can be written as

$$\widetilde{\mathcal{G}}_l = \sigma(\text{GraphSAGE}(\mathcal{G}_l)), \tag{3}$$

where $\widetilde{\mathcal{G}}_l$ denotes the generated graph. GraphSAGE represents the inductive graph convolution [23] used in our model, which allows the message passing in the spatial dimension of multi-level graph. It should be noted that other spatial graph convolutions with different massage passing mechanism also can be used to explore the different relationship between extracted entities. $\sigma(\cdot)$ denotes the activation function, such as ReLU.

Attentive Hierarchical Interaction. As shown in Fig. 1, based on the biological affiliation of cell and tissues, each cell entity has subordinate relation with a determinate tissue entity at every scale, forming $|\mathcal{V}_0|$ sequences in hierarchical dimension. Inspired by the long-range dependency modeling ability and attention mechanism of Transformer [24], we incorporate a vision transformer(ViT) paradigm [25] into our network to investigate the hierarchical interaction between the multi-level entities and selectively aggregate the interaction information to produce the final graph representation for classification. Specifically, each hierarchical sequence is tokenized and attached with positional embedding as the input of a Transformer encoder consisting of Multi-Headed Self-Attention [24], layer normalization (LN) [26] and MLP blocks. In addition, an extra learnable classification token is prepended to the hierarchical sequence, and its representation at the output layer of the Transformer encoder serves as the final representation. By inputting all hierarchical sequences to this ViT module, the multi-level graphs are transformed into a novel graph representation $\widetilde{\mathcal{G}}_{cls} \in \mathbb{R}^{|\mathcal{V}_0| \times D}$, where D is the output dimension of ViT. This process can be written as

$$\widetilde{\mathcal{G}}_{cls} = \text{ViT}(\widetilde{\mathcal{G}}_0, \widetilde{\mathcal{G}}_1, ..., \widetilde{\mathcal{G}}_{L-1}). \tag{4}$$

Classification Layer. Based on the graph $\widetilde{\mathcal{G}}_{cls}$ with spatial and hierarchical information of histological image, a more reliable output prediction can be obtained by:

$$\hat{Y} = \text{MLP}(\text{Readout}(\widetilde{\mathcal{G}}_{cls})), \tag{5}$$

where Readout is a global attention pooling layer [27] for generating representation for the final graph. For the network training, the cross-entropy loss is adopted for classification tasks and the objective loss is defined as

$$\mathcal{L} = -\frac{1}{N} \sum_{i=1}^{N} \sum_{j=1}^{T} Y_{ij} log(\hat{Y}_{ij}), \tag{6}$$

where N is the number of samples, T is the number of classes.

3   Experiments

3.1   Clinical Datasets and Evaluation Protocols

CRCS Dataset. CRCS dataset contains 5610 colorectal histological images with the fixed size of 512 px × 512 px. Based on strict proofs, all images were scanned at ×20 and manually marked by licensed clinicians, and have three types of labels: Normal, low grade intraepithelial neoplasia (LGIN) and high grade intraepithelial neoplasia (HGIN).

BRACS Dataset. BRACS [28] contains 4391 breast histological images scanned with an Aperio AT2 scanner at 0.25 μm/pixel resolution. The average size of images is 1778 px × 1723 px. The images were annotated as being Normal, Benign, Usual ductal hyperplasia (UDH), Atypical Ductal Hyperplasia (ADH), Flat Epithelial Atypia (FEA), Ductal Carcinoma In Situ (DCIS), and Invasive.

Experimental Setup. The area under the curve (AUC) is used as the evaluation metric. For each trial, five repeated 3-fold cross-validations (3-fold CVs) are adopted. All trials are conducted on a workstation with an Intel i9-9820X @ 4.1 GHz CPU and four NVIDIA GeForce RTX 2080Ti (11 GB) GPUs. The extraction of multi-level entities is implemented using Histocartography library [29]. Our GCN model is implemented by Pytorch Geometric [30]. Considering the resolution of histological images, the graph construction parameters of different data sets are set as follows. For CRCS, two-scale (200, 300 superpixels per image) tissue analysis is adopted ($L = 3$). For BRACS, one-scale (700 superpixels per image) tissue analysis is adopted ($L = 2$). The k was tuned from {3, 5, 7, 9}. The d_{min} was tuned from {1, 5, 10, 15}, respectively. The Adam optimizer was adopted, and the network was trained for 60 epochs. The learning rate is initially set to 1e−4 and decays to 1e−5 after 40 epochs.

3.2 Comparison with State-of-the-Arts

We first compare the proposed method with two CNN based methods: (1) GoogleNet [9], (2) ADN [10], as well as two GNN based methods: (3) CGC-Net [19], (4) HACT [11]. The comparative results on CRCS and BRACS datasets are shown in Table 1 and Table 2, respectively. Generally, due to the advantage of the biological entity oriented modeling, the overall performance of GNN based methods is better than that of CNN based methods. As our method not only considers the task-related information for graph structure design but also excavates the interaction information of the multi-level entities, our method outperforms the existing SOTAs on both two datasets.

Table 1. Comparison on the CRCS dataset. The mean AUC values are reported.

Method	Normal	LGIN	HGIN	Macro
GoogleNet [9]	89.27	98.97	89.58	92.61
ADN [10]	87.63	**99.26**	87.18	91.36
CGC-Net [19]	91.22	92.47	92.46	92.05
HACT [11]	92.58	95.11	96.13	94.61
Ours	**95.50**	96.08	**96.74**	**96.11**

Table 2. Comparison on the BRACS dataset. The mean AUC values are reported.

Method	Normal	Benign	UDH	ADH	FEA	DCIS	Invasive	Macro
GoogleNet [9]	93.86	87.33	75.19	80.78	96.25	91.90	98.80	89.16
ADN [10]	95.27	89.71	83.10	83.55	91.21	84.93	99.22	89.57
CGC-Net [19]	96.54	91.67	86.11	85.81	97.09	96.09	98.73	93.15
HACT [11]	96.49	93.40	86.22	85.52	**97.65**	96.70	99.27	93.61
Ours	**96.71**	**93.82**	**89.85**	**90.76**	97.50	**97.12**	**99.28**	**95.01**

3.3 Ablation Study

We first compare the DSL module with traditional fixed methods for graph structure design, including random adjacency matrix, space distance adjacency matrix and k-NN adjacency matrix [11,19], shown in Fig. 2(a). It can be observed that our DSL module is superior to the traditional fixed methods, as DSL module introduced the task-related information for enhancing the presentation capability of the graph. We also compare the attentive hierarchical interaction of SHGNN with add, multiplication, and concatenation forms [11], shown in Fig. 2(b). Overall, the proposed method consistently outperforms the fixed non-interactive methods, since the attention mechanism can adaptively select the useful multi-level entities for the task and hierarchical interaction can produce more abundant information for the decision-making.

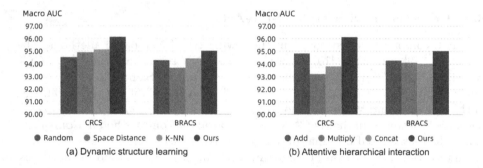

Fig. 2. Ablation study of the proposed framework.

3.4 Visualization of Proposed Framework

Figure 3 visualizes the learning process and attention map of the proposed framework. On the one hand, the middle figures show the evolution process of the cell graph structure, which indicates the proposed DSL module can dynamically refine the graph structure. On the other hand, the attention map (see right figures) can be obtained by the global attention pooling layer conducted on $\widetilde{\mathcal{G}}_{cls}$, which may aid clinical diagnosis and potentially lead to biomarker discoveries.

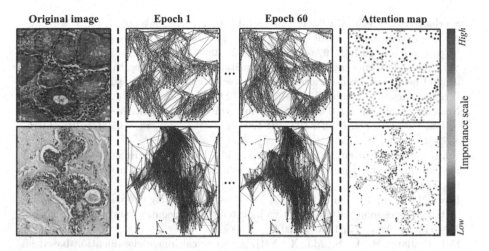

Fig. 3. Visualization of learning process and attention map of proposed framework. The first row: a sample from CRCS dataset. Second row: a sample from BRACS dataset.

4   Conclusion

In this paper, we propose a novel deep graph neural network for automatic histological image classification. The first advantage of the proposed model is to dynamically learn the connection structure of multi-level biological entities that better serves as the input of SHGNN for the classification task. Further, our proposed SHGNN combines spatial graph convolution with an attentive hierarchical interaction mechanism to simultaneously capture the spatial-hierarchical feature of the histological images, so that the potential of multi-level entities can be fully unleashed. Experimental results on two clinical datasets demonstrate our model achieves state-of-the-art performance over the existing models. The main limitation of our method lies in the relatively larger complexity comes from the extraction of multi-level entities. In the future, we will develop more computation-efficient strategies to accelerate the computation of the framework and evaluate our framework on other tasks.

Acknowledgement. This work was supported by Ministry of Science and Technology of the People's Republic of China (2021ZD0201900) (2021ZD0201903).

References

1. Yao, X.H., et al.: Pathological evidence for residual SARS-CoV-2 in pulmonary tissues of a ready-for-discharge patient. Cell Res. **30**(6), 541–543 (2020)
2. Cai, Z., et al.: A greater lymph node yield is required during pathological examination in microsatellite instability-high gastric cancer. BMC Cancer **21**(1), 1–9 (2021)
3. Kiesslich, R., et al.: Confocal laser endoscopy for diagnosing intraepithelial neoplasias and colorectal cancer in vivo. Gastroenterology **127**(3), 706–713 (2004)

4. Sterlacci, W., Vieth, M.: Early Colorectal Cancer. In: Baatrup, G. (ed.) Multidisciplinary Treatment of Colorectal Cancer, pp. 263–277. Springer, Cham (2021). https://doi.org/10.1007/978-3-030-58846-5_28
5. Shi, X., et al.: Genes involved in the transition from normal epithelium to intraepithelial neoplasia are associated with colorectal cancer patient survival. Biochem. Biophys. Res. Commun. **435**(2), 282–288 (2013)
6. Nowacki, T.M., et al.: The risk of colorectal cancer in patients with ulcerative colitis. Dig. Dis. Sci. **60**(2), 492–501 (2015). https://doi.org/10.1007/s10620-014-3373-2
7. He, K., Zhang, X., Ren, S., Sun, J.: Deep residual learning for image recognition. In: Proceedings of the IEEE Conference on Computer Vision and Pattern Recognition, pp. 770–778 (2016)
8. Hou, W., Wang, L., Cai, S., Lin, Z., Yu, R., Qin, J.: Early neoplasia identification in Barrett's esophagus via attentive hierarchical aggregation and self-distillation. Med. Image Anal. **72**, 102092 (2021)
9. Bai, J., Jiang, H., Li, S., Ma, X.: NHL pathological image classification based on hierarchical local information and GoogLeNet-based representations. Biomed. Res. Int. **2019**, 1065652 (2019)
10. Li, Y., Xie, X., Shen, L., Liu, S.: Reverse active learning based atrous DenseNet for pathological image classification. BMC Bioinform. **20**(1), 1–15 (2019)
11. Pati, P., et al.: Hierarchical graph representations in digital pathology. Med. Image Anal. **75**, 102264 (2022)
12. Zhou, J., et al.: Graph neural networks: a review of methods and applications. arXiv preprint arXiv:1812.08434 (2018)
13. Wu, Z., Pan, S., Chen, F., Long, G., Zhang, C., Philip, S.Y.: A comprehensive survey on graph neural networks. IEEE Trans. Neural Netw. Learn. Syst. **32**, 4–24 (2020)
14. Jia, Z., et al.: GraphSleepNet: adaptive spatial-temporal graph convolutional networks for sleep stage classification. In: IJCAI, pp. 1324–1330 (2020)
15. Lu, W., Graham, S., Bilal, M., Rajpoot, N., Minhas, F.: Capturing cellular topology in multi-gigapixel pathology images. In: Proceedings of the IEEE/CVF Conference on Computer Vision and Pattern Recognition Workshops, pp. 260–261 (2020)
16. Raju, A., Yao, J., Haq, M.M.H., Jonnagaddala, J., Huang, J.: Graph attention multi-instance learning for accurate colorectal cancer staging. In: Martel, A.L., et al. (eds.) MICCAI 2020. LNCS, vol. 12265, pp. 529–539. Springer, Cham (2020). https://doi.org/10.1007/978-3-030-59722-1_51
17. Anklin, V., et al.: Learning whole-slide segmentation from inexact and incomplete labels using tissue graphs. In: de Bruijne, M., et al. (eds.) MICCAI 2021. LNCS, vol. 12902, pp. 636–646. Springer, Cham (2021). https://doi.org/10.1007/978-3-030-87196-3_59
18. Chen, R.J., et al.: Pathomic fusion: an integrated framework for fusing histopathology and genomic features for cancer diagnosis and prognosis. IEEE Trans. Med. Imaging **41**, 757–770 (2022)
19. Zhou, Y., Graham, S., Alemi Koohbanani, N., Shaban, M., Heng, P.A., Rajpoot, N.: CGC-Net: cell graph convolutional network for grading of colorectal cancer histology images. In: Proceedings of the IEEE/CVF International Conference on Computer Vision Workshops, pp. 1–11 (2019)
20. Deng, J., Dong, W., Socher, R., Li, L.J., Li, K., Fei-Fei, L.: ImageNet: a large-scale hierarchical image database. In: 2009 IEEE Conference on Computer Vision and Pattern Recognition, pp. 248–255. IEEE (2009)

21. Graham, S., et al.: HoVer-Net: simultaneous segmentation and classification of nuclei in multi-tissue histology images. Med. Image Anal. **58**, 101563 (2019)
22. Achanta, R., Shaji, A., Smith, K., Lucchi, A., Fua, P., Süsstrunk, S.: SLIC superpixels compared to state-of-the-art superpixel methods. IEEE Trans. Pattern Anal. Mach. Intell. **34**(11), 2274–2282 (2012)
23. Hamilton, W., Ying, Z., Leskovec, J.: Inductive representation learning on large graphs. In: Advances in Neural Information Processing Systems, pp. 1024–1034 (2017)
24. Vaswani, A., et al.: Attention is all you need. In: Advances in Neural Information Processing Systems, vol. 30 (2017)
25. Dosovitskiy, A., et al.: An image is worth 16x16 words: transformers for image recognition at scale. In: International Conference on Learning Representations (2021)
26. Ba, J.L., Kiros, J.R., Hinton, G.E.: Layer normalization. arXiv preprint arXiv:1607.06450 (2016)
27. Li, Y., Tarlow, D., Brockschmidt, M., Zemel, R.: Gated graph sequence neural networks. arXiv preprint arXiv:1511.05493 (2015)
28. Brancati, N., et al.: BRACS: a dataset for breast carcinoma subtyping in H&E histology images. arXiv preprint arXiv:2111.04740 (2021)
29. Jaume, G., Pati, P., Anklin, V., Foncubierta, A., Gabrani, M.: HistoCartography: a toolkit for graph analytics in digital pathology. In: Proceedings of the MICCAI Workshop on Computational Pathology. In: Proceedings of Machine Learning Research, 27 September 2021, vol. 156, pp. 117–128. PMLR (2011)
30. Fey, M., Lenssen, J.E.: Fast graph representation learning with PyTorch Geometric. In: ICLR Workshop on Representation Learning on Graphs and Manifolds (2019)

Gigapixel Whole-Slide Images Classification Using Locally Supervised Learning

Jingwei Zhang[1(✉)], Xin Zhang[1], Ke Ma[2], Rajarsi Gupta[1], Joel Saltz[1],
Maria Vakalopoulou[3], and Dimitris Samaras[1]

[1] Stony Brook University, New York, USA
{jingwezhang,xin.zhang.3,samaras}@cs.stonybrook.edu,
{Rajarsi.Gupta,Joel.Saltz}@stonybrookmedicine.edu
[2] Snap Inc., California, USA
kemma@cs.stonybrook.edu
[3] CentraleSupélec, University of Paris-Saclay, Gif-sur-Yvette, France
maria.vakalopoulou@centralesupelec.fr

Abstract. Histopathology whole slide images (WSIs) play a very important role in clinical studies and serve as the gold standard for many cancer diagnoses. However, generating automatic tools for processing WSIs is challenging due to their enormous sizes. Currently, to deal with this issue, conventional methods rely on a multiple instance learning (MIL) strategy to process a WSI at patch level. Although effective, such methods are computationally expensive, because tiling a WSI into patches takes time and does not explore the spatial relations between these tiles. To tackle these limitations, we propose a locally supervised learning framework which processes the entire slide by exploring the entire local and global information that it contains. This framework divides a pre-trained network into several modules and optimizes each module locally using an auxiliary model. We also introduce a random feature reconstruction unit (RFR) to preserve distinguishing features during training and improve the performance of our method by 1% to 3%. Extensive experiments on three publicly available WSI datasets: TCGA-NSCLC, TCGA-RCC and LKS, highlight the superiority of our method on different classification tasks. Our method outperforms the state-of-the-art MIL methods by 2% to 5% in accuracy, while being 7 to 10 times faster. Additionally, when dividing it into eight modules, our method requires as little as 20% of the total gpu memory required by end-to-end training. Our code is available at https://github.com/cvlab-stonybrook/local_learning_wsi.

Keywords: Locally supervised learning · Whole slide image · Multiple instance learning · Classification

---

J. Zhang and X. Zhang—Contributed equally to this paper.

Supplementary Information The online version contains supplementary material available at https://doi.org/10.1007/978-3-031-16434-7_19.

1 Introduction

Computational pathology involving observation of tissue slides with a microscope, is the gold standard for cancer diagnosis. In recent years, digital pathology has emerged as a powerful technology for digitizing whole slide images (WSIs) for assessment, sharing and analysis [7]. This provides researchers a good opportunity to develop computer-aided analysis systems for various levels of applications, such as cell counting, gland segmentation, and WSI classification [6,9,13]. In particular, WSI-based cancer diagnosis faces unique challenges. The most typical characteristics of WSIs are their extremely large image size and high resolution. A WSI generally can be as large as $100,000 \times 100,000$ pixels at a 40X magnification, which makes it impractical to train deep neural networks in an end-to-end (E2E) manner. Consequently, the most popular methods nowadays follow a patch-based paradigm [4,12], i.e. each WSI is first tiled into thousands of small patches. Then a model extracts and aggregates patch-level features to make the final prediction [14,21,23].

Such methods follow a Multiple Instance Learning (MIL) scheme which is currently the state-of-the-art for solving histopathology classification tasks [3,10,14,21,25]. Zhang et al. [25] proposed a spatial and magnification based attention sampling strategy to extract informative patches, and directly learned a WSI classification model on these patches. DSMIL [14] jointly trained a patch and an image classifier, where the patches are selected softly with instance-level attention. More recently, TransMIL [21] presented a transformer-based MIL framework to explore both morphological and spatial information among instances. However, such a technical paradigm has some intrinsic shortcomings; these methods do not explore the spatial relations of each tile, by failing to properly combine the local and global information of the tumor's microenvironment. Moreover, these methods rely on pretrained features to represent the tiles since the current deep learning architecture cannot be trained in an end-to-end manner.

The end-to-end training of deep neural networks requires storing in memory the entire computational graph as well as the layer activations during the forward pass. Then the loss backpropagates and updates the weights layer by layer based on the chain rule. Storage of the graph and the gradients occupy a large amount of GPU memory, limiting the input image size. Some researchers [20,22] proposed to retain gradient information and train the model part by part to reduce memory consumption. Nevertheless, they still tiled images into patches, and trained networks on smaller regions with limited receptive field sizes.

Due to E2E training's limited scalability to large input and large architectures, recent research attempts to seek alternatives to mitigate the memory constraints, among which locally supervised learning attracts increasing interest [2,24]. Locally supervised learning aims to train each layer locally with a pre-defined objective function, without backpropagating the gradients end-to-end. The network training is free from storing *all* intermediate variables and the memory consumption is thus reduced. Belilovsky et al. [1] attached an auxiliary convolutional neural network classifier at each local module to predict the final target and evaluated it on ImageNet [5]. Nøkland et al. [18] proposed to use both classification loss and contrastive loss to supervise each local module and showed it was better than using a single loss.

In this paper, we introduce a locally supervised learning paradigm to train a classification network using the entire WSI. Our method splits a deep network into multiple gradient-isolated modules and each part is trained separately with local supervision. Thus we can use the entire WSI as input and do not have a patch size limited receptive field. Moreover, we further propose the Random Feature Reconstruction (RFR) model to boost the performance and optimize the GPU usage. To the best of our knowledge, we are the first to propose a locally supervised learning scheme coupled with RFR for the classification of entire WSIs. Our method has been extensively evaluated on three public WSI datasets, and achieves state-of-the-art performance compared to MIL-based methods. Moreover, without tiling, our method is significantly faster during inference.

2 Method

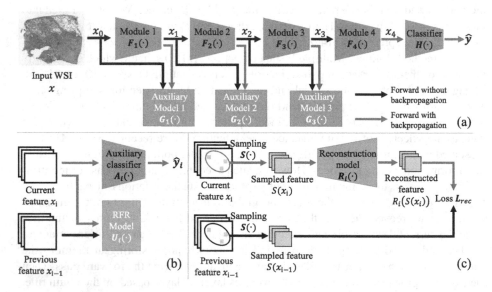

Fig. 1. Overview of the proposed method. (a) Overall structure of our locally supervised learning method. A network is divided into 4 modules and a classifier. The first 3 modules $F_i, i = 1, 2, 3$ are optimized using auxiliary models $G_i, i = 1, 2, 3$ respectively. The last module F_4 is optimized together with the classifier $H(\cdot)$. We assume $x_0 = x$. (b) Structure of the auxiliary model $G_i(\cdot)$. It has an auxiliary classifier $A_i(\cdot)$ and a Random Feature Reconstruction (RFR) model $U_i(\cdot)$. (c) Structure of the RFR model. It reconstructs randomly sampled regions in the previous feature map.

The key idea of our locally supervised learning is dividing a network layer by layer into several consecutive modules and optimizing them separately. Formally, let us assume without loss of generality, a network $F(\cdot)$ composed by K consecutive modules: $F(\cdot) = ((H \circ F_K) \circ F_{K-1} \circ \cdots \circ F_1)(\cdot)$, where $F_i(\cdot)$ represents the i-th network module. $H(\cdot)$ is a gated attention multiple instance learning [11] based classifier and $\circ$ is the function composition operation. Such a network is trained using pairs of (x, y) on which x denotes the entire WSI and y the corresponding label.

A network module contains several network layers of the original network, for example, the first 6 layers in a ResNet34. The input to a network module $F_i, i = 1, .., K$

is x_{i-1} and the output is x_i, assuming $x_0 = x$. An overview of our approach is presented in Fig. 1 on which the forward and backward passes are indicated.

In such a setup, each module is trained locally. More specifically, given a network module F_i and its input x_{i-1}, we use an auxiliary model G_i, and compute the loss as $\mathcal{L}_i = G_i(F_i(x_{i-1}), x_{i-1}, y) = G_i(x_i, x_{i-1}, y)$. We train F_i by minimizing the $\mathcal{L}_i$. Then, the trained module F_i is frozen and in an iterative process, the same technique is applied to F_{i+1} by minimizing $\mathcal{L}_{i+1} = G_{i+1}(x_{i+1}, x_i, y)$. The same process is applied to each of the $K - 1$ modules. Finally, the final module $F_K(\cdot)$ is optimized together with the classifier $H(\cdot)$ without an additional auxiliary model since the label y serves as the final supervision.

2.1 Auxiliary Model

The training of each model is performed using an auxiliary model with a greedy strategy [1]. As shown in Fig. 1(b), the auxiliary model has two parts: an auxiliary classifier $A_i(\cdot)$ and an RFR model $U_i(\cdot)$. The auxiliary classifier has a similar structure of classifier $H(\cdot)$ and computes a classification loss $\mathcal{L}_{cls}(\hat{y}_i, y)$ between the prediction $\hat{y}_i = A_i(x_i)$ and ground truth y. Such a design enables the training of the module $F_i(\cdot)$ locally. However, as discussed in [24], the shallower layers in a network have limited ability to extract discriminative features, making the training difficult.

To overcome this problem, the authors proposed to reconstruct the input image x from the feature map x_i and applied a reconstruction loss as a regularization to preserve the discriminative features. However, this strategy cannot be applied to WSIs as reconstructing an entire WSI is too costly.

To deal with this issue, we propose to use a RFR model instead of the reconstruction module. More specifically, a RFR model reconstructs randomly sampled regions from the previous feature map.

As shown in Fig. 1(c), the first step of a RFR model $U_i(\cdot)$ is to randomly sample ($S(\cdot)$), 10 corresponding spatial locations on the latent representations from the i-th module x_i as well as from the previous module x_{i-1}. Feature patches $S(x_i)$ and $S(x_{i-1})$ are cropped according to the sampled spatial locations. Then, a reconstruction network $R_i(\cdot)$ is applied to the cropped features from i-th module $S(x_i)$, aiming to reconstruct the target $S(x_{i-1})$. A reconstruction loss $\mathcal{L}_{rec}$ is used to minimize the distance between the reconstructed feature patches $R_i(S(x_i))$ and feature patches from its previous module in the corresponding spatial locations $S(x_{i-1})$. During training, this random sampling process eventually iterates over most locations and thus encourages the network to preserve discriminative features with limited GPU memory cost.

2.2 Optimization

In our framework, the first $K - 1$ modules are optimized locally with the following setting:

$$\mathcal{L}_i = \mathcal{L}_{cls}(A_i(F_i(x_{i-1})), y) + \alpha \mathcal{L}_{rec}(R_i(S(F_i(x_{i-1}))), S(x_{i-1})), \quad (1)$$

$$i = 1, \ldots, K - 1, \quad (2)$$

where x_{i-1} is the input feature of the i-th module $F_i(\cdot)$ and hyperparameter α is a regularization term. Since the last module $F_K(\cdot)$ is jointly optimized with the classifier $H(\cdot)$ the training scheme is changed to:

$$\mathcal{L}_K = \mathcal{L}_{cls}(H(F_K(x_{K-1})), y), \tag{3}$$

where x_{K-1} is the input feature of the last module. We used L1 loss as the reconstruction loss $\mathcal{L}_{rec}$ and cross entropy loss as the classification loss $\mathcal{L}_{cls}$. We set α to be 1 after grid search on the validation dataset. However, our methodological design is independent of these losses and different reconstruction and classification losses can be applied.

3   Experiments and Discussion

3.1   Datasets
TCGA-NSCLC. The TCGA-NSCLC (The Cancer Genome Atlas-Non-Small Cell Lung Cancer) dataset includes two sub-types of lung cancer, Lung Adenocarcinoma (LUAD) and Lung Squamous Cell Carcinoma (LUSC). The dataset contains a total of 1053 diagnostic WSIs. We randomly split them into 663 training slides, 166 validation slides and 214 testing slides (10 slides without magnification labels are discarded). We benchmarked the performance of our model on this dataset for the lung cancer sub-type classification task. The WSIs were on 5X magnification and the size of the slides ranges from 1581×1445 to 23362×11345.

TCGA-RCC. The TCGA-RCC (Renal Cell Carcinoma) dataset includes three sub-types of kidney cancer, Kidney Chromophobe Renal Cell Carcinoma (KICH), Kidney Renal Clear Cell Carcinoma (KIRC) and Kidney Renal Papillary Cell Carcinoma (KIRP). The dataset contains a total of 939 diagnostic digital slides. We randomly split them into 603 training slides, 150 validation slides and 186 testing slides. We benchmarked the performance of our model on this dataset for the classification of these three different kidney cancer types. The WSIs were on 5X magnification and the size of the slides ranges from 2610×1351 to 23849×10257.

LKS. The Liver-Kidney-Stomach(LKS) [17] dataset is a multi-tissue indirect immunofluorescence slides dataset. It includes four classes: Negative, Anti-Mitochondrial Antibodies (AMA), Vessel-Type Anti-Smooth Muscle Antibodies (SMA-V) and Tubule-Type Anti-Smooth Muscle Antibodies (SMA-T). The dataset contains a total of 684 slides, including 205 testing slides. To perform our experiments, we further split the rest into 383 training slides and 96 validation slides. Each slide in this dataset has the original size of 40000×40000. We further resized the images to 10000×10000 at 5X magnification.

3.2   Implementation Details

For all our experiments, we used ResNet34 [8] pretrained on ImageNet [5] as our backbone network $(F(\cdot))$. We froze the first 4 layers of ResNet34 and increased the stride of the first convolution from 2 to 3 to enlarge the receptive field. We set the batch size to be 1, since each WSI has a different size. To mitigate potential instability, we used the common optimization practice of accumulating the gradients of 8 batches before updating the parameters. All the batch normalization layers were frozen as well. In the RFR model, we sampled 10 patches of the size 128×128 for the first auxiliary model $G_1(\cdot)$ and the spatial dimensions sampled in the following modules depended on the size of the feature map. The number and size of patches are determined by the validation dataset. We used a gated attention multiple instance learning (GABMIL) [11] based network in the auxiliary classifier $A_i(\cdot)$ and classifier $H(\cdot)$.

We used AdamW [15] with weight decay 10^{-6} as the optimizer. For the two TCGA datasets, the learning rate was initially set to 1×10^{-5} for the pre-trained backbone modules $F_i(\cdot)$ and 2×10^{-5} for the randomly initialized auxiliary models $G_i(\cdot)$ and classifier $H(\cdot)$. Learning rates were decreased by a factor of 0.1 when the loss and validation accuracy plateaued. For the LKS dataset, the initial learning rates were doubled to 2×10^{-5} for pre-trained backbone modules and 4×10^{-5} for randomly initialized auxiliary models.

We used the PyTorch library [19] and trained our models on a NVIDIA Tesla V100 or a Nvidia Quadro RTX 8000 GPU.

3.3 Results

Evaluation of Overall Performance. We chose overall accuracy and area under Receiver Operating Characteristic curve (AUROC) as the main metrics to evaluate our method. Our baselines included ImageNet pre-trained ResNet34 with two different pooling methods: average pooling and max pooling. We also included the current state-of-the-art deep MIL models: the attention based multiple instance learning (ABMIL) [11] and its gated variant GABMIL [11], dual stream attention based model

Table 1. Comparison of accuracy and AUROC on three datasets. Our method, of both $K = 4$ and $K = 8$, outperforms existing state-of-art MIL models

Dataset	TCGA-NSCLC		TCGA-RCC		LKS	
Metric	Accuracy	AUROC	Accuracy	AUROC	Accuracy	AUROC
Max-pooling	0.8318	0.9036	0.8495	0.9306	0.8049	0.9366
Avg-pooling	0.7944	0.8669	0.8172	0.9309	0.6000	0.9086
ABMIL [11]	0.8037	0.8816	0.8495	0.9423	0.8341	0.9392
GABMIL [11]	0.8364	0.8762	0.8602	0.9535	0.8146	0.9399
MIL-RNN [3]	0.8178	0.9011	/	/	/	/
DSMIL [14]	0.8271	0.8909	0.8710	0.9590	0.8390	0.9328
CLAM-SB [16]	0.8224	0.9185	0.8763	0.9701	0.8293	0.9446
CLAM-MB [16]	0.8598	0.9131	0.8763	0.9716	0.8439	0.9448
StreamingCNN [20]	0.8692	0.9260	0.8817	0.9660	0.8927	**0.9652**
Ours (K=4)	**0.8785**	**0.9377**	**0.9140**	0.9740	**0.8976**	0.9562
Ours (K=8)	**0.8785**	0.9322	0.9032	**0.9760**	0.8829	0.9633

Table 2. Comparison of GPU memory consumption. Our method required around 20%($K = 8$) to 30%($K = 4$) GPU memory compared to E2E training. * is measured on CPU because of GPU memory limitation

Image size	8698×7496	12223×10057	23849×10257
E2E	17.89G	33.63G	78.14G*
Ours (K = 4)	5.35G	9.64G	18.32G
Ours (K = 8)	3.71G	6.47G	11.85G

DSMIL [14], single-attention-branch CLAM-SB [16], multi-attention-branch CLAM-MB [16], and also two-stage recurrent neural network based aggregation MIL-RNN [3], which considers binary classifications only. All these baselines are trained on 5X resolution and using ResNet34 for fair comparision. Our method was able to fine tune the ImageNet pretrained weights to adapt to the medical image domain, while other methods directly used the ImageNet pretrained features.

As shown in Table 1, our method ($K = 4$) outperformed all the compared methods in the overall accuracy and AUROC metrics. To the best of our knowledge the SOTA for the TCGA-NSCLC dataset is 96.3% AUROC (95% confidence interval: 93.7%-99.0%) reported by CLAM [16]. For experimental uniformity, we used the exact same splits on all comparisons and reported accuracy and AUROC, reporting a 91.9% AUROC for CLAM for the same resolution which is also higher than the rest of the compared methods. Our method achieved 1.87% higher accuracy than the best compared method CLAM-MB, and 2.46% higher AUROC. On the TCGA-RCC dataset, our method achieved 3.77% higher accuracy and 0.24% higher AUROC. On the LKS dataset, our method had 5.37% higher accuracy and 1.14% higher AUROC compared with the best performing method CLAM-MB. Also, comparing with the SOTA on this dataset, SOS [17], our method achieved comparable performance to it (90.73% accuracy).

Moreover, Table 1 highlights the robustness of our method with respect to the different modules. In particular, our model was divided into 8 modules and each of them trained locally using the proposed strategy performs as well as the $K = 4$ and outperformed the compared methods. Also, we compared our method with a non-MIL approach StreamingCNN [20], as shown in Table 1, our method ($K = 4$) outperformed it on TCGA-NSCLC and TCGA-RCC. On LKS dataset, our method achieved better accuracy and comparable AUROC.

Evaluation of GPU Memory Consumption. Another major advantage of our method is that our method significantly reduced the GPU memory required during training and thus enables training on the entire WSI. We compared the GPU memory consumption of our method (for $K = 4$ and $K = 8$) and that of the end-to-end (E2E) training. As the sizes of images in a WSI dataset usually vary a lot, instead of evaluating the memory consumption on three datasets, we evaluated it on three different sized images: a 23849×10257 image, the largest image in the TCGA-RCC dataset, a 12223×10057 image, and an 8698×7496 image. Note that for the 23848×10257 image, we performed the E2E measurement on the CPU since the GPU memory was not enough to perform

Table 3. Comparison of inference speed on three different sized inputs. Our method ran 7 to 10 times faster than GABMIL since we do not have the tilling and feature extraction step.

Image size	8698 × 7496			12223 × 10057			23849 × 10257		
Method	GABMIL	Ours	Speed gain	GABMIL	Ours	Speed gain	GABMIL	Ours	Speed gain
Tiling	0.3 s	/	/	0.7 s	/	/	1.8 s	/	/
Features	2.6s	/	/	3.7s	/	/	9.6s	/	/
Prediction	<0.1 s	0.3 s	/	<0.1 s	0.6 s	/	<0.1 s	1.2 s	/
Total	2.9 s	**0.3s**	9.7x	4.4 s	**0.6 s**	7.3x	11.4 s	**1.2s**	9.5x

this task. As shown in Table 2, when the input image size was 8698 × 7496, our 4 divided network required only 29.9% of the GPU memory that the E2E training needs. This number further dropped to 20.7% if we divided the network into $K = 8$ modules.

The same memory usage held for the other two input image sizes. In general, our 4 divided network required only around 30% memory and our 8 divided network required only around 20% memory compared to E2E training.

Evaluation of Time Efficiency. Besides the higher accuracy and the lower GPU memory cost, our method is faster in inference than the standard MIL approaches. We measured the total time (in seconds) that our method requires to infer an entire WSI and compared it with GABMIL [11], a high performance MIL model. We timed the whole inference pipeline including patch tiling, feature extraction, and final prediction. We reported the total inference time on WSIs in 3 different sizes. Table 3 highlights the time efficiency of our method. Our method took only 1.2 s to classify a 23849×10257 WSI, while GABMIL needed more than 11.4 s due to the time consuming step of feature extraction on the large amount of patches.

Ablation Study on RFR. We conducted an ablation study on the Random Feature Reconstruction (RFR) model. Table 4 shows the comparison on the accuracy of our method with and without RFR. On the TCGA-NSCLC dataset, using the RFR model improved the accuracy by 0.47% for $K = 4$ and 3.27% for $K = 8$. On the TCGA-RCC dataset, using the RFR model improved the accuracy by 2.15% for $K = 4$ and 3.22% for $K = 8$. On the LKS dataset, using the RFR model improved the accuracy by around 1% for both $K = 4$ and $K = 8$.

Table 4. Comparison of accuracy of our method with and without RFR. The RFR model improved the accuracy of our method by 1% to 3%.

Dataset	TCGA-NSCLC	TCGA-RCC	LKS
K = 4, w/o RFR	0.8738	0.8925	0.8829
K = 4, w. RFR	**0.8785**	**0.9140**	**0.8976**
K = 8, w/o RFR	0.8458	0.8710	0.8780
K = 8, w. RFR	**0.8785**	**0.9032**	**0.8829**

4   Conclusion

In this paper, we introduced a locally supervised learning framework to train using entire whole slide images. We evaluated it on three WSI datasets and achieved a 2% to 5% accuracy improvement compared to existing MIL methods. This significant performance gain was achieved by reducing GPU memory consumption and enabling fine-tuning of the feature extractor. Compared with end-to-end training, our method required only 20% to 30% of the memory. Moreover, our method did not require tiling as existing MIL methods do, thus it was 7 to 10 times faster during inference. We also demonstrated that the proposed random feature reconstruction (RFR) model improved the performance of our locally supervised learning framework by 1% to 3%. Our proposed approach showed the greater potential of locally supervised learning on classifying whole slide images and we will explore its applications on other tasks including segmentation.

Acknowledgements. This work was partially supported by the ANR Hagnodice ANR-21-CE45-0007, the NSF IIS-2123920 award, Stony Brook Cancer Center donors Bob Beals and Betsy Barton as well as the Partner University Fund 4D Vision award.

References

1. Belilovsky, E., Eickenberg, M., Oyallon, E.: Greedy layerwise learning can scale to imagenet. In: International Conference on Machine Learning, pp. 583–593. PMLR (2019)
2. Belilovsky, E., Eickenberg, M., Oyallon, E.: Decoupled greedy learning of cnns. In: International Conference on Machine Learning, pp. 736–745. PMLR (2020)
3. Campanella, G., et al.: Clinical-grade computational pathology using weakly supervised deep learning on whole slide images. Nat. Med. **25**(8), 1301–1309 (2019)
4. Coudray, N., et al.: Classification and mutation prediction from non-small cell lung cancer histopathology images using deep learning. Nat. Med. **24**(10), 1559–1567 (2018)
5. Deng, J., Dong, W., Socher, R., Li, L.J., Li, K., Fei-Fei, L.: Imagenet: a large-scale hierarchical image database. In: 2009 IEEE Conference on Computer Vision and Pattern Recognition, pp. 248–255. IEEE (2009)
6. Deng, S., et al.: Deep learning in digital pathology image analysis: a survey. Front. Med. **14**(4), 470–487 (2020). https://doi.org/10.1007/s11684-020-0782-9
7. Dimitriou, N., Arandjelović, O., Caie, P.D.: Deep learning for whole slide image analysis: an overview. Front. Med. **6**, 264 (2019)
8. He, K., Zhang, X., Ren, S., Sun, J.: Deep residual learning for image recognition. In: Proceedings of the IEEE Conference on Computer Vision and Pattern Recognition, pp. 770–778 (2016)
9. Hou, L., Agarwal, A., Samaras, D., Kurc, T.M., Gupta, R.R., Saltz, J.H.: Robust histopathology image analysis: to label or to synthesize? In: Proceedings of the IEEE/CVF Conference on Computer Vision and Pattern Recognition, pp. 8533–8542 (2019)
10. Hou, L., Samaras, D., Kurc, T.M., Gao, Y., Davis, J.E., Saltz, J.H.: Patch-based convolutional neural network for whole slide tissue image classification. In: Proceedings of the IEEE Conference on Computer Vision and Pattern Recognition (CVPR), June 2016
11. Ilse, M., Tomczak, J., Welling, M.: Attention-based deep multiple instance learning. In: International Conference on Machine Learning, pp. 2127–2136. PMLR (2018)

12. Le, H.: Utilizing automated breast cancer detection to identify spatial distributions of tumor-infiltrating lymphocytes in invasive breast cancer. Am. J. Pathol. **190**(7), 1491–1504 (2020)

13. Lerousseau, M., et al.: Weakly supervised multiple instance learning histopathological tumor segmentation. In: Martel, A.L., et al. (eds.) MICCAI 2020. LNCS, vol. 12265, pp. 470–479. Springer, Cham (2020). https://doi.org/10.1007/978-3-030-59722-1_45

14. Li, B., Li, Y., Eliceiri, K.W.: Dual-stream multiple instance learning network for whole slide image classification with self-supervised contrastive learning. In: Proceedings of the IEEE/CVF Conference on Computer Vision and Pattern Recognition, pp. 14318–14328 (2021)

15. Loshchilov, I., Hutter, F.: Decoupled weight decay regularization. In: International Conference on Learning Representations (2018)

16. Lu, M.Y., Williamson, D.F., Chen, T.Y., Chen, R.J., Barbieri, M., Mahmood, F.: Data-efficient and weakly supervised computational pathology on whole-slide images. Nat. Biomed. Eng. **5**(6), 555–570 (2021)

17. Maksoud, S., Zhao, K., Hobson, P., Jennings, A., Lovell, B.C.: SOS: selective objective switch for rapid immunofluorescence whole slide image classification. In: Proceedings of the IEEE/CVF Conference on Computer Vision and Pattern Recognition, pp. 3862–3871 (2020)

18. Nøkland, A., Eidnes, L.H.: Training neural networks with local error signals. In: Chaudhuri, K., Salakhutdinov, R. (eds.) Proceedings of the 36th International Conference on Machine Learning. Proceedings of Machine Learning Research, 09–15 June, vol. 97, pp. 4839–4850. PMLR (2019)

19. Paszke, A., et al.: Pytorch: an imperative style, high-performance deep learning library. In: Advances in Neural Information Processing Systems, vol. 32 (2019)

20. Pinckaers, H., van Ginneken, B., Litjens, G.: Streaming convolutional neural networks for end-to-end learning with multi-megapixel images. IEEE Trans. Pattern Anal. Mach. Intell. **44**, 1581–1590 (2020)

21. Shao, Z., et al.: Transmil: transformer based correlated multiple instance learning for whole slide image classification. In: Advances in Neural Information Processing Systems, vol. 34 (2021)

22. Takahama, S., et al.: Multi-stage pathological image classification using semantic segmentation. In: Proceedings of the IEEE/CVF International Conference on Computer Vision, pp. 10702–10711 (2019)

23. Tellez, D., Litjens, G., van der Laak, J., Ciompi, F.: Neural image compression for gigapixel histopathology image analysis. IEEE Trans. Pattern Anal. Mach. Intell. **43**, 567–578 (2019)

24. Wang, Y., Ni, Z., Song, S., Yang, L., Huang, G.: Revisiting locally supervised learning: an alternative to end-to-end training. In: International Conference on Learning Representations (2020)

25. Zhang, J., et al.: A joint spatial and magnification based attention framework for large scale histopathology classification. In: Proceedings of the IEEE/CVF Conference on Computer Vision and Pattern Recognition, pp. 3776–3784 (2021)

Whole Slide Cervical Cancer Screening Using Graph Attention Network and Supervised Contrastive Learning

Xin Zhang[1], Maosong Cao[2], Sheng Wang[1], Jiayin Sun[1], Xiangshan Fan[3], Qian Wang[2], and Lichi Zhang[1(✉)]

[1] School of Biomedical Engineering, Shanghai Jiao Tong University, Shanghai, China
lichizhang@sjtu.edu.cn
[2] School of Biomedical Engineering, ShanghaiTech University, Shanghai, China
[3] Department of Pathology, The Affiliated Drum Tower Hospital, Nanjing University Medical School, Nanjing, China

Abstract. Cervical cancer is one of the primary factors that endanger women's health, and Thin-prep cytologic test (TCT) has been widely applied for early screening. Automatic whole slide image (WSI) classification is highly demanded, as it can significantly reduce the workload of pathologists. Current methods are mainly based on suspicious lesion patch extraction and classification, which ignore the intrinsic relationships between suspicious patches and neglect the other patches apart from the suspicious patches, and therefore limit their robustness and generalizability. Here we propose a novel method to solve the problem, which is based on graph attention network (GAT) and supervised contrastive learning. First, for each WSI, we extract and rank a large number of representative patches based on suspicious cell detection. Then, we select the top-K and bottom-K suspicious patches to construct two graphs seperately. Next, we introduce GAT to aggregate the features from each node, and use supervised contrastive learning to obtain valuable representations of graphs. Specifically, we design a novel contrastive loss so that the latent distances between two graphs are enlarged for positive WSIs and reduced for negative WSIs. Experimental results show that the proposed GAT method outperforms conventional methods, and also demonstrate the effectiveness of supervised contrastive learning.

Keywords: Cervical cancer · Whole slide image classification · Graph attention network · Supervised contrastive learning

1 Introduction

Cervical cancer is one of the most common malignant cancers in women [14]. Many studies show that cytology screening can effectively reduce the incidence and mortality of cervical cancer [16,19]. At present, the most advanced screening method is Thin-prep cytologic test (TCT) [10]. During the diagnosis process, the cytopathology doctors need to spend a lot of time traversing all the cells, diagnosing the suspicious lesion cells among them, and grading the whole slide [13].

© The Author(s), under exclusive license to Springer Nature Switzerland AG 2022
L. Wang et al. (Eds.): MICCAI 2022, LNCS 13432, pp. 202–211, 2022.
https://doi.org/10.1007/978-3-031-16434-7_20

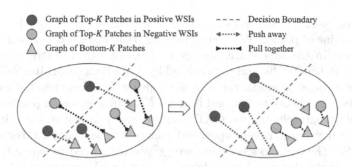

Fig. 1. The effect of supervised contrastive learning. **Left:** Some WSIs may be misclassified, which only depends on the graph of top-K patches. **Right:** In positive WSIs, the distances between graphs of top-K and bottom-K patches are expanded, while in negative WSIs, the distances are reduced, so that the WSIs can be properly classified.

Therefore, manual screening is labor-intensive and inevitably subjective. With the progress of digital whole-slide image-scanning instruments [18], accurate and efficient computer-aided cervical cancer screening becomes feasible.

Traditional methods, mainly based on morphological and textural characteristics, generally consist of cell segmentation [1,6], feature extraction [7], and cell classification [12]. With the development of deep learning [8], many attempts have been applied to the identification of cervical lesion cells based on convolutional neural networks (CNNs). For example, Yi et al. [20] proposed an automatic cervical cell detection method based on Dense-Cascade R-CNN. Du et al. [3] used CNN with attention-guided semi-supervised learning for the classification of cervical cell images. Zhou et al. [22] proposed a two-stage method based on CNN for cervical screening of pathology images. Shi et al. [15] used graph convolutional network (GCN) for the classification of cervical cell images. However, only a few studies tackled the whole slide image (WSI) diagnostic problem. Zhou et al. [21] proposed a three-stage method including cell-level detection, image-level classification, and case-level diagnosis obtained by an SVM classifier. Cheng et al. [2] designed a pipeline to find the most suspicious lesion cells in each slide and feed the features extracted by CNN to a recurrent neural network (RNN) to grade the whole slide.

The keynote of the methods mentioned above is finding the most suspicious lesion cells and integrating them to grade the WSIs. However, most methods ignore the intrinsic relationships between the suspicious lesion cells. Furthermore, in clinical practice, doctors not only focus on the suspicious lesion cells but also take the other cells into consideration. It is necessary due to the potential individual sample differences such as staining color variations. But the existing methods neglected information in the other areas which are not suspicious enough.

To solve the problems in WSI-level analysis, we propose a robust computer-aided diagnostic system for cervical cancer screening based on graph attention network (GAT) [17] and supervised contrastive learning. Our system focuses on distinguishing positive and negative classes of WSIs. Inspired by the standard screening routine of pathologists, our screening framework is developed in a two-stage manner. In the first stage, a large number of representative patches are extracted by RetinaNet [9] and then ranked by a pre-trained SE-ResNeXt-50 [5]. In the second stage, to model the intrinsic relationships between the suspicious lesion patches, we choose top-K and bottom-K suspicious lesion patches to construct graphs separately and use GAT to aggregate their features. As illustrated in Fig. 1, we develop a novel supervised contrastive learning strategy that in positive WSIs, the distances between two graphs are forced to expand, while in negative WSIs the distances are reduced. Therefore, the model can learn from the different distances between two graphs in negative and positive WSIs, which further improves the accuracy and robustness of our screening system.

2 Method

The proposed framework is shown in Fig. 2 which consists of two major stages. The first stage aims to generate a large number of suspicious lesion patches. These representative patches are further ranked by a pre-trained model. In the second stage, two different groups of patches are selected: one group contains top-K suspicious lesion patches in the WSI and the other one contains bottom-K suspicious lesion patches, which can be seen as the false positive patches generated in the detection process. The two groups of patches are aggregated into two graphs separately. The representations of graphs are computed by GAT and max-pooling layers, then in latent space, their feature vectors are optimized based on our designed contrastive loss. In the end, the screening system utilizes the graph representation of top-K patches to make the final prediction of the WSI.

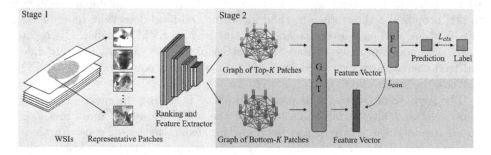

Fig. 2. The overview of our proposed framework. Stage 1 is to detect and extract all representative patches with their suspicious ranking information. Stage 2 is the proposed Graph Attention Network based on supervised contrastive learning for WSI-level classification.

2.1 Representative Patches Extraction and Ranking

Stage 1 aims to extract the representative patches based on the suspicious lesion cells detected in the WSI. Note that as it is impractical to directly implement detection on the WSI due to its enormous image size, we firstly crop every WSI into image tiles which are 1024×1024 in pixel. Usually, there are around 600 image tiles in one WSI. Then we adopt RetinaNet [9] as the detection model, which has demonstrated its effectiveness in this field. We train a RetinaNet which can automatically locate the suspicious lesion cervical cells by providing their bounding boxes, with the confidence scores as their initial suspicious ranking. For each bounding box of the detected cell, we extract a corresponding patch by starting from the center of the bounding box and expanding outward until reaching the patch size of 224×224 in pixel. We choose the top 200 patches as the representative patches according to confidence scores. The confidence scores output by the RetinaNet may not be accurate, so we need another classification model to regrade the representative patches. A large number of patches are collected in advance and manually divided by experienced pathologists into positive and negative classes, then we use SE-ResNext-50 [5] as the backbone and train the classification model. In this way, the suspicious ranking of the selected patches is updated by applying the classification model to them, experiments show that the results are more reliable than the initial ranking from the detection model.

2.2 WSI-Level Classification with GAT

The pipeline of the Graph Attention Network with supervised contrastive learning is shown in Stage 2 in Fig. 2. The inputs of the network are two graphs constructed by two groups of patches and the output is the prediction of the WSI.

Graph Construction. Let $S = \{(X_i, Y_i)\}, i = 1, 2, \ldots, N$ denote the dataset of WSIs. Here X_i represents the WSI, and Y_i represents the label of the WSI. After ranking the patches in Stage 1, we choose the top-K and bottom-K patches for further classification ($K = 20$). For negative WSIs, both groups of patches are negative and should share similar representations in latent space. For positive WSIs, the distances between two groups of patches in latent space should be large, because the confidence scores of the bottom-K patches are much smaller than 0.5 and can be seen as negative patches.

Through the pre-trained SE-ResNext-50, we can obtain the representations of the patches, which are all 2048-dim feature vectors. We construct two fully connected graphs based on two groups of patches for each WSI. Every node represents a patch and connects to the other nodes in the graph. The node features are the feature vectors of the corresponding patches. Here we define the graph of top-K patches in X_i as $G_i^+ = (V_i^+, E_i^+)$, and the graph of bottom-K patches as $G_i^- = (V_i^-, E_i^-)$ respectively. V_i includes a set of node features, $\boldsymbol{h}_i = \{\boldsymbol{h}_i^1, \boldsymbol{h}_i^2, \ldots, \boldsymbol{h}_i^K\}, \boldsymbol{h}_i^k \in \mathbb{R}^F$, where $\boldsymbol{h}_i^k$ is the output feature vector of the k-th patch in X_i, and F is the number of features in each node, which is 2048.

E_i represents the weights of edges. Each adjacency matrix of graphs is 20×20 where every number is initialized to 1.

Graph Attention Network. We propose a Graph Attention Network, which mainly includes two graph attention layers to solve the WSI analysis problem. For each X_i, the input to the network is G_i^+ and G_i^-. Both graphs are computed by the same graph attention layers.

Given $G_i = (V_i, E_i)$, the first graph attention layer produces a new set of node features, $\widehat{\boldsymbol{h}_i} = \left\{ \widehat{\boldsymbol{h}_i^1}, \widehat{\boldsymbol{h}_i^2}, \ldots, \widehat{\boldsymbol{h}_i^K} \right\}, \widehat{\boldsymbol{h}_i^k} \in \mathbb{R}^{F'}$, as its output ($F' = 512$). We firstly perform self-attention mechanism on the nodes to compute the attention coefficients e_{ijk}, which represents the importance of node j's features to k's in G_i:

$$e_{ijk} = \text{LeakyReLU}(\boldsymbol{a}^T[\mathrm{W}\boldsymbol{h}_i^j \parallel \mathrm{W}\boldsymbol{h}_i^k]), \tag{1}$$

where $\mathrm{W} \in \mathbb{R}^{F' \times F}$ is a learnable linear transformation, $\boldsymbol{a} \in \mathbb{R}^{2F'}$ is a single-layer feed-forward neural network, and $\parallel$ represents concatenation operation. To make coefficients comparable across different nodes, we normalize them across all of the nodes using the softmax function:

$$\alpha_{ijk} = \text{softmax}(e_{ijk}) = \frac{\exp(e_{ijk})}{\sum_{k=1}^{K} \exp(e_{ijk})}. \tag{2}$$

The normalized attention coefficients are used to compute a linear combination of the features corresponding to them, to serve as the output features for every node:

$$\widehat{\boldsymbol{h}_i^j} = \sigma(\sum_{k=1}^{K} \alpha_{ijk}\mathrm{W}\boldsymbol{h}_i^k), \tag{3}$$

where σ denotes the logistic sigmoid operation.

We perform multi-head attention on both layers with 8 heads. The aggregated features from each head are concatenated in the first layer and averaged in the last layer. Through graph attention layers, each node in graphs aggregates the information of the other nodes, and the weights of edges and node features are updated. Then we obtain the graph representations, $\boldsymbol{H}_i \in \mathbb{R}^{F'}$, by a simple max-pooling layer.

Let $\boldsymbol{H}_i^+$ denote the representation of G_i^+, and $\boldsymbol{H}_i^-$ denote the representation of G_i^-. The inference of our GAT model is based on $\boldsymbol{H}_i^+$, so we connect a fully-connected layer after $\boldsymbol{H}_i^+$ and obtain the classification results of the network, $f(\boldsymbol{H}_i^+)$, where f represents the transform function. Finally, we use cross-entropy loss to minimize the predicted errors for the GAT model, and the classification loss is therefore written as:

$$L_{cls} = \frac{1}{N} \sum_{i=1}^{N} CE(Y_i, f(\boldsymbol{H}_i^+)), \tag{4}$$

where CE denotes cross-entropy loss.

Supervised Contrastive Learning. H_i^+ is the representation of the most suspicious lesion cells in X_i and H_i^- is the representation of the least suspicious lesion cells in X_i. Here we define the cosine similarity of H_i^+ and H_i^- as:

$$sim(H_i^+, H_i^-) = \langle H_i^+, H_i^- \rangle = \frac{H_i^+ \cdot H_i^-}{|H_i^+| \cdot |H_i^-|}, \tag{5}$$

where $sim(H_i^+, H_i^-) \in [-1, 1]$ computes the cosine of the angle between H_i^+ and H_i^-. Let D_i denotes the distance between H_i^+ and H_i^-, and we obtain

$$D_i = 1 - sim(H_i^+, H_i^-). \tag{6}$$

If X_i is negative ($Y_i = 0$), both G_i^+ and G_i^- are constructed by negative patches, which indicates their latent distance D_i should be small. If X_i is positive ($Y_i = 1$), D_i should be large. So we propose a novel training strategy based on contrastive learning, which takes advantage of the prior knowledge that the distances between top-K and bottom-K patches are different in positive and negative WSIs. In this way, here we design a novel contrastive loss function L_i to decrease D_i in the negative WSI and increase D_i in the positive WSI:

$$L_i = \begin{cases} \alpha D_i, & Y_i = 0 \\ \beta(2 - D_i), & Y_i = 1 \end{cases} \tag{7}$$

where α and β denote the different weights of loss. The final contrastive loss is:

$$L_{con} = \frac{1}{N} \sum_{i=1}^{N} L_i. \tag{8}$$

Total Loss. The total loss for our framework is written as follows:

$$L_{total} = L_{cls} + L_{con}. \tag{9}$$

3   Experimental Results

Dataset. For the suspicious cervical cell detection, our training dataset includes 9000 images with the size of 1024×1024 pixels from WSIs. All abnormal cervical cells are manually annotated in the form of bounding boxes. Then we extract the suspicious lesion patches from both positive and negative WSIs using the detection model, and collect 5000 positive cell patches and 5000 negative cell patches. The patches are used to train the SE-ResNext-50 for updating the ranking information and feature extracting, as previously mentioned in Sect. 2.1. For the WSI-level classification model, we collect 3485 negative WSIs and 3462 positive WSIs. Note that there is no data overlap when training these models.

Implementation Details. The backbone of the suspicious cell detection network is RetinaNet [9] with ResNet-50 [4]. The backbone of the pre-trained patch classification network is SE-ResNeXt-50 [5]. All parameters are optimized by Adam with the initial learning rate of 4e-5. The network is trained for 100 epochs. The batch size is 128. The model is implemented by PyTorch on 2 Nvidia Tesla P100 GPUs.

Evaluation of the Proposed Method. Our framework includes two stages. The first stage aims to extract suspicious lesion patches and classify them, which is a common method for WSI-level classification [2,23]. The second stage is to aggregate the patches extracted before and make the final prediction of WSIs. In this paper, we focus on the second stage and propose to use GAT for aggregation. So we choose some common classification methods including SVM, MLP and RNN to compare with GAT. For the SVM method, we use the confidence scores of top-K patches output by the first stage as features and train an SVM classifier. For the MLP method, we aggregate the output features of top-K patches by max-pooling and feed the features to a fully connected layer to train the model. For the RNN method, the features of top-K patches are integrated and trained by the RNN model according to [2]. For the GAT method, we perform an ablation study to further evaluate the contributions of contrastive learning by adjusting α and β. α is the weight of contrastive loss for negative WSIs and β is for positive WSIs. If they are both set to 0, the graphs of bottom-K patches will not be involved during training. If $\alpha = 0$ and $\beta = 1$, the contrastive loss will only have effects on positive WSIs and vice versa.

We conduct a 5-fold cross-validation and testing experiment to evaluate the performance of the proposed method. All of the WSIs are equally and randomly divided into 5 groups. The ratio of training, validation and testing WSIs is 3:1:1. In each fold, one group is selected as the testing group and the other four are training and validation groups.

Table 1. The comparison of different methods and the ablation study for contrastive learning, α and β are the weights of contrastive loss for negative and positive WSIs, respectively. (%)

Method		ACC	AUC	REC	PREC	F1
SVM		76.82 ± 0.75	84.32 ± 1.07	73.49 ± 0.99	78.62 ± 1.20	75.96 ± 0.84
MLP		78.70 ± 1.94	85.60 ± 0.63	60.78 ± 4.11	84.52 ± 1.08	73.90 ± 3.11
RNN		80.89 ± 1.29	$87.17 \pm v1.42$	73.71 ± 2.52	84.08 ± 2.77	79.82 ± 0.96
GAT	$\alpha = 0, \beta = 0$	82.31 ± 1.62	90.77 ± 0.94	75.93 ± 5.75	87.21 ± 2.79	80.95 ± 2.50
	$\alpha = 0, \beta = 1$	84.93 ± 1.51	92.24 ± 1.08	82.09 ± 1.68	87.03 ± 2.42	84.46 ± 1.36
	$\alpha = 1, \beta = 0$	85.12 ± 0.99	$\mathbf{92.57 \pm 0.92}$	79.67 ± 1.37	$\mathbf{89.35 \pm 1.51}$	84.22 ± 0.94
	$\alpha = 1, \beta = 1$	$\mathbf{85.79 \pm 1.21}$	92.52 ± 0.91	$\mathbf{82.63 \pm 2.04}$	88.15 ± 1.39	$\mathbf{85.28 \pm 1.27}$

Table 1 shows the experimental results of other methods and the proposed method. It is observed that the basic GAT model without contrastive learning ($\alpha = 0, \beta = 0$) already outperforms other classifiers, which reaches 82.31% accuracy. Only performing contrastive learning on positive WSIs ($\alpha = 0, \beta = 1$) leads to higher sensitivity of the model, which raises the recall from 75.93% to 82.09%. Respectively, if we perform contrastive learning on negative WSIs, the precision increases from 87.21% to 89.35%, indicating the specificity of the model is enhanced. The GAT model with contrastive learning ($\alpha = 1, \beta = 1$) reaches the highest accuracy 85.79% with more balanced recall and precision.

We visualize the feature distribution of graphs in testing groups of WSIs by t-SNE [11]. The dimensional-reduced features are shown in Fig. 3. The graphs of bottom-K patches represent negative information of WSIs, so their features are aligned in Fig. 3(a), and the graphs of top-K patches in negative WSIs are separated from those in positive WSIs. It is noted that in Fig. 3(b), the distances between graphs of top-K and bottom-K patches in positive WSIs are expanded. And in Fig. 3(c), the distances between graphs of top-K and bottom-K patches in negative WSIs are reduced. Figure 3(d) achieves the goal that graphs of top-K patches of positive WSIs and negative WSIs are well separated, which demonstrates the effectiveness of contrastive learning.

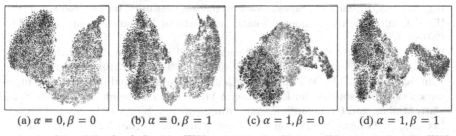

(a) $\alpha = 0, \beta = 0$ (b) $\alpha = 0, \beta = 1$ (c) $\alpha = 1, \beta = 0$ (d) $\alpha = 1, \beta = 1$

● Graph of Top-K Patches in Positive WSIs   ● Graph of Bottom-K Patches in Positive WSIs

● Graph of Top-K Patches in Negative WSIs   ● Graph of Bottom-K Patches in Negative WSIs

Fig. 3. The t-SNE visualizations of graphs in testing groups. (a) shows the feature distribution without contrastive learning. (b) shows the feature distribution with only applying contrastive learning in positive WSIs. (c) shows the feature distribution with only applying contrastive learning in negative WSIs. (d) shows the feature distribution with contrastive learning.

4   Conclusion

In this paper, a novel WSI classification method for cervical cancer with GAT and supervised contrastive learning is developed. Our method constructs graphs of the top-K and bottom-K suspicious lesion patches and aggregates node features into graph representations for WSI classification. Besides, the distances in latent space between top-K and bottom-K patches in positive and negative

WSIs are used for contrastive learning, which effectively improves the performance of GAT. Our work has great value in clinical applications, and can also be further applied to other WSI classification tasks in the computer-aided diagnosis of pathology images. Our source code and example data are available at https://github.com/ZhangXin1997/MICCAI-2022.

References

1. Chang, C.W., et al.: Automatic segmentation of abnormal cell nuclei from microscopic image analysis for cervical cancer screening. In: 2009 IEEE 3rd International Conference on Nano/Molecular Medicine and Engineering, pp. 77–80 (2009)
2. Cheng, S., et al.: Robust whole slide image analysis for cervical cancer screening using deep learning. Nature Commun. **12**, 5639 (2021)
3. Du, X., Huo, J., Qiao, Y., Wang, Q., Zhang, L.: False positive suppression in cervical cell screening via attention-guided semi-supervised learning. In: Rekik, Islem, Adeli, Ehsan, Park, Sang Hyun, Schnabel, Julia (eds.) PRIME 2021. LNCS, vol. 12928, pp. 93–103. Springer, Cham (2021). https://doi.org/10.1007/978-3-030-87602-9_9
4. He, K., Zhang, X., Ren, S., Sun, J.: Deep residual learning for image recognition. In: Proceedings of the IEEE Conference on Computer Vision and Pattern Recognition, pp. 770–778 (2016)
5. Hu, J., Shen, L., Sun, G.: Squeeze-and-excitation networks. In: Proceedings of the IEEE Conference on Computer Vision and Pattern Recognition, pp. 7132–7141 (2018)
6. Kale, A., Aksoy, S.: Segmentation of cervical cell images. In: 2010 20th International Conference on Pattern Recognition, pp. 2399–2402 (2010)
7. Kim, K.B., Song, D.H., Woo, Y.W.: Nucleus segmentation and recognition of uterine cervical pap-smears. In: International Workshop on Rough Sets, Fuzzy Sets, Data Mining, and Granular-Soft Computing, pp. 153–160 (2007)
8. LeCun, Y., Bengio, Y., Hinton, G.: Deep learning. Nature **521**(7553), 436–444 (2015)
9. Lin, T.Y., Goyal, P., Girshick, R., He, K., Dollár, P.: Focal loss for dense object detection. In: Proceedings of the IEEE international conference on computer vision, pp. 2980–2988 (2017)
10. Liu, Y., Zhang, L., Zhao, G., Che, L., Zhang, H., Fang, J.: The clinical research of Thinprep Cytology Test (TCT) combined with HPV-DNA detection in screening cervical cancer. Cell Mol. Biol. (Noisy-le-grand) **63**(2), 92–95 (2017)
11. Van der Maaten, L., Hinton, G.: Visualizing data using t-SNE. J. Mach. Learn. Res. **9**(86), 2579–2605 (2008)
12. Mariarputham, E.J., Stephen, A.: Nominated texture based cervical cancer classification. Comput. Math. Methods Med. **2015**, 1–10 (2015)
13. Nayar, R., Wilbur, D.C. (eds.): The Bethesda System for Reporting Cervical Cytology. Springer, Cham (2015). https://doi.org/10.1007/978-3-319-11074-5
14. Schiffman, M., Castle, P.E., Jeronimo, J., Rodriguez, A.C., Wacholder, S.: Human papillomavirus and cervical cancer. The Lancet **370**(9590), 890–907 (2007)
15. Shi, J., Wang, R., Zheng, Y., Jiang, Z., Zhang, H., Yu, L.: Cervical cell classification with graph convolutional network. Comput. Methods Programs Biomed. **198**, 105807 (2021)

16. Solomon, D., Breen, N., McNeel, T.: Cervical cancer screening rates in the united states and the potential impact of implementation of screening guidelines. CA Cancer J. clin. **57**(2), 105–111 (2007)
17. Veličković, P., Cucurull, G., Casanova, A., Romero, A., Liò, P., Bengio, Y.: Graph attention networks. In: International Conference on Learning Representations (ICLR)), pp. 1–12 (2017)
18. Wright, A.M., et al.: Digital slide imaging in cervicovaginal cytology: a pilot study. Arch. Pathol. Lab. Med. **137**(5), 618–624 (2013)
19. Yang, D.X., Soulos, P.R., Davis, B., Gross, C.P., Yu, J.B.: Impact of widespread cervical cancer screening: number of cancers prevented and changes in race-specific incidence. Am. J. Clin. Oncol. **41**(3), 289 (2018)
20. Yi, L., Lei, Y., Fan, Z., Zhou, Y., Chen, D., Liu, R.: Automatic detection of cervical cells using dense-cascade R-CNN. In: Chinese Conference on Pattern Recognition and Computer Vision (PRCV), pp. 602–613 (2020)
21. Zhou, M., et al.: Hierarchical pathology screening for cervical abnormality. Comput. Med. Imaging Graph. **89**, 101892 (2021)
22. Zhou, M., et al.: Hierarchical and robust pathology image reading for high-throughput cervical abnormality screening. In: International Workshop on Machine Learning in Medical Imaging, pp. 414–422 (2020)
23. Zhu, X., et al.: Hybrid AI-assistive diagnostic model permits rapid TBS classification of cervical liquid-based thin-layer cell smears. Nat. Commun. **12**(1), 1–12 (2021)

RandStainNA: Learning Stain-Agnostic Features from Histology Slides by Bridging Stain Augmentation and Normalization

Yiqing Shen[1] , Yulin Luo[2], Dinggang Shen[3,4], and Jing Ke[2,5,6(✉)]

[1] School of Mathematical Sciences, Shanghai Jiao Tong University, Shanghai, China
shenyq@sjtu.edu.cn
[2] School of Electronic Information and Electrical Engineering,
Shanghai Jiao Tong University, Shanghai, China
lyl010221@sjtu.edu.cn
[3] School of Biomedical Engineering, ShanghaiTech University, Shanghai, China
dgshen@shanghaitech.edu.cn
[4] Shanghai United Imaging Intelligence Co., Ltd., Shanghai, China
[5] School of Computer Science and Engineering, University of New South Wales,
Sydney, Australia
[6] BirenTech Research, Shanghai, China
kejing@sjtu.edu.cn

Abstract. Stain variations often decrease the generalization ability of deep learning based approaches in digital histopathology analysis. Two separate proposals, namely stain normalization (SN) and stain augmentation (SA), have been spotlighted to reduce the generalization error, where the former alleviates the stain shift across different medical centers using template image and the latter enriches the accessible stain styles by the simulation of more stain variations. However, their applications are bounded by the selection of template images and the construction of unrealistic styles. To address the problems, we unify SN and SA with a novel RandStainNA scheme, which constrains variable stain styles in a practicable range to train a stain agnostic deep learning model. The RandStainNA is applicable to stain normalization in a collection of color spaces *i.e.* HED, HSV, LAB. Additionally, we propose a random color space selection scheme to gain extra performance improvement. We evaluate our method by two diagnostic tasks *i.e.* tissue subtype classification and nuclei segmentation, with various network backbones. The performance superiority over both SA and SN yields that the proposed RandStainNA can consistently improve the generalization ability, that our models can cope with more incoming clinical datasets with unpredicted stain styles. The codes is available at https://github.com/yiqings/RandStainNA.

Y. Shen and Y. Luo—Equal contributions.

Supplementary Information The online version contains supplementary material available at https://doi.org/10.1007/978-3-031-16434-7_21.

Keywords: Histology image · Stain normalization · Stain augmentation

1 Introduction

Pathology visually exams across a diverse range of tissue types obtained by biopsy or surgical procedure under microscopes [6]. Stains are often applied to reveal underlying patterns to increase the contrast between nuclear components and their surrounding tissues [14]. Nevertheless, the substantial variance in each staining manipulation, *e.g.* staining protocols, staining scanners, manufacturers, batches of staining may eventually result in a variety of hue [10]. In contrast to pathologists who have adapted themselves to these variations with years' training, deep learning (DL) methods are prone to suffer from performance degradation, with the existence of inter-center stain heterogeneity [2]. Specifically, as color is a salient feature to extract for by deep neural networks, consequently, current successful applications for whole slide images (WSIs) diagnoses are subject to their robustness to color shift among different data centers [5]. There are two primary directions to reduce the generalization error, namely stain normalization and stain augmentation [22].

Stain normalization (SN) aims to reduce the variation by aligning the stain-color distribution of source images to a target template image [11,17,24]. Empirical studies regard stain normalization as an essential prerequisite of downstream applications [2,12,22]. Yet, the capability to pinpoint a representative template image for SN relies heavily on domain prior knowledges. Moreover, in real-world settings such as federated learning, the template-image selection is not feasible due to the privacy regularizations [10], as source images are inaccessible to the central processor as a rule. Some generative adversarial networks (GANs)

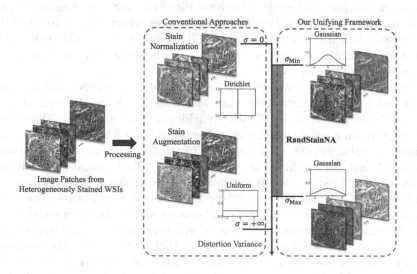

Fig. 1. The overall framework of the proposed RandStainNA.

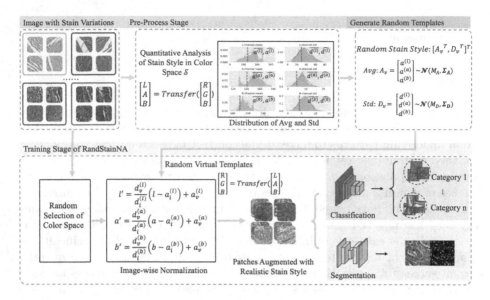

Fig. 2. The overall pipeline of the proposed RandStainNA that fuses stain normalization and stain augmentation. Prior to the training stage, random virtual template generation functions are defined *i.e.* $F_{\mathbf{M}}^{S} = \mathcal{N}(\mathbf{M}_A^S, \mathbf{\Sigma}_A^S)$ and $F_{\mathbf{D}}^{S} = \mathcal{N}(\mathbf{M}_D^S, \mathbf{\Sigma}_D^S)$. The three-step training stage comprises a random selection of color space S, the generated of an associated random stain style template $[\mathbf{M}_v^S, \mathbf{\Sigma}_v^S]$, and the normalization of a batch with the generated virtual template. Our approach is downstream task agnostic.

are proposed recently [17,18] for SN, yet remaining the phenotype recognizability is always problematic. A salient drawback of the sole stain style in SN is the restricted color-correlated features can be mined by deep neural networks. Stain augmentation (SA) seeks a converse direction to SN by simulating stain variations while preserving morphological features intact [21]. Tellz *et al.* [20] first tailored data augmentations from RGB color space to H&E color space. Afterward, in parallel with SN approaches, GAN is also widely adopted by stain augmentation applications *e.g.* HistAuGAN [23].

Previous works have compared the performance between SN and SA without interpretation of their differences [22]. Moreover, we have observed that the mathematical formulations of SN are coincidental with SA, where the transfer of SN depends on a prior Dirichlet distribution [25] and SA distorts images with a uniform distribution [20], depicted in Fig. 1. Hence, we make the first attempt to unify SN and SA for histology image analysis. Two primary contributions are summarized. First, a novel Random Stain Normalization and Augmentation (RandStainNA) method is proposed to bridge stain normalization and stain augmentation, consequently, images can be augmented with more realistic stain styles. Second, a random color space selection scheme is introduced to extend the target scope to various color spaces including HED, HSV, and LAB, to increase flexibility and produce an extra augmentation. The evaluation tasks include tissue classification and nuclei segmentation, and both show our method can consistently improve the performance with a variety of network architectures.

2   Methodology

Method Overview. Random Stain Normalization and **A**ugmentation (RandStainNA) is a hybrid framework designed to fuse stain normalization and stain augmentation to generate more realistic stain variations. It incorporates randomness to SN by automatically sorting out a random virtual template from pre-estimated stain style distributions. More specifically, from the perception of SN's viewpoint, stain styles 'visible' to the deep neural network are enriched in the training stage. Meanwhile, from the perception from the SA's viewpoint, RandStainNA imposes a restriction on the distortion range and consequently, only a constrained practicable range is 'visible' to CNN. The framework is a general strategy and task agonist, as depicted in Fig. 2.

Stain Style Creation and Characterization. Unlike the formulation of comprehensive color styles of nature images, stain style of histology remains to be a vague concept, which is primarily based on visual examination, restricting to obtain a precise objective for alleviating the stain style variation [16,24]. To narrow this gap, our work first qualitatively defines the stain style covering six parameter, namely the average and standard deviation of each channel in LAB color space [16]. We pick up LAB space for its notable capability to represent heterogeneous styles in medical images [16]. Novelly, we first transfer all histology slides in the training set from RGB space to LAB color space. Then the stain style of image x_i are depicted by $A_i = [a_i^{(l)}, a_i^{(a)}, a_i^{(b)}] \in \mathbb{R}^3$ and $D_i = [d_i^{(l)}, d_i^{(a)}, d_i^{(b)}] \in \mathbb{R}^3$, where $a_i^{(c)}, d_i^{(c)}$ are the average value and standard deviation of each channel $c \in \{l, a, b\}$ in image x_i, as shown in the pre-processing stage block in Fig. 2.

Virtual Stain Normalization Template. In routine stain normalization approaches [16,24], a source image is normalized to a pre-selected template image by aligning the average of A_s and standard deviation D_s of pixel values to the template A_t and D_t. Thus, it is sufficient to formulate a template image with $[A_t, D_t]$. In the proposed RandStainNA, we expand the uniformly shared one-template mode to a board randomly generated virtual templates $[A_v, D_v]$ scheme. To be more specific, iteratively, random A_v is sampled from distribution F_A, and likewise D_v is picked out from the other distribution F_D, which are jointly used as the target for every training sample normalization. Empirical results yield that eventual performance are robust to a wide range of distribution types of F_A and F_D, such as Gaussian and t-distribution. In the rest of this section, we simply leverage Gaussian distribution as the estimation *i.e.* setting $F_A = \mathcal{N}(M_A, \Sigma_A)$, $F_D = \mathcal{N}(M_D, \Sigma_D)$, where $\mathcal{N}(M, \Sigma)$ writes for the Gaussian distribution with expectation M and covariance matrix Σ. Notably, due to the orthogonality of channels, Σ is a diagonal matrix *i.e.* $\Sigma = \text{diag}(\sigma_1^2, \sigma_2^2, \sigma_3^2)$ for some σ_j with $j = 1, 2, 3$.

Statistics Parameters Estimation for Virtual Template Generation. The estimation of statistical parameters of $M_A, \Sigma_A, M_D, \Sigma_D$ are afterwards applied to the formation of stain style discussed above. A proper candidate is attributed to the sample channel mean values of all the training images for $\mathbf{M}_A$ and $\mathbf{M}_D$, as well as the standard deviations of samples for $\mathbf{\Sigma}_A$ and $\mathbf{\Sigma}_D$, based on the average value and standard deviation of the whole training set. However, two defects turn out in this discipline that one is the inefficiency to transverse the whole set, and the other is the special cases of infeasibility $e.g.$ federated learning or lifelong learning. Therefore, we provide a more computation-efficient alternative, by randomly curating a small number of patches from the training set and applying their sample mean and standard deviation as $\mathbf{M}_A, \mathbf{\Sigma}_A, \mathbf{M}_D, \mathbf{\Sigma}_D$. The empirical results suggest it can achieve competitive performance.

Image-Wise Normalization with Random Virtual Template. After transferring image $\mathbf{x}_i$ from RGB into LAB space, we write the pixel value as $[l, a, b]$. We denote the average and standard deviation (std) for each channel of this image as $\mathbf{A}_i = [a_i^{(l)}, a_i^{(a)}, a_i^{(b)}]$ and $\mathbf{D}_i = [d_i^{(l)}, d_i^{(a)}, d_i^{(b)}]$, and the generated random virtual template associated to $\mathbf{x}_i$ from F_A, F_D as $\mathbf{A}_v = [a_v^{(l)}, a_v^{(a)}, a_v^{(b)}]$ and $\mathbf{D}_i = [d_v^{(l)}, d_v^{(a)}, d_v^{(b)}]$. Then the image-wise normalization based on random virtual template is formulated as

$$
\begin{cases}
l' = \dfrac{d_v^{(l)}}{d_i^{(l)}}(l - a_i^{(l)}) + a_v^{(l)} \\[2ex]
a' = \dfrac{d_v^{(a)}}{d_i^{(a)}}(a - a_i^{(a)}) + a_v^{(a)} \\[2ex]
b' = \dfrac{d_v^{(b)}}{d_i^{(b)}}(b - a_i^{(b)}) + a_v^{(b)},
\end{cases}
\tag{1}
$$

Then, we transfer $[l', a', b']$ from LAB back to RGB space. Notably, we generate different virtual templates for images that vary at every epoch during the training stage. Therefore, RandStainNA can largely increase the data variations with the on-the-fly generate virtual templates.

Determine Random Color Space for Augmentation. By the computation of the stain style parameters $[\mathbf{M}, \mathbf{\Sigma}]$ of distinct color spaces, we can derive their associated F_A and F_D. Afterwards, we extend our RandStainNA from LAB to other color spaces $e.g.$ HED, HSV. This extension allows the proposal of a random color space selection scheme, which will further strengthen the regularization effect. The candidate pool comprises three widely-used color spaces in the domain of histology, $i.e.$ HED, HSV, LAB. Training iteratively, an initial color space $\mathcal{S}$ is an arbitrary decision with equal probability $i.e.$ $p = \frac{1}{3}$, or with manually-assigned values depending of the performance of each independent space. Subsequently, a virtual template is assigned to associate with $\mathcal{S}$ to perform image-wise stain normalization.

3   Experiments

Dataset and Evaluation Metrics. We evaluate our proposed RandStainNA on two image analysis tasks *i.e.* classification and segmentation. Regarding the patch-level classification task, we use a widely-used histology public dataset NCT-CRC-HE-100K-NONORM for training and validation, with the addition of the CRC-VAL-HE-7K dataset for external testing [9]. These two sets comprise a number of 100,000 and 7180 histological patches respectively, from colorectal cancer patients of multiple data centers with heterogeneous stain styles. We randomly pick up 80% from NCT-CRC-HE-100K-NONORM for training and the rest 20% for validation. The original dataset covers nine categories, but for the category of background, we can straightforwardly identify them in pre-processing stage with OTSU algorithm [15] and thus it is removed in our experiment for a more reliable result. The top-1 classification accuracy (%) is used as the metric for the 8-category classification task. For the nuclei segmentation task, we use a small public dataset of MoNuSeg [12], with Dice and IoU as the metrics.

Network Architecture and Settings. In the classification task, we employ six backbone architectures to perform the evaluations, namely the ResNet-18 [7], ResNet-50 [7], MobileNetV3-Small [8], EfficientNetB0 [19], ViT-Tiny [3] and SwinTransformer-Tiny [13]. These networks, including CNN and transformers, may represent a wide range of network capabilities, which effectively demonstrate the adaptability of our method in different settings. In the nuclei segmentation task, we use CIA-Net as the backbone [26] for its notable performance in small set processing. We use a consistent training scheme for distinct networks for performance comparison with stain augmentation and stain normalization methods. Detailed training schemes and hyper-parameter settings are shown in the supplementary material. We perform 3 random runs and compute the average for each experiments.

Compared Methods. All models are trained with morphology augmentation, namely the random vertical and horizontal flip. In both evaluation tasks, we compare our method with existing stain normalization [16] and stain augmentation [21,22] approaches performed in the three color spaces *i.e.* HED, HSV, LAB. Regarding the stain augmentation in HED, we employ a multiplication rule [22] that adds noise to each channel *i.e.* $p' = p * \varepsilon_1 + \varepsilon_2$, where p' is the augmented pixel value and p is the original pixel value, and ε_1 and ε_2 are uniform random noises, termed as stain augmentation scheme #1 (SA1). For the SA in HSV, we adopt an addition rule *i.e.* $p' = p + p * \varepsilon$ [22], termed as stain augmentation scheme #2 (SA2). We integrate the above two schemes for LAB stain augmentation, due to an absence of literature works for SA in LAB. We also configure two augmentation settings according to different degrees of distortion *i.e.* range of random noise, denoted as light (L) and strong (S) [21,22]. To fully retain recognizable morphological features, we do not take GAN-related approaches for comparison.

Table 1. Test accuracy (%) comparison on the tissue type classification task. We compare our method with stain augmentation (SA) [22] and stain normalization (SN) [16] in three color space *i.e.* LAB, HSV, HED [22]. In SA, we follow previous work [22] by leveraging two settings, namely light (L) and strong (S), determined by the degree of distortion. The best and second best are marked in boldface and with * respectively.

Method	ResNet18	ResNet50	MobileNet	EfficientNet	ViT	SwinTransformer
Baseline	84.20	72.07	80.25	79.62	72.85	71.06
SA1-L + LAB	84.62	77.24	84.09	81.71	75.17	69.42
SA1-S + LAB	89.35	87.97	90.79	90.81	84.77	76.76
SA2-L + LAB	93.55	92.81	92.72	93.66	89.90	88.42
SA2-S + LAB	90.77	90.50	89.13	89.64	84.84	75.13
SA1-L + HED	92.47	89.55	90.81	92.57	86.22	81.17
SA1-S + HED	88.77	87.92	86.58	88.67	87.42	76.50
SA2-L + HSV	91.39	88.97	88.97	91.10	82.80	78.70
SA2-S + HSV	91.93	90.06	90.22	91.76	85.81	77.83
SN + LAB	93.01	91.40	92.23	91.92	89.77	88.80
SN + HED	91.38	90.57	89.54	91.34	88.29	86.60
SN + HSV	93.85	93.86	92.38	93.90	90.63	86.21
Ours (LAB)	94.44*	93.97	93.94	93.54	90.30	91.01
Ours (HED)	93.28	93.61	91.69	92.67	91.41	90.03
Ours (HSV)	94.04	94.12*	94.06*	**94.81**	93.27*	**92.75**
Ours (Full)	**94.66**	**94.45**	**94.53**	94.62*	**93.34**	92.39*

Table 2. Performance comparison on nuclei segmentation in terms of Dice and IoU.

Metrics	Baseline	SA + LAB	SA + HED	SA + HSV	SN + LAB	SN + HED	SN + HSV	Ours
Dice	0.7270	0.7297	0.7354	0.7349	0.7792	0.7668	0.7780	**0.7802**
IoU	0.5564	0.5665	0.5758	0.5712	0.6302	0.6119	0.6291	**0.6335**

Results. Our method can consistently improve the baseline performance of the six backbone architectures in terms of test accuracy, with the implementation in three color spaces, as shown in Table 1. Therefore, it yields the effectiveness of RandStainNA. The hybrid architecture can outperform a sole deployment of either SN or SA. With the random color space selection scheme (denoted as 'full'), the RandStainNA achieves further performance improvement. To demonstrate the effects achieved with different approaches straightforwardly, we visualize the original raw images with stain variations, SN images, SA images, and images processed with our RandStainNA in Fig. 3. In the visualization graph, we use the results from SA and SN performed in HSV space as an example, which shows very similar outcomes in LAB and HED spaces. As shown, the SN unifies stain styles into a shared template that may leave out many useful features [22], and the SA may generate unrealistic images. In contrast, our method generates much more realistic images to reorganize by both human and deep learning techniques. The Fig. 4 provides the UMAP embedding of stain style parameters of $[\mathbf{M}, \boldsymbol{\Sigma}]$ in the associated solutions. The nuclei segmentation results are listed in

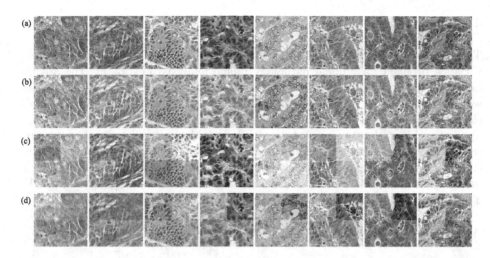

Fig. 3. The illustrative patch examples of (a) raw images (b) stain-normalized images (c) stain-augmented images (d) images processed with the proposed RandStainNA. We incorporate the results of four random runs into one image patch to demonstrate the different grades of randomness maybe achieved by the stain augmentation methods and our RandStainNA in (c) and (d).

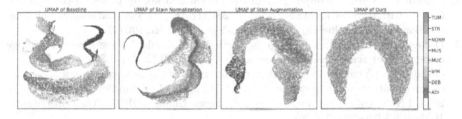

Fig. 4. UMAP [1] embedding of the stain style charactiersitic statistics *i.e.* $[\mathbf{M}, \mathbf{\Sigma}]$ of raw images, stain normalized images, stain augmented images and those augmented with our RandStainNA. As shown, our method can enrich the realistic stain styles in training CNNs.

the Table 2. For SN and SA in each color space, we pick up one configuration with higher performance in the classification task. Our method also achieves the best performance to demonstrate its effectiveness in various downstream tasks.

Ablation Study. The ablation study is performed on the classification task. First, we test the effect of the distribution style of $F_{\mathbf{A}}, F_{\mathbf{D}}$. The test accuracy is 93.98, 93.90, 93.04, 92.48 for Gaussian, t-distribution, uniform, and Laplace respectively. The effect of sample numbers to compute the sample mean and the standard deviation is also evaluated. The test accuracies are 93.42, 93.29, 94.08, 93.98 for the cases of computing the averages and standard deviations with 10 images per category, 100 images per category, 1000 images per category, and the whole training set respectively, which yields the robustness to $\mathbf{M}$ and $\mathbf{\Sigma}$.

4 Conclusion

The proposed RandStainNA framework aims to cope with the inevitable stain variance problem for clinical pathology image analysis. Leveraging the advantages of both stain normalization and stain augmentation, the proposed framework produces more realistic stain variations to train stain agnostic DL models. Additionally, RandStainNA is straightforward practically and efficient when applied as an on-the-fly augmentation technique, in comparison with most current GANs. Moreover, the result shows the feasibility to train robust downstream classification and segmentation networks on various architectures. One future direction of our current works is the expansion of color spaces, *e.g.* YUV, YCbCr, YPbPr, YIQ, XYZ [4], to further improve the generalization ability.

Acknowledgements. This work has been supported by NSFC grants 62102247.

References

1. Becht, E., et al.: Dimensionality reduction for visualizing single-cell data using umap. Nat. Biotechnol. **37**(1), 38–44 (2019)
2. Ciompi, F., et al.: The importance of stain normalization in colorectal tissue classification with convolutional networks. In: 2017 IEEE 14th International Symposium on Biomedical Imaging (ISBI 2017), pp. 160–163. IEEE (2017)
3. Dosovitskiy, A., et al.: An image is worth 16x16 words: Transformers for image recognition at scale. arXiv preprint arXiv:2010.11929 (2020)
4. Gowda, S.N., Yuan, C.: ColorNet: Investigating the importance of color spaces for image classification. In: Jawahar, C.V., Li, H., Mori, G., Schindler, K. (eds.) ACCV 2018. LNCS, vol. 11364, pp. 581–596. Springer, Cham (2019). https://doi.org/10.1007/978-3-030-20870-7_36
5. Gupta, V., Singh, A., Sharma, K., Bhavsar, A.: Automated classification for breast cancer histopathology images: Is stain normalization important? In: Cardoso, M.J., et al. (eds.) CARE/CLIP -2017. LNCS, vol. 10550, pp. 160–169. Springer, Cham (2017). https://doi.org/10.1007/978-3-319-67543-5_16
6. Gurcan, M.N., et al.: Histopathological image analysis: A review. IEEE Rev. Biomed. Eng. **2**, 147–171 (2009)
7. He, K., et al.: Deep residual learning for image recognition. In: Proceedings of the IEEE Conference on Computer Vision and Pattern Recognition, pp. 770–778 (2016)
8. Howard, A., et al.: Searching for mobilenetv3. In: Proceedings of the IEEE/CVF International Conference on Computer Vision, pp. 1314–1324 (2019)
9. Kather, J.N., et al.: Predicting survival from colorectal cancer histology slides using deep learning: A retrospective multicenter study. PLoS Med. **16**(1), e1002730 (2019)
10. Ke, J., et al.: Style normalization in histology with federated learning. In: 2021 IEEE 18th International Symposium on Biomedical Imaging (ISBI), pp. 953–956. IEEE (2021)
11. Khan, A.M., et al.: A nonlinear mapping approach to stain normalization in digital histopathology images using image-specific color deconvolution. IEEE Trans. Biomed. Eng. **61**(6), 1729–1738 (2014)

12. Kumar, N., et al.: A multi-organ nucleus segmentation challenge. IEEE Trans. Med. Imaging **39**(5), 1380–1391 (2019)
13. Liu, Z., et al.: Swin transformer: Hierarchical vision transformer using shifted windows. In: Proceedings of the IEEE/CVF International Conference on Computer Vision, pp. 10012–10022 (2021)
14. Nadeem, S., Hollmann, T., Tannenbaum, A.: Multimarginal Wasserstein Barycenter for stain normalization and augmentation. In: Martel, A.L., et al. (eds.) MICCAI 2020. LNCS, vol. 12265, pp. 362–371. Springer, Cham (2020). https://doi.org/10.1007/978-3-030-59722-1_35
15. Otsu, N.: A threshold selection method from gray-level histograms. IEEE Trans. Syst. Man Cybern. **9**(1), 62–66 (1979)
16. Reinhard, E., et al.: Color transfer between images. IEEE Comput. Graphics Appl. **21**(5), 34–41 (2001)
17. Salehi, P., et al.: Pix2pix-based stain-to-stain translation: a solution for robust stain normalization in histopathology images analysis. In: 2020 International Conference on Machine Vision and Image Processing (MVIP), pp. 1–7. IEEE (2020)
18. Shaban, M.T., et al.: Staingan: Stain style transfer for digital histological images. In: 2019 IEEE 16th International Symposium on Biomedical Imaging (Isbi 2019), pp. 953–956. IEEE (2019)
19. Tan, M., et al.: Efficientnet: Rethinking model scaling for convolutional neural networks. In: International Conference on Machine Learning, pp. 6105–6114. PMLR (2019)
20. Tellez, D., et al.: H and E stain augmentation improves generalization of convolutional networks for histopathological mitosis detection. In: Medical Imaging 2018: Digital Pathology, vol. 10581, p. 105810Z. International Society for Optics and Photonics (2018)
21. Tellez, D., et al.: Whole-slide mitosis detection in h&e breast histology using phh3 as a reference to train distilled stain-invariant convolutional networks. IEEE Trans. Med. Imaging **37**(9), 2126–2136 (2018)
22. Tellez, D., et al.: Quantifying the effects of data augmentation and stain color normalization in convolutional neural networks for computational pathology. Med. Image Anal. **58**, 101544 (2019)
23. Wagner, S.J., et al.: Structure-preserving multi-domain stain color augmentation using style-transfer with disentangled representations. In: de Bruijne, M., et al. (eds.) MICCAI 2021. LNCS, vol. 12908, pp. 257–266. Springer, Cham (2021). https://doi.org/10.1007/978-3-030-87237-3_25
24. Wang, Y.Y., et al.: A color-based approach for automated segmentation in tumor tissue classification. In: 2007 29th Annual International Conference of the IEEE Engineering in Medicine and Biology Society, pp. 6576–6579. IEEE (2007)
25. Zanjani, F.G., et al.: Stain normalization of histopathology images using generative adversarial networks. In: 2018 IEEE 15th International symposium on biomedical imaging (ISBI 2018), pp. 573–577. IEEE (2018)
26. Zhou, Y., Onder, O.F., Dou, Q., Tsougenis, E., Chen, H., Heng, P.-A.: CIA-Net: robust nuclei instance segmentation with contour-aware information aggregation. In: Chung, A.C.S., Gee, J.C., Yushkevich, P.A., Bao, S. (eds.) IPMI 2019. LNCS, vol. 11492, pp. 682–693. Springer, Cham (2019). https://doi.org/10.1007/978-3-030-20351-1_53

Identify Consistent Imaging Genomic Biomarkers for Characterizing the Survival-Associated Interactions Between Tumor-Infiltrating Lymphocytes and Tumors

Yingli Zuo[1], Yawen Wu[1], Zixiao Lu[2], Qi Zhu[1], Kun Huang[3], Daoqiang Zhang[1(✉)], and Wei Shao[1(✉)]

[1] MIIT Key Laboratory of Pattern Analysis and Machine Intelligence, College of Computer Science and Technology, Nanjing University of Aeronautics and Astronautics, Nanjing 211106, China
{dqzhang,shaowei20022005}@nuaa.edu.cn
[2] Department of Radiology, The Third Affiliated Hospital of Southern Medical University, Guangzhou 510630, China
[3] School of Medicine, Indiana University, Indianapolis, IN 46202, USA

Abstract. The tumor-infiltrating lymphocytes (TILs) and its correlation with tumors play a critical role in the development and progression of breast cancer. Existing studies have demonstrated that the combination of the whole-slide pathological images (WSIs) and genomic data can better characterize the immunological mechanisms of TILs and assess the prognostic outcome in breast cancer. However, it is still very challenging to characterize the intersections between TILs and tumors in WSIs because of their large size and heterogeneity patterns, and the high dimensional genomic data also brings difficulty for the integrative analysis with WSIs data. To address the above challenges, in this paper, we propose an interpretable multi-modal fusion framework, IMGFN, that can fuse the interaction information between TILs and tumors with the genomic data via an attention mechanism for prognosis predictions of breast cancer. Specifically, for WSIs data, we use the graph attention network (i.e., GAT) to describe the spatial interactions of TILs and tumor regions across WSIs. As to genomic data, we use co-expression network analysis algorithms to cluster genes into co-expressed modules followed by applying the Concrete Autoencoders to select survival-associated modules. Finally, a self-attention layer is adopted to combine both the imaging and genomic features for the prognosis prediction of breast cancer. The experimental results on The Cancer Genome Atlas(TCGA) dataset suggest that the proposed IMGFN can not only achieve better prognosis results than the comparing methods but also identify consistent survival-associated imaging and genomic biomarkers correlated strongly with the interaction between TILs and tumors.

Keywords: Tumor-infiltrating lymphocytes · Breast cancer · Graph attention network · Concrete Autoencoders · Prognosis prediction

© The Author(s), under exclusive license to Springer Nature Switzerland AG 2022
L. Wang et al. (Eds.): MICCAI 2022, LNCS 13432, pp. 222–231, 2022.
https://doi.org/10.1007/978-3-031-16434-7_22

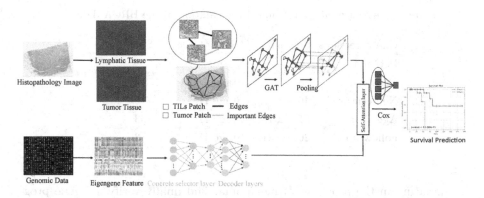

Fig. 1. The framework of the proposed method

1 Introduction

Recent studies demonstrate that the interactions between tumor and its microenvironment(TME) play a critical role for tumor growth and spread [1]. TME is consisted of heterogeneous cellular components including fibroblast cells and various types of immune cells that can influence cancer cell behavior [2]. Among different types of TME components, the tumour-infiltrating lymphocytes (TILs) is verified to have significant associations with the prognosis in various cancer types [3–5]. For example, recent studies [6] suggest the tumor-infiltrating B cells and T cells correlate with post-operative prognosis in triple-negative breast cancer. Fridman et al. [7] reports that the high TILs density in colorectal cancer usually enabled favorable clinical outcomes.

Early studies on the analysis of immunological mechanisms of TILs are either based on whole-slide pathological images (WSIs) or genomic data. On one hand, the recent advance of digital pathology makes the computerized quantitative analysis of TILs possible. For instance, Saltz et al. have presented global mappings of the spatial organization of TILs for over 5,000 H&E diagnostic WSIs from The Cancer Genome Atlas (TCGA) dataset [8]. However, it cannot reveal cellular information such as TIL counts and distribution in WSIs. Accordingly, Lu et al. [9] generate the cell-level TIL maps with 43 quantitative image features to perform the survival analysis on the breast cancer dataset. In addition, Wang et al. [10] present a cell-level spatial analysis pipeline of TILs on Whole-Slide Image, which reveals distinct clinical outcomes among multiple hepatocellular carcinoma subtypes. On the other hand, it is well known that cancer is caused by genomic mutations that can alter normal functions and biological processes in TILs, and several existing studies also explore the relationships between TILs and genomic data. Specifically, Zhou et al. [11] propose a machine learning-based computational framework for the recognition of the lncRNA signature of TILs. Liu et al. [12] analyze the TIL pattern of 993 melanoma samples and screened differential expression genes related to diverse immune sub-types. Other studies include [13] using the hierarchical clustering algorithm to explore the TIL-related

Table 1. Demographics and clinical information of the BRCA dataset

Characteristics	Summary	Characteristics	Summary
Patients:		Stage:	
Censored	381	Stage I	79
Non-censored	46	Stage II	252
Age (Y):	57.7 ± 13.2	Stage III	93
Follow-up (M):	26.4 ± 31.8	Stage IV	3

gene signature in the prognosis of melanoma, and finally verify a 7-gene prognostic signature associated with the TILs as a prognostic indicator.

Although much progress have been achieved, there still exists some limitations. Firstly, most of the studies predict the patients' survival only based on the spatial pattern of TIL indicated by WSI [8–10], which neglect to take the association between TILs and tumor into consideration. As a matter of fact, the intensity of the interactions between tumors and the host immune system is also an important indicator affecting survival of cancer patients [14,15]. In addition, to the best of our knowledge, all the existing studies only investigate the molecular or image profile of the TILs for the survival analysis task. Actually, different TIL bio-markers(i.e., image and gene) provide complementary information, which is useful for the prognosis task when used together [16,17].

To address the above limitations, we propose an interpretable multi-modal fusion framework, IMGFN, that can fuse the interactions between TILs and tumors with the genomic data via an attention mechanism for prognosis predictions of breast cancer. Specifically, for WSIs data, we use the graph attention network (i.e., GAT) to describe the spatial interactions of TILs and tumor regions across WSIs. As to genomic data, we apply the Concrete Autoencoders to identify survival-associated gene modules. Finally, a self-attention layer is adopted to combine both imaging and genomic features for the prognosis task on breast cancer.

2   Method

Figure 1 shows the framework of our study including four parts, *i.e.*, the preprocessing of the WSIs and genomic data, the characterization of the interaction between TILs and tumor patches by GAT, the identification of important eigengenes by Concrete Autoencoders, and the integrative analysis of imaging and genomic features for survival analysis of BRCA. We will firstly introduce the dataset used in this study.

Dataset: The Cancer Genome Atlas (TCGA) project has generated paired histology and genomic data and detailed clinical information for different types of cancer. In this work, we perform our experiments on the breast invasive carcinoma (BRCA) dataset derived from the TCGA. Specially, the TCGA-BRCA dataset contains pathological imaging, genomic, and clinical data including the corresponding survival information for 427 patients with breast invasive carcinoma. Among these patients, 46 of the them are non-censored patients. Table 1 summarizes the demographics of all the patients we use in this work.

Data Pre-processing: For the WSIs data, we first segment the WSIs into non-overlapping patches with 512×512 pixels and remove the background patches. Then, we construct a U-net++ network based on the annotated dataset released by Amgad M et al. [18] to segment the TIL and tumor tissues. By considering the uneven distribution of the different tissues, the Lovasz-Softmax loss [19] is used for U-net++ network training. Next, we feed the valid patches derived from WSIs into the U-net++ model to get the pixel-level prediction results.

For the genomic data, instead directly feeding them to our network, we use an algorithm called lmQCM [20] to obtain eigengene matrices of gene co-expression modules. Comparing with the initial genomic data, this algorithm reduces more than 99% of input features and simplify the networks significantly. For mRNA-seq data, we set lmQCM parameters $\gamma = 0.7, \lambda = 1, t = 1, \beta = 0.4$, minimum size of cluster $= 10$, and adopt Spearman's rank correlation coefficient to calculate gene-wised correlations. Finally, we get 57-dimensional eigengene feature for each sample.

Characterize the Interactions Between TILs and Tumor Patches by GAT: After getting the segmentation results of each valid patch, we calculate its tumor and TILs area ratios. Then, for each tissue type (i.e., TIL and tumor region) we select 200 patches with the largest tumor or TILs ratio. Based on the derived 400 patches, we construct a graph to describe the correlation among them. Specifically, let $G = (V, E)$ denotes a graph with nodes V and edges E. The 400 patches we selected are defined as our set of nodes V. We use the K-Nearest Neighbors (KNN) algorithm to find connections between adjacent patches to define our set of edges E and the adjacency matrix of our graph. In this work, we set $k = 20$. Meanwhile, we use a resnet-101 model pre-trained on ImageNet to extract 2048-dimension features from the selected patches as the graph node features. Then, we perform the principal component analysis (PCA) to reduce its dimensions to 64.

Next, we employ the graph-attention network (GAT) to learn the interactions among different node patches. It has been proved that graph-attention networks are versatile for different tasks and have fast computation speed as parallel computation can be performed on different nodes. If there is an edge from node j to node i, the attention coefficient e_{ij} is calculated as follows:

$$e_{ij} = a\left(W\boldsymbol{h}_i, W\boldsymbol{h}_j\right) \qquad (1)$$

where $W \in \mathbb{R}^{F' \times F}$ is a weight matrix, h_i and h_j are features of node i and node j, a is a shared attentional mechanism: $\mathbb{R}^{F'} \times \mathbb{R}^{F'} \rightarrow \mathbb{R}$. Then a softmax function across all the neighbor nodes $j \in N_i$ is used to normalize the attention coefficients of node i. Especially, there is a self-loop for each node to allow it update itself. This process can be expressed as:

$$\alpha_{ij} = \text{softmax}_j(e_{ij}) = \frac{\exp(e_{ij})}{\sum_{k \in N} \exp(e_{ij})} \qquad (2)$$

We feed graphs into the graph-attention network and a self-attention graph pooling layer is then adopted [21]. The key point of the pooling layer is that it uses a GNN to provide self-attention scores to attain the goal of graph hierarchical pooling. The self-attention score $Z \in \mathbb{R}^{N \times 1}$ is calculated as follows:

$$Z = \sigma(\widetilde{D}^{-\frac{1}{2}} \widetilde{A} \widetilde{D}^{-\frac{1}{2}} X \Theta_{att}) \qquad (3)$$

where σ is the activation function, $\widetilde{A} \in \mathbb{R}^{N \times N}$ is the adjacency matrix with self-connections, $\widetilde{D} \in \mathbb{R}^{N \times N}$ is the degree matrix of $\widetilde{A}$, $X \in \mathbb{R}^{N \times N}$ is the input features of the graph with N nodes and F-dimensional features, and $\Theta_{att} \in \mathbb{R}^{N \times 1}$ is the only parameter of the SAGPool layer. With the attention score derived from GAT and the graph pooling layer, we can easily get insight into the interactions between these TILs and tumor patches by the important edges we selected.

The Identification of Important Eigengenes by Concrete Autoencoders: With the gene co-expression modules derived from ImQCM, we employ the Concrete Autoencoders with a user-specified number of nodes, k, to identify survival associated features [22]. The Concrete Autoencoders is built based on Concrete random variables. Each element of sample m from the Concrete distribution is defined as:

$$m_j = \frac{exp((log\alpha_j + g_j)/T)}{\sum_{k=1}^{d} exp((log\alpha_k + g_k)/T)} \qquad (4)$$

where m_j refers to the jth element in a particular sample vector. T is a temperature parameter. g_j is a d-dimensional vector sampled from a Gumbel distribution. As the temperature of the layer approaches zero, the layer selects k individual input features. We feed gene co-expression modules data into the Concrete Autoencoders and extracted the genomic features. Meanwhile, by the pre-set k, we extract the most important k eigengene modules.

Integrative Analysis of Imaging and Genomic Features for Survival Analysis of BRCA: As we have already extracted the image and genomic features from GAT and Concrete Autoencoders, respectively, there still exists a data heterogeneity gap when combining them. To take full advantage of the inter-modality interactions between multi-modal data, we employ a self-attention layer [22] to fuse these features. The attention mechanism used is called "Scaled Dot-Product Attention". The input consists of queries and keys of dimension d_k,

Table 2. Comparisons of different survival analysis methods

Method	C-Index	AUC	Method	C-Index	AUC
IMGFN	0.743	0.753	Saltz [8]	0.586	0.618
OSCCA [17]	0.667	0.701	IMN	0.643	0.649
DGM2FS [16]	0.671	0.689	IGN	0.628	0.657
SALMON [23]	0.676	0.712	AIMGFN	0.714	0.721
Lu et al. [9]	0.597	0.614	JIMGFN	0.700	0.715

and values of dimension d_v and then pack them into a matrix Q, K and V. The output of the matrix is computing as:

$$Attention(Q, K, V) = softmax(\frac{QK^T}{\sqrt{d_k}})V \tag{5}$$

By the self-attention layer, we finally effectively fuse the image and genomic features for the following survival analysis task.

Prognosis Prediction: We feed the extracted feature to the Cox proportional hazards model for survival analysis. Here, we use the Area Under Curve (AUC) and Concordance Index (CI) values to measure our model performance. Besides, we also split patients into low-risk and high-risk groups via the median risk score predicted by the Cox proportional model, and use the KM-curves log-rank test to see if these two groups have distinct clinical outcomes.

3   Experiments and Results

Experimental Settings: In our experiment, we randomly divide all the patients into 3 groups, with 60% of the patients used for training, 20% for validation and 20% for testing. The proposed method is implemented using Pytorch and the models mentioned in this study were all trained on a single GPU (NVIDIA GeForce RTX3090). We optimize the proposed method via Adam algorithm, and the learning rate and batch size are set as 0.0001 and 64, respectively.

Results and Discussion: We compare our method with the following baseline methods by the measurement of CI and AUC. (1) OSCCA [17]: Integrate WSIs and genomic data for survival analysis via canonical correlation analysis method. (2) DGM2FS [16]: a diagnosis guided multi-modal feature selection method for survival analysis based on the combination of WSIs and genomic data (3) SALMON [23]: a deep-learning-based algorithm that can integrate multi-model genomics data for prognosis prediction. (4) An automatic pipeline that can extract cell-level TILs features from WSIs for survival analysis [9] (5) An

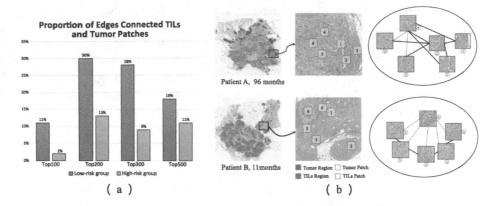

Fig. 2. (a): Proportion of Edges Connected TILs and Tumor patches (b): Interactions between TILs patches and tumor patches for long survival patients and short survival patients. The thick black line indicates the edges with higher weight.

automatic pipeline that can extract tissue-level TILs features from WSIs for survival analysis [8]. (6) IMN: A variant of IMGFN which only used the WSIs data. (7) IGN: A variant of IMGFN which only used the genomic data. (8) AIMGFN: A variant of IMGFN which fused the WSIs and genomic features by simply concatenating them together. (9) JIMGFN: A variant of IMGFN which combines the WSIs and genomic features together followed by a fully connected layer for prognosis predictions. The results are shown in Table 2.

As can be seen from Table 2, firstly, the methods (i.e., IMGFN, OSCCA, DGM2FS, AIMGFN, JIMGFN) that combine the both the image and genomic data can generally achieve higher CI and AUC values than the methods simply applying the single bio-marker (i.e., Lu et al. [9], Saltz [8], IMN, IGN). Secondly, the proposed IMGFN and its variants (i.e., AIMGFN. JIMGFN) can achieve better prognosis performance than other integrative analysis methods (i.e., OSCCA, DGM2FS, SALMON). The reasons lie in that our method considers the intrinsic correlation between the TILs and cancer patches in WSIs, which will benefit us in capturing the interactions between tumor and the host immune system. In comparison with the OSCCA and SALMON, the proposed method IMGFN applies the end-to-end deep learning framework to extract the image and genomic features that are more related to the following survival analysis task. Finally, the proposed method IMGFN is also superior to its two variants AIMGFN and JIMGFN, which shows the advantage of applying the self-attention layer for multi-modal data fusion.

In addition, we also compare the patient stratification performance of different methods. As can be seen from Fig. 3, IMGFN and OSCCA could achieve superior stratification performance than IMN and IGN which only use the WSIs or genomic data, proving that employing multi-modal data could achieve better performance in prognosis predictions. Moreover, we also observe that IMGFN outperforms OSCCA, indicating the advantage of applying the interaction

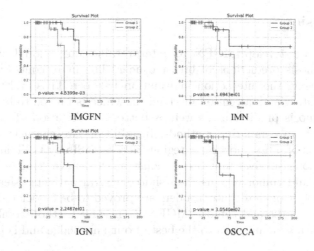

Fig. 3. Survival curves of IMGFN, IMN, IGN and OSCCA

information between TILs and tumor as well as the deep-learning-based method for the survival analysis. In addition, for the stratified patients in different groups, we check the important edges in each group according to their weights calculated via GAT. We select the top 100, 200, 300, 500 edges with the largest weights, and calculate the proportion of edges that connect TILs and tumor patches. As we can see from Fig. 2(a), the proportion of edges that connect TILs and tumor regions in low-risk group are higher than that in high-risk group, showing that the interactions of TILs and tumors play a critical role in prognosis prediction. In addition, as shown in Fig. 2(b), the weights of the edges that connect tumor and TIL regions are higher for patients in low survival risk group, which is also consistent with our knowledge that the brisk interaction between TIL and tumor regions will indicate a better clinical outcome.

Finally, as to genomic features, five eigengenes (Eigengenes 8, 21, 52, 15, 50) are identified with the highest score graded by the Concrete Autoencoders. Like the identified image features, the selected eigengenes in our model also show that the interactions between tumor and TILs will affect the prognosis of breast cancers. For example, Eigengene 8 is composed of 44 genes, and 7 of them (i.e., GATA3, BBS4, CELSR1, BCL2, FOXA1, ESR1, PGR) are correlated with epithelial tumor tube morphogenesis, which plays an essential role in breast tumor progression [24]. At the same time, 5 genes in Eigengene 8 are related to T cell differentiation, and it is reported that the co-culturing cancer cell lines with TILs increases epithelial cell migration and tube formation [25]. In addition, Eigengene 52 contains 11 genes, and HMBOX1 is widely accepted as the key genetic factor that promotes tumor immune escape via the immunosuppressive reprogramming of TILs [26]. PCM1 is one tumor-suppressor gene on chromosome arm 8p in early-onset and high-grade breast cancers [27].

4 Conclusion

In this paper, we develop IMGFN, an interpretable multi-modal fusion framework for prognosis predictions of breast cancer. The main contribution of our approach is fusing the interaction information between TILs and tumors with the genomic data via an attention mechanism, which is proved to be more accurately in prognosis predictions as well as better stratification of patients with breast cancer than comparing methods. In addition, we characterize the spatial interactions of TILs and tumor regions across WSIs by GAT and find that patients with long survival time are demonstrated to have stronger association between TILs and tumor regions than short survival patients. Meanwhile, the genes selected by Concrete Autoencoders are proved to be associated with interactions between TILs and tumor. IMGFN is the first method combining TILs information with genomic data to the best of our knowledge and is proved to be efficient.

Acknowledgements. This work was supported by the National Natural Science Foundation of China (Nos. 62136004, 61902183, 61876082, 61732006, 62076129), the National Key R&D Program of China (Grant Nos. 2018YFC2001600, 2018YFC20 01602).

References

1. Whiteside, T.L.: The tumor microenvironment and its role in promoting tumor growth. Oncogene **27**(45), 5904–5912 (2008)
2. Oya, Y., Hayakawa, Y., Koike, K.: Tumor microenvironment in gastric cancers. Cancer Sci. **111**(8), 2696–2707 (2020)
3. Yoneda, K., et al.: Alteration in tumoural PD-L1 expression and stromal CD8-positive tumour-infiltrating lymphocytes after concurrent chemo-radiotherapy for non-small cell lung cancer. Br. J. Cancer **121**(6), 490–496 (2019)
4. Wang, Z., et al.: Efficient recovery of potent tumour-infiltrating lymphocytes through quantitative immunomagnetic cell sorting. Nat. Biomed. Eng. **6**, 108–117 (2022)
5. Almangush, A., et al.: Tumour-infiltrating lymphocytes in oropharyngeal cancer: a validation study according to the criteria of the international immuno-oncology biomarker working group. Br. J. Cancer **126**(11), 1589–1594 (2022)
6. Kuroda, H., et al.: Tumor-infiltrating B cells and T cells correlate with postoperative prognosis in triple-negative carcinoma of the breast. BMC Cancer **21**(1), 1–10 (2021)
7. Fridman, W.H., Sautès-Fridman, C., Galon, J., et al.: The immune contexture in human tumours: impact on clinical outcome. Nat. Rev. Cancer **12**(4), 298–306 (2012)
8. Saltz, J., et al.: Spatial organization and molecular correlation of tumor-infiltrating lymphocytes using deep learning on pathology images. Cell Rep. **23**(1), 181–193 (2018)
9. Lu, Z., et al.: Deep-learning-based characterization of tumor-infiltrating lymphocytes in breast cancers from histopathology images and multiomics data. JCO Clin. Cancer Inform. **4**, 480–490 (2020)

10. Wang, H., Jiang, Y., Li, B., Cui, Y., Li, D., Li, R.: Single-cell spatial analysis of tumor and immune microenvironment on whole-slide image reveals hepatocellular carcinoma subtypes. Cancers **12**(12), 3562 (2020)

11. Zhou, M., et al.: Computational recognition of lncRNA signature of tumor-infiltrating B lymphocytes with potential implications in prognosis and immunotherapy of bladder cancer. Brief. Bioinform. **22**(3), bbaa047 (2021)

12. Liu, D., Yang, X., Wu, X.: Tumor immune microenvironment characterization identifies prognosis and immunotherapy-related gene signatures in melanoma. Front. Immunol. **12**, 663495 (2021)

13. Zeng, Y., et al.: Exploration of the immune cell infiltration-related gene signature in the prognosis of melanoma. Aging (Albany NY) **13**(3), 3459 (2021)

14. Yang, J., et al.: Assessing the prognostic significance of tumor-infiltrating lymphocytes in patients with melanoma using pathologic features identified by natural language processing. JAMA Netw. Open **4**(9), e2126337–e2126337 (2021)

15. Acs, B., et al.: An open source automated tumor infiltrating lymphocyte algorithm for prognosis in melanoma. Nat. Commun. **10**(1), 1–7 (2019)

16. Shao, W., et al.: Diagnosis-guided multi-modal feature selection for prognosis prediction of lung squamous cell carcinoma. In: Shen, D., et al. (eds.) MICCAI 2019. LNCS, vol. 11767, pp. 113–121. Springer, Cham (2019). https://doi.org/10.1007/978-3-030-32251-9_13

17. Shao, W., et al.: Ordinal multi-modal feature selection for survival analysis of early-stage renal cancer. In: Frangi, A.F., Schnabel, J.A., Davatzikos, C., Alberola-López, C., Fichtinger, G. (eds.) MICCAI 2018. LNCS, vol. 11071, pp. 648–656. Springer, Cham (2018). https://doi.org/10.1007/978-3-030-00934-2_72

18. Amgad, M., et al.: Structured crowdsourcing enables convolutional segmentation of histology images. Bioinformatics **35**(18), 3461–3467 (2019)

19. Berman, M., Triki, A.R., Blaschko, M.B.: The lovász-softmax loss: a tractable surrogate for the optimization of the intersection-over-union measure in neural networks. In: Proceedings of the IEEE Conference on Computer Vision and Pattern Recognition, pp. 4413–4421 (2018)

20. Zhang, J., Huang, K.: Normalized ImQCM: an algorithm for detecting weak quasi-cliques in weighted graph with applications in gene co-expression module discovery in cancers. Cancer Inform. **13**(CIN-S14021), 137–146 (2014)

21. Lee, J., Lee, I., Kang, J.: Self-attention graph pooling. In International conference on machine learning, pp. 3734–3743. PMLR (2019)

22. Abid, A., Balin, M.F., Zou, J.: Concrete autoencoders for differentiable feature selection and reconstruction. arXiv preprint arXiv:1901.09346 (2019)

23. Huang, Z., et al.: Salmon: survival analysis learning with multi-omics neural networks on breast cancer. Front. Genetics **10**, 166 (2019)

24. Ribatti, D.: Epithelial-mesenchymal transition in morphogenesis, cancer progression and angiogenesis. Exp. Cell Res. **353**(1), 1–5 (2017)

25. Cai, D.L., Jin, L.-P., Cai, D.L., Jin, L.-P.: Immune cell population in ovarian tumor microenvironment. J. Cancer **8**(15), 2915 (2017)

26. Zhou, C., et al.: Cancer-secreted exosomal miR-1468-5p promotes tumor immune escape via the immunosuppressive reprogramming of lymphatic vessels. Mol. Ther. **29**(4), 1512–1528 (2021)

27. Li, Y., Xu, Z., Li, J., Ban, S., Duan, C., Liu, W.: Interleukin-18 expression in oral squamous cell carcinoma: its role in tumor cell migration and invasion, and growth of tumor cell xenografts. FEBS Open Bio. **8**(12), 1953–1963 (2018)

Semi-supervised PR Virtual Staining for Breast Histopathological Images

Bowei Zeng[1], Yiyang Lin[1], Yifeng Wang[2], Yang Chen[1], Jiuyang Dong[1], Xi Li[3], and Yongbing Zhang[2(✉)]

[1] Tsinghua Shenzhen International Graduate School, Tsinghua University, Beijing, China
{zbw20,lyy20}@mails.tsinghua.edu.cn
[2] Harbin Institute of Technology (Shenzhen), Shenzhen, China
wangyifeng@stu.hit.edu.cn, ybzhang08@hit.edu.cn
[3] Department of Gastroenterology, Peking University Shenzhen Hospital, Shenzhen, China

Abstract. Progesterone receptor (PR) plays a vital role in diagnosing and treating breast cancer, but PR staining is costly and time-consuming, seriously hindering its application in clinical practice. The recent rapid development of deep learning technology provides an opportunity to address this problem by virtual staining. However, supervised methods acquire pixel-level paired H&E and PR images, which almost cannot be implemented clinically. In addition, unsupervised methods lack effective constraint information, and the staining results are not reliable sometimes. In this paper, we propose a semi-supervised PR virtual staining method without any pathologist annotation. Firstly, we register the consecutive slides and obtain the patch-level labels of H&E images from the registered consecutive PR images. Furthermore, by designing a Pos/Neg classifier and corresponding constraints, the output images maintain the Pos/Neg consistency with the input images, enabling the output images to be more accurate. Experimental results show that our method can effectively generate PR images from H&E images and maintain structural and pathological consistency with the reference. Compared with existing methods, our approach achieves the best performance.

Keywords: Semi-supervised learning · Generative adversarial network · Pathology consistency

1 Introduction

Histochemical staining is a crucial step in the workflow of histopathological analysis [5]. It can improve the color contrast between different tissue components and

B. Zeng, Y. Lin and Y. Wang—Co-first authors.

Supplementary Information The online version contains supplementary material available at https://doi.org/10.1007/978-3-031-16434-7_23.

facilitate the identification of different tissues and cells [1]. Among the histochemical stains, the most common one is H&E staining, which enables pathologists to observe tissues and cells' morphological features. However, it is difficult to accurately distinguish cancer subtypes based on H&E staining images alone. In contrast, immunohistochemistry (IHC) staining can detect protein expression qualitatively, quantitatively, and locally [11], which is vital for diagnosing cancers, histological classification, grading, staging, and prognosis of tumors [14].

As one type of IHC staining, progesterone receptor (PR) plays a vital role in diagnosing and treating breast cancer, which is considered one of the common IHC indicators [4]. However, the PR staining procedure is costly, tedious, and time-consuming and has not been fully used in clinical practice [3].

The rapid development of deep learning provides an opportunity to address this problem, and some image-to-image translation methods [2,7–9,13,16] have been successfully applied in virtual staining. Rivenson et al. used pix2pix to achieve virtual staining from bright-field images to H&E images. Moreover, they extended it to special stains such as Jones, Masson, and PAS [13]. Li et al. achieved virtual staining of unpaired images based on CycleGAN and introduced saliency constraints to avoid distortion of image content effectively [7]. Lin et al. accurately achieved the arbitrary transfer of multiple staining domains based on StarGAN [8]. In terms of IHC staining, Liu et al. proposed pathological consistency constraints and pathological representation networks to keep the same pathological properties of the generated and input images in different staining domains [9]; however, the quality of the generated images heavily depends on the expert annotation. In general, the existing virtual staining techniques are less studied in IHC staining. Virtual staining has been implemented only on Ki67 [16], which is still challenging for generating more specific IHC such as PR.

To solve the above-mentioned problems, we propose a virtual staining method from H&E images to PR images without paired data and expert annotation. We construct a semi-supervised model by the pathological consistency information of consecutive layer tissues to achieve virtual staining with high accuracy. The main contributions are listed as follows: (1) We register consecutive layers of tissues to obtain pathologically consistent information, fully exploiting valuable information and saving pathologists' time. (2) We design a Pos/Neg classification module and corresponding constraints, which helps the generated images to maintain the Pos/Neg consistency with the input images and thus be more accurate. (3) We achieve the transformation of H&E staining to PR staining of breast tissue for the first time. Meanwhile, the experimental results show that our method achieves excellent performance, which exceeds the existing methods.

2   Method

In the clinic, consecutive layers of tissue have similar information, which implies consistent pathological features. Inspired by this, we propose a virtual staining method for PR based on semi-supervised learning [10]. Our method is divided into two parts: 1. aligning consecutive layer images by a registration network and then assigning Pos/Neg labels to H&E images according to PR images character-istics; 2. introducing pathological consistency information into an unsupervised method according to the labels to improve staining accuracy.

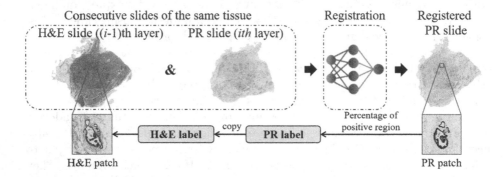

Fig. 1. Registration and label assignment.

2.1 Registration and Label Assignment

In clinical practice, pathologists can perform different stains on consecutive sec-tions of the same tissue to obtain H&E staining slides and PR staining slides, which contain associated information. Although these slides do not enable the pixel-level matching, the mapping relationship from H&E to PR can be observed at the slide-level. It is a pity for the traditional unsupervised method to treat them as independent slides and discard the information of consecutive slides completely. We utilize associated information through registration to make vir-tual staining more accurate.

We employ the registration network to align the consecutive slides (H&E slides and PR slides) [15], including preprocessing, initial alignment, affine transforma-tion, and nonlinear registration. Then, we obtain roughly matched slides, which are sliced into patches. The patches at corresponding regions of the slides are similar in histomorphology, having the same PR positive/negative (Pos/Neg) expression. Based on this property, we propose to use the information of approximately paired patches to assign the labels of PR patches to the corresponding H&E patches and realize the information transfer between consecutive layers, as shown in Fig. 1.

We can conveniently obtain positive/negative labels of PR patches based on their color characteristics. For each PR patch, the hematoxylin channel (blue) and the IHC channel (brown) can be separated by color deconvolution. In the IHC channel, we can calculate the percentage of the positive region in each PR patch and compare it with the threshold value. Patches with more than 10% positive region are labeled positive (+), patches with less than 2% positive region are labeled negative (−), and other patches are discarded. In this way, we can quickly obtain Pos/Neg labels of PR patches.

Further, we assign the label of each PR patch to the corresponding H&E patch as they have similar Pos/Neg expressions. Finally, we use the labels of patches as additional supervised information to construct a semi-supervised GAN to achieve PR virtual staining.

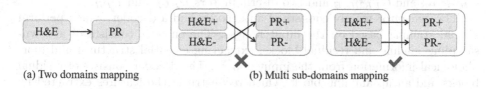

(a) Two domains mapping   (b) Multi sub-domains mapping

Fig. 2. Two domains mapping and multi sub-domains mapping.

2.2 PR Virtual Staining Based on Semi-supervised GAN

Multi Sub-domains Mapping. Unlike the general image-to-image translation, in the H&E-to-PR (H&E2PR) task, both H&E and PR are divided into positive and negative subclasses. Previously, only the style of the generated images and the real images is considered, but the Pos(+)/Neg(−) consistency is ignored as Fig. 2(a), which may cause H&E+ mapping to PR- or H&E- mapping to PR+, and this result is not consistent with the actual situation as Fig. 2(b). Therefore, we propose a semi-supervised GAN with a Pos/Neg classification module, constraining the input images and the generated images to maintain the Pos/Neg consistency through patch-level labels.

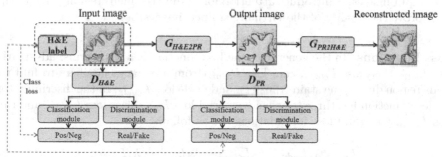

(a) H&E-PR-H&E virtual staining workflow

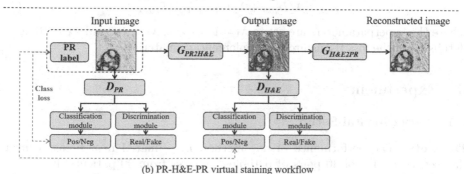

(b) PR-H&E-PR virtual staining workflow

Fig. 3. The structure of our PR virtual staining method.

Network Structure. We use the patch-level labels as additional supervised information that constrains the Pos/Neg property of the generated images. The structure of our network is shown in Fig. 3. It consists of two generators $G_{H\&E2PR}$ and $G_{PR2H\&E}$ and two discriminators $D_{H\&E}$ and D_{PR}.

The generator mainly consists of an encoder and a decoder, which perform virtual staining based on the input images. The encoder consists of a down-sampling module and residual blocks, extracting essential structural and morphological information from the input images. The decoder consists of residual blocks and an upsampling block, which reconstructs the features extracted by the encoder into the output images.

The discriminator mainly consists of a downsampling module, a discrimination module, and a classification module. The discrimination module aims to distinguish the real images from the generated images to confront the generator and make the generated image more realistic until Nash equilibrium. The role of the classification module is to classify the positive images and the negative images. In the process of class loss reduction, the generated images can learn the pathological characteristics of the input images and thus maintain the Pos/Neg consistency with the input images.

It is worth noting that our semi-supervised GAN does not use pixel-level ground truth in the virtual images generation. Relying on the Pos/Neg classification module and the corresponding patch-level label, we can maintain the same pathological properties between the input and output. Moreover, inspired by UGATIT [6], auxiliary classifier is used to learn the weight of the feature map from input images. It introduce attention for finding the focus region, which helps to improve the quality of the virtually stained images.

Loss Functions. In the generator, the loss function has four terms: adversarial loss L_{adv}, class loss L_{class}, cam loss L_{cam} (from auxiliary classifiers to find the focus region during the stain transfer), and cycle loss L_{cycle}. In the discriminator, the loss function has three terms: adversarial loss L_{adv}, class loss L_{class}, and cam loss L_{cam}. Our total loss formulations are as follows:

$$L_G = \lambda_1 L_{adv} + \lambda_2 L_{class} + \lambda_3 L_{cam} + \lambda_4 L_{cycle}, \tag{1}$$

$$L_D = \lambda_1 L_{adv} + \lambda_2 L_{class} + \lambda_3 L_{cam}, \tag{2}$$

where the hyperparameters are set to $\lambda_1 = 1$, $\lambda_2 = 1$, $\lambda_3 = 10$, and $\lambda_4 = 10$. The details of all the loss terms are in Supplementary materials.

3   Experiments

3.1   Experimental Setup

Datasets. The performance of our method is evaluated in a breast cancer dataset, consisting of 30 pairs of pathology images from 30 patients. Each pair includes 1 H&E slide and 1 PR slide, which are taken at ×5 magnification. The

Table 1. Comparison of CycleGAN, MUNIT, UGATIT and our method. We bold the highest value and underline the second highest value.

Method	CycleGAN	MUNIT	UGATIT	Our method
MAE↓	<u>7.032</u>	38.293	7.797	**4.927**
SSIM↑	0.961	0.611	<u>0.969</u>	**0.987**
MS-SSIM↑	<u>0.921</u>	0.472	0.897	**0.949**
PSNR↑	<u>28.306</u>	15.719	27.783	**31.225**
CSS↑	0.704	0.499	<u>0.707</u>	**0.715**

training and testing dataset contain 22 and 8 pairs of slides, respectively. Due to the memory limitation, all slides are cut into 256×256 patches with an overlap of 128. We randomly select 3,000 patches for each slide in the training set. After labelling, the patches with thresholds between 2% and 10% are removed, resulting in a training set containing 58,942 H&E patches and 62,218 PR patches.

Training Details. Our model is based on a PyTorch implementation on a computer with Intel(R) Xeon(R) Silver 4210R CPU, 128 GB RAM, and 1 NVidia RTX 3090 GPU. During training, each input image is passed through the data enhancement strategy of random horizontal flipping. Our model is trained for 200,000 iterations. During training, we use the Adam optimizer ($\beta_1 = 0.5$, $\beta_2 = 0.999$). The initial learning rate is set to 0.0001, and is decayed linearly after 100,000 iterations. In addition, the batch size is set to 1 during training.

Evaluation Metrics. We use MAE, SSIM, multi-scale SSIM (MS-SSIM), PSNR, and contrast-structure similarity (CSS) as quantitative evaluation metrics. The former four metrics are used to evaluate the quality of reconstructed images (as shown in Fig. 3). CSS is used to evaluate how much structural information of the input images is preserved in the output images.

3.2 Comparative Experiment Results and Analysis

We compare our method with CycleGAN [17], MUNIT [12], and UGATIT [6]. The results show that our method achieves the best performance. The results at the slide-level and patch-level are described in the following.

Patch-Level Performance. For vision evaluation, as shown in Fig. 4, none of the competing methods stain correctly over all the exhibited patches, while our method achieves the best performance. For quantitative evaluation, Table 1 summarizes the results for all methods. Compared with other comparison methods, our method obtains the highest accuracy in terms of MAE etc., indicating our method can ensure the consistency between the reconstructed and input images. Moreover, our method achieves the highest performance in CSS, indicating our results can preserve the structure and contrast of input H&E images well.

Slide-Level Performance. The most intuitive way to evaluate the PR staining is to stitch the generated PR patches into a slide and then compare it with the PR slide of the consecutive layer (considered as reference). In Fig. 4, we compare the generated PR slides with the reference. Our method can correctly stain the region of PR protein expression, which has a similar distribution to the reference PR slide.

In addition, a blind evaluation is employed, and the statistical results are shown in Fig. 5. We invite a pathologist to make a pathological determination of slides obtained by different methods. The positive slide and the negative slide are marked as PR+ and PR−, respectively. The slide-level results show a significant difference in the performance of the different methods for PR generation. Our method can better maintain the Pos/Neg consistency between the input images and output (generated) images.

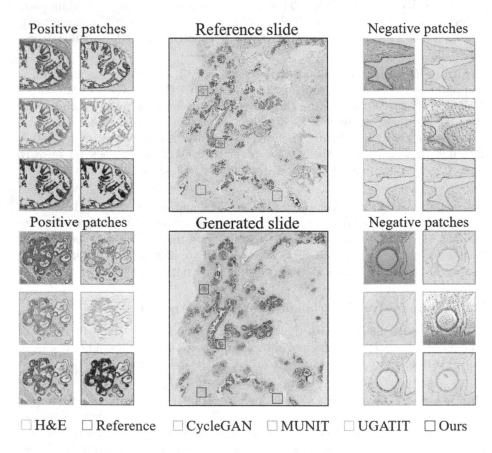

Fig. 4. Virtual PR staining results of different methods.

Virtual PR staining marks of different methods

		PR-	PR+	PR-	PR+	PR-	PR+	PR-	PR+
Reference marks	PR-	0	3	0	3	0	3	2	1
	PR+	2	3	0	5	0	5	0	5
		CycleGAN		MUNIT		UGATIT		Our method	

Fig. 5. Confusion matrices of PR marks. Each element in the matrices represents the number of slides with their PR marks evaluated by a board-certified pathologist (rows) based on: virtual PR staining, compared to the references (columns).

3.3 Ablation Experiment Results and Analysis

As shown in Fig. 6, the circled region is tumor-infiltrating tissue, which can be observed to be positive (brown) according to the reference. From the results without the classification module (Fig. 6(c)), it can be seen that the circled region is completely stained negative (blue). From the results without the registration process (Fig. 6(d)), it can be seen that the circled region tends to be stained positive (with some brown features), but the brown color is not apparent. From our results (Fig. 6(e)), the circled region can be clearly stained positive (brown). The results of ablation experiments show that both the classification module and the registration process are significant parts of our proposed method and play an indispensable role in achieving superior performance.

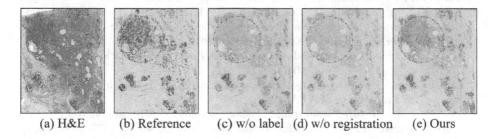

(a) H&E   (b) Reference   (c) w/o label   (d) w/o registration   (e) Ours

Fig. 6. Virtual PR-stained image results of ablation experiments. (Color figure online)

4   Conclusions

In conclusion, we propose a semi-supervised PR virtual staining method based on consecutive slides to realize the stain transformation between the H&E and PR domains. This method guarantees the images' structural and pathological consistency during virtual staining without any expert annotation, significantly reducing labor costs for pathologists. In our method, the stain transfer of unpaired patches is achieved based on the cycle-consistency framework. Moreover, roughly paired slides are obtained by the registration, which serves as additional supervised information to constrain the Pos/Neg property of the generated images to be consistent with the input images during transformation. Experiments are conducted on our breast cancer dataset to validate the performance; vision and quantitative analyses are provided. Numerous experiments validate our method's superiority, and the model performance is significantly better than that of the state-of-the-art methods.

Acknowledgements. This work was supported in part by the National Natural Science Foundation of China (61922048&62031023), in part by the Shenzhen Science and Technology Project (JCYJ20200109142808034), and in part by Guangdong Special Support (2019TX05X187).

References

1. BenTaieb, A., Hamarneh, G.: Adversarial stain transfer for histopathology image analysis. IEEE Trans. Med. Imaging **37**(3), 792–802 (2017)
2. Cai, Y., Hu, X., Wang, H., Zhang, Y., Pfister, H., Wei, D.: Learning to generate realistic noisy images via pixel-level noise-aware adversarial training. In: NeurIPS (2021)
3. Dabbs, D.J.: Diagnostic Immunohistochemistry E-Book: Theranostic and Genomic Applications. Elsevier Health Sciences (2017)
4. Daniel, A.R., Hagan, C.R., Lange, C.A.: Progesterone receptor action: defining a role in breast cancer. Expert Rev. Endocrinol. Metab. **6**(3), 359–369 (2011)
5. Feldman, A.T., Wolfe, D.: Tissue processing and hematoxylin and eosin staining. In: Day, C.E. (ed.) Histopathology. MMB, vol. 1180, pp. 31–43. Springer, New York (2014). https://doi.org/10.1007/978-1-4939-1050-2_3
6. Kim, J., Kim, M., Kang, H., Lee, K.: U-GAT-IT: unsupervised generative attentional networks with adaptive layer-instance normalization for image-to-image translation. arXiv preprint arXiv:1907.10830 (2019)
7. Li, X., et al.: Unsupervised content-preserving transformation for optical microscopy. Light Sci. Appl. **10**(1), 1–11 (2021)
8. Lin, Y., et al.: Unpaired multi-domain stain transfer for kidney histopathological images. In: Proceedings of AAAI (2022)
9. Liu, S., et al.: Unpaired stain transfer using pathology-consistent constrained generative adversarial networks. IEEE Trans. Med. Imaging **40**(8), 1977–1989 (2021)
10. Odena, A.: Semi-supervised learning with generative adversarial networks. arXiv preprint arXiv:1606.01583 (2016)
11. Ramos-Vara, J.: Technical aspects of immunohistochemistry. Vet. Pathol. **42**(4), 405–426 (2005)
12. Riesco, A.: MUnit: a unit framework for Maude. In: Rusu, V. (ed.) WRLA 2018. LNCS, vol. 11152, pp. 45–58. Springer, Cham (2018). https://doi.org/10.1007/978-3-319-99840-4_3
13. Rivenson, Y., et al.: Virtual histological staining of unlabelled tissue-autofluorescence images via deep learning. Nat. Biomed. Eng. **3**(6), 466–477 (2019)
14. Subik, K., et al.: The expression patterns of ER, PR, HER2, CK5/6, EGFR, KI-67 and AR by immunohistochemical analysis in breast cancer cell lines. Breast Cancer Basic Clin. Res. **4**, 117822341000400000 (2010)

15. Wodzinski, M., Müller, H.: DeepHistReg: unsupervised deep learning registration framework for differently stained histology samples. Comput. Methods Programs Biomed. **198**, 105799 (2021)
16. Xu, Z., Li, X., Zhu, X., Chen, L., He, Y., Chen, Y.: Effective immunohistochemistry pathology microscopy image generation using CycleGAN. Front. Mol. Biosci. **7**, 243 (2020)
17. Zhu, J.Y., Park, T., Isola, P., Efros, A.A.: Unpaired image-to-image translation using cycle-consistent adversarial networks. In: Proceedings of the IEEE International Conference on Computer Vision, pp. 2223–2232 (2017)

Benchmarking the Robustness of Deep Neural Networks to Common Corruptions in Digital Pathology

Yunlong Zhang[1,2], Yuxuan Sun[1,2], Honglin Li[1,2], Sunyi Zheng[2], Chenglu Zhu[2], and Lin Yang[2(✉)]

[1] College of Computer Science and Technology, Zhejiang University, Hangzhou, China
[2] School of Engineering, Westlake University, Hangzhou, China
yanglin@westlake.edu.cn

Abstract. When designing a diagnostic model for a clinical application, it is crucial to guarantee the robustness of the model with respect to a wide range of image corruptions. Herein, an easy-to-use benchmark is established to evaluate how deep neural networks perform on corrupted pathology images. Specifically, corrupted images are generated by injecting nine types of common corruptions into validation images. Besides, two classification and one ranking metrics are designed to evaluate the prediction and confidence performance under corruption. Evaluated on two resulting benchmark datasets, we find that (1) a variety of deep neural network models suffer from a significant accuracy decrease (double the error on clean images) and the unreliable confidence estimation on corrupted images; (2) A low correlation between the validation and test errors while replacing the validation set with our benchmark can increase the correlation. Our codes are available on https://github.com/superjamessyx/robustness_benchmark.

Keywords: Robustness · Digital pathology · Benchmark · Corruption

1 Introduction

Deep neural networks (DNNs) have recently made significant advances to a variety of computer vision tasks [8,13,22]. Nevertheless, it has been revealed that DNNs are vulnerable to input corruptions [1,7,11,14,25]. In digital pathology image analysis, DNNs will be further affected by corruptions compared to natural image processing due to the following reasons: (1) The complex imaging

---

Y. Zhang and Y. Sun—Equal contribution.

Supplementary Information The online version contains supplementary material available at https://doi.org/10.1007/978-3-031-16434-7_24.

processes, including tissue processing, cutting, staining, scanning, and storage [3], often generate more severe corruptions; (2) Interclass differences in pathology images are smaller and blurrier than those in natural images, causing the decision boundary relies more on details and is more susceptible to corruptions. Moreover, diagnostic systems must be robust to corruption since their predictions influence or even determine subsequent treatment decisions. Therefore, studying a robust model against image corruption is crucial for pathology image analysis.

It is pivotal to design a model evaluation criterion prior to building robust models. However, it is impossible to test models against all possible corruption types. To remedy this, we propose to evaluate models on certain types of corruptions that commonly occur in pathology images. More specifically, a new benchmark is presented to evaluate the model performance on nine types of common corruptions, each spanning five levels of severity. These corruptions are easy-to-use in practical settings since they are implemented by easy image processing techniques. We apply the proposed corruptions to the validation set of two large multi-center datasets, generating two benchmark datasets, Patchcamelyon-C and LocalTCT-C. Moreover, two classification and one ranking metrics are designed to evaluate the stability of the prediction (i.e., the accuracy of classification) and of the confidence (i.e., probabilities associated with the predicted class).

With the proposed benchmark, we evaluate the performance of ten convolutional neural networks (CNNs) and three vision transformers. Experimental results indicate that (1) the error rate on corrupted images is approximately doubled on clean images. Even though DNNs have been constantly improved over the past decade, their classification performance on corrupted pathology images changes slightly; (2) All models show unreliable confidence estimations while the robustness of the confidence seems to be slightly opposite to that of the prediction; (3) When applying models to practical scenarios, the validation error has a low correlation with the test error (Pearson's Correlation $r = -0.02$ on Patchcamelyon), failing in providing an unbiased evaluation of a model in general machine learning algorithms. The error on our benchmark is more correlated with the test error (improving Pearson's Correlation on Patchcamelyon to 0.45), illustrating our benchmark is better suited than the validation set in evaluating the generalization ability of the model.

Related work. Several studies have revealed that DNNs are vulnerable to common corruptions, such as blur and Gaussian noise [7] and translations [1]. In the field of digital pathology, few studies have also confirmed that the performance of DNNs drops a lot when encountering bubbles, uneven illumination, and so on [31]. To systematically study and improve the robustness of DNNs against corruptions, corruption benchmarks were first presented in the field of image recognition [14] and were further extended to object detection [20], semantic segmentation [16], pose estimation [30], and person Re-ID [5]. Our benchmark is inspired by them but is specially designed for pathology images in the aspects of the corruption type and metric choices.

The confidence plays an important role in clinical diagnosis. For instance, when confidence in a network for disease diagnosis is poor, control should be transferred to doctors [15]. However, the unreliable confidence becomes the critical weakness of most DNNs [12]. In our benchmark, a new metric to evaluate the stability of confidence under corruption is proposed.

2   Benchmark Design

2.1   Formulation

Prediction error under corruptions. Assume we have a classifier f trained on samples from a distribution $\mathcal{D}$. Most existing studies supposed test samples drawn from the same distribution, i.e., $\{(x, y)\} \sim \mathcal{D}$, and evaluated their methods by calculating $\mathbb{P}_{(x;y)}(f(x) = y)$. Yet in a vast range of cases the classifier is tasked with classifying low-quality or corrupted inputs. In this view, a more suitable way to evaluate the error of the classifier is

$$\mathbb{E}_{c \in C}[\mathbb{P}_{(x;y)}(f(c(x)) = y)]. \tag{1}$$

where C denotes a set of corruption functions that will occur in pathology images.

Confidence ranking under corruptions. Intuitively, corruptions will undermine the confidence, causing samples with more severe corruptions are predicted with less confidence. We would like the confidence estimation of DNNs, i.e., $\hat{p}(x) = \max \mathbb{P}(f(x)|x)$, to match human intuition. Thus, confidence values should obey

$$\hat{p}(c(x, s1)) > \hat{p}(c(x, s2)), s.t. 0 \leq s1 < s2 \leq 5, \tag{2}$$

where $c(x, s1)$ and $c(x, s2)$ denote corruption samples with severity levels $s1$ and $s2$, respectively. Besides, the sample with the severity level of 0 denotes the clean one, i.e., $c(x, 0) = x$.

The corruption functions C is the core in Eq. 1 and Eq. 2. However, defining all possible C is unfeasible because the computational cost grows proportionally to the number of corruption functions $|C|$. Hence, we design the corruption functions that often occur in pathology images in Sect. 2.2. Moreover, in Sect. 2.3, two classification and one ranking metrics are proposed to measure the stability of the prediction and of the confidence.

2.2   Corruption Setup

The presented corruptions consist of several types of Digitization: *JPEG* and *pixilation*; Blur: *defocus blur* and *motion blur*; Color: *brightness*, *saturation*, and *hue*; and Stain: *mark* and *bubble* (illustrated in Fig. 1). These types of corruptions are then introduced in detail.

The *JPEG* is a lossy image compression format and imitates the image distortion brought by different storage formats. The common image compression methods in digital slides include JPEG, JPEG2000, JPEG-XR, H.265, and JPEG-LS

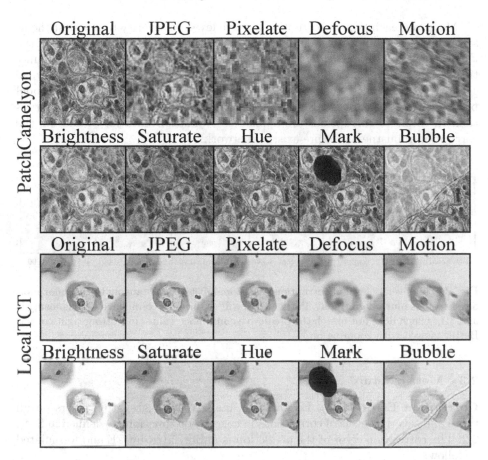

Fig. 1. Two examples from PatchCamelyon and LocalTCT are imposed to nine types of corruptions that commonly occur in pathology images.

[18]. The *pixilation* occurs when images are enlarged beyond the true resolution [21]. As an example, when the classifier is trained on the data at 40× magnification and tested on the data at 20× magnification, the *pixilation* will occur when test images are zoomed in twice in the evaluation process. The *defocus blur* occurs in the situation of insufficient focusing accuracy of the auto-focusing systems [10]. Similarly, the *motion blur* results from sample movement during camera exposure [10]. The *brightness, saturation,* and *hue* vary in the cases of different illuminations, scanners, stain concentration or even time elapse [6], severely degrading the generalization ability of DNNs [32]. The *mark* and *bubble* are two typical stains in pathology images. The *mark* appears when pathologists use marking pens to delineate regions of interest on a pathology slide, for measurement, or other uses [31]. The *bubble* is introduced by air getting underneath the coverslip [27].

Moreover, each type of corruption has five levels of severity to manifest themselves at varying intensities. One example with five different severity levels of the *defocus blur* is given in Fig. 2. All types of corruptions are implemented by functions so that they can be plugged into the dataloader for portability and storage saving. Although these corruptions are not equivalent to real-world ones, model performance on them can also reflect the adaptive ability of models to corruption. In total, 45 corruptions are applied to validation data for evaluating the corruption robustness of a pre-existing network.

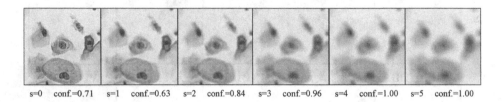

s=0   conf.=0.71   s=1   conf.=0.63   s=2   conf.=0.84   s=3   conf.=0.96   s=4   conf.=1.00   s=5   conf.=1.00

Fig. 2. The severity level of corruption rises from left to right, causing the cell morphology becomes blurred gradually. Pathologists will reduce the confidence in diagnosing it as LSIL, which does not match the predictive confidence values in bottom right corner. Better viewed with zooming in.

2.3   Metric Setup

Corruption Error (CE). Eq. 1 can be realized by aggregating errors on all types and severity levels of corruptions in corruption functions C defined in Sect. 2.2. The corruption error of the prediction is abbreviated by CE and formulated as follow:

$$\text{CE} = \frac{1}{N_c * N_s} \sum_{c=1}^{N_c} \sum_{s=1}^{N_s} E^{c,s}, \tag{3}$$

where $E^{c,s}$ denotes the error on corruption type c at level of severity s, while $N_c = 9$ and $N_s = 5$ indicate the number of corruptions and severity levels, respectively.

Relative Corruption Error (rCE). We also focus on the degraded performance resulting from corruptions. To measure the relative degradation of performance on corrupted data compared to clean data, the rCE is defined as

$$\text{rCE} = \frac{\text{CE}}{\text{Error}}, \tag{4}$$

where Error is the error on the validation set without corruption. Investigating which components are relative to the rCE is essential for further improving model robustness against corruptions.

Corruption Error of Confidence (CEC). Predictive confidence values may not match pathologist's intuition that confidence values fall with corruption severity levels increasing (e.g., the example in Fig. 2). To measure this mismatch, a new metric, CEC, based on the number of swap operations in the bubble sort method is presented. Specifically, with the confidence sequence $S(x)$ denoted by $\{\hat{p}(c(x,0)), \ldots, \hat{p}(c(x,N_s))\}$, the CEC is defined as

$$\text{CEC} = \frac{1}{N_v * N_c} \sum_{c=1}^{N_c} \sum_{x \in \mathcal{V}} \frac{K_\tau(S(x))}{C_{N_s}^2}, \tag{5}$$

where $\mathcal{V}$ denotes the validation set, Kendall Tau $K_\tau()$ [9] denotes the number of swap operations when sorting the confidence sequence from largest to smallest with the bubble sort method and $C_{N_s}^2$ is the comparison times between any two confidence values in S.

3 Experiments

3.1 Experimental Setup

Corruption implementation. Here, implementations of corruptions are introduced in brief. The *JPEG* saves the image to jpeg format and then reloads it. The *pixilation* zooms in the image and then zooms out it to its original shape. The *defocus blur* and *motion blur* filter the image with two customized kernels. The *brightness*, *saturation*, and *hue* modify the image in the corresponding channel of the HSV space. The *mark* and *bubble* mix the image with predefined matrix of mark and bubble examples, respectively.

Datasets. To evaluate the robustness against corruptions, one histopathological dataset, i.e., PatchCamelyon [29], and one cytological dataset, i.e., LocalTCT, are adopted. The PatchCamelyon is derived from the Camelyon 16 challenge [4]. It is divided into a training set of 262,144 examples, and a validation and test set both of 32,768 examples. Each example has the resolution of 96 × 96 and a binary label indicating the presence of metastatic tissue. The LocalTCT dataset is provided by the cervical cancer pathology screening of local hospitals, which contains about 16,902 WSIs at 20× magnification. Six categories patches with the resolution of 224 × 224 are collected and annotated by three professional pathologists, including 18,912 HSILs, 20,599 LSILs, 23,488 ASC-Hs, 21,869 ASC-USs, 2,743 AGCs and 87,592 negative cells. We divide them into train&validation&test datasets, consisting of 110,701, 32,253, and 32,249 patches, respectively. To be adaptive for application scenarios, the test set is sampled from more than 6 hospitals that are not included in the training and validation sets. Moreover, the proposed corruptions are applied to the validation set of these two datasets, generating two corruption benchmark datasets, PatchCamelyon-C and LocalTCT-C.

DNNs Choice. The robustness of ten CNNs and three vision transformers is investigated. Ten CNNs include classical (Alexnet [17], VGG16 [24], ResNet18 [13], ResNet34, ResNet50, and ResNet101), lightweight (MobileNetV2 [23] and shuffleNet [33]), and SOTA models (EffecientNetB0 [26] and EffecientNetB7). Vision transformers cover ViT [8] and its newest variants, SwinTransformer [19] and DeiT [28]. Three vision transformers are not applied to the PatchCamelyon due to their unstable training procedure at the resolution of 96 × 96.

3.2   Experimental Results

Proposed corruptions are close to reality while keeping the diagnostic information in human experts' opinion. In Sect. 2.2, corruption types have been discussed that they are common in reality. Herein, the design of the corruption severity level is also explored to ensure its clinical significance. Otherwise, the diagnostic information remaining in the corrupted images is also crucial to the clinical value of proposed corruptions. 3 images with 45 corruptions each (135 images in total) for two datasets are evaluated by experts. 127 Patchcamelyon and 130 LocalTCT patches are thought likely to appear in the real world. Meanwhile, 118 Patchcamelyon and 127 LocalTCT patches can be correctly recognized by experts.

Table 1. Robustness performance on the Patchcamelyon-C and LocalTCT-C. The first and second best results are emphasized by <u>**value**</u> and **value**, respectively. Results reported by aggregating MAE numbers over 3 different seeds.

Method	PatchCamelyon				LocalTCT			
	Error(%)	CE(%)	rCE	CEC(%)	Error(%)	CE(%)	rCE	CEC(%)
AlexNet	14.94	26.87	<u>**1.80**</u>	53.85	16.06	30.64	<u>**1.91**</u>	43.25
VGG16	10.34	**23.16**	2.24	48.56	13.51	30.24	2.24	44.16
ResNet18	11.12	24.84	2.23	44.70	13.23	30.48	2.30	41.41
ResNet34	11.22	**23.60**	2.10	43.47	12.92	28.38	2.20	**38.89**
ResNet50	12.54	28.84	2.30	47.00	12.96	31.61	2.44	41.41
ResNet101	12.00	25.15	2.09	**43.40**	13.25	29.64	2.24	**36.29**
MobileNetV2	9.68	26.60	2.75	44.30	12.81	30.24	2.36	43.61
ShuffleNet	13.53	26.15	**1.93**	53.56	14.53	32.91	2.26	46.98
EfficientNetb0	10.76	26.19	2.43	<u>**42.75**</u>	12.96	30.51	2.35	46.70
EfficientNetb7	10.39	24.89	2.39	43.75	12.56	<u>**26.36**</u>	2.10	44.11
ViT	–	–	–	–	15.30	30.91	2.02	48.23
Swin Trans	–	–	–	–	13.00	28.47	2.19	45.08
DeiT	–	–	–	–	13.85	**27.81**	**2.01**	43.36

Image corruptions decrease the prediction accuracy. The robustness performance of models is shown in Table 1. The related metrics on classification performance, Error, CE, and rCE, are first discussed. rCE values of all models range from 1.8 to 2.8. In other words, the error on corrupted images is 0.8 to 1.8 times larger than that on clean images, indicating the poor robustness of modern DNNs. On both datasets, AlexNet shows the worst Error on all CNNs while it has the best rCE value. Overall, its CE is comparable to the other CNNs.

That is, although CNNs are constantly improved in the past decade, their performance on corrupted images changes little while causing the incredibly worse robustness. Moreover, three vision transformers have smaller rCE values than most CNNs, illustrating their better robustness towards image corruptions.

Model confidence is unstable to image corruptions. We analyze the performance of the CEC and find that CEC values of all models range from 35% to 55%, which means nearly half of all confidence values are falsely ranked. This phenomenon manifests the terrible confidence estimation of modern DNNs. Comparing CEC values of CNNs and vision transformers, it is found that the confidence of vision transformers is less reliable than that of most CNNs. Another interesting observation is that the CEC and rCE seem to be in the opposite direction. In other words, if a model has better robustness of the prediction, its robustness of the confidence is worse.

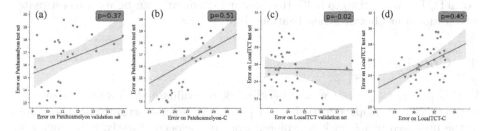

Fig. 3. Pearson correlation coefficients between the error on Patchcamelyon validation and test sets (a), Patchcamelyon-C and Patchcamelyon test set (b), LocalTCT validation and test sets (c), and LocalTCT-C and LocalTCT test set (d). Four correlation coefficients are all calculated by 30 points. Results show that the performance on our benchmark is more closely related to that on the test set.

Corruption types affect model performance. Comparing the performance on only one type of corruption (shown in Table A1 and Table A2 of Appendix), more phenomena deserve attention. Firstly, the architecture is robust to some corruptions while vulnerable to others. For example, as shown in Table A1, the accuracy of AlexNet changes slightly when encountering the *JPEG* (i.e., error of 20.99%), whereas *hue* will severely impair its accuracy (i.e., error of 38.50%). The reason causing this may be that AlexNet is sensitive to the statistical variation while is robust to texture details. Secondly, corruption type has effects on the performance of DNNs. The top half of Table A1 shows that most architectures' CE values below 20% on the corruption of *mark* while having CE values above 30% on the corruption of *defocus blur*. Thirdly, the performance of models, especially the CEC, varies widely on the same corruption. As shown in the top half of Table A2, the best CEC is 48.31% and the worst one is 72.54% when the *hue* varies.

Early-stopping helps improve robustness towards corruptions. The early-stopping is a regularization technique used to avoid overfitting when the validation error does not drop. We find that overfitting also harms the corruption robustness of models. As shown in Fig. A1 of Appendix, although the validation error has stabilized after the 4,000 iterations, CE values rise one to two points compared to the best results at the 4,000 iterations. Thus, early-stopping is also helpful for improving models' robustness with respect to image corruption.

Robustness against corruptions is related to the generalization ability of models. Figure 3(a)–(d) show the correlation between the error on the validation set or our benchmark, and the error on the test set. On the Patchcamelyon dataset, the proposed benchmark has a higher Pearson correlation coefficient than the clean validation set (0.51 v.s., 0.37). On the LocalTCT dataset, the correlation coefficient between the validation and test errors is −0.02, which means no correlation or even slightly negative correlation between them. In other words, the validation set loses its ability to choose the model with good generalization. In comparison, the correlation coefficient between the error on LocalTCT-C and LocalTCT test set rises to 0.45. Hence, our benchmark can be used to estimate which model has better generalization ability.

4   Conclusion

In this paper, we present a new benchmark to evaluate the robustness of current DNNs with respect to real-world pathology image corruptions. The value of the proposed benchmark is explored from two aspects. Firstly, it is crucial to guarantee the robustness of the model for pathology image analysis. However, there is still considerable room for improving the models' robustness against image corruption. Hence, we encourage more efforts to be devoted to improving the models' robustness using our benchmark. Secondly, experimental results show that the proposed benchmark is more reliable than the validation set in accurately evaluating the generalization behavior of models, which is useful for practitioners to design the right model for their task at hand.

Limitations and Future Work. Our goal is to investigate the performance of DNNs on corrupted images, but the role of input augmentation is neglected in this paper. In fact, augmentation is verified to be able to improve the robustness towards corruption in the field of digital pathology [32]. Moreover, strong augmentations may be the recipe of the big architectures in improving robustness [2]. Next, we will analyze the impact of augmentation on corruption robustness.

Acknowledgements. This work was funded by China Postdoctoral Science Foundation (2021M702922).

References

1. Azulay, A., Weiss, Y.: Why do deep convolutional networks generalize so poorly to small image transformations? arXiv preprint arXiv:1805.12177 (2018)
2. Bai, Y., Mei, J., Yuille, A.L., Xie, C.: Are transformers more robust than CNNs? Adv. Neural Inf. Process. Syst. **34** (2021)

3. Barisoni, L., Lafata, K.J., Hewitt, S.M., Madabhushi, A., Balis, U.G.: Digital pathology and computational image analysis in nephropathology. Nat. Rev. Nephrol. **16**(11), 669–685 (2020)
4. Bejnordi, B.E., et al.: Diagnostic assessment of deep learning algorithms for detection of lymph node metastases in women with breast cancer. JAMA **318**(22), 2199–2210 (2017)
5. Chen, M., Wang, Z., Zheng, F.: Benchmarks for corruption invariant person re-identification. arXiv preprint arXiv:2111.00880 (2021)
6. Clarke, E.L., Treanor, D.: Colour in digital pathology: a review. Histopathology **70**(2), 153–163 (2017)
7. Dodge, S., Karam, L.: Understanding how image quality affects deep neural networks. In: 2016 Eighth International Conference on Quality of Multimedia Experience (QoMEX), pp. 1–6. IEEE (2016)
8. Dosovitskiy, A., et al.: An image is worth 16x16 words: transformers for image recognition at scale. arXiv preprint arXiv:2010.11929 (2020)
9. Fagin, R., Kumar, R., Sivakumar, D.: Comparing top k lists. SIAM J. Discrete Math. **17**(1), 134–160 (2003)
10. Farahani, N., Parwani, A.V., Pantanowitz, L., et al.: Whole slide imaging in pathology: advantages, limitations, and emerging perspectives. Pathol. Lab. Med. Int. **7**(23–33), 4321 (2015)
11. Geirhos, R., Rubisch, P., Michaelis, C., Bethge, M., Wichmann, F.A., Brendel, W.: Imagenet-trained cnns are biased towards texture; increasing shape bias improves accuracy and robustness. arXiv preprint arXiv:1811.12231 (2018)
12. Guo, C., Pleiss, G., Sun, Y., Weinberger, K.Q.: On calibration of modern neural networks. In: International Conference on Machine Learning, pp. 1321–1330. PMLR (2017)
13. He, K., Zhang, X., Ren, S., Sun, J.: Deep residual learning for image recognition. In: Proceedings of the IEEE Conference on Computer Vision and Pattern Recognition, pp. 770–778 (2016)
14. Hendrycks, D., Dietterich, T.: Benchmarking neural network robustness to common corruptions and perturbations. arXiv preprint arXiv:1903.12261 (2019)
15. Jiang, X., Osl, M., Kim, J., Ohno-Machado, L.: Calibrating predictive model estimates to support personalized medicine. J. Am. Med. Inf. Assoc. **19**(2), 263–274 (2012)
16. Kamann, C., Rother, C.: Benchmarking the robustness of semantic segmentation models with respect to common corruptions. Int. J. Comput. Vis. **129**(2), 462–483 (2021)
17. Krizhevsky, A., Sutskever, I., Hinton, G.E.: Imagenet classification with deep convolutional neural networks. Adv. Neural Inf. Process. Syst. **25** (2012)
18. Liu, F., Hernandez-Cabronero, M., Sanchez, V., Marcellin, M.W., Bilgin, A.: The current role of image compression standards in medical imaging. Information **8**(4), 131 (2017)
19. Liu, Z., et al.: Swin transformer: hierarchical vision transformer using shifted windows. In: Proceedings of the IEEE/CVF International Conference on Computer Vision, pp. 10012–10022 (2021)
20. Michaelis, C., et al.: Benchmarking robustness in object detection: Autonomous driving when winter is coming. arXiv preprint arXiv:1907.07484 (2019)
21. Rohde, G.K., Ozolek, J.A., Parwani, A.V., Pantanowitz, L.: Carnegie mellon university bioimaging day 2014: challenges and opportunities in digital pathology. J. Pathol. Inf. **5** (2014)

22. Ronneberger, O., Fischer, P., Brox, T.: U-Net: convolutional networks for biomedical image segmentation. In: Navab, N., Hornegger, J., Wells, W.M., Frangi, A.F. (eds.) MICCAI 2015. LNCS, vol. 9351, pp. 234–241. Springer, Cham (2015). https://doi.org/10.1007/978-3-319-24574-4_28

23. Sandler, M., Howard, A., Zhu, M., Zhmoginov, A., Chen, L.C.: Mobilenetv 2: inverted residuals and linear bottlenecks. In: Proceedings of the IEEE Conference on Computer Vision and Pattern Recognition, pp. 4510–4520 (2018)

24. Simonyan, K., Zisserman, A.: Very deep convolutional networks for large-scale image recognition. arXiv preprint arXiv:1409.1556 (2014)

25. Szegedy, C., et al.: Intriguing properties of neural networks. arXiv preprint arXiv:1312.6199 (2013)

26. Tan, M., Le, Q.: Efficientnet: Rethinking model scaling for convolutional neural networks. In: International Conference on Machine Learning, pp. 6105–6114. PMLR (2019)

27. Taqi, S.A., Sami, S.A., Sami, L.B., Zaki, S.A.: A review of artifacts in histopathology. J. Oral Maxillof. Pathol. 22(2), 279 (2018)

28. Touvron, H., Cord, M., Douze, M., Massa, F., Sablayrolles, A., Jégou, H.: Training data-efficient image transformers & distillation through attention. In: International Conference on Machine Learning, pp. 10347–10357. PMLR (2021)

29. Veeling, B.S., Linmans, J., Winkens, J., Cohen, T., Welling, M.: Rotation equivariant CNNs for digital pathology. In: Frangi, A.F., Schnabel, J.A., Davatzikos, C., Alberola-López, C., Fichtinger, G. (eds.) MICCAI 2018. LNCS, vol. 11071, pp. 210–218. Springer, Cham (2018). https://doi.org/10.1007/978-3-030-00934-2_24

30. Wang, J., Jin, S., Liu, W., Liu, W., Qian, C., Luo, P.: When human pose estimation meets robustness: adversarial algorithms and benchmarks. In: Proceedings of the IEEE/CVF Conference on Computer Vision and Pattern Recognition, pp. 11855–11864 (2021)

31. Wang, N.C., Kaplan, J., Lee, J., Hodgin, J., Udager, A., Rao, A.: Stress testing pathology models with generated artifacts. J. Pathol. Inf. 12 (2021)

32. Yamashita, R., Long, J., Banda, S., Shen, J., Rubin, D.L.: Learning domain-agnostic visual representation for computational pathology using medically-irrelevant style transfer augmentation. IEEE Trans. Med. Imaging 40(12), 3945–3954 (2021)

33. Zhang, X., Zhou, X., Lin, M., Sun, J.: Shufflenet: an extremely efficient convolutional neural network for mobile devices. In: Proceedings of the IEEE Conference on Computer Vision and Pattern Recognition, pp. 6848–6856 (2018)

Weakly Supervised Segmentation by Tensor Graph Learning for Whole Slide Images

Qinghua Zhang and Zhao Chen[✉]

School of Computer Science and Technology, Donghua University, Shanghai 201620, China
chenzhao@dhu.edu.cn

Abstract. Semantic segmentation of whole slide images (WSIs) helps pathologists identify lesions and cancerous nests. However, training fully supervised segmentation networks usually requires plenty of pixel-level annotations, which consume lots of time and human efforts. Coming from tissues of different patients with large amounts of pixels, WSIs exhibit various patterns, resulting in intra-class heterogeneity and inter-class homogeneity. Meanwhile, most existing methods for WSIs focus on extracting a certain type of features, neglecting the relations between different features and their joint effect on segmentation. Therefore, we propose a novel weakly supervised network based on tensor graphs (WSNTG) for WSI segmentation. Using only sparse point annotations, it efficiently segments WSIs by superpixel-wise classification and credible node reweighting. To deal with the variability of WSIs, the proposed network represents multiple hand-crafted features and hierarchical features yielded by a pretrained Convolutional Neural Network (CNN). Particularly, it learns over the semi-labeled tensor graphs constructed on the hierarchical features to exploit nonlinear data structures and associations. It gains robustness via the tensor-graph Laplacian of the hand-crafted features superimposed on the segmentation loss. We evaluated WSNTG on two WSI datasets, DigestPath2019 and SICAPV2. Results show that it outperforms many fully supervised and weakly supervised methods with minimal point annotations in WSI segmentation. The codes are published at https://github.com/zqh 369/WSNTG.

Keywords: Weakly-supervised segmentation · Pathology image segmentation · Graph convolutional networks · Node reweighting

1 Introduction

Segmentation of cancerous region in medical images is one of the fundamental tasks in the field of medical image analysis. With the advent of gigapixel whole slide images

This work was funded by the "Chenguang Program" supported by Shanghai Education Development Foundation and Shanghai Municipal Education Commission under Grant 18CG38.

Supplementary Information The online version contains supplementary material available at https://doi.org/10.1007/978-3-031-16434-7_25.

L. Wang et al. (Eds.): MICCAI 2022, LNCS 13432, pp. 253–262, 2022.
https://doi.org/10.1007/978-3-031-16434-7_25

(WSIs), its digital nature allows automatic cancerous region segmentation with computer algorithms, which aims to improve efficiency and accuracy for cancer diagnosis, thus showing a high practical value. Traditional segmentation methods generally rely on a series of features extracted from WSI, yet the simple use of hand-crafted feature extraction lacks effectiveness and generalizability. In recent years, deep learning has been successfully applied to WSI segmentation, which allows for end-to-end training and better feature representation [1–4]. Although producing good results, most of the deep learning methods are trained on large annotated datasets. Since one WSI usually contains gigantic pixels while fine-grained annotation requires high-level expertise from experienced pathologists, it is exhausting and expensive to provide precise masks to train segmentation networks. Thus, weakly supervised methods for WSI semantic segmentation are proposed, which can be categorized as inexact [5–8], incomplete [9–11] and inaccurate supervision [12]. Generally, the incomplete supervision refers to the training condition whereas only parts of the images in the training set are labeled but the rest remain unlabeled. As a type of incomplete annotation, sparse point annotation is a good choice in terms of saving manual efforts [13].

Another major problem with WSI segmentation is that it is difficult to recognize variant patterns in WSIs. Recently, graph convolutional networks (GCNs) have been used for image segmentation [13, 14]. Graphs can naturally depict connective patterns, exploit irregular relationships and express arbitrarily structured data. They enable deep networks to represent long-range contextual information. For this reason, GCNs are applied to WSI segmentation and achieved satisfactory results [8, 15]. Studies show that learning from multiple graphs, instead of a single graph can discover extra nonlinear and intricate data relation [16, 17].

Therefore, we propose a novel weakly supervised framework based on tensor graph learning for WSI segmentation. Our contributions are as follows. 1) WSNTG only uses sparse point annotations as supervisory information and segments WSI by a credible-label-reweighted classifier; 2) to cope with the variability of WSIs, it learns tensor graphs of low-level and high-level features to represent multi-relational features and discover highly nonlinear data associations; 3) it constructs tensor-graph Laplacian regularization by hand-crafted features to gain robustness and generalizability. We compare our WSNTG with classical fully supervised segmentation methods and the latest weakly supervised methods to achieve state-of-the-art performance on two WSIs datasets, proving the effectiveness of our method.

2   Method

The proposed WSNTG framework is illustrated by Fig. 1. It contains three branches: superpixel classification with sparse point annotations, tensor-graph regularization based on hand-crafted features, and semi-labelled tensor-graph learning for hierarchical features. To train the third branch, a credible sample reweighting technique is employed. Let $\underline{\mathbf{X}}_n \in \mathbb{R}^{W \times H \times B}$ denote a WSI, where $n = 1, 2, ..., N$, N is the number of WSIs, and W, H, B is the width, height and channels, respectively. As WSI are real-color images, $B = 3$. The detailed description of the framework is as follows.

2.1 Superpixel Classification with Sparse Point Annotations

For WSNTG, superpixels are used as samples during model training. First, the original WSI $\underline{\mathbf{X}}_n$ are split into patches $\{\mathbf{X}_p\}_{p=1}^P$. Then, SLIC [18] is used to segment $\mathbf{X}_P$.

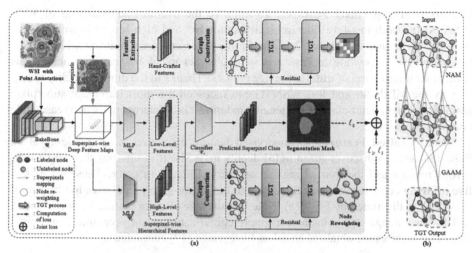

Fig. 1. (a) The proposed framework. (b) TGT block. The yellow nodes are the pixels with cancer nest labels and the purple nodes are the background samples. (Color figure online)

into superpixels $\{\mathbf{S}_m\}_{m=1}^M$, where M is the number of superpixels in $\mathbf{X}_P$. SLIC clusters similar pixels by multi-domain distances, which are more robust than single-domain distances. Its adherence to boundaries of variant objects of different shapes and sizes gives WSTGN extra robustness. To obtain superpixel labels $\{\mathbf{y}_m\}_{m=1}^{M^{(L)}}$, where $M^{(L)}$ is the number of superpixels with annotations, WSNTG diffuses the point annotations to the superpixels by majority voting. If a superpixel contains annotated pixels, its label is assigned to the class that occupies the majority of the annotated pixel members; otherwise, its label is set as null. Thus, the point-supervised segmentation problem is turned into superpixel-wise classification with only a few superpixel labels.

As shown in Fig. 1(a), the superpixel classification network comprises a backbone Ψ_0, two multi-layer perceptrons (MLPs) Ψ_1 and Ψ_2, and a classifier Ψ_3. The VGG-16 pretrained on ImageNet is used as Ψ_0 and the feature maps of each convolutional layer are upsampled to the same size as $\mathbf{X}_P$ by using bilinear interpolation. Next, all feature maps are concatenated to obtain the pixel-wise deep feature maps $\mathbf{f}^{(h)}$. Superpixel-wise deep feature $\mathbf{f}_m$ is produced by superimposing the contours of the superpixels $\{\mathbf{S}_m\}_{m=1}^M$ on $\mathbf{f}^{(h)}$ and averaging the deep features of the pixels within each superpixel. After that, WSNTG uses MLP Ψ_1 to reduce the dimensionality of the first half of $\mathbf{f}_m$ and obtain low-level feature $\mathbf{h}^{(l)}$ for superpixel $\mathbf{S}_m$. Likewise, it uses MLP Ψ_2 to process the second half of $\mathbf{f}_m$ and obtain high-level feature $\mathbf{h}^{(h)}$ for superpixel $\mathbf{S}_m$. Finally, $\mathbf{h}^{(l)}$ and $\mathbf{h}^{(h)}$ are concatenated to produce the hierarchical feature $\mathbf{h}_m$ for classifier Ψ_3 to predict the class $\hat{\mathbf{y}}_m$ (cancerous or not) for each superpixel $\mathbf{S}_m$, i.e., $\hat{\mathbf{y}}_m = \Psi_3(\mathbf{h}_m)$. The classification loss is defined as $\ell_0 = \sum_{m=1}^{M^{(L)}} \varsigma_m g(\mathbf{y}_m, \hat{\mathbf{y}}_m)$, where ς_m is the class-specific weight to handle class imbalance and $g(\,\cdot\,)$ is the cross-entropy loss.

2.2 Multiple Feature Extraction

Hierarchical Superpixel Features. To improve the overall understanding of WSI, WSNTG use both low-level hierarchical features $\mathbf{h}^{(l)}$ and high-level hierarchical features $\mathbf{h}^{(h)}$ as defined in Subsect. 2.1. The former represents local features which reflect finer details in WSIs while the latter represents abstract and global feature which reveals contextual information of different image regions. Thanks to the dimensionality reduction by the MLPs Ψ_1 and Ψ_2, WSNTG can focus on the most important superpixel features to handle inter-class homogeneity and intra-class heterogeneity at a reasonable computational speed.

Hand-Crafted Features. Unsupervised feature extraction is an efficient yet an important way to discover meaningful details in WSIs. It is obvious that target cancerous regions and the normal regions are very different in color. Thus, we extract five different color features and feed them to the tensor-graph regularization branch of WSNTG, as illustrated by Fig. 1(a). Note that the size of color feature vector is only 5 × 1 for each image so that the tensor-graph regularization is not very time-consuming. The color features are obtained based on histograms [19] computed by

$$H(i) = k_i / K, i = 0, 1, ..., L - 1 \tag{1}$$

where i represents a gray level, k_i is the number of pixels with gray level i and K is the total pixel number. The color features are as follows [19]. 1) Mean. It reflects the overall lightness/darkness of an image. 2) Standard Deviation. It shows the range of image color distribution. 3) Peak. It depicts the state of an image, whether it is highlighted or flat. 4) Energy. It reflects the texture coarseness and uniformity of image grayscale distribution. 5) Entropy, which represents the complexity of image grayscale distribution. By using the above hand-crafted features for tensor-graph regularization, WSTGN can leverage the statistical distributions of image colors and gain robustness to wide variations of tumor nests and tissues in WSIs. The details of tensor graph learning and regularization are introduced in the following.

2.3 Tensor Graph Learning

Inspired by reference [17], we design cascaded tensor-graph transformation (TGT) blocks to learn from related data such as different features of WSIs. As illustrated in Fig. 1(b), TGT can well represent nonlinear relations between intricate regions of WSIs by dynamically adapting to different connective patterns. Consider a tensor-graph $\underline{\mathbf{G}} = \{\mathbf{G}_1, ..., \mathbf{G}_n\}$ of N nodes, with nodal set $\mathbf{V} = \{\mathbf{v}_1, ..., \mathbf{v}_N\}$ connected through I relations. The adjacency matrices $\{\mathbf{A}_i\}_{i=1}^{I}$ define the edges between each pair of nodes and represent the multiple relations of the input data $\underline{\mathbf{X}} = [\mathbf{x}_1, ..., \mathbf{x}_N]^T$, where $\mathbf{x}_n$ is the nth node feature. For WSNTG, $\mathbf{x}_n$ can be the hand-crafted features defined in Subsect. 2.2, the low-level hierarchical feature $\mathbf{h}^{(l)}$ or the high-level hierarchical feature $\mathbf{h}^{(h)}$ in Subsect. 2.1.

To cope with the variability in WSIs, we use a residual layer that feeds $\mathbf{X}$ to each layer of TGT so that it can pick up the original image features. In general, the mapping of the input tensor $\underline{\mathbf{Z}}^{(l-1)}$ to $\underline{\mathbf{Z}}^{(l)}$ by the TGT module can be formulated as

$$\underline{\mathbf{Z}}^{(l)} = f(\underline{\mathbf{Z}}^{(l-1)}; \theta_z^{(l)}) + f(\mathbf{X}; \theta_x^{(l)}), \qquad (2)$$

where f is the combination of the two units, **neighborhood aggregation module (NAM) and graph adaptive and aggregation module (GAAM)**, and $\theta^{(l)}$ holds the learnable parameters of layer l. In our model, $l \in \{1,2\}$ and $\underline{\mathbf{Z}}^{(0)} = \mathbf{X}$. NAM linearly combines the information locally available in each neighborhood. Since the neighborhood depends on particular relations and nodes, TGT feeds $\underline{\mathbf{Z}}^{(l-1)}$ into the NAM to obtains the output $\underline{\mathbf{H}}^{(l)}$. By successive application of this operation across layers, TGT is able to transform the diffusion reach eventually spreading the WSI region information across the network. GAAM combines and adjusts between different relations encoded in multi-relational graphs. Since $\underline{\mathbf{H}}^{(l)}$ captures the diffused input per relation, with $\underline{\mathbf{H}}^{(l)}$ TGT should be able to cope with variant WSI patterns. The GAAM is thus designed to learn $\underline{\mathbf{Z}}^{(l)}$ from $\underline{\mathbf{H}}^{(l)}$ via layer l. Via GAAM, TGT can mix the features of each graph, and combine and adapt to different relations encoded by the multi-relational graph. For example, TGT can consider the relationship of low hierarchical feature $\mathbf{h}^{(l)}$ and high hierarchical feature $\mathbf{h}^{(h)}$ respectively, as well as the relationship between $\mathbf{h}^{(l)}$ and $\mathbf{h}^{(h)}$, so that specific decisions can be made based on each WSIs.

As illustrated by Fig. 1(a), the loss function of the hand-crafted feature learning branch of WSNTG is based on tensor-graph Laplacian, i.e., $\ell_1 = \text{Tr}(\mathbf{y}_h^T \mathbf{A}_h \mathbf{y}_h)$, where $\mathbf{y}_h$ is the TGT output learned from the statistical color features described in Subsect. 2.2, and $\mathbf{A}_h$ is the adjacency matrix. As the tensor-graph Laplacian regularization carries intricate relational information of different color features of WSIs, it gives WSNTG extra robustness to the variability of WSI patterns. In addition, another tensor-graph learning branch based on $\mathbf{h}^{(l)}$ and $\mathbf{h}^{(h)}$ is constructed for credible node reweighting, which can further increase segmentation accuracy.

2.4 Credible Node Reweighting and Optimization

It is assumed that nodes with similar features or nodes that are connected are very likely to share the same labels. To exploit highly nonlinear data associations as well as rich information in unlabeled superpixels, we propose a credible node reweighting approach on top of tensor-graph based classification.

First, WSNTG is pretrained on the tensor graphs only based on the labeled nodes. Specifically, the tensor graph $\underline{\mathbf{G}}^{(R)}$ is built on the hierarchical features $\mathbf{h}^{(l)}$ and $\mathbf{h}^{(h)}$. The $\underline{\mathbf{G}}^{(R)}$ is fed to the cascaded TGT blocks to capture the long-range intrinsic relationship between nodes, integrating the supervised information of labeled nodes by minimizing $\ell_2 = \sum_{m=1}^{M^{(L)}} g(\mathbf{y}_m, \tilde{\mathbf{y}}_m)$, where $M^{(L)}$ is the number of superpixels with labeled, $\tilde{\mathbf{y}}_m$ is the class predicted by TGT for superpixel $\mathbf{S}_m$ and g($\cdot$) is the cross-entropy loss.

Then, by using unlabeled samples for reweighting, the network can reduce the effect caused by too few labels, highlight the significant instances and their characteristics, and make the model focus more on representative instances. After the TGT blocks are trained up to E epochs, we consider that TGT can correctly classify the nodes. Moreover, motivated by reference [20], we propose dynamic credible node reweighting for WSNTG and define the reweighting factor as

$$\omega_m = \begin{cases} 1, & \text{epoch} > E \text{ and } \tilde{y}_m > \eta \\ 0, & \text{otherwise} \end{cases}, \tag{3}$$

where ω_m is the label weight of each node, η is a threshold. Thus, the credible node reweighting loss is defined as $\ell_3 = \sum_{m=M^{(L)}+1}^{M} \omega_m g(\hat{y}_m, \tilde{y}_m)$, where denotes the label predicted for superpixel S_m by classifier Ψ_3 as described in Subsect. 2.1.

Putting all the blocks together, we obtain the joint objective function,

$$\ell = \ell_0 + \lambda_1 \ell_1 + \lambda_2 \ell_2 + \lambda_3 \ell_3, \tag{4}$$

where $\lambda_1, \lambda_2, \lambda_3$ are the trade-off coefficients. With the joint loss function in Eq. (4), WSNTG adopts the stochastic gradient descent (SDG) algorithm with momentum to perform end-to-end training and update the parameters with sparse point annotations.

3 Experiments

3.1 Datasets

We evaluated model performance on three WSI datasets. One is the colonoscopy tissue segment dataset of MICCAI 2019 Challenge, namely, DigestPath2019[1]. The images were collected from four different medical centers. The average image size is 5000 × 5000 pixels. Each image is sliced into 800 × 800 patches. The training set consists of 250 positive samples containing malignant lesions from 93 WSIs and 410 negative samples from 231 WSIs. The test set contains 90 positive and 122 negative WSIs from 152 patients. All WSIs were acquired by scanning under a 20x objective. The second dataset, SICAPv2[2], contains 18783 patches of size 512 × 512, with pixel annotations. We recover 155 original WSIs at 10 × resolution from the dataset description file. Each WSI contains up to 11000 × 11000 pixels. We divide the WSIs into train, validation, and test sets, each with 108, 15 and 32 slides. The third dataset is CAMELYON16. Due to limited space, the experimental settings and results concerning this dataset are reported in the supplementary file.

3.2 Setup

Patch Sampling and Annotation Generation. Due to hardware limitations, only a few numbers of patches are randomly selected from each WSI as training samples. This procedure is viable and widely adopted. Sparse annotations are generated imitating what pathologists do in practice. First, the target and background are identified from the full-mask annotations of each training image. Then a very small amount of annotations (e.g., 0.01%) in the target and background are randomly selected to form the sparse annotation set. The amounts of point annotations for DigestPath2019 and SICAPv2 are approximately 7 points/patch and 20 points/patch, respectively.

---

[1] https://digestpath2019.grand-challenge.org/Dataset.
[2] https://data.mendeley.com/datasets/9xxm58dvs3/2s.

Hyperparameter Setting. Before fed to WSNTG, every rescaled input patch is augmented by blurring, color jittering, flipping, etc. The area of each superpixel is set to approximately 300 pixels and the compactness parameter is set to 40. In credible node reweighting, E is 8 and η is 0.92. For Eq. (4), $\lambda_1 = 0.25$, $\lambda_2 = 0.1$, $\lambda_3 = 0.2$ and $\varsigma_{\mathbf{y}_m} \in \{1, 2\}$, where the scale factor for background and target is 1 and 2, respectively. For SGD optimization, momentum is set as 0.9, weight decay is 0.001, mini batch size is 1 and the initial learning rate is 0.0008, which is halved if in the next 10 epochs the overall loss does not decrease. This process is repeated until the learning rate reaches 0.00001 or the overall loss stops decreasing completely.

Comparison Models and Evaluation Metrics. We compare WSNTG with recently proposed weakly supervised models, CDWS [21], SizeLoss [22] and WESUP [11]. We also compare the fully-supervised version of WSNTG with other fully supervised models, FCN-8 [23], U-net [24] and MedT [25] and YAMU [26]. We use the Dice index (DI), the overall pixel-level classification accuracy (OA) and the Jaccard Index (Jaccard) as evaluation metrics. Average results of five runs of each model are reported. All the models are implemented with pytorch on 64 GB RAM and NVIDIA GeForce RTX 3090. More details can be found in our codes and supplementary file.

3.3 Analysis

Efficacy. Several state-of-the-art methods were tested on the DigestPath2019 and SICAPv2 datasets under the same conditions. SizeLoss uses both points around (circle radius is set to 5) and individual bounds (IB) (margin is set to 0.1) label information, CDWS is supervised by image tags and area constraint (AC), and Wesup use point(p) annotation information. As shown in Table 1, WSNTG outperforms the other weakly supervised models, thus demonstrates that the hand-made features and the hie rarchical features generated by backbone have a good representation capability to cope with the variability and diversity of WSIs. Moreover, with the credible node reweighting of the TGT block, a large amount of unlabeled sample information can be exploited. It enables WSNTG to reach 82.83% in terms of DI and level with or even outperform some fully-supervised methods using only 7 points/patch for DigestPath2019. The qualitative evaluation is illustrated by Fig. 2. In such a complex WSI, our WSNTG can predict the target region very well.

Ablation study & Limitations. We completed ablation study on DigestPath2019, as shown in Table 2. The first ablated model is without fine-tuning, which freezes the parameters of the backbone and severely reduces the performance. It is because the backbone is pre-trained on ImageNet, which completely differs from WSIs. Moreover, the TGT module using credible node reweighting can exploit information of unlabeled samples to enhance the segmentation performance. However, the gain in accuracy yielded by the tensor-graph regularization based on the hand-crafted features exists, but not much, since only color features are considered. For future study, we shall construct tensor graphs by multiple types of spatial patterns of tumor nests.

Table 1. Comparison with SOTA methods on DigestPath2019 and SICAPV2.

Method	Supervision	DigestPath2019			SICAPV2		
		OA	DI	Jaccard	OA	DI	Jaccard
FCN-8S [23]	Full	95.65	79.82	70.88	96.46	68.31	55.61
U-Net [24]	Full	96.04	81.21	72.84	97.45	69.08	57.54
Wesup-F [11]	Full	95.68	82.10	73.49	97.41	70.51	59.08
MedT [25]	Full	96.20	80.60	72.03	96.71	68.12	55.17
YAMU [26]	Full	96.27	82.96	74.64	97.89	68.29	56.61
WSNTG-Full	Full	**96.69**	**83.42**	**75.12**	**97.47**	**71.54**	**59.64**
CDWS [21]	Tags+ AC	95.02	75.95	66.53	97.50	62.74	50.63
SizeLoss [22]	7/20p+ IB	95.12	75.85	66.90	97.18	61.06	49.35
Wesup [11]	7/20p	95.29	80.93	72.13	**97.51**	69.56	57.84
WSNTG	7/20p	**96.42**	**82.83**	**74.21**	97.39	**70.89**	**58.76**

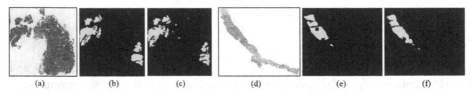

(a)   (b)   (c)   (d)   (e)   (f)

Fig. 2. Example of predicted segmentation on two datasets. (a)–(c) show an image from Digest-PathP2019, its ground truth and the mask predicted by WSNTG. (d)–(f) show an image from SICAPv2, its ground truth and the mask predicted by WSNTG.

Table 2. Ablation experiment on DigestPath2019.

Model	OA	DI	Jaccard
w/o fine-tuning	94.20	71.45	61.53
w/o TGT for node reweighting	95.41	80.89	72.09
w/o TGT for hand-crafted features	96.34	82.71	74.02
WSNTG	**96.42**	**82.83**	**74.21**

4   Conclusion

We propose a novel weakly supervised framework, which only uses sparse point annotations as supervisory information and efficiently segments WSIs by superpixel-wise classification and credible node reweighting. Moreover, our model leverages the tensor-graphs networks to discover nonlinear data associations and learn information about unlabeled regions. It constructs tensor-graph Laplacian regularization by adding un-supervised hand-crafted features to gain generalizability and robustness. Results on two WSIs datasets suggested that WSNTG achieves competitive WSIs segmentation performance even when compared to the fully-supervised counterparts.

References

1. Feng, R., Liu, X., Chen, J., Chen, D.Z., Gao, H., Wu, J.: A deep learning approach for colonoscopy pathology WSI analysis: accurate segmentation and classification. IEEE J. Biomed. Health Inform. **25**(10), 3700–3708 (2020)
2. Feng, Y., Hafiane, A., Laurent, H.: A deep learning based multiscale approach to segment the areas of interest in whole slide images. Comput. Med. Imaging Graph. **90**, 101923 (2021)
3. Ni, H., Liu, H., Wang, K., Wang, X., Zhou, X., Qian, Y.: WSI-Net: branch-based and hierarchy-aware network for segmentation and classification of breast histopathological whole-slide images. In: Suk, H.-I., Liu, M., Yan, P., Lian, C. (eds.) MLMI 2019. LNCS, vol. 11861, pp. 36–44. Springer, Cham (2019). https://doi.org/10.1007/978-3-030-32692-0_5
4. Wang, X., et al.: A hybrid network for automatic hepatocellular carcinoma segmentation in H&E-stained whole slide images. Med. Image Anal. **68**, 101914 (2021)
5. Xu, G., et al.: CAMEL: a weakly supervised learning framework for histopathology image segmentation. In: Proceedings of the IEEE/CVF International Conference on Computer Vision, pp. 10682–10691 (2019)
6. Xu, Y., Zhu, J.-Y., Eric, I., Chang, C., Lai, M., Tu, Z.: Weakly supervised histopathology cancer image segmentation and classification. Med. Image Anal. **18**, 591–604 (2014)
7. Lu, M.Y., Williamson, D.F., Chen, T.Y., Chen, R.J., Barbieri, M., Mahmood, F.: Data-efficient and weakly supervised computational pathology on whole-slide images. Nat. Biomed. Eng. **5**(6), 555–570 (2021)
8. Zhang, J., et al.: Joint fully convolutional and graph convolutional networks for weakly-supervised segmentation of pathology images. Med. Image Anal. **73**, 102183 (2021)
9. Qu, H., et al.: Weakly supervised deep nuclei segmentation using partial points annotation in histopathology images. IEEE Trans. Med. Imaging **39**(11), 3655–3666 (2020)
10. Tian, K., et al.: Weakly-supervised nucleus segmentation based on point annotations: a coarse-to-fine self-stimulated learning strategy. In: Martel, A.L., et al. (eds.) MICCAI 2020. LNCS, vol. 12265, pp. 299–308. Springer, Cham (2020). https://doi.org/10.1007/978-3-030-59722-1_29
11. Chen, Z., et al.: Weakly supervised histopathology image segmentation with sparse point annotations. IEEE J. Biomed. Health Inform. **25**(5), 1673–1685 (2021)
12. Li, S., Gao, Z., He, X.: Superpixel-guided iterative learning from noisy labels for medical image segmentation. In: de Bruijne, M., et al. (eds.) MICCAI 2021. LNCS, vol. 12901, pp. 525–535. Springer, Cham (2021). https://doi.org/10.1007/978-3-030-87193-2_50
13. Meng, Y., et al.: CNN-GCN aggregation enabled boundary regression for biomedical image segmentation. In: Martel, A.L., et al. (eds.) MICCAI 2020. LNCS, vol. 12264, pp. 352–362. Springer, Cham (2020). https://doi.org/10.1007/978-3-030-59719-1_35
14. Wolterink, J.M., Leiner, T., Išgum, I.: Graph convolutional networks for coronary artery segmentation in cardiac CT angiography. In: Zhang, D., Zhou, L., Jie, B., Liu, M. (eds.) GLMI 2019. LNCS, vol. 11849, pp. 62–69. Springer, Cham (2019). https://doi.org/10.1007/978-3-030-35817-4_8
15. Anklin, V., et al.: Learning whole-slide segmentation from inexact and incomplete labels using tissue graphs. In: de Bruijne, M., et al. (eds.) MICCAI 2021. LNCS, vol. 12902, pp. 636–646. Springer, Cham (2021). https://doi.org/10.1007/978-3-030-87196-3_59

16. Liu, X., You, X., Zhang, X., Wu, J., Lv, P.: Tensor graph convolutional networks for text classification. In: Proceedings of the AAAI Conference on Artificial Intelligence, vol. 34, no. 05, pp. 8409–8416 (2020)
17. Ioannidis, V.N., Marques, A.G., Giannakis, G.B.: Tensor graph convolutional networks for multi-relational and robust learning. IEEE Trans. Signal Process. **68**, 6535–6546 (2020)
18. Achanta, R., Shaji, A., Smith, K., Lucchi, A., Fua, P., Süsstrunk, S.: SLIC superpixels compared to state-of-the-art superpixel methods. IEEE Trans. Pattern Anal. Mach. Intell. **34**(11), 2274–2282 (2012)
19. Dong, N., Zhao, L., Wu, C.H., Chang, J.F.: Inception v3 based cervical cell classification combined with artificially extracted features. Appl. Soft Comput. **93**, 106311 (2020)
20. Cheng, L., Su, Y., Ye, L., Yuan, P., Han, S.: Learning from large-scale noisy web data with ubiquitous reweighting for image classification. IEEE Trans. Pattern Anal. Mach. Intell. **43**(5), 1808–1814 (2021)
21. Jia, Z., Huang, X., Chang, E.I.C., Xu, Y.: Constrained deep weak supervision for histopathology image segmentation. IEEE Trans. Med. Imaging **36**(11), 2376–2388 (2017)
22. Kervadec, H., Dolz, J., Tang, M., Granger, E., Boykov, Y., Ben Ayed, I.: Constrained-CNN losses for weakly supervised segmentation. Med. Image Anal. **54**, 88–99 (2019)
23. Shelhamer, E., Long, J., Darrell, T.: Fully convolutional networks for semantic segmentation. IEEE Trans. Pattern Anal. Mach. Intell. **39**, 640–651 (2017)
24. Ronneberger, O., Fischer, P., Brox, T.: U-Net: convolutional networks for biomedical image segmentation. In: Navab, N., Hornegger, J., Wells, W.M., Frangi, A.F. (eds.) MICCAI 2015. LNCS, vol. 9351, pp. 234–241. Springer, Cham (2015). https://doi.org/10.1007/978-3-319-24574-4_28
25. Valanarasu, J.M.J., Oza, P., Hacihaliloglu, I., Patel, V.M.: Medical transformer: gated axial-attention for medical image segmentation. In: de Bruijne, M., et al. (eds.) MICCAI 2021. LNCS, vol. 12901, pp. 36–46. Springer, Cham (2021). https://doi.org/10.1007/978-3-030-87193-2_4
26. Samanta, P., Singhal, N.: YAMU: yet another modified U-Net architecture for semantic segmentation. In: Proceedings of the 5th Conference on Medical Imaging with Deep Learning (2022)

Test Time Transform Prediction for Open Set Histopathological Image Recognition

Adrian Galdran[1,3]([✉]), Katherine J. Hewitt[2], Narmin Ghaffari Laleh[2],
Jakob N. Kather[2], Gustavo Carneiro[3], and Miguel A. González Ballester[1,4]

[1] BCN Medtech, Department of Information and Communication Technologies,
Universitat Pompeu Fabra, Barcelona, Spain
{adrian.galdran,ma.gonzalez}@upf.edu
[2] Department of Medicine III, University Hospital RWTH Aachen, Aachen, Germany
{khewitt,nghaffarilal,jkather}@ukaachen.de
[3] University of Adelaide, Adelaide, Australia
gustavo.carneiro@adelaide.edu
[4] Catalan Institution for Research and Advanced Studies (ICREA), Barcelona, Spain

Abstract. Tissue typology annotation in Whole Slide histological images
is a complex and tedious, yet necessary task for the development of computational pathology models. We propose to address this problem by applying Open Set Recognition techniques to the task of jointly classifying tissue that belongs to a set of annotated classes, *e.g.* clinically relevant tissue categories, while rejecting in test time Open Set samples, *i.e.* images
that belong to categories not present in the training set. To this end, we
introduce a new approach for Open Set histopathological image recognition based on training a model to accurately identify image categories
and simultaneously predict which data augmentation transform has been
applied. In test time, we measure model confidence in predicting this transform, which we expect to be lower for images in the Open Set. We carry
out comprehensive experiments in the context of colorectal cancer assessment from histological images, which provide evidence on the strengths of
our approach to automatically identify samples from unknown categories.
Code is released at https://github.com/agaldran/t3po.

Keywords: Histopathological image analysis · Open Set Recognition

1 Introduction and Related Work

Computational pathology has become fertile ground for deep learning techniques,
due to several factors like the availability of large scale annotated data coupled
with the increase in computational power, or the extremely time-consuming and
tedious nature of visual histology examination [6,14,18]. In this context, the
advanced pattern recognition capabilities of modern neural networks represents
a great match for the challenges posed by digital histopathology.

However, for each new dataset that a practitioner needs to analyze, there is a
requirement to annotate large whole slide images, which contain many different

L. Wang et al. (Eds.): MICCAI 2022, LNCS 13432, pp. 263–272, 2022.
https://doi.org/10.1007/978-3-031-16434-7_26

tissues, some of them relevant for the task at hand, whereas some others not. In this situation, this manual annotation processing can be focused only on the labeling of the relevant tissues. Hence, an algorithm that could automatically disregard data samples outside the set of categories initially labeled by the user would be greatly useful. Another plausible scenario arises if the practitioner has labeled all of the tissue typologies that might be of interest to them, but regions of anomalous appearance show up at a later stage. These could belong to a category of clinical interest, such as rare disease signs, or simply be acquisition artifacts, but manual review of these findings could be advisable to prevent potential misdiagnosis. An obvious solution to these problems would be to flag samples in test time for which the computational model is unconfident on its prediction, assuming this could point to atypical data. Unfortunately, deep neural networks are known to be incapable of associating anomalous inputs to meaningful low confidence values [8], and there is the need for specific solutions [15].

A suitable framework to solve the above problems is based on Open Set Recognition (OSR) techniques. These are a class of learning algorithms designed to handle the presence in test time of data out of the categories on which a model was trained. This is closely related to Out-of-Distribution (OoD) detection; for the sake of clarity, we stress that here we follow the definitions given in [24], and consider OoD detection as the problem of identifying in test time samples that do not belong to the data distribution where the model was trained, without the simultaneous goal of also performing classification on data belonging to known categories. For example, a popular approach to OoD detection involves training a model to solve some pretext task for which we know the solution beforehand, e.g. predicting the way in which an image has been geometrically transformed [7]. The rationale is that after training, for in-distribution data the model will be able to accurately predict the applied transformation, whereas for OoD data it will most likely fail to recognize it. Other common OoD detection methods include exposing the model to outliers during training [10], observing the maximum softmax probability [9], or adding extra branches to the model to account for predictive confidence [5]. These and most other techniques have been proposed in the context of natural images, and it has been shown that they may not translate satisfactorily for OoD detection in medical imaging [1,26].

OSR and OoD detection are also related to Domain Shift/Adaptation (DS/A), the task of training a model to accurately classify data collected in a particular domain, and having the same model generalize to data with the same categories but gathered from a different domain, e.g. a second hospital with a different tissue preparation protocol or acquisition device [11]. In histopathological image analysis, OoD detection and DS/A have been more studied in recent years than OSR. For instance, in [22] the effect of color augmentation techniques on domain generalization in image classification on slides acquired in 9 different pathology laboratories was analyzed, and in [25] unsupervised style transfer techniques from non-medical data were applied to enhance robustness to domain shift. Stacke et al. also studied domain shift in histological imaging in [20,21], defining a measure in the space of learned image representations to quantify it and using it to detect data for which a model may struggle to generalize. Ensembling techniques are also popular for uncertainty quantification in histological data, and can be put to use for identifying unreliable predictions, which can then be associated to OoD data [23]. This was proposed for instance in [16], where multi-head CNNs were shown to be superior to Monte Carlo dropout and deep ensembles for the task of flagging breast histologies containing lymph node tissue showing signs of diffuse large B-cell lymphoma, an anomaly that was not present in the training set. Self-supervision based on contrastive learning and multi-view consistency has also recently been leveraged for learning robust representations that may enable DA, namely in [4]. In [2], the authors used a similar approach to learn representations that could be useful for performing OoD detection under DS.

In this paper we introduce a novel method for OSR on histological images based on recycling information obtained during training regarding the kind of data augmentation operations that are applied online to the training data. We conjecture that for images belonging to known categories, a model trained to predict those operations will be more confident in test time, whereas for OoD data the model will be uncertain when solving this pretext task. We validate our hypothesis on two popular datasets related to colorectal cancer detection, where our experiments show that the proposed approach can accurately classify images from categories used for training and simultaneously reject clinically uninformative regions in an image without the need to manually label them.

2   Methodology

In this section, we introduce basic definitions related to the OSR setting and explain our data augmentation pipeline, which allows us to define transform prediction in a well-posed way. We then define our OSR method that jointly classifies in-distribution data and measures confidence in predicting if a data transform operation has been applied in order to declare a sample as OoD.

2.1   Open Set Recognition - Max over Softmax as a Strong Baseline

In an OSR scenario, we start from a labeled training set $\mathcal{C}_{\text{train}}$ with examples belonging to N known categories $\mathcal{K} = \{k_1, ..., k_N\}$, which compose the known, or *Closed Set*. However, in test time the classifier encounters samples from an *Open Set* $\mathcal{O}_{\text{test}}$ with M unknown categories $\mathcal{U} = \{u_1, ..., u_M\}$ not seen during training, *i.e.* $\mathcal{D}_{\text{test}} = \mathcal{C}_{\text{test}} \cup \mathcal{O}_{\text{test}}$. The goal of an open set classifier is to generate a reliable prediction on $\mathcal{C}_{\text{test}}$ while also rejecting samples from $\mathcal{O}_{\text{test}}$.

There exist many approaches to OSR [9]. However, it has been recently demonstrated in [24] that the simplest of all OSR methods, when optimized so as to maximize closed set accuracy with modern model architectures U_θ and training techniques, attains state-of-the-art OSR results. This baseline method consists of minimizing the cross-entropy loss between one-hot labels y and softmax probabilities $p_\theta(y|x)$ for $x \in \mathcal{C}_{\text{train}}$, and then define an OSR score as the maximum softmax probability $S(y \in \mathcal{C}_{\text{test}}|x) = \max_{y \in \mathcal{C}} p_\theta(y|x)$, assuming that U_θ will distribute probabilities with high entropy for unknown classes, resulting in a low $S(y \in \mathcal{O}_{\text{test}}|x)$ value.

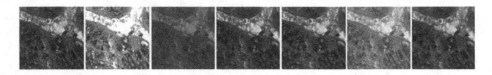

Fig. 1. Transform space $\mathcal{T}_{\text{app}}$, shown left to right: $\mathcal{T}_{\text{app}} = \{$Identity, Brightness, Contrast, Saturation, Hue, Gamma, Sharpness$\}$. Our model learns to predict the applied transform during training. In test time, the model only receives un-transformed images, and we measure its confidence on transform prediction.

2.2 Decoupled Color-Appearance Data Augmentation

Data augmentation operations (image transforms in computer vision), are a conventional technique to increase generalization and reduce overfitting when training deep neural networks. Recently, learned data augmentation, which learns an optimal transformation policy from a validation set, has gained popularity, with increasingly complex techniques being proposed. However, this comes at a noticeable training overhead that has been recently shown to be indeed unnecessary [17]: the simpler scheme of randomly selecting, for each optimization step, *a single image transform* (instead of a composition of transforms) from a fixed transform space $\mathcal{T}$, with a variable strength, works remarkably well.

Inspired by [17], we define a data augmentation policy with a single transform at a time, allowing us to pose the auxiliary problem of predicting which transform has been applied to a training sample. Also, noting that geometric transforms are hardly predictable on histological data (as opposed to natural images, there is no meaningful notion of top/bottom, rotations, etc.), we decouple geometry from appearance, and define our transform space as $\mathcal{T} = \mathcal{T}_{\text{geom}} \cup \mathcal{T}_{\text{app}}$, where $\mathcal{T}_{\text{geom}}$ contains geometric transformations - rotations, shears, and translations - whereas $\mathcal{T}_{\text{app}}$ contains only color transformations. These transforms are illustrated and listed in Fig. 1; definitions can be found in the standard Python Image Library https://github.com/python-pillow/Pillow.

2.3 Test-Time Transform Prediction and Open Set Recognition

We formulate the training of our model as a joint optimization of two tasks. During training, we sample an image x from $\mathcal{C}_{\text{train}}$, apply a random geometric transform $\tau_g \in \mathcal{T}_{\text{geom}}$, then an appearance transform $\tau_a \in \mathcal{T}_{\text{app}}$, and pass it through a CNN U_θ, which produces an internal representation x_θ. This is then sent to the main branch f_α, a fully connected layer followed by a softmax operation, which generates a probability of x belonging to a known category from $\mathcal{K}$, but also to an auxiliary branch g_β that predicts the actual appearance transform τ_a that was applied. Among these there is the Identity operation, meaning that the model needs to learn what an image $x \in \mathcal{C}$ looks like.

Finally, in test time, an image x is processed by U_θ without applying any transform, resulting in a classification score $f_\alpha(U_\theta(x))$, and we define as our OSR score the maximum of softmax probabilities on the transform prediction task:

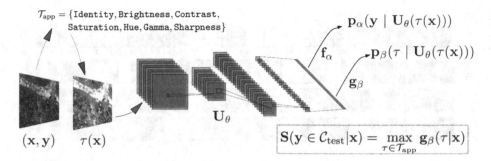

Fig. 2. Visual scheme of our OSR Test-Time Transform Prediction technique. A shared representation $U_\theta(\tau(x))$ is sent to two linear layers, f_α performs Closed Set classification and g_β predicts the applied transform τ. In test time, our OSR score is the confidence of the transform prediction branch g_β on its prediction.

$$S(y \in C_{\text{test}}|x) = \max_{\tau_a \in \mathcal{T}_{\text{app}}} g_\beta(\tau_a|x). \tag{1}$$

In essence, we expect the model to be more confident when predicting the transform on C_{test} than on O_{test}. Let us note that we could also generate and aggregate predictions on transformed test images (Test-Time Augmentation), although this would induce an inference overhead that we prefer to avoid in this work. An illustration of the proposed OSR approach is shown in Fig. 2.

3   Experimental Analysis

In this section we introduce our experimental setup: datasets, proposed OSR tasks, and detailed performance evaluation with a discussion on the numerical differences between compared methods, as well as limitations of our technique.

3.1   Datasets and Open Set Splits

We evaluate our technique on a clinically meaningful task, namely colorectal cancer (CRC) assessment. In this context, tumor tissue composition is heterogeneous, non-stationary, and its study is key to disease prognosis [13]. A common technique for CRC monitoring is quantification of tissue configuration by histological evaluation of Hematoxylin and Eosin (H&E) stained tissue sections.

We consider two publicly available datasets[1] that enable CRC tissue characterization, referred to as Kather-5k [13] and Kather-100k [12]. Examples of images from each tissue type in these datasets are shown in Fig. 3. Specifically:

---

[1] Kather-5k: http://doi.org/10.5281/zenodo.53169.
Kather-100k: http://doi.org/10.5281/zenodo.1214456.

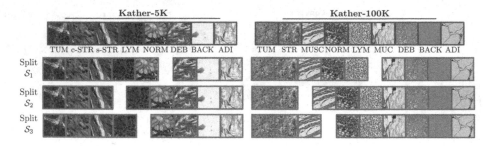

Fig. 3. Closed (green) and Open (orange) Set partitions defined on the two considered datasets, please see the text for acronym definitions and motivation. (Color figure online)

- Kather-5k contains 5,000 image patches extracted from 10 tumoral tissue slides with 8 classes: *tumor* epithelium (TUM), *simple stroma* (s-STR), homogeneous tissue, with tumoral and extra-tumoral stroma, but also muscle, *complex stroma* (c-STR), which may contain some immune cells, *immune cell conglomerates* (LYM), *debris* (DEB), which includes necrosis or mucus, *normal* colon mucosa (NORM), *adipose* tissue (ADI), and *background* tissue (BACK). Data is balanced, with 150×150 pixel size and $74\,\mu m$/px resolution.
- Kather-100k is larger, with 100,000 image patches extracted from 86 CRC tissue slides, originally used for overall CRC survival prediction. It has 9 different tissue types: *tumour* epithelium (TUM), cancer-related *stroma* (t-STR), smooth *muscle* (MUS), *immune cell conglomerates* (LYM), *debris/necrosis* (DEB), *mucus* (MUC), *normal* colon mucosa (NORM), *adipose* tissue (ADI), and *background* (BACK). Note some subtle differences with Kather-5k: the category debris is split into debris/necrosis and mucus; also, stroma is not divided into simple an complex: only tumoral stroma is considered, whereas muscle is a new category. Data is approximately balanced and color-normalized, with images of size 224×224 and $122\,\mu$/px resolution.

Next, following expert pathologist's advice, we define several Closed/Open set splits in each dataset, illustrated in Fig. 3. We first design a split $\mathcal{S}_1$ mimicking the hypothetical situation in which a practitioner decides to label only clinically informative tissue regions, and leaves uninformative regions unlabeled, expecting the OSR model to automatically identify it as part of the Open Set $\mathcal{O}$, while still achieving high accuracy in the Closed Set $\mathcal{C}$. Note that this is not a trivial task, since necrotic tissue, part of the debris category, can be infiltrated by inflammatory cells, and therefore the lymphocytes class acts as a confounder in the closed set. To supplement our experimental analysis and understand the weaknesses of OSR systems in this application, we also define two other splits $\mathcal{S}_2$ and $\mathcal{S}_3$. In $\mathcal{S}_2$ we aim at analyzing if an OSR classifier can classify tumoral regions while rejecting healthy tissue as well as uninformative samples in test time, so we include tumor and stroma patches in the closed set. Note that for both datasets there are now some confounders in the Open Set. Namely, in the

Table 1. Performance averaged over 10 training runs of our approach and other OSR techniques on several Open/Closed splits of the Kather-5k dataset. Best performance is underlined, results within its confidence interval are bold.

	Split 0		Split 1		Split 2	
	ACC	AUC	ACC	AUC	ACC	AUC
CE+	**93.03**	91.66	**94.27**	82.51	92.88	90.02
ARPL	**92.84**	88.96	92.51	80.28	**93.39**	82.39
MC-Dropout	**93.16**	91.52	**94.02**	82.19	92.80	85.45
T3PO (Ours)	92.54	**93.55**	**94.27**	**84.73**	91.80	**91.24**

Kather-5k dataset complex stroma images may include some immune cells, but the immune-cell conglomerate category is in the Open Set of S_2. On the other hand, in the Kather-100k dataset stroma images do not include immune cells, but the stroma and the muscle categories share a fibrous aspect, and muscle images belong to the Open Set. For comparison purposes, in the last split S_3 we move the lymphocites class to the Closed Set, which should result in an easier OSR task at the expense of a more challenging Closed Set classification task, since now C contains two similar classes.

3.2 Implementation Details and Performance Evaluation

We compare Test-Time Transform Prediction (T3PO) with the state-of-the-art ARPL technique [3], and CE+, the strong baseline proposed recently in [24], which consists of maximizing the Closed Set accuracy of the classifier and, instead of taking the maximum over the softmax probabilities as the OSR score, use the maximum over the logits, *i.e.* pre-softmax activations of the network. We also adopt the MC-Dropout baseline (applying dropout multiple times ($n = 32$) in test time and collecting the entropy of the resulting set of softmax probabilities as the OSR score), popular in medical image analysis problems [16].

Since previous work has shown that relatively small architectures are capable of achieving high accuracy on the two considered datasets, for the sake of quick experimentation we always train a MobileNet V2 network as our backbone [19], starting from ImageNet weights. Following [13], we split the data into 70% for training, 15% for validation and early-stopping, and 15% for testing. In all cases we train with a cyclical learning rate starting at $l = 0.01$ and a batch-size of 128, for 200 epochs in the Kather-5k dataset. Due to the larger amount of training samples, we only train for 20 epochs in the Kather-100k dataset, which is enough for all models to converge. We use the Adam optimizer, monitor the Closed Set accuracy during training, and keep the highest-performing checkpoint. After training, we collect model accuracy on the Closed test set, and OSR scores in the Closed and Open test sets. We perform ten training runs per split and report mean Closed Set accuracy and Closed/Open AUC.

Table 2. Performance averaged over 10 training runs of our approach and other OSR techniques on several Open/Closed splits of the Kather-100k dataset. Best performance is underlined, results within its confidence interval are bold.

	Split 0		Split 1		Split 2	
	ACC	AUC	ACC	AUC	ACC	AUC
CE+	**99.54**	96.50	**99.69**	**84.59**	**99.62**	82.96
ARPL	98.88	91.76	**99.33**	78.00	98.98	79.96
MC-Dropout	**99.57**	96.23	**99.64**	**84.93**	99.58	84.52
T3PO (Ours)	99.46	**96.57**	**99.66**	83.32	99.56	**92.42**

3.3 Results and Discussion

Tables 1 and 2 show the performance of the considered OSR techniques on the Kather-5k and Kather-100k datasets respectively. The first split, which in both cases sets out the task of classifying clinically relevant tissue categories, is successfully solved to a high accuracy by all approaches, with no statistically significant difference between our proposed T3PO and the top performer MC-Dropout. If we analyze the ability of each method to reject uninteresting data in test time, however, we see that T3PO outperforms the other techniques, by a relatively wide margin in the Kather-5k dataset, in terms of Closed/Open Set AUC, indicating that our method can better identify Open Set data in this case.

The second and third split in the Kather-5k dataset illustrate a limitation of OSR approaches. In the second split, the Open Set contains images from the immune cell category, and immune cells are also present on some images from the complex stroma class, which belongs to the Closed Set. This results in a generally lower AUC for all methods, although T3PO continues to outperform other techniques. In addition, when we move the immune-cell category from the Open to the Closed Set, we see a noticeable increase in AUC for all methods (and a decrease in accuracy, since two visually similar categories are now in the Closed Set), with T3PO still significantly attaining top performance in Open Set recognition. It should be noted that this is achieved at the cost of a modest, but statistically significant decrease in Closed Set accuracy for the third split.

Lastly, the second and third split in the Kather-100k dataset also show a similar phenomenon. In this case the muscle class belonging to the Open Set in the second split drives the Closed/Open AUC down for all methods, since it is confounded with the stroma category from the Closed set, and we see that T3PO is among the worst techniques now. However, when we move the muscle class into the Closed Set, T3PO increases the AUC by more than 9 points, outperforming all other methods, and losing very little accuracy.

3.4 Conclusion and Future Work

We have illustrated how a clinically meaningful task, disregard irrelevant image regions from histological slides without explicitly training a model to discriminate them, can be addressed with OSR techniques. We have also introduced T3PO, a new OSR method that outperforms several recent approaches in most cases. We have also discussed its limitations, namely T3PO consists of the identification of global image transformations in test time, thereby relying on low-level image characteristics like color and aspect, but not taking full advantage of other semantic cues, which may result in sub-optimal performance. We leave the integration of the knowledge of image content into our approach for future work.

Acknowledgments. This work was partially supported by a Marie Skłodowska-Curie Global Fellowship (No. 892297) and by Australian Research Council grants (DP180103232 and FT190100525).

References

1. Berger, C., Paschali, M., Glocker, B., Kamnitsas, K.: Confidence-based out-of-distribution detection: a comparative study and analysis. In: Sudre, C.H., et al. (eds.) UNSURE/PIPPI -2021. LNCS, vol. 12959, pp. 122–132. Springer, Cham (2021). https://doi.org/10.1007/978-3-030-87735-4_12

2. Bozorgtabar, B., Vray, G., Mahapatra, D., Thiran, J.P.: SOoD: self-supervised out-of-distribution detection under domain shift for multi-class colorectal cancer tissue types. In: 2021 IEEE/CVF International Conference on Computer Vision Workshops (ICCVW), pp. 3317–3326, October 2021. https://doi.org/10.1109/ICCVW54120.2021.00371. ISSN: 2473-9944

3. Chen, G., Peng, P., Wang, X., Tian, Y.: Adversarial reciprocal points learning for open set recognition. IEEE Trans. Pattern Anal. Mach. Intell. 1 (2021). https://doi.org/10.1109/TPAMI.2021.3106743

4. Ciga, O., Xu, T., Martel, A.L.: Self supervised contrastive learning for digital histopathology. Mach. Learn. App. **7**, 100198 (2022). https://doi.org/10.1016/j.mlwa.2021.100198

5. Devries, T., Taylor, G.W.: Learning Confidence for Out-of-Distribution Detection in Neural Networks. arXiv:1802.04865 [cs, stat], February 2018

6. Echle, A., Rindtor, N.T., Brinker, T.J., Luedde, T., Pearson, A.T., Kather, J.N.: Deep learning in cancer pathology: a new generation of clinical biomarkers. Br. J. Cancer. **124**(4), 686–696 (2021). https://doi.org/10.1038/s41416-020-01122-x 020-01122-

7. Golan, I., El-Yaniv, R.: Deep anomaly detection using geometric transformations. In: Advances in Neural Information Processing Systems, vol. 31 (2018)

8. Guo, C., Pleiss, G., Sun, Y., Weinberger, K.Q.: On Calibration of Modern Neural Networks. In: Precup, D., Teh, Y.W. (eds.) Proceedings of the 34th International Conference on Machine Learning. Proceedings of Machine Learning Research, vol. 70, pp. 1321–1330. PMLR (Aug 2017)

9. Hendrycks, D., Gimpel, K.: A baseline for detecting misclassified and out-of-distribution examples in neural networks. In: International Conference on Learning Representations. OpenReview.net (2017)

10. Hendrycks, D., Mazeika, M., Dietterich, T.: Deep anomaly detection with outlier exposure. In: International Conference on Learning Representations (2019)

11. Howard, F.M., et al.: The impact of site-specific digital histology signatures on deep learning model accuracy and bias. Nat. Commun. **12**(1), 4423 (2021). https://doi.org/10.1038/s41467-021-24698-1

12. Kather, J.N., et al.: Predicting survival from colorectal cancer histology slides using deep learning: a retrospective multicenter study. PLOS Med. **16**(1), e1002730 (2019). https://doi.org/10.1371/journal.pmed.1002730

13. Kather, J.N., et al.: Multi-class texture analysis in colorectal cancer histology. Sci. Rep. **6**(1), 27988 (2016). https://doi.org/10.1038/srep27988

14. van der Laak, J., Litjens, G., Ciompi, F.: Deep learning in histopathology: the path to the clinic. Nat. Med. **27**(5), 775–784 (2021). https://doi.org/10.1038/s41591-021-01343-4

15. Lee, K., Lee, H., Lee, K., Shin, J.: Training confidence-calibrated classifiers for detecting out-of-distribution samples. In: International Conference on Learning Representations (2018)

16. Linmans, J., Laak, J., Litjens, G.: Efficient out-of-distribution detection in digital pathology using multi-head convolutional neural networks. In: Medical Imaging with Deep Learning (2020)

17. Müller, S.G., Hutter, F.: TrivialAugment: Tuning-Free Yet State-of-the-Art Data Augmentation, pp. 774–782 (2021)

18. Picon, A., et al.: Novel pixelwise co-registered hematoxylin-eosin and multiphoton microscopy image dataset for human colon lesion diagnosis. J. Pathol. Inform. **13**, 100012 (2022). https://doi.org/10.1016/j.jpi.2022.100012

19. Sandler, M., Howard, A., Zhu, M., Zhmoginov, A., Chen, L.C.: MobileNetV2: inverted residuals and linear bottlenecks. In: 2018 IEEE/CVF Conference on Computer Vision and Pattern Recognition, pp. 4510–4520, June 2018

20. Stacke, K., Eilertsen, G., Unger, J., Lundström, C.: A closer look at domain shift for deep learning in histopathology. In: MICCAI COMPAY Workshop, July 2019

21. Stacke, K., Eilertsen, G., Unger, J., Lundström, C.: Measuring domain shift for deep learning in histopathology. IEEE J. Biomed. Health Inform. **25**(2), 325–336 (2021). https://doi.org/10.1109/JBHI.2020.3032060

22. Tellez, D., et al.: Quantifying the effects of data augmentation and stain color normalization in convolutional neural networks for computational pathology. Med. Image Anal. **58**, 101544 (2019). https://doi.org/10.1016/j.media.2019.101544

23. Thagaard, J., Hauberg, S., van der Vegt, B., Ebstrup, T., Hansen, J.D., Dahl, A.B.: Can you trust predictive uncertainty under real dataset shifts in digital pathology? In: Martel, A.L., et al. (eds.) MICCAI 2020. LNCS, vol. 12261, pp. 824–833. Springer, Cham (2020). https://doi.org/10.1007/978-3-030-59710-8_80

24. Vaze, S., Han, K., Vedaldi, A., Zisserman, A.: Open-Set Recognition: A Good Closed-Set Classifier is All You Need, September 2021

25. Yamashita, R., Long, J., Banda, S., Shen, J., Rubin, D.L.: Learning domain-agnostic visual representation for computational pathology using medically-irrelevant style transfer augmentation. IEEE Trans. Med. Imaging. **40**(12), 3945–3954 (2021). https://doi.org/10.1109/TMI.2021.3101985

26. Zhang, O., Delbrouck, J.-B., Rubin, D.L.: Out of distribution detection for medical images. In: Sudre, C.H., et al. (eds.) UNSURE/PIPPI -2021. LNCS, vol. 12959, pp. 102–111. Springer, Cham (2021). https://doi.org/10.1007/978-3-030-87735-4_10

Lesion-Aware Contrastive Representation Learning for Histopathology Whole Slide Images Analysis

Jun Li[1], Yushan Zheng[2(✉)], Kun Wu[1], Jun Shi[3(✉)], Fengying Xie[1], and Zhiguo Jiang[1]

[1] Image Processing Center, School of Astronautics, Beihang University, Beijing 102206, China
[2] School of Engineering Medicine, Beijing Advanced Innovation Center on Biomedical Engineering, Beihang University, Beijing 100191, China
yszheng@buaa.edu.cn
[3] School of Software, Hefei University of Technology, Hefei 230601, China
juns@hfut.edu.cn

Abstract. Image representation learning has been a key challenge to promote the performance of the histopathological whole slide images analysis. The previous representation learning methods followed the supervised learning paradigm. However, manual annotation for large-scale WSIs is time-consuming and labor-intensive. Hence, the self-supervised contrastive learning has recently attracted intensive attention. In this paper, we proposed a novel contrastive representation learning framework named Lesion-Aware Contrastive Learning (LACL) for histopathology whole slide image analysis. We built a lesion queue based on the memory bank structure to store the representations of different classes of WSIs, which allowed the contrastive model to selectively define the negative pairs during the training. Moreover, We designed a queue refinement strategy to purify the representations stored in the lesion queue. The experimental results demonstrate that LACL achieves the best performance in histopathology image representation learning on different datasets, and outperforms state-of-the-art methods under different WSI classification benchmarks. The code is available at https://github.com/junl21/lacl.

Keywords: Weakly supervised learning · Contrastive learning · WSI analysis

1 Introduction

In recent years, the research on the whole slide images (WSIs) analysis becomes popular in the field of digital pathology [7,12,18]. The accuracy performance of the models for WSI analysis is crucial for the different downstream tasks, such as WSIs classification, retrieval, and survival prediction. However, due to the limitation of hardware resources, WSIs are difficult to directly fed into deep

L. Wang et al. (Eds.): MICCAI 2022, LNCS 13432, pp. 273–282, 2022.
https://doi.org/10.1007/978-3-031-16434-7_27

neural networks for training. The typical solution is to generate WSI-level representations by aggregating local tissue representations before inference [7,15]. In this situation, local representation learning is a key challenge to promote the development of digital pathology [12,24]. The previous methods proposed learning representations in the supervised learning paradigm based on pathologists' manual annotations [1,5,9], but the development of these methods has hit a bottleneck because of the expensive cost of large-scale annotations.

To address this issue, transfer learning from ImageNet [14] is a well-adopted strategy to learn local representations [12]. However, The performance of these methods is limited by the semantic gap between the natural images and the histopathological images. Some weakly supervised learning methods tended to transfer the feature domain from natural scene to histopathology by multi-instance learning (MIL), but the upper bound of such methods is limited by the performance of the representation model trained outside the histopathology domain [8,10,19]. Moreover, MIL methods mainly focus on the positive vs. negative discrimination of the local representations, which makes it weak in describing the differences of subtype lesions.

In this case, self-supervised contrastive learning has been introduced for histopathology image representation learning. It learns image patterns based on large-scale unlabeled data, which has demonstrated superiority to the ImageNet-trained model in a variety of downstream vision tasks [2,4,6]. There are several works applying contrastive learning methods into the field of computational pathology [20,22].

The success of the contrastive learning depends on the design of informative of the positive and negative pairs [13]. However, the present sampling strategy introduces class collision problem [23] for the reason that it treats each instance as a single class. Specifically, common contrastive learning treats any two samples in the dataset as a negative pair, even though they belong to the same class semantically. It hurts the quality of the learned representation, especially for histopathological images where the image content is rather complex. Several works have tried to refine the sampling strategy [16,21], but there is lack of sampling strategies specifically designed for pathological images.

In this paper, we rethought the applicability of contrastive learning in digital pathology, and proposed a weakly supervised representations learning method named lesion-aware contrastive learning (LACL). A dynamic queue was built to refine the negative pairs selection in the LACL. Moreover, we designed a queue refinement strategy (QRS) to continuously purify queues during the training process. The experimental results on two WSIs classification benchmarks show that the representations learned by our method achieves significant improvement in both accuracy and AUC metrics, when compared to the state-of-the-art representation learning methods. The contribution of this paper can be summarized into two aspects:

- We propose a novel weakly supervised contrastive learning framework with a designed lesion queue. The lesion queue is a dynamic memory bank, which is used to replace the memory bank of MoCo [6] in storing the features from

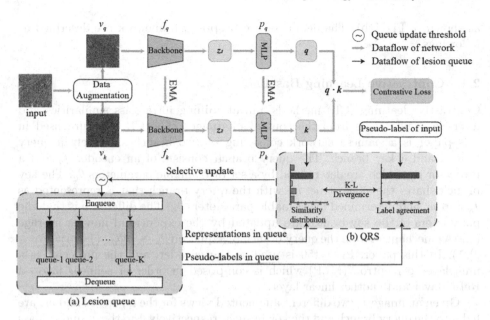

Fig. 1. The overview of the proposed lesion-aware contrastive learning (LACL) framework which takes MoCo v2 as the basic structure. (a) is the proposed lesion queue redesigned from memory bank in MoCo. It allows the model to selective construct the contrastive sample pairs and enables the model to embed the WSI lesion information to the representations. (b) represents the queue refinement strategy (QRS), which is designed for selecting typical samples for each class to update the lesion queue.

different types of WSIs. Based on the queue, the contrastive learning for each sample is restricted to the samples with different WSI labels, which enables the model to embed the WSI lesion information to the representations.

- We design a queue refinement strategy (QRS). In each step of training, the typical samples for each class are selected by the QRS to update the queue, which is different from MoCo [6] that simply updates the memory bank using all the batch samples. It makes the representations stored in the queue more representative to the lesion types, and therefore improves the effectiveness for WSI analysis.
- The experimental results show our LACL can outperform state-of-the-art representation learning methods for downstream whole slide images analysis.

2   Methods

The overview of the proposed framework is illustrated in Fig. 1. The architecture of the framework is constructed based on MoCo v2, where we have redesigned the original memory bank and renamed it as lesion queue, as shown in Fig. 1(a). In addition, a queue refinement strategy (QRS) is built for queue updating, as shown in Fig. 1(b). The details of the proposed framework are described as followings.

2.1 Contrastive Learning Baseline

Contrastive learning (CL) methods aim at mining intra-class similarities and inter-class differences from the content of images. The CL structure used in this paper is a siamese network consisting of two branches, namely a query branch and a key branch. The query branch consists of an encoder f_q and a projector p_q, which are determined by a set of trainable parameters θ_q. The key branch shares the same structure with the query branch that is represented as f_k and p_k and determined by trainable parameters θ_k. The difference is that the parameters of the key branch are updated by the exponential moving average (EMA) mechanism from the query branch by equation $\theta_k \leftarrow m\theta_q + (1-m)\theta_k, m \in [0,1)$. In this paper, ResNet50 is used as the encoder, and the projector is a multilayer perceptron (MLP) which is composed in order of a linear layer, a ReLU layer and another linear layer.

Given an image x, two different augmented views for the image, v_q and v_k, are fed into the query branch and the key branch, respectively. Firstly, v_q and v_k pass through the corresponding encoder to generate the representations $z_q = f_q(v_q)$ and $z_k = f_k(v_k)$. Then a projector $g(\cdot)$ is adopted to map the representations to the space where contrastive loss is applied. Here we defined the outputs of the projectors as $q = p_q(z_q)$ and $k_+ = p_k(z_k)$. Referring to MoCo, we define k_+ as the positive sample, and those representations from the memory bank as negative keys $\{k_0, k_1, \ldots, k_N\}$, and the objective function is optimized by minimizing the InfoNCE loss function

$$\mathcal{L} = -\log \frac{\exp(q^T k_+/\tau)}{\sum_{i=0}^{N} \exp(q^T k_i/\tau)}, \tag{1}$$

where τ is a temperature hyper-parameter, and the sum is over one positive and N negative samples.

2.2 Lesion Queue Construction

It is notable that the contrastive representation learning in the majority works are achieved in unsupervised paradigm without any level of supervision from the WSI type information. It makes the representations hard to aware the semantic gaps of histopathology image content involving intra-class variation and inter-class similarity. This problem does harm to the downstream WSI analysis tasks.

To tackle the problem, we propose to rebuilding the memory bank based on the WSI type information of the contrastive samples, and rename it as lesion queue. Specifically, we build a queue for each WSI class, and let each queue only stores the image representations obtained from its corresponding class of WSI. Based on the settings, we redesign the contrastive objective by dynamically select the negative samples for each positive sample with the modified InfoNCE loss function

$$\mathcal{L} = -\log \frac{\exp(\mathbf{q}^{\mathrm{T}}\mathbf{k}_{+}/\tau)}{\sum_{y\in\mathbb{C}} \sum_{i=0}^{M} \exp(\mathbf{q}^{\mathrm{T}}\mathbf{k}_{yi}/\tau)}, \tag{2}$$

where M is the capacity of each queue, $\mathbb{C}$ is the set of classes that need to be contrasted as negative samples, and $\mathbf{k}_{yi}$ denotes the i-th sample in the y-th queue.

In this paper, we set a pseudo-label for a certain sample as the WSI label to which the sample belongs. Then, for a sample x with pseudo-label $\tilde{y}$, we set $\mathbb{C} = \{y|y \neq \tilde{y}\}$. In this way, the type information of the samples are implicitly embedded into the contrastive learning process, which guides the image representations from the same lesion to allocate in the consistent direction of the feature space. It relives the class collision problems caused by the common contrastive representation learning and therefore will be more effective in representing histopathological images.

2.3 Queue Refinement Strategy

To ensure the samples in queues to be representative to the corresponding class during the training process, the queues need to be updated during the training. Here, we propose a novel queue refinement strategy (QRS). QRS purifies each queue with its most representative representations from each mini-batch by measuring the similarities between the to-be-updated representations and the queue representations. Specifically, we define $\mathcal{P}(x)$ to represent the similarity distribution between the to-be-updated k_+ and representations in queues, and $\mathcal{Q}(x)$ to represent the expected distribution with equations

$$\mathcal{P}(x_{yi}) = \frac{\exp(\mathbf{k}_{+}^{\mathrm{T}}\mathbf{k}_{yi})}{\sum_{y=1}^{K} \sum_{i=1}^{M} \exp(\mathbf{k}_{+}^{\mathrm{T}}\mathbf{k}_{yi})} \tag{3}$$

$$\mathcal{Q}(x_{yi}) = \frac{\exp(1(y = \tilde{y}))}{\sum_{y=1}^{K} \sum_{i=1}^{M} \exp(1(y = \tilde{y}))}, \tag{4}$$

where K is total number of classes of the WSIs, $1(\cdot)$ takes 1 when $y = \tilde{y}$, and 0, otherwise.

Then, we determine the collection of samples for updating basing on the consensus that the representation distance between the samples from the same class is smaller than those from the different classes. It can be achieved by examining the distribution consistency of $\mathcal{P}(x)$ and $\mathcal{Q}(x)$ with Kullback-Leibler (KL) divergence:

$$\mathbb{U} = \{\mathbf{k}_{+}|D_{KL}(\mathcal{P}(x)||\mathcal{Q}(x)) \leq \frac{1}{|\mathbb{B}|} \sum_{x\in\mathbb{B}} D_{KL}(\mathcal{P}(x)||\mathcal{Q}(x))\}, \tag{5}$$

$$D_{KL}(\mathcal{P}(x)||\mathcal{Q}(x)) = \sum_{y=1}^{K} \sum_{i=1}^{M} \mathcal{P}(x_{yi}) \log \frac{\mathcal{P}(x_{yi})}{\mathcal{Q}(x_{yi})}, \tag{6}$$

where $\mathbb{U}$ is the set of representations which needs to be updated into the queue from each mini-batch, $\mathbb{B}$ is the mini-batch and $D_{KL}(\cdot)$ is the K-L divergence.

3   Datasets

To verify the proposed method, we collected two datasets including different tasks: EGFR mutation identification for lung cancer and endometrial subtyping, which are introduced below.

EGFR is a dataset of lung adenocarcinoma whole slide images for epidermal growth factor receptor (EGFR) gene mutation identification. The dataset contains a total of 754 WSIs, which are categorized into 5 classes including EGFR 19del mutation, EGFR L858R mutation, none common driver mutations (wild type), other driver gene mutation, and cancer-free tissue (Normal).

Endometrium. Endometrium includes 698 histopathological WSIs of endometrial cases, which includes 5 categories, namely Normal, well differentiated endometrioid adenocarcinoma (WDEA), moderately differentiated endometrioid adenocarcinoma (MDEA), lowly differentiated endometrioid adenocarcinoma (LDEA), and Serous endometrial intraepithelial carcinoma (SEIC).

In each dataset, the WSIs were randomly split into train, validation and test parts following the ratio of 6:1:3 at the patient-level. The train part is used to train the models, and validation part is used to do early stop for the WSI classification benchmarks, and the final result is obtained within the test part. The WSIs were divided into non-overlapping patches in size of 256 × 256 for the representation learning and feature extraction. We assign a pseudo-label for each patch to the WSI label that the patch belongs.

4   Experiments and Results

4.1   Experimental Setup

For each model involved in the experiment, we trained it by 100 epochs on the training set with the batch size as 256. We set the capacity of each lesion queue $M = 65536/K$, to make the total length of the lesion queue is 65536 that is the same as MoCo's memory bank. Afterwards, we took over the backbone of the Resnet50 to extract features for the downstream WSI classification tasks.

In this paper, we evaluated the representation learning performance under two WSI classification benchmarks, CLAM [12] and TransMIL [15]. Both methods use the attention mechanism to aggregate features. The difference is that CLAM focuses on the parts of features in WSI that are most useful for diagnosis. While, TransMIL considers the spatial connections of the patches within the WSI and meanwhile extracts the long-term dependencies through the Transformer [17] architecture. For both of the datasets, we utilize evaluation metrics of accuracy, macro-average area under the curve (AUC) and macro-average F1-Score for the multi-class classification tasks.

All the models were implemented in Python 3.8 with PyTorch 1.7.1 and run on a computer with 4 Nvidia GTX 2080Ti GPUs.

Table 1. Ablation study on the EGFR dataset and the Endometrium dataset under the TransMIL benchmark, where the accuracy (ACC), the macro-average area under the curve (AUC) and the macro-average F1-Score are used as metrics.

Methods	EGFR			Endometrium		
	ACC	AUC	F1-score	ACC	AUC	F1-score
LACL-w/o-queue (MoCov2)	0.534	0.826	0.517	0.436	0.670	0.259
LACL-w/o-QRS	0.556	0.844	0.547	0.474	0.715	0.382
LACL	0.574	0.855	0.552	0.488	0.732	0.390

4.2 Structural Verification

We set up ablation experiments to investigate the impact of our proposed method. The results are shown in the Table 1. LACL-w/o-queue represents the contrastive learning without the proposed lesion queue and the corresponding QRS strategy. In this case, it degrades to the MoCov2. In LACL-w/o-QRS, we did not use QRS to update the lesion queue. Instead, we updated the queue with the strategy in MoCov2. Table 1 shows LACL-w/o-queue suffers from a decrease by 0.018 and 0.045 in AUC in the task for EGFR and Endometrium, respectively, compared to LACL-w/o-QRS. It demonstrates the effectiveness of the proposed lesion queue. When comparing the results of LACL-w/o-QRS and LACL, we found that the QRS further improves the AUC by 0.011 and 0.017. It demonstrates the necessity for a QRS strategy.

4.3 Comparisons with State-of-the-Art Methods

We compared the representations under 6 different WSI presenting strategies. (1) ImageNet denotes extracting the patch representations using the ResNet50 pre-trained on the ImageNet dataset [14]. (2) MoCov2 [3] is the widely applied contrastive learning framework, which is the basis of the proposed method. (3) SimSiam [4] is another popular self-supervised learning method based on positive pair contrasting. (4) SimTriplet [11] redesign the sampling strategy for positive pairs for pathological images, which allows the model to mine the relevance of adjacent tissues. (5) Pseudo-labels denote extracting the patch representations using the ResNet50 trained with pseudo-labels (WSI-level labels). (6) Lerousseau. et al. [10] is a weakly supervised patch representation learning and classification method.

The results are shown in Tables 2 and 3. It shows that the negative-independent methods, i.e., SimSiam and SimTriplet, perform worse on the Endometrium than on the EGFR. The main reason is that the class imbalance of Endometrium dataset is more serious than the EGFR. It indicates that negative-independent methods suffer from the long-tailed distribution dataset. In contrast, the negative-dependent methods, including MoCo and LACL, delivered better performance in accuracy and robustness. It is mainly because the

Table 2. Comparisons with state-of-the-art methods on the EGFR dataset, where the metrics are the same as Table 1

Methods	CLAM			TransMIL		
	ACC	AUC	F1-score	ACC	AUC	F1-score
ImageNet [14]	0.435	0.754	0.429	0.502	0.798	0.484
MoCo v2 [3]	0.462	0.803	0.447	0.534	0.826	0.517
SimSiam [4]	0.453	0.768	0.391	0.502	0.801	0.483
SimTriplet [11]	0.511	0.819	0.464	0.529	0.841	0.510
Pseudo-labels	0.426	0.776	0.403	0.466	0.802	0.421
Lerousseau et al. [10]	0.390	0.710	0.339	0.368	0.660	0.326
LACL (Ours)	**0.525**	**0.826**	**0.510**	**0.574**	**0.855**	**0.552**

Table 3. Comparisons with state-of-the-art methods on the Endometrium dataset, where the metrics are the same as Table 1.

Methods	CLAM			TransMIL		
	ACC	AUC	F1-score	ACC	AUC	F1-score
ImageNet [14]	0.483	0.675	0.404	0.427	0.662	0.258
MoCo v2 [3]	0.502	0.710	0.369	0.436	0.670	0.289
SimSiam [4]	0.483	0.663	0.368	0.436	0.639	0.233
SimTriplet [11]	0.422	0.639	0.258	0.408	0.636	0.181
Pseudo-labels	0.417	0.670	0.332	0.412	0.664	0.326
Lerousseau. et al. [10]	0.408	0.586	0.196	0.427	0.579	0.185
LACL (Ours)	**0.531**	**0.756**	**0.447**	**0.488**	**0.732**	**0.390**

negative pairs can provide more information to assist models in mining intra-class variation. At the same time, large-capacity memory bank could relieve the problem of class imbalance on models. It is obvious that the overall performance of SimTriplet on the EGFR dataset is significantly better than that on the Endometrium dataset. It may because the fact that the tissues of different differentiation stages usually intersect with each other, and thereby the usage of the adjacent tissues as positive pairs would introduce semantic ambiguity and hurt the quality of the representations. In comparison, the proposed LACL achieves consistent performance on the two datasets. It benefits from the design of equal-length lesion queue, and corresponding sampling strategy from the perspective of negative pairs.

Overall, the proposed LACL achieves the best representation learning performance on both the EGFR dataset and Endometrium dataset under both the CLAM and the TransMIL benchmarks. It demonstrates that the design of the lesion queue and the corresponding QRS have provided more discriminative and robust image representations for WSI analysis.

5 Conclusion

In this paper, we proposed a novel lesion-aware contrastive learning framework to generate robust and discriminative representations for the histopathological image analysis. We built the lesion queue module to address the class collision problems in the common contrastive learning methods. The lesion queue enables the model to dynamically select negative pairs during the training process. In addition, we designed a queue refinement strategy to refine the queue update process, which further improved the model performance. Experimental results on WSI sub-typing tasks have demonstrated the effectiveness and robustness of our proposed representation learning method. In future work, we will try to leverage the positive pair mining strategy to the proposed method, to further improve its performance for WSI analysis.

Acknowledgments. This work was partly supported by the National Natural Science Foundation of China [grant no. 61901018, 62171007, 61906058, and 61771031], partly supported by the Anhui Provincial Natural Science Foundation [grant no. 1908085MF210], and partly supported by the Fundamental Research Funds for the Central Universities of China [grant no. JZ2022HGTB0285].

References

1. Arvaniti, E., et al.: Automated Gleason grading of prostate cancer tissue microarrays via deep learning. Sci. Rep. **8**(1), 1–11 (2018)
2. Chen, T., Kornblith, S., Norouzi, M., Hinton, G.: A simple framework for contrastive learning of visual representations. In: International Conference on Machine Learning, pp. 1597–1607. PMLR (2020)
3. Chen, X., Fan, H., Girshick, R., He, K.: Improved baselines with momentum contrastive learning. arXiv preprint arXiv:2003.04297 (2020)
4. Chen, X., He, K.: Exploring simple Siamese representation learning. In: Proceedings of the IEEE/CVF Conference on Computer Vision and Pattern Recognition, pp. 15750–15758 (2021)
5. Han, L., Murphy, R.F., Ramanan, D.: Learning generative models of tissue organization with supervised GANs. In: 2018 IEEE Winter Conference on Applications of Computer Vision (WACV), pp. 682–690. IEEE (2018)
6. He, K., Fan, H., Wu, Y., Xie, S., Girshick, R.: Momentum contrast for unsupervised visual representation learning. In: Proceedings of the IEEE/CVF Conference on Computer Vision and Pattern Recognition, pp. 9729–9738 (2020)
7. Huang, Z., Chai, H., Wang, R., Wang, H., Yang, Y., Wu, H.: Integration of patch features through self-supervised learning and transformer for survival analysis on whole slide images. In: de Bruijne, M., et al. (eds.) MICCAI 2021. LNCS, vol. 12908, pp. 561–570. Springer, Cham (2021). https://doi.org/10.1007/978-3-030-87237-3_54
8. Ilse, M., Tomczak, J., Welling, M.: Attention-based deep multiple instance learning. In: International Conference on Machine Learning, pp. 2127–2136. PMLR (2018)
9. Jiang, Y., Chen, L., Zhang, H., Xiao, X.: Breast cancer histopathological image classification using convolutional neural networks with small SE-ResNet module. PLoS ONE **14**(3), e0214587 (2019)

10. Lerousseau, M., et al.: Weakly supervised multiple instance learning histopathological tumor segmentation. In: Martel, A.L., et al. (eds.) MICCAI 2020. LNCS, vol. 12265, pp. 470–479. Springer, Cham (2020). https://doi.org/10.1007/978-3-030-59722-1_45

11. Liu, Q., et al.: SimTriplet: simple triplet representation learning with a single GPU. In: de Bruijne, M., et al. (eds.) MICCAI 2021. LNCS, vol. 12902, pp. 102–112. Springer, Cham (2021). https://doi.org/10.1007/978-3-030-87196-3_10

12. Lu, M.Y., Williamson, D.F., Chen, T.Y., Chen, R.J., Barbieri, M., Mahmood, F.: Data-efficient and weakly supervised computational pathology on whole-slide images. Nat. Biomed. Eng. **5**(6), 555–570 (2021)

13. Robinson, J., Chuang, C.Y., Sra, S., Jegelka, S.: Contrastive learning with hard negative samples. arXiv preprint arXiv:2010.04592 (2020)

14. Russakovsky, O., et al.: ImageNet large scale visual recognition challenge. Int. J. Comput. Vis. **115**(3), 211–252 (2015)

15. Shao, Z., Bian, H., Chen, Y., Wang, Y., Zhang, J., Ji, X., et al.: TransMIL: transformer based correlated multiple instance learning for whole slide image classification. In: Advances in Neural Information Processing Systems 34 (2021)

16. Tian, Y., Sun, C., Poole, B., Krishnan, D., Schmid, C., Isola, P.: What makes for good views for contrastive learning? Adv. Neural. Inf. Process. Syst. **33**, 6827–6839 (2020)

17. Vaswani, A., et al.: Attention is all you need. In: Advances in Neural Information Processing Systems 30 (2017)

18. Le Vuong, T.T., Kim, K., Song, B., Kwak, J.T.: Ranking loss: a ranking-based deep neural network for colorectal cancer grading in pathology images. In: MICCAI 2021. LNCS, vol. 12908, pp. 540–549. Springer, Cham (2021). https://doi.org/10.1007/978-3-030-87237-3_52

19. Wang, S., et al.: RMDL: recalibrated multi-instance deep learning for whole slide gastric image classification. Med. Image Anal. **58**, 101549 (2019)

20. Wang, X., et al.: TransPath: transformer-based self-supervised learning for histopathological image classification. In: de Bruijne, M., et al. (eds.) MICCAI 2021. LNCS, vol. 12908, pp. 186–195. Springer, Cham (2021). https://doi.org/10.1007/978-3-030-87237-3_18

21. Xiao, T., Wang, X., Efros, A.A., Darrell, T.: What should not be contrastive in contrastive learning. arXiv preprint arXiv:2008.05659 (2020)

22. Yang, P., Hong, Z., Yin, X., Zhu, C., Jiang, R.: Self-supervised visual representation learning for histopathological images. In: de Bruijne, M., et al. (eds.) MICCAI 2021. LNCS, vol. 12902, pp. 47–57. Springer, Cham (2021). https://doi.org/10.1007/978-3-030-87196-3_5

23. Zheng, M., et al.: Weakly supervised contrastive learning. In: Proceedings of the IEEE/CVF International Conference on Computer Vision, pp. 10042–10051 (2021)

24. Zheng, Y., et al.: Diagnostic regions attention network (DRA-Net) for histopathology WSI recommendation and retrieval. IEEE Trans. Med. Imaging **40**(3), 1090–1103 (2020)

Kernel Attention Transformer (KAT) for Histopathology Whole Slide Image Classification

Yushan Zheng[1(✉)], Jun Li[2], Jun Shi[3], Fengying Xie[2], and Zhiguo Jiang[2]

[1] School of Engineering Medicine, Beijing Advanced Innovation Center on Biomedical Engineering, Beihang University, Beijing 100191, China
yszheng@buaa.edu.cn
[2] Image Processing Center, School of Astronautics, Beihang University, Beijing 102206, China
[3] School of Software, Hefei University of Technology, Hefei 230601, China

Abstract. Transformer has been widely used in histopathology whole slide image (WSI) classification for the purpose of tumor grading, prognosis analysis, etc. However, the design of token-wise self-attention and positional embedding strategy in the common Transformer limits the effectiveness and efficiency in the application to gigapixel histopathology images. In this paper, we propose a kernel attention Transformer (KAT) for histopathology WSI classification. The information transmission of the tokens is achieved by cross-attention between the tokens and a set of kernels related to a set of positional anchors on the WSI. Compared to the common Transformer structure, the proposed KAT can better describe the hierarchical context information of the local regions of the WSI and meanwhile maintains a lower computational complexity. The proposed method was evaluated on a gastric dataset with 2040 WSIs and an endometrial dataset with 2560 WSIs, and was compared with 6 state-of-the-art methods. The experimental results have demonstrated the proposed KAT is effective and efficient in the task of histopathology WSI classification and is superior to the state-of-the-art methods. The code is available at https://github.com/zhengyushan/kat.

Keywords: WSI classification · Transformer · Cross-attention

1 Introduction

Histopathology whole slide image (WSI) classification based on image processing and deep learning has proven effective to building computer-aided applications for cancer screening [11,17], tumor grading [1], prognosis analysis [5], gene mutant prediction [16], etc.

Supplementary Information The online version contains supplementary material available at https://doi.org/10.1007/978-3-031-16434-7_28.

Recently, Vision Transformer (ViT) [4], the extensively studied model in natural scene image recognition, was introduced to this problem. The WSI classification can be achieved by regarding the WSI local features as tokens. Theoretically, the self-attention mechanism of Transformer enables it to detect the useful relations of the local features for WSI recognition. The recent studies [3,6,8] have proven Transformer-based models can further improve the WSI classification accuracy when compared to the previous methods based on convolution neural network (CNN) [13], recurrent neural network (RNN) [2], and multiple instance learning (MIL) [9]. Nevertheless, the calculation flowchart of self-attention, the main operation in Transformer, occurs notable problem when applied for the WSI containing gigapixels. Firstly, the positional embedding strategy of ViT, which is designed for images in fixed size and shape, cannot consistently describe the structural information of WSI. Secondly, the self-attention operation permits equivalent conjunction of tokens in every stage of transformer. The equivalent conjunction usually causes over-smoothing in the token representations and thereby does harm the learning of the local patterns of the WSI. Furthermore, the computational complexity of the self-attention operation is $\mathcal{O}(n^2)$ to the number of tokens n. The inference of the Transformer becomes rather inefficient when facing a WSI with thousands of tokens. These problems have affected the efficiency and accuracy of the Transformer-based method for WSI classification.

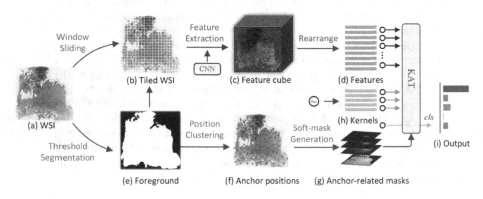

Fig. 1. The proposed framework for WSI classification, where (a–d) is the process of feature extraction for the WSI, (a–g) illustrates the flowchart of anchor position detection and mask generation, (h) is a set of trainable kernel vectors that related to the anchor positions, and KAT is the proposed kernel attention network that is detailed in Sect. 2.2 and Fig. 2.

In this paper, we propose a novel Transformer model named kernel attention Transformer (KAT) and an integrated framework for histopathology whole slide image classification, which is illustrated in Fig. 1. Compared to the common Transformer structure, the proposed KAT can describe hierarchical context information of the local regions of the WSI and thereby is more effective for histopathology WSI analysis. Meanwhile, the kernel-based cross-attention paradigm maintains a near-linear computational complexity to the size of the WSI. The proposed method was evaluated on a gastric dataset with 2040 WSIs and an endometrial dataset with 2560 WSIs, and was compared with 6 state-of-the-art methods [3,4,9,10,15,18]. The experimental results have demonstrated the proposed KAT is effective and efficient in the task of histopathology WSI classification and is superior to the state-of-the-art methods.

The contribution of the paper can be summarized in two aspects. (1) A novel Transformer-based structure named kernel attention Transformer (KAT) is proposed. Unlike the common Transformer, the information transmission of the tokens is achieved by cross-attention between the tokens and a set of kernels that are bounded to a set of positional anchors on the WSI. The experimental results show that the kernel-based cross-attention in KAT contributes to a competitive performance for WSI classification. Furthermore, it significantly relieves the burden of the computation device in both the training and the application stages. Furthermore, (2) We design a flowchart to generate hierarchical positional masks to define multi-scale WSI regions. The positional masks are calculated based on the spatial allocations of the tokens and then bound with the kernels in KAT. It makes the KAT able to learn hierarchical representations from the local to the global scale of the WSI and thereby delivers better WSI classification performance.

2   Method

2.1   Pre-processing and Data Preparation

The blank regions of the WSI are removed beforehand by a threshold on the intensity, for these regions are less informative for diagnosis. Then, a tissue mask for the WSI is generated by filling the cavities of the foreground of the threshold output (as shown in Fig. 1e). Based on the mask, the tissue region is divided into patches following the non-overlapping sliding window paradigm (Fig. 1b). Next, a CNN is trained to extract the patch features. The structure of CNN was EfficientNet-b0 [12] because of its lightweight and comprehensive performance. To meet the consensus of annotation-free modeling in the domain of histopathology WSI analysis, the EfficientNet-b0 is trained by contrastive representation learning proposed in BYOL [7].

One motivation for the kernel-based scheme is to refine the local information communication of the Transformer. Therefore, we designed a flowchart to generate hierarchical masks to guide information transmission in different stages. The features within the foreground of the tissue mask were rearranged to a feature matrix (as shown in Fig. 1d) which is formulated as $\mathbf{X} \in \mathbb{R}^{n_p \times d_f}$, where n_p denotes the number of tissue-related patches on the WSI, $\mathbf{x}_i \in \mathbb{R}^{d_f}$ is the i-th row of the $\mathbf{X}$ that represents the feature of the i-th tissue-related patch. Correspondingly, we define $p(\mathbf{x}_i) = (m_i, n_i)^{\mathrm{T}}$ to represent the patch-wise coordinate of the feature $\mathbf{x}_i$ on the WSI. Then, we extracted a set of anchors based on the spatially clustering property of the features. Specifically, the K-means algorithm is applied to clustering $\{p(\mathbf{x}_i)|i = 1, 2, ..., n_p\}$ into K centers. Then, the most nearest position to each center is recognized as an anchor position, which is represented as $\mathbf{c}_k = (m_k, n_k)^{\mathrm{T}}, k = 1, 2..., K$, as shown in Fig. 1f.

Afterward, we define weighting masks for each anchor position based on the spatial distance between features and the anchor. Specifically, the weight of the k-th anchor and the i-th feature is calculated by the equation

$$m_{ki}(\delta) = \exp(-\|p(\mathbf{x}_i) - \mathbf{c}_k\|_2^2 / 2\delta^2),\tag{1}$$

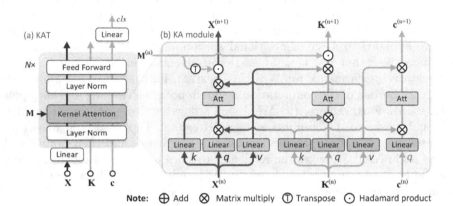

Fig. 2. The structure of kernel attention network (KAT), where Feed Forward is composed of two linear projection layers, Att denotes a scaling operation followed by a softmax operation, $\mathbf{M}^{(n)}$, $\mathbf{X}^{(n)}$, $\mathbf{K}^{(n)}$, and $\mathbf{c}^{(n)}$ denotes the anchor masks, the representations of the patch tokens, kernel tokens, and classification token, respectively.

where δ controls the scale of the Gaussian-like mask. By computing the weights between all the features and anchors, we obtain the mask matrix $\mathbf{M}(\delta) \in (0, 1)^{K \times n_p}$, where each row defines a soft-mask related to an anchor position to all the patch features, and each column records the weights of a feature to all the anchors. Moreover, we define multi-scale masks by adjusting δ, Finally, the hierarchical masks are represented by the collection $\mathbb{M} = \{\mathbf{M}(\delta_s) | s = 1, 2..., N\}$ with N representing the number of scales, as shown in Fig. 1g. The visualization of $\mathbb{M}$ can be found in the experiment section.

2.2   Kernel Attention Transformer (KAT)

The input of KAT includes the feature matrix $\mathbf{X}$ and the anchor masks $\mathbb{M}$ for each WSI. Each feature in $\mathbf{X}$ is regarded as a token. As shown in Fig. 2a, the basic structure of KAT follows the ViT. It is constructed by stacking N repeated blocks, which is composed of modules in the sequence of layer normalization, kernel attention, layer normalization, and feed-forward module, and the kernel attention and feed-forward module are with residual connections. Here, the kernel attention (KA) module is the core of KAT and is also the major difference of KAT to the common Transformer, which is detailed in this section.

As shown in Fig. 2b, the basic input of the n-th KA module includes the patch token representations $\mathbf{X}^{(n)} \in \mathbb{R}^{n_p \times d_e}$ and the classification token $\mathbf{c}^{(n)} \in \mathbb{R}^{d_e}$ with d_e denoting the embedding dimension. Besides, we further define a set of tokens $\mathbf{K}^{(n)} \in \mathbb{R}^{K \times d_e}$ (as shown in Fig. 1h) that serves as the kernels and correspondingly provides it the anchor masks $\mathbf{M}^{(n)} = \mathbf{M}(\delta_n) \in \mathbb{M}$. Instead of doing self-attention among the patch tokens, we propose to performing cross-attention between the kernels and the patch tokens. Namely, the information transmission in the KA module is achieved by a bi-direction message passing flow. One direction is the *information summary flow (ISF)*, which is defined by equation

$$\mathbf{K}^{(n+1)} = \sigma\left(\mathbf{K}^{(n)}\mathbf{W}_q^{(n)} \cdot (\mathbf{X}^{(n)}\mathbf{W}_k^{(n)})^{\mathrm{T}}/\tau\right) \odot \mathbf{M}^{(n)} \cdot \mathbf{X}^{(n)}\mathbf{W}_v^{(n)}, \qquad (2)$$

where the notations involving in $\mathbf{W}$ denote the trainable weights for linear projections, σ denotes the softmax function, and τ is the scaling factor that is set the same as ViT.

Another direction is the *information distribution flow (IDF)*. The definition of *IDF* is symmetric with *ISF* by equation

$$\mathbf{X}^{(n+1)} = \sigma\left(\mathbf{X}^{(n)}\mathbf{W}_q^{(n)} \cdot (\mathbf{K}^{(n)}\mathbf{W}_k^{(n)})^{\mathrm{T}}/\tau\right) \odot \mathbf{M}^{\mathrm{T}(n)} \cdot \mathbf{K}^{(n)}\mathbf{W}_v^{(n)}. \qquad (3)$$

Through ISF, the individual representations of the patch tokens are reported to their nearby kernels for information summary. Then, through the IDF, the regional information carried by the kernels will be broadcast back to their nearby patches. Based on the bi-directional message passing flow, communication among the feature tokens of the WSI can be accomplished.

Correspondingly, in each KA module, we set aside a token to sum up the information from all the kernels for the purpose of classification. The message passing is defined as

$$\mathbf{c}^{(n+1)} = \sigma\left(\mathbf{c}^{(n)}\mathbf{W}_q^{(n)} \cdot (\mathbf{K}^{(n)}\mathbf{W}_k^{(n)})^{\mathrm{T}}/\tau\right) \cdot \mathbf{K}^{(n)}\mathbf{W}_v^{(n)}. \qquad (4)$$

Supposing the number of the kernels is fixed, the computational complexity of KA module is $\mathcal{O}(n_p)$ to the token number n_p.

At the end of the KAT, we built a linear layer on the output of the classification token for WSI classification. The number of neurons of the last linear layer is the same as the type number of the WSIs. Finally, the entire KAT is trained end-to-end by cross-entropy loss function with Adam optimizer. The inputs of the kernel tokens and the classification token, i.e. $\mathbf{K}^{(0)}$ and $\mathbf{c}^{(0)}$, are randomly initialed and kept trainable in the training stage. To ensure all the kernels have consistent action for the same allocation of nearby features, we make all the kernels share the same set of trainable parameters. To further improve the performance of the KA module, we extended it to the Multi-head KA module following the paradigm of Transformer [4].

3   Experiment and Result

The proposed method was evaluated on two large-scale WSI datasets. (1) *Gastric-2K* contains 2040 WSIs of gastric histopathology from 2040 patients. These WSIs are categorized into 6 subtypes of gastric pathology, including Low/High-grade intraepithelial neoplasia, Adenocarcinoma, Mucinous adeno-carcinoma, Signet-ring cell carcinoma, and Normal. (2) *Endometrial-2K* contains 2650 WSIs of endometrium histopathology from 2650 patients. These WSIs are categorized into 5 subtypes of endometrial pathology, including Well/Moderately/Low-differentiated endometrioid adenocarcinoma, Serous endometrial intraepithelial carcinoma, and Normal.

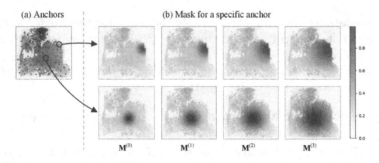

Fig. 3. An instance of the anchor position allocation and the corresponding hierarchical masks under the setting $\bar{n}_k = 144$ and $N = 4$.

In each dataset, the WSIs were randomly separated into train, validation, and test subset at the patient level by the proportion of 6:1:3. All the models discussed in the experiment were trained within the training set. The validation set was used to perform early stop and hyper-parameter tuning. And the results reported in the following sections were obtained on the test set by the final models.

The window sliding and CNN feature extraction were performed on the WSI under 20× lenses (the resolution is 0.48 μm/pixel). The window size, as well as the image patch size, was set to 224 × 224 and the feature dimension $d_f = 1280$ for the EfficientNet-b0 structure. The proposed method was implemented in Python 3.8 with torch 1.9 and Cuda 10.2, and run on a computer with 2 Xeon 2.66 GHz CPUs and 4 GPUs of Nvidia Geforce 3090. More details please refer to the source code on https://github.com/zhengyushan/kat.

3.1   Model Verification

We first conducted experiments to verify the design of the proposed KAT model. The number of kernels K is the main hyper-parameter that is additional to the common ViT. To make the proposed KAT be scalable to the size of WSI, we

Table 1. The results on the *Endometrial-2K* dataset for different settings of KAT, where the classification accuracy (Acc.), and macro/weighted area under the receiver operating characteristic curve (mAUC/wAUC) for the sub-typing, and the specificity (Spec.), sensitivity (Sens.), and AUC for the binary task are calculated. The floating-point operations (#FLOPs) and GPU memory cost (Mem.) per WSI are also provided.

Models	Sub-typing			Normal vs. Others				# FLOPs	Mem.
	Acc.	mAUC	wAUC	Acc.	Spec.	Sens.	mAUC	($\times 10^9$)	(MiB)
KAT ($\bar{n}_k = 16$)	0.575	0.811	0.866	0.941	**0.881**	0.967	0.973	0.227	899.71
KAT ($\bar{n}_k = 64$)	0.597	0.830	0.881	0.945	0.835	0.981	0.972	0.217	581.56
KAT ($\bar{n}_k = 144$)	**0.608**	**0.835**	**0.882**	**0.949**	0.867	0.975	**0.983**	0.213	569.31
KAT ($\bar{n}_k = 256$)	0.582	0.825	0.872	0.945	0.834	0.981	0.977	**0.208**	566.03
KAT w/o kernels	0.549	0.788	0.840	0.925	0.810	0.963	0.969	0.701	3655.1
KAT w/o masks	0.567	0.814	0.857	0.927	0.822	0.963	0.960	0.213	**563.24**
KAT w/o IDF	0.586	0.823	0.869	0.947	0.827	**0.983**	0.970	0.743	3953.2

assigned an adaptive K for each WSI by defining $K = [n_p/\bar{n}_k]$, where $\bar{n}_k$ is the desired number of patches processed per kernel. Correspondingly, we empirically set $\delta_n^2 = \bar{n}_k^2 \cdot 2^n$. It makes the intersection of the ($-\delta_0$, $+\delta_0$) area of all the anchors basically cover all the patches, as shown in Fig. 3. The performance of KAT with different $\bar{n}_k$ on the *Endometrial-2K* dataset is presented on Table 1. The results show that KAT performs relatively consistent when $\bar{n}_k \in [64, 256]$ and $\bar{n}_k = 144$ is the most appreciate for the dataset.

Then, we conducted the ablation study, for which the results are also summarized in Table 1. KAT w/o kernels denotes KAT without kernels and masks. In this situation, the KAT degrades to the common ViT structure. It causes a significant decrease in macro AUC for the subtyping from 0.835 to 0.788 and the AUC for the binary classification from 0.983 to 0.969. These results have demonstrated the effectiveness of the proposed kernel attention design and the corresponding anchor masking strategy. Furthermore, the FLOPs and GPU memory for the inference of a WSI respectively enlarge by 3.37× and 6.46×. It shows the efficiency advantage of KAT over the normal ViT. KAT w/o masks indicates KAT without the $\mathbf{M}^{(n)}$, where the spatial information passing control for the patches and the anchors are discarded. The results show that it achieves a comparable performance to KAT w/o kernels, i.e., ViT, while maintaining a low computational complexity. In this case, KAT w/o masks acts as a linear approximation model for ViT like Linformer [14], Nyströmformer [15], etc. In the model KAT w/o IDF, we use self-attention operations among patch tokens to substitute the *IDF* for patch token encoding. It causes a decrease of 0.012 to 0.013 in the AUCs. The results show that getting the information from the kernels is more efficient than that from individual patch tokens. It indicates the kernels contain higher-level semantics compared to the individual tokens.

3.2 Comparison with Other Methods

The proposed method was compared with 6 methods [3,4,9,10,15,18]. For all the Transformer-based models, we uniformly stacked four self-attention blocks with 8 heads and set the embedding dimension $d_e = 256$. The results are presented in Table 2.

Overall, the proposed method achieves the best performance with a mAUC/AUC of 0.835/0.983 in the sub-typing/binary classification task on the *Endometrial-2K* dataset, which is 2.4%/0.9% superior to the second-best methods, and a mAUC/AUC of 0.855/0.967 in the two tasks on the *Gastric-2K* dataset, which is 4.1%/0.9% superior to the second-best methods.

Table 2. Comparison of the state-of-the-art methods, where the *Speed* represents the number of WSI per second in the inference stage of the compared models.

Endometrial-2K	Sub-type classification			Normal vs. Others				Speed
	Accuracy	mAUC	mAUC	Accuracy	Specificity	Sensitivity	AUC	(WSI/s)
ViT [4]	0.549	0.788	0.840	0.925	0.810	0.963	0.969	15.2
Nyströmformer [15]	0.571	0.790	0.832	0.936	0.853	0.967	0.969	**45.3**
CLAM [9]	0.574	0.791	0.835	0.938	0.846	0.963	0.951	23.9
Patch-GCN [3]	0.534	0.799	0.832	0.918	0.840	0.943	0.958	8.1
TransMIL [10]	0.552	0.811	0.858	0.941	**0.855**	0.971	0.974	42.7
LAGE-Net [18]	0.598	0.801	0.855	0.938	0.852	0.963	0.974	14.5
KAT (Ours)	**0.608**	**0.835**	**0.882**	**0.949**	0.830	**0.985**	**0.983**	38.1
Gastric-2K	Sub-type classification			(Normal+LGIN) vs. Others				Speed
	Accuracy	mAUC	mAUC	Accuracy	Specificity	Sensitivity	AUC	(WSI/s)
ViT [4]	0.765	0.780	0.938	0.842	0.827	**0.913**	0.924	33.3
Nyströmformer [15]	0.819	0.784	0.935	0.900	**0.953**	0.760	0.934	**71.7**
CLAM [9]	0.788	0.790	0.915	0.898	0.909	0.868	0.929	28.2
Patch-GCN [3]	0.797	0.810	0.939	0.874	0.915	0.770	0.941	15.7
TransMIL [10]	**0.824**	0.791	0.944	0.902	0.940	0.796	0.958	64.7
LAGE-Net [18]	0.775	0.814	0.951	0.907	0.935	0.851	0.936	28.9
KAT (Ours)	0.819	**0.855**	**0.955**	**0.915**	0.941	0.866	**0.967**	61.2

Nyströmformer [15] provides a linear solution to approximate standard self-attention in Transformer. The computational complexity is reduced to $\mathcal{O}(n)$. Meanwhile, the better convergence makes Nyströmformer achieve higher classification accuracy than ViT [4]. Patch-GCN [3] is a typical spatial-graph-based WSI classification method, where the patches in the WSI are connected by a spatial graph. The adjacency information of the local patterns is considered by GCN in the encoding of the WSI. Therefore, it delivers comparable performance to ViT and Nyströmformer. LAGE-Net [18] is a composition model of ViT and GCN, where both the long-range and adjacency relationship are considered. However, the combination usage of ViT and GCN causes an even lower computational efficiency than ViT. TransMIL [10] utilizes the Nyströmformer module to catch the long-range relationship in high computational efficiency. Meanwhile, a pyramid position encoding generator (PPEG) is built to extract the spatial relationship, which contributes to a better performance than Nyströmformer. Nevertheless, the spatial relationship described by PPEG is inconsistent for different WSIs, especially for the gastric biopsy dataset where the tissue area varies a lot for different WSI. This made TransMIL be inferior to Patch-GCN and LAGE-Net on the gastric WSI sub-typing task.

In comparison, the proposed method builds uniformly distributed anchors that is adaptive to the shape and size of the tissue region and generates hierarchically region masks for the anchors to describe the local to the global relationship of the patches. The spatial relationship described by KAT is more complete and consistent compared to the previous methods and therefore achieves relatively better performance. Moreover, the kernel-based cross-attention computation in the KA module maintains a relatively high computational efficiency. The speed of inference is 38.1 WSIs per second on the endometrial dataset and 61.2 on the gastric dataset, which is comparable to TransMIL and Nyströmformer. (Please refer to the supplemental material for more details.)

4 Conclusion

In this paper, we have proposed a novel model named kernel attention Transformer (KAT) with the corresponding anchor mask generation approach for histopathology whole slide image classification. The experiments on two large-scale datasets have proven the KAT with the hierarchical anchor masks is both effective and efficient in the tasks of WSI sub-typing and binary classification, and achieves the state-of-the-art overall performance. Future work will develop representative region detection and encoding methods based on the kernel attention property of the KAT.

Acknowledgments. This work was partly supported by the National Natural Science Foundation of China [grant no. 61901018, 62171007, 61906058, and 61771031], partly supported by the Anhui Provincial Natural Science Foundation [grant no. 1908085MF210], and partly supported by the Fundamental Research Funds for the Central Universities of China [grant no. JZ2022HGTB0285].

References

1. Bulten, W., et al.: Artificial intelligence for diagnosis and Gleason grading of prostate cancer: the panda challenge. Nat. Med. **28**, 154–163 (2022)
2. Campanella, G., et al.: Clinical-grade computational pathology using weakly supervised deep learning on whole slide images. Nature medicine **25**(8), 1301–1309 (2019)
3. Chen, R.J., et al.: Whole slide images are 2D point clouds: context-aware survival prediction using patch-based graph convolutional networks. In: International Conference on Medical Image Computing and Computer-Assisted Intervention, pp. 339–349 (2021)

4. Dosovitskiy, A., et al.: An image is worth 16 × 16 words: transformers for image recognition at scale. In: International Conference on Learning Representations (2020)
5. Fu, Y., et al.: Pan-cancer computational histopathology reveals mutations, tumor composition and prognosis. Nat. Cancer **1**(8), 800–810 (2020)
6. Gao, Z., Hong, B., Zhang, X., Li, Y., Jia, C., Wu, J., Wang, C., Meng, D., Li, C.: Instance-based vision transformer for subtyping of papillary renal cell carcinoma in histopathological image. In: de Bruijne, M., et al. (eds.) MICCAI 2021. LNCS, vol. 12908, pp. 299–308. Springer, Cham (2021). https://doi.org/10.1007/978-3-030-87237-3_29
7. Grill, J.B., et al.: Bootstrap your own latent-a new approach to self-supervised learning. Adv. Neural. Inf. Process. Syst. **33**, 21271–21284 (2020)
8. Li, H., et al.: DT-MIL: deformable transformer for multi-instance learning on histopathological image. In: de Bruijne, M., et al. (eds.) MICCAI 2021. LNCS, vol. 12908, pp. 206–216. Springer, Cham (2021). https://doi.org/10.1007/978-3-030-87237-3_20
9. Lu, M.Y., Williamson, D.F., Chen, T.Y., Chen, R.J., Barbieri, M., Mahmood, F.: Data-efficient and weakly supervised computational pathology on whole-slide images. Nat. Biomed. Eng. **5**(6), 555–570 (2021)
10. Shao, Z., Bian, H., Chen, Y., Wang, Y., Zhang, J., Ji, X., et al.: TransMIL: transformer based correlated multiple instance learning for whole slide image classification. In: Advances in Neural Information Processing Systems, vol. 34 (2021)
11. Song, Z., et al.: Clinically applicable histopathological diagnosis system for gastric cancer detection using deep learning. Nat. Commun. **11**(1), 1–9 (2020)
12. Tan, M., Le, Q.: EfficientNet: rethinking model scaling for convolutional neural networks. In: International Conference on Machine Learning, pp. 6105–6114. PMLR (2019)
13. Tellez, D., Litjens, G., van der Laak, J., Ciompi, F.: Neural image compression for gigapixel histopathology image analysis. IEEE Trans. Pattern Anal. Mach. Intell. **43**(2), 567–578 (2019)
14. Wang, S., Li, B.Z., Khabsa, M., Fang, H., Ma, H.: Linformer: self-attention with linear complexity. arXiv preprint arXiv:2006.04768 (2020)
15. Xiong, Y., et al.: Nyströmformer: a nyStöm-based algorithm for approximating self-attention. In: AAAI Conference on Artificial Intelligence, p. 14138 (2021)
16. Yamashita, R., et al.: Deep learning model for the prediction of microsatellite instability in colorectal cancer: a diagnostic study. Lancet Oncol. **22**(1), 132–141 (2021)
17. Yu, H., et al.: Large-scale gastric cancer screening and localization using multi-task deep neural network. Neurocomputing **448**, 290–300 (2021)
18. Zheng, Y., et al.: Encoding histopathology whole slide images with location-aware graphs for diagnostically relevant regions retrieval. Med. Image Anal. **76**, 102308 (2022)

Joint Region-Attention and Multi-scale Transformer for Microsatellite Instability Detection from Whole Slide Images in Gastrointestinal Cancer

Zhilong Lv[1,2], Rui Yan[1,2], Yuexiao Lin[3], Ying Wang[4], and Fa Zhang[1(✉)]

[1] Institute of Computing Technology, Chinese Academy of Sciences, Beijing, China
zhangfa@ict.ac.cn
[2] University of Chinese Academy of Sciences, Beijing, China
[3] Department of General Surgery, Beijing Chaoyang Hospital, Capital Medical University, Beijing, China
[4] Department of Pathology, Beijing Chaoyang Hospital, Capital Medical University, Beijing, China

Abstract. Microsatellite instability (MSI) is a crucial biomarker to clinical immunotherapy in gastrointestinal cancer, while additional immunohistochemical or genetic tests for MSI are generally missing due to lack of medical resources. Deep learning has achieved promising performance in detecting MSI from hematoxylin and eosin (H&E) stained histopathology slides. However, these methods are primarily based on patch-supervised slide-label models and then aggregate patch-level results into the slides-level result, resulting unstable prediction due to noisy patches and aggregation ways.

In this paper, we propose a joint region-attention and multi-scale transformer (RAMST) network for microsatellite instability detection from whole slide images in gastrointestinal cancer. Specifically, we present a region-attention mechanism and a feature weight uniform sampling (FWUS) method to learn a representative subset of image patches from whole slide images. Moreover, we introduce the transformer architecture to fuse the multi-scale histopathology features consisting of patch-level features with region-level features to characterize the whole slide images for slide-level MSI detection. Compared to the existing MSI detection methods, the proposed RAMST shows the best performances on the colorectal and stomach cancer dataset from The Cancer Genome Atlas (TCGA) and provides an effective features representation learning method for WSI-label tasks.

Keywords: Microsatellite instability · Gastrointestinal cancer · Region attention · Transformer

---

Supplementary Information The online version contains supplementary material available at https://doi.org/10.1007/978-3-031-16434-7_29.

1 Introduction

Microsatellite instability (MSI) is a key predictive biomarker for therapeutic response to immune checkpoint inhibitors in gastrointestinal cancer patients [1]. The gold standard for microsatellite status (microsatellite instability (MSI) or microsatellite stability (MSS)) is based on immunohistochemistry (IHC) or genetic tests with subsequent polymerase chain reaction (PCR), but these additional tests are generally missing in clinical practice due to lack of medical resources [3]. The popularization of pathological examination provides an opportunity for MSI detection directly from hematoxylin and eosin (H&E) stained histopathology whole slide images (WSI), which show the immunologic microenvironment phenotypes of tumors. Compared with predictive systems merely relying on morphological phenotypic features such as lymphocytic infiltration, poor differentiation and mucinous differentiation, deep learning methods with powerful feature representation capability have achieved promising performance in detecting MSI from pathological images [7].

As the first deep learning-based MSI detection study in gastrointestinal cancer, in 2019, Kather et al. presented a patch-level classifier based on resnet18 network to classify MSI versus MSS from H&E histopathology slides [10]. After this initial study, Schmauch et al. explored MSI prediction from H&E images with pretrained model on RNA-sequencing data in 2020, further suggesting the potential correlation between transcriptomic phenotype and morphological patterns. They achieved a patch cluster-level neural network classifier and obtained final MSI prediction of whole slide image (WSI) by calculating a weighted mean of all patch clusters [14]. Cao et al. developed a multiple-instance learning (MIL)-based model to predict the microsatellite status from histopathology images, which aggregated the patch likelihoods through an ensemble classifier to obtain the WSI-level prediction [4]. Then, Echle et al. provided a lightweight deep learning system based on shufflenet network with the largest colorectal cancer patient cohort so far, averaging patch-level predictions to the WSI level [6]. In 2021, Yamashita et al. proposed a two-step method: a tissue-type classifier and a microsatellite status classifier, whose predictions were averaged to generate a WSI-level probability of MSI [18]. Bilat et al. advanced a weakly-supervised deep learning pipeline to predict the slide-level molecular status by aggregating the prediction scores of all patches into the average probability-based result [2]. Schirris et al. applied a self-supervised heterogeneity-aware multiple instance learning (DeepSMILE) to predict the WSI-level genomic label classification by the attention-weighted mean and variance of all patches feature representation [13].

Overall, these MSI detection models are primarily based on patch-supervised prediction and then aggregate these patch-level results as the slide-level result. Since the cellular and tissue morphology associated with the MSI are not entirely clear, the performances of these patch-supervised models are limited by noisy patches and aggregation ways. Then, WSI-supervised models are gradually introduced for MSI detection from H&E histopathology slides. However, the existing WSI-supervised methods basically predicted the microsatellite status from randomly sampled partial patches, which are difficult to obtain stable and representative the features of whole slide images.

In this paper, we propose a region-attention and multi-scale transformer (RAMST) network to detect the microsatellite status from whole slide images in gastrointestinal cancer. In the RAMST, we present a feature weight uniform sampling (FWUS) method based on the region-attention mechanism to learn a representative subset of image patches and to largely eliminate noisy and redundant patches. Furthermore, we combine patch-level features from the subset of image patches with region-level features from image regions as the multi-scale histopathology features to characterize the whole slide images, and then introduce the transformer architecture to fuse the multi-scale features for slide-level microsatellite status (MSI or MSS) detection. In addition, we utilize an extra classification objective function to facilitate the optimization of region-attention module, which is the basis of the feature weight uniform sampling method.

The main contributions of this work can be summarized as follows: 1) We propose a joint region-attention and multi-scale transformer (RAMST) to detect the microsatellite status from while slide images, which outperforms existing patch-supervision methods on the gastrointestinal cancer dataset from TCGA. 2) We provide an effective representation learning method based on the feature weight uniform sampling (FWUS) method for WSI-label tasks, which preserves representative features and largely removes noisy and redundant data.

2   Method

The key challenge of WSI supervision for MSI detection is how to extract representative features from thousands of patches in whole slide images. Although convolutional neural networks (CNNs) show excellent feature representation capabilities, it is difficult to solve above problems with CNNs alone [11]. As a successful architecture for natural language processing tasks, transformer has been migrated to computer vision tasks by transforming images into patches and has shown impressive performance [5,12,15,16]. Compared to CNN architecture, transformer has powerful sequence modeling capability to capture long-range relationships, but still cannot handle thousands of patches directly. Recently, He et al. presented a transformer-based masked autoencoder (MAE) to learn visual representation by reconstructing the original images from a random subset of patches, which provides a way of features representation learning [8]. However, due to the inhomogeneous distribution of features in histopathology slides, the random mask sampling strategy of the MAE is no longer applicable.

Therefore, we propose a joint region-attention and multi-scale transformer (RAMST) network to classify the microsatellite status (MSI or MSS) from whole slide images, which introduces a novel feature weight uniform sampling (FWUS) method to sample a subset of patches that preserves representative features of image regions. Furthermore, we integrate the region-level tissues features with patch-level cells features as the multi-scale histopathology features to characterize the whole slide images, and introduce the transformer to fuse the multi-scale features for WSI-level MSI detection. The proposed region-attention and multi-scale transformer (RAMST) can be further divided into the region-level RAMST (Reg-RAMST) and the WSI-level RAMST (WSI-RAMST), as shown in Fig. 1.

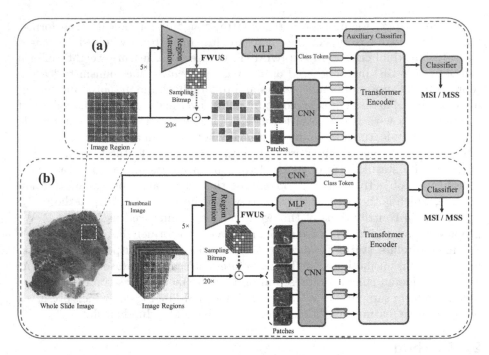

Fig. 1. The architecture of the proposed region-attention and multi-scale transformer (RAMST). (a) The region-level RAMST for MSI detection from the megapixel image regions. (b) The WSI-level RAMST for MSI detection from the gigapixel histopathology slides.

2.1 Region-Level Region-Attention and Multi-scale Transformer

The Reg-RAMST is proposed to detect the microsatellite status from megapixel image regions, while focusing on the optimization of the region-attention module and exploring the influence of sampling rate. Specifically, given a megapixel image region $\mathbf{X}^R$, we split it into non-overlapping patches of the same size, defined as $\mathbf{X}^P \in \mathbb{R}^{n \times n \times (p \times p \times 3)}$, where $p \times p$ is the resolution of image patches, $n \times n$ is the number of patches, and 3 is the number of image channels. Then, the region-attention module can extract the region-level feature map $\mathbf{M} \in \mathbb{R}^{n \times n \times c}$ from the image region $\mathbf{X}^R$, where c is the number of feature map channels. Through the channel pooling operation, the feature map $\mathbf{M}$ is transformed to the feature weight map $\mathbf{M}' \in \mathbb{R}^{n \times n}$, indicating the region-level feature distribution of $\mathbf{X}^P$. In this way, we construct the spatial relationship between $\mathbf{M}'$ and $\mathbf{X}^P$ based on the region-attention module, which is the basis for patches sampling.

To largely eliminate noisy and redundant patches, we propose a feature weight uniform sampling (FWUS) method, which ranks the feature weight value of $\mathbf{M}'$ and then performs uniform sampling from ranked result at rate r, to generate the binary sampling bitmap $\mathbf{M}'_{fwus} \in \mathbb{R}^{n \times n}$. Then, we can obtain the desired representative subset $\mathbf{M}_{fwus}^{P}$ sampled from $\mathbf{X}^{P}$ according to the bitmap $\mathbf{M}_{fwus}'$:

$$\mathbf{X}_{fwus}^{P} = \mathbf{X}^{P} \odot \mathbf{M}_{fwus}' \in \mathbb{R}^{s \times (p \times p \times 3)} \tag{1}$$

where $\odot$ indicates patch-level sampling according to the bitmap, and $s = \lceil r \times n^2 \rceil$ is the rounding sampling number of patches. By adjusting the sampling rate r, we can explore a balanced proportion to largely eliminate noisy and redundant patches while preserving sufficient features representation of image regions.

Moreover, we utilize the pretrained deep residual network [9] to extract features for all patches in $\mathbf{X}_{fwus}^{P}$ to generate a sequence of patch-level features representation $\mathbf{F}_{fwus}^{P} \in \mathbb{R}^{s \times d}$, where d is the dimension of features representation. In addition to the patch-level features representation $\mathbf{F}_{fwus}^{P}$, we further extract the region-level features representation $\mathbf{f}^{R} \in \mathbb{R}^{1 \times d}$ from feature map $\mathbf{M}$, and combine $\mathbf{f}^{R}$ and $\mathbf{F}_{fwus}^{P}$ as the multi-scale features sequence $\mathbf{F}_{ms} \in \mathbb{R}^{(1+s) \times d}$. Then, we introduce the transformer encoder to explore deep correlation information between multiple patch-level features and multi-scales features with multi-head self-attention module.

Following the standard process of input to transformer, the multi-scale features sequence $\mathbf{F}_{ms}$ is appended with a learnable class token $\mathbf{y}_{cls} \in \mathbb{R}^{1 \times d}$ and then added with 2D-aware sampling positional embeddings $\mathbf{E}_{pos}$ [5] to generate the sequence $\mathbf{Y}_{ms} \in \mathbb{R}^{(2+s) \times d}$:

$$\mathbf{Y}_{ms} = \left[\mathbf{y}_{cls}, \mathbf{f}^{R}, \mathbf{F}_{fwus}^{P}\right] + \mathbf{E}_{pos}. \tag{2}$$

Finally, we adopt standard transformer encoder to fuse the multi-scale feature sequence $\mathbf{Y}_{ms}$. Since the class token interacts with all feature tokens, it serves as the integrated multi-scale features representations of the image region $\mathbf{X}^{R}$ and as the input of the multilayer perception classifier to predict the microsatellite status.

Objective Function: The region-attention module is the basis for the feature weight uniform sampling method to learn a representative subset of patches. However, the Reg-RAMST is a deep hybrid architecture network and the region-attention module locates at the bottom, resulting in more difficult optimization based only on the prediction classification loss from multi-scale features.

Therefore, we introduce an auxiliary classifier based on region-level features to facilitate the optimization of the region-attention module. Moreover, we design a dynamic objective function to balance the primary classification loss and auxiliary classification loss, formulated as:

$$\mathcal{L} = \lambda \mathcal{L}_{BCE}(z_{ms}, z) + (1 - \lambda)\mathcal{L}_{BCE}(z_r, z) \tag{3}$$

where $\mathcal{L}_{BCE}$ is the binary cross entropy classification loss function, and $\lambda \in (0, 1]$ is the dynamic balance factor, z_{ms} is the predicted labels from multi-scale features, z_r is the predicted labels from region-level features, z is the ground-truth labels. Specifically, λ is set to a small value in the initial training phase to enforce the Reg-RAMST primarily optimize the region-attention module. Then, the value of λ is gradually increased to 1 with the increase of training epochs, thereby shifting the optimization focus from the region-attention module to the transformer-based multi-scale feature fusion module.

2.2 WSI-Level Region-Attention and Multi-scale Transformer

On the basis of the Reg-RAMST, we advance the WSI-RAMST to detect the microsatellite status for gigapixel whole slide images. Similar to the description in the Reg-RAMST, given a whole slide image $\mathbf{S}$, we split it into non-overlapping valid image regions of the same size, defined as $\mathbf{S^R} \in \mathbb{R}^{m \times (q \times q \times 3)}$, where $q \times q$ is the resolution of image regions, and m is the number of regions. The regions $\mathbf{S^R}$ can be further divided into image patches $\mathbf{S^P} \in \mathbb{R}^{m \times (n \times n) \times (p \times p \times 3)}$, where $p \times p$ is the resolution of image patch, and $m \times (n \times n)$ is the number of patches.

Then, we utilize the pretrained region-attention module to extract region-level feature maps $\mathbf{M} \in \mathbb{R}^{m \times (n \times n \times c)}$ from $\mathbf{S^R}$ and transfer it to feature weight map $\mathbf{M'} \in \mathbb{R}^{m \times (n \times n)}$ by the channel pooling, where c is the number of feature map channels. We still adopt the feature weight uniform sampling (FWUS) method to generate binary sampling bitmap $\mathbf{M'}_{fwus} \in \mathbb{R}^{m \times n \times n}$ from $\mathbf{M'}$ and obtain the representative subset $\mathbf{S^P}_{fwus}$ sampled from $\mathbf{S^P}$ with bitmap $\mathbf{M'}_{fwus}$:

$$\mathbf{S^P}_{fwus} = \mathbf{S^P} \odot \mathbf{M'}_{fwus} \in \mathbb{R}^{m \times s \times (p \times p \times 3)} \tag{4}$$

where $\odot$ indicates patch-level sampling according to the bitmap, and s is the sampling number of patches in a single region.

Moreover, we extract the patch-level features $\mathbf{F^P}_{fwus} \in \mathbb{R}^{m \times s \times d}$ from $\mathbf{S^P}_{fwus}$ and region-level features $\mathbf{F^R} \in \mathbb{R}^{m \times d}$ from $\mathbf{M}$, through pretrained convolutional neural networks respectively, where d is the dimension of features representation. To leverage slide-level features of histopathology images and facilitate the optimization of the WSI-RAMST, we initialize class token with the feature representation $\mathbf{f^S} \in \mathbb{R}^{1 \times d}$ extracted from the thumbnail of slide. The multi-scale features sequence $\mathbf{Y}_{ms}$ is added with two-level positional embeddings $\mathbf{E'}_{pos}$ consisting of region position and patch position as the input of the standard transformer encoder:

$$\mathbf{Y}_{ms} = \left[\mathbf{f^S}, \mathbf{F^R}, \mathbf{F^P}_{fwus}\right] + \mathbf{E'}_{pos} \in \mathbb{R}^{(1 + m + m \times s) \times d}. \tag{5}$$

Finally, the microsatellite status is detected by a multilayer perception classifier according to the learned histopathology representation from the multi-scale features sequence $\mathbf{Y}_{ms}$ via transformer encoder. Through such transformer-based sequence data process, the proposed WSI-RAMST can detect the microsatellite status from whole slide images of different shapes.

3   Experiments

We used 896 formalin-fixed paraffin-embedded (FFPE) diagnostic slides and 2675 snap-frozen slides of stomach cancer and colorectal cancer from 868 patients in The Cancer Genome Atlas (TCGA) cohort. To keep the test samples consistent with previous studies, we selected FFPE diagnostic slides of the same 206 patients as the test dataset, and divided the rest of FFPE slides and Snap-frozen slides into training set (85%) and validation set (15%). In practice, we obtained image regions from histopathology slides at 5× magnification and corresponding image patches from slides at 20× magnification with size of 224 × 224 and with resolution of 0.5 μm/px.

The RAMST was implemented based on PyTorch library (https://pytorch. org) and was trained on a deep learning workstation with ten NVIDIA GeForce GTX 2080Ti GPUs. The detailed implementation setting is appended in Supplementary Material.

3.1   Results

Performance Evaluation: To evaluate the performance of the proposed region-attention and multi-scale transformer (RAMST) for MSI detection, we used the area under receiver operating characteristic curve (AUC) as the evaluation metrics. Meanwhile, we selected multiple deep learning-based MSI detection methods for comparison [2,4,6,10,13,14,17,18]. The AUC results of different methods on the colorectal cancer and stomach cancer dataset are shown Table 1, where the RAMST represents the WSI-level RAMST with feature weight uniform sampling rate of 25%.

As shown in Table 1, the proposed RAMST achieved the best performance with AUC of 0.921 for MSI detection on the colorectal cancer dataset, exceeding the state-of-the-art method DeepSMILE [13] by 0.18%. Moreover, the RAMST performed well with AUC of 0.886 on the stomach cancer dataset. The experimental result demonstrates the superiority of the RAMST to existing methods in MSI detection.

Table 1. The AUC results of different models.

Methods	AUC (TCGA-CRC)	AUC (TCGA-STAD)
Kather et al. [10]	0.840	0.810
Schmauch et al. [14]	0.820	0.760
Cao et al. [4]	0.885	–
Echle et al. [6]	0.740	–
Yamashita et al. [18]	0.779	–
Yamashita et al. [17]	0.876	–
Bilat et al. [2]	0.860	–
DeepSMILE [13]	0.903	–
RAMST	**0.921**	**0.886**

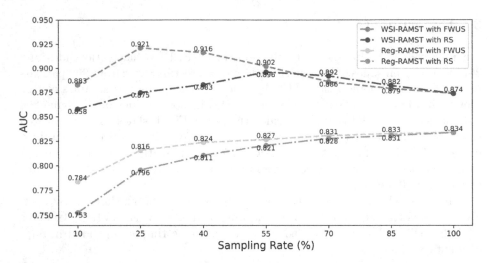

Fig. 2. The classification performance of RAMST with the feature weight uniform sampling (FWUS) and random sampling (RS) at different sampling rate.

Ablation Study: Furthermore, we conducted the experiments to explore the performance of the RAMST with the proposed feature weight uniform sampling (FWUS) and random sampling (RS) at different sampling rate, shown in Fig. 2. Specifically, we trained the region-level RAMST on fixed number of image patches, using two different sampling strategies at different sampling rate from 10% to 100%. The curves of region-level RAMST of two sampling strategies both showed that the detection performance advances as the sampling rate increases. However, the magnitude gradually decreases, especially starting from the sampling rate of 25%. This indicates that superfluous image patches of the same region contribute limitedly to the classification performance.

Then, we trained the WSI-level RAMST on a larger fixed number of image patches using two sampling strategies. As can be seen from Fig. 2, the best performance of WSI-level RAMST with feature weight uniform sampling (FWUS) corresponds to a sampling rate of 25%, and then the performance decreases as the sampling rate increases. The performance curve of WSI-level RAMST using random sampling is broadly similar, except for the optimal sampling rate. This shows that considering more image regions with an appropriate sampling rate in gigapixel whole slide images contributes remarkably to the classification performance.

Overall, the models using the proposed feature weight uniform sampling (FWUS) outperform the models with random sampling (RS), further demonstrating the excellent performance of RAMST in representation learning.

4 Conclusion

In this paper, we propose a joint region-attention and multi-scale transformer (RAMST) network to classify microsatellite instability (MSI) versus microsatellite stability (MSS) from whole slide images, which outperforms existing methods on the gastrointestinal cancer dataset from TCGA. Specifically, we present a feature weight uniform sampling (FWUS) method based on the region-attention mechanism to learn a representative subset of image patches from whole slide images. Meanwhile, we introduce the transformer architecture to fuse the multi-scale histopathology features consisting of patch-level features with region-level features to characterize the whole slide images. In the future, we will conduct the proposed RAMST method as a WSI-supervised representation learning method for more tasks.

Acknoledgements. The research is supported by the Strategic Priority Research Program of the Chinese Academy of Sciences (No. XDA16021400), and the NSFC Projects Grants (61932018, 62072441 and 62072280).

References

1. Bhargava, R., Madabhushi, A.: Emerging themes in image informatics and molecular analysis for digital pathology. Annu. Rev. Biomed. Eng. **18**, 387 (2016)
2. Bilal, M., et al.: Development and validation of a weakly supervised deep learning framework to predict the status of molecular pathways and key mutations in colorectal cancer from routine histology images: a retrospective study. Lancet Digital Health **3**(12), e763–e772 (2021)
3. Boland, C.R., Goel, A.: Microsatellite instability in colorectal cancer. Gastroenterology **138**(6), 2073–2087 (2010)
4. Cao, R., et al.: Development and interpretation of a pathomics-based model for the prediction of microsatellite instability in colorectal cancer. Theranostics **10**(24), 11080 (2020)
5. Dosovitskiy, A., et al.: An image is worth 16×16 words: transformers for image recognition at scale. In: International Conference on Learning Representations, ICLR (2021)
6. Echle, A., et al.: Clinical-grade detection of microsatellite instability in colorectal tumors by deep learning. Gastroenterology **159**(4), 1406–1416 (2020)
7. Echle, A., et al.: Deep learning for the detection of microsatellite instability from histology images in colorectal cancer: a systematic literature review. ImmunoInformatics **3–4**, 100008 (2021)
8. He, K., Chen, X., Xie, S., Li, Y., Dollár, P., Girshick, R.: Masked autoencoders are scalable vision learners. In: Proceedings of the IEEE/CVF Conference on Computer Vision and Pattern Recognition, pp. 16000–16009 (2022)
9. He, K., Zhang, X., Ren, S., Sun, J.: Deep residual learning for image recognition. In: Proceedings of the IEEE Conference on Computer Vision and Pattern Recognition, pp. 770–778 (2016)
10. Kather, J.N., et al.: Deep learning can predict microsatellite instability directly from histology in gastrointestinal cancer. Nat. Med. **25**(7), 1054–1056 (2019)

11. Krizhevsky, A., Sutskever, I., Hinton, G.E.: ImageNet classification with deep convolutional neural networks. In: Advances in Neural Information Processing Systems, vol. 25 (2012)

12. Liu, Z., et al.: Swin transformer: Hierarchical vision transformer using shifted windows. In: Proceedings of the IEEE/CVF International Conference on Computer Vision, pp. 10012–10022 (2021)

13. Schirris, Y., Gavves, E., Nederlof, I., Horlings, H.M., Teuwen, J.: DeepSMILE: self-supervised heterogeneity-aware multiple instance learning for DNA damage response defect classification directly from H&E whole-slide images. arXiv preprint arXiv:2107.09405 (2021)

14. Schmauch, B., et al.: A deep learning model to predict RNA-Seq expression of tumours from whole slide images. Nat. Commun. **11**(1), 1–15 (2020)

15. Vaswani, A., et al.: Attention is all you need. In: Advances in Neural Information Processing Systems, vol. 30 (2017)

16. Wang, W., et al.: Pyramid vision transformer: a versatile backbone for dense prediction without convolutions. In: Proceedings of the IEEE/CVF International Conference on Computer Vision, pp. 568–578 (2021)

17. Yamashita, R., Long, J., Banda, S., Shen, J., Rubin, D.L.: Learning domain-agnostic visual representation for computational pathology using medically-irrelevant style transfer augmentation. IEEE Trans. Med. Imaging **40**(12), 3945–3954 (2021)

18. Yamashita, R., et al.: Deep learning model for the prediction of microsatellite instability in colorectal cancer: a diagnostic study. Lancet Oncol. **22**(1), 132–141 (2021)

Self-supervised Pre-training for Nuclei Segmentation

Mohammad Minhazul Haq$^{(\boxtimes)}$ and Junzhou Huang

Department of Computer Science and Engineering,
The University of Texas at Arlington, Arlington, TX 76019, USA
mohammadminhazu.haq@mavs.uta.edu, jzhuang@uta.edu

Abstract. The accurate segmentation of nuclei is crucial for cancer diagnosis and further clinical treatments. For semantic segmentation of nuclei, Vision Transformers (VT) have the potentiality to outperform Convolutional Neural Network (CNN) based models due to their ability to model long-range dependencies (i.e., global context). Usually, VT and CNN models are pre-trained with large-scale natural image dataset (i.e., ImageNet) in fully-supervised manner. However, pre-training nuclei segmentation models with ImageNet is not much helpful because of morphological and textural differences between natural image domain and medical image domain. Also, ImageNet-like large-scale annotated histology dataset rarely exists in medical image domain. In this paper, we propose a novel region-level Self-Supervised Learning (SSL) approach and corresponding triplet loss for pre-training semantic nuclei segmentation model with unannotated histology images extracted from Whole Slide Images (WSI). Our proposed region-level SSL is based on the observation that, non-background (i.e., nuclei) patches of an input image are difficult to predict from surrounding neighbor patches, and vice versa. We empirically demonstrate the superiority of our proposed SSL incorporated VT model on two public nuclei segmentation datasets.

Keywords: Nuclei segmentation · Self-supervised learning · Transformers

1 Introduction

Nuclei segmentation is considered as a fundamental task of digital histopathology image analysis. For semantic segmentation of nuclei, Convolutional Neural Network (CNN) based approaches give very promising results [12,17,21,31]. However, due to the intrinsic locality nature and limited receptive fields of convolution operations, CNN based models are incapable of capturing the global context of the input [6,30]. Transformers, an alternative to CNNs, are powerful at modeling the global context of input images [30]. Also, Transformers show

---

Supplementary Information The online version contains supplementary material available at https://doi.org/10.1007/978-3-031-16434-7_30.

L. Wang et al. (Eds.): MICCAI 2022, LNCS 13432, pp. 303–313, 2022.
https://doi.org/10.1007/978-3-031-16434-7_30

superior transferability for downstream tasks, when pre-trained with large-scale dataset. However, Vision Transformers (VT) need lot of data for training, usually more than what is necessary to standard CNNs [16].

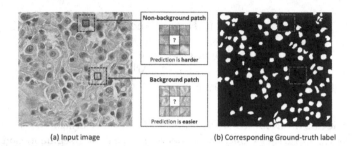

(a) Input image   (b) Corresponding Ground-truth label

Fig. 1. We divide the input image into kxk patches. We try to predict patch features using its 8-connected neighboring patches. We see that, predicting a non-background (i.e., nuclei) patch is much harder than predicting a background patch.

Usually, VT are pre-trained with large-scale annotated natural image dataset like ImageNet [8], and then fine-tuned to downstream tasks [10]. However, histology images are quite different from natural images due to the nuclei and background textures, morphological structures of nuclei, large variations in the shape and appearance of nuclei, clustered and overlapped nuclei, blurred nuclei boundaries, inconsistent staining methods, scanning artifacts, etc. [18,28]. Due to this domain gap between natural images and medical images, the ImageNet pre-trained models may yield marginal improvement over train-from-scratch models for nuclei segmentation tasks [27]. Unfortunately, in medical image domain, ImageNet-like large-scale annotated histopathology image datasets do not exist, and they are very difficult to produce, because of expensive, time-consuming and tedious labeling process of histology images [5,28].

In this work, we propose a Transformer-based Self-Supervised Learning (SSL) approach for pre-training so that the segmentation network implicitly acquires a better understanding of the nuclei and background using a large-scale unannotated histology image dataset extracted from Whole Slide Images (WSI). In computer vision, SSL is used to learn useful data representations without using any labels [3,4,20]. To achieve this goal, we first divide the image into $k \times k$ patches where $k = 32$. Then, we try to predict each of the patch features from its 8-connected neighboring patches. Figure 1 shows that predicting non-background patches (i.e. that contain nuclei) is much harder than background patch prediction. Based on this aforementioned observation, we design region-level triplet loss to pre-train the segmentation network. Our pre-trained SSL model learns to separate nuclei features from the background features in the embedding space. Additionally, our SSL approach involves the image-level sub-task of predicting the scale of image, which enables the segmentation network to implicitly acquire further knowledge of nuclei size and shape. Finally, we fine-tune the pre-trained network for nuclei segmentation with a small annotated dataset.

Thus, the main contributions of this paper are: (a) We propose a novel region-level Self-Supervised Learning (SSL) approach and corresponding triplet loss for pre-training semantic nuclei segmentation model with unannotated histology image dataset. (b) We incorporate our proposed pre-training technique into a Vision Transformer (VT). To the best of our knowledge, this is the first work focusing on Transformer-based SSL for semantic segmentation of nuclei. (c) Extensive experimental results demonstrate the superiority of our proposed SSL incorporated transformer model over baseline methods.

2 Related Works

Several Self-Supervised Learning (SSL) approaches have been proposed for nuclei segmentation. An instance-aware SSL model is proposed considering scale-wise triplet learning and count ranking as proxy sub-tasks [27]. Another self-supervised nuclei segmentation approach without requiring annotations is proposed utilizing scale classification as a self-supervision signal to locate nuclei [22].

In literature, Transformer has been employed in various computer vision problems [2,6,10,11,24–26,29,30]. For natural image segmentation, a pure transformer-based model named SEgmentation TRansformer (SETR) is proposed by treating semantic segmentation problem as a sequence-to-sequence prediction task [30]. For medical image segmentation, TransUNet is proposed to solve multi-organ segmentation task [6]. In recent times, SSL have been applied to Vision Transformers (VT). In Self-supervised vision Transformer (SiT), parts of the input image are corrupted using several local transformation operations, and original image is reconstructed later from the corrupted one [1]. An auxiliary self-supervised localization task also has been proposed which encourages the VTs to learn relative distances between patch embedding pairs [16].

3 Methodology

In semantic nuclei segmentation problem, we have nuclei histology image of size $H \times W \times 3$ as input, and we want to predict the segmentation output of size $H \times W$. We first pre-train our proposed model with unannotated image patches $D_s = \{(X_n)\}$. Then, we fine-tune the model with annotated images $D_t = \{(X_t, Y_t)\}$. In this work, since we propose Transformers-based Self-Supervised learning method for Nuclei segmentation, we name our proposed framework as TransNuSS. Figure 2 shows the complete architecture of TransNuSS.

In our work, we adopt TransUNet [6] as the segmentation network. The encoder of the segmentation network consists of a hybrid Convolutional Neural Network (CNN) - Transformer architecture. CNN works as a feature extractor to generate feature map F_x for the input. Then, patch embedding is applied to get embedding $Z_0 \in \mathbb{R}^{n_{patch} \times d}$, where $n_{patch} = \frac{H}{16} \times \frac{W}{16}$ and d is the dimension of embedding space which we set to 768. After that, transformer encoder appears which consists of L layers of Multi-head Self-Attention (MSA) and Multi-Layer

Perceptron (MLP) blocks. The final layer of the transformer encoder produces hidden features $Z_L \in \mathbb{R}^{n_{patch} \times d}$. In encoder, we use ResNet-50 [13] and ViT [10] as CNN and transformer, respectively. The decoder of the segmentation network consists of multiple upsampling steps. At first, hidden features Z_L is reshaped to the shape of $d \times \frac{H}{16} \times \frac{W}{16}$, which we denote as A. Then, a 3×3 convolution is applied to decrease the depth to 512. Finally, multiple upsampling blocks are used to generate the full resolution segmentation mask. We refer the reader to [6] for more details.

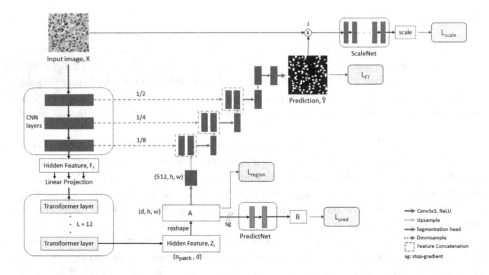

Fig. 2. Complete architecture of TransNuSS.

3.1 Self-supervised Pre-training with Unannotated Dataset

For each image $X_n \in D_s$ of size $H \times W \times 3$, we generate a same-size image X_s by cropping and scaling. To generate X_s, we first randomly select a scaling-factor z_s from a pool $\{1.0, 1.25, 1.5, 1.75, 2.0\}$. We denote this scale-pool as S_p. Now, we randomly crop a patch from X_n, and then scale the cropped patch z_s times so that the scaled patch becomes of size $H \times W \times 3$. Thus, for self-supervised pre-training, our input consists of $\{(X_n, X_s, z_s)\}$.

Region-Level Triplet Loss. For self-supervised pre-training, we consider that we have background and non-background image patches (see Fig. 1) in an input image. Then, we propose region-level triplet loss to learn the embedding space. We expect that, in the embedding space, feature should have similarity and dissimilarity among same and different types of patches, respectively. We design our triplet loss in a way so that the segmentation network can implicitly learn to separate background and non-background patch features in a given image. To generate triplet samples, we use feature map A which is of size $d \times h \times w$ where $h = \frac{H}{16}$ and $w = \frac{W}{16}$. Therefore, A contains $h \times w$ number (i.e., the number of patches) of d-dimensional feature vectors. As we mentioned before, our intuition and observation is that: in this embedding space, we can easily predict a background feature vector from its 8-connected neighboring features vectors, whereas predicting a non-background feature vector is comparatively harder.

We try to predict feature vector $A_{i,j} \in \mathbb{R}^d$ at each spatial location (i, j) of A, where $2 \leq i \leq h-1$ and $2 \leq j \leq w-1$. To compute the corresponding predicted feature vector $B_{i,j} \in \mathbb{R}^d$, we use PredictNet P which consists of two fully-connected layers with $2d$ and d output neurons, respectively. To predict $B_{i,j}$, we first concatenate 8-connected features of $A_{i,j}$ which is denoted as $e_{i,j} \in \mathbb{R}^{8d}$. Thus, $e_{i,j} = (A_{i-1,j-1}, ..., A_{i-1,j+1}, A_{i,j-1}, A_{i,j+1}, A_{i+1,j-1}, ..., A_{i+1,j+1})$. We forward $e_{i,j}$ through PredictNet to predict $B_{i,j}$. Now, we produce a hardness-to-predict matrix $Hard \in \mathbb{R}^{h \times w}$ which computes the prediction difficulty for each of the non-boundary patches. $Hard$ is computed as:

$$Hard_{i,j} = \begin{cases} d_{L1}(A_{i,j}, B_{i,j}), & \text{if } 2 \leq i \leq h-1 \text{ and } 2 \leq j \leq w-1 \\ 0, & \text{otherwise} \end{cases} \quad (1)$$

where $B_{i,j} = P(e_{i,j})$, and $d_{L1}(.)$ is the Mean Absolute Error (MAE) between two feature vectors. Now, we normalize $Hard$ matrix, and denote normalized matrix as $Hard'$. To avoid selecting boundary patch features later, we also replace boundary pixel values of $Hard'$ with the median of $Hard'$. For input image pair $\{X_n, X_s\}$, we denote corresponding feature map pair, predicted feature map pair, and normalized hardness matrix pair as $\{An, As\}$, $\{Bn, Bs\}$, and $\{HardN', HardS'\}$, respectively. Now, from $HardN'$ and $HardS'$ we generate following sets of feature vectors:

$$FG_n = \{An_{i,j} : HardN'_{i,j} \geq \tau_{fgn}\}; BG_n = \{An_{i,j} : HardN'_{i,j} \leq \tau_{bgn}\}$$
$$FG_s = \{As_{i,j} : HardS'_{i,j} \geq \tau_{fgs}\}; BG_s = \{As_{i,j} : HardS'_{i,j} \leq \tau_{bgs}\} \quad (2)$$

We empirically set the value of τ_{fgn} and τ_{fgs} to 95th percentile of $HardN'$ and $HardS'$, respectively. And, we set the value of τ_{bgn} and τ_{bgs} to 5th percentile of $HardN'$ and $HardS'$, respectively. In words, FG_n and BG_n set contain feature vectors from potential foreground (i.e., nuclei) and background patches of X_n, respectively. Similarly, FG_s and BG_s contain probable foreground and background patch features of scaled image X_s, respectively.

We now generate triplet samples $\{(a, p, n)\}$ from feature map pair $\{An, As\}$. We consider a, p and n as anchor, a positive sample, and a negative sample, respectively, each of which is a d-dimensional feature vector. To generate a triplet sample (a, p, n) from input pair $\{X_n, X_s\}$, we randomly sample feature vector from FG_n, FG_s and $(BG_n \cup BG_s)$, respectively. Thus, a contains the feature vector of a non-background patch from unscaled image X_n, and p contains the feature vector of a non-background patch from probably-scaled image X_s. And, n contains the feature vector of a background patch from either X_n or X_s. We randomly generate m number of triplet samples for an input pair $\{X_n, X_s\}$. We set, $m = 32$ in our experiments. We define our region-level triplet loss as:

$$L_{region}(X_n, X_s) = \frac{1}{m} \sum_{k=1}^{m} max(0, d_{L2}(a_k, p_k) - d_{L2}(a_k, n_k) + c) \qquad (3)$$

where $d_{L2}(.)$ is the squared L_2 distance between two features, and c is the margin value which is empirically set to 1.0. Triplet loss encourages features from the same class to be located nearby, and pushes apart features from different classes in the embedding space [7,23]. In other words, being pre-trained with proposed region-level triplet loss, the segmentation network can narrow down the distance between anchor and positive samples in the embedding space, and enlarges the semantic dissimilarity between the anchor and negative samples [27]. Note that, in the embedding space, we separate background and non-background patch features regardless of the corresponding scales of the patches of input image X_n and X_s. This design helps to map multi-scale nuclei features to be located nearby in the feature space. Similarly, multi-scale background features are also mapped so that they are located far from nuclei features, and remain close to each other in the embedding space. Finally, for accurately predicting the feature vectors, we train PredictNet with following loss function:

$$L_{pred}(X_n, X_s) = \frac{1}{(h-2) \times (w-2)} \sum_{i=2}^{h-1} \sum_{j=2}^{w-1} (d_{L1}(An_{i,j}, Bn_{i,j}) + d_{L1}(As_{i,j}, Bs_{i,j})) \qquad (4)$$

where $d_{L1}(.)$ is the Mean Absolute Error (MAE) between two features.

Scale Loss. According to [22], looking at the size and texture of nuclei should be enough to determine the magnification level (i.e., scale) of input image, and this identification of the scale can generate a preliminary self-supervision signal to locate nuclei. Similar to [22], we compute the attention map J_s for input X_s with $J_s = \hat{Y}_s \odot X_s$, where $\hat{Y}_s$ is segmentation output for X_s, and $\odot$ represents element-wise multiplication. We use a scale classification network ScaleNet C to predict the scale from J_s. For C, we use ResNet-34 [13]. The output of C is a 5-dimensional vector v which gives the scores for each magnification level. Therefore, $v = C(J_s)$. We use negative log-likelihood to train ScaleNet C, and in turn the segmentation network S. Thus, our scale loss is defined as:

$$L_{scale}(X_s, z_s) = -log(p_l) \qquad (5)$$

where l is the class label for z_s (i.e. index of z_s in S_p), and $p_l = [softmax(v)]_l$. Therefore, the total loss L_{PT} for pre-training TransNuSS is defined as:

$$L_{PT}(X_n, X_s) = L_{region}(X_n, X_s) + L_{pred}(X_n, X_s) + \lambda_{scale} L_{scale}(X_s, z_s) \qquad (6)$$

where, λ_{scale} is the weight to balance scale loss which is empirically set to 0.5.

3.2   Fine-Tuning with Annotated Dataset

After pre-training, we fine-tune our segmentation network S with a small annotated dataset. For fine-tuning, S takes image X_t as input, and produces the segmentation prediction $\hat{Y}_t$ of the same size as output. We denote the ground-truth label by Y_t. In practice, we found dice-coefficient loss to be more effective than the binary cross-entropy loss for nuclei segmentation tasks. Therefore, we choose dice-coefficient loss as our supervised segmentation loss for fine-tuning:

$$L_{FT}(X_t) = 1 - \frac{2.Y_t'.\hat{Y}_t'}{Y_t' + \hat{Y}_t'}, \tag{7}$$

where Y_t' and $\hat{Y}_t'$ are flattened Y_t and $\hat{Y}_t$, respectively.

3.3 Implementations

We train TransNuSS with batch size 16, and using four GPUs. To train segmentation network, we use SGD optimizer with learning rate 0.01, momentum 0.9 and weight decay 0.0001. We use SGD optimizer with learning rate 0.001 and 0.0001 to train PredictNet and ScaleNet, respectively. We pre-train our model for 20 epochs, and then fine-tune for 80 epochs.

Table 1. Nuclei segmentation results for Experiment-1 and Experiment-2. IoU denotes intersection over union. Results are from testing on TNBC-test and MoNuSeg-test for experiment-1 and experiment-2, respectively.

		Experiment-1 TNBC dataset		Experiment-2 MoNuSeg dataset	
Method	Pre-trained on	IoU%	Dice score	IoU%	Dice score
AttnSSL [22]	MoNuSegWSI	45.86	0.6018	59.93	0.7412
InstSSL w/o fine-tuning [27]	MoNuSegWSI	46.91	0.6136	61.05	0.7521
FCN [17]	–	63.01	0.7726	63.81	0.7803
U-Net [21]	–	64.65	0.7824	64.91	0.7982
UNet++ [31]	–	64.35	0.7813	65.38	0.7998
ResUNet-50 [9]	ImageNet	64.96	0.7863	65.79	0.8041
SETR-MLA [30]	ImageNet	64.87	0.7854	65.39	0.8021
TransUNet [6]	ImageNet	65.66	0.7905	66.02	0.8072
TransUNet + L_{drloc} [6,16]	ImageNet	65.73	0.7894	66.63	0.8101
InstSSL [27]	ImageNet	64.68	0.7831	66.57	0.8112
InstSSL [27]	MoNuSegWSI	65.85	0.7942	67.92	0.8244
InstSSL-ViT [6,27]	MoNuSegWSI	66.32	0.7991	68.11	0.8256
TransNuSS w/o fine-tuning	MoNuSegWSI	48.11	0.6252	63.43	0.7664
TransNuSS w/o L_{region}	MoNuSegWSI	66.28	0.7951	66.83	0.8147
TransNuSS w/o L_{scale}	MoNuSegWSI	66.72	0.8007	67.66	0.8236
TransNuSS (ours)	MoNuSegWSI	**67.02**	**0.8059**	**68.72**	**0.8307**

4 Experiments

4.1 Dataset

Pre-training Dataset (MoNuSegWSI). MoNuSeg [14,15] training dataset contains thirty 1000×1000 annotated image patches extracted from thirty Whole Slide Images (WSI) of different patients collected from The Cancer Genomic Atlas (TCGA). Similar to train-split of AttnSSL [22], we select 19 patients, and download corresponding 19 H&E stained WSIs from which we extract patches of size 512×512 at 40x magnification. Following AttnSSL [22], we perform a simple thresholding in HSV color space for each extracted patch to determine whether the patch contains tissue or not. Patches with less than 70% tissue cover are not used. Thus, a total of 178217 patches are selected for pre-training. In our experiments, we denote this unannotated pre-training dataset as MoNuSegWSI.

Fine-Tuning Dataset-1 (TNBC). The images of TNBC dataset [19] are collected at 40x magnification. This dataset consists of 50 H&E stained histology images of size 512×512. Labeling of this dataset is performed by expert pathologist and research fellows. In our experiments, we randomly split TNBC into 80% for training, 10% for validation, and 10% for testing.

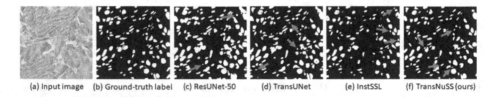

(a) Input image   (b) Ground-truth label   (c) ResUNet-50   (d) TransUNet   (e) InstSSL   (f) TransNuSS (ours)

Fig. 3. Visualization of the nuclei segmentation outputs of ResUNet-50 [9], TransUNet [6], InstSSL [27], and our proposed TransNuSS model. Input image is chosen from TNBC-test dataset. In (c)-(e), blue arrows indicate false positive nuclei that are removed in TransNuSS. In (f), yellow arrows denote missing nuclei from previous models. (Color figure online)

Fine-Tuning Dataset-2 (MoNuSeg). We split thirty 1000×1000 annotated images of MoNuSeg [14,15] training data into 80% for training, and 20% for validation. MoNuSeg-test consists of 14 images of MoNuSeg testing data. We refer this dataset as MoNuSeg in our experiments.

4.2 Experimental Results

Experiment-1. In our first experiment, we fine-tune our pre-trained TransNuSS model with TNBC dataset. We choose FCN [17], U-Net [21], UNet++ [31] and ResUNet-50 [9] as the representatives of Convolutional Neural Network (CNN) based approaches. SETR-MLA [30] and TransUnet [6] represent transformer-based semantic segmentation models. TransUnet + L_{drloc} shows the performance when auxiliary self-supervised localization loss [16] is utilized while training TransUNet. AttnSSL [22] and InstSSL [27] are chosen as representatives of Self-Supervised Learning (SSL) models for nuclei segmentation. We choose AttnSSL and InstSSL over the generic SSL models for two reasons: (1) AttnSSL and InstSSL were explicitly devised for nuclei segmentation problem, and (2) these two SSL methods perform significantly well for nuclei segmentation with better performance compared with generic self-supervised methods. We also employ TransUNet in InstSSL (i.e., replacing ResUNet backbone with TransUNet) model which is denoted as InstSSL-ViT in Table 1.

From Table 1, we see that our proposed TransNuSS model outperforms all other approaches in terms of IoU% and dice score. Our pre-trained model (see the second last row in Table 1) also achieves superiority over AttnSSL, and InstSSL without fine-tuning. The excellence of TransNuSS is mainly due to our proposed region-level triplet learning, which enables the segmentation network to separate nuclei from the backgrounds in a better manner in feature space. We also see that, MoNuSegWSI-pretrained and then fine-tuned InstSSL, InstSSL-ViT and TransNuSS models outperform ImageNet [8]-pretrained models, which proves the effectiveness of pre-training nuclei segmentation models with Whole Slide Image (WSI) patches. Figure 3 shows the visualization results of ResUNet-50, TransUNet, InstSSL and our proposed TransNuSS model. Figure 3 shows that, TransNuSS can significantly reduce false positive nuclei generated by other approaches. From Fig. 3(f), we see that TransNuSS is capable to segment nuclei which were missed out by InstSSL model. Also, our intuition and assumption is that, $HardN'_{i,j}$ and $HardS'_{i,j}$ will have larger values if corresponding patch contains nuclei (i.e., is non-background patch). Supplementary material shows the visualization of $HardN'$ matrices, which empirically validates our aforementioned intuition.

To understand the impact of each of the losses (i.e., region-level triplet loss, and scale loss), we also pre-train TransNuSS using a single (i.e., either triplet loss or scale loss) loss, and then we fine-tune the pre-trained model. From last three rows of Table 1, we see that the proposed TransNuSS outperforms both of TransNuSS w/o L_{region}, and TransNuSS w/o L_{scale}. The overall good performance of TransNuSS comes when both losses are applied together. In summary, both losses complement each other for the excellent performance of TransNuSS.

Experiment-2. We conduct second experiment with MoNuSeg dataset in the similar way to Experiment-1. This experiment again reflects the excellence of TransNuSS compared to other approaches (see last two columns of Table 1).

5   Conclusion

Due to a large domain gap between natural images and histology images, ImageNet-pretrained Vision Transformers (VT) does not transfer very well to nuclei segmentation tasks. In this paper, we propose Self-Supervised Learning (SSL) based region-level triplet learning for pre-training so that VT implicitly learns to separate nuclei from the backgrounds. Prominent experimental results validate the effectiveness of our proposed TransNuSS model.

Acknowledgments. This work was partially supported by the NSF CAREER grant IIS-1553687 and Cancer Prevention and Research Institute of Texas (CPRIT) award (RP190107).

References

1. Atito, S., Awais, M., Kittler, J.: Sit: self-supervised vision transformer. arXiv preprint arXiv:2104.03602 (2021)
2. Carion, N., et al.: End-to-end object detection with transformers. In: Vedaldi, A., Bischof, H., Brox, T., Frahm, J.-M. (eds.) ECCV 2020. LNCS, vol. 12346, pp. 213–229. Springer, Cham (2020). https://doi.org/10.1007/978-3-030-58452-8_13
3. Caron, M., Bojanowski, P., Joulin, A., Douze, M.: Deep clustering for unsupervised learning of visual features. In: Proceedings of the European Conference on Computer Vision (ECCV), pp. 132–149 (2018)
4. Caron, M., Misra, I., Mairal, J., Goyal, P., Bojanowski, P., Joulin, A.: Unsupervised learning of visual features by contrasting cluster assignments. arXiv preprint arXiv:2006.09882 (2020)
5. Chen, C., Dou, Q., Chen, H., Qin, J., Heng, P.A.: Synergistic image and feature adaptation: Towards cross-modality domain adaptation for medical image segmentation. In: Proceedings of the AAAI Conference on Artificial Intelligence, vol. 33, pp. 865–872 (2019)
6. Chen, J., et al.: Transunet: Transformers make strong encoders for medical image segmentation. arXiv preprint arXiv:2102.04306 (2021)
7. Chen, W., Chen, X., Zhang, J., Huang, K.: Beyond triplet loss: a deep quadruplet network for person re-identification. In: Proceedings of the IEEE Conference on Computer Vision and Pattern Recognition, pp. 403–412 (2017)
8. Deng, J., Dong, W., Socher, R., Li, L.J., Li, K., Fei-Fei, L.: Imagenet: a large-scale hierarchical image database. In: 2009 IEEE Conference on Computer Vision and Pattern Recognition, pp. 248–255. IEEE (2009)
9. Diakogiannis, F.I., Waldner, F., Caccetta, P., Wu, C.: Resunet-A: a deep learning framework for semantic segmentation of remotely sensed data. ISPRS J. Photogram. Rem. Sens. **162**, 94–114 (2020)
10. Dosovitskiy, A., et al.: An image is worth 16x16 words: transformers for image recognition at scale. arXiv preprint arXiv:2010.11929 (2020)
11. Han, K., et al.: A survey on visual transformer. arXiv preprint arXiv:2012.12556 (2020)
12. Haq, M.M., Huang, J.: Adversarial domain adaptation for cell segmentation. In: Medical Imaging with Deep Learning, pp. 277–287. PMLR (2020)
13. He, K., Zhang, X., Ren, S., Sun, J.: Deep residual learning for image recognition. In: Proceedings of the IEEE Conference on Computer Vision and Pattern Recognition, pp. 770–778 (2016)
14. Kumar, N., et al.: A multi-organ nucleus segmentation challenge. IEEE Trans. Med. Imaging **39**(5), 1380–1391 (2019)
15. Kumar, N., Verma, R., Sharma, S., Bhargava, S., Vahadane, A., Sethi, A.: A dataset and a technique for generalized nuclear segmentation for computational pathology. IEEE Trans. Med. Imaging **36**(7), 1550–1560 (2017)
16. Liu, Y., Sangineto, E., Bi, W., Sebe, N., Lepri, B., Nadai, M.: Efficient training of visual transformers with small datasets. Adv. Neural Inf. Process. Syst. **34** (2021)

17. Long, J., Shelhamer, E., Darrell, T.: Fully convolutional networks for semantic segmentation. In: Proceedings of the IEEE Conference on Computer Vision and Pattern Recognition, pp. 3431–3440 (2015)
18. Mahmood, F., et al.: Deep adversarial training for multi-organ nuclei segmentation in histopathology images. IEEE Trans. Med. Imaging **39**(11), 3257–3267 (2019)
19. Naylor, P., Laé, M., Reyal, F., Walter, T.: Segmentation of nuclei in histopathology images by deep regression of the distance map. IEEE Trans. Med. Imaging **38**(2), 448–459 (2018)
20. Oord, A.V.D., Li, Y., Vinyals, O.: Representation learning with contrastive predictive coding. arXiv preprint arXiv:1807.03748 (2018)
21. Ronneberger, O., Fischer, P., Brox, T.: U-Net: Convolutional networks for biomedical image segmentation. In: Navab, N., Hornegger, J., Wells, W.M., Frangi, A.F. (eds.) MICCAI 2015. LNCS, vol. 9351, pp. 234–241. Springer, Cham (2015). https://doi.org/10.1007/978-3-319-24574-4_28
22. Sahasrabudhe, M., et al.: Self-supervised nuclei segmentation in histopathological images using attention. In: Martel, A.L., et al. (eds.) MICCAI 2020. LNCS, vol. 12265, pp. 393–402. Springer, Cham (2020). https://doi.org/10.1007/978-3-030-59722-1_38
23. Schroff, F., Kalenichenko, D., Philbin, J.: Facenet: a unified embedding for face recognition and clustering. In: Proceedings of the IEEE Conference on Computer Vision and Pattern Recognition, pp. 815–823 (2015)
24. Vaswani, A., et al.: Attention is all you need. In: Advances in Neural Information Processing Systems, pp. 5998–6008 (2017)
25. Wang, X., et al.: TransPath: transformer-based self-supervised learning for histopathological image classification. In: de Bruijne, M., et al. (eds.) MICCAI 2021. LNCS, vol. 12908, pp. 186–195. Springer, Cham (2021). https://doi.org/10.1007/978-3-030-87237-3_18
26. Xie, E., Wang, W., Wang, W., Ding, M., Shen, C., Luo, P.: Segmenting transparent objects in the wild. In: Vedaldi, A., Bischof, H., Brox, T., Frahm, J.-M. (eds.) ECCV 2020. LNCS, vol. 12358, pp. 696–711. Springer, Cham (2020). https://doi.org/10.1007/978-3-030-58601-0_41
27. Xie, X., Chen, J., Li, Y., Shen, L., Ma, K., Zheng, Y.: Instance-aware self-supervised learning for nuclei segmentation. In: Martel, A.L., et al. (eds.) MICCAI 2020. LNCS, vol. 12265, pp. 341–350. Springer, Cham (2020). https://doi.org/10.1007/978-3-030-59722-1_33
28. Xu, Y., et al.: Large scale tissue histopathology image classification, segmentation, and visualization via deep convolutional activation features. BMC Bioinformatics **18**(1), 1–17 (2017)
29. Yang, J., et al.: Vision-language pre-training with triple contrastive learning. In: Proceedings of the IEEE/CVF Conference on Computer Vision and Pattern Recognition, pp. 15671–15680 (2022)
30. Zheng, S., et al.: Rethinking semantic segmentation from a sequence-to-sequence perspective with transformers. In: Proceedings of the IEEE/CVF Conference on Computer Vision and Pattern Recognition, pp. 6881–6890 (2021)
31. Zhou, Z., Rahman S., Md Mahfuzur, Tajbakhsh, N., Liang, J.: UNet++: a nested U-Net architecture for medical image segmentation. In: Stoyanov, D., et al. (eds.) DLMIA/ML-CDS -2018. LNCS, vol. 11045, pp. 3–11. Springer, Cham (2018). https://doi.org/10.1007/978-3-030-00889-5_1

LifeLonger: A Benchmark for Continual Disease Classification

Mohammad Mahdi Derakhshani[1(✉)], Ivona Najdenkoska[1], Tom van Sonsbeek[1], Xiantong Zhen[1,2], Dwarikanath Mahapatra[2], Marcel Worring[1], and Cees G. M. Snoek[1]

[1] University of Amsterdam, Amsterdam, The Netherlands
m.m.derakhshani@uva.nl
[2] Inception Institute of Artificial Intelligence, Abu Dhabi, United Arab Emirates

Abstract. Deep learning models have shown a great effectiveness in recognition of findings in medical images. However, they cannot handle the ever-changing clinical environment, bringing newly annotated medical data from different sources. To exploit the incoming streams of data, these models would benefit largely from sequentially learning from new samples, without forgetting the previously obtained knowledge. In this paper we introduce *LifeLonger*, a benchmark for continual disease classification on the MedMNIST collection, by applying existing state-of-the-art continual learning methods. In particular, we consider three continual learning scenarios, namely, task and class incremental learning and the newly defined cross-domain incremental learning. Task and class incremental learning of diseases address the issue of classifying new samples without re-training the models from scratch, while cross-domain incremental learning addresses the issue of dealing with datasets originating from different institutions while retaining the previously obtained knowledge. We perform a thorough analysis of the performance and examine how the well-known challenges of continual learning, such as the catastrophic forgetting exhibit themselves in this setting. The encouraging results demonstrate that continual learning has a major potential to advance disease classification and to produce a more robust and efficient learning framework for clinical settings. The code repository, data partitions and baseline results for the complete benchmark are publicly available[1] (https://github.com/mmderakhshani/LifeLonger).

Keywords: Medical continual learning · Disease classification · Medical image analysis

1 Introduction

Applying deep learning models to automate disease classification in medical images has a major potential to assist diagnosis in clinical practice and minimize labour [19,20]. Current deep learning models achieve best performance when

---

M. M. Derakhshani, I. Najdenkoska, T. van Sonsbeek—Equal contribution.

trained on large general datasets. However, adopting this to medical settings has additional challenges compared to when dealing with general data. Obtaining large enough datasets is difficult due to discrepancies in the imaging protocols and medical equipment across different hospitals. Additionally, learning from new incoming data requires constant retraining of existing models, which is less efficient. An ideal approach would be to update models as new data arrives, without forgetting the knowledge obtained from previously seen datasets, which is the objective of this paper.

In the machine learning parlance, the ability of a model to learn sequentially from incoming streams of data is known as *continual* or *lifelong learning* [22, 26, 29]. Unlike the conventional supervised learning of tasks by observing the whole dataset and its label space at once, this sequential learning of tasks is constantly updating the knowledge of the model as it processes more data. Applying this learning paradigm would make deep learning models much more versatile to the constant growth of medical datasets. Therefore, training models for disease classification to learn sequentially is highly desired. Despite the promise, very few efforts have been made to exploit continual learning in medical settings. Existing work tackles this paradigm in image segmentation [3, 9, 25, 39, 40], disease classification [6, 18, 37], domain adaptation [16] and domain incremental learning [32], showing that they are only approaching a small spectrum of continual learning scenarios. They are bypassing more challenging scenarios, which are already considered for well-curated general imagery datasets and tasks [21]. Consequently, no appropriate continual learning baselines exist to detect findings in medical images, creating additional challenges for this promising learning paradigm.

This paper introduces the first continual learning benchmark on medical images for multi-class disease classification, by adopting five popular approaches, namely *Elastic Weight Consolidation* (EWC) [15], *Learning without Forgetting* (LwF) [17], *Memory Aware Synapses* (MAS) [38], *Incremental Classifier and Representation Learning* (iCaRL) [28] and *End-to-End Incremental Learning* (EEIL) [5]. We train and evaluate models on the multi-class disease classification datasets of the publicly available MedMNIST [36], which represents a large-scale MNIST-like collection of biomedical images. Furthermore, we analyse the performance by reporting the average accuracy and forgetting criteria. This analysis also represents an effort to address the major challenge in continual learning, which causes performance degradation on previous tasks after the model is trained on new tasks, named catastrophic forgetting [10, 15, 17, 24].

In the scope of the benchmark, we introduce a new continual learning scenario, termed *cross-domain incremental learning* where each dataset is treated as a distinct domain. This way of learning is especially practical when dealing with datasets originating from different hospitals or imaging equipment. Instead of being retrained from scratch for each specific dataset, models can benefit from sharing the learned knowledge across different datasets. Particularly, to better mimic a future clinical scenario, where a complete diagnosis of a patient is required beyond a single medical modality, our cross-domain incremental learning setting also assumes that disease classification tasks can come

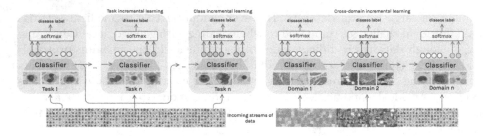

Fig. 1. Continual learning scenarios covered in the LifeLonger benchmark: task incremental learning, class incremental learning and cross-domain incremental learning. Each scenario uses a random subset of the incoming data stream and its label space and each domain is a separate dataset (see Table 1). The classifier is shared across all tasks and domains and it yields output logits (denoted by colored circles) representing the current task (and/or domain). We provide baseline results for all tasks. (Color figure online)

from different medical modalities. Moreover, the ability to aggregate knowledge from data coming from different institutions, without the need to re-train from scratch, provides another clear benefit for cross-domain incremental learning. Secondly, we examine two types of existing continual learning scenarios, namely, *task incremental* and *class incremental learning*. In these two scenarios, the disease labels are grouped as separate subsets, representing the "tasks". In task incremental learning, the model is able to relate each data sample to one specific task [23,33] since it is aware of which classification label appears within each task. In the more complex class incremental learning setting, it is not known which task the data sample belongs to, making this type of learning considerably more difficult. These scenarios are highly useful in clinical practise, since the model should be able to respond well to new labels i.e. diseases in a dataset, while preserving the performance on previously seen labels and without being trained from scratch on it.

The following is the summary of our contributions: (1) We introduce the first benchmark on the MedMNIST dataset, for task, class and cross-domain incremental learning, as an effort to advance the continual learning methods in disease classification of medical images. (2) We introduce a new setting, termed cross-domain incremental learning for multi-class disease classification to illustrate a highly relevant clinical scenario of sharing learned knowledge across different medical datasets. (3) We explore task and class incremental learning scenarios of continual learning, to respond well to new labels i.e. diseases for multi-class disease classification.

2   LifeLonger Benchmark Definition

Formally, continual learning for multi-class disease classification consists of a sequence of n non-stationary tasks $\{\mathcal{T}_1, \mathcal{T}_2, \mathcal{T}_3, \cdots, \mathcal{T}_n\}$, where each task $\mathcal{T}_i$ is represented by the training data $\mathcal{X}_i$ and its label space $\mathcal{Y}_i$, which refers to a

Table 1. Multi-class disease datasets used in the LifeLonger benchmark, adopted from MedMNIST [36]. We follow the splits defined by MedMNIST, but add the class per task division to allow for continual learning.

	Train	Val	Test	Class	Tasks	Classes per Task
BloodMNISTs [1]	11,959	1,712	3,421	8	4	[2, 2, 2, 2]
OrganaMNIST [4]	34,581	6,491	17,778	11	4	[3, 3, 3, 2]
PathMNIST [13]	89,996	10,004	7,180	9	4	[3, 2, 2, 2]
TissueMNIST [4]	165,466	23,640	47,280	8	4	[2, 2, 2, 2]

random subset of disease labels. The tasks are disjoint, and there is no overlap between tasks' label space ($\mathcal{Y}_i \cap \mathcal{Y}_j = \emptyset$ for $i \neq j$). During the training of task t, the learner only has access to the corresponding subset $\mathcal{X}_t$. The model is trained once on each task using online incremental learning techniques or multiple times using offline learning approaches. In this paper, we utilize offline incremental learning.

2.1 Multi-class Disease Datasets

We consider the MedMNIST collection [36] to define our benchmark, due to its balanced and standardized datasets spanning across various modalities. All images are normalized and rescaled to size 28×28 to enable fast computation and evaluation. We select subsets of the collection appropriate for multi-class disease classification, namely, BloodMNIST [1], OrganaMNIST [4], PathMNIST [13] and TissueMNIST [4]. We divide each dataset according to its label space $\mathcal{Y}$ into disjoint subsets $(\mathcal{X}_1, \mathcal{Y}_1), (\mathcal{X}_2, \mathcal{Y}_2), \cdots, (\mathcal{X}_n, \mathcal{Y}_n)$, such that $\mathcal{Y}_i \cap \mathcal{Y}_j = \emptyset$ for $i \neq j$, where each $(\mathcal{X}_i, \mathcal{Y}_i)$ is considered as a separate task. Dataset details are provided in Table 1.

2.2 Continual Learning Scenarios

We consider three continual learning scenarios to establish the benchmarks and to evaluate the model performance: task and class incremental learning [8, 28, 30] and the newly introduced cross-domain incremental learning.

The task incremental learning protocol uses knowledge of the task identifier t and evaluates the model exclusively on the label space $\mathcal{Y}_t$. This is in contrast to class incremental learning, as a more challenging scenario in which the performance of the model is evaluated on all observed classes $\cup_{i=1}^{t} \mathcal{Y}_i$.

The cross-domain incremental learning scenario allows to measure the ability of continual learning models in terms of transferring knowledge between different domains. In particular, each domain is defined as a separate dataset for multi-class disease classification. Formally, in this scenario, given a sequence of n distinct domains, multi-class disease classification datasets, $\mathcal{D}_1, \mathcal{D}_2, \cdots \mathcal{D}_n$, we consider each domain $\mathcal{D}_i$ as a separate task $\mathcal{T}_i$. The learner is then trained on this series of tasks, same as in task incremental learning and class incremental learning scenarios. Additionally, we define *domain-aware* and *domain-agnostic* incremental learning. In domain-aware incremental learning, the domain identifier is available during inference, whereas in domain-agnostic incremental learning, this information does not exist. Figure 1 illustrates these three continual learning scenarios.

2.3   Evaluation Criteria

We quantify continual learning performance by examining average accuracy and average forgetting criterion, following existing work [8,28]. When a training task t is complete, the average accuracy of a model is computed as $A_t = \frac{1}{t} \sum_{i=1}^{t} a_{t,i}$, where $a_{t,i}$ indicates the accuracy of the model on task i when training on task t is finished. Average forgetting quantifies the decline in the model performance between the highest and lowest accuracy for each task, calculated as $F = \frac{1}{T-1} \sum_{i=1}^{T-1} \max_{1,\dots,T-1} (a_{t,i} - a_{T,i})$.

3   Baseline Continual Learners

We provide implementation code for five state-of-the-art continual learners, covering all existing categories of continual learning methods, namely, regularization methods, rehearsal methods and bias correction methods. We establish a lower bound (LB) by simply fine-tuning the model on the current task, without relying on any specific continual learning strategy. Moreover, we provide the multi-task learning average accuracy for each benchmark as the upper bound (UB).

Regularization Methods. They reduce catastrophic forgetting by combining regularization term with the classification loss. While some algorithms such as *Elastic Weight Consolidation* (EWC) and *Memory Aware Synapses* (MAS) regularize the weights and estimate an importance measure for each parameter in the network [2,7,15,38], others, e.g. *Learning without Forgetting* (LwF), regularize the feature map and try to minimize activation drift via knowledge distillation [17].

Rehearsal-Based Methods These methods assume the availability of data from previous tasks via a fixed-size memory unit [5,28,34], a generative model capable of synthesizing samples [27,31] or pseudo samples [14,35] from previous tasks. Rehearsal systems aim to avoid forgetting by replaying previously stored or produced data from earlier tasks. From this category, we evaluate on *Incremental Classifier and Representation Learning* (iCaRL) [28].

Bias Correction Methods Regularization and rehearsal approaches are primarily affected by task recency bias, which refers to a network's inclination to be biased toward classes, associated with the most recently learnt task. This is partly because by the time the training is complete, the network has seen numerous instances of classes in the most recent task but none (or very few in the case of rehearsal) in the prior tasks. Methods for bias correction are meant to resolve this issue [5,12,34]. A

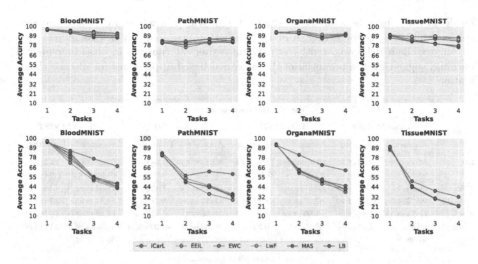

Fig. 2. LifeLonger benchmark results for four consecutive datasets in terms of average accuracy and average forgetting. The results show that all baselines for task incremental learning (top row) perform similarly, whereas for class incremental learning (bottom row) we observe better performance of iCarL, a conclusion that deviates from existing benchmarks for general imagery datasets [23].

simple yet effective approach is proposed by Castro et al. [5], termed *End-to-End Incremental Learning* (EEIL), in which they suggest a balanced training step at the end of each training session. This phase uses an equal number of exemplars from each class for a specified number of iterations.

3.1 Implementation Details

As the learner, we use a deep neural network parameterized by weights θ, to transform the input data x to the output logits o. We split this network into two parts: a feature extractor h parameterized by ψ, and a classifier f in particular a fully-connected layer with parameters ϕ. To predict the label, we apply a softmax layer on the network logits $\hat{y} = \sigma(o)$ where $o = f_\phi(h_\psi(x))$. For all baselines, we use a ResNet-18 [11] as h_θ (without the penultimate fully-connected layers), trained on five distinct random seeds across four sequential tasks. f_ϕ includes a set of fully-connected layers with 512 neurons. To provide fair comparisons, we train the model using the same hyperparameters for all baselines. All baseline runs have a batch size of 32. For each task, we train the model on one NVIDIA RTX 2080ti GPU for 200 epochs with the option of early stopping in the occurrence of overfitting.

4   Baseline Results

Task and Class Incremental Learning. To compare the various baselines, we provide the average accuracy and forgetting, for four sequential tasks on five

Table 2. LifeLonger benchmark results for the provided baselines in terms of average accuracy and average forgetting. All baselines perform comparably in task incremental learning, while iCarL consistently outperforms other alternatives in class incremental learning, suggesting the potential of the rehearsal-based approaches for disease classification.

	Task Incremental Learning							
Method	BloodMNIST		PathMNIST		OrganaMNIST		TissueMNIST	
	Accuracy ↑	Forgetting ↓	Accuracy ↑	Forgetting ↓	Accuracy ↑	Forgetting ↓	Accuracy ↑	Forgetting ↓
LB	88.49±4.09	9.84±7.10	82.40±10.18	12.60±19.80	89.21±7.59	2.58±4.75	77.56 ±10.61	12.1±7.16
EWC [15]	88.94±2.16	9.36±6.12	83.01±3.89	6.48±11.88	90.43±3.94	3.07±3.32	**86.99±3.71**	**1.54±0.94**
MAS [38]	86.63±7.27	10.72±6.02	80.87±5.63	4.64±5.77	90.29±5.12	2.41±2.61	75.54±9.82	5.16±3.38
LwF [17]	90.24±4.04	**0.97±1.06**	82.47±8.26	-2.24±4.88	**91.52±5.50**	-0.10±0.96	84.81±5.92	2.16±3.51
iCarL [28]	**91.74±3.22**	1.83±2.53	**85.66±7.95**	0.28±2.65	90.66±7.21	2.27±2.21	82.98±5.67	2.97±2.31
EEIL [5]	90.55±2.90	2.01±2.14	82.65±5.58	-0.24±6.18	90.30±8.68	**-0.27±3.14**	84.95±4.56	3.77±4.36
UB	97.98±0.18	-	93.52±1.91	-	95.22±0.37	-	91.27±0.87	-

	Class Incremental Learning							
Method	BloodMNIST		PathMNIST		OrganaMNIST		TissueMNIST	
	Accuracy ↑	Forgetting ↓	Accuracy ↑	Forgetting ↓	Accuracy ↑	Forgetting ↓	Accuracy ↑	Forgetting ↓
LB	46.59±6.46	68.26±8.13	32.29±6.74	77.54±16.40	41.21±7.39	54.20±23.97	21.63 ±2.55	90.69±1.77
EWC [15]	47.60±7.30	66.22±14.36	33.34±4.77	76.39±15.53	37.88±7.97	67.92±27.40	21.56±2.51	90.48±1.76
MAS [38]	43.94±6.96	69.43±12.90	34.22±6.17	74.98±15.79	44.99±5.61	55.13±24.43	21.11±2.56	89.38±1.72
LwF [17]	43.68±6.55	66.30±8.70	35.36±9.59	67.37±15.76	41.36±6.36	51.47±24.53	21.49±2.58	90.79±1.22
iCarL [28]	**67.70±8.67**	**14.52±6.93**	**58.46±8.79**	**-0.70±6.41**	**63.02±7.53**	**7.75±4.49**	**32.00±3.01**	**14.42±10.21**
EEIL [5]	42.17±7.05	71.25±12.90	28.42±5.43	79.39±15.79	41.03±11.53	62.47±24.43	21.69±2.43	91.35±1.72
UB	97.98±0.18	-	93.52±1.91	-	95.22±0.37	-	91.27±0.87	-

Table 3. LifeLonger benchmark results for the provided baselines on the domain-aware and domain-agnostic incremental learning tasks, in terms of average accuracy and average forgetting, where each domain is represented by a separate dataset. iCarL consistently outperforms alternatives in both cases, suggesting again the potential of the rehearsal-based approaches for continual disease classification.

	Domain-aware		Domain-agnostic	
Baselines	Accuracy ↑	Forgetting ↓	Accuracy ↑	Forgetting ↓
EWC [15]	28.61±4.99	50.49±1.95	21.59±5.33	58.34±5.86
LwF [17]	40.95±3.98	42.58±9.88	37.95±5.61	52.92±11.89
iCarL [28]	**51.22±1.49**	**22.00±0.75**	**50.78±1.51**	**21.78±1.29**
UB	93.28±0.28	-	93.28±0.28	-

distinct random seeds among four medical datasets, given in Table 2. In terms of accuracy, all benchmarks show comparable performance, whereas in terms of the forgetting it can be noticed a larger gap between some approaches, indicating the drop of performance over time. Additionally, in Fig. 2 we illustrate the running average accuracy to show the performance over time. In task incremental

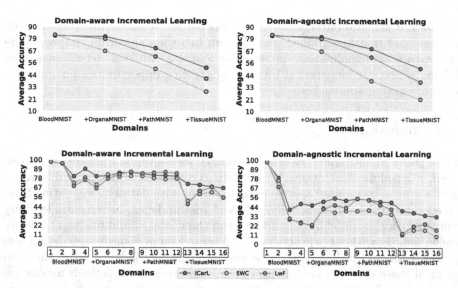

Fig. 3. LifeLonger benchmark results for cross-domain incremental learning. *Left* column presents the average accuracy of domain-aware incremental learning while *right* column indicates the average forgetting of domain-agnostic incremental learning.

learning, all baselines exhibit comparable performance, whereas, in class incremental learning the iCarL method highlights its great superiority and effectiveness over other alternatives across all benchmarks by a large margin. This is in contrast with the findings of previous work [23], showing that the EEIL method performs remarkably better than iCaRL in task and class incremental learning. Hence, this demonstrates the superiority of the rehearsal-based strategies for disease classification and indicates its potential for future study.

Cross-Domain Incremental Learning. We conduct two separate experiments to evaluate the performance for disease classification of domain-aware and domain-agnostic incremental learning. For the first experiment, we report the average accuracy and forgetting on the best performing approaches, namely, EWC, LwF and iCarL. We treat each dataset (domain) as a separate task and train a continual learning model and we report the results on Table 3. It can be observed that iCarL constantly outperforms LwF and EWC, once again proving its superiority for disease classification. Similarly as in the previous scenarios, we report the average accuracy across time of domain-aware and domain-agnostic models, in the top row of Fig. 3. This shows that both scenarios are similar in terms of complexity when we treat each domain as a separate task. The second experiment ablates a fine-grained version of cross-domain incremental learning by subdividing each domain into a sequence of tasks, for example, four tasks per domain. The bottom row of Fig. 3 shows the running average accuracy for domain-aware and domain-agnostic classification.

As shown, iCarL still outperforms other approaches. Additionally, these experiments suggest that fine-grained cross-domain incremental learning improves the performance of domain-aware incremental learning, while it deteriorates that of domain-agnostic incremental learning, suggesting opportunities for improvements of existing approaches.

5   Conclusion

In this paper we introduce the first benchmark for continual learning for disease classification of medical images. We introduce cross-domain incremental learning which shows to be a suited approach when dealing with datasets originating from different institutions. Additionally, we adopt task and class incremental learning to illustrate a relevant clinical scenario when the model should readjust to newly labeled samples without being trained from scratch on previously seen data. Last, but not least, we evaluate various state-of-the-art methods, showing that the rehearsal-based methods are the most promising category of methods for disease classification. The obtained results demonstrate the shortcomings of the current continual learning methods for disease classification of medical images, due to their inherent complexity, such as the spatial locality of diseases, compared to general images. Nevertheless, this paper represents an initial effort to establish the foundation of continual learning for disease classification of medical images.

Acknowledgements. This work is financially supported by the Inception Institute of Artificial Intelligence, the University of Amsterdam and the allowance Top consortia for Knowledge and Innovation (TKIs) from the Netherlands Ministry of Economic Affairs and Climate Policy.

References

1. Acevedo, A., Merino, A., Alférez, S., Molina, Á., Boldú, L., Rodellar, J.: A dataset of microscopic peripheral blood cell images for development of automatic recognition systems (2020)
2. Aljundi, R., Babiloni, F., Elhoseiny, M., Rohrbach, M., Tuytelaars, T.: Memory aware Synapses: Learning what (not) to forget. In: Ferrari, V., Hebert, M., Sminchisescu, C., Weiss, Y. (eds.) ECCV 2018. LNCS, vol. 11207, pp. 144–161. Springer, Cham (2018). https://doi.org/10.1007/978-3-030-01219-9_9
3. Baweja, C., Glocker, B., Kamnitsas, K.: Towards continual learning in medical imaging. arXiv preprint arXiv:1811.02496 (2018)
4. Bilic, P., et al.: The liver tumor segmentation benchmark (lits). arxiv 2019. ArXiv (2019)
5. Castro, F.M., Marín-Jiménez, M.J., Guil, N., Schmid, C., Alahari, K.: End-to-End incremental learning. In: Ferrari, V., Hebert, M., Sminchisescu, C., Weiss, Y. (eds.) ECCV 2018. LNCS, vol. 11216, pp. 241–257. Springer, Cham (2018). https://doi.org/10.1007/978-3-030-01258-8_15
6. Chakraborti, T., Gleeson, F., Rittscher, J.: Contrastive representations for continual learning of fine-grained histology images. In: International Workshop on Machine Learning in Medical Imaging (2021)

7. Chaudhry, A., Dokania, P.K., Ajanthan, T., Torr, P.H.S.: Riemannian walk for incremental learning: Understanding forgetting and intransigence. In: Ferrari, V., Hebert, M., Sminchisescu, C., Weiss, Y. (eds.) ECCV 2018. LNCS, vol. 11215, pp. 556–572. Springer, Cham (2018). https://doi.org/10.1007/978-3-030-01252-6_33

8. Derakhshani, M.M., Zhen, X., Shao, L., Snoek, C.: Kernel continual learning. In: ICML (2021)

9. Gonzalez, C., Sakas, G., Mukhopadhyay, A.: What is wrong with continual learning in medical image segmentation? ArXiv (2020)

10. Goodfellow, I.J., Mirza, M., Xiao, D., Courville, A., Bengio, Y.: An empirical investigation of catastrophic forgetting in gradient-based neural networks. ArXiv (2013)

11. He, K., Zhang, X., Ren, S., Sun, J.: Deep residual learning for image recognition. In: CVPR (2016)

12. Hou, S., Pan, X., Loy, C.C., Wang, Z., Lin, D.: Learning a unified classifier incrementally via rebalancing. In: CVPR (2019)

13. Kather, J.N., et al.: Predicting survival from colorectal cancer histology slides using deep learning: a retrospective multicenter study (2019)

14. Kemker, R., Kanan, C.: Fearnet: Brain-inspired model for incremental learning. In: ICLR (2018)

15. Kirkpatrick, J., et al.: Overcoming catastrophic forgetting in neural networks. Proc. Nat. Acad. Sci. **114**, 3521–3526 (2017)

16. Lenga, M., Schulz, H., Saalbach, A.: Continual learning for domain adaptation in chest x-ray classification. In: Medical Imaging with Deep Learning (2020)

17. Li, Z., Hoiem, D.: Learning without forgetting. In: PAMI (2017)

18. Li, Z., Zhong, C., Wang, R., Zheng, W.-S.: Continual learning of new diseases with dual distillation and ensemble strategy. In: Martel, A.L., et al. (eds.) MICCAI 2020. LNCS, vol. 12261, pp. 169–178. Springer, Cham (2020). https://doi.org/10.1007/978-3-030-59710-8_17

19. Litjens, G., et al.: A survey on deep learning in medical image analysis. Med. Image Anal. **42**, 60–88 (2017)

20. Liu, X., et al.: A comparison of deep learning performance against health-care professionals in detecting diseases from medical imaging: a systematic review and meta-analysis. Lancet Digital Health **1**, e271–e297 (2019)

21. Lomonaco, V., et al.: Avalanche: an end-to-end library for continual learning. In: CVPR (2021)

22. Lopez-Paz, D., Ranzato, M.: Gradient episodic memory for continual learning. In: NeurIPS (2017)

23. Masana, M., Liu, X., Twardowski, B., Menta, M., Bagdanov, A.D., van de Weijer, J.: Class-incremental learning: survey and performance evaluation on image classification. ArXiv (2020)

24. McCloskey, M., Cohen, N.J.: Catastrophic interference in connectionist networks: The sequential learning problem. In: Psychology of Learning and Motivation (1989)

25. Memmel, M., Gonzalez, C., Mukhopadhyay, A.: Adversarial continual learning for multi-domain hippocampal segmentation. In: Domain Adaptation and Representation Transfer, and Affordable Healthcare and AI for Resource Diverse Global Health (2021)

26. Nguyen, C.V., Li, Y., Bui, T.D., Turner, R.E.: Variational continual learning. In: ICLR (2018)

27. Ostapenko, O., Puscas, M., Klein, T., Jahnichen, P., Nabi, M.: Learning to remember: a synaptic plasticity driven framework for continual learning. In: CVPR (2019)

28. Rebuffi, S.A., Kolesnikov, A.I., Sperl, G., Lampert, C.H.: iCaRL: Incremental classifier and representation learning. In: CVPR (2017)
29. Ring, M.B.: Child: a first step towards continual learning. Learning to learn (1998)
30. Rusu, A.A., et al.: Progressive neural networks. In: NeurIPS (2016)
31. Shin, H., Lee, J.K., Kim, J., Kim, J.: Continual learning with deep generative replay. In: NeurIPS (2017)
32. Srivastava, S., Yaqub, M., Nandakumar, K., Ge, Z., Mahapatra, D.: Continual domain incremental learning for chest x-ray classification in low-resource clinical settings. In: Domain Adaptation and Representation Transfer, and Affordable Healthcare and AI for Resource Diverse Global Health (2021)
33. Van de Ven, G.M., Tolias, A.S.: Three scenarios for continual learning. ArXiv (2019)
34. Wu, Y., et al.: Large scale incremental learning. In: CVPR (2019)
35. Xiang, Y., Fu, Y., Ji, P., Huang, H.: Incremental learning using conditional adversarial networks. In: CVPR (2019)
36. Yang, J., Shi, R., Ni, B.: Medmnist classification decathlon: a lightweight automl benchmark for medical image analysis. In: ISBI (2021)
37. Yang, Y., Cui, Z., Xu, J., Zhong, C., Wang, R., Zheng, W.-S.: Continual learning with bayesian model based on a fixed pre-trained feature extractor. In: de Bruijne, M., et al. (eds.) MICCAI 2021. LNCS, vol. 12905, pp. 397–406. Springer, Cham (2021). https://doi.org/10.1007/978-3-030-87240-3_38
38. Zenke, F., Poole, B., Ganguli, S.: Continual learning through synaptic intelligence. In: ICML (2017)
39. Zhang, J., Gu, R., Wang, G., Gu, L.: Comprehensive importance-based selective regularization for continual segmentation across multiple sites. In: de Bruijne, M., et al. (eds.) MICCAI 2021. LNCS, vol. 12901, pp. 389–399. Springer, Cham (2021). https://doi.org/10.1007/978-3-030-87193-2_37
40. Zheng, E., Yu, Q., Li, R., Shi, P., Haake, A.: A continual learning framework for uncertainty-aware interactive image segmentation. In: AAAI (2021)

Unsupervised Nuclei Segmentation Using Spatial Organization Priors

Loïc Le Bescond[1,2,3]([✉]), Marvin Lerousseau[1,2], Ingrid Garberis[3],
Fabrice André[3], Stergios Christodoulidis[1], Maria Vakalopoulou[1,2],
and Hugues Talbot[1,2]

[1] CentraleSupélec, Université Paris-Saclay, 91190 Gif-sur-Yvette, France
`loic.le-bescond@centralesupelec.fr`
[2] Inria OPIS, 91190 Gif-sur-Yvette, France
[3] Gustave Roussy Cancer Campus, 94800 Villejuif, France

Abstract. In digital pathology, various biomarkers (e.g., KI67, HER2, CD3/CD8) are routinely analyzed by pathologists through immuno-histo-chemistry-stained slides. Identifying these biomarkers on patient biopsies allows for a more informed design of their treatment regimen. The diversity and specificity of these types of images make the availability of annotated databases sparse. Consequently, robust and efficient learning-based diagnostic systems are difficult to develop and apply in a clinical setting. Our study builds on the observation that the overall organization and structure of the observed tissues are similar across different staining protocols. In this paper, we propose to leverage both the wide availability of haematoxylin-eosin stained databases and the invariance of tissue organization and structure in order to perform unsupervised nuclei segmentation on immuno-histochemistry images. We implement and evaluate a generative adversarial method that relies on high-level nuclei distribution priors through comparison with largely available haematoxylin-eosin stained cell nuclei masks. Our approach shows promising results compared to classic unsupervised and supervised methods, as we quantitatively demonstrate on two publicly available datasets. Our code is publicly available to encourage further contributions (https://github.com/loic-lb/Unsupervised-Nuclei-Segmentation-using-Spatial-Organization-Priors).

Keywords: Precision medicine · Biomedical imaging · Digital pathology · Generative adversarial networks

1 Introduction

Learning nuclei segmentation models is a challenging problem for immunohisto-chemistry (IHC) stained histological images. In routine pathology, IHC images are used to provide a distinct readout for proteins at the surface of nuclei or cell

Supplementary Information The online version contains supplementary material available at https://doi.org/10.1007/978-3-031-16434-7_32.

L. Wang et al. (Eds.): MICCAI 2022, LNCS 13432, pp. 325–335, 2022.
https://doi.org/10.1007/978-3-031-16434-7_32

membranes or in the cytoplasm that would otherwise be invisible to the human eye, using immunostains [3]. IHC is widely used for diagnostic and for treatment selection, notably in cancer pathology, since it bypasses the need to perform expensive and time-consuming genetic testing. There are over 100 immunostains routinely used by pathologists, highlighting different proteins such as Ki67 and HER2, which can provide clues to tumor characterization. The segmentation of nuclei stained as such provides essential information for distinguishing benign cells from malignant cells or those which express a specific protein from those which do not. The ability to automatically identify and segment nuclei in IHC images is crucial since it could *(i)* accelerate the diagnosis time of cancers, *(ii)* reduce misdiagnosis in routine pathology, and *(iii)* improve the performance of cell-based learning system for therapy response prediction.

The most popular nuclei segmentation approaches currently rely on manually obtained, careful pixel-based annotations of nuclei [16,17,26]. However, producing such annotations is time-consuming, cumbersome, tedious and error-prone, which hampers the development of segmentation models for a wide range of immunostains. Some semi-supervised methods such as [11] have been proposed to alleviate this need, requiring however manual interactions making their use on whole slide level time-consuming. On the other hand, current unsupervised segmentation approaches, such as those based on color clustering, perform inadequately, preventing their application in clinical settings.

This study introduces an approach that revolves around a simple idea: we exploit the fact that the spatial organization and shape characteristics of cells within tissues do not change significantly with the type of coloration technique used to stain histological tissue slides. Specifically, we design and evaluate a powerful and highly versatile adversarial-based approach that leverages already publicly available nuclei annotations for haematoxylin-eosin (H&E) staining to learn segmentation models for potentially many types of immunostains. We show in our experiments that our approach is effective for two of the most prevalent types of nuclei-based and membranous-based immunostains. On these examples, our method obtains results which are close to fully supervised approaches quantitatively evaluated on two publicly available datasets, without requiring any additional annotation.

2   Related Work

Nuclei segmentation is attracting a lot of attention lately with different challenges focusing on methods that can provide accurate segmentation for the many and diverse nuclei present on histology slides [5,30]. These challenges however focus on fully supervised methods, mostly in the domain of H&E stains. Similar approaches relying on manually obtained pixel-based annotations on H&E sometime generalize to some IHC stains e.g., for HER2-stained segmentation [27] and StarDist [29]. However, these methods essentially use color augmentation strategies [18,24], which would be specific to each new staining. In practice, there is a trade-off between the available amount of annotated tiles and the expressive power of the annotations: a higher number of annotated tiles can improve the generalization performance of segmentation systems due to the higher variability of the training data.

Conversely, a variety of thresholding-based approaches have been investigated for unsupervised nuclei segmentation, either based on Otsu thresholding [12, 20] or constrained local thresholding [2, 19]. In [28], authors train a network to accurately classify the magnification of an input tile using an attention module, and show that the attention maps can be used to produce detection maps of nuclei in H&E staining which can be further converted into nuclei segmentation maps.

Cross-domain learning is a paradigm that consists of the adaptation of a model from one domain to another, for instance from the H&E domain to the IHC domain. In this vein, authors of [13] tackle H&E-IHC cross-domain learning by matching the distribution of high-level features obtained from both domains, for tissue segmentation. Other recent approaches have leveraged the use of generative adversarial networks (GANs) to train segmentation networks with various approaches. GANs can be used to generate images via style transfer and use annotations provided in one domain into another, which can then be used to train a supervised network like a U-Net or a Mask-RCNN [13,14]. Moreover, in [31] an auto-encoder like approach for image-to-image translation for style transfer is proposed, learning the segmentation and transfer simultaneously.

Contrary to these approaches, our method exploits the available information at the segmentation level by encoding and identifying the histological tissue characteristics that are independent of the explored staining. To the best of our knowledge, this is the first time that such a scheme has been explored, and shown to provide close to fully supervised performance.

3 Methodology

In this study, we propose an unsupervised method for nuclei segmentation incorporating priors from publicly available datasets. The intuition for our work is that the underlying spatial organization of cells within tissues is the same irrespective of staining. For a given immunostain, rather than relying on specific pixel-based annotations, our approach exploits generic pixel-based segmentation annotations from classical H&E-stained histological images.

Our architecture is composed of three different components trained jointly, as illustrated in Fig. 1. The first is a generator (S) that generates segmentation maps from the IHC inputs. The output of S is then processed by a discriminator (D_S), which predicts if the produced segmentation is plausible or not. Moreover, real, unpaired binary segmentation of nuclei from public datasets are given to the discriminator, in order to guide and encode real tissue characteristics. The last component of our method relies upon a reconstruction generator (R) which is trained to reconstruct IHC-looking nuclei from a segmentation. This way, our framework enforces consistency priors between the generated and the real tiles.

Formally, given an input IHC tile t from a training set T, the segmenter S produces a predicted segmentation map $S(t)$. Given a database $\mathcal{DB}$ of segmentation maps from any type of staining (e.g., H&E), a ground-truth segmentation

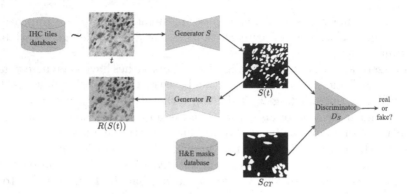

Fig. 1. An overview of our proposed framework. An IHC image t is fed to the generator S, outputting the corresponding segmentation map $S(t)$. This map is compared to a ground truth mask S_{GT} through discriminator D_S; and used by the generator R to reproduce the original image $R(S(t))$. Similarly, the same process is applied to S_{GT} to generate the corresponding IHC image (not represented here for clarity).

map S_{GT} is sampled from $\mathcal{DB}$ for each IHC tile t. The discriminator D_S is then asked to correctly predict that each S_{GT} is real (label 1) and that each predicted IHC segmentation map $S(t)$ is fake (label 0); this is done by minimizing $\mathcal{L}_D$:

$$\mathcal{L}_D = \big(D(S_{GT}) - 1\big)^2 + \big(D(S(t))\big)^2 \tag{1}$$

Conversely, the segmenter S is optimized by maximizing its ability to fool, i.e. by minimizing the loss function $\mathcal{MSE}_G$ that is:

$$\mathcal{L}_G = \big(D(S(t)) - 1\big)^2 \tag{2}$$

The two examined losses $\mathcal{L}_D$ and $\mathcal{L}_G$ should train S to produce segmentation maps that contain nuclei objects that resemble true nuclei segmentation (shape prior), and that display nuclei distribution similar to the nuclei distribution of $\mathcal{DB}$ (organization prior). In fact, with both losses $\mathcal{L}_D$ and $\mathcal{L}_G$ combined, the system is optimized when the distributions of $\mathcal{DB}$ and $\{S(t), t \in T\}$ are matched.

However, we found that the segmentation model S tended to produce false negatives by failing to segment some nuclei. The reconstructor R is intended to circumvent this by reconstructing the input IHC tile t from its predicted segmentation $S(t)$; nuclei that would be missed by S would then induce errors in the reconstruction $R(S(t))$, therefore inducing S to minimize the number of false negatives. R is trained by minimizing the reconstruction $\mathcal{L}_R$, where an ℓ_1 norm is used for sparsity:

$$\mathcal{L}_R = \big\|R(S(t)) - t\big\|_1 \tag{3}$$

Following CycleGAN [32], we add another discriminator D_R on the IHC and reconstructed IHC domains, in order to train R (and therefore S through backpropagation) with an additional loss more complex than pixel-based. For simplicity, we merge this discriminator loss within $\mathcal{L}_D$, and the corresponding adversarial loss of R within $\mathcal{L}_R$ and $\mathcal{L}_G$.

Furthermore, we introduce an additional consistency loss for robustness and to ensure that the segmentation network does not solely focus on color. For an IHC tile t, we consider a color augmentations c_1 (e.g. color jitter) and an augmented view $c_1(t)$ of t. The consistency loss is defined as the ℓ_1 norm between the predicted segmentation maps from both the original tile and the augmented view:

$$\mathcal{L}_C = \left\| S(t) - S(c_1(t)) \right\|_1 \tag{4}$$

Finally, we sharpen the predicted segmentation maps $S(t)$ by multiplying the predicted logits of S using a sharpening factor r = 60, similarly to [7]. This result in saturated values of 0 or 1 rather than float values in $[0, 1]$, which can be used by the discriminator D_S to easily identify fake segmentations.

The system is trained end-to-end, by optimizing both modules through minimization of the following loss function:

$$\mathcal{L}_{\text{system}} = \mathcal{L}_D + \mathcal{L}_G + \mathcal{L}_R + \mathcal{L}_C \tag{5}$$

4   Experimental Configuration

4.1   Databases

We performed extensive experiments on 3 immunohistochemistry datasets to measure the performance of all benchmarked approaches. In detail, we utilize the **DeepLIIF dataset** [6] with 1667 Ki67-stained fields of view of size 512×512 pixels at 40× magnification. Our experiments are based on the publicly available splitting of the dataset [6], excluding the immunofluorescence data. Each image is supplied with ground-truth annotations, which were used for testing purposes but never for our training except for the fully supervised benchmark comparisons. We also employ the **BCDataset** [8] which consists of 1338 Ki67-stained 640 pixel-width 40x fields of view. Each nucleus is annotated with a single point highlighting its center. These were never used for our training except for testing purposes. Lastly, we also use the **Warwick HER2 dataset** [22,23] which contains 84 HER2-stained whole slide images (WSI) split into 50 training and 34 testing slides. We extracted 512×512 patches and 256×256 patches from each slide for each set respectively after performing contours detection and filtering based on texture and lightness criteria [15]. To get a good representation of each tissue, we performed K-Means clustering on the Resnet18 features of each patch and selected for each one the closest to centroids [10]. As KMeans is sensitive to outliers, we applied an isolation forest algorithm to remove the few artifacts that may remain after our pre-processing steps. For the testing set, we divided the patch sets into 2 folds leading to 68 patches. Similarly, for the training set, we divided the patch sets into 14 folds leading to 700 patches. The testing tiles were finally annotated by an experienced anatomopathologist. Compared to Ki67, HER2-stained images are more challenging since HER2 marks the membranes of cells (and not their nuclei).

4.2 Baselines

We compare the performance of our proposed method with five competing methods, including two fully supervised approaches. Specifically: a fully supervised model based on **Unet** [9] was utilized. Moreover, **NuClick** [11] was also employed, a weakly supervised approach specifically designed to compute nuclei masks from point annotations at the center of each cell. To provide this supervision, an experienced pathologist manually annotated all nuclei centers in HER2 test images, and such centers were obtained by computing the centroid of each nuclei ground-truth mask for both DeepLIIF and BCDataset test sets. Furthermore, **StarDist** [29] is a supervised method originally trained on H&E images. For our problem, this approach can be considered unsupervised since it does not rely on extra annotations. StarDist was used as a plugin within QuPath [1]. **Thresholding** was performed by applying Otsu thresholding on the Gaussian filtered luminance image. For Warwick HER2 dataset, we applied the same protocol to the deconvolved haematoxylin images obtained through stain deconvolution [25]. The **proposed** approach was implemented with Unet-style architectures for S and R, and PatchGAN-based discrimators for D_R and D_S [9]. At each iteration, a segmentation map $S(t)$ is produced by S for an input IHC tile t. $S(t)$ is forwarded into D_S, along with a randomly sampled segmentation map S_{GT} from the Pannuke dataset [4,5] which contains nuclei instance masks of H&E tiles extracted at either 20× or 40× magnification. Similarly, R outputs from these masks simulated IHC images that are compared to the real ones through D_R. As we found that the reconstruction represents a key factor in the training of our method, we leveraged HER2 membranous nature to train our approach reconstructing only the deconvolved haematoxylin images as nucleus are only highlighted by this marker in this setting [25].

4.3 Implementation Details

We trained S and R using 64 filters in the last convolutional layer and a dropout of 0.5 and Adam optimizer with a learning rate of 0.0002 and $\beta_1 = 0.5$ and $\beta_2 = 0.999$. For the discriminators, we used 64 filters and 3 layers in total, with the same parameters for the optimizer. We exploited nuclei invariance to rotation and flipping to perform data augmentation. Moreover, as our datasets are all extracted from slides scanned at 40× magnifications, we performed random resizing to simulate 20× magnifications images and reproduce Pannuke distribution.

The fully supervised Unet based architecture was tuned using a Gaussian process algorithm during 50 iterations maximising the F1 score on the validation set after 10 training epochs. The parameters include the number of filters $\in$ {64, 128}, the dropout value $\in [0.3, 0.5]$, the learning rate $\in [10^{-5}, 10^{-2}]$, the decay rate $\in [10^{-10}, 10^{-3}]$ and the batch size $\in$ {10, 30, 60, 120, 140}.

Both fully supervised Unet and the unsupervised proposed approach were then trained on a single A100 GPU for up to 600 epochs with PyTorch v1.10 [21]. For Unet, the model with the highest validation score was inferred on the

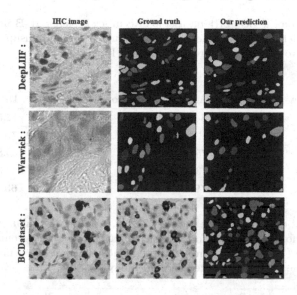

Fig. 2. Examples of predictions of our approach on the different datasets.

(shared) testing set of the DeepLIIF dataset (and was not trained on both other datasets because of missing ground-truth training data). For proposed, the final model was selected by finding the minimum of the loss: $\mathcal{L}_G + \mathcal{L}_R + \mathcal{L}_C$ after 250 epochs to discard early training instabilities. To improve our nuclei masks, we first applied a median filter with a window size of 5 to remove the noise that may remain on our final predictions. For HER2 images, we applied in addition an erosion operation with a radius of 5 to remove remaining artifacts. To obtain nuclei instance segmentation, we lastly applied opening and closing operations and a watershed transform with labeling [28]. To ensure a fair comparison, the same post-processing was applied to the Unet and Thresholding outputs.

5   Results and Discussion

Table 1 reports semantic and object-level results on the DeepLIIF dataset for Ki67-stained images. The proposed approach obtained the highest Dice score of 69.81 and the highest balanced accuracy of 79.65 among all unsupervised approaches, i.e. approaches that do not necessitate additional annotations. While StarDist [29] obtained a higher precision, the proposed obtained the best recall of unsupervised approaches with 66.30; trading recall for precision is better for clinical considerations as false negative could aggravate the course of the patient care, while false positive can be more easily corrected. The proposed approach obtained competitive results with the fully supervised Unet and the weakly supervised NuClick, which obtained no more than 5% of improvement on the balanced accuracy without requiring any further annotations.

Table 1. Results on the DeepLIIF dataset [6]. Accuracy is balanced. **Bold** indicates the top performing method for each metric, for both supervised and unsupervised groups. AJI corresponds to the Mean Aggregated Jaccard Index.

Method	Unsupervised	Semantic				Object		
		Dice	Accuracy	Precision	Recall	AJI	Dice	Hausdorff
Unet	✗	**77.28**	**84.30**	81.42	**73.67**	51.01	72.52	12.81
Nuclick	✗	76.14	82.65	**85.85**	68.62	**61.09**	**75.81**	**9.46**
Threshold	✓	64.21	75.65	76.86	56.42	37.08	58.85	17.30
StarDist	✓	61.92	73.04	**87.89**	48.00	40.80	60.38	**14.79**
Proposed	✓	**69.81**	**79.65**	74.54	**66.30**	**41.91**	**63.47**	16.18

Table 2. Results on the Warwick dataset [22,23]. Accuracy is balanced. **Bold** indicates the top performing method for each metric for unsupervised group. Unet results are not available (NA) since ground-truth segmentation maps were unavailable. AJI corresponds to the Mean Aggregated Jaccard Index.

Method	Unsupervised	Semantic				Object		
		Dice	Accuracy	Precision	Recall	AJI	Dice	Hausdorff
Unet	✗	NA	NA	NA	NA	NA	NA	NA
Nuclick	✗	70.63	89.08	64.10	82.79	56.61	70.88	7.39
Threshold	✓	43.03	67.46	**75.71**	34.65	25.49	44.56	9.87
StarDist	✓	51.95	71.32	72.41	42.71	35.44	54.95	**6.12**
Proposed	✓	**58.46**	**81.64**	64.01	**64.34**	**39.07**	**58.65**	8.71

The Table 2 outlines the results on the testing set extracted from the Warwick dataset. Our approach outperforms the other unsupervised methods on almost all metrics, showing great improvements in semantic metrics with a Dice score of 58.46 and a recall of 64.34 while the classic methods top at 51.95 and 42.71 respectively. Once again, our approach proved to be better tailored to clinical use with a higher recall and better object metrics. It is also advocating for a great adaptability of our method to the diversity of IHC staining. Indeed, providing minor changes in the training and post-processing, we successfully applied our method to two different staining conditions, thus underlying that our method can better leverage H&E information than directly applying pre-trained state-of-the-art algorithms.

Finally, we qualitatively assessed the generalization of the proposed approach trained on DeepLIIF to BCDataset dataset. As highlighted in Fig. 2, our approach managed to provide a segmentation matching many ground truth annotations without adding any additional knowledge.

We performed an ablation study that can be found in the supplementary material (Table 1. supplementary) by successively removing some key components of our method and computing the performances on both DeepLIIF (Ki67 staining) and Warwick (HER2 staining). On both datasets, removing the reconstruction loss decreased the performances significantly on almost all the metrics and produced masks uncorrelated to the input, thus underlying the key role of the proposed cycling architecture. For the consistency loss and the sharpening factor, we noticed that these two elements balanced each other, with a stronger precision but a lower recall when decreasing the sharpening factor, and inversely when removing the consistency loss.

6   Conclusion

In this paper, we introduced a simple yet effective and unsupervised framework for nuclei segmentation integrating spatial organization priors. Extensive experiments on 3 highly heterogeneous datasets highlight the potential of this approach. In particular, we found that our approach outperformed all other benchmarked unsupervised methods, closing the gap with supervised approaches.

There are several axes of improvement for this work. First, besides the nuclei segmentation and detection information, the type of nuclei is also an important information in routine pathology. The current formulation could integrate such information by outputting one segmentation mask per stain and counterstain of IHC images (e.g. HER2 and haematoxylin). Another very interesting direction includes the integration of additional datasets or segmentation masks, which would unravel further shape and organization priors for the nuclei.

Acknowledgments. This work was partially supported by the ANR project Hagnodice ANR-21-CE45-0007, and the PRISM project funded by France 2030 and grant number ANR-18-IBHU-0002.

References

1. Bankhead, P., Loughrey, M.B., Fernández, J.A., et al.: Qupath: Open source software for digital pathology image analysis. Sci. Rep. **7**(1), 1–7 (2017)
2. Di Cataldo, S., Ficarra, E., Acquaviva, A., Macii, E.: Automated segmentation of tissue images for computerized ihc analysis. Comput. Methods Programs Biomed. **100**(1), 1–15 (2010)
3. Duraiyan, J., Govindarajan, R., Kaliyappan, K., Palanisamy, M.: Applications of immunohistochemistry. J. Pharm. Bioallied Sci. 4(Suppl 2), S307 (2012)
4. Gamper, J., Alemi Koohbanani, N., Benet, K., Khuram, A., Rajpoot, N.: Pan-Nuke: an open pan-cancer histology dataset for nuclei instance segmentation and classification. In: Reyes-Aldasoro, C.C., Janowczyk, A., Veta, M., Bankhead, P., Sirinukunwattana, K. (eds.) ECDP 2019. LNCS, vol. 11435, pp. 11–19. Springer, Cham (2019). https://doi.org/10.1007/978-3-030-23937-4_2
5. Gamper, J., Koohbanani, N.A., Benes, K., et al.: Pannuke dataset extension, insights and baselines. arXiv preprint arXiv:2003.10778 (2020)
6. Ghahremani, P., Li, Y., Kaufman, A., et al.: Deep learning-inferred multiplex immunofluorescence for ihc image quantification. bioRxiv (2021)
7. Hou, L., Nguyen, V., Kanevsky, A.B., et al.: Sparse autoencoder for unsupervised nucleus detection and representation in histopathology images. Pattern Recogn. **86**, 188–200 (2019)

8. Huang, Z., et al.: BCData: a large-scale dataset and benchmark for cell detection and ounting. In: Martel, A.L., et al. (eds.) MICCAI 2020. LNCS, vol. 12265, pp. 289–298. Springer, Cham (2020). https://doi.org/10.1007/978-3-030-59722-1_28

9. Isola, P., Zhu, J., Zhou, T., Efros, A.A.: Image-to-image translation with conditional adversarial networks. In: 2017 IEEE Conference on Computer Vision and Pattern Recognition (CVPR), Los Alamitos, CA, USA, pp. 5967–5976. IEEE Computer Society, Jul 2017

10. Kalra, S., Tizhoosh, H., Choi, C., et al.: Yottixel - an image search engine for large archives of histopathology whole slide images. Med. Image Anal. **65**, 101757 (2020)

11. Koohbanani, N., Jahanifar, M., Tajadin, N.Z., Rajpoot, N.: Nuclick: a deep learning framework for interactive segmentation of microscopic images. Med. Image Anal. **65**, 101771 (2020)

12. Kuok, C.P., Wu, P.T., Jou, I.M., et al.: Automatic segmentation and classification of tendon nuclei from ihc stained images. In: Seventh International Conference on Graphic and Image Processing (ICGIP 2015), vol. 9817, p. 98170J. International Society for Optics and Photonics (2015)

13. Lin, Z., Li, J., Yao, Q., et al.: Adversarial learning with data selection for cross-domain histopathological breast cancer segmentation. Multimed. Tools Appli. **81**, 1–20 (2022)

14. Liu, D., Zhang, D., Song, Y., et al.: Unsupervised instance segmentation in microscopy images via panoptic domain adaptation and task re-weighting. In: Proceedings of the IEEE/CVF Conference on Computer Vision and Pattern Recognition, pp. 4243–4252 (2020)

15. Lu, M.Y., Williamson, D.F., Chen, T.Y., et al.: Data-efficient and weakly supervised computational pathology on whole-slide images. Nat. Biomed. Eng. **5**(6), 555–570 (2021)

16. Mahanta, L.B., Hussain, E., Das, N., et al.: Ihc-net: A fully convolutional neural network for automated nuclear segmentation and ensemble classification for allred scoring in breast pathology. Appl. Soft Comput. **103**, 107136 (2021)

17. Mao, K.Z., Zhao, P., Tan, P.H.: Supervised learning-based cell image segmentation for p53 immunohistochemistry. IEEE Trans. Biomed. Eng. **53**(6), 1153–1163 (2006)

18. Mi, H., Bivalacqua, T.J., Kates, M., et al.: Predictive models of response to neoadjuvant chemotherapy in muscle-invasive bladder cancer using nuclear morphology and tissue architecture. Cell Rep. Med. **2**(9), 100382 (2021)

19. Mouelhi, A., Rmili, H., Ali, J.B., et al.: Fast unsupervised nuclear segmentation and classification scheme for automatic allred cancer scoring in immunohistochemical breast tissue images. Comput. Methods Programs Biomed. **165**, 37–51 (2018)

20. Otsu, N.: A threshold selection method from gray-level histograms. IEEE Trans. Syst. Man Cybern. **9**(1), 62–66 (1979)

21. Paszke, A., Gross, S., Massa, F., et al.: Pytorch: an imperative style, high-performance deep learning library. In: Advances in Neural Information Processing Systems, vol. 32 (2019)

22. Qaiser, T., Mukherjee, A., Reddy PB, C., et al.: Her2 challenge contest: a detailed assessment of automated her2 scoring algorithms in whole slide images of breast cancer tissues. Histopathology **72**(2), 227–238 (2018)

23. Qaiser, T., Rajpoot, N.M.: Learning where to see: a novel attention model for automated immunohistochemical scoring. IEEE Trans. Med. Imaging **38**(11), 2620–2631 (2019)

24. Rassamegevanon, T., Feindt, L., Müller, J., et al.: Molecular response to combined molecular-and external radiotherapy in head and neck squamous cell carcinoma (hnscc). Cancers **13**(22), 5595 (2021)

25. Ruifrok, A.C., Johnston, D.A.: Quantification of histochemical staining by color deconvolution. Anal. Quant. Cytol. Histol. **23**(4), 291–299 (2001)
26. Saha, M., Arun, I., Ahmed, R., et al.: Hscorenet: a deep network for estrogen and progesterone scoring using breast ihc images. Pattern Recogn. **102**, 107200 (2020)
27. Saha, M., Chakraborty, C.: Her2net: a deep framework for semantic segmentation and classification of cell membranes and nuclei in breast cancer evaluation. IEEE Trans. Image Process. **27**(5), 2189–2200 (2018)
28. Sahasrabudhe, M., et al.: Self-supervised nuclei segmentation in histopathological images using attention. In: Martel, A.L., et al. (eds.) MICCAI 2020. LNCS, vol. 12265, pp. 393–402. Springer, Cham (2020). https://doi.org/10.1007/978-3-030-59722-1_38
29. Schmidt, U., Weigert, M., Broaddus, C., Myers, G.: Cell detection with star-convex polygons. In: Frangi, A.F., Schnabel, J.A., Davatzikos, C., Alberola-López, C., Fichtinger, G. (eds.) MICCAI 2018. LNCS, vol. 11071, pp. 265–273. Springer, Cham (2018). https://doi.org/10.1007/978-3-030-00934-2_30
30. Verma, R., Kumar, N., Patil, A., et al.: Monusac 2020: a multi-organ nuclei segmentation and classification challenge. IEEE Trans. Med. Imaging **40**(12), 3413–3423 (2021)
31. Yao, K., Huang, K., Sun, J., Jude, C.: AD-GAN: End-to-end unsupervised nuclei segmentation with aligned disentangling training. arXiv preprint arXiv:2107.11022 (2021)
32. Zhu, J.Y., Park, T., Isola, P., Efros, A.A.: Unpaired image-to-image translation using cycle-consistent adversarial networks. In: Proceedings of the IEEE International Conference on Computer Vision, pp. 2223–2232 (2017)

Visual Deep Learning-Based Explanation for Neuritic Plaques Segmentation in Alzheimer's Disease Using Weakly Annotated Whole Slide Histopathological Images

Gabriel Jimenez[2], Anuradha Kar[2], Mehdi Ounissi[2], Léa Ingrassia[2],
Susana Boluda[1], Benoît Delatour[2], Lev Stimmer[2],
and Daniel Racoceanu[2(✉)]

[1] Sorbonne University, Faculty of Medecine, Department of Neuropathology, DMU Neuroscience, 75013 Paris, France
[2] Sorbonne University, Faculty of Science and Engineering, Department of Engineering and Computer Science, 75013 Paris, France
daniel.racoceanu@sorbonne-universite.fr

Abstract. Quantifying the distribution and morphology of tau protein structures in brain tissues is key to diagnosing Alzheimer's Disease (AD) and its subtypes. Recently, deep learning (DL) models such as UNet have been successfully used for automatic segmentation of histopathological whole slide images (WSI) of biological tissues. In this study, we propose a DL-based methodology for semantic segmentation of tau lesions (i.e., neuritic plaques) in WSI of postmortem patients with AD. The state of the art in semantic segmentation of neuritic plaques in human WSI is very limited. Our study proposes a baseline able to generate a significant advantage for morphological analysis of these tauopathies for further stratification of AD patients. Essential discussions concerning biomarkers (ALZ50 versus AT8 tau antibodies), the imaging modality (different slide scanner resolutions), and the challenge of weak annotations are addressed within this seminal study. The analysis of the impact of context in plaque segmentation is important to understand the role of the micro-environment for reliable tau protein segmentation. In addition, by integrating visual interpretability, we are able to explain how the network focuses on a region of interest (ROI), giving additional insights to pathologists. Finally, the release of a new expert-annotated database and the code (https://github.com/aramis-lab/miccai2022-stratifiad.git) will be helpful for the scientific community to accelerate the development of new pipelines for human WSI processing in AD.

Keywords: Alzheimer's disease · Tau aggregates · Neuritic plaques · Deep learning · Visual explanation · Whole slide images · Segmentation

Supplementary Information The online version contains supplementary material available at https://doi.org/10.1007/978-3-031-16434-7_33.

1   Introduction

Accumulations of Amyloid-β and tau protein aggregates, such as plaques in the brain gray matter, are well-known biomarkers of the neurodegenerative Alzheimer's disease (AD) [2]. Quantitative estimation of plaques is typically done by pathologists manually or semi-automatically, using proprietary black-box software from histopathological images of the brain – a time and effort-intensive process prone to human observation variability and errors. In recent times, deep learning (DL) based methods have shown promising results in digital pathology [4] and incredibly high accuracy segmentation of digital whole slide images [6]. In [13], three different DL models were used to segment tau aggregates (tangles) and nuclei in postmortem brain Whole Slide Images (WSIs). The three models included a fully convolutional neural network (FCN), UNet, and Segnet, the latter achieving the highest accuracy in terms of IoU. In [10], an FCN was trained on a dataset of 22 WSIs for semantic segmentation of tangle objects from postmortem brain WSIs. Their model can segment tangles of varying morphologies with high accuracy under diverse staining intensities. An FCN model was also used in [12] to classify morphologies of tau protein aggregates in the gray and white matter regions from 37 WSIs representing multiple degenerative diseases. In [7], tau aggregate analysis was done on a dataset of 6 WSIs with a combined classification-segmentation framework which achieved an F1 score of 81.3% and 75.8% on detection and segmentation tasks, respectively. Several domains in DL-based histopathological analysis of AD tauopathy remain unexplored. Firstly, most existing studies have used DL to segment tangles rather than plaques, which are harder to identify against the background gray matter due to their diffuse/sparse appearance. Secondly, annotations of whole slide images are frequently affected by errors by human annotators. In such cases, a DL preliminary model may be trained using weakly annotated data and used to assist the expert in refining annotations. Thirdly, contemporary tau segmentation studies do not consider context information, which is essential in segmenting plaques from brain WSIs as these emerge as sparse objects against an extended background of gray matter. Finally, DL models with explainability features have not yet been applied in tau segmentation from WSIs. This is a critical requirement for DL models used in clinical applications [1] [14]. The DL models should not only be able to identify regions of interest precisely but also give clinicians and general users the knowledge about which image features the model found necessary that influenced its decision. Based on the above, a DL pipeline for the segmentation of plaque regions in brain WSIs is presented in our study. This pipeline uses context and explainability features with a UNet-based semantic segmentation model to identify plaque features from WSIs.

2   Methodology

2.1   Dataset Characteristics

In this work, we analyzed eight whole slide images containing histological sections from the frontal cortices of patients with AD, which were provided by the

French national brain biobank Neuro-CEB. Signed informed consent for autopsy and histologic analysis was obtained in all cases from the patients or their family members. The present cohort represents a common heterogeneity of AD cases, including slides with variable tau pathology (e.g., different object densities), variable staining quality, and variable tissue preservation. Sections of the frontal lobe were stained with AT8 antibody to reveal phosphorylated tau pathology, using a standardized immunohistochemistry protocol. Obtained slides were scanned using two Hamamatsu slide scanners (NanoZoomer 2.0-RS and NanoZoomer s60 with 227 nm/pixel and 221 nm/pixel resolution, respectively) at 40x initial magnification. The slides were used for human-CNN iterative object annotation resulting in about 4000 annotated and expert-validated Neuritic plaques. The labels, extracted in an XML format, constitute the segmentation ground truth.

2.2 Data Preparation

From the WSIs, at 20× magnification, patches with two levels of context information were generated using an ROI-guided sampling method. The larger patches (256 × 256 pixels) capture a broader context containing object neighborhood and background pixels, whereas the smaller (128 × 128 pixels) mainly focus on the plaque region without much context information. The amount of context present in each patch is quantified using a ratio of the area of annotated ROI to the total area of the patch. The plaque example in different patch sizes is shown in Fig. 1 (note that the bigger patch has additional objects-plaques). In addition, two different normalizations are used and compared: Macenko [5] and Vahadane [11] methods.

A new scheme for data augmentation was implemented based on ROI-shifting to prevent the networks' bias from focussing on the center location of plaques in the patches. Accordingly, the annotated plaque ROIs are shifted to four corners of a patch, producing a four-fold augmentation of each patch containing an object. This augmentation aims to train the UNet models robustly in the presence of variable neighborhood context information, especially when closely-spaced plaque objects are present. An example of this augmentation is shown in Fig. 2.

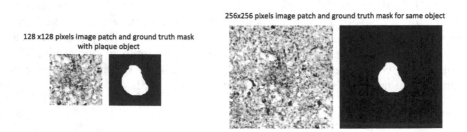

Fig. 1. Example of plaque image for different levels of context.

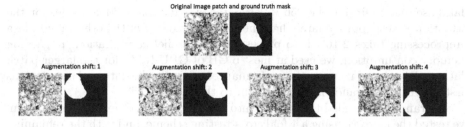

Fig. 2. Example of ROI shifting augmentation.

2.3 Deep Learning Architecture for Segmentation

In order to segment the neuritic plaques, a UNet model adapted from [9] is used with modifications for accommodating context information within the WSI patches during training and testing. The model architecture is modified to work with the two datasets containing different patch sizes – i.e., 128×128 (having low context information) and 256×256 pixels (having more information about the plaque neighborhood). For the first dataset, the UNet architecture consists of 3 downsampling and 3 upsampling convolutional blocks, in addition to the convolutional middle block. For the 256×256-patch-size dataset, we added a downsampling and upsampling convolutional block to the previous UNet model. For the downsampling block, we used a leaky ReLU activation function and ReLU for the upsampling block. In both blocks, we used batch-normalization following the suggestions in [3] and [7]. Dropout was used in each convolutional block with a probability of 0.5.

2.4 Deep Learning Architecture for Visual Interpretation

In addition to the segmentation, we focus on deriving locations within the patches where the DL model found significant features from the plaque objects. Therefore, we used an attention UNet described in [8], which allows us to visualize the activated features at each iteration and evaluate qualitatively where the network focuses during training. The attention UNet architecture was also modified for the two different patch-size datasets following a configuration similar to the one described for the UNet.

3 Experiments and Results

Data preparation and UNet experiments were executed on an 12-core Intel(R) Core i9-9920X @ 3.5GHz CPU with 128 GB RAM and two 12 GB RAM Nvidia GeForce RTX 2080 Ti GPUs. The attention UNet experiments run on a cluster (1 GPU Tesla V100S-PCIe-32GB, 12 CPU cores Intel(R) Xeon(R) Gold 6126 CPU @ 2.60GHz, and 80 GB of RAM). The average training and evaluation time of the UNet per epoch is approximately 2 min for the 128×128 patch-size database and 5 min for the 256×256 patch-size database. Meanwhile, for the attention UNet, approximately half the time is needed. On the other hand, data preprocessing takes 2 to 5 h to process using parallel computation. Regarding memory consumption, we used at most 6 GB of GPU RAM for the larger patch dataset. In order to increase the performance, we cache the data and annotations first in CPU RAM and then move them to the GPU.

We randomly divided the 8 WSIs into 4 folds for the DL experiments. Then, we tested the network using a 4-fold cross-testing scheme, and with the remaining data from each test fold, we also performed a 3-fold cross-validation. In addition, we run a series of tests (using these folds) to select the loss function and the best optimizer for the UNet and attention UNet. We tested 4 loss functions (i.e., Focal loss, BCEwithLogits, Dice, and BCE-Dice loss) and 4 different optimizers (i.e., SGD, Adam, RMSProp, and AdaDelta). After the hyperparameter tuning, we obtained the best performance using the BCE-Dice loss with a 50% balance between Dice and BCE (Binary Cross Entropy) and the Adadelta optimizer with $\rho = 0.9$ and a varying learning rate based on the evolution of the validation loss. Also, we implemented early stopping for training with a patience value of 15 epochs.

3.1 Results from UNet Architecture

The segmentation evaluation metric used for all of the experiments regarding the UNet is the Dice score which is equivalent to the F1 score for binary segmentation problems. In the first experiment, the UNet model was trained with two datasets having different patch sizes: 128×128 and 256×256 pixels. The mean and standard deviations of the Dice coefficient for cross-validation and cross-testing are reported in Table 1. The patches were previously normalized using the Macenko method and then separated in their corresponding fold for training, validation, and testing following the scheme described above. We observe a decrease in the Dice score for larger patches having additional environmental context from the neuritic plaque.

Table 1. UNet results (Dice score) for 4-fold cross testing and 3-fold cross validation for different patch sizes.

Patch size	Normalization	Cross validation	Cross testing
128×128	Macenko	0.6954 ± 0.0289	0.6852 ± 0.0260
256×256	Macenko	0.6600 ± 0.0420	0.6460 ± 0.0330

As described, the WSIs were acquired using two different scanners. Therefore, to study the impact of its properties, we divided the entire cohort into two independent datasets: 4 WSIs belonging to the NanoZoomer 2.0-RS and 4 WSIs scanned with the NanoZoomer s60. For both datasets, we only evaluate the performance of the DL architecture using 4-fold cross-validation and patches of 128×128 pixels size. Additionally, we normalize each dataset independently (i.e., using two reference patches: one for the NanoZoomer 2.0-RS and one for the NanoZoomer s60) using the Macenko method. The Dice score obtained using the images from the higher resolution Hamamatsu NanoZoomer S60 scanner was 0.6345 ± 0.0243, whereas that from the NanoZoomer 2.0-RS was 0.7342 ± 0.0063.

We also study the effect of normalization in the entire dataset (8 WSIs). We normalized the patches from the 128×128 dataset using Macenko and Vahadane methods, and we selected the best fold (i.e., highest Dice score in testing for the first experiment) to train, validate and test the UNet under different input color properties. Opposite to the results reported in [7], the Dice score obtained was higher using the Macenko method (0.7248 in testing) than the Vahadane (0.7098 in testing), even in validation (0.72313 for Macenko and 0.6864 for Vahadane). For a full list of results, see supplementary material.

3.2 Visual Deep Learning Interpretation

The attention UNet model was trained using the 128×128 and the 256×256 patch size dataset, and the results are summarized in Table 2. All images were normalized using the Macenko method, and we observed a similar trend as the UNet: better performance using patches containing less background information.

Table 2. Attention UNet results (Dice score) for 4-fold cross testing and 3-fold cross validation for different patch sizes.

Patch size	Normalization	Cross validation	Cross testing
128×128	Macenko	0.7516 ± 0.0334	0.6920 ± 0.0254
256×256	Macenko	0.6931 ± 0.0447	0.6342 ± 0.0301

An example segmentation result from the attention UNet model in a 128×128 patch containing a plaque object and its corresponding ground-truth mask is shown in Fig. 3. We observe that the attention UNet model finds significant activation features around the plaque object initially annotated by experts (see ground truth mask in Fig. 3). We also notice that the loss at iteration 100 increases over iteration 1; however, we clearly distinguish the region of the object (dark red color). After 1000 iterations, the loss decreases 50% due to the fact that the Dice part of the BCE-Dice loss function influences the network into detecting a pattern very similar to the given ground truth.

Another result from attention UNet is in Fig. 4. Here, the attention UNet focuses on 2 plaques initially annotated by a human expert. It also identifies strong activation features in regions with no ground truth annotations, which could indicate missed ROIs by human experts during the annotation process. Thus with the attention UNet, it is not only possible to segment the plaque objects but also to improve or refine the manual annotations by experts.

Weak and imprecise annotations are frequently observed in histopathology arising from human or software errors. In such cases, deep learning attention

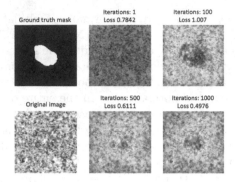

Fig. 3. Global coherence of attention-UNet result with human annotation.

maps could be useful to provide pathologists and biologists with refined annotations (e.g., precision on the boundaries of ROIs). An example is shown in Fig. 5 where DL attention maps are closer to the shape of actual ROIs compared to human-made annotations.

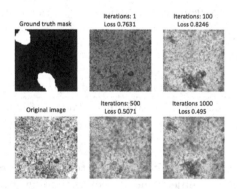

Fig. 4. Focus progression using successive activation layers of attention-UNet.

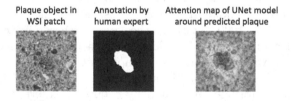

Fig. 5. Improving human annotations using attention-based DL models.

4   Discussion and Conclusion

In the presented work, we studied/evaluated a number of factors that contribute to the segmentation of plaques from whole slide images using DL models. The key observations are the following:

1. Use of biomarkers: the study in [7] uses the ALZ50 (used to discover compacted structures) biomarker, while our study uses the AT8 (majorly used in clinics, helps to discover all structures). We focus on AT8 in order to stay close to clinical protocols. The drawback is that this biomarker creates less compact structures meaning a slightly more difficult segmentation of the plaques, as our results support.
2. Use of different modalities: using the AT8 biomarker, we analyzed 2 types of WSI scanners (see Sect. 2.1) with different resolutions. High-resolution scanners amplify the annotation errors (human-software). Accordingly, some results concerning the high-resolution scanners have been affected, generating lower dice scores.
3. Context effect on results of DL models: We noticed that increasing the background information in the patches negatively affects the segmentation results, which can be explained by the imbalance between the foreground and background pixels. In future works, this will be addressed using adaptive loss functions to take advantage of context information around the ROIs.
4. Attention maps: We observed that using the attention UNet model helps us see the weakness in the human-made annotations (see Fig. 5), generating precious insights about the segmentation DL protocol, which can be used to refine the annotations by improving the border of the detected objects. These refined patterns can be used for a morphology and topology pipeline toward a robust AD patient's stratification proof. In addition, quantitative results show better performance of the same UNet architecture with attention blocks.
5. Comparison with state-of-the-art commercial software: We compared our WSI segmentation results with those generated by a commercial software. This software uses a UNet architecture with a VGG encoder which is different from our model. Our system outperforms this software (Dice score 0.63 for test), using the same WSI as the ones used in this paper. Besides, in this software, neither information about how patches are generated nor the type of normalization or pre-processing perfomed on the dataset is available.

Whole slide histopathology images whose sizes range in giga-pixels often contain thousands of objects per image. As seen for plaques in this study, it becomes more challenging when the objects being annotated do not have clear boundaries separating them from their surrounding environments, which may give rise to errors in human-made annotations. We saw an example of how DL models with visual explanation properties can help pathologists refine the ROI identification process. Our future challenge is to create deep learning assistive tools that can improve human-made few and weak annotations, a generic problem of a wide range of biomedical applications.

Acknowlegements. This research was supported by Mr Jean-Paul Baudecroux and The Big Brain Theory Program - Paris Brain Institute (ICM). The human samples were obtained from the Neuro-CEB brain bank (https://www.neuroceb.org/en/) (BRIF Number 0033-00011), partly funded by the patients' associations ARSEP, ARSLA, "Connaître les Syndromes Cérébelleux", France-DFT, France Parkinson and by Vaincre Alzheimer Fondation, to which we express our gratitude. We are also grateful to the patients and their families.

References

1. Border, S.P., Sarder, P.: From what to why, the growing need for a focus shift toward explainability of AI in digital pathology. Front. Physiol. **12** (2022)
2. Duyckaerts, C., Delatour, B., Potier, M.C.: Classification and basic pathology of Alzheimer disease. Acta Neuropathol. **118**(1), 5–36 (2009)
3. Ioffe, S., Szegedy, C.: Batch normalization: Accelerating deep network training by reducing internal covariate shift. arXiv preprint arXiv:1502.03167 (2015)
4. Janowczyk, A., Madabhushi, A.: Deep learning for digital pathology image analysis: a comprehensive tutorial with selected use cases. J. Pathol. Inform. **7**, 29 (2016)
5. Macenko, M., et al.: A method for normalizing histology slides for quantitative analysis. In: 2009 IEEE International Symposium on Biomedical Imaging: From Nano to Macro, pp. 1107–1110 (2009)
6. Madabhushi, A., Lee, G.: Image analysis and machine learning in digital pathology: challenges and opportunities. Med. Image Anal. **33**, 170–175 (2016)
7. Maňoušková, K., et al.: Tau protein discrete aggregates in Alzheimer's disease: neuritic plaques and tangles detection and segmentation using computational histopathology. In: Tomaszewski, J.E., Ward, A.D., M.D., R.M.L. (eds.) Medical Imaging 2022: Digital and Computational Pathology, vol. 12039, pp. 33–39. International Society for Optics and Photonics, SPIE (2022)
8. Oktay, O., et al.: Attention u-net: Learning where to look for the pancreas (2018)
9. Ronneberger, O., Fischer, P., Brox, T.: U-Net: convolutional networks for biomedical image segmentation. In: Navab, N., Hornegger, J., Wells, W.M., Frangi, A.F. (eds.) MICCAI 2015. LNCS, vol. 9351, pp. 234–241. Springer, Cham (2015). https://doi.org/10.1007/978-3-319-24574-4_28
10. Signaevsky, M., et al.: Artificial intelligence in neuropathology: deep learning-based assessment of tauopathy. Lab. Investig. **99**(7), 1019–1029 (2019)
11. Vahadane, A., et al.: Structure-preserved color normalization for histological images. In: 2015 IEEE 12th International Symposium on Biomedical Imaging (ISBI), pp. 1012–1015 (2015)
12. Vega, A.R., et al.: Deep learning reveals disease-specific signatures of white matter pathology in tauopathies. Acta Neuropathol. Commun. **9**(1), 170 (2021)
13. Wurts, A., Oakley, D.H., Hyman, B.T., Samsi, S.: Segmentation of tau stained Alzheimers brain tissue using convolutional neural networks. Annu. Int. Conf. IEEE Eng. Med. Biol. Soc. **2020**, 1420–1423 (2020)
14. Yamamoto, Y., et al.: Automated acquisition of explainable knowledge from unannotated histopathology images. Nat. Commun. **10**(1), 5642 (2019)

MaNi: Maximizing Mutual Information for Nuclei Cross-Domain Unsupervised Segmentation

Yash Sharma[✉], Sana Syed, and Donald E. Brown

University of Virginia, Charlottesville, VA, USA
ys4yh@virginia.edu

Abstract. In this work, we propose a mutual information (MI) based unsupervised domain adaptation (UDA) method for the cross-domain nuclei segmentation. Nuclei vary substantially in structure and appearances across different cancer types, leading to a drop in performance of deep learning models when trained on one cancer type and tested on another. This domain shift becomes even more critical as accurate segmentation and quantification of nuclei is an essential histopathology task for the diagnosis/prognosis of patients and annotating nuclei at the pixel level for new cancer types demands extensive effort by medical experts. To address this problem, we maximize the MI between labeled source cancer type data and unlabeled target cancer type data for transferring nuclei segmentation knowledge across domains. We use the Jensen-Shanon divergence bound, requiring only one negative pair per positive pair for MI maximization. We evaluate our set-up for multiple modeling frameworks and on different datasets comprising of over 20 cancer-type domain shifts and demonstrate competitive performance. All the recently proposed approaches consist of multiple components for improving the domain adaptation, whereas our proposed module is light and can be easily incorporated into other methods (Implementation: https://github.com/YashSharma/MaNi).

Keywords: Unsupervised domain adaptation · Contrastive learning · Histology · Instance segmentation · Semantic segmentation

1 Introduction

Nuclei are the fundamental organizational unit of life. Accurate assessment of these nuclei in histopathology slides provides critical morphological information necessary for the quantitative analysis of multiple diseases. In the last decade, Convolutional Neural Network-based approaches have emerged as a promising solution in medical imaging tasks, and nuclei segmentation tasks [7,21]. However, they require a large amount of annotated data for any reliable training. Moreover, even with a large dataset, models are prone to be poor at generalizing learned knowledge

---

S. Syed and D. E. Brown—Co-Corresponding Author.

from one cancer type to another. Pixel-level image annotations by a medical expert are required to expand to a new cancer type, making it difficult, expensive, and a time-consuming task. Therefore, there is a need for methods that can transfer learned information from existing cancer datasets to other domains without additional annotations. We tackle this problem, characterized as Unsupervised domain adaptation (UDA), to close the gap between the annotated source domain and unlabeled target domain by learning domain-invariant and task-relevant features.

It has been observed that trivially training a model on the source domain and evaluating on a target domain leads to sub-par performance owing to domain shift [8]. Moreover, the domain shift problem is widespread in medical image datasets due to different scanners, scanning protocols, and tissue types, among others. Hence, multiple strategies comprising of adversarial learning, pseudo-labeling, consistency regularization, or data-augmentation have been proposed to tackle this limitation [8]. Among these, self-training has emerged as a competitive approach. Various de-noising strategies such as confidence thresholding, uncertainty estimation, or distance penalty between domains have been proposed. These strategies have led to gains, but they all rely on unlabeled data points closer to labeled data points for pseudo-label training since those are the points with high confidence and attempts to push the target distribution closer to the source. However, forcing the target-domain distribution towards the source-domain distribution can destroy the latent structural patterns of the target domain, leading to a drop in performance. We hypothesize that instead of using these approaches, using an information-theoretic distance can lead to better alignment between the domains.

Contrastive learning (CL) has seen wide success in representation learning with applications ranging from unsupervised pre-training to multi-modal alignment [22]. The basic idea of CL is to push together the latent distribution of similar samples and push away the latent distribution of dissimilar samples. Wang et al. [25] adopted a supervised, pixel-wise contrastive learning algorithm and treated pixels belonging to the same class as positive pairs and pixels from dissimilar classes as negative pairs, observing significant gains in semantic segmentation performance. We take inspiration from their work and expand the idea of contrasting similar class pixels against dissimilar class pixels for UDA.

In summary, our paper makes the following contributions: 1) We propose a simple Jensen-Shannon Divergence-based contrastive loss for UDA in nuclei semantic and instance segmentation tasks. The proposed loss maximizes the mutual information between the representations of ground truth nuclei pixels from the labeled source dataset and the pseudo-labeled nuclei pixels in the target data. 2) We demonstrate our approach using different architectures and for over 20 cancer-type domain shifts establishing that the inclusion of the MI loss leads to competitive gain over recently proposed methods.

2   Related Works

2.1   Unsupervised Domain Adaptation

UDA is a well-studied problem in literature where two of the widely adopted techniques are adversarial learning and self-training. In Adversarial learning, researchers attempt to align source data representation with target data representation via discriminator training. Hoffman et al. [11] proposed a cycle-consistent adversarial domain adaptation (DA) method for enforcing cycle-consistency between domains. [17] used a category-level adversarial network for enforcing semantic consistency between each class. Tsai et al. [23] developed a patch alignment method for DA by adversarially pushing the feature representations of clustered patches together. Vu et al. [24] used an entropy-based adversarial training approach for aligning weighted self-information distributions of different domains. Yang et al. [26] showed improvement in domain alignment by iteratively defensing against pointwise adversarial perturbations for domains.

In Self-training, pseudo-labels are iteratively generated on target datasets using the model trained on labeled source datasets and used for retraining. Recent papers have incorporated different de-noising strategies for improving the accuracy of pseudo-labels. Zhang et al. [29] used category centroids from the source domain for pseudo-labeling the target data and used the distance to centroids for training. Zhang et al. [28] denoised pseudo-label by online correcting them according to the relative feature distance to the prototypes. Zou et al. [30] used class-wise normalized confidence scores for generating pseudo-labels with balanced class distribution for self-training. Zou et al. [31] proposed a confidence regularization for smoothing the prediction via regularizer loss minimization.

We highlight the relevant works extending the above approaches for UDA in nuclei segmentation. Yang et al. [27] used adversarial domain discriminator and cyclic adaptation with pseudo labels for UDA. Further, they utilized weak labels to improve nuclei instance segmentation and classification. Haq et al. [9] used adversarial learning loss and reconstruction loss on output space for UDA for cell segmentation. Li et al. [15] extended [9] and applied a self-ensembling method with a student-teacher framework for imposing consistency loss along with reconstruction and adversarial training. In another branch of works, [16] performed UDA from microscopy to histopathology images by synthesizing target-type images using CycleGAN followed by an inpainting module before applying adversarial adaptation. However, this approach requires pixel-level translation for synthesizing target-like images before a segmentation module and uses instance-level information for the mutual information-based feature alignment, constraining its adoption to only instance segmentation. Therefore, we limit our work and first test it extensively for tissue/cancer type domain shifts and leave microscopy to histopathology adaptation for future works. Further, our proposed MI-based feature alignment strategy can be used for both semantic and instance segmentation problems.

2.2   Contrastive Learning and Mutual Information

Contrastive learning (CL) methods are being widely adopted for classification and segmentation tasks of different modalities. For semi-supervised segmentation, Alonso et al. [1] used positive-only CL for enforcing the segmentation network to yield similar pixel-level feature representation for same-class samples between labeled and unlabeled datasets. Hu et al. [13] for MRI and CT image segmentation pretraining used global contrastive loss on unlabeled images and supervised local contrastive loss on limited labeled images. For volumetric medical segmentation, Chaitanya et al. [2] leveraged similarity across corresponding slices in different volumes for defining positive and negative pairs for contrastive loss. They used infoNCE bound for CL, requiring a large number of negative samples for training. For tackling this dependency, Peng et al. [20] maximized mutual information (MI) on categorical distribution by projecting the continuous feature embedding to clustering space. They used encoder representation for global regularization and, for local regularization, maximized MI between neighboring feature vectors at multiple intermediate levels.

Our work maximizes the MI between similar classes using labeled source images and pseudo-labeled target images. Concurrent to our work, Chaitanya et al. [3] proposed an end-to-end semi-segmentation framework by defining a local pixel-level contrastive loss between pseudo-labels of unlabeled sets and limited labeled sets. They randomly sample pixels from each image to address the computational limitations of running CL for all the pixels. In contrast, we use average pooling at the class level for considering all the pixels of labeled and unlabeled images. Further, we use JSD bound instead of InfoNCE for MI estimation and focus on domain adaptation tasks. Shrivastava et al. [22] in their work for visual representation learning from textual annotation, demonstrated that the JSD-based bound enables the MI maximization at a smaller batch size with just one negative sample. Also, [10] demonstrated in their extended analysis that JSD is insensitive to the number of negative samples, while infoNCE shows a decline as the number of negative samples decreases, motivating us to choose JSD bound for MI estimation.

3   Methods

3.1   Problem Set-Up

In our work, we tackle the problem of unsupervised domain adaptation for nuclei segmentation, where we have labeled source domain data and unlabeled target domain data coming from different cancer types. Our labeled source data has N_s images (x_s, y_s) and our unlabeled target domain has N_t images (x_t).

3.2   Segmentation Loss and Mutual Information Maximization

We use a combination of dice loss and binary cross-entropy loss for supervised segmentation training (L_{seg}). For mutual information (MI) maximization, we use Jensen-Shannon Divergence (JSD)-based lower bound proposed in [10]. This bound allows us to estimate the MI with just one negative example for each positive example. In our framework, we define nuclei pixels in the source domain with nuclei pixels in the target domain as positive pairs while background pixels in the source domain with nuclei pixels in the target domain as a negative pair.

We use a simple 1×1 convolution network with the same number of input and output channels, followed by batch normalization and ReLU as the projection head. The output of the backbone network is passed to the projection head for generating representation for MI loss. Projected feature representation and segmentation labels are used for MI maximization. Since labels are not available for the target domain, we use a segmentation network output from the same iteration as pseudo-labels. Typically, we would like to contrast all the positive pair pixels with negative pair pixels. However, for computational feasibility, we mean pool the projected representations using the segmentation labels to get aggregated background and nuclei pixel representations. Further, mean pooled source nuclei representation with mean pooled target nuclei representation is treated as a positive pair, whereas mean pooled background pixel representation with mean pooled target nuclei representation is treated as a negative pair. We define our JSD estimator as:

$$\hat{I}_\omega^{JSD}(Z_s; Z_t) := \mathbb{E}_{P(Z_s, Z_t)}[-sp(-T_\omega(z_s, z_t))] - \mathbb{E}_{P(Z_s)P(Z_t)}[sp(T_\omega(z'_s, z_t))] \quad (1)$$

where z_s is mean pooled source nuclei representation, z_t is mean pooled target nuclei representation, z'_s is mean pooled background representation for the source sample, and $sp(z) = log(1 + e^z)$ is the softplus function. Here, $T_\omega : Z_s \times Z_t \rightarrow \mathbb{R}$ is a discriminator network with trainable parameters ω which are jointly optimized to distinguish between a paired-sample from a joint distribution (positive pair) and a paired sample from product of marginals (negative pair). For discriminator network, we use the concat architecture proposed in [10].

3.3   Training

As shown in Fig. 1, our architecture is divided into 4 parts - 1) backbone encoder-decoder network (θ_b), 2) segmentation head (θ_s) for generating segmentation masks, 3) projection head (θ_p) for generating feature representations for MI maximization and 4) discriminator network (T_ω) for estimating MI.

We divide our training into 2 steps. In step 1, for warming up the model and achieving reasonable pseudo-labels for target data, we pretrain the backbone network (θ_b) and segmentation head (θ_s) using source data on segmentation loss.

$$(\hat{\theta}_b, \hat{\theta}_s) = \underset{\theta_b, \theta_s}{\operatorname{argmin}} \frac{1}{|X_s|} \sum_{(x_s, y_s)} L_{seg}(y_s, \hat{y_s}) \quad (2)$$

In step 2, we continue the training the model with the MI loss between labeled source data points and pseudo-labeled target data points.

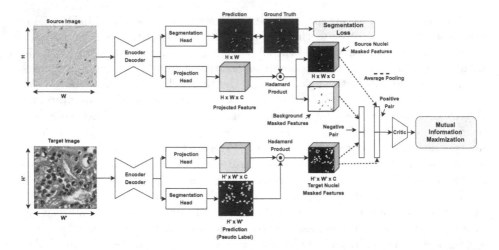

Fig. 1. Images pass through the backbone network and segmentation head for the segmentation training and projection head for contrastive training. Source image actual label is used for segmentation loss and to obtain the feature representation of nuclei and background area. Target image prediction is used as the pseudo label to get the feature representation of the nuclei area. Masked features are average pooled for generating positive and negative pairs for mutual information maximization.

$$(\hat{\theta}_b, \hat{\theta}_s, \hat{\theta}_p, \omega) = \underset{\theta_b, \theta_s}{\operatorname{argmin}} \frac{1}{|X_s|} \sum_{(x_s, y_s)} L_{seg}(y_s, \hat{y}_s) +$$
$$\underset{\omega, \theta_p, \theta_b, \theta_s}{\operatorname{argmax}} \frac{1}{|X_{pair}|} \sum_{(x_s, y_s), (x_t, \hat{y}_t)} \hat{I}_\omega^{JSD}(Z_s; Z_t) \tag{3}$$

where Z_s and Z_t are mean pooled nuclei representation for source and target respectively, and X_{pair} define randomly paired source and target image for MI maximization.

4 Experiments

4.1 Dataset and Implementation

We evaluate our approach using the similar setting used in [15] for Nuclei Semantic Segmentation and [27] for Nuclei Instance Segmentation. In [15], authors used the Kidney Renal Clear Cell Carcinoma (KIRC) dataset [14], Triple Negative Breast Cancer Cell (TNBC) dataset [18], and Stomach adenocarcinoma (STAD) [12] of the TCIA repository. There are 486 images of 400×400 pixel size in KIRC, 50 images of 512 × 512 pixel size in TNBC, and 99 images of 256 × 256 pixel size in STAD. [15] evaluated UDA Nuclei Semantic Segmentation for following cancer type domain shift - TNBC to KIRC/TCIA, and TCIA to KIRC/TNBC.

Table 1. Nuclei semantic segmentation results for UDA.

Source domain	TNBC		TCIA	
Target domain	KIRC	TCIA	KIRC	TNBC
Source Only	0.713	0.680	0.710	0.791
DA_ADV [4]	0.726	0.734	0.708	0.787
CellSegUDA [9]	0.728	0.765	0.705	0.805
SelfEnsemblingUDA [15]	0.727	0.761	0.715	0.816
MaNi	0.733	0.776	0.727	0.821

Following the same setup for comparison, we use standard U-Net architecture as the backbone encoder-decoder network and 80% of images for training, 10% for validation, and 10% for testing. We report average dice scores from five runs with different splits for accounting for sampling bias.

In [27], the authors used colorectal nuclear segmentation and phenotype dataset (CoNSep) [7] as the source domain and PanNuke dataset [5] comprising 19 cancer types as the target domain for UDA in nuclei instance segmentation and classification task. As used in their paper, we use labeled CoNSep and the first split of PanNuke for training, second split for validation, and third split for testing. We focused on the instance segmentation task and didn't use classification labels for training. We use HoverNet as the backbone encoder-decoder network with MI maximization module included in the nuclei segmentation branch. We report Dice Score, Aggregate Jaccard Index (AJI), Panoptic Quality (PQ), Detection Quality (DQ), and Segmentation Quality (SQ) for comparison.

All experiments are carried out in PyTorch using 1 A100 GPU for nuclei semantic segmentation and 4 A100 GPUs for nuclei instance segmentation. For the nuclei semantic segmentation experiment, we train the model for 1000 iterations using only segmentation loss and 9000 iterations with both segmentation and MI maximization loss. We use a batch size of 4, Adam optimizer with a learning rate of 1e−3, and rotation augmentation. We randomly pair labeled source images with unlabeled target images during the MI maximization step. For nuclei instance segmentation experiment, we follow the training details provided in [27] and [7]. We extend our approach only for nuclei instance segmentation and will focus on classification in our future work. First, we freeze the encoder and train the decoder for 50 epochs, with the first 10 epochs only using segmentation loss and the subsequent 40 epochs using both segmentation and MI loss. Then we unfreeze and train the whole network for 50 epochs with both losses. We use a batch size of 16 and Adam optimizer with a learning rate of 1e−4.

Table 2. Nuclei instance segmentation results for UDA from CoNSep to PanNuke.

Method	Dice	AJI	DQ	SQ	PQ
Source only	0.576	0.387	0.461	0.657	0.342
GRL [6]	0.723	0.509	0.587	0.756	0.450
Paul et al. [19]	0.731	0.501	0.600	0.751	0.446
Yang et al. [27]	0.740	0.516	0.602	0.753	0.460
MaNi	0.735	0.534	0.621	0.742	0.477

4.2 Evaluation

Nuclei Semantic Segmentation - Table 1 compares our approach with recently proposed approaches for UDA for nuclei semantic segmentation[1]. MaNi outperforms all other approaches for both TNBC to KIRC/TCIA shift and TCIA to KIRC/TNBC shift. The next best performing approach proposed in [15] uses multiple components consisting of a discriminator and a reconstruction network, consistency regularization between perturbed target images, and post-processing with CRF. While MaNi only uses the MI maximization module with segmentation loss for training, reducing the complexity of the architecture. We attribute high gains to the MI module's ability to transfer nuclei segmentation knowledge from labeled source pixels to pseudo-labeled target pixels.

Nuclei Instance Segmentation - Results for UDA in nuclei instance segmentation from CoNSep data to PanNuke data is reported in Table 2[2]. MaNi performs competitively to the best performing approach. MaNi demonstrates superior performance over PQ, DQ, and AJI, highlighting that our approach can detect and segment more nuclei accurately and suffers less from the issue of false negatives. While in terms of SQ and Dice Score, MaNi is competitive to other approaches (Table 4).

Table 3. Impact of MI loss weight.

Source domain	TNBC	TCIA
Target domain	TCIA	TNBC
1	0.776	0.821
0.1	0.769	0.765
0.01	0.751	0.765

Table 4. Impact of type of MI loss.

Source domain	TNBC	TCIA
Target domain	TCIA	TNBC
Mean-pooling	0.776	0.821
Max-pooling	0.751	0.817
Random pixels	0.771	0.809

---

[1] Other approach results reported using best self-implementation.
[2] Other approach results reported from [27].

4.3   Ablation Studies

We study the impact of different weightage on the MI loss for training. As shown in Table 3, the default choice of 1 performs best. The impact of MI loss dilutes with reduction in weight, leading to a drop in performance. Further, we study how replacing the average pooling approach with the max-pooling approach or sampling random pixels approach (N = 4), as done in [3], impacts performance. Average pooling performs superior to other approaches.

5   Conclusion

In this paper, we propose a JSD-based MI loss for UDA for Nuclei Semantic Segmentation and Instance Segmentation. We perform comprehensive experiments with different architecture - UNet and HoverNet and for different cancer-type domain shifts - TNBC to TCIA/KIRC, TCIA to KIRC/TNBC, and CoNSep to PanNuke. We highlight that our method leads to gain for both semantic segmentation and instance segmentation. We plan to extend this approach for nuclei classification tasks and subsequently to general imaging tasks in our future work.

Acknowledgements. This work was supported by NIDDK of the National Institutes of Health under award number K23DK117061-01A1 and Litwin IBD Pioneers Award of the Crohn's & Colitis Foundation.

References

1. Alonso, I., Sabater, A., Ferstl, D., Montesano, L., Murillo, A.C.: Semi-supervised semantic segmentation with pixel-level contrastive learning from a class-wise memory bank. In: Proceedings of the IEEE/CVF International Conference on Computer Vision, pp. 8219–8228 (2021)
2. Chaitanya, K., Erdil, E., Karani, N., Konukoglu, E.: Contrastive learning of global and local features for medical image segmentation with limited annotations. Adv. Neural Inf. Process. Syst. **33**, 12546–12558 (2020)
3. Chaitanya, K., Erdil, E., Karani, N., Konukoglu, E.: Local contrastive loss with pseudo-label based self-training for semi-supervised medical image segmentation. arXiv preprint arXiv:2112.09645 (2021)
4. Dong, N., Kampffmeyer, M., Liang, X., Wang, Z., Dai, W., Xing, E.: Unsupervised domain adaptation for automatic estimation of cardiothoracic ratio. In: Frangi, A.F., Schnabel, J.A., Davatzikos, C., Alberola-López, C., Fichtinger, G. (eds.) MICCAI 2018. LNCS, vol. 11071, pp. 544–552. Springer, Cham (2018). https://doi.org/10.1007/978-3-030-00934-2_61
5. Gamper, J., Alemi Koohbanani, N., Benet, K., Khuram, A., Rajpoot, N.: PanNuke: an open pan-cancer histology dataset for nuclei instance segmentation and classification. In: Reyes-Aldasoro, C.C., Janowczyk, A., Veta, M., Bankhead, P., Sirinukunwattana, K. (eds.) ECDP 2019. LNCS, vol. 11435, pp. 11–19. Springer, Cham (2019). https://doi.org/10.1007/978-3-030-23937-4_2
6. Ganin, Y., Lempitsky, V.: Unsupervised domain adaptation by backpropagation. In: International Conference on Machine Learning, pp. 1180–1189. PMLR (2015)

7. Graham, S., et al.: HoVer-Net: simultaneous segmentation and classification of nuclei in multi-tissue histology images. Med. Image Anal. **58**, 101563 (2019)
8. Guan, H., Liu, M.: Domain adaptation for medical image analysis: a survey. IEEE Trans. Biomed. Eng. **69**(3), 1173–1185 (2021)
9. Haq, M.M., Huang, J.: Adversarial domain adaptation for cell segmentation. In: Medical Imaging with Deep Learning, pp. 277–287. PMLR (2020)
10. Hjelm, R.D., et al.: Learning deep representations by mutual information estimation and maximization. arXiv preprint arXiv:1808.06670 (2018)
11. Hoffman, J., et al.: CyCADA: cycle-consistent adversarial domain adaptation. In: International Conference on Machine Learning, pp. 1989–1998. PMLR (2018)
12. Hou, L., et al.: Dataset of segmented nuclei in hematoxylin and eosin stained histopathology images of ten cancer types. Sci. Data **7**(1), 1–12 (2020)
13. Hu, X., Zeng, D., Xu, X., Shi, Y.: Semi-supervised contrastive learning for label-efficient medical image segmentation. In: de Bruijne, M., Cattin, P.C., Cotin, S., Padoy, N., Speidel, S., Zheng, Y., Essert, C. (eds.) MICCAI 2021. LNCS, vol. 12902, pp. 481–490. Springer, Cham (2021). https://doi.org/10.1007/978-3-030-87196-3_45
14. Irshad, H., et al.: Crowdsourcing image annotation for nucleus detection and segmentation in computational pathology. In: Pacific Symposium on Biocomputing Co-Chairs, pp. 294–305. World Scientific (2014)
15. Li, C., Zhou, Y., Shi, T., Wu, Y., Yang, M., Li, Z.: Unsupervised domain adaptation for the histopathological cell segmentation through self-ensembling. In: MICCAI Workshop on Computational Pathology, pp. 151–158. PMLR (2021)
16. Liu, D., et al.: PDAM: a panoptic-level feature alignment framework for unsupervised domain adaptive instance segmentation in microscopy images. IEEE Trans. Med. Imaging **40**(1), 154–165 (2020)
17. Luo, Y., Zheng, L., Guan, T., Yu, J., Yang, Y.: Taking a closer look at domain shift: Category-level adversaries for semantics consistent domain adaptation. In: Proceedings of the IEEE/CVF Conference on Computer Vision and Pattern Recognition, pp. 2507–2516 (2019)
18. Naylor, P., Laé, M., Reyal, F., Walter, T.: Segmentation of nuclei in histopathology images by deep regression of the distance map. IEEE Trans. Med. Imaging **38**(2), 448–459 (2018)
19. Paul, S., Tsai, Y.-H., Schulter, S., Roy-Chowdhury, A.K., Chandraker, M.: Domain adaptive semantic segmentation using weak labels. In: Vedaldi, A., Bischof, H., Brox, T., Frahm, J.-M. (eds.) ECCV 2020. LNCS, vol. 12354, pp. 571–587. Springer, Cham (2020). https://doi.org/10.1007/978-3-030-58545-7_33
20. Peng, J., Pedersoli, M., Desrosiers, C.: Boosting semi-supervised image segmentation with global and local mutual information regularization. arXiv preprint arXiv:2103.04813 (2021)
21. Ronneberger, O., Fischer, P., Brox, T.: U-Net: convolutional networks for biomedical image segmentation. In: Navab, N., Hornegger, J., Wells, W.M., Frangi, A.F. (eds.) MICCAI 2015. LNCS, vol. 9351, pp. 234–241. Springer, Cham (2015). https://doi.org/10.1007/978-3-319-24574-4_28
22. Shrivastava, A., Selvaraju, R.R., Naik, N., Ordonez, V.: CLIP-Lite: information efficient visual representation learning from textual annotations. arXiv preprint arXiv:2112.07133 (2021)
23. Tsai, Y.H., Sohn, K., Schulter, S., Chandraker, M.: Domain adaptation for structured output via discriminative patch representations. In: Proceedings of the IEEE/CVF International Conference on Computer Vision, pp. 1456–1465 (2019)

24. Vu, T.H., Jain, H., Bucher, M., Cord, M., Pérez, P.: ADVENT: adversarial entropy minimization for domain adaptation in semantic segmentation. In: Proceedings of the IEEE/CVF Conference on Computer Vision and Pattern Recognition, pp. 2517–2526 (2019)
25. Wang, W., Zhou, T., Yu, F., Dai, J., Konukoglu, E., Van Gool, L.: Exploring cross-image pixel contrast for semantic segmentation. In: Proceedings of the IEEE/CVF International Conference on Computer Vision, pp. 7303–7313 (2021)
26. Yang, J., et al.: An adversarial perturbation oriented domain adaptation approach for semantic segmentation. In: Proceedings of the AAAI Conference on Artificial Intelligence, vol. 34, pp. 12613–12620 (2020)
27. Yang, S., Zhang, J., Huang, J., Lovell, B.C., Han, X.: Minimizing labeling cost for nuclei instance segmentation and classification with cross-domain images and weak labels. In: Proceedings of the AAAI Conference on Artificial Intelligence, vol. 35, pp. 697–705 (2021)
28. Zhang, P., Zhang, B., Zhang, T., Chen, D., Wang, Y., Wen, F.: Prototypical pseudo label denoising and target structure learning for domain adaptive semantic segmentation. In: Proceedings of the IEEE/CVF Conference on Computer Vision and Pattern Recognition, pp. 12414–12424 (2021)
29. Zhang, Q., Zhang, J., Liu, W., Tao, D.: Category anchor-guided unsupervised domain adaptation for semantic segmentation. In: Advances in Neural Information Processing Systems 32 (2019)
30. Zou, Y., Yu, Z., Vijaya Kumar, B.V.K., Wang, J.: Unsupervised domain adaptation for semantic segmentation via class-balanced self-training. In: Ferrari, V., Hebert, M., Sminchisescu, C., Weiss, Y. (eds.) ECCV 2018. LNCS, vol. 11207, pp. 297–313. Springer, Cham (2018). https://doi.org/10.1007/978-3-030-01219-9_18
31. Zou, Y., Yu, Z., Liu, X., Kumar, B., Wang, J.: Confidence regularized self-training. In: Proceedings of the IEEE/CVF International Conference on Computer Vision, pp. 5982–5991 (2019)

Region-Guided CycleGANs for Stain Transfer in Whole Slide Images

Joseph Boyd[1]([✉]), Irène Villa[2], Marie-Christine Mathieu[2], Eric Deutsch[2], Nikos Paragios[3], Maria Vakalopoulou[1], and Stergios Christodoulidis[1]

[1] MICS Laboratory, CentraleSupélec, Université Paris-Saclay,
91190 Gif-sur-Yvette, France
{joseph.boyd,maria.vakalopoulou,
stergios.christodoulidis}@centralesupelec.fr
[2] Gustave Roussy Cancer Campus, 94800 Villejuif, France
{irene.villa,marie-Christine.mathieu,eric.deutsch}@gustaveroussy.fr
[3] Therapanacea, 75014 Paris, France
n.paragios@therapanacea.eu

Abstract. In whole slide imaging, commonly used staining techniques based on hematoxylin and eosin (H&E) and immunohistochemistry (IHC) stains accentuate different aspects of the tissue landscape. In the case of detecting metastases, IHC provides a distinct readout that is readily interpretable by pathologists. IHC, however, is a more expensive approach and not available at all medical centers. Virtually generating IHC images from H&E using deep neural networks thus becomes an attractive alternative. Deep generative models such as CycleGANs learn a semantically-consistent mapping between two image domains, while emulating the textural properties of each domain. They are therefore a suitable choice for stain transfer applications. However, they remain fully unsupervised, and possess no mechanism for enforcing biological consistency in stain transfer. In this paper, we propose an extension to CycleGANs in the form of a region of interest discriminator. This allows the CycleGAN to learn from unpaired datasets where, in addition, there is a partial annotation of objects for which one wishes to enforce consistency. We present a use case on whole slide images, where an IHC stain provides an experimentally generated signal for metastatic cells. We demonstrate the superiority of our approach over prior art in stain transfer on histopathology tiles over two datasets. Our code and model are available at https://github.com/jcboyd/miccai2022-roigan.

Keywords: Stain transfer · CycleGANs · Region-based discriminator

M. Vakalopoulou and S. Christodoulidis—These authors contributed equally to this work.

Supplementary Information The online version contains supplementary material available at https://doi.org/10.1007/978-3-031-16434-7_35.

1 Introduction

The use of histopathological whole slide images (WSI) is considered the gold standard for the diagnosis and prognosis of cancer patients. These slides contain biopsies of pathological tissue from patients and are typically stained in order to highlight different tissue structures. One of the most common tissue staining protocols is hematoxylin and eosin staining (H&E), sometimes augmented with saffron (HES) (Fig. 1a). Under the H&E protocol, the hematoxylin component stains cell nuclei with a purple-blue color, while the eosin component stains the extracellular matrix and cytoplasm in pink [20]. Another common staining is based on immunohistochemistry (IHC) (Fig. 1b). This staining involves the process of selectively identifying proteins in cells and highlighting them using a chromogen. One of the most common IHC stains is based on hematoxylin together with the diaminobenzidine (DAB) chromogen forming an H-DAB stain. Under this protocol, different staining configurations can be used, targeting different cell proteins (e.g., Ki67, HER2, hormone receptors). The resulting stained tissue can provide a distinct readout, for example with AE1/AE3, in which DAB localises on cancer cell membranes. In the case of breast cancer, the presence of metastatic cells in the axillary lymph nodes can greatly affect the prognosis of a patient. Lymph node status, assessed through the WSI inspection of dissected sentinel or axillary lymph nodes, is therefore a crucial diagnostic readout. In cases where the diagnosis is difficult to make (e.g. micro-metastasis or isolated tumor cells) IHC-stained slides that highlight cancer cells are necessary.

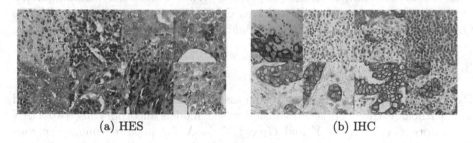

(a) HES   (b) IHC

Fig. 1. Stain transfer translates between unpaired HES (a) and IHC (b) tiles (Gustave Roussy dataset). Cancer cells visible in IHC by the golden DAB stain.

With the recent advances in deep learning, there is a growing interest in automatically processing digitised slides. We present a methodology to computationally transfer from H&E to IHC WSIs. Our main contribution is a region-based discriminator network within a CycleGAN framework, which utilises automatically extracted regions of interest to improve stain localisation. Unlike fully supervised schemes, our method learns from unpaired H&E and IHC slides and produces a stain transfer that can serve as a soft segmentation for metastasis detection. Experiments on two datasets illustrate the success of our method, while demonstrating that baseline models are unable to reliably localise the DAB stain and, consequently, cancer cells. To the best of our knowledge, this is the first work to propose such a region-guided CycleGAN, as well as the first to provide robust models for stain transfer on the WSI level. Synthesised IHC slides show the potential of our method as a clinical visualisation tool, as well as in metastasis segmentation pipelines for diagnosis.

2 Related Work

Generative adversarial networks (GANs) are a popular family of generative models in histopathology image analysis [21]. Various types of GANs have been applied to histopathology images for stain transfer [22], stain normalisation [1,2,18], cell segmentation [7], data augmentation [4] and representation learning [3]. A widely used variant of GANs are image-to-image translation networks, such as pix2pix [23], which learns to translate between image *pairs*, and CycleGANs [9], which relax the pairing assumption to enable *unpaired* and fully unsupervised image-to-image translation. CycleGANs have been used for stain transfer before, notably in [22], which augments the CycleGAN training criterion with additional priors, so as to guide an otherwise unsupervised model.

Region of interest (RoI) information is one possible enrichment to a generative learning task, in conjunction with attention mechanisms. In [19], a CoGAN-inspired setup [14] is used for joint generation of global and RoI images. In [17], pedestrians are edited into predefined scenes using pix2pix, with spatial pyramid pooling in the discriminator for direct scrutiny. Pre-trained R-CNN object detection systems have been used to propose regions during GAN training in [8], or as a feature extractor in object-driven GANs [12]. In contrast, we modify the GAN discriminator itself, and leverage automatically derived RoI data.

3 Method

CycleGANs [23] lend themselves to the task of stain transfer between unpaired histopathology tiles. These are unsupervised models incorporating two GAN generators, $G_{XY} : X \rightarrow Y$ and $G_{YX} : Y \rightarrow X$ for *unpaired* image domains X and Y. In an application of stain transfer between two stains, each stain represents a different domain. Although both generators are trained, in our case only one direction of transfer is desired (HES $\rightarrow$ IHC), and the other generator may be discarded after training. CycleGAN training is performed according to,

$$\min_{G_{XY}, G_{YX}} \max_{D_X, D_Y} \mathcal{L}_{CG} = \mathcal{L}_{GAN}(D_Y, G, X, Y) + \mathcal{L}_{GAN}(G_{XY}, D_Y, X, Y) \quad (1)$$

$$+ \lambda_{CYC}\mathcal{L}_{CYC}(G_{XY}, G_{YX}, X, Y) + \lambda_{ID}\mathcal{L}_{ID}(G_{XY}, G_{YX}, X, Y),$$

which combines least squares adversarial losses [16] $\mathcal{L}_{GAN}$, with PatchGAN discriminators D_X and D_Y, along with a cycle-consistency loss $\mathcal{L}_{CYC}$ to maintain pixel-wise consistency back and forth between domains, identity function losses $\mathcal{L}_{ID}$ for stability, and λ_{CYC} and λ_{ID} are hand-tuned weights.

3.1 Region of Interest Discrimination

Image photo-realism is enforced in a CycleGAN by a "PatchGAN" discriminator,

$$D_{patch} : X \rightarrow \{0,1\}^{h \times w}, \tag{2}$$

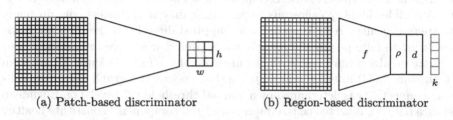

(a) Patch-based discriminator   (b) Region-based discriminator

Fig. 2. Conventional PatchGAN discriminates over a regular grid of overlapping receptive fields (a) while a region-based discriminator may discriminate an image on arbitrarily-sized regions (b).

which consists of a sequence of strided convolutions producing a $h \times w$ grid of outputs, with each grid element discriminating an overlapping patch of the inputs, as in Fig. 2a. The output grid is compared element-wise with a grid of ground truth labels. As will be quantified in Sect. 5, this purely unsupervised, standard CycleGAN setup fails to correctly localise DAB in a stain transfer application. This motivates a new type of discriminator, based on region of interest discrimination via a region of interest alignment (RoIAlign) layer. The RoIAlign layer was originally proposed in the Mask R-CNN object detection system [5], and is a generalisation of the classical MaxPool layer, and a way of quantising regions of activation maps of arbitrary size into a standardised dimension. Our proposed RoI discriminator consists of feature extraction layers f followed by a RoIAlign layer ρ, and a final discrimination layer d, as shown in Fig. 2b. We formalise it as,

$$D_{roi} : X \times B \rightarrow \{0,1\}^{k}, \tag{3}$$

for image domain X and bounding box domain B, where k is the number of bounding boxes. The adversarial loss thus becomes,

$$\mathcal{L}_{ROI}(G, D_{roi}, X, Y) = \frac{1}{2}\mathbb{E}_{\mathbf{x} \in X}[(D_{roi}(\mathbf{x}, \mathcal{B}(\mathbf{x}))-1)^2] + \frac{1}{2}\mathbb{E}_{\mathbf{y} \in Y}[D_{roi}(G(\mathbf{y}), \mathcal{B}(\mathbf{y}))^2] \tag{4}$$

that is, a least squares adversarial loss, where the operator $\mathcal{B}$ returns the set of bounding boxes of an image, provided by a previously generated object library. A pair of RoI discriminators (one for each domain) can then be trained alongside–or instead of–the PatchGAN discriminators (see Appendix A).

3.2   Library Generation for Region-Based Discrimination

To train our proposed region-based discriminator, we build a bounding box library by localising cancer and normal cells using an automatic image processing pipeline (see Appendix B). All input tiles (see Sect. 4) are first decomposed into their hematoxylin-eosin-DAB components. The expert annotations available for H&E slides identify cancerous regions that may nevertheless contain many interspersed healthy cells. Blob detection applied directly on the HES images is thus prone to false positives, precisely when precision is more important to our downstream algorithm than recall. To mitigate this effect, we apply a Laplacian of Gaussian (LoG) filter ($\sigma = \{1, 2\}$). We then construct a graph of healthy cells where connectivity is determined by a manual threshold (25 pixels) on Euclidean distance between detected cells. Graph connected components constitute healthy cell clusters, and the convex hull of each cluster is zeroed-out of the expert annotation. In a final step, a second pass of blob detection ($\sigma = \{10, \ldots, 12\}$) is applied to detect the larger, dimmer cancer cells in the unmasked regions. In the case of IHC tiles, we instead perform an Otsu threshold on the DAB channel to isolate the cancerous sub-regions. Cancer cell nuclei feature as elliptical discontinuities in the binarised DAB stain, and can again be detected using a LoG filter ($\sigma = \{7, \ldots, 10\}$). Smaller blobs ($\sigma = \{1, \ldots, 3\}$) outside the segmented region are taken to be normal cells. The library, consisting of over 100k cell bounding boxes, is then used for the training of the RoI discriminator.

3.3   Implementation and Training Details

In each experiment, the two CycleGAN generators follow the architecture of a baseline approach [22], itself based on a network proposed for style transfer [10]. The tile inputs are of size 256×256 with three (RGB) channels. The generators consist first of strided convolutions to lower the resolution. A sequence of residual blocks [6] of tunable length is then applied. We benchmark 6 and 9 residual blocks. Following this, fractionally-strided convolutions restore the input resolution. The PatchGAN discriminators consist of a standard sequence of five strided convolutions and an output layer. This reduces the input to a 8×8 patch-wise prediction. This architecture, hereafter referred to as CycleGAN 8×8, in reference to the discriminator output size, is trained according to Eq. 1. The baselines and proposed model are all modifications of this core baseline.

Given that our proposed discriminators have a selective receptive field, we control for the receptive field size of the PatchGAN discriminators by modifying the stride of their convolutions. We modify the stride of the first layer from 2 to 1 in baseline CycleGAN 16×16, doubling the patch output size, and the first two layers in baseline CycleGAN 32×32, doubling again. We also implement the conditional CycleGAN model [22]. This introduces two additional networks of its own, which are used to classify tiles in each domain. Here, Eq. 1 is supplemented with classification and cycle classification losses for the new networks, as well as novel photo-realism and structural similarity losses. Exceptionally, due to the speed and memory constraints of the photo-realism loss, we train this baseline with batch size 2. In addition, we test a plain conditional CycleGAN without these additional losses.

For our proposed model, the RoI discriminator resembles the PatchGAN, with four stride-2 feature convolutions f, followed by a RoIAlign layer ρ, and a final discrimination layer d. Without loss of generality, we restrict cell bounding box dimension to 48×48, centered on the library nuclei. Although the cell populations in each tile are often imbalanced, we sample balanced numbers of positives and negatives with replacement, whenever available, equaling $k = 8$ bounding boxes per tile, and we skip tiles containing no library cells. All model weights are randomly initialised and all models use the Adam optimiser [11] with maximum learning rate 2-e4 and $(\beta_0, \beta_1) = (0.5, 0.999)$. Models were trained for 20 epochs with a batch size of 8 randomly sampled tiles, consuming roughly two hours of processing time per model on an NVIDIA Tesla V100 GPU.

4 Datasets

To benchmark our method, we conducted experiments on two breast cancer datasets. One dataset was provided by the Gustave Roussy (GR) Institute consisting of 205 WSIs, corresponding to sentinel lymph node sections for patients of breast cancer. Each lymph node was imaged with both HES and cytokeratin AE1/AE3 IHC. Although the two stainings are performed on closely situated sections of tissue, the lack of precise alignment implies an unpaired image dataset. Metastatic regions of the HES slides were annotated with bounding contours by two expert pathologists. The dataset comprises cases of micro- and macro-metastases (resp. 0.2 mm–2 mm and ≥ 2 mm tumours), as well as negative cases. Non-overlapping tiles of size 256×256 pixels were extracted at a magnification of 20x from the segmented tissue regions of WSIs using CLAM [15]. For HES slides, the expert annotation is used to extract balanced samples of positive (metastatic tissue) and negative (normal tissue) tiles whereas, for IHC, the thresholded DAB stain substitutes as an experimentally-generated annotation.

CAMELYON16 [13] consists of 1399 hematoxylin-eosin-stained (H&E) slides. Among these, 111 slides were annotated in a fashion similar to the GR dataset. We processed and sampled tiles from these slides in the same way, yielding a dataset of 12000 tiles. Note that this dataset features a slightly different imaging modality, and furthermore contains no IHC slides. Nevertheless, we found that IHC tiles from the GR dataset were fully compatible with CAMELYON16 during model training (provided the imaging magnification), demonstrating that one can combine datasets of different origin for stain transfer.

5 Experimental Results

5.1 Tile-Level Quantitative Results

Our primary means of evaluating model performance is with the expert H&E annotations. This provides a good first approximation to the locations of the

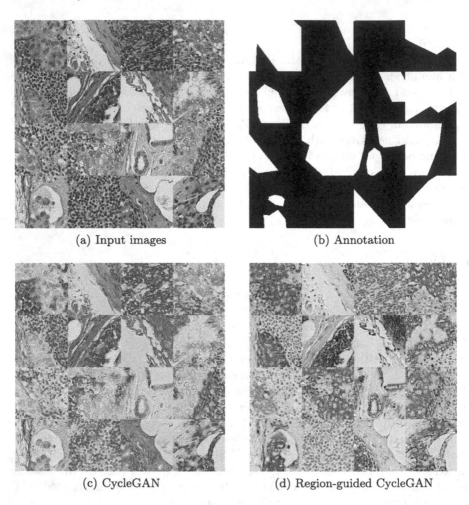

(a) Input images   (b) Annotation

(c) CycleGAN   (d) Region-guided CycleGAN

Fig. 3. Sample H&E tiles from the GR dataset (a); with corresponding ground truth annotation masks (b); baseline CycleGAN stain transfer (c); and proposed region-guided stain transfer (d).

cancer cells, and where the DAB should appear once the stain transfer has been performed, even though annotation contours often bisect healthy tissue regions or otherwise contain normal cells. For each of our trained generators, we first produce the IHC stain for each of a set of 500 held-out test H&E tiles. We visualise samples of these in Fig. 3 for both the proposed model and the baseline CycleGAN 8 × 8, alongside the annotation. One may observe the accuracy of our proposed model in localising the DAB stain. Although we observe a weak correlation between positive tiles and the presence of DAB, the baseline CycleGAN systematically misplaces the DAB stain. This localisation problem was observed across all competing models. We hypothesise our proposed model profits from the object-level supervision, with our proposed RoI discriminator performing discrimination directly centered on cells.

In pursuing a quantitative evaluation, we obtain a binary mask for each synthesised DAB stain in the same manner as was performed in Sect. 3.2 for real IHC tiles. This mask is then compared with the ground truth annotation by DICE similarity and balanced accuracy (BAC), and we report the mean and standard deviation for each metric across all test tiles in Table 1. We emphasise the ground truth is approximate, as it is intended to capture metastatic regions at a macro level, and often does not exclude healthy sub-regions. For each model, we select the best performing instance in a grid search over the number of generator residual blocks $(6, 9)$, and $\lambda_{cyc} = \{1, 10, 30\}$. Models generally performed better with 6 residual blocks, and with the standard $\lambda_{CYC} = 10$. Our proposed model performs significantly better for $\lambda_{CYC} = 30$, however, seemingly to compensate for the weight of the additional discriminators. We nevertheless note the superiority of our proposed model over all baselines, with 0.536 DICE and 0.634 BAC on the GR dataset, and 0.533 DICE and 0.615 BAC on CAMELYON16. Among the baselines, we observe that changing the discriminator outputs (16×16 and 8×8) can have a positive effect on BAC, but ultimately falls short on DICE. On the other hand, the conditional CycleGANs do not show improvement over the plain baselines. Finally, we observe that our high performance is sustained on CAMELYON16, even though in the absence of a IHC data, GR IHC tiles, of different clinical origin, were used as surrogate.

Table 1. DICE similarity and balanced accuracy (BAC) for all baselines and proposed model for GR dataset and CAMELYON16. Each entry reads mean ± std. Best results in bold.

Model	GR Dataset		CAMEYLON16	
	DICE	BAC	DICE	BAC
CycleGAN (8×8)	0.442 ± 0.370	0.490 ± 0.103	0.415 ± 0.372	0.501 ± 0.091
CycleGAN (16×16)	0.365 ± 0.330	0.520 ± 0.125	0.388 ± 0.349	0.502 ± 0.091
CycleGAN (32×32)	0.384 ± 0.324	0.511 ± 0.130	0.403 ± 0.358	0.503 ± 0.100
Conditional CycleGAN	0.341 ± 0.328	0.488 ± 0.120	0.412 ± 0.366	0.501 ± 0.100
Xu et al. (2019) [22]	0.325 ± 0.310	0.474 ± 0.107	0.260 ± 0.257	0.498 ± 0.115
Proposed	$\mathbf{0.536 \pm 0.360}$	$\mathbf{0.634 \pm 0.221}$	$\mathbf{0.533 \pm 0.371}$	$\mathbf{0.615 \pm 0.197}$

5.2   Slide-Level Qualitative Results

We further explore the capabilities of our method by generating whole slide outputs, as shown for a macrometastatic case (Appendix C, Fig. 3a, b, and c) and negative case (Appendix C, Fig. 3d, e, and f) from the GR dataset. One may observe that the HES and IHC ground truth slides are unregistered. Here, the model is applied tile-by-tile and the outputs are recombined to produce slide thumbnails. Inference times were 22 s for Appendix C Fig. 3b and 14 s for Appendix C Fig. 3e. We observe the overall consistency of our model outputs with the IHC ground truth. However, false positives, indicated by misplaced DAB signal, remain a problem for our model, and attenuating these will be the subject of future work. Surprisingly, though these test slides belong to the GR dataset, we found the model trained on CAMELYON16 data produced outputs (pictured) at least comparable to those from the GR model, indicating a readily transferable method.

6 Discussion

In this paper we have demonstrated a systematic localisation problem with unsupervised CycleGANs for stain transfer in histopathology tiles, and proposed an improved method using a region-based discriminator, leveraging a library of cell interest regions. We have further shown how datasets of different clinical origin may be successfully combined for learning stain transfer models. The proposed pipeline is a semi-automatic means for extracting additional supervision "for free", greatly improving the unsupervised baseline. Although for H&E data, we still rely on an expert annotation, our experiments revealed exciting possibilities for further automation. Firstly, due to a parsimonious design (only assumptions about cell size and clustering are made), the library building pipeline was equally applicable to both datasets and would likely generalise to others. Secondly, we found datasets could be combined and that a model trained on CAMELYON16 H&E transfers well to the GR dataset. In the latter case, only annotations from CAMELYON16 have been used, implying reusability of a library once computed on CAMELYON16, a free resource.

Acknowledgments. This work was partially supported by the ANR Hagnodice ANR-21-CE45-0007 and ARC SIGNIT201801286. Experiments have been conducted using HPC resources from the "Mésocentre" computing center of CentraleSupélec and École Normale Supérieure Paris-Saclay supported by CNRS and Région Île-de-France.

References

1. de Bel, T., Hermsen, M., Kers, J., van der Laak, J., Litjens, G.: Stain-transforming cycle-consistent generative adversarial networks for improved segmentation of renal histopathology. In: International Conference on Medical Imaging with Deep Learning-Full Paper Track (2018)
2. BenTaieb, A., Hamarneh, G.: Adversarial stain transfer for histopathology image analysis. IEEE Trans. Med. Imaging **37**(3), 792–802 (2017)
3. Boyd, J., Liashuha, M., Deutsch, E., Paragios, N., Christodoulidis, S., Vakalopoulou, M.: Self-supervised representation learning using visual field expansion on digital pathology. In: Proceedings of the IEEE/CVF International Conference on Computer Vision, pp. 639–647 (2021)
4. Claudio Quiros, A., Murray-Smith, R., Yuan, K.: Pathologygan: learning deep representations of cancer tissue. J. Mach. Learn. Biomed. Imaging **2021**(4), 1–48 (2021)
5. He, K., Gkioxari, G., Dollár, P., Girshick, R.: Mask r-CNN. In: Proceedings of the IEEE international conference on computer vision, pp. 2961–2969 (2017)

6. He, K., Zhang, X., Ren, S., Sun, J.: Deep residual learning for image recognition. In: Proceedings of the IEEE Conference on Computer Vision and Pattern Recognition, pp. 770–778 (2016)
7. Hou, L., Agarwal, A., Samaras, D., Kurc, T.M., Gupta, R.R., Saltz, J.H.: Robust histopathology image analysis: to label or to synthesize? In: Proceedings of the IEEE/CVF Conference on Computer Vision and Pattern Recognition, pp. 8533–8542 (2019)
8. Huang, W., Xu, Y., Oppermann, I.: Realistic image generation using region-phrase attention. arXiv preprint arXiv:1902.05395 (2019)
9. Isola, P., Zhu, J.Y., Zhou, T., Efros, A.A.: Image-to-image translation with conditional adversarial networks. In: Proceedings of the IEEE Conference on Computer Vision and Pattern Recognition, pp. 1125–1134 (2017)
10. Johnson, J., Alahi, A., Fei-Fei, L.: Perceptual losses for real-time style transfer and super-resolution. In: Leibe, B., Matas, J., Sebe, N., Welling, M. (eds.) ECCV 2016. LNCS, vol. 9906, pp. 694–711. Springer, Cham (2016). https://doi.org/10.1007/978-3-319-46475-6_43
11. Kingma, D.P., Ba, J.: Adam: A method for stochastic optimization. arXiv preprint arXiv:1412.6980 (2014)
12. Li, W., et al.: Object-driven text-to-image synthesis via adversarial training. In: Proceedings of the IEEE Conference on Computer Vision and Pattern Recognition, pp. 12174–12182 (2019)
13. Litjens, G., et al.: 1399 h&e-stained sentinel lymph node sections of breast cancer patients: the camelyon dataset. GigaScience 7(6), giy065 (2018)
14. Liu, M.Y., Tuzel, O.: Coupled generative adversarial networks. In: Advances in Neural Information Processing Systems, pp. 469–477 (2016)
15. Lu, M.Y., Williamson, D.F., Chen, T.Y., Chen, R.J., Barbieri, M., Mahmood, F.: Data-efficient and weakly supervised computational pathology on whole-slide images. Nat. Biomed. Eng. 5(6), 555–570 (2021)
16. Mao, X., Li, Q., Xie, H., Lau, R.Y., Wang, Z., Paul Smolley, S.: Least squares generative adversarial networks. In: Proceedings of the IEEE International Conference on Computer Vision, pp. 2794–2802 (2017)
17. Ouyang, X., Cheng, Y., Jiang, Y., Li, C.L., Zhou, P.: Pedestrian-synthesis-gan: generating pedestrian data in real scene and beyond. arXiv preprint arXiv:1804.02047 (2018)
18. Rana, A., Yauney, G., Lowe, A., Shah, P.: Computational histological staining and destaining of prostate core biopsy RGB images with generative adversarial neural networks. In: 2018 17th IEEE International Conference on Machine Learning and Applications (ICMLA), pp. 828–834. IEEE (2018)
19. Savioli, N., Vieira, M.S., Lamata, P., Montana, G.: A generative adversarial model for right ventricle segmentation. arXiv preprint arXiv:1810.03969 (2018)
20. Suvarna, K.S., Layton, C., Bancroft, J.D.: Bancroft's Theory and Practice of Histological Techniques E-Book. Elsevier Health Sciences (2018)
21. Tschuchnig, M.E., Oostingh, G.J., Gadermayr, M.: Generative adversarial networks in digital pathology: a survey on trends and future potential. Patterns 1(6), 100089 (2020)
22. Xu, Z., Moro, C.F., Bozóky, B., Zhang, Q.: Gan-based virtual re-staining: a promising solution for whole slide image analysis. arXiv preprint arXiv:1901.04059 (2019)
23. Zhu, J.Y., Park, T., Isola, P., Efros, A.A.: Unpaired image-to-image translation using cycle-consistent adversarial networks. In: Proceedings of the IEEE International Conference on Computer Vision, pp. 2223–2232 (2017)

Uncertainty Aware Sampling Framework of Weak-Label Learning for Histology Image Classification

Asmaa Aljuhani[1] , Ishya Casukhela[1] , Jany Chan[1] , David Liebner[4] ,
and Raghu Machiraju[1,2,3(✉)]

[1] Department of Computer Science and Engineering, The Ohio State University,
Columbus, OH, USA
{Aljuhani.2,Casukhela.4,Chan.206,Machiraju.1}@osu.edu
[2] Department of Biomedical Informatics, The Ohio State University
College of Medicine, Columbus, OH, USA
[3] Department of Pathology, The Ohio State University College of Medicine,
Columbus, OH, USA
[4] Division of Medical Oncology, Department of Internal Medicine, The Ohio State
University, Columbus, OH, USA
David.liebner@osumc.edu

Abstract. Advances in digital pathology and deep learning have
enabled robust disease classification, better diagnosis, and prognosis. In
real-world settings, readily available and inexpensive image-level labels
from pathology reports are weak, which seriously degrades the performance of deep learning models. Weak image-level labels do not represent the complexity and heterogeneity of the analyzed WSIs. This
work presents an importance-based sampling framework for robust
histopathology image analysis, Uncertainty-Aware Sampling Framework
(UASF). Our experiments demonstrate the effectiveness of UASF when
used to grade a highly heterogeneous subtype of soft tissue sarcomas.
Furthermore, our proposed model achieves better accuracy when compared to the baseline models by sampling the most relevant tiles.

Keywords: Histopathology image analysis · Uncertainty estimation ·
Weak label learning · Noisy label detection

1 Introduction

Whole slide images (WSI) are increasingly used in pathology labs for diagnosing
and monitoring diseases, including cancer. Diagnosis of WSI-level labels can be
obtained from clinical data which are readily available from patient records.
However, associated WSIs are very large, and there is limited notation as to

Supplementary Information The online version contains supplementary material
available at https://doi.org/10.1007/978-3-031-16434-7_36.

which regions within them explain the WSI-level diagnosed label. More often than not, a WSI with an accorded label includes several regions associated with other labels of diagnostic severity, as well as normal tissue and other artifacts as shown in Fig. 1. This incongruence is even more remarkable for certain complex cancers, like soft tissue sarcomas (STS) which are a rare group of aggressive cancers that account for one percent of the overall malignant tumors in adults. They are highly heterogeneous with more than 89 subtypes. Each subtype is manifested by distinct histological, molecular, and specific clinical characteristics [7], which poses significant challenges to pathologists in terms of annotation effort and accuracy.

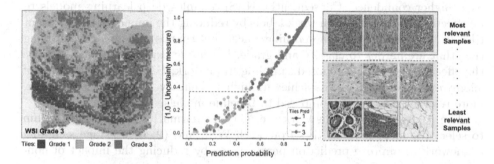

Fig. 1. Left: Example of a grade 3 WSI showing various tiles predicted as different grades that may not reflect the WSI-level label. **Middle:** Distribution of tiles based on estimated prediction probabilities and uncertainty measures. Solid box contains tiles associated with high predictive confidence and low uncertainty. Dashed-line box contains tiles with low predictive confidence and high uncertainty. **Right:** Most relevant samples are associated with the assigned WSI-level grade. The least relevant samples consist of non-tumor regions, tissue artifacts, or different grades than the assigned WSI-label.

The current gold standard for diagnosis of STS cases relies on a pathologist-assigned tumor grade using the French National Federation of Cancer Centers (FNCLCC) system [24]. Pathologists visually inspect H&E stained tissue under a high-power microscope to determine cancerous regions while avoiding non-relevant regions and other artifacts. A diagnosis grade $1-3$ (3 being most severe, 1 being the least) is then assigned by the aggregate score of tumor differentiation, necrosis, and mitotic rate.

Deep learning, particularly weakly supervised learning approaches that utilize only WSI-level labels, has had success with handling segmentation and classification [3,17,21]. These methodologies, however, depend on several thousands of WSIs to achieve performance comparable to supervised approaches. Promising results have been reported by assigning the same WSI-level label to all tiles (often square regions) [10]. However, not all tiles are equally representative of the assigned WSI label, generating noisy training labels that degrade the performance of deep learning models. Consequently, errors in diagnoses in addition to noise from pre-processing will accumulate and hinder the inferential and predictive performance of models. A reliable approach to identify relevant tiles from a large WSI has to be accurate and ideally provide a measure of uncertainty for its prediction. Uncertainty measures estimated by Bayesian neural networks [11] can not only identify samples that are hard to classify but can also detect samples that deviate from the data used for training the model.

This work presents an importance-based sampling framework on weak labels, which we name the Uncertainty-Aware Sampling Framework (UASF). This framework combines recent advances in Bayesian deep learning and weakly supervised techniques to systematically identify the most diagnostically relevant tiles of a WSI by estimating prediction uncertainty and retaining tiles with higher confidence. Consequently, UASF enables deep learning models to be effective when training on weak labels by reducing the impact of non-relevant tiles in the training set. The ensuing uncertainty maps also guide identifying tiles that are harder to classify and grade. Extensive experiments demonstrate the effectiveness of the proposed sampling framework, UASF, on the grading of leiomyosarcoma (LMS) WSIs achieving higher accuracy by sampling a smaller, more relevant subset tiles compared to baseline models.

The contributions of this work are: (1) an informative sampling algorithm to select the most relevant tiles from each WSI; and (2) a two-stage sampling framework to improve prediction performance by reducing the impact of non-relevant tiles.

The rest of the paper is organized as follows. Section 2 reviews the related work on deep learning with noisy labels. Section 3 details the proposed framework, USAF, while Sect. 4 presents the experimental results. Finally, Sect. 5 concludes this work.

2   Related Work

Recent studies have investigated various approaches to reduce the negative impact of label noise of prediction tasks [18]. Sampling-based methods focus on identifying and either relabeling or discarding samples with corrupted labels. A recent study by Naik et al. [20], followed a random sampling approach by selecting random tiles from each WSI to predict estrogen receptor status. Bilal et al. [2] presented a method that requires a tumor detection model to identify tumor tiles relevant as samples from a given WSI. Another approach proposed by Yao et al. [26] requires tiles to be sampled from generated clusters obtained from the application of the K-means algorithm for tissue morphology. The performance of this class of methods relies on sufficiently large datasets for the sampling technique to capture informative (relevant) tiles associated with the weak WSI-level label.

Model-based methods focus on model selection, loss functions, or training processes that are more robust to label noise. Ghosh et al. [14] showed that the mean absolute value of error (MAE) is tolerant of label noise in segmentation tasks. For classification tasks, the symmetric cross-entropy (SCE) loss [25] was proposed by combining reverse cross-entropy (RCE) together with the cross-entropy measure to overcome the risk of training error associated with weak labels: $L_{SCE} = L_{CE} + L_{RCE}$.

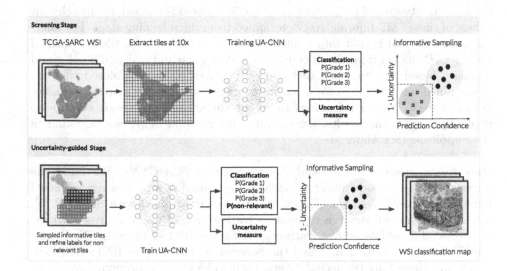

Fig. 2. Overview of the proposed Uncertainty-Aware Sampling Framework (UASF) for learning with weak labels. **Screening Stage:** screening model first predicts tile-level labels with corresponding uncertainties. Then, an informative sampling is performed to identify the most relevant tiles. **Uncertainty-guided Stage**: uncertainty-guided model trained on the refined training dataset.

Despite the success of CNN architectures, it is infeasible to quantify their uncertainty given the deterministic nature associated with their parameters. To address this limitation, Bayesian machine learning approaches have been employed to estimate the uncertainty associated with each prediction [19]. Gal and Ghahramani [12] showed that combining dropout regularization proposed by Srivastava et al. [22] with Bayesian modeling can derive uncertainty estimates in deep learning classification tasks. Thiagarajan et al. [23] proposed a Bayesian CNN (BCNN) to facilitate interpretation, visualization, and performance evaluation based on a predetermined uncertainty threshold for breast cancer images. However, BCNNs are computationally expensive compared to CNNs. Furthermore, a fixed threshold may not work for all WSIs in a collection. Given the tissue heterogeneity for WSIs, there is a need to optimize the uncertainty threshold for each WSI.

3   Methods

Uncertainty-Aware Sampling Framework (UASF): Inspired by the workflow of pathologists, our proposed two-stage framework is visualized in Fig. 2. In the first screening stage, training tiles (LMS-All) are provided to the Uncertainty Aware Convolutional Neural Network (UA-CNN) classifier (see below). Upon successful training, we perform the informative sampling algorithm (see below) to identify the most relevant tiles predictive of their WSI-level label. Then, in the uncertainty-guided stage, another UA-CNN model is trained on the relevant subset of tiles (LMS-Informative) determined from the screening stage. For inference, a given WSI is split into a set of smaller-sized tiles. Each tile is classified by UA-CNN model from the uncertainty-guided stage and assigned a color and intensity based on predicted label and uncertainty measure. Colored tiles are reassembled into a WSI to form an uncertainty classification map, so pathologists can make informed decisions to accept the automated classification or to manually inspect the results. Uncertainty classification maps can be found in the Supplementary Materials.

Uncertainty-Aware Convolutional Neural Network (UA-CNN): We build the uncertainty-aware model using a backbone composed of a previously published implementation of Resnet18 (RN18) [16] that is pre-trained with SimCLR [5], a framework for self-supervising contrastive learning of visual representations, on a total of 57 unlabeled histopathology datasets (RN18-HistoSSL) [8]. To create UA-CNN, we further modified the network architecture of RN18-HistoSSL by adding three fully connected layers, each followed by a dropout layer. The dropout layers are used to prevent overfitting [22], which in turn, allows us to apply Monte Carlo (MC) dropout during testing to obtain uncertainty estimation. In the baseline models, indicated by "RN18-HistoSSL+L" in Table 1, we remove the uncertainty estimation by deactivating these dropout layers at inference.

Monte Carlo (MC) Dropout: We adopted MC dropout [12] (dropout rate = 0.5) during inferencing in order to estimate uncertainties associated with neural network outputs. We perform variational inference for a given tile, leading to a collection of T different predictions. In our models, we used $T=10$. The final prediction for a sample is computed as the average of the variational predictions, providing a robust classification.

Predictive Entropy: Predictive entropy is a measure of the uncertainty of the model's predictive density function for the variational inference of each sample. It measures both epistemic uncertainty, i.e., uncertainty measure based on the underlying model, and aleatoric uncertainty, i.e., uncertainty based on the underlying noise in the data [11]. It is defined as: $H[P(y^*|x, D)] = -\sum_{c=1}^{C} P(y^* = c|x, D) \log P(y^* = c|x, D)$ where C is the total number of classes and $P(y^* = c|x, D)$ is the output softmax probability for input x belonging to class c. A higher entropy indicates that the model is less confident about its prediction and vice versa.

Loss Function: Robust loss functions are essential for training an accurate CNN in the presence of ambiguity and noisy labels. The reviewed loss functions in Sect. 2 assume that labels are mutually exclusive and do not account for the ordinal nature of the grading labels in our problem. If a model predicted a sample **grade 3** instead of **grade 1**, it should penalize more than if predicted **grade 2**. The Ordinal Regression (OR) loss function was introduced to adapt a traditional neural network to learn ordinal labels [6]. Each class output node O_c uses a standard sigmoid function $\sigma(z) = \frac{1}{1+e^{-z}}$ without the input from other class nodes. Thus, a sample x is predicted as class c if the output prediction is $O = (1, ..., 1, 0, ..., 0)$, in which the first c elements is 1 and the remaining are assigned 0. To evaluate the effectiveness of state-of-the-art loss functions for reducing the negative impact of label noise, we compare UA-CNN performance trained on the cross-entropy loss L_{CE} (baseline), symmetric cross-entropy loss L_{SCE}, and ordinal regression loss L_{OR}. Results are shown in Table 1.

Informative Sampling Algorithm: Figure 4(a) shows a plot of the uncertainty and prediction probability for the entirety of the training data. We first assume that the most relevant tiles have the same accorded label of the given WSI with high confidence, implying high prediction probability (found from the overall model) and low uncertainty (found from the variational Monte-Carlo inference). We model uncertainty using a quadratic function of prediction confidence for each WSI. Our next goal is to identify a threshold that allows the selection of the most relevant tiles with respect to the tile distribution of a WSI.

A straightforward approach is to set a hard threshold. Yet, given tissue heterogeneity, the variability of tile distribution makes it difficult to set fixed thresholds for all WSIs. Thus, it will be useful to select a threshold of the prediction probability and uncertainty measure that maximizes the number of true predicted tiles (tile labels matching WSI-level label) and minimizes the number of false predicted tiles (tile labels not matching WSI-level label). Two factors dictate the level of the optimal threshold for each WSI: (i) the overall uncertainty measure of the WSI samples and (ii) the variability of tile predictions. Let us note that this method is not practical to apply on the entire training data set because minority classes tend to show higher measures of uncertainty compared to majority classes, which leads to biased sampling.

To find the best trade-off between representative and non-representative tiles for each WSI, we compute the difference between the true predicted rate (TPR) and false predicted rate (FPR) at each threshold γ. We determine the optimal threshold by identifying the minimum of γ as shown in Fig. 3. (1 - *min*) was plotted for easily interpretable visualizations. We examine this informative sampling qualitatively in Fig. 3 and quantitatively in Table 1, which demonstrates the effectiveness of the informative policy as an indicator for relevant samples. A detailed pseudocode algorithm can be found in the Supplementary Materials.

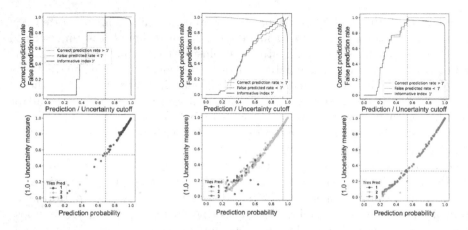

Fig. 3. Examples of identifying representative tiles for 3 WSIs across the three grades with the informative sampling algorithm. **Top row:** Determine the optimal threshold between the true predicted rate (TPR) and the false predicted rate (FPR) which provides the best trade-off between prediction probability and uncertainty. **Bottom row:** By using the determined threshold, we can isolate and sample the tiles that are truly representative of the WSI grade.

4   Experiments

Dataset: Our experiments employs the data collections from the Cancer Genome Atlas (TCGA). We especially consider 85 H&E stained WSIs of subjects diagnosed with leiomyosarcoma (LMS). This collection also consists of clinical data obtained from a comprehensive study of adult subjects [1]. Each WSI is assigned a grade label based on the FNCLCC grading system [15]. **Grade 1** counts 12 WSIs, **grade 2** counts 58 WSIs, while **grade 3** counts 15 WSIs. It is important to note that although the LMS cohort represents a single subtype, there is a wide range of variability in morphological structures due to different anatomic origins of tissue. To examine the generalizability of our proposed framework, we utilized 121 WSIs with tumor and non-tumor labels from the National Cancer Institute's Clinical Proteomic Tumor Analysis Consortium (CPTAC) database to predict whether a WSI has tumor or non-tumor regions.

Experimental Set Up: We perform three-fold cross-validation experiments. For each experiment, the dataset is randomly partitioned into a training set (80% of cases), validation set (10% of cases), and test set (10% of cases). For each fold, the model's performance on the validation set is monitored during training and used for hyper-parametric regularization while the test set is held out until the end of training to evaluate the model.

Implementation Details: All slides are preprocessed for tissue segmentation using the HistomicsTK API [9]. WSIs are sectioned into 256×256 px tiles at $10\times$ magnification level, giving a total number of 1.5M tiles. We adopt accuracy, precision, recall, and F1-score metrics as the evaluation criteria for predicting grade. We compare the performance of a baseline model, which is built on a Resnet18 backbone pre-trained on histological images (i.e., HistoSSL) and then trained on all training samples (LMS-All), to our UA-CNN model, which is the baseline with the dropout layers activated for variational inference and trained on relevant training samples (LMS-Informative). We keep the validation and testing sets identical in those experiments. The training takes 100 epochs with an early stop if the minimum validation loss did not improve for 15 epochs. The inference time for a WSI is highly affected by the variational inference parameter T. For $T = 10$, it takes 4 minutes to generate an uncertainty map for a single WSI on an NVIDIA Tesla P100 (Pascal) GPU. We utilized the Ohio Supercomputer Center [4] to run our experiments. The two-stage UASF framework is implemented in PyTorch and available as open-source code on Github: https://github.com/machiraju-lab/UA-CNN.

4.1 Results

The stated objectives of this work are two-fold: (i) effective identification of disease-representative tiles using informative sampling algorithm and (ii) enhanced prediction performance using an uncertainty-aware model trained on representative tiles. We report on how we effectively achieve both objectives.

Effectiveness of Informative Sampling Analysis: Figure 4(b) shows the uncertainty vs. prediction probability of informative sampled tiles. When representative tiles were isolated from non-representative tiles, all three grades improved in mean certainty, $(1.0 - uncertainty)$. To verify that UASF was able to identify diagnostically representative tiles, a subset of WSIs were annotated by pathologists into tumor and non-tumor regions. The UA-CNN assigned an uncertainty measure to tiles extracted from tumor and non-tumor regions. A paired two-sample $t - test$ was performed to compare the mean uncertainty measure of tumor tiles and non-tumor tiles. There was a significant difference in the uncertainty measure between tumor and non-tumor tiles; $t(47815) = -36.07$, $\alpha = 0.05$, $p - value < .001$, which further confirms the robustness of the informative policy (α denotes the level of significance).

Effectiveness of UASF: The performance comparison between models trained on the LMS-All and LMS-Informative datasets (see Sect. 3), ensured that the informative sampling technique was producing superior results by identifying disease-representative tiles. Table 1 demonstrates the effectiveness of UASF on the leiomyosarcoma (LMS) histological subtype grading task, achieving 83% accuracy as a result of filtering out 30% of samples as non-informative, which is a 12% relative improvement compared to the baseline scenario trained on all samples. When comparing performance across the different loss functions, UA-CNN models trained on LMS-Informative significantly outperformed their respective baseline model trained on LMS-All. Notably, OR loss outperformed SCE loss for LMS-Informative experiments. OR is not as robust as SEC at first, but when trained on clean labels, it can learn the monotonic property of the ordinal labels [13]. We use randomly selected samples from each WSI as a control group to demonstrate the importance and effectiveness of determining relevant samples to a WSI. All of the above-mentioned experiments were evaluated on the same validation and testing data for a fair comparison.

Table 1. Results of the proposed Uncertainty-Aware Sampling Framework compared to Ciga et al. [8] architecture on LMS dataset.

Network Architecture	Training Data	Accuracy	Precision	Recall	F1-score
RN18-HistoSSL+L_{CE}	LMS-ALL	0.70 ± 0.01	0.63 ± 0.01	0.70 ± 0.01	0.66 ± 0.01
RN18-HistoSSL+L_{SCE} [25]	LMS-ALL	0.72 ± 0.003	0.62 ± 0.01	0.72 ± 0.01	0.65 ± 0.01
RN18-HistoSSL+L_{OR} [6]	LMS-ALL	0.71 ± 0.001	0.61 ± 0.01	0.72 ± 0.01	0.65 ± 0.01
UASF+L_{CE}	LMS-ALL/Informative	0.72 ± 0.03	0.65 ± 0.03	0.72 ± 0.03	0.68 ± 0.03
UASF+L_{SCE}	LMS-ALL/Informative	0.77 ± 0.01	0.66 ± 0.04	0.77 ± 0.01	0.69 ± 0.01
UASF+L_{OR}	LMS-ALL/Informative	$\mathbf{0.83 \pm 0.09}$	$\mathbf{0.75 \pm 0.10}$	$\mathbf{0.83 \pm 0.09}$	$\mathbf{0.77 \pm 0.10}$
UASF	Random	0.57 ± 0.13	0.66 ± 0.02	0.57 ± 0.13	0.60 ± 0.08

Generalization of UASF: We applied the UA-CNN trained on LMS-Informative on the CPTAC dataset to verify the generalizability of UASF to predict the tumor and non-tumor regions of a WSI. We adapted our three grade classes to represent tumor tiles and a non-relevant class to represent non-tumor tiles. The WSI-level label was assigned to tiles based on the weighted majority of informative tiles in a given WSI. Our model that was not explicitly trained on tumor detection could classify WSIs into tumor vs. normal WSI with 87% accuracy (F1-score: 0.91 (normal), 0.76 (tumor)). The ability of UA-CNN to generalize offers the potential of handling "unseen" histopathology images, thereby facilitating its future use especially since fewer expert annotations are required. Please refer to the Supplementary section for more details on results pertaining to the generalization.

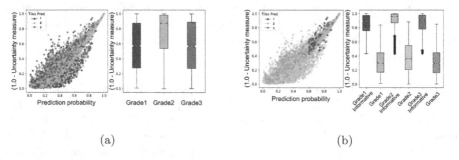

(a)   (b)

Fig. 4. (a) Distribution of certainty $(1 - Uncertainty)$ vs. prediction probability of all samples. **Grade 1** and **grade 3** exhibit high variability in uncertainty, whereas, **grade 2** has the least amount, given the higher number of samples. (b) Distribution of tiles after isolating tiles deemed relevant based on informative index. All grades improved in mean certainty once informative tiles are identified (opaque), in comparison to tiles deemed irrelevant (light)

5   Conclusion

This work proposed a two-stage Uncertainty-Aware Sampling Framework, UASF, to improve prediction performance of convolution neural networks for histopathology images by sampling the most relevant tiles and reducing the adverse impact of non-relevant tiles of a whole slide image. The framework utilized the model's uncertainty to determine a threshold at which disease-relevant regions would be prioritized. As a result, we achieved better performance by only sampling the most relevant training tiles, whereas the performance of the baseline models are degraded by irrelevant tiles and artifacts.

Acknowledgments. The results shown here are in whole or part based upon data generated by the TCGA Research Network: cancer.gov/tcga.

References

1. Abeshouse, A.A., Adebamowo, C., Adebamowo, S.N., et al.: Comprehensive and integrated genomic characterization of adult soft tissue sarcomas. Cell 950.e28–965.e28 (2017)
2. Bilal, M., et al.: Development and validation of a weakly supervised deep learning framework to predict the status of molecular pathways and key mutations in colorectal cancer from routine histology images: a retrospective study. The Lancet. Digital Health (2021)
3. Campanella, G., et al.: Clinical-grade computational pathology using weakly supervised deep learning on whole slide images. Nat. Med. 1–9 (2019)
4. Center, O.S.: Ohio Supercomputer Center (1987). http://osc.edu/ark:/19495/f5s1ph73
5. Chen, T., Kornblith, S., Norouzi, M., Hinton, G.E.: A simple framework for contrastive learning of visual representations. arXiv preprint arXiv:2002.05709 (2020)
6. Cheng, J., Wang, Z., Pollastri, G.: A neural network approach to ordinal regression. In: 2008 IEEE International Joint Conference on Neural Networks (IEEE World Congress on Computational Intelligence), pp. 1279–1284 (2008)
7. Choi, J., Ro, J.: The 2020 who classification of tumors of soft tissue: selected changes and new entities. Adv. Anatom. Pathol. 28, 44–58 (2020)
8. Ciga, O., Martel, A.L., Xu, T.: Self supervised contrastive learning for digital histopathology. arXiv preprint arXiv:2011.13971 (2020)
9. Cooper, L.: Histomicstk: developing an open-sourced platform for integrated histopathology analysis (2017)
10. Coudray, N., et al.: Classification and mutation prediction from non-small cell lung cancer histopathology images using deep learning. Nat. Med. 24, 1559–1567 (2018)
11. Gal, Y.: Uncertainty in deep learning (2016)
12. Gal, Y., Ghahramani, Z.: Dropout as a Bayesian approximation: representing model uncertainty in deep learning. arXiv preprint arXiv:1506.02142 (2016)
13. Garg, B., Manwani, N.: Robust deep ordinal regression under label noise. arXiv preprint arXiv:1912.03488 (2019)
14. Ghosh, A., Kumar, H., Sastry, P.S.: Robust loss functions under label noise for deep neural networks. In: AAAI (2017)
15. Hasegawa, T., et al.: Validity and reproducibility of histologic diagnosis and grading for adult soft-tissue sarcomas. Human Pathol. 111–115 (2002)

16. He, K., Zhang, X., Ren, S., Sun, J.: Deep residual learning for image recognition. In: 2016 IEEE Conference on Computer Vision and Pattern Recognition (CVPR), pp. 770–778 (2016)
17. Ianni, J.D., et al.: Tailored for real-world: a whole slide image classification system validated on uncurated multi-site data emulating the prospective pathology workload. Sci. Rep. **10** (2020)
18. Karimi, D., Dou, H., Warfield, S., Gholipour, A.: Deep learning with noisy labels: exploring techniques and remedies in medical image analysis. Med. Image Anal. **65**, 101759 (2020)
19. Kuleshov, V., Fenner, N., Ermon, S.: Accurate uncertainties for deep learning using calibrated regression. arXiv preprint arXiv:1807.00263 (2018)
20. Naik, N., et al.: Deep learning-enabled breast cancer hormonal receptor status determination from base-level h&e stains. Nat. Commun. **11** (2020)
21. Schmauch, B., et al.: A deep learning model to predict RNA-seq expression of tumours from whole slide images. Nat. Commun. **11** (2020)
22. Srivastava, N., Hinton, G.E., Krizhevsky, A., Sutskever, I., Salakhutdinov, R.: Dropout: a simple way to prevent neural networks from overfitting. J. Mach. Learn. Res. **15**, 1929–1958 (2014)
23. Thiagarajan, P., Khairnar, P., Ghosh, S.: Explanation and use of uncertainty quantified by Bayesian neural network classifiers for breast histopathology images. IEEE Trans. Med. Imaging **41**, 815–825 (2022)
24. Trojani, M., et al.: Soft-tissue sarcomas of adults; study of pathological prognostic variables and definition of a histopathological grading system. Int. J. Cancer **33** (1984)
25. Wang, Y., Ma, X., Chen, Z., Luo, Y., Yi, J., Bailey, J.: Symmetric cross entropy for robust learning with noisy labels. In: 2019 IEEE/CVF International Conference on Computer Vision (ICCV), pp. 322–330 (2019)
26. Yao, J., Zhu, X., Jonnagaddala, J., Hawkins, N., Huang, J.: Whole slide images based cancer survival prediction using attention guided deep multiple instance learning networks. Med. Image Anal. **65**, 101789 (2020)

Local Attention Graph-Based Transformer for Multi-target Genetic Alteration Prediction

Daniel Reisenbüchler[1,2]([✉]), Sophia J. Wagner[1,2], Melanie Boxberg[3], and Tingying Peng[2]

[1] Technical University Munich, Munich, Germany
[2] Helmholtz AI, Neuherberg, Germany
reisenbuechler@helmholtz-muenchen.de
[3] Institute of Pathology Munich-North, Munich, Germany

Abstract. Classical multiple instance learning (MIL) methods are often based on the identical and independent distributed assumption between instances, hence neglecting the potentially rich contextual information beyond individual entities. On the other hand, Transformers with global self-attention modules have been proposed to model the interdependencies among all instances. However, in this paper we question: Is global relation modeling using self-attention necessary, or can we appropriately restrict self-attention calculations to local regimes in large-scale whole slide images (WSIs)? We propose a general-purpose local attention graph-based Transformer for MIL (LA-MIL), introducing an inductive bias by explicitly contextualizing instances in adaptive local regimes of arbitrary size. Additionally, an efficiently adapted loss function enables our approach to learn expressive WSI embeddings for the joint analysis of multiple biomarkers. We demonstrate that LA-MIL achieves state-of-the-art results in mutation prediction for gastrointestinal cancer, outperforming existing models on important biomarkers such as microsatellite instability for colorectal cancer. Our findings suggest that local self-attention sufficiently models dependencies on par with global modules. Our LA-MIL implementation is available at https://github.com/agentdr1/LA_MIL.

Keywords: Multiple instance learning · Graph transformer · Local attention · Whole slide images · Mutation prediction

1 Introduction

Advances in slide-scanning microscopes and deep learning-based image analysis have significantly increased interest in computational pathology [2]. Whole slide images typically contain billions of pixels and reach up to several gigabytes in size. To mitigate the resulting computational burden, WSIs are commonly

Supplementary Information The online version contains supplementary material available at https://doi.org/10.1007/978-3-031-16434-7_37.

tessellated into smaller tiles [16]. However, patient diagnosis is typically only available as weakly-supervised slide-level annotation, e.g., cancer vs. non-cancer classification, cancer subtyping, or genomic analyses.

In histopathological image analysis, this task is formulated as multiple instance learning (MIL), where a WSI is considered as a bag, and tiles as contained instances. Hence, efficiently learning representations and aggregating them from tiles to a bag label is crucial. One simple solution for this is to pass the bag label onto each tile, reducing MIL to supervised learning. This approach is particularly favored because of its ease of implementation, e.g., to predict microsatellite instability or tumor mutational burden [10,22]. The final bag-level prediction is obtained by aggregating all instance-level predictions with average pooling. These methods have two drawbacks: (i) a fraction of instance labels may differ from the bag label and therefore form label noise in supervised learning, and (ii) no morphological or spatial correlation between tiles is taken into account.

To remedy (i), MIL can learn from bag-level annotation without assuming the same label for each tile. In particular, Ilse et al. [8] propose an attention-based pooling layer aiming to weight each tile individually for its relevance within the bag prediction task. To tackle (ii), recently, convolutional neural networks (CNNs) were combined with self-attention-based Transformers [21]. Here, the tiles are condensed into feature vectors and subsequently the resulting sequence is fed into a Transformer, where the interdependence between tiles is incorporated by self-attention mechanisms. For instance, Li et al. [11] propose a deformable Transformer-based encoder-decoder structure and evaluate it across encoder only based Transformer. Shao et al. [20] uses the Neyström method to approximate self-attention, aiming to decrease the computational complexity. Myronenko et al. [17] suggest incorporating feature vectors of different scales into an encoder-based Transformer.

However, general Transformer approaches suffer from quadratic complexity with respect to the sequence length. This complexity is a general problem across computer vision and neural language processing (NLP) domains. To alleviate this concern, Transformer using local attention in the NLP domain [15] showed that it is sufficient for a token to restrict the attention calculation to a local neighborhood inside the sequence, i.e., the surrounding words. On the other hand, in computer vision self-attention can be modified by introducing local windowed attention [12]. However, this approach for WSIs is not as conveniently applicable as for domain areas where the images have the same size, such as in well-curated datasets like ImageNet [4]. Whole slide images come with varying geometrical shapes and the representation obtained by using tiles while excluding some entities (e.g. due to artifacts, pen marks, etc.) leads to holes within the visual representation. A handcrafted selection of which entities participate in the key-to-query product is not generally applicable for all WSIs, as this would not effectively adapt to the varying local neighborhoods.

Combining the local windowed attention idea with Graph Transformer [5], we propose a computationally light training pipeline consisting of a CNN and local attention-based Transformer with the following contributions:

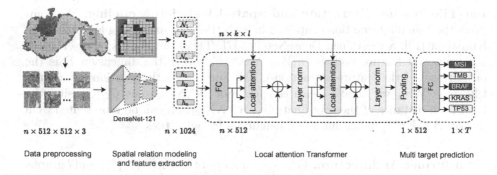

Fig. 1. LA-MIL overview: The pipeline consists of preprocessing, spatial relation modeling and feature extraction, and a local attention-based transformer.

- We present LA-MIL, a novel local attention graph-based Transformer that restricts self-attention calculations in Transformers by using k-nearest neighbor (kNN) graphs to model local regimes with respect to tiles inside the WSI.
- To our knowledge, LA-MIL is the first pipeline to predict microsatellite instability and tumor mutational burden jointly with genetic alterations as well as the first transformer-based approach for mutation prediction.
- An efficiently adapted loss function enables our approach to learn meaningful bag representations for a joint analysis of multiple imbalanced biomarkers.
- We evaluate our approach extensively on two datasets for gastrointestinal cancer and demonstrate that our local attention mechanism sufficiently leverages information on par with global self-attention modules.
- LA-MIL shows great modeling interpretability by visualizing local attention scores, consisting of spatial and morphological dependencies.

Our experiments indicate that LA-MIL outperforms state-of-the-art approaches or is on par for mutation prediction tasks in gastrointestinal cancer.

2   Method

The pipeline of our LA-MIL approach is visualized in Fig. 1. In the following, we introduce the key components of our algorithm.

2.1   LA-MIL Framework

Data Preprocessing. First, a given gigapixel WSI is tessellated into N tiles, where each tile $t_i \in \mathbb{R}^{H \times W \times C}$. Further, we extract the coordinates $c_i \in \mathbb{R}^2$ with respect to the WSI for each tile. Tiles containing background, artifacts, and non tumor-tissue are excluded using Otsu's method [18] and region of interest (RoI) annotations, reducing the number of tiles for downstream processing to $n < N$.

Per-Tile Feature Extraction and Spatial Relation Modeling. We compress the visual information contained in each tile t_i by extracting features using KimiaNet [19], a pretrained DenseNet-121 [7]. Thus, the WSI is represented as a sequence of feature vectors $\{h_i\}_{i=1}^n \in \mathbb{R}^{n \times D}$, where the dimension D is the output size of the feature extraction CNN. For the spatial relation among the tiles of a WSI, we build l k-nearest neighbor (kNN) graphs $\mathcal{G}_{kNN}^l$ using the Euclidean distance of the coordinates c_i. A kNN graph can be represented by a matrix $A \in \mathbb{R}^{n \times k}$, indicating the k neighbors for all n tiles.

Transformer Architecture. Given a sequence of features $\{h_i\}_{i=1}^n$ and l graphs $\mathcal{G}_{kNN}^l$, we further downscale the feature vectors from D to d by using a fully-connected (FC) layer. Subsequently, a Transformer with l blocks of local attention layers is applied. These layers utilize the kNN graphs to update neighboring tiles, thereby modeling local morphological and spatial correlations. Note that a graph can also be shared between layers. Applying a residual connection and layer normalization [1] after each attention layer aims to improve the gradient flow and generalization performance. Finally, the sequence is aggregated into a bag-embedding vector $b \in \mathbb{R}^d$ by mean pooling as done in [21]. Another FC layer projects the bag-embedding vector into a target vector $t \in \mathbb{R}^T$, where T is the number of targets to predict. The sigmoid function is applied element-wise on the target vector t to obtain the scores for each target individually. In the context of mutation prediction, the thresholded scores indicate whether a particular gene occurs as wildtype or mutated, respectively.

Loss Function. Mutation prediction is a challenging task since the targets often only occur in small frequencies (see Table 1). Hence, we use a loss which penalizes the model for wrong decisions about the prediction of underrepresented classes by weighting each binary cross-entropy (BCE) term individually. We take the mean of T BCE losses, thus treating each target equally:

$$L(\mathbf{x}, \mathbf{y}) = -\frac{1}{T} \sum_{t=1}^{T} \frac{n_t^{\text{neg}}}{n_t^{\text{pos}}} \left(y_t \log(\sigma(x_t)) + (1 - y_t) \log(1 - \sigma(x_t)) \right).$$

As mentioned in the introduction, most mutation prediction studies use tile-level supervised learning rather than bag-level MIL. Hence, a common strategy to tackle highly imbalanced classification is to apply downsampling to reach an equilibrium of classes in the dataset splits [9,10]. However, this may not be possible in the multi-target and bag-operating setup, as downsampling may exclude nearly all samples, depending on the individual class distributions.

2.2   Local Attention Layer

Self-attention is a key component in Transformer architectures, where each token h_i is updated with global information of the complete input sequence $\{h_1, \ldots, h_n\}$. In contrast, our local attention modules constrain the updates for

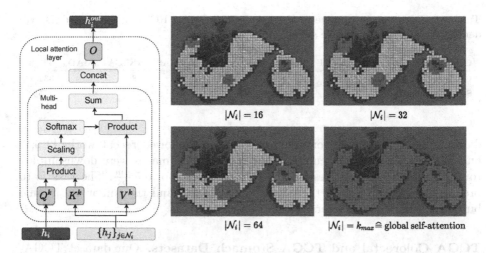

Fig. 2. Left: Computational block for a local attention layer. Right: Illustration of the spatial field of view for the attention calculations. Tiles in red visualize a query tile and blue colored tiles visualize the adaptive local neighborhoods of different sizes. (Color figure online)

each token h_i associated with node n_i to all tokens h_j with nodes $j \neq i$ that are connected with node n_i, as shown in Fig. 2. As input we consider a n-dimensional sequence of tokens h_i for $i = 1, \ldots, n$ associated with n nodes of a graph $\mathcal{G}$ where the nodes are connected by $n \times k$ edges. The update equation for token h_i is

$$h_i = O \cdot \text{Concat}_k \left(\sum_{j \in \mathcal{N}_j} w_{ij}^k V^k h_j \right), \qquad w_{i,j}^k = \text{softmax}_j \left(\frac{Q^k h_i \cdot K^k h_j}{\sqrt{d_k}} \right) \quad (1)$$

where $Q^k, K^k, V^k \in \mathbb{R}^{d_k \times d}$ and $O \in \mathbb{R}^{d \times d}$ with $k = 1, \ldots, H$ denoting the number of the respective attention head. The notation $j \in \mathcal{N}_i$ refers to a set of indices j of nodes connected to the ith node by j edges. The cardinality of $\mathcal{N}_i$ is equal to the number of neighbors for all tiles. To calculate local attention scores a_i for each tile from local attention layers, we first cache the intermediate outputs $w_{i,j}^k$ from Eq. 1 and sum them across heads and local regimes, i.e.

$$a_i = \sum_{k=1}^{H} \sum_{j \in \mathcal{N}_j} w_{i,j}^k. \quad (2)$$

Subsequently, we normalize all n attention values a_i into the range $[0, 1]$ and denote the outcomes as local attention scores for each tile.

3   Experiments

We applied the proposed method on diagnostic formalin-fixed paraffin-embedded diagnostic slides for two cohorts in The Cancer Genome Atlas (TCGA)

Table 1. Distribution of genetic alterations in TCGA-CRC and TCGA-STAD. We denote the number of positive samples for each target.

Cohort	n	MSI	TMB	BRAF	ALK	ERBB4	FBXW7	KRAS	PIK3CA	SMAD4	TP53
CRC	594	78	85	66	40	62	107	223	178	81	332
STAD	440	75	86	13	19	62	38	40	86	36	225

dataset [24]. From tissue contained in WSIs, we followed recent works [3,6,9] and include only tumor-occupied tissue regions. All images were downsampled to 20× magnification, corresponding to a resolution of $0.5 \frac{\mu m}{px}$. The task is to predict genetic alterations, the microsatellite status and the tumor mutational burden (TMB) as biomarkers [16] directly from WSIs.

TCGA Colorectal and TCGA Stomach Datasets. Our dataset TCGA-CRC consists of tiled WSIs from tumor regions of colorectal tissue. We used the preprocessed tumor tissue tiles from kather.ai. As a second dataset, we tiled WSIs of stomach tissue from TCGA, downloaded at portal.gdc.cancer.gov. After noise removal, we excluded all tiles which were not contained in the tumor region by using manual tumor annotations available at: kather.ai. We retrieved the genetic annotations matching the WSIs from xenabrowser.net. Annotations for the microsatellite stability/instability (MSS/MSI) and TMB are available at cbioportal.org. Following Luchini et al. [14], we binarized MSS and MSI-Low as MSS and MSI-High as MSI.

Implementation. Each tile was embedded into a 1024-dimensional feature space by a DenseNet-121 model that was pretrained on histopathological data. By using the coordinates of each tile, we built two kNN-Graphs with $k = 16$ and $k = 64$ for subsequent attention restriction in the first and second local attention module, respectively. In the training phase, each feature vector associated with the tiles was further compressed from 1024 to 512 by a FC layer. After a stack of two local attention layers, we averaged the feature vectors across all tiles. The resulting bag embedding was passed through a classification head, consisting of another fully connected layer from 512 to 10, to compute the logits. We applied the sigmoid activation function element-wise to calculate the probabilities for each individual target. For optimization, we employed the Lookahead optimizer [25] together with AdamW [13], and used a learning rate of 2e-05 and 2e-04 (for TCGA-CRC and TCGA-STAD, respectively) for 10 epochs, weight decay of 2e-05, and batch size 1. The LA-MIL model with 2.1M parameter was implemented in PyTorch and DGL [23], and trained on a single Tesla V100 GPU.

Evaluation. To evaluate the mutation prediction task on both datasets TCGA-CRC and TCGA-STAD, we compared the performance of LA-MIL with state-of-the-art methods. The fact that most of the recent advances predict T biomarkers individually results in training, validating, and hyperparameter tuning for T

Table 2. Mean AUROC scores for mutation prediction on the datasets TCGA-CRC and TCGA-STAD. For the competitive methods, we report results from the original publications; for our methods, we report the mean over five folds (see supplementary material for results with standard deviation).

Dataset	Method	MSI	TMB	BRAF	ALK	ERBB4	FBXW7	KRAS	PIK3CA	SMAD4	TP53
TCGA-CRC	Kather et al. [10]	0.77	–	–	–	–	–	–	–	–	–
	Wang et al. [22]	–	0.82	–	–	–	–	–	–	–	–
	Kather et al. [9]	–	–	0.66	0.51	–	0.49	0.60	**0.62**	**0.63**	**0.68**
	Fu et al. [6]	–	–	0.57	–	–	**0.66**	0.55	0.59	0.58	**0.68**
	T-MIL (Ours)	**0.85**	0.82	**0.73**	0.61	0.57	0.64	0.61	0.60	0.60	0.64
	LA-MIL (Ours)	**0.85**	**0.83**	0.72	**0.63**	**0.60**	**0.66**	**0.62**	0.61	0.58	0.63
TCGA-STAD	Kather et al. [10]	**0.81**	–	–	–	–	–	–	–	–	–
	Wang et al. [22]	–	0.75	–	–	–	–	–	–	–	–
	Kather et al. [9]	–	–	0.37	0.45	–	0.74	0.64	**0.67**	0.61	0.60
	Fu et al. [6]	–	–	–	–	–	–	–	0.47	0.49	**0.63**
	T-MIL (Ours)	0.80	**0.78**	**0.73**	0.52	0.47	0.71	0.65	0.58	0.62	0.57
	LA-MIL (Ours)	0.78	0.77	0.67	**0.52**	**0.47**	0.72	**0.70**	0.61	**0.64**	0.58

separate models, while we used a single model to predict all biomarkers. Moreover, we implemented a Transformer MIL approach where we exchanged all local attention blocks with global self-attention [21], denoted as T-MIL. To stick with common evaluation procedures for mutation prediction in recent works, we evaluated our pipeline with a 5-fold cross validation (CV). We split the datasets into folds such that individual class distributions in each fold were approximately the same and ensured that no patient appeared in the training and validation set at the same time. We measured the performance using the area under the receiver operating characteristic curve (AUROC) for each target individually.

4   Results

Current methods, such as Kather et al. [10] for MSI and Wang et al. [22] for TMB, predict the biomarkers instance-wise as single targets for each tile with the corresponding label inherited from its parent WSI. Similarly, Kather et al. [9] and Fu et al. [6] train one model for each target gene when predicting mutations, but evaluate their results on WSI-level by average pooling of tile-wise predictions. In contrast, we train and evaluate only one model on WSI-level to predict multiple biomarkers using a MIL transformer that aggregates features from all tiles with global or local self-attention layers.

Table 2 shows the AUROC scores of state-of-the-art instance-wise methods compared to our methods on the dataset TCGA-CRC. The results suggest that our models can leverage information from multiple targets to achieve better overall performance. Interestingly, this holds especially for the prediction of MSI, where our approach improves the score by 8% from 0.77 to 0.85. The prediction of TMB and most of the gene mutations (except for SMAD4 and TP53) are on par or marginally better (+1%).

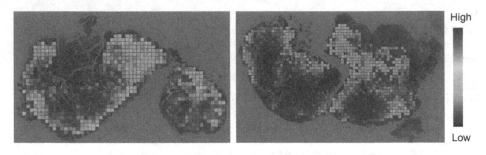

Fig. 3. Local attention scores visualization for the last local attention layer with restricted self-attention in a neighborhood of size 64.

The results for the TCGA-STAD dataset in MSI prediction are marginally worse (-1%). This could arise due to the fact that the compared work uses a slightly different label strategy for MSI-Low cases, which also affects the evaluation. The results for TMB improves by up to 3%. Similar as on the TCGA-CRC dataset, we observe an improvement of results using our Transformer-based approaches for the remaining targets except for a few genes.

Local Attention Visualization. As described in Eq. 2, we can calculate the local attention scores from the query-to-key product. In Fig. 3 we colorized the tiles according to their corresponding local attention score. The high attentive regions include the nuclear chromatin that seems to be hyperchromatic, as well as crowded glands or solid areas. Yet, to the best of our knowledge, there are no distinguishing patterns from WSI for mutated genes, which makes it difficult for a quantitative evaluation. Nevertheless, LA-MIL provides an interpretation based on the contribution of each tile for the bag-level prediction task and thus paves a way for a deeper investigation of highly scored tiles.

5   Conclusion

In this work, we proposed a novel MIL framework with local attention for WSI analysis. Local attention is achieved through a graph-based transformer that models region-wise inter-dependencies. As the size of the region can be set arbitrarily, our approach bridges the gap between instance-wise and global relation approaches by modeling local relations of arbitrary size. Moreover, an effective adapted loss enables us to learn multiple biomarkers at once, for low computational cost compared to CNN-only based methods.

However, there is often more than one WSI for a patient available in the TCGA database. Future work will investigate the strategy of combining all WSIs for a patient, while suitably scaling the coordinates for tiles of different WSIs. Thus, each tile will only be updated with local information from its direct parent WSI and transformed into a bag-embedding consisting of locally correlated tiles of all WSIs from a patient. We believe that our approach provides a base for further applications in other WSI analysis tasks where structured relation modeling is crucial.

Acknowledgements. S.J.W. was supported by the Helmholtz Association under the joint research school "Munich School for Data Science - MUDS".

References

1. Ba, J.L., Kiros, J.R., Hinton, G.E.: Layer normalization (2016). https://doi.org/10.48550/ARXIV.1607.06450
2. Cooper, L.A., Demicco, E.G., Saltz, J.H., Powell, R.T., Rao, A., Lazar, A.J.: Pan-Cancer insights from the cancer genome atlas: the pathologist's perspective. J. Pathol. **244**(5), 512–524 (2018)
3. Coudray, N., et al.: Classification and mutation prediction from non–small cell lung cancer histopathology images using deep learning. Nat. Med. **24**(10), 1559–1567 (2018)
4. Deng, J., Dong, W., Socher, R., Li, L.J., Li, K., Fei-Fei, L.: Imagenet: A large-scale hierarchical image database. In: 2009 IEEE Conference on Computer Vision and Pattern Recognition, pp. 248–255. IEEE (2009)
5. Dwivedi, V.P., Bresson, X.: A generalization of transformer networks to graphs. In: Methods and Applications, AAAI Workshop on Deep Learning on Graphs (2021)
6. Fu, Y., et al.: Pan-cancer computational histopathology reveals mutations, tumor composition and prognosis. Nat. Cancer **1**(8), 800–810 (2020). https://doi.org/10.1038/s43018-020-0085-8
7. Huang, G., Liu, Z., Pleiss, G., Van Der Maaten, L., Weinberger, K.: Convolutional networks with dense connectivity. IEEE Trans. Pattern Anal. Mach. Intell. (2019)
8. Ilse, M., Tomczak, J., Welling, M.: Attention-based deep multiple instance learning. In: Dy, J., Krause, A. (eds.) Proceedings of the 35th International Conference on Machine Learning. Proceedings of Machine Learning Research, vol. 80, pp. 2127–2136. PMLR (2018)
9. Kather, J.N., et al.: Pan-cancer image-based detection of clinically actionable genetic alterations. Nat. Cancer **1**(8), 789–799 (2020)
10. Kather, J.N., et al.: Deep learning can predict microsatellite instability directly from histology in gastrointestinal cancer. Nat. Med. **25**(7), 1054–1056 (2019)
11. Li, H., et al.: DT-MIL: deformable transformer for multi-instance learning on histopathological image. In: de Bruijne, M., et al. (eds.) MICCAI 2021. LNCS, vol. 12908, pp. 206–216. Springer, Cham (2021). https://doi.org/10.1007/978-3-030-87237-3_20
12. Liu, Z., et al.: Swin transformer: hierarchical vision transformer using shifted windows. In: International Conference on Computer Vision (ICCV) (2021)
13. Loshchilov, I., Hutter, F.: Decoupled weight decay regularization. In: 7th International Conference on Learning Representations, ICLR 2019, New Orleans, 6–9 May 2019. OpenReview.net (2019)
14. Luchini, C., et al.: ESMO recommendations on microsatellite instability testing for immunotherapy in cancer, and its relationship with PD-1/PD-l1 expression and tumour mutational burden: a systematic review-based approach. Ann. Oncol. **30**(8), 1232–1243 (2019)

15. Luong, T., Pham, H., Manning, C.D.: Effective approaches to attention-based neural machine translation. In: Proceedings of the 2015 Conference on Empirical Methods in Natural Language Processing, pp. 1412–1421. Association for Computational Linguistics, Lisbon (2015). https://doi.org/10.18653/v1/D15-1166
16. Murchan, P., et al.: Deep learning of histopathological features for the prediction of tumour molecular genetics. Diagnostics 11(8), 1406 (2021)
17. Myronenko, A., Xu, Z., Yang, D., Roth, H.R., Xu, D.: Accounting for Dependencies in Deep Learning Based Multiple Instance Learning for Whole Slide Imaging. In: de Bruijne, M., et al. (eds.) MICCAI 2021. LNCS, vol. 12908, pp. 329–338. Springer, Cham (2021). https://doi.org/10.1007/978-3-030-87237-3_32
18. Otsu, N.: A threshold selection method from gray-level histograms. IEEE Trans. Syst. Man Cybern. 9(1), 62–66 (1979). https://doi.org/10.1109/TSMC.1979.4310076
19. Riasatian, A., et al.: Fine-tuning and training of densenet for histopathology image representation using TCGA diagnostic slides. Med. Image Anal. 70, 102032 (2021)
20. Shao, Z., et al.: Transmil: transformer based correlated multiple instance learning for whole slide image classification (2021)
21. Vaswani, A., et al.: Attention is all you need. In: Guyon, I., et al. (eds.) Advances in Neural Information Processing Systems, vol. 30. Curran Associates, Inc. (2017)
22. Wang, L., Jiao, Y., Qiao, Y., Zeng, N., Yu, R.: A novel approach combined transfer learning and deep learning to predict TMB from histology image. Pattern Recogn. Lett. 135, 244–248 (2020)
23. Wang, M., et al.: Deep graph library: a graph-centric, highly-performant package for graph neural networks (2020)
24. Weinstein, J.N., et al.: The cancer genome atlas pan-cancer analysis project. Nat. Genet. 45(10), 1113–1120 (2013)
25. Zhang, M.R., Lucas, J., Hinton, G., Ba, J.: Lookahead optimizer: k steps forward, 1 step back (2019)

Incorporating Intratumoral Heterogeneity into Weakly-Supervised Deep Learning Models via Variance Pooling

Iain Carmichael[1,2], Andrew H. Song[1,2], Richard J. Chen[1,2],
Drew F. K. Williamson[1,2], Tiffany Y. Chen[1,2], and Faisal Mahmood[1,2(✉)]

[1] Department of Pathology, Brigham and Women's Hospital, Harvard Medical
School, Boston, MA, USA
{icarmichael,asong,rchen14,dwilliamson,tchen25,
faisalmahmood}@bwh.harvard.edu
[2] Department of Pathology, Massachusetts General Hospital, Harvard Medical
School, Boston, MA, USA

Abstract. Supervised learning tasks such as cancer survival prediction from gigapixel whole slide images (WSIs) are a critical challenge in computational pathology that requires modeling complex features of the tumor microenvironment. These learning tasks are often solved with deep multi-instance learning (MIL) models that do not explicitly capture intratumoral heterogeneity. We develop a novel variance pooling architecture that enables a MIL model to incorporate intratumoral heterogeneity into its predictions. Two interpretability tools based on "representative patches" are illustrated to probe the biological signals captured by these models. An empirical study with 4,479 gigapixel WSIs from the Cancer Genome Atlas shows that adding variance pooling onto MIL frameworks improves survival prediction performance for five cancer types.

Keywords: Computer vision · Computational pathology · Multiple instance learning · Intratumoral heterogeneity · Interpretability

1 Introduction

Cancer diagnosis and prognosis using *hematoxylin and eosin* (H&E) stained *whole slide images* (WSIs) are central tasks in computational pathology. These supervised learning problems are made difficult by the size and complexity of WSIs; these images can be gigapixels in scale and involve localizing subtle visual signals that expert pathologists are trained for years to identify. In recent years, weakly supervised deep learning algorithms have made significant progress in addressing some of these challenges [2, 5–7, 15, 21].

I. Carmichael and A.H. Song—These authors contributed equally.

Supplementary Information The online version contains supplementary material available at https://doi.org/10.1007/978-3-031-16434-7_38.

L. Wang et al. (Eds.): MICCAI 2022, LNCS 13432, pp. 387–397, 2022.
https://doi.org/10.1007/978-3-031-16434-7_38

Cancer cell morphology can vary greatly within a single tumor and it is increasingly recognized that *intratumoral heterogeneity* (ITH) plays an important role in prognostication for certain cancer types [1,17], though its exact role is still being elucidated. Furthermore, ITH complicates prognostication based on WSIs by increasing the range of morphologies that correspond to a particular prognosis. For example, pathologists often encounter *clear cell renal cell carcinoma* displaying significant heterogeneity within the same tumor, with some areas demonstrating classic clear cell morphology and others displaying morphologies bordering on diagnoses such as *chromophobe renal cell carcinoma* or *clear cell tubulopapillary renal cell carcinoma*.

Existing supervised algorithms that scale to WSIs do not generally incorporate histological ITH. These algorithms typically approach a supervised learning task such as survival prediction through a *multiple instance learning* (MIL) framework [11]. First, a WSI is represented as a *bag* of many smaller image patches. Next, neural network features are extracted from each patch. Finally, these patch features are aggregated for prediction. The standard MIL aggregation approaches capture only simple statistics (e.g. mean or max) and neglect higher-order information (e.g. variance), which can capture heterogeneity.

To this end, we develop a novel MIL aggregation component that scales to gigapixel WSIs and explicitly incorporates ITH into its predictions. We accomplish this through a *variance pooling* operation that quantifies ITH as the variance along a collection of low rank projections of patch features (Sect. 2.2). Moving beyond pre-specified measures of heterogeneity (e.g. the variance of tumor cell morphology), this architecture uses the data to determine how to measure heterogeneity (e.g. the projection vectors, along which the variance of the features are measured, are learned.) This operation can be seamlessly incorporated into existing MIL architectures, as we now demonstrate.

We demonstrate empirically in Sect. 3 that including this operation improves baseline MIL models' performance on survival prediction tasks across five cancer types from The Cancer Genome Atlas (TCGA). Through attention and a novel "variance projection contrast" visualization, we provide interpretable insights into what biological signals these architectures utilize to make the predictions in Sect. 4. Code: https://github.com/mahmoodlab/VARPOOL.

1.1   Related Work

Survival Analysis Using WSIs: Survival analysis in histopathology has been a longstanding problem in medical imaging. Early work required manual identification of regions of interest [10]. Other methods make use of hand-crafted tumor cell features (e.g. shape) to predict patient survival [14]. Most recent survival methods use MIL algorithms that are directly trained on WSIs without additional annotations [18,21,24,25]. Some of these methods use *graph convolutional networks* (GCNs), which learn more context-aware features [4,24].

Intratumoral Heterogeneity: Much of the previous work on ITH uses genomic data to identify and quantify subclones of tumor cells that share mutations [19]. There is growing interest in using machine learning to quantify the histologic ITH that pathologists observe on a daily basis [8].

2   Incorporating Heterogeneity with Variance Pooling

This section presents the novel variance pooling operation for weakly-supervised MIL tasks. In this setting, we observe a set of bags – an unordered collection of vectors (instances) – that we use to predict some bag level response. In computational pathology, each patient has a WSI which is used to predict the response (e.g. class label or survival outcome). Each patent's WSI[1] (the bag) is broken up into many small image patches and the instances are either the raw image patches or patch features extracted by a neural network.

We first define some notation. Suppose we have N patients. For the ith patient, we observe a response $y^{(i)}$ and a bag of instances (image patch features) $\mathcal{X}^{(i)} = \{x_1^{(i)}, \ldots, x_{n^{(i)}}^{(i)}\}$, where each $x_j^{(i)} \in \mathbb{R}^d$ and $n^{(i)}$ is the size of the bag. For classification tasks $y^{(i)}$ is a patient-level class label; for survival tasks $y^{(i)} = (t^{(i)}, c^{(i)})$ where $t^{(i)} \in \mathbb{R}_+$ is the observed survival time and $c^{(i)} \in \{0, 1\}$ indicates whether or not this time was censored. We want to learn a mapping $f(\mathcal{X}^{(i)}) = z^{(i)}$ that outputs a patient-level prediction minimizing a supervised loss function.

In the following two sections, we present the variance pool architecture in the context of the attention mean pooling model of [11]. We emphasize variance pooling can be easily incorporated into other MIL architectures. For notational simplicity we generally drop the patient superscript i.

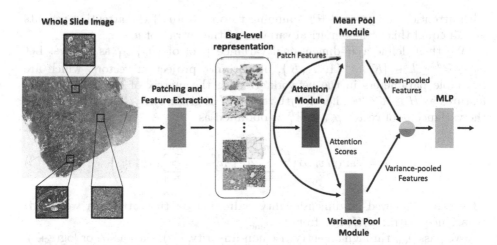

Fig. 1. Variance pooling framework. Zoomed-in WSI patches show examples of intratumoral heterogeneity, with the colonic adenocarcinoma displaying multiple moderately-to poorly-differentiated morphologies. The mean and variance pooling branches capture different statistical characteristics of the data and are aggregated to yield the final prediction.

---

[1] When a patient has multiple WSIs, the patches are unioned across the WSIs.

2.1 Attention Mean Pooling Architecture

The attention mean pool architecture of [11] reduces a bag of instances, $\{x_j\}_{j=1}^n$, to a vector through a weighted mean operation. Specifically, each instance is first passed through an (optional) encoding network, as $h_j = \phi(x_j) \in \mathbb{R}^{d_{enc}}$. The attention neural network α, takes in $\{h_j\}_{j=1}^n$ and computes the normalized attention weights $a = \alpha\left(\{h_j\}_{j=1}^n\right) \in \mathbb{R}_+^n$, which sum to 1. The attention mean pool vector p_{mean} is obtained as

$$p_{mean} = \sum_{j=1}^n a_j h_j. \tag{1}$$

Finally, the bag prediction (e.g. predicted survival risk) is obtained by passing p_{mean} through an additional multi-layer perceptron (MLP), $z = \rho(p_{mean})$.

2.2 Attention Variance Pooling

We incorporate within-bag heterogeneity (intratumoral heterogeneity) by computing the variance of learned projections of the instances. First, let us define the *attention variance function*, $\mathrm{Var}\,(\cdot\,;a) : \mathbb{R}^n \to \mathbb{R}$, of n numbers, $u \in \mathbb{R}^n$, as

$$\mathrm{Var}\,(u;a) := \sum_{j=1}^n a_j \left(u_j - \sum_{\ell=1}^n a_\ell u_\ell \right)^2 \tag{2}$$

with attention weights $a \in \mathbb{R}_+^n$ summing to one. Note, if the attention weights are all equal this is the empirical variance of the entries of u.

We then define a K-dimensional variance pool of $\{h_j\}_{j=1}^n$ as follows. Let $v_k \in \mathbb{R}^{d_{enc}}, k \in [K] := \{1, \ldots, K\}$, be variance projection vectors, which are learnable parameters in the network. Denote the matrix of encoded instance features as $H \in \mathbb{R}^{n \times d_{enc}}$, i.e. the jth row of H is given by h_j. The kth entry[2] of the variance pool vector $p_{var} \in \mathbb{R}_+^K$ is obtained as

$$p_{var,k} = \mathrm{Var}\,(Hv_k; \alpha) = \sum_{j=1}^n a_j \left(h_j^T v_k - \sum_{\ell=1}^n a_\ell h_\ell^T v_k \right)^2. \tag{3}$$

This can be viewed as dimensionality reduction on the (attention weighted) covariance matrix of H, i.e., from $O(d_{enc}^2)$ to K.

We pass p_{var} through an entrywise non-linearity, $\eta(\cdot)$, such as $\sqrt{\cdot}$ or $\log(\epsilon + \cdot)$. This non-linearity operation is required since linear combinations of several variance pools is equivalent to just a single variance pool. Finally, the first and second moment information of the attended $\{h_j\}_{j=1}^n$ are combined and the prediction is obtained by passing the concatenated mean and variance pool vector,

---

[2] Without the attention weights this would be the quadratic form $v_k^T \mathrm{cov}(H) v_k$.

$$p_{\text{cat}} = [p_{\text{mean}}; \eta(p_{\text{var}})] \in \mathbb{R}^{d_{\text{enc}}+K} \tag{4}$$

through the MLP, $z = \rho(p_{\text{cat}})$.

Figure 1 shows the entire architecture. The learnable parameters are the networks $\{\phi, \alpha, \rho\}$ and $\{v_k\}_{k=1}^{K}$. Several design choices can be modified including: no attention mechanism, separate attention mechanisms for the mean and variance pools, and different combination schemes for the mean/variance pools.

3 Experiments with Survival Prediction

Data: From the public TCGA dataset, we use: Breast Invasive Carcinoma (BRCA, $N = 1,061$), Glioblastoma & Lower Grade Glioma (GBMLGG, $N = 872$), Uterine Corpus Endometrial Carcinoma (UCEC, $N = 504$), Colon Adenocarcinoma & Rectum Adenocarcinoma (COADREAD, $N = 612$), and Bladder Urothelial Carcinoma (BLCA, $N = 386$). The choice of these types was based on the number of patients. We use *progression-free interval* (PFI) [13].

We use the concordance index (c-Index) to evaluate survival prediction models. The c-Index, which lies between 0 and 1 (larger is better), measures the agreement between predicted risk scores and actual survival outcomes using only order information (see discussion around (5) below.) We split each dataset into a 70%/30% train/test split. To ensure that our results are not sensitive to a particular data split, we randomly split the data into train/test folds 10 times.

Implementation Details: We extract $d = 1,024$ features from each WSI image patch (256×256 pixels at $20\times$ magnification) using an ImageNet-pretrained ResNet-50 CNN encoder, truncated after the third residual block and spatially averaged. We use a batch size of $B = 32$ patients[3]. To fit each mini-batch into GPU memory during training we cap–by random subsampling– the number of instances in each bag. For each cancer type, the maximum number of instances per bag is set to be the 75% quantile of the overall bag sizes (WSIs typically have $15 - 20,000$ patches). In the Supplemental information, we report the summary statistics for number of instances per WSI slide in the TCGA dataset. All patches in the bag are used at test time. We use the Adam optimizer with a learning rate of 2×10^{-4}, weight decay of 1×10^{-5}, and train for 30 epochs.

We use three MIL architectures: Deep Sets [23], Attention MeanPool [11], and DeepGraphConv [24]. For the Deep Sets framework, the attention weights are not learned and instead set to identical values of $1/n$. For the DeepGraph-Conv framework, the bag of features is first passed through two layers of graph convolutional neural network layers, the output of which are passed through the attention mean/variance pooling modules. These are some of the most popular MIL architectures used in computational pathology and thus provide great testbeds for variance pooling module extension.

---

[3] Note the patient batch size is not equal to the number of summands in (5); there are between 0 and $\binom{B}{2}$ summands depending on the number of comparable pairs.

We use $K = 10$ variance pooling projections and an $\eta(\cdot) = \log(0.01 + \cdot)$ non-linearity. We performed an internal ablation study for the nonlinearity comparing the logarithm, square root, and sigmoid functions, but did not find any significant difference in performance. We initialize the projection vectors $v_k \sim \mathcal{N}(0, 1/d_{\mathrm{enc}})$ to make them approximately orthonormal with high probability.

Loss Function: Suppose the bag prediction network, $f(\cdot)$, outputs a risk score for each patient. We train the network with the survival ranking loss [16,20], which is a continuous approximation of the negative c-Index given by

$$\mathcal{L}\left(\{\mathcal{X}^{(i)}, t^{(i)}, c^{(i)}\}_{i=1}^{N}\right) = -\frac{1}{|\mathcal{C}|} \sum_{(w,b)\in\mathcal{C}} \psi\left(f(\mathcal{X}^{(w)}) - f(\mathcal{X}^{(b)})\right), \qquad (5)$$

where $\mathcal{C} = \{(w, b) | c^{(w)} = 0 \text{ and } t^{(w)} < t^{(b)}, \text{ for } w, b \in [N]\}$ is the set of *comparable pairs* i.e. pairs of patients where we know one patient has worse survival than the other. If $\psi(\cdot) = \mathbf{1}(\cdot > 0)$ then (5) would be exactly the negative c-Index. We set $\psi(\cdot)$ to be a sigmoid, which is a differentiable approximation of this indicator.

We chose the ranking loss because it is separable, which allows the use of proper mini-batches unlike the Cox loss. Additionally, the c-Index is a natural objective for survival analysis. An alternative is the negative log-likelihood of a discrete time-to-event model [22]. This loss function coarsely bins the survival times and does not fully utilize the available survival ordering information.

Table 1. Test set c-Index performance (mean ± std) across 10 re-sampled data splits on the 100 point scale.

Frameworks	BRCA	GBMLGG	COADREAD
Deep Sets	59.5 ± 3.1	72.8 ± 1.0	50.8 ± 4.1
Deep Sets w/VarPool	$\mathbf{60.0 \pm 3.8}$	$\mathbf{73.8 \pm 0.9}$	$\mathbf{56.1 \pm 3.0}$
Attn MeanPool	59.2 ± 3.7	73.0 ± 1.2	52.0 ± 2.3
Attn MeanPool w/VarPool	$\mathbf{60.4 \pm 3.9}$	$\mathbf{73.6 \pm 1.0}$	$\mathbf{56.3 \pm 2.3}$
DeepGraphConv	57.9 ± 4.2	70.7 ± 2.3	51.4 ± 3.0
DeepGraphConv w/VarPool	$\mathbf{58.0 \pm 5.2}$	$\mathbf{70.9 \pm 2.3}$	$\mathbf{51.6 \pm 3.2}$
	BLCA	UCEC	Overall
Deep Sets	56.6 ± 5.3	51.3 ± 4.3	58.2
Deep Sets w/VarPool	$\mathbf{57.5 \pm 5.1}$	$\mathbf{54.1 \pm 3.0}$	**60.3**
Attn MeanPool	57.2 ± 5.3	50.7 ± 3.9	58.4
Attn MeanPool w/VarPool	$\mathbf{57.8 \pm 4.6}$	$\mathbf{52.5 \pm 3.7}$	**60.1**
DeepGraphConv	52.1 ± 7.7	54.2 ± 2.1	57.3
DeepGraphConv w/VarPool	$\mathbf{53.1 \pm 7.6}$	$\mathbf{55.0 \pm 2.0}$	**57.7**

Table 1 shows the results. We observe that for every cancer type and all models, the variance pooling versions outperform their counterparts, with up to 10.4% relative increase (Deep Sets for COADREAD). We conjecture that the smaller performance gain in DeepGraphConv comes from "feature smoothing" in GCNs, which reduces the heterogeneity in patch features. In the Supplemental information, we present an ablation study with the Cox loss and show that similar improvements are observed with the addition of variance pooling module.

The fact that explicitly incorporating intratumoral heterogeneity gives the greatest benefit in COADREAD and UCEC is interesting, since subsets of these tumor types have very high mutation rates due to microsatellite instability, a molecular change with impacts on survival [9,12]. This might lead to the development of multiple subclones of tumor cells that have different morphologies, as the effects of those mutations propagate from DNA to protein.

4   Interpretability and Biological Insights

This section presents two interpretability approaches to probe what biological signals the trained models learn. We focus on the Attention MeanPool and VarPool architectures, though similar approaches can be used for other architectures.

Interpretability via attention scores For each patient, we visualize the patches with the largest attention scores, i.e., the a in (1) and (3), as depicted in Fig. 2. Note that this interpretability approach is not possible for the Deep Sets framework, since the attention weights are set to be uniform.

Interpretability via variance projection scores For variance pooling, we can examine signals captured by each variance pool projection. Each projection can be viewed as sorting the patches of a WSI, the biological signal of which we aim to uncover. We project the patches onto a given projection vector and visualize the patches along the spectrum. A similar interpretability approach was taken in [3]. Following (3), for a projection vector v and jth instance, we define the *signed attention weighted squared residuals* (SAsqR) as

$$SAsqR_j = \text{sign}(r_j)a_j r_j^2, \text{ where } r_j := h_j^T v - \sum_{\ell=1}^{n} a_\ell h_\ell^T v.$$

These values can be used to sort the patches e.g. to identify the patches with the most extreme negative/positive SAsqR values.

4.1   Interpretability Visualizations

We illustrate the two interpretability tools discussed in the previous section. Our analysis outputs a large number of images based on these tools. The figures below illustrate the trends that were reviewed by two pathologists.

394   I. Carmichael et al.

Figure 2 compares the top attended patches for MeanPool and VarPool in one COADREAD patient. We observed that MeanPool attends to more compact, dense, and intact tumor with surrounding stroma, while VarPool attends to fragmented tumor, often with surrounding extracellular mucin and debris.

Figure 3 shows patches along a single variance projection for two COAD-READ patients. Figure 4 is similar for UCEC. We have sorted the patches by their SQsqR values and shown several patches for 11 quantiles: 0, 10, ..., 100. We might expect the rightmost and leftmost patches to represent visual contrast. We observe dense tumor region on one end of the spectrum and other micro-environment features, such as lymphocytes, muscle, or necrosis on the other end.

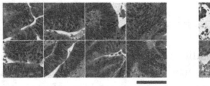 

(a) Top MeanPool patches.   (b) Top VarPool patches.

Fig. 2. The highest attended patches for the attention MeanPool and VarPool for a single COADREAD patient. Here, MeanPool typically attends to solid tumor while VarPool attends to fragmented, more poorly-differentiated tumor. The scale bar represents $100\,\mu m$.

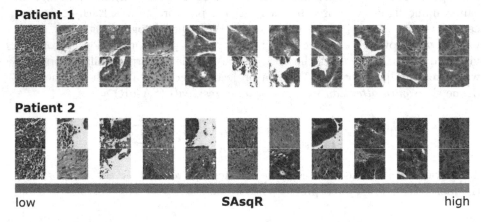

Patient 1

Patient 2

low   SAsqR   high

Fig. 3. Patches along one variance projection for two COADREAD patients. The patches are ordered from the most negative (left) SAsqR scores to most positive (right). The leftmost patches contain dense inflammatory infiltrate comprised mostly of lymphocytes, while the rightmost patches show denser tumor regions.

Patient 1

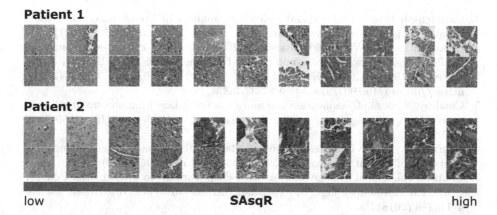

Patient 2

low   SAsqR   high

Fig. 4. Patches along one variance projection for two UCEC patients. This projection shows two patterns that are illustrated by these patients. For the first patient, the leftmost patches display necrosis and the right most patches display tumor. For the second patient, the leftmost patches display predominantly muscle and connective tissue and the right most patches display tumor.

5   Conclusion

We introduce a novel variance pooling module that can be incorporated into existing multiple instance learning (MIL) frameworks, to encode heterogeneity information through the second order statistics of low rank projections. We show that variance pooling can improve survival prediction across several cancer types. We also provide interpretability tools based on attention and projection scores to understand the heterogeneous biological signals captured by our framework. We hope this study will lead to further investigations of intratumoral heterogeneity – and other tumor microenvironment features – for computational pathology.

Acknowledgement. We thank Katherine Hoadley for helpful suggestions. This work was supported in part by internal funds from BWH Pathology, NIGMS R35GM138216 (F.M.), BWH President's Fund, MGH Pathology, BWH Precision Medicine Program, Google Cloud Research Grant, Nvidia GPU Grant Program and funding from the Fredrick National Lab. R.C. was additionally supported by the NSF graduate research fellowship. T.Y.C. was additionally funded by the NIH National Cancer Institute (NCI) Ruth L. Kirschstein National Service Award, T32CA251062. The content is solely the responsibility of the authors and does not reflect the official views of the NIH, NIGMS, NCI, or NSF.

References

1. Andor, N., et al.: Pan-cancer analysis of the extent and consequences of intratumor heterogeneity. Nat. Med. **22**(1), 105–113 (2016)
2. Campanella, G., et al.: Clinical-grade computational pathology using weakly supervised deep learning on whole slide images. Nat. Med. (2019)

3. Carmichael, I., et al.: Joint and individual analysis of breast cancer histologic images and genomic covariates. Ann. Appl. Statist. **15**(4), 1697–1722 (2021)

4. Chen, R.J., et al.: Whole slide images are 2D point clouds: context-aware survival prediction using patch-based graph convolutional networks. In: de Bruijne, M., et al. (eds.) MICCAI 2021. LNCS, vol. 12908, pp. 339–349. Springer, Cham (2021). https://doi.org/10.1007/978-3-030-87237-3_33

5. Coudray, N., et al.: Classification and mutation prediction from non-small cell lung cancer histopathology images using deep learning. Nat. Med. **24**(10), 1559–1567 (2018)

6. Courtiol, P., et al.: Deep learning-based classification of mesothelioma improves prediction of patient outcome. Nat. Med. **25**(10), 1519–1525 (2019)

7. Couture, H.D., et al.: Image analysis with deep learning to predict breast cancer grade, ER status, histologic subtype, and intrinsic subtype. NPJ Breast Cancer **4**(1), 1–8 (2018)

8. Faust, K., et al.: Unsupervised resolution of histomorphologic heterogeneity in renal cell carcinoma using a brain tumor-educated neural network. JCO Clin. Cancer Inf. **4**, 811–821 (2020)

9. Guinney, J., et al.: The consensus molecular subtypes of colorectal cancer. Nat. Med. **21**(11), 1350–1356 (2015)

10. Gurcan, M.N., Boucheron, L.E., Can, A., Madabhushi, A., Rajpoot, N.M., Yener, B.: Histopathological image analysis: a review. IEEE Rev. Biomed. Eng. **2**, 147–171 (2009)

11. Ilse, M., Tomczak, J., Welling, M.: Attention-based deep multiple instance learning. In: Proceedings of the 35th International Conference on Machine Learning. PMLR (2018)

12. Levine, D.A.: Integrated genomic characterization of endometrial carcinoma. Nature **497**(7447), 67–73 (2013)

13. Liu, J., et al.: An integrated tcga pan-cancer clinical data resource to drive high-quality survival outcome analytics. Cell **173**(2), 400–416 (2018)

14. Lu, C., et al.: Nuclear shape and orientation features from h&e images predict survival in early-stage estrogen receptor-positive breast cancers. Lab. Investig. **98**(11), 1438–1448 (2018)

15. Lu, M.Y., Williamson, D.F., Chen, T.Y., Chen, R.J., Barbieri, M., Mahmood, F.: Data-efficient and weakly supervised computational pathology on whole-slide images. Nat. Biomed. Eng. **5**(6), 555–570 (2021)

16. Luck, M., Sylvain, T., Cohen, J.P., Cardinal, H., Lodi, A., Bengio, Y.: Learning to rank for censored survival data. arXiv preprint arXiv:1806.01984 (2018)

17. Marusyk, A., Janiszewska, M., Polyak, K.: Intratumor heterogeneity: the Rosetta stone of therapy resistance. Cancer Cell **37**(4), 471–484 (2020)

18. Mobadersany, P., et al.: Predicting cancer outcomes from histology and genomics using convolutional networks. Proc. Natl. Acad. Sci. **115**(13), E2970–E2979 (2018)

19. Raynaud, F., Mina, M., Tavernari, D., Ciriello, G.: Pan-cancer inference of intra-tumor heterogeneity reveals associations with different forms of genomic instability. PLoS Genet. **14**(9), e1007669 (2018)

20. Steck, H., Krishnapuram, B., Dehing-Oberije, C., Lambin, P., Raykar, V.C.: On ranking in survival analysis: bounds on the concordance index. Adv. Neural Inf. Process. Syst. **20** (2007)

21. Wulczyn, E., et al.: Interpretable survival prediction for colorectal cancer using deep learning. NPJ Digit. Med. **4**(1), 1–13 (2021)

22. Zadeh, S.G., Schmid, M.: Bias in cross-entropy-based training of deep survival networks. IEEE Trans. Pattern Anal. Mach. Intell. **43**(9), 3126–3137 (2020)

23. Zaheer, M., Kottur, S., Ravanbakhsh, S., Poczos, B., Salakhutdinov, R.R., Smola, A.J.: Deep sets. In: Advances in Neural Information Processing Systems, vol. 30. Curran Associates, Inc. (2017)
24. Zhao, Y., et al.: Predicting lymph node metastasis using histopathological images based on multiple instance learning with deep graph convolution. In: Proceedings of the IEEE/CVF Conference on Computer Vision and Pattern Recognition, pp. 4837–4846 (2020)
25. Zhu, X., Yao, J., Zhu, F., Huang, J.: Wsisa: making survival prediction from whole slide histopathological images. In: Proceedings of the IEEE Conference on Computer Vision and Pattern Recognition, pp. 7234–7242 (2017)

Prostate Cancer Histology Synthesis Using StyleGAN Latent Space Annotation

Gagandeep B. Daroach[1], Savannah R. Duenweg[2], Michael Brehler[3],
Allison K. Lowman[3], Kenneth A. Iczkowski[4], Kenneth M. Jacobsohn[5],
Josiah A. Yoder[1(✉)], and Peter S. LaViolette[6]

[1] Department of Electrical Engineering and Computer Science,
Milwaukee School of Engineering, Milwaukee, WI 53202, USA
yoder@msoe.edu

[2] Departments of Biophysics, Medical College of Wisconsin,
Milwaukee, WI 53226, USA

[3] Departments of Radiology, Medical College of Wisconsin,
Milwaukee, WI 53226, USA

[4] Departments of Pathology and Urology,
Medical College of Wisconsin, Milwaukee, WI 53226, USA

[5] Departments of Urology, Medical College of Wisconsin,
Milwaukee, WI 53226, USA

[6] Departments of Radiology and Biomedical Engineering, Medical College of
Wisconsin, Milwaukee, WI 53226, USA
plaviole@mcw.edu

https://www.daraoch.net, https://www.msoe.edu, https://www.mcw.edu

Abstract. The latent space of a generative adversarial network (GAN) may model pathologically-significant semantics with unsupervised learning. To explore this phenomenon, we trained and tested a StyleGAN2 on a high quality prostate histology dataset covering the prostate cancer (PCa) diagnostic spectrum. Our pathologist annotated synthetic images to identify learned PCa regions in the GAN latent space. New points were drawn from these regions, synthesized into images, and given to a pathologist for annotation. 77% of the new points received the same annotation, and 98% of the latent points received the same or adjacent diagnostic stage annotation. This confirms the GAN network can accurately disentangle and model PCa features without exposure to labels in the training process.

Keywords: Generative adversarial networks · Prostate cancer · Histology · Latent space · Unsupervised deep learning

1 Introduction

Prostate cancer (PCa) is the most commonly diagnosed non-cutaneous cancer in men, accounting for 27% of new male cancer diagnoses. An estimated 268,000 new cases of PCa will be diagnosed in 2022 [23]. Prostate cancer is graded using

© The Author(s), under exclusive license to Springer Nature Switzerland AG 2022
L. Wang et al. (Eds.): MICCAI 2022, LNCS 13432, pp. 398–408, 2022.
https://doi.org/10.1007/978-3-031-16434-7_39

digital images and the Gleason grading scale, a purely visual system that assigns a score based on the two most predominant glandular patterns.

Digital pathology is becoming common in the research and clinical communities with applications in diagnosis, training, and decision support [10]. Generative adversarial networks (GANs) are a recent development in the field of artificial intelligence that are capable of autonomously forming complex feature representations and generating novel synthetic datapoints that generalize well while interpolating real data [5,6,11,13,15,25]. The GAN backpropagation driven training process embeds high-level concepts (semantic information) as deep representative features structured in its input numerical latent space [12,14,20].

Understanding the relationship between a GAN's latent space and real-world phenomena has many clinical applications. Capturing abstract underlying structures, GANs show promise as systems capable of image domain translation. GANs have been demonstrated to provide cutting-edge results in color normalization, ink removal, nuclei segmentation, and stain-to-stain translation [11]. In stained histology, discrete diagnostic latent spaces between stain modalities may exist. In digital pathology, AI systems could translate MRI images into histology images through the GAN latent space.

But more importantly, GANs have the potential to model and describe clinically-relevant features unknown to science [11], exposing mechanisms of cancer progression. In the present work, pathologist annotations validate the correspondence of regions of the GAN's latent space to clinically-relevant categories such as Gleason Scores. Knowing these latent space representations of different cancer grades will allow modeling the transition between them. Interpolation may also support the construction of 3D histology providing new insights into cellular structure.

Critical to interpretable AI, GANs can visually demonstrate interpretable variations to an image that change classification decisions [14]. Unlike a CNN producing the same latent code for many images, a GAN produces a unique image for every point in its latent space. When making a medical decision based on a latent space, pathologists have more than a set of arbitrary numbers. Instead, they can explore feature correlations in both latent space (via tuning across subspaces defined by covariance) and histology space (by producing a full image) to draw conclusions with real patient data.

A GAN can visually augment the decisions made by a classification network to strengthen the neural network – human interaction [14], separately modeling spatial and semantic content within an image [2,3,13]. The use of high-resolution (1024×1024) images allows structure to be captured at multiple levels of detail [2,13].

A trained GAN synthesizes an image from a latent point. Finding the latent point from an image – whether real or synthetic – is known as GAN inversion. While recent work improves GAN inversion [1,21,26], we found these approaches to not capture the key structures needed for digital pathology in the reconstructed images. Without a strong inverter, it is challenging to explore the latent-space of the GAN via real annotated histology. To avoid this complexity [2,11,13], in this work, a pathologist identifies the Gleason patterns on

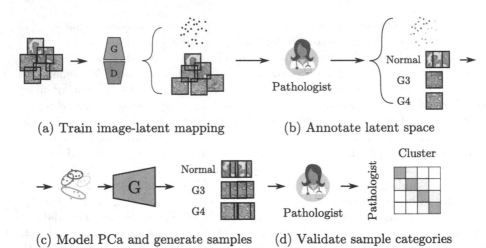

(a) Train image-latent mapping   (b) Annotate latent space

(c) Model PCa and generate samples   (d) Validate sample categories

Fig. 1. (a) First a StyleGAN2 is trained to learn an image to latent space mapping. (b) A pathologist annotates synthetic images, in turn annotating the latent space coordinates. (c) Clusters in latent space are formed around the labeled points, and new images are generated from within the cluster. (d) A pathologist annotates these new images, validating the integrity of the latent regions.

synthetic histology produced by a trained GAN, for which corresponding latent points are already known. In future work with improved invertable generators [7], real histology can be directly inverted into this latent space and analyzed quantitatively. Our work highlights the importance of improving GAN inversion techniques for histology.

In this paper, we propose a technique to characterize and validate PCa regions within the latent space of a GAN, based on pathologist annotations of Gleason patterns. The GAN can synthesize histology representative of a particular Gleason category by sampling from PCa regions annotated by the pathologist in latent space. A pathologist blind to the PCa latent regions selected the exact Gleason category used to generate the region in 77% of cases and a neighboring class in 98% of cases. This demonstrates that deep representations of PCa semantics are captured, isolated, and relationally modeled in the latent space of a StyleGAN network trained on PCa histology in unsupervised training.

2   Method

Our proposed technique is shown in Fig. 1. The pathologist categorizes only synthetic images produced by the GAN, in turn annotating the corresponding latent point from which the image was generated without needing to invert the network.

Considering all the points sharing the same category, we apply principal component analysis (PCA) to describe the variation of these points within a

Table 1. Patient demographics and training data breakdown.

(a) Patient demographics	Patients	(b) Training data breakdown — Category	Number of Images
Age at RP, years (mean, SD)		High Grade Cancer	
(n = 26)	60 (6.1)	G4FG	22,505
Ethnicity (n, %)		G4CG	6,687
African American	3 (12)	G5	5,808
White/Caucasian	22 (84)	**Total**	**35,000**
Asian	1 (4)	Low Grade Cancer	
Preoperative PSA, ng/mL (n, %)		G3	35,000
≤ 10	21 (81)	**Total**	**35,000**
10.1 – 20.0	4 (15)	Non-Cancerous	
≥ 20	3 (4)	Atrophy	28,943
Grade group at RP (n, %)		S. Vesicles	3,692
6	5 (19)	HGPIN	2,365
3+4	12 (45)	**Total**	**35,000**
4+3	3 (12)	Uncategorized	
8	3 (12)	Benign Tissue	35,000
9	3 (12)	**Total**	**35,000**
		Full Training Set	**140,000**

unimodal latent cluster. This cluster models a hyperelliptical region within latent space. Ideally, this region would have the same number of dimensions as the latent space, but in practice, it is limited to a hyperelliptical region within a subspace containing all the points labeled by the pathologist in that region. The PCA model is used to generate new images with the same annotation. Given a random point $\mathbf{n} \sim N(0, \mathbf{I})$ drawn from a standard normal distribution, we generate a new point according to

$$\mathbf{w}_{c_i} = V_{c_i}\mathbf{n} + \overline{\mathbf{w}} \qquad (1)$$

where $\overline{\mathbf{w}}$ is the mean and V_{c_i} is the matrix of the eigenvalues of the points in the ith cluster. From this point $\mathbf{w}_{c_i}$, we generate a new image that we hypothesize will have the same classification as the other images previously annotated by the pathologist. A board-certified genitourinary pathologist independently annotates the new synthetic image to validate this hypothesis.

3   Experiments and Results

3.1   Patient Population

Data from 26 prospectively recruited patients (mean age 60 years) with pathologically confirmed prostate cancer undergoing radical prostatectomy between

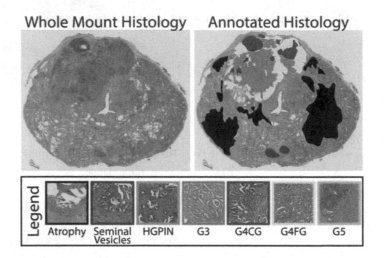

Fig. 2. Example of a pathologist-annotated prostate whole slide image. Tiles are extracted for GAN training.

2014 and 2018 were screened for inclusion in this institutional review board (IRB) approved study. Written informed consent was obtained from all patients. A summary of patient demographics and diagnoses is shown in Table 1a.

3.2   Tissue Processing

Prostatectomy was performed using the da Vinci robotic system (Intuitive Surgical, Sunnyvale, CA) by a single fellowship-trained surgeon (KMJ) [19,24]. Surgical specimens were fixed in formalin overnight, inked, and sectioned using a custom slicing jig, and 3D printed using a fifth-generation MakerBot (MakerBot Industries, Brooklyn, NY) [4,8,16–18,22].

Whole-mount tissue sections were paraffin embedded and slides from the sections were stained for hematoxylin and eosin (H&E) (Fig. 2). Slides were digitally scanned using a Nikon (Nikon Metrology, Brighton, MI) (n=12 patients, 117 slides) or Olympus (Olympus Corporation, Tokyo, Japan) (n=9 patients, 102 slides) sliding stage microscope at a resolution of 0.58 or 0.34 microns per pixel (40x magnification), respectively. An additional 5 patients had slides scanned on both the Nikon and Olympus microscopes.

3.3   Tissue Annotation

219 digitized whole slide images (WSI) were manually annotated for different Gleason patterns by a urological fellowship-trained pathologist (KAI) across all patients using a stylus on a Microsoft Surface Pro 4 (Microsoft, Seattle, WA) with a preloaded color palette. The annotations were isolated to create a single non-overlapping mask for each of eight possible classes: seminal vesicles, atrophy,

high-grade prostatic intraepithelial neoplasia (HGPIN), Gleason 3 (G3), Gleason 4 fused gland (G4FG), Gleason 4 cribriform gland (G4CG) [9], Gleason 5 (G5), and unannotated benign tissue. Non-tissue areas (i.e., background, lumen, and other artifacts) were removed from the annotation masks to ensure the most representative histology remained within the annotation.

WSI samples were divided into 2048×1536 pixels or 3000×3000 pixels tiles for the Nikon or Olympus scanners, respectively. The annotated image tiles and full-resolution WSI were aligned using Matlab's imregister function (Mathworks Inc., Natick, MA). Tiles more than 50% within a classification mask were annotated with that class, ensuring each tile has one primary annotation. A demonstration of the annotation segmentation and tile extraction is shown in Fig. 2.

3.4   GAN Training

The high resolution PCa tiles were further divided into 256×256 pixel patch PNGs. To create a balanced training distribution w.r.t. PCa, the annotation categories were divided into four meta-categories: high-grade cancer (G4FG, G4CG, and G5), low-grade cancer (G3), normal (Atrophy, Seminal Vesicles, and HGPIN), and uncategorized (Tissue). Each meta-category included 35,000 training images for a total of 140,000 distinct images in the GAN dataset. The total breakdown of images used per category and meta-category is shown in Table 1b. Although the meta-categories are balanced, the four sub-categories Benign Tissue, Atrophy, G3, and G4FG dominate the training set. Before this balancing, normal tissue dominated the training set. Training on the the balanced dataset shown in Table 1b dramatically increased the latent space representation and diversity for adenocarcinomic grandular patterns.

The StyleGAN2 Configuration F network architecture and training loop were selected from the authors' [13] Tensorflow source code without any adjustments[1]. The network topology, optimizer, learning rate, loss functions, validation metrics, multi-gpu training loop, and data preparation scripts were cloned from this code-base. One random latent point and random noise are input to the Generator to yield one 256×256 image. The unsupervised training loop disregarded the Gleason and meta-categories, using a Discriminator as the sole loss for the Generator. A Nvidia DGX-1 Workstation at the Milwaukee School of Engineering trained the GAN to convergence in approximately 5 d with 8 V100 Nvidia GPUs.

3.5   Pathologist Annotation of Synthetic Histology

After training, we generated 1500 random synthetic images. Due to limited annotation bandwidth, 4 lab researchers selected 40 samples each for pathologist (KAI) to annotate as: Healthy, Seminal Vesicles, Atrophy, HGPIN, G3, G4FG, G4CG, or G5. KAI found images of all categories except Seminal Vesicles, G4CG, and G5. Together, the unfound categories constitute 11.6% of GAN training dataset. The remaining categories are summarized in Table 2 (a).

---

[1] https://github.com/NVlabs/stylegan2.

G4FG	G3	HGPIN	Atrophy	Healthy

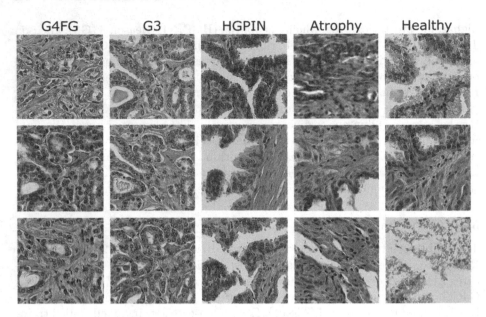

Fig. 3. Representative images generated from each category in latent space. All images were created with the same noise-channel seed thus sharing the same nuclear and gland layout.

3.6 Generating Categorized Synthetic Images

The mean and co-variance were derived for each category in Table 2 using all synthetic images within that category, creating PCa regions or latent clusters. Ten points were drawn randomly from each cluster with equation (1). Each latent point was truncated toward the mean of the cluster using factor of $\psi = 0.6$ [12],

$$\mathbf{w}_{c_i} = \psi V_{c_i} \mathbf{n} + \overline{\mathbf{w}} \tag{2}$$

reducing the number of unrepresentative features within the cluster while preserving diversity. Points nearer the boundaries of latent space are known to be more likely to contain unrealistic features [12]. The ten latent points are input to the Generator to produce ten synthetic images for each category. Examples from each category are shown in Fig. 3.

In addition to the $\mathbf{w}$ channel, the StyleGAN network has a random noise channel that influences the layout of features within the image [2]. While every layer is derived from the same is $\mathbf{w}$ channel, the noise channel provides random noise in the shape of each layer [12,13]. In generating images within a category, the noise channel was fixed so that the layout of glands, nuclei, etc., in the images would remain fixed while the classification of the images changed.

The images were shuffled, unlabeled, and then presented to KAI for annotation. Images from the Healthy and Atrophy categories are grouped into one Normal category in the results. The pathologist's resulting classifications are sum-

Table 2. (a) Pathologist-assigned categories (b) Confusion matrix comparing the histolological classifications from the GAN versus ground truth categorization provided from our pathologist.

(a)

Category	Number categorized
Healthy	84
Atrophy	16
HGPIN	4
G3	34
G4FG	22
Total	**160**

(b)

		Latent Cluster				
		Normal	HGPIN	G3	G4FG	Total
Pathologist	Normal	20	3	1		24
	HGPIN		3			3
	G3		2	9	5	16
	G4FG				5	5
	Total	**20**	**8**	**10**	**10**	**48**

marized in Fig. 2 (b). There were two images from the HGPIN category which are excluded from this figure, leaving 48 images that the pathologist classified. The pathologist considered these 2 HGPIN images on the borderline between cancerous and non-cancerous tissue.

4 Discussion

While it is widely believed that the latent space of a GAN captures semantic information from the training space, it is unknown whether clinically-significant categories such as Gleason grades are learned by a GAN when these categorizations are not provided during training.

Using a generative adversarial network, we found discrete pathologically relevant regions in the latent space from images of prostate cancer digitally annotated using the Gleason grading system. Independent classification of the images generated from these regions by our pathologist (KAI) shows that images in a region share similar Gleason scores.

These results can be interpreted in two ways: First, although the GAN was trained without classification categories, we find that its latent space automatically forms regions corresponding to these categories.

Second, the GAN provides a quantitative approach to comparing Gleason grades. Gleason patterns are often arranged from least- to most- cancerous tissues. The categories confused in Fig. 2 (b) follow this same scheme, for example, with the more-cancerous G4FG category being confused only with the less cancerous G3 category and not with any of the non-cancerous tissue categories. This provides further evidence that the Gleason system truly captures the morphology of an image on a scale. Only exposed to the morphologies, the GAN, without knowledge of the Gleason system, formed a similar orientation of semantic concepts with respect to cancer severity.

4.1 Limitations

This study included a relatively small 26 patient cohort, two slide scanners for digitization, and one pathologist for annotation of slides and GAN-output images. Beyond the scope of this study, future studies may use larger populations, additional pathologists, and additional scanners to enforce a more robust deep representations of PCa information in the learned GAN features. The identified latent clusters are based upon pathologist annotations of 160 slides, limiting the dimensionality of the subspaces explored in this work. Further experiments with a larger set of annotated synthetic images could provide additional insights into the structure of deep learning engineered latent space.

The GAN latent space models certain parts of the training data over others, e.g. large tissue features. Future studies should explore how techniques for preserving the diversity in the training set can be extended to histology representations.

This study considered only prostate histology. Future studies are required to confirm that GANs trained on other organs and modalities also capture clinically-import classifications.

5 Conclusions

This study confirmed the presence of regions of a GAN's latent space corresponding to Gleason categories. The consistency of these regions was confirmed through categorization of synthetic images by a pathologist blind to the category from which the images were produced. 77% of images were categorized in the exact same category as the region from which they were drawn and 98% of regions were categorized in the same region or an adjacent one. The high level of agreement between the pathologist's categories and the categories defining the regions of latent space from which the images were drawn suggests these regions are truly contiguous within latent space.

Future studies should look into the clinical [14] implications of the latent understanding in this work, the GAN may be paired with an accurate classifier to exemplify alternative realization of the same semantic concepts to explore additional perspectives of diagnosis.

References

1. Chen, J., et al.: Generative invertible networks (GIN): Pathophysiology-interpretable feature mapping and virtual patient generation. In: Medical Image Computing and Computer Assisted Intervention, pp. 537–545 (2018). https://doi.org/10.1007/978-3-030-00928-1_61
2. Daroach, G., Yoder, J., Iczkowski, K., LaViolette, P.: High-resolution controllable prostatic histology synthesis using StyleGAN. In: Proceedings of the International Joint Conference on Biomedical Engineering Systems and Technologies (2021). https://doi.org/10.5220/0010393901030112

3. Epstein, D., Park, T., Zhang, R., Shechtman, E., Efros, A.A.: BlobGAN: Spatially disentangled scene representations. arXiv preprint arXiv:2205.02837 (2022)
4. Epstein, J.I., et al.: A contemporary prostate cancer grading system: a validated alternative to the gleason score. Eur. Urol. **69**(3), 428–435 (2016). https://doi.org/10.1016/j.eururo.2015.06.046
5. Feldman, V.: Does learning require memorization? A short tale about a long tail. In: Proceedings of the Symposium on Theory of Computing, pp. 954–959 (2020)
6. Goodfellow, I., et al.: Generative adversarial nets. In: Advances in Neural Information Processing Systems, vol. 27 (2014)
7. Grover, A., Dhar, M., Ermon, S.: Flow-GAN: Combining maximum likelihood and adversarial learning in generative models. In: Proceedings of the AAAI conference on artificial intelligence, vol. 32 (2018)
8. Hurrell, S.L., et al.: Optimized b-value selection for the discrimination of prostate cancer grades, including the cribriform pattern, using diffusion weighted imaging. J. Med. Imaging **5**(01), 1 (2017). https://doi.org/10.1117/1.jmi.5.1.011004
9. Iczkowski, K.A., Paner, G.P., der Kwast, T.V.: The new realization about cribriform prostate cancer. Adv. Anat. Pathol. **25**(1), 31–37 (2018). https://doi.org/10.1097/pap.0000000000000168
10. Jahn, S.W., Plass, M., Moinfar, F.: Digital pathology: advantages, limitations and emerging perspectives. J. Clin. Med. **9**(11), 3697 (2020). https://doi.org/10.3390/jcm9113697
11. Jose, L., Liu, S., Russo, C., Nadort, A., Ieva, A.D.: Generative adversarial networks in digital pathology and histopathological image processing: a review. J. Pathol. Inform. **12**(1), 43 (2021). https://doi.org/10.4103/jpi.jpi_103_20
12. Karras, T., Laine, S., Aila, T.: A style-based generator architecture for generative adversarial networks. In: Proceedings of the IEEE/CVF Conference on Computer Vision and Pattern Recognition (CVPR) (June 2019)
13. Karras, T., Laine, S., Aittala, M., Hellsten, J., Lehtinen, J., Aila, T.: Analyzing and improving the image quality of StyleGAN. In: 2020 IEEE/CVF Conference on Computer Vision and Pattern Recognition (CVPR), pp. 8107–8116 (2020). https://doi.org/10.1109/CVPR42600.2020.00813
14. Lang, O., et al.: Explaining in style: training a GAN to explain a classifier in StyleSpace. In: 2021 IEEE/CVF International Conference on Computer Vision (ICCV), pp. 673–682 (2021). https://doi.org/10.1109/ICCV48922.2021.00073
15. Ma, S., Bassily, R., Belkin, M.: The power of interpolation: Understanding the effectiveness of SGD in modern over-parametrized learning. In: International Conference on Machine Learning, pp. 3325–3334 (2018)
16. McGarry, S.D., et al.: Radio-pathomic mapping model generated using annotations from five pathologists reliably distinguishes high-grade prostate cancer. J. Med. Imaging **7**(05) (2020). https://doi.org/10.1117/1.jmi.7.5.054501
17. McGarry, S.D., et al.: Gleason probability maps: a radiomics tool for mapping prostate cancer likelihood in MRI space. Tomography **5**(1), 127–134 (2019). https://doi.org/10.18383/j.tom.2018.00033
18. McGarry, S.D., et al.: Radio-pathomic maps of epithelium and lumen density predict the location of high-grade prostate cancer. Int. J. Radiat. Oncol.-Biol.-Phys. **101**(5), 1179–1187 (2018). https://doi.org/10.1016/j.ijrobp.2018.04.044
19. Menon, M., A.K.H.: Vattikuti institute prostatectomy: a technique of robotic radical prostatectomy: Experience in more than 1000 cases. J. Endourol. **18**(7), 611–619 (2004). https://doi.org/10.1089/end.2004.18.611

20. Quiros, A.C., Murray-Smith, R., Yuan, K.: PathologyGAN: Learning deep representations of cancer tissue. arXiv:1907.02644 [cs, eess, stat] (2020). arXiv: 1907.02644
21. Richardson, E., et al.: Encoding in style: a StyleGAN encoder for image-to-image translation. arXiv:2008.00951 (2020)
22. Shah, V., et al.: A method for correlatingin vivoprostate magnetic resonance imaging and histopathology using individualized magnetic resonance-based molds. Rev. Sci. Instrum. 80(10), 104301 (2009). https://doi.org/10.1063/1.3242697
23. Siegel, R.L., Miller, K.D., Fuchs, H.E., Jemal, A.: Cancer statistics, 2022. CA: a Cancer J. Clin. 72(1), 7–33 (2022). https://doi.org/10.3322/caac.21708
24. Sood, A., Jeong, W., Peabody, J.O., Hemal, A.K., Menon, M.: Robot-assisted radical prostatectomy. Urol. Clin. North Am. 41(4), 473–484 (2014). https://doi.org/10.1016/j.ucl.2014.07.002
25. Zhang, C., Bengio, S., Hardt, M., Recht, B., Vinyals, O.: Understanding deep learning (still) requires rethinking generalization. Commun. ACM 64(3), 107–115 (2021)
26. Zhu, J., Shen, Y., Zhao, D., Zhou, B.: In-domain GAN inversion for real image editing. arXiv:2004.00049 (2020)

Fast FF-to-FFPE Whole Slide Image Translation via Laplacian Pyramid and Contrastive Learning

Lei Fan[✉], Arcot Sowmya, Erik Meijering, and Yang Song

School of Computer Science and Engineering, University of New South Wales,
Sydney, NSW 2052, Australia
{lei.fan1,yang.song1}@unsw.edu.au

Abstract. Formalin-Fixed Paraffin-Embedded (FFPE) and Fresh Frozen (FF) are two major types of histopathological Whole Slide Images (WSIs). FFPE provides high-quality images, however the acquisition process usually takes 12 to 48 h, while FF with relatively low-quality images takes less than 15 min to acquire. In this work, we focus on the task of translating FF to FFPE style (FF2FFPE), to synthesize FFPE-style images from FF images. However, WSIs with giga-pixels impose heavy constraints on computation and time resources. To address these issues, we propose the fastFF2FFPE for translating FF into FFPE-style efficiently. Specifically, we decompose FF images into low- and high-frequency components based on the Laplacian Pyramid, wherein the low-frequency component at low resolution is transformed into FFPE-style with low computational cost, and the high-frequency component is used for providing details. We further employ contrastive learning to encourage similarities between original and output patches. We conduct FF2FFPE translation experiments on The Cancer Genome Atlas (TCGA) Glioblastoma Multiforme (GBM) and Lung Squamous Cell Carcinoma (LUSC) datasets, and verify the efficacy of our model on Microsatellite Instability prediction in gastrointestinal cancer. The code and models are released at https://github.com/hellodfan/fastFF2FFPE.

Keywords: Image translation · Histopathology · Laplacian pyramid · Whole Slide Images · Contrastive learning

1 Introduction

Whole Slide Images (WSIs) serve as the gold standard in diagnosis and prognosis of various diseases, since WSIs provide high-resolution molecular information that can be used for a wide variety of clinical purposes [9,17]. During the acquisition process, a set of glass slides are scanned and stitched together to produce digital WSIs. Generally, there are two common tissue preparation methods of WSIs: Formalin-Fixed Paraffin-Embedded (FFPE) and Fresh Frozen (FF). FFPE slides are obtained via a standard procedure in which specimens are processed sequentially in multiple steps [2], *e.g.*, dehydrated, saturated with formalin

L. Wang et al. (Eds.): MICCAI 2022, LNCS 13432, pp. 409–419, 2022.
https://doi.org/10.1007/978-3-031-16434-7_40

and stained with dyes, whereas FF slides are produced in ultra-low temperature freezers with liquid nitrogen [15]. FFPE provides highly accurate tissue morphology and is widely used for archiving biological material and long-term clinical follow-up research, but its acquisition is time-consuming (near 36 h). On the other hand, as the processing for FF only requires about 15 min, FF slides are overwhelmingly adopted for intra-operative consultation and decision-making. However, there are many artifacts in FF slides and variations between FF and FFPE slides [29, 32] (see Fig. 1.a).

To eliminate the effects caused by artifacts or disagreement between FF and FFPE, recent studies [8, 25] attempted to translate FF patches into FFPE style (named FF2FFPE) using Generative Adversarial Networks (GANs) [10]. GANs have achieved remarkable performance on style transfer, such as house to zebra [27, 39], photo-realistic image synthesis [24, 33], MR-to-CT synthesis [34, 35] and stain normalization in WSIs [6, 31]. As the FF2FFPE data are *unpaired* instances, existing studies [8, 25] are based on CycleGAN [39] where FF patches are encoded and decoded via encoder-decoder structures with fully convolutional layers. However, training CycleGAN-based models requires a high amount of computational resources. Moreover, these models cannot be directly applied to WSI-level translation since WSIs contain giga-pixels. These methods [8, 25] thus adopted a sampling strategy where a set of small patches (512 × 512 pixels) tiled from WSIs are translated individually. However, WSIs at high resolutions would produce numerous such small patches and hence impose heavy burden on computational resources and hinder the deployment of models.

To remedy this issue, we propose a highly efficient GAN-based model trained using unpaired data, called fastFF2FFPE, to translate FF into FFPE-style slides. Specifically, we leverage Laplacian Pyramid (LP) to disentangle WSI patches into low- and high-frequency components. The low-frequency component at low resolutions is transformed into FFPE-style based on a lightweight generator network with low computational cost. The high-frequency component including various resolution levels is used for supplying details hierarchically to obtain final translated images. In addition, we maintain a memory bank to store high-level features of all training examples, based on which we employ contrastive learning to encourage similarities between original and translated patches. The contributions of this paper are summarized as follows: (1) We propose fastFF2FFPE to translate FF into FFPE-style slides based on LP and contrastive learning. (2) Compared with previous methods, our model is capable of dealing with larger patches at resolutions (*e.g.*, 2048 × 2048 pixels) and hence the WSI-level translation can be much faster. (3) We conduct FF2FFPE translation experiments on TCGA-GBM and TCGA-LUSC datasets both quantitatively and qualitatively, and demonstrate the effectiveness of our generator network for downstream analysis on Microsatellite Instability prediction in gastrointestinal cancer.

2 Methodology

We propose fastFF2FFPE to translate FF slides into FFPE-style slides efficiently both in computational resources and time costs. As illustrated in Fig. 1.b,

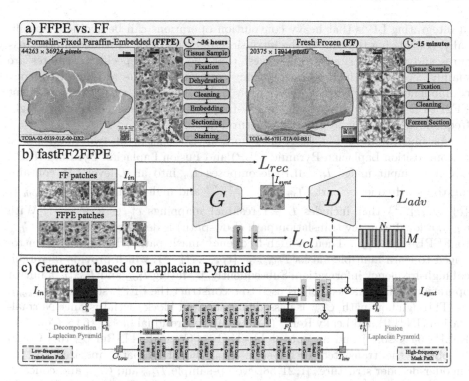

Fig. 1. a). Two slides from TCGA-GBM dataset (green lines indicate the tissue regions after pro-processing). b). Overall architecture of fastFF2FFPE. c). Detailed architecture of generator based on Laplacian Pyramid. (Color figure online)

fastFF2FFPE is based on a GAN model and consists of generator (see Fig. 1.c) and discriminator networks. Given the input domain (FF) $\mathbb{X} \in \mathbb{R}^{H \times W \times C}$ (H and W are the width and height and C denotes the number of channels) and target domain (FFPE) $\mathbb{Y} \in \mathbb{R}^{H \times W \times C}$, the goal of FF2FFPE is to translate images in $\mathbb{X}$ to appear like images in $\mathbb{Y}$, based on a dataset of unpaired images $X = \{x \in \mathbb{X}\}, Y = \{y \in \mathbb{Y}\}$. The input image $I_{in} \in X$ is fed to the generator G to synthesize an FFPE-style image I_{synt}. Then, we employ a discriminator to identify whether I_{synt} belongs to the target domain.

2.1 Frequency Decomposition via Laplacian Pyramid

For the FF2FFPE task, the majority of visual content in FF patches should remain unchanged, but some parts (especially artifacts) should be removed or translated; and the main goal is to enhance staining quality and nucleo-cytoplasmic contrast [25]. Recently, Laplacian Pyramid (LP) [3], one of the traditional computer vision techniques, has been adapted into various deep learning models, such as image generation [7], super-resolution [20], and high-resolution image-to-image translation [21]. As demonstrated by these studies, the merit of integrating LP is that heavy convolution operations can be avoided. Specifically, considering that one of the intrinsic properties of LP is to decompose textures and visual attributes, we suggest that the domain-specific attributes are mainly represented in the low-frequency component, while the high-frequency component contains texture information [3,21]. Therefore, we try to implement FF2FFPE translation based on the low-frequency component, and utilize high-frequency component to provide structural details.

As illustrated in Fig. 1.c, our generator G consists of two main parts: Decomposition Laplacian Pyramid (dLP) and Fusion Laplacian Pyramid (fLP). Given an input image I_{in}, dLP decomposes I_{in} into an L-level LP, containing the low-frequency part $C_{low} \in \mathbb{R}^{\frac{H}{2^L} \times \frac{W}{2^L} \times 3}$ and high-frequency part $C_{high} = \{c_h^1, \ldots, c_h^{L-1}\}$ that includes $L-1$ residual mappings $c_h^i \in \mathbb{R}^{\frac{H}{2^i} \times \frac{W}{2^i} \times 3}$. With C_{low}, a low-frequency translation path (Low-path) is designed to translate C_{low} to FFPE-style T_{low}. Then, a high-frequency mask path (High-path) is introduced to learn multiple masks $T_{mask} = \{t_h^1, \ldots, t_h^{L-1}\}$, which provide hierarchical high-frequency information. Subsequently, by fusing T_{low} and T_{mask}, a mirror operation of dLP, named fLP, is used to reconstruct the FFPE-style image I_{synt}.

Through Low-path, C_{low} is passed into an input block (with Instance Normalization (IN [14]) and Leaky ReLU (L-ReLU)), five residual blocks ($64 \times$ Conv+L-ReLU+$64 \times$ Conv) and an output block ($16 \times$ Conv+IN+L-ReLU+$16 \times$ Conv) to obtain the translated FFPE-style T_{low}. For High-path, inspired by the encoder-decoder structures [1,21,38], we up-sample T_{low} and C_{low} and concatenate them with c_h^{L-1}, which is then passed into an input block ($16 \times$ Conv+L-ReLU) and three residual blocks ($16 \times$ Conv+L-ReLU+$16 \times$ Conv), to generate a feature map $F_h^{L-1} \in \mathbb{R}^{\frac{H}{2^{L-1}} \times \frac{W}{2^{L-1}} \times 1}$. F_h^{L-1} is adjusted to obtain the mask t_h^{L-1} by performing pixel-wise multiplication with c_h^{L-1}. Similarly, for masks at other levels, each t_h^i is learned by up-sampling previous F_h^{L-1} and concatenating with F_h^i, and then passing into a block ($16 \times$ Conv+L-ReLU+$1 \times$ Conv).

Compared to most existing translation methods [24,26,27,33,36,39] that employ the encoder-decoder architecture with fully convolutional layers, our model utilizes LP to perform down-sampling or up-sampling operations and implements FF2FFPE style translation mainly based on the low-frequency part C_{low} at lower resolutions. Therefore, fastFF2FFPE can substantially reduce computational and time costs. In addition, by focusing the image translation on C_{low}, the generated image would naturally contain fewer artifacts.

2.2   Contrastive Learning via Memory Bank

The goal of FF2FFPE is to eliminate the effects caused by artifacts or disagreement between FF and FFPE. We consider that each FF patch should share the majority of content with the corresponding translated FFPE-style patch, and their feature representations should exhibit some consistencies. Recently, contrastive learning is widely used in multiple fields, such as image classification [4,11,18] and object detection [5,22]. We attempt to employ contrastive learning to encourage similarities between FF and translated patches.

Inspired by He *et al.* [11], we maintain a memory bank $\mathbb{M}$ to store the feature representations of all input patches, so that contrastive learning can be effectively performed. Given an unpaired dataset with N instances, $\mathbb{M}$ stores $\{v_0, \ldots, v_{N-1}\}$ feature representations of all FF patches, in which v is obtained by feeding the corresponding FF patch into G, which is further appended with a convolutional block and an MLP layer on top of Low-path for feature extraction. Here each v_i has a dimension of 256. During the training phase, for an FF patch I_{in}^k ($k \in \{0, \ldots, N-1\}$), we feed it to G to obtain feature representation f_k. We employ contrastive learning to encourage similarities between features representations of the same input image but from the current and previous training epochs by calculating the infoNCE loss L_{cl}:

$$L_{cl} = -\log \frac{\exp(f_k \cdot v_k)/\tau}{\sum_{i=0}^{N-1} \exp(f_k \cdot v_i/\tau)} \tag{1}$$

where τ is a temperature parameter (τ is set to 0.03) and v_k is the feature representation generated in the previous epoch. During each training epoch, we store feature representations of all FF patches to update the memory bank at the start of the next training epoch.

2.3   Optimization Objective

Since the FF2FFPE data are unpaired instances, we train our model in an unsupervised manner. The overall optimization objective consists of three parts: the reconstruction loss L_{rec}, adversarial loss L_{adv} and contrastive learning loss L_{cl}. For L_{rec}, we calculate $L_{rec} = \|I_{synt} - I_{in}\|_2^2$ in a pixel-wise way to keep the majority of content from the FF domain. Then, following the Least Squares GAN [24], we force our model to adapt the FFPE domain-specific distribution by optimizing the generator G and discriminator D iteratively. We train the generator G by minimizing $\mathbb{E}_{x \sim \mathbb{X}}[D(G(x)-1)^2]$, and then optimize the discriminator D to recognize real or synthesized patches by minimizing L_{adv} as follows:

$$L_{adv} = \mathbb{E}_{y \sim p_{data}(\mathbb{Y})}[(D(y)-1)^2] + \mathbb{E}_{x \sim p_{data}(\mathbb{X})}[D(G(x))^2] \tag{2}$$

Then, the overall objective is as follows:

$$L_{total} = L_{rec} + \alpha L_{adv} + \beta L_{cl} \tag{3}$$

where α and β are hyper-parameters for balancing the overall optimization objective. Overall, under the supervision of L_{total}, the generator G is expected to reconstruct translated images under restrictions both in image and feature spaces, and to synthesize FFPE-style patches that share the majority of content with FF patches while reducing artifacts.

3   Experiment

3.1   Dataset and Implementation Details

We conduct FF2FFPE translation experiments on two public datasets: glioblastoma multiforme (GBM) and lung squamous cell carcinoma (LUSC), retrieved from The Cancer Genome Atlas (TCGA) [16][1]. We cropped a set of patches from raw FF and FFPE slides, and removed patches that contain more than 60% area of background, or color pens. Overall, the patches were selected at three resolution levels: 512×512, 1024×1024 and 2048×2048 pixels with $20K$, $10K$ and $4K$ images for both FF and FFPE. We split all data into training and test sets with 90% and 10% proportions. We conducted all experiments on a workstation with 8×Nvidia 2080Ti with 11GB graphical memory and platform PyTorch1.10 [28]. We train models with 40 epochs, Adam optimizer [19], and step learning strategy (initial learning rate is 0.0001), $\alpha = 0.1$ and $\beta = 0.05$. Since FF2FFPE translation is an *unpaired* Image-to-Image task, we adopt the Fréchet Inception Distance (FID) [13] as our metric, which is a measure of similarity between two datasets by computing the Fréchet distance. A small value of FID means that the model has better translation performance. More importantly, we report the training memory and time cost per iteration, and the inference Frames Per Second(FPS)/time of each image by averaging 3000 iterations.

Table 1. Performance of various FF2FFPE methods.

Model	Resolution	TCGA-GBM	TCGA-LUSC	Training Sec/Iter (s) ↓	Memory (GB) ↓	Inference FPS (↑)/Time (s) ↓
		FID ↓				
vFFPE [8]	512×512	66.33	44.89	0.318	7.6	35.09/0.0285
	1024×1024	N/A				
	2048×2048					
AI-FFPE [25]	512×512	46.89	**34.81**	0.359	10.9	30.67/0.0326
	1024×1024	N/A				
	2048×2048					
fastFF2FFPE	512×512	49.67	51.71	0.085	2.8	204.1/0.0049
	1024×1024	**46.85**	43.64	0.101	4.4	192.3/0.0052
	2048×2048	75.58	80.12	0.180	7.9	51.8/0.0193

3.2 Results

We compare our model with two state-of-the-art methods: vFFPE [8] and AI-FFPE [25] (codes are publicly available), as shown in Table 1. The vFFPE method based on CycleGAN and AI-FFPE based on a large ResNet-based encoder network are designed to take input patches at 512×512 pixels due to the GPU memory limitations. Firstly, we verify the feasibility of our model. Under the same input resolution setting of 512×512 pixels, our fastFF2FFPE ($L = 3$) obtains comparable FID performance of 49.67 and 51.71 on TCGA-GBM and TCGA-LUSC respectively. However, our model has substantial advantages in training resources and inference time, in which our model can be trained under only 2.8 GB memory and much faster (near 7× speedup) than vFFPE and AI-FFPE. Moreover, our fastFF2FFPE is able to take patches at larger resolutions as data inputs. When the input resolution increases to 1024×1024 or

---

[1] https://portal.gdc.cancer.gov/.

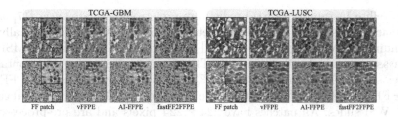

Fig. 2. Visualization results of three methods.

2048 × 2048 pixels, both vFFPE and AI-FFPE cannot be trained due to GPU memory limitations. Benefiting from the LP, our fastFF2FFPE is still trainable while requiring relatively lower training resources, which demonstrates the potential of our model in real-time application. For example, for an FF WSI with 20375 × 17914 pixels (see Fig. 1.a), the translation process of vFFPE and AI-FFPE requires about 39.9 and 45.6 s respectively, whereas our fastFF2FFPE only needs 6.86, 1.77 and 1.74 s under 512 × 512, 1024 × 1024 and 2048 × 2048 pixels settings. In addition, we also visualize some FF2FFPE translation results of these three methods (see Fig. 2), and observe that our model can overcome some artifacts.

We further conduct experiments on TCGA-LUSC to explore the different settings of our model. As shown in Table 2, we mainly investigate the number of layers of dLP (also fLP) and the effect of not using contrastive learning. When increasing layer number L, we observe that the FID performance fluctuates but the training resources and inference time reduce substantially, which is mainly because the resolution of low-frequency component C_{low} is exponentially shrunk. When training models without contrastive learning loss L_{cl}, models without using contrastive learning loss L_{cl} ($L = 3^*$) show apparent decreases of 2.5 and 4.6 of FID under 1024 × 1024 and 2048 × 2048 pixels settings.

Table 2. Ablation study of our model (* denotes w/o using contrastive learning L_{cl}).

	1024 × 1024 pixels				2048 × 2048 pixels			
	$L = 3$	$L = 3^*$	$L = 4$	$L = 5$	$L = 3$	$L = 3^*$	$L = 4$	$L = 5$
FID ↓	43.64	46.15	**39.95**	48.89	80.12	84.77	**63.64**	63.69
Sec/Iter (s) ↓	0.115	0.101	0.113	0.101	0.191	0.180	0.179	0.113
Memory (GB) ↓	4.5	4.4	4.4	2.9	7.9	7.9	4.7	4.6
FPS ↑	192.3	192.3	185.2	163.9	51.8	51.8	83.3	100.1

3.3 Microsatellite Instability Prediction

We additionally conduct experiments to explore the potential of using our model as a data augmentation technique with the trained generator. We select

Microsatellite Instability (MSI) prediction in gastrointestinal cancer [17] as our benchmarking task. MSI determines whether patients respond exceptionally well to immunotherapy, and prior study [17] has attempted to formulate MSI prediction as a binary classification task. The dataset released by [17]² contains a training set (60.9k FF and 93.4k FFPE patches) and test set (78.2k FF and 98.9k FFPE patches), and all patches are cropped from TCGA-colorectal cancer (CRC) WSI slides. All patches have 224×224 pixels and are pre-processed by stain normalization [23]. We augment the training set by feeding all FF patches into the generator (trained under 1024×1024 pixels on TCGA-LUSC) to synthesize 60.9k FFPE-style images.

We employ two common networks as our baselines: MobileNetv2 (Mv2) [30] and ResNet50 (R50) [12], and our synthesized data is used in combination with two kinds of data augmentation methods: colorjit and Mixup [37]. Based on a larger training set with adding synthesized FFPE-style images, both Mv2 and R50 produce considerable improvement, especially 4.84% when incorporated with Mixup based on R50. These experimental results demonstrate that our generator has the strong potential for data augmentation.

Table 3. F1-score of MSI prediction. Black numbers are results using the raw dataset, and *blue* and *red* numbers indicate results after combining raw and synthesized FFPE-style data. "Baseline" indicates no other data augmentation technique is incorporated. ([†] and [‡] denote significance tests when $p<0.05$ and $p<0.001$ respectively.)

Model	Baseline	Colorjit	Mixup [37]
Mv2 [30]	58.43%/59.74%[†]	58.51%/58.5%[‡]	58.49%/59.37%[†]
R50 [12]	63.01%/65.22%[‡]	66.84%/67.13%[†]	66.07%/67.85%[‡]

4 Conclusion

In this paper, we propose a GAN-based model, called fastFF2FFPE, to translate FF into FFPE-style patches efficiently. Specifically, we introduce Laplacian Pyramid to decompose an FF patch into low- and high-frequency components. The low-frequency component at low resolutions is translated into an FFPE-style image via a lightweight generator, and the high-frequency component provides detailed information to obtain the translated image. We further employ contrastive learning to encourage similarities between FF and translated FFPE-style patches. Compared with existing studies, our model can be trained under low computational and time costs. We demonstrated the effectiveness of our model by conducting extensive FF2FFPE experiments on two datasets: TCGA-GBM and TCGA-LUSC. In addition, we illustrated the efficacy of our generator as a data augmentation method for MSI prediction in gastrointestinal cancer.

---

² https://zenodo.org/record/2530835 and https://zenodo.org/record/2532612.

References

1. Badrinarayanan, V., Kendall, A., Cipolla, R.: SegNet: a deep convolutional encoder-decoder architecture for image segmentation. IEEE Trans. Pattern Anal. Mach. Intell. **39**(12), 2481–2495 (2017)
2. Brown, R.W.: Histologic Preparations: Common Problems and their Solutions. College of American Pathologists (2009)
3. Burt, P.J., Adelson, E.H.: The Laplacian pyramid as a compact image code. IEEE Trans. Commun. **3**(4), 532–540 (1983)
4. Chen, T., Kornblith, S., Norouzi, M., Hinton, G.: A simple framework for contrastive learning of visual representations. In: International Conference on Machine Learning (ICML), pp. 1597–1607. PMLR (2020)
5. Chen, X., He, K.: Exploring simple siamese representation learning. In: CVPR, pp. 15750–15758 (2021)
6. Cong, C., et al.: Semi-supervised adversarial learning for stain normalisation in histopathology images. In: de Bruijne, M., et al. (eds.) MICCAI 2021. LNCS, vol. 12908, pp. 581–591. Springer, Cham (2021). https://doi.org/10.1007/978-3-030-87237-3_56
7. Denton, E., Chintala, S., Szlam, A., Fergus, R.: Deep generative image models using a laplacian pyramid of adversarial networks. In: NeurIPS, vol. 28, pp. 1486–1494 (2015)
8. Falahkheirkhah, K., Guo, T., Hwang, M., et al.: A generative adversarial approach to facilitate archival-quality histopathologic diagnoses from frozen tissue sections. Lab. Investig. **102**(5), 554–559 (2022)
9. Fan, L., Sowmya, A., Meijering, E., Song, Y.: Learning visual features by colorization for slide-consistent survival prediction from whole slide images. In: de Bruijne, M., et al. (eds.) MICCAI 2021. LNCS, vol. 12908, pp. 592–601. Springer, Cham (2021). https://doi.org/10.1007/978-3-030-87237-3_57
10. Goodfellow, I., Pouget-Abadie, J., Mirza, M., et al.: Generative adversarial nets. In: NeurIPS, vol. 27 (2014)
11. He, K., Fan, H., Wu, Y., Xie, S., Girshick, R.: Momentum contrast for unsupervised visual representation learning. In: CVPR, pp. 9729–9738 (2020)
12. He, K., Zhang, X., Ren, S., Sun, J.: Deep residual learning for image recognition. In: CVPR, pp. 770–778 (2016)
13. Heusel, M., Ramsauer, H., Unterthiner, T., Nessler, B., Hochreiter, S.: GANs trained by a two time-scale update rule converge to a local nash equilibrium. In: NeurIPS, vol. 30 (2017)
14. Huang, X., Belongie, S.: Arbitrary style transfer in real-time with adaptive instance normalization. In: ICCV, pp. 1501–1510 (2017)
15. Jaafar, H.: Intra-operative frozen section consultation: concepts, applications and limitations. Malaysian J. Med. Sci. MJMS **13**(1), 4 (2006)
16. Kandoth, C., McLellan, M.D., Vandin, F., et al.: Mutational landscape and significance across 12 major cancer types. Nature **502**(7471), 333–339 (2013)
17. Kather, J.N., Pearson, A.T., Halama, N., et al.: Deep learning can predict microsatellite instability directly from histology in gastrointestinal cancer. Nat. Med. **25**(7), 1054–1056 (2019)
18. Khosla, P., Teterwak, P., Wang, C., et al.: Supervised contrastive learning. In: NeurIPS, vol. 33, pp. 18661–18673 (2020)

19. Kingma, D.P., Ba, J.: Adam: A method for stochastic optimization. In: International Conference for Learning Representations (ICLR) (2015)
20. Lai, W.S., Huang, J.B., Ahuja, N., Yang, M.H.: Deep Laplacian pyramid networks for fast and accurate super-resolution. In: CVPR, pp. 624–632 (2017)
21. Liang, J., Zeng, H., Zhang, L.: High-resolution photorealistic image translation in real-time: a Laplacian pyramid translation network. In: CVPR, pp. 9392–9400 (2021)
22. Liu, X., Zhang, F., Hou, Z., et al.: Self-supervised learning: generative or contrastive. IEEE Trans. Knowl. Data Eng. (2021). https://doi.org/10.1109/TKDE.2021.3090866
23. Macenko, M., Niethammer, M., Marron, J.S., et al.: A method for normalizing histology slides for quantitative analysis. In: IEEE International Symposium on Biomedical Imaging: From Nano to Macro (ISBI), pp. 1107–1110. IEEE (2009)
24. Mao, X., Li, Q., Xie, H., et al.: Least squares generative adversarial networks. In: ICCV, pp. 2794–2802 (2017)
25. Ozyoruk, K.B., Can, S., Gokceler, G.I., et al.: Deep learning-based frozen section to FFPE translation. arXiv preprint arXiv:2107.11786 (2021)
26. Pang, Y., Lin, J., Qin, T., Chen, Z.: Image-to-image translation: methods and applications. IEEE Trans. Multim. (2021). https://doi.org/10.1109/TMM.2021.3109419
27. Park, T., Efros, A.A., Zhang, R., Zhu, J.-Y.: Contrastive learning for unpaired image-to-image translation. In: Vedaldi, A., Bischof, H., Brox, T., Frahm, J.-M. (eds.) ECCV 2020. LNCS, vol. 12354, pp. 319–345. Springer, Cham (2020). https://doi.org/10.1007/978-3-030-58545-7_19
28. Paszke, A., Gross, S., Massa, F., et al.: PyTorch: an imperative style, high-performance deep learning library. In: NeurIPS, pp. 8024–8035 (2019)
29. Rolls, G.O., Farmer, N.J., Hall, J.B.: Artifacts in histological and cytological preparations. Leica Microsystems (2008)
30. Sandler, M., Howard, A., Zhu, M., et al.: MobileNetv2: Inverted residuals and linear bottlenecks. In: CVPR, pp. 4510–4520 (2018)
31. Shaban, M.T., Baur, C., Navab, N., Albarqouni, S.: StainGAN: stain style transfer for digital histological images. In: IEEE International Symposium on Biomedical Imaging: From Nano to Macro (ISBI), pp. 953–956. IEEE (2019)
32. Taqi, S.A., Sami, S.A., Sami, L.B., Zaki, S.A.: A review of artifacts in histopathology. J. Oral Maxillof. Pathol. 22(2), 279 (2018)
33. Wang, T.C., Liu, M.Y., Zhu, J.Y., et al.: High-resolution image synthesis and semantic manipulation with conditional GANs. In: CVPR, pp. 8798–8807 (2018)
34. Wolterink, J.M., Dinkla, A.M., Savenije, M.H.F., Seevinck, P.R., van den Berg, C.A.T., Išgum, I.: Deep MR to CT synthesis using unpaired data. In: Tsaftaris, S.A., Gooya, A., Frangi, A.F., Prince, J.L. (eds.) SASHIMI 2017. LNCS, vol. 10557, pp. 14–23. Springer, Cham (2017). https://doi.org/10.1007/978-3-319-68127-6_2
35. Yang, H., et al.: Unpaired brain MR-to-CT synthesis using a structure-constrained CycleGAN. In: Stoyanov, D., et al. (eds.) DLMIA/ML-CDS -2018. LNCS, vol. 11045, pp. 174–182. Springer, Cham (2018). https://doi.org/10.1007/978-3-030-00889-5_20
36. Yi, X., Walia, E., Babyn, P.: Generative adversarial network in medical imaging: a review. Med. Image Anal. 58, 101552 (2019)
37. Zhang, H., Cisse, M., Dauphin, Y.N., Lopez-Paz, D.: Mixup: beyond empirical risk minimization. In: International Conference for Learning Representations (ICLR) (2018)

38. Zhou, Z., Siddiquee, M.M.R., Tajbakhsh, N., Liang, J.: UNet++: redesigning skip connections to exploit multiscale features in image segmentation. IEEE Trans. Med. Imag. **39**(6), 1856–1867 (2020)
39. Zhu, J.Y., Park, T., Isola, P., Efros, A.A.: Unpaired Image-to-Image translation using cycle-consistent adversarial networks. In: ICCV, pp. 2223–2232 (2017)

Feature Re-calibration Based Multiple Instance Learning for Whole Slide Image Classification

Philip Chikontwe[1], Soo Jeong Nam[2], Heounjeong Go[2,3], Meejeong Kim[2], Hyun Jung Sung[2], and Sang Hyun Park[1(✉)]

[1] Department of Robotics and Mechatronics Engineering, DGIST, Daegu, Korea
{philipchicco,shpark13135}@dgist.ac.kr
[2] Department of Pathology, Asan Medical Center, Seoul, Korea
[3] Department of Pathology, University of Ulsan College of Medicine, Seoul, Korea

Abstract. Whole slide image (WSI) classification is a fundamental task for the diagnosis and treatment of diseases; but, curation of accurate labels is time-consuming and limits the application of fully-supervised methods. To address this, multiple instance learning (MIL) is a popular method that poses classification as a weakly supervised learning task with slide-level labels only. While current MIL methods apply variants of the attention mechanism to re-weight instance features with stronger models, scant attention is paid to the properties of the data distribution. In this work, we propose to re-calibrate the distribution of a WSI bag (instances) by using the statistics of the max-instance (critical) feature. We assume that in binary MIL, positive bags have larger feature magnitudes than negatives, thus we can enforce the model to maximize the discrepancy between bags with a metric feature loss that models positive bags as out-of-distribution. To achieve this, unlike existing MIL methods that use single-batch training modes, we propose balanced-batch sampling to effectively use the feature loss i.e., $(+/-)$ bags simultaneously. Further, we employ a position encoding module (PEM) to model spatial/morphological information, and perform pooling by multi-head self-attention (PSMA) with a Transformer encoder. Experimental results on existing benchmark datasets show our approach is effective and improves over state-of-the-art MIL methods https://github.com/PhilipChicco/FRMIL.

1 Introduction

Histopathology image analysis (HIA) is an important task in modern medicine and is the gold standard for cancer detection and treatment planning [17]. The development of whole slide image (WSI) scanners has enabled the digitization of tissue biopsies into gigapixel images and paved the way for the application of machine learning techniques in the field of digital pathology [3,22]. However, employing popular convolutional neural network (CNN) architectures for varied tasks in HIA is non trivial and has several challenges, ranging from the large size

© The Author(s), under exclusive license to Springer Nature Switzerland AG 2022
L. Wang et al. (Eds.): MICCAI 2022, LNCS 13432, pp. 420–430, 2022.
https://doi.org/10.1007/978-3-031-16434-7_41

of WSIs and extreme high resolution to lack of precise labeling and stain color variations [22]. This motivates the need for memory efficient methods that mitigate the need for fine-grained labels and are fairly interpretable. To address this, multiple instance learning (MIL) [1,31] is a popular formulation that considers diagnosis as a weakly supervised learning problem [29].

Through the recent advances in deep learning [16,30], MIL based histopathology [8,10,13,25,27] analysis has achieved notable success [11,18,24,28]. For instance, Li *et al.* [21] introduced non-local attention to re-weight instances relative the highest scoring instance (critical) in a bag, proving to be a simple yet effective approach. However, the critical instance is only employed for implicit instance re-weighting and the method is sensitive to both the choice of the instance feature encoder (i.e., pre-trained ImageNet or self-supervised), and the scale of patches used. In MIL-RNN [6], recurrent neural networks (RNN) are used to sequentially process instance features, partially encoding position and context, but is limited in the ability to capture long range dependences.

Thus, follow-up works [21,23,24,26] built on the latter with more complex attention-based variants using Transformer [12,30] inspired architectures to better model long range instance correlations via multi-head self-attention (MSA) with positional information encoding. Along this line of thought, TransMIL [26] highlights the importance of spatial positional encoding (PE) and single-scale learning over the latter, but is relatively sensitive to the depth of PE layers (i.e., ×3) and does not explicitly pool all instances to a single bag representation, instead uses a learnable class token for final bag-level prediction. Thus, the use of Transformers with several MSA blocks can be computationally prohibitive, and would be more desirable to have less over-parameterized designs.

To address these challenges, we propose a Feature Re-calibration based MIL framework (FRMIL), building upon prior MIL approaches [21,23,26] leveraging MSA with Transformer encoders. Here, we argue that re-calibrating the distribution of instance features can improve model performance towards better generalization by using the properties of the data distribution directly. In vision tasks such as few-shot learning, feature/distribution re-calibration is used to enable better generalization when learning from limited samples by transferring statistics from classes with sufficient examples [32]. However, in the MIL scenario, instances are not always i.i.d [26], especially since positive instances are often limited in a WSI i.e., ($\leq 10\%$). Thus, we consider a simpler form that uses the max instance to shift the original distribution towards better separability. Also, we consider MIL and anomaly detection [7,14,20] as closely related tasks. For instance, Lee *et al.* [20] leveraged MIL for weakly-supervised action localization by modeling background/normal actions as out-of-distribution using uncertainty by considering their inconsistency in a sequence with video-level labels only.

Inspired by these works, we hypothesize that features from positive and negative bags (binary MIL) exhibit larger and smaller feature magnitudes respectively, and this prior can be directly encoded into the learning framework for better representation learning [20]. In Fig. 1, we show this phenomena and our intuition to highlight how the standard MIL assumption of having at-least one (+) instance

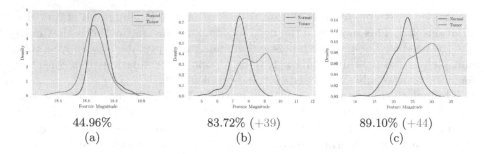

44.96%   83.72% (+39)   89.10% (+44)
(a)   (b)   (c)

Fig. 1. Normalized density plots of the mean feature magnitudes on the CAME-LYON16 [4] train-set, with test-set accuracy and improvements (red color). (a) Original feature magnitudes. (b) Max-instance calibrated based features. (c) Features learned by our FR-MIL model. (Color figure online)

in a bag can be used to make the distribution more separable. Herein, we establish a simple non-parametric baseline that re-calibrates features by subtracting the max instance per-bag, and then computes the probability of a bag-label as the normalized minimum between the mean magnitude and the estimated bag magnitude (see Sect. 2). Our evaluation shows that the baseline performance is comparable to classic MIL operators (i.e., max/mean-pooling) [31].

To incorporate this idea in our framework, we explicitly re-calibrate features with the aforementioned concept, and then feed the new features to a positional encoding module (PEM) [26] followed by a single pooling multi-head self-attention block (PMSA) [19] for bag classification. To effectively enforce feature magnitude discrepancy, we propose a feature embedding loss that maximizes the distance between positive and negative bag features, as well as the standard cross-entropy losses. The main contributions of this work are as follows: (i) We show that feature re-calibration using the max-critical instance embedding is a simple yet powerful technique for MIL, (ii) We introduce a feature magnitude loss to learn better instance/bag separation, (iii) To obtain robust bag embeddings, we leverage a positional encoder and a single self-attention block for instance aggregation, and (iv) Experimental results on a public benchmark and inhouse-curated datasets demonstrate the effectiveness of our method over state-of-the-art methods.

2 Methods

Overview. In this work, we consider a set of WSIs $\mathbf{X} = \{X_i\}$, each associated with a slide-level label $Y_i = \{0, 1\}$, and our goal predict the slide labels using MIL (see Fig. 2). We first extract instance features $\mathbf{H} \in \mathbb{R}^D$ using a neural network $\mathbf{F}_\theta$ i.e., $\mathbf{H_i} = \mathbf{F}_\theta(\mathbf{X_i})$, where $\mathbf{F}$ is either pre-trained on ImageNet or self-supervised learning [9,15]. In FR-MIL, we feed $\mathbf{H}$ to our max-instance selection module to obtain the highest instance (critical) as well as it's probability, then we re-calibrate the features $\mathbf{H}$ with the max-instance to obtain $\hat{\mathbf{H}}$. The position

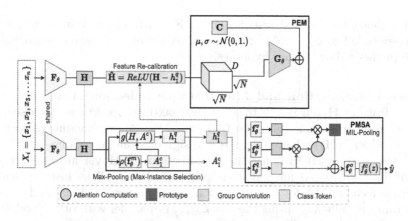

Fig. 2. Overview of the proposed FR-MIL framework.

encoding module (PEM) creates a spatial representation of $\hat{\mathbf{H}}$, applies a single group convolution $\mathbf{G}_\theta$ to obtain correlated features, and then concatenates with a learnable class token $\mathbf{C}$. Finally, we perform MIL Pooling by Multi-head Self-Attention (PSMA) using the max-instance as a query and the output of $\mathbf{G}_\theta$ as key-value pairs to obtain the bag feature. FR-MIL is trained to minimize the bag loss, max-instance loss, and feature magnitude loss between positive and negative instance features. We detail each step below.

Preliminaries: A Simple Baseline. Inspired by the work of Lee *et al.* [20] that employ feature magnitudes for uncertainty estimation of background actions in video sequences, we hypothesize that normal and positive bags should have different magnitudes and can serve as a simple MIL baseline. Herein, given instance features $\mathbf{H}_i^c = \{h_1, h_2, \ldots, h_n\}$, where c denotes the WSI class; the mean feature magnitude per WSI can be obtained as $\mu_i^c = \frac{1}{N} \sum \|\mathbf{H}_i^c\|_2^2$, where N denotes the number of instances in a bag. To obtain the probability $\mathbf{P}(y = 1.)$ of a bag, we formalize our assumption as:

$$\mathbf{P}(y = 1.|\mu_i^c) = \frac{\min(\tau, \mu_i^c)}{\tau}, \tag{1}$$

where τ is the pre-defined maximum feature magnitude determined on the train-set only i.e., point at which the distributions first meet (see Fig. 1). Also, Eq. 1 is ensured to fall between 0 and 1, i.e., $0 \le \mathbf{P}(y = 1.|\cdot) \le 1$. In Fig. 1, we show the magnitudes on a given train-set (Camelyon16 [4]) as a density plot. Note that while both normal and tumor slide curves appear to follow the Gaussian distribution (Fig. 1(a)), separation is non-trivial due to the presence of more normal than tumor instances ($\le 10\%$), and reports a low accuracy (44%) with $\tau = 18.8$. In Fig. 1(b), we show that re-calibrating the distribution by subtracting the max-instance feature before computing the magnitudes creates better separability. Formally, $\hat{\mu}_i^c = \frac{1}{N} \sum \|\hat{\mathbf{H}}_i^c\|_2^2$, where $\hat{\mathbf{H}}_i^c = \{\hat{\mathbf{H}} - h_{max}^c\}$ given $h_{max}^c = \text{argmax}_c \hat{\mathbf{H}}_i^c$. Notably, re-calibration improves the test-accuracy by +39 with $\tau = 8.2$. Finally,

Fig. 1(c) shows the learned distribution of FR-MIL when trained with a feature magnitude loss $\mathcal{L}_{fm}$ and re-calibration, with more significant improvements (+44), further validating our hypothesis.

Feature Re-calibration and Max-Instance Selection. Given the set of instance features $\mathbf{H}$, our goal is to select the max-instance h^q and it's associated score A^c using an instance classifier $\mathbf{f}_\theta^m$ in our Max-Pooling module (see Fig. 2). Here, $A^c = \rho(\mathbf{f}_\theta^m(\mathbf{H}))$ where ρ denotes the sigmoid function. Consequently, the sorted scores are used to index the max-instance in $\mathbf{H}$ via an operator $g(\cdot)$, with h^q later employed for feature re-calibration, as well as instance feature aggregation via PSMA for bag prediction. The max score A^c is used to train the instance classifier $\mathbf{f}_\theta^m$ using the loss $\mathcal{L}_{max}$, in parallel with other modules in FR-MIL. Formally, re-calibration of features can be modeled as

$$\hat{\mathbf{H}} = \text{ReLU}(\hat{\mathbf{H}} - h^q), \qquad (2)$$

similar to the intuition highlighted by the simple baseline. To further incorporate the concept of distribution re-calibration in our framework, we draw connections to prior work [20] for anomaly detection i.e., assumes the feature magnitudes of positive- and normal-bags are different, and can be modeled via uncertainty. Therefore, to effectively model the ambiguous normal/background features, the training procedure should employ both positive and negative bags simultaneously instead of selecting normal features within a single bag (single batch). Herein, counter to existing methods that use a single bag for training, we employ a sampling strategy to produce balanced bags per epoch i.e., we initialize a zero-tensor with the maximum bag size in during training, and fill the relevant bag instance features. Note that by '*balanced*', we imply 1-negative and 1-positive bag is sampled. Formally, to enforce feature discrepancy we propose feature magnitude loss $\mathcal{L}_{fm}$ as:

$$\mathcal{L}_{fm}(\hat{\mathbf{H}}_i^{pos}, \hat{\mathbf{H}}_i^{neg}, \tau) = \frac{1}{N} \sum_{n=1}^{N} (\max(0, \tau - ||\hat{\mathbf{H}}_i^{pos}||) + ||\hat{\mathbf{H}}_i^{neg}||), \qquad (3)$$

where $\hat{\mathbf{H}}^{pos}$, and $\hat{\mathbf{H}}^{neg}$ are the positive- and negative bag instance features, and τ is the pre-defined margin, respectively. While prior work [21] equally used max-pooling to select the max-instance, note that non-local masked attention was proposed for bag feature learning, whereas we use PSMA and propose feature re-calibration.

Positional Encoding Module (PEM). In the standard transformer [12,30] design, encoding spatial information has proved useful for recognition tasks. However, it is non-trivial for WSIs due to varying sizes. In this work, we employ a conditional position encoder (PEM) [23] that takes re-calibrated features $\hat{\mathbf{H}}$, performs zero-padding to provide absolute position for a convolution $\mathbf{G}_\theta$, and later concatenates the output with a class token $\mathbf{C}$ initialized from the normal distribution. Here, features $\hat{\mathbf{H}}$ are re-shaped into a 2D image by first computing $\{H, W\}$ i.e., $H = \sqrt{N} = \sqrt{n}$, where n is the number of instances in a bag. Thus,

$$\hat{\mathbf{H}} \in \mathbb{R}^D \rightarrow \hat{\mathbf{H}} \in \mathbb{R}^{B \times C \times H \times W}, \tag{4}$$

where B is the batch-size, $C = D$ are the instance feature dimensions, and $\mathbf{G}_\theta$ is 2D convolution layer that performs group convolution with kernel size 3×3, and 1×1 zero padding. Note that prior work [23] used different sized convolutions in a pyramidal fashion. Instead, we opt for a single layer to maintain computational feasibility. Finally, let $\acute{\mathbf{H}} = \text{concat}(\mathbf{C}_\theta, \mathbf{G}_\theta(\hat{\mathbf{H}}))$, where $\acute{\mathbf{H}} \in \mathbb{R}^{(N+1) \times D}$ are the flattened restored features i.e., in the case of a single bag.

MIL Pooling by Multi-head Self-Attention (PMSA). In order to pool instance features $\acute{\mathbf{H}}$ to a single bag feature, we employ a single multi-head Transformer encoder [19] that takes as input the max-instance feature h^q as a query and $\acute{\mathbf{H}}$ as key-value pairs i.e., $\text{PMSA}_\theta(h^q, \acute{\mathbf{H}})$. The formulation proposed by Lee *et al.* [19] for set-based tasks employs an attention function $\varphi(\mathbf{Q}, \mathbf{K}, \mathbf{V})$ to measure similarity between a query vector $\mathbf{Q}$ with key-value pairs $\mathbf{K}, \mathbf{V} \in \mathbb{R}^{d \times m}$ as: $\varphi(\mathbf{Q}, \mathbf{K}, \mathbf{V}) = \text{softmax}(\frac{\mathbf{Q}\mathbf{K}^T}{\sqrt{m}})\mathbf{V}$, where $\{d, m\}$ is the instance feature dimension. This can be easily extended to multi-head attention by first projecting vectors onto k different dimensions. The encoder consists of feed-forward networks $\{\mathbf{f}_\theta^q, \mathbf{f}_\theta^k, \mathbf{f}_\theta^v\}$, where $\mathbf{f}_\theta^o$ is fed the output of φ (prototype) together with residual connections and optional Layer Normalization [2] (LN). Formally, let $\hat{\varphi} = \varphi(\mathbf{Q}, \mathbf{K}, \mathbf{V}) + \mathbf{Q}$, then:

$$z = \text{PSMA}(h^q, \acute{\mathbf{H}}, \acute{\mathbf{H}}) = \text{LN}(\hat{\varphi} + \text{ReLU}(\mathbf{f}_\theta^o(\hat{\varphi}))), \tag{5}$$

to produce a bag feature z, later fed to the bag classifier $\mathbf{f}_\theta^c$ for WSI classification. Finally, FR-MIL is trained to minimize the bag-, max-pooling and feature losses. Thus, the final objective is:

$$\mathcal{L} = \gamma_1 \mathcal{L}_{bag}(\hat{y}, y) + \gamma_2 \mathcal{L}_{max}(A^c, y) + \gamma_3 L_{fm}(\hat{\mathbf{H}}_i^{pos}, \hat{\mathbf{H}}_i^{neg}, \tau), \tag{6}$$

where $\{\gamma_i\}$ are balancing weights and $\mathcal{L}_{\{bag, max\}}$ is the binary cross-entropy loss over the true WSI labels y given $\hat{y} = \mathbf{f}_\theta^c(z)$, respectively.

3   Experiments

Datasets. To demonstrate the effectiveness of FR-MIL, we conducted experiments on the publicly available dataset CAMELYON16 [4], and an in-house curated dataset termed COLON-MSI i.e., colorectal (adenocarcinoma) cancer slides involving microsatellite instable (MSI) molecular phenotypes [5]. CAMELYON16 dataset was proposed for metastasis detection in breast cancer, it consists of 271 training sets and 129 testing sets. After pre-processing, a total of 3.2 million patches at ×20 magnification, with an average of 8,800 patches per bag, and a maximum of 30,000 patches per bag on the training set. On the other hand,

Table 1. Evaluation of the proposed method on CAMELYON16 (CM16) and COLON-MSI sets. Metrics accuracy (ACC) and area under the curve (AUC) were employed. †: *denotes scores reported in the paper using ResNet50 as* $\mathbf{F}_\theta$ *with ImageNet features.*

Method	CM16		COLON-MSI	
	ACC	AUC	ACC	AUC
Mean-pooling [31]	0.7984	0.7620	0.624	0.830
Max-pooling [31]	0.8295	0.8641	0.763	0.859
ABMIL [18]	0.8450	0.8653	0.740	0.779
MIL-RNN [6]	0.8062	0.8064	0.630	0.631
CLAM-SB [24]	0.845	0.894	0.786	0.820
DSMIL [21]	0.8682	0.8944	0.734	0.811
TransMIL [23]	0.791	0.813	0.676	0.617
TransMIL† [23]	0.8837	0.9309	–	–
FR-MIL (w/$\mathcal{L}_{bag}$)	0.8600	0.8990	0.809	0.880
FR-MIL (w/$\mathcal{L}_{bag} + \mathcal{L}_{fm}$)	0.8760	0.8990	0.775	0.842
FR-MIL (w/$\mathcal{L}_{bag} + \mathcal{L}_{max}$)	0.8840	0.8940	0.780	0.831
FR-MIL (w/$\mathcal{L}_{bag} + \mathcal{L}_{max} + \mathcal{L}_{fm}$)	0.8910	0.8950	0.809	0.901

COLON-MSI consists of both microsatellite-stable (MSS) and microsatellite-instable (MSI), and is thus a subtyping task. It consists of 625 images, split as follows: 360 training, 92 validation, and 173 testing sets. Experts pathologists detected the presence of tumors with Immunohistochemical analysis (IHC) and PCR-based amplification and collectively agreed on the final slide-level label. Note that tumor ROIs are not used in this work. After pre-processing, a total of 3.5 million patches at ×20 magnification, an average of 6,000 patches/bag, and a maximum of 8900 patches in the train-set.

Implementation Settings. In the pre-processing step, we extracted valid patches of 256×256 after tissue detection and discard patches with $\leq 15\%$ tissue entropy. For the instance encoder $\mathbf{F}_\theta$, we employed the SimCLR [9] ResNet18 [16] encoder trained by Lee *et al.* [21] for the CAMELYON16 dataset. On the COLON-MSI set, we used an ImageNet pre-trained ResNet18. Thus, each instance feature is represented as $\mathbf{H}_i \in \mathbb{R}^{n \times 512}$. FR-MIL is trained with balanced batch sampling (B = 2), and learning rate of $1e-4$ with Adam optimizer for 100 epochs with 20% dropout as regularization, and PSMA has heads $k = 8$. Hyper-parameters $\{\gamma_{1,2,3}\} = 0.33$, with $\tau = 8.48$ for CAMELYON16, and $\tau = 57.5$ on COLON-MSI, respectively.

Comparison Methods. We compare FR-MIL to traditional MIL methods max- and mean-pooling [31], as well as existing state-of-the-art methods: ABMIL [18], DSMIL [21], CLAM-SB [24], MIL-RNN [6], and TransMIL [26]. All compared methods are trained for 200 epochs on COLON-MSI with similar settings.

4   Results and Discussion

Main Results. Table 1 presents the results of our approach against recent methods. On the CAMELYON16 dataset, FR-MIL reports +3% (ACC) improvement over DSMIL with comparable performance (+1%) to the reported TransMIL scores using a larger feature extractor. Given that only a small portion of a each positive bag contains tumors, using the max-instance for bag pooling with re-calibration is intuitively sound and shows better performance over other methods. Moreover, though we employ PEM similar to TransMIL, the use of a single PEM module on calibrated facilitates better correlation learning.

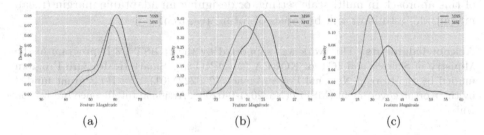

(a)   (b)   (c)

Fig. 3. Density plots of the mean feature magnitudes on the COLON-MSI train-set. (a) Original feature magnitudes. (b) Max-instance re-calibration based features. (c) Features learned by our FR-MIL model.

On the other hand, since the majority of slides contain relatively large tumor regions (averagely $\geq 75\%$) in COLON-MSI, max- and mean-pooling show high AUC but had inconsistent results (ACC). Overall, CLAM-SB reports the best ACC among the compared methods i.e., 78.6%. Interestingly, TransMIL performed poorly on this set, possibly due to over-parametrization, and the morphological similarities between MSS and MSI instances. Similar observations were drawn regarding MIL-RNN. Consequently, the proposed FR-MIL highlights the importance of calibration in subtyping problems, reporting +2% (ACC) and +5% (AUC) improvements achieving the best scores. See Fig. 3 for the distribution of features.

Ablations. To validate the effectiveness of the proposed losses on learning, we evaluated FR-MIL with/without certain losses (see Table 1). First, on CAMELYON16, we found $\mathcal{L}_{fm}$ was a crucial component to further boost the AUC score. Overall, when both $\mathcal{L}_{max}$ and $\mathcal{L}_{fm}$ were omitted, performance drops were noted. On the other hand, on COLON-MSI, using a $\mathcal{L}_{bag}$ only had the best scores, whereas the use of both $\mathcal{L}_{max}$ and $\mathcal{L}_{fm}$ resulted in a significant reduction (AUC). However, employing all the losses resulted in more stable scores.

5   Conclusion

In this work, we presented a MIL framework for Whole Slide Image classification that leverages Feature Re-calibration, applicable to both binary and sub-typing tasks. We show that: (i) by leveraging feature magnitude discrepancy between positive and negative bags as a probabilistic measure; a simple baseline is comparable in performance to classic MIL operators, (ii) explicitly re-calibrating the data distribution with max-instances during training by drawing connections to the standard MIL assumption is simple yet effective, and (iii) the use of a metric feature loss to encourage better feature separation in $(+/-)$ bags improves both Accuracy and AUC over state-of-the-art methods. Further exploring the utility of this approach in multi-scale setting, or designing an adaptable margin (mean magnitude) estimator will be topics of future research.

Acknowledgments. This work was supported by the DGIST R&D program of the Ministry of Science and ICT of KOREA (21-DPIC-08), Smart HealthCare Program funded by the Korean National Police Agency (220222M01), and IITP grant funded by the Korean government (MSIT) (No. 2021-0-02068, Artificial Intelligence Innovation Hub).

References

1. Amores, J.: Multiple instance classification: review, taxonomy and comparative study. Artif. Intell. **201**, 81–105 (2013)
2. Ba, J.L., Kiros, J.R., Hinton, G.E.: Layer normalization. arXiv preprint arXiv:1607.06450 (2016)
3. Banerji, S., Mitra, S.: Deep learning in histopathology: a review. Wiley Interdiscip. Rev. Data Min. Knowl. Disc. **12**(1), e1439 (2022)
4. Bejnordi, B.E., et al.: Diagnostic assessment of deep learning algorithms for detection of lymph node metastases in women with breast cancer. JAMA **318**(22), 2199–2210 (2017)
5. Boland, C.R., Goel, A.: Microsatellite instability in colorectal cancer. Gastroenterology **138**(6), 20732087 (2010)
6. Campanella, G., et al.: Clinical-grade computational pathology using weakly supervised deep learning on whole slide images. Nat. Med. **25**(8), 1301–1309 (2019)
7. Chalapathy, R., Chawla, S.: Deep learning for anomaly detection: a survey. arXiv preprint arXiv:1901.03407 (2019)
8. Chen, H., et al.: From pixel to whole slide: automatic detection of microvascular invasion in hepatocellular carcinoma on histopathological image via cascaded networks. In: de Bruijne, M., et al. (eds.) MICCAI 2021. LNCS, vol. 12908, pp. 196–205. Springer, Cham (2021). https://doi.org/10.1007/978-3-030-87237-3_19
9. Chen, T., Kornblith, S., Norouzi, M., Hinton, G.: A simple framework for contrastive learning of visual representations. In: ICML, pp. 1597–1607. PMLR (2020)
10. Chikontwe, P., Kim, M., Nam, S.J., Go, H., Park, S.H.: Multiple instance learning with center embeddings for histopathology classification. In: Martel, A.L., et al. (eds.) MICCAI 2020. LNCS, vol. 12265, pp. 519–528. Springer, Cham (2020). https://doi.org/10.1007/978-3-030-59722-1_50

11. Dimitriou, N., Arandjelović, O., Caie, P.D.: Deep learning for whole slide image analysis: an overview. Front. Med. **6**, 264 (2019)

12. Dosovitskiy, A., et al.: An image is worth 16x16 words: transformers for image recognition at scale. In: ICLR (2021)

13. Fan, L., Sowmya, A., Meijering, E., Song, Y.: Learning visual features by colorization for slide-consistent survival prediction from whole slide images. In: de Bruijne, M., et al. (eds.) MICCAI 2021. LNCS, vol. 12908, pp. 592–601. Springer, Cham (2021). https://doi.org/10.1007/978-3-030-87237-3_57

14. Feng, J.C., Hong, F.T., Zheng, W.S.: MIST: multiple instance self-training framework for video anomaly detection. In: CVPR, pp. 14009–14018 (2021)

15. Grill, J.B., et al.: Bootstrap your own latent-a new approach to self-supervised learning. In: NeurIPS, vol. 33, pp. 21271–21284 (2020)

16. He, K., Zhang, X., Ren, S., Sun, J.: Deep residual learning for image recognition. In: CVPR, pp. 770–778 (2016)

17. He, L., Long, L.R., Antani, S., Thoma, G.R.: Histology image analysis for carcinoma detection and grading. Comput. Methods Programs Biomed. **107**(3), 538–556 (2012)

18. Ilse, M., Tomczak, J., Welling, M.: Attention-based deep multiple instance learning. In: ICML, pp. 2127–2136. PMLR (2018)

19. Lee, J., Lee, Y., Kim, J., Kosiorek, A., Choi, S., Teh, Y.W.: Set Transformer: a framework for attention-based permutation-invariant neural networks. In: ICML, pp. 3744–3753. PMLR (2019)

20. Lee, P., Wang, J., Lu, Y., Byun, H.: Weakly-supervised temporal action localization by uncertainty modeling. In: AAAI, vol. 2 (2021)

21. Li, B., Li, Y., Eliceiri, K.W.: Dual-stream multiple instance learning network for whole slide image classification with self-supervised contrastive learning. In: CVPR, pp. 14318–14328 (2021)

22. Li, C., et al.: A comprehensive review of computer-aided whole-slide image analysis: from datasets to feature extraction, segmentation, classification, and detection approaches. arXiv preprint arXiv:2102.10553 (2021)

23. Li, H., et al.: DT-MIL: deformable transformer for multi-instance learning on histopathological image. In: de Bruijne, M., et al. (eds.) MICCAI 2021. LNCS, vol. 12908, pp. 206–216. Springer, Cham (2021). https://doi.org/10.1007/978-3-030-87237-3_20

24. Lu, M.Y., Williamson, D.F., Chen, T.Y., Chen, R.J., Barbieri, M., Mahmood, F.: Data-efficient and weakly supervised computational pathology on whole-slide images. Nat. Biomed. Eng. **5**(6), 555–570 (2021)

25. Rymarczyk, D., Borowa, A., Tabor, J., Zielinski, B.: Kernel self-attention for weakly-supervised image classification using deep multiple instance learning. In: IEEE Winter Conference on Applications of Computer Vision, pp. 1721–1730 (2021)

26. Shao, Z., et al.: TransMIL: transformer based correlated multiple instance learning for whole slide image classification. In: NeurIPS, vol. 34 (2021)

27. Sharma, Y., Shrivastava, A., Ehsan, L., Moskaluk, C.A., Syed, S., Brown, D.: Cluster-to-conquer: a framework for end-to-end multi-instance learning for whole slide image classification. In: Medical Imaging with Deep Learning, pp. 682–698. PMLR (2021)

28. Shi, X., Xing, F., Xie, Y., Zhang, Z., Cui, L., Yang, L.: Loss-based attention for deep multiple instance learning. In: AAAI, vol. 34, pp. 5742–5749 (2020)

29. Srinidhi, C.L., Ciga, O., Martel, A.L.: Deep neural network models for computational histopathology: a survey. Med. Image Anal. **67**, 101813 (2021)

30. Vaswani, A., et al.: Attention is all you need. In: NeurIPS, vol. 30 (2017)
31. Wang, X., Yan, Y., Tang, P., Bai, X., Liu, W.: Revisiting multiple instance neural networks. Pattern Recogn. **74**, 15–24 (2018)
32. Yang, S., Liu, L., Xu, M.: Free lunch for few-shot learning: distribution calibration. In: ICLR (2020)

Computational Anatomy and Physiology

Physiological Model Based Deep Learning Framework for Cardiac TMP Recovery

Xufeng Huang[1], Chengjin Yu[1], and Huafeng Liu[1,2,3]($\boxtimes$)

[1] State Key Laboratory of Modern Optical Instrumentation,
Zhejiang University, Hangzhou 310027, China
`liuhf@zju.edu.cn`
[2] Jiaxing Key Laboratory of Photonic Sensing and Intelligent Imaging,
Jiaxing 314000, China
[3] Intelligent Optics and Photonics Research Center, Jiaxing Research Institute,
Zhejiang University, Jiaxing 314000, China

Abstract. Recovering cardiac transmembrane potential (TMP) from body surface potential (BSP) plays an important role in the noninvasive diagnosis of heart diseases. However, most current solutions for TMP recovery are typically proposed and designed to follow a static mapping paradigm between TMP and BSP, which ignores the inherent dynamic activation process of cardiomyocytes during the cardiac cycle. In this paper, we propose to introduce the physiological information of this dynamic activation process in the objective functions. Based on this, we further establish a physiological model based deep learning framework for cardiac TMP recovery. First, the objective functions of our physiological model are deduced via a two-variable diffusion-reaction system, where the static mapping and the dynamic activation process of cardiomyocytes are jointly modeled. Then, a data-driven Kalman Filtering network (KFNet) is adopted to solve the proposed objective functions. Specifically, the KFNet consists of two components: a state transfer network (SSNet) is employed for directly predicting the prior estimation; furthermore, a Kalman gain network (KGNet) is employed for adaptively learning the gain coefficients. In our experiments, the proposed physiological model is verified on the 1200 simulated subjects. The quantified analysis shows the proposed method can accurately recover the TMP, with the low LE values 10.5 for the ectopic pacing location task and the high SSIM values 0.75 for the myocardial infarction detection task. These powerful performances completely verify the effectiveness of our model.

Keywords: TMP · Physiological model · Deep learning · Kalman filtering

1 Introduce

TMP recovery is of great clinical significance since it can directly detect the location of cardiac ectopic pacing and reconstruct the shape of myocardial infarction scar [1–3]. However, the TMP recovery is an ill-posed inverse problem due to the

L. Wang et al. (Eds.): MICCAI 2022, LNCS 13432, pp. 433–443, 2022.
https://doi.org/10.1007/978-3-031-16434-7_42

dimensions of the body surface potential are much smaller than the potential on the heart surface [4,5]. At present, there are two main methods for TMP recovery: (1) one category is traditional machine leaning methods [6], including graph-based total variational regularization [7], spatiotemporal regularization [8], unscented KF (UKF) [9], etc. (2) Another category is deep learning based methods [10,11], including variational autoencoder network (VAENet) [12], Spatial Temporal Modeling [13], LNISTANet [14], GISTANet [15], GFIS-TANet [16], etc.

However, most methods for TMP recovery ignore the physiological information of the dynamic activation process during the cardiac cycle. Those methods only model the static relationship from TMP-to-BSP at a single moment. For example, in the field of traditional methods, the Graph-TV [7] combines TMP with cardiac geometry structure. In [8], a novel spatiotemporal regularization approach is proposed. However, these traditional methods are still challenging by manually defined parameters and taking a lot of time for the iterative calculation. To deal with these challenges, many researchers propose to utilize the deep neural networks for TMP recovery. For example, in the LNISTANet, a learning nonlocal regularized Iterative Shrinkage-Thresholding Network is proposed. In the GISTANet, the geometry of the cardiac is introduced in conjunction with an iterative soft-threshold contraction algorithm [17]. Even so, both of those traditional methods and deep learning methods ignore the dynamic activation process of the cardiomyocytes, resulting in poor performance in TMP recovery. The dynamic activation process is considered in the latent space of the encoding [13], but the dynamic activation process of the TMP itself is not considered.

Recently, the work in [9] propose an interesting framework, where the dynamic activation model of the cardiomyocyte is considered for TMP recovery. Compared with the static mapping based models, the work in [9] completely models the prior physiological information of the heart, and also shows better performance. Despite this, the clinical application value of the [9] is still limited. This is because the model in [9] is solved through a traditional UKF method. During the optimization process of the UKF, it is necessary to introduce additional parameter to update the state transition equation, and resulting in the high computational complexity. Besides, the gaps between the different initialized parameters in UKF will propagate to the learning process of the model, and lead to unstable performance.

In this paper, considering the dynamic activation process, we further propose a physiological model based deep learning framework. Different from [9], we develop a data-driven KFNet to solve the proposed model. Firstly, the state transition equation is updated by SSNet. Then the KGNet is proposed to obtain the kalman gain coefficients. Finally, the reconstructed TMP is generated by the KF update [18]. The advantages of this paper can be summarized from three aspects:

1. We extend the existing static TMP recovery model to a dynamic space, and establish a physiological model by further modeling the dynamic activation process of cardiomyocytes.

2. We propose a deep Kalman Filtering network (KFNet) instead of the traditional KF method for solving the proposed physiological model. Via a data-driven form, the proposed KFNet can adaptively initialize and update the model parameters.
3. We provide a potential clinical tool for TMP recovery. Compared with the existing methods, the proposed tool can achieve more accurate TMP recovery in a time-saving and stable way.

2 Methodology

2.1 Physiological Model

The relationship between TMP(U) and BSP(Φ) can be modeled by the quasi-static equation of electromagnetic theory [19] as the following equation:

$$\Phi = HU \tag{1}$$

To consider a dynamic TMP distribution with F frames:$U \in R^{N*F}$, the corresponding dynamic mapping of BSP is $\Phi \in R^{M*F}$. M and N are the numbers of body surface nodes and heart surface nodes. $H \in R^{M*N}$ is the transform matrix, obtained by solving the relationship between the heart and the trunk using boundary element and finite element method [20].

By Eq. (1), we can obtain **the measurement equation:**

$$\phi_t = Hu_t \tag{2}$$

According to two-variable diffusion-reaction systems [19]:

$$\frac{\partial u}{\partial t} = \nabla \cdot (D_d \nabla u) + f_1(u, v) \tag{3}$$

$$\frac{\partial v}{\partial t} = f_2(u, v) \tag{4}$$

v is the conduction current. D_d is diffusion tensor, and $\nabla \cdot (D_d \nabla u)$ is the diffusion term. f_1 and f_2 produce different TMP shapes. It can be modeled as the following equation: $x_t = f(x_{t-1}), x_t = (u_t, v_t)$, but this formula contains the conduction current, the model is more complicated. Because the state transition equation of Kalman filter is inherently an inaccurate prediction process, we redefine **the state transition equation:**

$$u_t = f(u_{t-1}) \tag{5}$$

When solving a problem by using KF, we have to take into account the noise contained in the system, so the state space is:

$$u_t = f(u_{t-1}) + \alpha_t \tag{6}$$

$$\phi_t = Hu_t + \beta_t \tag{7}$$

α_t and β_t is the noise.

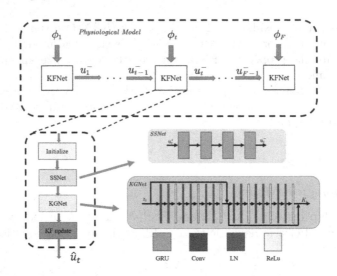

Fig. 1. The proposed physiological model and the KFNet structure. f is the state transfer network (SSNet), and κ is Kalman gain network (KGNet). GRU is a gate recurrent unit.

2.2   Kalman Update

KF modified prior the estimation of state transition equation [21–23]. KF is divided into two steps: (1) State prediction, (2) State update.

State Prediction

$$u_t^- = f(\hat{u}_{t-1}) \tag{8}$$

$$P_t^- = g(\hat{P}_{t-1}) \tag{9}$$

In Eq. (8), u_t^- which is a prior estimate can be predicted at t frame, and $\hat{u}_{t-1}$ is the posterior estimation at t−1 frame, which is a precise result. In Eq. (9), P_t^- is a prior estimate of variance at t frame, and $\hat{P}_{t-1}$ is a posterior estimate of variance at t−1 frame. No explicit formulation is derived for g

State Update

$$K_t = P_t^- H^T (H P_t^- H^T + R_t) \tag{10}$$

$$\hat{u}_t = u_t^- + K_t(\phi_t - H u_t^-) \tag{11}$$

$$\hat{P}_t = (I - K_t H) P_t^- \tag{12}$$

K_t is kalman gain coefficient which can be calculated by Eq. (10). R_t is the β_t covariance matrix. $\hat{P}_t$ are a posterior estimate of variance. I is the identity matrix.

2.3   KFNet

We propose to combine KF and deep learning to build a KFNet for TMP recovery. Figure 1 shows KFNet network structure. KFNet includes a SSNet and a

Kalman gain network. In the following equations, we use κ to represent the KGNet, and f to represent the SSNet. We replace state transfer equation which is nonlinear with SSNet.

$$u_t^- = f(u_{t-1}^-) \tag{13}$$

From the Kalman update Eqs. (10), (11) and (12), we know that calculation of a posterior estimate depends on the Kalman gain coefficient. The Kalman gain coefficient is not only related to the observation ϕ_t at t frame but also to the state transition equation. Therefore, we combine SSNet that replaces the state transition equation and kalman gain network, then obtain the Kalman gain coefficient.

We multiply ϕ_t and u_t^- to get $z_t = \phi_t * u_t^-$. Then K_t is estimated by using κ.

$$K_t = \kappa(z_t) \tag{14}$$

According to Eq. (11), We calculate the gain coefficient and combine the learned Kalman gain coefficient into the overall Kalman update flow.

$$\hat{u}_t = f(u_{t-1}^-) + \kappa(z_t)(\phi_t - Hf(u_{t-1}^-)) \tag{15}$$

Loss Function: Two requirements need to be considered when the loss function is established. First, in order to ensure the accuracy of the state transition equation, we set a constraint loss function. Second, it is necessary to ensure that the update result is close to the ground truth. For these reasons, the loss function is designed as the superposition of these two partial loss function

$$Loss = \frac{1}{F} \sum_{t=1}^{F} \|\hat{u}_t - u_t\|_2^2 + \frac{1}{F} \sum_{t=1}^{F} \|u_t^- - u_t\|_2^2 \tag{16}$$

u_t is the ground truth.

3 Experiments

3.1 Experimental Settings

Experiments. To verify the effectiveness of the proposed KFNet for TMP recovery, we perform the experiments from three aspects. 1) Performance studies: we test the performance of the KFNet on cardiac ectopic pacing task and the myocardial infarction detection task [28], since the former will cause abnormal conduction of the TMP, while the latter will cause local non-conduction of the TMP. 2) Comparison studies: In order to show the superiority of the KFNet, we compared it with Tikhonov regularization [25], TV [7] and VAENet [12]. Specifically, the comparison is conducted on the mentioned two tasks over the three measurement metrics. Besides, visual analysis, quantitative analysis, robustness analysis are also studied to prove the advantages of the KFNet. 3) Ablation studies: to study the effect of the data-driven Kalman coefficient learning, we compare the performance of our model without Kalman coefficient learning (SSNet).

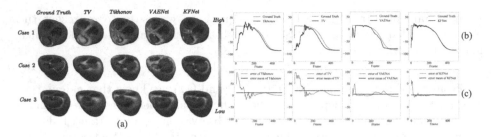

Fig. 2. The visualization results of the different methods on the ectopic pacing task. (a) shows the spatial distributions of TMP on three cases with different heart initiates ectopic pacing locations. (b) shows the temporal TMP curves of real and predicted results on case 1, and (c) shows the predicted error of temporal TMP on case 1.

Measurement Metrics. The experimental results are measured by three evaluation metrics: 1) correlation coefficient (CC) [26]: it describes the degree of linear correlation between ground-truth and predicted results; 2) structural similarity (SSIM) [27]: it evaluates the structure similarity between the real images and the reconstructed images, i.e., the real ectopic pacing images and reconstructed ectopic pacing images; 3) location error (LE) [15]: it evaluates the positioning accuracy of ectopic pacing via calculating the Euclidean distance.

Data Acquisition. Our experimental data are generated by ECGsim software [24]. In total, we simulated 1200 subjects, including 600 cases of ectopic pacing [29] and 600 cases of myocardial infarction [30]. In the ectopic pacing location task, 500 cases are used for model training and 100 cases are used for model testing. At the same time, we ensure that the ectopic pacing positions of all cases are not repeated, and set the complete activation TMP as −85 mv and the resting TMP as 15 mv. In the myocardial infarction detection task, 500 cases are used for model training and 100 cases are used for model testing. At the same time, we ensure that the myocardial infarction regions of all cases are not repeated, and set the TMP in myocardial infarction area as −85 mv.

3.2 Experimental Results

Powerful Performance of the KFNet. The last column of Fig. 2 (a) shows the visual results of the cardiac ectopic pacing location on three cases, in which we can find that the KFNet can accurately reconstruct the cardiac ectopic pacing location similar to the ground truth. The last column Fig. 2 (b) shows the comparison between the real TMP and the recovered TMP. Furthermore, we can find that the proposed method can accurately recovery the TMP with a small error as shown in the last column of Fig. 2 (c).

Figure 3 (a) shows the spatial distribution of myocardial infarction detected by KFNet on three different cases. In fact, the proposed KFNet preserves the shape details of the myocardial infarction area compared to the true distribution.

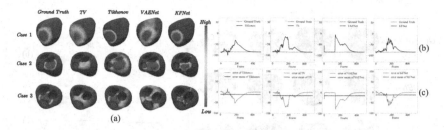

Fig. 3. The visualization results of the different methods on the myocardial infarction task. (a) shows the spatial distributions of TMP on three cases, where the red region represents normal area, and the blue region represents infarct scar. (b) shows the temporal TMP curves of real and predicted results on case 1, and (c) shows the predicted error of temporal TMP on case 1.

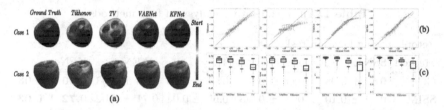

Fig. 4. (a) shows the myocardial activation time sequence on two different ectopic pacing locations. (b) show the linear regression analysis of four methods for TMP recovery. (c) shows the performance analysis on two metrics based on the box diagram (The left two pictures of the ectopic pacing location task and the right two pictures of the myocardial infarction detection task).

The last column Fig. 3 (b) and (c) also shows the KFNet can recovery resting TMP with small fluctuations.

Better Performance than the Existing TMP Recovery Methods.
Figure 2 and Fig. 3 show the visual analysis of four methods. Although Tikhonov and TV can roughly locate the source of ectopic pacing, the edges of the pacing area are blurred in Fig. 2 (a). On the contrary, our proposed KFNet can clearly show the details of the ectopic pacing position. As is shown Fig. 2 (b) and (c), KFNet and KFNet reconstructed temporal TMP from ectopic pacing positions perform better than TV and Tikhonov with smaller errors.

As is shown Fig. 3 (a), (b), and (c), KFNet achieved good results in four methods for reconstructing the area of myocardial infarction, in which the shape and detail of myocardial infarction can be reconstructed very well.

Table 1 shows the quantitative analysis of four methods. It can be seen from the table that the reconstruction effect of Tikhonov and TV is not as good as KFNet. Compared to VAEnet, KFNet also has higher CC, SSIM, and lower LE.

Figure 4 (a) shows the performance of different methods on two cases of reconstruction activation sequence. The activation time of the heart can reflect

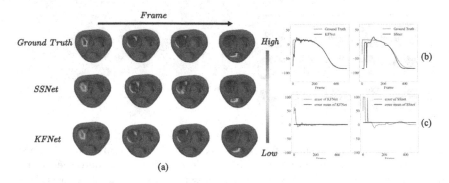

Fig. 5. Spatial distributions of TMP signal, temporal TMP signal and difference plot in pacemaker by the two methods in comparison to the ground truth.

Table 1. The quantitative analysis of four methods.

Ectopic pacing location task					
Method	SSNet	Tikhonov	TV	VAENet	KFNet
CC	0.62 ± 0.08	0.65 ± 0.02	0.61 ± 0.03	0.65 ± 0.03	**0.66 ± 0.03**
SSIM	0.64 ± 0.10	0.70 ± 0.06	0.65 ± 0.04	0.71 ± 0.02	**0.72 ± 0.03**
LE	18.07 ± 10.99	15.1 ± 11.6	20.3 ± 10.7	11.1 ± 7.2	**10.5 ± 7.7**
Myocardial infarction detection task					
CC	\	0.61 ± 0.020	0.60 ± 0.06	0.69 ± 0.02	**0.70 ± 0.05**
SSIM	\	0.71 ± 0.02	0.65 ± 0.07	0.74 ± 0.03	**0.75 ± 0.01**

the activation sequence of each point of the heart [31], which is helpful for the diagnosis of heart disease. From the start of activation to the end of activation, the activate time sequence of TV and Tikhonov fluctuates greatly. As is shown in Fig. 4 (a), the activate time sequence variation of VAENet and KFNet is stable. But KFNet is more stable than VAENet at the early activation time sequence.

Furthermore, Fig. 4 (b) and (c) shows the robustness analysis of four methods. It is show that our proposed method performs the best among the four methods.

The Benefits of the Data Driven Kalman Gain Coefficient Learning. Figure 5 shows the comparison results of KFNet and SSNet. This experiment verifies the effectiveness of our proposal to improve the reconstructed TMP signal by learning the Kalman gain coefficient through the network. As is shown in Table 1, the Kalman gain coefficients learned by the network can improve the reconstruction accuracy of TMP signals.

4   Conclusions

In this paper, we proposed a physiological model based deep learning framework. Our model fully considered the physiological information of the dynamic activation process of cardiomyocytes. To solve this model, we also designed a data-driven deep Kalman Filtering net to replace the traditional KF method. The experiments on simulated data indicates that the proposed method can accurately locate the source of ectopic pacing and reconstruct myocardial infarction area. In future work, we hope that the proposed model can be extended to real clinical data.

Acknowledgements. This work was supported in part by the National Natural Science Foundation of China (U1809204, 62101491), by the Talent Program of Zhejiang Province (2021R51004), by the National Key Technology Research and Development Program of China (2017YFE0104000).

References

1. Carmeliet, E.: Cardiac transmembrane potentials and metabolism. Circ. Res. **42**, 577–587 (1978)
2. Paul, T., et al.: Atrial reentrant tachycardia after surgery for congenital heart disease: endocardial mapping and radiofrequency catheter ablation using a novel, noncontact mapping system. Circulation **103**, 2266–2271 (2001)
3. Ramanathan, C., Ghanem, R., Jia, P., Ryu, K., Rudy, Y.: Noninvasive electrocardiographic imaging for cardiac electrophysiology and arrhythmia. Nat. Med. **10**, 422–428 (2004)
4. Wu, D., Ono, K., Hosaka, H., He, B.: Body surface Laplacian mapping during epicardial and endocardial pacing: a model study. Comput. Cardiol. **1996**, 725–728 (1996)
5. Dhamala, J., Ghimire, S., Sapp, J.L., Horáček, B.M., Wang, L.: High-dimensional Bayesian optimization of personalized cardiac model parameters via an embedded generative model. In: Frangi, A.F., Schnabel, J.A., Davatzikos, C., Alberola-López, C., Fichtinger, G. (eds.) MICCAI 2018. LNCS, vol. 11071, pp. 499–507. Springer, Cham (2018). https://doi.org/10.1007/978-3-030-00934-2_56
6. Pullan, A., Cheng, L., Nash, M., Bradley, C., Paterson, D.: Noninvasive electrical imaging of the heart: theory and model development. Ann. Biomed. Eng. **29**, 817–836 (2001)
7. Xie, S., Wang, L., Zhang, H., Liu, H.: Non-invasive reconstruction of dynamic myocardial transmembrane potential with graph-based total variation constraints. Healthc. Technol. Lett. **6**, 181–186 (2019)
8. Messnarz, B., Tilg, B., Modre, R., Fischer, G., Hanser, F.: A new spatiotemporal regularization approach for reconstruction of cardiac transmembrane potential patterns. IEEE Trans. Biomed. Eng. **51**, 273–281 (2004)
9. Wang, L., Zhang, H., Wong, K., Liu, H., Shi, P.: Physiological-model-constrained noninvasive reconstruction of volumetric myocardial transmembrane potentials. IEEE Trans. Biomed. Eng. **57**, 296–315 (2009)
10. Ghimire, S., Wang, L.: Deep generative model and analysis of cardiac transmembrane potential. In: 2018 Computing in Cardiology Conference (CinC), vol. 45, pp. 1–4 (2018)
11. Bacoyannis, T., Krebs, J., Cedilnik, N., Cochet, H., Sermesant, M.: Deep learning formulation of ECGI for data-driven integration of spatiotemporal correlations and imaging information. In: Coudière, Y., Ozenne, V., Vigmond, E., Zemzemi, N. (eds.) FIMH 2019. LNCS, vol. 11504, pp. 20–28. Springer, Cham (2019). https://doi.org/10.1007/978-3-030-21949-9_3

12. Ghimire, S., Dhamala, J., Gyawali, P.K., Sapp, J.L., Horacek, M., Wang, L.: Generative modeling and inverse imaging of cardiac transmembrane potential. In: Frangi, A.F., Schnabel, J.A., Davatzikos, C., Alberola-López, C., Fichtinger, G. (eds.) MICCAI 2018. LNCS, vol. 11071, pp. 508–516. Springer, Cham (2018). https://doi.org/10.1007/978-3-030-00934-2_57

13. Jiang, X., et al.: Label-free physics-informed image sequence reconstruction with disentangled spatial-temporal modeling. In: de Bruijne, M., et al. (eds.) MICCAI 2021. LNCS, vol. 12906, pp. 361–371. Springer, Cham (2021). https://doi.org/10.1007/978-3-030-87231-1_35

14. Xie, S., Cheng, L., Liu, H.: Lnista-Net: learning nonlocal regularized iterative shrinkage-thresholding network for noninvasive cardiac transmembrane potential imaging. In: 2021 IEEE 18th International Symposium on Biomedical Imaging (ISBI), pp. 183–186 (2021)

15. Mu, L., Liu, H.: Cardiac transmembrane potential imaging with GCN based iterative soft threshold network. In: de Bruijne, M., et al. (eds.) MICCAI 2021. LNCS, vol. 12906, pp. 547–556. Springer, Cham (2021). https://doi.org/10.1007/978-3-030-87231-1_53

16. Cheng, L., Liu, H.: Noninvasive cardiac transmembrane potential imaging via global features based FISTA network. In: 2021 43rd Annual International Conference of the IEEE Engineering in Medicine & Biology Society (EMBC), pp. 3149–3152 (2021)

17. Zhang, J., Ghanem, B.: ISTA-Net: interpretable optimization-inspired deep network for image compressive sensing. In: Proceedings of the IEEE Conference on Computer Vision and Pattern Recognition, pp. 1828–1837 (2018)

18. Simon, D.: Kalman filtering. Embed. Syst. Program. **14**, 72–79 (2001)

19. Aliev, R., Panfilov, A.: A simple two-variable model of cardiac excitation. Chaos Solitons Fractals **7**, 293–301 (1996)

20. Gulrajani, R.: The forward and inverse problems of electrocardiography. IEEE Eng. Med. Biol. Mag. **17**, 84–101 (1998)

21. Sinopoli, B., Schenato, L., Franceschetti, M., Poolla, K., Jordan, M., Sastry, S.: Kalman filtering with intermittent observations. IEEE Trans. Autom. Control **49**, 1453–1464 (2004)

22. Einicke, G., White, L.: Robust extended Kalman filtering. IEEE Trans. Signal Process. **47**, 2596–2599 (1999)

23. Revach, G., Shlezinger, N., Van Sloun, R., Eldar, Y.: KalmanNet: data-driven Kalman filtering. In: ICASSP 2021-2021 IEEE International Conference on Acoustics, Speech and Signal Processing (ICASSP), pp. 3905–3909 (2021)

24. Van Oosterom, A., Oostendorp, T.: ECGSIM: an interactive tool for studying the genesis of QRST waveforms. Heart **90**, 165–168 (2004)

25. Greensite, F., Huiskamp, G.: An improved method for estimating epicardial potentials from the body surface. IEEE Trans. Biomed. Eng. **45**, 98–104 (1998)

26. Ghodrati, A., Brooks, D., Tadmor, G., MacLeod, R.: Wavefront-based models for inverse electrocardiography. IEEE Trans. Biomed. Eng. **53**, 1821–1831 (2006)

27. Mu, L., Liu, H.: Noninvasive electrocardiographic imaging with low-rank and nonlocal total variation regularization. Pattern Recogn. Lett. **138**, 106–114 (2020)

28. Van Dam, P., Oostendorp, T., Linnenbank, A., Van Oosterom, A.: Non-invasive imaging of cardiac activation and recovery. Ann. Biomed. Eng. **37**, 1739–1756 (2009)

29. Rosa, A., et al.: Ectopic pacing at physiological rate improves postanoxic recovery of the developing heart. Am. J. Physiol. Heart Circ. Physiol. **284**, H2384–H2392 (2003)

30. Frangogiannis, N.: Pathophysiology of myocardial infarction. Compr. Physiol. **5**, 1841–1875 (2011)
31. Rosenqvist, M., Bergfeldt, L., Haga, Y., Ryden, J., Ryden, L., Öwall, A.: The effect of ventricular activation sequence on cardiac performance during pacing. Pacing Clin. Electrophysiol. **19**, 1279–1286 (1996)

DentalPointNet: Landmark Localization on High-Resolution 3D Digital Dental Models

Yankun Lang[1], Xiaoyang Chen[4], Hannah H. Deng[2], Tianshu Kuang[2],
Joshua C. Barber[2], Jaime Gateno[2,3], Pew-Thian Yap[1(✉)],
and James J. Xia[2,3(✉)]

[1] Department of Radiology and Biomedical Research Imaging Center (BRIC),
University of North Carolina at Chapel Hill, Chapel Hill, NC, USA
ptyap@med.unc.edu
[2] Department of Oral and Maxillofacial Surgery,
Houston Methodist Hospital, Houston, TX, USA
jxia@houstonmethodist.org
[3] Department of Surgery (Oral and Maxillofacial Surgery),
Weill Medical College, Cornell University, New York, NY, USA
[4] Department of Biomedical Engineering, University of North Carolina at Chapel
Hill, Chapel Hill, NC, USA

Abstract. Dental landmark localization is an essential step for analyzing dental models in orthodontic treatment planning and orthognathic surgery. Typically, more than 60 landmarks need to be manually digitized on a 3D dental surface model. However, most existing landmark localization methods are unable to perform reliably especially for partially edentulous patients with missing landmarks. In this work, we propose a deep learning framework, DentalPointNet, to automatically locate 68 landmarks on high-resolution dental surface models. Landmark area proposals are first predicted by a curvature-constrained region proposal network. Each proposal is then refined for landmark localization using a bounding box refinement network. Evaluation using 77 real-patient high-resolution dental surface models indicates that our approach achieves an average localization error of 0.24 mm, a false positive rate of 1% and a false negative rate of 2% on subjects both with or without partial edentulous, significantly outperforming relevant start-of-the-art methods.

Keywords: 3D dental surface · Landmark localization · Region proposal generation

1 Introduction

Dental landmark localization is the first step in dental model analysis for patients with jaw and teeth deformities. To quantify the deformity and plan orthodontic or surgical treatment [1], the current standard of care requires 68 commonly used

L. Wang et al. (Eds.): MICCAI 2022, LNCS 13432, pp. 444–452, 2022.
https://doi.org/10.1007/978-3-031-16434-7_43

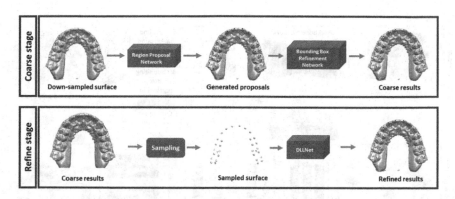

Fig. 1. Coarse-to-fine framework for dental landmark localization on a 3D surface. The generated proposals are illustrated by the center points.

dental landmarks to be digitized on high-resolution surface models that are generated by a three-dimensional (3D) intraoral surface scanner. Manual landmark digitalization is time-consuming and labor-intensive. On the other hand, automatic dental landmark digitalization on a high-resolution 3D model poses the following challenges: 1) processing the 3D surface model is computationally intensive due to the large number of triangles, typically in the order of 100,000; 2) clinically, a very high accuracy is needed for the central incisor landmarks; and 3) localization of landmarks on molars is affected by normal wear, poor restoration, and gums.

Over the years, deep learning methods have been developed for locating anatomical landmarks on medical images [2–5]. However, the applicability of these methods to 3D surface models is limited. This limitation can be overcome by more recent deep learning methods [6,8,9] that focus on analyzing 3D surfaces, represented as point clouds or meshes. PointNet++ [6] was proposed for 3D point cloud segmentation, where hierarchical geometric features are learned by applying PointNet [7] on grouped points. PointConv [8] calculates continuous weight and density functions via multi-layer perceptron (MLP), making the convolution kernels permutation/translation-invariant in the 3D point cloud segmentation tasks. MeshSegNet [9] uses a dynamic graph-constrained learning module to hierarchically extract multi-scale local contextual features for tooth segmentation task from 3D dental models. These segmentation methods can be applied for landmark detection by replacing the classification layer with a heatmap regression layer. However, these methods are not tailored for learning edge features in landmark areas and hence might perform with low accuracy in dental landmark detection.

In the past, DLLNet [10] was proposed to detect 68 dental landmarks on 3D dental surface by extending MeshSegNet with an attention mechanism to further improve the localization accuracy. However, DLLNet still suffers from two limitations. First, DLLNet cannot automatically determine whether there are missing teeth, and is significantly impacted for patients with jaw deformity or partial edentulous. Second, DLLNet relies on pre-segmented tooth partitions for landmark localization and is sensitive to segmentation errors.

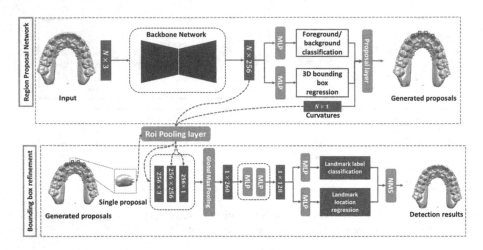

Fig. 2. The architecture of the proposed DentalPointNet.

In this paper, we propose an end-to-end deep learning method, DentalPoint-Net, to automatically locate dental landmarks on 3D high-resolution dental models represented as point clouds. A two-stage coarse-to-fine strategy is applied to detect the entire 68 commonly used dental landmarks (Fig. 1). In the coarse localization stage, DentalPointNet takes the raw point cloud as input, and outputs a coarse localization result of each landmark. In the refinement stage, DLLNet is applied to small groups of points sampled in the vicinity of the coarse localization results to refine landmark locations. The contribution of our work is threefold. First, we propose a balanced focal loss function to train the region proposal network (RPN) for generating reliable proposals to cover each landmark area. Second, we apply curvature constraints to ensure that the proposals are accurately centered on landmark locations. Third, we solve the landmark localization problem as an object detection task, which significantly reduces false negatives on patients who are partially edentulous, compared with state-of-the-art methods.

2   Methods

DentalPointNet consists of two sub-networks (Fig. 2). The first sub-network is a RPN that takes down-sampled point clouds as input for foreground/background classification and 3D bounding box regression based on the proposals. A balanced foreground/background loss function is applied to further improve the classification accuracy. The second sub-network is a 3D bounding box refinement network that takes the points inside the proposals as input, and outputs the regression result of the offset from the center of the bounding box to the target landmark. Finally, non-maximum suppression (NMS) is applied to reduce redundant proposals.

2.1   RPN for Dental Landmarks

Each dental landmark is located on either cusp or fossa of a dental model. We view each landmark as an abstract object and treat landmark localization as an object detection task. To train the RPN, a ground truth bounding box with a non-overlapped size is centered on each landmark. Specifically, the size of the bounding boxes used as ground truth is 2.5 mm and 3.0 mm for landmarks on the molars and other teeth, respectively. Points inside the box are viewed as the ground truth of foreground. Specifically, our RPN applies PointNet++ [6] as the backbone network, which takes a coordinate matrix $\mathbf{F}^0 \in R^{N\times 3}$ as input, where N is the volume of the point cloud. Four set-abstraction layers with multi-scale grouping are used to subsample points into groups with sizes 4,096, 1,024, 256, 64. The backbone network outputs a high-level contextual feature matrix $\mathbf{F}^1 \in R^{N\times 256}$, which is shared by two tasks: 1) a classification task that assigns foreground/background label to each point; and 2) a regression task for generating proposals as 3D bounding boxes.

The loss for dental landmark RPN is

$$L^{\text{RPN}}(\{c_i\}, \{p_i\}) = \lambda_c L^{\text{RPN}}_{\text{cls}}(c_i, c_i^*) + \lambda_r L^{\text{RPN}}_{\text{reg}}(\mathbf{p}_i, \mathbf{p}_i^*). \tag{1}$$

where $L^{\text{RPN}}_{\text{reg}}$ and $L^{\text{RPN}}_{\text{cls}}$ are the losses for classification and regression, respectively. λ_c and λ_r are training weights. c is the predicted classification score and $\mathbf{p}$ is a 6-dimensional vector, indicating the offset from the current point to the target landmark (3-dimensional) and the regressed size of the bounding box (3-dimensional). $\mathbf{p}^*$ is the corresponding ground truth. The classification ground truth is defined as $c_i^* = 1$ (foreground) if the i-th point is inside the ground truth bounding box, otherwise it will be defined as $c_i^* = 0$ (background). Additionally, we define c_i^* of the i-th point as

$$c_i^* = \begin{cases} 1, & \text{IoU} > 0.65, \\ -1, & 0.35 < \text{IoU} < 0.65, \\ 0, & \text{otherwise}, \end{cases} \tag{2}$$

where Intersection over Union (IoU) calculates the volume of intersection of the current bounding box of point i and the target landmark bounding box, indicating the overlap of them. Points assigned with $c_i^* = -1$ will not participate in the calculation of the training loss.

$L^{\text{RPN}}_{\text{cls}}$ can be defined as a binary cross-entropy loss for foreground/background classification. However, in the real cases, the background points are more numerous than the foreground points, directly applying binary cross-entropy may achieve a low accuracy of foreground classification. To solve this problem, we randomly select 512 points from the ground truth that are assigned with background and foreground labels, respectively, then calculate loss with the loss function defined as

$$L^{\text{RPN}}_{\text{cls}} = \frac{1}{2}\left(\frac{1}{N^{\text{f}}}\sum_{i=0}^{N^{\text{f}}} L(c_i, (c_i^*=1)) + \frac{1}{N^{\text{b}}}\sum_{i=0}^{N^{\text{b}}} L(c_i, (c_i^*=0))\right), \tag{3}$$

where $N^f = 512$ and $N^b = 512$ are the number of foreground and background points, respectively. $L(c_i, c_i^*)$ is a focal loss with multiplicative factor $\alpha = 0.25$ and power $\gamma = 0.75$.

Since the classification results may be interfered by gums or poor restoration of the 3D dental model, curvature constraints are applied to further increase the reliability of the generated proposals. Specifically, only points with curvature value higher than an empirically pre-defined threshold (0.65) are considered proposals. Finally, NMS with a threshold (0.85) is applied to reduce redundant proposals.

2.2   Bounding Box Refinement Network

We selected 128 proposals with the highest classification scores from the 3D proposals generated by RPN. 256 points are randomly selected from the points inside each proposal. A fusion strategy is employed to concatenate the point coordinates $\mathbf{F}_s^0 \in R^{256 \times 3}$, feature matrix from the backbone network $\mathbf{F}_s^1 \in R^{256 \times 256}$ and curvature matrix $\mathbf{F}_s^2 \in R^{256 \times 1}$ as a feature matrix $\mathbf{F}_s^3 \in R^{256 \times 260}$. A global max pooling operation is applied on $\mathbf{F}_s^3$ to generate a feature vector $\mathbf{F}_s^4 \in R^{1 \times 260}$. Followed by two MLPs with the output size of 128 and 128, the generated feature vector $\mathbf{F}_s^5 \in R^{1 \times 128}$ is shared by two tasks: 1) multi-classification tasks that assigns label $c^r = \{0, 1, 2, ...M\}$ for each proposal box, where M is the number of involved landmarks. $c^r = 0$ indicates that the landmark does not exist; and 2) a bounding box regression that outputs a 3-dimensional displacement vector $\mathbf{p}^r$ indicating the offset from the proposal box center to the target landmark. The loss function is defined as

$$L^B(\{c_i^b\}, \{\mathbf{p}_i^b\}) = \lambda_{bc} L_{cls}^B(c_i^b, c_i^{b*}) + \lambda_{br} L_{reg}^B(\mathbf{p}_i^b, \mathbf{p}_i^{b*}), \tag{4}$$

where c_i^{b*} is the ground truth label of the i-th proposal defined by (2). λ_{bc} and λ_{br} are the training weights. We apply cross-entropy and L_1 loss for L_{cls}^B and L_{reg}^B, respectively. Finally, NMS with a threshold of 0.35 is applied to reduce redundant 3D bounding boxes.

2.3   Implementation and Inference

In the coarse stage, each tooth surface is down-sampled to a volume of 16, 500 points. The RPN is trained by Adam optimizer with an initial rate of 0.002 for 400 epochs with the batch size of 16. The bounding box refinement network is also trained by Adam optimizer with an initial rate of 0.001 for 100 epochs with the batch size of 4. We empirically set $\lambda_{bc} = 1.0$, $\lambda_{br} = 1.0$, $\lambda_c = 1.0$ and $\lambda_r = 0.5$. In the refinement stage, DLLNet is adopted to further refine the accuracy of each detected landmark. Specifically, 300 points around each predicted landmark with various offset (≤ 0.5 mm) are sampled to train DLLNet as inputs. Other training parameter setting is kept same as reported in [10].

During inference, all landmarks are located by directly using the coarse-to-fine strategy with the trained networks. In the coarse stage, we only keep 100

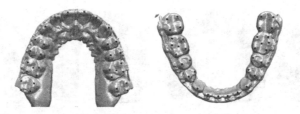

Fig. 3. Landmark annotation on the maxillary (left) and mandibular (right) dental models.

proposals with the highest classification scores to improve the inference speed. Our approach takes about 15 seconds to process a single (maxillary or mandibular) dental model in an environment of Intel Core i7-8700K CPU with a 12 GB GeForce GTX 1080Ti GPU. All procedures are implemented using Pytorch.

3   Experiments

3.1   Data

We evaluated our approach quantitatively using 77 sets of high-resolution digital dental models randomly selected from our clinical digital archive, in which 15 sets were partially edentulous (missing tooth/teeth). All personal information were de-identified prior to the study. For each set of the dental models, 32 maxillary and 36 mandibular dental landmarks were digitized by experienced oral surgeons. The dental landmarks on each of the maxillary and mandibular models were trained in two separate groups marked with different colors (Fig. 3). Each dental surface has roughly $100,000–300,000$ triangles, with a resolution of $0.2–0.4$ mm (the average length of the edge in a mesh triangle). Prior to training, data augmentation (30 times) was performed by randomly rotation ($[-\frac{\pi}{20}, \frac{\pi}{20}]$), translation ($[-20, 20]$) and re-scaling ($[0.8, 1.2]$) along the three orthogonal directions. The input feature matrix was normalized by Gaussian normalization constant (GNC).

3.2   Evaluation Methods

We compared DentalPointNet quantitatively with PointConv [8], DLLNet [10] and PointRCNN [11] using the same network architectures described in their original papers. In order to evaluate the effectiveness of the balanced focal loss and the curvature constraints, which are the main differences between our DentalPointNet and PointRCNN, we performed an ablation study by comparing PointRCNN to two variants: Variant-1 where the classification loss used in RPN was the proposed balanced focal loss, and no curvature-constraint was applied; and Variant-2 where the loss function used in the RPN was same as the one used in PointRCNN.

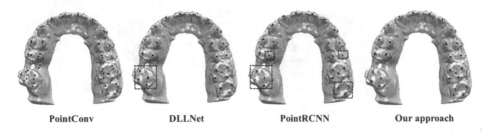

PointConv   DLLNet   PointRCNN   Our approach

Fig. 4. Dental landmark localization using the four methods (Red: predictions; Green: Ground truth). (Color figure online)

The results of landmark localization were quantitatively evaluated using Root Mean Squared Errors (RMSEs). In addition, false positive (FP) and false negative (FN) rates were used to evaluate if the missing tooth/teeth could be correctly identified on partially edentulous patients. The accuracy was calculated separately based on five anatomical regions: central incisors (CI), lateral incisors and canines (LC), 1st and 2nd premolars (PM), first molars (FM), and second molars (SM). All competing methods were trained under the same environment with coarse-to-fine strategy and data augmentation.

3.3 Results

Quantitative results in terms of RMSE, and FP and FN rates are summarized in Table 1 for normal patients and Table 2 for partially edentulous patients. Point-Conv results in the largest errors for both patient types since curvature features are not considered. A large FP rate can be observed for partially edentulous patients. DLLNet achieves good accuracy for both types of patients due to the attention mechanism. However, the FP rate is significantly increased in partially edentulous patients due to the low accuracy in pre-segmentation. PointConv and DLLNet result in large FP and FN rates associated with landmark misidentifications. PointRCNN yields the largest FN rate on both patient types since the foreground and background are significantly unbalanced. Due to the overwhelming number of background points, the loss calculated by binary cross-entropy is maintained at an extreme low value during training, resulting in a low fore-

Table 1. RMSD (mm) for landmark localization (Mean ± SD) on normal patients.

Method	CI	LC	PM	FM	SM	FP	FN
PointConv	0.82 ± 0.52	0.66 ± 0.41	1.40 ± 0.54	1.39 ± 0.48	1.41 ± 0.58	18%	17%
DLLNet	0.24 ± 0.18	0.30 ± 0.11	0.37 ± 0.27	0.44 ± 0.31	0.45 ± 0.38	11%	12%
PointRCNN	0.49 ± 0.41	0.31 ± 0.24	0.44 ± 0.41	0.43 ± 0.41	0.47 ± 0.48	9%	25%
Variant-1	0.33 ± 0.31	0.24 ± 0.25	0.26 ± 0.32	0.41 ± 0.31	0.45 ± 0.40	7%	6%
Variant-2	0.31 ± 0.25	0.21 ± 0.27	0.23 ± 0.22	0.31 ± 0.38	0.29 ± 0.28	4%	14%
Our approach	**0.20 ± 0.17**	**0.18 ± 0.11**	**0.19 ± 0.16**	**0.29 ± 0.21**	**0.27 ± 0.23**	**1%**	**2%**

Table 2. RMSD (mm) for landmark localization (Mean ± SD) on edentulous patients.

Method	CI	LC	PM	FM	SM	FP	FN
PointConv	0.87 ± 0.56	0.64 ± 0.43	1.47 ± 0.59	1.42 ± 0.48	1.51 ± 0.53	60%	20%
DLLNet	0.21 ± 0.15	0.29 ± 0.12	0.33 ± 0.24	0.56 ± 0.36	0.51 ± 0.28	30%	18%
PointRCNN	0.42 ± 0.33	0.33 ± 0.21	0.41 ± 0.35	0.47 ± 0.46	0.54 ± 0.41	11%	27%
Variant-1	0.31 ± 0.36	0.21 ± 0.26	0.23 ± 0.372	0.33 ± 0.24	0.48 ± 0.44	9%	15%
Variant-2	0.24 ± 0.23	0.17 ± 0.21	0.19 ± 0.24	0.34 ± 0.33	0.32 ± 0.25	8%	19%
Our approach	**0.18 ± 0.13**	**0.16 ± 0.11**	**0.19 ± 0.26**	**0.26 ± 0.25**	**0.28 ± 0.33**	**1%**	**1%**

Fig. 5. Landmark localization by DentalPointNet on normal patients (left two) and edentulous patients (right two).

ground classification outcome. The low foreground classification accuracy results in the inability of the generated proposals to cover all landmark areas, causing missed detections. Finally, DentalPointNet achieves the highest localization accuracy among the compared methods, and also gained the lowest FP and FN rates for edentulous patients without requiring any additional post-processing. DentalPointNet meets clinical requirements with high localization accuracy in each region, especially in CI. Figure 4 shows qualitative results of the compared methods on a randomly selected edentulous patient.

The results for the ablation study are summarized in Tables 1 and 2. Compared with PointRCNN, Variant-1 reduces the FN rate because the balanced focal loss results in great proposal confidence, and thus yields reliable proposals that cover more tooth areas. However, interference of gums or poor restoration might affect the RPN results, causing the landmarks to be misidentified in areas such as premolars and molars. Compared with Variant-1, Variant-2 results in a relatively lower RMSE on average for all anatomical regions due to the curvature constraints. However, the higher FN rates indicate that the generated proposals do not cover all landmark areas. Finally, DentalPointNet achieves the lowest FN rates due to the balanced focal loss. Utilizing the curvature constraints yields the highest localization accuracy. These results further confirm the effectiveness of DentalPointNet. Figure 5 shows randomly selected results given by Dental-PointNet for both types of patients.

4   Conclusion

The proposed DentalPointNet can automatically and accurately locate 68 commonly used dental landmarks on 3D dental surface models. Our approach first generates reliable proposals to cover all dental landmark areas from a RPN that is trained by a proposed balanced classification function, then further refines the localization results by curvature constraints. Experimental results show that our method significantly outperforms competing methods with a lowest average MSE of 0.24 mm. Most importantly, DentalPoinNet achieves superior performance on partially edentulous patients and meets clinical requirements in terms of localization accuracy.

Acknowledgment. This work was supported in part by United States National Institutes of Health (NIH) grants R01 DE022676, R01 DE027251, and R01 DE021863.

References

1. Xia, J.J., Gateno, J., Teichgraeber, J.F.: A new clinical protocol to evaluate craniomaxillofacial deformity and to plan surgical correction. J. Oral Maxillofac. Surg. **67**(10), 2093–2106 (2009)
2. Payer, C., Štern, D., Bischof, H., Urschler, M.: Regressing heatmaps for multiple landmark localization using CNNs. In: Ourselin, S., Joskowicz, L., Sabuncu, M.R., Unal, G., Wells, W. (eds.) MICCAI 2016. LNCS, vol. 9901, pp. 230–238. Springer, Cham (2016). https://doi.org/10.1007/978-3-319-46723-8_27
3. Zhang, J., et al.: Joint craniomaxillofacial bone segmentation and landmark digitization by context-guided fully convolutional networks. In: Descoteaux, M., Maier-Hein, L., Franz, A., Jannin, P., Collins, D.L., Duchesne, S. (eds.) MICCAI 2017. LNCS, vol. 10434, pp. 720–728. Springer, Cham (2017). https://doi.org/10.1007/978-3-319-66185-8_81
4. Chen, X., et al.: Fast and accurate craniomaxillofacial landmark detection via 3D faster R-CNN. IEEE Trans. Med. Imaging **40**(12), 3867–3878 (2021)
5. Wang X., Yang, X., Dou, H., Li, S., Heng, P.A., Ni, D.: Joint segmentation and landmark localization of fetal femur in ultrasound volumes. In: IEEE International Conference on Biomedical & Health Informatics, pp. 1–5 (2019)
6. Qi, C.R., Yi, L., Su, H., Guibas, L.J.: PointNet++: deep hierarchical feature learning on point sets in ametric space. In: NeurIPS, pp. 5099–5108 (2017)
7. Qi, C.R., Su, H., Mo, K., Guibas, L.J.: PointNet: deep learning on point sets for 3D classification and segmentation. In: CVPR, pp. 652–660 (2017)
8. Wu, W., Qi, Z., Fuxin, L.: PointConv: deep convolutional networks on 3D point clouds. In: CVPR, pp. 9621–9630 (2019)
9. Lian, C., et al.: Deep multi-scale mesh feature learning for automated labeling of raw dental surfaces from 3D intraoral scanners. IEEE Trans. Med. Imaging **39**(7), 2440–2450 (2020)
10. Lang, Y., et al.: DLLNet: an attention-based deep learning method for dental landmark localization on high-resolution 3D digital dental models. In: de Bruijne, M., et al. (eds.) MICCAI 2021. LNCS, vol. 12904, pp. 478–487. Springer, Cham (2021). https://doi.org/10.1007/978-3-030-87202-1_46
11. Shi, S., Wang, X., Li, H.: PointRCNN: 3D object proposal generation and detection from point cloud. In: Proceedings of the IEEE/CVF Conference on Computer Vision and Pattern Recognition, pp. 770–779 (2019)

Landmark-Free Statistical Shape Modeling Via Neural Flow Deformations

David Lüdke[1], Tamaz Amiranashvili[1,2,3(✉)], Felix Ambellan[1,4], Ivan Ezhov[3],
Bjoern H. Menze[2,3], and Stefan Zachow[1]

[1] Zuse Institute Berlin, Berlin, Germany
[2] University of Zurich, Zurich, Switzerland
`tamaz.amiranashvili@uzh.ch`
[3] Technical University of Munich, Munich, Germany
[4] Freie Universität Berlin, Berlin, Germany

Abstract. Statistical shape modeling aims at capturing shape variations of an anatomical structure that occur within a given population.
Shape models are employed in many tasks, such as shape reconstruction
and image segmentation, but also shape generation and classification.
Existing shape priors either require dense correspondence between training examples or lack robustness and topological guarantees. We present
FlowSSM, a novel shape modeling approach that learns shape variability without requiring dense correspondence between training instances.
It relies on a hierarchy of continuous deformation flows, which are
parametrized by a neural network. Our model outperforms state-of-the-
art methods in providing an expressive and robust shape prior for distal
femur and liver. We show that the emerging latent representation is discriminative by separating healthy from pathological shapes. Ultimately,
we demonstrate its effectiveness on two shape reconstruction tasks from
partial data. Our source code is publicly available (https://github.com/
davecasp/flowssm).

Keywords: Representation learning · Statistical shape analysis ·
Shape prior

1 Introduction

Statistical shape models (SSMs) are an important tool in medical image analysis
and computational anatomy. Application examples include diagnosis, pathology
detection and segmentation, outlier detection, shape reconstruction, etc. (cf. e.g.
[1]). For this purpose, shape models capture variations in shape that occur within
the population of a given anatomical structure. The model is typically learned

---

D. Lüdke and T. Amiranashvili—Equal contribution.

Supplementary Information The online version contains supplementary material
available at https://doi.org/10.1007/978-3-031-16434-7_44.

in an automated fashion from example data. This results in a generative model, which can be, among others, used as a regularizer for ill-posed tasks. Furthermore, shape models provide a low-dimensional statistics-driven latent representation of shapes, which allows clustering, classification and shape regression.

The most established statistical shape model in the medical domain is a *point distribution model* (PDM) [9,15]. While PDMs are simple and effective, they employ linear statistics, which restricts their capacity to fully capture the high variability of anatomical structures [11]. There exists a variety of non-linear statistical shape models [13,16,25] that have been shown to increase the flexibility and can handle large, non-linear deformations well, such as the recently developed *fundamental coordinate model* (FCM) [4]. However, most of these models still require consistently parametrized training shapes, i.e. shapes which are in dense correspondence to each other. This limits the learned shape model to the resolution of the given training data. Furthermore, generating well-defined dense correspondence typically requires manual landmark annotation that is tedious to obtain. Moreover, establishing exact dense correspondence is faulted by generally undefined true dense correspondence of biological shapes [15]. Lastly, as these models work on uncoupled primitives, such as mesh triangles, they have no inherent safeguards to avoid the generation of unnatural shapes with self-intersections.

Another popular tool in computational anatomy is *large deformation diffeomorphic metric mapping* (LDDMM) [12,22,26]. It allows estimating a template from a population of training shapes, as well as deformations that map the template to individual subjects. These deformations are continuous, however they are parametrized by a finite set of momentum vectors, providing a compact latent representation. While the template is population-wide, the subject-specific latent representations result from independent, pair-wise registration of each subject to the template. In context of shape modeling, LDDMMs have several advantages over PDMs and FCMs. First, LDDMMs do not rely on dense correspondence between training shapes. Second, being formulated as a diffeomorphism, they are less prone to producing self-intersections. Recently, novel parametrizations of approximately diffeomorphic deformation flows through a multilayer perceptron (MLP) were proposed [14,17,23]. The MLP's parameters are estimated on the training data, hence representing a population-wide prior. In this work, we extend neurally parametrized deformation fields to create *FlowSSM* – a novel hierarchical, continuous shape model, that is able to accurately capture variations in shapes of anatomical structures without requiring dense correspondence between training shapes. Our main contributions can be summarized as follows:

- We propose a novel shape model FlowSSM, which is based on continuous neural flows and produces natural shape deformations without relying on a given dense correspondence between training shapes.
- Our model outperforms state-of-the-art methods in capturing variability in anatomical shapes variation on liver and distal femur, as measured in generalization ability and specificity.

– We demonstrate the discriminative nature of our learned latent representation by classifying knee osteoarthritis.
– We qualitatively show that our model provides anatomically plausible reconstructions from partial and sparse shapes on both anatomical structures.

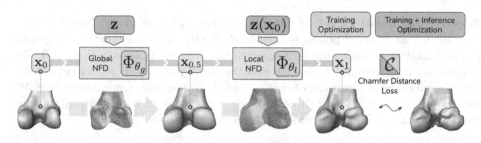

Fig. 1. We model shapes by template deformations, defined by two sequential, continuous neural flow deformers (NFD). The model is trained as an auto-decoder with correspondence-free Chamfer distance loss. The bottom row visualizes the template deformation through the velocity fields.

2 Methodology

2.1 Neural Flow Deformer

We model shapes by a continuous deformation of a template surface (cf. Fig. 1). A shape X is obtained by deforming each point x_0 on a template $\mathcal{T}$ along a trajectory $x : [0,1] \rightarrow \mathbb{R}^3$, where $x(0) = x_0$ and $x(1) \in X$. We model these trajectories by a time-dependent velocity field $v : \mathbb{R}^3 \times [0,1] \rightarrow \mathbb{R}^3$, that relates to $x(\cdot)$ through the following ordinary differential equation:

$$\frac{\mathrm{d}x(t)}{\mathrm{d}t} = v(x(t), t). \tag{1}$$

For each initial condition $x_0 \in \mathcal{T}$, the solution of this ODE describes a trajectory that starts in x_0. All solutions for different starting points are summarized as the flow function $\Phi : \mathbb{R}^3 \times [0,1] \rightarrow \mathbb{R}^3$, for which holds:

$$\Phi(x_0, \tau) = x_0 + \int_0^{\tau} v(\Phi(x_0, t), t)\, dt. \tag{2}$$

Hence, the flow Φ describes the trajectory of a point x_0 which tangentially follows the velocity field v. The target shape is described by $\{\Phi(x_0, 1) \mid x_0 \in \mathcal{T}\}$.

Velocity Field Parametrization. Following recent advances in modeling continuous neural flows [7,17,23], we propose to parametrize the velocity field $v(\cdot, \cdot)$ through an MLP that is conditional on a shape-specific latent representation $z \in \mathbb{R}^d$. Similar to [17], we define the deformation velocity field as:

$$v_\theta(x(t), t) = f_\theta(x(t), t \cdot z) \cdot \|z\|_2, \tag{3}$$

where f is the flow function parametrized by an MLP (IM-Net [8]) and then scaled by a flow magnitude proportional to the euclidean vector norm of z. For architectural detail of the applied flow function, we refer the reader to Fig. S1 in the supplements.

Global and Local Level of Detail. In Eq. (3), one global latent vector $z \in \mathbb{R}^d$ for all starting points is employed. While being compact, such global parametrization tends to produce smooth, low-frequency deformations [17]. To extend the deformations' frequency spectrum, we propose to model the latent representation as a continuous function in $\mathbb{R}^3$. In particular, we interpolate M latent weights $z_k \in \mathbb{R}^d$ at their control point positions $c_k \in \mathbb{R}^3$ via radial basis functions, using a Gaussian kernel with an inverse width ε_k:

$$z(x) = \sum_{k=1}^{M} z_k \varphi_k(\|c_k - x\|_2),$$

$$\varphi_k(r) = e^{-(\varepsilon_k \cdot r)^2}.$$

(4)

When solving (2) to obtain a deformation trajectory for a starting point $x_0 \in \mathcal{T}$, we compute $z(x)$ via (4) only at the starting point x_0, using a constant $z(x_0)$ for the whole resulting trajectory. This allows us to sample $\{c_k\}$ equidistantly on the template surface, instead of the whole volume, making for a more compact parametrization.

To disentangle global, low frequency shape characteristics from local, high frequency details, we apply two deformers sequentially. The first one uses a global latent vector, while the second one uses the localized formulation (4). Each deformer has its own set of MLP parameters θ_g and θ_l respectively.

In summary, a global latent vector z, M local control points $(z_k, c_k, \varepsilon_k)$ and MLP parameters θ_g and θ_l parametrize a continuous, time-dependent velocity field, which defines deformation trajectories for every surface point on a template, yielding a single target shape.

2.2   Training

Given a set of N arbitrarily parametrized but topologically equivalent training surfaces $\mathcal{X} = \{X_1, \cdots, X_N\}$ and a template surface $\mathcal{T}$, our model is trained without given dense correspondence. Every shape X_i is represented by $M + 1$ latent vectors $(z^i, \{z_k^i\})$. The MLP parameters, $\{c_k\}$, ε_k and $\mathcal{T}$ are shared across all training surfaces, representing a population-wide prior. We train our model as an auto-decoder [17,24]. That is, in training, the latent representations are randomly initialized from $\mathcal{N}(0, 0.1^2)$ and jointly optimized with the MLP parameters, without learning an encoder. The global and local deformers are trained consecutively with the same target surfaces $\mathcal{X}$. The loss is the correspondence-free, symmetric point-set to point-set Chamfer distance $\mathcal{C}$ between randomly sampled surface points of the target $P_i \subset X_i$ and deformed, sampled surface points of the template $P_\Phi = \Phi^i(P_\mathcal{T} \subset \mathcal{T}, 1)$:

$$\mathcal{C}(P_i, P_\Phi) = \frac{1}{2|P_i|} \sum_{x_i \in P_i} \min_{x \in P_\Phi} \|x_i - x\|_2 + \frac{1}{2|P_\Phi|} \sum_{x \in P_\Phi} \min_{x_i \in P_i} \|x_i - x\|_2 . \quad (5)$$

After training, we estimate the probability distribution of the latent vectors by performing principal component analysis (PCA) [28] on the emerging latent representations of training shapes. The PCA is performed separately for the global and local latent representations, keeping all modes of variation.

2.3 Inference

To embed unseen shape instances in the learned shape space, e.g. for reconstruction, one needs to obtain a latent representation that best describes a given observation. For this, a new latent embedding is initialized from $\mathcal{N}(0, 0.1^2)$. We fix the trained MLP parameters and $\{\varepsilon_k\}$, while the latent representations are optimized with the correspondence-free loss (5). Within this process, the latent embedding is restricted to the subspace, i.e. span of the training representations, defined by the PCA. The global and local latent representations are trained consecutively.

3 Experiments

We conduct experiments on three datasets: liver, distal femur bone, as well as the condyle region of the distal femur (a dataset summary can be found in Table S1 in the supplements). Both femur datasets cover the full spectrum of osteoarthritis severity. The liver, being a deformable soft tissue organ, exhibits a much higher degree of nonlinear variability, yielding a particularly challenging dataset for shape modeling.

Liver and Femur Datasets. The datasets consist of correspondingly 112 and 253 surfaces. The surfaces were obtained from manually segmented CT scans of liver [18] and MRI scans of knee [3]. For correspondence-based methods, consistently meshed surfaces were obtained semi-automatically following [18,25]. Both datasets are split into 70% training, 10% validation, and 20% test data.

Classification Dataset. We adopt the *Osteoarthritis Initiative*[1] - *right distal femur* dataset from [4,25]. The dataset consists of 116 femur surfaces with 58 healthy cases and 58 severe cases of osteoarthritis, according to their Kellgren and Lawrence [20] score of 0/1 and 4, respectively. For further information on the dataset and its construction, cf. [4,25].

Template Generation. For liver and femur datasets, we generate a correspondence free template per dataset by applying the hub-and-spokes approach of ShapeFlow [17]. This results in non-rigidly aligned training shapes in a canonical space. These are used for the template surface generation by applying an unscreened Poisson surface reconstruction [19]. Finally, the template meshes are

---

[1] nda.nih.gov/oai.

simplified to attain approximately the same number of faces as in the training data. For the classification dataset, the template is directly constructed by unscreened Poisson surface reconstruction from given shapes.

Data Preprocessing. Although our method randomly samples points on training surfaces and therefore does not use correspondences, we further emphasize this fact by re-meshing the surfaces to destroy correspondences. Each mesh is aligned to its template via Iterative Closest Points [5]. All meshes are then isotropically rescaled to fit $[-1, 1]$ based on the largest training instance and centred around the origin in alignment with the template shape. The classification dataset is left unchanged for comparability to previous works [4,25].

Table 1. Generality (measured as average symmetric surface distance in mm), specificity (measured as average Chamfer distance in mm) and number of self-intersecting meshes (SIM) for distal femur and liver. Bold numbers indicate statistically significant improvements to baselines (paired t-test, $p < 0.05$).

Femur	Generality [mm] ↓	Specificity [mm] ↓	SIM Gen. [#] ↓	SIM Spec. [#] ↓
PDM	0.26 ± 0.04	1.12 ± 0.12	1	25
FCM	0.26 ± 0.04	1.15 ± 0.16	0	1
LDDMM	0.27 ± 0.04	1.19 ± 0.12	0	0
FlowSSM (ours)	**0.24 ± 0.04**	**0.97 ± 0.09**	0	0
Liver				
PDM	1.57 ± 0.30	4.98 ± 0.59	18	871
FCM	1.52 ± 0.26	5.91 ± 0.90	7	668
LDDMM	1.75 ± 0.36	5.16 ± 0.60	4	86
FlowSSM (ours)	**1.20 ± 0.18**	**4.00 ± 0.48**	5	4

3.1   Experimental Setup

In the following, we compare FlowSSM to two correspondence-based models – the linear PDM [9] and a non-linear statistical shape model, the FCM [2,4]. Furthermore, we compare to an LDDMM-based approach [12], where the emerging latent shape space is estimated by a PCA on the learned initial momentum vectors of training shapes. This is motivated by [6,27], who used a PCA on momenta for disease classification. For comparability, we use the same template and control points as in our method. We emphasize that the PDM and FCM baselines require corresponding meshes for training, in contrast to LDDMM and ours. We run all experiments on an NVIDIA A100 40 GB GPU. The training takes about 2 h and 4 h for liver and femur data, respectively, while generating a single shape given a latent representation takes about 0.14 s per shape. For further implementation details and hyperparameters, refer to Tables S2 and S4 in the supplements.

3.2   Generality and Specificity

To quantitatively assess the quality of our generative model in the light of statistical shape modeling, we apply two standard measures, generalization ability and specificity, as introduced by Davies [10]. Here, generality refers to the ability of a statistical shape model to fit unseen instances of the class of shapes. It is evaluated by the average symmetric surface distance between all test shapes and their reconstructions. To ensure comparability between the methods, we fit the correspondence-based models to the test shape by minimizing the average surface distance. In contrast to generality, specificity measures the restrictiveness of a model to generate shapes that are close to training instances. To generate random samples, we utilize the distributions described by all PCA modes of each model. We randomly sample 1000 surfaces by sampling latent representations and computing the surfaces. We then calculate their average surface distance to the closest example in the training set. For computational reasons, the surface distance is approximated by symmetric Chamfer distance.

The results in Table 1 show that FlowSSM exhibits the lowest generality error for both liver and femur, i.e., best fit to unseen shape instances. Further, FlowSSM is more specific than the baselines and generates samples closest to the training population. All methods are less precise on the liver dataset, which can be explained by larger, nonlinear variability in the deformable liver. Generally, dense correspondence between livers is not clearly defined and thus poses an additional challenge for PDM and FCM. The femur, on the other hand, has better defined correspondences and less variation between shapes, which we conjecture to be the main reason for similar performance between all methods. Furthermore, self-intersections degrade the resulting mesh quality and suggest that a model produces unnatural shape deformations. FlowSSM exhibits by far the lowest total number of self-intersecting meshes out of the four models, indicating smooth and natural shape deformations.

Lastly, our localized deformer allows us to nearly half the generalization error, when compared to the global parametrization of [17,23] (cf. Table S3 in the supplements).

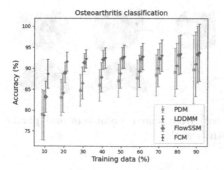
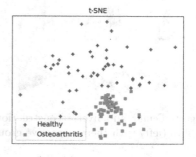

Fig. 2. Left: Osteoarthritis classification accuracy indicated by mean and standard deviation of the 10,000 balanced split samples per partitioning. Right: Unsupervised 2D t-SNE visualization of the learned PCA weights of FlowSSM shows a clustering of diseased cases.

3.3   Osteoarthritis Classification

A discriminative emerging latent space is an important property of a shape model. Following the experimental setup of [4,25], we evaluate our model's ability to classify knee osteoarthritis (OA) – a degenerative disease of the joints which causes pathological malformities of the femur. To this end, FlowSSM is trained to best reconstruct the complete classification data of the condyle region. Note that this does not involve the OA labels and is therefore to be considered unsupervised. Ultimately, we classify the respective PCA weights of our model and the baselines with a linear support vector machine. We evaluate the average classification accuracy of a stratified Monte-Carlo cross-validation for 10,000 samples per partitioning with training set sizes from 10% to 90%.

In Fig. 2, the high average classification accuracy of our model across all partitionings is indicative of the discriminative nature of the unsupervisedly learned latent space. This is further exemplified through the emerging clustering in the t-distributed Stochastic Neighbor Embedding (t-SNE) [21] visualization. The FCM provides slightly more robust classification, especially for smaller training sets, indicating a more distinct linear separability of the weights. Still, our model shows comparable performance for larger training sets, without relying on given correspondence in representation learning.

3.4   Shape Reconstruction

Our model can be fitted to various target parametrizations. We fit our trained model from Sect. 3.2 to a partial mesh and a sparse point-cloud (200 surface points) from unseen subjects and reconstruct full meshes. In contrast to the shape inference in the generality experiment, a one-sided Chamfer distance is minimized to obtain a latent embedding. Reconstructions in Fig. 3 qualitatively highlight our model's specificity by displaying anatomically plausible reconstructions. At the same time, our model's generality is demonstrated by preserving patient-specific details, present in the targets.

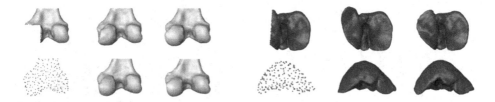

Fig. 3. Femur and liver reconstructions (center) from sparse point-sets and partial meshes (left) with their respective ground truth (right).

4   Conclusion

We present a novel landmark-free shape model that captures variability of a given population of anatomical shapes. This is achieved through a novel, localized neural flow parametrization. Our model exhibits good generalization ability to unseen shapes without sacrificing specificity, demonstrated on two anatomical structures. Additionally, in contrast to established methods, our model does not require any given dense correspondences. Furthermore, the emerging latent space is discriminative, as demonstrated by classification of osteoarthritis.

In practice, our method simplifies building robust and expressive shape priors by utilizing large pools of heterogeneous training data, independent of their parametrization and resolution. The emerging latent representation is useful in discriminating various shape-correlated features. As the flow parametrization of our model makes it well suited for studying temporal shape trajectories, this poses an exciting future research direction.

Acknowledgements. This work was supported by the Bundesministerium für Bildung und Forschung (BMBF) through the research campus MODAL (ref. 3FO18501) and The Berlin Institute for the Foundations of Learning and Data (BIFOLD) - (ref. 01IS18025A and ref. 01IS18037A). We are grateful for the open-access dataset OAI. (The Osteoarthritis Initiative is a public-private partnership comprised of five contracts (N01-AR-2-2258; N01-AR-2-2259; N01-AR-2-2260; N01-AR-2-2261; N01-AR-2-2262) funded by the National Institutes of Health, a branch of the Department of Health and Human Services, and conducted by the OAI Study Investigators. Private funding partners include Merck Research Laboratories; Novartis Pharmaceuticals Corporation, GlaxoSmithKline; and Pfizer, Inc. Private sector funding for the OAI is managed by the Foundation for the National Institutes of Health. This manuscript was prepared using an OAI public use data set and does not necessarily reflect the opinions or views of the OAI investigators, the NIH, or the private funding partners.)

References

1. Ambellan, F., Lamecker, H., von Tycowicz, C., Zachow, S.: Statistical shape models: understanding and mastering variation in anatomy. In: Rea, P.M. (ed.) Biomedical Visualisation. AEMB, vol. 1156, pp. 67–84. Springer, Cham (2019). https://doi.org/10.1007/978-3-030-19385-0_5
2. Ambellan, F., Hanik, M., von Tycowicz, C.: Morphomatics: geometric morphometrics in non-Euclidean shape spaces (2021). https://doi.org/10.12752/8544
3. Ambellan, F., Tack, A., Ehlke, M., Zachow, S.: Automated segmentation of knee bone and cartilage combining statistical shape knowledge and convolutional neural networks: data from the osteoarthritis initiative. Med. Image Anal. **52**, 109–118 (2019)
4. Ambellan, F., Zachow, S., von Tycowicz, C.: Rigid motion invariant statistical shape modeling based on discrete fundamental forms: Data from the osteoarthritis initiative and the Alzheimer's disease neuroimaging initiative. Med. Image Anal. **73**, 102178 (2021)
5. Besl, P.J., McKay, N.D.: Method for registration of 3-D shapes. In: Sensor Fusion IV: Control Paradigms and Data Structures, vol. 1611, pp. 586–606. SPIE (1992)

6. Charon, N., Islam, A., Zbijewski, W.: Landmark-free morphometric analysis of knee osteoarthritis using joint statistical models of bone shape and articular space variability. J. Med. Imaging **8**(4), 044001 (2021)
7. Chen, R.T.Q., Rubanova, Y., Bettencourt, J., Duvenaud, D.: Neural ordinary differential equations. In: Advances in Neural Information Processing Systems (2018)
8. Chen, Z., Zhang, H.: Learning implicit fields for generative shape modeling. In: Proceedings of the IEEE/CVF Conference on Computer Vision and Pattern Recognition, pp. 5939–5948 (2019)
9. Cootes, T.F., Taylor, C.J., Cooper, D.H., Graham, J.: Active shape models-their training and application. Comput. Vis. Image Unders. **61**(1), 38–59 (1995)
10. Davies, R.H.: Learning shape: optimal models for analysing natural variability. The University of Manchester, United Kingdom (2002)
11. Davis, B.C., Fletcher, P.T., Bullitt, E., Joshi, S.: Population shape regression from random design data. Int. J. Comput. Vis. **90**(2), 255–266 (2010)
12. Durrleman, S., et al.: Morphometry of anatomical shape complexes with dense deformations and sparse parameters. NeuroImage **101**, 35–49 (2014)
13. Fletcher, P.T., Lu, C., Pizer, S.M., Joshi, S.: Principal geodesic analysis for the study of nonlinear statistics of shape. IEEE Trans. Med. Imaging **23**(8), 995–1005 (2004)
14. Gupta, K., Chandraker, M.: Neural mesh flow: 3D manifold mesh generation via diffeomorphic flows. Adv. Neural Inf. Process. Syst. **33**, 1747–1758 (2020)
15. Heimann, T., Meinzer, H.P.: Statistical shape models for 3D medical image segmentation: a review. Med. Image Anal. **13**(4), 543–563 (2009)
16. Huckemann, S., Hotz, T., Munk, A.: Intrinsic shape analysis: geodesic PCA for riemannian manifolds modulo isometric lie group actions. Statistica Sinica **20**(1), 1–58 (2010). ISSN 10170405, 19968507. http://www.jstor.org/stable/24308976. Accessed 06 Sept 2022
17. Jiang, C., Huang, J., Tagliasacchi, A., Guibas, L.J.: ShapeFlow: learnable deformation flows among 3D shapes. In: Larochelle, H., Ranzato, M., Hadsell, R., Balcan, M.F., Lin, H. (eds.) Advances in Neural Information Processing Systems, vol. 33, pp. 9745–9757. Curran Associates, Inc. (2020)
18. Kainmüller, D., Lange, T., Lamecker, H.: Shape constrained automatic segmentation of the liver based on a heuristic intensity model. In: Proceedings of the MICCAI Workshop 3D Segmentation in the Clinic: A Grand Challenge, vol. 109, p. 116 (2007)
19. Kazhdan, M., Hoppe, H.: Screened Poisson surface reconstruction. ACM Trans. Graph. (ToG) **32**(3), 1–13 (2013)
20. Kellgren, J.H., Lawrence, J.: Radiological assessment of osteo-arthrosis. Ann. Rheumatic Dis. **16**(4), 494 (1957)
21. Van der Maaten, L., Hinton, G.: Visualizing data using t-SNE. J. Mach. Learn. Res. **9**(11) (2008)
22. Miller, M.I., Trouvé, A., Younes, L.: Geodesic shooting for computational anatomy. J. Math. Imaging Vis. **24**(2), 209–228 (2006)
23. Niemeyer, M., Mescheder, L., Oechsle, M., Geiger, A.: Occupancy flow: 4D reconstruction by learning particle dynamics. In: Proceedings of the IEEE/CVF International Conference on Computer Vision, pp. 5379–5389 (2019)
24. Park, J.J., Florence, P., Straub, J., Newcombe, R., Lovegrove, S.: DeepSDF: learning continuous signed distance functions for shape representation. In: Proceedings of the IEEE/CVF Conference on Computer Vision and Pattern Recognition, pp. 165–174 (2019)

25. von Tycowicz, C., Ambellan, F., Mukhopadhyay, A., Zachow, S.: An efficient rie-
    mannian statistical shape model using differential coordinates: with application to
    the classification of data from the osteoarthritis initiative. Med. Image Anal. **43**,
    1–9 (2018)
26. Vaillant, M., Qiu, A., Glaunès, J., Miller, M.I.: Diffeomorphic metric surface map-
    ping in subregion of the superior temporal gyrus. NeuroImage **34**(3), 1149–1159
    (2007)
27. Wang, L., et al.: Large deformation diffeomorphism and momentum based hip-
    pocampal shape discrimination in dementia of the Alzheimer type. IEEE Trans.
    Med. Imaging **26**(4), 462–470 (2007)
28. Wold, S., Esbensen, K., Geladi, P.: Principal component analysis. Chemom. Intell.
    Lab. Syst. **2**(1–3), 37–52 (1987)

Learning Shape Distributions from Large Databases of Healthy Organs: Applications to Zero-Shot and Few-Shot Abnormal Pancreas Detection

Rebeca Vétil[1,2]([✉]), Clément Abi-Nader[2], Alexandre Bône[2],
Marie-Pierre Vullierme[3], Marc-Michel Rohé[2], Pietro Gori[1],
and Isabelle Bloch[1,4]

[1] LTCI, Télécom Paris, Institut Polytechnique de Paris, Palaiseau, France
[2] Guerbet Research, Villepinte, France
rebeca.vetil@guerbet.com
[3] Department of Radiology, Hospital of Annecy-Genevois,
Université de Paris, Paris, France
[4] Sorbonne Université, CNRS, LIP6, Paris, France

Abstract. We propose a scalable and data-driven approach to learn shape distributions from large databases of healthy organs. To do so, volumetric segmentation masks are embedded into a common probabilistic shape space that is learned with a variational auto-encoding network. The resulting latent shape representations are leveraged to derive zero-shot and few-shot methods for abnormal shape detection. The proposed distribution learning approach is illustrated on a large database of 1200 healthy pancreas shapes. Downstream qualitative and quantitative experiments are conducted on a separate test set of 224 pancreas from patients with mixed conditions. The abnormal pancreas detection AUC reached up to 65.41% in the zero-shot configuration, and 78.97% in the few-shot configuration with as few as 15 abnormal examples, outperforming a baseline approach based on the sole volume.

Keywords: Shape analysis · Anomaly detection · Pancreas

1 Introduction

Anatomical alterations of organs such as the brain or the pancreas may be informative of functional impairments. For instance, hippocampal atrophy and duct dilatation are well-known markers of Alzheimer's disease and pancreatic ductal adenocarcinoma, respectively [9,15]. In these examples, quantifying anatomical differences bears therefore a great potential for determining the patient's clinical status, anticipating its future progression or regression, and supporting the treatment planning.

Supplementary Information The online version contains supplementary material available at https://doi.org/10.1007/978-3-031-16434-7_45.

Since the seminal work of Thompson [19], the computational anatomy literature proposed several Statistical Shape Modeling (SSM) approaches, which embed geometrical shapes into metric spaces where notions of distance and difference can be defined and quantified [2,5,12]. Taking advantage of these representations, statistical shape models were then proposed to perform group analyses of shape collections. In particular, atlas models [16] learn geometrical distributions in terms of an "average" representative shape and associated variability, generalizing the Euclidean mean-variance analysis. In medical imaging, learning atlases from healthy examples allows for the definition of normative models for anatomical structures or organs, such as brain MRIs or subcortical regions segmented from neuroimaging data [10,22], thus providing a natural framework for the detection of abnormal anatomies.

In practice, leveraging an atlas model to compute the likelihood of a given shape to belong to the underlying distribution either requires to identify landmarks [6], or to solve a registration problem [3]. To circumvent the computational cost of this shape embedding operation, the authors in [21] proposed to train an encoder network to predict registration parameters from image pairs. In [7,14], the authors built on this idea and used the variational autoencoder (VAE) of [13] to learn the embedding space jointly with the atlas model, instead of relying on pre-determined parametrization strategies. However, the structure of the decoding network remained constrained by hyperparameter-rich topological assumptions, enforced via costly smoothing and numerical integration operators from a computational point of view.

Alternative approaches proposed to drop topological hypotheses by relying on variations of the AE or its variational counterparts [13] to learn normative models that are subsequently used to perform Anomaly Detection (AD). These methods compress and reconstruct images of healthy subjects to capture a normative model of organs [1,23]. Yet, they are usually applied on the raw imaging data, thus they entail the risk of extracting features related to the intensity distribution of a dataset which are not necessarily specific to the organ anatomy. Therefore, regularization constraints [1,4] are introduced to improve the detection performances compared to the vanilla AE. To further reduce the overfitting risk, these methods artificially increase the dataset size by working on 2D slices.

Given this context, we propose a VAE-based method to learn a normative model of organ shape that can subsequently be used to detect anomalies, thus bridging the gap between SSM and AD models. Although SSM methods with explicit modeling constraints proved effective to learn relevant shape spaces from relatively small collections of high-dimensional data, we propose to further reduce the set of underlying hypotheses and leave the decoding network unconstrained in its architecture. With the objective to learn normative shape models from collections of healthy organs, we argue that sufficiently large databases of relevant medical images can be constructed by pooling together different data sources, see [8] for instance. To reduce the risk of overfitting and focus on the anatomy of organs, the VAE is learned from 3D binary segmentation masks and is coupled with a shape-preserving data augmentation strategy consisting of translations, rotations and scalings. An approach to study and visualize group differences is also proposed.

Section 2 details the proposed method, which is then illustrated on a pancreas shape problem in Sect. 3. Section 4 discusses the results and concludes.

2   Methods

Modeling Organ Shape. We consider an image acquired via a standard imaging technique. For a given organ in the image, its anatomy can be represented by a binary segmentation mask $\mathbf{X} = \{x_i, i = 1...d\}$ with $x_i \in \{0, 1\}$ and d the number of voxels in the image. We are interested in studying the shape of this organ, and assume that it is characterized by a set of underlying properties that can be extracted from the segmentation mask. Therefore, we hypothesize the following generative process for the segmentation mask:

$$p_\theta(\mathbf{X} \mid \mathbf{z}) = \prod_{i=1}^{d} f_\theta(\mathbf{z})_i^{x_i} (1 - f_\theta(\mathbf{z})_i)^{1-x_i} \tag{1}$$

where $0^0 = 1$ by convention, and $\mathbf{z}$ is a latent variable generated from a prior distribution $p(\mathbf{z})$. This latent variable provides a low-dimensional representation of the segmentation mask embedding its main shape features. The function f_θ is a non-linear function mapping $\mathbf{z}$ to a predicted probabilistic segmentation mask.

We are interested in inferring the parameters θ of the generative process, as well as approximating the posterior distribution of the latent variable $\mathbf{z}$ given a segmentation mask $\mathbf{X}$. We rely on the VAE framework [13] to estimate the model parameters. Hence, we assume that $p(\mathbf{z})$ is a multivariate Gaussian with zero mean and identity covariance. We also introduce the approximate posterior distribution $q_\phi(\mathbf{z} \mid \mathbf{X})$ parameterized by ϕ, and optimize a lower bound $\mathcal{L}$ of the marginal log-likelihood, which can be written for the segmentation mask $\mathbf{X}^p$ of a subject p as:

$$\mathcal{L} = \mathbb{E}_{q_\phi(\mathbf{z}\mid\mathbf{X}^p)}[\log p_\theta(\mathbf{X}^p \mid \mathbf{z})] - KL[q_\phi(\mathbf{z} \mid \mathbf{X}^p) \mid p(\mathbf{z})], \tag{2}$$

where $q_\phi(\mathbf{z} \mid \mathbf{X}^p)$ follows a Gaussian distribution $\mathcal{N}(\mu_\phi(\mathbf{X}^p), \sigma_\phi^2(\mathbf{X}^p)\mathbf{I})$ with $\mathbf{I}$ the identity matrix, and KL is the Kullback-Leibler divergence.

To capture shape features, we rely on a convolutional network and adopt the U-Net [17] encoder-decoder architecture without skip connections.[1] In practice, the number of convolutional layers and the convolutional blocks are automatically inferred thanks to the nnU-Net self-configuring procedure [11] (see Section A in the supplementary material for details). Due to this encoder-decoder architecture, the segmentation masks are progressively down-sampled to obtain low-resolution feature maps which are mapped through a linear transformation to the latent variable $\mathbf{z}$. The latent code is subsequently decoded by a symmetric path to reconstruct the original masks.

---

[1] Code available at https://github.com/rebeca-vetil/HealthyShapeVAE.

Anomaly Detection. We propose to learn a normative model of organ shapes by applying the VAE framework previously presented on the segmentation masks of a large cohort of N healthy patients, allowing the model to capture a low-dimensional embedding characteristic of a normal organ anatomy. In addition, we use a data augmentation procedure consisting of random translations, rotations and scalings, in order to be invariant to these transformations and force the network to extract shape features. Based on this learned model, we propose two approaches to perform Anomaly Detection (AD) by leveraging the latent representation of normal organ shapes.

Zero-Shot Learning Method. After training, the recognition model $q_\phi(\mathbf{z} \mid \mathbf{X})$ can be used to project the segmentation maps $\mathbf{X}^p$ of the cohort of healthy subjects and obtain an empirical distribution of normal shapes in the latent space. We rely on this low-dimensional distribution of normality to detect abnormal shapes. To do so, we compute the mean of the healthy subjects projection, and define abnormality through the L2 distance to this mean latent representation.

Few-Shot Learning Method. Another approach is to classify normal and abnormal shapes based on their low-dimensional representations. In practice, we project the segmentation maps from a set of healthy and pathological subjects in the latent space using the recognition model $q_\phi(\mathbf{z} \mid \mathbf{X})$. Therefore, we obtain for all these subjects a set of low-dimensional organ shape features that we can use to learn any type of classifier (*e.g.*, linear SVM).

Studying Organ Shapes Differences. Our framework can also be used to study organ differences between groups. Let us consider a set of healthy and pathological subjects, as well as their segmentation masks. Based on the recognition model $q_\phi(\mathbf{z} \mid \mathbf{X})$, we can compute the average of the subject's latent projection for each group, denoted by $\mathbf{z}_{normal}$ and $\mathbf{z}_{abnormal}$, respectively. We consider the line of equation $(1 - t) \times \mathbf{z}_{normal} + t \times \mathbf{z}_{abnormal}$ with $t \in \mathbb{R}$. When moving along this line with increasing values of t, we progress from a healthy mean latent shape representation to a pathological one, and can reconstruct the corresponding segmentation mask using the probabilistic decoder $p_\theta(\mathbf{X} \mid \mathbf{z})$.

3   Experiments

In this section, we applied our method in the case of the pancreas. A normative model of pancreas shape was learned on a large cohort of healthy subjects, and was then leveraged for AD on an independent test cohort. Several configurations were proposed to assess the model performances, including the impact of the number of training subjects and of the latent space dimensionality on the AD performances. Detection with the few-shot learning method was performed using Support Vector Machine (SVM). Finally, we showed how the proposed framework can be used to visualize differences between the healthy and pathological pancreas.

Training. The training dataset $\mathcal{D}^{Train}$ was created from our private cohort containing 2606 abdominal Portal CT scans of patients with potential liver cancer. To ensure the healthy condition and shape of the pancreas, several exclusion criteria were applied (see Section B in the supplementary material). Finally, 1200 portal CT scans were retained. To explore the influence of the number of samples seen during training, subsets $\mathcal{D}_N$ with a growing number of subjects were created (see Table 1 in the supplementary material). For each $\mathcal{D}_N$, 80% and 20% of the samples were used for training and validation, respectively. Splitting was done such that the pancreas volume distribution was balanced across the splits.

Fig. 1. Examples of normal and abnormal pancreas shapes from $\mathcal{D}^{Test}$. Green and red figures are examples taken from $\mathcal{D}^{Test}_{normal}$ and $\mathcal{D}^{Test}_{abnormal}$, respectively. (Color figure online)

Testing. The test database $\mathcal{D}^{Test}$ was obtained by combining two datasets: i) a private dataset $\mathcal{D}^{Test}_{abnormal}$ containing 144 cases diagnosed with pancreatic cancer, and for whom the pancreas shape was evaluated as abnormal by an expert radiologist; ii) a public dataset $\mathcal{D}^{Test}_{normal}$ from The Cancer Imaging Archive (TCIA) containing 80 CT scans [18] of patients who neither had abdominal pathologies nor pancreatic lesions, and for whom the assumption of normal pancreas shape held. Centers, machines and protocols differed among the three datasets. Examples of normal and abnormal shapes can be seen in Fig. 1.

Preprocessing. The first step consisted in obtaining the pancreas segmentation masks. For the public dataset $\mathcal{D}^{Test}_{normal}$, we used the reference pancreas segmentation masks provided by TCIA. For $\mathcal{D}^{Train}_{normal}$ and $\mathcal{D}^{Test}_{abnormal}$, the masks were obtained semi-automatically using an in-house segmentation algorithm derived from the nnU-Net, and validated by a radiologist with 25 years of expertise in abdominal imaging. Finally, all the masks were resampled to $1 \times 1 \times 2$ mm^3 in (x, y, z) directions, and centered in a volume of size $192 \times 128 \times 64$ voxels.

Zero-Shot AD. We trained our model on the different datasets $\mathcal{D}^{Train}_N$, with a growing number of latent dimensions L ranging from 16 to 1024 (denoted by $L_{16}...L_{1024}$). For each experiment, we applied the zero-shot AD procedure, as previously explained, on $\mathcal{D}^{Test}$. We report the Area Under the Curve (AUC), in %, in Table 1. Increasing the dimension of the latent space L improved the classification performances on each dataset $\mathcal{D}_N$. Moreover, for each dataset size the best result was consistently obtained when L was set at the maximum value L_{1024}. We also observed that the effect of the latent space dimension on the performances seemed to attenuate as the dataset size increased. Indeed, we observed

Table 1. Results for zero-shot AD. For each experiment, corresponding to a specific training size $\mathcal{D}$ and latent space dimension L, we report the mean and standard deviation of AUC scores (in %) obtained by bootstrapping with 10000 repetitions. Best results by line are <u>underlined</u> and by column are in **bold**.

	L_{16}	L_{64}	L_{256}	L_{1024}
$\mathcal{D}_{300}$	51.51 ±0.37	59.08 ±0.37	62.16 ±0.37	<u>62.17</u> ±0.37
$\mathcal{D}_{600}$	59.24 ±0.38	60.97 ±0.36	**64.32** ±0.36	65.11 ±0.36
$\mathcal{D}_{900}$	60.77 ±0.37	**62.64** ±0.37	64.04 ±0.36	<u>64.81</u> ±0.36
$\mathcal{D}_{1200}$	**62.28** ±0.36	61.74 ±0.37	62.58 ±0.37	<u>**65.41**</u> ±0.36

that when going from L_{16} to L_{1024}, the mean AUC for $\mathcal{D}_{300}$, $\mathcal{D}_{600}$, $\mathcal{D}_{900}$, $\mathcal{D}_{1200}$ improved by 10.7, 5.9, 4.0 and 3.1 points, respectively. Regarding the effect of the database size, we observed that increasing the training set size seemed to globally improve the AUC scores. For instance, going from $\mathcal{D}_{300}$ to $\mathcal{D}_{600}$ increased the classification performances for all the experiments, particularly for L_{16} which gained 9.3 points. This beneficial effect of both larger training sets and latent dimension was also observed on the Dice score between the original and reconstructed segmentation masks (see Table 2 in the supplementary material). Thus, for the following experiments, we chose the model trained on $\mathcal{D}_{1200}$ with a latent dimension L_{1024} as it gave the best results in terms of AUC and Dice scores.

To visualize the separation between normal and abnormal shapes, we projected each subject from $\mathcal{D}^{test}$ using the recognition model $q_\phi(\mathbf{z}|\mathbf{X})$. Based on the subjects' latent representation, we applied three dimensionality reduction techniques, namely Principal Components Analysis (PCA), t-distributed Stochastic Neighbor Embedding (t-SNE) and Isomap. Results are displayed in Fig. 2, on which each point represents the latent projection of a test subject reduced on a 2D plane. We observed that, independently of the projection technique, normal and abnormal shapes tended to be separated in two different clusters.

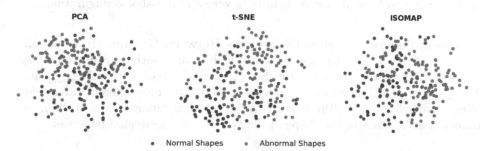

Fig. 2. 2D reduction of the latent representation of the test subjects. The 80 samples from $\mathcal{D}_{normal}^{Test}$ are in green, and the 144 samples from $\mathcal{D}_{abnormal}^{Test}$ are in red. (Color figure online)

Few-Shot AD. We trained a linear SVM classifier on the latent representation of $\mathcal{D}^{Test}$ with stratified k-fold cross-validation. We varied the number k of folds to test the performances of the classifier depending on the train/test samples ratio. Experiments ranged from a 0.05 train/test ratio to a leave-one-out cross-validation and are presented in Table 2. We noticed that using only 8 healthy and 15 abnormal training samples increased the performance to 78.9%. We also observed that the AUC scores and the balanced accuracy increased with the number of training samples, reaching a maximum of 91.1% and 83.2% respectively in the leave-one-out configuration.

Table 2. Results for few-shot AD. For each experiment, we indicate the number of training samples, as well as the number of abnormal samples (in brackets). We report the means and standard deviations for AUC (in %) and balanced accuracy (in %), obtained by bootstrapping with 10000 repetitions.

Train/Test ratio	0.05	0.11	0.25	1	223
Number of training samples	*12 (8)*	*23 (15)*	*45 (29)*	*112 (72)*	*223 (144)*
AUC	66.02 $\pm$0.02	78.97 $\pm$0.03	81.87 $\pm$0.07	86.95 $\pm$0.23	91.18 $\pm$0.19
Balanced accuracy	67.78 $\pm$0.03	70.88 $\pm$0.05	73.96 $\pm$0.10	75.49 $\pm$0.37	83.26 $\pm$0.34

Comparison with a Baseline Method. We compared our approach with a baseline method classifying shapes based on their volume. We applied this method on $\mathcal{D}^{Test}$ with bootstrap sampling and obtained an average AUC of 51% with a 95% confidence interval of [49.9; 51.7], below the maximum AUC scores of 65.4% and 91.1% previously reported in the zero-shot and few-shot cases, respectively. We also compared the proposed method to two SSM methods: active shape models (ASM) [6] and Large Deformation Diffeomorphic Metric Mapping (LDDMM) using the Deformetrica software [3]. Details and results, reported in Section D in the supplementary material, show that our approach outperforms these two state-of-the-art methods in both zero and few-shot configurations.

Studying Pancreas Shapes Differences Between Groups. To model differences in the pancreas shape between healthy and pathological groups, we applied the procedure presented in Sect. 2 on the subjects from $\mathcal{D}^{Test}_{normal}$ and $\mathcal{D}^{Test}_{abnormal}$. Figure 3 shows the pancreas shapes obtained for different values of t. When going from a healthy towards a pathological latent representation, we observed a shrinkage of the shape in the body for the generated pancreas.

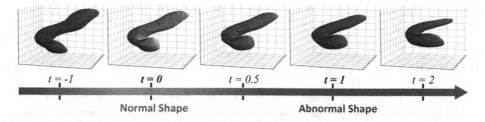

Fig. 3. Generated pancreas shapes. Pancreas shapes generated by decoding latent representations lying on the line of equation $(1 - t) \times z_{normal} + t \times z_{abnormal}$.

4   Discussion and Conclusion

We presented a method based on a VAE to learn a normative model of organ shape. We hypothesized that such a model could be learned from large databases of healthy subjects. The method was applied in the case of the pancreas, for which morphological changes can be a marker of disease.

We empirically observed that large training sets and latent dimensions were beneficial to the model in terms of AD performances. Our results also demonstrated that the model captured features that distinguished between normal and abnormal shapes in the latent space, as illustrated in Fig. 2. From a quantitative point of view, we observed in the zero-shot case - *i.e.* without supervision - that the best model obtained an AUC score of $65.41 \pm 0.36\%$, which significantly outperformed a naive model classifying shapes based on their volume. In the few-shot experiments, we obtained a mean AUC score of 77.4% by training a SVM with only 8 healthy subjects and 15 pathological subjects. These findings highlight the discriminating properties of the latent normative model of pancreas shape estimated by our model. Moreover, classification performances reached up to 91.1% AUC and 83.2% balanced accuracy when training the classifier on 223 samples in a leave-one-out fashion. These results are in line with [15], where the authors reported a balanced accuracy of 85.2% on their private dataset. Yet, our approach differs from theirs by its paradigm. Instead of training a supervised model for joint shape representation and classification, we propose to learn a normative model of shape. The advantage of this approach is that it does not require different types of patients to be trained but solely a database of healthy subjects. Moreover, it can be used in an unsupervised manner (*cf.* zero-shot) or with few labeled data (*cf.* few-shot), with good performances in both cases.

Finally, we also showed that our framework could be used to study and visualize the morphological differences between the organ shape of different clinical groups, based on an exploration of the latent space. The anatomical changes observed in Fig. 3 seemed to concur with clinical evidence as the shrinkage suggests partial parenchymal atrophy [20]. This hypothesis would require further medical evaluation, and could be the subject of a proper clinical validation.

Acknowledgments. This work was partly funded by a CIFRE grant from ANRT # 2020/1448.

References

1. Baur, C., Denner, S., Wiestler, B., Navab, N., Albarqouni, S.: Autoencoders for unsupervised anomaly segmentation in brain MR images: a comparative study. Med. Image Anal. **69**, 101952 (2021)
2. Beg, M., Miller, M., Trouvé, A., Younes, L.: Computing large deformation metric mappings via geodesic flows of diffeomorphisms. IJCV **61**(2), 139–157 (2005). https://doi.org/10.1023/B:VISI.0000043755.93987.aa
3. Bône, A., Louis, M., Martin, B., Durrleman, S.: Deformetrica 4: an open-source software for statistical shape analysis. In: Reuter, M., Wachinger, C., Lombaert, H., Paniagua, B., Lüthi, M., Egger, B. (eds.) ShapeMI 2018. LNCS, vol. 11167, pp. 3–13. Springer, Cham (2018). https://doi.org/10.1007/978-3-030-04747-4_1
4. Chen, X., Konukoglu, E.: Unsupervised detection of lesions in brain MRI using constrained adversarial auto-encoders. In: MIDL (2018)
5. Christensen, G.E., Rabbitt, R.D., Miller, M.I.: Deformable templates using large deformation kinematics. IEEE Trans. Image Process. **5**(10), 1435–1447 (1996)
6. Cootes, T.F., Taylor, C.J., Graham, J.: Active shape models-their training and application. Comput. Vis. Image Underst. **61**(1), 38–50 (1995)
7. Dalca, A.V., Balakrishnan, G., Guttag, J., Sabuncu, M.R.: Unsupervised learning for fast probabilistic diffeomorphic registration. In: Frangi, A.F., Schnabel, J.A., Davatzikos, C., Alberola-López, C., Fichtinger, G. (eds.) MICCAI 2018. LNCS, vol. 11070, pp. 729–738. Springer, Cham (2018). https://doi.org/10.1007/978-3-030-00928-1_82
8. Dufumier, B., et al.: Contrastive learning with continuous proxy meta-data for 3D MRI classification. In: de Bruijne, M., et al. (eds.) MICCAI 2021. LNCS, vol. 12902, pp. 58–68. Springer, Cham (2021). https://doi.org/10.1007/978-3-030-87196-3_6
9. Fox, N., et al.: Presymptomatic hippocampal atrophy in Alzheimer's disease: a longitudinal MRI study. Brain **119**(6), 2001–2007 (1996)
10. Gori, P., et al.: A Bayesian framework for joint morphometry of surface and curve meshes in multi-object complexes. Med. Image Anal. **35**, 458–474 (2017)
11. Isensee, F., et al.: nnU-Net: a self-configuring method for deep learning-based biomedical image segmentation. Nat. Methods **18**(2), 203–211 (2021)
12. Kendall, D.G.: Shape manifolds, procrustean metrics, and complex projective spaces. Bull. Lond. Math. Soc. **16**(2), 81–121 (1984)
13. Kingma, D.P., Welling, M.: Auto-encoding variational Bayes. In: 2nd International Conference on Learning Representations, ICLR 2014, Banff, AB, Canada (2014)
14. Krebs, J., Delingette, H., Mailhé, B., Ayache, N., Mansi, T.: Learning a probabilistic model for diffeomorphic registration. IEEE Trans. Med. Imaging **38**(9), 2165–2176 (2019)
15. Liu, F., Xie, L., Xia, Y., Fishman, E., Yuille, A.: Joint shape representation and classification for detecting PDAC. In: Suk, H.-I., Liu, M., Yan, P., Lian, C. (eds.) MLMI 2019. LNCS, vol. 11861, pp. 212–220. Springer, Cham (2019). https://doi.org/10.1007/978-3-030-32692-0_25
16. Pennec, X.: Intrinsic statistics on Riemannian manifolds: basic tools for geometric measurements. J. Math. Imaging Vis. **25**(1), 127–154 (2006)

17. Ronneberger, O., Fischer, P., Brox, T.: U-Net: convolutional networks for biomedical image segmentation. In: Navab, N., Hornegger, J., Wells, W.M., Frangi, A.F. (eds.) MICCAI 2015. LNCS, vol. 9351, pp. 234–241. Springer, Cham (2015). https://doi.org/10.1007/978-3-319-24574-4_28
18. Roth, H., et al.: Data from pancreas-CT. Cancer Imaging Arch. (2016). https://doi.org/10.7937/K9/TCIA.2016.tNB1kqBU
19. Thompson, D.W.: On Growth and Form. Cambridge University Press, Cambridge (1917)
20. Yamao, K., et al.: Partial pancreatic parenchymal atrophy is a new specific finding to diagnose small pancreatic cancer (≤ 10 mm) including carcinoma in situ: comparison with localized benign main pancreatic duct stenosis patients. Diagnostics **10**(7), 445 (2020)
21. Yang, X., Kwitt, R., Styner, M., Niethammer, M.: Quicksilver: fast predictive image registration - a deep learning approach. Neuroimage **158**, 378–396 (2017)
22. Zhang, M., Singh, N., Fletcher, P.T.: Bayesian estimation of regularization and atlas building in diffeomorphic image registration. In: Gee, J.C., Joshi, S., Pohl, K.M., Wells, W.M., Zöllei, L. (eds.) IPMI 2013. LNCS, vol. 7917, pp. 37–48. Springer, Heidelberg (2013). https://doi.org/10.1007/978-3-642-38868-2_4
23. Zimmerer, D., Isensee, F., Petersen, J., Kohl, S., Maier-Hein, K.: Unsupervised anomaly localization using variational auto-encoders. In: Shen, D., et al. (eds.) MICCAI 2019. LNCS, vol. 11767, pp. 289–297. Springer, Cham (2019). https://doi.org/10.1007/978-3-030-32251-9_32

From Images to Probabilistic Anatomical Shapes: A Deep Variational Bottleneck Approach

Jadie Adams[1,2]([✉]) and Shireen Elhabian[1,2]

[1] Scientific Computing and Imaging Institute,
University of Utah, Salt Lake City, UT, USA
{jadie,shireen}@sci.utah.edu
[2] School of Computing, University of Utah, Salt Lake City, UT, USA

Abstract. Statistical shape modeling (SSM) directly from 3D medical images is an underutilized tool for detecting pathology, diagnosing disease, and conducting population-level morphology analysis. Deep learning frameworks have increased the feasibility of adopting SSM in medical practice by reducing the expert-driven manual and computational overhead in traditional SSM workflows. However, translating such frameworks to clinical practice requires calibrated uncertainty measures as neural networks can produce over-confident predictions that cannot be trusted in sensitive clinical decision-making. Existing techniques for predicting shape with aleatoric (data-dependent) uncertainty utilize a principal component analysis (PCA) based shape representation computed in isolation of the model training. This constraint restricts the learning task to solely estimating pre-defined shape descriptors from 3D images and imposes a linear relationship between this shape representation and the output (i.e., shape) space. In this paper, we propose a principled framework based on the variational information bottleneck theory to relax these assumptions while predicting probabilistic shapes of anatomy directly from images without supervised encoding of shape descriptors. Here, the latent representation is learned in the context of the learning task, resulting in a more scalable, flexible model that better captures data non-linearity. Additionally, this model is self-regularized and generalizes better given limited training data. Our experiments demonstrate that the proposed method provides an accuracy improvement and better calibrated aleatoric uncertainty estimates than state-of-the-art methods.

Keywords: Uncertainty quantification · Statistical shape modeling · Bayesian deep learning

1 Introduction

Statistical shape modeling (SSM) is an enabling tool in medicine and biology to quantify population-specific anatomical shape variation. SSM can detect pathological morphologies tied to impaired function and answer clinical hypotheses regarding anatomical cohorts (e.g., [3,4,11]). Two effective representations of

© The Author(s), under exclusive license to Springer Nature Switzerland AG 2022
L. Wang et al. (Eds.): MICCAI 2022, LNCS 13432, pp. 474–484, 2022.
https://doi.org/10.1007/978-3-031-16434-7_46

shape in SSM are deformation fields and *landmarks* - the former captures implicit transformations between images/shapes and a pre-defined atlas, while the latter are sets of explicit points defined on the shape surface to be in correspondence across the population [20,21]. While the proposed framework is agnostic to the choice of shape representation, we demonstrate the approach using landmarks, both to be consistent with existing methods and because landmarks are more intuitive and interpretable for statistical analyses and visualization [20,26]. Existing computational workflows, such as ShapeWorks [8,9], automatically place dense sets of landmarks or *correspondence points* on shapes segmented from 3D medical images. However, generating such a set of points or *point distribution model* (PDM) requires expert-driven, data-intensive steps: segmenting the anatomy of interest from 3D images, data preprocessing, shape registration, and correspondence optimization along with hyperparameter tuning. Deep learning has alleviated these burdens by providing end-to-end solutions for mapping unsegmented 3D images (i.e., CT or MRI) to PDM with little preprocessing [1,5,6,23]. While the traditional SSM pipelines take hours, trained networks can discover statistical representations of anatomies directly from new images in seconds, creating the potential to streamline the adoption of SSM in research and practice. DeepSSM [5,6] is one such state-of-the-art framework that provides SSM estimates that perform statistically similar to traditional methods in downstream tasks [7]. DeepSSM relies on a supervised latent representation computed using principal component analysis (PCA) in advance of model training to enable data augmentation and incorporate prior shape knowledge, as has been done in related image-based tasks (e.g., [6,14,18,25,27]). However, PCA supervision imposes a linear relationship between the latent and the output space and restricts the learning task to strictly SSM prediction. Additionally, PCA does not scale in the case of large sets of high-dimensional shape data.

Another caveat of DeepSSM, and deep learning models at large, is that they can produce overconfident estimates that can not be blindly assumed to be accurate, especially in sensitive decision-making settings such as clinical practice. There are two forms of uncertainty in such frameworks; aleatoric (or data-dependent) and epistemic (or model-dependent uncertainty, which can be explained away given enough training data) [15]. Learning from medical imaging data poses a challenge because scans can vary widely in quality and often suffer from coarse resolution, artifacts, and noise. These factors signify a strong need to capture uncertainty inherent in the input data; thus here, we chose to focus on aleatoric uncertainty quantification. Progress has been made in inferring probabilistic SSM from images to capture aleatoric uncertainty measures [1,23]. However, existing probabilistic SSM models share the same limitations as DeepSSM in that they rely on a predetermined PCA-based latent representation.

Here, we present a novel formulation for inferring statistical representations of anatomies from unsegmented images that mitigates these limitations by learning a latent representation in tandem via a variational information bottleneck [2]. In information bottleneck (IB) theory, a stochastic encoding $\mathbf{z}$ captures the minimal sufficient statistics required of input $\mathbf{x}$ to predict the output $\mathbf{y}$ [22]. The encoding $\mathbf{z}$ and model parameters Θ are estimated by maximizing the IB objective:

$$\text{argmax}_\Theta \, I(\mathbf{y}, \mathbf{z}; \Theta) - \beta I(\mathbf{x}, \mathbf{z}; \Theta) \tag{1}$$

where I is the mutual information and β, is a Lagrangian multiplier that controls the trade-off between predictive accuracy (encouraging $\mathbf{z}$ to be maximally expressive about $\mathbf{y}$) and model complexity (encouraging $\mathbf{z}$ to be maximally compressive about $\mathbf{x}$). By leveraging this theory to learn a latent representation in our proposed model, we achieve better accuracy and uncertainty calibration than existing state-of-the-art techniques. The advantages of this formulation include the following.

- The latent representation is learned in the context of the learning task rather than in isolation, resulting in better accuracy and a more scalable framework.
- The proposed model better captures the true shape distribution by allowing for a non-linear relationship between the latent encoding and output space.
- This formulation is self-regularized and thus generalizes better under limited training data without ad-hoc regularization methods.
- Because the latent space is unsupervised, the proposed model is general enough to accommodate other learning tasks. For example, it could be used to predict SSM plus additional clinically relevant quantities of interest.
- The proposed model outperforms existing state-of-the-art methods in both predictive accuracy and uncertainty calibration.

2   Methods

Given an unsegmented image $\mathbf{x}_n \in \mathbb{R}^{H \times W \times D}$, the task is to predict a statistical representation of an anatomy-of-interest in the form of a PDM $\mathbf{y}_n \in \mathbb{R}^{3M}$, which is a set of M 3D correspondence points, and the associated point-wise estimates of aleatoric uncertainty $\mathbf{a}_n \in \mathbb{R}^{3M}$. This task is solved by training a model with parameters Θ using a population of $N-$unsegmented 3D images $\mathcal{X} = \{\mathbf{x}_n\}_{n=1}^N$ and their corresponding PDMs denoted $\mathcal{Y} = \{\mathbf{y}_n\}_{n=1}^N$. The proposed method and state-of-the-art models used in comparison utilize a bottleneck and latent encoding $\mathcal{Z} = \{\mathbf{z}_n\}_{n=1}^N$ where $\mathbf{z}_n \in \mathbb{R}^L$ and $L \ll 3M$.

2.1   VIB-DeepSSM Formulation

In the proposed method, denoted **VIB-DeepSSM**, the latent encoding is learned by minimizing the IB objective (Eq. 1). As direct calculation of mutual information is ill-posed in this context, variational inference provides a way to approximate the problem given an empirical data distribution. In "Deep Variational Information Bottleneck" [2], the IB model is parameterized via a neural network by minimizing the derived theoretical lower bound on the IB objective:

$$\mathcal{L}_{VIB} = \frac{1}{N} \sum_{n=1}^N \mathbb{E}_{\epsilon \sim p(\epsilon)} \left[-\log q_\phi(\mathbf{y}_n | \mathbf{z}_{n,\epsilon}) \right] + \beta \, \text{KL} \left[p_\theta(\mathbf{z}_n | \mathbf{x}_n) \| r(\mathbf{z}) \right] \tag{2}$$

This loss balances a Kullback-Leibler divergence (KL) and a data fidelity (or reconstruction) term formulated as negative log-likelihood (NLL) with the Lagrangian multiplier $\beta \in [0,1]$ to learn model parameters $\Theta = \{\phi, \theta\}$. The KL term encourages maximal compression of $\mathbf{x}$, while the NLL term encourages maximal expression of $\mathbf{y}$. We define a stochastic encoder of the form $p_\theta(\mathbf{z}|\mathbf{x}) = \mathcal{N}(\mathbf{z}|f_e^\mu(\mathbf{x};\theta), f_e^\Sigma(\mathbf{x};\theta))$, where f_e is a convolutional network parameterized by θ that maps an input image to a Gaussian latent distribution. Here, $r(\mathbf{z})$ is a prior to the marginal distribution of $\mathbf{z}$, which is set to be a fixed L-dimensional spherical unit Gaussian, $r(\mathbf{z}) = \mathcal{N}(\mathbf{z}|\mathbf{0}, \mathbb{I})$. This method is self-regularized in a principled way as the KL term prevents the latent representation from overfitting, allowing for better generalization under limited data. The decoder, $q_\phi(\mathbf{y}|\mathbf{z})$, serves as a variational approximation to the intractable $p(\mathbf{y}|\mathbf{z})$. We define it as $q_\phi(\mathbf{y}|\mathbf{z}) = f_d(\mathbf{z};\phi)$, where f_d is an MLP parameterized by the weights ϕ (with non-linear activation) that maps the latent representation to correspondence points (Fig. 1). To enable gradient calculation, posterior samples $\mathbf{z}_{n,\epsilon}$ are acquired using the reparameterization trick [17]: $\mathbf{z}_{n,\epsilon} = f_e^\mu(\mathbf{x}_n;\theta) + \epsilon f_e^\Sigma(\mathbf{x}_n;\theta)$ where $\epsilon \sim \mathcal{N}(\mathbf{0}, \mathbb{I})$. In our experiments, the expectation is estimated using 30 samples. The uncertainty is quantified as the entropy of this distribution $p(\mathbf{y}|\mathbf{z})$.

2.2 Baseline Models in Comparison

We compare the proposed model[1] against the state-of-the-art deterministic formulation that does not predict uncertainty, PCA-DeepSSM [6], as well as two state-of-the-art stochastic formulations that do provide predicted uncertainty: PPCA-DeepSSM [1] and PPCA-Offset-DeepSSM [23] (Fig. 1).

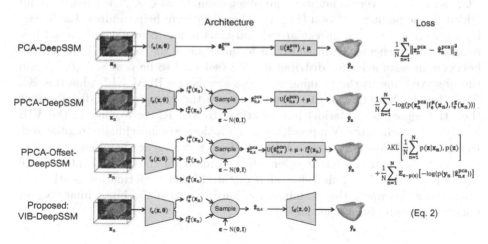

Fig. 1. Model Variants: Architecture and loss of the proposed method and baseline models. All encoders $f_e^\mu(\mathbf{x};\theta)$ have the same architecture as in DeepSSM [6] (five convolutional layers with batch normalization followed by two fully connected layers) only the output size of the last layer is variant-dependent (L-dimensional for PCA-DeepSSM, otherwise $2L$). In VIB-DeepSSM, the decoder $f_d(\mathbf{z};\phi)$ is comprised of three fully connected layers with non-linear activation.

---

[1] The source code is publicly available at: https://github.com/jadie1/VIB-DeepSSM.

In these frameworks, the latent representation is supervised via PCA scores computed from the training correspondence points $\mathbf{y}_n$. The latent space dimension, L, is chosen such that 95% of variability is preserved. We denote the PCA scores $\mathcal{Z}^{pca} = \{\mathbf{z}_n^{pca}\}_{n=1}^N$ where $\mathbf{z}_n^{pca} \in \mathbb{R}^L$. Thus $\mathbf{y}_n \approx \mathbf{U}\mathbf{z}_n^{pca} + \boldsymbol{\mu}$ where $\mathbf{U} \in \mathbb{R}^{3M \times L}$ is the matrix of eigenvectors and $\boldsymbol{\mu} \in \mathbb{R}^{3M}$ is the mean of the training correspondence points. In the proposed model, VIB-DeepSSM, the latent space is not supervised, but its dimensionality should be predefined. PCA provides a reasonable, reproducible way to do define this dimension size, thus in VIB-DeepSSM, we use the same L-value, though this is not a requirement.

PCA-DeepSSM [6] is a deterministic framework that uses PCA scores as a supervised latent space. The decoder is a single **fixed**, fully connected layer without activation with the PCA basis as weights and mean shape as bias. The loss function is mean square error (MSE) between true and predicted PCA scores.

PPCA-DeepSSM [1] is equivalent to Uncertain-DeepSSM [1], except dropout is removed as we are not analyzing epistemic uncertainty quantification. Here the latent space is supervised and the encoder is stochastic, where PCA variance serves as a regularization term and is learned implicitly via the loss (NLL of the true PCA scores given the predicted distribution). The decoder is fixed PCA reconstruction, as it is in PCA-DeepSSM [6], but here the predicted correspondence points are acquired by averaging over posterior samples.

PPCA-Offset-DeepSSM [23] is based on the approach in Tóthová *et al.* [23], but here the architecture is altered to predict 3D PDM instead of 2D shape vertices. In this formulation, the encoder also predicts a distribution of PCA scores; however, in addition, an offset term $f_e^s(\mathbf{x}) \in \mathbb{R}^{3M}$ is predicted and added to the point prediction (Fig. 1). The offset term helps address the linearity restriction, but it is unregularized and thus prone to overshoot. An ad hoc regularization scheme is utilized in this formulation in the form of KL divergence between an assumed prior distribution of $\mathbf{z}$ (selected to be $p(\mathbf{z}) = \mathcal{N}(0, I)$) and the observed one in the training set. The loss is the PDM NLL plus this KL term (Fig. 1). Note that in this loss, the sum of the N $\mathbf{z}$ predicted distributions (i.e., the aggregate posterior) is regularized by the KL term, and in the VIB loss (Eq. 2), each of the N $\mathbf{z}$ predicted distributions are individually regularized. Hence, the VIB loss effectively minimizes the KL divergence between the aggregate posterior and the latent prior while minimizing the mutual information between $\mathbf{x}$ and $\mathbf{z}$ [13]. This behavior is dictated by the information bottleneck; learn the $\mathbf{z}$ descriptor that is minimally informative of the input image $\mathbf{x}$ but maximally predictive of the shape $\mathbf{y}$.

3   Results

To best analyze accuracy and uncertainty calibration across model variants, we select a large, highly variable dataset for experiments. In the original DeepSSM [6] formulation, a data augmentation scheme is used to create additional training samples. However, this technique relies on PCA, which we intend to remove as a requirement; thus here training is done without augmentation.

3.1   Left Atrium Dataset

In experiments, we use a set of 1001 anonymized LGE MRI images of the left atrium (LA) from unique atrial fibrillation patients. The images were manually segmented by experts at the University of Utah Division of Cardiovascular Medicine with spatial resolution $0.65 \times 0.65 \times 2.5$ mm^3 and the endocardium wall was used to cut off pulmonary veins. Significant morphological variations are expected to be in the left atrium appendage or LAA (varies immensely in size across patients), the pulmonary veins (vary in number and size across patients), and in the mitral valve (for which there are no defining image features for segmentation). This dataset is appropriate for aleatoric uncertainty analysis because, in addition to the large shape variation, the input images vary widely in intensity and quality, and LA boundaries are blurred and have low contrast with the surrounding structures (Fig. 2). To enable calibration analysis, we define a specific testing set of images with high uncertainty using an outlier degree computed on input images that combines within- and off-subspace distances [1,19]. By thresholding on outlier degree at 3 (Fig. 2), we define an *outlier test* set of size 78. We randomly split the remaining samples (90%, 10%, 10%) to get a training set of 739, a validation set of 92, and an *inlier test* set of 92.

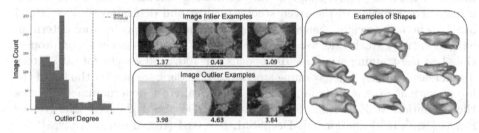

Fig. 2. The distribution of image outlier degrees is displayed with examples of image slices and corresponding outlier degree. Outlier images tend to be over-exposed with low contrast or contain artifacts. Examples of ground truth meshes are displayed from the top view to demonstrate the significant shape variability.

Acquiring target correspondence points for the training images requires generating a PDM via the traditional SSM pipeline (i.e., segmentation, preprocessing, and optimization). We employ the open-source *ShapeWorks* software [8] to align and crop the images and binary segmentations and optimize a PDM with 1024 landmarks per shape. The resulting input images are size (166, 120, 125). Given the optimized training PDM, we generate target PDMs for the validation and test sets for analysis by optimizing landmarks positions on these samples with the training landmarks fixed so that the statistics of the validation and test samples are not reflected in the training PDM. The first two modes of variations in the training PDM are shown in Fig. 3.

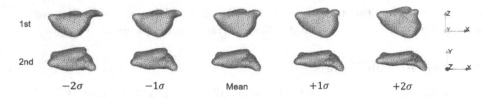

Fig. 3. Modes of variation from the training PDM generated using ShapeWorks. The primary mode shown from anterior view captures the LAA elongation. The secondary mode shown from top view captures the LA sphericity.

3.2 Training Scheme

VIB-DeepSSM and the baseline methods are trained on 100%, 80%, 40%, 20%, and 10% of the training data to analyze robustness in low-sample-size scenarios. We select subsets of the training data using stratified random sampling by clustering the training PDMs and selecting data subsets so that each cluster is equally represented. All variants are implemented in PyTorch and training is run on GTX1080Ti GPUs with Adam optimization [16], a fixed learning rate of $5e^{-5}$, a batch size of 6, Xavier weight initialization [10], and Parametric ReLU [12] activation. Models are trained until the validation PDM MSE has not decreased in 50 epochs. A loss burn-in scheme is used for stochastic variants to allow the model to learn to predict shape before estimating variance. This is done using a linear combination of the given stochastic loss and deterministic loss (PDM MSE), where the weight changes over a given number of epochs from deterministic to entirely stochastic. We set the number of burn-in epochs to be proportional to the training size (i.e., 100 epochs for 100%, 80 epochs for 80%, etc.). To increase stability when training stochastic encoders, we predict the log of the latent variance (as is done in [15]). We empirically set hyperparameters using the validation MSE and find for PPCA-Offset-DeepSSM [23], $\lambda = 100$ (tested range: $[1e^{-4}, 1e^4]$) and for VIB-DeepSSM, $\beta = 0.01$ (tested range: $[1e^{-8}, 1]$).

3.3 Accuracy Analysis

Prediction accuracy is evaluated by calculating the relative root mean square error (RRMSE) between the true and predicted correspondence points. This is evaluated sample-wise, **RRMSE** $= \sqrt{(\|\mathbf{y}_n - \hat{\mathbf{y}}_n\|^2)/3M}$, and point-wise where for point i, **Point-RRMSE** $= \sqrt{(\|\mathbf{y}_n^i - \hat{\mathbf{y}}_n^i\|^2)/3}$. We also analyze accuracy using the **surface-to-surface** distance between the expert-segmented mesh and one constructed from the predicted PDM. This predicted mesh is obtained by finding the closest example in the training set and applying the warp between points to its mesh using [24]. Figure 4 illustrates the proposed method has a similar or better accuracy on both testing inliers and outliers than the baseline methods given any training size. Note that for PPCA-Offset-DeepSSM [23], accuracy does not significantly improve with increased training data, suggesting the model is over-regularized. However decreasing the λ parameter results

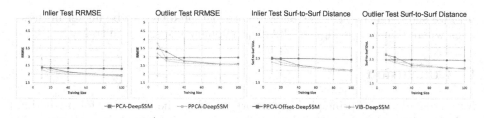

Fig. 4. Accuracy: The mean accuracy is shown for each model variant with error bars representing standard deviation on inlier and outlier test sets. Overall, VIB-DeepSSM performs best, and most notably when training data is limited.

in unstable training. VIB-DeepSSM provides a more principled way to capture data non-linearity and self-regularize.

3.4   Uncertainty Calibration Analysis

To assess uncertainty calibration, we consider the correlation between (1) the input image outlier degree and entropy of $p(\mathbf{y}|\mathbf{z})$, (2) RRMSE and entropy of $p(\mathbf{y}|\mathbf{z})$, and (3) point-RRMSE and predicted point-wise standard deviation (volume of the 3D Gaussian for each landmark/point). We quantify correlation using the Pearson correlation coefficient, where a higher value suggests the model more effectively identifies input with high uncertainty and areas of low prediction confidence. Our models predicted uncertainty is better calibrated both in relation to outlier degree and error (Fig. 5). The heat maps generated via interpolation

	Outlier Degree vs Entropy	RRMSE vs Entropy	Point-RRMSE vs Predicted Point Standard Deviation	
PPCA-DeepSSM	Outliers / Inliers			
Corr. Coefficient:	0.119	0.278	0.376	
PPCA-Offset DeepSSM	Outliers / Inliers			
Corr. Coefficient:	0.118	0.002	0.318	
VIB-DeepSSM	Outliers / Inliers			
Corr. Coefficient:	0.369	0.782	0.522	

Fig. 5. Uncertainty Calibration Plots and correlation coefficients show the uncertainty calibration of each model variant. Heat maps show average quantities on a representative mesh.

in Fig. 5 show that point uncertainty is correctly predicted to be higher in these areas where the error is highest (LAA, pulmonary veins, and mitral valve).

4 Conclusion

We presented a novel principled framework based on the IB theory for predicting probabilistic SSM from unsegmented 3D images and demonstrated that it provides better calibrated aleatoric uncertainty quantification than existing state-of-the-art techniques without sacrificing accuracy. By learning a latent representation in the context of the task, we provide a more scalable, flexible framework that better captures data non-linearity. Additionally, the proposed method is self-regularized and generalizes better under limited training data. These contributions increase the feasibility of using SSM in research and medicine by both bypassing the time and cost-prohibitive steps of traditional SSM and providing the necessary safeguard against model over-confidence. This has the potential to improve medical standards and increase patient accessibility to statistic-based diagnosis. In future work, we plan to analyze the effectiveness of this model for predicting SSM with clinically relevant quantities, and to explore techniques for learning the optimal latent dimension size in tandem with the task.

Acknowledgements. This work was supported by the National Institutes of Health under grant numbers NIBIB-U24EB029011, NIAMS-R01AR076120, NHLBI-R01HL135568, NIBIB-R01EB016701, and NIGMS-P41GM103545. The content is solely the responsibility of the authors and does not necessarily represent the official views of the National Institutes of Health. The authors would like to thank the University of Utah Division of Cardiovascular Medicine for providing left atrium MRI scans and segmentations from the Atrial Fibrillation projects.

References

1. Adams, J., Bhalodia, R., Elhabian, S.: Uncertain-DeepSSM: from images to probabilistic shape models. In: Reuter, M., Wachinger, C., Lombaert, H., Paniagua, B., Goksel, O., Rekik, I. (eds.) ShapeMI 2020. LNCS, vol. 12474, pp. 57–72. Springer, Cham (2020). https://doi.org/10.1007/978-3-030-61056-2_5
2. Alemi, A., Fischer, I., Dillon, J., Murphy, K.: Deep variational information bottleneck. In: ICLR (2017). https://arxiv.org/abs/1612.00410
3. Atkins, P.R., et al.: Quantitative comparison of cortical bone thickness using correspondence-based shape modeling in patients with cam femoroacetabular impingement. J. Orthop. Res. **35**(8), 1743–1753 (2017)
4. Bhalodia, R., Dvoracek, L.A., Ayyash, A.M., Kavan, L., Whitaker, R., Goldstein, J.A.: Quantifying the severity of metopic craniosynostosis: a pilot study application of machine learning in craniofacial surgery. J. Craniofac. Surg. **31**, 697 (2020)
5. Bhalodia, R., Elhabian, S., Adams, J., Tao, W., Kavan, L., Whitaker, R.: DeepSSM: a blueprint for image-to-shape deep learning models (2021)
6. Bhalodia, R., Elhabian, S.Y., Kavan, L., Whitaker, R.T.: DeepSSM: a deep learning framework for statistical shape modeling from raw images. CoRR arXiv:1810.00111 (2018)

7. Bhalodia, R., et al.: Deep learning for end-to-end atrial fibrillation recurrence estimation. In: Computing in Cardiology, CinC 2018, Maastricht, The Netherlands, 23–26 September 2018
8. Cates, J., Elhabian, S., Whitaker, R.: ShapeWorks: particle-based shape correspondence and visualization software. In: Statistical Shape and Deformation Analysis, pp. 257–298. Elsevier (2017)
9. Cates, J., Fletcher, P.T., Styner, M., Shenton, M., Whitaker, R.: Shape modeling and analysis with entropy-based particle systems. In: Karssemeijer, N., Lelieveldt, B. (eds.) IPMI 2007. LNCS, vol. 4584, pp. 333–345. Springer, Heidelberg (2007). https://doi.org/10.1007/978-3-540-73273-0_28
10. Glorot, X., Bengio, Y.: Understanding the difficulty of training deep feedforward neural networks. In: Proceedings of the Thirteenth International Conference on Artificial Intelligence and Statistics. Proceedings of Machine Learning Research, 13–15 May 2010, vol. 9, pp. 249–256. PMLR (2010)
11. Harris, M.D., Datar, M., Whitaker, R.T., Jurrus, E.R., Peters, C.L., Anderson, A.E.: Statistical shape modeling of cam femoroacetabular impingement. J. Orthop. Res. **31**(10), 1620–1626 (2013). https://doi.org/10.1002/jor.22389
12. He, K., Zhang, X., Ren, S., Sun, J.: Delving deep into rectifiers: surpassing human-level performance on ImageNet classification. CoRR arXiv:1502.01852 (2015)
13. Hoffman, M.D., Johnson, M.J.: ELBO surgery: yet another way to carve up the variational evidence lower bound. In: Workshop in Advances in Approximate Bayesian Inference, NIPS, vol. 1 (2016)
14. Huang, W., Bridge, C.P., Noble, J.A., Zisserman, A.: Temporal HeartNet: towards human-level automatic analysis of fetal cardiac screening video. In: Descoteaux, M., Maier-Hein, L., Franz, A., Jannin, P., Collins, D.L., Duchesne, S. (eds.) MICCAI 2017. LNCS, vol. 10434, pp. 341–349. Springer, Cham (2017). https://doi.org/10.1007/978-3-319-66185-8_39
15. Kendall, A., Gal, Y.: What uncertainties do we need in Bayesian deep learning for computer vision? CoRR arXiv:1703.04977 (2017)
16. Kingma, D., Ba, J.: Adam: a method for stochastic optimization. In: International Conference on Learning Representations (2014)
17. Kingma, D.P., Welling, M.: Auto-encoding variational Bayes. CoRR arXiv:1312.6114 (2014)
18. Milletari, F., Rothberg, A., Jia, J., Sofka, M.: Integrating statistical prior knowledge into convolutional neural networks. In: Descoteaux, M., Maier-Hein, L., Franz, A., Jannin, P., Collins, D.L., Duchesne, S. (eds.) MICCAI 2017. LNCS, vol. 10433, pp. 161–168. Springer, Cham (2017). https://doi.org/10.1007/978-3-319-66182-7_19
19. Moghaddam, B., Pentland, A.: Probabilistic visual learning for object representation. IEEE Trans. Pattern Anal. Mach. Intell. **19**(7), 696–710 (1997)
20. Sarkalkan, N., Weinans, H., Zadpoor, A.A.: Statistical shape and appearance models of bones. Bone **60**, 129–140 (2014)
21. Thompson, D.: On Growth and Form. Cambridge University Press, Cambridge (1917)
22. Tishby, N., Pereira, F.C., Bialek, W.: The information bottleneck method (2000)
23. Tóthová, K., et al.: Uncertainty quantification in CNN-based surface prediction using shape priors. CoRR arXiv:1807.11272 (2018)
24. Wang, Y., Jacobson, A., Barbič, J., Kavan, L.: Linear subspace design for real-time shape deformation. ACM Trans. Graph. (TOG) **34**(4), 1–11 (2015)

25. Xie, J., Dai, G., Zhu, F., Wong, E.K., Fang, Y.: DeepShape: deep-learned shape descriptor for 3D shape retrieval. IEEE Trans. Pattern Anal. Mach. Intell. **39**(7), 1335–1345 (2017)
26. Zachow, S.: Computational planning in facial surgery. Facial Plast. Surg. **31**(05), 446–462 (2015)
27. Zheng, Y., Liu, D., Georgescu, B., Nguyen, H., Comaniciu, D.: 3D deep learning for efficient and robust landmark detection in volumetric data. In: Navab, N., Hornegger, J., Wells, W.M., Frangi, A.F. (eds.) MICCAI 2015. LNCS, vol. 9349, pp. 565–572. Springer, Cham (2015). https://doi.org/10.1007/978-3-319-24553-9_69

Opthalmology

Structure-Consistent Restoration Network for Cataract Fundus Image Enhancement

Heng Li[1]([✉]), Haofeng Liu[1], Huazhu Fu[2], Hai Shu[3], Yitian Zhao[4], Xiaoling Luo[5], Yan Hu[1]([✉]), and Jiang Liu[1,6,7]

[1] Department of Computer Science and Engineering, Southern University of Science and Technology, Shenzhen, China
{lih3,huy3}@sustech.edu.cn
[2] IHPC, A*STAR, Singapore, Singapore
[3] Department of Biostatistics, School of Global Public Health, New York University, New York, USA
[4] Cixi Institute of Biomedical Engineering, Chinese Academy of Sciences, Beijing, China
[5] Shenzhen People's Hospital, Shenzhen, China
[6] Guangdong Provincial Key Laboratory of Brain-Inspired Intelligent Computation, Southern University of Science and Technology, Shenzhen, China
[7] Research Institute of Trustworthy Autonomous Systems, Southern University of Science and Technology, Shenzhen, China

Abstract. Fundus photography is a routine examination in clinics to diagnose and monitor ocular diseases. However, for cataract patients, the fundus image always suffers quality degradation caused by the clouding lens. The degradation prevents reliable diagnosis by ophthalmologists or computer-aided systems. To improve the certainty in clinical diagnosis, restoration algorithms have been proposed to enhance the quality of fundus images. Unfortunately, challenges remain in the deployment of these algorithms, such as collecting sufficient training data and preserving retinal structures. In this paper, to circumvent the strict deployment requirement, a structure-consistent restoration network (SCR-Net) for cataract fundus images is developed from synthesized data that shares an identical structure. A cataract simulation model is firstly designed to collect synthesized cataract sets (SCS) formed by cataract fundus images sharing identical structures. Then high-frequency components (HFCs) are extracted from the SCS to constrain structure consistency such that the structure preservation in SCR-Net is enforced. The experiments demonstrate the effectiveness of SCR-Net in the comparison with state-of-the-art methods and the follow-up clinical applications. The code is available at https://github.com/liamheng/Annotation-free-Fundus-Image-Enhancement.

Keywords: Cataract · Fundus image enhancement · High-frequency components · Structure consistency

L. Wang et al. (Eds.): MICCAI 2022, LNCS 13432, pp. 487–496, 2022.
https://doi.org/10.1007/978-3-031-16434-7_47

1   Introduction

High-quality medical images are the foundation for modern diagnosis and monitoring. The advantages in safety and cost have made fundus photography become a routine examination in clinics to diagnose and monitor ocular diseases [8,19]. More recently, automatic algorithms have been developed to assist the clinical screening and diagnosis based on fundus images [17,18,21]. Unfortunately, as a pathological characteristic, low quality is unavoidable for the fundus images collected from cataract patients. The degradation in cataract images not only impacts the performance of automatic algorithms, but also prevents reliable diagnosis by ophthalmologists [12,20]. Therefore, cataracts lead to uncertainty in clinical observation and the risk of misdiagnosis.

To improve the certainty in ophthalmic diagnosis and treatment, the medical imaging community has strived to overcome the degradation of fundus images caused by missing focus, uneven illumination, as well as cataracts [8]. Histogram equalization [13], spatial filtering [3], and frequency filtering [1] were imported to develop fundus image enhancement algorithms. However, these methods are not sensitive to retinal details or not generalizable in clinical scenarios. In recent years, deep learning has been employed to adaptively learn restoration models for fundus images [2,5,10]. To overcome the limitation caused by the requirement of vast supervised data, unsupervised algorithms and data augmentation techniques have been developed to implement fundus image restoration. Cycle-GAN [22] and contrastive unpaired translation (CUT) [14] were modified [4] to learn suitable mappings from a low-quality domain to a high-quality domain from unpaired data. Alternatively, low-high quality paired data were synthesized for the training of fundus enhancement networks [9,11,16]. Considering the gap between synthesized and real data, domain adaptation [6,7] was also introduced to further promote the performance of the restoration model based on synthesized data.

Although the previous studies have achieved outstanding performances, the deployment of the restoration algorithms remains a challenging task. 1) It is impractical to collect low-high quality paired cataract images, since the high-quality one is only available from post-operation eyes. 2) Retinal details are always neglected by the model learned from unpaired data, and the deployment of domain adaptation is limited by the requirement of target data. 3) Preserving retinal structures with image guidance, such as segmentation aggravates the requirement of annotations and impacts the robustness of the algorithm. 4) Existing algorithms focus on enhancing image quality, while ignoring the performance improvement of clinical applications from the enhancement.

To address these problems, a cataract restoration network, called SCR-Net, is proposed to enhance cataract fundus images in the absence of supervised data. Specifically, to enforce the training of SCR-Net, SCS is generated by synthesizing cataract fundus images with identical structures according to the imaging principle, and then HFCs are extracted to constrain the structure consistency of SCS as well as enforce the structure preservation in the restoration. Our main contributions are summarised as follows:

- A restoration network, called SCR-Net[1], is proposed to enhance the quality of cataract fundus images based on synthesized training data.
- According to the fundus imaging principle, a synthesis model of cataract images is proposed, and the cataract images sharing identical structures are hence synthesized to compose the SCS.
- The structure consistency in the HFCs of the SCS is introduced to boost the model training and structure preservation.
- Experiments demonstrate the effectiveness of the proposed approach, by which data requirement is alleviated and superior performance are presented when compared with state-of-the-art algorithms in the cataract image enhancement and the follow-up clinical applications of segmentation and diagnosis.

2 Methodology

Considering the challenges in enhancing fundus images from cataract patients, the SCR-Net is developed to restore cataract images, as shown in Fig. 1. As the foundation of fundus assessment, preserving retinal structures is prioritized in fundus image restoration. Following this consensus, capturing cataract-invariant features of retinal structures is essential to an efficient restoration model. Thus an SCS sharing identical structures is firstly acquired by simulating multiple cataract fundus images from an individual clear image. Subsequently, through the HFCs in fundus images, structure consistency in the SCS is leveraged to boost the learning of the restoration model and structure preservation. Specifically, the proposed SCR-Net imports invariant features from HFC alignment to robustly restore fundus images and preserve retinal structures.

2.1 Synthesized Cataract Set with Identical Structures

In [15], the fundus imaging through a lens with cataracts is formulated as:

$$I(i,j) = \alpha \cdot L \cdot \gamma(i,j) \cdot t(i,j) + L(1 - t(i,j)), \tag{1}$$

where $I(i,j)$ is the pixel at (i,j) in the fundus image I taken through cataracts, and α denotes the attenuation of retinal illumination caused by cataracts. L is the illumination of the fundus camera, and $\gamma(i,j)$ and $t(i,j)$ are the reflectance function of fundus and the transmission function of cataracts, respectively.

Based on Eq. 1, we design a cataract simulation model given by:

$$s'_c = \alpha \cdot s_c * g_B(r_B, \sigma_B) + \beta \cdot J * g_L(r_L, \sigma_L) \cdot (L_c - s_c), \tag{2}$$

where s_c and s'_c, with $c \in \{r, g, b\}$, are one RGB channel of the clear and cataract images, respectively. Notations g_B and g_L represent the Gaussian filters for clear image smooth and cataractous panel, where $g(r, \sigma)$ denotes a filter with a radius of r and spatial constant σ. Specifically, $r_B, r_L \in \{1, 2, 3\}$,

---

[1] Code is public available.

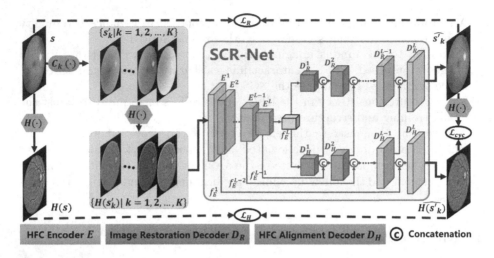

Fig. 1. Overview of the proposed restoration algorithm. From an identical clear image s, $C_k(\cdot)$ synthsizes the SCS $\{s'_k \mid k = 1, 2, ..., K\}$ with various cataract parameters, and then $H(\cdot)$ extracts the HFCs from the clear and cataract images for structure alignment as well as image restoration. The architecture of SCR-Net is composed of an HFC encoder E, an image restoration decoder D_R, and an HFC alignment decoder D_H. The middle layer features f_E^l of E are forward to D_H for aligning $\widehat{H(s'_k)}$ to $H(s)$. Decoder D_R loads the multi-level features f_H^l from D_H to restore the fundus image.

$\sigma_B, \sigma_L \in [10, 30]$. Parameter β is a weight coefficient. A transmission panel $J_{ij} = \sqrt{(i-a)^2 + (j-b)^2}$ is introduced to model the uneven transmission of $t(i, j)$ with the center of (a, b). The illumination of a channel L_c is given by the maximum intensity of s_c. The simulated cataract image is finally defined as $s' = [s'_r, s'_g, s'_b]$.

According to Eq. 2, discrepant cataract fundus images can be simulated by changing the parameters, such as (a, b), α, and β. As demonstrated in the orange box of Fig. 2, an SCS $\{s'_k = C_k(s) \mid k = 1, 2, ..., K\}$ is thus simulated from a clear fundus image s, where $C_k(\cdot)$ denotes the kth simulation with random parameters and K was set as 16. Accordingly, the various cataract images in an SCS share identical structures, which is leveraged to enforce structure preservation in the following sections.

2.2   High-Frequency Components with Structure Consistency

Intuitively, the SCS $\{s'_k \mid k = 1, 2, ..., K\}$ contains the retinal structures consistent with the clear image s. This structure consistency can be leveraged to boost the restoration model training and structure preservation.

Motivated by the Retinex theory [6], the blur caused by cataracts is considered as a low-frequency noise. Thus removing the low-frequency components (LFCs) can suppress the fundus image degradation results from cataracts, while the retinal structures in fundus images are carried by the rest HFCs. Consequently, the structure consistency is imported by the HFCs, which not only suppress the degradation from cataracts, but also preserve the retinal structures.

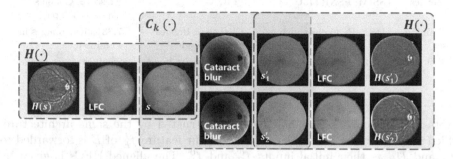

Fig. 2. Examples for the SCS and HFCs. Randomly simulated cataract blur is imported into the clear image s to acquire the cataract images s'_1 and s'_2. The HFCs are extracted by removing the LFCs from s, s'_1, and s'_2.

The LFCs are extracted by a Gaussian filter, which is a common low-pass filter in signal and image processing. Then the HFCs are straightforwardly captured by removing the LFCs from the fundus image as presented in the turquoise boxes of Fig. 2. This calculation is given by

$$H(I) = I - I * g_P(r_P, \sigma_P), \tag{3}$$

where $H(\cdot)$ denotes the HFCs, and the low-pass Gaussian filter g_P with radius r_P of 26 and spatial constant σ_P of 9, is used to capture the LFCs from image I. Hence, $\{H(s'_k) \mid k = 1, 2, ..., K\}$ and $H(s)$, denoting the HFCs in the SCS and the clear image, are employed to introduce structure consistency in the training of the restoration network.

2.3 SCR-Net Architecture

Based on the SCS and HFCs the SCR-Net is hence proposed, in which HFC alignment is implemented to constrain the structure consistency in the HFCs, and features from the alignment are forwarded to optimize the restoration model. As shown in the khaki box of Fig. 1, SCR-Net contains three modules. The feature encoder E, embedding $H(s'_k)$, is shared by the HFC alignment decoder D_H and the image restoration decoder D_R. Following the structure consistency, decoder D_H aligns $H(s'_k)$ to $H(s)$, and decoder D_R attempts to restore a clear fundus image $\widehat{s'_k}$. The latent features from E are forwarded to D_H, and the multi-level features in D_H are used in D_R.

Decomposing encoder E as a composition of convolution layers, the feature output from a specific layer is given by $f_E^l = E^l(E^{l-1}(...E^1(H(s'_k))...))$, $l = 1, 2, ..., L$, where l denotes the index of layers and L is the total number of

Table 1. Datasets and evaluation metrics used in the experiments

Evaluation	With reference		Without reference	
	Restoration	Segmentation	Restoration	Diagnosis
Metrics	SSIM, PSNR	IoU	FIQA	F1-score, Cohen's kappa (Ckappa)
Training set	DRIVE: 40 clear images		300 clear images from Kaggle	7,331 clear images in Fundus-iSee
Test set	RCF: 26 pre- and post-operative image pairs		100 cataract images from Kaggle	2,669 cataract images in Fundus-iSee

layers in E. Decoders D_H and D_R are constructed by the same architecture, which is symmetrical to encoder E. The output feature f_E^L of E is forwarded to D_H and D_R as their initial inputs f_H^0 and f_R^0. The aligned HFCs is given by $\widehat{H(s_k')} = D_H^L(f_H^{L-1})$, where $f_H^l = [D_H^l(f_H^{l-1}), f_E^{L-l}]$, $l = 1, 2, ..., L-1$, refers to the concatenation of the outputs of the lth later in D_H and the outputs of the symmetrical $(L-l)$th layer in E. Thus, an alignment loss is calculated to enforce the learning of invariant features, which is given by

$$\mathcal{L}_H(E, D_H) = \mathbb{E}\left[\sum_{k=1}^{K}\left\|H(s) - \widehat{H(s_k')}\right\|_1\right]. \tag{4}$$

Simultaneously, decoder D_R generates the restored image $\widehat{s_k'}$. To construct a robust restoration network, D_R loads f_H^l for reconstructing the restored image with invariant features. Thus $\widehat{s_k'} = D_R^L(f_R^{L-1})$, where $f_R^l = [D_R^l(f_R^{l-1}), D_H^l(f_H^{l-1})]$, $l = 1, 2, ..., L-1$. The restoration loss is given by

$$\mathcal{L}_R(E, D_H, D_R) = \mathbb{E}\left[\sum_{k=1}^{K}\left\|I - \widehat{I_k'}\right\|_1\right]. \tag{5}$$

Moreover, once the fundus image is properly restored by D_R, its HFCs should be consistent with the HFCs aligned by D_H. Consequently, a cycle-consistency loss $\mathcal{L}_{cyc}$ is computed between $\widehat{H(s_k')}$ and the HFCs of $\widehat{s_k'}$ to optimize the network:

$$\mathcal{L}_{cyc}(E, D_H, D_R) = \mathbb{E}\left[\sum_{k=1}^{K}\left\|H\left(\widehat{s_k'}\right) - \widehat{H(s_k')}\right\|_1\right]. \tag{6}$$

The overall objective function is as follows:

$$\mathcal{L}_{total} = \mathcal{L}_H(E, D_H) + \mathcal{L}_R(E, D_H, D_R) + \mathcal{L}_{cyc}(E, D_H, D_R). \tag{7}$$

Therefore, SCR-Net is optimized with explicit objective function rather than adversarial learning so that the training is easier to achieve convergence.

3   Experiments

Implementation: Four fundus image datasets were used to verify the effectiveness of SCR-Net. Evaluations and datasets used in the experiment are summarized in Table 1, where paired training data were generated from the training

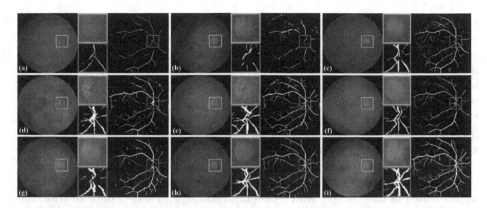

Fig. 3. Comparison between the cataract restoration algorithms: (a) cataract fundus image (b) SGRIF [3], (c) CycleGAN [22], (d) Luo et al. [11], (e) CofeNet [16], (f) Li et al. [7], (g) I-SECRET [4], (h) SCR-Net (ours), and (i) clear image after surgery.

sets by Eq. 2. Four kinds of evaluations were implemented. 1) Restoration and 2) segmentation were conducted with the public dataset DRIVE[2] and the private dataset RCF to conduct evaluations with reference. The intersection over union (IoU) metric for segmentation was calculated between the restored image and reference. 3) A fundus image dataset from Kaggle[3] was collected to evaluate the restoration without reference, where the fundus image quality assessment (FIQA) from [4] was used as the metric. 4) A diagnostic evaluation was presented with the private dataset Fundus-iSee, which contains 10,000 images sorted into five categories of fundus status. The diagnosis model was learned by ResNet-50 from 5,000 images, and the rest are for testing.

The training data for comparative algorithms were individually synthesized by Eq. 2. The input images had the size 256×256, and the training batch size was 8. The model was trained by the Adam optimizer for 150 epochs with a learning rate of 0.001 plus 50 epochs with the learning rate decaying to 0 gradually. The total number of layers in the encoder E was 8. The comparison experiment was conducted under the same setting.

Comparison and Ablation Study: To demonstrate the effectiveness of the proposed SCR-Net, comparisons with state-of-the-art methods and an ablation study were conducted. The recent methods, SGRIF [3], CycleGAN [22], Luo et al. [11], CofeNet [16], Li et al. [7], and I-SECRET [4] were included into comparison. Table 1 reports the used datasets. In the ablation study, the SCS achieved by cataract simulation, the HFCs extracted by $H(\cdot)$, and D_H for domain alignment are respectively removed from the proposed algorithm. The restoration results are visualized in Fig. 3 and summarized in Table 2.

---

(1) Comparison The comparison of SCR-Net with the competing methods is shown in Fig. 3, where the restored images and corresponding segmentation results are exhibited. Cataracts severely degrade the quality of the example image, and thus only a few of the vessels are identified. Through image filtering SGRIF [3] enhances the retinal structures, but the appearance color in the restored image is considerably different from the common ones, which impacts the segmentation. The model learned from unpaired data by CycleGAN [22] presents inferior structure preservation. Guided by segmentation masks, fundus vessels are enhanced by Luo et al. [11] and CofeNet [16]. However, vessel disconnection and pigment disorder are observed in the restored optic disks. To bridge the gap between the synthesized and real data, domain adaptation is implemented in Li et al. [7], which uses both source and target data to train the restoration model. Although domain adaptation boosts the generalization from the source to the target domain, the access to target data aggravates the burden of data collection. Though implemented with unpaired data, the importance map in I-SECRET [4] promises it a decent performance. The proposed SCR-Net learns a restoration model for cataract images from the synthesized data, and the restoration and segmentation results validate its superior performance on real cataract data.

Table 2. Comparisons and ablation study of SCR-Net with state-of-the-art methods on restoration, segmentation, and diagnosis.

	SSIM	PSNR	IoU	FIQA	F1-score	Ckappa
Clear	–	–	–	0.99	0.838	0.448
Cataract	0.673	15.76	0.179	0.15	0.730	0.310
SGRIF [3]	0.609	15.07	0.194	0.17	0.760	0.420
CycleGAN [22]	0.732	17.25	0.336	0.50	0.724	0.286
Luo et al. [11]	0.704	17.29	0.383	0.32	0.712	0.370
CofeNet [16]	0.754	18.03	0.401	0.54	0.754	0.416
Li et al. [7]	0.755	18.07	0.376	0.52	0.747	0.405
I-SECRET [4]	0.748	17.63	0.380	0.46	0.734	0.382
SCR-Net w/o SCS, $H(\cdot)$, D_H	0.729	17.47	0.314	0.18	0.685	0.353
SCR-Net w/o $H(\cdot)$, D_H	0.731	17.80	0.386	0.40	0.730	0.398
SCR-Net w/o D_H	0.755	18.02	0.393	0.48	0.734	0.425
SCR-Net (ours)	**0.773**	**18.39**	**0.417**	**0.65**	**0.770**	**0.445**

Quantitative evaluations on restoration, segmentation, and diagnosis are presented in Table 2. As shown in the evaluation metrics, cataracts degrade the fundus image quality and disturb the segmentation and diagnosis. By applying the restoration algorithms, the quality of cataract images is enhanced and thus the precision of fundus assessment is further boosted. As a result of the unusual appearance color, though received remarkable results in the diagnosis,

SGRIF [3] receives an inferior assessment in the quantitative metrics of restoration and segmentation. Mediocre performances are provided by CycleGAN [22] in the segmentation and diagnosis. Acceptable performance in the restoration and the follow-up applications is presented by Luo et al. [11]. Among the existing algorithms, by importing structure guidance the recent algorithms, CofeNet [16], Li et al. [7] and I-SECRET [4] perform prominently, while our SCR-Net has the best performance in all considered evaluation metrics.

(2) Ablation Study Also from Table 2, the effectiveness of the proposed three modules of SCR-Net is validated by the ablation study. The training of the restoration model is enhanced by synthesizing cataract data with sufficient variation. Then the HFCs are extracted to preserve retinal structures, as well as constrain structure consistency cooperating with D_H. Additionally, the objective function of SCR-Net consists of explicit losses so that the model is efficiently optimized. Therefore the learned restoration model can be favorably applied to real cataract data.

4   Conclusion

Due to the impact of cataracts, diagnosing and monitoring fundus diseases for cataract patients is a challenging task, and supervised data are unavailable to develop restoration algorithms of cataract fundus images. To increase the certainty of fundus examination, based on structure consistency this paper develops a restoration model for cataract fundus images from synthesized data. Thanks to its independence from annotations and test data, the proposed algorithm is convenient to deploy in clinics. In the experiments, the comparison and ablation study on restoration, segmentation, and diagnosis demonstrate the superior performance and effectiveness of the proposed algorithm.

Acknowledgment. This work was supported in part by Basic and Applied Fundamental Research Foundation of Guangdong Province (2020A1515110286), The National Natural Science Foundation of China (8210072776), Guangdong Provincial Department of Education (2020ZDZX3043), Guangdong Provincial Key Laboratory (2020B121201001), Shenzhen Natural Science Fund (JCYJ20200109140820699, 20200925174052004), and A*STAR AME Programmatic Fund (A20H4b0141).

References

1. Cao, L., Li, H., Zhang, Y.: Retinal image enhancement using low-pass filtering and α-rooting. Sign. Process. **170**, 107445 (2020)
2. Chen, J., Tan, C.H., Hou, J., Chau, L.P., Li, H.: Robust video content alignment and compensation for rain removal in a cnn framework. In: Proceedings of the IEEE Conference on Computer Vision and Pattern Recognition, pp. 6286–6295 (2018)
3. Cheng, J., et al.: Structure-preserving guided retinal image filtering and its application for optic disk analysis. IEEE Trans. Med. Imaging **37**(11), 2536–2546 (2018)

4. Cheng, P., Lin, L., Huang, Y., Lyu, J., Tang, X.: I-SECRET: importance-guided fundus image enhancement via semi-supervised contrastive constraining. In: de Bruijne, M. (ed.) MICCAI 2021. LNCS, vol. 12908, pp. 87–96. Springer, Cham (2021). https://doi.org/10.1007/978-3-030-87237-3_9

5. Huang, T., Li, S., Jia, X., Lu, H., Liu, J.: Neighbor2neighbor: Self-supervised denoising from single noisy images. arXiv preprint arXiv:2101.02824 (2021)

6. Li, H., et al.: An annotation-free restoration network for cataractous fundus images. IEEE Transactions on Medical Imaging (2022)

7. Li, H., et al.: Restoration of cataract fundus images via unsupervised domain adaptation. In: 2021 IEEE 18th International Symposium on Biomedical Imaging (ISBI), pp. 516–520. IEEE (2021)

8. Li, T., et al.: Applications of deep learning in fundus images: A review. Medical Image Analysis p. 101971 (2021)

9. Liu, H., et al.: Domain generalization in restoration of cataract fundus images via high-frequency components. In: 2022 IEEE 19th International Symposium on Biomedical Imaging (ISBI), pp. 1–5. IEEE (2022)

10. Lore, K.G., Akintayo, A., Sarkar, S.: Llnet: a deep autoencoder approach to natural low-light image enhancement. Pattern Recogn. **61**, 650–662 (2017)

11. Luo, Y., et al.: Dehaze of cataractous retinal images using an unpaired generative adversarial network. IEEE J. Biomed. Health Inform. **24**(1), 3374–3383 (2020)

12. MacGillivray, T.J., et al.: Suitability of UK biobank retinal images for automatic analysis of morphometric properties of the vasculature. PLoS ONE **10**(5), e0127914 (2015)

13. Mitra, A., Roy, S., Roy, S., Setua, S.K.: Enhancement and restoration of non-uniform illuminated fundus image of retina obtained through thin layer of cataract. Comput. Methods Programs Biomed. **156**, 169–178 (2018)

14. Park, T., Efros, A.A., Zhang, R., Zhu, J.-Y.: Contrastive learning for unpaired image-to-image translation. In: Vedaldi, A., Bischof, H., Brox, T., Frahm, J.-M. (eds.) ECCV 2020. LNCS, vol. 12354, pp. 319–345. Springer, Cham (2020). https://doi.org/10.1007/978-3-030-58545-7_19

15. Peli, E., Peli, T.: Restoration of retinal images obtained through cataracts. IEEE Trans. Med. Imaging **8**(4), 401–406 (1989)

16. Shen, Z., Fu, H., Shen, J., Shao, L.: Modeling and enhancing low-quality retinal fundus images. IEEE Trans. Med. Imaging **40**(3), 996–1006 (2020)

17. Wang, S., Yu, L., Yang, X., Fu, C.W., Heng, P.A.: Patch-based output space adversarial learning for joint optic disc and cup segmentation. IEEE Trans. Med. Imaging **38**(11), 2485–2495 (2019)

18. Zhang, W., Zhong, J., Yang, S., Gao, Z., Hu, J., Chen, Y., Yi, Z.: Automated identification and grading system of diabetic retinopathy using deep neural networks. Knowl.-Based Syst. **175**, 12–25 (2019)

19. Zhang, X., Hu, Y., Xiao, Z., Fang, J., Higashita, R., Liu, J.: Machine learning for cataract classification/grading on ophthalmic imaging modalities: a survey. Mach. Intell. Res. **19**, 184–208 (2022)

20. Zhang, X., et al.: Adaptive feature squeeze network for nuclear cataract classification in as-oct image. J. Biomed. Inform. **128**, 104037 (2022)

21. Zhao, R., Chen, X., Liu, X., Chen, Z., Guo, F., Li, S.: Direct cup-to-disc ratio estimation for glaucoma screening via semi-supervised learning. IEEE J. Biomed. Health Inform. **24**(4), 1104–1113 (2019)

22. Zhu, J.Y., et al.: Unpaired image-to-image translation using cycle-consistent adversarial networks. In: Proceedings of the IEEE international conference on computer vision. pp. 2223–2232 (2017)

Unsupervised Domain Adaptive Fundus Image Segmentation with Category-Level Regularization

Wei Feng[1,2,3], Lin Wang[1,2,3], Lie Ju[1,2,3], Xin Zhao[4], Xin Wang[4], Xiaoyu Shi[4], and Zongyuan Ge[1,2,3(✉)]

[1] Monash Medical AI Group, Monash University, Melbourne, Australia
zongyuan.ge@monash.edu
[2] Airdoc Monash Research Centre, Monash University, Clayton, Australia
[3] Monash eResearch Center, Monash University, Clayton, Australia
[4] Airdoc LLC, Beijing, China
https://www.monash.edu/mmai-group

Abstract. Existing unsupervised domain adaptation methods based on adversarial learning have achieved good performance in several medical imaging tasks. However, these methods focus only on global distribution adaptation and ignore distribution constraints at the category level, which would lead to sub-optimal adaptation performance. This paper presents an unsupervised domain adaptation framework based on category-level regularization that regularizes the category distribution from three perspectives. Specifically, for inter-domain category regularization, an adaptive prototype alignment module is proposed to align feature prototypes of the same category in the source and target domains. In addition, for intra-domain category regularization, we tailored a regularization technique for the source and target domains, respectively. In the source domain, a prototype-guided discriminative loss is proposed to learn more discriminative feature representations by enforcing intra-class compactness and inter-class separability, and as a complement to traditional supervised loss. In the target domain, an augmented consistency category regularization loss is proposed to force the model to produce consistent predictions for augmented/unaugmented target images, which encourages semantically similar regions to be given the same label. Extensive experiments on two publicly fundus datasets show that the proposed approach significantly outperforms other state-of-the-art comparison algorithms[1](Our code is available at https://github.com/fengweie/UDA_CLR.).

Keywords: Unsupervised domain adaptation · Category level regularization · Fundus image segmentation

1 Introduction

Recently deep neural networks have dominated several medical image analysis tasks and have achieved good performance [7,10,18]. However, a well-trained

L. Wang et al. (Eds.): MICCAI 2022, LNCS 13432, pp. 497–506, 2022.
https://doi.org/10.1007/978-3-031-16434-7_48

model usually underperform when tested directly on an unseen dataset due to domain shift [15]. In clinical practice, this phenomenon is prevalent and remains unresolved. To this end, domain adaptation strategies have received a lot of attention, aiming to transfer knowledge from a label-rich source domain to a label-rare target domain. Recent adversarial training-based domain adaptation methods have shown promising performance, focusing mainly on global distribution adaptation at the input space [23], feature space [4] or output space [16]. Despite the significant performance gains achieved, they all ignore the category distribution constraints. This may result in a situation where although global distribution differences between domains have been reduced, the pixel features of different categories in the target domain are not well separated. This is because some categories are similar to others in terms of appearance and texture. There have been several studies try to address this issue. For example, Liu et al. [11] proposed a prototype alignment loss to reduce the mismatch between the source and target domains in the feature space. Xie et al. [19] proposed a semantic alignment loss to learn semantic feature representations by aligning the category centres of the labelled source domain and the category centres of the pseudo-labelled target domain. However, the shortcoming of these methods is that there is no explicit constraint on the distance between different category features, resulting in categories that look similar in the source domain also being distributed similarly in the target domain, which would potentially lead to incorrect prediction results, especially in edge regions and low-contrast regions.

In this paper, we propose an unsupervised domain adaptation framework based on category-level regularization to accurately segment the optic disc and cup from fundus images. We perform category regularization from both intra-domain and inter-domain perspectives. Specifically, for intra-domain category regularization, on the source domain side, we first propose a prototype-guided discriminative loss to enhance the separability of inter-class distributions and the compactness of intra-class distributions, thus learning more discriminative feature representations; on the target domain side, we propose an augmented consistency-based category regularization loss to constrain the model to produce consistent predictions for perturbed and unperturbed target images, thus encouraging semantically similar regions to have the same labels. For inter-domain category regularization, we propose an adaptive prototype alignment module to ensure that pixels from the same class but different domains can be mapped nearby in the feature space. Experiment results on two public fundus datasets and ablation studies demonstrate the effectiveness of our approach.

2   Methodology

Figure 1 shows an overview of our proposed unsupervised domain adaptation framework based on category-level regularization. It consists of three main components, prototype-guided source domain category regularization, augmented consistency-based target domain category regularization, and inter-domain category regularization, performing category-level regularization from different perspectives.

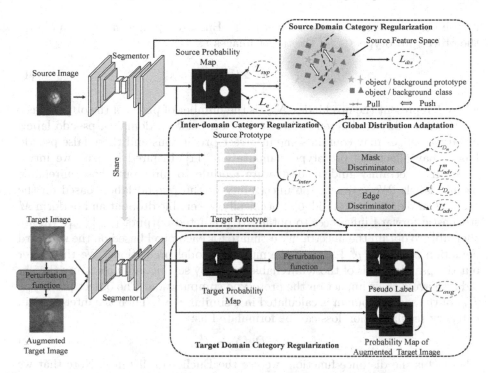

Fig. 1. Overview of an unsupervised domain adaptation framework based on category-level regularization. We first align global distributions between domains by adversarial learning. Then we perform fine-grained level category distribution adaptation from three perspectives: source domain, target domain and inter-domain, via three category regularization methods.

2.1 Inter-domain Category Regularization

In an typical unsupervised domain adaptation (UDA) setting, we are given a source domain image set $\{x_i^s\}_{i=1}^{N_s}$ and its corresponding pixel-wise annotation $\{y_i^s\}_{i=1}^{N_s}$, and a target domain image set $\{x_i^t\}_{i=1}^{N_t}$ without annotation. To regularize the category distributions between domains, we propose an adaptive prototype alignment module that aligns prototypes of pixels of the same category in the labelled source domain and the pseudo-labelled target domain, thus guaranteeing that features of the same category in different domains are mapped nearby.

Specifically, we feed the target images x^t into the segmentation model G to obtain the pseudo-label $\widehat{y}^t = \mathbb{1}[p^t \geqslant \beta]$, where p^t is the predicted probability and $\mathbb{1}$ is the indicator function. β is a probability threshold. We denote the feature map before the last convolution layer as h^t. Based on $\hat{y}^t$ and h^t, we can obtain the object prototype f_{obj}^t of the target images as:

$$f_{obj}^t = \frac{1}{N_{obj}} \sum_k \mathbb{1}\left(\hat{y}_k^t = 1\right) h_k^t, \tag{1}$$

where k represent the pixel index, N_{obj} is the number of pixels of the object class.

However, due to differences in distribution between domains, pseudo labels of target images may contain some incorrect predictions and these false pseudo labels may affect the prototype computation [11]. Inspired by [20], we introduce an uncertainty-guided noise-aware module to filter out those unreliable pseudo labels. We estimate the uncertainty of the pseudo labels based on the Monte Carlo dropout method [6]. Specifically, we enable dropout and perform M stochastic forward inferences to obtain M predicted outputs $\{p_m^t\}_{m=1}^M$. We are then able to obtain the uncertainty estimate for each pixel based on the standard deviation $S = std(\{p_m^t\}_{m=1}^M)$ of the multiple model predictions. We then filter out the pseudo labels of those unreliable pixels by setting an uncertainty threshold ξ to avoid their impact on the prototype computation. The object prototype f_{obj}^s of the source domain is calculated in a similar way[2]. Then the inter-domain category regularization loss can be formulated as:

$$L_{inter} = D(f_{obj}^s - f_{obj}^t), \tag{2}$$

where D is the distance function, we use the Euclidean distance. Note that we only align the prototypes of object class between domains, as object class has more domain shared features than background class [22].

2.2   Intra-domain Category Regularization

In order to further regularize the distributions of the different categories in the feature space, we perform intra-domain category regularization to learn discriminative feature representations by using the category information within the source and target domains, which also works as a complement of inter-domain category regularization.

Source Domain Category Regularization. On the source domain side, we propose a prototype-guided discriminative loss to regularize the category distribution. Specifically, we use the category feature prototype to provide supervised signals, explicitly constraining pixel features to be closer to their corresponding category prototypes, while being farther away from other category prototypes. The prototype-guided discriminative loss is formulated as:

$$\begin{aligned} L_{dis} = &\sum_k \mathbb{1}\left(y_k^s = 1\right) \max\left(\left\|h_k^s - f_{obj}^s\right\| - \left\|h_k^s - f_{bg}^s\right\| + \delta, 0\right) \\ &+ \sum_k \mathbb{1}\left(y_k^s = 0\right) \max\left(\left\|h_k^s - f_{bg}^s\right\| - \left\|h_k^s - f_{obj}^s\right\| + \delta, 0\right), \end{aligned} \tag{3}$$

---

[2] Note that since source domain annotation information is available, we use ground truth labels to compute the source domain prototypes.

where δ is a predefined distance margin. $f_{bg}^s = \frac{1}{N_{bg}} \sum_k \mathbb{1} \left(y_k^s = 0 \right) h_k^s$ is the prototype of the background class. h^s is the pixel-wise deep feature of the source domain images. This loss would be 0 when the distance between each pixel feature and its corresponding prototype is less than its distance from other classes of prototypes by a margin δ.

Target Domain Category Regularization. In the target domain, since we do not have access to the ground truth labels and therefore the discriminative loss can not be applied as the same way as in the source domain. To perform category-level feature regularization, inspired by the dominant consistency training strategy in semi-supervised learning [17], we propose an augmented consistency-based regularization method that constrains the predictions of the augmented target images to be consistent with the pseudo labels of the original target images, which encourages semantically similar parts of the target images to have the same labels and thus regularize the category-level feature distributions.

Specifically, we apply a perturbation function to $(x^t, \hat{y}^t)$ to generate a perturbed pair $(x^{pert}, \hat{y}^{pert})$. The augmented consistency loss can be formulated as:

$$L_{aug} = - \sum_k \mathbb{1} \left(S_k < \mu \right) \ell \left(G(x_k^{pert}), \hat{y}_k^{pert} \right), \tag{4}$$

where $\ell(\cdot)$ is the cross-entropy loss. Note that here we only calculate the augmented consistency loss for those pseudo-labelled pixels for which the uncertainty estimate S_k is less than a threshold μ to avoid error accumulation due to incorrect pseudo labels [14].

2.3   Training Procedure

In addition to category-level regularization, we also perform global distribution alignment by adversarial learning. Following [15], we build two discriminators, D_m and D_e, to align the predicted probability distribution (p_m^s, p_m^t) and the edge structure distribution (p_e^s, p_e^t) of the source and target domains respectively. At the same time the training goal of the segmentation model is to learn domain invariant features to deceive the discriminators. In summary, the training objective of the segmentation network can be formulated as:

$$L_{total} = L_{sup} + L_e + \lambda_1 L_d + \lambda_2 L_{inter} + \lambda_3 L_{dis} + \lambda_4 L_{aug}$$

$$L_e = \sum_k \left(y_{e,k}^s - p_{e,k}^s \right)^2 \tag{5}$$

$$L_d = L_{adv}^m + L_{adv}^e = \frac{1}{N_t} \sum_{i=1}^{N_t} L_D \left(p_{m,i}^t, 1 \right) + \frac{1}{N_t} \sum_{i=1}^{N_t} L_D \left(p_{e,i}^t, 1 \right),$$

where L_{sup} is the supervised loss on the labelled source domain image. L_e and L_d are the edge regression loss and the adversarial loss respectively, L_D is the binary cross-entropy loss. y_e^s is the edge ground truth labels. $\lambda_1, \lambda_2, \lambda_3, \lambda_4$ are balance coefficients.

The training objectives of the two discriminators are:

$$
\begin{aligned}
L_{D_m} &= \frac{1}{N_s} \sum_{i=1}^{N_s} L_D \left(p_{m,i}^s, 1 \right) + \frac{1}{N_t} \sum_{i=1}^{N_t} L_D \left(p_{m,i}^t, 0 \right) \\
L_{D_e} &= \frac{1}{N_s} \sum_{i=1}^{N_s} L_D \left(p_{e,i}^s, 1 \right) + \frac{1}{N_t} \sum_{i=1}^{N_t} L_D \left(p_{e,i}^t, 0 \right),
\end{aligned}
\tag{6}
$$

where L_{D_m} and L_{D_e} are the adversarial loss of the mask discriminator and the adversarial loss of the edge discriminator, respectively.

3   Experiments

Dataset and Evaluation Metric. In order to evaluate the proposed method, we use three datasets: the training part of the REFUGE challenge[1] [12], RIMONE-r3 [5] and Drishti-GS [13]. Following [15], we choose the REFUGE challenge as the source domain and RIMONE-r3 and Drishti-GS as the target domains, respectively. The training set of the REFUGE challenge contains 400 images with annotations, and the RIMONE-r3 and Drishti-GS contain 99/60 and 50/51 training/testing images respectively. Following [15], we crop a 512×512 optic disc region as input of the model. In addition, we use the commonly used Dice coefficient to evaluate the segmentation performance of the optic disc and cup [15].

Implementation Details. We use the MobileNetV2 modified Deeplabv3+ [2] network as the segmentation backbone [15]. The Adam algorithm is used to optimize the segmentation model and SGD algorithm is used to optimize the two discriminators [15]. The learning rate of the segmentation network is set as $1e-3$ and divided by 0.2 every 100 epochs and we train a total of 500 epochs. The learning rate of the two discriminators is set as $2e-5$. The probability threshold β is set as 0.75 [15]. In the uncertainty estimation part, we perform 10 stochastic forward passes, and the uncertainty threshold μ is set as 0.05 [1]. We empirically set the distance margin δ to 0.01 and found that it worked well on different datasets. The loss balance coefficients $\lambda_1, \lambda_2, \lambda_3, \lambda_4$ are set as 0.01, 0.01, 0.01,0.01. For the perturbation function, we use the perturbation function used in [3], which includes: color jittering and gaussian blur. We use the feature map of the previous layer of the last convolutional layer to calculate the prototype. All experiments are performed using the Pytorch framework and 8 RTX 3090 GPUs.

---

[1] https://refuge.grand-challenge.org/

Table 1. Comparison of different methods on the target domain datasets

Method	RIM-ONE-r3 [5]		Drishti-GS [13]	
	Dice disc	Dice cup	Dice disc	Dice cup
Oracle	0.968	0.856	0.974	0.901
Baseline	0.779	0.744	0.944	0.836
TD-GAN [21]	0.853	0.728	0.924	0.747
Hoffman et al. [8]	0.852	0.755	0.959	0.851
Javanmardi et al. [9]	0.853	0.779	0.961	0.849
OSAL-pixel [16]	0.854	0.778	0.962	0.851
pOSAL [16]	0.865	0.787	0.965	0.858
BEAL [15]	0.898	0.810	0.961	0.862
Ours	**0.905**	**0.841**	**0.966**	**0.892**

Comparison with State-of-the-Art Methods. We compare the proposed method with Baseline method (without adaptation), fully supervised methods (Oracle), and several state-of-the-art unsupervised domain adaptation algorithms, including TD-GAN [21], high-level alignment [8], output space adaptation [9,16], BEAL [15]. As can be seen from the experimental results in Table 1, the proposed method achieves significant performance gains on both datasets, especially for the segmentation of the optic cup. Compared to the best comparison algorithm BEAL, our method achieves 3.1% and 3% Dice improvement for the optic cup segmentation on the RIM-ONE-r3 and Drishti-GS datasets, respectively. Furthermore, the segmentation performance of our method is very close to that of fully supervised performance. This indicates that our method is able to achieve good performance in scenarios with varying degrees of domain shift.

We also show the segmentation results of the different algorithms on the two datasets in Fig. 2. It can be seen that in some regions that are obscured or blurred by blood vessels, the segmentation results of other comparison algorithms are poor, while our method is able to accurately identify the boundaries of the optic cup and optic disc, while being very close to the ground truth labels.

Ablation Study. We conduct ablation experiments to investigate the effectiveness of each component of the proposed method. In Table 2, +src_reg represents source domain category regularization, +trg_reg denotes target domain category regularization, and +inter_reg represents inter-domain category regularization. As seen in Table 2, inter-domain category regularization and both intra-domain regularization techniques lead to performance gains, which justifies the need for performing global distribution regularization and category regularization simultaneously. In addition, from Table 3 we can also observe that using uncertainty-guided noise-aware (UGNA) modules to filter out unreliable pseudo-labels can benefit inter-domain category distribution regularization. By combining multiple category regularization techniques, our approach further improves segmentation performance on both datasets.

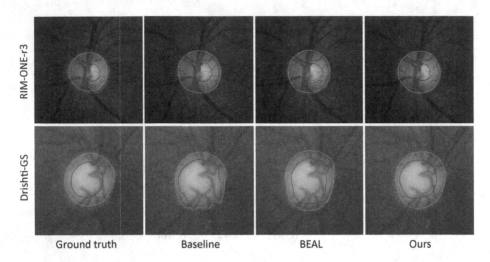

Fig. 2. Quantitative comparison of segmentation results of different methods

Table 2. Ablation study of different components of our method

Method				Target domain			
				RIM-ONE-r3[5]		Drishti-GS[13]	
baseline	+src_reg	+trg_reg	+inter_reg	Dice disc	Dice cup	Dice disc	Dice cup
✓				0.779	0.744	0.944	0.836
✓	✓			0.899	0.829	0.958	0.871
✓		✓		0.898	0.837	0.963	0.875
✓			✓	0.901	0.833	0.961	0.881
✓	✓	✓		0.900	0.839	0.965	0.880
✓	✓		✓	0.903	0.836	0.964	0.883
✓		✓	✓	0.902	0.838	0.963	0.887
✓	✓	✓	✓	**0.905**	**0.841**	**0.966**	**0.892**

Table 3. The impact of UGNA in inter-domain category regularization

Method	RIM-ONE-r3 [5]		Drishti-GS [13]	
	Dice disc	Dice cup	Dice disc	Dice cup
+inter_reg(W/o UGNA)	0.898	0.824	0.959	0.870
+inter_reg	**0.901**	**0.833**	**0.961**	**0.881**

4   Conclusion

In this paper, we propose an unsupervised domain adaptation framework based on category-level regularization for cross-domain fundus image segmentation.

Three category regularization methods are developed to simultaneously regularize the category distribution from three perspectives: inter-domain, source and target domains, thus making the model better adapted to the target domain. Our method significantly outperforms state-of-the-art comparison algorithms on two public fundus datasets, demonstrating its effectiveness, and it can be applied to other unsupervised domain adaptation tasks as well.

References

1. Chen, C., Liu, Q., Jin, Y., Dou, Q., Heng, P.-A.: Source-free domain adaptive fundus image segmentation with denoised pseudo-labeling. In: de Bruijne, M. (ed.) MICCAI 2021. LNCS, vol. 12905, pp. 225–235. Springer, Cham (2021). https://doi.org/10.1007/978-3-030-87240-3_22
2. Chen, L.C., Zhu, Y., Papandreou, G., Schroff, F., Adam, H.: Encoder-decoder with atrous separable convolution for semantic image segmentation. In: Proceedings of the European Conference on Computer Vision (ECCV), pp. 801–818 (2018)
3. Chen, T., Kornblith, S., Norouzi, M., Hinton, G.: A simple framework for contrastive learning of visual representations. In: International Conference on Machine Learning, pp. 1597–1607. PMLR (2020)
4. Dou, Q., Ouyang, C., Chen, C., Chen, H., Heng, P.A.: Unsupervised cross-modality domain adaptation of convnets for biomedical image segmentations with adversarial loss. arXiv preprint arXiv:1804.10916 (2018)
5. Fumero, F., Alayón, S., Sanchez, J.L., Sigut, J., Gonzalez-Hernandez, M.: Rimone: An open retinal image database for optic nerve evaluation. In: 2011 24th International Symposium on Computer-Based Medical Systems (CBMS), pp. 1–6. IEEE (2011)
6. Gal, Y., Ghahramani, Z.: Dropout as a bayesian approximation: Representing model uncertainty in deep learning. In: international conference on machine learning, pp. 1050–1059. PMLR (2016)
7. Hang, w, et al.: Local and global structure-aware entropy regularized mean teacher model for 3D left atrium segmentation. In: Martel, A.L. (ed.) MICCAI 2020. LNCS, vol. 12261, pp. 562–571. Springer, Cham (2020). https://doi.org/10.1007/978-3-030-59710-8_55
8. Hoffman, J., Wang, D., Yu, F., Darrell, T.: FCNs in the wild: Pixel-level adversarial and constraint-based adaptation. arXiv preprint arXiv:1612.02649 (2016)
9. Javanmardi, M., Tasdizen, T.: Domain adaptation for biomedical image segmentation using adversarial training. In: 2018 IEEE 15th International Symposium on Biomedical Imaging (ISBI 2018), pp. 554–558. IEEE (2018)
10. Ju, L., et al.: Improving medical images classification with label noise using dual-uncertainty estimation. IEEE Trans. Med. Imaging 41(6), 1533–1546 (2022)
11. Liu, Y., Deng, J., Gao, X., Li, W., Duan, L.: BAPA-Net: Boundary adaptation and prototype alignment for cross-domain semantic segmentation. In: Proceedings of the IEEE/CVF International Conference on Computer Vision, pp. 8801–8811 (2021)
12. Orlando, J.I., et al.: Refuge challenge: a unified framework for evaluating automated methods for glaucoma assessment from fundus photographs. Med. Image Anal. 59, 101570 (2020)
13. Sivaswamy, J., Krishnadas, S., Chakravarty, A., Joshi, G., Tabish, A.S., et al.: A comprehensive retinal image dataset for the assessment of glaucoma from the optic nerve head analysis. JSM Biomed. Imaging Data Papers 2(1), 1004 (2015)

14. Sohn, K., et al.: Fixmatch: simplifying semi-supervised learning with consistency and confidence. Adv. Neural. Inf. Process. Syst. **33**, 596–608 (2020)
15. Wang, S., Yu, L., Li, K., Yang, X., Fu, C.-W., Heng, Pheng-Ann.: Boundary and entropy-driven adversarial learning for fundus image segmentation. In: Shen, D. (ed.) MICCAI 2019. LNCS, vol. 11764, pp. 102–110. Springer, Cham (2019). https://doi.org/10.1007/978-3-030-32239-7_12
16. Wang, S., Yu, L., Yang, X., Fu, C.W., Heng, P.A.: Patch-based output space adversarial learning for joint optic disc and cup segmentation. IEEE Trans. Med. Imaging **38**(11), 2485–2495 (2019)
17. Wang, X., Chen, H., Xiang, H., Lin, H., Lin, X., Heng, P.A.: Deep virtual adversarial self-training with consistency regularization for semi-supervised medical image classification. Med. Image Anal. **70**, 102010 (2021)
18. Wu, Y., Xia, Y., Song, Y., Zhang, Y., Cai, W.: Multiscale network followed network model for retinal vessel segmentation. In: Frangi, A.F., Schnabel, J.A., Davatzikos, C., Alberola-López, C., Fichtinger, G. (eds.) MICCAI 2018. LNCS, vol. 11071, pp. 119–126. Springer, Cham (2018). https://doi.org/10.1007/978-3-030-00934-2_14
19. Xie, S., Zheng, Z., Chen, L., Chen, C.: Learning semantic representations for unsupervised domain adaptation. In: International Conference on Machine Learning, pp. 5423–5432. PMLR (2018)
20. Yu, L., Wang, S., Li, X., Fu, C.-W., Heng, P.-A.: Uncertainty-aware self-ensembling model for semi-supervised 3D left atrium segmentation. In: Shen, D. (ed.) MICCAI 2019. LNCS, vol. 11765, pp. 605–613. Springer, Cham (2019). https://doi.org/10.1007/978-3-030-32245-8_67
21. Zhang, Y., Miao, S., Mansi, T., Liao, R.: Task driven generative modeling for unsupervised domain adaptation: application to x-ray image segmentation. In: Frangi, A.F., Schnabel, J.A., Davatzikos, C., Alberola-López, C., Fichtinger, G. (eds.) MICCAI 2018. LNCS, vol. 11071, pp. 599–607. Springer, Cham (2018). https://doi.org/10.1007/978-3-030-00934-2_67
22. Zheng, Y., Huang, D., Liu, S., Wang, Y.: Cross-domain object detection through coarse-to-fine feature adaptation. In: Proceedings of the IEEE/CVF Conference on Computer Vision and Pattern Recognition, pp. 13766–13775 (2020)
23. Zhu, J.Y., Park, T., Isola, P., Efros, A.A.: Unpaired image-to-image translation using cycle-consistent adversarial networks. In: Proceedings of the IEEE International Conference on Computer Vision, pp. 2223–2232 (2017)

Degradation-Invariant Enhancement of Fundus Images via Pyramid Constraint Network

Haofeng Liu[1,2], Heng Li[2(✉)], Huazhu Fu[3], Ruoxiu Xiao[4], Yunshu Gao[1,2], Yan Hu[2(✉)], and Jiang Liu[1,2,5]

[1] Guangdong Provincial Key Laboratory of Brain-inspired Intelligent Computation, Southern University of Science and Technology, Shenzhen, China
[2] Department of Computer Science and Engineering, Southern University of Science and Technology, Shenzhen, China
{lih3,huy3}@sustech.edu.cn
[3] IHPC, A*STAR, Singapore, Singapore
[4] The School of Computer and Communication Engineering, University of Science and Technology Beijing, Beijing, China
[5] Singapore Eye Research Institute, Singapore National Eye Centre, Singapore, Singapore

Abstract. As an economical and efficient fundus imaging modality, retinal fundus images have been widely adopted in clinical fundus examination. Unfortunately, fundus images often suffer from quality degradation caused by imaging interferences, leading to misdiagnosis. Despite impressive enhancement performances that state-of-the-art methods have achieved, challenges remain in clinical scenarios. For boosting the clinical deployment of fundus image enhancement, this paper proposes the pyramid constraint to develop a degradation-invariant enhancement network (PCE-Net), which mitigates the demand for clinical data and stably enhances unknown data. Firstly, high-quality images are randomly degraded to form sequences of low-quality ones sharing the same content (SeqLCs). Then individual low-quality images are decomposed to Laplacian pyramid features (LPF) as the multi-level input for the enhancement. Subsequently, a feature pyramid constraint (FPC) for the sequence is introduced to enforce the PCE-Net to learn a degradation-invariant model. Extensive experiments have been conducted under the evaluation metrics of enhancement and segmentation. The effectiveness of the PCE-Net was demonstrated in comparison with state-of-the-art methods and the ablation study. The source code of this study is publicly available at https://github.com/HeverLaw/PCENet-Image-Enhancement.

Keywords: Fundus image · Degradation-invariant enhancement · Laplacian pyramid feature · Feature pyramid constraint

---

Supplementary Information The online version contains supplementary material available at https://doi.org/10.1007/978-3-031-16434-7_49.

1   Introduction

Due to the convenience, economy, and safety, fundus photography has widely served as a routine clinical examination. Fundus photography is taken by a specialized low-power microscope with an attached CCD (Charge Coupled Device) camera designed to photograph the interior of the eye, including the retina, optic disc, macula, and posterior pole (i.e., the fundus) [20,21]. Unfortunately, collecting fundus images under non-ideal light conditions is a frustrating experience. The causation of image quality degradation includes imperfections in the fundus camera optics, aberrations of the human eye, improper camera adjustment, flash lighting, or focusing during the exam. Therefore fundus observation is prone to be impacted by the degradation, resulting in the uncertainty of diagnosis.

Efforts have been long made to enhance the quality of fundus images [13,15]. Contrast limited adaptive histogram equalization (CLAHE) and Fourier transforms have been collaborated to restore degraded fundus images [17]. Inheriting the guided image filtering (GIF), Cheng et al. [2] designed a structure-preserving guided retinal image filtering (SGRIF) to correct the fundus images from cataract patients. With filtering technique and root domain in frequency, Cao et al. [1] proposed an enhancement method for the retinal images. More recently, with the advance of deep learning techniques, fundus image enhancement has achieved state-of-the-art performances. Segmentation networks were introduced to preserve retinal vessels in enhancement [19]. Based on unpaired image translation [18,22], importance-guided semi-supervised contrastive constraining (I-SECRET) [3] as well as structure and illumination constrained GAN (StillGAN) [16] were proposed to learn the enhancing mappings from unpaired data. Considering the gap between synthesized and clinical data, domain adaptation [11,12] was leveraged to generalize the restoration model from synthesized data to real ones by accessing the clinical data.

Despite existing enhancement methods performed decently in the laboratory, challenges remain in the clinical scenarios. i) Due to the complexity of clinical imaging interference, it is impractical for the model to traverse every possible degradation in training. ii) Unpaired data tends to drive enhancement models to abandon some fundus characteristics (such as vessels and abnormality), while synthesized data probably result in performance-drop on real data. iii) As the foundation of fundus assessment, retinal structures need to be more efficiently preserved in the enhancement. iv) Access to clinical data is still necessary for domain adaptation to bridge the gap between synthesized and clinical domains.

To circumvent the above issues, a degradation-invariant fundus enhancement method, termed PCE-Net, is developed in this paper via pyramid constraint. SeqLCs are generated from identical images as the training data with content consistency. Then, the LPF is employed to preserve the retinal structures in the enhancement, and FPC is proposed to constrain the consistency of embeddings for enforcing the learning of a degradation-invariant model. The main contributions of this paper are summarised as follows:

- For boosting the enhancement of clinical fundus images, the PCE-Net is developed to learn the degradation-invariant enhancement model from simulated data.
- The SeqLC and FPC are married to enforce the training of a degradation-invariant model, and the LPF is employed to preserve retinal structures.
- Three evaluations are presented in the experiment to verify the effectiveness of the PCE-Net, and superior performance to state-of-the-art algorithms is achieved in the enhancement of clinical fundus images.

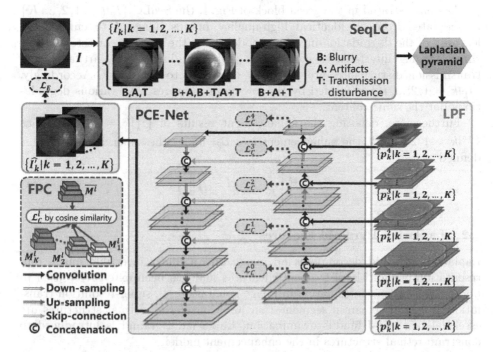

Fig. 1. Overview of PCE-Net. Given a high-quality image I, the SeqLC $\{I'_k | k = 1, 2, ..., K\}$ is randomly synthesized. Then I'_k is decomposed as the LPF $\{p^l_k | l = 0, 1, ..., L\}$ to boost structure-preserving in PCE-Net. Subsequently, the FPC is quantified by the consistency loss $\mathcal{L}^l_C$ at each encoding layer to enforce the model to learn degradation-invariant representations. (Color figure online)

2   Methodology

As exhibited in Fig. 1, SeqLC, LPF, and FPC are implemented in the proposed PCE-Net. Specifically, the SeqLC is randomly degraded from an identical high-quality image for the training of the enhancement network. The LPF is adopted to forward multi-level inputs to boost structure-preserving of the enhancement network. The FPC leads the network to learn the degradation-invariant enhancement model.

2.1   Sequence of Low-Quality Images with the Same Content

In clinics, fundus images often suffer from quality degradations caused by imaging interferences [19]. Unfortunately, the enormous cost of collecting high-low quality fundus image pairs and the limited volume of available data prevent the development of enhancement models. To collect training data and boost the learning of degradation-invariant models, high-quality images are randomly degraded to generate low-quality ones with the same content. SeqLCs are thus acquired to import content consistency into the model training.

As demonstrated in the green block of Fig. 1, the SeqLC $\{I'_k|k = 1, 2, ..., K\}$ is generated from an identical high-quality fundus image I to enforce the learning of the degradation-invariant model using the content consistency. The three imaging interferences modeled in [19], including blurry, artifacts, and transmission disturbance, are randomly combined to degrade I. Accordingly, $\{I'_k|k = 1, 2, ..., K\}$ is formed by the low-quality images with various degradations but the same content.

Furthermore, denoting the enhancement results of $\{I'_k|k = 1, 2, ..., K\}$ as $\{\widehat{I'_k}|k = 1, 2, ..., K\}$, the enhancement loss $\mathcal{L}_E$ under the supervision from I is defined as:

$$\mathcal{L}_E = \mathbb{E}\left[\frac{1}{K}\sum_{k=1}^{K}\left\|I - \widehat{I'_k}\right\|_1\right]. \tag{1}$$

2.2   Laplacian Pyramid Features

Laplacian Pyramid decomposes an image into a linear invertible image representation of multi-level frequency features and has been extensively used to boost the structure information in image generation [4], super-resolution translation [14], and semantic segmentation [6]. Considering retinal structures are essential in clinical fundus examination, Laplacian Pyramid is introduced to constrain retinal structures in the enhancement model.

Laplacian Pyramid is implemented with down-sampling and up-sampling operations. For an image I with the size of $s \times s$, the down-sampling operation $\delta(\cdot)$ is carried out by smoothing with a Gaussian filter and then down-sampling to $\frac{s}{2} \times \frac{s}{2}$. Subsequently, the up-sampling operation $\mu(\cdot)$ is performed by resizing the image back to $s \times s$. To acquire an L-level Laplacian pyramid feature (LPF) from an image I, a Gaussian pyramid $\mathcal{G}(I) = \{g^l|l = 0, 1, ..., L\}$ is firstly computed, where $g^0 = I$ and g^n denotes the output of I underwent n times $\delta(\cdot)$. Then the LPF $\mathcal{P}(I) = \{p^l|l = 0, 1, ..., L\}$ is achieved, where $p^l = g^l - \mu(g^{l+1})$ and $p^L = g^L$.

As shown in the yellow block of Fig. 1, an LPF with the L of 4 is extracted for retinal structure preservation in the proposed PCE-Net. LPFs $\{\mathcal{P}(I'_k)|k = 1, 2, ..., K\}$ are calculated from $\{I'_k|k = 1, 2, ..., K\}$, and then the LPFs are forwarded to the network by concatenating with the output of the corresponding layers. Denote f^l as the output from the l-th layer in PCE-Net, the output of the next layer is given by

$$f_k^{l+1} = \text{Conv}([p_k^{l+1}, f_k^l]), l = 0, 1..., L-1, k = 1, 2, ..., K, \qquad (2)$$

where $[\cdot]$ is the concatenation operation, $\text{Conv}(\cdot)$ refers to the convolution operation at each layer, and $f_k^0 = \text{Conv}(p_k^0)$.

2.3 Feature Pyramid Constraint

The underlying content consistency in SeqLC enables the learning of an enhancement model invariant to degradations. Concretely, for a degradation-invariant enhancement model, corresponding consistency should share in the features embedded from $\{I_k'|k = 1, 2, ..., K\}$. However, straightly constraining the numerical consistency of the feature maps in PCE-Net is too inflexible to converge at the optimal solution. Therefore, the FPC is proposed to boost the enhancement model training effectively.

The FPC replaces the numerical consistency constraint to learn the representations invariant to degradations, which leads to a degradation-invariant model. Concretely, spatial pyramid pooling (SPP) [7], a multi-scale pooling operation, is employed to quantify the FPC. Denote SPP as $\sigma(\cdot)$, where the pooling scales of 2×2, 4×4, and 8×8 are conducted. The feature map extracted by SPP is defined as $M_k^l = \sigma(f_k^l)$, where f_k^l denotes the output at the l-th layer in PCE-Net from I_k'. Subsequently, as exhibited by the purple blocks in Fig. 1, the feature maps extracted with SPP are adopted to calculate the consistency loss $\mathcal{L}_C^l$ at each encoding layer of PCE-Net using cosine similarity:

$$\mathcal{L}_C^l = \mathbb{E}\left[\frac{1}{K}\sum_{k=1}^{K}\left(1 - \frac{M_k^l \cdot \overline{M^l}}{\|M_k^l\|\|\overline{M^l}\|}\right)\right], \qquad (3)$$

where $\overline{M^l} = \frac{1}{K}\sum_{k=1}^{K} M_k^l$. The FPC is hence given by $\mathcal{L}_C = \sum_{l=0}^{L}\mathcal{L}_C^l$.

Accordingly, the total loss function is defined as:

$$\mathcal{L}_{total} = \mathcal{L}_E + \lambda_C \mathcal{L}_C, \qquad (4)$$

where λ_C is the weight to balance the total loss and set to 0.1 in training.

3 Experiments

3.1 Implementation Details

To demonstrate the effectiveness of the proposed PCE-Net, a comparison and ablation study were implemented in three evaluations, including enhancement evaluations with and without reference, and vessel segmentation.

Table 1. Datasets used in the experiments

Evaluation	Training set	Test set	Metrics
Full reference enhancement	Good subset in EyeQ: 16,817 high-quality fundus images	FIQ: 196 low-high quality fundus image pairs	SSIM, PSNR
Non-reference enhancement		Usable & Reject subset in EyeQ test dataset: 6,435 mediocre- and 5,540 low-quality fundus images	FIQA, WFQA
Segmentation		FIQ	IoU, DSC

As reported in Table 1, the public dataset of EyeQ[1] and a private fundus dataset FIQ were used in the experiments. Six state-of-the-art enhancement methods, including Cao et al. [1], pix2pix [9], CycleGAN [22], I-SECRET [3], CofeNet [19], Li et al. [12] were compared with PCE-Net. The 'Good' subset in EyeQ was employed as the high-quality images to construct paired data for the model training. High-low quality image pairs are contained FIQ, serving as the test data for the full reference evaluation of enhancement and segmentation. The non-reference evaluation was tested on the 'Usable' and 'Reject' subsets in EyeQ. The enhancement performance was quantified by structural similarity (SSIM) and peak signal-to-noise ratio (PSNR) [8] in the full reference evaluation, while by fundus image quality assessment (FIQA) [3] and weighted FIQA (WFQA) in the non-reference one. FIQA was defined as the ratio of the test images predicted as 'Good' by MCF-Net [5], and WFQA was calculated by assigning the weights of {2, 1, 0} to the images predicted as {'Good', 'Usable', 'Reject'}. The segmentation was measured by the metrics of intersection over union (IoU) and Dice score (DSC) [10]. The segmentation results were obtained from enhanced images and the reference using a U-Net trained on the DRIVE dataset.

In the experiments, a U-Net was designed to construct PCE-Net illustrated in Fig. 1. Note that low-quality images are individually degraded from high-quality ones without the SeqLC. The model trained 200 epochs with Adam optimizer, which the learning rate was 0.001 for the first 150 epochs and decayed gradually to 0 for the following 50 epochs. The batch size was 16, and instance normalization was applied. The input image was resized to 256×256. The same training strategy and augmentation data were applied to all algorithms.

3.2 Comparison and Ablation Study

Comparison of enhancement and segmentation with the state-of-the-art algorithms is visualized in Fig. 2. And quantitative evaluations of the comparison and ablation study are summarized in Table 2.

Comparison. As illuminated in Fig. 2 (a), as a result of the quality degradation, it is difficult to observe the fundus, and the segmentation is also severely

[1] https://github.com/HzFu/EyeQ.

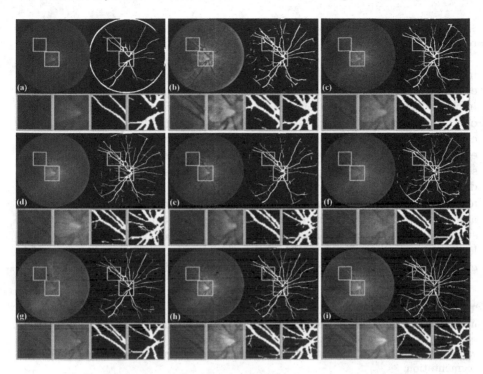

Fig. 2. Visual comparison on the fundus image with full reference. PCE-Net outstandingly enhances the clinical degraded fundus image and outperforms the state-of-the-art methods. (a) Low-quality real image. (b) Cao et al. [1]. (c) pix2pix [9]. (d) Cycle-GAN [22]. (e) I-SECRET [3]. (f) CofeNet [19]. (g) Li et al. [12]. (h) PCE-Net (ours). (i) Reference.

impacted. Based on image filtering, Cao et al. [1] improved the image clarity in Fig. 2 (b), but the enhancement result was apparently different from the common ones. Due to the grievous interferences, the detailed structures are abandoned in the enhancement by pix2pix [9]. Thanks to training on unpaired images, Cycle-GAN [22] and I-SECRET [3] are more convenient to deploy in clinical scenarios. However, their preservation of retinal structures is limited by the unpaired data, such that artifacts appear in the enhancement and segmentation result of Fig. 2 (d) and (e). Using vessel annotations as the structure guidance, promises CofeNet [19] remarkable preservation for fundus vessels, but leads to neglect of the unannotated structures. To suppress the gap between the synthesized and real data, Li et al. [12] introduces domain adaptation to generalize the enhancement model from synthesized images to real ones. Despite the advance in the performance of Fig. 2 (g), access to real data is required in the model training. Though only learning from synthesized data, superior performance on clinical image enhancement is presented by PCE-Net in Fig. 2 (h). An enhanced image with prominent structure visualization is provided by PCE-Net, and the corresponding segmentation result is highly consistent with that of the high-quality reference in Fig. 2 (i).

Table 2 summarizes the quantitative performances in the comparison. As the image clarity is improved by Cao et al. [1], decent segmentation is achieved. However, the appearance different from common images leads to inferior performance in the enhancement evaluation. Although the image-to-image translation methods of pix2pix [9] and CycleGAN [22] present reasonable performances in the enhancement evaluation with reference, the mediocre results in the non-reference evaluation and segmentation demonstrate their limitations on enhancing retinal structures. Because an importance map and contrastive constraint are introduced in I-SECRET [3] to boost structure preservation and local consistency, advantages in the enhancement and segmentation are exhibited. CofeNet [19] and Li et al. [12] respectively employ vessel segmentation and edge detection as structure guidance, achieving reasonable segmentation performance. Nevertheless, as a restoration method of cataract fundus images, the performance of Li et al. [12] has been impacted in the enhancement of degraded images.

Table 2. Comparisons and ablation study of PCE-Net on evaluations of full-reference, non-reference enhancement, and segmentation. Clear and degraded denote the high-quality images and the low-quality ones before enhancement. N.A. denotes the results were not available. PCE-Net achieves superior performance in the enhancement and segmentation.

	Full reference		Non-reference		Segmentation	
	SSIM	PSNR	FIQA	WFQA	IoU	DSC
Clear	N.A	N.A	0.95	1.95	N.A	N.A
Degraded	0.766	16.55	0.09	0.67	0.350	0.518
Cao et al. [1]	0.741	20.17	0.27	0.68	0.431	0.602
pix2pix [9]	0.846	21.96	0.18	0.87	0.420	0.592
CycleGAN [22]	0.844	21.36	0.25	0.90	0.420	0.591
I-SECRET [3]	0.841	21.85	0.43	1.18	0.423	0.593
CofeNet [19]	0.857	22.41	0.45	1.26	0.427	0.599
Li et al. [12]	0.839	21.88	0.37	1.15	0.435	0.606
PCE-Net w/o SeqLC, LPF, FPC	0.849	21.46	0.11	0.73	0.400	0.572
PCE-Net w/o LPF, FPC	0.854	22.35	0.24	0.99	0.424	0.596
PCE-Net w/o FPC	0.860	22.55	0.50	1.32	0.447	0.618
PCE-Net (ours)	**0.871**	**23.09**	**0.55**	**1.38**	**0.464**	**0.634**

Owing to the degradation-invariant representation and multi-level structure preservation, PCE-Net achieves outstanding quantification results in each evaluation compared to the state-of-the-art methods.

Ablation Study. The ablation study is also provided in Table 2 to verify the effectiveness of the proposed modules. The SeqLC not only prepares sufficient training data for the enhancement model, but also imports content consistency for enforcing the degradation invariance. By decomposing the images into multi-level inputs to the network, the LPF boosts the structure preservation in the enhancement and thus performs remarkably in the enhancement and segmentation. Based on the underlying consistency from the SeqLC, the model in training is constrained by the FPC to learn degradation-invariant representations. Consequently, a prominent enhancement model invariant to various degradations is acquired with the proposed modules.

4 Conclusion

To address the impact of quality degradation on clinical fundus examination, a fundus image enhancement network via pyramid constraint, called PCE-Net, is proposed to construct the degradation-invariant model from generated data. The SeqLCs are first formed by low-quality images degraded from identical high-quality ones for training the enhancement model. Then the degraded images are decomposed into the LPFs to boost the retinal structure preservation of the enhancement model. Furthermore, FPC is proposed to enforce the learning of degradation-invariant representations based on the underlying content consistency in the SeqLCs. The qualitative and quantitative experiments in enhancement and vessel segmentation demonstrate that PCE-Net presents superior performance compared to state-of-the-art methods. And the ablation study verifies the effectiveness of the proposed modules.

Acknowledgment. This work was supported in part by Basic and Applied Fundamental Research Foundation of Guangdong Province (2020A1515110286), The National Natural Science Foundation of China (8210072776), Guangdong Provincial Department of Education (2020ZDZX3043), Guangdong Provincial Key Laboratory (2020B121201001), Shenzhen Natural Science Fund (JCYJ20200109140820699, 20200925174052004), and A*STAR AME Programmatic Fund (A20H4b0141).

References

1. Cao, L., Li, H., Zhang, Y.: Retinal image enhancement using low-pass filtering and α-rooting. Signal Process. **170**, 107445 (2020)
2. Cheng, J., et al.: Structure-preserving guided retinal image filtering and its application for optic disk analysis. IEEE Trans. Med. Imaging **37**(11), 2536–2546 (2018)
3. Cheng, P., Lin, L., Huang, Y., Lyu, J., Tang, X.: I-SECRET: importance-guided fundus image enhancement via semi-supervised contrastive constraining. In: de Bruijne, M., et al. (eds.) MICCAI 2021. LNCS, vol. 12908, pp. 87–96. Springer, Cham (2021). https://doi.org/10.1007/978-3-030-87237-3_9
4. Denton, E., Chintala, S., Szlam, A., Fergus, R.: Deep generative image models using a laplacian pyramid of adversarial networks. Adv. Neural Inf. Process. Syst. **2015**, 1486–1494 (2015)

5. Fu, H., et al.: Evaluation of retinal image quality assessment networks in different color-spaces. In: Shen, D., et al. (eds.) MICCAI 2019. LNCS, vol. 11764, pp. 48–56. Springer, Cham (2019). https://doi.org/10.1007/978-3-030-32239-7_6

6. Ghiasi, G., Fowlkes, C.C.: Laplacian pyramid reconstruction and refinement for semantic segmentation. In: Leibe, B., Matas, J., Sebe, N., Welling, M. (eds.) ECCV 2016. LNCS, vol. 9907, pp. 519–534. Springer, Cham (2016). https://doi.org/10.1007/978-3-319-46487-9_32

7. He, K., Zhang, X., Ren, S., Sun, J.: Spatial pyramid pooling in deep convolutional networks for visual recognition. IEEE Trans. Pattern Anal. Mach. Intell. **37**(9), 1904–1916 (2015)

8. Hore, A., Ziou, D.: Image quality metrics: PSNR vs. SSIM. In: 2010 20th International Conference on Pattern Recognition, pp. 2366–2369. IEEE (2010)

9. Isola, P., et al.: Image-to-image translation with conditional adversarial networks. In: Proceedings of the IEEE Conference on Computer Vision and Pattern Recognition, pp. 1125–1134 (2017)

10. Jadon, S.: A survey of loss functions for semantic segmentation. In: 2020 IEEE Conference on Computational Intelligence in Bioinformatics and Computational Biology (CIBCB), pp. 1–7. IEEE (2020)

11. Li, H., et al.: An annotation-free restoration network for cataractous fundus images. IEEE Trans. Med. Imaging (2022)

12. Li, H., et al.: Restoration of cataract fundus images via unsupervised domain adaptation. In: 2021 IEEE 18th International Symposium on Biomedical Imaging (ISBI), pp. 516–520. IEEE (2021)

13. Li, T., et al.: Applications of deep learning in fundus images: a review. Med. Image Anal. **69**, 101971 (2021)

14. Liang, J., Zeng, H., Zhang, L.: High-resolution photorealistic image translation in real-time: a laplacian pyramid translation network. In: Proceedings of the IEEE/CVF Conference on Computer Vision and Pattern Recognition, pp. 9392–9400 (2021)

15. Liu, H., et al.: Domain generalization in restoration of cataract fundus images via high-frequency components. In: 2022 IEEE 19th International Symposium on Biomedical Imaging (ISBI), pp. 1–5. IEEE (2022)

16. Ma, Y., et al.: Structure and illumination constrained GAN for medical image enhancement. IEEE Trans. Med. Imaging (2021)

17. Mitra, A., Roy, S., Roy, S., Setua, S.K.: Enhancement and restoration of non-uniform illuminated fundus image of retina obtained through thin layer of cataract. Comput. Methods Programs Biomed. **156**, 169–178 (2018)

18. Park, T., Efros, A.A., Zhang, R., Zhu, J.-Y.: Contrastive learning for unpaired image-to-image translation. In: Vedaldi, A., Bischof, H., Brox, T., Frahm, J.-M. (eds.) ECCV 2020. LNCS, vol. 12354, pp. 319–345. Springer, Cham (2020). https://doi.org/10.1007/978-3-030-58545-7_19

19. Shen, Z., Fu, H., Shen, J., Shao, L.: Modeling and enhancing low-quality retinal fundus images. IEEE Trans. Med. Imaging **40**(3), 996–1006 (2020)

20. Zhang, X.Q., Hu, Y., Xiao, Z.J., Fang, J.S., Higashita, R., Liu, J.: Machine learning for cataract classification/grading on ophthalmic imaging modalities: a survey. Mach. Intell. Res. **19**(3), 184–208 (2022)

21. Zhang, X., et al.: Adaptive feature squeeze network for nuclear cataract classification in AS-OCT image. J. Biomed. Inform. **128**, 128 (2022)

22. Zhu, J.Y., et al.: Unpaired image-to-image translation using cycle-consistent adversarial networks. In: Proceedings of the IEEE International Conference on Computer Vision, pp. 2223–2232 (2017)

A Spatiotemporal Model for Precise and Efficient Fully-Automatic 3D Motion Correction in OCT

Stefan Ploner[1,2]([✉]), Siyu Chen[2], Jungeun Won[2], Lennart Husvogt[1], Katharina Breininger[1], Julia Schottenhamml[1], James Fujimoto[2], and Andreas Maier[1]

[1] Friedrich-Alexander-Universität Erlangen-Nürnberg, Erlangen, Germany
stefan.ploner@fau.de
[2] Massachusetts Institute of Technology, Cambridge, MA, USA

Abstract. Optical coherence tomography (OCT) is a micrometer-scale, volumetric imaging modality that has become a clinical standard in ophthalmology. OCT instruments image by raster-scanning a focused light spot across the retina, acquiring sequential cross-sectional images to generate volumetric data. Patient eye motion during the acquisition poses unique challenges: Non-rigid, discontinuous distortions can occur, leading to gaps in data and distorted topographic measurements. We present a new distortion model and a corresponding fully-automatic, reference-free optimization strategy for computational motion correction in orthogonally raster-scanned, retinal OCT volumes. Using a novel, domain-specific spatiotemporal parametrization of forward-warping displacements, eye motion can be corrected continuously for the first time. Parameter estimation with temporal regularization improves robustness and accuracy over previous spatial approaches. We correct each A-scan individually in 3D in a single mapping, including repeated acquisitions used in OCT angiography protocols. Specialized 3D forward image warping reduces median runtime to <9 s, fast enough for clinical use. We present a quantitative evaluation on 18 subjects with ocular pathology and demonstrate accurate correction during microsaccades. Transverse correction is limited only by ocular tremor, whereas submicron repeatability is achieved axially (0.51 µm median of medians), representing a dramatic improvement over previous work. This allows assessing longitudinal changes in focal retinal pathologies as a marker of disease progression or treatment response, and promises to enable multiple new capabilities such as supersampled/super-resolution volume reconstruction and analysis of pathological eye motion occurring in neurological diseases.

Keywords: Optical coherence tomography · Motion compensation · Non-rigid registration · Forward warping

---

Supplementary Information The online version contains supplementary material available at https://doi.org/10.1007/978-3-031-16434-7_50.

L. Wang et al. (Eds.): MICCAI 2022, LNCS 13432, pp. 517–527, 2022.
https://doi.org/10.1007/978-3-031-16434-7_50

1   Introduction

Imaging the eye is particularly challenging because three types of involuntary eye movements continuously occur even during fixation [16]: *Microsaccades* (occasional fast movements lasting $< \sim 25$ ms), *drift* (slow, random walk-like motion causing distortion throughout), and *tremor* (aperiodic transverse vibration below the resolution of non-adaptive optics retinal imaging). Fixation capabilities decrease with age and in pathology. Optical coherence tomography (OCT) is a non-invasive 3D imaging modality and standard of care in ophthalmology [10]. By raster-scanning a laser beam across the retina, OCT assembles a volume of quasi-instantaneous depth profiles of backscattering (A-scans). A line of A-scans forms a 2D cross-sectional image (B-scan) with minimal distortion due to a millisecond acquisition (Fig. 1). In contrast, volume acquisition requires seconds and is correspondingly more distorted in slow scan direction. Microsaccades appear as discontinuities and cause gaps if performed opposite to the slow scan direction. OCT angiography (OCTA) visualizes microvasculature by performing repeated B-scans at the same retinal location and detecting motion contrast from moving blood cells [20]. However, scan time and distortion are further increased.

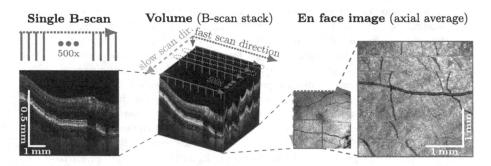

Fig. 1. A volume is composed of A-scans (red lines, in *axial* direction). The *transverse* scanned trajectory indicated in the volumetric scan, consisting of B-scans (blue arrows) and flyback (orange lines), defines continuity of image distortion. Microsaccade discontinuities (pink markers) are best visible after axial averaging, in *en face* images. (Color figure online)

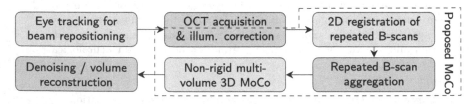

Fig. 2. Classic OCT processing pipeline. Steps related to motion correction (MoCo) in light blue, steps related to signal reconstruction and illumination (illum.) correction in red. Repeated B-scan registration is limited to 2D and increases gap size (see Fig. 5B). (Color figure online)

Previous motion correction methods are based on a three-step procedure outlined in Fig. 2. Eye tracking compensates motion and, thus, gap size during acquisition, but is insufficient as typically only transverse motion is corrected, and accuracy is fundamentally limited by latency in the range of a microsaccade duration [19]. Secondly, repeated B-scans are affinely registered. This step is limited to correcting in-plane (2D) motion by its 2D nature [20]. Subsequently, repeated B-scans are aggregated by averaging (OCT) or variance computation (OCTA). Lastly, two or more volumes are coregistered, allowing latency-free 3D distortion correction. Additional scans increase acquisition time, but enable data fusion for gap filling and signal-to-noise ratio enhancement [20].

For the volumetric correction, typically a pair of volumes with orthogonally oriented B-scans is used. This allows correcting distortion along the slow scan direction with the B-scans of the orthogonal volume and vice-versa. The main challenges are lack of a distortion-free reference, and the spatial discontinuity in distortion due to raster-scanning. Brea et al. reviewed existing methods and concluded that current models are insufficient to accurately correct fine features [21]. More recently, Ploner et al. integrated utilization of OCTA data [17] into the method of Kraus et al. [11], which is in commercial use. A special feature of these methods is that they are reference-free: displacement fields for each scan are jointly estimated in an axial, followed by a 3D, iterative optimization. This avoids propagation of drift motion from a reference to the result. Axial undistortion is achieved reliably, but correction is limited by use of backward warping: B-scan shearing must be estimated and compensated in the initial axial optimization, but this introduces inaccuracies because it lacks correction of transverse motion. Discontinuities in the distorted inputs (pink markers in Fig. 1) may cause spurious gradients in the similarity metric (during optimization). Furthermore, backward-warped displacements are defined at *target* grid voxels, limiting continuity regularization to target grid axes. However, B-scans acquired during slow scan direction motion or torsional eye motion (around the optical axis) are no longer axis-aligned with the target grid. This must be compensated by discontinuities in the displacement fields which *violate* the regularizer. Consequently, issues occur in datasets with head tilt (many volumes or widefield), and misregistration persists especially near slow scan direction microsaccades. While, e. g., the method of Athwal et al. compensates torsional motion [2], its local undistortion is limited (see discussion). The more promising forward warping was avoided for iterative OCT motion correction because the necessary scattered data interpolation was assumed computationally infeasible for clinical settings.

Contribution. We present the first spatiotemporal motion model and a corresponding fully-automatic, reference-free optimization strategy for volumetric distortion correction in OCT. Our approach introduces numerous *advances* over the state of the art: By using a displacement field *parametrization with respect to time*, discontinuities in optimization are remedied. Compared to prior work, a *drastically reduced parameter density* suffices without compromising accuracy, and *smoothness regularization* no longer contradicts with discontinuities. Two features are critical to enable time-continuous modeling: First, in order to infer consistent displacements despite distinct A-scan locations, motion is described for the eye as a whole, by a spatially rigid 3D transform. Remaining change is assumed to be of temporal origin. Secondly, to be able to derive the displacement of each A-scan based on its acquisition time, the transform must be defined at the input voxels, i.e. formulated via *forward warping*. While forward warping (FW) is fundamentally more complex to compute than backward warping, it enables image warping using a *single, direct mapping*. This allows estimation of *all parameters* in a single optimization, towards the (iteratively) *fully corrected* orthogonal dataset. A further advantage of FW is its *correct handling of overlaps*, which enables individual registration of repeated B-scans during volume registration. This not only removes the necessity for prior registration and intermediate averaging of B-scan repeats, but more importantly, enables their *correction in all three spatial dimensions*. Besides improving accuracy, this can substantially reduce gap size compared to prior in-plane registration methods. Finally, FW enables direct integration of *head tilt compensation*, effective *compensation of displacement bias* from aliasing effects during resampling, and gradient computation in the iteratively *motion-corrected targets*, thereby bypassing spurious gradients in the input volumes. Our model is suited for volume-pair, many-volume and widefield imaging, and is more reliable, dramatically more accurate, and converges faster. As discussed at the end, a range of new applications is enabled. Lastly, by exploiting the structure of possible distortion in the model, we formulate a domain-specific, *separable forward interpolation scheme* to enable iterative optimization in clinically feasible runtimes. While adding all described advantages, previously reported runtimes are reduced by a factor of 5.

2   Methods

Our approach jointly motion corrects two or more volumes with orthogonal B-scans. The log-scale B-scans are preprocessed with a radius 1 px median filter and factor 2 axial downsampling. OCT volumes are displayed in a grid where x, y displacements are within the coronal plane and z corresponds to depth. We assume the image to be distorted by the 3D affine, temporally varying transform

$$\mathcal{T}(\boldsymbol{x}, \tau, \boldsymbol{p}) = \begin{pmatrix} \cos(-\alpha(\tau)+\alpha_0) & -\sin(-\alpha(\tau)+\alpha_0) & 0 & -t^{\mathrm{x}}(\tau) \\ \sin(-\alpha(\tau)+\alpha_0) & \cos(-\alpha(\tau)+\alpha_0) & 0 & -t^{\mathrm{y}}(\tau) \\ -m^{\mathrm{x}}(\tau) & -m^{\mathrm{y}}(\tau) & 1 & -t^{\mathrm{z}}(\tau) \end{pmatrix} \begin{pmatrix} | \\ \boldsymbol{x} \\ | \\ 1 \end{pmatrix}. \quad (1)$$

Here, $\boldsymbol{x}$ and τ are the 3D position and acquisition time of a voxel and $\boldsymbol{p} = (t^{\mathrm{x}}, t^{\mathrm{y}}, t^{\mathrm{z}}, m^{\mathrm{x}}, m^{\mathrm{y}}, \boldsymbol{\alpha})$ is the vector of motion parameters for all scans. $t^{\mathrm{x/y/z}}$ is the transverse (x, y) and axial (z) displacement of the retina. Depending on the fast scan direction, either m^{x} or m^{y} is nonzero and describes axial shearing of B-scans originating from scanning beam to pupil center alignment [11]. The transverse rotation $\boldsymbol{\alpha}$ corresponds to torsional motion [13], which we assume constant within each scan. For all other parameter types, parameters (e.g. t^{x}) are estimated for the time points corresponding to the centers of each B-scan repeat and then interpolated along time using a cubic hermite spline $(t^{x}(\tau))$ to attain A-scan-specific values. To reduce displacement bias from equidistant resampling of the registration target grid to the axes-aligned moving B-scans [1], a constant $\alpha_0 \approx 45°$ is added. Lastly, besides other effects, illumination can vary with beam alignment/motion, and potentially confound registration. Therefore, based on a (log-scale) voxel intensity s, change in illumination is modeled as

$$\mathcal{I}(s, \tau, c) = s + I(s > s_{\min}) \cdot c(\tau), \tag{2}$$

where $c(\tau)$ is a spline given by parameters c, I is the indicator function, and $s_{\min}$ is a threshold to ignore the background, which is not affected by illumination.

Parameters are optimized jointly by minimization of the objective function

$$\mathcal{J}(p, c) = \sum_{M \in \mathcal{V}} \mathcal{D}(p, c, M) + \mathcal{R}(p, c) \quad \text{s.t.} \quad \mathcal{C}(p, c) = 0, \tag{3}$$

comprised of data terms $\mathcal{D}$ for all volumes $M \in \mathcal{V}$, and a smoothness regularization term $\mathcal{R}$, which penalizes the squared difference between sequential parameters with parameter type-specific weighting factors. Optimization is performed via momentum gradient descent with parameter type-specific step sizes until the maximum change falls below a threshold. The constraint $\mathcal{C}$ enforces parameters to have zero mean (by mean subtraction after each optimizer step). Optimization is performed in a 4-level coarse-to-fine multi-resolution pyramid of the (preprocessed) input, created by consecutive factor 2 downsamplings in axial direction. Axial displacement parameters are initialized to the average depth of the voxels of temporally neighboring A-scans, weighted by their cubed intensity. This aligns the bright horizontal band corresponding to the retinal pigment epithelium (see B-scan in Fig. 1). Other parameters are initialized with zeros.

Each data term $\mathcal{D}$ operates on the illumination-corrected voxels $\tilde{s}_{i,k}^{M}(c) := \mathcal{I}(s_{i,k}^{M}, \tau_i^{M}, c)$ of a moving volume M, where i, k, $s_{i,k}^{M}$ and τ_i^{M} are a voxel's A-scan index, depth index, intensity and acquisition time. To compute the corresponding squared difference loss for each target T, target volumes $\tilde{S}^{T}$ are interpolated to the voxel's motion-corrected location $\tilde{x}_{i,k}^{M}(p) := \mathcal{T}(x_{i,k}^{M}, \tau_i^{M}, p)$, where $x_{i,k}^{M}$ is the original voxel position, via 3D cubic hermite spline interpolation $\mathcal{W}$:

$$\mathcal{D}(p, c, M) = \sum_{\substack{T \in \mathcal{V} \\ \text{dir}(T) \neq \text{dir}(M)}} \sum_{i=1}^{wh} \sum_{\substack{k=1 \\ \text{valid}(\tilde{S}^{T}, \tilde{x}_{i,k}^{M}(p))}}^{d} \left(\tilde{s}_{i,k}^{M}(c) - \mathcal{W}(\tilde{S}^{T}, \tilde{x}_{i,k}^{M}(p)) \right)^2 \tag{4}$$

Only volumes with orthogonal B-scan orientation (given by $\text{dir}(\cdot)$) are used as targets. wh and d are the number of A-scans and their depth. Target volumes $\tilde{S}^{T}$ are assumed constant within each data term evaluation, to limit computational demands of the gradient evaluation. The implementation for forward-warping the targets' A-scans by $\mathcal{T}$ is detailed later. Due to use of forward warping, gaps in $\tilde{S}^{T}$ are known. Consequently, $\mathcal{W}$ is only defined if the 4^3 neighborhood around the moving voxel's location is valid, and ignored otherwise, as determined by $\text{valid}(\tilde{S}^{T}, x)$. In the final multi-resolution level, the target volume is computed with similar resolution as the preprocessed input, and is reduced in factor 2 steps in all dimensions for the smaller levels. Again, to avoid displacement bias during resampling [1], pseudo-random subpixel offsets are introduced by a slightly lower transverse resolution and z-position offsets (detailed in supplementary Fig. 1).

Besides accuracy, a primary concern for algorithm design was a small memory footprint, to allow joint registration of many volumes on a single GPU. Under these preconditions, the algorithm was designed for massively parallel computing throughout and implemented in CUDA 11.1. The most demanding step is the forward-resampling of the target volume. Naive mapping to a 4^3 neighborhood in the target grid necessitates complex computations to determine each voxel-specific weight, rendering the method infeasible for clinical use. We utilize the absence of axial distortion within A-scans in two critical ways: First, we perform a cubic hermite spline-weighted warping only in axial direction of each A-scan, such that data points are axially aligned with the target grid voxels. This limits the complexity of scattered-data warping to the 2 transverse dimensions only, where we use a truncated Gaussian weighting (sidelength 4, $\sigma = 0.5$, in target pixels). Secondly, we precompute and share coefficients across the axial direction. For a volume with sidelength N, separability and precomputation dramatically reduce the number of coefficient computations from $N^3 \cdot 4^3$ to $N^2 \cdot (4 + 4^2)$.

3   Experiments and Results

A dataset of 18 patients was acquired on a prototype spectral domain OCT scanner with 128 kHz A-scan rate over a 6 × 6 mm field with 500 × 500 A-scans without B-scan repeats. The axial resolution was 3 µm FWHM, axial pixel spacing was 1.78 µm, A-scans had 775 pixels. For each subject, in one eye, 4 volumes were acquired at the fovea with alternating B-scan orientation. Eye tracking was not available. The study cohort is detailed in the supplementary material, Table 1. We used 6 subjects to tune hyperparameters, mainly step size and convergence tolerance, and report our results on the remaining 12 subjects.

Evaluation of OCT motion correction accuracy is challenging [21], ground truth motion is not available. Discontinuities limit the definition of landmarks, as well as error computation between backward displacements, to pixel accuracy. Positional ambiguities arise due to overlaps/gaps. This doesn't apply to the axial direction, which was evaluated in [11] via reproducibility of segmented retinal layers, but localization accuracy (~3 µm [9]) is worse than registration accuracy. In contrast, forward-warped displacements allow *direct* computation of exact differences. We register each scan to both orthogonally acquired scans *independently*. Local distortion is independent from the coregistered scan used, so both estimated displacement fields should be identical up to global differences from scanner-to-eye alignment, which must be compensated. We used two transforms: Eq. (1), fixed to a single time-point τ, only removes *rigid* movement in the optical setup, and describes (all) residual distortion. The *affine-like* transform removes two further types of global linear distortion, leaving only local distortion and providing a descriptor of misalignment. This transform, and prevention of bias from resampling effects, are described in the supplementary material.

Images and estimated displacements are shown for a representative scan in Fig. 3. Tiny discontinuities prove absence of overregularization, and consistent transverse vibration indicates partial correction of ocular tremor. For quantitative analysis, we computed the median distance between the aligned A-scan displacements, and the fraction of displacements with a distance above 0.5 (problematic for supersampling) and 1 pixels (misalignments). The first and last 5% of B-scans were excluded, because they might not overlap with the orthogonal data, preventing registration. As the distributions are heavily skewed, we present box plots in Fig. 4. The three outliers in each direction in the right plot originate from the same subject, which is shown in supplementary Fig. 2. It is critical to note that the parameter density (B-scan 205 Hz) of the hermite splines is insufficient to fully correct ocular tremor (frequency up to $\sim$100 Hz [16]). Therefore, this aperiodic, wave-like motion (amplitude $\sim$30″ $\equiv$ $\sim$1.6 µm on the retina [16])

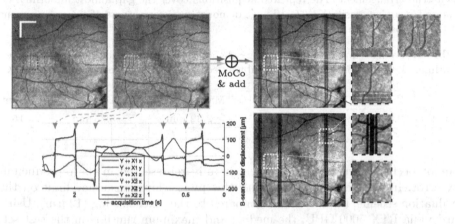

Fig. 3. Top: Input X- and Y-fast en face images, and red/cyan composite image after motion correction (MoCo). Bottom: Red/cyan composite of a scan Y registered to targets X1/X2, after affine-like alignment. Plot: The x, y, z displacements of the B-scan centers, computed with X1 (colored) and X2 (black), as compared in the quantitative evaluation (Fig. 4). Saccades consistently overshoot in this subject. Scalebars 1 mm. (Color figure online)

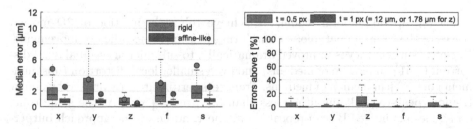

Fig. 4. Box plot and means (circles) of scan reproducibility metrics in x, y, z, fast and slow direction. Left: Median A-scan displacement distance. The y-axis range is one transverse pixel spacing. Right: Fraction of distances >0.5 and 1 px (affine-like).

524   S. Ploner et al.

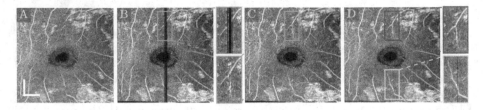

Fig. 5. Demonstration of individual B-scan repeat registration and gap filling in an example swept-source OCT dataset with 8 B-scan repeats. A: Uncorrected Y-fast volume, projected over the superficial capillary plexus. White spots originate from nerve fiber layer segmentation inaccuracies. B: Corrected using only 1 (constant) displacement parameter set for all B-scan repeats, limiting repeated A-scans to a single position, like previous methods. A gap appears at a slow scan direction microsaccade. C: Registration with individual displacements for each A-scan-repeat reveals their true arrangement: The repeated acquisitions cover the gap almost uniformly. D: The red/cyan composite X/Y-fast image demonstrates correctness of the arrangement in C. Scalebars 1 mm.

Table 1. Average runtime for registering $\sim 2 \times 500^2$ A-scans. Not all prior work reported runtime. [1]I/O time not reported, we subtracted 10 s. [2]2D transverse correction only.

	Zang ('17) [22][1]	Ploner ('21) [17]	Makita ('21) [14][1,2]	Cheng ('21) [3][1]	ours
Runtime	6.83 min	84 s	$\geq$ 2.32 min	5.83 min	**15 s**

cannot be fully corrected, and neither is fully represented in the reproducibility error. In the transverse directions, this puts a lower accuracy limit on the evaluation scheme, but it is small compared to the pixel spacing (12 μm). Using an Nvidia RTX 5000 GPU, the median and maximum runtime in the test set, excluding disk I/O which is irrelevant in clinical routine, was 8.6 s and 31.3 s. Table 1 compares average runtimes of various methods. Lastly, registration of individual B-scan repeats is demonstrated on a swept-source scanner in Fig. 5.

4 Discussion

Using our spatiotemporal model, we achieve robust estimation of 3D motion traces of the retina in pathology even during fast microsaccadic eye movements. Registration accuracy is improved dramatically, to sub-micron residual axial distortion (0.51 μm median of medians) and even smaller local distortion (misalignment) of 0.20 μm median of medians. Transverse errors are only limited by ocular tremor (peak-to-peak amplitude less than 3.2 μm $\approx \frac{1}{4}$ px). At the same time, on single- or merged-B-scan-repeat data, the runtime of our approach outperforms published methods by a factor of 5 and more. Whereas runtime increases with additional B-scan repeats, the necessity for prior registration of repeated B-scans is removed. We presented the first metric/distance-based 3D error quantification in OCT motion correction. Due to lack of such evaluation of previous methods, a direct comparison is not possible (see Sect. 3). However, by investigating algorithm properties, lower bounds for accuracy can be derived: Athwal et al. create a registration target by stitching saccade-free segments [2]. Drift motion in the reference segment is not corrected, resulting in residual transverse distortion in the range of $6' \approx \sim 19.1$ μm on the retina [16] and alignment is computed in whole-pixel steps only (12 μm in our dataset, typically ≥ 6 μm). Axial registration is limited by segmentation accuracy (ca. 3 μm [9]) and reliability is limited in pathology [2]. In [11] and [17], performing the B-scan shear estimation before transverse motion compensation puts a limit on overall axial registration accuracy. 7.0 and 3.7 μm were reported for axial reproducibility and misalignment errors. However, the evaluation compared retinal layer positions, whose segmentation introduces additional error. As detailed in the introduction, these methods are further limited by model inaccuracies in the transverse directions, and are unreliable near microsaccades [17]. Incompatibility with head rotation limits applicability to many-volume and widefield registration [13]. Displacement bias from resampling was not discussed in prior 3D OCT registration literature.

The advances of our model open up various new possibilities for exploration that go beyond motion correction: Subpixel-accuracy and direct forward warping allow *supersampling* using repeated volume scans [8], enabling a new paradigm for high-density widefield OCT imaging that is more robust to saccadic eye motion. OCT-derived blood flow signals like OCTA [20] can not only be merged and analyzed at capillary vasculature scale, but the maintained temporal dependency allows cardiac cycle-aware *4D spatiotemporal analysis and reconstruction* of flow speeds via Doppler-OCT [12] and VISTA-OCTA [18]. For both OCT intensity and derived signals, *advanced 3D signal reconstruction* allows probabilistic maximum a-posteriori modeling of the non-Gaussian noise distribution [4] in the reconstruction loss, or deblurring [5], *directly based on raw voxel data*. The reconstructed eye motion trace extends OCT with potential for accessible *screening of neurological diseases* that manifest in oculomotor dysfunction [6,7,15].

Given the variety of ocular pathologies and OCT scanners, performance should be reaffirmed in a larger cohort. Hardware tracking could be included to improve reliability and prevent longer runtimes in subjects with severe motion. To make optimal use of the motion correction, we are working on an iterative reconstruction and plan a release of the complete framework in the future.

Acknowledgements. DFG MA 4898/12-1, NIH 5-R01-EY011289-35.

References

1. Aganj, I., Yeo, B.T.T., Sabuncu, M.R., Fischl, B.: On removing interpolation and resampling artifacts in rigid image registration. IEEE Trans. Image Process. **22**(2), 816–827 (2013). https://doi.org/10.1109/TIP.2012.2224356
2. Athwal, A., Balaratnasingam, C., Yu, D.Y., Heisler, M., Sarunic, M., Ju, M.: Optimizing 3D retinal vasculature imaging in diabetic retinopathy using registration and averaging of OCT-A. Biomed. Opt. Express **12**(1), 553–570 (2021). https://doi.org/10.1364/BOE.408590

3. Cheng, Y., Chu, Z., Wang, R.K.: Robust three-dimensional registration on optical coherence tomography angiography for speckle reduction and visualization. Quant. Imaging Med. Surg. **11**(3) (2021). https://doi.org/10.21037/qims-20-751

4. Dubose, T.B., Cunefare, D., Cole, E., Milanfar, P., Izatt, J.A., Farsiu, S.: Statistical models of signal and noise and fundamental limits of segmentation accuracy in retinal optical coherence tomography. IEEE Trans. Med. Imaging **37**(9), 1978–1988 (2018). https://doi.org/10.1109/TMI.2017.2772963

5. Farsiu, S., Robinson, M., Elad, M., Milanfar, P.: Fast and robust multiframe super resolution. IEEE Trans. Image Process. **13**(10), 1327–1344 (2004). https://doi.org/10.1109/TIP.2004.834669

6. Fletcher, W.A., Sharpe, J.A.: Saccadic eye movement dysfunction in Alzheimer's disease. Ann. Neurol. **20**(4), 464–471 (1986). https://doi.org/10.1002/ana.410200405

7. Gitchel, G.T., Wetzel, P.A., Baron, M.S.: Pervasive ocular tremor in patients with Parkinson disease. Arch. Neurol. **69**(8), 1011–1017 (2012). https://doi.org/10.1001/archneurol.2012.70

8. Greenspan, H.: Super-resolution in medical imaging. Comput. J. **52**(1), 43–63 (2008). https://doi.org/10.1093/comjnl/bxm075

9. He, Y., et al.: Fully convolutional boundary regression for retina OCT segmentation. In: Shen, D., et al. (eds.) MICCAI 2019. LNCS, vol. 11764, pp. 120–128. Springer, Cham (2019). https://doi.org/10.1007/978-3-030-32239-7_14

10. Huang, D., et al.: Optical coherence tomography. Science **254**(5035), 1178–1181 (1991). https://doi.org/10.1126/science.1957169

11. Kraus, M., et al.: Quantitative 3D-OCT motion correction with tilt and illumination correction, robust similarity measure and regularization. Biomed. Opt. Express **5**(8), 2591–2613 (2014). https://doi.org/10.1364/BOE.5.002591

12. Leitgeb, R.A., Werkmeister, R.M., Blatter, C., Schmetterer, L.: Doppler optical coherence tomography. Prog. Retinal Eye Res. **41**, 26–43 (2014). https://doi.org/10.1016/j.preteyeres.2014.03.004

13. Lezama, J., Mukherjee, D., McNabb, R., Sapiro, G., Kuo, A., Farsiu, S.: Segmentation guided registration of wide field-of-view retinal optical coherence tomography volumes. Biomed. Opt. Express **7**(12), 4827–4846 (2016). https://doi.org/10.1364/BOE.7.004827

14. Makita, S., Miura, M., Azuma, S., Mino, T., Yamaguchi, T., Yasuno, Y.: Accurately motion-corrected Lissajous OCT with multi-type image registration. Biomed. Opt. Express **12**(1), 637–653 (2021). https://doi.org/10.1364/BOE.409004

15. Mallery, R.M., et al.: Visual fixation instability in multiple sclerosis measured using SLO-OCT. Invest. Ophthalmol. Vis. Sci. **59**(1), 196–201 (2018). https://doi.org/10.1167/iovs.17-22391

16. Martinez-Conde, S., Macknik, S., Hubel, D.: The role of fixational eye movements in visual perception. Nat. Rev. Neurosci. **5**(3), 229–240 (2004). https://doi.org/10.1038/nrn1348

17. Ploner, S.B., et al.: Efficient and high accuracy 3-D OCT angiography motion correction in pathology. Biomed. Opt. Express **12**(1), 125–146 (2021). https://doi.org/10.1364/BOE.411117

18. Ploner, S.B., et al.: Toward quantitative optical coherence tomography angiography. Retina **36**, S118–S126 (2016). https://doi.org/10.1097/IAE.0000000000001328

19. Schwarzhans, F., et al.: Generating large field of view en-face projection images from intra-acquisition motion compensated volumetric OCT data. Biomed. Opt. Express **11**(12), 6881–6904 (2020). https://doi.org/10.1364/BOE.404738

20. Spaide, R., Fujimoto, J., Waheed, N., Sadda, S., Staurenghi, G.: Optical coherence tomography angiography. Prog. Retinal Eye Res. **64**, 1–55 (2018). https://doi.org/10.1016/j.preteyeres.2017.11.003
21. Sánchez Brea, L., Andrade De Jesus, D., Shirazi, M.F., Pircher, M., van Walsum, T., Klein, S.: Review on retrospective procedures to correct retinal motion artefacts in OCT imaging. Appl. Sci. **9**(13) (2019). https://doi.org/10.3390/app9132700
22. Zang, P., et al.: Automated three-dimensional registration and volume rebuilding for wide-field angiographic and structural optical coherence tomography. J. Biomed. Opt. **22**(2), 26001 (2017). https://doi.org/10.1117/1.JBO.22.2.026001

DA-Net: Dual Branch Transformer and Adaptive Strip Upsampling for Retinal Vessels Segmentation

Changwei Wang[1,3], Rongtao Xu[1,3], Shibiao Xu[2(✉)], Weiliang Meng[1,3(✉)], and Xiaopeng Zhang[1,3]

[1] National Laboratory of Pattern Recognition, Institute of Automation, Chinese Academy of Sciences, Beijing, China
[2] School of Artificial Intelligence, Beijing University of Posts and Telecommunications, Beijing, China
shibiaoxu@bupt.edu.cn
[3] School of Artificial Intelligence, University of Chinese Academy of Sciences, Beijing, China
weiliang.meng@ia.ac.cn

Abstract. Since the morphology of retinal vessels plays a pivotal role in clinical diagnosis of eye-related diseases and diabetic retinopathy, retinal vessels segmentation is an indispensable step for the screening and diagnosis of retinal diseases, yet it is still a challenging problem due to the complex structure of retinal vessels. Current retinal vessels segmentation approaches roughly fall into image-level and patches-level methods based on the input type, while each has its own strengths and weaknesses. To benefit from both of the input forms, we introduce a Dual Branch Transformer Module (DBTM) that can simultaneously and fully enjoy the patches-level local information and the image-level global context. Besides, the retinal vessels are long-span, thin, and distributed in strips, making the square kernel of classic convolutional neural network false as it is only suitable for most natural objects with bulk shape. To better capture context information, we further design an Adaptive Strip Upsampling Block (ASUB) to adapt to the striped distribution of the retinal vessels. Based on the above innovations, we propose a retinal vessels segmentation **Net**work with **D**ual Branch Transformer and **A**daptive Strip Upsampling (**DA-Net**). Experiments validate that our DA-Net outperforms other state-of-the-art methods on both DRIVE and CHASE-DB1 datasets.

Keywords: Retinal vessels segmentation · Dual branch transformer module · Adaptive strip upsampling block

---

C. Wang and R. Xu—Contributed equally.

Supplementary Information The online version contains supplementary material available at https://doi.org/10.1007/978-3-031-16434-7_51.

1 Introduction

Accurate retinal vessels segmentation is essential for clinical retinal degenerative diseases diagnosis such as Diabetic Retinopathy [5], Macular Edema, and Cytomegalovirus Retinitis [14]. As the number of medical images has been increasing in recent years, time-consuming and laborious manual segmentation method by doctors is not feasible to large-scale disease screening and diagnosis [25]. Therefore, the automatic retinal vessels segmentation methods have become a research hot topic of medical image processing. Traditional automatic retinal vessels segmentation methods including line detection [11], hand-crafted feature extraction [26] and wavelet transform [1] cannot cope with retinal vessels segmentation well, especially for the thin and low-contrast retinal vessels. In recent years, deep learning based methods have been rapidly developed and have surpassed these traditional methods in retinal vessels segmentation. For example, the most famous work U-Net [12] employed an encoder to capture context information and a decoder for enabling precise localization, and its derivative works [8, 10, 17, 21–24] have achieved advanced segmentation results on retinal vessels segmentation. In order to further improve the accuracy of retinal vessels segmentation, CE-Net [7] utilized a U-Net-like method with context extractor, which can improve the segmentation by context information. Wang et al. [16] proposed a variant of U-Net with dual encoders to capture richer context features. CTF-Net [19] gave a coarse-to-fine supervised framework for retinal vessels segmentation. CGA-Net [18] used spatial attention guidance and hard sample mining training strategy. SCS-Net [20] provided a scale and context sensitive network to mine more effective semantic representations.

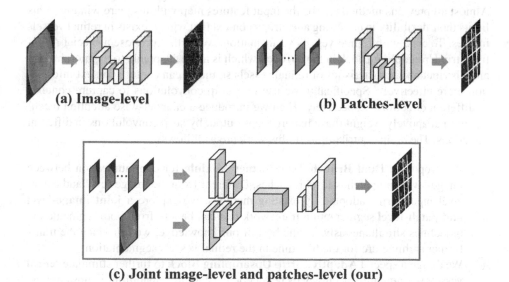

(a) Image-level   (b) Patches-level

(c) Joint image-level and patches-level (our)

Fig. 1. Various input forms of retinal vessels segmentation methods. In this work, we propose a novel joint image-level and patches-level segmentation framework.

Above deep learning based methods can be roughly divided into two categories according to the different input types: i) image-level methods [2,7,8,10,18,20,25] feed the entire retinal image into the network, as shown in Fig. 1 (a). ii) patches-level methods [16,19,21,24] crop the image into patches and then feed them into the network, as shown in Fig. 1 (b). Both types of input forms have their pros and cons. On one side, image-level methods retain the long-range context information that is helpful for the network to perceive the morphological and structural information of retinal vessels. In contrast, patches-level methods make the geometric features and semantic correlations of vessels cannot be well-presented in a single local patch as retinal vessels usually span multiple patches. On the other side, patches-level methods effectively enrich the diversity of samples by cropping the image into multiple patches, which alleviates the problem of insufficient training data of image-level methods and can reduce overfitting to improve the segmentation performance.

Inspired by the above different input types, we propose a new joint image-level and patch-level vessels segmentation framework which aims to combine the advantages of these two input forms, as shown in Fig. 1 (c). The philosophy behind our proposed framework is that the image-level and patches-level input forms are complementary, so we can combine them to further stimulate the segmentation performance. Specifically, our proposed method has two branches at image-level and patches-level respectively, and these two branches are communicated through a well-designed Dual Branch Transformer Module, which uses the transformer layers [4] to capture the long-range context correlations between them.

Different from other medical image segmentation tasks, retinal vessels are usually long, thin with striped distribution, which also brings challenges for segmentation [18]. Almost all previous methods probe the input features map within square windows, this limits their flexibility in capturing anisotropy context that widely exists in retinal vessels images. To cope with retinal vessels segmentation, we further propose a special Adaptive Strip Upsampling Block in the decoder, which is more adaptable to the morphology and distribution characteristics of retinal vessels so that it can capture context information more effectively. Specifically, we use four strip convolutions to capture contexts in different directions respectively. Then we introduce a channel-wise attention mechanism to adaptively weight these feature maps output by strip convolutions in different directions. The main contributions of this work are as follows:

(1) We propose a **Dual Branch Transformer Module** for communication between image-level and patches-level branches. Different from the image-level and patch-level input forms adopted by existing methods, we explore a **joint image-level and patch-level** segmentation framework that can benefit from both segmentation modalities simultaneously. To the best of our knowledge, we introduce the transformer architecture for the first time in the retinal vessels segmentation.
(2) We design a special **Adaptive Strip Upsampling Block** to further stimulate retinal vessels segmentation accuracy by better context capture capabilities in upsampling.
(3) We provide a retinal vessels segmentation network named **DA-Net** based on the above innovations. We implement comprehensive experiments, validating that our DA-Net has achieved the state-of-the-art performance on both public DRIVE and CHASE-DB1 datasets.

2 Our Proposed Method

In this section, we first illustrate the architecture of our DA-Net in Sect. 2.1, and then describe the designed Dual Branch Transformer Module in Sect. 2.2 and Adaptive Strip Upsampling Block in Sect. 2.3. Finally, we give the implementation details in Sect. 2.4.

2.1 Framework Overview

As illustrated in Fig. 2, our DA-Net consists of a shared encoder backbone, a Dual Branch Transformer Module (DBTM) and a decoder with Adaptive Strip Upsampling Block (ASUB). First, we crop the input image into patches $I^{(i)} \in \mathbb{R}^{H \times W \times 3}$, $i \in N^2$ and downsample the image to $1/N$ ($h \times w$) obtaining $I' \in \mathbb{R}^{H/N \times W/N \times 3}$. Then, we feed them into the shared encoder and get the corresponding feature maps $F^{(i)}, F'$. Note that the patches-level branch and the image-level branch use the same encoder backbone with shared weights. Two branches can be operated in parallel by merging batches. This means that the encoding of an input image can be completed in one forward inference without adding additional parameters and time consumption. Specifically, We employ a VGG [13] like encoder with five Conv Blocks to extract feature maps, as shown in Fig. 2. The outputs of these two branches communicate through our **DBTM** which can broadcast the long-range global context information to each patch. Finally, the predicted segmentation result is obtained after passing through a decoder with our **ASUB**.

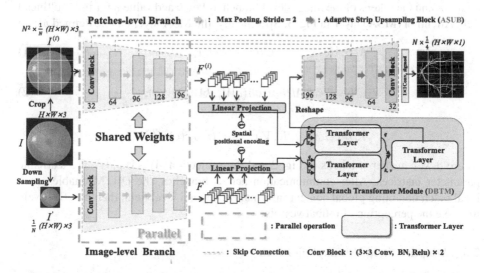

Fig. 2. The overall architecture of our **DA-Net**. The shared encoder contains five convolution blocks, while the **DBTM** and decoder with **ASUB** follow the encoder.

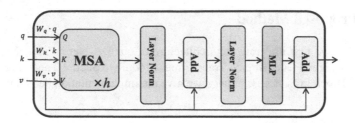

Fig. 3. Transformer layer in Dual Branch Transformer Module. Here MSA denotes Multihead Self-Attention and MLP denotes Multi-Layer Perceptron block, while h is the number of attention heads. We refer the readers to [4] and code in supplementary material for more details.

2.2 Dual Branch Transformer Module: Local Patches Meet Global Context

First, we take flattened and projected feature maps $F^{(i)}, F'$ as input tokens, where trainable position embeddings are added to retain the positional information. Then the input tokens are fed to the transformer layer as shown in Fig. 3. Different from previous classic vision transformer methods [4], we design a special **self-then-cross** pipeline to communicate the input from two branches called Dual Branch Transformer Module. Firstly, the input tokens of these two branches model the long-range dependence in the image-level and patches-level with the self-attention mechanism respectively. Then, the cross-attention mechanism are used for communication between tokens of both branches. In the cross-attention mechanism, we denote the tokens from patches-level branch as query q, and the tokens of the image-level branch as key k and value v for the Multihead Self-Attention (MSA) layer in Fig. 3. Specifically, the MSA layer can be defined as:

$$MSA(q, k, v) = Concat(head_1, ...head_h), \qquad (1)$$

$$head_i = Attention(qW_q, kW_k, vW_v), \qquad (2)$$

$$Attention(Q, K, V) = softmax(QK^T)V, \qquad (3)$$

where q, k, v are input tokens in Fig. 2 and the projections W_q, W_k, W_v are learnable parameter matrices. After communication across branches, the DBTM enables each local patch obtaining global context information beyond local field, thereby effectively improve the perception of retinal vessels.

2.3 Adaptive Strip Upsampling Block

Some inherent characteristics of retinal vessels lead to difficulty for its segmentation: the branches of retinal vessels are slender, the boundaries are difficult to distinguish, and the relationship between retinal vessels is complicated. In these cases, the context information around the retinal vessels is vital to the retinal vessels segmentation. However, traditional square convolution kernels in normal upsampling block cannot capture linear features well and inevitably introduce irrelevant information from neighboring pixels as shown in Fig. 4 (a). To better gather the context information around retinal vessels, we propose the Adaptive Strip Upsampling Block (ASUB) that is suitable for the distribution of long and thin retinal vessels.

As illustrated in Fig. 5, our ASUB employs four strip convolution kernels to capture the context information around revessels in the horizontal (S_1), vertical (S_2), left diagonal (S_3), and right diagonal ((S_4)) directions, respectively. First, we use a 1×1 Conv to halve the dimension of the feature maps to reduce computational cost. Then, we leverages four strip convolutions to capture long-range context information from different directions. In addition, we also utilize the Global Average Pooling (GAP) to obtain feature vectors in the channel dimension of feature maps, and use fully connected layers to learn channel-wise attention vectors for each strip convolution. After that, the softmax function are applied to produce the channel-wise fusion weights $W_i, i \in \{1, 2, 3, 4\}$. Finally, we weight the output of each strip convolution F_i with the learned adaptive weights W_i to obtain the feature maps $F'_{out} = \sum_i^4 F_i W_i$. Then we upsample F'_{out} and restore the dimension with a 1×1 Conv to get the final output F_{out}.

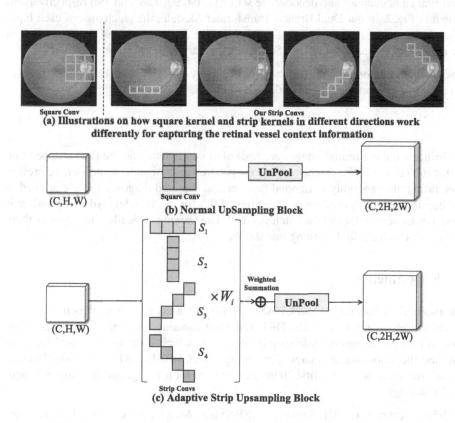

(a) Illustrations on how square kernel and strip kernels in different directions work differently for capturing the retinal vessel context information

(b) Normal UpSampling Block

(c) Adaptive Strip Upsampling Block

Fig. 4. Schematic diagram of Normal UpSampling Block and our **ASUB**.

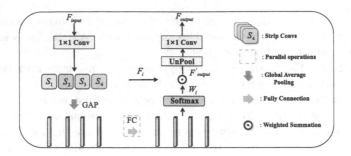

Fig. 5. Details of our **Adaptive Strip UpSampling Block (ASUB)**.

2.4 Implementation Details

Network Structure: The number of feature maps for each Conv Block of the patches-level branch of encoder and decoder are set to 32, 64, 96, 128, and 196 respectively, as shown in Fig. 2. In our Dual Branch Transformer Module, the patch size of each input token is set to 1×1, the number of heads h in Fig. 3 is set to 4, and the dimension of the embedded tokens is set to 196. See supplementary material for more details.

Loss Function: Both classic Binary Cross-Entropy loss $\mathcal{L}_{bce}$ and Dice loss [9] $\mathcal{L}_{dice}$ are used to construct the total loss $\mathcal{L}_{total}$ as follows:

$$\mathcal{L}_{total} = \mathcal{L}_{bce} + \mathcal{L}_{dice} \tag{4}$$

Training: All input retinal images are resized to 640×640, and are then cropped into 160×160 $(1/4\ H \times W)$ patches to feed the patches-level branch of encoder. To prevent over-fitting, the randomly horizontal flip, vertical flip, and diagonal flip are applied to the training data with random probabilities of 0.5 for all. Besides, Adam optimizer is used to train our model and the batch size is 2. The training typically converges in about 400 epochs with a initial learning rate 0.0002.

3   Experiments

Datasets: The DRIVE [15] and CHASE-DB1 [6] datasets are common benchmark for retinal vessels segmentation. The DRIVE dataset contains 40 color fundus images and ground-truth masks manually labeled by experts, in which 20 images are used for training, and the remaining 20 images for testing. The CHASE-DB1 dataset has 28 color retinal images, in which the first 20 images are used for training, and the other 8 images are for testing.

Metrics: Accuracy (ACC), Sensitivity (SEN) and Area Under Curve (AUC) are used to evaluate each method. For convenient, we use the following denotations: TP for true positive; TN for true negative; FP for false positive; FN for false negative. Then, $ACC = \frac{TP+TN}{TP+TN+FP+FN}$, $SEN = \frac{TP}{TP+FN}$, while AUC is a quantitative indicator of the receiver operating characteristic (ROC) curve.

Table 1. Comparison with advanced methods on the DRIVE and CHASE-DB1 datasets. The best results are marked in **bold** and second best are marked in <u>underline</u>.

Method	Pub.	Input type	DRIVE			CHASE-DB1		
			SEN	ACC	AUC	SEN	ACC	AUC
Maninis et al. [8]	MICCAI 2016	Image	82.80	95.41	98.01	76.51	96.57	97.46
Orlando et al. [10]	T-BME 2016	Image	78.97	–	95.07	72.77	–	95.24
JL-UNet [24]	T-BME 2018	Patches	77.92	95.56	97.84	76.33	96.10	97.81
MS-NFN [21]	MICCAI 2018	Patches	78.44	95.67	98.07	75.38	96.37	98.25
CE-Net [7]	TMI 2019	Image	<u>83.09</u>	95.45	97.79	81.52	96.89	98.30
Wang et al. [16]	MICCAI 2019	Patches	79.40	95.67	97.72	80.74	96.61	98.12
CTF-Net [19]	ISBI 2020	Patches	78.49	95.67	97.88	79.48	96.48	98.47
CGA-Net [18]	ISBI 2021	Image	83.05	96.47	<u>98.65</u>	<u>86.78</u>	97.06	98.12
SCS-Net [20]	MIA 2021	Image	82.89	<u>96.97</u>	98.37	83.65	<u>97.44</u>	<u>98.67</u>
DA-Net (our)	MICCAI 2022	**Joint**	**85.57**	**97.07**	**99.03**	**87.04**	**97.66**	**99.08**

3.1 Comparison with Advanced Methods

The quantitative comparison between our DA-Net and other state-of-the-art methods on DRIVE and CHASE-DB1 is given in Table 1. Our **DA-Net** achieves the highest AUC, SEN, and ACC on both datasets. Besides, Fig. 6 shows some visual segmentation results of our **DA-Net** on the DRIVE and the CHASE-DB1 datasets. We can clearly see that our **DA-Net** can obtain better segmentation visual results.

3.2 Ablation Study

Table 2 shows the results of our ablation experiments on DRIVE dataset. We use the classic U-Net [12] as the baseline, and employ two input forms mentioned in Fig. 1 to train the models respectively. The results show that our **DBTM** and **ASUB** can significantly improve the scores of ACC and AUC individually. Finally, the best segmentation performance is obtained after we apply all the proposed components. To investigate the additional cost brought by the proposed components, we also report 'FLOPs' and 'Parameters' for each variant in ablation study. Since the increments by our DA-Net are lightweight (e.g. encoder with shared weights and parallel operations in Sect. 2.1; low resolution input in Sect. 2.2 reducing feature map dimension in Sect. 2.3), they bring only slight memory and computational consumption. Due to space constraints, more ablation studies about parameter settings are provided in the supplementary material.

Table 2. Ablation study on DRIVE dataset. **DBTM** means Dual Branch Transformer Module proposed in Sect. 2.2.**ASUB** means Adaptive Strip Upsampling Block proposed in Sect. 2.3.

Methods	ACC	AUC	FLOPs	Parameters
Baseline w/image-level input	95.68	97.60	**21.5 G**	**8.2 MB**
Baseline w/patches-level input	96.01	97.51	**21.5 G**	**8.2 MB**
Baseline + **DBTM**	96.56	98.44	22.6 G	8.9 MB
Baseline + **ASUB**	96.71	98.54	23.5 G	10.3 MB
Baseline + all (our **DA-Net**)	**97.07**	**99.03**	24.3 G	11.2 MB

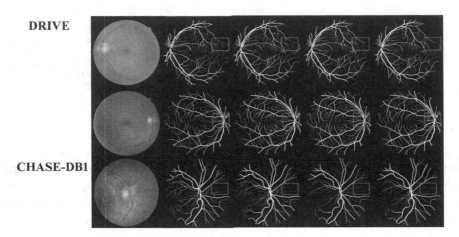

Fig. 6. Visualization of segmentation results on DRIVE and CHASE-DB1 datasets. **From Left to Right**: Retina images, Ground truths, proposed DA-Net, CGANet [18] and CENet [7] outputs.

4   Conclusion

We propose a retinal vessels segmentation method **DA-Net**, in which the image-level context information is introduced in local patches via a well-designed Dual Branch Transformer Module. Furthermore, we designed an Adaptive Strip Upsampling Block in the decoder of our DA-Net to capture the context information that adapts to the distribution of retinal vessels more flexibly and effectively. Our **DA-Net** significantly outperforms other state-of-the-art methods for retinal vessels segmentation on both DRIVE and CHASE-DB1 datasets, and can be applied to other high-resolution or strip objects and lesions segmentation tasks potentially.

5   Future Work

Note that the strip convolution direction set by ASUB is not necessarily exactly the same as the direction of some small blood vessels, we will further improve the context modeling ability of these small blood vessels by introducing deformable convolution [27] or deformable transformer [3] in future work.

Acknowledgements. This work is supported by the National Key R&D Program of China (No. 2020YFC2008500, 2020YFC2008503), the National Natural Science Foundation of China (Nos. 61972459, 61971418 and 62071157), the Open Research Fund of Key Laboratory of Space Utilization, Chinese Academy of Sciences (No. LSU-KFJJ-2020-04).

References

1. Bankhead, P., Scholfield, C.N., McGeown, J.G., Curtis, T.M.: Fast retinal vessel detection and measurement using wavelets and edge location refinement. PLoS ONE **7**(3), e32435 (2012)
2. Chen, D., Yang, W., Wang, L., Tan, S., Lin, J., Bu, W.: PCAT-UNet: UNet-like network fused convolution and transformer for retinal vessel segmentation. PLoS ONE **17**(1), e0262689 (2022)
3. Chen, Z., et al.: DPT: deformable patch-based transformer for visual recognition. In: Proceedings of the 29th ACM International Conference on Multimedia, pp. 2899–2907 (2021)
4. Dosovitskiy, A., et al.: An image is worth 16x16 words: transformers for image recognition at scale. arXiv preprint arXiv:2010.11929 (2020)
5. Fraz, M.M., et al.: Blood vessel segmentation methodologies in retinal images-a survey. Comput. Methods Programs Biomed. **108**(1), 407–433 (2012)
6. Fraz, M.M., et al.: An ensemble classification-based approach applied to retinal blood vessel segmentation. IEEE Trans. Biomed. Engin. **59**(9), 2538–2548 (2012)
7. Gu, Z., et al.: CE-Net: context encoder network for 2D medical image segmentation. IEEE Trans. Med. Imaging **38**(10), 2281–2292 (2019)
8. Maninis, K.-K., Pont-Tuset, J., Arbeláez, P., Van Gool, L.: Deep retinal image understanding. In: Ourselin, S., Joskowicz, L., Sabuncu, M.R., Unal, G., Wells, W. (eds.) MICCAI 2016. LNCS, vol. 9901, pp. 140–148. Springer, Cham (2016). https://doi.org/10.1007/978-3-319-46723-8_17
9. Milletari, F., Navab, N., Ahmadi, S.A.: V-Net: fully convolutional neural networks for volumetric medical image segmentation. In: 2016 Fourth International Conference on 3D Vision (3DV), pp. 565–571 (2016). https://doi.org/10.1109/3DV.2016.79
10. Orlando, J.I., Prokofyeva, E., Blaschko, M.B.: A discriminatively trained fully connected conditional random field model for blood vessel segmentation in fundus images. IEEE Trans. Biomed. Eng. **64**(1), 16–27 (2016)
11. Ricci, E., Perfetti, R.: Retinal blood vessel segmentation using line operators and support vector classification. IEEE Trans. Med. Imaging **26**(10), 1357–1365 (2007)
12. Ronneberger, O., Fischer, P., Brox, T.: U-Net: convolutional networks for biomedical image segmentation. In: Navab, N., Hornegger, J., Wells, W.M., Frangi, A.F. (eds.) MICCAI 2015. LNCS, vol. 9351, pp. 234–241. Springer, Cham (2015). https://doi.org/10.1007/978-3-319-24574-4_28
13. Simonyan, K., Zisserman, A.: Very deep convolutional networks for large-scale image recognition. arXiv preprint arXiv:1409.1556 (2014)
14. Son, J., Park, S.J., Jung, K.H.: Retinal vessel segmentation in fundoscopic images with generative adversarial networks. arXiv preprint arXiv:1706.09318 (2017)
15. Staal, J., Abràmoff, M.D., Niemeijer, M., Viergever, M.A., Van Ginneken, B.: Ridge-based vessel segmentation in color images of the retina. IEEE Trans. Med. Imaging **23**(4), 501–509 (2004)
16. Wang, B., Qiu, S., He, H.: Dual encoding U-Net for retinal vessel segmentation. In: Shen, D., Liu, T., Peters, T.M., Staib, L.H., Essert, C., Zhou, S., Yap, P.-T., Khan, A. (eds.) MICCAI 2019. LNCS, vol. 11764, pp. 84–92. Springer, Cham (2019). https://doi.org/10.1007/978-3-030-32239-7_10

17. Wang, C., et al.: Accurate lung nodules segmentation with detailed representation transfer and soft mask supervision. arXiv preprint arXiv:2007.14556 (2020)
18. Wang, C., Xu, R., Zhang, Y., Xu, S., Zhang, X.: Retinal vessel segmentation via context guide attention net with joint hard sample mining strategy. In: 2021 IEEE 18th International Symposium on Biomedical Imaging (ISBI), pp. 1319–1323. IEEE (2021)
19. Wang, K., Zhang, X., Huang, S., Wang, Q., Chen, F.: CTF-Net: retinal vessel segmentation via deep coarse-to-fine supervision network. In: 2020 IEEE 17th International Symposium on Biomedical Imaging (ISBI), pp. 1237–1241. IEEE (2020)
20. Wu, H., Wang, W., Zhong, J., Lei, B., Wen, Z., Qin, J.: SCS-Net: a scale and context sensitive network for retinal vessel segmentation. Med. Image Anal. **70**, 102025 (2021)
21. Wu, Y., Xia, Y., Song, Y., Zhang, Y., Cai, W.: Multiscale network followed network model for retinal vessel segmentation. In: Frangi, A.F., Schnabel, J.A., Davatzikos, C., Alberola-López, C., Fichtinger, G. (eds.) MICCAI 2018. LNCS, vol. 11071, pp. 119–126. Springer, Cham (2018). https://doi.org/10.1007/978-3-030-00934-2_14
22. Xu, R., Li, Y., Wang, C., Xu, S., Meng, W., Zhang, X.: Instance segmentation of biological images using graph convolutional network. Eng. Appl. Artif. Intell. **110**, 104739 (2022)
23. Xu, R., Wang, C., Xu, S., Meng, W., Zhang, X.: DC-Net: dual context network for 2D medical image segmentation. In: de Bruijne, M., Cattin, P.C., Cotin, S., Padoy, N., Speidel, S., Zheng, Y., Essert, C. (eds.) MICCAI 2021. LNCS, vol. 12901, pp. 503–513. Springer, Cham (2021). https://doi.org/10.1007/978-3-030-87193-2_48
24. Yan, Z., Yang, X., Cheng, K.T.: Joint segment-level and pixel-wise losses for deep learning based retinal vessel segmentation. IEEE Trans. Biomed. Eng. **65**(9), 1912–1923 (2018)
25. Yang, T., Wu, T., Li, L., Zhu, C.: SUD-GAN: deep convolution generative adversarial network combined with short connection and dense block for retinal vessel segmentation. J. Digit. Imaging **33**(4), 946–957 (2020)
26. Zhang, B., Zhang, L., Zhang, L., Karray, F.: Retinal vessel extraction by matched filter with first-order derivative of gaussian. Comput. Biol. Med. **40**(4), 438–445 (2010)
27. Zhu, X., Hu, H., Lin, S., Dai, J.: Deformable ConvNets V2: more deformable, better results. In: Proceedings of the IEEE/CVF Conference on Computer Vision and Pattern Recognition, pp. 9308–9316 (2019)

Visual Explanations for the Detection of Diabetic Retinopathy from Retinal Fundus Images

Valentyn Boreiko[✉], Indu Ilanchezian, Murat Seçkin Ayhan, Sarah Müller,
Lisa M. Koch, Hanna Faber, Philipp Berens, and Matthias Hein

University of Tübingen, Tübingen, Germany
valentyn.boreiko@uni-tuebingen.de

Abstract. In medical image classification tasks like the detection of diabetic retinopathy from retinal fundus images, it is highly desirable to get
visual explanations for the decisions of black-box deep neural networks
(DNNs). However, gradient-based saliency methods often fail to highlight the diseased image regions reliably. On the other hand, adversarially
robust models have more interpretable gradients than plain models but
suffer typically from a significant drop in accuracy, which is unacceptable for clinical practice. Here, we show that one can get the best of both
worlds by ensembling a plain and an adversarially robust model: maintaining high accuracy but having improved visual explanations. Also, our
ensemble produces meaningful visual counterfactuals which are complementary to existing saliency-based techniques. Code is available under
https://github.com/valentyn1boreiko/Fundus_VCEs.

Keywords: Interpretability · Counterfactual explanations ·
Adversarial robustness · Trustworthy AI · Diabetic retinopathy

1 Introduction

In many medical domains, deep learning systems have been shown to perform
close to or even better than domain experts in detecting disease from images
[21]. For clinicians and patients to trust such systems in practice, they need
to be interpretable [14,15]. Current techniques for interpreting model decisions,
however, have critical shortcomings. For instance, post-hoc interpretability techniques such as saliency maps are often used to generate explanations for a classifier's decision. These have been evaluated for clinical relevance, e.g. in ophthalmology [2,5,33], with some methods producing more meaningful visualizations
than others. As DNNs can rely on spurious features and are not necessarily

---

V. Boreiko and I. Ilanchezian–Equal Contribution.

Supplementary Information The online version contains supplementary material
available at https://doi.org/10.1007/978-3-031-16434-7_52.

Model	Orig.(GT:DR)	T-GBP [29]	T-IG [30]	$l_{1.5}$-VCE, ϵ=30	T-VSM
	DR:1.00	**0.10**	**0.12**	→DR: 1.00	**0.10**
Plain					
	DR:0.99	**0.19**	**0.20**	→DR: 1.00	**0.20**
Robust					
	DR:1.00	**0.20**	**0.22**	→DR: 1.00	**0.21**
Ensemble (proposed)					

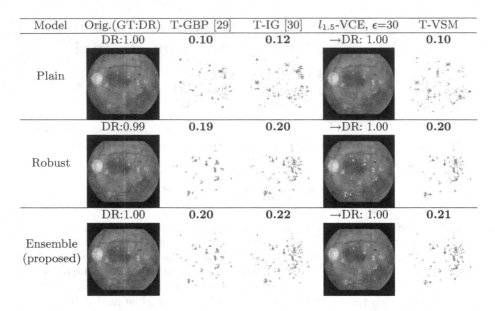

Fig. 1. Visual explanations of decisions are better for robust and ensemble models than for plain models, as shown by intersection over union (IoU) between saliency maps (P) and ground truth (GT) masks ($\mathbf{IoU}(P, GT) := \frac{|P \cap GT|}{|P \cup GT|}$) (in bold). We show an image correctly classified as DR (left), post-hoc explanations for the decision using thresholded Guided Backprop (T-GBP), Integrated Gradients (T-IG) and visual counterfactual examples (VCEs) for enhancing the classifiers' confidence into DR as well as the corresponding saliency map: thresholded VCE Saliency Map (T-VSM). Numerical evaluation of these maps in comparison to the ground truth segmentation can be found in Table 2.

learning all class-relevant features [11,12], saliency maps may also have limited usefulness in clinical settings [2,28]: for standard classifiers they sometimes just highlight high-frequency components of an image [5]. Especially for healthy cases, these are often hard to interpret during screening for timely intervention.

Interestingly, models trained to provide inherent robustness against adversarial attacks [7,22], have also been shown to yield better saliency maps [10,23]. Also, these robust models allow to generate visual counterfactual explanations (VCEs) [3,6], an alternative image-wise interpretability technique that shows the minimal changes necessary to maximize the confidence of the classifier in a desired class (Fig. 1). But, the gain of these models in adversarial robustness comes at the price of a loss in accuracy [32,35] which is unacceptable especially in medical applications. Thus, adversarially robust models have not seen widespread use in practice.

Here we show that an ensemble of a plain and an adversarially robust model yields improved saliency maps and allows for the computation of VCEs to further explore the basis of the model's decision. Further, it achieves almost the same accuracy as the plain model. We demonstrate this new approach to explainability for medical image classifiers for the case of diabetic retinopathy (DR) detection from retinal fundus images and propose a new type of the saliency map.

2 Methods

2.1 Datasets

We used three publicly available datasets of retinal fundus images for which DR grades were available: the Kaggle DR detection challenge data [1] for method development and main results, the Messidor dataset [9] for additional external validation, and a portion of the Indian Diabetic Retinopathy Image Dataset (IDRiD) [26] for quantitative evaluation of visual explanations, as these data additionally had DR lesion annotations at pixel level. We pre-processed the images using contrast limited adaptive histogram equalization (CLAHE) [36], and by tightly cropping the circular mask of the retinal fundus, which was detected by iterative least-squares fitting of a circular shape to image edges. For the Kaggle dataset, we filtered out poor quality images using an ensemble of EfficientNets [31] trained on the ISBI2020 challenge dataset[1]. This quality filtering model achieved 87.50% accuracy for image gradability. After quality filtering, the resulting dataset contained $45,923$ images (at a final resolution of 224×224 pixels): $33,783$ in class 'no DR', $3,598$ in 'mild DR', $6,765$ in 'moderate DR', $1,186$ in 'severe DR' and 591 in 'proliferative DR'. The Messidor dataset contained 1200 retinal fundus images, and the IDRiD 81 images along with annotations for microaneuryms, haemorrhages, hard and soft exudates. We combined the annotations of these lesion types to obtain a single ground truth mask.

2.2 Plain, Robust and Ensemble Models

As mild DR is a transitional stage between no DR and moderate-to-advanced stages of DR [34], these images lead to high uncertainty in decisions of both DNNs and clinicians [4]. Therefore, to obtain a clear separation of 'no DR' and DR classes, we excluded the 'mild DR' cases. We then trained binary classifiers $f : \mathbb{R}^d \to \mathbb{R}^2$ to predict whether a fundus image x was in the 'no DR' class or belonged to moderate-to-advanced stages of DR, with $\hat{p}_f(y = 1|x)$ indicating the predicted probability of disease. We used 75% of the Kaggle data for training, 15% for validation, 4% for temperature scaling [16] and 6% for testing.

For the plain model we used a ResNet-50 [17] which was trained with cross-entropy loss. We used batch size of 128, with oversampling of the DR cases to account for class imbalance. We first trained the model for 500 epochs with learning rate of 0.01 and a cosine learning rate schedule. This model was further fine-tuned for 3 epochs with a cyclic triangle schedule for one cycle. We chose the model with the best balanced accuracy on the validation set.

The robust model used the same architecture but was trained using TRADES [35] for l_2-adversarial robustness, where one minimizes for the given training set $(x_i, y_i)_{i=1}^n$ the objective:

$$\frac{1}{n} \sum_{i=1}^{n} \left[-\log\left(\hat{p}_f(y_i|x_i)\right) + \beta \max_{x \in B_2(x_i,\epsilon)} D_{KL}\left(\hat{p}_f(\cdot|x) \,\|\, \hat{p}_f(\cdot|x_i)\right) \right], \qquad (1)$$

---

[1] https://isbi.deepdr.org/challenge2.html.

where D_{KL} denotes the Kullback-Leibler divergence, $\hat{p}_f(\cdot|x)$ is the predicted probability distribution over the classes at x, β controls the trade-off between adversarial and plain training schemes, and $B_p(x,\epsilon) := \{\hat{x} \in \mathbb{R}^d | \|x - \hat{x}\|_p \leq \epsilon\}$. For training we used $p = 2$ and $\epsilon = 0.25$ and set $\beta = 6$.

In our experience, tuning β down during training can increase accuracy but negatively affects interpretability. Hence, we built the following ensemble of plain and robust models, which preserves both accuracy and interpretable gradients for the given β:

$$\hat{p}_{f,ensemble}(k|x) := \frac{1}{2}[\hat{p}_{f,plain}(k|x) + \hat{p}_{f,robust}(k|x)], \quad k = 0, 1. \tag{2}$$

As saliency methods often require logits f instead of probabilities, we defined logits for the ensemble as $f_k := \log\left(\hat{p}_{f,ensemble}(k|x)\right)$. All models are calibrated via temperature scaling by minimizing the expected calibration error [16].

Experiments were done on an Nvidia Tesla V100 GPU with 32 GB RAM, using PyTorch. Code for pre-processing and training as well as the trained models will be available upon acceptance.

2.3   Generating Visual Counterfactual Explanations (VCEs)

Following [6], a VCE $\tilde{x}$ should have high probability $\hat{p}_f(k|\tilde{x})$ in a chosen class k ("validity"). It should be similar to the starting image x_0 ("sparsity") and close to the data manifold ("realism"). For generating an l_p-VCE $\tilde{x}$ for a classifier f we solved

$$\tilde{x} = \underset{x \in B_p(x_0,\epsilon) \cap [0,1]^d \cap \mathcal{M}}{\arg\max} \log\left(\hat{p}_f(k|x)\right) \tag{3}$$

where $\mathcal{M}$ is the mask for the region of the eye obtained by our pre-processing. The formulation of VCEs suggests that some "robustness" is required as Eq. 3 is similar to the formulation of adversarial examples [6]. Compared to saliency maps the advantage of VCE is that the generated images are purely based on the behavior of the classifier. We used adaptive projected gradient descent (APGD) [7] and Frank-Wolfe [19,24] based schemes as optimizers. APGD requires projections onto l_p-balls which are available in closed form for l_2 and l_∞ or can be computed efficiently for l_1 [8]. However, for $p \notin \{1, 2, \infty\}$, there is no such projection available and thus we used for the generation of l_p-VCEs the Auto-Frank-Wolfe scheme of [6].

2.4   Saliency Maps

We used Guided Backprop (GBP) [29] and Integrated Gradients (IG) [30] from a public repository [25] to generate saliency maps for the models' decisions. GBP and IG are among the best saliency techniques for DR detection [5,33]. Based on our VCEs, we also introduced the VCE Saliency Map (VSM) as the difference between VCE and the original image. For all saliency methods, we used absolute saliency values summed over color channels in order to better

Table 1. Evaluation of plain and robust classifier and their ensemble in terms of standard, balanced and l_2-robust accuracy. The ensemble maintains the accuracy but gains sufficient robustness required for better interpretability (see Table 2).

	Kaggle			Messidor		
	acc.	bal. acc.	rob. acc.	acc.	bal. acc.	rob. acc.
Plain	89.5	85.8	15.2	89.5	89.5	20.6
Robust	78.4	71.6	66.6	66.1	66.5	60.9
Ensemble	89.7	85.2	19.4	87.9	87.9	24.4

cover salient regions [5]. Then, saliency scores were normalized to $[0, 1]$ via min-max normalization and thresholded at the τ-quantile for sparsity. The threshold τ was optimized for each method on 40 out of 81 images in the IDRiD dataset by computing the intersection over union (IoU) with respect to the pixel-wise annotation of DR lesions. This yielded $\tau = 0.98$ for GBP, $\tau = 0.96$ for both IG and VSM. For the VSMs we additionally optimized over the norm $p \in \{1.5, 2, 4\}$ and different ϵ per norm and found $p = 1.5$, $\epsilon = 30$ to be the best.

2.5   Model Evaluation

We evaluated the performance of models on the Kaggle test set and Messidor images using accuracy (acc.), and balanced accuracy (bal. acc., mean of TPR and TNR). Additionally, we reported l_2-robust accuracy (rob. acc.) for a perturbation budget of $\epsilon = 0.1$ which we evaluated using 9 restarts of 100 iterations of APGD [7] maximizing the confidence in the wrong class. The robust accuracy is the fraction of test inputs where the decision could not be changed by the attack.

For a quantitative evaluation of our visual explanations, we used the 41 images on which τ had not been optimized from the IDRiD dataset. Table 2 shows the mean IoU for all models and saliency techniques (including T-VSMs for different p-norms) with the pixel-level DR lesion annotations.

This evaluation indicates that the saliency maps derived from VCEs are on par with state-of-the-art techniques, such as GBP and IG. However, VCEs go beyond those techniques as they can be used to generate images and even animations that illustrate how an image would have to change to affect the prediction of the classifier.

3   Results

First, we analyzed the properties of the plain and robust classifiers, and the ensemble introduced in Eq. 2. Then, we explored VCEs as an alternative for explaining classifier decisions and studied the sparsity-realism trade-off for VCEs. Finally, we show the effect of different perturbation budgets on VCEs.

Table 2. Evaluation of saliency maps and T-VSMs on IDRiD. The IoU-score of the ensemble is higher than for the plain model for all interpretability methods including VCEs (higher is better, mean ± std).

	GBP	IG	$l_{1.5}, \epsilon = 30$	$l_2, \epsilon = 6$	$l_4, \epsilon = 0.2$
Plain	0.09 ± 0.03	0.08 ± 0.03	0.07 ± 0.03	0.07 ± 0.03	0.07 ± 0.03
Robust	0.15 ± 0.06	0.14 ± 0.06	0.13 ± 0.06	0.12 ± 0.06	0.12 ± 0.05
Ensemble	0.15 ± 0.06	0.14 ± 0.06	0.13 ± 0.06	0.12 ± 0.06	0.12 ± 0.05

3.1   Ensembling Plain and Adversarially Trained DNNs

We found that the plain model achieved good standard and balanced accuracy for classifying DR from fundus images (Table 1), but with comparably low robust accuracy (see Sect. 2.5). In contrast, the robust classifier achieved high robust accuracy, but suffered a large drop in accuracy of more than 10–20%. Interestingly, and in line with the literature [10,23], the saliency maps of the robust model were much better than those of the plain model (Table 2, Fig. 1) for both of the tested saliency methods, Guided Backprop (GBP) and Integrated Gradients (IG). In fact, the saliency maps of the plain classifier were of rather low quality, focusing on less prominent disease-related regions of the image (Fig. 1).

We found that an ensemble of the plain and robust models (Eq. 2) combined their advantages: It had about equal standard and improved robust accuracy compared to the plain model (Table 1) and its saliency maps were as good as those of the robust model (Table 2, Fig. 1).

3.2   VCEs as an Alternative to Saliency Maps

We next explored VCEs (Eq. 3) as an alternative for explaining classifier decisions. The properties of the VCEs depend on the chosen model for the perturbation, which in this paper was always an l_p-ball, and the perturbation budget in form of the radius of l_p-ball. Small values of p close to one lead to sparse changes whereas for larger p one can realize much more outspread changes affecting larger parts of the image. As discussed in Sect. 2.4 we chose $l_{1.5}$-VCEs of radius $\epsilon = 30$ as they produced the best quality of T-VSMs.

We found that the robust model and the ensemble allowed for the computation of realistic VCE (Eq. 3, Fig. 1). T-VSMs (see Sect. 2.4) also provided good explanations for the classifiers' decision (Table 2), highlighting exudates and haemorrhages. In contrast, the VCE of the plain model was not very meaningful as its main changes were only vaguely related to the diseased regions.

3.3   Sparsity Versus Realism of VCEs

We then analyzed the effect of different perturbation models in terms of different l_p-balls (Fig. 2). We first studied the VCEs for enhancing the correct decision for a DR image. We found that the changes of $l_{1.5}$-perturbation model were

Orig.(GT:DR)	$l_{1.5}$-VCE, $\epsilon=30$	l_2-VCE, $\epsilon=6$	l_4-VCE, $\epsilon=0.2$
DR:0.97	→DR: 1.00	→DR: 1.00	→DR: 1.00

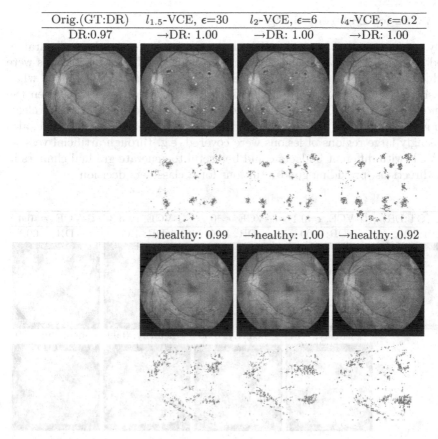

Fig. 2. VCEs for the ensemble with varying degree of sparsity: $p \in \{1.5, 2, 4\}$. For a correctly classified DR image, we show VCEs when transformed further into the DR or the healthy class. Below VCEs, T-VSMs are shown. The VCE radius was adapted to the sparsity condition. In addition, the confidence of the classifier is reported above the image.

sparser and thus looked more cartoon-like than for l_4. The VCEs of the l_4 model appeared much more natural although they even introduced new diseased regions not present in the original image. Thus the classifier seems to have picked up certain disease signs very well and can integrate even new disease patterns in a natural fashion into fundus images. We next studied the VCE for changing the decision of the classifier to 'no DR'. Here, all l_p-perturbation models attempted to "smooth out" the main lesions as well as the exudates. This provides complementary evidence that the classifier picked up the right disease signal in the data. Note that the artefact around the optic nerve was not changed in the VCE, showing that the classifier has correctly identified it as a feature which is not discriminatory for the disease decision. Not all VCEs, however, provided by our method are perfectly realistic: for example, the algorithm often tried to cover lesions with vessels when creating a VCE turning a diseased image into a healthy one. Further failure cases are discussed in Appendix A.

3.4 VCEs for Different Budgets

Finally, we investigated how the VCEs changed with increasing budget parameterized with ϵ (Fig. 3). We found that an increasing number of new lesions were introduced for both the sparse $l_{1.5}$-VCE as well as the realistic l_4-VCE, when increasing the budget for more DR evidence. Here, the difference between the two models—that l_4-VCEs appeared more realistic—became even more clear. When generating VCEs for turning the diseased image into an healthy one, also increasingly large regions of lesions were covered, e.g. through artificial vessels. Such VCE with different budgets could be useful to generate gradual changes in either directions, providing good intuitions for a classifiers decision.

Orig.(GT:DR)	l_4-VCE, ϵ=0.1	l_4-VCE, ϵ=0.2	l_4-VCE, ϵ=0.3	l_4-VCE, ϵ=0.4
DR:0.95	→DR: 1.00	→DR: 1.00	→DR: 1.00	→DR: 1.00

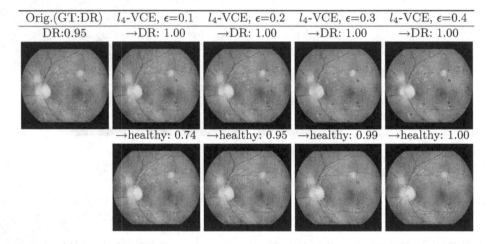

| | →healthy: 0.74 | →healthy: 0.95 | →healthy: 0.99 | →healthy: 1.00 |

Fig. 3. VCEs show increasingly strong modification for different radii. For one correctly classified DR image, we show for the ensemble the l_4-VCEs for $\epsilon \in \{0.1, 0.2, 0.3, 0.4\}$ when transforming into the DR and healthy class, respectively.

4   Discussion

We showed that the ensemble of plain and robust models can preserve accuracy of plain models, yet provide better visual explanations. In agreement with the literature [10,23], the resulting saliency maps highlight clinically relevant lesions more reliably. Therefore, the explanations obtained for diseased images are often satisfying, while those for healthy images are less so—showing the absence of lesions is difficult in this framework. The ensemble model allowed us to compute also realistic VCEs [6], to yield interpretable explanations of the classifier's decision, pinpointing the features in the image the classifier picks up on.

In related work, iterative augmentation of saliency maps has been used to improve saliency-based visual explanations [13]. Also, VCEs have been generated using GANs [20] (no models/code is available) but the advantage of our VCE is that they depend only on the classifier and thus there is no danger that the prior of the GAN "hides" undesired behavior of the classifier. Finally, models interpretable-by-design such as BagNets [18] have been advocated for medical imaging tasks [27]. As many high-performing DNNs do not fall into this category, we view our work as complementary.

We believe realistic VCEs and derived T-VSMs will be a useful tool to better understand the behavior of DNN-based classifiers in medical imaging, in particular when gradually morphing an image from one class to the other which is the main complementary strength of VCEs compared to saliency maps. As the sparseness and the degree of changes allowed can be precisely controlled, it is straightforward to yield more or less natural VCEs. Even extreme and therefore less natural VCEs can be useful, as they provide a "cartoon" version of what the classifier believes the disease looks like.

Acknowledgement. We acknowledge support by the German Ministry of Science and Education (BMBF, 01GQ1601 and 01IS18039A) and the German Science Foundation (BE5601/8-1 and EXC 2064, project number 390727645). The authors thank the International Max Planck Research School for Intelligent Systems (IMPRS-IS) for supporting I.I.

References

1. Kaggle competition on diabetic retinopathy detection (2015). https://www.kaggle.com/c/diabetic-retinopathy-detection/data. Accessed 02 Feb 2022
2. Arun, N., et al.: Assessing the trustworthiness of saliency maps for localizing abnormalities in medical imaging. Radiol. Artif. Intell. **3**(6), e200267 (2021)
3. Augustin, M., Meinke, A., Hein, M.: Adversarial robustness on in- and out-distribution improves explainability. In: Vedaldi, A., Bischof, H., Brox, T., Frahm, J.-M. (eds.) ECCV 2020. LNCS, vol. 12371, pp. 228–245. Springer, Cham (2020). https://doi.org/10.1007/978-3-030-58574-7_14
4. Ayhan, M.S., Kühlewein, L., Aliyeva, G., Inhoffen, W., Ziemssen, F., Berens, P.: Expert-validated estimation of diagnostic uncertainty for deep neural networks in diabetic retinopathy detection. Med. Image Anal. **64**, 101724 (2020)
5. Ayhan, M.S., et al.: Clinical validation of saliency maps for understanding deep neural networks in ophthalmology. Med. Image Anal. **77**, 102364 (2022)
6. Boreiko, V., Augustin, M., Croce, F., Berens, P., Hein, M.: Sparse visual counterfactual explanations in image space. arXiv preprint arXiv:2205.07972 (2022)
7. Croce, F., Hein, M.: Reliable evaluation of adversarial robustness with an ensemble of diverse parameter-free attacks. In: ICML (2020)
8. Croce, F., Hein, M.: Mind the box: l_1-APGD for sparse adversarial attacks on image classifiers. In: ICML (2021)
9. Decencière, E., et al.: Feedback on a publicly distributed database: the Messidor database. Image Anal. Stereol. **33**(3), 231–234 (2014). https://doi.org/10.5566/ias.1155
10. Etmann, C., Lunz, S., Maass, P., Schönlieb, C.B.: On the connection between adversarial robustness and saliency map interpretability. In: ICML (2019)
11. Geirhos, R., Rubisch, P., Michaelis, C., Bethge, M., Wichmann, F.A., Brendel, W.: ImageNet-trained CNNs are biased towards texture; increasing shape bias improves accuracy and robustness. In: ICLR (2019)

12. Geirhos, R., et al.: Shortcut learning in deep neural networks. Nat. Mach. Intell. **2**(11), 665–673 (2020)
13. González-Gonzalo, C., Liefers, B., van Ginneken, B., Sánchez, C.I.: Iterative augmentation of visual evidence for weakly-supervised lesion localization in deep interpretability frameworks. IEEE Trans. Med. Imaging (2019)
14. González-Gonzalo, C., et al.: Trustworthy AI: closing the gap between development and integration of AI systems in ophthalmic practice. Prog. Retinal Eye Res., 101034 (2021)
15. Grote, T., Berens, P.: On the ethics of algorithmic decision-making in healthcare. J. Med. Ethics **46**(3), 205–211 (2020)
16. Guo, C., Pleiss, G., Sun, Y., Weinberger, K.Q.: On calibration of modern neural networks. In: ICML (2017)
17. He, K., Zhang, X., Ren, S., Sun, J.: Deep residual learning for image recognition. In: CVPR. pp. 770–778 (2016)
18. Ilanchezian, I., Kobak, D., Faber, H., Ziemssen, F., Berens, P., Ayhan, M.S.: Interpretable gender classification from retinal fundus images using BagNets. In: de Bruijne, M., et al. (eds.) MICCAI 2021. LNCS, vol. 12903, pp. 477–487. Springer, Cham (2021). https://doi.org/10.1007/978-3-030-87199-4_45
19. Jaggi, M.: Revisiting Frank-Wolfe: projection-free sparse convex optimization. In: ICML (2013)
20. Lang, O., et al.: Explaining in style: training a GAN to explain a classifier in stylespace. arXiv preprint arXiv:2104.13369 (2021)
21. Liu, X., et al.: A comparison of deep learning performance against health-care professionals in detecting diseases from medical imaging: a systematic review and meta-analysis. Lancet Digit. Health **1**(6), e271–e297 (2019)
22. Madry, A., Makelov, A., Schmidt, L., Tsipras, D., Vladu, A.: Towards deep learning models resistant to adversarial attacks. In: ICLR (2018)
23. Margeloiu, A., Simidjievski, N., Jamnik, M., Weller, A.: Improving interpretability in medical imaging diagnosis using adversarial training. arXiv preprint arXiv:2012.01166 (2020)
24. Moraru, V.: An algorithm for solving quadratic programming problems. Comput. Sci. J. Moldova (1997)
25. Ozbulak, U.: PyTorch CNN visualizations. https://github.com/utkuozbulak/pytorch-cnn-visualizations (2019)
26. Porwal, P., et al.: Indian diabetic retinopathy image dataset (IDRiD): a database for diabetic retinopathy screening research. Data **3**(3), 25 (2018)
27. Rudin, C.: Stop explaining black box machine learning models for high stakes decisions and use interpretable models instead. Nat. Mach. Intell. **1**(5), 206–215 (2019)
28. Saporta, A., et al.: Deep learning saliency maps do not accurately highlight diagnostically relevant regions for medical image interpretation. medRxiv (2021)
29. Springenberg, J.T., Dosovitskiy, A., Brox, T., Riedmiller, M.: Striving for simplicity: the all convolutional net. In: ICLR (Workshop Track) (2014)
30. Sundararajan, M., Taly, A., Yan, Q.: Axiomatic attribution for deep networks. In: ICML (2017)
31. Tan, M., Le, Q.: EfficientNet: rethinking model scaling for convolutional neural networks. In: ICML (2019)
32. Tsipras, D., Santurkar, S., Engstrom, L., Turner, A., Madry, A.: Robustness may be at odds with accuracy. In: ICLR (2019)

33. Van Craenendonck, T., Elen, B., Gerrits, N., De Boever, P.: Systematic comparison of heatmapping techniques in deep learning in the context of diabetic retinopathy lesion detection. Transl. Vis. Sci. Technol. 9(2), 64–64 (2020). https://doi.org/10.1167/tvst.9.2.64

34. Younis, N., Broadbent, D.M., Vora, J.P., Harding, S.P.: Incidence of sight-threatening retinopathy in patients with type 2 diabetes in the liverpool diabetic eye study: a cohort study. Lancet 361(9353), 195–200 (2003)

35. Zhang, H., Yu, Y., Jiao, J., Xing, E.P., Ghaoui, L.E., Jordan, M.I.: Theoretically principled trade-off between robustness and accuracy. In: ICML (2019)

36. Zuiderveld, K.: Contrast limited adaptive histogram equalization. Graph. Gems, 474–485 (1994)

Multidimensional Hypergraph on Delineated Retinal Features for Pathological Myopia Task

Bilha Githinji[1], Lei Shao[2], Lin An[1], Hao Zhang[1], Fang Li[1], Li Dong[2], Lan Ma[1], Yuhan Dong[1], Yongbing Zhang[1], Wen B. Wei[2], and Peiwu Qin[1(✉)]

[1] Tsinghua Shenzhen International Graduate School, Shenzhen, China
pwqin@sz.tsinghua.edu.cn
[2] Beijing Tongren Hospital, Beijing, China

Abstract. Vision-threatening pathological myopia presents several lesions affecting various retinal anatomical structures. Detection approaches, however, either focus on one anatomical feature or are not intentional. This study uses hypergraph learning to modulate delineated retinal anatomical features from fundus images and capitalize on hidden associations between them. Experiments are conducted to assess prediction performance when targeting a particular anatomical trait versus using a mixture of select anatomical features, and in comparison to a ResNet34-based convolutional neural network classifier. Results indicate better prediction with hypergraph learning on a mix of the delineated features (F1 score 89.75%, AUC score 95.39%). A choroid tessellation segmentation method is also included.

Keywords: Multidimensional hypergraph · Pathological myopia · Fundus

1 Introduction

It is estimated that by 2050 about 50% of the world population will have myopia and 10% will have high myopia compared to 23% and 3% respectively in the year 2000; there is a significant increase in prevalence globally and a need for prevention and management of vision-threatening myopia conditions such as pathological myopia (PM) [8]. PM exhibits structural changes in the posterior segment of the eye, and progressive degeneration of the choroid and retinal pigment epithelium (RPE) [12]. A primary sign of the initial changes associated with PM and its subsequent progression is a tessellated fundus, which is a fundus with visible choroidal vessels due to thinning of the RPE [12,18]. Tessellation is more common at the posterior pole, which includes the optic nerve and macula

Supplementary Information The online version contains supplementary material available at https://doi.org/10.1007/978-3-031-16434-7_53.

regions [15]. Other observable changes include posterior staphyloma, optic disc changes (tilting, parapapillary atrophy (PPA)), and bright lesions like lacquer cracks. The resulting range of PM-associated retinal and choroidal lesions are referred to as myopic maculopathy and are often clinically diagnosed via examination of fundus photographs. Limited contrast, quality concerns and narrow optical angle of view in fundus imaging, however, make clinical use laborious and challenging [7].

While several studies apply machine learning and deep learning methods on fundus images, PM-specific studies are relatively fewer, suffering from small datasets, and fundus-based exploration of the choroid layer is low [10]. Some of the PM studies take a targeted approach and focus on elements of the optic nerve head region [4,11], while the others do not target any particular retinal anatomical feature [2,3,21]. One study integrates fundus image data with clinical data and genotyping data to set up a multimodal learning problem using machine learning techniques [21]. Furthermore, where deep learning techniques are employed, the choice is convolutional neural networks (CNNs), with increasing depth and need for larger datasets [2–4]. Unlike CNNs, graph learning does not impose structure on the data, and presents the opportunity to exploit higher-order correlations and leverage hidden topological information more efficiently [16,17,20].

This study utilizes a unique PM dataset from a large population study to identify early or mild PM using fundus images. To take advantage of the anatomical diversity in retinal fundus images, several prominent retinal structures (as opposed to targeting one structure) are extracted and multidimensional hypergraph learning is employed to leverage potential hidden associations. Blood vessels, general optic nerve region (optic disc, optic cup, surrounding atrophies), bright regions, and choroid tessellation are considered. Specific contributions are, 1) We implement a pipeline that employs multidimensional hypergraph learning to learn higher-order associations and modulate delineated retinal features, 2) Through comparison experiments, we demonstrate that this approach has the potential to improve prediction performance, 3) Additionally, given the limited literature on the segmentation of choroidal structures on fundus images, we share an intensity-thresholding approach for extracting choroid tubular patterns.

2   Method

We hypothesize that learning on a set of delineated retinal anatomical features, as distinct dimensions, may enhance prediction results as opposed to targeting one retinal structure or not targeting at all. We use hypergraph learning to capitalize on any hidden relationships between the different retinal features and dynamically modulate their interaction. Figure 3 shows our proposed pipeline.

2.1   Feature Extraction

Since the goal is to separate key anatomical features into distinct components so that we can dynamically drive their interaction for the task at hand, any

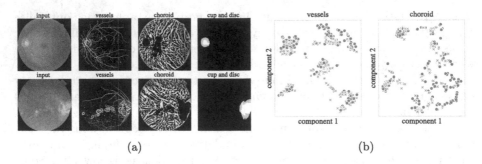

(a)   (b)

Fig. 1. a) illustrates some of the extracted features while figure b) shows t-SNE results for blood vessels and choroid segmentation (circles represent low expert PM grading, crosses represent high PM grading).

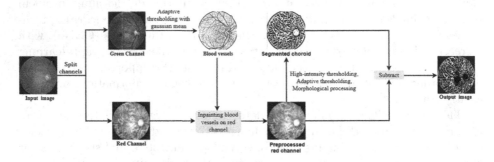

Fig. 2. Choroid segmentation process.

reasonable feature extraction method of choice should suffice. Additionally, a mix of machine learning and deep learning extraction methods may be used as desired or for different anatomical features. Traditional machine learning methods have the added advantage of reduced computational complexity. Visual inspection and statistical analysis may be used to review extracted samples. Figure 1 illustrates some of the extracted retinal features, which are obtained from a mix of machine learning and deep learning segmentation methods. Additionally, t-SNE plots do not highlight strong PM-level associations for any particular feature.

Furthermore, the extracted features are compacted to save on computational resources since graph generation and graph learning may operate on the entire dataset simultaneously. Consequently, we use a combination of deep learning and statistical features to encode the input images and retain as much discriminative capacity as possible. We first encode the input images using a ResNet34 [6] CNN encoder. The CNN embeddings are then used to generate statistical features. A disadvantage of this strategy, however, is the loss of interpretability.

Method for Extracting Choroidal Tubular Structures. Choroid tessellation is a critical indicator of the early development of PM [12]. To extract choroid tessellation and tubular structures, an intensity-based thresholding technique is applied. The general approach is to apply intensity thresholding on a preprocessed version of the red color channel where choroidal details are prominent [9]. We improve on the prior method by 1) Using a dehazing [1] step to enhance illumination, particularly because of cataracts and other conditions that alter corneal opacity, 2) Eliminating bright regions through additional intensity thresholding, and 3) Morphological post-processing to clean up any artifacts from the previous steps. Figure 2 is a schematic flow and example results are shown in Fig. 1. Additional example results are included in the supplementary material. Moreover, at the choroid tessellation delineation step, an edge-based technique such as multi-scale hessian may be employed in place of intensity thresholding and this is also included in the code, which will be publicly released via Github.

2.2 Hypergraph Learning

A hypergraph $G = (V, E, W)$ is a set of vertices V and a set of hyperedges E with weights W, where vertices represent nodes or entities and hyperedges represent relationships or correlations between those nodes. In this case, we model each fundus image (or its extracted features) as a node and the association between images with similar retinal characteristics as the edges, where the similarity score, by Euclidean distance, is the edge weight. The resulting graph and edge weights are estimated using k-NN and k-Means distance-based methods when a vertex is connected to many other vertices. We adopt inductive learning using the graph Laplacian (denoted by Δ) to predict the PM label. The objective is to estimate a matrix M that projects the input features X onto the label space F, where $F = X^T M$. The associated hypergraph objective function is shown in Eq. (1), where $\mathcal{R}_{emp}(M)$ is the empirical loss term, $\Phi(M)$ is a tunable regularization term to avoid over-fitting and $\Omega(M)$ is the Laplacian-based graph smoothing term, which can be solved as $tr(M^T X \Delta X^T M)$ [5]. The resulting multidimensional setup is as per Eq. (2) where i indexes the graph for each dimension, and the label prediction task is concurrently learned with an optimal set of m mixture weights, such that $\sum_{i=1}^{m} \alpha_i = 1$. Prediction on a new instance v is then achieved by $F(v) = \sum_{i=1}^{m} \alpha_i X^i(v)^T M_i$.

$$argmin_F \Psi(M) = \lambda \, \mathcal{R}_{emp}(M) + \eta \, \Phi(M) + \Omega(M) \tag{1}$$

$$argmin_F \Psi(M, \alpha) = \sum_{i=1}^{m} \alpha_i \{ \Omega(M_i) + \lambda \, \mathcal{R}_{emp}(M_i) + \eta \, \Phi(M_i) \} + \mu \sum_{i=1}^{m} \alpha_i^2$$

$$s.t. \sum_{i=1}^{m} \alpha_i = 1 \tag{2}$$

Loss Function. We set the empirical loss to the sum of Frobenius norm and L1 norm, and apply Lasso regularization on the projection matrix M (Φ is Lasso). The resulting empirical loss term for each modality graph is as per Eq. (3). The

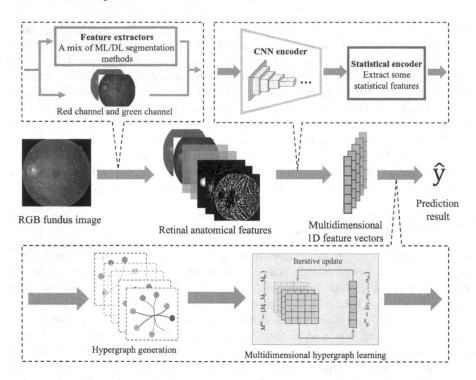

Fig. 3. Proposed multidimensional hypergraph learning on a set of delineated retinal anatomical features. Anatomical channels are preferred over RGB color channels.

combination of Frobenius norm and L1 norm is empirically found to have less performance variability across randomized samples, given our small dataset.

$$\mathcal{R}_{emp}(M_i) = \|F_i - Y\|_{frob} + \|F_i - Y\|_1 \tag{3}$$

3   Experiments

3.1   Dataset

A total of 449 fundus images (from 73 participants) are available from a longitudinal population study for PM progression, which contained 4439 adult participants older than 40 years [19]. These selected images exhibited high myopia (refractive error ≤ -6.0 diopters, axial length ≥ 26.5 mm) at both the baseline and end-line of the population study. The study was approved according to the Declaration of Helsinki and all participants gave written informed consent. Two expert measurements for the degree of fundus tessellation are present - a macula-centered measure and an optic disc-centered measure. The population study graded PM almost exclusively using the fundus photographs. A trained examiner obtained the measurements under the regular supervision of a panel of two experienced ophthalmologists. On average, each participant has about three images per year from a combination of right eye and/or left eye images for macula and/or disc-centered measurements. All the images are 45° color fundus photographs. Additionally, Drishti-GS1 dataset [14], a public dataset for validation of optic disc and optic cup segmentation, is used to train a BGA-Net model [13] for optic cup and disc regions extraction.

3.2 Inputs Setup

An observation is defined as a fundus image for a given participant, for the left or right eye, and for the macula or disc centered assessment. 396 of the 449 fundus images have an associated ground truth measurement. The expert-assessed degree of fundus tessellation (the ground truth metric) ranges from 0 to 3.5. We group the degree of fundus tessellation into 1) Low tessellation ($0 \leq y \leq 1.725$) and 2) High tessellation ($1.725 < y \leq 3.5$). A distribution plot is included in the supplementary material.

Feature Extraction. Two catch-all dimensions are extracted, one for retinal surface structures (green color channel) and one for structures that are just below the retinal surface (red color channel). Choroid tessellation, blood vessels, high-intensity regions, optic disc and optic cup regions (and surrounding atrophies) are also segmented. The retrieved features are then encoded and compacted using a ResNet34 encoder and statistical methods, yielding a 1088 long 1D vector for each image of size 256×256. The statistical features include gray-level co-occurrence matrix (GLCM) and descriptive statistics (mean, median, standard deviation). All images are enhanced and normalized using the mean and standard deviation of each cohort to account for equipment differences. Resolution is also reduced to 128×128 when training on the comparison CNN model. Note that, the same pre-trained CNN encoder (ResNet34 in this case) is used in the baseline model, allowing us to focus on the modulation aspect irrespective of the CNN encoding scheme.

Comparison Groups. We identify three comparison groups - 1) Using the RGB fundus images as-is, 2) Targeted mode, where only the choroid tessellation segmentation image is used, and 3) Retinal mix mode, where a combination of retinal structures is employed as distinct channels or dimensions.

3.3 Hypergraph Learning and Evaluation

Two hypergraph configurations are defined based on the method of estimating the hypergraph from the input fundus images. Distance-based k-nn and k-means hypergraph estimation methods are defined for when a vertex is connected to many other vertices. Through earlier exploration, we identify a neighborhood size of 128 for the k-nn method and 4 clusters for the k-means method. Moreover, the hypergraph parameters in Eq. (2) are determined for the dataset as $\lambda = 1$,

$\eta = 100$, $\mu = .5$ when learning on a single dimension, and $\mu = 1$ for multiple dimensions case.

Model Implementation and Evaluation. We implement using PyTorch and a python hypergraph learning toolkit [5]. The baseline CNN model consists of a ResNet34 [6] encoder pre-trained on imagenet data, three fully connected layers with ReLU activation, and an output linear layer. This CNN model is trained on the PM dataset using cross-entropy loss and Adam optimizer for up to 50 iterations. We adopt F1 score as the primary metric for assessing the prediction accuracy of the models. In addition, the area under the ROC (receiver operator curve) or AUC score is available. The dataset is randomly split into 80% training and 20% testing sets, and 100 experiment runs are conducted for each model configuration.

3.4   Results

Table 1 summarizes the prediction results and visualized comparisons are shown in Fig. 4. Hypergraph learning on a mixture of retinal structures, and using k-nn graph estimation approach, achieves a prediction accuracy of 89.75%. This is the highest F1 score observed and it is found to be statistically different from using a CNN on the RGB images directly (p-value $< 10^{-1}$) or hypergraph learning on the targeted choroidal tessellation (p-value $< 10^{-3}$). P-value tables are provided in the supplementary material.

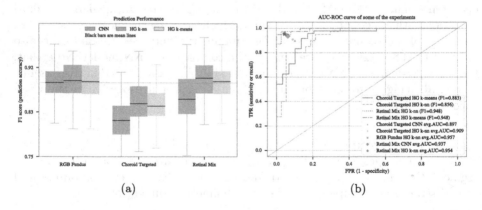

(a)   (b)

Fig. 4. Model performance. a) compares prediction accuracy (F1 score) for different models on the three input cases. b) is a plot of the AUC-ROC curves for some of the iterations and with the average AUC scores for the comparison groups and models marked on it.

Training the k-nn hypergraph on the encoded RGB images has similar performance to applying the CNN model on the RGB images (p-value $> 10^{-1}$) indicating a comparable baseline. Unlike the hypergraph, the CNN model has

Table 1. Model performance results for different input comparison groups and learning models.

	Model	F1-score	AUC score	Precision	Sensitivity
RGB	CNN	0.8887 ±0.03		0.8931 ±0.03	0.8888 ±0.03
	HG k-means	0.8903 ±0.03	0.9620 ±0.02	0.8969 ±0.03	0.8911 ±0.03
	HG k-nn	**0.8921** ±0.03	0.9571 ±0.02	0.8988 ±0.03	0.8930 ±0.03
Choroid	CNN	0.8177 ±0.04	0.8975 ±0.04	0.8239 ±0.04	0.8183 ±0.04
	HG k-means	0.8448 ±0.04	0.9091 ±0.04	0.8521 ±0.04	0.8463 ±0.04
	HG k-nn	**0.8493** ±0.04	0.9093 ±0.04	0.8584 ±0.04	0.8512 ±0.04
Retinal mix	CNN	0.8580 ±0.06	0.9372 ±0.03	0.8663 ±0.04	0.8593 ±0.05
	HG k-means	0.8910 ±0.03	0.9527 ±0.03	0.8975 ±0.03	0.8920 ±0.03
	HG k-nn	**0.8975** ±0.04	0.9539 ±0.03	0.9065 ±0.03	0.8989 ±0.04

The measure of variability is standard deviation.

a significant drop in performance, by 3.07% (p-value $< 10^{-3}$), when trained on the retinal mix of features. The multimodal hypergraph setup appears to better leverage associations between the multiple channels or dimensions. Additionally, while the hypergraph has a numerically higher F1 score on the retinal mix of features, this is not statistically different from running it on the RGB images directly (p-value $> 10^{-1}$). This suggests that, the multimodal hypergraph is more amenable to the idea of combining selected features or offline generated segmentation results, in place of color fundus images, in a pipeline as presented here and when using fundus images for PM.

Regarding targeting a particular retinal anatomical structure, both CNN and hypergraph models experience a drop in performance when applied to the choroid tessellation segmentation. However, the best performing choroid targeting model (hypergraph learning with k-nn graph estimation) achieves an F1 score of 84.93% and an AUC score of 90.93%. This positive performance may imply that 1) The models need more information, which the hypergraph demonstrates by increasing prediction performance by 4.82% (p-value $< 10^{-3}$) with the retinal mix, and 2) The segmentation quality of the choroid tessellation segmentation method is reasonably associated with PM.

Overall, dynamically modulating multiple retinal features using a multi-dimensional hypergraph model seems to best exploit associations between the features when identifying early PM in tessellated fundus images. In effect, this is akin to replacing the dense layers (classifier-head) of a CNN model, which simply concatenate the encoded features, with a multi-dimensional hypergraph classifier-head to better exploit any higher-order correlations in the data.

An underlying limitation of this work is the small dataset. In addition, the population study from which the dataset is collected targeted mature adults, with an inclusion criterion of 40 years or older, further impacting generalizability. Furthermore, an area of future work is building in interpretability in an end-to-end manner.

4   Conclusion

In this study, we submit a method for extracting choroid tessellation and tubular patterns from fundus images. This is of potential importance given the difficulty of manually examining fundus images for choroid-related characteristics and the seeming scarcity of studies focusing on their extraction from fundus images. In addition, we present an approach for predicting the degree of PM that utilizes hypergraph learning to capitalize on and modulate the diverse retinal anatomical structures in fundus images. Multidimensional hypergraph learning using k-nn graph generation method achieves an F1-score of 89.75% (AUC score of 95.39%), which is statistically different from using a ResNet34-based classifier on the RGB images directly.

Acknowledgements. This work was supported in part by Science, Technology, Innovation Commission of Shenzhen Municipality (JSGG20191129110812708; JSGG 20200225150707332; WDZC20200820173710001; JCYJ20190809180003689), National Natural Science Foundation of China (31970752), Shenzhen Bay Laboratory Open Funding (SZBL2020090501004), China Postdoctoral Science Foundation (2020M680023), and General Administration of Customs of the People's Republic of China (2021HK007).

References

1. Cai, B., Xu, X., Jia, K., Qing, C., Tao, D.: DehazeNet: an end-to-end system for single image haze removal. IEEE Trans. Image Process. **25**(11), 5187–5198 (2016). https://doi.org/10.1109/TIP.2016.2598681
2. Cen, L.P., et al.: Automatic detection of 39 fundus diseases and conditions in retinal photographs using deep neural networks. Nat. Commun. **12**(1), 4828 (2021). https://doi.org/10.1038/s41467-021-25138-w, https://www.nature.com/articles/s41467-021-25138-w
3. Dai, S., Chen, L., Lei, T., Zhou, C., Wen, Y.: Automatic detection of pathological myopia and high myopia on fundus images. In: 2020 IEEE International Conference on Multimedia and Expo (ICME), London, United Kingdom, pp. 1–6. IEEE, July 2020. https://doi.org/10.1109/ICME46284.2020.9102787, https://ieeexplore.ieee.org/document/9102787/
4. Devda, J., Eswari, R.: Pathological myopia image analysis using deep learning. Procedia Comput. Sci. **165**, 239–244 (2019). https://doi.org/10.1016/j.procs.2020.01.084. https://linkinghub.elsevier.com/retrieve/pii/S1877050920300922
5. Gao, Y., Zhang, Z., Lin, H., Zhao, X., Du, S., Zou, C.: Hypergraph learning: methods and practices. IEEE Trans. Pattern Anal. Mach. Intell. **44**, 2548–2566 (2020). https://doi.org/10.1109/TPAMI.2020.3039374
6. He, K., Zhang, X., Ren, S., Sun, J.: Deep residual learning for image recognition. CoRR abs/1512.03385 (2015). http://arxiv.org/abs/1512.03385
7. Hoang, Q.V., Chua, J., Ang, M., Schmetterer, L.: Imaging in myopia. In: Ang, M., Wong, T.Y. (eds.) Updates on Myopia, pp. 219–239. Springer, Singapore (2020). https://doi.org/10.1007/978-981-13-8491-2_10
8. Holden, B.A., et al.: Global prevalence of myopia and high myopia and temporal trends from 2000 through 2050. Ophthalmology **123**(5), 1036–1042 (2016). https://doi.org/10.1016/j.ophtha.2016.01.006

9. Komuku, Y., et al.: Choroidal thickness estimation from colour fundus photographs by adaptive binarisation and deep learning, according to central serous chorioretinopathy status. Sci. Rep. **10**(1), 5640 (2020). https://doi.org/10.1038/s41598-020-62347-7, https://www.nature.com/articles/s41598-020-62347-7

10. Li, T., et al.: Applications of deep learning in fundus images: a review. Med. Image Anal. **69**, 101971 (2021). https://doi.org/10.1016/j.media.2021.101971, https://www.sciencedirect.com/science/article/pii/S1361841521000177

11. Liu, J., et al.: Detection of pathological myopia by PAMELA with texture-based features through an SVM approach. J. Healthc. Eng. **1**(1), 1–12 (2010). https://doi.org/10.1260/2040-2295.1.1.1, http://www.hindawi.com/journals/jhe/2010/657574/

12. Ohno-Matsui, K., et al.: META-analysis for pathologic myopia (META-PM) study group: international photographic classification and grading system for myopic maculopathy. Am. J. Ophthalmol. **159**(5), 877.e7–883.e7 (2015). https://doi.org/10.1016/j.ajo.2015.01.022

13. Sivaswamy, J., Chakravarty, A., Joshi, G.D., Syed, T.A.: A comprehensive retinal image dataset for the assessment of glaucoma from the optic nerve head analysis. JSM Biomed. Imaging Data Papers **2**, 1004 (2015). https://www.semanticscholar.org/paper/A-Comprehensive-Retinal-Image-Dataset-for-the-of-Sivaswamy-Chakravarty/04b45aeaa59a19340652ad28d650429054d3e7fd

14. Sivaswamy, J., Krishnadas, S.R., Datt Joshi, G., Jain, M., Syed Tabish, A.U.: Drishti-GS: retinal image dataset for optic nerve head (ONH) segmentation. In: 2014 IEEE 11th International Symposium on Biomedical Imaging (ISBI), pp. 53–56 (2014). https://doi.org/10.1109/ISBI.2014.6867807

15. Terasaki, H., et al.: Location of tessellations in ocular fundus and their associations with optic disc tilt, optic disc area, and axial length in young healthy eyes. PLOS ONE **11**(6), e0156842 (2016). https://doi.org/10.1371/journal.pone.0156842, https://dx.plos.org/10.1371/journal.pone.0156842

16. Wolf, M.M., Klinvex, A.M., Dunlavy, D.M.: Advantages to modeling relational data using hypergraphs versus graphs. In: 2016 IEEE High Performance Extreme Computing Conference (HPEC), pp. 1–7, September 2016. https://doi.org/10.1109/HPEC.2016.7761624

17. Xia, F., et al.: Graph learning: a survey. IEEE Trans. Artif. Intell. **2**(2), 109–127 (2021). https://doi.org/10.1109/TAI.2021.3076021

18. Yan, Y.N., Wang, Y.X., Xu, L., Xu, J., Wei, W.B., Jonas, J.B.: Fundus tessellation: prevalence and associated factors: the Beijing eye study 2011. Ophthalmology **122**(9), 1873–1880 (2015). https://doi.org/10.1016/j.ophtha.2015.05.031

19. Yan, Y.N., et al.: Ten-year progression of myopic maculopathy: the Beijing eye study 2001–2011. Ophthalmology **125**(8), 1253–1263 (2018). https://doi.org/10.1016/j.ophtha.2018.01.035

20. Zhang, X.M., Liang, L., Liu, L., Tang, M.J.: Graph neural networks and their current applications in bioinformatics. Front. Genet. **12**, 1073 (2021). https://doi.org/10.3389/fgene.2021.690049, https://www.frontiersin.org/article/10.3389/fgene.2021.690049

21. Zhang, Z., et al.: Automatic diagnosis of pathological myopia from heterogeneous biomedical data. PLOS ONE **8**(6), e65736 (2013). https://doi.org/10.1371/journal.pone.0065736, https://dx.plos.org/10.1371/journal.pone.0065736

Unsupervised Lesion-Aware Transfer Learning for Diabetic Retinopathy Grading in Ultra-Wide-Field Fundus Photography

Yanmiao Bai[1], Jinkui Hao[1], Huazhu Fu[3], Yan Hu[4], Xinting Ge[5], Jiang Liu[4], Yitian Zhao[1,2(✉)], and Jiong Zhang[1,2(✉)]

[1] Cixi Institute of Biomedical Engineering, Ningbo Institute of Materials Technology and Engineering, Chinese Academy of Sciences, Ningbo, China
{yitian.zhao,zhangjiong}@nimte.ac.cn
[2] Affiliated Ningbo Eye Hospital of Wenzhou Medical University, Ningbo, China
[3] Institute of High Performance Computing, A*STAR, Singapore, Singapore
[4] Southern University of Science and Technology, Shenzhen, China
[5] School of Information Science and Engineering, Shandong Normal University, Jinan, China

Abstract. Ultra-wide-field (UWF) fundus photography is a new imaging technique with providing a broader field of view images, and it has become a popular and effective tool for the screening and diagnosis for many eye diseases, such as diabetic retinopathy (DR). However, it is practically challenging to train a robust deep learning model for DR grading in UWF images, due to the limited scale of data and manual annotations. By contrast, we may find large-scale high-quality regular color fundus photography datasets in the research community, with either image-level or pixel-level annotation. In consequence, we propose an **Unsupervised Lesion-aware TRA**nsfer learning framework (ULTRA) for DR grading in UWF images, by leveraging a large amount of publicly well-annotated regular color fundus images. Inspired by the clinical identification of DR severity, i.e., the decision making process of ophthalmologists based on the type and number of associated lesions, we design an adversarial lesion map generator to provide the auxiliary lesion information for DR grading. A Lesion External Attention Module (LEAM) is introduced to integrate the lesion feature into the model, allowing a relative explainable DR grading. Extensive experimental results show the proposed method is superior to the state-of-the-art methods.

Keywords: Unsupervised · UWF imaging · Diabetic retinopathy

Supplementary Information The online version contains supplementary material available at https://doi.org/10.1007/978-3-031-16434-7_54.

1   Introduction

Diabetic Retinopathy (DR) is a chronic complication of diabetes, and has been one of the major causes of visual impairment and blindness [1]. The severity of DR can be graded into five stages: normal, mild, moderate, severe non-proliferative and proliferative, according to international protocol [2]. The presence of peripheral retinal pathology, such as microaneurysms (MA), hemorrhages (HE), soft exudates (SE) and hard exudates (EX) is highly associated with the DR stage grading [3,4]. Timely identification of DR stages or retinal lesion detection is of great importance to reduce the risk of visual loss.

Recent years have witnessed the rapid development of methods for automated screening or grading severity of DR on Color Fundus Photography (CFP), with evidenced by extensive reviews [5–8]. Ultra-wide-field (UWF) fundus photography is a new imaging technique. Compared with the 30°–60° imaging range of regular color fundus imaging, UWF imaging covers 200° of the retina, allowing for a better detection of peripheral retinal pathology [3]. Recently, the deep learning models have been employed in UWF images, aim to detect central retinal vein occlusion [9], branch retinal vein occlusion [10] and rhegmatogenous retinal detachments [11], respectively.

Although these studies [12,13] have shown that UWF images have significant strength over the CFP images in the monitoring of these disease, it is relatively unexplored due to the limited dataset and annotations, thus only a few works have been developed for the automatic DR grading by using UWF images. For example, Nagasawa et al. [14] used the VGG-16 to detect proliferative diabetic retinopathy (PDR). Xie et al. [15] proposed a attention-based multi-disease classification network to distinguish DR from healthy control in UWF images. In contrast, there are a number of well-annotated and high-quality CFP datasets for DR grading purpose. For example, the EyePACS dataset [16] consists of 88,702 CFP with five labeled DR categories. The IDRID dataset [17] not only contains DR grading labels, but also provides pixel-level multi-lesion annotations.

Transfer learning was developed to tackle the domain-shift issue between the source and target domain, and has shown its capacity in the field of computer vision [18–20]. Therefore, it gives potential opportunity to train a robust UWF grading model by incorporating rich labeled CFP images. For instance, Ju et al. [13] proposed a method based on the modified cycle generative adversarial network (CycleGAN) to translate a large number of CFP images into UWF-style images, and trained a DR grading model with the synthetic and realistic UWF images. However, they treated image synthesis and DR diagnosis as two independent processes, and the accuracy of the diagnostic model depends on the quality of the synthetic images, which makes it difficult to transfer the diagnostic knowledge of the annotated CFP mages to the UWF images diagnostic model.

In addition, although remarkable results have been achieved by using deep learning with accuracy of $\geq 90.0\%$ for DR grading from CFP images [21,22], most existing learning-based methods are based on a end-to-end model, and lack the ability to explain the decision, a common issue that haunts deep learning community. To this end, it is ever imperative to develop an interpretable approach for DR grading, such as exploiting the lesion features.

In this paper, we propose an **U**nsupervised **L**esion-aware **TRA**nsfer learning framework (ULTRA) for DR grading in UWF images. We aim to leverage a large amount of well-annotated CFP images to train a more robust UWF grading model. The main contributions of this work are: 1) It is the first attempt to use unsupervised approach for DR grading in UWF images. 2) Considering the fact that the severity grading of DR is closely related to different lesion types, an adversarial lesion map generation module is proposed to provide multi-lesion features to improve the grading accuracy. 3) A lesion external attention module is proposed to embed fine lesion knowledge from CFP images into the UWF images grading model, to achieve a more accurate and interpretable result.

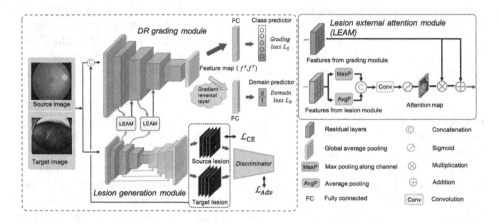

Fig. 1. Framework of the proposed method.

2   Methodology

The retina images from different datasets have various illuminations, we therefore adopt a image pre-processing method [23] to normalize the image and enhance the texture details. In addition, since UWF images are often obstructed by eyelids and eyelashes, we trained a U-net [24] to mask out such artifacts.

2.1   Overall Architecture

We aim to leverage the high-quality annotated CFP images to train a robust DR grading model for UWF images in an unsupervised manner. The main body of our framework is an unsupervised DR grading module with lesion attention. The additional adversarial lesion generation can provide multi-lesion information to the grading module via an external lesion attention module (LEAM). The overall architecture of the proposed framework is illustrated in Fig. 1.

We assume that the grading module works with an input image $x \in X$ and its label $y \in Y$, where X is certain input domain and Y is the corresponding label space. We define the domain of CFP images as the source domain $S(x,y)$ and the domain of UWF images as the target domain $T(x,y)$. The encoder of ResNet50 [25] is employed as the backbone of our grading module for the feature extraction. Different from the original feature extractor, we re-weight the feature maps of layer-1 and layer-2 using the lesion attention information provided by the LEAM. The feature extractor can obtain n-dimensional feature vectors f^S and f^T, denoting the source domain and target domain feature representations, respectively. Then, class label predictor consisting of two fully connected (FC) layers can output DR severity grading probability based on the feature f. Features from CFP images and UWF images present different domain properties. In order to transfer the disease-related knowledge from the CFP image to the unlabeled UFW image efficiently, the extracted feature f should be discriminative and invariant to the change of domains. Therefore, we utilize a domain predictor to make the learned feature domain-invariant. The domain predictor consists of two FC layers: one is followed by batch normalization (BN) and ReLU activation layers, and another is followed by BN and Softmax activation layers. The feature vector f is mapped to $d = 0$ (if input is from the source domain S) or $d = 1$ (if input is from the target domain T) by the domain predictor, ensuring the feature distributions over the two domains are similar. The domain predictor is connected to the feature extractor via a gradient reversal layer [26], which allows us to train the class predictor and domain predictor using standard backpropagation algorithms in a gradient descent manner. Notably, the class predictor is used during both training and testing procedures to obtain grading labels, and the domain predictor is only used during training.

2.2 Adversarial Lesion Generation Module

In real clinical scenario, the human experts perform DR diagnosis by observing detailed characteristics of lesions. To simulate this procedure, we design an adversarial multi-lesion generation module to obtain a prior knowledge of the related lesions. Considering the fact that the UWF images are provided without any pixel-level lesion annotations available, we thus need to utilize CFP images with pixel-level annotations to train the lesion generation module. We build the multi-lesion generation module based on domain adaption [27], which obtains different types of lesions, i.e., MA, HE, SE, EX. This consists of two parts: a multi-lesion map generator $G_L(\cdot)$ and a discriminator $D(\cdot)$. The $G_L(\cdot)$ has an encoder-decoder structure, with skip connections to preserve the details of the decoding process. To optimize the multi-lesion generation module, we use a binary cross-entropy loss $\mathcal{L}_{CE}$ to minimize the distance between the prediction and pixel-level annotation of CFP images.

To generate better lesions maps for the UWF data, we employ a $D(\cdot)$, which optimizes the $G_L(\cdot)$ by means of adversarial training [28]. The essential goal of the $D(\cdot)$ is to make the generated sample close to the real data. In our implementation, we take the source lesion maps predicted by the $G_L(\cdot)$ from the CFP data as the real data branch and those target lesion maps predicted from the UWF data as the fake data branch. We use the two lesion predictions obtained from the $G_L(\cdot)$ as input of the $D(\cdot)$, with the adversarial loss to ensure the UWF lesion prediction closer to the CFP lesion prediction. The adversarial loss enables the unsupervised learning to use $\mathcal{L}_{CE}$ on unlabeled UWFs by taking advantage of the labeled CFP lesion information. Similar ideas have been successfully applied to unsupervised semantic segmentation [26] and medical image segmentation [29]. The total loss for optimizing the multi-lesion generation task can be defined as

$$\mathcal{L}_{Total} = \mathcal{L}_{Adv} + \lambda \mathcal{L}_{CE}, \tag{1}$$

where λ is the balance weight of the adversarial loss, $\mathcal{L}_{CE}$ is a pixel-level loss of the $G_L(\cdot)$. Once the adversarial multi-lesion generation module has been trained, pixel-level lesion maps can be predicted for images from two domains, which are then concatenated with the input images and taken as inputs for the grading model to obtain more accurate classification results.

2.3 Lesion External Attention Module

Although we fed the generated lesion maps as input to the grading module, the lesion information cannot effectively guide the learning of the grading module due to that the lesion generation module and grading module are two independent modules. Otherwise, The disease grading task is not only restricted by the multiple lesion types of different clinical significances, but also suffered from the complicated background artifacts (e.g., eyelash and eyelids) and noise from UWF images, particularly in an unsupervised manner. In order to better embed the filtered lesion knowledge into the grading module, we design a lesion external attention module (LEAM). Unlike the previous self-attention mechanism [30], we obtain the lesion attention map from the external module (i.e. lesion generation module) to re-weight the features of the grading module. The LEAM can be used as a bridge to allow the lesion information obtained by the lesion generation module to guide the learning of the grading module. It might be useful to assist the grading module in a human-like manner for classification, i.e., automatically extracting task-specific lesion regions and ignoring irrelevant information to improve the grading accuracy.

The details of LEAM are shown in Fig. 1. We first obtain the feature maps f_i^L from lesion generation module, i denotes the i-th intermediate layer of the generator $G_L(\cdot)$ in lesion generation module. After average-pooling and max-pooling operations along the channel, we cascade the two obtained spatial lesion descriptors. The cascaded descriptors are then fed into a convolution layer followed by a sigmoid activation layer to obtain the lesion attention map m_i^L. Then we multiply the feature maps f_i^G from the grading module (i denotes the i-th intermediate layer of the grading module) by m_i^L and perform an element-wise sum operation with f_i^G to obtain the new feature maps $\widetilde{f}_i^G$. The overall attention process can be summarized as follows:

$$m_i^L = \sigma \left(\mathbf{Conv} \left(\mathbf{AvgPool} \left(f_i^L \right) \parallel \mathbf{MaxPool} \left(f_i^L \right) \right) \right),$$
$$\widetilde{f}_i^G = (f_i^G \otimes m_i^L) \oplus f_i^G, \tag{2}$$

where $\parallel$ denotes the concatenation operation, σ denotes the sigmoid activation function. $\otimes$ and $\oplus$ demote the element-wise multiplication and element-wise sum, respectively. This design allows more multi-scale pathological information to be extracted from UWF images, which helps our unsupervised transfer learning framework to be more accurate and robust.

3 Experimental Results

3.1 Data Description

The experiment involves two public CFP images dataset (EyePACS [16] and IDRID [17]) and one in-house UWF images dataset. **EyePACS** dataset contains 88,702 CFP images, and provides five categories image-level grading annotation. In order to accelerate the training, we randomly selected 8,000 images (about 1,600 images per category) from EyePACS to establish a new subset as the source domain to train the grading . **IDRID** dataset is a CFP images dataset which provides pixel-level multi-lesion annotations, includes MA, HE, SE and EX. This dataset contains 81 CFP images with DR, which we used as the source domain set for training the adversarial lesion generation module.

We established a **UWF** dataset as the target domain set in this work, which consists of 904 images collected from local hospital and contained different levels (i.e. 440 nomal, 195 mild, 103 moderate, 79 severe non-proliferative DR and 81 proliferative DR). All the images were captured by Optos 200Tx with an imaging resolution of 3900×3072 pixels, and then they were randomly divided into 60% for training, 40% for test.

3.2 Implementation Details

In our implementation, all images were resized into 512×512 pixels. Data augmentations including random flip and rotation were conducted. The proposed networks were implemented using Python based on the Pytorch package. The Adam optimizer with recommended parameters was used to optimize the model, and the batch size was set as 32. The maximum epoch was 150.

3.3 Ablation Study

To evaluate the DR grading performance of our ULTRA method and the effectiveness of each component, we set different baselines for comparison. $M_{\mathbf{CFP}}$: A ResNet-50 grading model that was trained using only EyePACS subset and tested on the UWF dataset. $M_{\mathbf{UWF}}^{\star}$: Training a grading model based on ResNet-50 in a fully supervised manner using UWF data and testing on the UWF dataset. $M_{\mathbf{Transfer}}$: A baseline model that was jointly trained on the EyePACS and UWF dataset in an unsupervised manner, without explicitly using lesion information in this process. $M_{\mathbf{Lesion}}$: We explore the improvement of the grading module by integrating the lesion information. The lesion map obtained from the lesion generation module was fed into the grading module. $M_{\mathbf{ULTRA}}$: The LEAM was integrated into the framework to provide the fine lesion information, which was used as our final method. In this work, we used four metrics to evaluate the DR grading performance: average accuracy (ACC), precision (PRE), F1-score and *Kappa*.

Table 1 shows the classification performance of different methods. Overall, our method achieves the highest scores in all the metrics among all unsupervised methods. The model trained with labeled CFP images, i.e., $M_{\mathbf{CFP}}$, only receives an Acc = 28.81%, which indicates the large domain gap between CFP images and UWF images. Although $M_{\mathbf{UWF}}^{\star}$ is trained using labeled UWF images, our method still outperforms it, with ACC, Pre, F1 and Kappa improved by 3.61%, 3.94%, 4.31%, 4.19%, respectively. This is mainly due to the limited number of UWF images used for training (543 images in total). As shown in the row of the $M_{\mathbf{Transfer}}$, compared to $M_{\mathbf{CFP}}$, joint training of CFP and UWF images using transfer learning increases the ACC of grading by 33.52%. In particular, an increase of approximate 2.21% in ACC for $M_{\mathbf{Lesion}}$ is achieved when compared to $M_{\mathbf{Transfer}}$. This indicates that the lesion generation module can improve the grading results. In Fig. 2, we show the lesion maps obtained by the lesion generation module. Although there are some false detection (e.g., bright spots and eyelashes wrongly segmented as lesions), the module still accurately detects most lesions and provides guidance information related to lesions for the grading model. When LEAM is employed, a significant improvement can be observed on $M_{\mathbf{ULTRA}}$, which implies that the proposed LEAM can finely embed the lesion knowledge into the grading module. The confusion matrices of different methods are shown in the **supplementary material**.

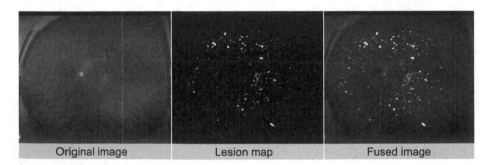

Fig. 2. A sample of UWF image and the lesion detection result of our method. (green: MA, yellow: HE, purple: SE, red: EX) (Color figure online)

3.4   Comparisons with State-of-the-Art Methods

We evaluate the effectiveness of the following state-of-the-art domain adaptation methods: Domain Separation Networks (**DSN**) [31], Adversarial Discriminative Domain Adaptation (**ADDA**) [32], **CycleGAN** [13]. Notably, **Cycle-GAN** method is the only method that uses CFP images to aid the training of UWF images, which is fully supervised and requires labeled UWF images for training. Although our method is unsupervised, fully supervised training can also be performed when the labels of the UWF images are available, which we define as $M_{\text{ULTRA}}^{\star}$.

Table 1. The DR grading results over the UWF dataset. C and U denotes the CFP and UWF datasets, respectively. $\star$ indicates the method is fully supervised, i.e., the grading labels of UWF images are used in the training phase.

Methods	Training	ACC(%)	PRE(%)	F1(%)	Kappa(%)
M_{CFP}	C_{label}	28.81	45.23	26.00	11.43
$M_{\text{UWF}}^{\star}$	C_{label}	63.43	64.39	63.26	46.82
M_{Transfer}	$C_{label}/U_{unlabel}$	62.33	67.55	60.97	46.54
M_{Lesion}	$C_{label}/U_{unlabel}$	64.54	63.8 7	66.69	47.25
DSN [31]	$C_{label}/U_{unlabel}$	51.33	37.26	63.82	13.00
ADDA [32]	$C_{label}/U_{unlabel}$	62.33	51.62	70.16	41.89
CycleGAN* [13]	C_{label}/U_{label}	63.16	48.21	72.02	40.76
M_{ULTRA}	$C_{label}/U_{unlabel}$	67.04	68.33	67.57	51.01
$M_{\text{ULTRA}}^{\star}$	C_{label}/U_{label}	70.08	70.22	70.46	55.98

As shown in Table 1, the proposed method outperforms these methods in most metrics. For example, our method exhibits a large advantage over **Cycle-GAN** method by an increase of Acc, Pre and *Kappa* of approximate 6.92%, 22.01%, 15.22%, respectively. The main reason is that **CycleGAN** method generates UWF images from CFP images by style transfer, and the performance of the grading model depends on the quality of the synthesized images. It is essentially a data enhancement method and does not achieve effective knowledge transfer. In addition, although the **DSN** method adds a reconstruction loss to learn more generalised features, this simultaneously makes the model prone to ignore image details, such as lesions in CFP and UWF images, which makes the **DSN** perform poorly on this task.

3.5   Effect of Number of CFP Images

In this section, we investigate the effect of the number of CFP images on the grading performance by our ULTRA. Specifically, we incrementally use 2,000, 5,000, 8,000 and 15,000 CFP images to train the model. The results is summarized in Table 2. Generally, we can observe that the values of all metrics increase when change number of CFP images from 2,000 to 8,000. Particularly, we receive ACC = 63.17%, and *Kappa* = 45.96% when number is 15,000, which is 3.33%, 5.05% lower compared to 8,000, respectively. This suggests that as the number of images in the source domain increases, the model may learn to extract more robust feature, but choosing an appropriate amount of source data is also crucial. And it also shows that the availability of large-scale high-quality CFP images makes it a feasible and effective idea to train a UWF images grading model with the aid of such database.

Table 2. Results of DR grading obtained by our ULTRA method in term of different number of CFP images.

–	Image Number	ACC(%)	PRE(%)	F1(%)	Kappa(%)
No.1	2000	59.00	55.00	66.53	33.00
No.2	5000	62.05	66.58	61.72	44.86
No.3	8000	67.04	68.33	67.57	51.01
No.4	15000	63.71	69.13	68.33	45.96

4   Conclusion

In this paper, we have investigated an unsupervised learning method for DR grading using UWF images and proposed a novel framework, called ULTRA, which utilizes well-labeled CFP images to assist the DR grading in UWF images. Specifically, the ULTAR can transfer disease-related information from CFP images to UWF images using a domain adaption method with gradient reversal layers. In addition, we have also designed an adversarial lesion map generator and a lesion external attention module to provide rich lesion information for DR grading, with the goal of mimicking the decision making process of ophthalmologists. Experimental validations have demonstrated that our method achieves competitive performance for DR grading.

Acknowledgment. This work was supported in part by the National Science Foundation Program of China (62103398), Zhejiang Provincial Natural Science Foundation of China (LR22F020008), in part by the Youth Innovation Promotion Association CAS (2021298), in part by the Ningbo major science and technology task project (2021Z054) and the AME Programmatic Fund (A20H4b0141).

References

1. Yong, J.K., Kim, B.H., Bo, M.C., Sun, H.J., Choi, K.S.: Bariatric surgery is associated with less progression of diabetic retinopathy: a systematic review and meta-analysis. Surg. Obes. Relat. Dis. **13**(2), 352 (2017)
2. Chilamkurthy, S., et al.: Development and validation of deep learning algorithms for detection of critical findings in head CT scans (2018)

3. Ju, L., Wang, X., Zhou, Q., Zhu, H., Ge, Z.: Bridge the domain gap between ultra-wide-field and traditional fundus images via adversarial domain adaptation (2020)
4. Zhao, Y., et al.: Uniqueness-driven saliency analysis for automated lesion detection with applications to retinal diseases. In: Frangi, A.F., et al. (eds.) MICCAI 2018. LNCS, vol. 11071, pp. 109–118. Springer, Cham (2018). https://doi.org/10.1007/978-3-030-00934-2_13
5. Ting, D., et al.: Development and validation of a deep learning system for diabetic retinopathy and related eye diseases using retinal images from multiethnic populations with diabetes. Jama **318**(22), 2211 (2017)
6. Sayres, R., et al.: Using a deep learning algorithm and integrated gradients explanation to assist grading for diabetic retinopathy. Ophthalmology (2018)
7. Foo, A., Hsu, W., Lee, M.L., Lim, G., Wong, T.Y.: Multi-task learning for diabetic retinopathy grading and lesion segmentation. Proc. AAAI Conf. Artif. Intell. **34**(8), 13267–13272 (2020)
8. Sun, R., Li, Y., Zhang, T., Mao, Z., Wu, F., Zhang, Y.: Lesion-aware transformers for diabetic retinopathy grading. In: Proceedings of the IEEE/CVF Conference on Computer Vision and Pattern Recognition, pp. 10938–10947 (2021)
9. Nagasato, D., et al.: Deep neural network-based method for detecting central retinal vein occlusion using ultrawide-field fundus ophthalmoscopy. J. Ophthalmol. **2018**, 1–6 (2018)
10. Daisuke, N., Hitoshi, T., Hideharu, O., Hiroki, M., Hiroki, E.: Deep-learning classifier with ultrawide-field fundus ophthalmoscopy for detecting branch retinal vein occlusion. Int. J. Ophthalmol. **12**(1), 6 (2019)
11. Ohsugi, H., Tabuchi, H., Enno, H., Ishitobi, N.: Accuracy of deep learning, a machine-learning technology, using ultra-wide-field fundus ophthalmoscopy for detecting rhegmatogenous retinal detachment. Sci. Rep. **7**, 9425 (2017)
12. Singh, R.P., et al.: Protecting vision in patients with diabetes with ultra-widefield imaging: a review of current literature. Ophthal. Surg. Lasers Imag. Retina **50**(10), 639–648 (2019)
13. Ju, L., Wang, X., Zhao, X., Bonnington, P., Drummond, T., Ge, Z.: Leveraging regular fundus images for training UWF fundus diagnosis models via adversarial learning and pseudo-labeling. IEEE Trans. Med. Imaging (2021)
14. Nagasawa, T., et al.: Accuracy of ultrawide-field fundus ophthalmoscopy-assisted deep learning for detecting treatment-naïve proliferative diabetic retinopathy. Int. Ophthalmol. **39**(10), 2153–2159 (2019). https://doi.org/10.1007/s10792-019-01074-z
15. Xie, H., et al.: Cross-attention multi-branch network for fundus diseases classification using SLO images. Med. Image Anal. **71**, 102031 (2021)
16. Graham, B.: Kaggle Diabetic Retinopathy Detection Competition Report. University of Warwick (2015)
17. Porwal, P., et al.: Indian diabetic retinopathy image dataset (IDRID): a database for diabetic retinopathy screening research. Data **3**(3), 25 (2018)
18. Long, M., Wang, J., Ding, G., Sun, J., Yu, P.S.: Transfer feature learning with joint distribution adaptation. In: Proceedings of the IEEE International Conference on Computer Vision (ICCV) (2013)
19. Wang, P., Lu, L., Li, J., Gan, W.: Transfer learning with joint distribution adaptation and maximum margin criterion (2018)
20. Xiao, N., Zhang, L.: Dynamic weighted learning for unsupervised domain adaptation. In: Proceedings of the IEEE/CVF Conference on Computer Vision and Pattern Recognition, pp. 15242–15251 (2021)

21. Abdelmaksoud, E., El-Sappagh, S., Barakat, S., Abuhmed, T., Elmogy, M.: Automatic diabetic retinopathy grading system based on detecting multiple retinal lesions. IEEE Access **9**, 15939–15960 (2021)
22. Zhou, Y., et al.: Collaborative learning of semi-supervised segmentation and classification for medical images. In: Proceedings of the IEEE/CVF Conference on Computer Vision and Pattern Recognition, pp. 2079–2088 (2019)
23. Grinsven, M.V., Ginneken, B.V., Hoyng, C., Theelen, T., Sanchez, C.: Fast convolutional neural network training using selective data sampling: application to hemorrhage detection in color fundus images. IEEE Transactions on Medical Imaging, pp. 1273–1284 (2016)
24. Ronneberger, O., Fischer, P., Brox, T.: U-Net: convolutional networks for biomedical image segmentation. In: Navab, N., Hornegger, J., Wells, W.M., Frangi, A.F. (eds.) MICCAI 2015. LNCS, vol. 9351, pp. 234–241. Springer, Cham (2015). https://doi.org/10.1007/978-3-319-24574-4_28
25. He, K., Zhang, X., Ren, S., Sun, J.: Deep residual learning for image recognition. In: Proceedings of the IEEE Conference on Computer Vision and Pattern Recognition, pp. 770–778 (2016)
26. Ganin, Y., Lempitsky, V.: Unsupervised domain adaptation by backpropagation. In: International Conference on Machine Learning, PMLR, pp. 1180–1189 (2015)
27. Tsai, Y.H., Hung, W.C., Schulter, S., Sohn, K., Yang, M.H., Chandraker, M.: Learning to adapt structured output space for semantic segmentation. In: Proceedings of the IEEE Conference on Computer Vision and Pattern Recognition, pp. 7472–7481 (2018)
28. Goodfellow, I., et al.: Generative adversarial nets. Adv. Neural Inf. Process. Syst. **27** (2014)
29. Kamnitsas, K., et al.: Unsupervised domain adaptation in brain lesion segmentation with adversarial networks. In: Niethammer, M., et al. (eds.) IPMI 2017. LNCS, vol. 10265, pp. 597–609. Springer, Cham (2017). https://doi.org/10.1007/978-3-319-59050-9_47
30. Fu, J., et al.: Dual attention network for scene segmentation. In: Proceedings of the IEEE/CVF Conference on Computer Vision and Pattern Recognition, pp. 3146–3154 (2019)
31. Bousmalis, K., Trigeorgis, G., Silberman, N., Krishnan, D., Erhan, D.: Domain separation networks (2016)
32. Tzeng, E., Hoffman, J., Saenko, K., Darrell, T.: Adversarial discriminative domain adaptation (2017)

Local-Region and Cross-Dataset Contrastive Learning for Retinal Vessel Segmentation

Rui Xu[1,2], Jiaxin Zhao[1], Xinchen Ye[1,2(✉)], Pengcheng Wu[1], Zhihui Wang[1,2], Haojie Li[1,2], and Yen-Wei Chen[3]

[1] DUT-RU International School of Information Science and Engineering, Dalian University of Technology, Dalian, China
yexch@dlut.edu.cn
[2] DUT-RU Co-Research Center of Advanced ICT for Active Life, Dalian, China
[3] College of Information Science and Engineering, Ritsumeikan University, Kusatsu, Japan

Abstract. Retinal vessel segmentation is an essential preprocessing step for computer-aided diagnosis of ophthalmic diseases. Many efforts have been made to improve vessel segmentation by designing complex deep networks. However, due to some features related to detailed structures are not discriminative enough, it is still required to further improve the segmentation performance. Without adding complex network structures, we propose a local-region and cross-dataset contrastive learning method to enhance the feature embedding ability of a U-Net. Our method includes a local-region contrastive learning strategy and a cross-dataset contrastive learning strategy. The former aims to more effectively separate the features of pixels that are easily confused with their neighbors inside local regions. The latter utilizes a memory bank scheme that further enhances the features by fully exploiting the global contextual information of the whole dataset. We conducted extensive experiments on two public datasets (DRIVE and CHASE_DB1). The experimental results verify the effectiveness of the proposed method that has achieved the state-of-the-art performances.

Keywords: Retinal vessel segmentation · Contrastive learning

1 Introduction

Retinal vessel segmentation is an essential preprocessing step for quantitative analysis of some systemic and ophthalmic diseases. Morphological properties of

This work was supported by National Natural Science Foundation of China (NSFC) under Grant 61772106, Grant 61702078 and Grant 61720106005, and by the Fundamental Research Funds for the Central Universities of China.

Supplementary Information The online version contains supplementary material available at https://doi.org/10.1007/978-3-031-16434-7_55.

retinal vessels, such as vessel diameter, tortuosity, bifurcation pattern and so on, are important biomarkers for these diseases [15]. Thus, it is required to segment retinal vessels with high accuracy. A lot of efforts have been dedicated for this by proposing deep neural network based methods [2,8,11,19,20]. Many of them have tried to improve U-Net [12] by adding some carefully designed specific network modules. Although they can improve the segmentation, they introduce lots of extra network parameters, increasing the burden of network training and testing. We notice that a basic U-Net trained by a cross-entropy loss has already achieved relatively good performance on the segmentation. However, it is hard to segment some detailed structures, whose features are not discriminative enough. Inspired from the idea of supervised contrastive learning (SCL) originally proposed for semantic segmentation of natural images [17], we address this problem by applying a local-region and cross-dataset contrastive learning method. Without adding complex network modules that have a large number of extra parameters, we introduce two supervised contrastive learning losses, which can enhance the basic U-Net by learning a more effective feature embedding space.

Due to the structural complexity of fundus images, automatic retinal vessel segmentation faces many difficulties, such as the great scale variation of vessels, insufficient illumination, pathological exudates and periodic noise [16,18]. These factors make it difficult for the U-Net trained by a cross-entropy loss to accurately segment some detailed structures related to vessel connectivity, especially for the pixels surrounding to capillaries, vessel boundaries and bifurcations. These hard pixels are located in tiny regions that only takes a small proportion of the fundus images. However, the cross-entropy loss is uniformly conducted on all pixels of the images. This results in that the training of a U-Net can relatively ignore the information from these hard pixels while more focusing on the easier ones. Thus, the features learnt by the U-Net are not discriminative enough on these hard pixels and their surrounding local regions. Besides, the deep model is trained by a mini-batch based manner, which only takes information of the samples in the current mini-batch and ignores the information of the whole dataset. Thus, the learnt features are less discriminative for retinal vessel segmentation.

To extract discriminative features, we propose a local-region and cross-dataset contrastive learning method. Together with the original cross-entropy loss, we introduce two supervised contrastive learning losses to train a U-Net for exploring a more powerful feature embedding space. We design a quality-aware anchor sampler, selecting hard pixels as anchors by comparing current predictions with the ground-truth, and a local contrastive sample selector, producing suitable positive and negative samples for each hard pixel inside the corresponding local regions. A local-region contrastive learning loss is conducted in a supervised pixel-to-pixel manner, to ensure that the hard pixels should be similar as the positive samples and dissimilar as the negative ones. Besides, region-level positive and negative samples are summarized and stored in a memory bank, by which information from different mini-batches can be provided for a cross-dataset contrastive learning loss. Thus, the features of the hard pixels can be further enhanced by exploiting the contextual information crossing the whole dataset. Our method differs from the work [17] in several aspects. To adapt

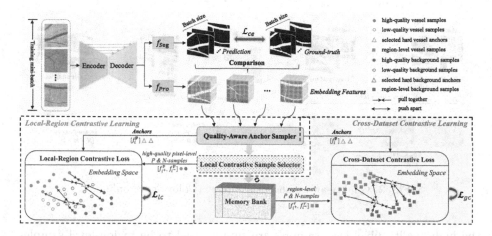

Fig. 1. Overview of the proposed local-region and cross-dataset contrastive learning. (Color figure online)

the SCL for retinal vessel segmentation, we design a different strategy to select anchors and positive/negative samples. Besides, we exploit the adapted SCL at the last layer of a decoder, rather than at the deepest layer of an encoder in [17].

In summary, the contributions of this paper are summarized as follows: 1) We propose a local-region contrastive learning strategy that can more effectively separate the features of pixels that are easily confused with their neighbors inside local regions. 2) We propose a cross-dataset contrastive learning strategy to further enhance the features by fully exploiting the global contextual information of the whole dataset. 3) Extensive experiments demonstrate that our approach obtains remarkable performance on two public datasets.

2 Local-Region and Cross-Dataset Contrastive Learning

2.1 Overview of the Proposed Method

We propose a local-region and cross-dataset contrastive learning method to enhance the feature embedding ability of a basic U-Net. Figure 1 illustrates an overview of the proposed method. We use a basic U-Net consisting of an encoder and a decoder to extract local features and feed them into a segmentation head and a projection head. For the segmentation head f_{seg}, we supervise the model by using a standard cross-entropy loss $\mathcal{L}_{ce}$. For the projection head f_{pro}, we utilize two supervised contrastive learning losses ($\mathcal{L}_{lc}$ and $\mathcal{L}_{gc}$) to train the model for exploring a more powerful feature embedding space. A quality-aware anchor sampler is designed to select hard pixels as anchors by comparing the ground-truth and the prediction of the segmentation head. A local contrastive sample selector is also designed to produce high-quality pixel-level positive and negative samples for each anchor surrounding its local region. These anchors and their corresponding high-quality pixel-level samples are imported into the local-region contrastive learning loss to enhance features of the hard pixels. Besides,

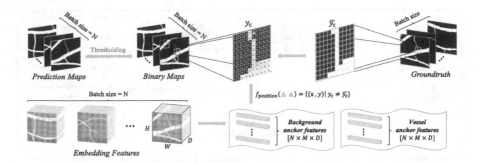

Fig. 2. Quality-aware anchor sampler. (Color figure online)

the high-quality pixel-level samples are summarized to be region-level samples that are stored in a memory bank. Then, anchors and these region-level samples are used in the cross-dataset contrastive learning loss to produce further enhanced features by exploiting cross-dataset information.

2.2   Local-Region Contrastive Learning

The basic U-Net trained by the cross-entropy loss is difficult to accurately segment some detailed structures, especially for some hard pixels around capillaries, vessel boundaries and bifurcations. Since the U-Net has already perform relatively well, the hard pixels are not so many and scattered around detailed structures. Inside the corresponding local region surrounding a hard pixel, there are often some pixels that are quite similar as the hard one but correctly segmented by the U-Net. These correctly segmented pixels can be treated as high-quality samples, providing valuable cues for optimizing the segmentation of the hard pixel. Based on this observation, we design a local-region contrastive learning strategy. It includes a quality-aware anchor sampler to detect the hard pixels and a local contrastive sample selector to select the corresponding high-quality samples. Then, a contrastive loss is exploited to guide the U-Net to learn better features for the hard pixels based on the cues from the high-quality samples.

Quality-Aware Anchor Sampler is illustrated by Fig. 2. The hard pixels are detected according to the quality of the current U-Net prediction in the segmentation head. In a mini-batch with the batch size N, prediction maps are conducted by a thresholding to obtain binary maps, denoted as y_c. The ground truth, denoted as $\bar{y}_c$, is compared with the binary maps to find the wrongly predicted pixels. These are the hard pixels, which can be grouped into vessels and background by checking their ground-truth labels. For each category c of these hard pixels, we randomly sample M points as the anchors on each map. Totally, we can get $N \times M$ anchors respectively for vessels and background in the mini-batch. Then, we overlay these anchors onto the embedding features of the projection head to obtain the anchor features.

Local Contrastive Sample Selector produces high-quality pixel-level positive and negative samples for each hard anchor inside the corresponding local regions. Each region is centered on an anchor point, and its size is $S \times S$. We randomly select P positive samples and Q negative samples in each region for the corresponding anchor. The positive samples are defined as the pixels that are correctly segmented in the current prediction and have the same ground-truth label as the anchor inside the region. The negative samples are defined in a similar manner but with different ground-truth label.

We employ the InfoNCE loss [9] to simultaneously pull each anchor towards to the corresponding high-quality pixel-level positive samples, and push them apart from the negative samples. For each input image $I \in R^{W \times H \times C}$, the local-region contrastive learning loss is defined by Eq. 1.

$$\mathcal{L}_{lc} = \frac{1}{|\mathcal{A}|} \sum_{i \in \mathcal{A}} \frac{1}{|\mathcal{P}(i)|} \sum_{i^+ \in \mathcal{P}(i)} - \log \frac{e^{\cos\left(f_i^p, f_{i+}^p\right)/\tau}}{e^{\cos\left(f_i^p, f_{i+}^p\right)/\tau} + \sum_{i^- \in \mathcal{N}(i)} e^{\cos\left(f_i^p, f_{i-}^p\right)/\tau}} \quad (1)$$

where $\mathcal{A}$ is the set of anchors, $\mathcal{P}(i)$ and $\mathcal{N}(i)$ denote the high-quality pixel-level positive and negative samples of the i-th anchor, $cos(\cdot)$ is the cosine similarity function, $f^p \in R^D$ denotes the D-dimensional feature obtained from the projection head f_{pro}, τ is a temperature hyper-parameter.

2.3 Cross-Dataset Contrastive Learning

Due to the anisotropy of fundus images in terms of structure and contrast, there is a domain shift problem between regions of different images. It should be better to fully explore the global contextual information contained in the training data instead of only focusing on local regions of the image. We implement this by exploiting a memory bank that is similar to a queue operation. This memory bank stores the region-level samples (f^r) that are calculated from the high-quality pixel-level samples (f^p) obtained from the local contrastive sample selector, according to Eq. 2.

$$f^r = \frac{\sum_{j \in \Omega_i} f_j^p \mathbb{1}[\bar{y}_c = c]}{\sum_{j \in \Omega_i} \mathbb{1}[\bar{y}_c = c]}, \quad c \in \{0, 1\} \quad (2)$$

where Ω_i denotes the set of high-quality pixel-level samples in the $S \times S$ local region centered on the i-th anchor, $\bar{y}_c$ is the class label of ground-truth, $\mathbb{1}(\cdot)$ is the indicator function.

The region-level samples can be seen as the generalized version of the corresponding multiple high-quality pixel-level samples. They are not only more robust but also can reduce the computation cost [4]. In each mini-batch, the memory bank is updated like a queue that discards the oldest region-level samples and stores new ones. Then, the region-level samples and the anchors are imported into the cross-dataset contrastive loss, defined by Eq. 3, to fully exploit the cross-dataset information for further enhancing the feature embedding ability of the model.

$$\mathcal{L}_{gc} = \frac{1}{|\mathcal{A}|} \sum_{i \in \mathcal{A}} \frac{1}{|\mathcal{P}_b(i)|} \sum_{i^+ \in \mathcal{P}_b(i)} - \log \frac{e^{\cos\left(f_i^p, f_{i+}^r\right)/\tau}}{e^{\cos\left(f_i^p, f_{i+}^r\right)/\tau} + \sum_{i^- \in \mathcal{N}_b(i)} e^{\cos\left(f_i^p, f_{i-}^r\right)/\tau}}$$

$$(3)$$

Table 1. Ablation study of the proposed method with different losses for retinal vessel segmentation on the DRIVE dataset.

Method	$\mathcal{L}_{ce}$	$\mathcal{L}_{lc}$	$\mathcal{L}_{gc}$	ACC	SE	SP	AUC	DICE	COR ↑	INF↓	Params(M)
baseline	✓			0.9699	0.8205	**0.9845**	0.9870	0.8262	0.4952	0.4229	8.6279
method-a	✓	✓		0.9703	0.8355	0.9834	0.9886	0.8304	0.4956	0.4269	8.6301
method-b	✓	✓	✓	**0.9705**	**0.8441**	0.9828	**0.9890**	**0.8328**	**0.5467**	**0.3775**	8.6301

where $\mathcal{P}_b(i)$ and $\mathcal{N}_b(i)$ denote the memory bank collecting a set of positive and negative samples for the i-th anchor.

In summary, the total loss of the proposed method is formulated as Eq. 4.

$$\mathcal{L}_{total} = \mathcal{L}_{ce} + \alpha\mathcal{L}_{lc} + \beta\mathcal{L}_{gc} \tag{4}$$

where α and β are hyperparameters used to balance the various losses.

3 Experiments

3.1 Dataset and Implementation

Dataset Details. We conduct extensive experiments on two public datasets to evaluate the proposed method: DRIVE [13] and CHASE_DB1 [10]. The DRIVE dataset consists of 40 fundus images with the resolution of 565×584, of which 7 images show signs of mild early diabetic retinopathy. It is officially divided into a training set and a test set, both containing 20 images. The CHASE_DB1 dataset contains 28 images with the resolution of 999×960 from the left and right eyes of 14 children. Like other methods, we divide the first 20 images for training and the last 8 images for testing. To avoid model overfitting, the training images of DRIVE datasets and CHASE_DB1 datasets are randomly cropped into 64×64 and 128×128 image patches, respectively. All image patches are augmented by horizontal flipping, vertical flipping, and rotation.

Evaluation Metrics. To quantitatively analyze the segmentation performance of the proposed method, we utilize five metrics to evaluate the segmentation accuracy of the model: accuracy (ACC), sensitivity (SE), specificity (SP), the area under the receiver operating characteristic curve (AUC), dice similarity coefficient (DICE). Moreover, we also employ the correct (COR) and infeasible (INF) metrics [1] to quantify the connectivity of the segmented vessels. Note that higher COR and lower INF indicate better segmented vessel connectivity.

Implement Settings. The entire framework is implemented by pytorch1.7.0 on NVIDIA TITAN RTX. The network is initialized randomly and directly trained by using an Adam optimizer with the learning rate of 0.0015. The hyperparameters $N = 64$, $D = 32$, $S = 10$, $\tau = 0.07$, $\alpha = \beta = 0.001$, M is set to 32 for DRIVE dataset and 128 for CHASE_DB1 dataset. The memory bank stores 5000 region-level features for each class and updates 10 per iteration.

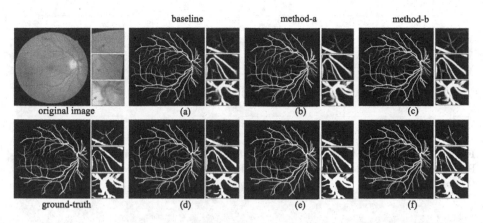

Fig. 3. Visualization results of segmentation results for different methods in the ablation study. (a)–(c) probability maps. (d)–(f) binary maps. (Color figure online)

3.2 Ablation Study

We perform the ablation study to illustrate the effectiveness of the proposed method. Table 1 summarizes the segmentation results of different methods on the DRIVE dataset. The baseline method is the U-Net trained with cross-entropy loss. The method-a utilizes the local-region contrastive learning strategy based on the baseline, while the method-b utilizes both the local-region contrastive learning strategy and the cross-dataset contrastive learning strategy. The results show that jointly applying the cross-entropy loss and the two contrastive losses significantly improves the segmentation performance of the model on the six evaluation metrics, while increasing only about 2,000 (0.025%) parameters over the baseline method. The INF is decreased by 4.54% and the COR is increased by 5.15%, which means that the connectivity of segmented vessels is largely enhanced due to better segmentation of detailed structures. Besides, we also give the visualization results in Fig. 3 to show how these methods are visually different on probability maps and binary maps. Compared to the baseline method, the method-a can discriminate a few of hard pixels of detailed structures (capillaries and vessel boundaries), but breakpoints still exist on the binary segmentation results. Meanwhile, the method-b extracts more vessel pixels with insignificant feature differences, and the connectivity of the segmented vessels is greatly enhanced.

In order to evaluate the embedding ability of the model, we visualize the embedding features learned by different models via the t-SNE [7]. As shown in Fig. 4, compared with the baseline method, the pixels of the same class are more clustered for the method-a, but there are still a few less discriminative vessels (red dots) spreading inside the region of the background (green dots).

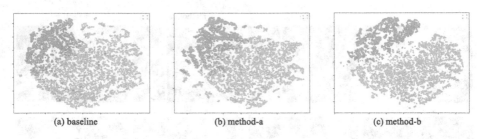

(a) baseline   (b) method-a   (c) method-b

Fig. 4. Visualization of embedding features for different methods in the ablation study. Red and green dots denote vessel and background embedding features, respectively. (Color figure online)

The method-b further improves the intra-class affinity and inter-class separability of the embedding space, pulling less discriminative vessel pixels closer to the same class. Therefore, the joint supervision of $\mathcal{L}_{ce}$, $\mathcal{L}_{lc}$ and $\mathcal{L}_{gc}$ remarkably benefits the training of the U-Net in learning a more effective feature embedding space.

3.3   Comparison with Other Advanced Methods

The experimental results in Table 2 verify the effectiveness of the proposed method. We compare the proposed method with other advanced methods. Dual E-Unet [14], IterNet [6] and RC-Net [5] design a unique U-Net variant to fully exploit the spatial and semantic information of images. HANet [15] dynamically locates the thick and thin vessels in fundus images and processes them separately. SA-UNet [3] and CAR-UNet [2] introduce spatial and channel attention module to improve the feature representation ability of U-Net. BEFD-Unet [21] proposes a boundary enhancement and feature denoising module to extract more boundary information. Genetic U-Net [18] utilizes an improved genetic algorithm to search for the optimal network structure. Compared with these methods, the proposed method achieves better segmentation results in SE, AUC, and DICE metrics, which means that the model can correctly predicts more hard vessel pixels located in tiny regions. In particular, AUC metric does not relate to the threshold, the higher AUC reflects that the proposed method trains the model with better segmentation ability. Furthermore, SCL-UNet, which directly adopts the contrastive learning strategy described in [17], can even lower the performance of the U-Net. These results show that the proposed method enhances the feature embedding ability of U-Net and improves the segmentation performance. More results can be found in the supplementary material.

Table 2. Comparison of the proposed method with other advanced methods for retinal vessel segmentation on the DRIVE, CHASE_DB1 dataset.

Dataset	Method	Year	ACC	SE	SP	AUC	DICE
DRIVE	Dual E-Unet [14]	2019	0.9567	0.7940	0.9816	0.9772	0.8270
	IterNet [6]	2019	0.9574	0.7791	0.9831	0.9813	0.8218
	HANet [15]	2020	0.9581	0.7991	0.9813	0.9823	0.8293
	SA-Unet [3]	2020	0.9698	0.8212	0.9840	0.9864	0.8263
	BEFD-Unet [21]	2020	0.9701	0.8215	0.9845	0.9867	0.8267
	CAR-UNet [2]	2021	0.9699	0.8135	**0.9849**	0.9852	0.8253
	RC-Net [5]	2021	0.9694	0.8319	0.9826	0.9864	0.8262
	Genetic U-Net [18]	2021	**0.9707**	0.8300	0.9843	0.9885	0.8314
	SCL-UNet [17]	2021	0.9678	0.8086	0.9833	0.9820	0.8140
	Our proposed	2022	0.9705	**0.8441**	0.9828	**0.9890**	**0.8328**
CHASE_DB1	Dual E-Unet [14]	2019	0.9661	0.8074	0.9821	0.9812	0.8037
	IterNet [6]	2019	0.9655	0.7970	0.9823	0.9851	0.8073
	HANet [15]	2020	0.9673	0.8186	0.9844	0.9881	0.8191
	SA-UNet [3]	2020	0.9755	**0.8573**	0.9835	0.9905	0.8153
	CAR-UNet [2]	2021	0.9751	0.8439	0.9839	0.9898	0.8098
	Genetic U-Net [18]	2021	0.9769	0.8463	0.9857	0.9914	0.8223
	SCL-UNet [17]	2021	0.9751	0.8162	**0.9859**	0.9879	0.8046
	Our proposed	2022	**0.9771**	0.8543	0.9855	**0.9919**	**0.8243**

4   Conclusion

In this paper, without adding complex modules, we propose a local-region and cross-dataset contrastive learning method to enhance the U-Net by learning a more effective feature embedding space. The local-region contrastive learning strategy aims to effectively separate the features of pixels that are easily confused with their neighbors inside local regions. The cross-dataset contrastive learning strategy aims to further enhance the features by fully exploiting the contextual information of the whole dataset. Experimental results verify that the proposed method achieves remarkable segmentation performance.

References

1. Araújo, R.J., Cardoso, J.S., Oliveira, H.P.: A deep learning design for improving topology coherence in blood vessel segmentation. In: Shen, D., et al. (eds.) MICCAI 2019. LNCS, vol. 11764, pp. 93–101. Springer, Cham (2019). https://doi.org/10.1007/978-3-030-32239-7_11
2. Guo, C., Szemenyei, M., Hu, Y., Wang, W., Zhou, W., Yi, Y.: Channel attention residual U-Net for retinal vessel segmentation. In: ICASSP 2021–2021 IEEE International Conference on Acoustics, Speech and Signal Processing (ICASSP), pp. 1185–1189 (2021)

3. Guo, C., Szemenyei, M., Yi, Y., Wang, W., Chen, B., Fan, C.: SA-UNet: spatial attention U-Net for retinal vessel segmentation. In: 2020 25th International Conference on Pattern Recognition (ICPR), pp. 1236–1242 (2021)
4. Hu, H., Cui, J., Wang, L.: Region-aware contrastive learning for semantic segmentation. In: Proceedings of the IEEE/CVF International Conference on Computer Vision, pp. 16291–16301 (2021)
5. Khan, T.M., Robles-Kelly, A., Naqvi, S.S.: RC-Net: a convolutional neural network for retinal vessel segmentation. In: 2021 Digital Image Computing: Techniques and Applications (DICTA), pp. 01–07. IEEE (2021)
6. Li, L., Verma, M., Nakashima, Y., Nagahara, H., Kawasaki, R.: IterNet: retinal image segmentation utilizing structural redundancy in vessel networks. In: Proceedings of the IEEE/CVF Winter Conference on Applications of Computer Vision, pp. 3656–3665 (2020)
7. Van der Maaten, L., Hinton, G.: Visualizing data using t-SNE. J. Mach. Learn. Res. **9**(11) (2008)
8. Mou, L., et al.: CS2-Net: deep learning segmentation of curvilinear structures in medical imaging. Med. Image Anal. **67**, 101874 (2021)
9. Van den Oord, A., Li, Y., Vinyals, O.: Representation learning with contrastive predictive coding. arXiv e-prints, arXiv-1807 (2018)
10. Owen, C.G., et al.: Measuring retinal vessel tortuosity in 10-year-old children: validation of the computer-assisted image analysis of the retina (CAIAR) program. Invest. Ophthalmol. Vis. Sci. **50**(5), 2004–2010 (2009)
11. Park, K.B., Choi, S.H., Lee, J.Y.: M-GAN: retinal blood vessel segmentation by balancing losses through stacked deep fully convolutional networks. IEEE Access **8**, 146308–146322 (2020)
12. Ronneberger, O., Fischer, P., Brox, T.: U-Net: convolutional networks for biomedical image segmentation. In: Navab, N., Hornegger, J., Wells, W.M., Frangi, A.F. (eds.) MICCAI 2015. LNCS, vol. 9351, pp. 234–241. Springer, Cham (2015). https://doi.org/10.1007/978-3-319-24574-4_28
13. Staal, J., Abràmoff, M.D., Niemeijer, M., Viergever, M.A., Van Ginneken, B.: Ridge-based vessel segmentation in color images of the retina. IEEE Trans. Med. Imaging **23**(4), 501–509 (2004)
14. Wang, B., Qiu, S., He, H.: Dual encoding U-Net for retinal vessel segmentation. In: Shen, D., et al. (eds.) MICCAI 2019. LNCS, vol. 11764, pp. 84–92. Springer, Cham (2019). https://doi.org/10.1007/978-3-030-32239-7_10
15. Wang, D., Haytham, A., Pottenburgh, J., Saeedi, O., Tao, Y.: Hard attention net for automatic retinal vessel segmentation. IEEE J. Biomed. Health Inform. **24**(12), 3384–3396 (2020)
16. Wang, W., Zhong, J., Wu, H., Wen, Z., Qin, J.: RVSeg-Net: an efficient feature pyramid cascade network for retinal vessel segmentation. In: Martel, A.L., et al. (eds.) MICCAI 2020. LNCS, vol. 12265, pp. 796–805. Springer, Cham (2020). https://doi.org/10.1007/978-3-030-59722-1_77
17. Wang, W., Zhou, T., Yu, F., Dai, J., Konukoglu, E., Van Gool, L.: Exploring cross-image pixel contrast for semantic segmentation. In: Proceedings of the IEEE/CVF International Conference on Computer Vision, pp. 7303–7313 (2021)
18. Wei, J., et al.: Genetic U-Net: automatically designed deep networks for retinal vessel segmentation using a genetic algorithm. IEEE Trans. Med. Imaging **41**(2), 292–307 (2022)
19. Wu, H., Wang, W., Zhong, J., Lei, B., Wen, Z., Qin, J.: SCS-Net: a scale and context sensitive network for retinal vessel segmentation. Med. Image Anal. **70**, 102025 (2021)

20. Zhang, J., Zhang, Y., Xu, X.: Pyramid U-Net for retinal vessel segmentation. In: ICASSP 2021–2021 IEEE International Conference on Acoustics, Speech and Signal Processing (ICASSP), pp. 1125–1129 (2021)
21. Zhang, M., Yu, F., Zhao, J., Zhang, L., Li, Q.: BEFD: boundary enhancement and feature denoising for vessel segmentation. In: Martel, A.L., et al. (eds.) MICCAI 2020. LNCS, vol. 12265, pp. 775–785. Springer, Cham (2020). https://doi.org/10.1007/978-3-030-59722-1_75

Y-Net: A Spatiospectral Dual-Encoder Network for Medical Image Segmentation

Azade Farshad[1($\boxtimes$)], Yousef Yeganeh[1], Peter Gehlbach[2], and Nassir Navab[1,2]

[1] Technical University of Munich, Munich, Germany
azade.farshad@tum.de
[2] Johns Hopkins University, Baltimore, USA

Abstract. Automated segmentation of retinal optical coherence tomography (OCT) images has become an important recent direction in machine learning for medical applications. We hypothesize that the anatomic structure of layers and their high-frequency variation in OCT images make retinal OCT a fitting choice for extracting spectral domain features and combining them with spatial domain features. In this work, we present Y-Net, an architecture that combines the frequency domain features with the image domain to improve the segmentation performance of OCT images. The results of this work demonstrate that the introduction of two branches, one for spectral and one for spatial domain features, brings very significant improvement in fluid segmentation performance and allows outperformance as compared to the well-known U-Net model. Our improvement was 13% on the fluid segmentation dice score and 1.9% on the average dice score. Finally, removing selected frequency ranges in the spectral domain demonstrates the impact of these features on the fluid segmentation outperformance. Code: github.com/azadef/ynet

Keywords: OCT segmentation · Frequency domain in OCT · U-Net

1 Introduction

Ocular Optical Coherence Tomography (OCT) is among the heavily utilized clinical imaging modalities by ophthalmologists and retina specialists. Segmentation of OCT images now drives the diagnosis and treatment of eye diseases such as diabetic macular edema [32] (DME) and age-related macular degeneration (AMD). Segmentation of intraretinal fluid pockets is especially useful as it determines the presence, extent and response of retina to treatment. However, despite the importance of fluid segmentation in OCT images, existing methods fail to segment this area efficiently. In this work, we propose to extract

---

A. Farshad and Y. Yeganeh—Equal Contribution.

Supplementary Information The online version contains supplementary material available at https://doi.org/10.1007/978-3-031-16434-7_56.

L. Wang et al. (Eds.): MICCAI 2022, LNCS 13432, pp. 582–592, 2022.
https://doi.org/10.1007/978-3-031-16434-7_56

and process information from the spectral domain due to the existence of spectral features in OCT images, that may otherwise be missed in existing spatial neural networks. Furthermore, it has been shown in previous work [1] that spatial information only focuses on local information and fails to target the global information across all the pixels in an image. This problem is solved here by combining features from both spectral and spatial domains.

To summarize our contributions: 1) We propose Y-Net, an end-to-end autoencoder based architecture, with two encoder branches for automated retinal layer and fluid segmentation, in OCT images. 2) Our proposed spectral encoder is designed for extracting frequency domain features from the images. 3) Y-Net outperforms the well-known U-Net [25] architecture and other related work by a minimum of 13% in fluid segmentation, and 1.9% on average in terms of dice score. 4) The Y-Net architecture has less parameters compared to U-Net.

2   Related Work

Many of the early methods for segmentation of retinal OCT images [3] relied on graph-based techniques (e.g., graph cut, shortest path). Subsequently, some works focused on the combination of neural networks and graph-based methods for estimating the final retinal layer boundaries [5] or combining graph convolutional networks with other neural networks [15].

He et al. studied OCT segmentation in a series of works [7–9] considering OCT scan topology. Utilizing fully convolutional networks (FCN) has been explored [10,13] for predicting segmentation maps and correcting the topology based on a specific topology criterion.

A number of recent methods in medical image segmentation focus on using autoencoder based deep neural networks [12,26] for end-to-end segmentation. One of the earliest and best-known autoencoder based architectures for 2D medical image segmentation is U-Net [25]. The evolution of U-shaped networks for image segmentation has been of high research interest in recent years. Many works, such as MDAN-U-Net [17] try to use multiscale features or an attention mechanism to improve the segmentation performance of existing methods. Feature Pyramid Networks (FPNs), which are commonly used in the computer vision community, have also been of interest in medical image segmentation for global feature extraction [6,16]. Other lines of work focus on networks designed specifically for the OCT segmentation task [12,24,33], using Gaussian process [22], feature alignment [4,18], or epistemic uncertainty [21].

Using Recurrent Neural Networks (RNNs) for OCT segmentation has been explored in [14,31]. While [14] considered sequences between different scans, Tran et al. [31] modeled OCT retinal layers using natural language and developed an OCT segmentation method using RNNs for processing pixel sequences. An autoencoder network with two encoder branches has been previously used for polyp detection [19] by taking advantage of a pre-trained VGG network. The purpose of this application is considerably different than ours. A combination of U-Net [25] and fast Fourier transforms (FFT) [20] has been explored for reducing the computational costs of convolutional networks. Recently fast Fourier convolutions [1] were integrated into the image inpainting task [29] by the computer vision community. The purpose was to use the global patterns that exist in images which may not be well extracted by regular convolutional layers. This inspired us to take advantage of the fast Fourier convolutions for the task of OCT segmentation due to the existence of high-frequency speckles, which are a function of the tissue and its layers [27]. The existence of these speckles can harm the model performance when using only spatial features; Therefore, we hypothesize that by extracting spectral features from the OCT images, our network will be able to disentangle features from different frequency distributions. This enables the model to attend to more important frequency ranges in the features using adaptive learnable kernels in FFT Convolutions and to be able to model the high-frequency variation and distribution within each layer.

3   Method

In this section, we present the core principles of our work. First, we explain the overall structure of the segmentation framework; we then describe the components of our proposed spectral encoder and, at its core, the Fourier unit that performs the spectral feature extraction function. Finally, the loss functions used in this work are presented.

3.1   Segmentation Framework

The segmentation network predicts the segmentation map $\hat{y}$ given an input image $x \in \mathbb{R}^{H \times W}$ and its corresponding segmentation label $y \in \mathbb{Z}^{H \times W}$, where H and W are the image height and width, respectively. As shown in Fig. 1-a, the segmentation network, Y-Net consists of two encoder branches E_c, E_f, where E_c is the spatial encoder with convolutional blocks, and E_f is our proposed spectral encoder with fast Fourier convolutional (FFC) blocks [1]. The decoder network $G(.)$, receives the combined spatial and spectral features from the encoder networks and generates the segmentation map $\hat{y}$, where $\hat{y} = G(E_c(x), E_f(x))$. Similar to U-Net [25], Y-Net has an autoencoder based structure with skip connections from spatial encoder blocks to decoder blocks. The role of the proposed spectral encoder is to extract and process global features from the frequency domain that may have been missed by the spatial convolutions. This section explains each of our network's components and the objective functions in detail.

Spatial Encoder. The spatial encoder in our network is the same as the original U-Net [25] with four convolutional blocks. Each convolutional block consists of a convolutional layer, batch normalization layer (BN), an activation function (ReLU) and a max pooling (MP) layer. The input to the first convolutional block is the input image, and the output of each block is fed to the next block as shown in Fig. 1-a.

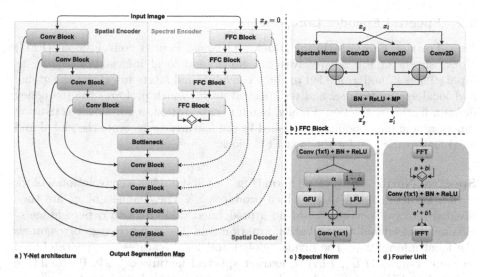

Fig. 1. a) Y-Net: Our proposed network has two branches, one for processing spatial features similar to previous works and our proposed branch for extracting spectral features. The spectral encoder has four FFC blocks which gets the local and global features x_l, x_g as input and generates the processed features x'_l, x'_g. **b) FFC Block:** The FFC blocks process the local features using Conv2D layers and process the global features using the spectral norm. **c) Spectral Norm:** The global information is divided into two portions which are fed to a Fourier unit. **d) Fourier Unit:** Here, the fast Fourier transform, followed by a conv layer, is applied to the features to get the frequency domain features. Finally, the processed features are brought back to the spatial domain using inverse FFT.

Spectral Encoder. Here we introduce our spectral encoder, to extract spectral domain features from the data. Our spectral encoder receives the same input as the spatial encoder. The input image x is fed to the first FFC block as local information x_l. The value of x_g is set to zeros for the first block since the input image pixels are considered local information, and there are no global features in the input image. Similar to the spatial encoder, there are in total four FFC blocks in the spectral encoder.

Spatial Decoder. The spatial decoder network G has four up convolutional blocks in total. It receives the spectral and spatial features and concatenates them before passing them to the bottleneck layer. Then, the features from the previous decoder block and features from the skip connections are up-scaled using a convolutional block similar to the spatial encoder, followed by transpose convolutional layers. The final segmentation map is generated by the final decoder block.

3.2   Spectral Encoder Components

Fast Fourier Convolutional Block. The Fast Fourier convolutional (FFC) block, shown in Fig. 1-b receives the global and local information x_g, x_l as input. Then x_g and x_l are fed to three convolutional layers to extract the global and local spatial features and the spectral norm, which performs the frequency domain feature extraction. Finally, batch normalization, a non-linear activation function, and max pooling are applied to the features to generate the global and local features, x'_g, x'_l for the next FFC block.

Spectral Norm. The spectral norm (Fig. 1-c) first applies a convolutional block with a kernel size of 1 to x_g, which produces x''. The channels of x'' are then divided into two portions based on a predefined value α, with α percentage of channels considered the global information and $1 - \alpha$ percentage of channels the local information. The divided global and local features are separately fed to Fourier units (FU_g, FU_l) to extract spectral features x''_g, x''_l. It should be noted that FU_g and FU_l share the same architectural design. Finally, x'' and the output of global and local Fourier units x''_g, x''_l are summed and fed to a convolutional layer with kernel size 1.

Fourier Unit. The Fourier unit (Fig. 1-d) receives a portion of x'' as input, then fourier transform is applied to those features to obtain real and imaginary parts $a + bi \in \mathbb{C}$. The real and imaginary parts a, b are stacked and then fed to a convolutional layer with a kernel size of 1. An activation layer and a batch normalization layer are applied to the output of the convolutional layer. The output is then split into two parts, namely the real and imaginary parts a', b', which are then fed to the inverse Fourier transform to convert the features back to the spatial domain.

3.3   Losses

Our models are trained with a combination [30] of dice loss [28] and cross-entropy loss. The combo loss is widely used for medical image segmentation . The loss between each ground truth segmentation label y and the predicted segmentation map $\hat{y}$ is computed as follows:

$$\mathcal{L}_{Dice}(y, \hat{y}) = 1 - \frac{2y\hat{y} + \epsilon}{y + \hat{y} + \epsilon} \tag{1}$$

The dice Loss considers the intersection over union (IoU) and is computed as shown in Eq. 1. To ensure the numerical stability, a very small value, ϵ is used for computing the dice loss. The cross-entropy loss as shown in Eq. 2 maximizes the cross-entropy information between the true and predicted labels.

$$\mathcal{L}_{CE}(y, \hat{y}) = -\frac{1}{N} \sum_{i=0}^{N} y_i \log(\hat{y}_i) \tag{2}$$

Table 1. Mean and per layer dice score compared to related works on the publicly available Duke OCT dataset [2]

Method	ILM	NFL-IPL	INL	OPL	ONL-ISM	ISE	OS-RPE	Fluid	Mean
RelayNet [26]	0.84	0.85	0.70	0.71	0.87	0.88	0.84	0.30	0.75
Language [31]	0.85	0.89	0.75	0.75	0.89	**0.90**	**0.87**	0.39	0.78
Alignment [18]	0.85	0.89	0.75	0.74	0.90	**0.90**	**0.87**	0.56	0.81
U-Net [25]	0.84	0.89	0.77	**0.76**	0.89	0.89	0.85	0.80	0.836
Y-Net (Ours)	**0.86**	**0.89**	**0.78**	0.75	**0.90**	0.88	0.85	**0.93**	**0.855**

with λ_{Dice}, λ_{CE} being the weighting factor for each loss term, the total loss then becomes:

$$\mathcal{L}_{total} = \lambda_{Dice}\mathcal{L}_{Dice} + \lambda_{CE}\mathcal{L}_{CE} \qquad (3)$$

4   Experiments

In this section, we evaluate our proposed method and compare it to the existing literature and known baselines. First, we discuss our experimental setup, and then present a comparison of our model to prior work, and finally, we show an ablation study of the components in our model. As discussed in previous sections, we tackle the problem of retinal layer and fluid segmentation using OCT images. We train and test our proposed method on the publicly available Duke OCT dataset [2] and compare it against multiple previous works on OCT segmentation. All reported results except U-Net [25] are taken from the original

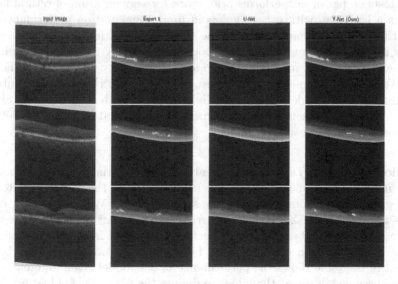

Fig. 2. Some qualitative results of Y-Net compared to U-Net [25]

values reported in the papers. The results of RelayNet [26] are taken from [31] based on the 6-2-2 split for the evaluation. Please refer to the supplementary material for the results on the UMN dataset [23] and based on the mIoU metric on both datasets.

4.1 Experimental Setup

We follow the same experimental protocol for training and evaluation of our method on the Duke OCT dataset, as in prior works [18,31]. The Duke OCT dataset consists of OCT scans from 10 patients, which are annotated by two experts. The scans from the first six subjects are used for training, subjects 7 and 8 for validation, and the scans from the remaining two subjects are used for testing. Our models are trained and tested on the annotations from expert 1, similar to previous works. All our models and the U-Net [25] were trained with a batch size of 10, a learning rate of 5e−4, weight decay of 1e−4, maximum 80 epochs of training and Adam optimizer. The number of training epochs was chosen based on the best validation accuracy for all models. The values of $\lambda_{Dice}, \lambda_{CE}$ were found empirically and set to 1 for both. The images were resized to (224×224). The evaluations are reported using dice score values for all retinal layers, fluid and their average. The number of model parameters for U-Net and Y-Net are 7.76M, 7.46M respectively.

4.2 Results

Table 1 shows the dice score of our proposed method for various retinal layers and their fluid pockets, as compared to previously reported approaches. Our model tests on par or outperforms prior work for segmentation of retinal layers, and has a large gap with other models in fluid segmentation performance. We argue that this performance gain is due to existence of features in certain frequency ranges that relate to the fluid pockets. We verify this hypothesis in one of our experiments by modifying the range of frequency values in the Fourier unit. We also show some qualitative results to compare the fluid segmentation performance of our model to U-Net in Fig. 2. We report that our model is able to segment the fluid pockets similar to expert one's annotation, while U-Net fails to segment the fluid in some regions.

Ablation Study. In Table 2, we present an ablation study of the components in our model. The first row shows the performance of the Y-Net architecture with regular convolutional blocks in the second branch. We evaluate our model on this architecture to show that the current improvement in average dice score, and especially the fluid segmentation performance is not from merely increasing the size of the network, and is affected by the introduction of the FFC blocks. The rest of the table shows the performance of our model given different values of α. As discussed in the methodology, α defines the percentage of features in the global and local Fourier units. As it can be seen in Table 2, the best performance

Table 2. Ablation study on the FFC blocks and the value of α

FFC Block	α	ILM	NFL-IPL	INL	OPL	ONL-ISM	ISE	OS-RPE	Fluid	Mean
–	–	**0.87**	**0.90**	0.77	0.75	0.89	0.88	**0.86**	0.89	0.851
✓	0	0.86	0.89	0.76	0.75	**0.90**	**0.89**	0.85	0.86	0.845
✓	0.25	0.86	0.89	0.77	0.74	0.89	**0.89**	0.86	**0.93**	0.854
✓	0.5	0.86	0.89	**0.78**	0.75	**0.90**	0.88	0.85	**0.93**	**0.855**
✓	0.75	0.84	0.87	0.76	0.73	0.89	0.88	**0.86**	0.90	0.841
✓	1	0.85	0.89	0.77	**0.76**	0.89	0.88	0.85	0.88	0.846

Table 3. Effect of variation in frequency ranges

Spectral features range	ILM	NFL-IPL	INL	OPL	ONL-ISM	ISE	OS-RPE	Fluid	Mean
No change	0.85	**0.89**	0.77	**0.75**	0.90	**0.89**	0.85	0.93	0.854
Keep (−10, 10)	**0.86**	**0.89**	**0.78**	**0.75**	0.90	0.88	0.85	**0.93**	**0.855**
Remove (−10, 10)	0.84	0.88	0.76	0.74	0.90	0.88	0.85	0.78	0.829

is gained by the α values of 0.25 and 0.5 with both models reaching a dice score of 0.93 in fluid segmentation while being on par with other models in retinal layer segmentation. We argue that both local and global features have valuable information that our model could learn. By having a value of α which is neither too large (1) nor too small (0), our model is able to correlate the global and local features to achieve the best performance.

We further explore the effect of the FFC blocks in Table 3 by varying the range of frequencies processed by the Fourier units in specific ranges. The first row in Table 3 shows the regular model without any changes to the frequency range, which is usually between −40 and 40. In the second row, we clip the range of the frequency values to (−10, 10), which slightly increases the overall segmentation performance. In the last row, we remove the frequencies between (−10, 10) by setting the value of the frequencies from −10 to 0 to −10 and setting the positive values between 0 and 10 to 10. As it can be seen, the fluid segmentation performance drops to 0.78 in this setting, while the retinal layer segmentation performance drops very slightly. Based on these experiments, we can argue that the high segmentation performance of the fluid pockets by our model is affected by the spectral domain features and that the features used for the fluid segmentation belong to a specific range of frequencies (here close to (−10, 10)).

In our experiments, we also tried using focal frequency loss [11] and adding skip connection from the spectral encoder to the spatial decoder, but this did not improve model performance. We believe that adding skip connections from the spectral domain to the spatial domain does not convey significant advantage since the spectral features and global information may not correlate well with the segmentation map.

4.3   Discussions and Conclusion

In this work, we present an end-to-end autoencoder based architecture for the segmentation of retinal layers and fluid pockets in ocular OCT images. Our proposed network Y-Net extracts spectral domain features in a second encoder branch proposed by us in addition to the spatial encoder used in previous works. We hypothesized that by extracting spectral domain features from OCT images, that have high-frequency non-uniform speckles that are dependent on the tissue and retinal layers, our model would learn features that would improve OCT segmentation performance. Learning features in the frequency domain would enable our network to model and learn the distribution of speckles within each layer. Our experiments showed that the model would be highly affected by varying the range of frequencies in the Fourier units in the core of our FFC blocks. This could verify our hypothesis that certain frequencies in the OCT images may correlate with specific layers or fluid pockets. We compared our final proposed model to multiple previous works and showed that our model outperforms existing models by 13% in fluid segmentation, reaching a value of 0.93 in dice score, while achieving on par or better performance in retinal layer segmentation.

Acknowledgement. We gratefully acknowledge the Munich Center for Machine Learning (MCML) with funding from the Bundesministerium für Bildung und Forschung (BMBF) under the project 01IS18036B.

References

1. Chi, L., Jiang, B., Mu, Y.: Fast Fourier convolution. In: Advances in Neural Information Processing Systems (2020)
2. Chiu, S.J., Allingham, M.J., Mettu, P.S., Cousins, S.W., Izatt, J.A., Farsiu, S.: Kernel regression based segmentation of optical coherence tomography images with diabetic macular edema. Express Biomed. Opt. (2015)
3. Chiu, S.J., Li, X.T., Nicholas, P., Toth, C.A., Izatt, J.A., Farsiu, S.: Automatic segmentation of seven retinal layers in SDOCT images congruent with expert manual segmentation. Express Opt. (2010)
4. Duan, W., et al.: A generative model for OCT retinal layer segmentation by groupwise curve alignment. IEEE Access (2018)
5. Fang, L., Cunefare, D., Wang, C., Guymer, R., Li, S., Farsiu, S.: Automatic segmentation of nine retinal layer boundaries in OCT images of non-exudative AMD patients using deep learning and graph search. Biomed. Opt. Express (2017)
6. Feng, S., et al.: CPFNet: context pyramid fusion network for medical image segmentation. IEEE Trans. Med. Imaging **39**, 3008–3018 (2020)
7. He, Y., et al.: Topology guaranteed segmentation of the human retina from OCT using convolutional neural networks (2018)
8. He, Y., et al.: Deep learning based topology guaranteed surface and MME segmentation of multiple sclerosis subjects from retinal OCT. Express Biomed. Opt. (2019)
9. He, Y., et al.: Fully convolutional boundary regression for retina OCT segmentation. In: Shen, D., et al. (eds.) MICCAI 2019. LNCS, vol. 11764, pp. 120–128. Springer, Cham (2019). https://doi.org/10.1007/978-3-030-32239-7_14

10. He, Y., et al.: Towards topological correct segmentation of macular OCT from cascaded FCNs. In: Cardoso, M.J., et al. (eds.) FIFI/OMIA -2017. LNCS, vol. 10554, pp. 202–209. Springer, Cham (2017). https://doi.org/10.1007/978-3-319-67561-9_23

11. Jiang, L., Dai, B., Wu, W., Loy, C.C.: Focal frequency loss for image reconstruction and synthesis. In: Proceedings of the IEEE/CVF International Conference on Computer Vision (2021)

12. Kiaee, F., Fahimi, H., Rabbani, H.: Intra-retinal layer segmentation of optical coherence tomography using 3D fully convolutional networks. In: 2018 25th IEEE International Conference on Image Processing (ICIP) (2018)

13. Kugelman, J., et al.: Automatic choroidal segmentation in OCT images using supervised deep learning methods. Sci. Rep. **9**, 1–13 (2019)

14. Kugelman, J., Alonso-Caneiro, D., Read, S., Vincent, S., Collins, M.: Automatic segmentation of OCT retinal boundaries using recurrent neural networks and graph search. Biomed. Opt. Express **9**, 5759–5777 (2018)

15. Li, J., et al.: Multi-scale GCN-assisted two-stage network for joint segmentation of retinal layers and discs in peripapillary oct images. Biomed. Opt. Express **12**, 2204-2220 (2021)

16. Li, Q., et al.: DeepRetina: layer segmentation of retina in OCT images using deep learning. Transl. Vis. Sci. Technol. **9**, 61 (2020)

17. Liu, W., Sun, Y., Ji, Q.: MDAN-UNet: multi-scale and dual attention enhanced nested U-Net architecture for segmentation of optical coherence tomography images. Algorithms **13**, 60 (2020)

18. Maier, H., Faghihroohi, S., Navab, N.: A line to align: deep dynamic time warping for retinal OCT segmentation. In: International Conference on Medical Image Computing and Computer-Assisted Intervention (2021)

19. Mohammed, A., Yildirim, S., Farup, I., Pedersen, M., Hovde, Ø.: Y-Net: a deep convolutional neural network for polyp detection. arXiv preprint arXiv:1806.01907 (2018)

20. Nair, V., Chatterjee, M., Tavakoli, N., Namin, A., Snoeyink, C.: Optimizing CNN using fast Fourier transformation for object recognition (2020)

21. Orlando, J.I., et al.: U2-Net: a Bayesian U-Net model with epistemic uncertainty feedback for photoreceptor layer segmentation in pathological OCT scans. In: 2019 IEEE 16th International Symposium on Biomedical Imaging (ISBI 2019). IEEE (2019)

22. Pekala, M., Joshi, N., Liu, T.A., Bressler, N.M., DeBuc, D.C., Burlina, P.: Deep learning based retinal OCT segmentation. Comput. Biol. Med. **114**, 103445 (2019)

23. Rashno, A., et al.: Fully-automated segmentation of fluid regions in exudative age-related macular degeneration subjects: kernel graph cut in neutrosophic domain. PLoS ONE **12**(10), e0186949 (2017)

24. Guru Pradeep Reddy, T., Ashritha, K.S., Prajwala, T.M., Girish, G.N., Kothari, A.R., Koolagudi, S.G., Rajan, J.: Retinal-layer segmentation using dilated convolutions. In: Chaudhuri, B.B., Nakagawa, M., Khanna, P., Kumar, S. (eds.) Proceedings of 3rd International Conference on Computer Vision and Image Processing. AISC, vol. 1022, pp. 279–292. Springer, Singapore (2020). https://doi.org/10.1007/978-981-32-9088-4_24

25. Ronneberger, O., Fischer, P., Brox, T.: U-Net: convolutional networks for biomedical image segmentation. In: Navab, N., Hornegger, J., Wells, W.M., Frangi, A.F. (eds.) MICCAI 2015. LNCS, vol. 9351, pp. 234–241. Springer, Cham (2015). https://doi.org/10.1007/978-3-319-24574-4_28

26. Roy, A.G., et al.: ReLayNet: retinal layer and fluid segmentation of macular optical coherence tomography using fully convolutional networks. Biomed. Opt. Express **8**, 3627–3642 (2017)
27. Schmitt, J.M., Xiang, S., Yung, K.M.: Speckle in optical coherence tomography. J. Biomed. Opt. **4**(1), 95–105 (1999)
28. Sudre, C.H., Li, W., Vercauteren, T., Ourselin, S., Jorge Cardoso, M.: Generalised dice overlap as a deep learning loss function for highly unbalanced segmentations. In: Cardoso, M.J., Arbel, T., Carneiro, G., Syeda-Mahmood, T., Tavares, J.M.R.S., Moradi, M., Bradley, A., Greenspan, H., Papa, J.P., Madabhushi, A., Nascimento, J.C., Cardoso, J.S., Belagiannis, V., Lu, Z. (eds.) DLMIA/ML-CDS -2017. LNCS, vol. 10553, pp. 240–248. Springer, Cham (2017). https://doi.org/10.1007/978-3-319-67558-9_28
29. Suvorov, R., : Resolution-robust large mask inpainting with Fourier convolutions. In: Proceedings of the IEEE/CVF Winter Conference on Applications of Computer Vision (2022)
30. Taghanaki, S.A., et al.: Combo loss: handling input and output imbalance in multi-organ segmentation. Comput. Med. Imaging Graph. **75**, 24–33 (2019)
31. Tran, A., Weiss, J., Albarqouni, S., Faghi Roohi, S., Navab, N.: Retinal layer segmentation reformulated as OCT language processing. In: Martel, A.L., Abolmaesumi, P., Stoyanov, D., Mateus, D., Zuluaga, M.A., Zhou, S.K., Racoceanu, D., Joskowicz, L. (eds.) MICCAI 2020. LNCS, vol. 12265, pp. 694–703. Springer, Cham (2020). https://doi.org/10.1007/978-3-030-59722-1_67
32. Virgili, G., et al.: Optical coherence tomography (OCT) for detection of macular oedema in patients with diabetic retinopathy. Cochrane Database Syst. Rev. (2015)
33. Wei, H., Peng, P.: The segmentation of retinal layer and fluid in SD-OCT images using mutex dice loss based fully convolutional networks. IEEE Access **8**, 60929–60939 (2020)

Camera Adaptation for Fundus-Image-Based CVD Risk Estimation

Zhihong Lin[1], Danli Shi[2], Donghao Zhang[1], Xianwen Shang[3], Mingguang He[3], and Zongyuan Ge[1,4(✉)]

[1] Monash University, Clayton, VIC 3800, Australia
zongyuan.Ge@monash.edu
[2] Zhongshan Ophthalmic Center, Sun Yat-sen University, Guangzhou, China
[3] University of Melbourne, Parkville, VIC 3010, Australia
[4] Monash Airdoc Research, Monash eResearch Centre, Clayton, VIC 3800, Australia

Abstract. Recent studies have validated the association between cardiovascular disease (CVD) risk and retinal fundus images. Combining deep learning (DL) and portable fundus cameras will enable CVD risk estimation in various scenarios and improve healthcare democratization. However, there are still significant issues to be solved. One of the top priority issues is the different camera differences between the databases for research material and the samples in the production environment. Most high-quality retinography databases ready for research are collected from high-end fundus cameras, and there is a significant domain discrepancy between different cameras. To fully explore the domain discrepancy issue, we first collect a Fundus Camera Paired (FCP) dataset containing pair-wise fundus images captured by the high-end Topcon retinal camera and the low-end Mediwork portable fundus camera of the same patients. Then, we propose a cross-laterality feature alignment pre-training scheme and a self-attention camera adaptor module to improve the model robustness. The cross-laterality feature alignment training encourages the model to learn common knowledge from the same patient's left and right fundus images and improve model generalization. Meanwhile, the device adaptation module learns feature transformation from the target domain to the source domain. We conduct comprehensive experiments on both the UK Biobank database and our FCP data. The experimental results show that the CVD risk regression accuracy and the result consistency over two cameras are improved with our proposed method. The code is available here: https://github.com/linzhlalala/CVD-risk-based-on-retinal-fundus-images

Keywords: Retinal fundus image · Cardiovascular diseases · Domain adaptation · Domain generalization

© The Author(s), under exclusive license to Springer Nature Switzerland AG 2022
L. Wang et al. (Eds.): MICCAI 2022, LNCS 13432, pp. 593–603, 2022.
https://doi.org/10.1007/978-3-031-16434-7_57

1   Introduction

Cardiovascular diseases (CVD) are the leading causes of mortality around the world [17]. Early screening and identification of the at-risk populations are necessary for CVD prevention and control. The existing CVD risk estimation guidelines (for example, the WHO-CVD score [12]) are based on the patient physical measures and laboratory testing, such as body massive index (BMI) and high-density lipoprotein (HDL). However, some inputs are difficult to acquire in scenarios where medical professionals and laboratory testing are not accessible. A prospective solution is to predict fundus-image-based CVD risk with an automated CAD algorithm using a portable fundus camera. Recent studies [4,16] have revealed the associations between the retinal fundus and its CVD risk factors. The fundus-image-based CVD risk estimation on a portable camera can significantly reduce the examination cost and the requirement of medical professionals. It will also improve medical democratization and let more people benefit from medical AI. Despite this prospective application, there still exist issues to be solved to achieve successful implementation. One of the most challenging problems is the domain discrepancy between fundus cameras. The ideal high-quality retinal samples for CVD risk inference are mainly captured by expensive clinical devices. For example, the retinal images from the UK Biobank [19] (UKB) are collected using the Topcon 3D OCT-1000 MKII. Meanwhile, the retinal samples in the practical scenario are sometimes captured by low-cost portable fundus cameras. The key components of the fundus camera, such as light source, lens, and camera sensor, are all different. The impacts on images quality and style can lead to the problem of domain discrepancy.

To tackle the problem of fundus camera adaptation, the existing efforts have mainly focused on feature and image alignment. The CFEA [14] exploited collaborative adversarial learning and self-ensembling for feature adaptation on the optic disc (OD) and optic cup (OC) segmentation task. The CSFA [13] concentrated on the content and style feature consistency among source domain images, target-like query images and target domain images also for the disc and cup segmentation task. Yang et al. [21] proposed a camera-oriented residual-CycleGAN to pre-process the images and improve the diabetic retinopathy prediction performance on multiple cameras data. Ju et al. [11] proposed a modified CycleGAN to bridge the domain gap between regular and ultra-widefield fundus images for several tasks. However, these solutions only consider the target domain performance with abundant training images from the target domain required, which is impossible to collect in our task. Furthermore, these methods also ignore the cross-domain consistency, which may lead to disastrous outcomes for CVD risk evaluation.

In this work, we collect a Fundus Camera Paired (FCP) dataset containing the pair-wise fundus images of the same patients using two cameras (Topcon upright camera and Mediwork portable camera).[1] Our strategy on the task is

---

[1] We do not provide CVD risk ground-truth for the FCP dataset due to the absence of patient information.

two-fold: domain generalization [20] and domain adaptation [9]. The domain generalization is to improve the adaptability with the unseen target domain. Inspired by the contrastive learning [2,3,8], we propose a cross-laterality feature alignment (CLFA) pre-training scheme to utilize the images of both lateralities, which are believed to share the invariant representation for the CVD risk. Besides the supervised CVD risk regression, we introduce an asymmetric feature alignment task for domain generalization by comparing the pair-wise image features and letting the superior one teach the other one to enhance the learning on domain-invariant representation. Domain adaptation is to adapt the model to the target domain given. To maintain the model knowledge on the CVD task, we adopt a plug-in camera adaptor module based on multi-head self-attention. The camera adaptor can transform the target domain image feature to match its source domain edition. The experiment shows that our two-step strategy improves the CVD risk regression performance on the UKB dataset and the prediction consistency between the two cameras on our FCP dataset. Moreover, we conduct ablation studies on our pre-training method and camera adaptor. We find that our CLFA pre-training reduces the feature-space discrepancy between the UKB dataset and the other cameras. Meanwhile, our camera adaptor can significantly improve the CVD result coefficient on different pre-trained models.

2   Method

2.1   Cross-Laterality Feature Alignment Pre-training

Our cross-laterality feature alignment (CLFA) pre-training is inspired by the domain generalization research [20] and contrastive learning [2,3,8]. The UKB provides both left and right fundus photos for each patient, which can be utilized as natural positive sample pairs. We hypothesize that the visual clues of CVD risk have invariant representation over the two eyes. A deep learning model would have better generalization when identifying the invariant representation. As shown in Fig. 1, our pre-training adopts the siamese network [5] and lets both lateralities share the backbone model (a vision transformer model in this paper). The model is simultaneously trained with two branches.

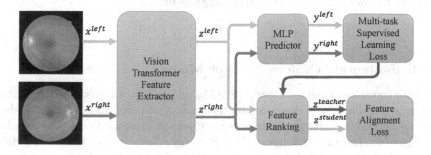

Fig. 1. The cross-laterality feature alignment pre-training has two branches: a multi-task supervised learning branch and an asymmetric feature alignment branch.

In the supervised learning branch, we jointly train the model on the WHO-CVD score as well as seven clinical variables explicitly related to the WHO-CVD, including age, systolic blood pressure (SBP), total cholesterol (TC), body massive index (BMI), gender, smoking status, and diabetes status. The aim is to improve the model generalization by sharing representations between the tasks [22]. Let $S = \left\{ x_i^{left}, x_i^{right}, y_i^{rgs}, y_i^{cls} \right\}_{i=1}^{n}$ $(rgs = 1, 2, 3, 4, 5; cls = 1, 2, 3)$ denote the training set, where the x_i^{left} denotes the left fundus photo, x_i^{right} denotes the right fundus photo, y_i^{rgs} denotes the regression labels, and y_i^{cls} denotes the binary classification labels. The backbone model is defined as the function of $f_\theta : \mathcal{X} \rightarrow (\mathcal{Y}^{rgs}, \mathcal{Y}^{cls})$. The mean squared error (MSE) and binary cross-entropy (BCE) are used as the loss functions for the regression and binary classification. The weighting of tasks are denoted as $W = \left\{ w^{rgs}, w^{cls} \right\}$ $(r = 1, 2, ..., 5; c = 1, 2, ..., 3)$. The $\sigma(\cdot)$ denotes the *sigmoid* function. The loss function of branch is defined as follows:

$$\ell_{sup.}(\theta) = \sum_{rgs=1}^{5} w^{rgs} \cdot MSE\left(y_i^{rgs}, f_\theta^{rgs}(x_i)\right) + \sum_{cls=1}^{3} w^{cls} \cdot BCE\left(y_i^{cls}, \sigma(f_\theta^{cls}(x_i))\right) \quad (1)$$

Note that both eyes are used as laterality-agnostic inputs. Hence, for every patient we have two supervised loss $\{\ell_{sup.}^{left}, \ell_{sup.}^{right}\}$.

The feature alignment learning branch is designed to enable the interaction between two fundus image features from the same patient. With the input pair $\{x_i^{left}, x_i^{right}\}$, the two supervised learning loss $\{\ell_{sup.}^{left}, \ell_{sup.}^{right}\}$ will have a larger one and a smaller one. The feature with the smaller loss is selected as the teacher while the other is selected as the student. This operation can be regarded as a feature-level knowledge distillation. The backbone model function can be split into two steps: the feature extractor function $g_\theta : \mathcal{X} \rightarrow \mathcal{Z}$ and the predict function $p_\theta : \mathcal{Z} \rightarrow (\mathcal{Y}^{rgs}, \mathcal{Y}^{cls})$. The $SD(\cdot)$ means the stop-gradient operation. The loss function is defined as follows:

$$\ell_{ali.}(\theta) = \begin{cases} MSE\left(g_\theta(x_i^l eft), SD(g_\theta(x_i^r iht))\right) & \ell_{sup.}^{left} \geq \ell_{sup.}^{right}, \\ MSE\left(g_\theta(x_i^r ight), SD(g_\theta(x_i^l eft))\right) & \ell_{sup.}^{left} < \ell_{sup.}^{right} \end{cases} \quad (2)$$

Hence the overall loss function of the CLFA pre-training is as follows, where the λ denotes the weighting for the feature alignment branch:

$$L_S(\theta) = L_S^{sup.}(\theta) + \lambda \cdot L_S^{ali.}(\theta) \quad (3)$$

2.2 Self-attention Camera Adaptor Module

Our self-attention camera adaptor (SACA) module is inspired by the feature learning approaches [9] in domain adaptation research. We freeze the pre-trained model to anchor the outcome of the source domain. Meanwhile, we add an adaptor module for the target domain. This strategy allows us to utilize the pairing information in our FCP dataset and establish the benchmark based on cross-domain consistency.

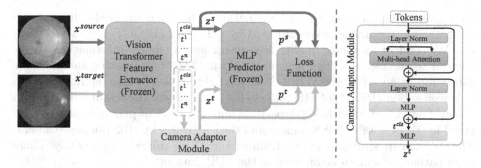

Fig. 2. The left part of the figure illustrates the workflow of prediction. The blue arrows represent the prediction procedure of the source domain, while the yellow arrows represent the prediction procedure of the target domain. The right part of the figure shows the structure of the camera adaptor module. (Color figure online)

The module network is shown in Fig. 2. Based on our early performance comparison, we choose the vision transformer [6] (ViT) as our backbone model. The ViT feature extractor outputs the classification token and image patch tokens as $T^{out} = \{t^{cls}, t^1, t^2, ..., t^N\}$. Generally, the classification token (t^{cls}) is used as the image feature (denoted as $\mathcal{Z}$ in the Sect. 2.1). However, the image patch embeddings are also informative and can be utilized in our task. We adopt the block design of ViT, including the multiheaded self-attention (MSA), multilayer perceptron (MLP), Layernorm (LN), and residual connections. Besides the block, we apply an extra MLP projector. The camera adaptor module ($k_\beta : T \rightarrow \mathcal{Z}_a$) can be described as follow:

$$T' = MSA(LN(T_{out})) + T_{out}$$
$$T_a = MLP(LN(T')) + T' = \{t_a^{cls}, t_a^1, t_a^2, ..., t_a^N\} \qquad (4)$$
$$\mathcal{Z}_a = MLP(t_a^{cls})$$

To train the camera adaptor module, we use pair-wise data which is denoted as $P = \{x_i^s, x_i^t\}_{i=1}^n$. For each image pair $\{x^s, x^t\}$ fed in the source model and the adapted model, we have the WHO-CVD prediction $\{p^s, p^t\}$. We define the training loss function as:

$$L_P(\beta) = \frac{1}{n} \sum_{i=1}^{N} MSE\left(p_i^s, p_i^t\right) \qquad (5)$$

3 Experiment

3.1 Dataset

In this work, we use the UK Biobank retinal photography dataset (UKB) [19] for backbone model pre-training and our Fundus Camera Paired (FCP) dataset for camera adaptor training and evaluation. The UKB originally had 58,700 patients, and the images were captured by a Topcon 3D OCT-1000 MKII camera. We conduct an image quality assessment and a clinical information assessment. The selected 41,530 patients are split into 33,224 for training and 8,306 for validation balanced by the WHO-CVD score. From the validate split, we slice a balanced subset (UKB*) of 416 patients (741 images) for the feature distribution study. The FCP dataset has 227 patients and 415 pairs of pair-wise photos captured by Topcon TRC-NW8 camera and the Mediwork FC-162 portable camera. The patients are split into 182 for training and 45 for validation randomly. There is no patient information collected in the FCP dataset.

3.2 Implementation Details and Metrics

For the UKB dataset, we calculate the WHO-CVD score according to the WHO guideline [12] and transform it into the logarithmic scale to normalize the distribution. Our backbone vision transformer (ViT) model structure is as the "R26+S/32" in the AugReg [18]. The model loads the ImageNet pre-trained [18] as the initial state. The default task weighting w^c, w^r, λ mentioned in Sect.2.1 are all set to 1.0 for default. For backbone model pre-training, the batch size is 16, and the start learning rate is 1e−4. The augmentation includes resize, crop, color jitter, and grayscale. For the camera adaptor module, the batch size is 32, and the start learning rate is 1e−2. All experiments in this study use the Adam optimizer with momentum 0.9 and weight decay 1e−4.

coefficient of determination (R^2) is used to evaluate the WHO-CVD regression performance and the WHO-CVD result consistency between cameras with the Topcon result as pseudo target and the Mediwork result as the prediction. We also experimentally introduce the **Multi-Kernel Maximum Mean Discrepancy (MK-MMD)** [7] to measure the feature-distribution discrepancy between domains.

3.3 Ablation Study

We perform an ablation study to show the effectiveness of each design in our backbone model pre-training and camera adaptation.

Backbone Model Pre-training In this experiment, we pre-train several backbone models on the UKB dataset and then train the camera adaptor[2] for each backbone model. Table 1 shows our experiment result of the backbone model pre-training. The baseline model is the ViT model with only the supervised learning branch and the WHO-CVD regression task. In "Weight1" the eight tasks describe in Sect. 2.1 are equally weighted. With "Weight1", we observe the R^2_{CVD} degrades and the R^2 scores of systolic blood pressure (SBP), total cholesterol (TC), and body massive index (BMI) regression

---

[2] As our uniform self-attention camera adaptor.

Table 1. Ablation study on the pre-training (CVD = WHO-CVD regression on the UKB; T=Topcon data in FCP; M = Mediwork data in FCP; U* = A balanced subset of the UKB validate set.)

Method	R^2_{CVD}	$R^2_{(T,M)}$		MK-MMD (Pre-Ada.)		
		Pre-ada.	Post-ada.	T↔M	U*↔M	U*↔T
Baseline	0.5586	**0.3610**	0.4071	**0.3028**	0.4898	0.1836
Weight1	0.5319	0.3263	0.4373	0.3996	0.3789	0.3372
Weight2	0.5643	0.1572	0.4176	0.3456	0.3972	0.2333
Weight2+SimSiam	0.0267	-0.0128	0	0.0002	4.2678	0.0003
Weight2+CLFA	**0.5703**	0.2144	**0.4937**	0.3741	**0.3557**	**0.1597**

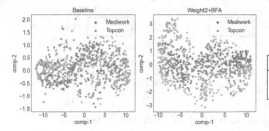

Model	$AUC_{lat.}$	AUC_{camera}
Baseline	0.5270	0.6414
Weight2+CLFA	**0.7322**	**0.9722**

(a) The t-SNE features visualization on the FCP dataset

(b) Laterality and camera prediction performance on the FCP dataset

Fig. 3. Study of features extracted from the pre-training models

are very low. Therefore, in "Weight2," we remove the SBP, TC, BMI and increase the weight of WHO-CVD and achieve an increased R^2_{CVD}. Based on the "Weight2" supervised learning branch, we add the second branch of contrastive learning [2] or our Cross-Laterality Feature Alignment (CLFA). Surprisingly, the "Weight2+SimSiam" has obtained a collapsing performance while the "Weight2+CLFA" achieves the highest R^2_{CVD} and post-adaptation $R^2_{(T,M)}$. It indicates that our "Weight2+CLFA" provides the best potential and adaptability. The MK-MMD comparison shows the "Weight2+CLFA" has the lowest feature-distribution discrepancy between UKB and Mediwork as well as between UKB and Topcon. These two variables show a negative correlation to the $R^2_{(T,M)}$. However, the pre-adaptation $R^2_{(T,M)}$ and feature-distribution discrepancy between Topcon and Mediwork shows no strong relation to post-adaptation $R^2_{(T,M)}$. The relation between MK-MMD and post-adaptation $R^2_{(T,M)}$ indicates the MK-MMD can be a metric to evaluate model adaptability in future research.

To further investigate the factors for model adaptability, we visualize the image feature of the FCP dataset extracted by "Baseline" and "Weight2+CLFA" through t-SNE as shown in Fig. 3a. We figure out "Weight2+CLFA" has better feature clustering over different cameras. To quantify this observation, we train a single layer fully connected neural network on the image feature to pre-

Table 2. Ablation study on the camera adaptor (SA = Self-attention.)

Module	$R^2(T, M)$			
	ℓ_{CVD}	$\ell_{feature}$	ℓ_{MK-MMD}	$\ell_{CVD} + \ell_{feature}$
MLP	0.3831	0.3479	0.1349	**0.3602**
SA Block	0.3229	0.3097	**0.3052**	0
SA Block+MLP	**0.4937**	**0.4885**	0.2113	0.3458

Table 3. The overall performance comparison (CVD = WHO-CVD regression on UKB; T = Topcon data in FCP; M = Mediwork data in FCP.)

Method	R^2(CVD)	$R^2(T, M)$
Baseline	0.5586	0.3610
Baseline+DAN [15]	0.5586	0.3243
Baseline+DANN [1]	−0.0253	0.0254
Baseline+MDD [23]	−0.0104	1.000
Baseline+Pix2Pix GAN [10]	0.5586	0.3183
Baseline+Cycle GAN [24]	0.5586	0.3594
Ours (CLFA Pre-training + Adaptation Module)	**0.5703**	**0.4732**

dict the eye laterality and camera. The result is as Fig. 3b, and it proves the "Weight2+CLFA" feature can support better discrimination of laterality and camera. Furthermore, it indicates that discrimination on camera may positively affect post-adaptation result consistency Table 3.

Camera Adaptor Module. To verify the design of our camera adaptor module, we test it under several different settings with a range of loss functions. The results in Table 2 demonstrate that both the self-attention block and the MLP projector are essential for our camera adaptor module. The comparison of the loss function shows that the WHO-CVD score-focused loss function has the best results. We also observe that optimizing the feature distribution discrepancy (MK-MMD) between features does not improve the prediction result consistency.

3.4 Quantitative Analysis

To compare our proposed method and other approaches, we select several typical approaches of feature-alignment and image-alignment. The baseline model in this experiment is as Sect. 3.3 and is without the adaptor. For feature-alignment, we test the DAN [15] which optimize the MK-MMD between transformed features, the DANN [1] which apply the adversairal training, and the MDD [23] which using an auxiliary classifier to optimize the discrepancy between the two domains. For image alignment, we select the Pix2Pix GAN [10] and Cycle GAN [24] as the generators. The comparison shows that our method improves the result consistency over the two cameras. However, DAN, DANN, Cycle GAN, and Pix2Pix GAN lead to a lower consistency than baseline. The MDD reach $R^2 = 1.0$ as the model output a collapsed result. For the DAN, the reason for degrading may be DAN is designed for unpaired data and its MK-MMD-based loss function have no advantage when pair-wise data is available, which has also been proved in our ablation study (Sect. 2). The DANN and MDD require the parameter updating on the backbone model and lead to the degrading of backbone model. For the Pix2Pix GAN, we check its generated images and find the generator focusing on color toning or image style adjustment with a loss of the microvascular vessels' detail, which is supposed to be an essential visual representation of CVD. The Cycle GAN learns some image style transformation but fails to improve the prediction outcome. The advantage of our CLFA pretraining plus camera adaptor method is that both generalization and adaptation are considered to improve the model's adaptability.

4 Conclusion

This paper researches the domain discrepancy problem in developing a fundus-image-based CVD risk predicting algorithm. We observe that the deep learning model trained conventionally will have a variant representation on photos from different fundus cameras. Therefore, we propose a cross-laterality feature learning training method and a camera adaptor module. The experiments show that our design has improved on the prediction result consistency. Also, we find that the feature-space distribution discrepancy between pre-training and target domain data may be the key factor of model transportability. Future research will explore the data augmentation in adaption to overcome the data lacking and utilize the FCP data in the backbone model pre-training.

References

1. Ajakan, H., Germain, P., Larochelle, H., Laviolette, F., Marchand, M.: Domain-adversarial neural networks. arXiv preprint arXiv:1412.4446 (2014)
2. Chen, X., He, K.: Exploring simple Siamese representation learning. In: IEEE Conference on Computer Vision and Pattern Recognition, CVPR 2021, Virtual, 19–25 June 2021, pp. 15750–15758. Computer Vision Foundation/IEEE (2021)
3. Chen, X., Xie, S., He, K.: An empirical study of training self-supervised vision transformers. arXiv preprint arXiv:2104.02057 (2021)
4. Cheung, C.Y., et al.: Retinal vascular fractal dimension and its relationship with cardiovascular and ocular risk factors. Am. J. Ophthalmol. **154**(4), 663–674 (2012)
5. Chicco, D.: Siamese neural networks: an overview. Artif. Neural Netw., 73–94 (2021)
6. Dosovitskiy, A., et al.: An image is worth 16x16 words: transformers for image recognition at scale. In: 9th International Conference on Learning Representations, ICLR 2021, Virtual Event, Austria, 3–7 May 2021. OpenReview.net (2021)

7. Gretton, A., et al.: Optimal kernel choice for large-scale two-sample tests. In: Advances in Neural Information Processing Systems 25 (2012)

8. Grill, J., et al.: Bootstrap your own latent - a new approach to self-supervised learning. In: Larochelle, H., Ranzato, M., Hadsell, R., Balcan, M., Lin, H. (eds.) Advances in Neural Information Processing Systems 33: Annual Conference on Neural Information Processing Systems 2020, NeurIPS 2020, 6–12 December 2020, virtual (2020)

9. Guan, H., Liu, M.: Domain adaptation for medical image analysis: a survey. IEEE Trans. Biomed. Eng. (2021)

10. Isola, P., Zhu, J.Y., Zhou, T., Efros, A.A.: Image-to-image translation with conditional adversarial networks. In: Proceedings of the IEEE Conference on Computer Vision and Pattern Recognition, pp. 1125–1134 (2017)

11. Ju, L., Wang, X., Zhao, X., Bonnington, P., Drummond, T., Ge, Z.: Leveraging regular fundus images for training UWF fundus diagnosis models via adversarial learning and pseudo-labeling. IEEE Trans. Med. Imaging 40(10), 2911–2925 (2021). https://doi.org/10.1109/TMI.2021.3056395

12. Kaptoge, S., et al.: World health organization cardiovascular disease risk charts: revised models to estimate risk in 21 global regions. Lancet Glob. Health 7(10), e1332–e1345 (2019)

13. Lei, H., et al.: Unsupervised domain adaptation based image synthesis and feature alignment for joint optic disc and cup segmentation. IEEE J. Biomed. Health Inform. 26(1), 90–102 (2022). https://doi.org/10.1109/JBHI.2021.3085770

14. Liu, P., Kong, B., Li, Z., Zhang, S., Fang, R.: CFEA: collaborative feature ensembling adaptation for domain adaptation in unsupervised optic disc and cup segmentation. In: Shen, D., Liu, T., Peters, T.M., Staib, L.H., Essert, C., Zhou, S., Yap, P.-T., Khan, A. (eds.) MICCAI 2019. LNCS, vol. 11768, pp. 521–529. Springer, Cham (2019). https://doi.org/10.1007/978-3-030-32254-0_58

15. Long, M., Cao, Y., Wang, J., Jordan, M.: Learning transferable features with deep adaptation networks. In: International Conference on Machine Learning, pp. 97–105. PMLR (2015)

16. Poplin, R., et al.: Prediction of cardiovascular risk factors from retinal fundus photographs via deep learning. Nat. Biomed. Eng. 2(3), 158–164 (2018)

17. Roth, G.A., et al.: Global burden of cardiovascular diseases and risk factors, 1990–2019: update from the GBD 2019 study. J. Am. Coll. Cardiol. 76(25), 2982–3021 (2020)

18. Steiner, A., Kolesnikov, A., Zhai, X., Wightman, R., Uszkoreit, J., Beyer, L.: How to train your ViT? data, augmentation, and regularization in vision transformers. CoRR abs/2106.10270 (2021)

19. Sudlow, C., et al.: UK biobank: an open access resource for identifying the causes of a wide range of complex diseases of middle and old age. PLoS Med. 12(3), e1001779 (2015)

20. Wang, J., Lan, C., Liu, C., Ouyang, Y., Zeng, W., Qin, T.: Generalizing to unseen domains: a survey on domain generalization. arXiv preprint arXiv:2103.03097 (2021)

21. Yang, D., Yang, Y., Huang, T., Wu, B., Wang, L., Xu, Y.: Residual-CycleGAN based camera adaptation for robust diabetic retinopathy screening. In: Martel, A.L., Abolmaesumi, P., Stoyanov, D., Mateus, D., Zuluaga, M.A., Zhou, S.K., Racoceanu, D., Joskowicz, L. (eds.) MICCAI 2020. LNCS, vol. 12262, pp. 464–474. Springer, Cham (2020). https://doi.org/10.1007/978-3-030-59713-9_45

22. Zhang, Y., Yang, Q.: A survey on multi-task learning. IEEE Trans. Knowl. Data Eng. (2021)

23. Zhang, Y., Liu, T., Long, M., Jordan, M.: Bridging theory and algorithm for domain adaptation. In: International Conference on Machine Learning, pp. 7404–7413. PMLR (2019)
24. Zhu, J.Y., Park, T., Isola, P., Efros, A.A.: Unpaired image-to-image translation using cycle-consistent adversarial networks. In: Proceedings of the IEEE International Conference on Computer Vision, pp. 2223–2232 (2017)

Opinions Vary? Diagnosis First!

Junde Wu, Huihui Fang, Dalu Yang, Zhaowei Wang, Wenshuo Zhou,
Fangxin Shang, Yehui Yang, and Yanwu Xu[✉]

Intelligent Healthcare Unit, Beijing, China
ywxu@ieee.org

Abstract. With the advancement of deep learning techniques, an
increasing number of methods have been proposed for optic disc and
cup (OD/OC) segmentation from the fundus images. Clinically, OD/OC
segmentation is often annotated by multiple clinical experts to mitigate
the personal bias. However, it is hard to train the automated deep learning models on multiple labels. A common practice to tackle the issue is
majority vote, e.g., taking the average of multiple labels. However such
a strategy ignores the different expertness of medical experts. Motivated
by the observation that OD/OC segmentation is often used for the glaucoma diagnosis clinically, in this paper, we propose a novel strategy to
fuse the multi-rater OD/OC segmentation labels via the glaucoma diagnosis performance. Specifically, we assess the expertness of each rater
through an attentive glaucoma diagnosis network. For each rater, its
contribution for the diagnosis will be reflected as an expertness map. To
ensure the expertness maps are general for different glaucoma diagnosis
models, we further propose an Expertness Generator (ExpG) to eliminate the high-frequency components in the optimization process. Based
on the obtained expertness maps, the multi-rater labels can be fused as
a single ground-truth which we dubbed as Diagnosis First Ground-truth
(*DiagFirst*GT). Experimental results show that by using *DiagFirst*GT
as ground-truth, OD/OC segmentation networks will predict the masks
with superior glaucoma diagnosis performance.

Keywords: Multi-rater learning · Optic disc/cup segmentation ·
Glaucoma diagnosis

1 Introduction

Accurate optic disc and cup (OD/OC) segmentation on fundus images is important for the clinical assessment of glaucoma. It has been increasingly popular to
develop automated OD/OC segmentation [13,14]ß, which is especially accelerated by the exciting breakthroughs of deep neural networks and publicly available
datasets [2,7,24]. Different from the natural image dataset, OD/OC segmentation datasets are often annotated by multiple clinical experts (e.g., RIGA [2],
REFUGE-2 [7]) to mitigate the subjective bias of particular rater. However, this
multi-rater scenario also brings challenges to the deployment of deep learning

© The Author(s), under exclusive license to Springer Nature Switzerland AG 2022
L. Wang et al. (Eds.): MICCAI 2022, LNCS 13432, pp. 604–613, 2022.
https://doi.org/10.1007/978-3-031-16434-7_58

models, since they are commonly trained by a single ground-truth. For training the neural network in multi-rater scenario, a common practice is to take the average of multiple labels, i.e., majority vote. Although this fusion strategy is simple and easy to implement, it comes at the cost of ignoring the different expertness of multiple experts [9].

It is thus necessary to estimate the rater expertness for the fusion of multi-rater annotations. A popular way is to estimate the expertness based on the raw image prior [5,18,25]. However, we note that OD/OC segmentation is clinically established for the glaucoma diagnosis. Specifically, the Cup-to-Disc Ratio (CDR) calculated from the segmentation masks is an essential clinical parameter for the glaucoma diagnosis [10]. This inspires us to take glaucoma diagnosis as a gold standard to estimate the multi-rater expertness and fuse the multi-rater labels. The fused label then can be used as the ground-truth for the segmentation training.

Specifically, we use a glaucoma diagnosis network to evaluate the multi-rater expertness. The evaluation diagnosis network is implemented by a segmentation attentive diagnosis network, following [31]. We optimize an expertness map for each rater to maximize the glaucoma diagnosis performance of the network. The ground-truth fused according to this multi-rater expertness maps is named as Diagnosis First Ground-truth ($DiagFirst$GT). In order to make $DiagFirst$GT general for different diagnosis networks, we further propose Expertness Generator (ExpG) to generate the expertness maps. ExpG helps to constrain the high-frequency components by the continuity nature of neural network, so as to promise the effectiveness of $DiagFirst$GT across different diagnosis networks.

In brief, three major contributions are made with this paper. First, we propose a novel strategy to fuse the ground-truth from multiple OD/OC segmentation labels. The obtained ground-truth is called $DiagFirst$GT, which can significantly facilitate the glaucoma diagnosis. Secondly, in order to reinforce the generalization of $DiagFirst$GT, we further propose ExpG to generate the expertness maps in the optimization process. ExpG eliminates the high-frequency components by the continuity of neural network. Finally, the experimental results show the OD/OC segmentation models trained on $DiagFirst$GT estimates the masks with a clear 3% AUC improvement on standard glaucoma diagnosis network. Such a method can be freely applied to any model architecture and gains general improvement without external data.

2   Methodology

2.1   Motivation

In clinical research, a better segmentation often lead to a better diagnosis. In the neural network models, many prior work [4,27,31] also show that lesions segmentation masks can bring diagnosis networks with solid improvement. Move a step further, a natural question is that whether the segmentation masks with better qualities are better for the disease diagnosis?

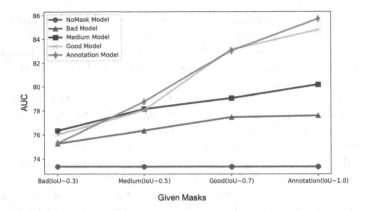

Fig. 1. Diagnosis performance of segmentation masks with different qualities. It shows the OD/OC mask quality and glaucoma diagnosis performance are positively correlated.

We design a simple experiment on fundus images to answer this question. We train ResNet50 [12] to diagnose glaucoma from the fundus images, with OD/OC segmentation masks as the auxiliary information. The fundus image and its segmentation mask are concatenated as the input of the network. The network is supervised by the glaucoma classification labels on a private dataset with 1600 samples. Segmentation masks with different qualities are collected from early-stop training, which are denoted as Bad (average IOU of segmentation is 0.3), Medium (= 0.5), Good (= 0.7), and Annotation. We use these masks to train the corresponding diagnosis networks, denoted as Bad Model, Medium Model, Good Model, and Annotation Model. Then the segmentation masks with different qualities are given to each model for the inference. The final diagnosis performance measured by AUC score (%) is shown in Fig. 1. In the figure, NoMask Model denotes training the diagnosis network only on the raw images.

It is clear to see that better segmentation masks promote the diagnosis performance more than the worse. The diagnosis networks trained on better segmentation masks show better average diagnosis performance. In the inference, the diagnosis performance is also gradually improved with the improvement of the segmentation quality. This result suggests, like what in clinical research, better OD/OC segmentation is also more conducive to the glaucoma diagnosis in the neural network models.

2.2 Learning *DiagFirst*GT

Motivated by this relationship between OD/OC segmentation and glaucoma diagnosis, we want to find the optimal OD/OC segmentation label toward the glaucoma diagnosis when multiple labels are collected. Such a label, based on the results above, may be closer to the potential gold segmentation. To fuse

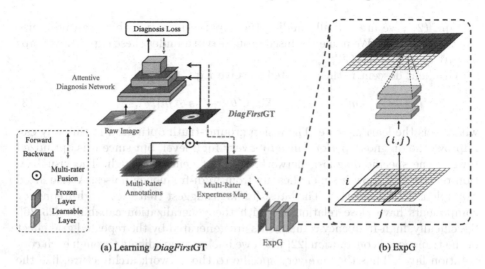

Fig. 2. Overall flow of proposed method. Blue denotes static parameters. Orange denotes learnable parameters. (Color figure online)

multiple labels to one ground-truth, we weighted sum the multiple labels by the expertness of each rater:

$$\text{Groundtruth} = s \odot m = \sum_{i=1}^{n} s_i * m_i, \tag{1}$$

where $*$ denotes the element-wise multiplication, s_i and m_i are the annotation and the expertness map of the rater i, respectively.

We then assess the rater expertness through the glaucoma diagnosis. In other words, the rater contributes more to the correct diagnosis would be given higher expertness. Toward that end, we take the multi-rater expertness maps as the learnable variables to maximize the diagnosis performance of a OD/OC attentive diagnosis network. The network is pre-trained on the same data so as to correctly evaluate the diagnosis contribution. The optimization is solved by the gradient descent to activate the target class in diagnosis network. We dubbed the label fused as $DiagFirst$GT.

The overflow of learning $DiagFirst$GT is shown in Fig. 2 (a). Formally, consider each raw image $x \in \mathbb{R}^{h \times w \times c}$ is annotated by n raters, resulting in n segmentation masks $s \in \mathbb{R}^{h \times w \times n}$, and the image is diagnosed as $y \in [0, 1]$. Let θ denotes the set of diagnosis model parameters. $L(\theta, x, y)$ denotes the loss function of a standard classification task. Our goal is to find an optimal expertness map $m \in \mathbb{R}^{h \times w \times n}$ by solving the following optimization problem:

$$m^* = \arg \min_m L(\theta, x \oplus [s \odot m], y), \tag{2}$$

where $\oplus$ denotes concatenation operation, m^* denotes the optimal expertness maps. Note that we applied Softmax on m to normalize the weights. According to Eqn. (2) , we are actually finding the expertness maps which can minimize the diagnosis loss. We name the fused ground-truth under these expertness maps $s \odot m^*$ as $DiagFirst$GT.

Gradient descent is then adopted to solve Eqn. (2)

$$m^{t+1} = m^t + \alpha \nabla_m L(\theta, x \oplus [s \odot m], y), \tag{3}$$

where α is the learning rate. The fusion ground-truth optimized in this way can improve the diagnosis performance to a very high level, but since it is optimized toward one specific diagnosis network, it is not general enough. The visualization results also show it suffers heavily from high-frequency noises. A visualized example is shown in Fig. 3. The latest findings suggest that these high-frequency components have close relationship with the generalization capability [23,26]. Specifically, high-frequency components are generated by the repeated grid effect of the transposed convolution [22] when we backprop gradients through each convolution layer. Thus they are very specific to the network architecture, like the number of the layers, the stride of the convolution, etc.

2.3   ExpG

Therefore, a possible approach to improve generalization of $DiagFirst$GT is to constrain the high-frequency components in the optimization process. We tried several methods to achieve the goal, including Transformation Robustness (TransRob), Fourier Transform (Fourier) and proposed Expertness Generator (ExpG). Transformation Robustness constrains high-frequency gradients by applying small transformations to the expertness map before optimization. In practice, we rotate, scale and jitter the maps. Fourier Transform transforms the expertness map parameters to frequency domain, thus decorrelated the relationship between the neighbour pixels.

ExpG constrains the high-frequency components by the continuity nature of the neural network, which is implemented by a tiny CNN based pixel generator. An illustration of ExpG is shown in Fig. 2 (b). The network scans one pixel at a time. For each pixel it predicts the pixel value given the position of the pixel. The input of ExpG is the coordinate vector (i, j) and the output is the pixel value. ExpG is optimized to generate expertness maps which are able to minimize the diagnosis loss. Denote the parameters of ExpG as ϕ, our goal is to solve:

$$\arg\min_{\phi} L(\theta, x \oplus [s \odot \{ExpG_\phi(i,j)\}_{i=1\sim h}^{j=1\sim w}], y), \tag{4}$$

where $\{ExpG_\phi(i,j)\}_{i=1\sim h}^{j=1\sim w}$ denotes generated expertness map with size $h \times w \times n$ by ExpG. Since the continuity of the neural network mapping function, similar inputs tend to cause similar outputs, which lead the element values in expertness maps variant smoothly between the positions and thus eliminate the high-frequency components.

The visualized results of all high-frequency elimination methods are shown in Fig. 3. The first line is a non-glaucoma example and the second line is a glaucoma

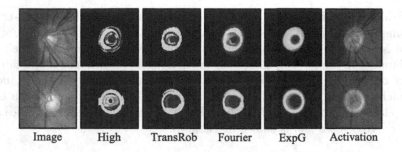

Fig. 3. Visualized results of various high-frequency elimination methods and ExpG. From left to right are raw fundus image, original high-frequency results, TransRob, Fourier, ExpG low-frequency results and activation results of ExpG.

example. We can see the visualized effects of TransRob and Fourier are obviously improved comparing with high-frequency examples. But ExpG achieves much better visualized effects than both of them. Thus, we adopt ExpG to eliminate the high-frequency components in the experiments.

3 Experiment

3.1 Experimental Settings

All the experiments are implemented with the PyTorch platform and trained/tested on 4 T P40 GPU with 24GB of memory. All images are uniformly resized to the dimension of 256×256 pixels. The networks are trained in an end-to-end manner using Adam optimizer with a mini-batch of 16 for 80 epochs. The learning rate is initially set to 1×10^{-4}. The detailed hyper-parameters and architectures can be found in the code.

We conduct the experiments on REFUGE-2 [7] dataset. REFUGE-2 is a publicly available dataset for retinal cup and disc segmentation annotated by multiple glaucoma experts. REFUGE-2 contains in total 2000 color fundus images, including three sets each with 1200 images for training, 400 for validation, and 400 for testing. Seven glaucoma experts from different organizations labeled the optic cup and disc contour masks manually for the REFUGE-2 benchmark. 200 samples correspond to glaucomatous subjects, and the others correspond to non-glaucomatous subjects. The glaucomatous subjects are distributed equally to the training, validation, and test set. It is worth noting that the diagnosis network is pre-trained on REFUGE-2 training set to generate $DiagFirst$GTs, thus no external data is used.

3.2 Comparing with SOTA

To verify the glaucoma diagnosis effect of $DiagFirst$GT, we compare it with state-of-the-art (SOTA) multi-rater fusion strategies on REFUGE-2 dataset.

Specifically, we train standard UNet on various multi-rater fusion ground-truths, including random fusion (Random), majority vote (MV), STAPLE [22], AggNet [1] and Max-Mig [5]. We then evaluate the diagnosis performance of their estimated masks on the test set. The glaucoma diagnosis performance is evaluated by a range of OD/OC segmentation-assisted glaucoma prediction methods, including which based on vertical Cup-to-Disc Ratio (vCDR) [6,19] and which based on deep learning models [15,17,27,28]. The obtained diagnosis performance measured by AUC score (%) is shown in Table 1a.

Table 1. Comparison of $DiagFirst$GT and SOTA multi-rater fused ground-truths on a range of diagnosis models (a) and segmentation models (b).

| Ground Truth | Diagnosis Models | | | | | |
| | vCDR | | Deep Learning | | | |
	[6]	[19]	[17]	[15]	[28]	[27]
NoMask	-	-	77.45	79.21	80.06	79.18
Random	68.79	73.34	79.74	82.76	84.34	85.07
MV	72.20	76.04	80.54	83.65	85.55	86.23
STAPLE	71.66	77.41	81.23	84.17	86.18	87.00
AggNet	71.25	75.91	80.42	83.80	85.75	87.50
Max-Mig	70.14	75.02	80.31	83.88	85.73	86.76
$DiagFirst$GT	**74.12**	**79.23**	**82.20**	**86.27**	**88.86**	**89.62**

| | MV | | | $DiagFirst$GT | | |
	$\mathcal{D}_{disc}$	$\mathcal{D}_{cup}$	AUC	$\mathcal{D}_{disc}$	$\mathcal{D}_{cup}$	AUC
AGNet	91.30	**77.38**	80.18	**91.65**	75.14	**81.58**
CENet	**91.70**	**80.34**	80.46	91.05	78.63	**83.41**
pOSAL	**94.52**	**82.42**	81.53	93.64	82.32	**84.07**
BEAL	93.84	**83.51**	81.66	**93.88**	81.93	**84.35**
ATTNet	**96.10**	**84.91**	81.75	95.78	84.65	**84.82**

(a) Comparison of $DiagFirst$GT and SOTA multi-label fusion methods. Taking $DiagFirst$GT as the ground-truth, the segmentation model estimates better masks for glaucoma diagnosis. The results are verified on vCDR and deep learning based diagnosis methods by AUC (%).

(b) Comparison of majority vote (MV) and $DiagFirst$GT ground-truth on various segmentation models measured by Dice (%) and AUC (%). Although $DiagFirst$GT is more difficult to learn, it supervises the segmentation models to learn more glaucoma diagnosis knowledge.

We can see $DiagFirst$GT significantly improves the diagnosis performance on all of the methods, no matter it is vCDR based [6,19], attentive CNN based [15,17,28] or transfer learning CNN based [27]. On vCDR based, attentive network based and transfer learning based methods, it outperforms the previous best ground-truths (MV, STAPLE and LFC) by a 1.82%, 2.68% and 2.12% AUC, respectively. This demonstrates $DiagFirst$GT is a general and effective ground-truth for the glaucoma diagnosis algorithms, and also indicates its significant potential value in clinical diagnosis of glaucoma.

To verify $DiagFirst$GT is also an effective ground-truth for various segmentation models. We train SOTA segmentation models on $DiagFirst$GT, and compare it with traditional majority vote ground-truth (MV). The SOTA segmentation models include AGNet [29], CENet [11], pOSAL [21], BEAL [20] and ATTNet [30]. The segmentation performance measured by optic disc Dice score ($\mathcal{D}_{diusc}$) and optic cup Dice score ($\mathcal{D}_{cup}$) is shown in Table 1b. We can see the segmentation models perform better on MV than $DiagFirst$GT. That is because MV is a simple average of multiple labels which is easy to learn, while the fusion of $DiagFirst$GT is based on the diagnosis prior knowledge that is more difficult to learn. We also report the glaucoma diagnosis performance of their estimated masks measured by AUC (%). The diagnosis performance is evaluated by [31] pre-trained on a large glaucoma detection dataset (LAG [15]). It is shown although the segmentation models perform better on MV, the diagnosis performance of the estimated masks is worse than that of *DiagFirst*GT. With the improvement of the segmentation capabilities, the glaucoma diagnosis AUC on *DiagFirst*GT increase about 3%, also outperforms the counterpart on MV (about 1%), indicating the supervision of *DiagFirst*GT can improve the diagnosis performance of estimated masks to a larger extent.

3.3 Ablation Study on ExpG

ExpG is proposed in the paper to improve generalization of *DiagFirst*GT. In order to verify the effectiveness of ExpG, we compare the *DiagFirst*GT before and after the application of ExpG on REFUGE-2 dataset. The diagnosis performance measured by AUC (%) is shown in Table 2. Experiment is conducted on a range of OD/OC-assisted diagnosis models to evaluate the generalization capability. Six different models are selected, including DualStage [3], DENet [8], AGCNN [15], ColNet [31], L2T-KT [27], and Swin Transformer [16] with mask-concated input.

As shown in Table 2, comparing with original high-frequency *DiagFirst*GT, ExpG generated *DiagFirst*GT consistently achieves higher performance on different diagnosis methods, especially on stronger networks. Concretely, ExpG generated *DiagFirst*GT outperforms the counterpart by a 3.95% AUC on DENet, a 4.93% AUC on AGCNN, a 6.06% AUC on Swin-cat and a 7.94% AUC on L2T-KT. It is obvious that ExpG generated *DiagFirst*GT is more robust for different diagnosis networks.

Table 2. The ablation study of ExpG. High-frequency *DiagFirst*GT and ExpG generated low-frequency *DiagFirst*GT are compared on different diagnosis backbones. The diagnosis performance is evaluated by AUC (%).

	Original	ExpG
DualStage [3]	79.36	**80.78**
DENet [8]	81.21	**85.16**
AGCNN [15]	79.35	**84.28**
Swin-cat [16]	78.66	**84.72**
ColNet [31]	81.69	**87.34**
L2T-KT [27]	83.67	**91.61**

4 Conclusion

OD/OC segmentation is often annotated by multiple experts. For training standard deep learning models, the multiple labels need to be fused to one ground-truth. The existed fusion methods often ignore the different expertness of each rater. In the paper, we take glaucoma diagnosis as the gold standard to assess the multi-rater expertness, which enable the fused ground-truth $DiagFirst$GT to facilitate the glaucoma diagnosis. Detailed experiments revealed that by training on $DiagFirst$GT, the OD/OC segmentation networks can produce the masks with high glaucoma diagnosis performance. The results are verified on a variety of glaucoma diagnosis networks to promise the generalization. Since OD/OC segmentation is often used to assist the glaucoma diagnosis clinically, we believe the proposed method is in line with the original intention of OD/OC segmentation task and has great significance for the clinical glaucoma diagnosis.

References

1. Albarqouni, S., Baur, C., Achilles, F., Belagiannis, V., Demirci, S., Navab, N.: Aggnet: deep learning from crowds for mitosis detection in breast cancer histology images. IEEE Trans. Med. Imaging **35**(5), 1313–1321 (2016)
2. Almazroa, A., et al.: Retinal fundus images for glaucoma analysis: The RIGA dataset. In: SPIE Conference on Medical Imaging (2018)
3. Bajwa, M.N., et al.: Two-stage framework for optic disc localization and glaucoma classification in retinal fundus images using deep learning. BMC Med. Inform. Decis. Mak. **19**(1), 1–16 (2019)
4. Bechar, M.E.A., Settouti, N., Barra, V., Chikh, M.A.: Semi-supervised superpixel classification for medical images segmentation: application to detection of glaucoma disease. Multidimension. Syst. Signal Process. **29**(3), 979–998 (2018)
5. Cao, P., Xu, Y., Kong, Y., Wang, Y.: Max-MIG: an information theoretic approach for joint learning from crowds. arXiv preprint arXiv:1905.13436 (2019)
6. Chandrika, S., Nirmala, K.: Analysis of cdr detection for glaucoma diagnosis. Int. J. Eng. Res. Appl. **2**(4), 23–27 (2013)
7. Fang, H., et al.: Refuge2 challenge: Treasure for multi-domain learning in glaucoma assessment. arXiv preprint arXiv:2202.08994 (2022)
8. Fu, H., et al.: Disc-aware ensemble network for glaucoma screening from fundus image. IEEE Trans. Med. Imaging **37**(11), 2493–2501 (2018)
9. Fu, H., et al.: A retrospective comparison of deep learning to manual annotations for optic disc and optic cup segmentation in fundus photographs. Translational vision science & technology 9(2), 33–33 (2020)
10. Garway-Heath, D.F., Ruben, S.T., Viswanathan, A., Hitchings, R.A.: Vertical cup/disc ratio in relation to optic disc size: its value in the assessment of the glaucoma suspect. Br. J. Ophthalmol. **82**(10), 1118–1124 (1998)
11. Gu, Z., et al.: Ce-net: Context encoder network for 2D medical image segmentation. IEEE Trans. Med. Imaging **38**(10), 2281–2292 (2019)
12. He, K., Zhang, X., Ren, S., Sun, J.: Deep residual learning for image recognition. In: Proceedings of the IEEE Conference on Computer Vision and Pattern Recognition, pp. 770–778 (2016)
13. Held, K., Kops, E.R., Krause, B.J., Wells, W.M., Kikinis, R., Muller-Gartner, H.W.: Markov random field segmentation of brain MR images. IEEE Trans. Med. Imaging **16**(6), 878–886 (1997)
14. Ji, W., et al.: Learning calibrated medical image segmentation via multi-rater agreement modeling. In: Proceedings of the IEEE/CVF Conference on Computer Vision and Pattern Recognition. pp. 12341–12351 (2021)

15. Li, L., Xu, M., Wang, X., Jiang, L., Liu, H.: Attention based glaucoma detection: A large-scale database and cnn model. In: Proceedings of the IEEE/CVF Conference on Computer Vision and Pattern Recognition, pp. 10571–10580 (2019)

16. Liu, Z., et al.: Swin transformer: Hierarchical vision transformer using shifted windows. In: Proceedings of the IEEE/CVF International Conference on Computer Vision. pp. 10012–10022 (2021)

17. Luo, Y., Huang, Q., Li, X.: Segmentation information with attention integration for classification of breast tumor in ultrasound image. Pattern Recogn. **124** 108427 (2021)

18. Raykar, V.C., et al.: Learning from crowds. J. Mach. Learn. Res. **11** 1297–1322 (2010)

19. Thangaraj, V., Natarajan, V.: Glaucoma diagnosis using support vector machine. In: 2017 International Conference on Intelligent Computing and Control Systems (ICICCS), pp. 394–399. IEEE (2017)

20. Wang, S., Yu, L., Li, K., Yang, X., Fu, C.-W., Heng, Pheng-Ann.: Boundary and entropy-driven adversarial learning for fundus image segmentation. In: Shen, D. (ed.) MICCAI 2019. LNCS, vol. 11764, pp. 102–110. Springer, Cham (2019). https://doi.org/10.1007/978-3-030-32239-7_12

21. Wang, S., Yu, L., Yang, X., Fu, C.W., Heng, P.A.: Patch-based output space adversarial learning for joint optic disc and cup segmentation. IEEE Trans. Med. Imaging **38**(11), 2485–2495 (2019)

22. Warfield, S.K., Zou, K.H., Wells, W.M.: Simultaneous truth and performance level estimation (staple): an algorithm for the validation of image segmentation. IEEE Trans. Med. Imaging **23**(7), 903–921 (2004)

23. Wojna, Z., et al.: The devil is in the decoder. In: British Machine Vision Conference 2017, BMVC 2017, pp. 1–13. BMVA Press (2017)

24. Wu, J., et al.: Gamma challenge: glaucoma grading from multi-modality images. arXiv preprint arXiv:2202.06511 (2022)

25. Wu, J., et al.: Learning self-calibrated optic disc and cup segmentation from multi-rater annotations (2022)

26. Wu, J., Fu, R.: Universal, transferable and targeted adversarial attacks. arXiv preprint arXiv:2109.07217 (2019)

27. Junde, W., et al.: Leveraging undiagnosed data for glaucoma classification with teacher-student learning. In: Martel, A.L. (ed.) MICCAI 2020. LNCS, vol. 12261, pp. 731–740. Springer, Cham (2020). https://doi.org/10.1007/978-3-030-59710-8_71

28. Zhang, J., Xie, Y., Xia, Y., Shen, C.: Attention residual learning for skin lesion classification. IEEE Trans. Med. Imaging **38**(9), 2092–2103 (2019)

29. Zhang, S., et al.: Attention guided network for retinal image segmentation. In: Shen, D. (ed.) MICCAI 2019. LNCS, vol. 11764, pp. 797–805. Springer, Cham (2019). https://doi.org/10.1007/978-3-030-32239-7_88

30. Zhao, X., Wang, S., Zhao, J., Wei, H., Xiao, M., Ta, N.: Application of an attention u-Net incorporating transfer learning for optic disc and cup segmentation. SIViP **15**(5), 913–921 (2021)

31. Zhou, Y., et al.: Collaborative learning of semi-supervised segmentation and classification for medical images. In: Proceedings of the IEEE/CVF Conference on Computer Vision and Pattern Recognition, pp. 2079–2088 (2019)

Learning Self-calibrated Optic Disc and Cup Segmentation from Multi-rater Annotations

Junde Wu, Huihui Fang, Zhaowei Wang, Dalu Yang, Yehui Yang,
Fangxin Shang, Wenshuo Zhou, and Yanwu Xu[✉]

Intelligent Healthcare Unit, Baidu Inc., Beijing, China
ywxu@ieee.org

Abstract. The segmentation of optic disc (OD) and optic cup (OC) from fundus images is an important fundamental task for glaucoma diagnosis. In the clinical practice, it is often necessary to collect opinions from multiple experts to obtain the final OD/OC annotation. This clinical routine helps to mitigate the individual bias. But when data is multiply annotated, standard deep learning models will be inapplicable. In this paper, we propose a novel neural network framework to learn OD/OC segmentation from multi-rater annotations. The segmentation results are self-calibrated through the iterative optimization of multi-rater expertness estimation and calibrated OD/OC segmentation. In this way, the proposed method can realize a mutual improvement of both tasks and finally obtain a refined segmentation result. Specifically, we propose Diverging Model (DivM) and Converging Model (ConM) to process the two tasks respectively. ConM segments the raw image based on the multi-rater expertness map provided by DivM. DivM generates multi-rater expertness map from the segmentation mask provided by ConM. The experiment results show that by recurrently running ConM and DivM, the results can be self-calibrated so as to outperform a range of state-of-the-art (SOTA) multi-rater segmentation methods.

Keywords: Multi-rater learning · Optic disc and cup segmentation · Recurrent learning

1 Introduction

Accurate annotation of the optic disc and cup (OD/OC) on fundus image can significantly facilitate the glaucoma diagnosis [11,27]. With the development of deep learning methods, automated OD/OC segmentation from the fundus images become more and more popular recently [5,6,17]. Training the deep learning models often requires the a single ground-truth for each instance. However, in order to mitigate the individual bias, it is common to collect the annotations

Supplementary Information The online version contains supplementary material available at https://doi.org/10.1007/978-3-031-16434-7_59.

from multiple clinical experts clinically. It makes the deep learning models which work well on nature images can not be directly applied to this task. This problem is called 'multi-rater problem' by the prior works [14,16,26]. A common practice toward the problem is to take majority vote, i.e., taking the average of multiple labels. Being simple and easy to implement, this strategy, however, comes at the cost of ignoring the varied expertise-level of multiple experts [10].

Recently, the problem of multi-rater labels start to attract research attention. A part of methods are proposed to learn calibrated results which aware the inter-observer variability [8,12–14]. It is shown the calibrated results will achieve better performance on a variety of ground-truths fused from multi-rater labels. However, they still need rater expertness provided to guide the calibration. As a result, in most cases, they are still limited to predict traditional majority vote.

We can see besides the learning of the calibrated models, estimating the multi-rater expertness indicating which rater is more credible is also necessary. A few previous methods proposed to assign multi-rater expertness based on the prior knowledge that reflects the confidence of the raters [1,3,19–21,25,26]. One general and reliable prior knowledge is the segmentation prior of raw images [1,19,20]. In OD/OC segmentation, it means that labels are more consistent with the OD/OC structure of fundus images should be given more confidence. However, these methods learned fused ground-truth without calibration. Therefore, the multi-rater expertness cannot be dynamically adjusted in the inference stage, which causes the results to be either overconfident or ambiguous.

In order to make up for the shortcomings of these two branches of study, we propose a novel recurrent neural network to jointly calibrate OD/OC segmentation and estimate the multi-rater expertness maps. We dubbed the process as self-calibrated segmentation. In the recurrence, multi-rater expertness maps can provide as a guidance for the calibration and the calibrated masks can be used in turn for the multi-rater expertness evaluation. By the regularization of fundus image prior, the two tasks can mutually improve through the iterative optimization and eventually achieve convergence. Specifically, we propose Converging Model (ConM) and Diverging Model (DivM) to learn the two tasks respectively. ConM learns calibrated OD/OC segmentation based on the multi-rater expertness maps provided by DivM. It is achieved by the feature integration based on the attention mechanism [22]. DivM learns to separate multi-rater labels from the OD/OC masks provided by ConM. We theoretically prove this separation process is equivalent the estimation of multi-rater expertness. By the iterative optimization of DivM and ConM, it can be proved both calibrated segmentation and multi-rater expertness will converge to the optimal solutions. The experimental results also show the results can be gradually improved with the recurrence of ConM and DivM.

Three major contributions are made with this paper. First, toward the multi-rater OD/OC segmentation, we propose a novel recurrent learning framework for the self-calibrated segmentation. The framework jointly learns calibrated segmentation and estimates multi-rater expertness, which gains mutual improvement on both tasks. Second, in this recurrent learning framework, we propose ConM and DivM for the calibrated segmentation and multi-rater expertness assignment. Attention is adopted to integrate the expertness maps into segmentation decoder. Finally, we validate the proposed method on th OD/OC segmentation. Our method shows superior performance compared with SOTA multi-rater learning strategies.

2   Theoretical Premises

Suppose that there are M raters, K classes, e.g. optic disc, optic cup, background in OD/OC segmentation task. Denote by a matrix $z^m \in \mathbb{R}^{H \times W \times K}$ the observed label of rater m, H and W are the height and width of the item respectively. Denote by a matrix $w^m \in \mathbb{R}^{H \times W \times K}$ the expertness map of rater m. Let $z^{[M]}$ denotes $z^1, z^2, ..., z^M$. The data point x and multi-rater labels $z^{[M]}$ are assumed to be drawn i.i.d. from random variables X and $Z^1, Z^2...Z^M$.

Denote by y that the fusion of $z^{[M]}$ by multi-rater expertness maps $w^{[M]}$, which can be expressed as:

$$y = softmax(\sum_{m=1}^{M} w^m \cdot z^m + p),   (1)$$

where $\cdot$ represents element-wise multiplication, p is the prior. We softmax the matrix dimension which represents the classes, to make sure the sum of the possibility is 1. Denote by y^* the potentially correct label and w^* the optimal expertness maps to attain it. There has:

Proposition 1. *If and only if* $w^{*m} = logP(z^m|y^*)$, *it has* $P(y^*|z^{[M]}) = softmax(\sum_{m=1}^{M} w^{*m} \cdot z^m + p)$.

Proposition 1 is proved in supplementary material. It implies learning optimal expertness w^{*m} is equivalent to learn $P(z^m|y^*)$. This enables us to supervise DivM by the observed multi-rater labels z^M. The estimated masks $\tilde{z}^{[M]}$ of DivM can be used as w^m to self-fuse the multi-rater labels:

$$y^{self} = \tilde{z}^{[M]} \odot z^{[M]} = softmax(\sum_{m=1}^{M} log(\tilde{z}^m) \cdot z^m + p_u),   (2)$$

where $\odot$ denotes the self-fusion operation, p_u is the uniform distribution prior, y^{self} is self-fusion label. We construct ConM to estimate y^{self} from raw fundus image and $\tilde{z}^m$, and construct DivM to estimate $z^{[M]}$ from $\tilde{y}$ produced by ConM. It can be proved this iterative optimization will converge to the optimal solution $w^{*[M]}$ and y^* (shown in supplementary material).

3   Methodology

In this paper, we propose a recurrent model to learn self-calibrated segmentation from multi-rater annotations. The overall flow of the proposed method is shown

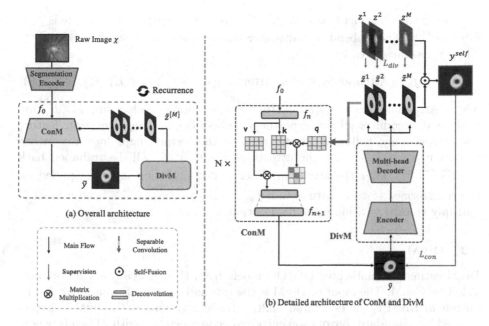

Fig. 1. Overall architecture of the proposed self-calibration segmentation method. Green denotes ConM modules. Orange denotes DivM modules. (Color figure online)

in Fig. 1 (a). Raw image x is first sent into a CNN-based encoder to obtain a deep embedding $f_0 \in \mathbb{R}^{\frac{H}{r} \times \frac{W}{r} \times C}$, where r is the down sample rate, C is the channel number of the embedding. Then ConM will use f_0 and given expertness maps $\tilde{w}^{[M]}$ to estimate a fused segmentation mask $\tilde{y} = softmax(\sum_{m=1}^{M} \tilde{w}^m \cdot z^m + p_x)$, where p_x is the raw image prior implicitly learned by network itself. Obtained $\tilde{y}$ will be taken as potential accurate segmentation mask y^* and be sent to DivM. DivM would then separate it to multi-rater segmentation masks, by estimating $P(z^{[M]}|y^*)$. Each head of DivM will estimate its corresponding rater's annotation. Multi-rater expertness maps can be represented by these estimated probability maps as shown in Proposition 1. Multi-rater expertness maps will then be embedded by separable convolution [7] and sent to ConM in the next iteration. ConM and DivM will recurrently run several times until converge.

3.1   ConM

We propose ConM to estimate calibrated segmentation mask based on given multi-rater expertness maps. The basic structure is shown in Fig. 1 (b). The input of ConM is the raw image embedding f_0 and the output is the segmentation mask $\tilde{y}$. Multi-rater expertness maps $\tilde{w}^{[M]}$ produced by DivM are integrated into ConM by attention mechanism to calibrate the segmentation. In ConM, attention are inserted into each two deconvolution layers. It takes embedded multi-rater expertness as *query*, segmentation features as *key* and *value*. In this way, the segmentation features can be selected and enhanced based on the given multi-rate expertness maps.

Specifically, consider ConM at the nth layer, the segmentation feature is $f_n \in \mathbb{R}^{\frac{H}{r_n} \times \frac{W}{r_n} \times C_n}$. The embedded multi-rater expertness map is $\bar{w}_n \in \mathbb{R}^{\frac{H}{r_n} \times \frac{W}{r_n} \times C_n}$. Then f_n is transferred by:

$$\bar{f}_n = \text{Attention}(q, k, v) = \text{Attention}(\bar{w}_n + E_w, f_n + E_f, f_n). \tag{3}$$

where $\text{Attention}(query, key, value)$ denotes attention mechanism, E_w, E_f are positional encodings [4] for expertness embedding and segmentation feature map respectively. Following [9], we reshape the feature maps into a sequence of flattened patches before the attention. Similarly, $\bar{f}_n$ will be reshaped back to $\mathbb{R}^{\frac{H}{r_n} \times \frac{W}{r_n} \times C_n}$ after the attention. Then a deconvolution layer is applied on the transformed feature $\bar{f}_n$ to obtain $f_{n+1} \in \mathbb{R}^{\frac{H}{r_{n+1}} \times \frac{W}{r_{n+1}} \times C_{n+1}}$. Such a block is multiply stacked to achieve the final output $\tilde{y}$.

3.2   DivM

DivM estimates multi-rater OD/OC labels from the segmentation masks provided by ConM. The input of DivM is the estimated segmentation mask $\tilde{y}$. The output of DivM is the estimated multi-rater annotations $\tilde{z}^{[M]}$. DivM is implemented by a standard convolution encoder-decoder network with M heads, where each head estimates one rater's segmentation annotation.

The estimated probability maps can be represented by the multi-rater expertness maps according Proposition 1. In order to integrate the expertness into ConM by attention, these maps are embedded to the same size as the target segmentation feature. We use separable convolution [7] which contains a pair of point-wise convolution and depth-wise convolution to embed multi-rater expertness maps. Pointwise convolution keeps the scale of the maps but deepen the channels, while depth-wise convolution downsamples the features but keeps the channel number. These layers not only reshape the maps but also embed the maps to the feature level for the integration.

3.3   Supervision

Consider ConM and DivM run once each, i.e., from f_0 to $\tilde{z}^{[M]}$, as one recurrence. Each instance will run τ recurrences in a single epoch. We backforward the gradients of the model after τ times of recurrence. The total loss function is represented as:

$$\mathcal{L}_{total} = \sum_{i=1}^{\tau} \mathcal{L}_{div}^i + \mathcal{L}_{con}^i, \tag{4}$$

where $\mathcal{L}_{con}$ and $\mathcal{L}_{div}$ are the loss functions for ConM and DivM, respectively.

$\mathcal{L}_{div}$ is the loss function for DivM. The estimation of each head is supervised by the corresponding multi-rater label, which is:

$$\mathcal{L}_{div} = \sum_{m=1}^{M} \mathcal{L}_{CE}(\tilde{z}^m, z^m), \tag{5}$$

where $\mathcal{L}_{CE}$ denotes the cross-entropy loss function.

$\mathcal{L}_{con}$ constraints ConM to estimate the self-fusion label, which is $y^{self} = softmax(\sum_{m=1}^{M} log(\tilde{z}^m) \cdot z^m + p_u)$. However, note that ConM is supposed to learn the raw image prior p_x that cannot be supervised. Therefore, instead of the pixel-level supervision, we adopt Structural Similarity Index (SSIM) as the loss function. SSIM constraints the estimated mask to have a similar structure with self-fusion label but also allows the slight difference caused by the raw image prior. Formally, $\mathcal{L}_{con}$ for the ith recurrence is represented as:

$$\mathcal{L}_{con}^{i} = \text{SSIM}(\tilde{y}_i, y_{i-1}^{self}). \tag{6}$$

The gradients are backforward individually in each recurrence, which means the gradients of the ith recurrence will not effect the $(i-1)^{th}$ recurrence.

4 Experiment

4.1 Implement Details

In the experiments, we initialize the recurrence by the expertness maps sampled from uniform distribution. We use ResUnet [29] as the backbone for ConM and DivM. Segmentation encoder is jointly trained with ConM and DivM in the experiments. All the experiments are implemented with the PyTorch platform and trained/tested on 4 T P40 GPU with 24GB of memory. All training and test images are uniformly resized to the dimension of 256 × 256 pixels. The networks are trained in an end-to-end manner using Adam optimizer [15] with a mini-batch of 16 for 80 epochs. The learning rate is initially set to 1×10^{-4}. If not specifically mentioned, we use the results of the 4th recurrence for the comparison. The detailed hyper-parameters and model architectures can be found in the supplementary material and open-source code.

4.2 Main Results

To verify the proposed model dynamically calibrated the segmentation results in the recurrence, we show the results in different recurrences for the comparison. The results are verified on REFUGE [18] OD/OC segmentation dataset (1200 samples), which is annotated by seven medical experts. The segmentation performance measured by dice score of OD ($\mathcal{D}_{disc}$) and OC ($\mathcal{D}_{cup}$) is shown in Table 1. The outputs of DivM are compared with multi-rater labels, and the output of ConM is compared with the self-fusion label. In practice, we conduct four times of recurrence since the results are stable since then.

In Table 1, we can see the performance of DivM keeps increasing on Rater1, Rater2 and Rater4 (R1, R2, R4) in the recurrence, while dropping on Rater5, Rater6 and Rater7 (R5, R6, R7). It indicates the model consistently calibrates the results in the recurrence. Constraint by the raw image prior, some raters become more and more credible in the recurrence. We can also see the results of

Table 1. The performance of DivM and ConM in different recurrences. DivM is evaluated by multi-rater labels. ConM is evaluated by self-fusion ground-truth.

Models	DivM														ConM	
Raters	R1		R2		R3		R4		R5		R6		R7		Self-fusion	
Dice	$\mathcal{D}_{disc}$	$\mathcal{D}_{cup}$	$\mathcal{D}_{disc}$	$\mathcal{D}_{cup}$	$\mathcal{D}_{disc}$	$\mathcal{D}_{cup}$	$\mathcal{D}_{disc}$	$\mathcal{D}_{cup}$	$\mathcal{D}_{disc}$	$\mathcal{D}_{cup}$	$\mathcal{D}_{disc}$	$\mathcal{D}_{cup}$	$\mathcal{D}_{disc}$	$\mathcal{D}_{cup}$	$\mathcal{D}_{disc}$	$\mathcal{D}_{cup}$
Rec1	96.06	84.45	95.56	83.13	94.64	81.55	**94.50**	77.71	95.00	87.52	**94.60**	80.56	94.67	75.45	95.48	87.80
Rec2	96.14	85.05	95.35	85.28	**94.71**	81.00	94.33	80.46	95.62	**88.07**	94.11	78.12	94.28	74.44	95.60	88.63
Rec3	96.58	86.27	96.20	86.17	94.42	**81.63**	94.35	81.12	95.42	86.76	94.30	77.39	94.66	73.48	96.24	89.55
Rec4	**96.77**	**86.49**	**96.39**	**86.39**	94.53	81.19	94.41	**81.34**	**95.89**	86.72	94.14	76.88	94.46	73.30	**96.33**	**89.71**

ConM are gradually improved on self-fusion labels, indicating the increasing consistency of DivM and ConM with the recurrence. Both the results of DivM and ConM become stable in the 4th recurrence, indicating the results have converged.

We also show the visualization results in Fig. 2. We find the model predicts uncertain masks first, then calibrate the results to be more confident through the recurrence, to an end of confident and calibrated result.

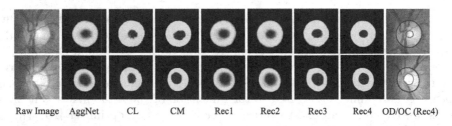

Raw Image   AggNet   CL   CM   Rec1   Rec2   Rec3   Rec4   OD/OC (Rec4)

Fig. 2. Visualized comparison of OD/OC segmentation. Column 2–4 are the results of AggNet [1], CL [20] and CM [21], respectively. Column 5–9 are self-calibrated results in recurrence 1, 2, 3, 4 and the final OD/OC boundary, respectively.

4.3 Compared with SOTA

To verify the calibration ability of the proposed method, we compare it with SOTA calibrated/non-calibrated segmentation methods on REFUGE and RIGA [2] dataset. RIGA is a OD/OC segmentation dataset contains 750 samples annotated by six raters. We compare the non-calibrated methods, including AGNet [28], BEAL [23] and pOSAL [24]. and the calibrated methods, including WDNet [12], UECNN [13] and MRNet [14]. The models are measured on different combinations of multi-rater labels, including majority vote (MV), STAPLE [25], LFC [19], and Diag [26] to verify the generalization. The quantitative results are shown in Table 2a and 2b. We can see calibrated methods basically work better than non-calibrated one, and the proposed self-calibrated method outperforms the calibrated ones on various multi-rater ground-truths. The improvement is especially prominent on OC segmentation where the inter-observer variability is significant. In addition, we also note most segmentation models can achieve

Table 2. Quantitative comparison results of SOTA calibrated/non-calibrated segmentation methods. Results are measured by Dice score (%).

		MV		STAPLE		LFC		Diag		Self fusion	
		$\mathcal{D}_{disc}$	$\mathcal{D}_{cup}$	$\mathcal{D}_{disc}$	$\mathcal{D}_{cup}$	$\mathcal{D}_{disc}$	$\mathcal{D}_{cup}$	$\mathcal{D}_{disc}$	$\mathcal{D}_{cup}$	$\mathcal{D}_{disc}$	$\mathcal{D}_{cup}$
No Calibrated	AGNet	90.21	71.86	89.45	70.30	88.40	69.65	88.98	68.57	91.26	72.83
	pOSAL	94.52	83.81	93.97	83.08	93.06	81.86	92.82	80.32	94.30	83.05
	BEAL	94.84	84.92	94.28	84.14	93.49	83.27	92.88	81.93	95.14	84.66
Calibrated	WDNet	94.63	84.46	95.32	84.32	93.14	80.55	92.53	81.03	94.67	83.60
	UECNN	94.42	84.80	94.53	84.26	94.22	82.79	94.07	80.71	95.47	84.87
	MRNet	95.00	86.40	94.13	85.25	93.71	84.14	93.53	82.14	95.43	86.42
Self-calibrate	Ours	**95.23**	**87.75**	**95.34**	**88.14**	**94.67**	**86.82**	**94.20**	**85.25**	**96.33**	**89.71**

(a) Performance on REFUGE dataset.

		MV		STAPLE		LFC		Diag		Self fusion	
		$\mathcal{D}_{disc}$	$\mathcal{D}_{cup}$	$\mathcal{D}_{disc}$	$\mathcal{D}_{cup}$	$\mathcal{D}_{disc}$	$\mathcal{D}_{cup}$	$\mathcal{D}_{disc}$	$\mathcal{D}_{cup}$	$\mathcal{D}_{disc}$	$\mathcal{D}_{cup}$
No Calibrated	AGNet	96.31	78.05	95.30	77.02	95.37	75.82	95.23	72.45	95.32	77.40
	pOSAL	95.85	84.07	95.37	83.25	95.07	83.75	96.22	79.28	96.10	85.61
	BEAL	97.08	85.97	96.13	84.16	95.87	84.82	95.06	81.06	96.28	86.89
Calibrated	WDNet	96.81	82.17	96.15	81.25	96.11	82.78	95.18	80.31	95.53	84.38
	UECNN	96.37	85.52	95.88	83.59	96.16	84.34	95.60	82.73	95.48	85.92
	MRNet	**97.55**	87.20	96.26	86.37	**96.58**	85.77	95.11	82.55	96.33	86.83
Self-calibrate	Ours	97.22	**88.24**	**96.34**	**88.50**	96.23	**88.48**	**96.63**	**85.78**	**97.82**	**90.15**

(b) Performance on RIGA dataset.

Table 3. Ablation study on attentive integration and SSIM loss function

SSIM	Attentive Integration	MV		STAPLE		LFC		Diag	
		$\mathcal{D}_{disc}$	$\mathcal{D}_{cup}$	$\mathcal{D}_{disc}$	$\mathcal{D}_{cup}$	$\mathcal{D}_{disc}$	$\mathcal{D}_{cup}$	$\mathcal{D}_{disc}$	$\mathcal{D}_{cup}$
		94.51	84.12	94.58	84.31	94.33	84.03	93.26	81.48
✓		94.72	84.73	95.03	84.90	94.56	84.61	93.77	81.70
	✓	94.89	85.71	95.35	85.41	94.38	85.27	93.96	82.63
✓	✓	**95.23**	**87.75**	**95.34**	**88.14**	**94.67**	**86.82**	**94.20**	**85.25**

better performance on the self-fusion ground-truth, which demonstrates the self-fusion label is easier to learn on account of the awareness of raw image prior.

Not only the multi-rater expertness helps to improve calibration, the calibration can also facilitate the multi-rater expertness estimation. We compare the self-calibration with SOTA self-fusion supervised segmentation methods, including CL [20], CM [21] and AggNet [1]. The visual comparisons is shown in Fig. 2. We can see the CL and CM who explicitly learn the multi-rater expertness, will be overconfident over the inaccurate results, while AggNet who implicitly learns the multi-rater expertness is prone to obtain ambiguous results. The proposed self-calibrated segmentation is able to estimate the result from uncertain to confident with the recurrence, to an end of confident and calibrated result.

4.4 Ablation Study

Ablation studies are performed over attentive integration and SSIM loss function on REFUGE dataset, as listed in Table 3. The experiments are evaluated on a range of ground-truths. Simple feature concatenation is used to replace attention in the ablation study. In Table 3, as we sequentially adding SSIM and attention, the model performance is gradually improved. It also shows the combination usage of SSIM and attention boosts the performance more than the individual components, indicating the awareness of fundus image prior and multi-rater expertness are mutually improved.

5 Conclusion

Toward learning OD/OC segmentation from multi-rater labels, we propose a self-calibrated segmentation model to recurrently calibrated the segmentation and estimate the multi-rater expertness. In this way, the shortcomings of the two independent tasks are complemented, thus gain the mutual improvement. Extensive empirical experiments demonstrated the self-calibrated segmentation outperforms both the calibrated segmentation methods and expertness-aware segmentation methods. Future works will continue to exploit the potential of the proposed method and extend it to the other multi-rater segmentation tasks.

References

1. Albarqouni, S., Baur, C., Achilles, F., Belagiannis, V., Demirci, S., Navab, N.: Aggnet: deep learning from crowds for mitosis detection in breast cancer histology images. IEEE Trans. Med. Imaging **35**(5), 1313–1321 (2016)
2. Almazroa, A., et al.: Agreement among ophthalmologists in marking the optic disc and optic cup in fundus images. Int. Ophthalmol. **37**(3), 701–717 (2017)
3. Cao, P., Xu, Y., Kong, Y., Wang, Y.: Max-MIG: an information theoretic approach for joint learning from crowds. arXiv preprint arXiv:1905.13436 (2019)
4. Carion, N., Massa, F., Synnaeve, G., Usunier, N., Kirillov, A., Zagoruyko, Sergey: End-to-end object detection with transformers. In: Vedaldi, A., Bischof, H., Brox, T., Frahm, J.-M. (eds.) ECCV 2020. LNCS, vol. 12346, pp. 213–229. Springer, Cham (2020). https://doi.org/10.1007/978-3-030-58452-8_13
5. Chen, C., Dou, Q., Jin, Y., Chen, H., Qin, J., Heng, P.-A.: Robust multimodal brain tumor segmentation via feature disentanglement and gated fusion. In: Shen, D. (ed.) MICCAI 2019. LNCS, vol. 11766, pp. 447–456. Springer, Cham (2019). https://doi.org/10.1007/978-3-030-32248-9_50
6. Chen, S., Ding, C., Liu, M.: Dual-force convolutional neural networks for accurate brain tumor segmentation. Pattern Recogn. **88**, 90–100 (2019)
7. Chollet, F.: Xception: Deep learning with depthwise separable convolutions. In: Proceedings of the IEEE conference on computer vision and pattern recognition, pp. 1251–1258 (2017)
8. Chou, H.C., Lee, C.C.: Every rating matters: Joint learning of subjective labels and individual annotators for speech emotion classification. In: ICASSP 2019–2019 IEEE International Conference on Acoustics, Speech and Signal Processing (ICASSP), pp. 5886–5890. IEEE (2019)

9. Dosovitskiy, A., et al.: An image is worth 16x16 words: Transformers for image recognition at scale. arXiv preprint arXiv:2010.11929 (2020)

10. Fu, H., et al.: A retrospective comparison of deep learning to manual annotations for optic disc and optic cup segmentation in fundus photographs. Translational vision science & technology 9(2), 33–33 (2020)

11. Garway-Heath, D.F., Ruben, S.T., Viswanathan, A., Hitchings, R.A.: Vertical cup/disc ratio in relation to optic disc size: its value in the assessment of the glaucoma suspect. Br. J. Ophthalmol. 82(10), 1118–1124 (1998)

12. Guan, M.Y., Gulshan, V., Dai, A.M., Hinton, G.E.: Who said what: Modeling individual labelers improves classification. In: Thirty-Second AAAI Conference on Artificial Intelligence (2018)

13. Jensen, M.H., Jørgensen, D.R., Jalaboi, R., Hansen, M.E., Olsen, M.A.: Improving uncertainty estimation in convolutional neural networks using inter-rater agreement. In: Shen, D. (ed.) MICCAI 2019. LNCS, vol. 11767, pp. 540–548. Springer, Cham (2019). https://doi.org/10.1007/978-3-030-32251-9_59

14. Ji, W., et al.: Learning calibrated medical image segmentation via multi-rater agreement modeling. In: Proceedings of the IEEE/CVF Conference on Computer Vision and Pattern Recognition, pp. 12341–12351 (2021)

15. Kingma, D.P., Ba, J.: Adam: A method for stochastic optimization. arXiv preprint arXiv:1412.6980 (2014)

16. Liao, Z., Hu, S., Xie, Y., Xia, Y.: Modeling human preference and stochastic error for medical image segmentation with multiple annotators. arXiv preprint arXiv:2111.13410 (2021)

17. Liu, Q., Dou, Q., Yu, L., Heng, P.A.: Ms-Net: multi-site network for improving prostate segmentation with heterogeneous MRI data. IEEE Trans. Med. Imaging 39(9), 2713–2724 (2020)

18. Orlando, J.I., et al.: Refuge challenge: a unified framework for evaluating automated methods for glaucoma assessment from fundus photographs. Med. Image Anal. 59, 101570 (2020)

19. Raykar, V.C., et al.: Learning from crowds. J. Mach. Learn. Res. 11 1297–1322 (2010)

20. Rodrigues, F., Pereira, F.C.: Deep learning from crowds. In: Thirty-Second AAAI Conference on Artificial Intelligence (2018)

21. Tanno, R., Saeedi, A., Sankaranarayanan, S., Alexander, D.C., Silberman, N.: Learning from noisy labels by regularized estimation of annotator confusion. In: Proceedings of the IEEE/CVF Conference on Computer Vision and Pattern Recognition, pp. 11244–11253 (2019)

22. Vaswani, A., et al.: Attention is all you need. In: Advances in neural information processing systems, pp. 5998–6008 (2017)

23. Wang, S., Yu, L., Li, K., Yang, X., Fu, C.-W., Heng, P.-A.: Boundary and entropy-driven adversarial learning for fundus image segmentation. In: Shen, D. (ed.) MICCAI 2019. LNCS, vol. 11764, pp. 102–110. Springer, Cham (2019). https://doi.org/10.1007/978-3-030-32239-7_12

24. Wang, S., Yu, L., Yang, X., Fu, C.W., Heng, P.A.: Patch-based output space adversarial learning for joint optic disc and cup segmentation. IEEE Trans. Med. Imaging 38(11), 2485–2495 (2019)

25. Warfield, S.K., Zou, K.H., Wells, W.M.: Simultaneous truth and performance level estimation (staple): an algorithm for the validation of image segmentation. IEEE Trans. Med. Imaging 23(7), 903–921 (2004)

26. Wu, J., Fang, H., Wu, B., Yang, D., Yang, Y., Xu, Y.: Opinions vary? diagnosis first! arXiv preprint arXiv:2202.06505 (2022)

27. Wu, J., et al.: Leveraging undiagnosed data for glaucoma classification with teacher-student learning. In: Martel, A.L. (ed.) MICCAI 2020. LNCS, vol. 12261, pp. 731–740. Springer, Cham (2020). https://doi.org/10.1007/978-3-030-59710-8_71
28. Zhang, S., et al.: Attention guided network for retinal image segmentation. In: Shen, D. (ed.) MICCAI 2019. LNCS, vol. 11764, pp. 797–805. Springer, Cham (2019). https://doi.org/10.1007/978-3-030-32239-7_88
29. Zhang, Z., Liu, Q., Wang, Y.: Road extraction by deep residual u-net. IEEE Geosci. Remote Sens. Lett. **15**(5), 749–753 (2018)

TINC: Temporally Informed Non-contrastive Learning for Disease Progression Modeling in Retinal OCT Volumes

Taha Emre[✉], Arunava Chakravarty, Antoine Rivail, Sophie Riedl, Ursula Schmidt-Erfurth, and Hrvoje Bogunović

Department of Ophthalmology and Optometry, Medical University of Vienna, Vienna, Austria
{taha.emre,hrvoje.bogunovic}@meduniwien.ac.at

Abstract. Recent contrastive learning methods achieved state-of-the-art in low label regimes. However, the training requires large batch sizes and heavy augmentations to create multiple views of an image. With non-contrastive methods, the negatives are implicitly incorporated in the loss, allowing different images and modalities as pairs. Although the meta-information (i.e., age, sex) in medical imaging is abundant, the annotations are noisy and prone to class imbalance. In this work, we exploited already existing temporal information (different visits from a patient) in a longitudinal optical coherence tomography (OCT) dataset using temporally informed non-contrastive loss (**TINC**) without increasing complexity and need for negative pairs. Moreover, our novel pair-forming scheme can avoid heavy augmentations and implicitly incorporates the temporal information in the pairs. Finally, these representations learned from the pretraining are more successful in predicting disease progression where the temporal information is crucial for the downstream task. More specifically, our model outperforms existing models in predicting the risk of conversion within a time frame from intermediate age-related macular degeneration (AMD) to the late wet-AMD stage.

1 Introduction

The scarcity of manually annotated labels is a major limitation for the classification tasks in medical image analysis. Self-supervised learning (SSL) showed a great promise in exploiting the availability of unlabeled medical data by outperforming models trained from random weights or pretrained with non-medical images in difficult supervised settings [1]. Traditional SSL methods rely on pretext tasks that are believed to be semantically relevant to the downstream task, such as jigsaw-puzzle solving, and rotation angle prediction.

In recent years, contrastive learning (CL) methods surpassed the pretext-based SSL in unsupervised representation learning. They learn similar representations of two heavily augmented views (*positive pairs*) of a sample while pushing

L. Wang et al. (Eds.): MICCAI 2022, LNCS 13432, pp. 625–634, 2022.
https://doi.org/10.1007/978-3-031-16434-7_60

away the others in the representation space as *negatives*. The goal is to find representations that are semantically meaningful and robust to image perturbations. Following this, CL methods have also been adapted for medical images. Li et al. [11] addressed the class imbalance problem by sample re-weighting during contrastive training and devised an augmentation scheme for 3D volumes. Chen et al. [7] proposed a sampling strategy by feeding two frames as pairs from an ultrasound video to encode the temporal information for the CL. They found that sampling and augmentation strategies were crucial for the downstream task. Azizi et al. [1] showed that if two different images of a patient included the same pathology, they formed more informative positive pairs than the heavily augmented pairs. Also, they reported that if the supervised and the unsupervised data were mixed for the CL, the downstream task's performance was increased. These methods were based on contrastive InfoNCE loss [12]. However, the success of the CL largely depends on the quality of the negative samples [8]. This introduces two challenges for medical imaging; (i) large batch sizes, and (ii) explicit negatives in a batch. Furthermore, particularly in longitudinal studies, the large batch sizes (over a thousand) are not compatible with the number of patients (a few hundred) and would create negative pairs from the same patient.

The developments in non-contrastive learning methods [3,6,20] avoid the need for explicit negatives and consequently for large batch sizes. They implicitly learn to push the negatives with stop-gradient [6,9], clustering [5], or creating discrepancy between pairs through a specific loss [3,20]. Barlow Twins' [20] loss function achieves that by making the correlation matrix of the embeddings of the two views close to identity matrix and VICReg [3] by calculating a Huber variance loss within a batch of embeddings. Especially, VICReg requires no architectural trick, large batch sizes, or normalization. Both of them use a simple Siamese Network and a multi-layer perceptron (MLP) projector on the representations for the embeddings. They also allow constructing pairs from different images, and unlike contrastive methods, it is even possible to use multiple modalities.

In this paper, we focus on non-contrastive SSL in longitudinal imaging datasets, and we propose a new similarity loss to exploit the temporal meta-information without increasing the complexity of the non-contrastive training. Also, we introduce a new pair-forming strategy by using scans from different visits of a patient as inputs to the model. In this regard, our work is one of the first to build on non-contrastive learning with continuous labels (time difference between visits).

Clinical Background. The optical coherence tomography (OCT) imaging is widely used in clinical practice to provide a 3D volume of the retina as a series of cross-sectional slices called *B-scans*. Age-related macular degeneration (AMD) is the leading cause of vision loss in the elderly population [4]. It progresses from the early/intermediate stage with few visual symptoms to a late stage with severe vision loss. Conversion to late-stage could take two forms, wet and dry AMD. Wet-AMD is defined by the formation of new vessels. An intravitreal injection can improve the patients' vision, but it is most effective when applied soon upon conversion to wet-AMD. This motivated the medical imaging research communities to develop risk estimation models for conversion to wet-AMD. AMD progression prediction in OCT has been studied using statistical methods [15,16,18] based on biomarkers and genomics. Schmidt-Erfurth et al. [15] approached the conversion prediction as a survival problem and used a cox model. Initial deep learning models works showed the importance of standardized preprocessing in B-scans [14]. Recently, [19] exploited surrogate tasks like retinal biomarker segmentation in OCT volumes to improve the performance. On the other hand, [2] used imaging biomarkers and demographics to train an RNN on sequential data. As an SSL approach, Rivail et al. [13] pre-trained a Siamese network by predicting the time difference between the branches.

Contribution. We improve on learning representations such that they (a) capture temporal meta-information in longitudinal imaging data (b) do not suffer from dimensional collapse (only a small part of representation space is useful [10]). Our contribution is two-folds. First, we proposed a simple yet effective similarity loss called TINC to implicitly embed the temporal information without increasing the non-contrastive loss complexity. We hypothesized that the B-scans acquired closer in time should be close in the representation space. We chose VICReg [3] to use TINC with because its similarity loss explicitly reduces the distance between representations and allows alternatives in its place. Second, instead of aggressive augmentation for pair generation from a single B-scan, we formed pairs by picking two moderately augmented versions of two different B-scans from a patient's OCT volumes acquired at different times. Finally, TINC had increased performance in the difficult task of predicting conversion from the intermediate to wet-AMD within a clinically-relevant time interval of 6 months.

2 Method

We modified the VICReg's invariance (similarity) term by constraining it with the normalized absolute time difference (no temporal order among the inputs) between the input images. The original invariance term is the mean-squared error (MSE) between two unnormalized embeddings. The time difference acts as a margin on how low the invariance term can get. As the time difference between two visits increases, the similarity between a pair of the respective B-scans should decrease. Thus, the distance measure should lie within a margin, not on a point like the VICReg invariance term does. In other terms, the representations should slightly differ due to the time difference between the scans of a patient.

Given a batch of n patients with multiple visits, let visits v_1 and v_2 be the components of n pair of time points randomly sampled from each available patients' visit dates within a certain time interval. Randomly selected B-scans from the OCT volumes at times v_1 and v_2, are augmented by random augmentations t_1 and t_2 for the two views X_1 and X_2. First, the encoder produces n representations Y_1 and Y_2, then the projector (also called expander) expands the representations to embeddings Z_1 and Z_2 with embedding dimension d (Fig. 1).

The loss terms of the original VICReg works as follows: S (Eq. 1) is the invariance term or the similarity loss, V (Eq. 2) is the variance term to keep a

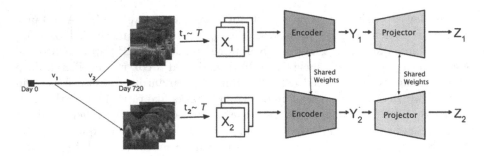

Fig. 1. The overall workflow. Two B-scans sampled from different visits of a patient are fed to the network. t_1 and t_2 are the transformations for the views X_1 and X_2. An encoder produces representations Y_1 and Y_2, then a projector expands them to embeddings Z_1 and Z_2, on which the loss is calculated.

variance margin between different pairs of embeddings (prevents representation collapse), and C (Eq. 3) is the covariance term that forces each component to be as informative as possible (prevents dimensional collapse).

$$S(Z_1, Z_2) = \frac{1}{n} \sum_i \|z_{1i} - z_{2i}\|_2^2, \tag{1}$$

$$V(Z) = \frac{1}{d} \sum_{j=1}^{d} \max(0, \gamma - \text{std}(z^j, \epsilon)), \tag{2}$$

$$C(Z) = \frac{1}{d} \sum_{i \neq j} [Cov(Z)]_{i,j}^2, \quad \text{where} \quad Cov(Z) = \frac{1}{n-1} \sum_{i=1}^{n} (z_i - \bar{z})(z_i - \bar{z})^T \tag{3}$$

where in V, std is the standard deviation of the z^j which is a vector of the jth embedding component values along the batch. For V, we used γ as 1. In covariance term C, Cov is the covariance matrix of an embedding vector. C and V are calculated for Z_1 and Z_2 separately. S is the MSE between two vectors. Finally, the total loss is the weighted sum of these three.

Temporally Informed Non-contrastive Loss. The temporal label is defined as the difference between visit dates v_1 and v_2. Δv is the absolute value of the difference scaled to 0–1 using a Min-Max scaler with given $v_{\min}$ and $v_{\max}$. We use Δv as a margin, where the distance between the two embeddings should not be greater than it. Inspired by the epsilon insensitive loss from support vector regression, the invariance term S in VICReg is replaced with our TINC loss:

$$\ell_{\text{TINC}}(Z_1, Z_2) = \frac{1}{n} \sum_i max(0, \|z_{1i} - z_{2i}\|_2^2 - \Delta v_i) \tag{4}$$

The TINC term forces the distance between the two representations to be within a non-zero margin, set proportionally to the time difference between visits. As

Δv gets close to 1, the margin becomes wider, and the loss does not enforce a strict similarity. On the other hand, when Δv is close to 0, TINC loss becomes similar to MSE between the two representations. In principle, the values of the embedding components could diminish, resulting in a collapse. Then the distance would be smaller than the margin, not contributing to the overall loss. However, the variance term in VICReg counteracts it by enforcing a standard deviation between different pairs, preventing the components from having infinitesimal values. We kept the variance and covariance losses from VICReg unmodified.

3   Experiments and Results

Dataset. The self-supervised and supervised trainings were performed and evaluated on a longitudinal dataset of OCT volumes of 1,096 patients *fellow* eyes[1] from a clinical trial[2] studying the efficacy of wet-AMD treatment of the *study* eyes. Patients had both eyes scanned monthly over two years with Cirrus OCT (Zeiss, Dublin, US) on monthly basis. The volumes consisted of 128 B-scans with a resolution of 512×1024 px covering a volume of $6 \times 6 \times 2$ mm^3.

For the wet-AMD conversion prediction task, we selected fellow eyes that either remained in the intermediate AMD stage throughout the trial, or converted to wet-AMD during the trial, excluding those that had late AMD from baseline or converted to late dry-AMD. The final supervised dataset consisted of 463 eyes and 10,096 OCT scans with 117 converter eyes, and 346 non-converters. The rest of the eyes were included in the unsupervised dataset, which consisted of 541 eyes and 12,494 volumes. Following [2,13,17,19], wet-AMD conversion was defined as a binary classification task, i.e., predicting whether an eye is going to convert to wet-AMD within a clinically-relevant 6 months time-frame. For the supervised training, eyes were split into 60% for training, 20% for validation, and 20% for testing, stratified by the detected conversion. The evaluation is reported on the scan level.

Preprocessing and Augmentations. In the supervised setting, we extracted from each OCT volume a set of 6 B-scans covering the central 0.28 mm, whereas 9 B-scans covering the central 0.42 mm were extracted for the SSL. To standardize the view, the retina in each B-scan was flattened with a quadratic fit to the RPE layer (segmentations are obtained with IOWA Reference Algorithm [21]). Then, each B-scan was cropped to 6×0.6 mm^2 and resized to 224×224 pixels, with intensities normalized between 0–1. All B-scans from an OCT volume were assigned the same conversion label for the supervised training. But during validation and testing, conversion probability of a volume was computed by picking the B-scan with maximum probability among the B-scans.

For the supervised training augmentations, random translation, rotation (max 10°C) and horizontal flip were used. When forming the pairs for the SSL, we followed [1,3] but with an increased minimum area ratio for the random

---

[1] The other eye that is not part of the interventional study.
[2] NCT00891735. https://clinicaltrials.gov/ct2/show/NCT00891735.

cropping from 0.08 to 0.4, because in OCT volumes the noise ratio is higher than in natural images (Fig. 2), which makes small crops uninformative. Also, random grayscaling augmentation is not applicable. We picked the B-scans of the same patient from different visits with the time difference in the range of $90-540$ days. The time difference acts an additional augmentation, which makes the task non-trivial. Additionally, two large crops from two B-scans yield similar color histograms, preventing network to memorize color histograms and overfit (Fig. 2(d)). Following the protocol in [1], the supervised and unsupervised data were combined for the SSL.

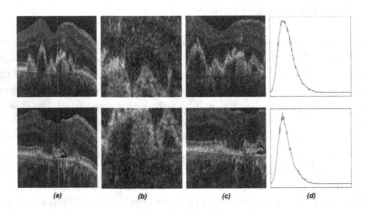

Fig. 2. Two examples of different random crop strategies. **a**: flattened B-scans, **b**: small crop area ratio [3], **c**: big crop area ratio between 0.4–0.8, **d**: color histograms of c

Setup. ResNet-50 was chosen as the encoder backbone, and an MLP with two hidden layers with batch normalization as the projector, similar to [3] except the dimensions were chosen as 4096 for all the SSL steps. In SSL, we used AdamW with batch size of 128, learning rate of $5 * 10^{-4}$ and a weight decay of 10^{-6} for 400 epochs. Following [3,6], a cosine learning rate scheduler with a warm-up of 10 epochs was used. In VICReg, the coefficient of the invariance term was fixed to 25, and we found improved performance when the coefficients of the variance and the covariance terms were set to 5 and 1, respectively. For the Barlow Twins, the coefficient for the redundancy reduction term was kept at 0.005.

For the downstream task, we provided the results from both the linear evaluation and the fine-tuning. The performance was evaluated with area under the receiver operating curve (AUROC) and the precision-recall curve (PRAUC). The linear evaluation was conducted by training a linear layer on top of the pre-trained & frozen encoder. It is trained with Adam optimizer, batch size of 128, learning rate of 10^{-4}, and 5-to-1 class weights in the cross-entropy loss for 10 epochs. Fine-tuning had the same parameters with the addition of weight decay for 100 epochs. When training from scratch, the model was trained for 300 epochs. The best epoch was selected as the one with the highest AUROC score on the validation set. The learning rate was selected between 10^{-2}–10^{-5}. The weight decay was selected between 10^{0}–10^{-7} including 0.

Experiments. We report results for wet-AMD conversion prediction task from linear evaluation and fine-tuning. We compared TINC against popular non-contrastive learning methods Barlow Twins and VICReg, which can accept different images as input pairs. When testing our new pair-forming scheme, we used the original VICReg and Barlow Twins along with their modified versions. In order to show the performance of TINC, we compared it against ResNet50 trained from scratch, VICReg and Barlow Twins modified with our new input scheme, and VICReg with additional explicit time difference prediction loss term.

Table 1. Linear evaluation results of SSL approaches with ResNet50 backbone. $VICReg_{TINC}$ is the proposed VICReg with TINC loss. "*w. two visits*" indicates the model modified with new pair-forming scheme.

Self-supervised learning	AUROC	PRAUC
VICReg [3]	Representational collapse	
Barlow Twins [20]	0.686	0.103
VICReg w. two visits	0.685	0.085
Barlow Twins w. two visits	0.708	0.098
VICReg + Explicit Time Difference	0.701	0.107
VICReg$_{TINC}$	**0.738**	**0.112**

Table 2. Model performances for the finetuning and training from scratch

Method	AUROC	PRAUC
Backbone (random initialization)	0.713	0.110
AMDNet [14] (random initialization)	0.676	0.087
Barlow Twins w. two visits	0.692	0.091
VICReg w. two visits	0.737	0.117
VICReg$_{TINC}$	**0.756**	**0.142**

Although random crop & resize are the most crucial augmentations for non-contrastive learning, small crop area may not be ideal for OCT images due to the loss in contextual information. To verify this, we first tested Barlow Twins and VICReg with their original augmentations and input scheme as baselines followed by training them with the proposed pair-forming scheme and larger random crops. We observed (first section of Table 1) that with vanilla VICReg, its similarity loss quickly reached close to zero, and the representations collapsed. A significant improvement in performance was observed for both the methods with the proposed input scheme. The AUROC of Barlow Twins increased from 0.686 to 0.708 and VICReg achieved 0.685 AUROC score on linear evaluation.

On linear evaluation, TINC loss clearly outperformed both Barlow Twins and VICReg even after modifying them with our novel pair-forming scheme (1). TINC achieved 0.738 AUROC, while modified VICReg and Barlow Twins achieved 0.708 and 0.685 respectively. TINC captures the temporal information better with its temporally induced margin based approach leading to these improvements.

With end-to-end fine-tuning (Table 2) the performance improvement due to the proposed TINC loss is more apparent, even after optimizing VICReg and Barlow Twins with our input pair scheme. We also compared our results against AMDNet [14], an architecture specifically designed for 2D B-scans. Interestingly, AMDNet could not outperform a ResNet-50 initialized with random weights.

In order to demonstrate that the temporal information is crucial in the conversion prediction task, we added time difference as an additional loss term to VICReg. For this, we concatenated the two embeddings and fed them to an MLP to obtain the time difference predictions. The labels are calculated as $v_1 - v_2$ w.r.t input order and scaled between -1 and 1. The MSE between the labels and the predictions is added besides the other VICReg loss terms. This clearly improved AUROC (Table 1, line 1–4), but the additional term increased the complexity of VICReg training. Whereas TINC implicitly uses the temporal information with its margin so that the representation capture the anatomical changes due to the disease progression. The experiments demonstrated that the TINC approach performs better in the downstream AMD conversion prediction task than adding the time difference as a separate term.

Additionally, we modified our loss as a squared epsilon insensitive loss to have smoother boundaries, but it degraded the performance. With Barlow Twins, we observed that the fine-tuning AUROC performance was worse than its linear evaluation by 0.016. This can be explained by the fact that in Barlow Twins, the fine-tuning reached the peak validation score within 10 epochs, same as the number of linear training epochs.

4 Discussion and Conclusion

The temporal information is one of the key factors to correctly model disease progression. However, popular contrastive and non-contrastive methods are not designed specifically to capture that. Additionally, they require strong augmentations to create two views of an image, which are not always applicable to medical images. We proposed TINC as a modified similarity term of the recent non-contrastive method VICReg, without increasing its complexity. Models trained with TINC outperformed the original VICReg and Barlow Twins in the task of predicting conversion to wet-AMD. Also TINC is not task or dataset specific, it is applicable to any longitudinal imaging dataset. Moreover, we proposed a new input pair-forming scheme for OCT volumes from different time points, which replaced the heavy augmentations required in the original VICReg and Barlow Twins and improved the performance.

Acknowledgements. The work has been partially funded by FWF Austrian Science Fund (FG 9-N), and a Wellcome Trust Collaborative Award (PINNACLE Ref. 210572/Z/18/Z).

References

1. Azizi, S., et al.: Big self-supervised models advance medical image classification. In: Proceedings of the IEEE/CVF International Conference on Computer Vision, pp. 3478–3488 (2021)
2. Banerjee, I., et al.: Prediction of age-related macular degeneration disease using a sequential deep learning approach on longitudinal sd-oct imaging biomarkers. Sci. Rep. **10**(1), 15434 (2020). https://doi.org/10.1038/s41598-020-72359-y
3. Bardes, A., Ponce, J., LeCun, Y.: VICReg: variance-invariance-covariance regularization for self-supervised learning. In: International Conference on Learning Representations (2022)
4. Bressler, N.M.: Age-related macular degeneration is the leading cause of blindness. JAMA **291**(15), 1900–1901 (2004). https://doi.org/10.1001/jama.291.15.1900
5. Caron, M., Misra, I., Mairal, J., Goyal, P., Bojanowski, P., Joulin, A.: Unsupervised learning of visual features by contrasting cluster assignments. Adv. Neural. Inf. Process. Syst. **33**, 9912–9924 (2020)
6. Chen, X., He, K.: Exploring simple siamese representation learning. In: Proceedings of the IEEE/CVF Conference on Computer Vision and Pattern Recognition, pp. 15750–15758 (2021)
7. Chen, Y., et al.: USCL: Pretraining deep ultrasound image diagnosis model through video contrastive representation learning. In: de Bruijne, M., et al. (eds.) MICCAI 2021. LNCS, vol. 12908, pp. 627–637. Springer, Cham (2021). https://doi.org/10.1007/978-3-030-87237-3_60
8. Ermolov, A., Siarohin, A., Sangineto, E., Sebe, N.: Whitening for self-supervised representation learning. In: International Conference on Machine Learning, pp. 3015–3024. PMLR (2021)
9. Grill, J.B., et al.: Bootstrap your own latent-a new approach to self-supervised learning. Adv. Neural. Inf. Process. Syst. **33**, 21271–21284 (2020)
10. Jing, L., Vincent, P., LeCun, Y., Tian, Y.: Understanding dimensional collapse in contrastive self-supervised learning. In: International Conference on Learning Representations (2022)
11. Li, H., et al.: Imbalance-aware self-supervised learning for 3D radiomic representations. In: de Bruijne, M., et al. (eds.) MICCAI 2021. LNCS, vol. 12902, pp. 36–46. Springer, Cham (2021). https://doi.org/10.1007/978-3-030-87196-3_4
12. van den Oord, A., Li, Y., Vinyals, O.: Representation learning with contrastive predictive coding (2019)
13. Rivail, A., et al.: Modeling disease progression in Retinal OCTs with longitudinal self-supervised learning. In: Rekik, I., Adeli, E., Park, S.H. (eds.) PRIME 2019. LNCS, vol. 11843, pp. 44–52. Springer, Cham (2019). https://doi.org/10.1007/978-3-030-32281-6_5
14. Russakoff, D.B., Lamin, A., Oakley, J.D., Dubis, A.M., Sivaprasad, S.: Deep learning for prediction of amd progression: a pilot study. Invest. Ophthalmol. Visual Sci. **60**(2), 712–722 (2019)
15. Schmidt-Erfurth, U., et al.: Prediction of individual disease conversion in early amd using artificial intelligence. Invest. Ophthalmol. Visual Sci. **59**(8), 3199–3208 (2018)

16. Wu, Z., Bogunović, H., Asgari, R., Schmidt-Erfurth, U., Guymer, R.H.: Predicting progression of age-related macular degeneration using oct and fundus photography. Ophthalmol. Retina **5**(2), 118–125 (2021). https://doi.org/10.1016/j.oret.2020.06.026

17. Yan, Q., et al.: Deep-learning-based prediction of late age-related macular degeneration progression. Nat. Mach. intell. **2**(2), 141–150 (2020)

18. Yang, J., et al.: Two-year risk of exudation in eyes with nonexudative age-related macular degeneration and subclinical neovascularization detected with swept source optical coherence tomography angiography. Am. J. Ophthalmol. **208**, 1–11 (2019). https://doi.org/10.1016/j.ajo.2019.06.017

19. Yim, J., et al.: Predicting conversion to wet age-related macular degeneration using deep learning. Nat. Med. **26**(6), 892–899 (2020)

20. Zbontar, J., Jing, L., Misra, I., LeCun, Y., Deny, S.: Barlow twins: self-supervised learning via redundancy reduction. In: International Conference on Machine Learning, pp. 12310–12320. PMLR (2021)

21. Zhang, L., et al.: Validity of Automated Choroidal Segmentation in SS-OCT and SD-OCT. Investigative Ophthalmol. Visual Sci. **56**(5), 3202–3211 (2015). https://doi.org/10.1167/iovs.14-15669

DRGen: Domain Generalization in Diabetic Retinopathy Classification

Mohammad Atwany$^{(\boxtimes)}$ and Mohammad Yaqub

Mohamed Bin Zayed University of Artificial Intelligence, Abu Dhabi, UAE
{mohammad.atwany,mohammad.yaqub}@mbzuai.ac.ae
https://mbzuai.ac.ae/biomedia

Abstract. Domain Generalization is a challenging problem in deep learning especially in medical image analysis because of the huge diversity between different datasets. Existing papers in the literature tend to optimize performance on single target domains, without regards to model generalizability on other domains or distributions. High discrepancy in the number of images and major domain shifts, can therefore cause single-source trained models to under-perform during testing. In this paper, we address the problem of domain generalization in Diabetic Retinopathy (DR) classification. The baseline for comparison is set as joint training on different datasets, followed by testing on each dataset individually. We therefore introduce a method that encourages seeking a flatter minima during training while imposing a regularization. This reduces gradient variance from different domains and therefore yields satisfactory results on out-of-domain DR classification. We show that adopting DR-appropriate augmentations enhances model performance and in-domain generalizability. By performing our evaluation on 4 open-source DR datasets, we show that the proposed domain generalization method outperforms separate and joint training strategies as well as well-established methods. Source Code is available at https://github.com/BioMedIA-MBZUAI/DRGen.

Keywords: Deep learning · Diabetic retinopathy · Domain generalization · Regularization

1 Introduction

The common assumption of independent and identically distributed (i.i.d.) data may not hold in real-world scenarios, and in our case, Diabetic Retinopathy (DR) classification. Therefore, domain generalization (DG) [26] aims at dealing with domain shift induced by the difference in training and testing distributions or image modalities. However, the main idea behind DG techniques is to train a model that is able to generalize well on data from unseen target distributions. Work in the DG literature includes reducing latent space domain gaps explicitly by meta-learning framework for transfer learning [16], causal capturing [2] and data augmentation to increase the number of images and its variations [27].

© The Author(s), under exclusive license to Springer Nature Switzerland AG 2022
L. Wang et al. (Eds.): MICCAI 2022, LNCS 13432, pp. 635–644, 2022.
https://doi.org/10.1007/978-3-031-16434-7_61

Table 1. Datasets used for DR detection and classification models.

Dataset	Img. Count	Img. Size (px)	Train+Val, Test size
EyePACS 2015 [10]	88,702	433 × 289 to 5184 × 3456	{35126, 53576}
APTOS 2019 [1]	3,660	Varies	–
Messidor [5]	1,200	1440 × 960 to 2304 × 1536 (24-bit)	–
Messidor-2 [5]	1,748	1440 × 960 to 2304 × 1536 (24-bit)	–
IDRiD [23]	516	4288 × 2848	{413, 103}
DRIVE [3]	40	565 × 584 (24-bit)	{20, 20}
DIARETDB1 [12]	89	1500 × 1152 (24-bit)	{28, 61}
DIARETDB0 [11]	130	1500 × 1152 (24-bit)	–
ODIR [13]	10,000	–	{9000, 1000}
DDR [18]	13,673	Varies	{9568, 4105}
RFMiD [21]	3200	2144 × 1424	{1920, 1280}

In this paper, we investigate DG in medical image analysis and assess the proposed method on the challenging classification of Diabetic Retinopathy datasets. Table 1 provides an overview of common publicly available DR datasets.

Diabetic Retinopathy (DR) is a complication of Diabetes Mellitus, in which glucose buildup can block blood vessels, causing swelling/leaking of fluids or blood; resulting in an irreversible eye damage. The retinal central swelling can therefore lead to detrimental vision loss. Generally, the four types of lesions that are indicators for diagnosis are Microaneurysms (MA), Haemorrhages (HM), soft and hard exudates (EX). DR is typically categorized into 5 classes, namely no DR, mild DR, moderate DR, severe DR and proliferative DR [9]. Figure 1 shows examples from the 5 DR classes/grades.

In this paper, we propose a DG method and apply it to the challenging task of DR classification. Our contributions are as follows:

- We propose a new method that utilizes flatness in domain generalization training for iteration-wise weight averaging, coupled with domain-level gradient variance regularization.
- We demonstrate the effectiveness of the proposed solution on the challenging DR classification task on 4 diverse DR datasets. We show how our method outperforms different methods such as joint training and Fishr [24] based models, independently.
- We provide detailed insights on the thorough evaluation we performed in the discussion and results sections, which shall hopefully help attract more DG research in the medical image analysis community.

2 Related Work

In this section, we review DG research in the medical image analysis domain. We then describe two important DG techniques that we build our proposed algorithm on, for the sake of making this paper self-contained.

Grade 0   Grade 1   Grade 2   Grade 3   Grade 4

Fig. 1. Example of Different Diabetic Retinopathy Grades obtained from APTOS [1] dataset.

2.1 DG in Medical Imaging

Although DG is crucial in medical image analysis to ensure robustness of deep learning models on data from unseen domains, it is well under-studied in this community. Variability and scarcity of annotated source domains are among different reasons why DG in medical imaging is crucial. Motivated by this issue, a meta-learning based scheme of episodic training with task augmentation on medical imaging classification [14], introduces task-specific augmentations to increase image variety during training. Another approach [17], uses variational encoding to learn a representative feature space through linear-dependency regularization. This allows the capturing of the shareable information. Thus, models trained under this regularization are able to better generalize on unseen target domains. DG in medical imaging has also been explored in the context of Federated Learning (FL). A novel Episodic Learning in Continuous Frequency Space (ELCFS) approach [19] leverages FL, by enabling privacy protected distribution of information between clients (e.g. hospitals).

2.2 Stochastic Weight Averaging Densely

Stochastic Weight Averaging Densely (SWAD) [4] finds a flat minima by averaging a dense sample of model weights with an over-fit criteria based on the validation loss. In this method, weights are essentially collected for iterations rather than epochs. Weights are sampled by searching the start and end iterations, for which the validation loss reaches a local optimum for the first time, and when it no longer decreases. This allows selectivity, to only average specific iteration weights where the validation loss decreases. This has shown to improve model generalizability in different domains [4], but has not been tested or utilized in medical imaging.

2.3 Fishr

Fishr [24] is a regularization technique which matches the gradients domain level variances across different source domains. This method exploits the gradient covariance, the Hessian of the loss and Fisher information relationship. Fishr only enforces domain invariance in the classifier's weights with an exponential moving

Table 2. Diabetic Retinopathy datasets and their class distribution as percentages of the total number of images.

Database	Grade 0	Grade 1	Grade 2	Grade 3	Grade 4	Total images
EyePACs	73.67%	7.00%	14.83%	2.35%	2.15%	88702
APTOS	49.25%	10.12%	27.29%	5.28%	8.06%	3657
Messidor	45.50%	12.75%	20.58%	21.17%	0.00%	1200
Messidor 2	58.31%	15.48%	19.90%	4.30%	2.01%	1744

average after a specified warm-up period, which is set as a hyperparameter. This warmup period is when the network initially learns predictive features. After the warmup threshold is reached, regularization comes into effect, ultimately, forcing domain-level gradient invariance in the classifier.

To achieve the task of reduction of domain shift, the gradient covariances at the domain level are to be made close, therefore the Fishr loss equation can be represented as:

$$\mathcal{L}_{\text{Fishr}} = \frac{1}{|\mathcal{E}|} \sum_{e \in \mathcal{E}} \|C_e - C\|_F^2 \qquad (1)$$

where C_e in Eq. 1 is the covariance matrix for each domain $e \in \mathcal{E}$ in the Fishr loss equation. The Frobenius difference squared between covariance matrices of all domains is taken with $C = \frac{1}{|\mathcal{E}|} \sum_{e \in \mathcal{E}} C_e$, which is the mean covariance matrix. The Fishr loss is then multiplied by a hyperparameter λ that is greater than zero, the total loss to be minimized is illustrated in Eq. 2:

$$\mathcal{L}_{Total} = \frac{1}{|\mathcal{E}|} \sum_{e \in \mathcal{E}} \mathcal{R}_e + \lambda \mathcal{L}_{\text{Fishr}} \qquad (2)$$

where the first summation term in Eq. 2, represents the average empirical risk averaged for all training domains.

3   Methodology

3.1   Baseline Adoption

In order to solve the issue of out-of-domain generalizability, we utilize the four most common datasets in DR literature, namely EyePACs [10], Aptos [1], Messidor and Messidor 2 [20]. All the aforementioned datasets are classified into 5 classes with grade 0 being the lowest form of DR and grade 4 being the most proliferative. Joint training was performed, in which the datasets were combined during training into 3 groups with the testing performed on the entire left-out dataset, similar to the DomainBed generalization on PACs [15], VLCS [6], DomainNet [22] etc. that are normally used for Domain Generalization studies (Fig. 2).

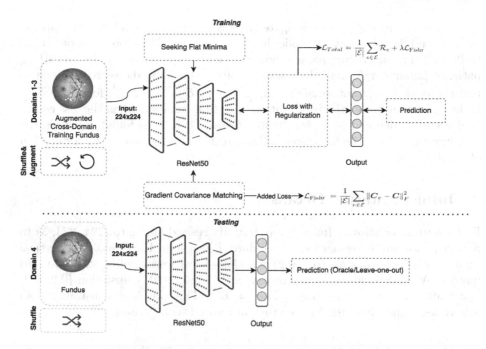

Fig. 2. High level process diagram of our proposed method implementation: fundus images of size (224, 224, 3) of 3 source domains are shuffled, weight sampled and then passed through a ResNet50 architecture. Iteration-wise averaging of weights is done in conjunction with regularized loss minimization. This is repeated for each dataset as a target domain and then the results are averaged.

Due to limited training samples, in most of the datasets in comparison to Eye-PACS [10] as can be seen in Table 2, data augmentations were adopted. Weighted imbalanced class sampler was used to mitigate the effect of class imbalance in the source datasets. All fundus images were resized to $(224, 224)$ to normalize the different spatial resolutions. The baseline was taken as the average of the results of each respective testing dataset when the model is trained on the other 3 datasets as shown in Table 3.

3.2 Stochastic Weighted Domain Invariance

We adapted Fishr [24] loss to enforce invariance based on the difference in covariance matrices as represented in Eq. 2. Three hyperparameters were searched to optimize the loss. The first is the lambda (λ) coefficient which is used to control the regularization strength. The second is the warmup iteration, which decides when the regularization is activated, so the model learns enough predictive features beforehand. Then, exponential moving average is used to compute stable gradient variances while the penalty anneal iteration γ coefficient helps moderate the update speed at each time-step.

We also leverage stochastic weighted averaging [4] which is a heuristic approximation and does not rely on model hyperparameters. Therefore, it is only controlled by three averaging parameters: a patience parameter N_s, an overfitting patience parameter N_e and the tolerance rate r. Initially, the search is done to find the value for t_s that satisfies $\min_{i \in [0,...,N_s-1]} \mathcal{E}_{\text{val}}^{(t_s+i)} = \mathcal{E}_{\text{val}}^{(t_s)}$, for which $\mathcal{E}_{\text{val}}^{(i)}$ is the validation loss at the ith iteration. The first iteration when the loss ceases to decrease is denoted by t_s for N_s iterations. Then, t_e is found, which is the first iteration where the loss exceeds the threshold or tolerance r for a duration of N_e iterations.

4   Implementation Details

Data Augmentations. Images were initially resized offline to (224, 224, 3) to normalize the spatial resolution to standard dimensions. Horizontal flip, vertical flipping, random grayscale (p = 0.2) and ColorJitter were applied on the fundus images. We also performed random rotation $(-180, 180)$, translation $(0.2, 0.2)$ and Gaussian blur (kernel size = 7, σ = 0.5). This was kept constant for all experiments and ablations for a consistent and fair comparison.

Backbone and Base Hyperparameters. ResNet50 [8] is used as the backbone. The network parameters were initialized with ImageNet [25] weights and the validation split was set to 20%. An initial learning rate of 0.001 is used and then decayed to 5e−5 using a step learning rate scheduler coupled with Cosine Annealing warmup and an Adam optimizer, with 10 warmup epochs. These parameters were experimentally chosen. The base joint model was trained for 200 epochs, that were sufficient to reach saturation.

Iteration-Wise Stochastic Weight Averaging and Domain Invariance Training. We set the total number of steps at 15000 with 15 steps per epoch, to be consistent with the original Fishr model. We fix the validation split at 20% with 5 fold cross-validation. ResNet-50 is initialized with ImageNet [25] weights, then used with a 64 batch size, a fixed learning rate of 5e−5 and Adam optimizer. We experimentally set stochastic weight averaging hyperparameters N_s, N_e and r to 3, 6 and 1.3, respectively.

4.1   Model Selection Method

Leave-one-domain-out cross-validation is used for joint training, where the validation set is different from the test distribution. We then test our method and Fishr models using Oracle method where validation set follows the same distribution as the test domain [7], in order to be consistent with the original Fishr model reporting.

Table 3. Joint training baseline: 3 datasets for training, 1 dataset for testing.

Joint combined training datasets	Testing dataset	Average accuracy %
Messidor, Messidor 2 and APTOS	EyePACs	59.27 %
Messidor, Messidor 2 and EyePACs	APTOS	69.98%
Messidor 2, APTOS and EyePACs	Messidor	55.58%
Messidor, APTOS and EyePACs	Messidor 2	64.45%
–	–	**62.32 ± 5.43**

5 Experiments and Results

Evaluation Metric. We leverage out-of-domain accuracy for evaluation, under the Oracle and leave-one-out model selection techniques. The results for joint training as a baseline are reported in Table 3. We evaluate the performance of our method under different hyperparameters. Table 4 conjectures the results for the Fishr [24] model for different hyperparameters on the 4 domains.

Table 4. Oracle method ablation results based on Fishr [24] model only for a fixed learning rate of 5e-5.

Hyperparameter name (Hp)	Hp value	Average accuracy %
Lambda (λ)	1000	**69.40**
Lambda (λ)	500	63.43
Lambda (λ)	1500	64.27
Penalty anneal iteration (γ)	1000	64.36
Penalty anneal iteration (γ)	2000	64.20
Exponential Moving Average (EMA)	0.85	63.70
Exponential Moving Average (EMA)	0.75	64.13

To assess the performance of our method, we compare it with both the joint training baseline and Fishr based methods, based on the leave-one-out and Oracle methods, respectively. We report results on all aforementioned datasets individually and collectively, as shown in Tables 3 and 5.

Table 5. Comparison between Fishr [24] and proposed method results (average accuracy) for each dataset (Oracle) for a learning rate of 5e−5 with a ResNet50 architecture

Testing dataset	Fishr accuracy %	Proposed method accuracy %
EyePACs	69.00	74.31
Aptos	68.72	70.34
Messidor	73.70	66.70
Messidor 2	66.11	70.53
Average	**69.40 ± 2.74**	**70.47 ± 2.69**

6 Discussion

In Table 3, a strict leave-one-out method evaluation was adopted to report results on the baseline. Since the EyePACs dataset represents the largest portion of any given training set, when included as part of the 3 source domains, results tend to be relatively close when the target domain is either APTOS or Messidor 2. However, it performs poorly when the target domain is Messidor [20]. This relates to its small training/testing subsets, since the total number of images is around 1200 and is further affected by the absence of grade 0 images from the dataset, therefore inducing a substantial domain shift. A prominent indicator of this shift is the high standard deviation with a value of 5.43%, influenced by large variations in the classification accuracy.

Moreover, the overall objective is to attain a better out-of-distribution accuracy, therefore, the balance between densely learning predictive features and gradient invariance can be observed by the accuracy of the model during inference on different testing datasets. Simultaneously, the lower standard variation in this context is used to suggest a more consistently performing model.

As for Table 4, the optimal performance for the Fishr only model was empirically observed for the same hyperparameter setting for the PACs [15] dataset used for DG benchmarking in DomainBed [7]. When compared to the baseline, better performance is observed in terms of accuracy and standard deviation with an increase and reduction of 7.08% and 2.69%, respectively. The Fishr model outperforms the baseline for all datasets individually, but most importantly a significant improvement when testing on Messidor with an increase from 55.58% to 73.70% accuracy, virtue of domain shift reduction by regularization. As observed in Table 5, Fishr achieves higher results for the Messidor dataset compared to the proposed method, but compromises the accuracy on the remaining 3 datasets, therefore increasing the standard deviation. This is possibly because Messidor has a complete absence of Grade 4 DR and there exists a scarcity of Grade 4 DR images in the other datasets as well, with percentages of around 2%, 8% and 2% for EyePACs, Aptos and Messidor 2 datasets, respectively. Therefore, when the Fishr alone is trained on the three other datasets, it becomes biased towards Grades 0, 1, 2 and 3, for which Messidor is completely comprised and therefore achieves a high average testing accuracy for Messidor.

Fishr alone focuses on reducing the domain shift through gradient invariance. This reduces the domain shift but not necessarily mitigating class imbalance directly. So dense weight averaging is then utilized to mitigate the aforementioned class imbalance.

Ultimately, our method outperforms Fishr in terms of average accuracy (+1.07%) and has a lower standard deviation (−0.05%). This is can be attributed to seeking a flatter minima empirically [4] with selective weight averaging. When compared to the baseline, the proposed method outperforms on all datasets individually, with the highest increase in accuracy for Messidor with 11.12%, as can be seen in Tables 3 and 5. The standard deviation was reduced by 2.74% as well. To ensure fair comparison, Fishr parameters where kept constant for all experiments.

7 Conclusion

In this paper, we addressed Diabetic Retinopathy classification for out of distribution generalization in medical imaging. We empirically demonstrate that seeking flat minima, while simultaneously matching gradient domain level variances as a domain generalization approach, achieves desirable results on the most common Diabetic Retinopathy datasets. Experiments against joint training and Fishr baselines show superior performance, even under a highly varying number of images per dataset. This work aims to potentially promote the benchmarking of DR classification results under the DomainBed genre. Ultimately, although our method achieves lower standard deviation and higher average accuracy, it may slightly reduce accuracy of a specific dataset. This opens up new perspectives for future work, such as the coupling of weight averaging while seeking network-level domain invariance.

References

1. APTOS: APTOS 2019 Blindness Detection, June 2018. https://kaggle.com/c/aptos2019-blindness-detection
2. Arjovsky, M., Bottou, L., Gulrajani, I., Lopez-Paz, D.: Invariant Risk Minimization. arXiv:1907.02893 [cs, stat], July 2019. version: 1
3. Asad, A.H., Azar, A.T., El-Bendary, N., Hassaanien, A.E.: Ant colony based feature selection heuristics for retinal vessel segmentation. arXiv:1403.1735 [cs], March 2014
4. Cha, J., Cho, H., Lee, K., Park, S., Lee, Y., Park, S.: Domain generalization needs stochastic weight averaging for robustness on domain shifts. CoRR arXiv:2102.08604 (2021)
5. Decencière, E., et al.: Feedback on a publicly distributed image database: the messidor database. Image Anal. Stereol. **33**(3), 231–234 (2014). https://doi.org/10.5566/ias.1155, https://www.ias-iss.org/ojs/IAS/article/view/1155
6. Fang, C., Xu, Y., Rockmore, D.N.: Unbiased metric learning: on the utilization of multiple datasets and web images for softening bias. In: Proceedings of the 2013 IEEE International Conference on Computer Vision, ICCV 2013, pp. 1657–1664. IEEE Computer Society, USA (2013). https://doi.org/10.1109/ICCV.2013.208
7. Gulrajani, I., Lopez-Paz, D.: In search of lost domain generalization. CoRR arXiv:2007.01434 (2020)
8. He, K., Zhang, X., Ren, S., Sun, J.: Deep residual learning for image recognition. In: 2016 IEEE Conference on Computer Vision and Pattern Recognition (CVPR), pp. 770–778, June 2016. https://doi.org/10.1109/CVPR.2016.90. ISSN: 1063-6919
9. Kempen, J.H., et al.: The prevalence of diabetic retinopathy among adults in the United States. Arch. Ophthalmol. (Chicago, Ill.: 1960) **122**(4), 552–563 (2004). https://doi.org/10.1001/archopht.122.4.552, https://europepmc.org/article/med/15078674
10. Kaggle: Diabetic Retinopathy Detection - EYEPACS Dataset. https://kaggle.com/c/diabetic-retinopathy-detection
11. Kauppi, T., et al.: DIARETDB 0: Evaluation Database and Methodology for Diabetic Retinopathy Algorithms (2007). https://www.paper/DIARETDB-0-%3A-Evaluation-Database-and-Methodology-Kauppi-Kalesnykiene/bd7d2380e76fb9dfd367d669e311d4913f67f7d2

12. Kauppi, T., et al.: DIARETDB1 diabetic retinopathy database and evaluation protocol. In: Proceedings of the British Machine Vision Conference, vol. 2007, January 2007. https://doi.org/10.5244/C.21.15
13. Larxel: Ocular Disease Recognition, April 2020. https://kaggle.com/andrewmvd/ocular-disease-recognition-odir5k, https://odir2019.grand-challenge.org/
14. Li, C., Qi, Q., Ding, X., Huang, Y., Liang, D., Yu, Y.: Domain generalization on medical imaging classification using episodic training with task augmentation. CoRR arXiv:2106.06908 (2021)
15. Li, D., Yang, Y., Song, Y.Z., Hospedales, T.M.: Deeper, broader and artier domain generalization. In: 2017 IEEE International Conference on Computer Vision (ICCV), pp. 5543–5551 (2017)
16. Li, D., Yang, Y., Song, Y.Z., Hospedales, T.M.: Learning to generalize: meta-learning for domain generalization. arXiv:1710.03463 [cs], October 2017
17. Li, H., Wang, Y., Wan, R., Wang, S., Li, T., Kot, A.C.: Domain generalization for medical imaging classification with linear-dependency regularization. CoRR arXiv:2009.12829 (2020)
18. Li, T., Gao, Y., Wang, K., Guo, S., Liu, H., Kang, H.: Diagnostic assessment of deep learning algorithms for diabetic retinopathy screening. Inf. Sci. **501**, 511–522 (2019). https://doi.org/10.1016/j.ins.2019.06.011, https://linkinghub.elsevier.com/retrieve/pii/S0020025519305377
19. Liu, Q., Chen, C., Qin, J., Dou, Q., Heng, P.: FedDG: federated domain generalization on medical image segmentation via episodic learning in continuous frequency space. CoRR arXiv:2103.06030 (2021)
20. Maffre, G.G., et al.: Messidor. https://www.adcis.net/en/third-party/messidor/
21. Pachade, S., et al.: Retinal Fundus Multi-Disease Image Dataset (RFMiD): a dataset for multi-disease detection research. Data **6**(2), 14 (2021). https://doi.org/10.3390/data6020014, https://www.mdpi.com/2306-5729/6/2/14
22. Peng, X., Bai, Q., Xia, X., Huang, Z., Saenko, K., Wang, B.: Moment matching for multi-source domain adaptation. CoRR arXiv:1812.01754 (2018)
23. Porwal, P., et al.: Indian Diabetic Retinopathy Image Dataset (IDRiD): a database for diabetic retinopathy screening research. Data **3**(3), 25 (2018). https://doi.org/10.3390/data3030025, https://www.mdpi.com/2306-5729/3/3/25
24. Ramé, A., Dancette, C., Cord, M.: Fishr: invariant gradient variances for out-of-distribution generalization. CoRR arXiv:2109.02934 (2021)
25. Russakovsky, O., et al.: ImageNet large scale visual recognition challenge. Int. J. Comput. Vis. **115**(3), 211–252 (2015). https://doi.org/10.1007/s11263-015-0816-y
26. Zhou, K., Liu, Z., Qiao, Y., Xiang, T., Loy, C.C.: Domain generalization in vision: a survey. arXiv:2103.02503 [cs], March 2021. version: 1
27. Zhou, K., Yang, Y., Qiao, Y., Xiang, T.: MixStyle neural networks for domain generalization and adaptation. arXiv:2107.02053 [cs], July 2021

Frequency-Aware Inverse-Consistent Deep Learning for OCT-Angiogram Super-Resolution

Weiwen Zhang[1]([⊠]), Dawei Yang[2], Carol Y. Cheung[2], and Hao Chen[1]([⊠])

[1] Department of Computer Science and Engineering,
The Hong Kong University of Science and Technology, Hong Kong, China
wzhangbu@connect.ust.hk
[2] Department of Ophthalmology and Visual Sciences,
The Chinese University of Hong Kong, Hong Kong, China

Abstract. Optical Coherence Tomography Angiography (OCTA) is a novel imaging modality that captures the retinal and choroidal microvasculature in a non-invasive way. So far, $3\,\text{mm} \times 3\,\text{mm}$ and $6\,\text{mm} \times 6\,\text{mm}$ scanning protocols have been the two most widely-used field-of-views. Nevertheless, since both are acquired with the same number of A-scans, resolution of $6\,\text{mm} \times 6\,\text{mm}$ image is inadequately sampled, compared with $3\,\text{mm} \times 3\,\text{mm}$. Moreover, conventional supervised super-resolution methods for OCTA images are trained with pixel-wise registered data, while clinical data is mostly unpaired. This paper proposes an Inverse-consistent generative adversarial network (GAN) for archiving $6\,\text{mm} \times 6\,\text{mm}$ OCTA images with super-resolution. Our method is designed to be trained with unpaired $3\,\text{mm} \times 3\,\text{mm}$ and $6\,\text{mm} \times 6\,\text{mm}$ OCTA image datasets. To further enhance the super-resolution performance, we introduce frequency transformations to refine high-frequency information while retaining low-frequency information. Compared with other state-of-the-art methods, our approach outperforms them on various performance metrics.

Keywords: OCTA · Image Super-Resolution · GAN · Frequency-aware · Inverse-consistency

1 Introduction

Optical coherence tomography angiography (OCTA) is a novel imaging technique that can provide depth-resolved angiographic flow images by utilizing motion contrast [13]. It has been used in clinics for the assessment of different retinal diseases, such as diabetic retinopathy (DR) [12,21] and age-related macular degeneration (AMD) [14,19], as it provides retinal and choroidal microvasculature visualization and perfusion estimation without the need of dye injection. Typically, $3\,\text{mm} \times 3\,\text{mm}$ and $6\,\text{mm} \times 6\,\text{mm}$ scanning protocols are two most widely-used field-of-views in the clinics. However, since both scans are acquired with the same number of A-scans due to the limited scanning speed of most commercial

L. Wang et al. (Eds.): MICCAI 2022, LNCS 13432, pp. 645–655, 2022.
https://doi.org/10.1007/978-3-031-16434-7_62

OCTA devices, it has been a common issue that the under-sampled 6 mm × 6 mm OCTA images are presented with an inadequate resolution. Hereinafter in this paper, 6 mm × 6 mm images are referred as low-resolution (LR) (B, Fig. 1), and 3 mm × 3 mm images are high-resolution (HR) capturing fovea-centered (C) and parafoveal area ($D_1 \sim D_4$). Since above LR and HR have the same image size while the ratio of field-of-view is 4:1, LR is upscaled ×2 to have the same size of parafoveal and fovea-center area (A, Fig. 1). Clinical studies have shown that HR images can provide better diagnosis performance for different retinal and choroidal diseases [4, 26]. However, due to the trade-off between field-of-view and image resolution, only 3 mm × 3 mm images have been largely used. Therefore, the development of 6 mm × 6 mm OCTA image super-resolution is highly demanded in clinical practice. However, the existing super-resolution networks of OCTA images are supervised learning approaches [7, 8], which strongly rely on pixel-wise registered images between LR and HR. It leads to challenges in collecting datasets in a large-scale way and application of these methods in clinics.

Unpaired Image Super-Resolution. eliminates the dependence of supervised learning on paired datasets in training process. Generative Adversarial Network (GAN) [9] has been deployed in unsupervised domain transformation in medical images analysis [2, 3]. Inspired by Cycle-Consistent GAN (CycleGAN) [29], unsupervised super-resolution approaches were proposed to improve the resolution of the LR image using unpaired datasets [15–17, 25, 28]. Super-resolution is essentially inferring missing high-frequency information from low-resolution images [6]. Therefore, except for the spatial domain perspective, several approaches also took advantage of frequency domain perspective [15, 25]. Existing supervised OCTA image super-resolution algorithms can only be trained on the paired dataset [7, 8]. Unpaired OCTA image super-resolution methods can mitigate this limitation, but study on this topic remains to be further explored.

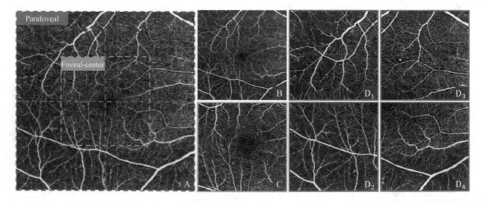

Fig. 1. Illustration of OCTA imaging on different field-of-views. Red: Fovea-center area. Blue: Parafoveal area. Dashed box: LR patches. Solid box: HR. A: Upscaled LR image. B: Raw LR image. C: Fovea-center HR image. $D_1 \sim D_4$: Parafoveal HR images.

To address above challenges, this paper proposes an inverse-consistent deep learning method that can be trained on unpaired datasets to improve the resolution of the LR OCTA images. To better exploit image super-resolution in the frequency domain, we conduct the feature transformations in both spatial and frequency domains. Finally, by integrating features from above two domains, our approach quantitatively outperforms other methods and achieves satisfactory visual results.

2   Method

Our motivation is to enhance the resolution of LR images using the unpaired dataset by exploiting spatial and frequency information. In our work, a restoration GAN is proposed to enhance resolution of LR with unpaired data. To preserve the microvasculature during restoration, a degradation GAN is deployed under the constraint of inverse consistency (see Fig. 2). By utilizing frequency transformation and decomposition, our method flexibly integrates frequency and spatial components to achieve more robust performance.

2.1   Frequency-Aware Based Restoration and Degradation

High-frequency details should be refined in restoration network, denoted as $G_{res}(LR) = LR^{\uparrow}$. Then the degradation network reduces the resolution of HR by mainly retaining the low-frequency information, denoted as $G_{deg}(HR) = HR^{\downarrow}$. The input is initially divided into high- and low-frequency components by

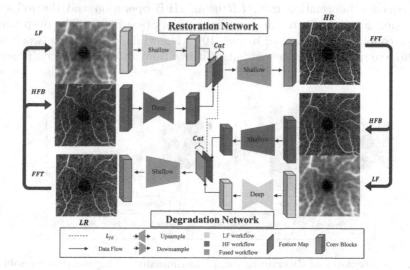

Fig. 2. The overview of our method. FFT followed by HFB and LF decomposes frequency information. G_{res} and G_{deg} process high- and low-frequency components separately. Then, feature maps are concatenated to reconstruct the images.

fast Fourier transformation (FFT), following high- and low-pass Gaussian filters (see Fig. 2). To maintain the structural integrity of the vessels while focusing on high-frequency information, we employ high-frequency boosting (HFB):

$$X^* = (X + f_{hp}(X))/2 \tag{1}$$

where X represents the original input, X^* represents the high-frequency boosted input, $f_{hp}(\cdot)$ represents the high-pass filter. Meanwhile, the low-frequency features are decomposed from low-pass filter (LF). Regarding discriminators, their prediction should also be based on frequency and spatial domains. We employed Haar discrete wavelet transformation (DWT) in horizontal and vertical directions with high- and low-pass filters [5] (see Fig. 3). Therefore, the DWT decomposition produces four components: one pure low-frequency component, denoted as Low-Low (LL), and three components containing high-frequency, denoted as Low-High (LH), High-Low (HL), and High-High (HH). Because the high-frequency information in HR is stronger than that in LR, discriminator should distinguish real or generated HR regarding high-frequency information and vice versa.

2.2 Inverse-Consistency via CycleGAN

Restoration and Degradation. Our method aims to construct the restoration (G_{res}) which is trained on the unpaired dataset. To let G_{res} maintain the structure of the vessels, a coupled degradation network (G_{deg}) and the inverse-consistency loss is deployed. In G_{res} and G_{deg}, high- and low-frequency information are treated in reverse ways. Specifically, G_{res} decomposes and boosts high-frequency information from LR using HFB operation and the following information is input into the deep neural network (see Fig. 2). The deep neural network contains eight residual blocks [10]. Meanwhile, a shallow network with only three convolutional layers extracts features from low-frequency components.

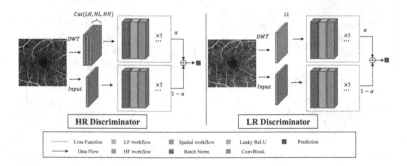

Fig. 3. Architecture of discriminators. Discriminators of high- and low-resolution images are denoted as D_{hr} and D_{lr}. Two pipelines of discriminator separately process spatial information and frequency components decomposed by DWT. Final discrimination is aggregated in a weighted way.

Then, an upsampling module consisting of three residual blocks fuses high- and low-frequency feature maps to reconstruct HR image. Conversely, G_{deg} processes low-frequency components from HR through the deep neural network, while the boosted high-frequency is processed by the shallow network. Then, features are also fused and reconstructed to the LR image through the upsampling module.

Discriminators. The introduction of discriminators, D_{hr} and D_{lr}, is to distinguish HR and LR in views of both spatial and frequency domain [25] (see Fig. 3). In the spatial domain, original LR and HR images are directly provided for spatial discriminator. Meanwhile, components decomposed by DWT are provided for frequency discriminators. In D_{lr}, the pure low-frequency component LL decomposed by DWT is the input of the frequency discriminator of D_{lr}. Similarly, D_{hr} distinguishes results with components containing high-frequency, which is the concatenation of (LH, HL, HH). The final discrimination is aggregated in a weighted way ($\alpha = 0.3$) from results of spatial and frequency discriminators.

2.3   Loss Function and Optimization

Adversarial Loss: We adopt the adversarial loss (L_{adv}) following least-square GAN (LSGAN) [18]. Since our labelling scheme for images is that 1 indicates the real image and 0 represents the generated image, the output of the discriminator ranges from 0 to 1. L_{adv} computes the mean square error between the discriminating result and the image label.

$$\mathcal{L}_{adv}\left(G_{res}, D_{hr}, lr, hr\right) = \mathbb{E}\left[\left\|D_{hr}\left(hr\right) - 1\right\|^2\right] + \mathbb{E}\left[\left\|D_{hr}\left(lr^\uparrow\right)\right\|^2\right] \quad (2)$$

$$\mathcal{L}_{adv}\left(G_{deg}, D_{lr}, lr, hr\right) = \mathbb{E}\left[\left\|D_{lr}\left(lr\right) - 1\right\|^2\right] + \mathbb{E}\left[\left\|D_{lr}\left(hr^\downarrow\right)\right\|^2\right] \quad (3)$$

Inverse-Consistency Loss: Inverse consistency loss (L_{inv}) measures L_1 norm loss between one lr and the reconstructed image $G_{deg}(lr^\uparrow)$, and similarly for hr and $G_{res}(hr^\downarrow)$ [29]. Since the generative model simulates the mapping between the source and target domains, the inverse consistency prevents the model from mapping various inputs to identical output, which is the regularization to the mode collapse of the GAN [9].

$$\mathcal{L}_{inv}\left(G_{res}, G_{deg}\right) = \mathbb{E}\left[\left\|G_{deg}\left(lr^\uparrow\right) - lr\right\|_1\right] + \mathbb{E}\left[\left\|G_{res}\left(hr^\downarrow\right) - hr\right\|_1\right] \quad (4)$$

Feature Distribution Loss: Feature distribution loss (L_{fd}) calculates the cross-entropy between features maps from the high-frequency branches of G_{res} and G_{deg}. It enables the feature distributions between two models as identical as possible. $\phi(\cdot)$ denotes the feature map (see Eq. 5).

$$\mathcal{L}_{fd} = -\beta_1\left[\phi\left(G_{deg}\right)\log\left(\phi\left(G_{res}\right)\right)\right] - \left[\phi\left(G_{res}\right)\log\left(\phi\left(G_{deg}\right)\right)\right] \quad (5)$$

Identity Loss: Identity loss (L_{idt}) constrains the model to maintain content in LR (or HR) that is similar to HR (or LR) domain [29]. It calculates the L_1 norm loss of an image, lr or hr, and its identical mapping, $G_{deg}(lr)$ or $G_{res}(hr)$. The ideal output should be identical to the original input.

$$\mathcal{L}_{idt} = \mathbb{E}\left[\|G_{res}(hr) - hr\|_1\right] + \mathbb{E}\left[\|G_{deg}(lr) - lr\|_1\right] \tag{6}$$

Total Loss: Above terms are combined as our total loss (L_{Total}) (see Eq. 7). Coefficients are set as $\beta_1 = 0.25$, $\beta_2 = 10$, $\beta_3 = 2.0$, $\beta_4 = \beta_5 = 0.5$. Then, the optimization objective is a min-max game [9] on L_{Total} (see Eq. 8). It maximizes the probability of discriminator to distinguish real LR and HR, while minimizing the loss of $G_{res}(lr)$ and $G_{deg}(hr)$.

$$\mathcal{L}_{Total}(G_{res}, G_{deg}, D_{lr}, D_{hr}) = \mathcal{L}_{fd} + \beta_2\mathcal{L}_{idt} + \beta_3\mathcal{L}_{inv}(G_{res}, G_{deg})$$
$$+ \beta_4\mathcal{L}_{adv}(G_{res}, D_{hr}, lr, hr) + \beta_5\mathcal{L}_{adv}(G_{deg}, D_{lr}, hr, lr) \tag{7}$$

$$G^*res, G^*deg = arg \min_{G_{res}, G_{deg}} \max_{D_{lr}, D_{hr}} \mathcal{L}_{Total}(G_{res}, G_{deg}, D_{lr}, D_{hr}) \tag{8}$$

3   Experiments

3.1   Dataset and Pre-processing

The dataset was retrospectively collected from the Chinese University of Hong Kong Sight-Threatening Diabetic Retinopathy (CUHK-STDR) study, which was an observational clinical study for studying diabetic retinal disease in subjects with Type 1 or Type 2 Diabetes Mellitus (DM) recruited from CUHK Eye Centre, Hong Kong Eye Hospital [22,23,27]. All participants underwent OCTA using a swept-source optical coherence tomography (DRI OCT Triton; Topcon, Tokyo, Japan). A total of 296 fovea-centered HR (C), 58 parafoveal HR (D$_1$ ∼ D$_4$) and 296 LR images (B) were used to train the model (see Fig. 1). For the testing set, 279 groups of paired HR (C, D$_1$ ∼ D$_4$) and LR (B) images were collected. For each group, five HR images, including one fovea-center (C) and four parafoveal (D$_1$ ∼ D$_4$), were acquired to generate a whole HR 6 mm × 6 mm montage registered for the original LR 6 mm × 6 mm image [1]. Notably, our model is trained with unpaired dataset but evaluated with paired images after proper registration. For pre-processing of training, images are randomly cropped into 128 × 128 for LR and 256 × 256 for HR first. Then we upscale LR to 256 × 256 by bi-cubic interpolation. To prepare pixel-wise aligned dataset for quantitative evaluation, each LR has a paired HR from the same eye of the same patients. To mitigate slight structural changes due to time interval in capturing images, we utilized non-rigid registration to align the paired images.

3.2   Implementation Details

We implemented our method with Python and PyTorch on a Tesla P100-PCIe with 16 GB memory. To train the inverse-consistenct GAN, we randomly selected one unaligned group of LR and HR images as input to the network for every iteration. We utilized AdamW as our optimizer. The parameters were initialized following standard normal distribution, and the initial learning rate was set to be 2e-4 for the first 30 epochs and then decayed by cosine annealing scheduler to 0.

3.3 Comparison with State-of-the-Art Methods

Regarding the quantitative evaluation, we utilized Peak Signal-to-Noise Ratio (PSNR) [11], Structural Similarity Index Measure (SSIM) [24] and Normalized Mutual Information (NMI) as our metrics. We compared our method with CycleGAN [29] with ResNet [10] and UNet [20] as backbones, the inner cycle of Cycle-in-Cycle GAN (CinCGAN) that aims to restores degraded LR [28], and UnpairedSR using pseudo pairs [17] in experiments. Since the dataset of CinC-GAN required an extra group of clean LR, its outer cycle was not applicable to our work. The comparisons were illustrated in both quantitative and visual results. Our results showed that our method outperformed other methods in all metrics (see Table 1). Higher NMI revealed that more information in high-resolution images was recovered. Moreover, our method visually depressed noises in foveal avascular zone (FAZ) as well (see Fig. 4). Furthermore, the evaluation results for the whole area showed that our method achieved better performance not only in the fovea-central area but also in the parafoveal areas (see Table 1). We also visualized the reconstruction results on a whole 6 mm × 6 mm image (see Fig. 5), which indicated the details of vessel structures were well recovered.

Table 1. Quantitative results of different methods on the CUHK-STDR of fovea-central area and whole area. ↑ means the higher the better.

Method	Fovea-central area			Whole area		
	↑ PSNR	↑ SSIM	↑ NMI	↑ PSNR	↑ SSIM	↑ NMI
CycleGAN-UNet [20]	16.803	0.447	1.051	16.920	0.462	1.055
CycleGAN-ResNet [10]	16.821	0.450	1.052	17.039	0.481	1.058
CinCGAN-Inner [28]	17.035	0.473	1.052	16.753	0.462	1.054
UnpairedSR [17]	16.886	0.348	1.048	17.196	0.411	1.056
Ours	**17.401**	**0.484**	**1.058**	**17.622**	**0.499**	**1.061**

Table 2. Ablation study on the CUHK-STDR of fovea-central area and whole area. ↑ means the higher the better.

Method	Fovea-central area			Whole area		
	↑ PSNR	↑ SSIM	↑ NMI	↑ PSNR	↑ SSIM	↑ NMI
Ours	**17.401**	**0.484**	**1.058**	**17.622**	**0.499**	**1.061**
$w\backslash o$ DWT	17.208	0.434	1.055	17.222	0.465	1.058
$w\backslash o$ L_{fd}	17.116	0.471	1.055	16.838	0.486	1.058
$w\backslash o$ HFB	16.294	0.336	1.047	15.638	0.359	1.044

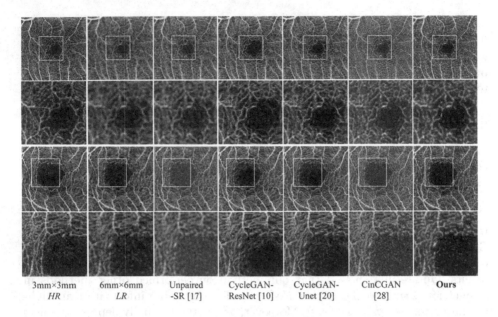

| 3mm×3mm | 6mm×6mm | Unpaired | CycleGAN- | CycleGAN- | CinCGAN | **Ours** |
| HR | LR | -SR [17] | ResNet [10] | Unet [20] | [28] | |

Fig. 4. Visual comparison results of different methods.

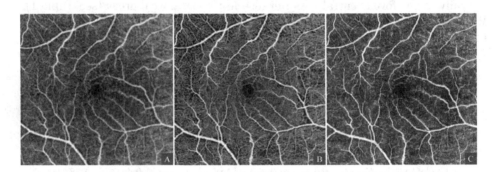

Fig. 5. Visual results of whole 6 mm × 6 mm OCTA image. A: LR 6 mm × 6 mm OCTA image, B: HR 6 mm × 6 mm OCTA image, C: Our restored whole 3 mm × 3 mm OCTA image.

We conducted ablation studies by removing L_{fd} and DWT in discriminator, and replacing HFB with pure high-frequency components. The decrease of quantitative measurements indicated that the above designs in the network were necessary to retain the useful information while depressing noises (see Table 2).

4   Conclusion

This paper proposes a frequency-aware inverse-consistent GAN to improve the resolution of OCTA images using unpaired dataset. The restoration GAN is coupled with a degradation version under the constraint of inverse-consistency. By employing frequency decomposition, we separate and fuse high- and low-frequency components to restore HR. We conducted comparison experiments and ablation studies to validate the efficacy of the proposed method. To our best knowledge, this is the first study on unpaired OCTA super-resolution by frequency-decomposition and inverse-consistency. It could mitigate the challenges of large-scale paired data collection. In our future work, we plan to introduce regularization on the vessel coherence to further improve the performance.

Acknowledgments. This work was supported by funding from Center for Aging Science, Hong Kong University of Science and Technology, and Shenzhen Science and Technology Innovation Committee (Project No. SGDX20210823103201011), and Direct Grants from The Chinese University of Hong Kong (Project Code: 4054419 & 4054487).

References

1. de Carlo, T.E., Salz, D.A., Waheed, N.K., Baumal, C.R., Duker, J.S., Witkin, A.J.: Visualization of the retinal vasculature using wide-field montage optical coherence tomography angiography. Ophthal. Surg. Lasers Imaging Retina **46**(6), 611 (2015)
2. Chen, C., Dou, Q., Chen, H., Qin, J., Heng, P.A.: Synergistic image and feature adaptation: towards cross-modality domain adaptation for medical image segmentation. In: Proceedings of the AAAI Conference on Artificial Intelligence, vol. 33, pp. 865–872 (2019)
3. Chen, C., Dou, Q., Chen, H., Qin, J., Heng, P.A.: Unsupervised bidirectional cross-modality adaptation via deeply synergistic image and feature alignment for medical image segmentation. IEEE Trans. Med. Imaging **39**(7), 2494–2505 (2020)
4. Cheung, C.M.G., et al.: Diabetic macular ischaemia-a new therapeutic target? Prog. Retinal Eye Res. 101033 (2021)
5. Cotter, F.: Uses of Complex Wavelets in Deep Convolutional Neural Networks. Ph.D. thesis, University of Cambridge (2020)
6. Fritsche, M., Gu, S., Timofte, R.: Frequency separation for real-world super-resolution. In: 2019 IEEE/CVF International Conference on Computer Vision Workshop (ICCVW), pp. 3599–3608. IEEE (2019)
7. Gao, M., Guo, Y., Hormel, T., Sun, J., Hwang, T., Jia, Y.: Reconstruction of high-resolution 6×6-mm oct angiograms using deep learning. Biomed. Opt. Exp. **11**, 3585–3600 (2020). https://doi.org/10.1364/BOE.394301
8. Gao, M., et al.: An open-source deep learning network for reconstruction of high-resolution oct angiograms of retinal intermediate and deep capillary plexuses. Investigat. Ophthalmol. Vis. Sci. **62**, 1032–1032 (2021). https://doi.org/10.1167/tvst.10.13.13
9. Goodfellow, I., et al.: Generative adversarial nets. Adv. Neural Inf. Process. Syst. **27** (2014)
10. He, K., Zhang, X., Ren, S., Sun, J.: Deep residual learning for image recognition. In: Proceedings of the IEEE Conference on Computer Vision and Pattern Recognition, pp. 770–778 (2016)

11. Hore, A., Ziou, D.: Image quality metrics: Psnr vs. ssim. In: 2010 20th International Conference on Pattern Recognition, pp. 2366–2369. IEEE (2010)
12. Hwang, T.S., et al.: Optical coherence tomography angiography features of diabetic retinopathy. Retina **35**(11), 2371 (2015)
13. Jia, Y., et al.: Quantitative optical coherence tomography angiography of vascular abnormalities in the living human eye. Proc. Natl. Acad. Sci. **112**(18), E2395–E2402 (2015)
14. Jia, Y., et al.: Quantitative optical coherence tomography angiography of choroidal neovascularization in age-related macular degeneration. Ophthalmology **121**(7), 1435–1444 (2014)
15. Kim, G., et al.: Unsupervised real-world super resolution with cycle generative adversarial network and domain discriminator. In: Proceedings of the IEEE/CVF Conference on Computer Vision and Pattern Recognition Workshops, pp. 456–457 (2020)
16. Lugmayr, A., Danelljan, M., Timofte, R.: Unsupervised learning for real-world super-resolution. In: 2019 IEEE/CVF International Conference on Computer Vision Workshop (ICCVW), pp. 3408–3416. IEEE (2019)
17. Maeda, S.: Unpaired image super-resolution using pseudo-supervision. In: Proceedings of the IEEE/CVF Conference on Computer Vision and Pattern Recognition, pp. 291–300 (2020)
18. Mao, X., Li, Q., Xie, H., Lau, R.Y., Wang, Z., Paul Smolley, S.: Least squares generative adversarial networks. In: Proceedings of the IEEE International Conference on Computer Vision, pp. 2794–2802 (2017)
19. Roisman, L., et al.: Optical coherence tomography angiography of asymptomatic neovascularization in intermediate age-related macular degeneration. Ophthalmology **123**(6), 1309–1319 (2016)
20. Ronneberger, O., Fischer, P., Brox, T.: U-Net: convolutional networks for biomedical image segmentation. In: Navab, N., Hornegger, J., Wells, W.M., Frangi, A.F. (eds.) MICCAI 2015. LNCS, vol. 9351, pp. 234–241. Springer, Cham (2015). https://doi.org/10.1007/978-3-319-24574-4_28
21. Rosen, R.B., et al.: Earliest evidence of preclinical diabetic retinopathy revealed using optical coherence tomography angiography perfused capillary density. Am. J. Ophthalmol. **203**, 103–115 (2019)
22. Sun, Z.,et al.: Oct angiography metrics predict progression of diabetic retinopathy and development of diabetic macular edema: a prospective study. Ophthalmology **126**(12), 1675–1684 (2019)
23. Tang, F.Y., et al.: Determinants of quantitative optical coherence tomography angiography metrics in patients with diabetes. Sci. Rep. **7**(1), 1–10 (2017)
24. Wang, Z., Bovik, A.C., Sheikh, H.R., Simoncelli, E.P.: Image quality assessment: from error visibility to structural similarity. IEEE Trans. Image Process. **13**(4), 600–612 (2004)
25. Wei, Y., Gu, S., Li, Y., Timofte, R., Jin, L., Song, H.: Unsupervised real-world image super resolution via domain-distance aware training. In: Proceedings of the IEEE/CVF Conference on Computer Vision and Pattern Recognition, pp. 13385–13394 (2021)
26. Wong, T.Y., Cheung, C.M.G., Larsen, M., Sharma, S., Simó, R.: Diabetic retinopathy. Nat. Rev. Dis. Primers **2**(1), 16012 (2016)
27. Yang, D.W., et al.: Clinically relevant factors associated with a binary outcome of diabetic macular ischaemia: an octa study. Br. J. Ophthalmol. (2022). https://doi.org/10.1136/bjophthalmol-2021-320779

28. Yuan, Y., Liu, S., Zhang, J., Zhang, Y., Dong, C., Lin, L.: Unsupervised image super-resolution using cycle-in-cycle generative adversarial networks. In: Proceedings of the IEEE Conference on Computer Vision and Pattern Recognition Workshops, pp. 701–710 (2018)
29. Zhu, J.Y., Park, T., Isola, P., Efros, A.A.: Unpaired image-to-image translation using cycle-consistent adversarial networks. In: Computer Vision (ICCV), 2017 IEEE International Conference on (2017)

A Multi-task Network with Weight Decay Skip Connection Training for Anomaly Detection in Retinal Fundus Images

Wentian Zhang[1,2], Xu Sun[2(✉)], Yuexiang Li[2], Haozhe Liu[2], Nanjun He[2],
Feng Liu[1(✉)], and Yefeng Zheng[2]

[1] Computer Vision Institute, College of Computer Science and Software Engineering,
Shenzhen University, Shenzhen, China
feng.liu@szu.edu.cn
[2] Jarvis Lab, Tencent, Shenzhen, China
ericxsun@tencent.com

Abstract. By introducing the skip connection to bridge the semantic gap between encoder and decoder, U-shape architecture has been proven to be effective for recovering fine-grained details in dense prediction tasks. However, such a mechanism cannot be directly applied to reconstruction-based anomaly detection, since the skip connection might lead the model overfitting to an identity mapping between the input and output. In this paper, we propose a weight decay training strategy to progressively mute the skip connections of U-Net, which effectively adapts U-shape network to anomaly detection task. Thus, we are able to leverage the modeling capabilities of U-Net architecture, and meanwhile prevent the trained model from bypassing low-level features. Furthermore, we formulate an auxiliary task, namely histograms of oriented gradients (HOG) prediction, to encourage the framework to deeply exploit contextual information from fundus images. The HOG feature descriptors with three different resolutions are adopted as the auxiliary supervision signals. The multi-task framework is dedicated to enforce the model to aggregate shared significant commonalities and eventually improve the performance of anomaly detection. Experimental results on Indian Diabetic Retinopathy image Dataset (IDRiD) and Automatic Detection challenge on Age-related Macular degeneration dataset (ADAM) validate the superiority of our method for detecting abnormalities in retinal fundus images. The source code is available at https://github.com/WentianZhang-ML/WDMT-Net.

Keywords: Skip connection · Anomaly detection · Feature prediction · Fundus image

---

W. Zhang, X. Sun, and Y. Li—Equal Contribution.
This work is done when Wentian Zhang is an intern at Jarvis Lab, Tencent.

1   Introduction

With the rapid development of artificial intelligence techniques in the past decades, deep supervised learning has proven its potential for automatic ocular disease screening or diagnosis using retinal fundus images [10,18]. However, training a highly accurate supervised classifier usually requires a fairly large amount of labeled data, which is extremely expensive and difficult to acquire due to the privacy issue of medical data. Even if the labeled data is available, the model often easily suffers from the class imbalance problem, as the data from healthy subjects is prevalent therefore easier to collect in a large quantity. For those reasons, anomaly detection, aiming to identify abnormalities with only normal images at the training stage, has drawn increasing attentions from the community [21,23,24]. Current anomaly detection methods can mainly be divided into two categories: the reconstruction-based and non-reconstruction-based methods. The former methods are established upon the assumption: the well-trained model can excellently reconstruct normal images while yield large reconstruction error for abnormal images. The latter ones rely on other techniques, such as transfer learning [12] and discriminative learning [5]. Compared to the non-reconstruction-based methods, the reconstruction-based ones are verified to achieve more robust anomaly detection performance. Hence, in this paper, we focus on the reconstruction-based anomaly detection for retinal fundus images.

By introducing skip connection in the encoder-decoder architecture, U-Net and its variants have achieved wide successes in biomedical image segmentation and image-to-image translation [7–9,14]. However, it is surprising to find that most existing reconstruction-based anomaly detection methods are built upon auto-encoder architecture without skip connections. Therefore, it remains an interesting question: *whether the skip connection can be helpful for improving the anomaly detection performance?* From another aspect, a recent research has revealed the effectiveness of histograms of oriented gradients (HOG) prediction for self-supervised representation learning [19]. For normal fundus images, large HOG values can be obtained from the areas around the blood vessels and optic disc, which contain the anatomical structure of the retina. Therefore, we raise a second question: *whether the HOG prediction task can serve the image reconstruction (main task) as auxiliary and assist the anomaly detection?*

To address the aforementioned two questions, we propose to train a multi-task encoder-decoder network with weight decay skip connection (WDMT-Net) for anomaly detection with retinal fundus images. The main contributions of this work can be summarized as follows. First, we explore the applicability of skip connection to reconstruction-based anomaly detection. Specifically, a weight decay skip connection training strategy is presented to mitigate the identity mapping problem of the U-Net architecture and meanwhile leverage its advantage on feature representation learning. Second, we integrate an auxiliary task, *i.e.*, HOG prediction, to the anomaly detection framework, which can fully exploit the significant commonalities of normal fundus images. Last but not least, our WDMT-Net outperforms the state-of-the-art methods on Indian Diabetic Retinopathy Image Dataset (IDRiD) [13], which demonstrates its effectiveness for detecting abnormal regions in retinal fundus images.

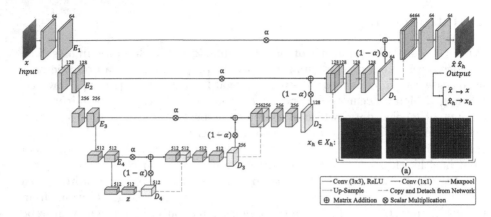

Fig. 1. The overall architecture of our proposed WDMT-Net for anomaly detection in retinal fundus images. (a) Examples of HOG features with different cell sizes: images from left to right are the HOG features obtained by cell sizes of 4×4, 8×8, and 16×16 pixels, respectively.

2   Method

Figure 1 shows the overall architecture of our proposed WDMT-Net. The main components consist of a weight decay skip connection training strategy to leverage the modeling capabilities of U-Net architecture and a dual-output decoder to exploit shared commonalities between two related tasks (*i.e.*, image reconstruction and HOG prediction).

2.1   Weight Decay Skip Connection Training

By introducing skip connections to bridge the semantic gap between encoder and decoder, U-Net architecture has been proven to be effective in recovering fine-grained details of the target subjects. However, such a mechanism is rarely utilized in current reconstruction-based anomaly detection methods. The underlying reason may be that the skip connections at early stages tend to mislead the model to bypass the lower levels of features and essentially learn an identity mapping function. Such a dilemma significantly degrades the performance of U-Net for anomaly detection.

To mitigate this problem, we develop a simple-yet-effective weight decay training strategy to gradually mute the skip connections. Different from the original U-Net architecture, where the different levels of features in the encoder are directly concatenated to the corresponding decoded features, in WDMT-Net, we first formulate the weighted feature map at each spatial resolution as follows:

$$M_i = (\alpha \otimes E_i) \oplus ((1 - \alpha) \otimes D_i), \tag{1}$$

where $\alpha \in [0, 1]$ is a weight factor; E_i and D_i represent the feature maps from the ith level of the encoder and decoder, respectively; $\oplus$ denotes feature addition;

and $\otimes$ denotes scalar multiplication. Then, M_i is concatenated to a detached counterpart of D_i, which yields

$$D'_i = Concat(M_i, \bar{D}_i), \tag{2}$$

where $Concat(\cdot)$ denotes the concatenation operation and $\bar{\cdot}$ denotes the detach operation. Note that we detach D_i from the network learning to restrict the gradients to propagate backward through the weighted feature path illustrated in Eq. (1).

During the training phase, the weight factor α in Eq. (1) is first initialized to 1, and then gradually decayed to 0. As shown in Fig. 1, when $\alpha = 1$, E_i is directly skip connected to $\bar{D}_i$ and our WDMT-Net is of the same structure to U-Net. However, since $\bar{D}_1$ is detached from the network learning flow, the computed gradients are not able to propagate from the upper layers to the lower layers in the decoder, which means only the network parameters at the first learning stage can be updated. As α decreases, the focus of optimization gradually varies from the horizontal decoder-encoder skip connection direction to the up-down direction. Therefore, the lower-level features learned at the early stage gradually aggregate to the higher-level features. Finally, when $\alpha = 0$, M_i is in fact a copy of D_i and our WDMT-Net degrades to an encoder-decoder network without skip connection. In the final network, D'_i contains two copies of D_i and this redundancy can be removed by re-organizing the weights.

2.2 HOG Prediction as an Auxiliary Task

As revealed by a recent research, HOG prediction could be an exceedingly effective way for self-supervised representation learning [19]. Meanwhile, large HOG values can be yielded around the blood vessels and optic disc, which provide the useful anatomical structure information for the representation learning of normal retinal fundus images. Based on such observation, we propose to formulate a multi-task network [15] to simultaneously regress the pixel intensity and the HOG feature of the input images, which enforces the model to learn the shared commonalities beneficial for anomaly detection. Let x denote an input image, the proposed WDMT-Net can then be formulated as:

$$\langle \hat{x}, \hat{x}_h \rangle = Dec(Enc(x)), \tag{3}$$

where the $Enc(\cdot)$ and $Dec(\cdot)$ are the encoder and decoder of the WDMT-Net, respectively; $\hat{x}$ is the reconstruction of the input image; and $\hat{x}_h$ is the predicted HOG feature map. The overall learning objective is defined as:

$$\mathcal{L} = \|\hat{x} - x\|_2^2 + \|\hat{x}_h - x_h\|_2^2, \tag{4}$$

where the training sample x is merely drawn from the normal images; the ground-truth of the corresponding HOG feature map $x_h \in X_h$ is randomly drawn from a pool X_h that contains HOG features computed with different cell resolutions; and $\|\cdot\|_2$ denotes the L_2-norm.

In essence, HOG is a feature descriptor, which describes the distribution of gradient orientations or edge directions over the local cells [3], and with different local cell size one can obtain HOG features in different scales. Figure 1 (a) shows the computed HOG features with three different spatial cell sizes, which are used in the feature prediction label pool during the training phase. There are two reasons for this setting: First, the use of multi-scale HOG features reflects the fact that the internal structure of fundus images is of varying sizes. Second, the random selection of HOG target label works as an effective data augmentation strategy that increases the diversity of input-output data pairs being fed to the model.

2.3 Anomaly Detection

Similar to existing reconstruction-based anomaly detection methods, our WDMT-Net is built based on the assumption that the abnormal images cannot be well reconstructed by a model trained merely with the normal images. Taking a gray image x_t as an input at the test stage, the proposed method can reconstruct a new image $\hat{x}_t$. We compute the the anomaly score map for the pixel-level anomaly detection in the image space as

$$\mathcal{A}_M = |\hat{x}_t - x_t| . \tag{5}$$

The larger the reconstruction error is, the higher possibility of the corresponding region to be abnormal.

3 Experiments

3.1 Dataset and Implementation Details

In this section, we adopt two publicly available datasets, namely Indian Diabetic Retinopathy Image Dataset (IDRiD) [13] and Automatic Detection challenge on Age-related Macular degeneration dataset (ADAM) [4], for performance evaluation. Following [23], we only choose the normal class from the original training set to train the proposed model and use the lesion detection dataset as the test set. In IDRiD dataset, there are 134 normal images for training, and 81 abnormal images for testing. The pixel-level annotation of abnormal images contains four different lesions, including haemorrhages, microaneurysms, hard and soft exudates. For ADAM dataset, it contains 282 normal images and 118 abnormal images with five different lesions and corresponding pixel-level annotations, including drusen, exudate, hemorrhage, scars and other lesions. Since the original images of both dataset are very large (*i.e.*, 4,288×2,848 pixels and 2124×2056 pixels), we resize each image to 768×768 pixels and then crop them into 3×3 non-overlapping patches. After that, we transform each patch to gray-scale image for training and test. To supervise the HOG prediction task, we extract the HOG features with three different cell sizes, as mentioned in Sect. 2.2.

Table 1. Ablation study of our WDMT-Net. SC, WD, and HOG represent the use of skip connection, weight decay training strategy and HOG prediction, respectively.

Model	Combination			IDRiD [13]			ADAM [4]		
	SC	WD	HOG	AUC	ACC	F1-score	AUC	ACC	F1-score
Auto-Encoder [2]				0.686	0.627	0.537	0.659	0.637	0.469
U-Net [14]	✓			0.553	0.564	0.532	0.610	0.619	**0.530**
WDMT-Net w/o HOG	✓	✓		0.725	0.667	0.680	0.670	0.654	0.484
Auto-Encoder			✓	0.715	0.655	0.664	0.662	0.643	0.470
U-Net	✓		✓	0.640	0.597	0.539	0.656	0.641	0.451
WDMT-Net (*Ours*)	✓	✓	✓	**0.748**	**0.694**	**0.711**	**0.687**	**0.660**	0.474

In our implementation, the proposed method is trained by the Adam optimizer with a learning rate of 1×10^{-4} and a weight decay of 5×10^{-5}. All code is implemented with PyTorch on a single NVIDIA RTX 3090 GPU with 24GB of memory and the batch size is set as 32. For simplicity, the weight factor α is initialized to 1 and decayed by Δ per epoch, where Δ is set as 0.05 by default. The decaying procedure stops when α reaches 0. Following previous work [23], the anomaly detection results are evaluated quantitatively by the area under the curve (AUC), balanced accuracy (ACC), and F1-score.

3.2   Ablation Study

We perform an ablation study to investigate the contribution made by different components of the proposed WDMT-Net to anomaly detection in retinal fundus images. To make a fair comparison, the network architectures of Auto-Encoder [2] and U-Net [14] are set the same as our WDMT-Net, except for the setting of skip connection. It is worthwhile to mention that models under different settings are trained with the same protocol stated in Sect. 3.1.

Weight Decay Skip Connection Training. As shown in Table 1, the performance of U-Net is worse than Auto-Encoder, no matter with or without the auxiliary HOG prediction task. This indicates that directly applying skip connection to encoder-decoder network deteriorates the performance of anomaly detection. Nevertheless, by using the proposed weight decay skip connection training strategy, WDMT-Net consistently achieves better results with and without HOG prediction, which indicates the effectiveness of the proposed training strategy.

Moreover, in order to illustrate the role of skip connection in anomaly detection network, we visualize the image reconstruction loss versus training epoch on IDRiD dataset in Fig. 2. From the reconstruction loss curves, we observe that U-Net consistently achieves the lowest loss, which means skip connections do enable U-Net to reconstruct the training images more accurately. However, the same rule does not hold for anomaly detection at the test stage. Thus, we can conclude that the naive utilization of skip connections do raise the issue of identity mapping. In contrast, our WDMT-Net can mitigate this problem by using the weight decay training strategy.

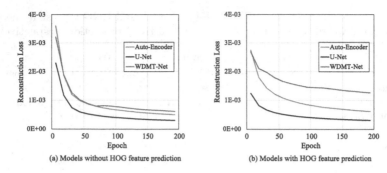

(a) Models without HOG feature prediction   (b) Models with HOG feature prediction

Fig. 2. The image reconstruction loss vs. training epochs on IDRiD dataset.

Table 2. Impact of the decay rate Δ of the skip connection in our WDMT-Net.

Decay setting	IDRiD [13]			ADAM [4]		
	AUC	ACC	F1-score	AUC	ACC	F1-score
$\Delta = 0.005$	0.729	0.661	0.687	0.676	0.663	0.451
$\Delta = 0.01$	0.738	0.685	0.692	0.678	0.662	**0.482**
$\Delta = 0.025$	0.731	0.674	0.680	0.673	**0.663**	0.465
$\Delta = 0.05$	**0.748**	**0.694**	**0.711**	**0.687**	0.660	0.474
$\Delta = 0.1$	0.724	0.669	0.709	0.674	0.660	0.471

The setting of hyper-parameters is also an important factor, which may affect the model performance. To this end, we conduct experiments to evaluate the model performance with different decay rate of the skip connections. As shown in Table 2, we set Δ as 0.005, 0.01, 0.025, 0.05 and 0.1 for comparison. It can be observed that our WDMT-Net model with $\Delta = 0.05$ achieves the best results.

Multi-task Learning. To extensively evaluate the contribution of HOG prediction for anomaly detection, we also apply the same multi-task learning scheme for Auto-Encoder and U-Net. Due to the extra information provided by the HOG prediction task, the anomaly detection performances of all multi-task models are consistently improved as shown in Table 1.

The proposed method learns the multi-resolution HOG features from a label pool that contains HOG features obtained by cell sizes of 4×4, 8×8, and 16×16 pixels, respectively. To verify the effectiveness of such a setting, we perform the following experiments based on WDMT-Net. First, we formulate three models where each of them only uses a single-scale of HOG features as the learning target. As shown in Table 3, among these three models, the one learned with HOG of the 16×16 cell size obtains the best results, However, it still underperforms our proposed method, which indicates the advantage of using multi-scale targets in WDMT-Net. Moreover, we also compare the performance of WDMT-Net with two alternative models in which the multi-scale HOG features are utilized in different ways (*i.e.*, to predict HOG at different resolutions simultaneously, and to

Table 3. Impact of auxiliary HOG prediction task setting of the proposed WDMT-Net.

Setting of the prediction target	IDRiD [13]			ADAM [4]		
	AUC	ACC	F1-score	AUC	ACC	F1-score
HOG features with 4×4 cells	0.736	0.668	0.704	0.677	0.653	0.468
HOG features with 8×8 cells	0.736	0.674	0.696	0.682	0.649	0.460
HOG features with 16×16 cells	0.738	0.671	0.685	0.682	0.660	**0.493**
Three HOG features as three outputs	0.731	0.678	**0.720**	0.660	0.647	0.439
The average of three HOG features	0.733	0.669	0.700	0.648	0.631	0.395
Three HOG features as a label pool	**0.748**	**0.694**	0.711	**0.687**	**0.660**	0.474

Table 4. Quantitative comparison of the proposed WDMT-Net with the state-of-the-art methods.

Method	IDRiD [13]			ADAM [4]		
	AUC	ACC	F1-score	AUC	ACC	F1-score
Auto-Encoder [2]	0.686	0.627	0.537	0.659	0.637	0.469
MemAE [6]	0.647	0.592	0.567	0.667	0.647	0.439
BiO-Net [20]	0.606	0.563	0.519	0.642	0.612	0.481
Attn U-Net [11]	0.581	0.555	0.558	0.645	0.617	0.408
AnoGAN [17]	0.630	0.618	0.579	0.677	**0.661**	0.455
f-AnoGAN [16]	0.698	0.686	0.637	0.662	0.638	0.455
GANomaly [1]	0.652	0.633	0.658	0.673	0.618	**0.539**
Sparse-GAN [22]	0.663	0.638	0.651	0.667	0.627	0.500
ProxyAno [23]	0.701	0.682	0.649	0.675	0.648	0.451
WDMT-Net (*Ours*)	**0.748**	**0.694**	**0.711**	**0.687**	0.660	0.474

predict the average of them). As shown in Table 3, our method outperforms these two alternative settings too in terms of AUC and ACC, which further indicates the effectiveness of our random sampling method.

3.3 Comparison to State-of-the-Art Methods

To further validate the superiority of our method, we compare our method with several state-of-the-art anomaly detection methods, including Auto-Encoder [2], MemAE [6], Attn U-Net [11], BiO-Net [20], AnoGAN [17], f-AnoGAN [16], GANomaly [1], Sparse-GAN [22], and ProxyAno [23]. It can be seen that, the proposed WDMT-Net outperforms the state-of-the-art methods. We further provide some results in Fig. 3. It can be seen that, the normal patches can be reconstructed with a small error, while the abnormal patches (*i.e.*, patches with lesion) are reconstructed with a large error. The prediction $\mathcal{A}_M$ matches the pixel-level lesion ground truth pretty well. These results further validate the superiority of our method.

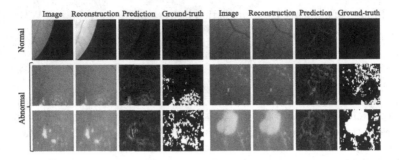

Fig. 3. The qualitative results of WDMT-Net on IDRiD retinal fundus images.

4 Conclusion

In the work, we explored the applicability of skip connection and multi-task learning to anomaly detection tasks. Concretely, a weight decay training strategy was proposed to effectively adapt U-shape network for the anomaly detection task, which prevented the model from overfitting to the identity mapping introduced by skip connections. Furthermore, an auxiliary task, *i.e.,* HOG prediction, was integrated to our framework to explore the effectiveness of multi-task learning. Such a multi-task framework was dedicated to enforce the model to aggregate shared commonalities between these two tasks and finally improve the performance of anomaly detection. Extensive experiments on publicly available IDRiD and ADAM fundus image datasets demonstrated the superiority of our framework to the state-of-the-art anomaly detection methods. In the future, we plan to expand the applicability of our WDMT-Net to more medical imaging modalities.

Acknowledgements. This work was supported in part by the National Natural Science Foundation of China (Grant 62076163 and Grant 91959108), the Shenzhen Fundamental Research Fund (Grant JCYJ20190808163401646), Key-Area Research and Development Program of Guangdong Province, China (No. 2018B010111001), National Key R&D Program of China (2018YFC2000702) and the Scientific and Technical Innovation 2030-"New Generation Artificial Intelligence" Project (No. 2020AAA0104100).

References

1. Akcay, S., Atapour-Abarghouei, A., Breckon, T.P.: GANomaly: semi-supervised anomaly detection via adversarial training. In: Jawahar, C.V., Li, H., Mori, G., Schindler, K. (eds.) ACCV 2018. LNCS, vol. 11363, pp. 622–637. Springer, Cham (2019). https://doi.org/10.1007/978-3-030-20893-6_39
2. Baur, C., Wiestler, B., Albarqouni, S., Navab, N.: Deep autoencoding models for unsupervised anomaly segmentation in brain MR images. In: Crimi, A., Bakas, S., Kuijf, H., Keyvan, F., Reyes, M., van Walsum, T. (eds.) BrainLes 2018. LNCS, vol. 11383, pp. 161–169. Springer, Cham (2019). https://doi.org/10.1007/978-3-030-11723-8_16

3. Dalal, N., Triggs, B.: Histograms of oriented gradients for human detection. In: IEEE Conference on Computer Vision and Pattern Recognition, vol. 1, pp. 886–893. IEEE (2005)

4. Fang, H., et al.: ADAM challenge: detecting age-related macular degeneration from fundus images. IEEE Trans. Med. Imaging (2022)

5. Golan, I., El-Yaniv, R.: Deep anomaly detection using geometric transformations. Adv. Neural Inf. Process. Syst. **31** (2018)

6. Gong, D., et al.: Memorizing normality to detect anomaly: memory-augmented deep autoencoder for unsupervised anomaly detection. In: Proceedings of the IEEE/CVF International Conference on Computer Vision, pp. 1705–1714 (2019)

7. Gu, Z., et al.: CE-Net: Context encoder network for 2D medical image segmentation. IEEE Trans. Med. Imaging **38**(10), 2281–2292 (2019)

8. Isola, P., Zhu, J.Y., Zhou, T., Efros, A.A.: Image-to-image translation with conditional adversarial networks. In: Proceedings of the IEEE Conference on Computer Vision and Pattern Recognition, pp. 1125–1134 (2017)

9. Ji, W., et al.: Learning calibrated medical image segmentation via multi-rater agreement modeling. In: Proceedings of the IEEE/CVF Conference on Computer Vision and Pattern Recognition, pp. 12341–12351 (2021)

10. Li, T., Bo, W., Hu, C., Kang, H., Liu, H., Wang, K., Fu, H.: Applications of deep learning in fundus images: A review. Med. Image Anal. **69**, 101971 (2021)

11. Oktay, O., et al.: Attention U-Net: Learning where to look for the pancreas. arXiv preprint arXiv:1804.03999 (2018)

12. Ouardini, K., et al.: Towards practical unsupervised anomaly detection on retinal images. In: Wang, Q., et al. (eds.) DART/MIL3ID -2019. LNCS, vol. 11795, pp. 225–234. Springer, Cham (2019). https://doi.org/10.1007/978-3-030-33391-1_26

13. Porwal, P., et al.: IDRiD: Diabetic retinopathy-segmentation and grading challenge. Med. Image Anal. **59**, 101561 (2020)

14. Ronneberger, O., Fischer, P., Brox, T.: U-Net: convolutional networks for biomedical image segmentation. In: Navab, N., Hornegger, J., Wells, W.M., Frangi, A.F. (eds.) MICCAI 2015. LNCS, vol. 9351, pp. 234–241. Springer, Cham (2015). https://doi.org/10.1007/978-3-319-24574-4_28

15. Ruder, S.: An overview of multi-task learning in deep neural networks. arXiv preprint arXiv:1706.05098 (2017)

16. Schlegl, T., Seeböck, P., Waldstein, S.M., Langs, G., Schmidt-Erfurth, U.: f-AnoGAN: fast unsupervised anomaly detection with generative adversarial networks. Med. Image Anal. **54**, 30–44 (2019)

17. Schlegl, T., Seeböck, P., Waldstein, S.M., Schmidt-Erfurth, U., Langs, G.: Unsupervised anomaly detection with generative adversarial networks to guide marker discovery. In: Niethammer, M., et al. (eds.) IPMI 2017. LNCS, vol. 10265, pp. 146–157. Springer, Cham (2017). https://doi.org/10.1007/978-3-319-59050-9_12

18. Son, J., Shin, J.Y., Kim, H.D., Jung, K.H., Park, K.H., Park, S.J.: Development and validation of deep learning models for screening multiple abnormal findings in retinal fundus images. Ophthalmology **127**(1), 85–94 (2020)

19. Wei, C., Fan, H., Xie, S., Wu, C.Y., Yuille, A., Feichtenhofer, C.: Masked feature prediction for self-supervised visual pre-training. arXiv preprint arXiv:2112.09133 (2021)

20. Xiang, T., Zhang, C., Liu, D., Song, Y., Huang, H., Cai, W.: BiO-Net: learning recurrent bi-directional connections for encoder-decoder architecture. In: Martel, A.L., et al. (eds.) MICCAI 2020. LNCS, vol. 12261, pp. 74–84. Springer, Cham (2020). https://doi.org/10.1007/978-3-030-59710-8_8

21. Zhao, H., Li, Y., He, N., Ma, K., Fang, L., Li, H., Zheng, Y.: Anomaly detection for medical images using self-supervised and translation-consistent features. IEEE Trans. Med. Imag. **40**(12), 3641–3651 (2021)
22. Zhou, K., et al.: Sparse-GAN: sparsity-constrained generative adversarial network for anomaly detection in retinal OCT image. In: IEEE 17th International Symposium on Biomedical Imaging, pp. 1227–1231. IEEE (2020)
23. Zhou, K., et al.: Proxy-bridged image reconstruction network for anomaly detection in medical images. IEEE Trans. Med. Imag. (2021)
24. Zimmerer, D., Isensee, F., Petersen, J., Kohl, S., Maier-Hein, K.: Unsupervised anomaly localization using variational auto-encoders. In: Shen, D., et al. (eds.) MICCAI 2019. LNCS, vol. 11767, pp. 289–297. Springer, Cham (2019). https://doi.org/10.1007/978-3-030-32251-9_32

Multiscale Unsupervised Retinal Edema Area Segmentation in OCT Images

Wenguang Yuan[1], Donghuan Lu[2(✉)], Dong Wei[2], Munan Ning[2], and Yefeng Zheng[2]

[1] Computer Science and Technology, South China University of Technology, Guangzhou, China
[2] Jarvis Lab, Tencent Healthcare Co., Shenzhen, China
caleblu@tencent.com, ludonghuan9@gmail.com

Abstract. Retinal edema area, which can be observed in the non-invasive optical coherence tomography image, is essential for the diagnosis and treatment of many retinal diseases. Due to the demand of professional knowledge for its annotation, acquiring sufficient labeled data for the usual data-driven learning-based approaches is time-consuming and laborious. To alleviate the intensive workload for manual labeling, unsupervised learning technique has been widely explored and adopted in different applications. However, the corresponding research in medical image segmentation is still limited and the performance is unsatisfactory. In this paper, we propose a novel unsupervised segmentation framework, which consists of two stages: the image-level clustering to group images into different categories and the pixel-level segmentation which leverages the guidance of the clustering network. Based on the observation that smaller lesions are more obvious on large scale images with detail texture information and larger lesions are easier to capture on small scale images for the large field-of-view, we introduce multiscale information into both stages through a scale-invariant regularization and a multiscale Class Activation Map (CAM) fusing strategy, respectively. Experiments on the public retinal dataset show that the proposed framework achieves a 76.28% Dice score without any supervision, which outperforms state-of-the-art unsupervised approaches by a large margin (more than 20% improvement in Dice score).

Keywords: Unsupervised segmentation · Optical coherence tomography · Retinal edema area segmentation · Multiscale

1 Introduction

The segmentation of Retinal Edema Area (REA) in non-invasive Optical Coherence Tomography (OCT) images plays an important role regarding the diagnosis and treatment of many retinal diseases, such as diabetic macular edema

Supplementary Information The online version contains supplementary material available at https://doi.org/10.1007/978-3-031-16434-7_64.

and age-related macular degeneration [6]. Benefiting from the recent development of deep learning, several automatic segmentation methods [3,7,14–16] for the retinal OCT images have been proposed to alleviate the intensive annotation workload of ophthalmologists. However, the requirement of large amount of accurately labeled data limits their application due to the expertise-demanding and time-consuming process to acquire pixel-wise annotation.

To get rid of the dependency on manual annotation, several efforts have been made on unsupervised image segmentation [4,10,11]. Xia et al. [19] concatenated two fully Convolutional Neural Networks (CNN) into an autoencoder and jointly minimized the normalized cut and reconstruction errors. Kanezaki [12] presented a self-training process using the backpropagation of the softmax loss and a superpixel refinement process. Chen et al. [2] parameterized the framework of active contour without edges through a recurrent CNN. However, these methods relied upon clear boundary of the object, leading to inferior performance regarding the segmentation of regions with obscure boundary, e.g., REA. Another stream of unsupervised segmentation approaches focuses on pixel-level clustering based on the small region cropped around each pixel [17]. Chen et al. [1] performed left ventricle segmentation via adaptive K-means clustering and knowledge-based morphological operations. Ji et al. [9] maximized the mutual information between the category assignments of input images and their augmentations. However, without global information, these pixel-level clustering methods could easily be distracted by intensity difference rather than meaningful structural variation, i.e., distinguishing retinal and background pixels rather than segmenting REA from retinal as shown in the third column of Fig. 2.

To address the above issues, we present a novel Multiscale Unsupervised Image Segmentation (MUIS) framework for the REA segmentation task. The framework consists of two stages: image-level clustering to group the images into two categories to provide guidance for the downstream segmentation task, and pixel-level segmentation to obtain pixel-wise labels for each image. Based on the observation that smaller lesions are more obvious on large scales images with sufficient texture information and larger lesions are easier to capture on small scale images for the large filed-of-view, we propose to introduce multiscale information in both stages for superior and robust performance. Specifically, for clustering, a simple yet effective scale-invariant regularization is introduced to improve the network's discriminative ability for images with only local difference instead of global diversity. Then, based on the clustering network, the Class Activation Maps (CAMs) at different scales can be obtained and fused to generate the pseudo mask for the supervision of the segmentation network. Extensive experiments are conducted to demonstrate the superiority of the proposed framework and the effectiveness of the multiscale information regarding the unsupervised segmentation task.

2   Methods

As displayed in Fig. 1, the overall architecture of the proposed MUIS framework consists of four sub-networks: the discriminator D, the critic C, the encoder Q

and the decoder S. Two steps, i.e., image-level clustering about the existing of REA and pixel-wise segmentation of REA, are performed for the optimization of the network. In the first step, we adopt the state-of-the-art Deep Clustering using Category-Style Representation (DCCS) approach [20] as backbone method to train the clustering network, including discriminator D, critic C and encoder Q. Despite DCCS's superior performance for natural images, it focus too much on global patterns while the difference of normal and abnormal OCT scans are more local. By additionally introducing the scale-invariant regularization, the network can gain better discriminative ability for local difference. Then, with the guidance of the pseudo masks obtained by fusing the CAMs at different scales, the encoder Q and the decoder S can be optimized to deliver pixel-wise segmentation for REA. In the following sections, we first briefly introduce the DCCS approach, and then present our image-level clustering and pixel-wise segmentation methods, respectively.

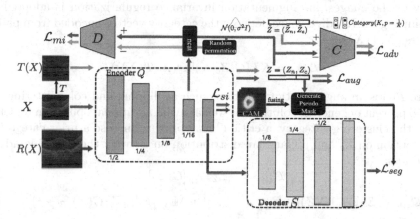

Fig. 1. The framework of the proposed method. The discriminator D and critic C are only applied to train the clustering network, while encoder Q and decoder S are adopt to deliver the segmentation results.

2.1 Primary DCCS

The key idea of Deep Clustering using Category-Style Representation [20] is to transform the input image into a category-style latent representation and disentangle the category information from image style for indicating the cluster assignment directly. To be more precise, given an input image X, DCCS aims to learn the disentangled latent representation $Z = (Z_c, Z_s)$, in which the category vector Z_c represents the probabilities of assigning X to each class and the style vector Z_s represents the intra-class style information. Three regularization terms, including the mutual information regularization, the disentanglement regularization and the prior distribution regularization, are introduced to train an appropriate encoder Q for such transformation.

To prevent the deep neural network from mapping the input to arbitrary representation, a mutual information regularization, which maximizes the mutual information between the input image X and its latent representation Z, is imposed via a discriminator D to retain the essential discriminative information. The loss of the mutual information regularization is defined as:

$$\mathcal{L}_{mi} = -(\mathbb{E}_{(X,Z)\sim Q(Z|X)P_X(X)}[\log S(D(X,Z))] \\ +\mathbb{E}_{(X,Z)\sim Q_Z(Z)P_X(X)}[\log(1 - S(D(X,Z)))]) \tag{1}$$

where P_X is the prior distribution of the images, $Q(Z|X)$ represents the encoding distribution of Z given X and $Q_Z = \mathbb{E}_{P_X}[Q(Z|X)]$ is the aggregated posterior distribution.

A disentanglement regularization is introduced to separate Z_c from Z_s to avoid the negative effect of intra-class style variation on the cluster assignment. Based on the assumption that certain augmentation should not change the category of the images, an augmentation invariance regularization is adopted by minimizing the KL-divergence between the category vectors encoded from paired images $(X, T(X))$:

$$\mathcal{L}_{Aug} = KL(Q(Z_c|X)||Q(Z_c|T(X))) \tag{2}$$

where $T(\cdot)$ is an augmentation function, such as flipping and color jittering.

To prevent degenerate solutions as well as avoid additional operation to determine the clustering category, a critic C is applied to impose a prior categorical distribution on Z_c and a Gaussian distribution on Z_s with the following adversarial loss:

$$\mathcal{L}_{Adv}^Q = -\mathbb{E}_{Z\sim Q_Z}[C(Z)], \tag{3}$$

$$\mathcal{L}_{Adv}^C = \mathbb{E}_{Z\sim Q_Z}[C(Z)] - \mathbb{E}_{\tilde{Z}\sim P_Z}[C(\tilde{Z})] + \lambda\mathbb{E}_{\hat{Z}\sim P_{\hat{Z}}}[(\|\nabla_{\hat{Z}}C(\hat{Z})\|_2 - 1)^2] \tag{4}$$

where $\widehat{Z}$ is the latent representation sampled from the prior distribution, and λ is the hyperparameter for gradient penalty, typically set to 10. Q_Z and P_Z represent the aggregated posterior distribution and the prior distribution, respectively. For more details about DCCS, please refer to the original study [20].

2.2   Unsupervised Image Clustering

DCCS achieves state-of-the-art performance for various natural image clustering tasks. However, the clustering of these images is based on global patterns, while the distinguishing of OCT scans in this study should focus more on local abnormal regions. To further improve the accuracy and robustness of the clustering network, we propose to utilize the multiscale information based on the assumption that lesions of different sizes could be better captured with different image scales, i.e., the small lesion are more obvious on large scale images for its detail texture information, while the large lesion are easier to capture with small scale images because the relatively large field-of-view enables a convolutional kernel cover most if not all lesion area. Specifically, we propose to introduce a scale-invariant regularization to ensure the consistency of the CAMs from the same image at different scales, which is defined as:

$$\mathcal{L}_{si} = \|F(X) - R^{-1}F(R(X))\|_1, \tag{5}$$

where $F(\cdot)$ denotes the bottleneck features of encoder Q before the final Global Average Pooling (GAP) layer, $R(\cdot)$ represents the rescale operation and $R^{-1}(\cdot)$ denotes its reverse operation to rescale the bottleneck features to the original size for the calculation of the scale-invariant loss. Note that unlike the disentanglement regularization, which is imposed on the final latent representation, the scale-invariant regularization is imposed on the bottleneck feature (feature used to obtain CAM) to ensure the CAMs can provide more accurate supervision for the downstream segmentation task. In summary, the overall objective function of the clustering network can be written as:

$$\min_{C} \beta_{adv}\mathcal{L}_{Adv}^{C},$$
$$\min_{Q,D} \mathcal{L}_{Adv}^{Q} + \beta_{mi}\mathcal{L}_{mi} + \beta_{Aug}\mathcal{L}_{Aug} + \beta_{si}\mathcal{L}_{si} \tag{6}$$

where β_{MI}, β_{Aug}, β_{Adv} and β_{si} are the weights used to balance each term. Note that similar to DCCS, the encoder Q and the discriminator D are jointly optimized, while the critic C is trained alternately.

2.3   Pseudo-Mask-Guided Pixel-Wise Segmentation

In the pixel-wise segmentation stage, once the clustering model has been trained, the bottleneck feature of the encoder Q can be used to generate the pseudo mask. To get more precise pseudo masks for the optimization of the segmentation decoder S, we further utilize the multiscale information to obtain an adapted CAM. If we use M to represent the CAM, the adapted CAM can be obtained by fusing the CAMs at different scales:

$$\overline{M} = \frac{1}{N} \sum_{i=1}^{n} R_i^{-1}M(R_i(X)), \ \overline{M} \in [0,1]. \tag{7}$$

where N represents the number of CMAs at different scales.

The adapted CAM $\overline{M}$ is further binarized via thresholding (setting as 0.5 empirically) and refined by an active contour model [13] to obtain the one-hot pseudo mask $\widehat{Y}$ for segmentation supervision. Then, we train the segmentation network with the supervision of pseudo mask $\widehat{Y}$ to distinguish the pixels of REA and the background through the pixel-wise cross entropy loss:

$$\min_{Q,S} \mathcal{L}_{seg} = -\widehat{Y}log(S(Q(X))). \tag{8}$$

Note that for inference, the segmentation network (encoder Q and decoder S) can directly deliver the segmentation result without other processing.

Table 1. Quantitative evaluation (mean ± standard deviation) of different segmentation methods. '†' denotes fully supervised learning with the ground truth masks (upper bound). Best unsupervised results are shown in bold.

Methods	Dice score↑	Precision↑	Recall↑	ASSD (mm)↓
nnU-Net [8]†	0.8868 ± 0.0194	0.9148 ± 0.0249	0.8720 ± 0.0329	2.6175 ± 0.7667
Kanezaki [12]	0.5038 ± 0.0001	0.4344 ± 0.0002	0.6516 ± 0.0001	10.6141 ± 0.0020
IIC [9]	0.5295 ± 0.0049	0.3915 ± 0.0058	$\mathbf{0.9290 \pm 0.0061}$	18.3256 ± 1.8729
MUIS (Proposed)	$\mathbf{0.7628 \pm 0.0153}$	$\mathbf{0.7585 \pm 0.0297}$	0.8020 ± 0.0187	$\mathbf{5.3127 \pm 0.3899}$

3 Experiments

3.1 Materials and Experimental Settings

The data used in this study is from the AI Challenger 2018[1] with a total of 85 OCT volumes of patients suffering from retinal edema lesion. There are 128 slices (B-scans) in each volume with the same size of 1024×512 pixels. Among them, a total of 5,498 slices contain REA while the rest 5,382 ones do not. To reduce the distraction of the unrelated area, the center 512×512 region of each slice is cropped and resized to 256×256.

The encoder Q consists of five residual blocks [5], a GAP layer and a fully connected layer, while both the discriminator and the critic are multi-layer perceptions. For the training of the clustering network, the batch size is 64, the size of the rescaled images is 96×96 and the weights β_{adv}, β_{mi}, β_{Aug} and β_{si} are set as 1, 0.5, 6 and 5, respectively. For more details regarding the clustering network and its optimization, please refer to [20]. The decoder S contains four residual blocks with skip connections to the corresponding blocks of the encoder, followed by a convolution layer with kernel size 1×1. For its optimization, slices at three different scales, 96×96, 128×128 and 192×192, are fed to the clustering network to generate the pseudo mask. The batch size for segmentation is 16, and the training process stops at 20 epochs. We use the Adam optimizer for training with a learning rate of 0.001 which decays by 5% after each epoch. The proposed framework is implemented on PyTorch1.4 with an NVIDIA Tesla V100 GPU. The pytorch implementation is publicly available at https://github.com/mangoyuan/MUIS.

The experiments are repeated three times for a more reliable evaluation. Three widely used metrics, including unsupervised clustering ACCuracy (ACC), Normalized Mutual Information (NMI), and Adjusted Rand Index (ARI) [18], are applied to evaluate the image-level clustering performance based on whether the clustering network can separate the images with REA from the normal images. Four metrics, including Dice score, Precision, Recall, and Average Symmetric Surface Distance (ASSD), are employed for the evaluation of the pixelwise segmentation. Note that two segmentation masks can be obtained corresponding to the two categories (normal and abnormal), but only the metrics

---

[1] https://github.com/AIChallenger/AI_Challenger_2018.

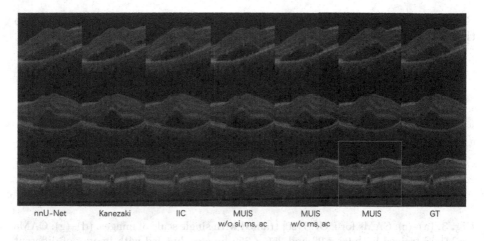

nnU-Net   Kenezaki   IIC   MUIS   MUIS   MUIS   GT
                                       w/o si, ms, ac   w/o ms, ac

Fig. 2. The visualization of segmentation results of different methods, where GT denotes the ground truth mask.

based on the mask which has the largest overlay with the ground truth REA annotation are presented here.

Table 2. Clustering performance (mean ± standard deviation) with different scales of images. Single number x in a cell represents using $x \times x$ image without scale-invariant regularization, while two numbers x/y in a cell denotes using both $x \times x$ and $y \times y$ images with scale-invariant regularization.

Scale	ACC↑	NMI↑	ARI↑
96	0.8183 ± 0.0135	0.3176 ± 0.0284	0.4058 ± 0.0341
192	0.7977 ± 0.0354	0.2775 ± 0.0733	0.3579 ± 0.0870
256	0.7899 ± 0.0008	0.2584 ± 0.0014	0.3360 ± 0.0017
96/192	$\mathbf{0.9284 \pm 0.0006}$	$\mathbf{0.6292 \pm 0.0022}$	$\mathbf{0.7341 \pm 0.0021}$
96/256	0.9276 ± 0.0020	0.6262 ± 0.0068	0.7314 ± 0.0070

3.2 Comparison Study

Due to limited efforts made on the unsupervised segmentation task and the difficulty of segmenting REA with obscure boundary, only a few methods can deliver meaningful results. Here, two state-of-the-art unsupervised segmentation methods, Kenezaki [12] and IIC [9], which have decent performance, are applied for comparison, along with the fully-supervised nnU-Net [8] as the upper bound. As shown in Table 1, the proposed method outperforms both unsupervised segmentation approaches by large margins on all metrics. As displayed in Fig. 2, neglecting the image-level information, Kenezaki and IIC are misled by the intensity variation, thus prone to segment the retinal and the background rather than the

REA, while the failure cases of the proposed MUIS approach are mostly due to the too small size of lesion.

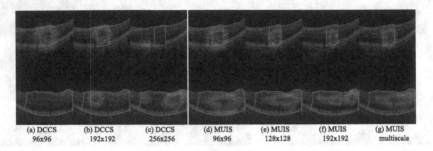

| (a) DCCS 96x96 | (b) DCCS 192x192 | (c) DCCS 256x256 | (d) MUIS 96x96 | (e) MUIS 128x128 | (f) MUIS 192x192 | (g) MUIS multiscale |

Fig. 3. (a)–(c): CAMs for DCCS [20] trained with single scale of images. (d)–(g): CAMs for MUIS trained with 96 × 96 and 256 × 256 images, but fed with images of different scales to obtain the bottleneck CAMs of the same size for visualization. "Multiscale" represents the fused CAM. The red curves denote the boundaries of the ground truth masks. (Color figure online)

3.3   Ablation Study

Ablation Study for Clustering. To demonstrate the effectiveness of the multiscale information, we first explore its impact on the image-level clustering. As shown in Table 2, the clustering accuracy with single scale input is close to each other (±0.03 in ACC) under different image resolutions, while the scale-invariant regularization can largely improve the performance (more than 0.11 in ACC). The visualization of CAMs from two example slices is displayed in Fig. 3, demonstrating our observation that lesions with different sizes could be better captured under different scales.

Ablation Study for Segmentation. The effectiveness of three components, i.e., the scale-invariant regularization (si), the multiscale CAM fusing (ms) and the active contour based refinement (ac), regarding the segmentation task is presented in Table 3 and Fig. 2. Note that MUIS without si, ms and ac is equivalent to using the CAM of DCCS [20] to train another segmentation network. As expected, introducing the multiscale information can significantly improve the segmentation performance.

Table 3. Quantitative evaluation (mean ± standard deviation) of different components in the proposed MUIS. *"si"*, *"ms"* and *"ac"* represent the scale-invariant regularization, the multiscale CAM fusing and active contour based refinement, respectively.

Methods	Dice score↑	Precision↑	Recall↑	ASSD (mm)↓
MUIS w/o si, ms, ac	0.533 ± 0.028	0.650 ± 0.033	0.613 ± 0.040	12.963 ± 0.795
MUIS w/o ms, ac	0.697 ± 0.019	0.716 ± 0.039	0.725 ± 0.025	7.195 ± 0.456
MUIS w/o ac	0.707 ± 0.022	0.736 ± 0.032	0.692 ± 0.037	6.774 ± 0.509
MUIS	$\mathbf{0.763 \pm 0.015}$	$\mathbf{0.759 \pm 0.030}$	$\mathbf{0.802 \pm 0.019}$	$\mathbf{5.313 \pm 0.390}$

4 Conclusion

In this paper, we proposed a novel framework regarding the challenging unsupervised segmentation of REA in OCT images. Through the two-stage framework, the distraction of intensity difference between retinal and the background pixels could be alleviated. Based on the observation that REAs with different sizes could be better captured under different image scales, multiscale information was introduced into both the clustering and segmentation stages to further improve the performance. Extensive experiments were conducted to verify the superiority of the proposed framework as well as the effectiveness of the proposed scale-invariant regularization and the multiscale CAM fusing strategy.

Acknowledgements. This work was funded by the Scientific and Technical Innovation 2030-'New Generation Artificial Intelligence' (No. 2020AAA0104100).

References

1. Chen, C.W., Luo, J., Parker, K.J.: Image segmentation via adaptive K-mean clustering and knowledge-based morphological operations with biomedical applications. IEEE Trans. Image Process. **7**(12), 1673–1683 (1998)
2. Chen, J., Frey, E.C.: Medical image segmentation via unsupervised convolutional neural network. In: Proceedings of the International Conference on Medical Imaging with Deep Learning (2020)
3. Girish, G., Thakur, B., Chowdhury, S.R., Kothari, A.R., Rajan, J.: Segmentation of intra-retinal cysts from optical coherence tomography images using a fully convolutional neural network model. IEEE J. Biomed. Health Inform. **23**(1), 296–304 (2018)
4. Gulrajani, I., Ahmed, F., Arjovsky, M., Dumoulin, V., Courville, A.: Improved training of Wasserstein GANs. In: Advances in Neural Information Processing Systems, pp. 5769–5779 (2017)
5. He, K., Zhang, X., Ren, S., Sun, J.: Deep residual learning for image recognition. In: Proceedings of the IEEE Conference on Computer Vision and Pattern Recognition, pp. 770–778 (2016)
6. Hee, M.R., et al.: Optical coherence tomography of the human retina. Arch. Ophthalmol. **113**(3), 325–332 (1995)

7. Hu, K., Shen, B., Zhang, Y., Cao, C., Xiao, F., Gao, X.: Automatic segmentation of retinal layer boundaries in OCT images using multiscale convolutional neural network and graph search. Neurocomputing **365**, 302–313 (2019)
8. Isensee, F., Jaeger, P.F., Kohl, S.A., Petersen, J., Maier-Hein, K.H.: nnU-Net: a self-configuring method for deep learning-based biomedical image segmentation. Nat. Methods **18**(2), 203–211 (2021)
9. Ji, X., Henriques, J.F., Vedaldi, A.: Invariant information clustering for unsupervised image classification and segmentation. In: Proceedings of the IEEE International Conference on Computer Vision, pp. 9865–9874 (2019)
10. Ji, Z., et al.: Beyond retinal layers: a large blob detection for subretinal fluid segmentation in SD-OCT images. In: Frangi, A.F., Schnabel, J.A., Davatzikos, C., Alberola-López, C., Fichtinger, G. (eds.) MICCAI 2018. LNCS, vol. 11071, pp. 372–380. Springer, Cham (2018). https://doi.org/10.1007/978-3-030-00934-2_42
11. Joyce, T., Chartsias, A., Tsaftaris, S.A.: Deep multi-class segmentation without ground-truth labels. In: Proceedings of the International Conference on Medical Imaging with Deep Learning (2018)
12. Kanezaki, A.: Unsupervised image segmentation by backpropagation. In: IEEE International Conference on Acoustics, Speech and Signal Processing, pp. 1543–1547 (2018)
13. Kass, M., Witkin, A., Terzopoulos, D.: Snakes: active contour models. Int. J. Comput. Vision **1**(4), 321–331 (1988)
14. Liu, W., Sun, Y., Ji, Q.: MDAN-UNet: multi-scale and dual attention enhanced nested U-Net architecture for segmentation of optical coherence tomography images. Algorithms **13**(3), 60 (2020)
15. Lu, D., et al.: Deep-learning based multiclass retinal fluid segmentation and detection in optical coherence tomography images using a fully convolutional neural network. Med. Image Anal. **54**, 100–110 (2019)
16. Montuoro, A., Waldstein, S.M., Gerendas, B.S., Schmidt-Erfurth, U., Bogunović, H.: Joint retinal layer and fluid segmentation in OCT scans of eyes with severe macular edema using unsupervised representation and auto-context. Biomed. Opt. Express **8**(3), 1874–1888 (2017)
17. Moriya, T., et al.: Unsupervised segmentation of 3D medical images based on clustering and deep representation learning. In: Medical Imaging 2018: Biomedical Applications in Molecular, Structural, and Functional Imaging, vol. 10578, p. 20. International Society for Optics and Photonics (2018)
18. Wu, J., et al.: Deep comprehensive correlation mining for image clustering. In: Proceedings of the IEEE International Conference on Computer Vision, pp. 8150–8159 (2019)
19. Xia, X., Kulis, B.: W-Net: a deep model for fully unsupervised image segmentation. arXiv preprint arXiv:1711.08506 (2017)
20. Zhao, J., Lu, D., Ma, K., Zhang, Yu., Zheng, Y.: Deep image clustering with category-style representation. In: Vedaldi, A., Bischof, H., Brox, T., Frahm, J.-M. (eds.) ECCV 2020. LNCS, vol. 12359, pp. 54–70. Springer, Cham (2020). https://doi.org/10.1007/978-3-030-58568-6_4

SeATrans: Learning Segmentation-Assisted Diagnosis Model via Transformer

Junde Wu[1], Huihui Fang[1], Fangxin Shang[1], Dalu Yang[1], Zhaowei Wang[1], Jing Gao[2], Yehui Yang[1], and Yanwu Xu[1(✉)]

[1] Intelligent Healthcare Unit, Baidu Inc., Shanghai, China
ywxu@ieee.org
[2] Purdue University, West Lafayette, USA

Abstract. Clinically, the accurate annotation of lesions/tissues can significantly facilitate the disease diagnosis. For example, the segmentation of optic disc/cup (OD/OC) on fundus image would facilitate the glaucoma diagnosis, the segmentation of skin lesions on dermoscopic images is helpful to the melanoma diagnosis, etc. With the advancement of deep learning techniques, a wide range of methods proved the lesions/tissues segmentation can also facilitate the automated disease diagnosis models. However, existing methods are limited in the sense that they can only capture static regional correlations in the images. Inspired by the global and dynamic nature of Vision Transformer, in this paper, we propose Segmentation-Assisted diagnosis Transformer (SeATrans) to transfer the segmentation knowledge to the disease diagnosis network. Specifically, we first propose an asymmetric multi-scale interaction strategy to correlate each single low-level diagnosis feature with multi-scale segmentation features. Then, an effective strategy called SeA-block is adopted to vitalize diagnosis feature via correlated segmentation features. To model the segmentation-diagnosis interaction, SeA-block first embeds the diagnosis feature based on the segmentation information via the encoder, and then transfers the embedding back to the diagnosis feature space by a decoder. Experimental results demonstrate that SeATrans surpasses a wide range of state-of-the-art (SOTA) segmentation-assisted diagnosis methods on several disease diagnosis tasks.

Keywords: Segmentation-assisted diagnosis · Transformer · Classification

1 Introduction

Clinically, the disease diagnosis is usually conducted based on critical biomarkers derived from an analysis of the images. For example, on fundus images, the vertical Cup-to-Disc Ratio (vCDR) parameter computed from the optic cup/disc

---

Supplementary Information The online version contains supplementary material available at https://doi.org/10.1007/978-3-031-16434-7_65.

L. Wang et al. (Eds.): MICCAI 2022, LNCS 13432, pp. 677–687, 2022.
https://doi.org/10.1007/978-3-031-16434-7_65

(OD/OC) masks is one of the most important clinical parameters for the glaucoma diagnosis [12]. In melanoma diagnosis, an unusual shape of the skin lesions is a major biomarker indicating melanoma [11]. In order to derive these important biomarkers, an essential step is to identify lesions or tissues in an image and segment these areas of interest from the rest of the image [9,17].

Motivated by this observation, methods have been proposed to utilize segmentation information to facilitate the automated disease diagnosis [4,10,18,26–28]. The common practices include region of interest (ROI) extraction [4,10], input concatenation, channel attention [18,28], and transfer learning [27]. These methods have two main limitations. First, the methods proposed for specific medical tasks are not general enough. They are often inapplicable or have unsatisfactory performance on other medical tasks. Second, most methods simply assume that the segmentation and diagnosis features are regional correlated, which is an invalid assumption in most cases. Traditional techniques they applied, like convolution layers and channel attentions are difficult to model this non-regional feature interaction, since these tools are largely local-focused. With the rise of vision transformer [7], such a research gap can be possibly addressed by its global and dynamic nature.

In this paper, we propose a novel transformer-based model to better capture the interaction of segmentation and diagnosis features. In order to address the scale-level discrepancy between segmentation and diagnosis features, we propose asymmetric multi-scale interaction to correlate multi-scale segmentation features with each single low-level diagnosis feature. A one-to-one coarse interaction and a one-against-rest fine-grain interaction are fused to produce the final feature. An effective approach, called SeA-block, is proposed to model the segmentation-diagnosis interaction, which is constructed by an encoder-decoder pair. The encoder first embeds the diagnosis feature through the calculated segmentation affinity map. Then a decoder maps the embeddings back to the diagnosis feature space through the calculated diagnosis affinity map. Through SeA-block, diagnosis features can be vitalized by the correlated segmentation information.

In brief, we have made three major contributions. First, we propose a general segmentation-assisted diagnosis model, named SeATrans, for integrating segmentation and diagnosis based on medical images. Thanks to the global and dynamic nature of transformer mechanism, SeATrans can achieve superior and robust performance comparing with state-of-the-art counterparts. Second, we propose asymmetric multi-scale interaction to correlate each low-level diagnosis feature with multi-scale segmentation features. In this way, diagnosis feature can be vitalized by both coarse and fine-grain segmentation information. Last but not the least, we propose a new strategy, i.e., SeA-block, for the segmentation-diagnosis interaction. A transformer-based encoder-decoder architecture is constructed to learn across the segmentation and diagnosis feature space. The experimental results show SeATrans outperforms previous best method by at least a 2% AUC over three different disease diagnosis tasks. Meanwhile, it shows competitive robustness to the domain shift of segmentation model.

2   Methodology

In this paper, we propose a general segmentation-assisted diagnosis framework. Given a raw image x and its lesions/tissues segmentation features f_m extracted from a segmentation network (joint-trained or pre-trained), our goal is to predict the disease y (0 for benign, 1 for malignant) of the image. Our basic idea is to integrate the segmentation information into diagnosis model on the feature level. The interaction module and diagnosis model are jointly optimized to predict the correct diagnosis. An illustration of the overflow is shown in Fig. 1 (a). Raw fundus image x is first sent into a UNet to obtain the deep segmentation embedding. The segmentation features in the UNet decoder are used to interact with the diagnosis features of a disease diagnosis network. In the diagnosis model, convolution layer and SeA-block based Interaction alternatively abstracts and vitalizes the features. The final disease probability is supervised by the binary disease label through binary cross-entropy (BCE) loss function.

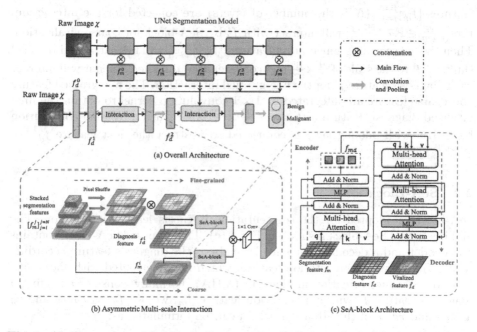

Fig. 1. An illustration of SeATrans framework, which starts from (a) an overview of the processing pipeline, and continues with zoomed-in diagrams of individual modules, including (b) the asymmetric multi-scale interaction and (c) the SeA-block.

2.1   Asymmetric Multi-scale Interaction

Note that the diagnosis network abstracts the low-level structure features to the deep semantic features, while the segmentation model abstracts multi-scale structural features. In order to align the diagnosis and segmentation features, we correlate multi-scale segmentation features to each single low-level diagnosis feature. As shown in Fig. 1 (b), stacked multi-scale segmentation features are collected for a single low-level diagnosis feature. The segmentation feature with the largest scale will first interact with the target diagnosis feature. As large-scale feature contains more specific but artifact structure information [25], this one-to-one interaction will produce a coarse vitalized diagnosis feature. Other segmentation features with smaller scales are fused together for the interaction with the diagnosis feature. Since these features contain more fine-grained and abstract features, this interaction will produce a fine-grained vitalized diagnosis feature. The coarse and fine-grained features are fused by 1×1 convolution layer to produce the final result.

In practice, the second and third layers of the diagnosis model will interact with the multi-scale features in UNet decoder. Consider the deep segmentation feature and diagnosis feature are f_m and f_d. To instill segmentation information into $f_d^i \in \mathbb{R}^{\frac{H}{r} \times \frac{W}{r} \times C}$ (i is the index of layer, H, W, r, C are height, width, down-sample rate and channel number respectively), stacked multi-scale segmentation features $[f_m^j]_{j=i}^{j=N}$ (N is the number of layers) are collected for the interaction. First, $f_m^i \in \mathbb{R}^{\frac{H}{r} \times \frac{W}{r} \times C}$ will interact with f_d^i by SeA-block for coarse vitalization. Then the subsequent segmentation features $[f_m^j]_{j=i+1}^{j=N}$ will be rearranged by pixel shuffle [23] to the scale of $\frac{H}{r} \times \frac{W}{r}$ and concatenated together. Then it will interact with diagnosis feature f_d^i for the fine-grained interaction. The fine-grained feature and coarse feature are integrated by 1×1 convolution kernel to obtain the final vitalized diagnosis feature with shape $\frac{H}{r} \times \frac{W}{r} \times C$. Then a residual convolution block [16] with pooling layer is connected to abstract the next feature $f_d^{i+1} \in \mathbb{R}^{\frac{H}{2r} \times \frac{W}{2r} \times 2C}$.

2.2   SeA-Block

SeA-block is adopted for the segmentation-diagnosis feature interaction. The architecture of SeA-block is shown in Fig. 1 (c). The proposed SeA-block contains an encoder and a decoder. The encoder embeds the diagnosis feature according to its affinity with segmentation feature, which is implemented with the multi-head dot-product attention mechanism (MHA). Formally, consider encoding a diagnosis feature f_d with segmentation feature f_m, we use f_m as *query* and f_d as *key* and *value* of the attention, which can be formulated as:

$$\text{MHA}(q, k, v) = \text{MHA}(f_m + E_m, f_d + E_d, f_d), \tag{1}$$

where E_m, E_d are positional encodings [5] for segmentation feature and diagnosis feature respectively. The features are all reshaped into a sequence of flattened patches following ViT. In this attention mechanism, the normalized affinity weights is first calculated between *query* and *key* to reflect the correlation between diagnosis and segmentation feature globally. Then the affinity weights are used to select and reinforce the diagnosis feature through the dot production of *value*. After the attention, the Layer Normalization [3] with residual connection is applied before and after the MLP layer. The embedded diagnosis feature, which we denoted as f_{md}, is outputted with the same shape as the inputs.

A decoder is connected after the encoder to map f_{md} back to diagnosis feature space. There are two inputs for the decoder, diagnosis embedding f_{md} and original diagnosis feature f_d. Being symmetrical to the encoder, decoder is implemented by the multi-head attention with diagnosis feature f_d as *query* and diagnosis embedding f_{md} as *key* and *value*, which can be formulated as:

$$\mathrm{MHA}(q, k, v) = \mathrm{MHA}(f_d + E_d, f_{md} + E_{md}, f_{md}), \tag{2}$$

where E_d, E_{md} are positional encodings for diagnosis feature and diagnosis embedding respectively. The decoder transfers f_{md} to a diagnosis feature by enhancing its affinity with f_d. A self-attention block is connected after the decoder to refine the representations. The obtained sequence will be reshaped back as a vitalized diagnosis feature $\hat{f}_d$ with the same shape as f_d.

3 Experiment

3.1 Diagnosis Tasks

We evaluate SeATrans on three different disease diagnosis tasks: glaucoma diagnosis, thyroid cancer diagnosis and melanoma diagnosis. Glaucoma is predicted from fundus images and is assisted by OD/OC segmentation. Thyroid cancer is predicted from ultrasound images and is assisted by the thyroid nodule segmentation. Melanoma is predicted from dermoscopic images and is assisted by skin lesions segmentation. The experiments of glaucoma, thyroid cancer and melanoma diagnosis are conducted on REFUGE-2 dataset [8], TNMIX dataset [13,24] and ISIC dataset [15], which contain 1200, 8046, 1600 samples, respectively. The datasets are publicly available with both segmentation and diagnosis labels. Train/validation/test sets are split following the default settings of the dataset.

3.2 Experimental Settings

In our experiments, the main framework utilizes the UNet [22] architecture as the segmentation model and ResNet50 [16] as the diagnosis model. The segmentation network is pre-trained on heterologous data distribution. All the experiments are implemented with the PyTorch platform and trained/tested on 4 T P40 GPU with 24 GB of memory. All images are uniformly resized to the dimension of 256×256 pixels. The networks are trained in an end-to-end manner using Adam optimizer with a mini-batch of 16 for 80 epochs. The learning rate is initially set to 1×10^{-4}. The detailed configurations can be found in the code.

To verify the effectiveness of SeATrans, we compare it with several baselines. The vanilla baseline is a standard classification model implemented by

ResNet50 with no segmentation mask provided. Three other baselines are implemented by commonly used segmentation-assisted diagnosis techniques [2], which are denoted as 'Base-cat', 'Base-multi', and 'Base-ROI', respectively. 'Base-cat' concatenates the estimated masks with the raw images as the input of the diagnosis model. 'Base-multi' learns a single network for both segmentation and diagnosis. 'Base-ROI' crops the region of interest (ROI) based on the estimated segmentation masks. In order to verify the generalization of the models, we train segmentation network on homologous (-homo) and heterologous (-hetero) data, respectively. '-homo' means segmentation and diagnosis network are trained on the same source of data. '-hetero' means segmentation model is trained on an external dataset, which is RIGA [1], DDIT [21] and PH2 [20] for glaucoma, thyroid cancer and melanoma diagnosis, respectively.

3.3 Main Results

Comparing SeATrans with baselines in Table 1, we can see significant improvement on all three diagnosis tasks. Concretely, comparing with the best baseline by AUC, SeATrans improves 6.56%, 6.78% and 8.14% on glaucoma, thyroid cancer and melanoma diagnosis respectively, indicating SeATrans can gain general and considerable improvement comparing with the present commonly used techniques. SeATrans also achieves the highest sensitivity with competitive accuracy and specificity, indicating it is more applicable to the real clinical scenarios, since sensitivity is commonly of great concern in clinical scenes.

Comparing vanilla baseline with the other methods, we can see except 'Base-multi', the segmentation more or less improves the diagnosis performance. It demonstrates the segmentation information of lesions/tissues is definitely useful for the automated diagnosis models. However, the improvement it can bring depends largely on the way we use it. Multi-task learning based methods seemed to be invalid according to our experimental results. This may be due to the large discrepancy between segmentation and diagnosis features. The segmentation encoder extract the low-level structure features while the diagnosis needs the high-level semantic features, it is thus hard to learn the universal features

Table 1. Comparing with the baselines. Accuracy, specificity, sensitivity and AUC (%) are measured on three different diagnosis tasks. Segmentation model performance measured by Dice score (%) is also reported.

Tasks		Glaucoma						Thyroid cancer					Melanoma				
Metrics		D_{disc}	D_{cup}	ACC	SPE	SEN	AUC	Dice	ACC	SPE	SEN	AUC	Dice	ACC	SPE	SEN	AUC
No mask	Baseline	–	–	82.95	94.06	37.97	77.29	–	79.29	93.75	68.62	77.08	–	78.53	92.23	22.22	72.49
-homo	Base-cat	94.73	81.77	78.95	82.18	65.82	81.91	86.76	81.74	**95.42**	70.76	80.06	82.35	77.72	87.84	36.11	76.42
	Base-multi	94.73	81.77	82.20	**92.50**	40.50	74.73	86.76	77.25	84.58	65.75	72.37	82.35	80.98	**95.27**	22.22	71.72
	Base-ROI	94.73	81.77	75.18	77.18	67.08	79.88	86.76	83.25	90.26	74.92	77.50	82.35	79.35	90.88	31.94	72.70
	SeATrans	94.73	81.77	**86.96**	90.93	**70.88**	**88.47**	86.76	**85.54**	91.75	**78.84**	**86.84**	82.35	**85.56**	93.77	**62.74**	**84.56**
-hetero	Base-cat	94.60	78.31	82.95	92.19	50.63	80.70	85.17	82.13	88.93	73.58	80.15	80.07	79.89	92.91	26.39	74.41
	Base-multi	94.60	78.31	76.19	90.31	55.70	72.40	85.17	81.35	**94.81**	67.79	72.21	80.07	80.98	**95.27**	22.22	68.70
	Base-ROI	94.60	78.31	**83.20**	**94.06**	39.24	77.52	85.17	82.39	87.74	78.65	76.73	80.07	72.28	77.03	52.78	72.22
	SeATrans	94.60	78.31	80.20	80.62	**78.48**	**87.61**	85.17	84.60	90.26	**80.45**	**86.23**	80.07	84.42	87.20	**57.35**	83.16

in one encoder. SeATrans fuses the multi-scale segmentation features to first few layers of the diagnosis model. In this way, these structure-focused layers are enhanced by the awareness of lesions/tissues structures, and the later layers can still abstract the high-level diagnosis feature. As a result, SeATrans outperforms the other segmentation-assisted diagnosis methods by a large margin.

To verify the generalization of the methods, we also conduct the experiment on heterologous data, where the segmentation model is pre-trained on external dataset. Due to the domain shift, the segmentation masks/features would be inferior to '-homo', thus disturb the diagnosis models. Comparing '-homo' with '-hetero', we can see a drop on the AUC performance over all of the methods. But SeATrans shows very competitive generalization ability, dropping only about 1% AUC on '-hetero'.

3.4   Comparing with SOTA

To demonstrate the advantage of SeATrans, we compare it with SOTA methods for segmentation-assisted diagnosis. Table 2 quantitatively compare SeATrans with nine SOTA segmentation-assisted diagnosis methods.

SeATrans vs Transformers. Present SOTA transformer-based diagnosis architectures: ConViT [6] and Swin Transformer [19] are involved for the comparison. Segmentation masks are concatenated as the inputs of the models. It shows SeATrans clearly outperforms these transformer architectures, increases about 5.60%, 5.82% and 7.10% AUC on glaucoma, thyroid and melanoma, respectively. It demonstrates a large proportion of the improvement comes from the proposed feature fusion strategy, but not the transformer-like architecture.

SeATrans vs ROI. We compare SeATrans with ROI based segmentation-assisted diagnosis methods: DualStage [4] and DENet [10]. It shows [4] only gains marginal improvement compared with vanilla baseline. Although [10] achieves better performance, it is only applicable on glaucoma diagnosis. SeATrans outperforms ROI based methods by an average 4% AUC on a range of tasks.

SeATrans vs Channel Attention. We also compare SeATrans with SOTA channel attention based segmentation-assisted diagnosis methods: AGCNN [18] and ColNet [28], who adopted channel-attention to enhance the diagnosis feature by the segmentation masks/features. We observe that SeATrans can surpass AGCNN and ColNet by 6.31% and 3.10% AUC on glaucoma, 3.99% and 2.40% on thyroid cancer, and 4.39% and 3.84% on melanoma diagnosis, indicating the superiority of SeATrans comparing with regional-correlated channel attention.

SeATrans vs Multi-task. Multi-task learning methods MagNet [14] and CMSNET [29] are involved for the comparison. SeATrans consistently outperforms both methods, especially on thyroid cancer diagnosis, which outperforms MagNet and CMSVNET by 11.16% and 10.13% AUC respectively.

SeATrans vs Transfer-Learning. L2T-KT [27] uniquely processed the task by teacher-student based transfer learning and achieved competitive performance. Comparing the AUC, SeATrans outperforms L2T-KT by 2.23%, 2.55% and 2.66% on glaucoma, thyroid cancer and melanoma diagnosis, respectively. SeATrans also achieves better sensitivity-speficity trade-off than L2T-KT. For example, SeATrans achieves 79.66% F1 score which surpasses 77.43% F1 score of L2T-KT on glaucoma diagnosis.

Heterologous Data Generalization. Comparing with '-homo' and '-hetero', we can see ROI-based methods (Dual-stage, DENet) show the best generalization, since they used less segmentation information than the others. SeATrans and Transformer-based methods (ConViT, Swin) also show competitive generalization capability, which drop only about 1% AUC on a range of tasks. Channel-attention based methods (AGCNN, ColNet) are more sensitive since their regional correlated assumption is vulnerable to the domain shift. Thanks to the dynamic and global nature of SeATrans, it gains high performance with very competitive generalization ability comparing with the other methods.

Table 2. Comparing with SOTA segmentation-assisted diagnosis methods. Accuracy, specificity, sensitivity and AUC (%) are measured on three different diagnosis tasks.

		Glaucoma				Thyroid cancer				Melanoma			
		ACC	SPE	SEN	AUC	ACC	SPE	SEN	AUC	ACC	SPE	SEN	AUC
-homo	ConViT [6]	80.45	86.56	55.69	82.87	80.85	90.31	64.67	81.02	79.89	90.87	34.72	77.46
	Swin [19]	81.95	91.56	43.03	82.32	82.76	85.70	73.82	80.34	80.76	89.11	47.29	76.75
	DualStage [4]	80.20	90.31	39.24	80.37	79.56	85.64	70.93	77.15	78.26	87.84	38.89	72.34
	DENet [10]	80.04	85.00	59.49	84.70	-	-	-	-	-	-	-	-
	AGCNN [18]	81.20	89.68	41.77	82.16	84.78	88.69	71.05	82.85	82.60	92.20	43.83	80.17
	ColNet [28]	79.69	79.69	79.74	85.36	**87.60**	**94.08**	72.47	84.43	85.21	**98.31**	30.98	80.72
	MagNet [14]	83.20	**94.06**	39.24	77.52	78.91	86.71	69.25	75.68	75.54	81.08	52.77	71.77
	CMSNET [29]	64.16	73.41	61.85	80.86	74.52	87.03	67.32	76.71	82.88	98.32	17.14	78.55
	L2T-KT [27]	80.20	80.62	78.48	86.24	81.49	90.31	75.59	84.29	79.34	84.69	58.10	81.90
	SeATrans	**86.96**	90.93	**70.88**	**88.47**	85.54	91.75	**78.84**	**86.84**	**85.59**	93.77	**62.74**	**84.56**
-hetero	ConViT [6]	80.45	91.56	35.44	82.37	77.46	93.75	60.11	81.02	79.34	85.42	54.79	76.55
	Swin [19]	72.18	83.54	69.37	81.85	80.34	83.45	76.18	80.34	79.89	87.11	50.68	75.28
	DualStage [4]	75.18	67.08	77.18	80.22	80.70	88.69	75.71	77.15	81.79	92.56	37.50	72.63
	DENet [10]	78.94	84.81	77.50	84.12	-	-	-	-	-	-	-	-
	AGCNN [18]	66.16	62.81	79.74	80.94	82.29	93.41	70.58	82.85	76.08	78.98	64.38	77.38
	ColNet [28]	61.40	**97.46**	52.50	82.78	**84.93**	91.19	73.82	84.43	82.33	**93.91**	34.72	77.95
	MagNet [14]	70.42	70.31	70.88	75.44	78.15	87.74	77.36	75.68	79.34	90.50	33.33	69.67
	CMSNET [29]	60.15	77.21	55.93	78.17	81.75	84.60	78.14	76.71	72.82	73.73	69.01	76.39
	L2T-KT [27]	79.95	85.00	59.49	84.98	83.89	**94.04**	76.18	84.29	82.06	88.51	55.56	80.75
	SeATrans	**80.70**	80.62	**78.48**	**87.61**	84.60	90.26	**80.45**	**86.23**	**84.42**	87.20	**57.35**	**83.16**

3.5   Ablation Study

Ablation studies are performed over each component of SeATrans, including multi-scale, asymmetric interaction and SeA-Block, as listed in Table 3. The experiments are conducted on glaucoma diagnosis task. Feature concatenation is adopted to replace SeA-block. In Table 3, as we sequentially adding the proposed modules on vanilla baseline, the model performance is gradually improved. First, by applying multi-scale segmentation-diagnosis integration, the AUC value is increased by 2% on homologous data while only 0.6% on heterologous data. This indicates that multi-scale integration can improve the diagnosis performance with limited generalization. Then, the asymmetric multi-scale interaction is applied to further focus the integration on the low-level features, which boosts the AUC by a 3.53% and a 3.42% on '-homo' and '-hetero' respectively. Finally, SeA-Block is utilized for the segmentation-diagnosis interaction. It can be observed the diagnosis performance is remarkably improved, which gains 5.09% and 6.34% AUC improvement on '-homo' and '-hetero', respectively. It indicates SeA-block gains significant and general improvement by its dynamic and global interaction.

Table 3. Ablation study on glaucoma diagnosis task. The diagnosis performance is measured by AUC (%)

Multi-scale	Asymmetric	SeA-block	-homo	-hetero
			77.29	77.29
✓			79.85	77.84
✓	✓		83.38	81.27
✓	✓	✓	**88.47**	**87.61**

4   Conclusion

In this work, we proposed SeATrans to overcome the shortcomings of existing segmentation-assisted diagnosis models. In SeATrans, asymmetric multi-scale interaction is proposed to address the segmentation-diagnosis scale level discrepancy. Then SeA-block is constructed for the global and dynamic feature interaction between segmentation and diagnosis space. Extensive empirical experiments demonstrated the general and superior performance of the proposed SeATrans on a range of medical image diagnosis tasks.

References

1. Almazroa, A., et al.: Agreement among ophthalmologists in marking the optic disc and optic cup in fundus images. Int. Ophthalmol. **37**(3), 701–717 (2016). https://doi.org/10.1007/s10792-016-0329-x
2. Anwar, S.M., Majid, M., Qayyum, A., Awais, M., Alnowami, M., Khan, M.K.: Medical image analysis using convolutional neural networks: a review. J. Med. Syst. **42**(11), 1–13 (2018)
3. Ba, J.L., Kiros, J.R., Hinton, G.E.: Layer normalization. arXiv preprint arXiv:1607.06450 (2016)
4. Bajwa, M.N., et al.: Two-stage framework for optic disc localization and glaucoma classification in retinal fundus images using deep learning. BMC Med. Inform. Decis. Mak. **19**(1), 1–16 (2019)
5. Carion, N., Massa, F., Synnaeve, G., Usunier, N., Kirillov, A., Zagoruyko, S.: End-to-end object detection with transformers. In: Vedaldi, A., Bischof, H., Brox, T., Frahm, J.-M. (eds.) ECCV 2020. LNCS, vol. 12346, pp. 213–229. Springer, Cham (2020). https://doi.org/10.1007/978-3-030-58452-8_13
6. d'Ascoli, S., Touvron, H., Leavitt, M., Morcos, A., Biroli, G., Sagun, L.: ConViT: improving vision transformers with soft convolutional inductive biases. arXiv preprint arXiv:2103.10697 (2021)
7. Dosovitskiy, A., et al.: An image is worth 16 × 16 words: transformers for image recognition at scale. arXiv preprint arXiv:2010.11929 (2020)
8. Fang, H., et al.: Refuge2 challenge: treasure for multi-domain learning in glaucoma assessment. arXiv preprint arXiv:2202.08994 (2022)
9. Fu, H., Cheng, J., Xu, Y., Wong, D.W.K., Liu, J., Cao, X.: Joint optic disc and cup segmentation based on multi-label deep network and polar transformation. IEEE Trans. Med. Imaging **37**(7), 1597–1605 (2018)
10. Fu, H., et al.: Disc-aware ensemble network for glaucoma screening from fundus image. IEEE Trans. Med. Imaging **37**(11), 2493–2501 (2018)
11. Gachon, J., et al.: First prospective study of the recognition process of melanoma in dermatological practice. Arch. Dermatol. **141**(4), 434–438 (2005)
12. Garway-Heath, D.F., Ruben, S.T., Viswanathan, A., Hitchings, R.A.: Vertical cup/disc ratio in relation to optic disc size: its value in the assessment of the glaucoma suspect. Br. J. Ophthalmol. **82**(10), 1118–1124 (1998)
13. Gong, H., et al.: Multi-task learning for thyroid nodule segmentation with thyroid region prior. In: 2021 IEEE 18th International Symposium on Biomedical Imaging (ISBI), pp. 257–261. IEEE (2021)
14. Gupta, S., Punn, N.S., Sonbhadra, S.K., Agarwal, S.: MAG-Net: multi-task attention guided network for brain tumor segmentation and classification. In: Srirama, S.N., Lin, J.C.-W., Bhatnagar, R., Agarwal, S., Reddy, P.K. (eds.) BDA 2021. LNCS, vol. 13147, pp. 3–15. Springer, Cham (2021). https://doi.org/10.1007/978-3-030-93620-4_1
15. Gutman, D., et al.: Skin lesion analysis toward melanoma detection: a challenge at the international symposium on biomedical imaging (ISBI) 2016, hosted by the international skin imaging collaboration (ISIC). arXiv preprint arXiv:1605.01397 (2016)
16. He, K., Zhang, X., Ren, S., Sun, J.: Deep residual learning for image recognition. In: Proceedings of the IEEE Conference on Computer Vision and Pattern Recognition, pp. 770–778 (2016)

17. Ji, W., et al.: Learning calibrated medical image segmentation via multi-rater agreement modeling. In: Proceedings of the IEEE/CVF Conference on Computer Vision and Pattern Recognition, pp. 12341–12351 (2021)
18. Li, L., Xu, M., Wang, X., Jiang, L., Liu, H.: Attention based glaucoma detection: a large-scale database and CNN model. In: Proceedings of the IEEE/CVF Conference on Computer Vision and Pattern Recognition, pp. 10571–10580 (2019)
19. Liu, Z., et al.: Swin transformer: hierarchical vision transformer using shifted windows. In: Proceedings of the IEEE/CVF International Conference on Computer Vision, pp. 10012–10022 (2021)
20. Mendonça, T., Ferreira, P.M., Marques, J.S., Marcal, A.R., Rozeira, J.: PH 2-a dermoscopic image database for research and benchmarking. In: 2013 35th Annual International Conference of the IEEE Engineering in Medicine and Biology Society (EMBC), pp. 5437–5440. IEEE (2013)
21. Pedraza, L., Vargas, C., Narváez, F., Durán, O., Muñoz, E., Romero, E.: An open access thyroid ultrasound image database. In: 10th International Symposium on Medical Information Processing and Analysis, vol. 9287, p. 92870W. International Society for Optics and Photonics (2015)
22. Ronneberger, O., Fischer, P., Brox, T.: U-Net: convolutional networks for biomedical image segmentation. In: Navab, N., Hornegger, J., Wells, W.M., Frangi, A.F. (eds.) MICCAI 2015. LNCS, vol. 9351, pp. 234–241. Springer, Cham (2015). https://doi.org/10.1007/978-3-319-24574-4_28
23. Shi, W., et al.: Real-time single image and video super-resolution using an efficient sub-pixel convolutional neural network. In: Proceedings of the IEEE Conference on Computer Vision and Pattern Recognition, pp. 1874–1883 (2016)
24. Shusharina, N., Heinrich, M.P., Huang, R. (eds.): MICCAI 2020. LNCS, vol. 12587. Springer, Cham (2021). https://doi.org/10.1007/978-3-030-71827-5
25. Wojna, Z., et al.: The devil is in the decoder. In: British Machine Vision Conference 2017, BMVC 2017, pp. 1–13. BMVA Press (2017)
26. Wu, J., et al.: Gamma challenge: glaucoma grading from multi-modality images. arXiv preprint arXiv:2202.06511 (2022)
27. Wu, J., et al.: Leveraging undiagnosed data for glaucoma classification with teacher-student learning. In: Martel, A.L., et al. (eds.) MICCAI 2020. LNCS, vol. 12261, pp. 731–740. Springer, Cham (2020). https://doi.org/10.1007/978-3-030-59710-8_71
28. Zhou, Y., et al.: Collaborative learning of semi-supervised segmentation and classification for medical images. In: Proceedings of the IEEE/CVF Conference on Computer Vision and Pattern Recognition, pp. 2079–2088 (2019)
29. Zhou, Y., et al.: Multi-task learning for segmentation and classification of tumors in 3D automated breast ultrasound images. Med. Image Anal. **70**, 101918 (2021)

Screening of Dementia on OCTA Images via Multi-projection Consistency and Complementarity

Xingyue Wang[1,2], Heng Li[2], Zunjie Xiao[1,2], Huazhu Fu[3], Yitian Zhao[4], Richu Jin[2], Shuting Zhang[5], William Robert Kwapong[5], Ziyi Zhang[5], Hanpei Miao[1,2(✉)], and Jiang Liu[1,2,6(✉)]

[1] Research Institute of Trustworthy Autonomous Systems, Southern University of Science and Technology, Shenzhen 518055, China
miaohp@mail.sustech.edu.cn, liuj@sustech.edu.cn
[2] Department of Computer Science and Engineering, Southern University of Science and Technology, Shenzhen 518055, China
[3] Agency for Science, Technology and Research (A*STAR), Singapore, Singapore
[4] Cixi Institute of Biomedical Engineering, Chinese Academy of Sciences, Beijing, China
[5] West China Hospital Sichuan University, Chengdu, China
[6] Guangdong Provincial Key Laboratory of Brain-Inspired Intelligent Computation, Southern University of Science and Technology, Shenzhen, China

Abstract. It has been suggested that the retinal vasculature alternations are associated with dementia in recent clinical studies, and the eye examination may facilitate the early screening of dementia. Optical Coherence Tomography Angiography (OCTA) has shown its superiority in visualizing superficial vascular complex (SVC), deep vascular complex (DVC), and choriocapillaris, and it has been extensively used in clinical practice. However, the information in OCTA is far from fully mined by existing methods, which straightforwardly analyze the multiple projections of OCTA by average or concatenation. These methods do not take into account the relationship between multiple projections. Accordingly, a Multi-projection Consistency and complementarity Learning Network (MUCO-Net) is proposed in this paper to explore the diagnosis of dementia based on OCTA. Firstly, a consistency and complementarity attention (CsCp) module is developed to understand the complex relationships among various projections. Then, a cross-view fusion (CVF) module is introduced to combine the multi-scale features from the CsCp. In addition, the number of input flows of the proposed modules is flexible to boost the interactions across the features from different projections. In the experiment, MUCO-Net is implemented on two OCTA datasets to screen for dementia and diagnose fundus diseases. The effectiveness of MUCO-Net is demonstrated by its superior performance to state-of-the-art methods.

Keywords: Dementia · OCTA · Deep learning · Multi-projection

© The Author(s), under exclusive license to Springer Nature Switzerland AG 2022
L. Wang et al. (Eds.): MICCAI 2022, LNCS 13432, pp. 688–698, 2022.
https://doi.org/10.1007/978-3-031-16434-7_66

1   Introduction

The diagnosis of dementia is still a challenging problem nowadays. It is a cognitive disorder characterized by mental decline and often associated with aging [15]. Clinically, the initial detection of dementia includes cognitive function, neuroimaging (magnetic resonance imaging, cerebrospinal fluid) [10]. However, screening of dementia is also a complicated problem in the medical field because neuroimaging examination is expensive and takes a long time, and it is not suitable for everyone. For example, cerebrospinal fluid is an invasive examination, magnetic resonance imaging takes a long time, and some patients with metal foreign bodies or claustrophobia cannot undergo magnetic resonance imaging examination.

Studies have found that changes in ophthalmic features are associated with dementia, and automatically screening for dementia through ophthalmic images is a field worthy of exploration. Eyes and brains have homology in tissue origin and similarity in structure and functional mechanism, making it possible to study the brain through eyes [9]. Moreover, the ophthalmic examination is more convenient than neuroimaging examination. Studies have shown that fundus vascular pathologies detected through optical coherence tomography angiography (OCTA) can be used as a new biomarker in diagnosing dementia disease [1]. OCTA is an emerging non-invasive technique to generate high-resolution images of fundus vessels. Compared with other ophthalmic examinations, OCTA can observe different layers of blood flow. OCTA images are produced by projection over regions of selective depth and can be generally divided into superficial vascular complex (SVC), deep vascular complex (DVC), and choriocapillaris. These vascular changes are associated with dementia disease. For instance, patients with dementia have lower vessel density in their choriocapillaris, superficial and deep vascular [24,25], and their foveal avascular zone (FAZ) regions have shown enlargement in both SVC and DVC [1,25]. Therefore, it is of great clinical value to effectively combine SVC, DVC, and choriocapillaris OCTA images for auxiliary diagnosis of dementia diseases.

Several automatic multi-projection OCTA images classification algorithms have been proposed in the past few years, mainly divided into two categories. The first category is traditional methods based on machine learning algorithms. For instance, De et al. employed several methods, such as SVM, with vascular features obtained from retinal and choriocapillaris, and found that OCTA features with different projections can enhance the effect of disease diagnosis [3]. The second category is deep-learning-based algorithms, which achieved overwhelming performance in computer vision fields. Several works for multi-projection OCTA images diagnosis based on deep learning have been reported [7,17,22]. These studies have shown that information fusion from different projections can enhance diagnostic performance. Despite the progress, these approaches still have limitations. First, they usually ignore consistency and complementarity information mining among multiple projections. The OCTA information of different projections describes the fundus vessels at the same position but with different thicknesses, so consistency and complementarity information may exist

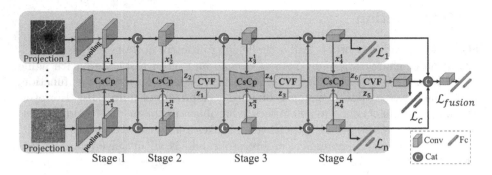

Fig. 1. An illustration of our proposed MUCO-Net for OCTA images classification. For clarity, we show only two projections in the figure. In practice, the number of network inputs for projection can be flexible.

among different projections. For example, SVC and DVC both have the characteristics of the FAZ, namely consistency information. In addition, SVC has obvious information about large vessels, and DVC can clearly describe capillaries, which are complementarity information. Similarly, in multi-view analysis, consistency and complementarity information extraction are also continuously studied to bring more prior information into the learning process, thus further boosting the learning performance [4,14]. Secondly, these methods generally do not consider the different scales of information extraction and combination. For OCTA images, ophthalmologists need to observe pathologies at multiple scales (e.g., from capillaries at the micrometer level, FAZ at the millimeter level, to large vessels through the whole eye). It has been suggested that these different information scales are helpful for disease diagnosis [1,24,25].

To address the above issues, we propose a multi-projection consistency and complementarity learning network (MUCO-Net) for OCTA images classification of dementia disease. At first, a consistency and complementarity attention (CsCp) module is proposed to fully exploit the underlying consistency and complementarity among multi-projection OCTA images, and the number of inputs in the design can be flexible. Besides, a cross-view fusion (CVF) module that marries multi-scale interactive information is used to combine features of different receptive fields. So the multi-scale features of CsCp can fully interact in our network. The experimental results show that the proposed method is superior to other state-of-the-art methods and has better performance on two OCTA datasets[1].

2 Method

The proposed MUCO-Net for OCTA images is shown in Fig. 1. In the network, each projection has its branch to extract specific information. After features

---

[1] We will make our code available after our paper is accepted https://github.com/Wangxingyue98/MUCO-Net-for-OCTA-images.

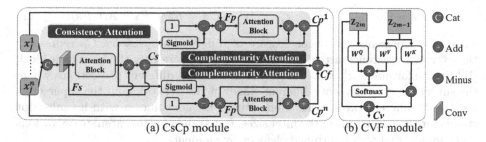

Fig. 2. Two modules in MUCO-Net, namely (a) CsCp module and (b) CVF module. The number of inputs to the CsCp module can be variable, two of which are drawn for clarity. In the figure, the attention block references the Bottleneck Attention Module [16]. W^Q, W^K, and W^V are Learnable vectors. z_{2m} and z_{2m-1} are multi-scales outputs of CsCp modules of different depths in the network.

are fetched at different stages of the network, the CsCp extracts the consistent and complementary information of multiple projections. It can obtain the characteristics of different receptive fields by CVF combined with information of different scales in the upper layer. The output of CVF will be integrated with the individual characteristics of each projection to realize the interaction between different projections. The network can be flexibly adjusted according to the different number of inputs. It has two essential building modules: the CsCp and the CVF modules. Each module will be described in the following subsections.

2.1 The Consistency and Complementarity Attention (CsCp)

In multi-projection OCTA image learning, consistency and complementarity from multiple projections are expected to boost the learning performance. Thus, it is critical to exploit the underlying correlations among multiple images while also capturing the specific information to preserve their properties. To achieve this goal, we construct the CsCp module in the right of Fig. 2. We first construct a consistent network for multi-projection images. We concatenate the feature from multi-projection OCTA images and then use one attention block to extract the consistent information from different projections. In the design of this module, we get the attention map from the attention block references the Bottleneck Attention Module [16]. Then combine the consistency attention map with the merged image. Besides, we also reverse the consistency attention map for effectively complementarity information extracting. Each projection has a complementarity attention module for better getting its specific feature respectively. After that, all the consistent and complementary features from different projections OCTA images are fused in this module. The number of inputs to the CsCp can be flexibly adjusted to accommodate the projections.

Consistency Attention. The consistency is implemented by using an attention block after fusing the information of different layers. The mathematical notation of the consistency attention calculation is:

$$Fs = \text{Conv}_{1\times1}(\text{Cat}(x_j^1, x_j^2, \ldots, x_j^n)), Cs = Fs + Fs \otimes \text{Att}(Fs). \tag{1}$$

where Fs represents the fusion feature of different projections, Cs represents the overall consistency attention block, and Att represents the attention block [16]. In the formulas, $x_j^1, x_j^2, \ldots, x_j^n$ are features from different projections, where the subscript of x represents different stages of the network, and the superscript represents different projections. Conv stands for convolution with its subscript stands for the magnitude of the filter sizes, Cat stands for concatenate operations on channels, and $\otimes$ is multiplied element by element.

Complementarity Attention. In order to efficiently capture the specific information of each projection, we first invert the attention feature map of the consistency information to obtain the remaining information. Then, the characteristic information of this part was obtained through each projection's respective attention networks. Given a feature x_j^i and the attention map of consistency attention block, namely $\text{Att}(Fs)$. In addition, σ is sigmoid function. The output Cp of complementarity attention block is formulated as:

$$Fp = x_j^i \otimes (1 - \sigma(\text{Att}(Fs))), \quad Cp(x_j^i) = Fp + Fp \otimes \text{Att}(Fp). \tag{2}$$

It is worth emphasizing that the number of inputs can be variable, and we assume that the number of inputs is n as shown in Fig. 2. The final output Cf is the sum of Cs and Cp of different projections.

2.2   The Cross-View Fusion (CVF)

Multi-scale processing is necessary for the CsCp modules to highlight the discriminative region at different scales in OCTA images. Our model directly takes the different scale outputs of the CsCp modules and feeds them into cross-view encoders. In this way, the consistency and complementarity information of the previous layer at different scales is combined and applied to the branch network of each projection.

We sequentially fuse information between pairs of two adjacent views, $2m$ and $2m-1$ ($m \geq 1, m \in \mathbb{Z}$), where the views are the outputs of CsCp ordered as the network deeper. Concretely, to update the output from the deeper projections z_{2m}, we compute its attention where the queries are z_{2m}, and the keys and values are z_{2m-1}. As the hidden dimensions of the feature between the two views can be different, we first project the keys and values to the same dimension. The module also includes a residual connection around the cross-view attention operation to make better use of context information, as denoted by

$$Cv = z_{2m} + \text{Softmax}(\frac{W^Q z_{2m} W^K (z_{2m-1})^T}{\sqrt{dk}}) W^V z_{2m-1} \tag{3}$$

Note that W^Q, W^K and W^V are the query-, key- and value-view matrices used in the attention operation [2,19,21], dk is the embedding dimension. This structure can obtain the characteristics of different receptive fields at the same level and then transfer them to the next layer after fusion, which can balance computational load and model capability more flexibly.

2.3 Objective Function

For this model, we assume that the number of input is n $(n \geq 2, n \in \mathbb{Z})$. We define three loss functions as $\mathcal{L}_c$, $\mathcal{L}_i(i \leq n)$, and $\mathcal{L}_{fusion}$, respectively. As shown in Fig. 1, $\mathcal{L}_c$ represents the loss of multi-scale consistency and complementarity information extraction branch, $\mathcal{L}_i$ is the loss for each OCTA images branch, and $\mathcal{L}_{fusion}$ represents the loss of fusion of all branches. The cross-entropy loss function is used in these three types of loss functions to guide the training process. And λ_c, λ_i are hyper parameters to adjust the weight of four different losses. In our dementia experiment, $n = 3$, and we set $\lambda_c = 0.4$, $\lambda_1 = \lambda_2 = \lambda_3 = 0.2$. In the training process, the goal of model is to minimize the main loss function $\mathcal{L}_{total}$, as shown in Eq. (4).

$$\mathcal{L}_{total} = \mathcal{L}_{fusion} + \lambda_c \mathcal{L}_c + \sum_{i=1}^{n} \lambda_i \mathcal{L}_i \tag{4}$$

3 Experiments

3.1 Dementia Experiment

Dataset. The 114 OCTA images of dementia patients in our private dataset were collected in the neurology department of West China Hospital; patients met the criteria National Institute on Aging and Alzheimer's Association (NIA-AA) criteria. We also enrolled controls (286 OCTA images). Imaging of the retinal microvasculature was done with the swept-source optical coherence tomography angiography, SS-OCTA (VG200; SVision Imaging, Limited); the tool has a scan rate of 200,000 A-scans per second, a central wavelength of 1050nm which could image the retina and choriocapillaris. A 3×3 mm area around the fovea was captured for all participants, and an inbuilt software in the tool segmented the retinal microvasculature into SVC and DVC.

Implementation. We resize images to the same size, which is 192×192, and adopt data augmentation methods including random rotation, flipping, contrast adjustment, adding Gaussian noise, etc. We use the SGD optimization strategy during model training. The initial learning rate is 0.00001, epochs is 200, and the number of batch size is 4. The learning rate optimization strategy is MultiStepLR. The models are trained and tested with PyTorch on the NVIDIA GeForce TITAN XP. We split each dataset into 80% and 20% for training and testing. Five-fold cross-validation is used for fair comparison in all settings.

Table 1. Quantitative evaluation of different methods, and ablation study on different stages of the CsCp and CVF on dementia experiment.

Model	ACC %	F1-score %	Kappa %
Resnet50 (superficial) [6]	79.75 ± 0.08	78.58 ± 0.11	45.57 ± 0.80
Resnet50 (deep) [6]	81.75 ± 0.10	79.78 ± 0.15	48.27 ± 0.98
Resnet50 (choriocapillaris) [6]	81.75 ± 0.05	80.66 ± 0.06	50.78 ± 0.39
Early fusion [5,8]	83.25 ± 0.03	82.78 ± 0.04	57.30 ± 0.44
Late fusion [7]	82.50 ± 0.09	81.07 ± 0.15	52.00 ± 0.38
Middile fusion [20,26]	82.25 ± 0.04	80.79 ± 0.12	51.19 ± 1.27
MCC [27]	83.25 ± 0.07	83.04 ± 0.07	57.99 ± 0.63
CRBM [23]	83.50 ± 0.03	83.07 ± 0.04	57.48 ± 0.36
MUCO-stage1	84.25 ± 0.02	83.52 ± 0.02	58.52 ± 0.24
MUCO-stage2	83.50 ± 0.06	82.84 ± 0.07	56.49 ± 0.66
MUCO-stage3	82.50 ± 0.02	81.47 ± 0.02	53.54 ± 0.31
MUCO-stage4	83.50 ± 0.07	82.33 ± 0.11	54.98 ± 1.15
MUCO-Merge	85.75 ± 0.05	85.95 ± 0.05	66.29 ± 0.19
MUCO(ours)	**86.00 ± 0.06**	**86.19 ± 0.06**	**66.67 ± 0.31**

Evaluation. We first compare the single-projection OCTA image method with resnet50 [6]. Then we compare performance of the proposed method with some multi-projection fusion methods like early fusion [5,8], late fusion [7], middile fusion [20,26], MCC [27], CRBM [23]. As shown in Table 1, The proposed method has obtained the best overall performance on our dementia experiment. All methods are evaluated using three metrics, i.e., accuracy (ACC), F1-score, and kappa. The results show that the performance of a single-projection method is generally inferior to those of multiple projections. Early fusion [5,8], late fusion [7], middile fusion [20,26] are common multiple image fusion methods, according to the different fusion stages. But these methods do not take into account the relationship between different projection images. MCC [27] and CRBM [23] consider the consistency between different projection images. However, they ignore the complementarity information.

The ablation experiment is also shown in Table 1. In this process, we gradually added the CsCp after each feature extraction stage as shown in Fig. 1 and

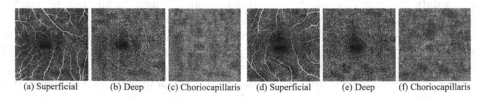

(a) Superficial   (b) Deep   (c) Choriocapillaris   (d) Superficial   (e) Deep   (f) Choriocapillaris

Fig. 3. Grad-CAMs for (a)(d) Superficial vascular complex, (b)(e) Deep vascular complex, (c)(f) Choriocapillaris on Dementia Dataset. In this case, (a)(b)(c) is an example of a control person, and (d)(e)(f) is an example of a person with dementia.

found that all of their classification results increased. Results were also improved when we simply merged multi-scale information from different stages into the same size and then integrated it (MUCO-Merge). The multi-scale method was further optimized, and the results were further improved after adding CVF.

Our method has achieved better performance. It is mainly due to the following advantages. 1) It takes advantage of the consistency between different projections because the data describe the same location from different perspectives. Moreover, it considers the complementarity of different projections because OCTA describes layers of different thickness positions. 2) Cross-view fusion combines the information between views of different scales and carries out feature extraction and fusion under different receptive fields. 3) Information from different projections fully interacts in the network, and a new loss is designed to take full advantage of each projection or branch.

Representative Grad-CAM [18] visualizations are shown in Fig. 3 for the case of two subjects. The large vascular area on superficial vascular complex, FAZ on superficial vascular complex and deep vascular complex, and part of the ischemic area on choriocapillaris greatly influence the classification of the dementia disease. It is enlightening to see if these blood flow changes are associated with dementia disease.

3.2 Extended Experiment

Dataset. Since there are no publicly available datasets to analyze dementia using OCTA images, we conducted extended experiments on the open OCTA-500 Dataset [11,12] to verify the method's reliability. In OCTA-500, we only use data from three categories (251 normal, 64 diabetic retinopathy, and 49 age-related macular degeneration) each with a sample size greater than 20. We use both superficial and deep vascular in this dataset. Since the additional layer given by the dataset is a superposition of these two layers, it is not used here.

Implementation. To enlarge the sample size and better evaluate the classification performance, we combine images with different spatial resolutions via resizing and center cropping by referring to the work of others [13]. The remaining implementation details are basically consistent with the dementia experiment.

Evaluation. We also compare the single-projection method and some multi-projection fusion methods on the extended experiment. In addition, BSDA [13] method, which the highest classification score in OCTA-500 Dataset, is compared. As shown in Table 2, The proposed method has obtained the best overall performance.

Table 2. Quantitative evaluation of different methods on the extended experiment.

Model	ACC %	F1-score %	Kappa %
Resnet50 (superficial) [6]	87.90 ± 0.10	87.70 ± 0.11	73.58 ± 0.49
Resnet50 (deep) [6]	89.01 ± 0.10	88.68 ± 0.11	76.47 ± 0.31
Early fusion [5,8]	90.11 ± 0.11	89.69 ± 0.12	78.45 ± 0.40
Late fusion [7]	89.29 ± 0.16	88.70 ± 0.20	76.71 ± 0.71
Middile fusion [20,26]	90.12 ± 0.14	89.14 ± 0.19	78.29 ± 0.63
MCC [27]	89.28 ± 0.07	89.05 ± 0.07	76.86 ± 0.17
CRBM [23]	89.01 ± 0.10	88.42 ± 0.11	75.97 ± 0.40
BSDA [13]	94.23	\	87.68
MUCO(ours)	**94.50 ± 0.01**	**94.44 ± 0.01**	**88.23 ± 0.03**

4 Conclusion

This paper proposes a multi-projection consistency and complementarity learning network (MUCO-Net) for dementia screening on OCTA images. Specifically, a consistency and complementarity attention (CsCp) module is designed to effectively exploit OCTA images' underlying information. The network also combines multi-scale features from the CsCp through the cross-view fusion (CVF) module because of the multi-scales pathologies on OCTA images. Our method achieves superior performance to various state-of-the-art methods on dementia diagnosis and other diseases. The ablation study shows that both the CsCp and CVF contribute to improved performance.

Acknowledgement. This work was supported in part by China Postdoctoral Science Foundation (2021M691437), the National Natural Science Foundation of China (62101236), Guangdong Provincial Department of Education (2020ZDZX3043), the Science and Technology Innovation Committee of Shenzhen City (20200925174052004 and JCYJ20200109140820699), and Guangdong Provincial Key Laboratory (2020B121201001).

References

1. Bulut, M., et al.: Evaluation of optical coherence tomography angiographic findings in Alzheimer's type dementia. Br. J. Ophthalmol. **102**(2), 233–237 (2018)
2. Chen, C.F.R., Fan, Q., Panda, R.: CrossViT: cross-attention multi-scale vision transformer for image classification. In: Proceedings of the IEEE/CVF International Conference on Computer Vision, pp. 357–366 (2021)
3. De Jesus, D.A., et al.: Octa multilayer and multisector peripapillary microvascular modeling for diagnosing and staging of glaucoma. Transl. Vis. Sci. Technol. **9**(2), 58–58 (2020)
4. Fu, H., Geng, Y., Zhang, C., Li, Z., Hu, Q.: RED-Nets: redistribution networks for multi-view classification. Inf. Fusion **65**, 119–127 (2021)

5. Guo, Z., Li, X., Huang, H., Guo, N., Li, Q.: Medical image segmentation based on multi-modal convolutional neural network: study on image fusion schemes. In: 2018 IEEE 15th International Symposium on Biomedical Imaging (ISBI 2018), pp. 903–907. IEEE (2018)
6. He, K., Zhang, X., Ren, S., Sun, J.: Deep residual learning for image recognition. In: Proceedings of the IEEE Conference on Computer Vision and Pattern Recognition, pp. 770–778 (2016)
7. Heisler, M., et al.: Ensemble deep learning for diabetic retinopathy detection using optical coherence tomography angiography. Transl. Vis. Sci. Technol. 9(2), 20–20 (2020)
8. Hermessi, H., Mourali, O., Zagrouba, E.: Multimodal medical image fusion review: theoretical background and recent advances. Signal Process. 183, 108036 (2021)
9. Hughes, S., Yang, H., Chan-Ling, T.: Vascularization of the human fetal retina: roles of vasculogenesis and angiogenesis. Invest. Ophthalmol. Visual Sci. 41(5), 1217–1228 (2000)
10. Hugo, J., Ganguli, M.: Dementia and cognitive impairment: epidemiology, diagnosis, and treatment. Clin. Geriatr. Med. 30(3), 421–442 (2014)
11. Li, M., et al.: Image projection network: 3D to 2D image segmentation in octa images. IEEE Trans. Med. Imaging 39(11), 3343–3354 (2020)
12. Li, M., et al.: IPN-V2 and octa-500: methodology and dataset for retinal image segmentation. arXiv preprint arXiv:2012.07261 (2020)
13. Lin, L., et al.: BSDA-Net: a boundary shape and distance aware joint learning framework for segmenting and classifying OCTA images. In: de Bruijne, M., et al. (eds.) MICCAI 2021. LNCS, vol. 12908, pp. 65–75. Springer, Cham (2021). https://doi.org/10.1007/978-3-030-87237-3_7
14. Liu, M., Zhang, D., Shen, D.: Relationship induced multi-template learning for diagnosis of Alzheimer's disease and mild cognitive impairment. IEEE Trans. Med. Imaging 35(6), 1463–1474 (2016)
15. Livingston, G., et al.: Dementia prevention, intervention, and care. Lancet 390(10113), 2673–2734 (2017)
16. Park, J., Woo, S., Lee, J.Y., Kweon, I.S.: BAM: bottleneck attention module. arXiv preprint arXiv:1807.06514 (2018)
17. Ryu, G., Lee, K., Park, D., Park, S.H., Sagong, M.: A deep learning model for identifying diabetic retinopathy using optical coherence tomography angiography. Sci. Rep. 11(1), 1–9 (2021)
18. Selvaraju, R.R., Cogswell, M., Das, A., Vedantam, R., Parikh, D., Batra, D.: Grad-CAM: visual explanations from deep networks via gradient-based localization. In: Proceedings of the IEEE International Conference on Computer Vision, pp. 618–626 (2017)
19. Vaswani, A., et al.: Attention is all you need. In: Advances in Neural Information Processing Systems, vol. 30 (2017)
20. Wang, X., Shu, K., Kuang, H., Luo, S., Jin, R., Liu, J.: The role of spatial alignment in multimodal medical image fusion using deep learning for diagnostic problems. In: 2021 the 3rd International Conference on Intelligent Medicine and Health, pp. 40–46 (2021)
21. Yan, S., et al.: Multiview transformers for video recognition. arXiv preprint arXiv:2201.04288 (2022)
22. Zang, P., et al.: DcardNet: diabetic retinopathy classification at multiple levels based on structural and angiographic optical coherence tomography. IEEE Trans. Biomed. Eng. 68(6), 1859–1870 (2020)

23. Zhang, N., Ding, S., Liao, H., Jia, W.: Multimodal correlation deep belief networks for multi-view classification. Appl. Intell. **49**(5), 1925–1936 (2018). https://doi.org/10.1007/s10489-018-1379-8
24. Zhang, S., et al.: Choriocapillaris changes are correlated with disease duration and MoCa score in early-onset dementia. Front. Aging Neurosci. **13**, 192 (2021)
25. Zhang, Y.S., et al.: Parafoveal vessel loss and correlation between peripapillary vessel density and cognitive performance in amnestic mild cognitive impairment and early Alzheimer's disease on optical coherence tomography angiography. PLoS ONE **14**(4), e0214685 (2019)
26. Zhou, T., et al.: Deep multi-modal latent representation learning for automated dementia diagnosis. In: Shen, D., et al. (eds.) MICCAI 2019. LNCS, vol. 11767, pp. 629–638. Springer, Cham (2019). https://doi.org/10.1007/978-3-030-32251-9_69
27. Zhou, T., Canu, S., Vera, P., Ruan, S.: 3D medical multi-modal segmentation network guided by multi-source correlation constraint. In: 2020 25th International Conference on Pattern Recognition (ICPR), pp. 10243–10250. IEEE (2021)

Noise Transfer for Unsupervised Domain Adaptation of Retinal OCT Images

Valentin Koch[1,3,5], Olle Holmberg[1,2], Hannah Spitzer[2], Johannes Schiefelbein[4], Ben Asani[4], Michael Hafner[4], and Fabian J. Theis[1,2(✉)]

[1] Technical University of Munich, Munich, Germany
fabian.theis@helmholtz-muenchen.de
[2] Institute of Computational Biology, Helmholtz Munich, Munich, Germany
[3] Institute of AI for Health, Helmholtz Munich, Munich, Germany
[4] Department of Ophthalmology, Ludwig-Maximilians-University, Munich, Germany
[5] Munich School for Data Science, Munich, Germany

Abstract. Optical coherence tomography (OCT) imaging from different camera devices causes challenging domain shifts and can cause a severe drop in accuracy for machine learning models. In this work, we introduce a minimal noise adaptation method based on a singular value decomposition (SVDNA) to overcome the domain gap between target domains from three different device manufacturers in retinal OCT imaging. Our method utilizes the difference in noise structure to successfully bridge the domain gap between different OCT devices and transfer the style from unlabeled target domain images to source images for which manual annotations are available. We demonstrate how this method, despite its simplicity, compares or even outperforms state-of-the-art unsupervised domain adaptation methods for semantic segmentation on a public OCT dataset. SVDNA can be integrated with just a few lines of code into the augmentation pipeline of any network which is in contrast to many state-of-the-art domain adaptation methods which often need to change the underlying model architecture or train a separate style transfer model. The full code implementation for SVDNA will be made available at https://github.com/ValentinKoch/SVDNA.

Keywords: Style-transfer · Unsupervised domain adaptation · Semantic segmentation

1 Introduction

Diseases in the Human retina are among the leading reasons for reduced vision and blindness globally. Estimates are that currently roughly 170 million people are affected by Age-related Macular Degeneration [1], while Diabetic Retinopathy is recognized as a global epidemic with the numbers increasing at ever higher

---

Supplementary Information The online version contains supplementary material available at https://doi.org/10.1007/978-3-031-16434-7_67.

L. Wang et al. (Eds.): MICCAI 2022, LNCS 13432, pp. 699–708, 2022.
https://doi.org/10.1007/978-3-031-16434-7_67

rates [2]. Optical coherence tomography (OCT) is a powerful technique used in many medical applications to generate real time and non-invasive cross-sectional images of live biological tissues [3]. In the field of Ophthalmology, OCT images help doctors to make therapy decisions and monitor the treatment outcome. As eye diseases are becoming more and more prevalent due to the increased age of populations [4], the need for research in automating diagnosis and aiding doctors is increasing.

Recently, deep learning methods are showing promising results in areas such as disease prediction [5,6], semantic segmentation [7,8] or improving quality [9] of retinal OCT images. Although a lot of progress has been made, challenges remain in applying artificial intelligence methods on real-world OCT data, where image characteristics such as signal-to-noise ratio, brightness, and contrast can vary and cause changes in data distribution, so-called domain shifts. For OCT images, a particular domain shift is introduced from different OCT imaging devices being used, which have different image-quality properties. While for a medical doctor those differences are only a mild annoyance, machine learning models can quickly fail when faced with only small disturbances in the underlying data distribution. One solution is to label images from all possible devices, but as manually labeling images is very costly and needs highly skilled specialists, other methods need to be developed.

Domain adaptation methods offer a solution to the reduced performance of AI algorithms that are caused by the difference in data distribution [10,11]. Domain adaptation has also been used for shifting domains between different device manufacturers for OCT imaging devices. Yang et al. [12] detect lesions in OCT images from different camera devices using an adversarial approach, several recent works use CycleGAN approaches to transfer style between domains [13–15]. In particular, Romo-Bucheli et al. train a CycleGAN and measure the improved performance on a segmentation task, which makes it the most comparable work to ours [13]. While GAN architectures are performant when dealing with domain shifts where the structural difference between the domains is much larger than between OCT camera devices [16], we argue that for domain adaptation between retinal OCT devices these models are unnecessarily complex and can through small changes to image content even be decremental to the performance.

In this work, we present a novel method for unsupervised domain adaptation (UDA) for semantic segmentation of retinal OCT images from multiple devices. The underlying observation motivating our approach is twofold. First, we observe that the noise structure is a key difference between images from different OCT cameras and needs to be specifically modeled. Second, we observe that many UDA methods are often developed for unsupervised domain adaptation between synthetic and real-world data and are not necessarily optimal for retinal OCT images. We therefore develop and evaluate a simple but effective unsupervised domain adaptation method using a singular value decomposition-based noise adaptation approach (SVDNA). We train a semantic segmentation model by using SVDNA and show that the model generalizes to unseen OCT devices and even performs on par with supervised methods trained with manual labels. Further, we show that the SVDNA method is comparable or even outperforms other state-of-the-art UDA methods that often require more complex training schemes or implementation and usage of separate style transfer models. Further, to the best of our knowledge previous work evaluated on private datasets, making comparisons difficult, whereas we benchmark SVDNA on publicly available OCT datasets from multiple devices.

Contributions. We make the following contributions to OCT imaging analysis and biomedical unsupervised domain adaptation:

- We present SVDNA, a minimal method for unsupervised domain adaptation method that transfers style between images by using a singular value decomposition-based noise transfer model.
- We demonstrate that our method performs on par or even outperforms more complex state-of-the-art UDA methods as well as models trained with supervised labels, while considerably reducing training complexity.

2 Proposed Method

First we introduce our Singular Value Decomposition-based noise adaptation method. In the second part, we describe how we trained our segmentation network with the help of the SVDNA restyled images (Fig. 1).

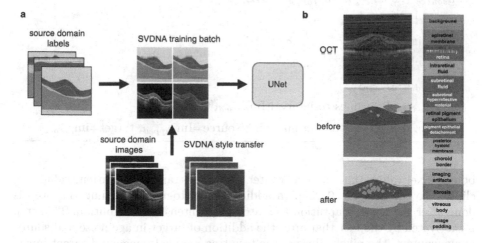

Fig. 1. (a): We train a segmentation network with images from the Spectralis device which are randomly restyled to the style of the Cirrus, Topcon or Bioptigen OCT device using SVDNA, thereby enabling unsupervised adaptation to multiple domains. (b) Comparisons between segmentations before and after SVDNA domain adaptation.

2.1 Singular Value Decomposition-Based Noise Adaptation (SVDNA)

SVDNA achieves style transfer between a source and target domain image by decomposing both images of size $n \times n$ into their respective singular value decompositions $U\Sigma V^T$, where U corresponds to the left singular vectors, V to the right singular vectors and Σ to the singular values. Then, the reconstructed noise from the target domain image is added to the reconstructed content of the source image. Therefore, we use the first k singular values and their corresponding right and left singular vectors from the source image, where the content is encoded, and add the noise that is encoded in the $k+1, ..., n$ singular values and their corresponding vectors from the target image. The resulting image can be expressed as a matrix multiplication as can be seen in Algorithm 1. The parameter k must be chosen by hand but is in our experience not very sensitive to variation. In practice, values between $k = 20$ and $k = 50$ were used to train our network with images of 256×256 pixels. For more details on the feasibility of the used values of k see supplementary figure 2. To account for possible out of

---

Algorithm 1. SVDNA

Let $U\Sigma V^T$ be the singular value decomposition of the respective images im_{source}, $\text{im}_{target} \in \mathbb{R}^{n \times n}$ and k the noise transfer threshold.

$\text{im}_{source} = U_s \Sigma_s V_s^T, \quad \text{im}_{target} = U_t \Sigma_t V_t^T,$

$U_r \leftarrow u_s^1, ..., u_s^k, u_t^{k+1}, ..., u_t^n$

$\Sigma_r \leftarrow \text{diag}(\sigma_s^1, ..., \sigma_s^k, \sigma_t^{k+1}, ..., \sigma_t^n)$

$V_r^T \leftarrow v_s^{1^T}, ..., v_s^{k^T}, v_t^{k+1^T}, ..., v_t^{n^T}$

$\text{Im}_{noised} \leftarrow U_r \Sigma_r V_r^T$

$\text{Im}_{clipped} \leftarrow \text{clip\_values\_to\_interval}(\text{Im}_{noised}, [0, 255])$

$\text{Im}_{restyled\_final} \leftarrow \text{histogram\_matching}(\text{source}=\text{Im}_{clipped}, \text{target}=\text{im}_{target})$

---

bound pixel values that can occur after this noise transfer operation, values are clipped to the interval $[0, 255]$. In addition, a histogram matching [17] step is done after the noise adaptation to match pixel intensity distribution. This step is motivated by the fact that after the addition of target image noise and source image content, the pixel values of the resulting restyled image and target image are still differently distributed. The effect of this step can be seen in the ablation study in table 1 of the supplementary material.

Combined, this does not only achieve a visually good style transfer, but we are also able to match different noise-related metrics of the target domain well as seen in Fig. 2. We evaluate the noise transfer from our private source domain dataset, where images were taken with a Spectralis device, on three different datasets: Two datasets from the RETOUCH challenge [18][1] who use Cirrus and Topcon devices as well as a dataset with images taken with a Bioptigen device [19].[2]

2.2 Training the Segmentation Network with SVDNA

SVDNA can be used to train any segmentation network and is applied before augmenting the training images. When loading an image, either no style transfer (probability $p = 1/n$), or an SVDNA style transfer to a randomly chosen target domain ($p = 1 - 1/n$) is applied, where n is the total number of domains, including the source domain. When a target domain is chosen, one image is randomly selected and used as a style target for the input image. When the source domain is chosen, no style transfer is applied. To maximize style variability, the hyperparameter k, determining the amount of noise to be transferred, is randomly sampled for each style transfer individually within range [20, 50]. As the content of the source image is combined with the style of the target image, the annotated labels of the source dataset can be used as ground truth to train the network.

3 Results

We compare our SVDNA against state-of-the-art domain adaptation approaches that we trained with the same segmentation model architecture, data processing pipeline, and augmentations. As the baseline, we use a network without any domain adaptation, which we compare to Fourier Domain Adaptation (FDA) [21], Confidence regularized self-training (CRST) [22], the CycleGAN approach [13] and an SVDNA trained model. For each method, the main hyperparameters were individually optimized to include each models best possible results in the comparison. Training details of all methods can be seen in the supplementary material.

3.1 Data

Our source domain training set consists of 462 OCT scans of the macula, taken with a Spectralis device (Spectralis; Heidelberg Engineering GmbH, Heidelberg, Germany) from different patients suffering from age-related macular degeneration. It is a private dataset annotated by three retinal experts of the Department of Ophthalmology, Ludwig-Maximilians-University, Munich (B.A., J.S. and M.H.), where each pixel of an OCT scan is labeled with one of 14 classes following the Consensus Nomenclature for Reporting Neovascular Age-Related Macular Degeneration Data of the AAO (American Academy of Ophthalmology) [23]: Intraretinal Fluid, Subretinal Fluid, Pigment Epithelium Detachments, Fibrosis,

---

[1] Access can be requested at https://retouch.grand-challenge.org/.
[2] https://www.kaggle.com/paultimothymooney/farsiu-2014.

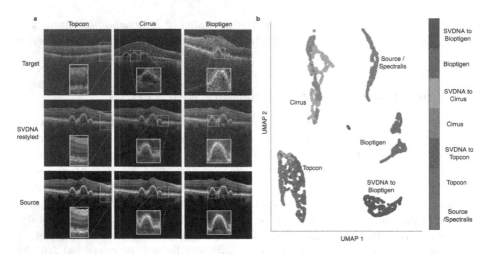

Fig. 2. (a): Sample SVDNA restyling to Topcon, Cirrus, and the Bioptigen device from a single source domain image (bottom row) for $k = 30$. (b): Noise statistics UMAP [20] between datasets of different domains and SVDNA adapted datasets.

Epiretinal Membrane, Posterior Hyaloid Membrane, Subretinal Hyper Reflective Material, Neurosensory Retina, Choroid layers, Choroid Border, Vitreous and Subhyaloid Space, Retinal Pigment Epithelium, imaging artifacts, image padding. For the quantitative evaluation, the RETOUCH challenge dataset is used, where images are taken from the Topcon (2688 images) and Cirrus (3072 images) device and are annotated with Subretinal Fluid, Intraretinal Fluid, Pigment Epithelium Detachments. The OCT images annotations were not used in training any algorithms but only for evaluating performance.

3.2 Evaluation

For all experiments a Unet++ [24] with a ResNet18 [25] encoder is used as the segmentation model. In Fig. 2a, SVDNA is applied to images of three different domains, showing how one image can be fitted to the style characteristics of different target domain images. Figure 2b shows a noise representation UMAP [20] embedding. For the embedding, three different noise statistics (signal-to-noise ratio [26], noise variance estimator [27], and wavelet noise standard deviation estimator [28]) are used. After SVDNA, the noise embeddings of the restyled Spectralis images align closely with those of the target domains Topcon and Cirrus. Only with Bioptigen, a domain with a very high noise level, there is still a gap between the respective embeddings. Additionally, we compare SVDNA against state-of-the-art domain adaptation approaches for the task of semantic segmentation on two datasets consisting of images of a Topcon or Cirrus device respectively in Fig. 3. As the baseline, a network without any domain adaptation is used, which is compared to Fourier Domain Adaptation (FDA) [21], Confidence regularized self-training (CRST) [22], the CycleGAN approach of

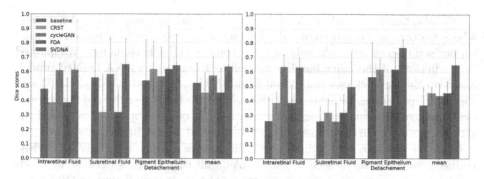

Fig. 3. 5-fold cross-validation comparison of different state-of-the-art methods, the SVDNA method, and the baseline network on the RETOUCH challenge datasets Cirrus (left) and Topcon (right). The SVDNA trained model outperforms the baseline and compares or outperforms all other tried methods across all datasets and classes.

Romo-Bucheli et al. [13] as well as our SVDNA trained model. For each method, the individual hyperparameter were optimized to include each models best possible results in the comparison. For further training details of all methods, we refer to the supplementary material. The evaluation is done on a 5-fold cross-validation over both datasets, using 80% of the target domain images as style targets for SVDNA or the Fourier Domain Adaptation or as training images for Self-Training and evaluate on the 20% remaining images and iterate this until the algorithm has been evaluated on all data samples. The CycleGAN method was, due to its complicated proposed evaluation scheme, trained on all of the images. As done in the RETOUCH challenge, we measure the performance with the dice score. The largest performance gain over the baseline can be seen for images from the Topcon device, where the SVDNA model consistently outperformed all other methods segmenting subretinal fluid and PED and is on par with the CycleGAN method for intraretinal fluid. When considering the mean performance difference across all classes, the SVDNA model performs better than all other methods.

Table 1. SVDNA and baseline model compared to the best supervised trained models from 8 teams in the RETOUCH challenge [18] on a non-public testset of Topcon (left) and Cirrus (right).

Name	SRF	IRF	PED	Mean	Rank	Name	SRF	IRF	PED	Mean	Rank
SFU [29]	0.80	0.72	0.74	0.75	1	SFU [29]	0.72	0.83	0.73	0.76	1
SVDNA	0.80	0.61	0.72	0.710	2	SVDNA	0.66	0.61	0.74	0.67	7
Baseline	0.42	0.17	0.66	0.42	10	Baseline	0.42	0.39	0.71	0.51	10

We also benchmark SVDNA on the separate hold-off non-public test datasets, where we compare our domain adaptation method to results achieved by fully supervised trained networks submitted in the RETOUCH challenge. We handed in predictions of the naive baseline as well as from our SVDNA trained model, again on the three classes Subretinal Fluid (SRF), Intraretinal Fluid (IRF) and Pigment Epithelium Detachments (PED). With SVDNA we achieved the second-best result of 10 submitted segmentation methods on the Topcon dataset and the sixth-best on the Cirrus dataset. SVDNA achieved a large improvement over the baseline, as well as a very competitive performance compared to fully supervised trained models as can be seen in Table 1. A qualitative analysis between methods can be seen in supplementary figure 1, where the three retinal experts (B.A., J.S. and M.H.) annotated all 14 classes on images from the two domains Topcon and Cirrus, as well as on the dataset of the manufacturer Bioptigen. There, accurate segmentations of the SVDNA model can be seen, whereas other methods often struggle to segment correctly.

4   Discussions and Limitations

We demonstrate that the minimal SVDNA method outperforms or performs on par with state-of-the-art UDA methods and allows for accurate cross-device segmentation of OCT Images without using any additional labeled data. The other main benefit of the SVDNA method is that it integrates directly to the regular training pipeline of semantic segmentation networks and does not need any modifications to the models architecture or training of a separate style transfer model as done in the CycleGAN approach [13], which can influence the feasibility of applying a method in practice. One possible limitation of the SVDNA method could be that it does not necessarily denoise images well. This would mean that domain adaptation from Spectralis, a less noisy domain, to Topcon, Cirrus, or Bioptigen works well but the opposite direction might not be as successful. One possible solution would then be to do test time SVDNA style transfer, meaning that when predicting low noise images on a high noise image trained model, one could add noise to the images before feeding it into the model, similar to the idea used by the CycleGAN approach where they restyle images from the target to the source domain at test time. The other benchmarked state-of-the-art domain adaptation methods did not consistently perform well for all devices. In our experiments with the CycleGAN model, we sometimes found it can slightly alter the content of the image or sometimes even fail completely to produce images similar to the input OCT image. As OCT biomarkers such as intraretinal cysts and PEDs are often represented by ambiguous and hard to detect textual features, even the slightest distortion to the morphology of the tissue can cause incorrect segmentation results, for examples of content distortions achieved by an optimized CycleGAN see supplementary figure 4. It is worth noting that in other domains such as on natural images, small context distortions might have a smaller effect on the segmentation performance. The features distinguish objects such as cars, houses, and trees or are considerably different from those representing OCT biomarkers. The FDA method [21] does not directly distort the content of the source image, however, we were not able to improve meaningfully over the baseline. Depending on the hyperparameter settings, either little to no style transfer was achieved for small beta values or image distorting artifacts got introduced into images for higher beta values, as can be seen in supplementary figure 3. Finally using a self-training-based domain adaptation method did not work well in our experiments which might be due to the limited size of the datasets.

Acknowledgements. The present contribution is supported by the Helmholtz Association under the joint research school "Munich School for Data Science - MUDS". H.S. and F.J.T. acknowledge support by the BMBF (grant number: 031L0210A) and by the Helmholtz Association's Initiative and Networking Fund through Helmholtz AI (grant number: ZT-I-PF-5-01). We want to thank Dr. Carsten Marr for his support and Dr. Hrvoje Bogunović for his help in evaluating our results on the non-public testset.

References

1. Pennington, K.L., DeAngelis, M.M.: Epidemiology of age-related macular degeneration (AMD): associations with cardiovascular disease phenotypes and lipid factors. Eye Vis. (Lond.) **3**, 34 (2016)
2. Lee, R., Wong, T.Y., Sabanayagam, C.: Epidemiology of diabetic retinopathy, diabetic macular edema and related vision loss. Eye Vis. (Lond.) **2**, 17 (2015)
3. Al-Mujaini, A., Wali, U.K., Azeem, S.: Optical coherence tomography: clinical applications in medical practice. Oman Med. J. **28**(2), 86–91 (2013)
4. Fricke, T.R., et al.: Global prevalence of presbyopia and vision impairment from uncorrected presbyopia: systematic review, meta-analysis, and modelling. Ophthalmology **125**(10), 1492–1499 (2018)
5. Banerjee, I., et al.: Prediction of age-related macular degeneration disease using a sequential deep learning approach on longitudinal SD-OCT imaging biomarkers. Sci. Rep. **10**(1), 15434 (2020)
6. Holmberg, O.G., et al.: Self-supervised retinal thickness prediction enables deep learning from unlabelled data to boost classification of diabetic retinopathy. Nat. Mach. Intell. **2**(11), 719–726 (2020)
7. Borkovkina, S., Camino, A., Janpongsri, W., Sarunic, M.V., Jian, Y.: Real-time retinal layer segmentation of OCT volumes with GPU accelerated inferencing using a compressed, low-latency neural network. Biomed. Opt. Express **11**(7), 3968–3984 (2020)
8. Hassan, B., et al.: Deep learning based joint segmentation and characterization of multi-class retinal fluid lesions on OCT scans for clinical use in anti-VEGF therapy. Comput. Biol. Med. **136**, 104727 (2021)
9. Cheong, H., et al.: OCT-GAN: single step shadow and noise removal from optical coherence tomography images of the human optic nerve head. Biomed. Opt. Express **12**(3), 1482–1498 (2021)
10. Guan, H., Liu, M.: Domain adaptation for medical image analysis: a survey. IEEE Trans. Biomed. Eng. **69**, 1173–1185 (2021)
11. Patel, V.M., Gopalan, R., Li, R., Chellappa, R.: Visual domain adaptation: a survey of recent advances. IEEE Signal Process. Mag. **32**(3), 53–69 (2015)

12. Yang, S., et al.: Unsupervised domain adaptation for cross-device OCT lesion detection via learning adaptive features. In: 2020 IEEE 17th International Symposium on Biomedical Imaging (ISBI), pp. 1570–1573 (2020)
13. Romo-Bucheli, D., et al.: Reducing image variability across OCT devices with unsupervised unpaired learning for improved segmentation of retina. Biomed. Opt. Express **11**(1), 346–363 (2020)
14. Zhang, T., et al.: Noise adaptation generative adversarial network for medical image analysis. IEEE Trans. Med. Imaging **39**(4), 1149–1159 (2020)
15. Manakov, I., Rohm, M., Kern, C., Schworm, B., Kortuem, K., Tresp, V.: Noise as domain shift: denoising medical images by unpaired image translation. In: Wang, Q., et al. (eds.) DART/MIL3ID -2019. LNCS, vol. 11795, pp. 3–10. Springer, Cham (2019). https://doi.org/10.1007/978-3-030-33391-1_1
16. Yang, Y., Lao, D., Sundaramoorthi, G., Soatto, S.: Phase consistent ecological domain adaptation. In: Proceedings of the IEEE/CVF Conference on Computer Vision and Pattern Recognition, pp. 9011–9020 (2020)
17. Gonzalez, R.C., Woods, R.E., Masters, B.R.: Digital image processing. J. Biomed. Opt. **14**(2), 029901 (2009)
18. Bogunović, H., et al.: RETOUCH: the retinal OCT fluid detection and segmentation benchmark and challenge. IEEE Trans. Med. Imaging **38**(8), 1858–1874 (2019)
19. Farsiu, S., et al.: Quantitative classification of eyes with and without intermediate age-related macular degeneration using optical coherence tomography. Ophthalmology **121**(1), 162–172 (2014)
20. McInnes, L., Healy, J., Melville, J.: UMAP: uniform manifold approximation and projection for dimension reduction (2020)
21. Yang, Y., Soatto, S.: FDA: Fourier domain adaptation for semantic segmentation. In: Proceedings of the IEEE/CVF Conference on Computer Vision and Pattern Recognition, pp. 4085–4095 (2020)
22. Zou, Y., et al.: Confidence regularized self-training. In: ICCV (2019)
23. Spaide, R.F., et al.: Consensus nomenclature for reporting neovascular age-related macular degeneration data: consensus on neovascular age-related macular degeneration nomenclature study group. Ophthalmology **127**(5), 616–636 (2020). https://doi.org/10.1016/j.ophtha.2019.11.004. ISSN 0161-6420
24. Zhou, Z., Siddiquee, M.M.R., Tajbakhsh, N., Liang, J.: UNet++: redesigning skip connections to exploit multiscale features in image segmentation. IEEE Trans. Med. Imaging **39**(6), 1856–1867 (2020)
25. He, K., Zhang, X., Ren, S., Sun, J.: Deep residual learning for image recognition. In: Proceedings of the IEEE Conference on Computer Vision and Pattern Recognition, pp. 770–778 (2016)
26. Janesick, J.R.: DN to [lambda]: Press Monographs. In: SPIE (2007). ISBN 9780819467225
27. Immerkaer, J.: Fast noise variance estimation. Comput. Vis. Image Underst. **64**(2), 300–302 (1996)
28. Donoho, D.L., Johnstone, I.M.: Ideal spatial adaptation by wavelet shrinkage. Biometrika **81**(3), 425–455 (1994)
29. Lu, D., et al.: Deep-learning based multiclass retinal fluid segmentation and detection in optical coherence tomography images using a fully convolutional neural network. Med. Image Anal. **54**, 100–110 (2019). https://doi.org/10.1016/j.media.2019.02.011. ISSN 1361-8415

Long-Tailed Multi-label Retinal Diseases Recognition via Relational Learning and Knowledge Distillation

Qian Zhou, Hua Zou$^{(\boxtimes)}$, and Zhongyuan Wang

Wuhan University, Wuhan, China
zouhua@whu.edu.cn

Abstract. More and more people are suffering from ocular diseases, which may cause blindness if not treated promptly. However, it is not easy to diagnose these diseases for the barely visible clinical symptoms. Even though some computer-aided approaches have been developed to help ophthalmologists make an accurate diagnosis, there still exist some challenges to be solved. For example, one patient may suffer from more than one retinal disease and these diseases often exhibit a long-tailed distribution, making it difficult to be automatically classified. In this work, we propose a novel framework that utilizes the correlations among these diseases in a knowledge distillation manner. Specifically, we apply the correlations from three main aspects (*i.e.*, multi-task relation, feature relation, and pathological region relation) to recognize diseases more exactly. Firstly, we take diabetic retinopathy (DR) lesion segmentation and severity grading as the downstream tasks to train the network backbone for the findings that segmentation may improve the classification. Secondly, the long-tailed dataset is divided into several subsets to train multiple teacher networks according to semantic feature relation, which can help reduce the label co-occurrence and class imbalance. Thirdly, an improved attention mechanism is adopted to explore relations among pathological regions. Finally, a class-balanced distillation loss is introduced to distill the multiple teacher models into a student model. Extensive experiments are conducted to validate the superiority of our proposed method. The results have demonstrated that we achieve state-of-the-art performance on the publicly available datasets. Code will be available at: https://github.com/liyiersan/RLKD.

Keywords: Retinal disease recognition · Long-tailed classification · Knowledge distillation

1 Introduction

Over the past decades, ocular diseases have become one of the main causes of blindness [1]. It is of great importance to detect and treat ocular diseases

---

Supplementary Information The online version contains supplementary material available at https://doi.org/10.1007/978-3-031-16434-7_68.

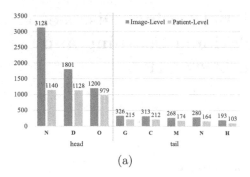
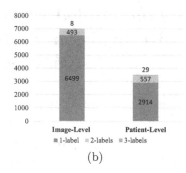

(a)   (b)

Fig. 1. Statistics for the ODIR-5K [23] dataset. (a) is the number of eight diseases; (b) is the number of multi-label images/patients. Overall, the whole dataset exhibits a long-tailed distribution and an image may contain multiple labels.

timely. However, the coexistence of multiple symptoms makes accurate diagnosis difficult. As shown in Fig. 1, in the real world, one patient may suffer from more than one retinal disease and these diseases follow a long-tailed distribution.

Many efforts have been done for computed-aided retinal diseases recognition, most of them mainly focus on a specific disease, especially on the DR [2–4]. Nevertheless, multi-label retinal diseases diagnosis under long-tailed distribution remains a big challenge. Some researchers mainly concentrate on multi-label classification [5,11] while the long-tailed distribution is not well considered. [11] introduces the task of transferring knowledge from single-disease diagnosis to enhance multi-disease diagnosis. Others aim to address the long-tailed recognition [6,12,13]. [6] leverages knowledge distillation to enhance feature representations for long-tailed recognition. Different from long-tailed multi-label recognition of natural images, there are strong associations among retinal diseases. For example, if the cataract is not treated immediately, it may cause the accumulation of aqueous humor and increase the intraocular pressure, which can lead to glaucoma [7]. However, most methods ignore the correlations among diseases. Even if some methods like [9,16] leverage the prior knowledge or relations among diseases, they require experts with extensive clinical experience to pre-process the data such as dividing the dataset into related subsets manually.

In this paper, we propose a new framework that utilizes the relations among diseases for long-tailed multi-label retinal diseases classification. In particular, the correlations are considered from three main aspects. Firstly, inspired by the finding that the lesion segmentation may contribute to the diagnosis of retinal diseases [14], we conduct two downstream tasks simultaneously to pre-train the network backbone. Please note that our work is unique to [11]. We design two parallel branches for the two downstream tasks, while in [11] the tasks are carried out in a sequential transfer learning manner. Secondly, the original long-tailed dataset is automatically divided into several relational subsets and we train teacher models on them. This is quite different from [16], in which the relational subsets are obtained manually, thus requiring experts to complete. Thirdly, we introduce an improved spatial attention mechanism to explore correlations of

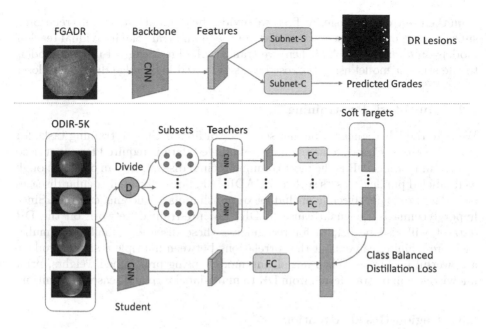

Fig. 2. Pipeline of the proposed framework. Above the line is the multi-task pre-trained model, the Subnet-S is designed for lesions segmentation and the Subset-C is used for severity grading. Below the line is the target model for retinal diseases recognition. Teacher models and student models are initialized with the pre-trained weights.

pathological areas. Finally, the knowledge of teacher models will be transferred into a unified student model with our proposed class-balanced distillation loss.

The main contributions of this work can be summarized as follows: (1) We develop a novel framework that fully leverages the relations among diseases from three aspects. (2) A novel class-balanced distillation loss is adopted to distill the multiple teacher models trained on subsets into a student model. (3) Extensive experiments are conducted to prove the effectiveness of our method. We also visualize the experimental results and analyze the interpretability of our method.

2   Method

2.1   Framework Overview

As shown in Fig. 2, our framework contains two stages, named multi-task pre-training and multi-label fine-tuning. When pre-training, we take the DR lesion segmentation and DR severity grading as the downstream tasks and design two branches respectively. The two parallel branches share the same bottom network, followed by another subnet, *i.e.*, 'Subnet-S' for segmentation and 'Subnet-C' for grading. We use ResNet-50 [15] as the bottom network and take U-net [19] for segmentation, while the classification network is a fully connected (FC) layer.

Regarding the long-tailed multi-label classification at the fine-tuning stage, the Subnet-S is dropped and we initialize the network with the weights obtained from the pre-training stage. At first, we divide the original dataset into relational subsets using our proposed automated approach and train the individual teacher models on each subset. And then, we transfer the knowledge of teacher models to the student model using proposed class-balanced knowledge distillation loss.

2.2 Multi-task Pre-training

We take the DR segmentation and severity grading as the pre-training tasks for several reasons. Firstly, a large amount of labeled data is required for supervised pre-training. Since DR is the most common retinal disease, we can obtain enough well-labeled public datasets such as FGADR [10]. Secondly, many ocular diseases are related to hyperglycemia, including xerophthalmia, glaucoma, cataract. Since hyperglycemia is the main cause of DR, the pre-trained network on the DR dataset will also be helpful for recognizing these diseases. Finally, the multi-task pre-training can exploit the correlations between multiple tasks to produce a powerful backbone. When initializing models using pre-trained weights, prior knowledge will be transferred from DR to multi-label retinal diseases recognition.

2.3 Region-Based Attention

Attention mechanisms like CBAM [20] can greatly improve performance. However, the localization ability of important regions is enabled by the global average/max pooling operation, which is not trainable and may fail to localize some valuable regions. In this work, the trainable convolutional layer is combined with the non-parameter pooling layer. To be specific, for the input features F, we use the pooling layer and the 1×1 convolution layer to obtain the global representation of features and then feed them into the convolutional layer with the sigmoid activation to calculate the weight map. Finally, we multiply the input features with the map. In short, the spatial attention weights is computed as:

$$M_s(F) = \sigma(f^{7 \times 7}([AvgPool(F), f^{1 \times 1}(F), MaxPool(F)])) \qquad (1)$$

where σ denotes the sigmoid function, $f^{7 \times 7}$ and $f^{1 \times 1}$ represent a convolution operation with the filter size of 7×7 and 1×1, $AvgPool$ and $MaxPool$ mean average pooling operation and max pooling operation on channel respectively. See supplementary material for more detailed structure of the region-based attention.

2.4 Relational Subsets Generation

There exist strong relations among ocular diseases, many diseases share similar semantic features. For example, DR and hypertension can both lead to abnormal retinal blood vessels. We propose an automated algorithm to group the diseases which share similar semantics into the same subset. And then we train teacher models on every subset so that both common and unique features can be learned. Specifically, We use the ResNet-50 [15] pre-trained on ImageNet as the feature extractor, and then we perform principal component analysis (PCA) to project the features of each category to the shared latent space. Finally, we take the K-Means [8] algorithm to cluster each sample and divide diseases into subsets. Since label 'N' (normal) contains no diseases and label 'O' (other) contains more than one disease, we group 'N' and 'O' into one subset. The final three subsets are {D, AMD, H, M}, {G, C}, {N, O}, respectively. The visualization results of features are shown in supplementary material.

When training teacher models on relational subsets, both label co-occurrence and class imbalance can be alleviated. For example, for a retinal image x with label $y_1 = 1$ and $y_2 = 1$, if y_1 and y_2 are divided into two different subsets, then x is no longer a multi-label image. Moreover, the class imbalance ratio of every subset (defined as the ratio between the largest and the smallest number of classes: $\rho = \frac{N_{max}}{N_{min}}$) is less or equal than the original long-tailed dataset.

2.5 Knowledge Distillation

After obtaining all teacher models, we can distill them into a uniform student model. Specifically, for the i-th image x_i, let z_i and $\hat{z}_i$ be the output logits of the teacher model and student model, the soft targets q_i and $\hat{q}_i$ are computed as:

$$q_i = \frac{exp(z_i/T)}{\sum exp(z_i/T)}, \quad \hat{q}_i = \frac{exp(\hat{z}_i/T)}{\sum exp(\hat{z}_i/T)} \tag{2}$$

where T is set to 5 as distillation temperature. The distillation loss of x_i is:

$$L_{KD_i} = KL(\hat{q}_i||q_i) = \hat{q}_i log\frac{\hat{q}_i}{q_i} \tag{3}$$

Now we need to integrate L_{KD_i} into a unified loss. The simplest way is to add them together, but this may lead to some problems caused by label co-occurrence. Regarding a multi-label image x with label $y_1 = 1$ and $y_2 = 1$, if y_1 and y_2 are divided into two different subsets, then x will be sampled twice to train two different teacher models. Since most multi-label images belong to the head classes, the head categories will be over-sampled, exacerbating class imbalance. To solve this problem, we define a class-balanced distillation loss. For class-balanced sampling strategy without label co-occurrence, all classes are assigned with an equal sampling probability $p = \frac{1}{C}$, where C is the number of classes. For each sample in the j-th class, they have the same probability $p_j = \frac{1}{N_j}$, where N_j is the number of the j-th class samples. Therefore, the instance-level sampling probability of the i-th image belongs to the j-th class is $p_i^j = \frac{1}{C}\frac{1}{N_j}$. Considering the multi-label sample, the instance-level sampling probability becomes the sum of each positive class j it contains: $p_i^A = \frac{1}{C}\sum_{j=0}^{C} \frac{1}{N_j}|x_i \in class_j$. Then, we define a class-balanced weight for each sample denoted as $w_i^j = \frac{p_i^j}{p_i^A}$. Finally, the class-balanced distillation loss is given as:

$$L_{KD} = \sum_{j}^{C}\sum_{i}^{N_i} KL(\hat{q}_i^j||q_i^j) \cdot w_i^j = \sum_{j}^{C}\sum_{i}^{N_i} \hat{q}_i^j log\frac{\hat{q}_i^j}{q_i^j} \cdot w_i^j \tag{4}$$

The final loss to train student model on the whole long-tailed dataset is:

$$L = L_{BCE} + \alpha L_{KD} \tag{5}$$

where L_{BCE} is the binary cross-entropy loss between the predicted labels of the student model and the ground-truth, α is a hyper-parameter and set to 1.

2.6 Implementation Details

To validate the effectiveness of the proposed method, we have conducted extensive experiments implemented with Pytorch and 4×RTX 3090 GPUs. The input color fundus images are resized to 512×512. We randomly crop 448×448 patches for training. For testing, center cropping of 448×448 patches is performed instead. The Adam optimizer is adopted with an initial learning rate of 0.001 and $\beta_1 = 0.9$, $\beta_2 = 0.99$. The mini-batch size is set to 64. Besides, we randomly split all samples to 80% for training and 20% for testing. All experiments are conducted with 5-fold cross-validation to produce more solid results.

3 Experiments

3.1 Datasets and Evaluation Metrics

FGADR [10] is a fine-grained annotated DR dataset containing 1,842 images with both pixel-level lesion annotations and image-level grading labels. Following [11], to convert pixel-level labels to image-level labels, if the ground-truth mask of a category has annotated spots, the corresponding image-level label is marked as positive, and negative otherwise. ODIR-5K [23] consists of 7000 images with patient-level annotations and image-level diagnostic keywords. The ocular diseases include normal (N), diabetes (D), glaucoma (G), cataract (C), age-related macular degeneration (AMD), hypertension (H), myopia (M), and other diseases (O). We relabel the ODIR-5K [23] to obtain image-level annotations according to the image-level diagnostic keywords. We use Cohen's kappa coefficient, F_1 score, and area under the receiver operating curve (AUC) as the metrics for evaluation on multi-label retinal diseases recognition.

3.2 Quantitative Performance

We have compared the results on ODIR-5K [23] dataset with other approaches. The compared methods include state-of-the-art methods which aim to recognize multi-label retinal diseases like CCT-Net [11], SCFKD [5], and other algorithms considering long-tailed classification such as Instance-Balanced Sampling, Class-Balanced Sampling, Focal Loss [17], RSKD [16], and Distribution-Balanced Loss [18]. When compared with [16], we only re-implement the "Multiple Weighted Knowledge Distillation" strategy because of the unavailable manual subsets division. To fairly compared with CCT-Net [11], we also take Dense-121 [21] as backbone following the setting in CCT-Net [11].

Table 1. Long-tailed multi-label retinal diseases classification results on ODIR-5K [23].

Backbone	Methods	Kappa	F1	AUC
ResNet-50 [15]	SCFKD [5]	0.635 ± 0.009	0.911 ± 0.007	0.927 ± 0.014
	IB Sampling	0.553 ± 0.010	0.974 ± 0.009	0.887 ± 0.012
	CB Sampling	0.601 ± 0.013	0.886 ± 0.011	0.920 ± 0.015
	Focal Loss [17]	0.625 ± 0.011	0.895 ± 0.009	0.930 ± 0.012
	RSKD [16]	0.660 ± 0.014	0.920 ± 0.013	0.935 ± 0.014
	DB Loss [18]	0.673 ± 0.008	0.930 ± 0.007	0.940 ± 0.009
	Ours	$\mathbf{0.712 \pm 0.011}$	$\mathbf{0.935 \pm 0.013}$	$\mathbf{0.944 \pm 0.012}$
DenseNet-121 [21]	CCT-Net [11]	0.749 ± 0.007	0.952 ± 0.011	0.960 ± 0.013
	Ours	0.744 ± 0.010	0.960 ± 0.013	0.964 ± 0.010
	Ours + Focal Loss [17]	$\mathbf{0.767 \pm 0.012}$	$\mathbf{0.965 \pm 0.008}$	$\mathbf{0.970 \pm 0.014}$

From Table 1, we can see that our proposed framework achieves the best performance when using ResNet-50 [15] as the backbone. Specifically, we have improved Distribution-Balanced Loss [18] and shown a sharp rise compared to Instance-Balanced Sampling (IB Sampling). When taking DenseNet-121 [21] as our backbone, the performance is improved greatly, and we achieve competitive performance to CCT-Net [11]. We attribute the big gap between ResNet-50 [15] and DenseNet-121 [21] to the dense connections that are more suitable to transfer the prior knowledge from DR to other diseases. What's more, our framework can be easily integrated with other methods addressing the long-tailed classification to further improve the performance. As shown in Table 1, our method are further improved when combined with Focal Loss [17].

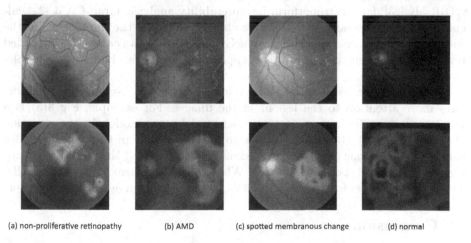

(a) non-proliferative retinopathy   (b) AMD   (c) spotted membranous change   (d) normal

Fig. 3. Class activation maps (CAM) of four typical diseases. The first row is the original image, the second row is the heat map. The circled areas in the first row are lesions.

3.3 Ablation Study

Effectiveness of Each Component. To investigate the contribution of each component, we design a series of ablation experiments. As shown in Table 2, the proposed framework mainly benefits from the multi-task pre-training and relational subsets division while the region-based attention module improves the performance slightly. Multi-task pre-training transfer DR-related prior knowledge to the multi-label diseases recognition, meanwhile, the relational subset division helps reduce the label co-occurrence and class imbalance. When combining the three modules, we achieve the best performance on multi-label retinal diseases recognition. In addition, when adopting the CBAM [20] attention mechanism, the performance will be dropped. It demonstrates the superiority of our proposed region-based attention.

Table 2. Ablation study results on ODIR-5K [23]. We compare our proposed modules with the original ResNet-50 [15] backbone.

Model	Kappa	F1	AUC
ResNet-50 [15]	0.553 ± 0.010	0.974 ± 0.009	0.887 ± 0.012
ResNet-50 [15] + attentions	0.579 ± 0.012	0.890 ± 0.011	0.915 ± 0.010
ResNet-50 [15] + pre-training	0.650 ± 0.014	0.922 ± 0.013	0.923 ± 0.012
ResNet-50 [15] + subsets	0.652 ± 0.011	0.915 ± 0.015	0.920 ± 0.015
ResNet-50 [15] + CBAM [20] + others	0.697 ± 0.013	0.930 ± 0.015	0.935 ± 0.017
ResNet-50 [15] + all	$\mathbf{0.712 \pm 0.011}$	$\mathbf{0.935 \pm 0.013}$	$\mathbf{0.944 \pm 0.012}$

Visualization Analysis. We use Grad-CAM [22] to visualize the results on ODIR-5K [23] dataset to perform interpretability analysis. Grad-CAM [22] calculates gradients concerning a specific class to calculate the importance of the spatial locations in each layer. Using the Grad-CAM [22], we can see the attended regions clearly from the output heat map. More results can be found in supplementary material.

From the generated heat map shown in Fig. 3, we can observe that the model pays more attention to the lesions in the images. For example, Fig. 3(a) is a DR image, most lesions are correctly detected by our model. In the situation of AMD (Fig. 3(b)), our model is able to observe lesions in the macula. As for spotted membranous change (classified into other diseases) shown in (Fig. 3(c)), the scattered small spots are detected. When taking is a normal image (Fig. 3(d)) as input, our model focuses on the whole image to make a accurate prediction.

4 Conclusion

In this paper, we present a new framework for multi-label retinal diseases recognition on the long-tailed datasets. We take full advantage of medical prior knowledge from three main aspects, that is multi-task relation, pathological feature relation, and lesion region relation. We first combine the segmentation and classification into a unified network for pre-training the backbone. Meanwhile, the original dataset is automatically divided into relational subsets. We train teacher models with a region-based mechanism on these subsets to reduce the label co-occurrence and class imbalance. Finally, all teacher models are transferred to a student model with a class-balanced distillation loss. Extensive experiments have proved the effectiveness and superiority of our method.

Acknowledgements. This work is supported by Science and Technology Cooperation Project of The Xinjiang Production and Construction Corps (No. 2019BC008, 2017DB004).

References

1. Rahmani, B., et al.: The cause-specific prevalence of visual impairment in an urban population: the Baltimore Eye Survey. Ophthalmology **103**(11), 1721–1726 (1996)
2. Abramoff, M.D., Fort, P.E., Han, I.C., Jayasundera, K.T., Sohn, E.H., Gardner, T.W.: Approach for a clinically useful comprehensive classification of vascular and neural aspects of diabetic retinal disease. Invest. Ophthal. Visual Sci. **59**(1), 519–527 (2018)
3. Li, X., Jia, M., Islam, M.T., Yu, L., Xing, L.: Self-supervised feature learning via exploiting multi-modal data for retinal disease diagnosis. IEEE Trans. Med. Imaging **39**(12), 4023–4033 (2020)
4. Li, X., et al.: Rotation-oriented collaborative self-supervised learning for retinal disease diagnosis. IEEE Trans. Med. Imaging **40**(9), 2284–2294 (2021)
5. He, J., Li, C., Ye, J., Qiao, Y., Gu, L.: Self-speculation of clinical features based on knowledge distillation for accurate ocular disease classification. Biomed. Signal Process. Control **67**, 102491 (2021)
6. Iscen, A., Araujo, A., Gong, B., Schmid, C.: Class-balanced distillation for long-tailed visual recognition. arXiv preprint arXiv:2104.05279 (2021)
7. Weinreb, R.N., Aung, T., Medeiros, F.A.: The pathophysiology and treatment of glaucoma: a review. JAMA **311**(18), 1901–1911 (2014)
8. Hartigan, J.A., Wong, M.A.: Algorithm AS 136: K-means clustering algorithm. J. Royal Stat. Soc. Ser. C (Appl. Stat.) **28**(1), 100–108 (1979)
9. Ju, L., Wang, X., Yu, Z., Wang, L., Zhao, X., Ge, Z.: Long-tailed multi-label retinal diseases recognition using hierarchical information and hybrid knowledge distillation. arXiv preprint arXiv:2111.08913 (2021)
10. Zhou, Y., Wang, B., Huang, L., Cui, S., Shao, L.: A benchmark for studying diabetic retinopathy: segmentation, grading, and transferability. IEEE Trans. Med. Imaging **40**(3), 818–828 (2020)
11. Zhou, Y., Huang, L., Zhou, T., Shao, L.: CCT-Net: category-invariant cross-domain transfer for medical single-to-multiple disease diagnosis. In: Proceedings of the IEEE/CVF International Conference on Computer Vision, pp. 8260–8270 (2021)
12. Sharma, S., Yu, N., Fritz, M., Schiele, B.: Long-tailed recognition using class-balanced experts. In: Akata, Z., Geiger, A., Sattler, T. (eds.) DAGM GCPR 2020. LNCS, vol. 12544, pp. 86–100. Springer, Cham (2021). https://doi.org/10.1007/978-3-030-71278-5_7

13. Xiang, L., Ding, G., Han, J.: Learning from multiple experts: self-paced knowledge distillation for long-tailed classification. In: Vedaldi, A., Bischof, H., Brox, T., Frahm, J.-M. (eds.) ECCV 2020. LNCS, vol. 12350, pp. 247–263. Springer, Cham (2020). https://doi.org/10.1007/978-3-030-58558-7_15

14. Foo, A., Hsu, W., Lee, M.L., Lim, G., Wong, T.Y.: Multi-task learning for diabetic retinopathy grading and lesion segmentation. In: Proceedings of the AAAI Conference on Artificial Intelligence, pp. 13267–13272 (2020)

15. He, K., Zhang, X., Ren, S., Sun, J.: Deep residual learning for image recognition. In: Proceedings of the IEEE Conference on Computer Vision and Pattern Recognition, pp. 770–778 (2016)

16. Ju, L., et al.: Relational subsets knowledge distillation for long-tailed retinal diseases recognition. In: de Bruijne, M., et al. (eds.) MICCAI 2021. LNCS, vol. 12908, pp. 3–12. Springer, Cham (2021). https://doi.org/10.1007/978-3-030-87237-3_1

17. Lin, T. Y., Goyal, P., Girshick, R., He, K., Dollár, P.: Focal loss for dense object detection. In: Proceedings of the IEEE International Conference on Computer Vision, pp. 2980–2988 (2017)

18. Wu, T., Huang, Q., Liu, Z., Wang, Yu., Lin, D.: Distribution-balanced loss for multi-label classification in long-tailed datasets. In: Vedaldi, A., Bischof, H., Brox, T., Frahm, J.-M. (eds.) ECCV 2020. LNCS, vol. 12349, pp. 162–178. Springer, Cham (2020). https://doi.org/10.1007/978-3-030-58548-8_10

19. Ronneberger, O., Fischer, P., Brox, T.: U-Net: convolutional networks for biomedical image segmentation. In: Navab, N., Hornegger, J., Wells, W.M., Frangi, A.F. (eds.) MICCAI 2015. LNCS, vol. 9351, pp. 234–241. Springer, Cham (2015). https://doi.org/10.1007/978-3-319-24574-4_28

20. Woo, S., Park, J., Lee, J.-Y., Kweon, I.S.: CBAM: convolutional block attention module. In: Ferrari, V., Hebert, M., Sminchisescu, C., Weiss, Y. (eds.) ECCV 2018. LNCS, vol. 11211, pp. 3–19. Springer, Cham (2018). https://doi.org/10.1007/978-3-030-01234-2_1

21. Huang, G., Liu, Z., Van Der Maaten, L., Weinberger, K. Q.: Densely connected convolutional networks. In: Proceedings of the IEEE Conference on Computer Vision and Pattern Recognition, pp. 4700–4708 (2017)

22. Selvaraju, R.R., Cogswell, M., Das, A., Vedantam, R., Parikh, D., Batra, D.: Grad-CAM: visual explanations from deep networks via gradient-based localization. In: Proceedings of the IEEE International Conference on Computer Vision, pp. 618–626 (2017)

23. International competition on ocular disease intelligent recognition. https://odir2019.grand-challenge.org

Fetal Imaging

Weakly Supervised Online Action Detection for Infant General Movements

Tongyi Luo[1], Jia Xiao[1], Chuncao Zhang[3], Siheng Chen[1], Yuan Tian[3], Guangjun Yu[3], Kang Dang[2], and Xiaowei Ding[1,2(✉)]

[1] Shanghai Jiao Tong University, Shanghai, China
dingxiaowei@sjtu.edu.cn
[2] VoxelCloud, Inc., Los Angeles, USA
[3] Department of Health Management,
Shanghai Children's Hospital, Shanghai, China

Abstract. To make the earlier medical intervention of infants' cerebral palsy (CP), early diagnosis of brain damage is critical. Although general movements assessment (GMA) has shown promising results in early CP detection, it is laborious. Most existing works take videos as input to make fidgety movements (FMs) classification for the GMA automation. Those methods require a complete observation of videos and can not localize video frames containing normal FMs. Therefore we propose a novel approach named WO-GMA to perform FMs localization in the weakly supervised online setting. Infant body keypoints are first extracted as the inputs to WO-GMA. Then WO-GMA performs local spatio-temporal extraction followed by two network branches to generate pseudo clip labels and model online actions. With the clip-level pseudo labels, the action modeling branch learns to detect FMs in an online fashion. Experimental results on a dataset with 757 videos of different infants show that WO-GMA can get state-of-the-art video-level classification and clip-level detection results. Moreover, only the first 20% duration of the video is needed to get classification results as good as fully observed, implying a significantly shortened FMs diagnosis time. Code is available at: https://github.com/scofiedluo/WO-GMA.

Keywords: Online action detection · Weakly supervised · General movements assessment · Fidgety movements (FMs)

1 Introduction

Clinical and public health problems of surviving high-risk infants are common worldwide. Taking preterm infants with the highest proportion of high-risk infants as an example, they may face various complications that affect the quality of life, such as delayed growth in language, cognition, motor, intelligence, and even cause cerebral palsy (CP) [16]. Diagnoses of CP are critical for early intervention of such high-risk preterm infants.

K. Dang and X. Ding—Co-corresponding author.

L. Wang et al. (Eds.): MICCAI 2022, LNCS 13432, pp. 721–731, 2022.
https://doi.org/10.1007/978-3-031-16434-7_69

Studies indicate that general movements assessment (GMA) with high sensitivity (98%) and specificity (91%) is the most cost-effective and accurate tool for early diagnoses of CP [10]. Fidgety movements (FMs) is an important stage of general movements (GMs). Normal FMs (F+) are smoothly circular movements involving the whole body, including the neck, trunk, and limbs. These movements are small in amplitude, moderate in speed, and variable in all directions [5,20]. The absence or sporadic occurrence of FMs (F−) is a strong indicator for infants' CP risk [4]. Qualified assessors usually watch the videos of infants to identify the absence or sporadic occurrence of FMs.

Though GMA is highly accurate, there is a great shortage of qualified assessors, and the assessment is time-consuming. Many works use machine learning or deep learning methods to make GMA automated. Generally, according to the sensors type, automated GMA can be categorized into vision-sensor-based and motion-sensor-based [11]. Since 2D camera data is easier to collect, we focus on vision-based methods. RGB frames are directly processed by VGG followed by LSTM to capture temporal information in [21]. However, RGB frames data contains lots of irrelevant noise in GMA scenes, such as illumination, background, and camera properties. Most vision-based works [3,17,18,22] claim that extracting body keypoints from video data followed by keypoints motion feature analyzer is more robust. Existing works focus on video classification after fully observing the video, leaving two critical problems unaddressed. First, for the real-world application of automated GMA, deep learning methods need greater interpretability. Since unhealthy infants would not exhibit normal FMs for a long time, we can assess infants by localizing when the normal FMs occur. Besides, if the assessment can be completed by partially observing the video, the record time (diagnosis time) can be shortened.

This paper addresses the above two key challenges by proposing a framework in the weakly supervised online action detection setting named WO-GMA. Most online action detection methods [6,8,23,24] rely on frame-level annotations of action boundaries for training. Annotating action boundaries may involve ambiguous decisions and is laborious, especially for FMs mixed with other movements; hence weakly supervised methods are preferred for FMs detection. Many weakly supervised action detection methods [7,19,25] utilize multiple instance learning [26] or contrastive learning [9] to train models with video-level labels. Following previous works, we first extract infants' 2D poses from videos as input of WO-GMA. The pipeline of our method is as follows. WO-GMA contains one local spatio-temporal extraction module followed by two branches to generate pseudo labels and model online action. The local module uses a 3D graph convolution network [15] to capture complex spatio-temporal features based on the extracted infant poses. Supervised by video-level labels, clip-level pseudo labels generating branch mines temporal labels by mixing local feature and long-range information. The online action modeling branch utilizes the generated pseudo labels to conduct clip-level action detection without future information.

Contributions: (1) We are the first to develop an online action detection method on this task and report frame-level recognition results. (2) We validate WO-GMA on our dataset with 757 videos of different infants. Experiments show that the video-level FMs prediction of our method outperforms existing automated GMA models. (3) Experiments demonstrate that we can obtain accurate video level results when only the first 20% of full video frames are used, implying a shortened FMs diagnosis time.

2   Methodology

We use a sequence of 2D keypoints estimated from the RGB video frames as our network input. Figure 1 shows the network architecture of our proposed skeleton-based weakly supervised online action detection model. It consists of three main components. First, a local feature extraction module (LFEM), containing a spatio-temporal graph network followed by joints fusing, is used to extract complex local features from the skeletons. Then, we capture bidirectional long-range information with a clip-level pseudo labels generating branch (CPGB) supervised by video-level labels. Third, the online action modeling branch (OAMB) supervised by the generated pseudo labels is used to detect action without future information. These components will be detailed in this section.

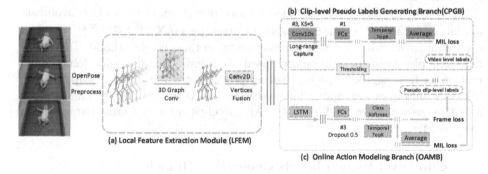

Fig. 1. Overall framework architecture of WO-GMA. Kernel Size (KS), Layers (#)

2.1   Local Feature Extraction Module

Human pose keypoints named skeleton is usually denoted as $\mathcal{G} = (\mathcal{V}, \mathcal{E})$, where nodes set $\mathcal{V} = \{v_i | 1 \leq i \leq N\}$ represents joints, and edges set $\mathcal{E} = \{e_i | 1 \leq i \leq E\}$ represents connectivity between joints. Formally, we use adjacency matrix $\mathbf{A} \in \mathbb{R}^{N \times N}$ to denote the edges set where $A_{i,j} = 1$ if there is an edge between v_i and v_j, otherwise 0. Assume that we are given a skeleton sequence $\mathcal{X} = \{\mathbf{x}_{t,n} \in \mathbb{R}^C | t, n \in \mathbb{Z}, 1 \leq t \leq T, 1 \leq n \leq N\}$, where T is the sequence length, and C denotes the feature vector dimension for one joint. Then the feature of this sequence can be written as $\mathbf{X} \in \mathbb{R}^{T \times N \times C}$.

As detailed in Sect. 1, FMs have complex movement patterns. To well modeling the local spatio-temporal information, we need to capture the relation between different joints in one frame and the variations of joints over time. Multi-scale graph convolution is often used to fuse long-range relations in one graph [14]. MS-G3D [15] utilized cross-spacetime skip connections to construct a spatio-temporal subgraph and proposed a disentangled multi-scale graph convolution to model human action dynamics. We extend the feature extractor in MS-G3D with vertices fusing to capture the local spatio-temporal information of FMs.

In detail, we first split the pose sequence $\mathcal{X}$ into clip-level set $\{C_1, C2, \cdots, C_L\}$ with a sliding window of temporal size τ and stride size s, where $C_1 \cup C_2 \cup \cdots \cup C_L = \mathcal{X}$. Then a spatio-temporal graph $(\mathcal{V}_\tau, \mathcal{E}_\tau)$ is constructed by tiling $\mathbf{A}$ into a block adjacency matrix $\mathbf{A}_\tau \in \mathbb{R}^{\tau N \times \tau N}$. A multi-scale graph convolution is applied to each clip feature tensor $\mathbf{X}_{(\tau)}^{in} \in \mathbb{R}^{1 \times \tau N \times C_{in}}$ as

$$\mathbf{X}_{(\tau)}^{out} = \sigma \left(\sum_{m=0}^{M} \tilde{\mathbf{D}}_{(\tau,m)}^{-\frac{1}{2}} \tilde{\mathbf{A}}_{(\tau,m)} \tilde{\mathbf{D}}_{(\tau,m)}^{-\frac{1}{2}} \mathbf{X}_{(\tau)}^{in} \boldsymbol{\Theta}_{(m)} \right), \tag{1}$$

where $\mathbf{X}_{(\tau)}^{out} \in \mathbb{R}^{1 \times \tau N \times C_{out}}$ is output feature, σ is activation function, $M \in \mathbf{R}$ is the number of scales to aggregate. $\tilde{\mathbf{D}}_{(\tau,m)}$ is the corresponding diagonal degree matrix of disentangled $\tilde{\mathbf{A}}_{(\tau,m)}$. $\boldsymbol{\Theta}_{(m)} \in \mathbb{R}^{C_{in} \times C_{out}}$ denotes the learnable parameter matrix.

For each clip, $\mathbf{X}_{(\tau)}^{out}$ will be collapsed into one skeleton by a 3D convolution operator with kernel size $(1, \tau, 1)$ to get a feature tensor $\mathbf{X}^{out} \in \mathbb{R}^{1 \times N \times C_{out}}$. Then each joint in $\mathbf{X}^{out}$ has got rich information from their neighborhood. To extract more complex local spatio-temporal fused feature, we will aggregate joints information as $\mathbf{f}_i = \text{agg}(\mathbf{X}_i^{out})$, where subscript i denotes the index of clip. We use 2D convolution as aggregator followed with ReLU in this paper. Then we get a feature sequences as $[\mathbf{f}_1, \mathbf{f}_2, \cdots, \mathbf{f}_L]$. All the clips share the same parameter in this module.

2.2   Clip-Level Pseudo Labels Generating Branch

For inference of weakly supervised online action detection, only accumulated history information is available. We introduce a branch to generate pseudo labels with future information and long-range information during training. Since infants' FMs are continual and hard to distinguish from other mixed movements [5], combination future information with long time receptive field is helpful for better classification and detection.

Take the features $\mathbf{F}^0 = [\mathbf{f}_1, \mathbf{f}_2, \cdots, \mathbf{f}_L] \in \mathbb{R}^{L \times C_{out}}$ extracted from LFEM as input, we use the 1D temporal convolutions followed by ReLU to aggregate long-range temporal information from neighbour clips features, i.e. $\mathbf{F}^{i+1} = \text{Relu}(\text{Conv1D}(\mathbf{F}^i))$. The output feature of the last 1D convolution layer is $\mathbf{F}_{out}$. Then for each clip, fully connected layers are used to get the action scores $\mathbf{S} = [\mathbf{s}_1, \mathbf{s}_2, \cdots, \mathbf{s}_L]$, where $\mathbf{s}_i \in \mathbb{R}^{n_c}$ is the score of n_c actions of clip i.

Multiple Instance Learning Loss (MILL) is widely used to get accurate actions scores [7,19]. In this paper, we consider the entire video clip-level sequence set $\{C_1, C2, \cdots, C_L\}$ as a bag of instances, where each instance denotes one clip. To use the video-level labels, we compute video-level scores with Top-K strategy for each action class. That is $s^c = \frac{1}{K}\sum_{j\in\mathcal{M}} s_j^c$, where $\mathcal{M}$ is the Top-K indices set of clips over class c, and K is got by $\max(1, \lfloor\frac{L}{\kappa}\rfloor)$ with hyper parameter κ. Then, to obtain the action class probabilities $\mathcal{P}$, sigmoid or softmax (multi-class dataset) is applied to the video-level scores. The MILL is computed as

$$\mathcal{L}_{MIL}^p = -\sum_{c=1}^{n_c} y_c \log(p_c), \tag{2}$$

where y_c and p_c is the ground truth label and prediction probability of class c. Supervised by $\mathcal{L}_{MIL}^p$, the network can learn clip-level scores which will be used to generate clip-level pseudo labels with future information by a two-stage threshold strategy [7]. First, action class will be discarded if video-level score is less than a threshold θ_{class}. Then, for the remaining action classes, a second threshold, θ_{score}, is applied on clip-level action scores $\mathbf{S}$ to get pseudo labels L_P. After that, the video-level ground truth labels are used to filter out wrong pseudo labels.

2.3 Online Action Modeling Branch

As shown above, CPGB can utilize future information during training. However, future information is not available during inference. LSTM is used to accumulate the historical temporal information in this branch.

Given one clip-level feature $\mathbf{f}_i$, previous hidden state $\mathbf{h}_{i-1}$ and cell state $\mathbf{c}_{i-1}$ as input, updated states is got by $\mathbf{h}_i, \mathbf{c}_i = \text{LSTM}(\mathbf{h}_{i-1}, \mathbf{c}_{i-1}, \mathbf{f}_i)$. For ith clip, online action score is computed as $\mathbf{a}_i = \text{softmax}(\mathbf{W}_a^\top \mathbf{h}_i)$, where $\mathbf{a}_i \in \mathbb{R}^{n_c+1}$ is the action scores including a background class. Then, cross entropy loss is applied to $\mathbf{a}_i$ over all clips with pseudo labels L_P to get frame loss, i.e.

$$\mathcal{L}_{FML} = -\frac{1}{L}\sum_{i=1}^{L}\sum_{c=0}^{n_c} L_{P,i}^c \log \mathbf{a}_i^c \tag{3}$$

To further utilize the ground truth video level information, another MILL is used in this branch. As shown in Fig. 1, we use the same top-K strategy as CPGB to get video-level scores for each action class. Here, $\mathcal{L}_{MIL}^o$ is used to denote MILL in this branch.

2.4 Training and Inference

In the training stage, two branches and the local feature extraction module are jointly optimized by $\mathcal{L}_{MIL}^p + \mathcal{L}_{FML} + \mathcal{L}_{MIL}^o$. During inference, the future information is not available for online action detection tasks, so we only use the feature extraction module and online action modeling branch.

3   Experiments

Dataset. For this study, ethical approval was provided by the Ethics Committee of Children's Hospital of Shanghai (Review number: 2021RY053-E01). Written informed consent was obtained from the parents/legal guardians in accordance with the Declaration of Helsinki. Our original dataset provided by three hospitals contains 792 videos. Two certified observers, who had got the GMs Trust qualification, made the video-level GMs classification. In case of disagreement, the third certified observer re-assessed the video. The eligible participants were high-risk (premature birth, low birth weight, suspected or brain injury, birth with chronic disease, genetic or genetic metabolic disease). Video recording was conducted according to standard protocol [5]. After deleting the repetitive videos, the dataset remains 757 different videos of 757 different infants at around 46–70 weeks gestational age (average: 55 weeks), including 353 F− videos and 404 F+ videos, 434 male and 323 female infants. The resolution of 678 videos is 1920 × 1080, others are 1280 × 720, 1440 × 1080, 960 × 540, 720 × 576. The average number of frames is 7787 (590–16322), and the average time duration is 307 s (24–653 s). We split the training and test sets with a ratio of 8:2, which ensures videos with different labels and of different hospitals are divided evenly.

Evaluation Metrics. For video-level performance, we report the classification accuracy, F1-score, and Area Under Curve(AUC). For detection results, following previous works [19,25], we use standard evaluation protocol by reporting mean Average Precision (mAP) values under different intersection over union (IoU) thresholds.

Implementation Details. OpenPose [1] is used to extract skeletons with 18 joints from videos and skeletons preprocessing method in [3] is adopted. For convenience, we truncate the first 6000 frames for the skeleton sequences more than 6000 frames; otherwise, pad 0 at the end of each skeleton sequence to 6000 frames. We implemented our WO-GMA in PyTorch, and performed experiments on a system with Nvidia 3090 GPUs. We train our network with 100 epochs by using Adam [13] with learning rate 5×10^{-5} and weight decay 5×10^{-4}. The window size τ and stride size s are set to be 20. And the parameter κ in the Top-K strategy of both branches is 8. Video threshold and frame threshold in pseudo labels generating are 0.4 and 0.3 respectively. The dimension of hidden state $\mathbf{h}_i$ in LSTM is 1024. Since we only focus on F+, the class number $n_c = 1$.

3.1   Main Results

Video-Level Classification Performance . For our model, one video is classified as F+ if the video level score got by Top-K strategy is greater than 0.5 in the seen video. For STAM [18], MS-G3D [15], Zhu et al. [27], the classification threshold is set to 0.5. Since action detection tasks also include classification, we also report the video-level performance of WOAD [7] and W-TALC [19]. Following previous appearance-based methods [7,25], the image features and optical

Table 1. Comparison with other video-level classification works and action detection works on our datasets. Here fusion is the concatenation of image and optical flow features among channel dimensions. The skeleton-based video-level performances are evaluated with 5-fold cross-validation. The proposed WO-GMA outperforms previous works by a lot margin.

Input	Method	Video level			Detection – mAP@IoU (%)					
		Accuracy	F1	AUC	0.1	0.2	0.3	0.4	0.5	Mean
Image	WOAD [7]	53.2	69.3	48	2.7	1.5	1.5	0.3	0.3	1.3
	W-TALC [19]	52.6	42.5	49.4	2.1	1.00	0.2	0.0	0.0	0.7
Optical flow	WOAD [7]	54.5	63.5	51	11.5	7.8	5.0	3.2	1.9	5.9
	W-TALC [19]	57.8	67.9	55.9	5.6	1.1	0.1	0.0	0.0	1.4
Fusion	WOAD [7]	55.2	69.9	49.4	11.5	8.7	5.5	3.9	1.7	6.3
	W-TALC [19]	54.5	61.5	50.5	1.0	0.2	0.0	0	0	0.2
Skeleton	Zhu et al. [27]	84.5 (2.0)	85.1 (2.0)	84.7 (2.0)	–					
	MS-G3D [15]	88.4 (1.5)	89.1 (1.6)	92.5 (0.7)	–					
	STAM [18]	86.5 (2.6)	86.5 (3.0)	93.1 (1.8)	–					
	WO-GMA	**93.8** (1.0)	**94.4** (0.9)	**96.9** (0.7)	**31.7**	**22.4**	**17.9**	**11.4**	**5.2**	**17.7**

features are extracted by I3D [2] pre-trained on Kinetics [12], a huge dataset contains 306k videos. For a fair comparison, none-skeleton based methods also use the first 6000 frames. Both the clip window size and window stride are 20. Other experiments settings are the same as original papers.

Results are shown in the left part of Table 1. For skeleton-based methods, we report the 5-fold cross-validation results. For other methods, since the results perform much worse than skeleton-based methods and calculating image and optical flow features requires a lot of computing power, we only report results of the fifth fold with frame-level annotations. Though only accumulated history information is used, video-level results of our model outperform previous works by a lot margin, demonstrating the superiority of WO-GMA. Moreover, for both WOAD [7] and W-TALC [19], the model with the image input feature performs worse than the optical flow input feature. This result indicates that motion information is more important than appearance information in this task.

Online Action Detection Performance. To the best of our knowledge, we are the first to develop weakly supervised online action detection method for GMA. 60 F+ samples in the fifth dataset split-fold were annotated by experts with frame-level labels, and 56 valid samples are used as ground truth to report detection results. The right part of Table 1 shows that our model achieves the best detection performance. Compared with the image features, the detection results using the optical flow features are better, which further demonstrates the importance of motion information. Since the skeleton contains only motion information, this result also proves the necessity of using the skeleton as input. The performance gap between left part and right part of Table 1 shows that detection is much more difficult than classification in this task. There are two main possible reasons. First, only video-level supervision information may not enough. Second, compared with everyday life actions like shaking hands, the boundary of FMs is even harder to determine for annotators accurately. Figure 2 demonstrates that our model can get video-level performance as good as fully observed when only the first 20% video frames are observed. This result shows a significant benefit of our model: the assessment time of automated GMA for real-world applications can be greatly shortened. The visualisation detection results in the top subplot of Fig. 3 shows the acceptable detection performance.

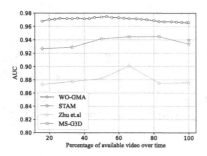

Fig. 2. Video-level performance comparison of AUC on our datasets when only part of frames is considered.

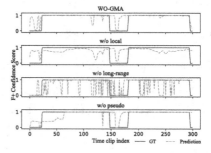

Fig. 3. An example of the comparison between detection results and ground truth frame-level annotations.

3.2   Ablation Study

Since the complex movements pattern of FMs, we argue that both local spatio-temporal information and long-range information are critical in this task. This part will analyze the effect each component in the fifth dataset split-fold with frame-level annotations.

To study the effect of CPGB which can combine future information, we remove this branch (w/o pseudo). As shown in Table 2, both the classification and detection performance will drop compared with WO-GMA, demonstrating the necessity to generate pseudo clip labels for training. We replace the LFEM with only clip skeletons vertices features concatenation to get results without complex local features (w/o local). As shown in the second row of Table 2, the video level accuracy will drop by 2%, and the detection results will drop when IoU is higher. Furthermore, to analyze the effect of long-range information, we remove the 1D convolutions used to capture long-range information in CPGB (w/o long-range). Results in Table 2 imply the importance of long-range information.

To better illustrate the influence of different modules, we plot three more curves of the same infant in Fig. 3 and report the number of detection instances in Table 2. These results show that the detection action instances are fragmented without long-range information, which is unsuitable for detecting continuous FMs. Without local feature extraction, the detection score is less confident than

Table 2. Ablation analysis of our proposed WO-GMA

Method	Video level			Detection - mAP@IoU (%)						Instances
	Accuracy	F1-score	AUC	0.1	0.2	0.3	0.4	0.5	Mean	
W/o pseudo	92.2	92.9	95.7	35.1	21.6	14.7	8.0	2.4	16.4	260
W/o local	92.8	93.6	95.8	**33.7**	**24.6**	**19.4**	10.6	4.7	18.6	296
W/o long-range	93.5	93.9	95.4	10.2	7.0	2.9	1.4	0.6	4.4	1000
Our model	**94.8**	**95.1**	**96.6**	31.7	22.4	17.9	**11.4**	**5.2**	17.7	420

WO-GMA. Without pseudo, the model may ignore the gap between intermittent FMs, which the long-range information in CPGB will make up. Moreover, generating pseudo labels without long-range information will bring the noise. The detection results further show the difficulty of detection task mentioned in previous subsection. Compared with appearance-based methods, our skeleton-based methods achieve better performance.

4 Conclusion

We are the first to propose WO-GMA to address online action detection for general movements assessment using weak supervision and evaluate it on a large dataset. Unlike previous methods that only focus on video classification, our WO-GMA can detect the occurrence of FMs in an online fashion without frame-level labels. Experiments results demonstrate that WO-GMA significantly outperforms state-of-the-art both in the classification and detection tasks.

References

1. Cao, Z., Simon, T., Wei, S.E., Sheikh, Y.: Realtime multi-person 2D pose estimation using part affinity fields. In: Proceedings of the IEEE Conference on Computer Vision and Pattern Recognition, pp. 7291–7299 (2017)
2. Carreira, J., Zisserman, A.: Quo vadis, action recognition? A new model and the kinetics dataset. In: proceedings of the IEEE Conference on Computer Vision and Pattern Recognition, pp. 6299–6308 (2017)
3. Chambers, C., et al.: Computer vision to automatically assess infant neuromotor risk. IEEE Trans. Neural Syst. Rehabil. Eng. **28**(11), 2431–2442 (2020)
4. Einspieler, C., Peharz, R., Marschik, P.B.: Fidgety movements-tiny in appearance, but huge in impact. Jornal de Pediatria **92**, 64–70 (2016)
5. Einspieler, C., Prechtl, H.F., Ferrari, F., Cioni, G., Bos, A.F.: The qualitative assessment of general movements in preterm, term and young infants-review of the methodology. Early Human Dev. **50**(1), 47–60 (1997)
6. Eun, H., Moon, J., Park, J., Jung, C., Kim, C.: Learning to discriminate information for online action detection. In: Proceedings of the IEEE/CVF Conference on Computer Vision and Pattern Recognition, pp. 809–818 (2020)
7. Gao, M., Zhou, Y., Xu, R., Socher, R., Xiong, C.: WOAD: weakly supervised online action detection in untrimmed videos. In: Proceedings of the IEEE/CVF Conference on Computer Vision and Pattern Recognition, pp. 1915–1923 (2021)

8. De Geest, R., Gavves, E., Ghodrati, A., Li, Z., Snoek, C., Tuytelaars, T.: Online action detection. In: Leibe, B., Matas, J., Sebe, N., Welling, M. (eds.) ECCV 2016. LNCS, vol. 9909, pp. 269–284. Springer, Cham (2016). https://doi.org/10.1007/978-3-319-46454-1_17
9. Gutmann, M., Hyvärinen, A.: Noise-contrastive estimation: a new estimation principle for unnormalized statistical models. In: Proceedings of the Thirteenth International Conference on Artificial Intelligence and Statistics, pp. 297–304. JMLR Workshop and Conference Proceedings (2010)
10. Herskind, A., Greisen, G., Nielsen, J.B.: Early identification and intervention in cerebral palsy. Dev. Med. Child Neurol. **57**(1), 29–36 (2015)
11. Irshad, M.T., Nisar, M.A., Gouverneur, P., Rapp, M., Grzegorzek, M.: Ai approaches towards Prechtl's assessment of general movements: a systematic literature review. Sensors **20**(18), 5321 (2020)
12. Kay, W., et al.: The kinetics human action video dataset. arXiv preprint arXiv:1705.06950 (2017)
13. Kingma, D.P., Ba, J.: Adam: a method for stochastic optimization. arXiv preprint arXiv:1412.6980 (2014)
14. Li, M., Chen, S., Chen, X., Zhang, Y., Wang, Y., Tian, Q.: Actional-structural graph convolutional networks for skeleton-based action recognition. In: Proceedings of the IEEE/CVF Conference on Computer Vision and Pattern Recognition, pp. 3595–3603 (2019)
15. Liu, Z., Zhang, H., Chen, Z., Wang, Z., Ouyang, W.: Disentangling and unifying graph convolutions for skeleton-based action recognition. In: Proceedings of the IEEE/CVF Conference on Computer Vision and Pattern Recognition, pp. 143–152 (2020)
16. Malcolm, W.F.: Beyond the NICU: Comprehensive Care of the High-Risk Infant. McGraw-Hill Education, Columbus (2015)
17. McCay, K.D., et al.: Towards explainable abnormal infant movements identification: a body-part based prediction and visualisation framework. In: 2021 IEEE EMBS International Conference on Biomedical and Health Informatics (BHI), pp. 1–4. IEEE (2021)
18. Nguyen-Thai, B., Le, V., Morgan, C., Badawi, N., Tran, T., Venkatesh, S.: A spatio-temporal attention-based model for infant movement assessment from videos. IEEE J. Biomed. Health Inform. **25**(10), 3911–3920 (2021)
19. Paul, S., Roy, S., Roy-Chowdhury, A.K.: W-TALC: weakly-supervised temporal activity localization and classification. In: Proceedings of the European Conference on Computer Vision (ECCV), pp. 563–579 (2018)
20. Prechtl, H.F., Hopkins, B.: Developmental transformations of spontaneous movements in early infancy. Early Human Dev. **14**(3–4), 233–238 (1986)
21. Schmidt, W., Regan, M., Fahey, M., Paplinski, A.: General movement assessment by machine learning: why is it so difficult? J. Med. Artif. Intell. **2** (2019)
22. Wu, Q., et al.: Automatically measure the quality of infants' spontaneous movement via videos to predict the risk of cerebral palsy. IEEE Trans. Instrum. Meas. **70**, 1–11 (2021)
23. Xu, M., Gao, M., Chen, Y.T., Davis, L.S., Crandall, D.J.: Temporal recurrent networks for online action detection. In: Proceedings of the IEEE/CVF International Conference on Computer Vision, pp. 5532–5541 (2019)
24. Xu, M., et al.: Long short-term transformer for online action detection. In: Advances in Neural Information Processing Systems, vol. 34 (2021)

25. Zhang, C., Cao, M., Yang, D., Chen, J., Zou, Y.: CoLA: weakly-supervised temporal action localization with snippet contrastive learning. In: Proceedings of the IEEE/CVF Conference on Computer Vision and Pattern Recognition, pp. 16010–16019 (2021)
26. Zhou, Z.H.: Multi-instance learning: a survey. Technical Report 1. Department of Computer Science & Technology, Nanjing University (2004)
27. Zhu, M., Men, Q., Ho, E.S., Leung, H., Shum, H.P.: Interpreting deep learning based cerebral palsy prediction with channel attention. In: 2021 IEEE EMBS International Conference on Biomedical and Health Informatics (BHI), pp. 1–4. IEEE (2021)

Super-Focus: Domain Adaptation for Embryo Imaging via Self-supervised Focal Plane Regression

Chloe He[1,2]([✉]), Céline Jacques[2], Jérôme Chambost[2], Jonas Malmsten[4],
Koen Wouters[5], Thomas Fréour[6,7], Nikica Zaninovic[4], Cristina Hickman[2,3],
and Francisco Vasconcelos[1]

[1] Wellcome/EPSRC Centre for Interventional and Surgical Sciences,
University College London, London, UK
chloe.he@apricity.life
[2] Apricity, Paris, France
[3] Institute for Reproductive and Developmental Biology,
Imperial College London, London, UK
[4] Ronald O. Perelman and Claudia Cohen Center for Reproductive Medicine,
Weill Cornell Medicine, New York, USA
[5] Brussels IVF, University Hospital Brussels, Brussels, Belgium
[6] Department of Reproductive Biology, Nantes University Hospital, Nantes, France
[7] Department of Reproductive Medicine, Dexeus University Hospital,
Barcelona, Spain

Abstract. In recent years, the field of embryo imaging has seen an
influx of work using machine learning. These works take advantage of
large microscopy datasets collected by fertility clinics as routine practice through relatively standardised imaging setups. Nevertheless, systematic variations still exist between datasets and can harm the ability
of machine learning models to perform well across different clinics. In
this work, we present Super-Focus, a method for correcting systematic
variations present in embryo focal stacks by artificially generating focal
planes. We demonstrate that these artificially generated planes are realistic to human experts and that using Super-Focus as a pre-processing step
improves the ability of a cell instance segmentation model to generalise
across multiple clinics.

Keywords: Domain adaptation · Super-resolution · Embryology ·
Microscopy

1 Introduction

The analysis of human embryos under the microscope constitutes an important task in the clinical embryology workflow, feeding into decisions about which

Supplementary Information The online version contains supplementary material
available at https://doi.org/10.1007/978-3-031-16434-7_70.

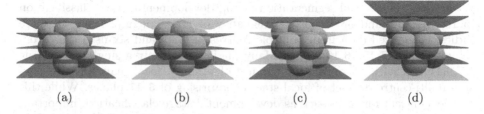

(a)   (b)   (c)   (d)

Fig. 1. Some of the systematic variations seen among embryo imaging datasets. Blue planes represent planes present in the original data. Yellow planes represent planes that can be artificially generated by our method. (a) **Ideal case** - the embryo is centered in the focal stack and the maximum number of planes are captured. (b) **Missing edge planes** - the focal stack is missing the planes that would have been in the upper and lower extremities of the ideal focal stack. (c) **Missing intermediate planes** - the distance between the planes is larger than in the ideal case. In practice, this is usually by a factor of 2. (d) **Plane misalignment** - the embryo is not centered in the focal stack.

embryos to use in a certain treatment cycle. In recent years, a number of works have attempted to accelerate the process of embryo analysis by using deep learning for tasks such as automated developmental stage classification [15,16,18,19,22]. Though many of these works analysed data derived from single centres retrospectively, some works make use of data from multiple centres, taking advantage of the fact many fertility clinics use similar (if not the same) imaging equipment.

In spite of this relative standardisation in terms of equipment, embryo imaging datasets can nevertheless be noticeably heterogeneous. The number of focal planes routinely captured at different centres can vary, as can the distance between different focal planes. Moreover, the location of the embryo within focal stacks can vary between centres - in some datasets, the embryos' equators coincide with the middle focal plane; in others, the embryo may only occupy the top half of the stack. Such variations among datasets (illustrated and categorised in Fig. 1) may prove damaging to the performance of deep learning systems, especially when evaluated on datasets from different centres to the ones in their training set.

In this paper, we present Super-Focus, a method for the standardisation of embryo focal stacks captured through Hoffman modulation contrast (HMC) microscopy [10]. We train deep neural networks in a self-supervised fashion to predict "missing" planes in focal stacks and use these predictions to construct standardised focal stacks. We demonstrate that these standardised stacks are not only realistic in qualitative studies with expert embryologists, but also improve the ability of a cell instance segmentation model to adapt to different embryo imaging datasets. Code can be found at https://github.com/PeterTheHe/Super-Focus.

2   Related Work

Deep Learning in Embryo Imaging. Convolutional neural networks (CNNs) have been applied to many key tasks in embryo imaging including blastocyst grading [11,13], cell segmentation [9,16], developmental stage classification [15,16,18,19,22] and prediction of pregnancy or miscarriage [2,7,29]. Of these studies, three used data from multiple centres [2,9,29] and six used data from a single centre [7,15,16,19,20,22]. Many made use of only a single focal plane [2,7,9,15,29], with [2] opting for the use of a single focal plane despite having a multi-centre dataset of focal stacks comprising of 3–11 planes. While this may be sufficient for tasks such as developmental stage classification, important 3-dimensional information is lost. Such information may be useful for more fine-grained tasks such as cell segmentation as noted in [9]. Moreover, even within the developmental stage classification literature, the most recent state-of-the-art models are increasingly relying on use of multiple focal planes [16,20,22]. To our knowledge, there haven't been any studies in the deep learning embryo imaging literature involving multiple focal planes and multiple data centres.

Domain Adaptation in Microscopy. Slight variations in imaging setups and procedures is well-documented in microscopy, leading to the need for strategies to ensure the robustness of deep learning models across different labs [28]. Most works in the area focus on the problem of standardising microscopy data with respect to variations in staining procedures [3,26,28] or illumination [21]. They typically concern single focal planes and their approaches mostly involve the use of CycleGAN-like models [32] augmented with structural similarity objectives such as SSIM [30]. To our knowledge, no works have tackled the problem of standardising microscopy data with respect to the systematic variations specific to working with focal stacks that we identified.

Super-resolution of Sliced Medical Imaging Data. Much work has gone into artificially increasing the spatial resolution of medical imaging data, mostly focusing on the magnetic resonance imaging (MRI), computerised tomography (CT) and positron emission tomography (PET) domains [1,5,6,14,23,27,31]. Many of these works make use of adversarial training setups to improve the perceptual quality of generated images [1,6,14,27]. Only few of these works, however, focus on super-resolving along the slice axis [14,31]. While [14] approaches the task by directly enhancing an image reconstructed from thick slices to look like it was generated from thin slices, [31] explicitly generates intermediate slices by super-resolving images in which one of the spatial axes runs parallel to the slice axis. Nevertheless, the aforementioned imaging modalities are quite different to optical microscopy. In particular, obtaining images in which the slice axis runs parallel to one of the images' spatial axes is not feasible in standard optical microscopy setups. To the best of our knowledge, no works have examined applying such approaches to optical microscopy.

3 Methods

We consider an arbitrary focal stack x_i drawn from a embryo imaging dataset $\mathcal{D}$. x_i is comprised of n focal planes x_i^k equally spaced at intervals of d where k is the focal depth. We train three deep neural networks: G^{up} which maps the

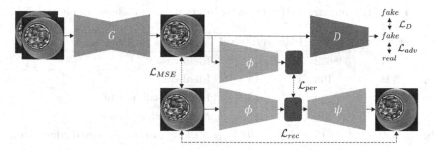

Fig. 2. Training our network. Arrows represent the flow of data between the various networks. Dotted arrows represent the computation of losses with respect to the lines' endpoints.

pair (x_i^k, x_i^{k+d}) to x_i^{k+2d}, G^{down} which maps the pair (x_i^{k+2d}, x_i^{k+d}) to x_i^k and G^{mid} which maps the pair (x_i^k, x_i^{k+2d}) to x_i^{k+d}. These networks can be used to correct the systematic variations described in Fig. 1 in other datasets captured using the same imaging equipment:

- If there are missing edge planes, artificial edge planes can be generated using G^{up} and G^{down} (Fig. 1b).
- If there are missing intermediate planes, artificial intermediate planes can be generated using G^{mid} (Fig. 1c).
- If the planes are misaligned with the embryo, artificial edge planes can be generated in the direction in which the embryo is offset using G^{up} or G^{down}. Edge planes in the opposite direction can be discarded to ensure that the total number of focal planes remains at n (Fig. 1d).

In this section, we introduce the networks in more detail and cover the training procedure (depicted in Fig. 2).

Generator Network. We use the same U-Net architecture [25] for the generator networks G^{up}, G^{down} and G^{mid}. The architecture we use is almost identical to that outlined in [25] bar three changes: (1) we use batch normalisation after each convolutional layer; (2) we end our downsampling pathway one convolutional block earlier such that our bottleneck only contains 512 channels (instead of 1024); and (3) our input is a $W \times H$ image with two channels while our output is a $W \times H$ image consisting of only a single channel. We train an arbitrary generator network G using triplets $(x_i^k, x_i^{k+d}, x_i^{k+2d})$ sampled from $x_i \sim \mathcal{D}$. Two of these images (the exact selection depending on G) comprise the input to G, while the remaining image becomes the target y. From the inputs, G generates an image $\hat{y}$ and its weights are updated to minimise the generator loss $\mathcal{L}_G = \mathcal{L}_{MSE} + \lambda_{per}\mathcal{L}_{per} + \lambda_{adv}\mathcal{L}_{adv}$ where $\mathcal{L}_{MSE}$ is the mean squared error between y and $\hat{y}$, $\mathcal{L}_{per}$ is a perceptual loss term with respect to a pre-trained feature extractor ϕ, $\mathcal{L}_{adv}$ is an adversarial loss term with respect to some discriminator D, and λ_{per} and λ_{adv} are weighting terms.

Table 1. Summary of the datasets. Intervals are measured in micron.

Dataset	Clinic	Stacks	Planes	Interval	Variations present
$\mathcal{D}_A$	A	348622	11	15	Ideal case
$\mathcal{D}_B$	B	108	11	15	Ideal case
$\mathcal{D}_C$	C	20	11	15	Plane misalignment
$\mathcal{D}_D$	D	146	7	15	Missing edge planes
$\mathcal{D}_E$	A	10	3	30	Missing intermediate and edge planes

Self-supervised Perceptual Loss. We use a self-supervised perceptual loss using the features extracted by the downsampling pathway of an autoencoder [17]. The advantage of such a setup is that it allows the model to learn features pertinent to the specific imaging domain without requiring additional labelling. In this work, the downsampling pathway ϕ consists of 3 convolutional layers with 64, 128 and 256 filters respectively; kernel sizes of 8, 5 and 5; strides of 4, 2 and 2; and padding of 2. The upsampling pathway ψ consists of 3 tranposed convolutional layers with 128, 64 and 1 filter respectively; kernel sizes of 4, 4 and 6; strides of 2, 2 and 4; and padding of 1. ϕ and ψ are pre-trained on single focal planes x_i^k sampled from $x_i \sim \mathcal{D}$ with the objective to minimise the loss $\mathcal{L}_{rec} = \frac{||x_i^k - \psi(\phi(x_i^k))||_F^2}{WH}$ where $|| \cdot ||_F$ is the Frobenius norm. Once pre-training is complete, we can discard ψ and our perceptual loss between our predicted plane $\hat{y}$ and the ground truth y takes the form $\mathcal{L}_{per} = \frac{||\phi(y) - \phi(\hat{y})||_F^2}{WHC}$ where C is the number of feature maps extracted by ϕ.

Adversarial Loss. The use of adversarial losses is well-documented in both the super-resolution and the domain adaptation literature, particularly for improving the realism of generated textures [3,5,23,26–28]. In this work, we use a ResNet-50 [8] discriminator D trained to differentiate between *fake* images generated by G and *real* images drawn from focal stacks in the dataset. G and D are optimised concurrently with D minimising the loss $\mathcal{L}_D = -\log(D(y)) - \log(1 - D(\hat{y}))$ and G trying to minimise the adversarial loss $\mathcal{L}_{adv} = \log(1 - D(\hat{y}))$.

4 Experiments

We evaluated our method through a combination of quantitative experiments and user studies. The user studies involved a panel of four clinical embryologists (referred to with the numbers 1–4) and a research associate in a reproductive medicine department specialising in embryo imaging. Embryologists 1, 2 and 3 were lead embryologists at their respective clinics with over 40 years of experience between them; embryologist 4 was a trainee embryologist.

Datasets. Experiments were performed on five de-identified private embryo imaging datasets (referred to as $\mathcal{D}_{A-E}$) sourced from four IVF clinics (referred to with the letters A-D) across four different countries (further details in Supplementary Materials). The datasets consisted of HMC focal stacks captured on

Table 2. Mean ratings for each dataset across stack standardisation (SS) and super-resolution (SR) tasks. Standard deviations are provided in parentheses.

Task	Dataset	Rating
SS	$\mathcal{D}_A$	4.4 (0.7)
	$\mathcal{D}_C$	3.6 (1.1)
	$\mathcal{D}_D$	3.6 (1.2)
	$\mathcal{D}_E$	3.2 (0.9)
SR	$\mathcal{D}_A$	4.4 (0.5)

Table 3. Comparison of segmentation model performance on standardised and non-standardised focal stacks. Standard deviations are provided in parentheses where possible.

Dataset	Method	Accuracy	Dice
$\mathcal{D}_C$	No action	0.45	0.84 (0.03)
	Ours	**0.50**	**0.96 (0.02)**
$\mathcal{D}_D$	Zero-padded	0.61	0.92 (0.04)
	Ours	**0.66**	**0.93 (0.04)**

Embryoscope time-lapse incubators. While $\mathcal{D}_A$ contained focal stacks covering the entirety of pre-implantation development, $\mathcal{D}_{B-E}$ only contained up 4-cell embryos. Details on the size, number of focal planes and interval between planes can be found in Table 1 along with information on the variations between them. Only $\mathcal{D}_A$ was used for training, with 263024 focal stacks earmarked for training and 20 for validation. The remaining 85578 stacks were used for testing. Focal stacks in each dataset were resized to dimensions 400×400. Contrast limited adaptive histogram equalisation [24] was applied to each focal stack and a circular mask was applied to hide the edges of the microscope well.

Training Details. All models were implemented using PyTorch (v1.10.0) and trained on a Ubuntu 20.04 machine with an NVIDIA Titan X GPU. The generator and discriminator models were trained for 30 epochs on a subset of $\mathcal{D}_A$ consisting of 10468 focal stacks for training and and 20 focal stacks for validation. Though initially intended to only be used in early experiments with our architecture, we found that using a smaller subset of the training dataset led to superior performance, given the same training time. We document this phenomenon more thoroughly in Sect. 4.4. A batch size of 4 was used and the process took 10GB VRAM and 30 h per generator-discriminator pair. The autoencoder used in the perceptual loss was trained for one epoch on the entire $\mathcal{D}_A$ training set taking 1 GB VRAM and 22 h. We used the Adam [12] optimiser with the default learning rate of 0.001 which was reduced by an order of magnitude every 15000 batches for the generator models, and every 3000 batches for the autoencoder. The values of λ_1 and λ_2 used were 100 and 10 respectively, such that all terms in $\mathcal{L}_G$ were within the same order of magnitude of 10^0.

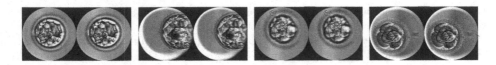

Fig. 3. Pairs of real and generated focal planes. In each pair, the left image corresponds to the ground truth focal plane and the right image corresponds to the generated focal plane.

4.1 Qualitative Evaluation of Generated Image Quality

Procedure. Each panellist was shown 40 standardised focal stacks. 30 of these stacks were generated from datasets $\mathcal{D}_{C-E}$; 10 were generated from the $\mathcal{D}_A$ test set with 4 planes randomly selected from a uniform distribution over planes being replaced with artificially generated planes. In addition, panellists were shown 10 super-resolved stacks consisting of 21 planes at intervals of 7.5 micron generated from the $\mathcal{D}_A$ test set. The panellists were asked to rate each focal stack on the following 1–5 scale: 1 (very unrealistic), 2 (major issues such as missing cells or artefacts), 3 (usable - only minor issues such as texture being slightly off), 4 (realistic - very minor flaws) and 5 (highly realistic - hard to tell it's fake). Examples of generated focal planes from $\mathcal{D}_A$ can be seen in Fig. 3. Further examples for this and other experiments can be found in the Supplementary Materials.

Results. A breakdown of results for each dataset is provided in Table 2. The standardised stacks were, on average, above the "usable" threshold with the best performance seen on $\mathcal{D}_A$ and the lowest performance seen on $\mathcal{D}_E$ (for which 8 planes had to be generated). Moreover, the super-resolved stacks were rated highly indicating the robustness of our method for slice axis super-resolution.

4.2 Impact on Embryo Grading

Procedure. Each of the clinical embryologists in the panel was shown 120 focal stacks of 5-day old embryos derived from the $\mathcal{D}_A$ test set. They were asked to grade each embryo into one of four categories using the Gardner scale [4], a routine task in clinical embryology. These 120 stacks were composed thus: 50 of these were ground-truth focal stacks; the next 50 depicted the same embryos as the first 50, but with every plane artificially generated using our model; the remaining 20 focal stacks were identical copies of 20 random focal stacks from the first 100. The stacks were presented to the embryologists in a random order. In this way, the embryologists (who were not informed of this setup) would annotate each embryo at least twice: once from a stack of real planes, once from a stack of artificially generated planes and perhaps once from one of the 20 copies. The agreement between the embryologists' annotations between real and artificially generated versions of each embryo was compared with the agreement between the annotations of identical copies using Fischer's exact test with two tails at 95% confidence.

Table 4. Comparison of agreement between embryologist annotations of the same images and embryologist annotations between real and generated stacks.

Embryologist	1	2	3	4
Agreement (Identical)	95%	100%	90%	80%
Agreement (Real vs generated)	96%	95%	82%	90%

Results. Results for each embryologist can be seen in Table 4. No statistically significant differences were found between the agreement on the annotations of identical stacks and the annotations of real and artificially generated stacks. This implies that the use of artificially generated stacks does not impact embryo assessment by human experts.

4.3   Impact on Cell Instance Segmentation

Procedure. Using $\mathcal{D}_B$, a model for cell instance segmentation on 11-plane focal stacks was trained following the architecture in [9]. The performance of the model was evaluated on $\mathcal{D}_C$ and $\mathcal{D}_D$ with respect to the mean Dice coefficient between predicted and ground-truth segmentation masks, as well as the model's accuracy at counting the number of cells present in a stack. For $\mathcal{D}_C$, we compare the model's performance on misaligned stacks and standardised stacks generated using our method. For $\mathcal{D}_D$, we compare the model's performance on stacks padded with zeros (to compensate for the lack of edge planes) and standardised stacks with edge planes generated using our method. The mean Dice coefficients were compared using two-tailed two-sample t-tests at 95% confidence.

Results. The standardised focal stacks led to increases in both cell counting accuracy and mean Dice coefficient in both datasets (see Table 3). For both $\mathcal{D}_C$ and $\mathcal{D}_D$, the increases in mean Dice coefficient were statistically significant ($p < 0.0001$ and $p = 0.03$ respectively). These results demonstrate that our method leads to better domain adaptation.

4.4   Impact of the Training Dataset

Procedure. As mentioned previously, we used a subset of our original training dataset in our final model after noticing that using the whole dataset led to qualitatively poorer results. We thus decided to run some ablations on the dataset to see which aspects of the full dataset were causing poor performance. Starting with a restricted subset of the dataset consisting of only up to 8-cell embryos and planes from the upper half of the focal stack, we gradually introduced the use of more stages and more planes. Four G^{up} models were trained on the different datasets for 77000 batches, using the same batch size and learning rates as previously described. The quality of the model outputs were evaluated over 10000 images using three well-established metrics: structural similarity index (SSIM), peak signal-to-noise ratio (PSNR) and Fréchet Inception distance (FID).

Table 5. Comparison of metrics on different subsets of the $\mathcal{D}_A$ training set. ↑ denotes that higher scores are better; ↓ denotes that lower scores are better.

Dataset	Stacks	SSIM ↑	PSNR ↑	FID ↓
Restricted (used in final model)	10468	0.828 (0.038)	24.5 (2.6)	**14.6**
All planes	10468	0.849 (0.031)	25.8 (2.4)	20.3
All stages	44656	0.843 (0.035)	25.3 (2.5)	20.1
All stages and planes	263024	**0.850 (0.031)**	**25.9 (2.4)**	20.9

Results. A breakdown of results can be found in Table 5. There was a distinct lack of agreement between the metrics - the best-performing model according to SSIM and PSNR was the worst-performing model according to FID (and vice versa). In light of this disagreement, an additional user study was conducted in which panellists were shown 30 focal planes generated by the model with the highest SSIM and the model with the highest FID. They were asked to select the highest quality image with reference to the ground truth, voting in favour of the model with the highest FID on 87% of the images. These results imply not only that training on a larger dataset does not necessarily lead to improved performance, but that SSIM and PSNR are poor metrics for image quality in the embryo imaging domain. Though interesting, further investigation is beyond the scope of this paper.

5   Conclusions

In this paper, we introduced Super-Focus, a novel method for correcting systematic variations present in embryo imaging datasets. Through user studies, we demonstrated that the focal planes generated by our approach are realistic while also illustrating the shortcomings of the SSIM and PSNR image quality metrics when applied to the embryo imaging domain. In addition, we provided evidence that our method can help ML models generalise across multiple clinics. Our work solves a key issue faced when working with embryo datasets from multiple clinics and thus opens the door to many exciting avenues for future work involving the use of multiple focal planes collected from multiple clinics.

References

1. Belov, A., Stadelmann, J., Kastryulin, S., Dylov, D.V.: Towards ultrafast MRI via extreme k-space undersampling and superresolution. In: de Bruijne, M., et al. (eds.) MICCAI 2021. LNCS, vol. 12906, pp. 254–264. Springer, Cham (2021). https://doi.org/10.1007/978-3-030-87231-1_25
2. Berntsen, J., et al.: Robust and generalizable embryo selection based on artificial intelligence and time-lapse image sequences. PLOS ONE **17**(2), e0262661 (2022)

3. de Bel, T., et al.: Stain-transforming cycle-consistent generative adversarial networks for improved segmentation of renal histopathology. In: Proceedings of The 2nd International Conference on Medical Imaging with Deep Learning. Proceedings of Machine Learning Research, vol. 102, pp. 151–163. PMLR, 08–10 July 2019

4. Gardner, D.K.: In-vitro culture of human blastocyst. In: Towards Reproductive Certainty: Infertility and Genetics Beyond 1999, pp. 378–388 (1999)

5. Georgescu, M.I., et al.: Convolutional neural networks with intermediate loss for 3D super-resolution of CT and MRI scans. IEEE Access 8, 49112–49124 (2020)

6. Gu, Y., et al.: MedSRGAN: medical images super-resolution using generative adversarial networks. Multimedia Tools Appl., 21815–21840 (2020). https://doi.org/10.1007/s11042-020-08980-w

7. Hariharan, R., et al.: Artificial intelligence assessment of time-lapse images can predict with 77% accuracy whether a human embryo capable of achieving a pregnancy will miscarry. Fertility Steril. 112(3), e38–e39 (2019)

8. He, K., et al.: Deep residual learning for image recognition. In: 2016 IEEE Conference on Computer Vision and Pattern Recognition (CVPR), pp. 770–778 (2016)

9. He, P., et al.: Machine learning for automated cell segmentation in embryos. Hum. Reprod. 36(Suppl._1), 211 (2021)

10. Hoffman, R., Gross, L.: Modulation contrast microscope. Appl. Opt. 14(5), 1169–1176 (1975)

11. Khosravi, P., et al.: Deep learning enables robust assessment and selection of human blastocysts after in vitro fertilization. npj Digit. Med. 2(1) (2019)

12. Kingma, D.P., Ba, J.: Adam: a method for stochastic optimization. CoRR abs/1412.6980 (2015)

13. Kragh, M.F., et al.: Automatic grading of human blastocysts from time-lapse imaging. Comput. Biol. Med. 115, 103494 (2019)

14. Kudo, A., Kitamura, Y., Li, Y., Iizuka, S., Simo-Serra, E.: Virtual thin slice: 3D conditional GAN-based super-resolution for CT slice interval. In: Knoll, F., Maier, A., Rueckert, D., Ye, J.C. (eds.) MLMIR 2019. LNCS, vol. 11905, pp. 91–100. Springer, Cham (2019). https://doi.org/10.1007/978-3-030-33843-5_9

15. Lau, T., et al.: Embryo staging with weakly-supervised region selection and dynamically-decoded predictions. In: Proceedings of the 4th Machine Learning for Healthcare Conference. Proceedings of Machine Learning Research, vol. 106, pp. 663–679. PMLR, 09–10 August 2019

16. Leahy, B.D., et al.: Automated measurements of key morphological features of human embryos for IVF. In: Martel, A.L., et al. (eds.) MICCAI 2020. LNCS, vol. 12265, pp. 25–35. Springer, Cham (2020). https://doi.org/10.1007/978-3-030-59722-1_3

17. Li, M., et al.: SACNN: self-attention convolutional neural network for low-dose CT denoising with self-supervised perceptual loss network. IEEE Trans. Med. Imaging 39(7), 2289–2301 (2020)

18. Liu, Z., et al.: Multi-task deep learning with dynamic programming for embryo early development stage classification from time-lapse videos. IEEE Access 7, 122153–122163 (2019)

19. Lockhart, L., Saeedi, P., Au, J., Havelock, J.: Automating embryo development stage detection in time-lapse imaging with synergic loss and temporal learning. In: de Bruijne, M., et al. (eds.) MICCAI 2021. LNCS, vol. 12905, pp. 540–549. Springer, Cham (2021). https://doi.org/10.1007/978-3-030-87240-3_52

20. Lukyanenko, S., et al.: Developmental stage classification of embryos using two-stream neural network with linear-chain conditional random field. In: de Bruijne, M., et al. (eds.) MICCAI 2021. LNCS, vol. 12908, pp. 363–372. Springer, Cham (2021). https://doi.org/10.1007/978-3-030-87237-3_35

21. Ma, Y., et al.: Cycle structure and illumination constrained GAN for medical image enhancement. In: Martel, A.L., et al. (eds.) MICCAI 2020. LNCS, vol. 12262, pp. 667–677. Springer, Cham (2020). https://doi.org/10.1007/978-3-030-59713-9_64

22. Malmsten, J., Zaninovic, N., Zhan, Q., Rosenwaks, Z., Shan, J.: Automated cell division classification in early mouse and human embryos using convolutional neural networks. Neural Comput. Appli. **33**(7), 2217–2228 (2020). https://doi.org/10.1007/s00521-020-05127-8

23. Peng, C., Zhou, S.K., Chellappa, R.: DA-VSR: domain adaptable volumetric super-resolution for medical images. In: de Bruijne, M., et al. (eds.) MICCAI 2021. LNCS, vol. 12906, pp. 75–85. Springer, Cham (2021). https://doi.org/10.1007/978-3-030-87231-1_8

24. Pizer, S.M., et al.: Adaptive histogram equalization and its variations. Comput. Vis. Graph. Image Process. **39**(3), 355–368 (1987)

25. Ronneberger, O., Fischer, P., Brox, T.: U-Net: convolutional networks for biomedical image segmentation. In: Navab, N., Hornegger, J., Wells, W.M., Frangi, A.F. (eds.) MICCAI 2015. LNCS, vol. 9351, pp. 234–241. Springer, Cham (2015). https://doi.org/10.1007/978-3-319-24574-4_28

26. Shaban, M.T., et al.: StainGAN: stain style transfer for digital histological images. In: 2019 IEEE 16th International Symposium on Biomedical Imaging (ISBI 2019), pp. 953–956 (2019)

27. Song, T.A., et al.: Pet image super-resolution using generative adversarial networks. Neural Netw. **125**, 83–91 (2020)

28. Thebille, A.-K., et al.: Deep learning-based bias transfer for overcoming laboratory differences of microscopic images. In: Papież, B.W., Yaqub, M., Jiao, J., Namburete, A.I.L., Noble, J.A. (eds.) MIUA 2021. LNCS, vol. 12722, pp. 322–336. Springer, Cham (2021). https://doi.org/10.1007/978-3-030-80432-9_25

29. VerMilyea, M., et al.: Development of an artificial intelligence-based assessment model for prediction of embryo viability using static images captured by optical light microscopy during IVF. Hum. Reprod. **35**(4), 770–784 (2020)

30. Wang, Z., et al.: Image quality assessment: from error visibility to structural similarity. IEEE Trans. Image Process. **13**(4), 600–612 (2004)

31. Yun, H.R., et al.: Improvement of inter-slice resolution based on 2D CNN with thin bone structure-aware on head-and-neck CT images. In: Medical Imaging 2021: Image Processing, vol. 11596, pp. 600–605. SPIE (2021)

32. Zhu, J.Y., Park, T., Isola, P., Efros, A.A.: Unpaired image-to-image translation using cycle-consistent adversarial networks. In: Proceedings of the IEEE International Conference on Computer Vision (ICCV), pp. 2223–2232 (2017)

SUPER-IVIM-DC: Intra-voxel Incoherent Motion Based Fetal Lung Maturity Assessment from Limited DWI Data Using Supervised Learning Coupled with Data-Consistency

Noam Korngut[1]([✉]), Elad Rotman[1], Onur Afacan[2]📷, Sila Kurugol[2]📷,
Yael Zaffrani-Reznikov[1], Shira Nemirovsky-Rotman[1]📷, Simon Warfield[2]📷,
and Moti Freiman[1]📷

[1] Faculty of Biomedical Engineering, Technion, Haifa, Israel
noam.korngut@campus.technion.ac.il
[2] Boston Children's Hospital, Boston, MA, USA

Abstract. Intra-voxel incoherent motion (IVIM) analysis of fetal lungs Diffusion-Weighted MRI (DWI) data shows potential in providing quantitative imaging bio-markers that reflect, indirectly, diffusion and pseudo-diffusion for non-invasive fetal lung maturation assessment. However, long acquisition times, due to the large number of different "b-value" images required for IVIM analysis, precluded clinical feasibility. We introduce SUPER-IVIM-DC a deep-neural-networks (DNN) approach which couples supervised loss with a data-consistency term to enable IVIM analysis of DWI data acquired with a limited number of b-values. We demonstrated the added-value of SUPER-IVIM-DC over both classical and recent DNN approaches for IVIM analysis through numerical simulations, healthy volunteer study, and IVIM analysis of fetal lung maturation from fetal DWI data. Our numerical simulations and healthy volunteer study show that SUPER-IVIM-DC estimates of the IVIM model parameters from limited DWI data had lower normalized root mean-squared error compared to previous DNN-based approaches. Further, SUPER-IVIM-DC estimates of the pseudo-diffusion fraction parameter from limited DWI data of fetal lungs correlate better with gestational age compared to both to classical and DNN-based approaches (0.555 vs. 0.463 and 0.310). SUPER-IVIM-DC has the potential to reduce the long acquisition times associated with IVIM analysis of DWI data and to provide clinically feasible bio-markers for non-invasive fetal lung maturity assessment.

Keywords: Fetal DWI · Intra-voxel incoherent motion ·
Deep-neural-networks

This research was supported in part by a grant from the United States-Israel Binational Science Foundation (BSF), Jerusalem, Israel.

1 Introduction

Normal fetal lung parenchyma development starts in the second trimester and progresses through multiple phases before becoming fully functional at full term. The first phase of development, the embryonic and pseudoglandular stage, is followed by the canalicular phase which starts at 16 weeks, then the saccular stage which starts at 24 weeks, and ends with the alveolar stage which starts at 36 weeks gestation. [18]. The progression through these phases is characterized with the formation of a dense capillary network and a progressive increase in pulmonary blood flow, leading to an increased perfusion [6]. Maldevelopment of the fetal lung parenchyma, however, may lead to life-threatening physiologic dysfunction due to pulmonary hypoplasia and pulmonary hypertension [13]. The ability to accurately assess lung maturation prior to delivery is therefore critical as newborns with inadequate in-utero lung development are at risk for post-natal respiratory failure or death [2].

In current practice, the non-invasive assessment of fetal lung parenchyma development is delivered by two anatomical imaging modalities: ultrasonography [15], and magnetic resonance imaging (MRI) [5]. Unfortunately, these modalities fail to provide adequate insight into lung function and are therefore suboptimal in assessing fetal lung maturity.

Diffusion-weighted MRI (DWI) is a non-invasive imaging technique sensitive to the random movement of individual water molecules. The displacement of individual water molecules results in signal attenuation in the presence of magnetic field encoding gradient pulses. This attenuation increases with the degree of sensitization-to-diffusion of the MRI pulse sequence (the "b-value") [1].

It is well established that the DWI signal attenuation essentially encapsulates not just thermally driven water diffusion, but also pseudo-diffusion that results from the randomness of the collective motion of blood water molecules in the randomly oriented network of micro-capillaries [14]. Specifically, the pseudo-diffusion phenomenon is known to attenuate the DWI signal acquired with low b-values (0–200 s/mm^2) [8].

Several studies demonstrated the potential role of diffusion and pseudo-diffusion imaging biomarkers derived from fetal lung DWI data with the so-called "intra-voxel incoherent motion" (IVIM) bi-exponential signal decay model in assessing lung maturity [6,10]. However, long acquisition times required to collect multiple b-values suitable for IVIM-based analysis of fetal lungs diffusion and pseudo-diffusion from DWI data (up to 16 different b-values [10]) hinder DWI-based analysis of fetal lung maturation in the clinical setting.

Previously, Bayesian approaches were proposed to address the challenge of obtaining reliable IVIM analyses from low SNR DW-MRI data. Neil et al. [16] and Orton et al. [17] suggested using a Bayesian shrinkage prior. Freiman et al. proposed a spatial homogeneity prior [7] and recently Spinner et al. [19] combined spatial and hierarchical priors. However, their heavy computational burdens hampered their utilization in practice.

In the past few years, state-of-the art deep-neural-networks (DNN)-based methods were introduced for IVIM parameter estimates. Bertleff et al. [4] demonstrated the ability of supervised DNN to predict the IVIM model parameters from low signal to noise ratio (SNR) DW-MRI data. Barbieri et al. [3] proposed an unsupervised physics-informed DNN (IVIM-NET) with results comparable to Bayesian methods with further optimizations by Kaandorp et al. [11] (IVIM-NET$_{optim}$). Recently, Vasylechko et al. used unsupervised convolutional neural networks (CNN) to improve the reliability of IVIM parameter estimates by leveraging spatial correlations in the data [20]. Specifically, Zhang et al. used a multi-layer perceptron with an amortized Gaussian posterior to estimate the IVIM model parameters from fetal lung DW-MRI data [21]. Yet, long acquisition times due to the large number of different b-value images required for fetal lung IVIM analysis with DNN-based methods (for example 16 in [10,21]) again precluded clinical feasibility.

In this work, we address the challenge of IVIM parameter estimates from clinical DWI data acquired with a limited number of b-values (i.e. up to 6 b-values) by presenting SUPER-IVIM-DC, a supervised DNN coupled with a data-consistency term that enables the analysis of diffusion and pseudo-diffusion biomarkers. We demonstrated the added value of SUPER-IVIM-DC compared to both the classical least-squares approach and recently proposed DNN-based approaches in assessing diffusion and pseudo-diffusion biomarkers through numerical simulations and a healthy volunteer study. Finally, we demonstrated clinical significance in fetal lung maturity analysis with the pseudo-diffusion fraction parameter of the IVIM model computed from DWI data with a limited number of b-values.

2   Method

2.1   The "Intra-voxel Incoherent Motion" Model of DWI

The "Intra-voxel Incoherent motion" model (IVIM) proposed by Le-Bihan [14], models the overall MRI signal attenuation as a sum of the diffusion and pseudo-diffusion components taking the shape of a bi-exponential decay:

$$s_i = s_0 \left(f \exp\left(-b_i \left(D^* + D\right)\right) + (1 - f) \exp\left(-b_i D\right) \right) \tag{1}$$

where s_i is the signal at b-value b_i; s_0 is the signal without sensitizing the diffusion gradients; D is the diffusion coefficient, an indirect measure of tissue cellularity; D^* is the pseudo-diffusion coefficient, an indirect measure of blood flow in the micro-capillaries network; and f is the fraction of the contribution of the pseudo-diffusion to the signal decay, which is related to the percentage volume of the micro-capillary network within the voxel.

Classical methods aim to estimate the IVIM model parameters from the observed data by using either a maximum-likelihood approach:

$$\hat{\theta} = \underset{\theta}{\text{argmax}}\, L\left(\theta | \{s_i\}_{i=0}^N\right) = \underset{\theta}{\text{argmax}}\, P\left(\{s_i\}_{i=0}^N | \theta\right) \tag{2}$$

where $\{s_i\}_{i=0}^N$ is the set of the observed signals at the different b-values and $\theta = \{D, D^*, f\}$ are the unknown IVIM model parameters, or a maximum a posterior approach:

$$\hat{\theta} = \underset{\theta}{\operatorname{argmax}} P\left(\theta| \{s_i\}_{i=0}^N\right) \propto P\left(\{s_i\}_{i=0}^N |\theta\right) P\left(\theta\right) \tag{3}$$

where $P(\theta)$ is the prior assumed on the distribution of the IVIM model parameters.

In contrast, DNN-based methods formalized the IVIM model parameters estimation problem as a prediction problem:

$$\hat{\theta} = g_\Phi\left(\{s_i\}_{i=0}^N\right) \tag{4}$$

where Φ are the DNN weights. The DNN weights are obtained through the minimization of some loss function over a training dataset. Bertleff et al. [4] used a supervised approach to obtain the DNN weights Φ:

$$\hat{\Phi} = \underset{\Phi}{\operatorname{argmin}} \sum_{k=1}^K \left\| g_\Phi\left(\{s_i^k\}_{i=0}^N\right) - \theta_{ref}^k \right\|^2 \tag{5}$$

where $k \in \{1, ..., K\}$ is the index of the DWI signal sample, Φ are the DNN weights for which the optimization is applied, by using simulated data generated from the reference parameters θ_{ref} with Eq. 1. More recently, Barbieri et al. [3] and Kaandorp et al. [11] used IVIM-NET, an unsupervised approach to obtain the DNN weights Φ:

$$\hat{\Phi} = \underset{\Phi}{\operatorname{argmin}} \sum_{k=1}^K \sum_{i=1}^N \left\| f_{g_\Phi\left(\{s_i^k\}_{i=0}^N\right)} \left(s_0^k, b_i\right) - s_i^k \right\|^2 \tag{6}$$

where $f_{g_\Phi\left(\{s_i^k\}_{i=0}^N\right)} \left(s_0^k, b_i\right)$ is the signal generated by the IVIM forward model (Eq. 1) given the parameter estimates predicted by the DNN $g_\Phi\left(\{s_i\}_{i=0}^N\right)$ for a given DWI signal s_0^k and a specific "b-value" $b_i, i \in \{1, ..., N\}$.

However, these methods may converge to a local minimum during the training process - resulting in suboptimal IVIM predictions when applied to new unseen data. Therefore, DWI data acquired with a large number of b-values are required to sufficiently constrain the DNN training process, and to obtain accurate IVIM model parameters predictions.

2.2   SUPER-IVIM-DC

In a shift from previous approaches, we propose to alleviate the need to acquire DWI data with a large number of "b-values" by constraining the DNN training process through a supervised loss function coupled with a data consistency term. Formally, our training process is defined as:

$$\hat{\Phi} = \underset{\Phi}{\mathrm{argmin}} \sum_{k=1}^{K} \left(L_{super}\left(\widehat{\theta^k}, \theta_{ref}^k\right) + \alpha_{dc} L_{dc}\left(\left\{\widehat{s_i^k}\right\}_{i=0}^{N}, \left\{s_{i,ref}^k\right\}_{i=0}^{N}\right) \right) \quad (7)$$

where $\widehat{\theta^k}$ are the IVIM model parameters predicted by the DNN for sample k, θ_{ref}^k are the reference parameters used to simulate the DWI data, $\left\{\widehat{s_i^k}\right\}_{i=0}^{N}$ are the DWI signals at the different "b-values" generated with the IVIM forward model (Eq. 1) using the predicted parameters $\widehat{\theta^k}$ and the $\left\{s_{i,ref}^k\right\}_{i=0}^{N}$ are the corresponding reference DWI signals simulated from the reference parameters θ_{ref}^k. To accommodate the differences in the IVIM model parameters magnitudes we decomposed $L_{super}\left(\widehat{\theta^k}, \theta_{ref}^k\right)$ into a weighted sum of the squared of the errors in the different IVIM model parameters estimates:

$$L_{super}\left(\widehat{\theta^k}, \theta_{ref}^k\right) = \alpha_D \left\|\widehat{D^k} - D_{ref}^k\right\|^2 + \alpha_f \left\|\widehat{f^k} - f_{ref}^k\right\|^2 + \alpha_{D*} \left\|\widehat{D*^k} - D*_{ref}^k\right\|^2 \tag{8}$$

in which our data-consistency term is defined as:

$$L_{dc}\left(\left\{\widehat{s_i^k}\right\}_{i=0}^{N}, \left\{s_i^k\right\}_{i=0}^{N}\right) = \sum_{i=1}^{N} \left\|f_{g_\Phi\left(\left\{s_i^k\right\}_{i=0}^{N}\right)}\left(s_0^k, b_i\right) - s_i^k\right\|^2 \tag{9}$$

2.3 Implementation Details

We modified the original IVIM-NET$_{optim}$ implementation [11] to include our SUPER-IVIM-DC loss function[1]. The scaling parameters in the SUPER-IVIM-DC loss function ($\{\alpha_D, \alpha_{D*}, \alpha_f, \alpha_{dc}\}$) were considered as hyperparameters. We used a one-dimensional grid search to determine the best values for these hyperparameters. We sampled sets of IVIM parameters at relevant ranges for each experiment, and used Eq. 1 to simulate DWI signals. To better mimic real data we added Rician Noise, at relevant pre-defined SNR levels, to those datasets. We split the simulated data into 90% for training and 10% for validation. We implemented our models on Spyder 4.2.0., Python 3.8.5 with PyTorch 1.6.0. We used an Adam optimizer [12] with learning-rate of 10^{-4}, and a batch-size of 128 to train the DNN. After 10 epochs with no improvement on the validation loss the networks stopped the training and the best performing model was saved for the evaluation.

2.4 Evaluation Methodology

Numerical Simulations. We conducted a simulation study to analyze the estimation errors for using a various undersampled b-values. First, we generated one million simulated signals using Eq. 1 with various undersampled b-values from

---

[1] Our code and trained models are available on GitHub:https://github.com/
TechnionComputationalMRILab/SUPER-IVIM-DC.

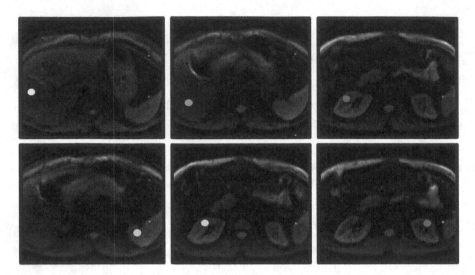

Fig. 1. Abdominal ROI from different slices

the following low b-values: (0,15,30,45,60,75,90,105,120,135,150,175) s/mm^2 concatenated with four high b-values: (200,400,600,800) s/mm^2 and pseudo-random values of Dt, Fp, and Dp. We sampled every k^{th} b-value from the low b-values vector according to a sampling factor $k \in \{1, ..., 6\}$, where when $k = 1$ represents a full sampling with all b-values. The b-values 0, 200 s/mm^2 remain part of the sampled b-values vector. We added noise to the simulated signals such that the SNR will be 10. Then, we trained SUPER-IVIM-DC and the baseline method IVIM-NET$_{optim}$ using the training data.

We then simulated 1000 samples of test data using the same approach as we used for training data generation. We estimated the model parameters from the noisy DW-MRI data as a function of the b-values sampling factor. We compared the estimation error of SUPER-IVIM-DC by means of normalized root-mean-squared error (NRMSE) in comparison to the baseline method IVIM-NET$_{optim}$.

Healthy Volunteer Study. We assessed the added-value of SUPER-IVIM-DC in estimating the IVIM model parameter values from limited DWI data in a clinical setting. We first acquire high-quality DWI data of a human volunteer with 22 b-values: (0, 12.5, 25, 37.5, 50, 62.5, 75, 87.5, 100, 112.5, 125, 150, 175, 200, 225, 250, 375, 500, 625, 750, 875, 1000) s/mm^2 using a multi-slice single shot echo planar imaging (EPI) sequence with 6 directions. We calculated trace-weighted images from the different directions at each b-value using geometric averaging. We annotated 6 different regions of interest in the kidneys, liver and spleen selected from different slices. (Fig. 1).

We estimated reference IVIM model parameters from the entire DWI data using standard least-squares approach. Next, we sampled the low b-value images (b-value $\leq$ 200 s/mm^2) in the DWI data in a similar way as in our numerical simulations above. We trained SUPER-IVIM-DC and the baseline method IVIM-NET$_{optim}$ using simulated data as described above and use them to predict IVIM model parameters from the human volunteer sampled data.

We compared the estimation error of SUPER-IVIM-DC for the 6 ROI by means of NRMSE in comparison to the baseline method IVIM-NET$_{optim}$ with the high-quality estimates as the reference.

Clinical Impact - Correlation Between Fetal Lung Maturation and Pseudo-diffusion Fraction. We used a legacy fetal lungs DWI data with reference gestational age from a study by Afacan et al. [1]. We used 38 cases of DWI data consisted of 6 b-values: (0, 50, 100, 200, 400, 600 s/mm^2). Detailed description of the acquisition protocol is provided in Afacan et al. [1]. We trained SUPER-IVIM-DC and the baseline method IVIM-NET$_{optim}$ using simulated data as described above with the same b-values used in the acquisition and SNR of 10. We estimated the pseudo-diffusion fraction parameter of the IVIM model (f) using classical least-squares approach [9], the IVIM-NET$_{optim}$ approach and SUPER-IVIM-DC.

We assessed Pearson-correlation between the estimated pseudo-diffusion fraction parameter of the IVIM model (f) obtained with the different approaches and the gestational age (GA) for different developmental stages.

3 Results

Numerical Simulations. Figure 2 summarizes our numerical simulations results. SUPER-IVIM-DC had a lower NRMSE for all IVIM model parameter estimates in all sampling factors compared to IVIM-NET$_{optim}$. The reduced NRMSE obtained with SUPER-IVIM-DC suggests a better generalization of the IVIM model by SUPER-IVIM-DC compared to IVIM-NET$_{optim}$.

Healthy Volunteer Study. Figure 3 summarizes our healthy volunteer study results. SUPER-IVIM-DC achieved lower NRMSE compared to IVIM-NET$_{optim}$ for both the D and the f parameters of the IVIM model in all sampling factors. For D^*, the improvement was evident in sampling factors 1,2, and 6, while in sampling factors 3–5 the difference was negligible.

The reduction in NRMSE achieved by SUPER IVIM DC was statistically significant ($p \ll 0.01$) for D and f parameters in experiments 1 and 2. The difference in D* was not statistically significant.

Clinical Impact - Correlation Between Fetal Lung Maturation and Pseudo-diffusion Fraction. Figure 4 depicts the correlations between the pseudo-diffusion-fraction of the IVIM model f as estimated by the different methods and the reference GA. By dividing the GA axis into two stages of the fetal lung development - the Canalicular phase (weeks 16–25) and the Saccular phase (week 26–34) our approach demonstrated a better correlation between the

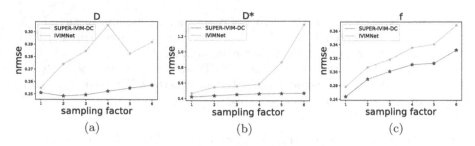

Fig. 2. Numerical simulations results. The NRMSE of the IVIM model parameter estimates obtained with SUPER-IVIM-DC and IVIM-NET$_{optim}$ as a function of the sampling factor.

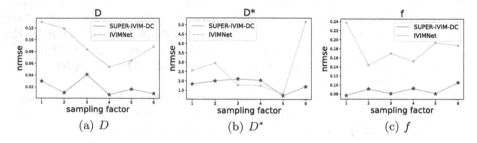

Fig. 3. Healthy volunteer study. SUPER-IVIM-DC reduced IVIM model parameter estimates NRMSE for D, f for all sampling factors. For D^*, the reduction was evident only in sampling factors 1,2, and 6.

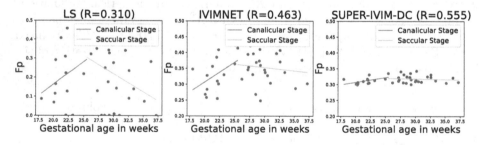

Fig. 4. Correlation between the pseudo-diffusion-fraction parameter (f) estimated with the different approaches and the gestational age (GA).

f parameter and the GA (0.555 with our SUPER-IVIM-DC vs. 0.463 and 0.310 with IVIMNET and LS) for the Canalicular phase of development (note that LS is in a different scale due to large distribution). This result correlates with the intensive angiogenesis starts the formation of a dense capillary network in the Canalicular phase.

4   Conclusions

In this work, we introduced SUPER-IVIM-DC, a DNN approach for the estimation of the IVIM model parameters from DWI data acquired with limited number of b-values. We demonstrated the added-value of SUPER-IVIM-DC over previously proposed DNN-based approach using numerical simulations and healthy volunteer study. Further, we show the potential clinical impact of SUPER-IVIM-DC in assessing fetal lung maturity from DWI data acquired with limited number of b-values. Thus, SUPER-IVIM-DC has the potential to reduce the overall acquisition times required for IVIM analysis of DWI data in various clinical applications. Specifically, SUPER-IVIM-DC has the potential to serve as a noninvasive prenatal diagnostic tool to study lung development and to quantify fetal growth. In turn, these data could have clinical relevance as benchmark values to distinguish normal fetuses from pathological fetuses with abnormal lung development.

References

1. Afacan, O., et al.: Fetal lung apparent diffusion coefficient measurement using diffusion-weighted MRI at 3 Tesla: correlation with gestational age. J. Magn. Reson. Imaging **44**(6), 1650–1655 (2016). https://doi.org/10.1002/jmri.25294
2. Ahlfeld, S.K., Conway, S.J.: Assessment of inhibited alveolar-capillary membrane structural development and function in bronchopulmonary dysplasia. Birth Defects Res. A **100**(3), 168–179 (2014)
3. Barbieri, S., Gurney-Champion, O.J., Klaassen, R., Thoeny, H.C.: Deep learning how to fit an intravoxel incoherent motion model to diffusion-weighted MRI. Magn. Reson. Med. **83**(1), 312–321 (2020)
4. Bertleff, M., et al.: Diffusion parameter mapping with the combined intravoxel incoherent motion and kurtosis model using artificial neural networks at 3 T. NMR Biomed. **30**(12), e3833 (2017)
5. Deshmukh, S., Rubesova, E., Barth, R.: MR assessment of normal fetal lung volumes: a literature review. Am. J. Roentgenol. **194**(2), W212–W217 (2010)
6. Ercolani, G., et al.: IntraVoxel Incoherent Motion (IVIM) MRI of fetal lung and kidney: can the perfusion fraction be a marker of normal pulmonary and renal maturation? Eur. J. Radiol. 139, 109726 (2021). https://doi.org/10.1016/J.EJRAD.2021.109726
7. Freiman, M., et al.: Reliable estimation of incoherent motion parametric maps from diffusion-weighted MRI using fusion bootstrap moves. Med. Image Anal. **17**(3), 325–336 (2013)
8. Freiman, M., Voss, S.D., Mulkern, R.V., Perez-Rossello, J.M., Callahan, M.J., Warfield, S.K.: In vivo assessment of optimal B-value range for perfusion-insensitive apparent diffusion coefficient imaging. Med. Phys. **39**(8), 4832–4839 (2012)
9. Gurney-Champion, O.J., et al.: Comparison of six fit algorithms for the intra-voxel incoherent motion model of diffusion-weighted magnetic resonance imaging data of pancreatic cancer patients. PLoS ONE **13**(4), e0194590 (2018)
10. Jakab, A., et al.: Microvascular perfusion of the placenta, developing fetal liver, and lungs assessed with intravoxel incoherent motion imaging. J. Magn. Reson. Imaging **48**(1), 214–225 (2018)

11. Kaandorp, M.P., et al.: Improved unsupervised physics-informed deep learning for intravoxel incoherent motion modeling and evaluation in pancreatic cancer patients. Magn. Reson. Med. **86**(4), 2250–2265 (2021)
12. Kingma, D.P., Ba, J.: Adam: a method for stochastic optimization. arXiv preprint arXiv:1412.6980 (2014)
13. Lakshminrusimha, S., Keszler, M.: Persistent pulmonary hypertension of the newborn. NeoReviews **16**(12), e680–e692 (2015)
14. Le Bihan, D.: What can we see with IVIM MRI? Neuroimage **187**, 56–67 (2019)
15. Moeglin, D., Talmant, C., Duyme, M., Lopez, A.C.: Fetal lung volumetry using two- and three-dimensional ultrasound. Ultrasound Obstet. Gynecol. 25(2), 119–127 (2005). https://doi.org/10.1002/UOG.1799
16. Neil, J.J., Bretthorst, G.L.: On the use of Bayesian probability theory for analysis of exponential decay date: an example taken from intravoxel incoherent motion experiments. Magn. Reson. Med. **29**(5), 642–647 (1993)
17. Orton, M.R., Collins, D.J., Koh, D.M., Leach, M.O.: Improved intravoxel incoherent motion analysis of diffusion weighted imaging by data driven Bayesian modeling. Magn. Reson. Med. **71**(1), 411–420 (2014)
18. Schittny, J.C.: Development of the lung. Cell Tissue Res. **367**(3), 427–444 (2017). https://doi.org/10.1007/s00441-016-2545-0
19. Spinner, G.R., Federau, C., Kozerke, S.: Bayesian inference using hierarchical and spatial priors for intravoxel incoherent motion MR imaging in the brain: analysis of cancer and acute stroke. Med. Image Anal. **73**, 102144 (2021)
20. Vasylechko, S.D., Warfield, S.K., Afacan, O., Kurugol, S.: Self-supervised IVIM DWI parameter estimation with a physics based forward model. Magn. Reson. Med. **87**(2), 904–914 (2022)
21. Zhang, L., Vishnevskiy, V., Jakab, A., Goksel, O.: Implicit modeling with uncertainty estimation for intravoxel incoherent motion imaging. In: 2019 IEEE 16th International Symposium on Biomedical Imaging (ISBI 2019), pp. 1003–1007. IEEE (2019)

Automated Classification of General Movements in Infants Using Two-Stream Spatiotemporal Fusion Network

Yuki Hashimoto[1]($\boxtimes$), Akira Furui[1], Koji Shimatani[2], Maura Casadio[3], Paolo Moretti[4], Pietro Morasso[5], and Toshio Tsuji[1]

[1] Hiroshima University, Hiroshima, Japan
{yukihashimato,akirafurui,toshiotsuji}@hiroshima-u.ac.jp
[2] Prefectural University of Hiroshima, Hiroshima, Japan
[3] University of Genoa, Genova, Italy
[4] Istituto G. Gaslini Pediatric Hospital, Genova, Italy
[5] Italian Institute of Technology, Genova, Italy

Abstract. The assessment of general movements (GMs) in infants is a useful tool in the early diagnosis of neurodevelopmental disorders. However, its evaluation in clinical practice relies on visual inspection by experts, and an automated solution is eagerly awaited. Recently, video-based GMs classification has attracted attention, but this approach would be strongly affected by irrelevant information, such as background clutter in the video. Furthermore, for reliability, it is necessary to properly extract the spatiotemporal features of infants during GMs. In this study, we propose an automated GMs classification method, which consists of preprocessing networks that remove unnecessary background information from GMs videos and adjust the infant's body position, and a subsequent motion classification network based on a two-stream structure. The proposed method can efficiently extract the essential spatiotemporal features for GMs classification while preventing overfitting to irrelevant information for different recording environments. We validated the proposed method using videos obtained from 100 infants. The experimental results demonstrate that the proposed method outperforms several baseline models and the existing methods.

Keywords: General movements · Infant · Motion classification · Spatiotemporal fusion · Two-stream network

1 Introduction

Neurodevelopmental disorders (NDs) are impairments of brain function and nervous system development. Patients with NDs may experience real-life difficulties due to biases and problems in cognition, movement, social skills, and attention. Meanwhile, the brain is capable of modifying the structure and function of

Y. Hashimoto and A. Furui—Equal contribution.

the central nervous system, known as plasticity, and the younger the brain, the greater the plasticity. Therefore, early detection of the signs of NDs followed by effective intervention is crucial.

General movements (GMs) assessment is one of the most predictive and valid methods for early detection of NDs [9,19]. GMs are spontaneous movements observed during early infancy that reflect the state of the central nervous system. In general, experts observe video recordings of infants and assess the quality of GMs, especially abnormalities in movements or the lack of specific movement patterns. Qualitative abnormalities in GMs are closely related to the risk of cerebral palsy and various NDs [3,12]. However, GMs assessment relies on visual inspection, which requires a high level of expertise and places a heavy burden on experts because of the need for prolonged observation; thus, an automated solution for GMs classification is eagerly awaited.

Recently, automated classification of GMs based on video recognition has attracted significant attention [1,2,17,18,22,26]. In this approach, the following is important. (i) Separation of infant and irrelevant information: The cost of GMs recording in a medical setting is very high, and it is not easy to obtain a large dataset. Additionally, the number of high-risk infants with abnormal GMs is generally small and often concentrated in specific medical institutions, which can lead to bias in the recording environment depending on the types of GMs. The use of these recordings possesses the risk of overfitting the recognition model to irrelevant information, such as background clutter (e.g., wrinkles in the sheets or bed frame) and differences in the relative body sizes in the videos. (ii) Appropriate extraction of spatiotemporal features: Experts assess GMs by comprehensively evaluating the infant's spatial features (appearance) and their temporal evolution (movement). Temporal features such as motor intensity and velocity would be the most important factors characterizing GMs, and abnormal GMs lack fluency and complexity [8]. Spatial features such as the body shape and posture may also contribute to the reliability of GMs assessment [14]. Therefore, if we can extract and integrate the effective spatial and temporal components from a video while removing irrelevant visual artifacts, an accurate and reliable recognition architecture for GMs classification can be developed.

In this study, we propose an automated GMs classification method that can remove irrelevant information from videos and efficiently learn the spatiotemporal features of infants during spontaneous movements. The proposed method consists of preprocessing networks and a motion classification network. First, the preprocessing networks receive the measured video and extract only the infant's body area from each frame using the mask obtained by salient object detection. The relative size and angle of the infant's body in the video are then unified among different individuals utilizing the joint coordinates obtained from the pose estimation model. Subsequently, we construct a single-frame image and stacked multi-frame optical flow from the preprocessed video, and the motion classification network with a two-stream architecture extracts temporal and spatial features to predict the types of GMs.

The main contributions of this study are as follows:

- We introduce preprocessing networks to remove irrelevant information from the videos automatically, thereby preventing overfitting to non-essential elements for GMs classification.
- We introduce a motion classification network based on a two-stream architecture. By fusing a spatial stream with a single-frame image and a temporal stream with a multi-frame optical flow, this network can efficiently learn the spatiotemporal features that characterize the GMs.

2   Related Work

GMs are whole-body spontaneous movements that appear 8–9 weeks after fertilization and are observed until 15–20 weeks of corrected age, giving an impression of fluency and grace [9,19]. These movements are generated by a central pattern generator that is believed to reside between the brainstem and spinal cord and reflect the state of the infant's nervous system. Writhing movements (WMs) observed in the post-term period are characterized by elliptical movements of the limbs, sometimes with large extensions of the upper limbs [9]. At the post-term ages of 6–9 weeks, WMs gradually disappear and fidgety movements (FMs) emerge, in which the head, trunk, and limbs move in all directions in tiny movements [20]. In contrast, movements that are absent or qualitatively different from normal movements are considered abnormal GMs. For example, poor repertoire GMs (PR) are classified if the sequence of successive movement components is monotonous, and the intensity, velocity, and range of motion lack the normal variability as seen in WMs [8]. Qualitative abnormalities of these GMs are a good predictor of cerebral palsy, autism spectrum disorders, and delayed cognitive and language development [3,8].

Video-based GMs classification methods that do not interfere with infants' natural movements have been studied to develop automated early screening tools for NDs. Various methods have been developed to design features of spontaneous movements in infants based on image processing [16,24], and some of these methods have been applied to GMs classification [1,2,26]. However, these feature engineering-based approaches have difficulty in comprehensively capturing the discriminative features specific to GMs classification. Recently, the automatic extraction of spatiotemporal features that characterize GMs based on deep neural networks, including a convolutional neural network (CNN)-based method [22] and a combination of pose estimation and attention mechanisms [18], has been shown to be effective. These video-based methods, however, involve the problem of being strongly affected by irrelevant information, such as background clutter and relative positions of the infant's body. The pose-based approach [5,18] may mitigate this problem, but its performance depends on the accuracy of the pose estimation algorithm. Therefore, we propose a video-based GMs classification method that can remove irrelevant, distracting information from the video and learn spatial and temporal features based on a two-stream architecture to extract effective features related to GMs.

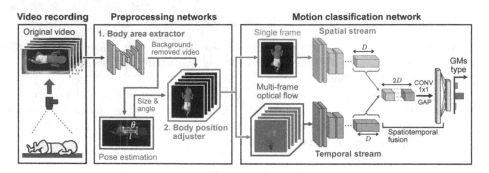

Fig. 1. Overview of the proposed GMs classification method. The abbreviations GAP and CONV 1×1 denote global average pooling and pointwise convolution, respectively.

3   Proposed GMs Classification Method

Figure 1 shows an overview of the proposed method. The proposed method consists of the preprocessing networks and motion classification network. The preprocessing networks extract the infant's body area and adjust the relative body size and position in the image to remove the effects of visual artifacts. The motion classification network predicts the types of GMs based on a two-stream architecture to efficiently extract the spatial and temporal features of infants during GMs.

3.1   Preprocessing Networks

In general, video recording of GMs is performed using a single RGB camera fixed above the bed to capture the movements of an infant lying supine, which has two difficulties. First, the video contains irrelevant information other than the infant's body, such as wrinkles in sheets, the bed frame, and the floor. Second, the relative scale and orientation of the infant with respect to the camera may differ for each recording period. It is difficult to completely standardize these conditions among different medical institutions. In the preprocessing networks, the former problem is solved by a body area extractor, and the latter problem is solved by a body position adjuster.

Body area extractor separates the infant's body and background information. We use U^2-Net [21] pretrained on the DUST-TR dataset, which has shown good segmentation results for various tasks. We apply the segmentation based on U^2-Net for each frame and extract the infant's body by masking the output saliency maps to the original video frames. **Body position adjuster** unifies the scale and orientation of the infant across different videos. This adjuster utilizes OpenPose [4], a pose estimation network. Out of the 18 joints output from this network, we use four coordinates for both shoulders and hips. The vector passing through the midpoints of both shoulders and hips is defined as the approximate body-axis direction and is used for adjustment.

The adjustment is performed in the following two steps. In the first step, pose estimation is applied to the first frame of the video and obtain the angle of the body axis relative to the vertical direction of the video. We then rotate all the video frames using this angle to roughly align the body orientation. In the second step, pose estimation is applied again to each frame of the rotated video, and the following three quantities at frame t are calculated: the angle θ_t of the body axis, center coordinate $\mathbf{c}_t$ of the line segment connecting the midpoints of both shoulders and hips, and length l_t of the line segment. To consistently adjust the video frames, the averages of the quartile range of the above quantities are calculated for every frame and defined as $\bar{\theta}$, $\bar{\mathbf{c}}$, and $\bar{l}$, respectively. The body orientation is readjusted by rotating all the frames using $\bar{\theta}$, and each video frame is cropped or uncropped with a square such that $\bar{\mathbf{c}}$ coincides with the center position of the video frame after rotation. We set the length of one side of the square to $R = 3\bar{l}/\alpha$, where $\alpha > 0$ is an arbitrary parameter that fits the infant's body in the video at a reasonable scale. Finally, all video frames are resized by $W \times H$ because R has a different value for each video.

3.2   Motion Classification Network with Two-Stream Architecture

We construct the motion classification network based on the two-stream approach [11,23] consisting of two CNNs: spatial and temporal streams. The feature maps in the output layer of each stream are fused, and the softmax scores are finally calculated through the fully connected layer.

The spatial and temporal streams receive a single-frame image and a stacked multi-frame optical flow, respectively. Here, the optical flow is a set of displacement vector fields between consecutive pairs of frames, t and $t + 1$, reflecting the infant's motion information between frames. Dense optical flow is calculated from each frame of the RGB video $\mathbf{x}_t \in \mathbb{R}^{W \times H \times 3}$ output from the preprocessing networks using the Farneback method [10], and the horizontal and vertical components of the vector field, $\mathbf{d}_t^h \in \mathbb{R}^{W \times H}$ and $\mathbf{d}_t^v \in \mathbb{R}^{W \times H}$, are extracted.

To represent motion across a sequence of frames, the input of each stream is given by a temporal chunk consisting of L consecutive frames. Each chunk is separated by τ frames. For the n-th chunk, the input of the spatial stream, $\mathbf{x}_n^s$, is a single-frame image at the center of the chunk, as follows:

$$\mathbf{x}_n^s = \mathbf{x}_{(n-1)\tau+\frac{L}{2}-1}. \tag{1}$$

The input of the temporal stream, $\mathbf{x}_n^t \in \mathbb{R}^{W \times H \times 2L}$, is constructed by stacking the flow components $\mathbf{d}_t^h$ and $\mathbf{d}_t^v$ in the chunk along the channel direction:

$$\mathbf{x}_n^t(2k - 1) = \mathbf{d}_{(n-1)\tau+k-1}^h, \quad \mathbf{x}_n^t(2k) = \mathbf{d}_{(n-1)\tau+k-1}^v, \tag{2}$$

where $k = 1, 2, \ldots, L$ and $\mathbf{x}_n^t(c)$ is the explicit element of $\mathbf{x}_n^t$ in channel c.

For both streams, we use CNNs pretrained on a large-scale dataset. Each CNN stream is combined after the activation function of the final convolutional layer. Because the input of the temporal stream has a channel size of $2L$, the first layer of the temporal CNN is modified to fit the dimensionality.

The feature maps output from the spatial and temporal streams, $\mathbf{y}_n^s \in \mathbb{R}^{W' \times H' \times D}$ and $\mathbf{y}_n^t \in \mathbb{R}^{W' \times H' \times D}$, are combined to create the final feature vector, where W', H', and D are the width, height, and the number of channels of the respective feature maps. First, we stack the two feature maps at the same spatial locations across the feature channels to form $\mathbf{y}_n^{cat} \in \mathbb{R}^{W' \times H' \times 2D}$. We then transform $\mathbf{y}_n^{cat}$ by pointwise convolution using the filters $\mathbf{f} \in \mathbb{R}^{1 \times 1 \times 2D \times D}$ and biases $\mathbf{b} \in \mathbb{R}^D$ to learn the correspondence between the two feature maps:

$$\widetilde{\mathbf{y}}_n = \mathbf{y}_n^{cat} * \mathbf{f} + \mathbf{b}, \tag{3}$$

where $*$ denotes the operator for convolution. After global average pooling is applied to the fused feature map $\widetilde{\mathbf{y}}_n$, the prediction score is calculated via a fully connected layer and softmax activation. Because the prediction score is calculated for each temporal chunk, the video-wise prediction of the GMs class is finally determined by averaging the scores over all the chunks in the video.

4   Experiments

To evaluate the validity of the proposed method, we conducted GMs classification experiments. In the experiments, we used a dataset of videos of infants captured in medical institutions at Japan and Italy. The aim of the study was fully explained to each infant's parents, and informed consent was obtained before participation in the experiment. All experiments were approved by the Ethics Committee of the Gaslini Pediatric Hospital and Hiroshima University (registration numbers: IGGPM01-2013 and E-1150-2). Our code is available at https:// github.com/uoNuM/two-stream-gma.

Dataset and Implementation Details: The dataset consisted of videos obtained from 100 infants; each video was captured at a frame rate of 30 fps and resolution of 1280×720 pixels. The length of the original videos ranged from 60 to 210 s, and we clipped consecutive 60 s frames during GMs from each original video, avoiding periods of sleep and crying. The infants' gestational ages ranged from 210 to 295 days, and their birth weight range was from 1400 to 3985 g. GMs labels were attached to each video based on annotations by well-trained experts with GMs evaluation licenses. The resulting labels are as follows: WMs, 37; FMs, 36; and PR, 27. Here, WMs and FMs are normal GMs, and PR is abnormal. To evaluate the classification performance, we performed a stratified infant-wise 5-fold cross-validation on the dataset.

We used ResNet-50 [13] that was pretrained on the ImageNet dataset for each CNN stream. Accordingly, the resize in the body position adjuster was set to $W = H = 224$, and the body scale parameter was set to $\alpha = 0.8$. Each video was downsampled to 6 fps and the length and interval of the temporal chunks were set to $L = \tau = 30$. The entire motion classification network was fine-tuned on our GMs dataset using the AdamW [15] optimizer, with a learning rate of 10^{-5}. During fine-tuning, we performed horizontal flipping data augmentation, which involved the inversion of the horizontal component of the optical flow.

Table 1. Quantitative evaluation results (*mean ± standard deviation*)

Method	Accuracy	MCC	Precision	Recall
Existing method				
Tsuji *et al.* [26]	0.556 ± 0.010	0.331 ± 0.016	0.556 ± 0.005	0.539 ± 0.013
STAM [18]	0.640 ± 0.032	0.408 ± 0.044	0.646 ± 0.046	0.427 ± 0.034
Baseline				
CNN + LSTM [7]	0.694 ± 0.031	0.563 ± 0.051	0.621 ± 0.057	0.659 ± 0.035
C3D [25]	0.700 ± 0.009	0.556 ± 0.016	0.684 ± 0.012	0.678 ± 0.010
Ours				
Only spatial	0.742 ± 0.029	0.628 ± 0.039	0.750 ± 0.022	0.723 ± 0.026
Only temporal	0.696 ± 0.019	0.551 ± 0.033	0.693 ± 0.030	0.670 ± 0.018
Two-stream fusion	**0.752 ± 0.013**	**0.647 ± 0.015**	**0.780 ± 0.010**	**0.737 ± 0.011**

Experimental Conditions: We compared the proposed method with two existing methods for GMs classification. One is an image processing-based system proposed by Tsuji *et al.* that uses 25 domain-dependent features calculated from background subtractions and inter-frame differences [26]. The other is STAM [18], which is a state-of-the-art method for infant movement classification using graph neural networks with features obtained from pose estimation as input. Both existing methods were retrained from scratch using our GMs dataset. As baselines, two types of action recognition networks, CNN + LSTM [7] and C3D [25], were used instead of the motion classification network of the proposed method. The preprocessing networks were also applied to these baselines. We used ResNet-50 pretrained on ImageNet for the former CNN and the latter was pretrained on the Sports-M1 dataset. Both were finetuned in the same way as the proposed method. In addition, we conducted an ablation study to evaluate the effectiveness of the body area extractor and the body position adjuster in the preprocessing networks.

We used accuracy, the Matthews correlation coefficient (MCC), precision, and recall as performance measures. For robust results, we repeated the analysis by changing the random seed five times and calculated the mean and standard deviation of each measure. We did not perform statistical tests due to the small sample size.

Results: Table 1 shows the quantitative evaluation results of each method. Our method also shows the results of using each stream individually. The proposed method with two-stream fusion achieves the best performance for all performance measures. The performance decreases when the structure of the motion classification network was changed to a single stream or a baseline. Therefore, the network based on the two-stream architecture was effective for extracting the spatiotemporal features of infants during GMs.

Table 2 shows the results of the ablation study. The combination of each element of the preprocessing networks shows the best performance except for

Table 2. Results of the ablation study for the preprocessing networks with the body area extractor and body position adjuster (*mean ± standard deviation*). The absence of ✓ means that the corresponding element is removed from the proposed method.

Extractor	Adjuster	Accuracy	MCC	Precision	Recall
		0.754 ± 0.016	0.636 ± 0.024	0.760 ± 0.016	0.734 ± 0.017
✓		0.734 ± 0.010	0.623 ± 0.013	0.742 ± 0.025	0.724 ± 0.012
✓	✓	0.752 ± 0.013	**0.647 ± 0.015**	**0.780 ± 0.010**	**0.737 ± 0.011**

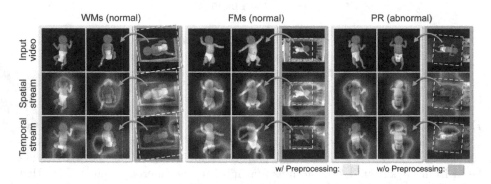

Fig. 2. Visualization of activation maps using Grad-CAM++. The results of the proposed method with the preprocessing networks are shown with two examples for each GMs class. The rightmost column for each class is an example without the preprocessing networks, corresponding to the second example with the preprocessing networks.

accuracy. Although the performance without the preprocessing networks is also relatively high, this is because the model focuses on irrelevant information other than the infant (as shown later in Fig. 2). Overfitting to such non-essential but class-related components may cause ostensibly high validation performance in the limited dataset. In fact, when only the extractor is applied, such components are not referred, resulting in a loss of performance. In contrast, incorporating the adjuster to unify the scale and orientation of the infant's body enables appropriate feature extraction and improves overall performance.

Figure 2 shows some typical examples of class activation maps using Grad-CAM++ [6]. These activation maps were calculated for each stream in the proposed two-stream architecture. The results demonstrate that the proposed method with the preprocessing networks adequately captures different aspects of infants during GMs in each stream. The spatial stream focuses on the infant's overall appearance, including body shape and posture, while the temporal stream pays more attention to the limbs, which greatly influences the impression of movement. In contrast, the proposed method without the preprocessing networks focuses on the bed frame or floor texture, irrelevant to the infant.

5 Conclusion

This study proposed a classification method for GMs in infants based on spatiotemporal fusion. In the proposed method, we introduce preprocessing networks to remove irrelevant information from the video and adjust the infant's body position. To capture spatiotemporal feature representations of infants during GMs, we also introduced a two-stream network with a single-frame image and stacked optical flow as the input of each stream to classify the types of GMs. The experimental results show that the proposed method outperforms existing GMs classification methods and suppresses overfitting to irrelevant elements in the video owing to the preprocessing networks.

One of the limitations of this study is that no quantitative evaluation of the reliability of the calculated optical flows has been made, which should be demonstrated in future work. We will also introduce a disentangle representation learning to explore the spatial and temporal features that are most strongly associated with GMs assessment. Furthermore, we plan to extend the proposed framework to a wider range of spontaneous movement assessments, such as longitudinal assessments.

References

1. Adde, L., Helbostad, J.L., Jensenius, A.R., Taraldsen, G., Grunewaldt, K.H., Støen, R.: Early prediction of cerebral palsy by computer-based video analysis of general movements: a feasibility study. Dev. Med. Child Neurol. **52**(8), 773–778 (2010)
2. Adde, L., et al.: Characteristics of general movements in preterm infants assessed by computer-based video analysis. Physiother. Theor. Pract. **34**(4), 286–292 (2018)
3. Beccaria, E., et al.: Poor repertoire general movements predict some aspects of development outcome at 2 years in very preterm infants. Early Hum. Dev. **88**(6), 393–396 (2012)
4. Cao, Z., Simon, T., Wei, S.E., Sheikh, Y.: Realtime multi-person 2D pose estimation using part affinity fields. In: Proceedings of the IEEE Conference on Computer Vision and Pattern Recognition (CVPR), pp. 7291–7299 (2017)
5. Chambers, C., et al.: Computer vision to automatically assess infant neuromotor risk. IEEE Trans. Neural Syst. Rehabil. Eng. **28**(11), 2431–2442 (2020)
6. Chattopadhay, A., Sarkar, A., Howlader, P., Balasubramanian, V.N.: Grad-CAM++: generalized gradient-based visual explanations for deep convolutional networks. In: Proceedings of the IEEE Winter Conference on Applications of Computer Vision (WACV), pp. 839–847 (2018)
7. Donahue, J., et al.: Long-term recurrent convolutional networks for visual recognition and description. In: Proceedings of the IEEE Conference on Computer Vision and Pattern Recognition (CVPR), pp. 2625–2634 (2015)
8. Einspieler, C., Bos, A.F., Libertus, M.E., Marschik, P.B.: The general movement assessment helps us to identify preterm infants at risk for cognitive dysfunction. Front. Psychol. **7**, 406 (2016)
9. Einspieler, C., Prechtl, H.F.: Prechtl's assessment of general movements: a diagnostic tool for the functional assessment of the young nervous system. Ment. Retard. Dev. Disabil. Res. Rev. **11**(1), 61–67 (2005)

10. Farnebäck, G.: Two-frame motion estimation based on polynomial expansion. In: Bigun, J., Gustavsson, T. (eds.) SCIA 2003. LNCS, vol. 2749, pp. 363–370. Springer, Heidelberg (2003). https://doi.org/10.1007/3-540-45103-X_50
11. Feichtenhofer, C., Pinz, A., Zisserman, A.: Convolutional two-stream network fusion for video action recognition. In: Proceedings of the IEEE Conference on Computer Vision and Pattern Recognition (CVPR), pp. 1933–1941 (2016)
12. Ferrari, F., Cioni, G., Prechtl, H.: Qualitative changes of general movements in preterm infants with brain lesions. Early Hum. Dev. 23(3), 193–231 (1990)
13. He, K., Zhang, X., Ren, S., Sun, J.: Deep residual learning for image recognition. In: Proceedings of the IEEE Conference on Computer Vision and Pattern Recognition (CVPR), pp. 770–778 (2016)
14. Hesse, N., et al.: Learning an infant body model from RGB-D data for accurate full body motion analysis. In: Frangi, A.F., Schnabel, J.A., Davatzikos, C., Alberola-López, C., Fichtinger, G. (eds.) MICCAI 2018. LNCS, vol. 11070, pp. 792–800. Springer, Cham (2018). https://doi.org/10.1007/978-3-030-00928-1_89
15. Loshchilov, I., Hutter, F.: Decoupled weight decay regularization. In: Proceedings of the International Conference on Learning Representations (ICLR) (2017)
16. Maggi, E., et al.: A new method for early detection of infants at risk of long-term neuromotor disabilities. Gait Posture 57, 23–24 (2017)
17. McCay, K.D., Ho, E.S., Shum, H.P., Fehringer, G., Marcroft, C., Embleton, N.D.: Abnormal infant movements classification with deep learning on pose-based features. IEEE Access 8, 51582–51592 (2020)
18. Nguyen-Thai, B., Le, V., Morgan, C., Badawi, N., Tran, T., Venkatesh, S.: A spatio-temporal attention-based model for infant movement assessment from videos. IEEE J. Biomed. Health Inform. 25(10), 3911–3920 (2021)
19. Prechtl, H.F.: Qualitative changes of spontaneous movements in fetus and preterm infant are a marker of neurological dysfunction. Early Hum. Dev. 23(3), 151–158 (1990)
20. Prechtl, H.F.: State of the art of a new functional assessment of the young nervous system. An early predictor of cerebral palsy. Early Hum. Dev. 50(1), 1–11 (1997)
21. Qin, X., Zhang, Z., Huang, C., Dehghan, M., Zaiane, O.R., Jagersand, M.: U^2-Net: going deeper with nested U-structure for salient object detection. Pattern Recogn. 106, 107404 (2020)
22. Schmidt, W., Regan, M., Fahey, M., Paplinski, A.: General movement assessment by machine learning: why is it so difficult? J. Med. Artif. Intell. 2, 1–10 (2019)
23. Simonyan, K., Zisserman, A.: Two-stream convolutional networks for action recognition in videos. In: Proceedings of the 27th International Conference on Neural Information Processing Systems (NIPS), pp. 568–576 (2014)
24. Tacchino, C., et al.: Spontaneous movements in the newborns: a tool of quantitative video analysis of preterm babies. Comput. Meth. Programs Biomed. 199, 105838 (2021)
25. Tran, D., Bourdev, L., Fergus, R., Torresani, L., Paluri, M.: Learning spatiotemporal features with 3D convolutional networks. In: Proceedings of the IEEE International Conference on Computer Vision (ICCV), pp. 4489–4497 (2015)
26. Tsuji, T., et al.: Markerless measurement and evaluation of general movements in infants. Sci. Rep. 10(1), 1422 (2020)

Author Index

Abi-Nader, Clément 464
Adams, Jadie 474
Afacan, Onur 743
Aichert, Andre 88
Aljuhani, Asmaa 366
Ambellan, Felix 453
Amiranashvili, Tamaz 453
An, Lin 550
André, Fabrice 325
Asani, Ben 699
Atwany, Mohammad 635
Ayhan, Murat Seçkin 539

Bai, Yanmiao 560
Barber, Joshua C. 444
Berens, Philipp 539
Bloch, Isabelle 464
Bogunović, Hrvoje 625
Bohnenberger, Hanibal 88
Boluda, Susana 336
Bône, Alexandre 464
Boreiko, Valentyn 539
Boxberg, Melanie 99, 377
Boyd, Joseph 356
Brehler, Michael 398
Breininger, Katharina 517
Brown, Donald E. 345

Cao, Maosong 202
Carmichael, Iain 387
Carneiro, Gustavo 263
Casadio, Maura 753
Casukhela, Ishya 366
Chakravarty, Arunava 625
Chambost, Jérôme 732
Chan, Jany 366
Chang, Eric I-Chao 160
Chen, Hanbo 35
Chen, Hao 140, 645
Chen, Junliang 109
Chen, Richard J. 387
Chen, Siheng 721
Chen, Siyu 517
Chen, Tiffany Y. 387

Chen, Xiaoyang 444
Chen, Yang 232
Chen, Yen-Wei 571
Chen, Zhao 253
Cheng, Kwang-Ting 140
Cheung, Carol Y. 645
Chikontwe, Philip 420
Christodoulidis, Stergios 325, 356
Couzinié-Devy, Florent 120
Cui, Hui 3

Dang, Kang 721
Daroach, Gagandeep B. 398
Delatour, Benoît 336
Deng, Hannah H. 444
Derakhshani, Mohammad Mahdi 314
Deutsch, Eric 356
Ding, Xiaowei 721
Doan, Tan Nhu Nhat 171
Dong, Jiuyang 232
Dong, Li 550
Dong, Yuhan 550
Du, Shiyi 56
Duenweg, Savannah R. 398

Elhabian, Shireen 474
Emre, Taha 625
Ezhov, Ivan 453

Faber, Hanna 539
Fan, Lei 409
Fan, Xiangshan 202
Fan, Yubo 160
Fang, Huihui 604, 614, 677
Fang, Zhenyu 3
Farshad, Azade 582
Feng, Wei 497
Freiman, Moti 743
Fréour, Thomas 732
Fu, Huazhu 487, 507, 560, 688
Fuchs, Moritz 14
Fujimoto, James 517
Furui, Akira 753

Gaitskell, Kezia   130
Galdran, Adrian   263
Gao, Jing   677
Gao, Xiangbo   109
Gao, Yunshu   507
Garberis, Ingrid   325
Gateno, Jaime   444
Ge, Xinting   560
Ge, Zongyuan   497, 593
Gehlbach, Peter   582
Ghaffari Laleh, Narmin   263
Githinji, Bilha   550
Go, Heounjeong   420
González Ballester, Miguel A.   263
Gori, Pietro   464
Gupta, Rajarsi   192

Hafner, Michael   699
Hao, Jinkui   560
Haq, Mohammad Minhazul   303
Hashimoto, Yuki   753
He, Chloe   732
He, Lei   35
He, Mingguang   593
He, Nanjun   656
Heimann, Tobias   88
Hein, Matthias   539
Hewitt, Katherine J.   263
Hickman, Cristina   732
Holmberg, Olle   699
Hou, Wentai   181
Hu, Yan   487, 507, 560
Hu, Yang   130
Huang, Helong   181
Huang, Junzhou   66, 303
Huang, Kun   222
Huang, Xufeng   433
Husvogt, Lennart   517

Iczkowski, Kenneth A.   398
Ilanchezian, Indu   539
Ingrassia, Léa   336

Jacobsohn, Kenneth M.   398
Jacques, Céline   732
Jiang, Zekun   56
Jiang, Zhiguo   273, 283
Jimenez, Gabriel   336
Jin, Qiangguo   3

Jin, Richu   688
Ju, Lie   497

Kang, Qingbo   56
Kar, Anuradha   336
Kather, Jakob N.   263
Ke, Jing   212
Kim, Kyungeun   171
Kim, Meejeong   420
Koch, Lisa M.   539
Koch, Valentin   699
Korngut, Noam   743
Kuang, Tianshu   444
Kurugol, Sila   743
Kwak, Jin Tae   171
Kwapong, William Robert   688

Lai, Maode   160
Lang, Yankun   444
Lao, Qicheng   56
LaViolette, Peter S.   398
Le Bescond, Loïc   325
Lerousseau, Marvin   325
Li, Fang   550
Li, Haojie   571
Li, Heng   487, 507, 688
Li, Honglin   242
Li, Jun   273, 283
Li, Kailu   160
Li, Kang   56
Li, Qingli   46
Li, Xi   232
Li, Xuechen   109
Li, Yiyue   56
Li, Yuexiang   656
Liebner, David   366
Lin, Yi   140
Lin, Yiyang   232
Lin, Yuexiao   293
Lin, Zhenyu   66
Lin, Zhihong   593
Liu, Feng   656
Liu, Haofeng   487, 507
Liu, Haozhe   656
Liu, Huafeng   433
Liu, Jiang   487, 507, 560, 688
Liu, Minmin   109
Liu, Shaolei   24
Liu, Zhiwen   150
Lowman, Allison K.   398

Lu, Donghuan   667
Lu, Zixiao   222
Lüdke, David   453
Luo, Tongyi   721
Luo, Xiaoling   487
Luo, Xiaoyuan   24
Luo, Yulin   212
Lv, Zhilong   293

Ma, Ke   192
Ma, Lan   550
Machiraju, Raghu   366
Mahapatra, Dwarikanath   314
Mahmood, Faisal   387
Maier, Andreas   517
Malmsten, Jonas   732
Mathieu, Marie-Christine   356
Meijering, Erik   409
Meng, Weiliang   528
Meng, Zhaopeng   3
Menze, Bjoern H.   453
Miao, Hanpei   688
Morasso, Pietro   753
Moretti, Paolo   753
Mukhopadhyay, Anirban   14
Müller, Sarah   539
Myronenko, Andriy   77

Najdenkoska, Ivona   314
Nam, Soo Jeong   420
Navab, Nassir   582
Nemirovsky-Rotman, Shira   743
Ning, Munan   667

Ounissi, Mehdi   336

Paragios, Nikos   356
Park, Sang Hyun   420
Peng, Qiong   181
Peng, Tingying   99, 377
Ploner, Stefan   517

Qian, Ziniu   160
Qin, Peiwu   550
Qu, Linhao   24

Racoceanu, Daniel   336
Reisenbüchler, Daniel   377
Riedl, Sophie   625
Rittscher, Jens   130

Rivail, Antoine   625
Rohé, Marc-Michel   464
Roth, Holger R.   77
Rotman, Elad   743

Saltz, Joel   192
Samaras, Dimitris   192
Scalbert, Marin   120
Schiefelbein, Johannes   699
Schmidt-Erfurth, Ursula   625
Schottenhamml, Julia   517
Shang, Fangxin   604, 614, 677
Shang, Xianwen   593
Shao, Lei   550
Shao, Wei   222
Sharma, Yash   345
Shen, Dinggang   212
Shen, Linlin   109
Shen, Yiqing   212
Shi, Danli   593
Shi, Jun   273, 283
Shi, Xiaoyu   497
Shimatani, Koji   753
Shu, Hai   487
Sirinukunwattana, Korsuk   130
Snoek, Cees G. M.   314
Song, Andrew H.   387
Song, Boram   171
Song, Yang   409
Song, Zhijian   24
Sowmya, Arcot   409
Spitzer, Hannah   699
Stimmer, Lev   336
Ströbel, Philipp   88
Su, Ran   3
Sun, Changming   3
Sun, Jiayin   202
Sun, Kai   66
Sun, Xu   656
Sun, Yuxuan   242
Sung, Hyun Jung   420
Syed, Sana   345

Talbot, Hugues   325
Teichmann, Marvin   88
Theis, Fabian J.   699
Tian, Yuan   721
Tolkach, Yuri   14

Tran, Manuel   99
Tsuji, Toshio   753

Vakalopoulou, Maria   120, 192, 325, 356
van Sonsbeek, Tom   314
Vasconcelos, Francisco   732
Verrill, Clare   130
Vétil, Rebeca   464
Villa, Irène   356
Vullierme, Marie-Pierre   464

Wagner, Nicolas   14
Wagner, Sophia J.   99, 377
Wang, Changwei   528
Wang, Liansheng   66, 181
Wang, Lin   497
Wang, Manning   24
Wang, Qian   202
Wang, Sheng   202
Wang, Xiaosong   77
Wang, Xin   497
Wang, Xingyue   688
Wang, Yan   46
Wang, Yifeng   232
Wang, Ying   293
Wang, Zeyu   140
Wang, Zhaowei   604, 614, 677
Wang, Zhihui   571
Wang, Zhongyuan   709
Warfield, Simon   743
Wei, Bingzheng   160
Wei, Dong   667
Wei, Leyi   3
Wei, Wen B.   550
Wen, Ziqi   150
Williamson, Drew F. K.   387
Won, Jungeun   517
Wood, Ruby   130
Worring, Marcel   314
Wouters, Koen   732
Wu, Huisi   109
Wu, Junde   604, 614, 677
Wu, Kun   273
Wu, Pengcheng   571
Wu, Yawen   222

Xia, James J.   444
Xiao, Jia   721
Xiao, Ruoxiu   507
Xiao, Zunjie   688

Xie, Fengying   273, 283
Xie, Xingran   46
Xu, Chundan   150
Xu, Daguang   77
Xu, Rongtao   528
Xu, Rui   571
Xu, Shibiao   528
Xu, Yan   160
Xu, Yanwu   604, 614, 677
Xu, Ziyue   77

Yan, Rui   293
Yang, Dalu   604, 614, 677
Yang, Dawei   645
Yang, Dong   77
Yang, Fan   35
Yang, Jiawei   35
Yang, Lin   242
Yang, Yehui   604, 614, 677
Yao, Jianhua   35, 66
Yap, Pew-Thian   444
Yaqub, Mohammad   635
Ye, Chuyang   150
Ye, Xinchen   571
Yeganeh, Yousef   582
Yoder, Josiah A.   398
Yu, Chengjin   433
Yu, Guangjun   721
Yu, Lequan   181
Yu, Rongshan   181
Yuan, Wenguang   667

Zachow, Stefan   453
Zaffrani-Reznikov, Yael   743
Zaninovic, Nikica   732
Zeng, Bowei   232
Zhang, Chuncao   721
Zhang, Daoqiang   222
Zhang, Donghao   593
Zhang, Fa   293
Zhang, Hao   550
Zhang, Jingwei   192
Zhang, Jiong   560
Zhang, Lichi   202
Zhang, Qinghua   253
Zhang, Shuting   688
Zhang, Weiwen   645
Zhang, Wentian   656
Zhang, Xiaopeng   528
Zhang, Xin   192, 202

Zhang, Yao 35
Zhang, Yidan 66
Zhang, Yongbing 232, 550
Zhang, Yunlong 242
Zhang, Ziyi 688
Zhao, Can 77
Zhao, Jiaxin 571
Zhao, Xin 497
Zhao, Yanfeng 56
Zhao, Yitian 487, 560, 688
Zhao, Yu 35, 66

Zhen, Xiantong 314
Zheng, Jiangbin 3
Zheng, Sunyi 242
Zheng, Yefeng 656, 667
Zheng, Yushan 273, 283
Zhou, Qian 709
Zhou, Wenshuo 604, 614
Zhu, Chenglu 242
Zhu, Qi 222
Zou, Hua 709
Zuo, Yingli 222

Printed in the United States
by Baker & Taylor Publisher Services

Printed in the United States
by Baker & Taylor Publisher Services